THE K&W GUIDE TO
COLLEGES

FOR STUDENTS
WITH LEARNING DIFFERENCES

14TH EDITION

From the Authors of The K&W Guide......

Both Marybeth and Imy have been working with students and families facing important individual education decisions for a combined total of over 70 years of experience. Marybeth has been in the College Counseling profession for over 40 years and is currently the Director of College Counseling for Wolcott School. Additionally, Marybeth also has a private Educational Consulting Practice. Imy has her own Consulting group as well, entering its 29th year that helps families identify appropriate education and/or therapeutic alternatives for young children, adolescents and young adults. Imy and Marybeth believe that there should never be a "closed door" to one's hopes and dreams. Each child's journey is unique. Success is about discovering the best and appropriate pathway on which to travel forward.

Each time we update our edition of the *K&W Guide*, we remember our original concerns in the early 1990's about how to figure out what support there was provided on college campuses and how little information was available. Colleges have come a long way since our first edition in 1991. Students are more informed about their learning issues and parents are more educated about how to understand their children's learning style. Colleges have so many different types and levels of support that it's become more important than ever to be able to distinguish what is and isn't necessary for the college student.

This book was created to help students feel confident about what they can expect from a college and for parents and professionals to be able to understand if the college is truly a "good match." It's very difficult for any parent to see their student as they are today and not for whom they hope they will be one day. It's very important that when looking for a college, and a college support program, that the parent takes a step back, looks at the child in front of them and recognizes what they need in the immediate.

It's much easier today, many editions later, for Marybeth and Imy to feel confident and comfortable approaching colleges and requesting detailed information from the vast number offering programs and support when once there was only but a few. Today students have so many college options to explore. Do your homework; identify priorities; ask lots of questions; determine what level of support is needed; pick carefully; look at courses required to matriculate, and courses required to graduate from a college; keep in mind that getting in is the first hurdle; successfully staying in and graduating is the true challenge; the journey can be circuitous; and the diploma on the wall identifies where you graduated from and not necessarily where you entered; the glue is understanding and accepting the Learning Difference, being a self-advocate, and congratulating yourself on reaching new accomplishments. The world is waiting for you and all that you will contribute. We wish you a safe and successful journey.

Marybeth Kravets and Imy Wax

Co-authors of the *K&W Guide*.

The
Princeton
Review®

PrincetonReview.com

THE K&W GUIDE TO
COLLEGES

FOR STUDENTS
WITH LEARNING DIFFERENCES

14TH EDITION

MARYBETH KRAVETS, MA

AND IMY F. WAX, MS

Penguin
Random
House

The Princeton Review
110 E. 42nd Street, 7th floor
New York, NY 10017
E-mail: editorialsupport@review.com

A Penguin Random House Company.

ISBN: 978-0-525-56789-9
ISSN: 1934-4775

Printed in the United States of America.

9 8 7 6 5 4 3 2 1

14th Edition

The Princeton Review is not affiliated with Princeton University.

Editorial

Robert Franek, Editor-in-Chief

David Soto, Director of Content Development

Danielle Correa, Editor

Stephen Koch, Student Survey Manager

Random House Publishing Team

Tom Russell, VP, Publisher

Alison Stoltzfus, Publishing Director

Ellen L. Reed, Production Manager

Amanda Yee, Associate Managing Editor

Suzanne Lee, Designer

DEDICATION & ACKNOWLEDGMENTS

This book is a labor of love. It is written to help individuals throughout the world who have been identified as having Attention Deficit Hyperactivity Disorder, Autism Spectrum Disorder or any other Learning Difference and who are seeking the right match and fit for life after high school. The KW Guide is an educational tool for all of the families, professionals, and friends who know someone who has a learning difference or other learning issues.

Our gratitude to the families of Marybeth Kravets and Imy Wax for their patience and support in this continued endeavor: Wendy, Steve, Allison, Connor, Isabel, Cooper, Mark, Sara, David, Robbie, Bennett, Cathy (in loving memory), Dan, Andrea, BJ, Matthew, Leia, Maise, Blue, Dr. Jack, Howard, Lisa, Bill, Niaya, Ellis, Gary, Tamar, Jordan, Eli, Debrah, Greg, Jamie, Joe, Benji, Goldie, Sadie, and Judy.

Our appreciation to all of the colleges who provide services and programs to promote the educational endeavors and dreams of students with learning differences or attention deficit hyperactivity disorder or are on the Autism Spectrum. We would like to thank all of the contributors in the *K&W Guide* who share their thoughts and experiences with learning differences and attention deficit/hyperactivity disorder. Our appreciation to Dr. Miriam Pike, Head of School for Wolcott School, Chicago, Illinois for her professional guidance, Linda Jamrozy, Wendy Perlin and Carol Sharp for their support in researching information and to Karen Rodgers Photography for the authors' pictures on the back cover of the book. karenrodgersphot@sbcglobal.net

CONTENTS

FOREWORD

Opening Doors and Opening Minds

By Kevin M.R. Mayne

They say when opportunity knocks you'd better answer. As educators, we see opportunities around us daily. Not only in the form of young minds eager to expand and learn, but also in our own ability to stretch our understanding of pre-existing concepts and industry standards. We all are aware that the field of higher education itself has changed dramatically over time. The education landscape has not only seen peaks and valleys, but has also been witness to several new emerging challenges and opportunities on the horizon. This is particularly true with the field of learning disabilities.

The concept of "learning disability" dates to 1964, and legal protections that assure access and fair treatment for students who learn differently have been on the books for more than four decades. In this time, great strides have been made. A research basis for various forms of neurodevelopmental differences such as dyslexia, ADHD, and ASD has been established, and learning challenges that seemed mysterious during earlier periods now are more fully understood. When it comes to learning challenges, there is an emerging consensus regarding effective educational practices. Many of our colleges and universities around the country offer strong comprehensive support programs, while others offer programs of basic accommodations and supplemental support services.

Here's where opportunity comes "a knocking." More recently, there has been a paradigm shift from a deficit management model that saw students with learning disabilities as broken and needing to be fixed, to a framework focused on the concept of "neurodiversity" - a model emphasizing human asset development whereby all learners can benefit from universal design for instruction and also for development of skills and strategies outside of the classroom.

No one disputes that neurodevelopmental differences such as dyslexia, ADHD and ASD present real challenges to students in conventional academic settings. The frustrations of learning to read, learning how to organize work and motivate to action, or how to interpret social cues and get along in group contexts are all real, and can represent true hurdles to academic accomplishment in postsecondary settings. At the same time, it has become clear that these diverse expressions of the human genome can not only be managed in the right settings with the right support, but also enable students to succeed, flourish, and contribute in ways traditional learners may not.

How so? There is growing recognition through anecdotal evidence and emerging research that the cognitive traits subsumed under the heading of neurodiversity represent adaptive strengths in many contexts, including the business world, technology, the arts, and the STEM fields. In particular, prominent companies such as SAP, Microsoft, HP, Deloitte, IBM, and others are recognizing the wisdom of having a more neurodiverse workforce. SAP believes that its Autism at Work program has created a diverse, inclusive, and bias-free culture that makes it a better company. These companies have expanded their human resources processes in order to identify and access this important talent.

Higher education, on the other hand, hasn't been as proactive. Isn't it time that we lead by example? The key point is that students within the broad range of cognitive processing differences that fall under the heading of neurodiversity must be seen for their strengths and abilities, not their challenges alone. They are human assets, not liabilities. They may need support, but they are not broken, and do not need to be fixed or "cured."

We have learned so much since the term "learning disability" was first coined more than five decades ago. The work of so many fine researchers, educators, and technology innovators has allowed us now to see a new paradigm, one that may still be emerging, but is putting down deep roots. One that is opening doors – and opening minds.

We understand the nature of dyslexia now, and that there are educational approaches that work, combining phonics-based reading instruction, effective use of reading and study skills, and the use of assistive technologies such as screen readers and voice recognition. We know that individuals who have experienced life-long struggle with print literacy can succeed in college and at the graduate level, go on to successful careers, and make innovative marks on the world.

We know that the executive challenges that come with ADHD – distractibility, challenges in activating work, difficulty with personal self-regulation – all can be helped through a process that includes the development of metacognition and the use of specific strategies for reading, studying, writing, and staying organized. Executive function coaching can provide a platform for ongoing development even as it helps to stabilize self-regulation and assure action-oriented strategies.

We know that the social challenges that typically accompany ASD can be addressed through explicit training in social pragmatics along with strategies and ongoing support for managing executive functioning and social behavior in group settings. And we know that individuals with ASD often do astonishing work in the area on which they have chosen to focus.

We know that students with different cognitive traits can do well in college and succeed at work and life, often at very high levels of accomplishment. The list of careers in which individuals who fall under the neurodiversity umbrella is essentially endless—from forest rangers and state troopers, to early childhood specialists and social workers, to business leaders and entrepreneurs, to the designers of new algorithms and new ways of digitally capturing information.

Likewise, while students with learning differences are each unique, so is every learner in every classroom. Rather than focusing on their disabilities, we are now more focused on their individual abilities. Universal Design for Instruction is still more of a general concept than a research-based educational approach, but it answers to common sense. Every classroom contains students who may struggle with language or with social skills; every classroom contains students who struggle with organization and executive functions; every classroom contains students who may learn best through auditory, or visual, or kinesthetic and tactile means.

The advent of two new concepts, neurodiversity and universal design for learning, marks a paradigm shift in the world of LD. In earlier days, it was a truism in the LD world that students with learning differences are each as unique and strong as a snowflake's intricate construction, and neurodiversity provides a way of realizing a deeper meaning and value in this idea.

What we have learned about effective teaching in the past five decades is strong and widely agreed on, and the power that new technologies give us as educators would have been unimaginable not so long ago. We truly are entering into a new era; a new door is opening. As we do, perhaps we should keep in mind that human assets are what make a nation strong, which is why so many small nations with few natural resources are able to perform so well on our new global economic stage. America's postsecondary educational system is the envy of the world, and the diversity of the nation's citizenship has been a core strength since it first became a republic. It is time to add the thread of neurodiversity to the great American tapestry.

While some evidence suggests that our communities are increasingly siloed and our discourse often divided, America's colleges and universities are one place where diversity is embraced and the idea of the melting pot (or at least the encounters students have across diverse backgrounds, racial and ethnic identities, gender and sexual orientation) is still honored in deep and meaningful ways. Neurodiversity should be an important piece of that. The types of educational supports and the students served do vary greatly. As such, educators should be leading the charge of embracing neurodiversity. After all, schools are educating individuals who will become future world problem solvers. Do we want to create learners who all think and act the same way? Who approach problems in the same manner? No, we want to help students to maximize their individual potential, to approach these problems from different viewpoints, and to feel comfortable developing and contributing innovative solutions.

For more than 30 years, The *K&W Guide* has been an invaluable resource for students, parents, and educators. As our industry has adapted and grown in its recognition, depth and breadth of learning disabilities, so has the guide. As we seek to embrace neurodiversity, the guide is an excellent means of discerning which program best meets an individual student's needs. In addition to highlighting important guidelines for documentation of a learning disability and how best to plan for the college search, the guide's main focus is showcasing the wide range of support programs available at colleges and universities across the country. The guide has been, and continues to be, a true champion of neurodiverse learners.

Education offers us opportunity. Let us not close the door on possibility or just focus on one predetermined pathway. Instead, let us answer that knock. Open up our minds to new ways of thinking, new ways of understanding, new ways of educating, and new ways of learning.

Kevin M.R. Mayne is the Vice President for Enrollment Management at Landmark College in Putney, Vermont. A disruptive innovator and student advocate, he has over 36 years of successful higher education experience in the areas of learning disabilities, admissions, marketing, advancement, global citizenship, and program development.

THOUGHTS FROM . . .

THOUGHTS FROM . . .

A PARENT OF A STUDENT WITH LEARNING CHALLENGES

After 7 years and 7 failed, in-vitro attempts, I admit it, I had lost hope that we would ever have our own children. I had started looking into adoption. My husband, Barry, forever the optimist, had other plans. He begged me to try, "just one more time." He still held out hope that attempt number 8 would be the magic number. He said he "knew it would work this time." It was that hope, that indomitable belief that inspired me to give it one more try. He was right, our dreams came true, times two. We welcomed twins, a boy and a girl on May 18th, 1997. Our lives were officially perfect.

Unfortunately, that perfect life would be all too brief. At the age of 7, our twin daughter, Danielle, was diagnosed with a malignant brain tumor. Barry and I went into action, we found one of the world's leading pediatric brain surgeons and wouldn't take no for an answer. However, after brain surgery, she had no physical abilities, none. She couldn't walk, talk, use her arms or legs; her vision was impaired as well as her hearing.

Hopeless? Some might think so, but we knew, from our previous experiences, that there is always hope if you look in the right places, connect with the right people and never give up. Eventually, through hard work and the belief that she could do anything she set her mind to, Danielle learned to walk, talk, and regain almost all of her abilities.

One thing we weren't completely prepared for, although we were warned about the possible long-term ramifications, was the toll the chemotherapy would take on her cognitive and learning abilities. This once bright child, who learned easily and had no apparent learning issues, was now a child with learning differences. Not only did she have to beat cancer, which she did, (she is now 13 years cancer free), not only did she have to spend endless hours in physical, occupational, speech and eye therapy but now she had trouble learning the way most kids learn. We were lucky to have the resources in Chicago, in the form of schools that were specifically for kids with learning differences. Again, finding these schools, gave us the hope we needed to believe that someday, she would gain the skills, through the diligence of teachers with specific knowledge and techniques that would help her get to college.

As I write this, she is a freshman at the University of Arizona and doing very well. When we started thinking about what schools would be right for Danielle, supporting her very special set of needs, again we were given hope. We were incredibly fortunate to have one of the writers of this book, Marybeth Kravets, as Danielle's college guidance counselor. Her book is the ultimate resource for anyone trying to find just the right school for their student with learning differences. It guides you through every detail, compares programs and services at each school so you can make an informed and therefore confident decision. For all parents facing the very difficult task of finding a college or university that is right for their child, think of this as a very special book of hope.

Judy Faulkner Krause, Parent
Creative Director at The Suite Imagination Arts Lab, Chicago IL

A STUDENT

"Let's just say she's not going to Harvard"—sounds pretty harsh right? You may have heard those words in a group poem for Louder Than a Bomb. Those were the words that were said by the head of radiation at Northwestern in a discussion with my parents after I had 13 hours of brain surgery. She was talking about what I would be like after standard photon radiation, the only kind they offered. It would leave me pretty much a vegetable, an underachiever. Those words did not go over well with my mom and dad.

Luckily, in my family, we don't take the first answer as the only answer. My dad worked for hours that night researching alternative types of radiation therapy. Finally, he discovered Proton Beam Therapy, a type of therapy that targets the tumor instead of the healthy tissue. That means less damage and fewer side effects down the road. That is why I am here today, able to speak to you, and heading off to the University of Arizona with great grades. Oh, and I made it to Harvard, for Proton Beam Radiation.

I've been at Wolcott for four successful years. I think people tend to make assumptions about people by the way they look, sound, or even move. I still have balance issues, my speech sounds different and I'm a bit shy but that's not really who I am. When I was 6, I was modeling for American Girl, I was a hell of a gymnast, actress, and singer. I was outgoing and talkative. That's what made losing all that so hard. I was old enough to know the girl I had been. But since I'm talking to you right now, you've probably guessed, that didn't stop me. I had to learn to walk, talk, and accomplish pretty much everything all over again. It wasn't fair, but it's made me a much stronger, caring, compassionate, and understanding person. That was the light at the end of this tunnel.

Dani Krause
Wolcott School 2017
University of Arizona 2021

THOUGHTS FROM . . .

DIRECTOR OF ASD COLLEGE SUPPORT PROGRAM

Because the challenges for individuals with Autism Spectrum Disorder (ASD) face are so unique and individualized, in order for college students with ASD to have the best chance at success, they need a defined on-campus support program that is designed specifically to offer support with the many issues that they will likely deal with. This program must be separate from the Office of Disability Support Services, where all students can receive academic and testing accommodations, which is most often not enough support for this population.

In 2007, when I started the Bridges to Adelphi Program (BAP) at Adelphi University in Garden City, NY, there were very few college support programs available for students with ASD. There was little research available, and from what I could tell from most of the college administrators that I spoke with, there was something between denial that there were students with (what was then known as) Asperger Syndrome on their campuses, and no best practices or resources to consult. That program that I started in 2007 with 3 students who were referred to me from the Office of Disability Support Services, now offers comprehensive, individualized, academic, social, and vocational support services to over 100 current Adelphi undergraduate and graduate students from all over the United States, the Caribbean, and China, who have self-disclosed with what is now diagnosed as ASD.

With the continuing rise in prevalence of ASD, now at 1 in 45 (Center for Disease Control, 2015), a greater awareness of the condition, increased research, and improved and earlier interventions and strategies for individuals with ASD have set the stage for increasing numbers of individuals with ASD to enroll in institutions of higher education. However, while these students may have the cognitive ability to successfully process college level academics, they may also experience significant challenges with communication, executive functioning, sensory issues, understanding social interactions, and managing their anxieties and emotions(Nagler & Shore, 2013).

The Bridges to Adelphi Program, which is fee-based, is based on social learning theory (Bandura, 1977) and cognitive behavioral principles (Beck, Rush, Shaw, & Emery, 1979) as theoretical foundations. A unique feature of BAP is that the staff consists almost exclusively of Adelphi graduate students who are studying psychology, social work, education, or communication disorders. Each student who enrolls in BAP is assigned at least two staff members to work with them a minimum of four times per week on academic issues. These meetings focus on executive functioning strategies to help the student remain aware of, and plan for, upcoming assignments, exams and meetings; and assignment completion, exam preparation, and research. In their meetings, staff is very interested in assessing how students think, learn, and work, so that we can design their supports to meet each student's individual strength and needs.

BAP also offers a variety of socialization opportunities, which are overseen by the staff. Two evenings a week, "Open Group" meetings are offered. These groups are driven by student interests. Students are also offered weekly "Men's" and "Women's" groups. These groups are more focused on subjects that college students need to talk about; and offer rich discussions on relationships, dating, romance, and associated topics. As well, twice a month students are offered group events, both on and off campus. These events include trips to a bowling alley or pool hall, Dave & Busters, or a local restaurant. BAP students are also offered the opportunity to meet weekly with a Peer Mentor, a volunteer undergraduate student who is asked to encourage BAP student's to attend campus activities or join campus clubs.

However, the most important social opportunity for students may occur in the BAP office, which is open Mondays through Fridays from 8am-8pm, and on Saturdays from 9am-4pm. Students are encouraged to hang around and socialize with each other in a safe and predictable environment. They often order food in together, play video games; talk about their classes; and over the years many friendships have been made.

Our research show outstanding outcomes. In 2014–15, BAP retained 95 percent of the students enrolled in the program. And the average GPA for the past four semesters has consistently been approximately 3.30. But these are not the only goals of BAP. We are also focused on developing independent and successful adults who, when they graduate, will find meaningful employment in their areas of study, at competitive wages.

To address these goals, we have developed a vocational program that offers BAP students complete vocational testing batteries, individual and group vocational meetings, assistance with resume writing and job interview skills, and help finding both on and off campus internships. BAP has also entered in partnerships with outside agencies that have programs that help adults with ASD find jobs and provide training for the employers, and on the job support for the employees.

This (very) brief outline of the services that the Bridges to Adelphi offers can serve as a guideline to parents of students with ASD. It is strongly advised that you go to each school that you and your child are considering. Take a campus tour when classes are in session to make certain that your child can feel comfortable there. Meet with an admissions officer. Meet with the Office of Disability Support Services to learn the criteria and documentation needed to receive services. And most importantly meet with the people that run the ASD support program on the campus. One last suggestion. Start early; don't wait for senior year to begin preparing for the transition from high school to college.

Mitch Nagler MA, LMHC, Director, Bridges to Adelphi Program
Assistant Director, Student Counseling Center
p – 516.877.3665
e – mnagler@adelphi.edu

10 Things College Students with Disabilities Need to Know About their Rights
By Matt Cohen

1) What schools are covered by the disability laws? Section 504 applies to all colleges and universities that receive federal financial assistance. The Americans with Disabilities Act applies to all colleges and universities unless they're religiously controlled. The IDEA (the special education law) does not apply to colleges and universities at all.

2) Can colleges and universities ask you about your medical conditions or disabilities in your admissions application? No. You may choose to disclose that you have a disability if you wish to, but cannot be required to disclose your disability prior to admission.

3) Is it a good idea for me to disclose that I have a disability on my application? There is no right or wrong answer to this question. Some students decide it will be helpful to their application to disclose their disability and perhaps write about it. Others feel it may dispose the school to reject them.

4) Is it the responsibility of the college to determine if I have a disability and require accommodations after I have been accepted? No. Unlike public elementary and secondary schools, colleges and universities are not responsible for discovering if a student has a disability. The burden is on the student to self-disclose that they have a disability and are seeking accommodations. This is done by notifying the college disability services office. Sometimes students decide not to seek accommodations because they are embarrassed or feel they don't need them, then seek help when they are experiencing academic or disciplinary problems. It is generally more difficult to get help and to obtain the protection of the law if students wait until they are in trouble to disclose their disability and seek help.

5) Who is entitled to accommodations? A person is entitled to reasonable accommodations if they meet a number of criteria. First, the person must have a physical or mental impairment that substantially limits a major life activity, such as learning, reading, concentrating, thinking, and communicating. Second, the person must meet the general qualifications for participation in the program or activity that they are applying for, either with or without accommodations. Third, they must establish that they: a) have a physical or mental impairment, b) need specific accommodations, and c) that these accommodations are "reasonable."

6) What if my disability is controlled by medication or other measures that allow me to function normally? Schools are not allowed to use the effect of mitigating measures as a basis to deny eligibility.

7) What am I entitled to if I have a disability? You are not entitled to the same level of services in college that you may have been eligible for in elementary and secondary school. You are only entitled to "reasonable accommodations," as long as they are not unduly burdensome and do not result in a fundamental alteration of the college's programs. These can include things like extended time on deadlines and tests, preferentially seating, access to lecture notes, or use of assistive technology to allow the student to more easily complete the work.

8) If I had an IEP or 504 plan in high school, am I automatically entitled to accommodations in college? No. The college has a right to review your clinical documentation and history of prior support. Prior eligibility does not automatically mean you will be eligible in college, but it does help to support the need for ongoing accommodations.

9) Does the absence of eligibility for an IEP or 504 plan in high school disqualify me from receiving accommodations in college? No. It makes it somewhat harder to obtain the right to accommodations, but not impossible. You will need to provide current clinical documentation of the disability along with an explanation of why the disability was not diagnosed and/or accommodated previously. Generally, you will need to provide recent testing that documents the presence of your disability, especially if you have learning disabilities, AD/HD or other disabilities that may change in their impact over time.

10) What can I do if the school denies that I have a disability or refuses my request for a specific accommodation? If that happens, you have the right to file a grievance or appeal within the college and you can also file a complaint with the US Department of Education Office for Civil Rights or the US Department of Justice Civil Rights Division, Disability Rights Unit.

Matt Cohen is the founder of Matt Cohen and Associates, a Chicago based disability rights law firm, and has over 35 years of experience advocating on behalf of people with disabilities. Matt can be reached at 866-787-9270 or mdcspedlaw@gmail.com. His website is: www.mattcohenandassociates.com.

GENERAL GUIDELINES FOR DOCUMENTATION OF A LEARNING DISABILITY

1. A comprehensive psycho-educational or neuropsychological evaluation that provides a diagnosis of a learning disability must be submitted. The report should indicate the current status and impact of he learning disability in an academic setting. If another diagnosis is applicable (e.g., ADHD, mood disorder), it should be stated.

2. The evaluation must be conducted by a professional who is certified/licensed in the area of learning disabilities, such as a clinical or educational psychologist, school psychologist, and neuropsychologist or learning disabilities specialist. The evaluator's name, title, and professional credentials and affiliation should be provided.

3. The evaluation must be based on a comprehensive assessment battery:

   - **Aptitude**: Average broad cognitive functioning must be demonstrated on an individually administered intelligence test, preferably administered during high school or beyond, such as the WAIS, WISC, Woodcock-Johnson Cognitive Battery, and Kaufman Adolescent and Adult Intelligence Test. Subtest scaled scores/subtest scores should be listed.

   - **Academic Achievement**: A comprehensive academic achievement battery, such as the WJ and WIAT should document achievement deficits relative to potential. The battery should include current levels of academic functioning in relevant areas, such as reading, oral and written language, and mathematics. Standard scores and percentiles for administered subtests should be stated. Specific achievement tests can also be included, such as the Nelson-Denny Reading Test and Test of Written Language (TOWL), as well as informal measures (e.g., informal reading inventories and writing samples).

   - **Information Processing**: Specific areas of information processing (e.g., short- and long-term memory, auditory and visual perception/processing, executive functioning) should be assessed.

   - **Social-Emotional Assessment**: To rule out a primary emotional basis for learning difficulties and provide information needed to establish appropriate services, a social-emotional assessment, using formal assessment instruments and/or clinical interview, should be conducted.

   - **Clinical Summary**: A diagnostic summary should present a diagnosis of a specific learning disability; provide impressions of the testing situation; interpret the testing data; and indicate how patterns in the student's cognitive ability, achievement, and information processing reflect the presence of a learning disability. Recommendations should be provided for specific accommodations based on disability-related deficits. For students just graduating high school, an evaluation reflecting current levels of academic skills should have been administered while in high school; for students who have been out of school for a number of years, documentation will be considered on a case-by-case basis. Additional documents that do not constitute sufficient documentation, but that may be submitted in addition to a psychological, psycho-educational or neuropsychological evaluation include an individualized education plan (IEP), a 504 plan, and/or an educational assessment.

GENERAL GUIDELINES FOR DOCUMENTATION OF ATTENTION DEFICIT/HYPERACTIVITY DISORDER (ADHD)

Students requesting accommodations and services on the basis of an Attention Deficit/Hyperactivity Disorder (AD/HD) are required to submit documentation that establishes a disability and supports the need for the accommodations recommended and requested.

1. A *qualified* professional must conduct the evaluation. Professionals who conduct the assessment, make the diagnosis of ADHD, detail symptoms, provide relevant history, determine functional limitations, and provide recommendations for accommodation must be qualified professionals defined as licensed mental health professionals. Primary care or general practice physicians are not considered qualified to complete an AD/HD evaluation.

2. Documentation must be current (typically within three years. The provision of accommodations is based upon an assessment of the current impact of the student's disability on learning in the college setting.

3. Documentation *must* be comprehensive. Requirements for any diagnostic report are:
   - A medical or clinical diagnosis of AD/HD based on DSM criteria
   - Assessment/testing profile and interpretation of the assessment instruments used that supports the diagnosis. Acceptable measures include objective measures of attention and discrimination or valid and reliable observer or self-report. Acceptable measures are
     - Conner's Continuous Performance Task (CPT)
     - Test of Variables of Attention (TOVA)
     - Behavioral Assessment System for Children
     - Conner's Adult AD/HD Rating Scale (CAARS)
     - CAARS-L; the long version of the self-report form
     - CARRS-O; the observer form
     - Brown Attention Deficit Disorder Scale
   - A clear description of the functional limitations in the educational setting, specifying the major life activities that are affected to a substantial degree because of the disability
   - Relevant history, including developmental, family, medical, psychosocial, pharmacological, educational and employment. AD/HD is by definition first exhibited in childhood. Therefore, the assessment should include historical information establishing symptoms of AD/HD throughout childhood, adolescence and into adulthood.
   - A description of the specific symptoms manifesting themselves at the present time that may affect the student's academic performance
   - Medications the student is currently taking, as well as a description of any limitations that may persist even with medication
   - Co-existing conditions, including medical and learning disabilities that should be considered in determining reasonable accommodations

General Guidelines for documentation of Autism Spectrum Disorder

A. Persistent deficits in social communication and social interaction across multiple contexts, as manifested by the following, currently or by history
1. Deficits in social-emotional reciprocity, ranging, for example, from abnormal social approach and failure of normal back-and-forth conversation; to reduced sharing of interests, emotions, or affect; to failure to initiate or respond to social interactions.
2. Deficits in nonverbal communicative behaviors used for social interaction, ranging, for example, from poorly integrated verbal and nonverbal communication; to abnormalities in eye contact and body language or deficits in understanding and use of gestures; to a total lack of facial expressions and nonverbal communication.
3. Deficits in developing, maintaining, and understand relationships, ranging, for example, from difficulties adjusting behavior to suit various social contexts; to difficulties in sharing imaginative play or in making friends; to absence of interest in peers.

Specify current severity:

Severity is based on social communication impairments and restricted, repetitive patterns of behavior.

B. Restricted, repetitive patterns of behavior, interests, or activities, as manifested by at least two of the following, currently or by history (examples are illustrative, not exhaustive; see text):
1. Stereotyped or repetitive motor movements, use of objects, or speech (e.g., simple motor stereotypes, lining up toys or flipping objects, echolalia, idiosyncratic phrases).
2. Insistence on sameness, inflexible adherence to routines, or ritualized patterns of verbal or nonverbal behavior (e.g., extreme distress at small changes, difficulties with transitions, rigid thinking patterns, greeting rituals, need to take same route or eat same food every day).
3. Highly restricted, fixated interests that are abnormal in intensity or focus (e.g., strong attachment to or preoccupation with unusual objects, excessively circumscribed or perseverative interests).
4. Hyper- or hyporeactivity to sensory input or unusual interest in sensory aspects of the environment (e.g. apparent indifference to pain/temperature, adverse response to specific sounds or textures, excessive smelling or touching of objects, visual fascination with lights or movement).

Specify current severity:

Severity is based on social communication impairments and restricted, repetitive patterns of behavior.

C. Symptoms must be present in the early developmental period (but may not become fully manifest until social demands exceed limited capacities or may be masked by learned strategies in later life).
D. Symptoms cause clinically significant impairment in social, occupational, or other important areas of current functioning.
E. These disturbances are not better explained by intellectual disability (intellectual developmental disorder) or global developmental delay. Intellectual disability and autism spectrum disorder frequently co-occur; to make comorbid diagnoses of autism spectrum disorder and intellectual disability, social communication should be below that expected for general developmental level.

Note: Individuals with a well-established DSM-IV diagnosis of autistic disorder, Asperger's disorder, or pervasive developmental disorder not otherwise specified should be given the diagnosis of autism spectrum disorder. Individuals who have marked deficits in social communication, but whose symptoms do not otherwise meet criteria for autism spectrum disorder, should be evaluated for social (pragmatic) communication disorder.

Specify if:
    With or without accompanying intellectual impairment
    With or without accompanying language impairment
    Associated with a known medical or genetic condition or environmental factor
    Associated with another neurodevelopmental, mental, or behavioral disorder
    With catatonia (refer to the criteria for catatonia associated with another mental disorder)

GETTING READY

The purpose of *The K&W Guide* is to help students with learning differences such as Specific Learning Disabilities (LD), Attention Deficit Hyperactivity Disorder (ADHD) or Asperger Syndrome Disorder (ASD) acquire the basic knowledge necessary to begin the college exploration process and get ready to make appropriate college selections.

To get ready students need to:
- Understand their strengths and weaknesses.
- Be able to articulate the nature of their learning disabilities.
- Understand the compensatory skills developed to accommodate the learning differences.
- Describe the services they received in high school.
- Identify short-term and long-term goals.
- Select appropriate college choices to match individual needs.

GUIDELINES FOR THE SEARCH AND SELECTION PROCESS
Self-Assessment
- What is the student's disability?
- When was the disability diagnosed?
- What is the student's level of performance in high school?
- Is the student enrolled in college-prep courses, modified courses, or individualized, special- education courses?
- What are the student's individual strengths and weaknesses?
- Is it easier for the student to learn from a lecture, reading the material, or having the material read to her?
- Does the student perform better on written assignments or oral presentations?
- Which subjects are easier, and which are more difficult?
- What are the student's favorite and least favorite courses and why?
- What are the student's short-term and long-term goals?
- Are these goals realistic?
- Is the student striving to improve in academic areas?
- What accommodations are being provided?
- Is the student actively utilizing resource assistance and learning compensatory strategies?
- What does the student plan to study in college?
- What skills and competencies are required for the career goals being pursued?
- When were the last diagnostic tests given?
- What level of services/accommodations is needed in college? Structured programs, comprehensive services, or basic services?

Articulation

- Does the student understand the disability?
- Can the student describe the disability?
- Does the student comprehend how the disability impacts learning?
- Can the student explain the nature of the disability?
- Can the student explain the accommodations being utilized as well as any curriculum modifications received?
- Can the student explain necessary accommodations to teachers?

ACADEMIC ASSESSMENT

Does the student have difficulty with written language?

- using appropriate words
- organizing thoughts
- writing lengthy compositions
- using correct punctuation and sentence structure
- expressing thoughts clearly

Does the student have trouble with verbal expression?

- retrieving appropriate words
- understanding what others are saying
- using words in the correct context
- carrying on conversations

Does the student have a problem with hand-eye coordination?

- finding certain information on a page
- performing tasks that require fine motor coordination

Does the student get frustrated reading?

- decoding unfamiliar words
- understanding reading assignments
- completing reading assignments within a time frame

Does the student often misspell words?

- mix up the sequence of letters
- become confused when spelling irregular words

Does the student experience difficulty performing mathematics?

- multiplication table and fractions
- sequencing of steps of various mathematical questions

Does the student have difficulty concentrating?

- fidgets or squirms
- distracted by noises
- difficulty following instructions
- difficulty finishing assignments

What are the student's study habits?

- attentive in class for an extended period of time
- easily distracted
- needs extra time to respond to questions
- note-taking skills
- memory
- time management
- time orientation
- organization

How is the student's handwriting ability?

- assignments are difficult to read
- appropriate capitalization used
- stays within the lines when writing
- leaves enough space between words

EXPLORATION AND TIMELINES

FRESHMAN YEAR

- Maintain an academic mindset
- Develop a four-year academic plan
- Meet with guidance counselor
- Know that grades are cumulative- stay focused
- Become familiar with college resources and websites
- Understand basic factors considered in college admission
- Understand your learning differences
- Zone in on learning time management skills, assertiveness training, stress management and exam preparation strategies
- Consider developing a digital portfolio
- Identify personal academic goals and benchmarks
- Read, read, and read. This is the best way to increase your vocabulary as you begin an early preparation for taking standardized tests.
- Become an active listener
- Become skilled at moving knowledge from short term memory to long term memory
- Become a skilled note taker
- Learn how to use assistive technology
- Set goals
- Register for sophomore year—take college prep core courses

SOPHOMORE YEAR

- Explore options.
- Consider taking the ACT Aspire (if available)- request appropriate testing accommodations
- Meet with counselor and case manager.
- Review testing and documentation.
- Review course registration for junior year
- Students considering four year colleges/universities should be enrolled in as many mainstreamed, college preparatory courses as possible.
- Use college web sites to explore for information.
- Register online as a prospective student
- Contact the service providers on the college campus.
- Work on developing good self-advocacy skills
- Understand learning style and strengths and challenges
- Understand the disability

JUNIOR YEAR

- Consider taking the PSAT—request appropriate testing accommodations
- Review achievement level.
- Review course registration for senior year
- Students considering four-year colleges/universities should be enrolled in as many mainstreamed, college preparatory courses as possible.
- Use college web sites to explore for information
- Review the level of services in high school.
- Identify the level of services needed in college.
- Be able to articulate the disability.
- Be comfortable asking for support and accommodations.
- Participate in the IEP process and be actively involved in the IEP meeting.
- Be involved in writing your Summary of Performance (SOP)
- Visit colleges.
- Register for the ACT/SAT, standardized or non-standardized.
- Request necessary updated psycho-educational testing. (Including the most current version of The Wechsler Adult Intelligence Scale)

SENIOR YEAR

- Submit general applications.
- Submit special applications (if required).
- Schedule interviews (if appropriate).
- Write a personal statement and self-disclose the disability.
- Answer essay questions (if required).
- Be involved in writing your Summary of Performance (SOP)
- Release current psycho-educational testing if required for a Support Program; otherwise release after determining what college the student will attend
- Release documentation of other health-related disabilities once it has been determined what college the student will attend.
- Be sure that the documentation includes a description of the disability and recommended accommodations.
- Be sure to get copies of the entire special education file including testing assessments and IEP summaries to have in your personal files after graduation.
- Students under the age of eighteen must have their parents' signature to release documentation to each of the colleges.

CAMPUS VISITS

- The student should call to make an arrangement for a visit.
- Visit while classes are in session.
- Meet with admissions and special support service providers.
- Take a guided tour.
- Attend a class.
- Eat a meal on campus.
- Drive around the boundaries of the campus.
- Take pictures, take notes, and talk to students on campus.
- Take parents or family members along (but not in the interview).
- Get available information on disability services
- E-mail or write thank-you notes.

INTERVIEWS

To prepare for interviews, students should know:
- Strengths and weaknesses
- The accommodations needed
- How to describe learning differences

If an interview is required prior to an admission decision:
- View the interview as an opportunity.
- Prepare a list of questions.
- Know that interviews, if required, are either required of all applicants or required for a special program or special admission practice.

QUESTIONS THE DIRECTOR OF SUPPORT SERVICES MAY ASK:

- When was the learning difference first diagnosed?
- What type of assistance has the student been receiving in high school?
- What kind of accommodations will the student need in college?
- Can the student describe the learning difficulties?
- Can the student articulate strengths and weaknesses?
- How has the learning difference affected the student's learning?
- What high school courses were easy (or more difficult)?
- Is the student comfortable self-identifying the learning difference?
- Can the student self-advocate?
- What does the student plan to choose as a major?
- Is the student motivated?

QUESTIONS STUDENTS AND/OR PARENTS MAY ASK:

- What are the admission requirements?
- Is there any flexibility in admission policy? Course substitutions? GPA?
- What is the application procedure?
- Is a special application required?
- What auxiliary testing is required?
- Are there extra charges or fees for the special programs or services?
- Are there remedial or developmental courses?
- What is the procedure for requesting course waivers or substitutions?
- Who is the contact person for learning differences?
- What are the academic qualifications of the individual who provides services to students with learning differences?
- What services and accommodations are available: Testing accommodations? Note takers? Books on tape? Skills classes? Support groups? Priority registration? Professional tutors? Peer tutors? Advising? Computer-aided technology? Scribes? Proctors? Oral tests? Use of computers and spell-checker in class? Use of calculators in class? Distraction-free environment for tests? Learning differences specialists? Advocacy with professors? Faculty in-services?
- How long has the program been in existence?
- How many students are receiving services?
- How long can students access services?
- What is the success rate of students receiving services?

FOR A SUCCESSFUL INTERVIEW:

- Develop a list of questions.
- Know the accommodations needed.
- Provide new information.
- Practice interviewing.
- Be able to describe strengths and weaknesses.
- Talk about extracurricular activities.
- Take notes.
- Get the business card of the interviewer.
- Try to relax.
- Have fun!

LETTERS OF RECOMMENDATION

- Obtain descriptive letters from counselors, teachers, and case managers.
- Have recommenders address learning style, degree of motivation, level of achievement, abilities, attitudes, self-discipline, determination, creativity, mastery of subject matter, academic risks, and growth.
- Have a teacher describe the challenge in a difficult course.
- Advise recommenders when letters are due.

We have just highlighted some of the areas of importance. Now it is time to begin to use the information in this guide that describes the various programs and services at various colleges and universities in the United States.

COLLEGE INTERVIEW PREPARATION FORM FOR STUDENTS WITH LEARNING DISABILITIES/ADHD

NAME: _____ DATE: _____

ADDRESS: _____

PHONE: _____

Description of Disability:

_____

_____

When Diagnosed:

_____

_____

Special Help Received:

Tutoring_____

LD Resource _____

Remedial Reading_____

Study Skills _____

Other _____

Which were helpful and why?

_____

_____

Current high school:

_____

Describe this school:

_____

_____

_____

GPA _____

SAT _____

ACT _____

Comment on your abilities in the following areas and describe:

Memory:

_____

Attention:

_____

Time Management:

_____

Time Orientation:

_____

Describe strategies you have used to compensate for your Learning Disability:

_____

Why were these strategies successful/unsuccessful for you?

_____

_____

What is taking these kinds of tests like for you?

_____

_____

Describe your skills in the following areas. If your learning disability interferes in any of these areas, describe strategies you have used to compensate:

_____

Reading

_____

Writing

_____

Spelling

_____

Math

_____

Test Taking

_____

Note Taking

_____

What is your favorite subject? Least favorite?

_____

How would your favorite teacher describe you?

_____

_____

How would your least favorite teacher describe you?

_____

_____

What do you see as your own personal strengths?

_____

_____

What are your weaknesses?

_____

_____

What kinds of activities are you involved in?

_____

_____

What do you hope to get out of college?

_____

_____

What do you want in an LD College Program?

_____

_____

Which of the following services will be appropriate for you?

Extended Time Tests _____

Distraction Reduced
Environment for Tests   _____

Taped Texts   _____

LD Specialist   _____

Skills Courses in Time
Management/Test Taking/
Organization/Note taking   _____

Tutors   _____

Note takers   _____

Counseling   _____

Reduced Course Load   _____

Study Skills   _____

Support Group   _____

What are your career interests?

_____

_____

PLANNING A COLLEGE VISIT:

- The student should call to arrange for a visit.
- Visit while classes are in session.
- Meet with admissions and special support service providers.
- Take a guided tour.
- Attend a class.
- Eat a meal on campus.
- Drive around the boundaries of the campus.
- Take pictures, take notes, and talk to students on campus.
- Take parents or family members along (but not in the interview).
- Get available information on disability services.
- E-mail or write thank-you notes.

HOW TO USE THIS GUIDE

The K&W Guide to Colleges for Students with Learning Differences includes information on colleges and universities that offer services to students with learning differences such as specific learning disabilities, Attention Deficit Hyperactivity Disorder or Asperger Syndrome Disorder.

Learning Disability (LD): A learning disability is a neurological condition that interferes with an individual's ability to store, process, or produce information.

Attention Deficit Hyperactive Disorder (ADHD): ADHD individuals generally have problems paying attention or concentrating. They can't seem to follow directions and are easily bored or frustrated with tasks. They also tend to move constantly and are impulsive, not stopping to think before they act. These behaviors are generally common in children. But they occur more often than usual and are more severe in a child with ADHD.

Autism Spectrum Disorder (ASD): are a group of developmental disabilities that can cause significant social, communication and behavioral challenges.

No two colleges are identical in the programs or services they provide, but there are some similarities. For the purpose of this guide, the services and programs at the various colleges have been grouped into three categories.

STRUCTURED PROGRAMS (SP)

Colleges with Structured Programs offer the most comprehensive services for students with learning disabilities. The director and/or staff are certified in learning disabilities or related areas. The director is actively involved in the admission decision and, often, the criteria for admission may be more flexible than general admission requirements. Services are highly structured and students are involved in developing plans to meet their particular learning styles and needs. Often students in Structured Programs sign a contract agreeing to actively participate in the program. There is usually an additional fee for the enhanced services. Students who have participated in a Structured Program or Structured Services in high school such as the Learning Disabilities Resource Program, individualized or modified coursework, tutorial assistance, academic monitoring, note-takers, test accommodations, or skill classes might benefit from exploring colleges with Structured Programs or Coordinated Services.

COORDINATED SERVICES (CS)

Coordinated Services differ from Structured Programs in that the services are not as comprehensive. These services are provided by at least one certified learning disability specialist. The staff is knowledgeable and trained to provide assistance to students to develop strategies for their individual needs. The director of the program or services may be involved in the admission decision, be in a position to offer recommendations to the admissions office on the potential success of the applicant, or to assist the students with an appeal if denied admission to the college. Receiving these services generally requires specific documentation of the learning disability—students are encouraged to self-identify prior to entry. Students voluntarily request accommodations or services in the Coordinated Services category, and there may be specific skills courses or remedial classes available or required for students with learning disabilities who are admitted probationally or conditionally. High school students who may have enrolled in some modified or remedial courses, utilized test accommodations, or required tutorial assistance, but who typically requested services only as needed, might benefit from exploring colleges with Coordinated Services or Services.

SERVICES (S)

Services are the least comprehensive of the three categories. Colleges offering Services generally are complying with the federal mandate requiring reasonable accommodations to all students with appropriate and current documentation. These colleges routinely require documentation of the disability in order for the students with LD/ADHD to receive accommodations. Staff and faculty actively support the students by providing basic services to meet the needs of the students. Services are requested on a voluntarily basis, and there may be some limitations as to what is reasonable and the degree of services available. Sometimes, just the small size of the student body allows for the necessary personal attention to help students with learning disabilities succeed in college. High school students who require minimum accommodations, but who would find comfort in knowing that services are available, knowing who the contact person is, and knowing that this person is sensitive to students with learning disabilities, might benefit from exploring colleges providing Services or Coordinated Services.

CATEGORIES USED TO DESCRIBE THE PROGRAMS AND SERVICES AT COLLEGES AND UNIVERSITIES

The categories on the following pages describe the topics of information used in this guide. Each college in the book is covered on two pages, beginning with pertinent information describing the learning disability program or services. This is followed by special admission procedures, specific information about services offered, and concludes with general college information. Please note the statement preceding the section on services and accommodations which states "Services and Accommodations are determined individually for each student based on current and appropriate documentation." Some categories are answered with: N/A (not applicable) because not all colleges were able to fit into every category included in this guide; NR (not reported) because some colleges were unable to provide the information we requested; and Y/N (Yes/No) because the answer is dependent on individual situations. The authors have made a conscientious effort to provide the most current information possible. However, names, costs, dates, policies, and other information are always subject to change, and colleges of particular interest or importance to the reader should be contacted directly for verification of the data.

The K&W Guide to Colleges for Students with Learning Differences includes information on colleges and universities that offer services to students with learning differences such as specific learning disabilities, Attention Deficit Hyperactivity Disorder or Asperger Syndrome Disorder. The colleges are arranged in State order and alphabetized within each state.

Nota Bene: The score ranges published in this edition are from the old SAT, administered prior to March 2016. For the most up-to-date information on SAT score concordance, college and university admission policies, and the new SAT, please visit PrincetonReview.com.

SCHOOL PROFILES

Auburn University at Montgomery

P.O. Box 244023, Montgomery, AL 36124-4023 • Admissions: 334-244-3615 • Fax: 334-244-3795

CAMPUS

Type of school	Public
Environment	City
Support	S

STUDENTS

Undergrad enrollment	4,234
% male/female	36/64
% from out of state	6
% frosh live on campus	39

FINANCIAL FACTS

Annual in-state tuition	$7,536
Annual out-of-state tuition	$16,944
Room and board	$6,980
Required fees	$700

GENERAL ADMISSIONS INFO

Regular application deadline	8/1

Nonfall registration accepted.

Range SAT EBRW	490–565
Range SAT Math	475–545
Range ACT Composite	19–24

ACADEMICS

Student/faculty ratio	15:1
% students returning for sophomore year	68
% students graduating within 4 years	9
% students graduating within 6 years	28

Most classes have 10–19 students.
Most lab/discussion sessions have
 10–19 students.

PROGRAMS/SERVICES FOR STUDENTS WITH LEARNING DIFFERENCES

AUM and the Center for Disability Services assist in the implementation of special accommodations in academic and campus life activities. Students needing accommodation may contact the center regarding documentation guidelines and services.

ADMISSIONS

If applying as a Bridge student, a minimum 17 ACT or 820 SAT score (taken before March 2016) or 900 SAT (taken March 2016 or after) and 2.3 GPA is required. Even if a student does not fully meet all the requirements for admission to Auburn Montgomery, the student still may find a home through the Bridge Program. This program is designed for students who meet specific academic criteria in order to enroll in courses designed to prepare them for full admission. The Bridge program provides qualified students with extra academic support for one semester prior to gaining full admission to AUM. During the Bridge semester, students will be enrolled in courses designed specifically for "bridging the gap" to a continued and successful college career. Bridge courses consist of a University Success course, as well as a Math and/or English course. Throughout the semester, faculty and staff on the Bridge team will assist students by implementing skill-building exercises for success in college. The Bridge program is designed to help familiarize students with our campus resources, while showing students how to thrive at AUM.

Additional Information

Contact Center for Disability Services for accommodations and academic support services. A student registered with the Center for Disability Services (CDS) may request a program modification or course substitution. Students with disabilities are encouraged to provide reasonable notification to instructors for exam accommodations. If CDS proctors the exam, it is the student's responsibility to contact CDS at least five days prior to an exam. Other Accommodations and Services:

ADMISSIONS INFO FOR STUDENTS WITH LEARNING DIFFERENCES

SAT/ACT required: Yes
Interview required: Not Applicable
Essay required: Not Applicable
Additional application required: Yes
Documentation required for:
 LD: Psychoeducational based on DSM-V standards, to include IQ and achievement standard test scores.
 ADHD: Psychoeducational based on DSM-V standards, to include IQ and achievement and behavioral checklist scores.
 ASD: Neuropsychological and/or psychoeducational evaluation based on DSM-V standards.
Documentation submitted to: Support Program/Services
Special Ed. HS course work accepted: Yes
Separate application required for Programs/Services: No
Contact Information
Name of program or department: Center for Disability Services
Telephone: 334-244-3631
Fax: 334-244-3907
Email: cds@aum.edu

Auburn University at Montgomery

Test accommodations including extended time frames: Proctored exams; Specialized equipment; Priority registration; Note-taking assistance; Tutor referral; Computer training; and Referral to outside sources.

GENERAL ADMISSIONS

Very important factors considered include: rigor of secondary school record, academic GPA, standardized test scores. *Freshman Admission Requirements:* High school diploma is required and GED is accepted. *Academic units recommended:* 3 English, 3 math, 2 science, 2 science labs, 2 foreign language, 2 social studies, 2 history, 2 academic electives.

ACCOMMODATIONS OR SERVICES

Accommodations are decided upon an individual basis after a thorough review of appropriate, current documentation. The accommodations requests must be supported through the documentation provided and must be logically linked to the current impact of the condition on academic functioning.

FINANCIAL AID

Students should submit: FAFSA. Applicants will be notified of awards on a rolling basis beginning 4/15. The Princeton Review suggests that all financial aid forms be submitted as soon as possible after October 1. *Need-based scholarships/grants offered:* College/university scholarship or grant aid from institutional funds; Federal Pell; SEOG; State scholarships/grants. *Loan aid offered:* Direct PLUS loans; Direct Subsidized Stafford Loans; Direct Unsubsidized Stafford Loans. Federal Work-Study Program available. Institutional employment available.

CAMPUS LIFE

Activities: Campus Ministries; Drama/theater; International Student Organization; Literary magazine; Music ensembles; Musical theater; Student government; Student newspaper.. **Organizations:** 50 registered organizations, 10 honor societies, 7 religious organizations. 3 fraternities, 6 sororities. **Athletics (Intercollegiate):** *Men:* baseball, basketball, cheerleading, soccer, tennis. *Women:* basketball, cheerleading, soccer, softball, tennis. **On-Campus Highlights:** Wellness Center, Warhawk Academic Success Center, Taylor Center/Student Union, Warhawk Alley Lounge, The Roost.

ACCOMMODATIONS

Allowed in exams:	
Calculators	Yes
Dictionary	Yes
Computer	Yes
Spell-checker	Yes
Extended test time	Yes
Scribe	Yes
Proctors	Yes
Oral exams	Yes
Note-takers	Yes
Support services for students with	
LD	Yes
ADHD	Yes
ASD	Yes
Distraction-reduced environment	Yes
Recording of lecture allowed	Yes
Reading technology:	Yes
Audio books	Yes
Other assistive technology	
Alternate test, to include Braille, e-text, Livescribe Pens, digital recorders, AT software (JAWS, Window Eyes, Zoomtext)	
Priority registration	Yes
Added costs for services:	
For LD:	No
For ADHD:	No
For ASD:	No
LD specialists	No
ADHD & ASD coaching	Yes
ASD specialists	No
Professional tutors	Yes
Peer tutors	Not Applicable
Max. hours/week for services	Varies
How professors are notified of student approved accommodations	Student

COLLEGE GRADUATION REQUIREMENTS

Course waivers allowed	Yes
In what courses	
Math (as a course substitution, no waiver)	
Course substitutions allowed	Yes
In what courses	Math

The University of Alabama in Huntsville

01 SPARKMAN DRIVE, HUNTSVILLE, AL 35899 • ADMISSIONS: 256-824-2773 • FAX: 256-824-4539

CAMPUS

Type of school	Public
Environment	City
Support	S

STUDENTS

Undergrad enrollment	6,338
% male/female	58/42
% from out of state	16
% frosh live on campus	62

FINANCIAL FACTS

Annual in-state tuition	$8,996
Annual out-of-state tuition	$19,766
Room and board	$9,603
Required fees	$846

GENERAL ADMISSIONS INFO

Application fee	$30
Regular application deadline	8/20

Nonfall registration accepted. Admission may be deferred for a maximum of 1 year.

Range SAT EBRW	520–650
Range SAT Math	540–680
Range ACT Composite	25–31

ACADEMICS

Student/faculty ratio	17:1
% students returning for sophomore year	83

Most classes have 10–19 students.

PROGRAMS/SERVICES FOR STUDENTS WITH LEARNING DIFFERENCES

The Office of Student Development Services offers a variety of services and accommodations to assist students with disabilities in eliminating barriers they encounter in pursuing higher education. The office's main objective is to provide access to academic, social, cultural, recreational, and housing opportunities at the university. A student is considered registered with Disability Support Services (DSS) when they have completed all application paperwork, their intake/registration paperwork has been approved, and they have had an interview with a 504 Coordinator. The services offered through this office encourage students to achieve and maintain autonomy.

ADMISSIONS

Each applicant is evaluated based on individual merit and demonstrated success in a rigorous academic environment. High school coursework, grade point average, and ACT/SAT scores are weighed heavily; however, these criteria do not constitute the entire foundation for an admission decision. An applicant with a grade point average of 2.9 and a composite score of 20 on the ACT or an equivalent SAT score, for example, is considered a strong candidate for admission. UAH does not require letters of recommendation or an essay for admission consideration. There is no special LD admission process. If a student becomes subject to academic suspension, the suspension is for a minimum of one term, and the student must petition the Admissions Committee for approval to reenroll.

Additional Information

The Academic Coaching Program helps UAH students improve their performance in and out of class by offering sessions on study, learning, and self-management strategies. Academic coaches can help students: Learn how to prioritize and manage their time; Set clear and relevant goals; Utilize strategies that reflect their learning preferences; Engage in effective study and learning habits; Reflect on strategies to help them stay motivated; Prepare for tests.

ADMISSIONS INFO FOR STUDENTS WITH LEARNING DIFFERENCES

SAT/ACT required: Yes
Interview required: No
Essay required: No
Additional application required: No
Documentation required for:
 LD: Psycho ed evaluation
 ADHD: Diagnosis based on DSM-V; history of behaviors impairing functioning in academic setting; diagnostic interview; history of symptoms; evidence of ongoing behaviors.
 ASD: Diagnosis based on DSM-V; history of behaviors impairing functioning in academic setting; diagnostic interview; history of symptoms; evidence of ongoing behaviors.
Documentation submitted to: Disability Support Services
Special Ed. HS course work accepted: Yes
Separate application required for Programs/Services: Yes
Contact Information
Name of program or department: Disability Support Services
Telephone: 256-824-1997
Fax: 256-824-5655
Email: dssproctor@uah.edu

The University of Alabama in Huntsville

GENERAL ADMISSIONS

Very important factors considered include: academic GPA, standardized test scores. *Other factors considered include:* level of applicant's interest. *Freshman Admission Requirements:* High school diploma is required and GED is accepted. *Academic units required:* 4 English, 3 math, 3 science, 4 social studies, 6 academic electives. *Academic units recommended:* 4 English, 4 math, 4 science, 2 science labs, 2 foreign language, 4 social studies, 6 academic electives.

ACCOMMODATIONS OR SERVICES

Accommodations are decided upon an individual basis after a thorough review of appropriate, current documentation. The accommodations requests must be supported through the documentation provided and must be logically linked to the current impact of the condition on academic functioning.

FINANCIAL AID

Students should submit: FAFSA. Applicants will be notified of awards on a rolling basis beginning 4/1. The Princeton Review suggests that all financial aid forms be submitted as soon as possible after October 1. *Need-based scholarships/grants offered:* College/university scholarship or grant aid from institutional funds; Federal Nursing Scholarships; Federal Pell; Private scholarships; SEOG; State scholarships/grants. *Loan aid offered:* Direct PLUS loans; Direct Subsidized Stafford Loans; Direct Unsubsidized Stafford Loans. Federal Work-Study Program available. Institutional employment available.

CAMPUS LIFE

Activities: Campus Ministries; Choral groups; Concert band; Dance; Drama/theater; International Student Organization; Jazz band; Model UN; Music ensembles; Musical theater; Opera; Pep band; Student government; Student newspaper. **Organizations:** 52 registered organizations, 24 honor societies, 5 religious organizations. 7 fraternities, 4 sororities. **Athletics (Intercollegiate):** *Men:* baseball, basketball, cheerleading, cross-country, ice hockey, soccer, tennis, track/field (outdoor), track/field (indoor). *Women:* basketball, cheerleading, cross-country, soccer, softball, tennis, track/field (outdoor), track/field (indoor), volleyball. **On-Campus Highlights:** Charger Union, University Fitness Center, Charger Village, Central Campus Residence Hall, Shelby Center.

ACCOMMODATIONS

Allowed in exams:

Calculators	Yes
Dictionary	Yes
Computer	Yes
Spell-checker	Yes
Extended test time	Yes
Scribe	Yes
Proctors	Yes
Oral exams	Yes
Note-takers	Yes

Support services for students with

LD	Yes
ADHD	Yes
ASD	Yes
Distraction-reduced environment	Yes
Recording of lecture allowed	Yes
Reading technology:	Yes
Audio books	No
Other assistive technology	Yes
Priority registration	Yes

Added costs for services:

For LD:	No
For ADHD:	No
For ASD:	No
LD specialists	No
ADHD & ASD coaching	Academic Coaching Program through Student Success Center
ASD specialists	No
Professional tutors	No
Peer tutors	No
Max. hours/week for services	Unlimited
How professors are notified of student approved accommodations	Student and Director

COLLEGE GRADUATION REQUIREMENTS

Course waivers allowed	Yes
In what courses	
Individual case-by-case decisions	
Course substitutions allowed	Yes
In what courses	
Individual case-by-case decisions	

The University of Alabama–Tuscaloosa

Box 870100, Tuscaloosa, AL 35487-0132 • Admissions: 205-348-5666 • Fax: 205-348-9046

CAMPUS

Type of school	Public
Environment	City
Support	S

STUDENTS

Undergrad enrollment	32,387
% male/female	44/56
% from out of state	60
% frosh live on campus	95

FINANCIAL FACTS

Annual in-state tuition	$10,780
Annual out-of-state tuition	$29,230
Room and board	$10,102

GENERAL ADMISSIONS INFO

Application fee	$40
Priority deadline	2/1

Nonfall registration accepted. Admission may be deferred for a maximum of one year.

Range SAT EBRW	530–640
Range SAT Math	520–640
Range ACT Composite	23–32

ACADEMICS

Student/faculty ratio	23:1
% students returning for sophomore year	87
% students graduating within 4 years	44
% students graduating within 6 years	68

Most classes have 20–29 students.
Most lab/discussion sessions have 20–29 students.

PROGRAMS/SERVICES FOR STUDENTS WITH LEARNING DIFFERENCES

Documented physical or mental condition that substantially limits one or more major life activities may be eligible for services and accommodations. Those seeking services for LD and/or ADHD must provide documentation including a narrative report of a psychoeducational or neuropsychological evaluation; a summary of areas of testing; actual test scores; overall summary and diagnosis; and recommendations and suggested strategies for student, professors, and academic advisors. The Office of Disability Services may request further testing. Complete documentation requirements can be found at www.ods.ua.edu.

ADMISSIONS

All students must meet regular entrance requirements. Decisions about the potential for academic success at UA are based on performance on the ACT and/or SAT, GPA, and courses. EX: A student with a 21 ACT or 1000 SAT [critical reading and math scores only] along with a GPA of 3.0 should be successful at the University. ACT with Writing or SAT with Writing required. 4 yrs. English, 4 years Social Sciences, 3 yrs. Math, 3 yrs. Natural Sciences, 1 unit of foreign language, and 4 units of academic courses (recommend courses in fine arts or computer literacy, with additional courses in mathematics, natural sciences, and foreign language.) Students who exceed the minimum number of units in math, natural sciences, or foreign language will be given additional consideration. An interview with the Office of Disability Services is recommended.

Additional Information

Accommodations are tailored to individual needs according to diagnostic testing. Accommodations may include: early registration; testing modifications; academic aids such as taping lectures, use of calculators, dictionaries, spell checkers, note takers, and materials in alternative formats. UA-ACTS program provides individualized services to help students develop appropriate skills for self-advocacy, daily living, and social interaction that will contribute to their success as an independent adult.

ADMISSIONS INFO FOR STUDENTS WITH LEARNING DIFFERENCES

SAT/ACT required: Yes
Interview required: No
Essay required: Not Applicable
Additional application required: Yes
Documentation required for:
 LD: Yes
 ADHD: Yes
 ASD: No
Documentation submitted to: Office of Disability Services
Special Ed. HS course work accepted: No
Separate application required for Programs/Services: For LD.
Contact Information
Name of program or department: Office of Disability Services
Telephone: 205-348-4285
Fax: 205-348-0804
Email: ods@ua.edu

The University of Alabama–Tuscaloosa

GENERAL ADMISSIONS

Very important factors considered include: rigor of secondary school record, academic GPA, standardized test scores. *Important factors considered include:* class rank. *Other factors considered include:* application essay, recommendation(s), interview, extracurricular activities, talent/ ability, character/personal qualities, first generation, alumni/ae relation, volunteer work, work experience. *Freshman Admission Requirements:* High school diploma is required and GED is accepted. *Academic units required:* 4 English, 3 math, 3 science, 2 science labs, 1 foreign language, 4 social studies, 5 academic electives. *Academic units recommended:* 4 English, 3 math, 3 science, 2 science labs, 2 foreign language, 4 social studies, 5 academic electives.

ACCOMMODATIONS OR SERVICES

Accommodations are decided upon an individual basis after a thorough review of appropriate, current documentation. The accommodations requests must be supported through the documentation provided and must be logically linked to the current impact of the condition on academic functioning.

FINANCIAL AID

Students should submit: FAFSA. Applicants will be notified of awards on a rolling basis beginning 4/1. The Princeton Review suggests that all financial aid forms be submitted as soon as possible after October 1. *Need-based scholarships/grants offered:* College/university scholarship or grant aid from institutional funds; Federal Nursing Scholarships; Federal Pell; Private scholarships; SEOG; State scholarships/grants. *Loan aid offered:* Direct PLUS loans; Direct Subsidized Stafford Loans; Direct Unsubsidized Stafford Loans. Federal Work-Study Program available. Institutional employment available.

CAMPUS LIFE

Activities: Campus Ministries; Choral groups; Concert band; Dance; Drama/theater; International Student Organization; Jazz band; Literary magazine; Marching band; Model UN; Music ensembles; Musical theater; Opera; Pep band; Radio station; Student government; Student newspaper; Student-run film society; Symphony orchestra; Television station. **Organizations:** 294 registered organizations, 66 honor societies, 30 religious organizations. 31 fraternities, 23 sororities. **Athletics (Intercollegiate):** *Men:* baseball, basketball, cross-country, diving, football, golf, swimming, tennis, track/field (outdoor), track/field (indoor). *Women:* basketball, crew/rowing, cross-country, diving, golf, gymnastics, soccer, softball, swimming, tennis, track/field (outdoor), track/field (indoor), volleyball. **On-Campus Highlights:** Ferguson Center Student Union, Amelia Gayle Gorgas Library, Bryant-Denny Stadium, Malone-Hood Plaza/Foster Auditorium, Museum of Natural History.

ACCOMMODATIONS

Allowed in exams:	
Calculators	Yes
Dictionary	Yes
Computer	Yes
Spell-checker	Yes
Extended test time	Yes
Scribe	Yes
Proctors	Yes
Oral exams	Yes
Note-takers	Yes
Support services for students with	
LD	Yes
ADHD	Yes
ASD	Yes
Distraction-reduced environment	Yes
Recording of lecture allowed	Yes
Reading technology:	Yes
Audio books	Yes
Other assistive technology	
E-text conversion; training in the use of certain assistive technology programs.	
Priority registration	Yes
Added costs for services:	
For LD:	No
For ADHD:	No
For ASD:	No
LD specialists	No
ADHD & ASD coaching	Yes
ASD specialists	Yes
Professional tutors	Yes
Peer tutors	Not Applicable
Max. hours/week for services	Varies
How professors are notified of student approved accommodations	Student

COLLEGE GRADUATION REQUIREMENTS

Course waivers allowed	No
Course substitutions allowed	Yes
In what courses	

Substitutions are sometimes granted, but no courses are waived. Courses cannot be substituted if doing so would substantially alter the nature of the program or if the course is required as part of the student's major.

University of Alaska Anchorage

3211 PROVIDENCE DRIVE, ANCHORAGE, AK 99508-8046 • ADMISSIONS: 907-786-1480 • FAX: 907-786-4888

CAMPUS

Type of school	Public
Environment	City
Support	S

STUDENTS

Undergrad enrollment	13,390
% male/female	42/58
% from out of state	10

FINANCIAL FACTS

Annual in-state tuition	$4,950
Annual out-of-state tuition	$17,400
Room and board	$9,827
Required fees	$832

GENERAL ADMISSIONS INFO

Application fee	$50
Regular application deadline	7/1

Nonfall registration accepted. Admission may be deferred for a maximum of 1 year.

Range SAT EBRW	430–580
Range SAT Math	440–570
Range ACT Composite	NR

ACADEMICS

Student/faculty ratio	12:1
% students returning for sophomore year	73

Most classes have 10–19 students.
Most lab/discussion sessions have 20–29 students.

PROGRAMS/SERVICES FOR STUDENTS WITH LEARNING DIFFERENCES

The University of Alaska—Anchorage provides equal opportunities for students who have disabilities. Academic support services are available to students with learning disabilities. Staff trained to work with students with disabilities coordinate these services. To allow time for service coordination, students are encouraged to contact the Disability Support Services (DSS) office several weeks before the beginning of each semester. Ongoing communication with the staff throughout the semester is encouraged.

ADMISSIONS

All students must meet the same admission requirements. The university has an open enrollment policy. However, admission to specific programs of study may have specific course work or testing criteria that all students will have to meet. While formal admission is encouraged, the university has an open enrollment policy that allows students to register for courses in which they have the adequate background. Open enrollment does not guarantee subsequent formal admission to certificate or degree programs. Individuals with learning disabilities are admitted via the standard admissions procedures that apply to all students submitting applications for formal admission. Students with documentation of a learning disability are eligible to receive support services once they are enrolled in the university. LD students who selfdisclose during the admission process are referred to DSS for information about services and accommodations.

Additional Information

Classes are available for all students in the areas of vocabulary building and study skills. There is no separate tutoring for students with learning disabilities. Tutorial help is available for all students in the reading and writing labs and the Learning Resource Center. With appropriate documentation, students with LD or ADHD may have access to accommodations such as testing modifications, distraction-free testing environments, scribes, proctors, note-takers, calculators, dictionaries, and computers in exams, and access to assistive technology. Services and accommodations are available for undergraduate and graduate students. The Academic Coach Center helps students develop academic skills. It is offered in individual sessions with a peer coach.

ADMISSIONS INFO FOR STUDENTS WITH LEARNING DIFFERENCES

SAT/ACT required: Yes
Interview required: No
Essay required: No
Additional application required: No
Documentation required for:
 LD: Psycho ed evaluation
 ADHD: Diagnosis based on DSM-V; history of behaviors impairing functioning in academic setting; diagnostic interview; history of symptoms; evidence of ongoing behaviors.
 ASD: Psycho ed evaluation
Documentation submitted to: Disability Support services
Special Ed. HS course work accepted: Yes
Separate application required for Programs/Services: No
Contact Information
Name of program or department: Disability Support Services
Telephone: 907-786-4530
Fax: 907-786-4531

University of Alaska Anchorage

General Admissions
Very important factors considered include: rigor of secondary school record. *Other factors considered include:* class rank, standardized test scores, talent/ability. *Freshman Admission Requirements:* High school diploma is required and GED is accepted.

Accommodations or Services
Accommodations are decided upon an individual basis after a thorough review of appropriate, current documentation. The accommodations requests must be supported through the documentation provided and must be logically linked to the current impact of the condition on academic functioning.

Financial Aid
Students should submit: FAFSA; Institution's own financial aid form. Applicants will be notified of awards on a rolling basis beginning 3/15. The Princeton Review suggests that all financial aid forms be submitted as soon as possible after October 1. *Need-based scholarships/grants offered:* College/university scholarship or grant aid from institutional funds; Federal Pell; Private scholarships; SEOG; State scholarships/grants. *Loan aid offered:* Federal Work-Study Program available. Institutional employment available.

Campus Life
Activities: Campus Ministries; Choral groups; Dance; Drama/theater; International Student Organization; Jazz band; Literary magazine; Model UN; Music ensembles; Musical theater; Opera; Radio station; Student government; Student newspaper; Student-run film society. **Organizations:** 70 registered organizations, 5 honor societies, 5 religious organizations. 1 fraternity, 2 sororities. **Athletics (Intercollegiate):** *Men:* basketball, cross-country, ice hockey, skiing (downhill/alpine), skiing (nordic/cross-country). *Women:* basketball, cross-country, gymnastics, skiing (downhill/alpine), skiing (nordic/cross-country), volleyball. **On-Campus Highlights:** Campus Center, Wells Fargo Sports Center, Creakside Eatery, Cuddy Center, Student Health Center.

ACCOMMODATIONS

Allowed in exams:

Calculators	Yes
Dictionary	Yes
Computer	Yes
Spell-checker	Yes
Extended test time	Yes
Scribe	Yes
Proctors	Yes
Oral exams	Yes
Note-takers	Yes

Support services for students with

LD	Yes
ADHD	Yes
ASD	Yes
Distraction-reduced environment	Yes
Recording of lecture allowed	Yes
Reading technology:	Yes
Audio books	No
Other assistive technology	Yes
Priority registration	Yes

Added costs for services:

For LD:	No
For ADHD:	No
For ASD:	No
LD specialists	No
ADHD & ASD coaching	No
ASD specialists	No
Professional tutors	No
Peer tutors	Yes
Max. hours/week for services	Unlimited
How professors are notified of student approved accommodations	By student

initiated letters sent through Disability Support

COLLEGE GRADUATION REQUIREMENTS

Course waivers allowed	Yes
In what courses	
Individual case-by-case basis	
Course substitutions allowed	Yes
In what courses	
Individual case-by-case basis	

University of Alaska Fairbanks

PO Box 757500, Fairbanks, AK 99775-7480 • Admissions: 907-474-7500 • Fax: 907-474-5379

CAMPUS
Type of school	Public
Environment	City
Support	S

STUDENTS
Undergrad enrollment	5,445
% male/female	45/55
% from out of state	14
% frosh live on campus	53

FINANCIAL FACTS
Annual in-state tuition	$7,020
Annual out-of-state tuition	$23,190
Room and board	$8,930
Required fees	$1,780

GENERAL ADMISSIONS INFO
Application fee	$50
Priority deadline	2/15
Regular application deadline	6/15

Nonfall registration accepted. Admission may be deferred for a maximum of 1 year.

Range SAT EBRW	480–610
Range SAT Math	480–610
Range ACT Composite	18–26

ACADEMICS
Student/faculty ratio	11:1
% students returning for sophomore year	75

Most classes have 10–19 students.

PROGRAMS/SERVICES FOR STUDENTS WITH LEARNING DIFFERENCES

The University of Alaska is committed to providing equal opportunity to students with disabilities. Disability Services at The University of Alaska—Fairbanks provides assistance to students with documented disabilities. The purpose of Disability Services (DS) is to provide equal access to higher education for students with disabilities. Campus services include the Academic Advising Center, which is responsible for advising incoming freshmen and students with undeclared majors. It provides explanations of programs and their requirements and assists students with choosing majors, selecting electives, and choosing classes consistent with their academic and career goals. Student Support Services provides academic and personal support, including developmental classes and tutoring for students who are economically disadvantaged, do not have a parent who graduated from college, or have a documented disability. Disabled Students of UAF is an organization that provides peer support groups for UAF students experiencing disabilities. The Student Development and Learning Center provides tutoring, individual instruction in basic skills and counseling, career-planning services, and assessment testing. Disability Services welcomes inquiries and seeks to make the college experience a success for students with disabilities.

ADMISSIONS

To enter as a freshman for a baccalaureate degree there are two options: 1) high school diplomas, 2.5 in core courses and GPA 3.0 and no cut-off on ACT/SAT; 2) high school diploma, 2.5 in core courses, a minimum 2.5 GPA and ACT 18 or SAT 1290. Core curriculum 4 years English, 3 years math, 3 years social sciences, and 3 years natural or physical sciences. Foreign languages are recommended. Students can be provisionally accepted if they make up course deficiencies with a C or better in each of the developmental or university courses and complete nine credits of general degree requirements with a C or better.

Additional Information

Services include individual counseling to determine necessary accommodations; arrangements for special services such as readers, scribes, and note-takers; advocacy with faculty and staff; assistance to faculty and staff in determining appropriate accommodations; help in determining specific needs for students with learning disabilities; and referral to campus and community agencies for additional services. Basic

ADMISSIONS INFO FOR STUDENTS WITH LEARNING DIFFERENCES

SAT/ACT required: Yes
Interview required: No
Essay required: No
Additional application required: No
Documentation required for:
  LD: Psycho ed evaluation
  ADHD: Diagnosis based on DSM-V; history of behaviors impairing functioning in academic setting; diagnostic interview; history of symptoms; evidence of ongoing behaviors.
  ASD: Psycho ed evaluation
Documentation submitted to: Disability services
Special Ed. HS course work accepted: Yes
Separate application required for Programs/Services: No
Contact Information
Name of program or department: UAF Office of Disability Services
Telephone: (907) 474-5655
Fax: (907) 474-5688
Email: mcmatthews@alaska.edu

University of Alaska Fairbanks

study-skills classes are offered for all students and may be taken for credit. Services and accommodations are provided for any student registered for at least 1 credit.

GENERAL ADMISSIONS

Very important factors considered include: academic GPA, standardized test scores. *Freshman Admission Requirements:* High school diploma is required and GED is not accepted. *Academic units required:* 4 English, 3 math, 3 science, 1 science lab, 3 social studies. *Academic units recommended:* 2 foreign language.

ACCOMMODATIONS OR SERVICES

Accommodations are decided upon an individual basis after a thorough review of appropriate, current documentation. The accommodations requests must be supported through the documentation provided and must be logically linked to the current impact of the condition on academic functioning.

FINANCIAL AID

Students should submit: FAFSA; Institution's own financial aid form. Applicants will be notified of awards on a rolling basis beginning 3/1. The Princeton Review suggests that all financial aid forms be submitted as soon as possible after October 1. *Need-based scholarships/grants offered:* College/university scholarship or grant aid from institutional funds; Federal Pell; Private scholarships; SEOG; State scholarships/grants. *Loan aid offered:* Direct PLUS loans; Direct Subsidized Stafford Loans; Direct Unsubsidized Stafford Loans. Federal Work-Study Program available. Institutional employment available.

CAMPUS LIFE

Activities: Campus Ministries; Choral groups; Dance; Drama/theater; International Student Organization; Jazz band; Literary magazine; Model UN; Music ensembles; Radio station; Student government; Student newspaper; Symphony orchestra. **Organizations:** 122 registered organizations, 11 honor societies, 10 religious organizations, 1 fraternity, 1 sorority. **Athletics (Intercollegiate):** *Men:* basketball, cross-country, ice hockey, riflery, skiing (nordic/cross-country). *Women:* basketball, cross-country, riflery, skiing (nordic/cross-country), volleyball. **On-Campus Highlights:** Wood Center (includes food court), Student Recreation Center (SRC), Rasmuson Library, Groomed cross-country ski trails on campus, Hess Recreation Center.

ACCOMMODATIONS

Allowed in exams:	
Calculators	No
Dictionary	Yes
Computer	Yes
Spell-checker	Yes
Extended test time	Yes
Scribe	Yes
Proctors	Yes
Oral exams	Yes
Note-takers	Yes
Support services for students with	
LD	Yes
ADHD	Yes
ASD	Yes
Distraction-reduced environment	Yes
Recording of lecture allowed	Yes
Reading technology:	Yes
Audio books	No
Other assistive technology	Yes
Priority registration	Yes
Added costs for services:	
For LD:	No
For ADHD:	No
For ASD:	No
LD specialists	No
ADHD & ASD coaching	No
ASD specialists	No
Professional tutors	No
Peer tutors	No
Max. hours/week for services	N/A
How professors are notified of student approved accommodations	Student

COLLEGE GRADUATION REQUIREMENTS

Course waivers allowed	No
Course substitutions allowed	Yes
In what courses	
Depends on documentation	

Arizona State University at the Tempe campus

Admissions Office, Tempe, AZ 85287-0112 • Admissions: 480-965-7788 • Fax: 480-965-3610

CAMPUS
Type of school	Public
Environment	Metropolis
Support	S

STUDENTS
Undergrad enrollment	42,181
% male/female	57/43
% from out of state	25
% frosh live on campus	72

FINANCIAL FACTS
Annual in-state tuition	$10,104
Annual out-of-state tuition	$27,618
Room and board	$12,648
Required fees	$718

GENERAL ADMISSIONS INFO
Application fee	$50
Priority deadline	2/1

Nonfall registration accepted. Admission may be deferred for a maximum of 2 years.

Range SAT EBRW	560–670
Range SAT Math	560–680
Range ACT Composite	22–29

ACADEMICS
Student/faculty ratio	22:1
% students returning for sophomore year	87
% students graduating within 4 years	45
% students graduating within 6 years	63

Most classes have 10–19 students. Most lab/discussion sessions have 10–19 students.

PROGRAMS/SERVICES FOR STUDENTS WITH LEARNING DIFFERENCES

The Disability Resource Center provides services to qualified students with disabilities on all ASU campuses. For convenience, students will find offices located at the Downtown, Polytechnic, Tempe, and West locations. The Arizona State University (ASU) Disability Resource Centers (DRC) on each ASU campus facilitate access to educational, social, and career opportunities for qualified ASU students with disabilities, including but not limited to students with learning disabilities and attention deficit hyperactivity disorder. Qualified DRC professional staff on each ASU campus are recommending and implementing reasonable and effective disability accommodations, resources, services, and auxiliary aids upon student request to facilitate student access. DRC services and accommodations are recommended individually for each student. DRC students are provided with self-advocacy training and academic resources and referrals, e.g., Student Success Centers, Writing Centers, Career Services, Enrollment Services, Student Financial Assistance, academic advising referrals, and encouraged to seek out methods for attaining the highest possible goals and achievement.

ADMISSIONS

All students are required to meet the same admissions requirements for the university. Students with LD submit the ASU application, self-disclose and submit documentation. Courses required: 4 English, 4 math, 3 science, 2 social science, 2 foreign language and 1 fine arts. Applicants must meet at least one of the following: Top 25 percent or 3.0 GPA or 22 ACT (24 ACT non-resident) or SAT 1040 (1110 non-resident). All applicants not meeting these standards are evaluated through an Individual Review process.

ADMISSIONS INFO FOR STUDENTS WITH LEARNING DIFFERENCES
SAT/ACT required: No
Interview required: Not Applicable
Essay required: Not Applicable
Additional application required: Not Applicable
Documentation required for:
  LD: The DRC will accept diagnoses of a Learning Disability that is based on comprehensive, age-appropriate, psychoeducational evaluations that demonstrate current functional limitations of the disability.
  ADHD: The DRC will accept diagnoses of ADHD that is based on comprehensive, age-appropriate, psychoeducational evaluations that demonstrate current functional limitations of the disability.
  ASD: The DRC will accept diagnoses of an Autism Spectrum Disorder that is based on comprehensive, age-appropriate, psychoeducational evaluations that demonstrate current functional limitations of the disability.
Documentation submitted to: Support Program/Services
Special Ed. HS course work accepted: Not Applicable
Separate application required for Programs/Services: For LD, ADHD, ASD.
Contact Information
Name of program or department: Disability Resource Center
Telephone: (480)727-1368
Fax: (480) 727-5459
Email: drc@asu.edu

Arizona State University at the Tempe campus

Additional Information
Contact the Disability Resource Center for further information. https://eoss.asu.edu/drc. Autistics on Campus is a new social hangout for students with Autism Spectrum Disorder looking to get involved in social activities across campus and create opportunities for future activities.

GENERAL ADMISSIONS
Very important factors considered include: class rank, academic GPA, standardized test scores. *Important factors considered include:* rigor of secondary school record. *Other factors considered include:* state residency. *Freshman Admission Requirements:* High school diploma is required and GED is accepted. *Academic units required:* 4 English, 4 math, 3 science, 3 science labs, 2 foreign language, 1 social studies, 1 history, and 1 unit from above areas or other academic areas.

ACCOMMODATIONS OR SERVICES
Accommodations are decided upon an individual basis after a thorough review of appropriate, current documentation. The accommodations requests must be supported through the documentation provided and must be logically linked to the current impact of the condition on academic functioning.

FINANCIAL AID
Students should submit: FAFSA. Applicants will be notified of awards on a rolling basis beginning 3/1. The Princeton Review suggests that all financial aid forms be submitted as soon as possible after October 1. *Need-based scholarships/grants offered:* College/university scholarship or grant aid from institutional funds; Federal Pell; Private scholarships; SEOG; State scholarships/grants; United Negro College Fund. *Loan aid offered:* Direct PLUS loans; Direct Subsidized Stafford Loans; Direct Unsubsidized Stafford Loans. Federal Work-Study Program available. Institutional employment available.

CAMPUS LIFE
Activities: Campus Ministries; Choral groups; Concert band; Dance; Drama/theater; International Student Organization; Jazz band; Literary magazine; Marching band; Model UN; Music ensembles; Musical theater; Opera; Pep band; Student government; Student newspaper; Student-run film society; Symphony orchestra. **Organizations:** 675 registered organizations, 16 honor societies, 51 religious organizations. 32 fraternities, 22 sororities. **Athletics (Intercollegiate):** *Men:* baseball, basketball, cross-country, diving, football, golf, swimming, track/field, wrestling. *Women:* basketball, cross-country, diving, golf, gymnastics, soccer, softball, swimming, tennis, track/field, volleyball, water polo. **On-Campus Highlights:** ASU Memorial Union, Grady Gammage Memorial Auditorium, Barrett Honors Complex, Hayden Library, Sun Devil Fitness Complex.

ACCOMMODATIONS

Allowed in exams:	
Calculators	Yes
Dictionary	Yes
Computer	Yes
Spell-checker	Yes
Extended test time	Yes
Scribe	Yes
Proctors	Yes
Oral exams	Yes
Note-takers	Yes
Support services for students with	
LD	Yes
ADHD	Yes
ASD	Yes
Distraction-reduced environment	Yes
Recording of lecture allowed	Yes
Reading technology:	Yes
Audio books	Yes
Other assistive technology	
All accommodations listed depend on the impact of the disability and the reasonableness of the accommodaitons based on the circumstances to ensure access.	
Priority registration	Yes
Added costs for services:	
For LD:	No
For ADHD:	No
For ASD:	No
LD specialists	Yes
ADHD & ASD coaching	Yes
ASD specialists	No
Professional tutors	Yes
Peer tutors	Yes
Max. hours/week for services	Varies
How professors are notified of student approved accommodations	
Director and Student	

COLLEGE GRADUATION REQUIREMENTS

Course waivers allowed	No
Course substitutions allowed	Yes
In what courses	Math, Foreign Language

Northern Arizona University

PO Box 4084, Flagstaff, AZ 86011-4084 • Admissions: 928-523-5511 • Fax: 928-523-6023

CAMPUS

Type of school	Public
Environment	Town
Support	CS

STUDENTS

Undergrad enrollment	26,974
% male/female	40/60
% from out of state	29
% frosh live on campus	87

FINANCIAL FACTS

Annual in-state tuition	$10,038
Annual out-of-state tuition	$24,654
Room and board	$10,282
Required fees	$1,174

GENERAL ADMISSIONS INFO

Application fee	$25

Nonfall registration accepted. Admission may be deferred.

Range SAT EBRW	520–620
Range SAT Math	510–610
Range ACT Composite	20–25

ACADEMICS

Student/faculty ratio	19:1
% students returning for sophomore year	76
% students graduating within 4 years	40
% students graduating within 6 years	55

Most classes have 20–29 students.
Most lab/discussion sessions have 20–29 students.

PROGRAMS/SERVICES FOR STUDENTS WITH LEARNING DIFFERENCES

In order to evaluate accommodation and service requests, Disability Resources will need information about how your disability is likely to impact you here at Northern Arizona University. We want to understand the relevant impacts of your disability on tasks like communication, reading, writing, housing, technology, dining, the physical environment, classroom and laboratory and on line learning, etc. Information on the impacts of physical (mobility, dexterity, endurance, etc.), perceptual, cognitive (attention, distractibility, communication, etc.), and behavioral abilities may be helpful as well. Any information/documentation students can readily share during or prior to the first meeting is helpful and can save the need for follow up meetings with Disability Resources.

ADMISSIONS

To be a qualified individual with a disability, students must meet our academic and technical standards required for admission. General admission requirements for unconditional admission include: 4 years of English, 4 years of math; 2 years of social science with 1 year being American history; 2–3 years of science lab with additional requirements; 1 year of fine arts; and 2 years of a foreign language. (Students may be admitted conditionally with course deficiencies, but not in both math and science). In-state residents should have a 2.5 GPA, be in the top 50 percent of their high school class (a 3.0 GPA or being in the upper 25 percent of their graduating class is required for non-residents), or earn an SAT combined score of 930 (1010 for non-residents) or an ACT score of 22 (24 for non-residents). Conditional admissions is possible with a 2.5–2.99 GPA or being in the top 50 percent of their graduating class and strong ACT/SAT scores. Exceptional admission may be offered to 10 percent of the new freshmen applicants or transfer applicants. The Writing section of the ACT is not required.

ADMISSIONS INFO FOR STUDENTS WITH LEARNING DIFFERENCES

SAT/ACT required: No
Interview required: No
Essay required: Not Applicable
Additional application required: Yes
Documentation required for:
 LD: Psychoeducational evaluation
 ADHD: Psychoeducational evaluation
 ASD: Psychoeducational evaluation
Documentation submitted to: Disability Resources
Special Ed. HS course work accepted: Yes
Separate application required for Programs/Services: For LD, ADHD, ASD.
Contact Information
Name of program or department: Disability Resources
Telephone: 928-523-8773
Fax: 928-523-8747
Email: DR@nau.edu

Northern Arizona University

Additional Information

Skills classes are available in note-taking, study techniques, reading, memory and learning, overcoming math anxiety, speed reading, time management, test-taking strategies. The university offers the following courses: How to Make Math Easy, How to Get Started Writing, How to Edit Writing, and How to Prepare for Final Exams. All services and accommodations are available for undergraduate and graduate students.

GENERAL ADMISSIONS

Very important factors considered include: rigor of secondary school record, academic GPA. *Important factors considered include:* class rank, standardized test scores. *Freshman Admission Requirements:* High school diploma is required and GED is accepted. *Academic units required:* 4 English, 4 math, 3 science, 3 science labs, 2 foreign language, 1 social studies, 1 history, and 1 unit from above areas or other academic areas.

ACCOMMODATIONS OR SERVICES

Accommodations are decided upon an individual basis after a thorough review of appropriate, current documentation. The accommodations requests must be supported through the documentation provided and must be logically linked to the current impact of the condition on academic functioning.

FINANCIAL AID

Students should submit: FAFSA. Applicants will be notified of awards on a rolling basis beginning 2/1. The Princeton Review suggests that all financial aid forms be submitted as soon as possible after October 1. *Need-based scholarships/grants offered:* College/university scholarship or grant aid from institutional funds; Federal Nursing Scholarships; Federal Pell; Private scholarships; SEOG; State scholarships/grants. *Loan aid offered:* Direct PLUS loans; Direct Subsidized Stafford Loans; Direct Unsubsidized Stafford Loans. Federal Work-Study Program available. Institutional employment available.

CAMPUS LIFE

Activities: Campus Ministries; Choral groups; Concert band; Dance; Drama/theater; International Student Organization; Jazz band; Marching band; Model UN; Music ensembles; Musical theater; Opera; Pep band; Radio station; Student government; Student newspaper; Symphony orchestra; Television station.. **Organizations:** 193 registered organizations, 20 honor societies, 7 religious organizations. 14 fraternities, 9 sororities. **Athletics (Intercollegiate):** *Men:* basketball, cheerleading, cross-country, football, tennis, track/field (outdoor). *Women:* basketball, cheerleading, cross-country, diving, golf, soccer, swimming, tennis, track/field (outdoor), volleyball. **On-Campus Highlights:** University Union, Historic Main Quadrangle, Health and Learning Center, Cline Library, NAU Skydome.

ACCOMMODATIONS

Allowed in exams:

Calculators	Yes
Dictionary	Yes
Computer	Yes
Spell-checker	Yes
Extended test time	Yes
Scribe	Yes
Proctors	Yes
Oral exams	Yes
Note-takers	Yes

Support services for students with

LD	Yes
ADHD	Yes
ASD	Yes
Distraction-reduced environment	Yes
Recording of lecture allowed	Yes
Reading technology:	Yes
Audio books	Yes
Other assistive technology	Whatever a student might require for effective access.
Priority registration	Yes

Added costs for services:

For LD:	No
For ADHD:	No
For ASD:	No
LD specialists	No
ADHD & ASD coaching	Yes
ASD specialists	No
Professional tutors	Yes
Peer tutors	Yes
Max. hours/week for services	
How professors are notified of student approved accommodations	Student

COLLEGE GRADUATION REQUIREMENTS

Course waivers allowed	No
Course substitutions allowed	Yes

In what courses

What ever courses necessary based on the disability, granted it does not fundamentally alter the program

University of Arizona

PO Box 210066, Tucson, AZ 85721-0073 • Admissions: 520-621-3237 • Fax: 520-621-9799

CAMPUS

Type of school	Public
Environment	Metropolis
Support	SP

STUDENTS

Undergrad enrollment	34,049
% male/female	48/52
% from out of state	31
% frosh live on campus	72

FINANCIAL FACTS

Annual in-state tuition	$10,860
Annual out-of-state tuition	$34,290
Room and board	$12,648
Required fees	$718

GENERAL ADMISSIONS INFO

Application fee	$50
Priority deadline	5/1
Regular application deadline	5/1
Nonfall registration accepted.	

Range SAT EBRW	540–650
Range SAT Math	560–690
Range ACT Composite	21–28

ACADEMICS

Student/faculty ratio	15:1
% students returning for sophomore year	83
% students graduating within 4 years	45
% students graduating within 6 years	64

Most classes have 10–19 students.
Most lab/discussion sessions have 10–19 students.

Programs/Services for Students with Learning Differences

The SALT Center (Strategic Alternative Learning Techniques) is a fee-based academic support program that provides a comprehensive range of enhanced services to University of Arizona students who have learning and/or attention challenges. The SALT Center's innovative approach is recognized nationwide as one of the most successful for empowering students in the university setting. The range of services in the SALT Center facilitates student learning, self-advocacy, and independence. Students take ownership of their education through working with a Strategic Learning Specialist to create an Individualized Learning Plan; engaging in strategies for time management, organization, reading and writing; utilizing tutoring by peer tutors who are internationally certified by the College Reading and Learning Association; and accessing assistive technology in the SALT Center's technology lab.

Admissions

Students must submit a general application to the University and a SALT application. Students may check the box on the general application indicating they are interested in SALT. Students are admitted to the University and then reviewed by SALT. General admission criteria include: 4 English, 4 math, 3 science, 2 social studies, 2 foreign language, 1 fine art. Deficiencies can be made up in English with ACT sub score of 21, Math ACT sub score 24 and science ACT sub score 20. Most applicants are admissible with required courses and either 24 ACT (22 ACT resident) or SAT 1110) SAT 1040 resident) or top ¼ of the class. SALT application should be submitted early in the process. All SALT applicants should answer 3 essay questions: 1) Why are you applying to SALT and how do you plan to use the services; 2) Describe a difficult situation you have encountered in your life, and tell how you handled the situation; 3) Tell about your strengths, skills and talents. Students can submit documentation of a disability to Admissions and to SALT or answer SALT question #4 which asks for a description of academic challenges and the support services used to manage those challenges.

ADMISSIONS INFO FOR STUDENTS WITH LEARNING DIFFERENCES

SAT/ACT required: Yes
Interview required: No
Essay required: Yes
Additional application required: No
Documentation required for:
  LD: Psycho Ed Evaluation
  ADHD: Diagnosis based on DSM-V; history of behaviors impairing functioning in academic setting; diagnostic interview; history of symptoms; evidence of ongoing behaviors.
  ASD: Psycho ed evaluation
Documentation submitted to: SALT Center
Special Ed. HS course work accepted: Not Applicable
Separate application required for Programs/Services: Not Applicable
Contact Information
Name of program or department: Disability Resource Center
Telephone: 520-621-3268
Fax: 520-621-9423
Email: drc-info@email.arizona.edu

University of Arizona

Additional Information

The SALT program provides comprehensive services for four years. The fee for the lower division is $5,600 per year (includes tutoring) and for upper division the fee is $2,600 plus $21 per hour for tutoring. Life and ADHD coaching is $1350 for three months. The SALT program includes: 1) Tutoring that models learning strategies specific to the subject matter; most UA courses are supported; schedule tutors online through TutorTrac™; meet with tutors individually; attend a group review session for courses; 2) Strategic Learning Specialist is a point person for SALT and campus resources; designs Individualized Learning Plan; teaches strategies to help improve academics; monitors academic progress; and 3) Educational Technology to print, study and research; draft essays using dictation software; listen to course readings; brainstorm and organize thoughts using the latest learning apps. Life and ADHD Coaching is designed for students who benefit from the support, structure and accountability coaches provide in this partnership.

GENERAL ADMISSIONS

Very important factors considered include: rigor of secondary school record, academic GPA. *Important factors considered include:* standardized test scores, extracurricular activities, talent/ability, character/personal qualities, level of applicant's interest. *Other factors considered include:* class rank, application essay, recommendation(s), first generation, volunteer work, work experience. *Freshman Admission Requirements:* High school diploma is required and GED is accepted. *Academic units required:* 4 English, 4 math, 3 science, 3 science labs, 2 foreign language, 2 social studies, 1 visual/performing arts. *Academic units recommended:* 4 English, 4 math, 3 science, 3 science labs, 2 foreign language, 2 social studies, 1 visual/performing arts.

ACCOMMODATIONS OR SERVICES

Accommodations are decided upon an individual basis after a thorough review of appropriate, current documentation. The accommodations requests must be supported through the documentation provided and must be logically linked to the current impact of the condition on academic functioning.

FINANCIAL AID

Students should submit: FAFSA. Applicants will be notified of awards on a rolling basis beginning 2/1. The Princeton Review suggests that all financial aid forms be submitted as soon as possible after October 1. *Need-based scholarships/grants offered:* College/university scholarship or grant aid from institutional funds; Federal Pell; Private scholarships; SEOG; State scholarships/grants. *Loan aid offered:* Direct PLUS loans. Direct Subsidized Stafford Loans; Direct Unsubsidized Stafford Loans. Federal Work-Study Program available. Institutional employment available.

CAMPUS LIFE

Activities: Campus Ministries; Choral groups; Concert band; Dance; Drama/theater; International Student Organization; Jazz band; Literary magazine; Marching band; Model UN; Music ensembles; Musical theater; Opera; Pep band; Radio station; Student government; Student newspaper; Symphony orchestra; Television station; Yearbook.. **Organizations:** 504 registered organizations, 13 honor societies, 13 religious organizations. 25 fraternities, 20 sororities. **Athletics (Intercollegiate):** *Men:* baseball, basketball, cross-country, diving, football, golf, swimming, tennis, track/field (outdoor). *Women:* basketball, cross-country, diving, golf, gymnastics, soccer, softball, swimming, tennis, track/field (outdoor), track/field (indoor), volleyball. **On-Campus Highlights:** Flandrau Science Center, Center for Creative Photography, UA Museum of Art, Athletics Events, Arizona State Museum.

ACCOMMODATIONS

Allowed in exams:

Calculators	Yes
Dictionary	Yes
Computer	Yes
Spell-checker	Yes
Extended test time	Yes
Scribe	Yes
Proctors	Yes
Oral exams	Yes
Note-takers	Yes

Support services for students with

LD	Yes
ADHD	Yes
ASD	Yes
Distraction-reduced environment	Yes
Recording of lecture allowed	Yes
Reading technology:	Yes
Audio books	Yes
Other assistive technology	Yes
Priority registration	No

Added costs for services:

For LD:	Yes, for SALT
For ADHD:	Yes, for SALT
For ASD:	Yes, for SALT
LD specialists	Yes
ADHD & ASD coaching	Yes
ASD specialists	No
Professional tutors	Yes
Peer tutors	Yes
Max. hours/week for services	Varies
How professors are notified of student approved accommodations	Student and SALT

COLLEGE GRADUATION REQUIREMENTS

Course waivers allowed	No
Course substitutions allowed	Yes
In what courses	Case per case basis.

Arkansas State University

PO Box 600, State University, AR 72467 • Admissions: 870-972-3024 • Fax: 870-972-3406

CAMPUS

Type of school	Public
Environment	Town
Support	S

STUDENTS

Undergrad enrollment	8,909
% male/female	43/57
% from out of state	11
% frosh live on campus	72

FINANCIAL FACTS

Annual in-state tuition	$6,060
Annual out-of-state tuition	$12,120
Room and board	$8,540
Required fees	$2,140

GENERAL ADMISSIONS INFO

Application fee	$15
Regular application deadline	8/24
Nonfall registration accepted.	

Range SAT EBRW	400–540
Range SAT Math	470–540
Range ACT Composite	21–26

ACADEMICS

Student/faculty ratio	17:1
% students returning for sophomore year	76

Most classes have 10–19 students.
Most lab/discussion sessions have 20–29 students.

PROGRAMS/SERVICES FOR STUDENTS WITH LEARNING DIFFERENCES

Arkansas State Disability Services' goal is to provide students with disabilities access to resources that will enable them to manage daily activities in the university setting. Disability Services is committed to providing opportunities in higher education for students with disabilities who demonstrate the reasonable ability for college success. Although A-State does not offer a specialized curriculum for persons with disabilities or assume the role of a rehabilitation center, A-State offers a variety of support services so that students with disabilities are admitted and integrated as completely as possible into the university.

ADMISSIONS

General admission requires High School GPA of 2.75. Students must submit either a minimum ACT composite score of 21 or SAT score of 990 on the Reading and Math or combined score of 1060. To be considered for conditional admission to Arkansas State University, an applicant must meet the following requirements: High School GPA (or comparable GED). High School GPA of 2.30 and a minimum ACT composite score of 19 or SAT score of 910-989 on the Reading and Math. All incoming freshmen who have an ACT c omposite score of 28 (or higher) AND a high school GPA of 3.5 (or higher) will be formally admitted to the Honors College. All students formally admitted to Arkansas State University will be automatically screened for admission to The Honors College; there is not a separate application for the Honors College

Additional Information

The Learning Commons offers free drop-in, peer one-on-one, and small group tutoring. Support services provided by the Office of Disability Services includes: orientation and registration, intake and assessment, note taking, test administration with accommodations, E-Texts (texts in alternate format), computer and technology demonstrations for all students, physical adaptations inside and outside of the classroom, guidance and counseling, priority registration, and Interpreter Services. Every fall term, students are required to make an appointment to meet with their Disability Services Counselor to review and request their accommodations. For the spring and summer terms, the student may simply log into AIM and choose their accommodations from a list of pre-approved accommodations chosen specifically for that particular student. Alternative books are also called audio books and e-text. Students are required to own the physical copy of the textbook.

ADMISSIONS INFO FOR STUDENTS WITH LEARNING DIFFERENCES

SAT/ACT required: Yes
Interview required: No
Essay required: Not Applicable
Additional application required: Yes
Documentation required for:
  LD: Documentation of disability from a professional
  ADHD: Documentation of disability from a professional
  ASD: Documentation of disability from a professional
Documentation submitted to: Support Program/Services
Special Ed. HS course work accepted: Not Applicable
Separate application required for Programs/Services: No
Contact Information
Name of program or department: Disability Services
Telephone: 870-972-3964
Fax: 870-972-3351
Email: jrmason@astate.edu

Arkansas State University

GENERAL ADMISSIONS

Very important factors considered include: rigor of secondary school record, standardized test scores. *Important factors considered include:* class rank. *Other factors considered include:* recommendation(s), talent/ability. *Freshman Admission Requirements:* High school diploma is required and GED is accepted. *Academic units required:* 4 English, 4 math, 3 science, 3 science labs, 1 social studies, 2 history. *Academic units recommended:* 2 foreign language.

ACCOMMODATIONS OR SERVICES

Accommodations are decided upon an individual basis after a thorough review of appropriate, current documentation. The accommodations requests must be supported through the documentation provided and must be logically linked to the current impact of the condition on academic functioning.

FINANCIAL AID

Students should submit: FAFSA; Institution's own financial aid form. Applicants will be notified of awards on a rolling basis beginning 6/1. The Princeton Review suggests that all financial aid forms be submitted as soon as possible after October 1. *Need-based scholarships/grants offered:* College/university scholarship or grant aid from institutional funds; Federal Pell; Private scholarships; SEOG; State scholarships/grants. *Loan aid offered:* Direct PLUS loans; Direct Subsidized Stafford Loans; Direct Unsubsidized Stafford Loans. Federal Work-Study Program available. Institutional employment available.

CAMPUS LIFE

Activities: Campus Ministries; Choral groups; Concert band; Dance; Drama/theater; International Student Organization; Jazz band; Marching band; Model UN; Music ensembles; Musical theater; Opera; Pep band; Radio station; Student government; Student newspaper; Symphony orchestra; Television station; Yearbook.. **Organizations:** 192 registered organizations, 42 honor societies, 16 religious organizations. 22 fraternities, 9 sororities. **Athletics (Intercollegiate):** *Men:* baseball, basketball, cross-country, football, golf, track/field (outdoor), track/field (indoor). *Women:* basketball, cross-country, golf, soccer, tennis, track/field (outdoor), track/field (indoor), volleyball. **On-Campus Highlights:** Student Union, Fowler Center, Convocation Center, Red Wolf Center, Centennial Bank Stadium.

ACCOMMODATIONS

Allowed in exams:	
Calculators	Yes
Dictionary	Yes
Computer	Yes
Spell-checker	Yes
Extended test time	Yes
Scribe	Yes
Proctors	Yes
Oral exams	Yes
Note-takers	Yes
Support services for students with	
LD	Yes
ADHD	Yes
ASD	Yes
Distraction-reduced environment	Yes
Recording of lecture allowed	Yes
Reading technology:	Yes
Audio books	Yes
Other assistive technology	Yes
Priority registration	Yes
Added costs for services:	
For LD:	No
For ADHD:	No
For ASD:	No
LD specialists	Yes
ADHD & ASD coaching	Yes
ASD specialists	Yes
Professional tutors	Yes
Peer tutors	No
Max. hours/week for services	Varies
How professors are notified of student approved accommodations	Director and Student

COLLEGE GRADUATION REQUIREMENTS

Course waivers allowed	Yes
In what courses	
Accommodations for physical education requirement.	
Course substitutions allowed	Yes
In what courses	
College Algebra and Foreign Language.	

University of Arkansas

125 ADMIN, FAYETTEVILLE, AR 72701 • ADMISSIONS: 479-575-5346 • FAX: 479-575-7515

CAMPUS

Type of school	Public
Environment	City
Support	S

STUDENTS

Undergrad enrollment	22,756
% male/female	47/53
% from out of state	45
% frosh live on campus	90

FINANCIAL FACTS

Annual in-state tuition	$7,204
Annual out-of-state tuition	$21,552
Room and board	$10,332
Required fees	$1,616

GENERAL ADMISSIONS INFO

Application fee	$40
Priority deadline	11/1
Regular application deadline	8/1

Nonfall registration accepted.

Range SAT EBRW	560–640
Range SAT Math	550–640
Range ACT Composite	23–29

ACADEMICS

Student/faculty ratio	19:1
% students returning for sophomore year	82
% students graduating within 4 years	42
% students graduating within 6 years	62

Most classes have 10–19 students.

PROGRAMS/SERVICES FOR STUDENTS WITH LEARNING DIFFERENCES

The Center for Educational Access (CEA) is the office responsible for facilitating campus access and accommodations for students with disabilities. The philosophy of the CEA is to provide an environment in which students are encouraged to develop independence, the ability to self-advocate, and knowledge of resources that will enable them to take advantage of opportunities available in the modern world. The Enhanced Learning Center offers tutoring services to all University of Arkansas students free of charge. Supplemental Instruction (SI) is an academic enrichment program that increases student performance and retention. SI offers enrolled students regularly scheduled, out-of-class review sessions in historically difficult courses. Sessions are led by experienced students who excel in the difficult subject matter. SI is free to all UA students.

ADMISSIONS

Guaranteed general admission to the University of Arkansas requires a minimum GPA of 3.0 and an ACT score of 20 (or SAT of 930). Students who do not meet qualifications may be admitted on the basis of individual review of their application portfolios. Course requirements include 4 years of English, 4 years of math, 3 years of social studies, 3 years of science, and 2 electives to be chosen from English, foreign languages, oral communication, mathematics, computer science, natural sciences, and social studies.

Additional Information

EMPOWER offers a four-year, non-degree college experience program for students with cognitive disabilities that incorporates functional academics, independent living, employment, social/leisure skills, and health/wellness skills in a public university setting with the goal of producing self sufficient young adults. The University of Arkansas program is offered for students who demonstrate the ability to safely live independently, sustain employment, and socially integrate during their enrollment. The program progresses with an emphasis on workplace experience, community integration, and independent living with transitionally reduced supports. Students who successfully complete the program will receive a certificate of program completion.

ADMISSIONS INFO FOR STUDENTS WITH LEARNING DIFFERENCES

SAT/ACT required: No
Interview required: No
Essay required: Not Applicable
Additional application required: No
Documentation required for:
Documentation submitted to: Support Program/Services
Special Ed. HS course work accepted: Not Applicable
Separate application required for Programs/Services: No
Contact Information
Name of program or department: Center for Educational Access
Telephone: 479-575-3104
Fax: 479-575-7445
Email: ada@uark.edu

University of Arkansas

GENERAL ADMISSIONS

Very important factors considered include: academic GPA, standardized test scores. *Other factors considered include:* rigor of secondary school record, class rank, application essay, recommendation(s), extracurricular activities, talent/ability, character/personal qualities, first generation, alumni/ae relation, geographical residence, state residency, volunteer work. *Freshman Admission Requirements:* High school diploma is required and GED is accepted. *Academic units required:* 4 English, 4 math, 3 science, 1 science lab, 1 social studies, 2 history, 2 academic electives, 0.5 visual/performing arts. *Academic units recommended:* 4 English, 4 math, 3 science, 1 science lab, 2 foreign language, 1 social studies, 2 history, 2 academic electives, 0.5 visual/performing arts.

ACCOMMODATIONS OR SERVICES

Accommodations are decided upon an individual basis after a thorough review of appropriate, current documentation. The accommodations requests must be supported through the documentation provided and must be logically linked to the current impact of the condition on academic functioning.

FINANCIAL AID

Students should submit: FAFSA. Applicants will be notified of awards on or about 4/1. The Princeton Review suggests that all financial aid forms be submitted as soon as possible after October 1. *Need-based scholarships/grants offered:* College/university scholarship or grant aid from institutional funds; Federal Pell; Private scholarships; SEOG; State scholarships/grants. *Loan aid offered:* Direct PLUS loans; Direct Subsidized Stafford Loans; Direct Unsubsidized Stafford Loans. Federal Work-Study Program available. Institutional employment available.

CAMPUS LIFE

Activities: Campus Ministries; Choral groups; Concert band; Dance; Drama/theater; International Student Organization; Jazz band; Literary magazine; Marching band; Model UN; Music ensembles; Musical theater; Opera; Pep band; Radio station; Student government; Student newspaper; Symphony orchestra; Television station; Yearbook.. **Organizations:** 340 registered organizations, 39 honor societies, 32 religious organizations. 16 fraternities, 11 sororities. **Athletics (Intercollegiate):** *Men:* baseball, basketball, cross-country, football, golf, tennis, track/field (outdoor), track/field (indoor). *Women:* basketball, cross-country, diving, golf, gymnastics, soccer, softball, swimming, tennis, track/field (outdoor), track/field (indoor), volleyball. **On-Campus Highlights:** Old Main: Iconic Image of Higher Education in the State of Arkansas., Steven L. Anderson Design Center: State-Of-The-Art Architectural Building, Senior Walk (every graduate's name engraved), The Nanoscale Material Science and Engineering Buidling, Reyno.

ACCOMMODATIONS

Allowed in exams:

Calculators	Yes
Dictionary	Yes
Computer	Yes
Spell-checker	Yes
Extended test time	Yes
Scribe	Yes
Proctors	Yes
Oral exams	Yes
Note-takers	Yes

Support services for students with

LD	Yes
ADHD	Yes
ASD	Yes
Distraction-reduced environment	Yes
Recording of lecture allowed	Yes
Reading technology:	Yes
Audio books	Yes
Other assistive technology	No
Priority registration	Yes

Added costs for services:

For LD:	No
For ADHD:	No
For ASD:	No
LD specialists	No
ADHD & ASD coaching	Not Applicable
ASD specialists	Yes
Professional tutors	No
Peer tutors	No
Max. hours/week for services	Varies

How professors are notified of student approved accommodations
Director and Student

COLLEGE GRADUATION REQUIREMENTS

Course waivers allowed	No
Course substitutions allowed	Yes
In what courses	Math and Foreign Language

University of the Ozarks

415 N. College Avenue, Clarksville, AR 72830 • Admissions: 479-979-1227 • Fax: 479-979-1417

CAMPUS

Type of school	Private (nonprofit)
Environment	Village
Support	SP

STUDENTS

Undergrad enrollment	615
% male/female	45/55
% from out of state	29
% frosh live on campus	86

FINANCIAL FACTS

Annual tuition	$21,450
Room and board	$6,500
Required fees	$600

GENERAL ADMISSIONS INFO

Application fee	$30
Priority deadline	4/1

Nonfall registration accepted.
  Admission may be deferred.

Range SAT EBRW	450–570
Range SAT Math	443–560
Range ACT Composite	19–25

ACADEMICS

Student/faculty ratio	11:1
% students returning for sophomore year	64

Most classes have 20–29 students.

PROGRAMS/SERVICES FOR STUDENTS WITH LEARNING DIFFERENCES

The University of the Ozarks has a comprehensive program called The Jones Learning Center that serves students with learning disabilities.. Serving these students was not done as a result of the law, but as a part of the college's mission. Students with documented disabilities are totally integrated into campus life in both curricular and extra-curricular activities. To receive services, students must provide documentation from a licensed professional that includes specific accommodation recommendations that are based on test results. The service model that is used is one that includes an academic support coordinator that the student meets with daily who is responsible for the individualized planning and implementation of the students' program of study, helps the student with executive functioning skills, acts as a secondary adviser, and monitors' the students' progress. Students receive help in understanding their learning styles, utilizing their strengths, circumventing deficits, building skills, and becoming independent learners. Enhanced services include testing accommodations (one-to-one if needed), assistive technology (including text-to-speech, speech-to-text, and other technology to meet specific needs), peer tutoring, notetakers, and audiotexts.

ADMISSIONS

The general admissions criteria for the University is an 18 on the ACT or SAT equivalent and a 2.00 high school GPA.. Students can elect to not submit an ACT or SAT as the university is Test Optional. For applicants applying with out a test score they must submit their Transcript, 2 letters of recommendation, an academic writing sample, have an interview with a member of the Admission Committee, and choose 1 additional requirement from 1) Community Service or Involvement 2) Extracurricular activities or 3) Personal or Group Achievements.

ADMISSIONS INFO FOR STUDENTS WITH LEARNING DIFFERENCES

SAT/ACT required: No (Test Optional)
Interview required: No
Essay required: Recommended
Additional application required: Yes
Documentation required for: Yes
  LD: Psychoeducational assessment that includes the most current WAIS, a comprehenive individually administered achievement measure, and processing assessment as well as behavioral information.
  ADHD: Medical evaluation. Psychoeducational assessment is recommended.
  ASD: Psychoeducational assessment
Documentation submitted to: Both
Special Ed. HS course work accepted: Yes
Contact Information
Name of program or department: Jones Learning Center
Telephone: 479-979-1403
Fax: 479-979-1429
Email: jlc@ozarks.edu

Additional Information

A decision about admission into the JLC is made at the time of general admission. The student then completes pre-registration for their first semester with the JLC's assistant director. The Living and Learning Community is for students who need more support with social and independent living skills, the LLC is for college students with learning disabilities, ADHD, ASD, and a variety of other learning differences. It teaches social thinking and offers individualized support for the challenges of college life. This program combines the academic services of the JLC with an enhanced residential life component. Trained staff help students acquire and apply social thinking and independent living and designed to help first year students ease their transitions to college life. Services include individual and group consultation, academic support and advocacy, skills teaching and practice, and social programming. The LLC is designed for highly capable students who may need additional residential support, social and communication skills teaching, and stress management assistance during freshman year. Support after freshman year is provided through the JLC coordinator of ASD Services.

GENERAL ADMISSIONS

Important factors considered include: standardized test scores. *Other factors considered include:* rigor of secondary school record, academic GPA, application essay, recommendation(s), interview, extracurricular activities, talent/ability, character/personal qualities, alumni/ae relation, volunteer work, work experience, level of applicant's interest. *Freshman Admission Requirements:* High school diploma is required and GED is accepted. *Academic units recommended:* 4 English, 4 math, 3 science, 2 science labs, 2 foreign language, 1 social studies, 2 history.

ACCOMMODATIONS OR SERVICES

Accommodations are decided upon an individual basis after a thorough review of appropriate, current documentation. The accommodations requests must be supported through the documentation provided and must be logically linked to the current impact of the condition on academic functioning.

FINANCIAL AID

Students should submit: FAFSA. Applicants will be notified of awards on a rolling basis beginning 3/1. The Princeton Review suggests that all financial aid forms be submitted as soon as possible after October 1. *Need-based scholarships/grants offered:* College/university scholarship or grant aid from institutional funds; Federal Nursing Scholarships; Federal Pell; Private scholarships; SEOG; State scholarships/grants; United Negro College Fund. *Loan aid offered:* Federal Work-Study Program available. Institutional employment available.

CAMPUS LIFE

Activities: Campus Ministries; Choral groups; Drama/theater; International Student Organization; Literary magazine; Music ensembles; Radio station; Student government; Student-run film society; Television station; Yearbook.. **Organizations:** 40 registered organizations, 5 honor societies, 6 religious organizations. **Athletics (Intercollegiate):** *Men:* baseball, basketball, cheerleading, cross-country, soccer, tennis. *Women:* basketball, cheerleading, cross-country, soccer, softball, tennis. **On-Campus Highlights:** Seay Student Center, Walton Fine Arts Center, Walker Education and Communications Buil, Robson Library, Rogers Conference Center.

ACCOMMODATIONS

Allowed in exams:	
Calculators	Yes
Dictionary	No
Computer	Yes
Spell-checker	Yes
Extended test time	Yes
Scribe	Yes
Proctors	Yes
Oral exams	Yes
Note-takers	Yes
Support services for students with	
LD	Yes
ADHD	Yes
ASD	Yes
Distraction-reduced environment	Yes
Recording of lecture allowed	Yes
Reading technology:	Yes
Audio books	Yes
Other assistive technology	Text-to-speech

and speech-to-text technology is available for students to install on their personal computers. Apps are recommended for students based on their specific needs.

Priority registration	Yes
Added costs for services:	
For LD:	No
For ADHD:	No
For ASD:	No
LD specialists	Yes
ADHD & ASD coaching	Yes
ASD specialists	Yes
Professional tutors	Yes
Peer tutors	Yes
Max. hours/week for services	
How professors are notified of student approved accomodations	
Director and Student	

COLLEGE GRADUATION REQUIREMENTS

Course waivers allowed	No
Course substitutions allowed	Yes
In what courses	

Course substitutions are not needed for foreign language because alternatives are given for all students.

California Polytechnic State University

1 GRAND AVENUE, SAN LUIS OBISPO, CA 93407-0031 • ADMISSIONS: 805-756-2311 • FAX: 805-756-5400

CAMPUS

Type of school	Public
Environment	Town
Support	CS

STUDENTS

Undergrad enrollment	21,249
% male/female	52/48
% from out of state	14
% frosh live on campus	99

FINANCIAL FACTS

Annual in-state tuition	$5,742
Annual out-of-state tuition	$264 per unit
Room and board	$13,115
Required fees	$3,690

GENERAL ADMISSIONS INFO

Application fee	$55
Regular application deadline	11/30
Nonfall registration accepted.	

Range SAT EBRW	610–690
Range SAT Math	610–710
Range ACT Composite	26–31

ACADEMICS

Student/faculty ratio	19:1
% students returning for sophomore year	95
% students graduating within 4 years	47
% students graduating within 6 years	82
Most classes have 10–19 students.	

PROGRAMS/SERVICES FOR STUDENTS WITH LEARNING DIFFERENCES

The goal of the program is to assist students with learning disabilities using their learning strengths. The Disability Resource Center (DRC) assists students with disabilities in achieving access to higher education, promotes personal and educational success, and increases the awareness and responsiveness of the campus community. DRC is actively involved with students and faculty and provides a newsletter and open house to keep the university population aware of who it is and what it does. Incoming students are encouraged to meet with college advisors, in conjunction with DRC staff, to receive assistance in the planning of class schedules. This allows for the selection of appropriate classes to fit particular needs and personal goals. It is the responsibility of each student seeking accommodations and services to provide a written, comprehensive psychological and/or medical evaluation verifying the diagnosis. The Cal Poly Student Learning Outcomes model promotes student personal growth and the development of self-advocacy for full inclusion of qualified students with verified disabilities. The promotion of student self-reliance and responsibility are necessary adjuncts to educational development.

ADMISSIONS

Admission is competitive in all majors. Students must declare a major when applying.. Cal Poly comprehensively reviews all applications for students who have strong academic records and are active in and outside the classroom. Cal Poly considers other factors for admission deemed important to the campus. All candidates are objectively evaluated by the cognitive and non-cognitive variables under the faculty-mandated Multi-Criteria Admission (MCA) process. Admissions consider:s intended program of study (the major to which the application is made); college-prep courses; GPA in college-preparatory courses; Standardized test scores; extra-curricular activities and work experience; Coursework with a Grade of C or Better.

ADMISSIONS INFO FOR STUDENTS WITH LEARNING DIFFERENCES

SAT/ACT required: Yes
Interview required: No
Essay required: No
Additional application required: No
Documentation required for:
 LD: Psycho ed evaluation
 ADHD: Psycho ed evaluation
 ASD: Psycho ed evaluation
Documentation submitted to: Support program/services
Special Ed. HS course work accepted: No
Separate application required for Programs/Services: N/A
Contact Information
Name of program or department: Disability Resource Center (DRC)
Telephone: 805-756-1395
Fax: 805-756-5451

California Polytechnic State University

Additional Information

Incoming students should contact the DRC for assistance. Supportive services may include: alternative format materials, assistive listening devices, note taking, taped textbooks, test accommodations, tutorial services and writing assistance. The Academic Skills Center (ASC) offers a variety of academic enrichment programs consisting of Supplemental Workshops and Study Session in addition to online study strategies available 24 hours a day. Cal Poly's Supplemental Workshops (SW) Program develops academic enrichment environments of active learners who ascend the levels of Bloom's Taxonomy. Guided by trained peer facilitators, enrolled students participate in discussions, compare notes, develop study strategies and challenge their understanding with practice exams, worksheets and more. Workshops meet twice a week and earn one unit of academic credit.

GENERAL ADMISSIONS

Very important factors considered include: rigor of secondary school record, academic GPA, standardized test scores. *Other factors considered include:* extracurricular activities, talent/ability, first generation, geographical residence, volunteer work, work experience. *Freshman Admission Requirements:* High school diploma is required and GED is accepted. *Academic units required:* 4 English, 3 math, 2 science, 2 science labs, 2 foreign language, 1 social studies, 1 history, 1 academic elective, 1 visual/performing arts. *Academic units recommended:* 4 English, 4 math, 4 science, 2 science labs, 4 foreign language, 1 social studies, 1 history, 1 academic elective, 2 visual/performing arts.

ACCOMMODATIONS OR SERVICES

Accommodations are decided upon an individual basis after a thorough review of appropriate, current documentation. The accommodations requests must be supported through the documentation provided and must be logically linked to the current impact of the condition on academic functioning.

FINANCIAL AID

Students should submit: FAFSA. Applicants will be notified of awards on a rolling basis beginning 3/15. The Princeton Review suggests that all financial aid forms be submitted as soon as possible after October 1. *Need-based scholarships/grants offered:* College/university scholarship or grant aid from institutional funds; Federal Pell; Private scholarships; SEOG; State scholarships/grants. *Loan aid offered:* Direct PLUS loans; Direct Subsidized Stafford Loans; Direct Unsubsidized Stafford Loans. Federal Work-Study Program available. Institutional employment available.

CAMPUS LIFE

Activities: Campus Ministries; Choral groups; Concert band; Dance; Drama/theater; International Student Organization; Jazz band; Literary magazine; Marching band; Model UN; Music ensembles; Musical theater; Opera; Pep band; Radio station; Student government; Student newspaper; Student-run film society; Symphony orchestra; Television station.. **Organizations:** 400 registered organizations, 14 religious organizations. 25 fraternities, 14 sororities. **Athletics (Intercollegiate):** *Men:* baseball, basketball, cross-country, football, golf, soccer, swimming, tennis, track/field (outdoor), wrestling. *Women:* basketball, cross-country, golf, soccer, softball, swimming, tennis, track/field (outdoor), track/field (indoor), volleyball. **On-Campus Highlights:** Performing Arts Center, Recreation Center, Julian's Cafe Bistro, Spanos Stadium, University Union.

ACCOMMODATIONS

Allowed in exams:	
Calculators	Yes
Dictionary	Yes
Computer	Yes
Spell-checker	Yes
Extended test time	Yes
Scribe	Yes
Proctors	Yes
Oral exams	Yes
Note-takers	Yes
Support services for students with	
LD	Yes
ADHD	Yes
ASD	Yes
Distraction-reduced environment	Yes
Recording of lecture allowed	Yes
Reading technology:	Yes
Audio books	Yes
Other assistive technology	Yes
Priority registration	Yes
Added costs for services:	
For LD:	No
For ADHD:	No
For ASD:	No
LD specialists	Yes
ADHD & ASD coaching	No
ASD specialists	No
Professional tutors	No
Peer tutors	No
Max. hours/week for services	0
How professors are notified of student approved accommodations	Student

COLLEGE GRADUATION REQUIREMENTS

Course waivers allowed	No
Course substitutions allowed	Yes

In what courses

On a case-by-case basis, individuals may be granted course substitutions (not waivers) in quantitative reasoning (in very limited non-math related majors) by the VP of Academic Affairs and foreign language substitutions with department approval.

California State Polytechnic University, Pomona

3801 W TEMPLE AVE, POMONA, CA 91768 • ADMISSIONS: 909-869-5299 • FAX: 909-869-4529

CAMPUS
Type of school	Public
Environment	City
Support	CS

STUDENTS
Undergrad enrollment	24,205
% male/female	54/46
% from out of state	1
% frosh live on campus	44

FINANCIAL FACTS
Annual in-state tuition	$5,742
Annual out-of-state tuition	$17,622
Room and board	$17,358
Required fees	$1611

GENERAL ADMISSIONS INFO
Application fee	$55
Priority deadline	11/30
Regular application deadline	11/30
Nonfall registration accepted.	

Range SAT EBRW	500–610
Range SAT Math	510–630
Range ACT Composite	20–27

ACADEMICS
Student/faculty ratio	25:1
% students returning for sophomore year	87
% students graduating within 4 years	18
% students graduating within 6 years	66

Most classes have 20–29 students.
Most lab/discussion sessions have 10–19 students.

PROGRAMS/SERVICES FOR STUDENTS WITH LEARNING DIFFERENCES
The Disability Resource Center (DRC) uses an integrated online system for students to access their accomodations. Although the DRC's primary focus is accomodative services, the DRC also provides individualized guidance to students to address their disability-related, academic, ad psychosocial barriers. The DRC's dual focus on both accommodations and supplemental advising allows the DRC student to be able to be suucessful at the University.

ADMISSIONS
Students must meet the university's regular entrance requirements, including C or better in the subject requirements of 4 years of English, 3 years of math, 1 year of U.S. history, 2 years of science lab, 2 years of a foreign language, 1 year of visual or performing arts, and 3 years of academic electives and a qualifiable eligibility index based on high school GPA and scores on either ACT or SAT. Special admits are very limited. Applicants with LD are encouraged to complete collegeprep courses. However, if students are unable to fulfill a specific course requirement because of a learning disability, alternative college-prep courses may be substituted. Substitutions may be granted in foreign language, science lab, and math. Substitutions may be authorized on an individual basis after review and recommendation by applicant's guidance counselor in consultation with the Director of DSS. Course substitutions could limit access to some majors. Students are encouraged to self-disclose a learning disability if it would help to explain lower grades. Students who self-disclose are reviewed by DSS, which provides a recommendation to admissions.

Additional Information
Support services include counseling, advocacy services, registration, note-takers, readers, tutors, testing accommodations, and specialized equipment. Skills classes are not offered through DSS, but are available in other departments in the areas of reading skills, test preparation, test-taking strategies, and study skills. Services and accommodations are available to undergraduate and graduate students. Cal Poly offers a summer program for any high school student.

ADMISSIONS INFO FOR STUDENTS WITH LEARNING DIFFERENCES
SAT/ACT required: Yes
Interview required: No
Essay required: No
Additional application required: No
Documentation required for:
  LD: Report with scores for aptitude and achievement testing. Visit Documentation Standards at: www.cpp.edu/~drc/
  ADHD: Diagnostic information and historical data should be summarized in a report. Visit Documentation Standards at: www.cpp.edu/~drc/
  ASD: Psycho ed evaluation
Documentation submitted to: Disability Resource Center
Special Ed. HS course work accepted: No
Separate application required for Programs/Services: No
Contact Information
Name of program or department: Disability Resource Center
Telephone: 909-869-3333
Fax: 909-869-3271
Email: drc@cpp.edu

California State Polytechnic University, Pomona

GENERAL ADMISSIONS
Very important factors considered include: rigor of secondary school record, academic GPA, standardized test scores. *Freshman Admission Requirements:* High school diploma is required and GED is accepted. *Academic units required:* 4 English, 3 math, 2 science, 2 science labs, 2 foreign language, 1 social studies, 1 history, 1 academic elective, 1 visual/performing arts. *Academic units recommended:* 4 math.

ACCOMMODATIONS OR SERVICES
Accommodations are decided upon an individual basis after a thorough review of appropriate, current documentation. The accommodations requests must be supported through the documentation provided and must be logically linked to the current impact of the condition on academic functioning.

FINANCIAL AID
Students should submit: FAFSA. Applicants will be notified of awards on a rolling basis beginning 4/1. The Princeton Review suggests that all financial aid forms be submitted as soon as possible after October 1. *Need-based scholarships/grants offered:* College/university scholarship or grant aid from institutional funds; Federal Pell; Private scholarships; SEOG; State scholarships/grants. *Loan aid offered:* Direct PLUS loans; Direct Subsidized Stafford Loans; Direct Unsubsidized Stafford Loans. Federal Work-Study Program available. Institutional employment available.

CAMPUS LIFE
Activities: Campus Ministries; Choral groups; Concert band; Dance; Drama/theater; International Student Organization; Jazz band; Literary magazine; Model UN; Music ensembles; Musical theater; Opera; Pep band; Student government; Student newspaper; Symphony orchestra; Yearbook. **Organizations:** 280 registered organizations, 26 honor societies, 10 religious organizations. 12 fraternities, 8 sororities. **Athletics (Intercollegiate):** *Men:* baseball, basketball, cheerleading, cross-country, soccer, tennis, track/field (outdoor). *Women:* basketball, cheerleading, cross-country, soccer, tennis, track/field (outdoor), volleyball. **On-Campus Highlights:** The Farmstore at Kellogg Ranch, Rain Bird Aquatic,Ethnobotony&Rainforest, W. K. Kellogg Arabian Horse Center, Kellogg House Pomona, John T. Lyle Center for Regenerative Studies.

ACCOMMODATIONS
Allowed in exams:	
Calculators	Yes
Dictionary	Yes
Computer	Yes
Spell-checker	Yes
Extended test time	Yes
Scribe	Yes
Proctors	Yes
Oral exams	Yes
Note-takers	Yes
Support services for students with	
LD	Yes
ADHD	Yes
ASD	Yes
Distraction-reduced environment	Yes
Recording of lecture allowed	Yes
Reading technology:	Yes
Audio books	No
Other assistive technology	Dragon Software
Priority registration	Yes
Added costs for services:	
For LD:	No
For ADHD:	No
For ASD:	No
LD specialists	Yes
ADHD & ASD coaching	No
ASD specialists	No
Professional tutors	No
Peer tutors	No
Max. hours/week for services	Varies
How professors are notified of student approved accommodations	Director and Student

COLLEGE GRADUATION REQUIREMENTS
Course waivers allowed	No
Course substitutions allowed	Yes
In what courses	

It depends on the student and the disability. However, there have been course substitutions for Math.

California State University, Fresno

5241 N. Maple Ave, Fresno, CA 93740-8026 • Admissions: 559-278-2261 * Fax: 559-278-4812

CAMPUS

Type of school	Public
Environment	Metropolis
Support	CS

STUDENTS

Undergrad enrollment	18,784
% male/female	43 /57
% from out of state	0
% frosh live on campus	22

FINANCIAL FACTS

Annual in-state tuition	$5,742
Annual out-of-state tuition	$11,160
Room and board	$10,550
Required fees	$790

GENERAL ADMISSIONS INFO

Application fee	$55
Regular application deadline	11/30
Nonfall registration accepted.	

Range SAT EBRW	400–510
Range SAT Math	410–530
Range ACT Composite	16–22

ACADEMICS

Student/faculty ratio	22:1
% students returning for sophomore year	86
% students graduating within 4 years	
% students graduating within 6 years	

Most classes have 20-29 students. Most lab/ discussion sessions have 20-29 students.

Programs/Services for Students with Learning Differences

There are a wide range of services provided by services for students with disabilities (SSD). The student will meet with a disability management specialist to determine which accommodations will best support their specific needs and develop an accommodation plan of resources. There is an ability to accessible instructional materials through SSD including electronic and printed textboooks and related core materials that can be designed to be more user-friendly. Fresno students who verified a disabity mist complete an application form and make an appointment with the Disabiity Management Specialist. Additional appointments may be necessary for training & orientation in using specific accommodations.

Admissions

Students are admitted on an eligibility index based on high school GPA in college-prep courses and scores on ACT or SAT. Lower GPA requires higher scores on the test. Other factors such as impaction and residency status are also considered. The foreign language requirement may be waived in rare cases when supported by the testing data supporting a relevant learning disability. ACT or SAT required. All applicants must have 2 social science, 4 English, 3 math, 2 science (science with a lab, 1 biological and 1 physical), and 2 foreign language. The GPA is calculated based on the college-prep courses completed in grades 10, 11, and if available, 12. Students must have at least a C in these courses. Grades of D or less cannot be validated by a higher second semester grade in any of the following disciplines: social science/history, English, laboratory science, visual/performing arts, and electives. Students must have C or higher in all semesters of English, other lab sciences than chemistry, social sciences/history, and visual/performing arts to have the course counted toward the required preparatory units. Applicants within the local area will be required to meet the minimum eligibility requirement of 2900 based on GPA and SAT result or a 694 based on GPA and ACT result. Students outside of the local area should not anticipate receiving an admissions decision until late January or February.

APPLICATION REQUIREMENTS FOR SERVICES

SAT/ACT required: Yes
Interview required: Yes
Essay required: Yes
Additional application required: No
Documentation required for:
 LD: Psycho ed evaluation
 ADHD: Diagnosis based on DSM-V; history of behaviors impairing functioning in academic setting; diagnostic interview; history of symptoms;evidence of ongoing behaviors.
 ASD: Psycho ed evaluation
Documentation submitted to: Disabled Student Services
Special Ed. HS course work accepted: No
Separate application required for Programs/Services: No
Contact Information
Name of program or department: Services for Students with Disabilities
Telephone: 559-278-2811
Fax: 559-278-4214
Email: ssdstaff@csufresno.edu

California State University, Fresno

Additional Information

Assistive technology, a piece of equipment that is used to increase the functional capabilities of a student can be accessed. In the classroom , notetakers are volunteers who will tak the notes and send them to the student in the class that has completed the forms trhough SSD. It is also possible to have TO have approval of a digital recorder or Laptop i the classroom. For students with a diagnosis of ASD there is a Mentoring and Peer Support program offered through SSD.

GENERAL ADMISSIONS

Very important factors considered inclue: rigor of secondary school record, academic GPA, standardized test scores. Freshman Admission Requirements: High school diploma is required and GED is accepted Academic units required: 4 English, 3 math, 1 science, 1 science labs, 2 foreign language, 1 social studies, 1 history, 1 academic electives, 1 visual/performing arts,

ACCOMMODATIONS OR SERVICES

Accommodations are decided upon an individual basis after a thorough review of appropriate, current documentation. The accommodations requests must be supported through the documentation provided and must be logically linked to the current impact of the condition on academic functioning.

FINANCIAL AID

Students should submit: FAFSA. Applicants will be notified of awards on a rolling basis beginning 4/1.. The Princeton Review suggests that all financial aid forms be submitted as soon as possible after October 1. Need-based scholarships/grants offered: College/university scholarship or grant aid from institutional funds; Federal Pell; Private scholarships; SEOG; State scholarships/grants Loan aid offered: Direct PLUS loans; Direct Subsidized Stafford Loans; Direct Unsubsidized Stafford Loans Federal Work-Study Program available. Institutional employment available.

CAMPUS LIFE

Activities: Choral groups; Concert band ; Dance ; Drama/theater; International Student Organization; Jazz band; Marching band; Music ensembles; Musical theater; Radio station ; Student government; Student newspaper; Symphony orchestra ; Television station; Yearbook Organizations: 250 registered organizations, 21 honor societies, 11 religious organizations. 19 fraternities, 13 sororities, Athletics (Intercollegiate): Men: baseball, basketball, cheerleading, cross-country, football, golf, tennis, track/field (outdoor) Women: basketball, cheerleading, cross-country, diving, equestrian sports, golf, lacrosse, light weight football, soccer, softball, swimming, tennis, track/field (outdoor), volleyball. On-Campus Highlights: Savemart Events Center, Downing Planetarium, Kennel Bookstore, New Ciminology Center, Henry Madden Library.

ACCOMMODATIONS

Allowed in exams:

Calculators	Yes
Dictionary	Yes
Computer	Yes
Spell-checker	Yes
Extended test time	Yes
Scribe	Yes
Proctors	Yes
Oral exams	Yes
Note-takers	Yes

Support services for students with

LD	Yes
ADHD	Yes
ASD	Yes
Distraction-reduced environment	Yes
Recording of lecture alowed	Yes
Reading technology:	Yes
Audio books	Yes
Other assistive technology	Yes
Priority registration	Yes

Added costs of services:

For LD:	No
For ADHD:	No
For ASD:	No
LD specialists	Yes
ADHD & ASD coaching	Yes
ASD specialists	Yes
Professional tutors	Yes
Peer tutors	Yes
Max. hours/week for services	Varies
How professors are notified of student approved accomodations	Student

COLLEGE GRADUATION REQUIREMENTS

Course waivers allowed	No
Course substitutions allowed	No

California State University, Fullerton

800 North State College Boulevard, Fullerton, CA 92834-6900 • Admissions: 657-278-7788 • Fax: 657-278-7699

CAMPUS

Type of school	Public
Environment	City
Support	CS

STUDENTS

Undergrad enrollment	38,672
% male/female	51/49
% from out of state	1
% frosh live on campus	7

FINANCIAL FACTS

Annual in-state tuition	$5,742
Annual out-of-state tuition	$16,632
Room and board	$15,642
Required fees	$1,108

GENERAL ADMISSIONS INFO

Application fee	$55
Priority deadline	10/30
Regular application deadline	11/30
Nonfall registration accepted.	

Range SAT EBRW	457.5–570
Range SAT Math	490–590
Range ACT Composite	19–24

ACADEMICS

Student/faculty ratio	27:1
% students returning for sophomore year	87
% students graduating within 4 years	22
% students graduating within 6 years	66
Most classes have fewer than 10 students.	

PROGRAMS/SERVICES FOR STUDENTS WITH LEARNING DIFFERENCES

The Office of Disability Support Services provides Counselors to help plan a CSUF experience to meet their individual needs. The program is designed to increase retention and graduation rates for underrepresented students. Students are encouraged to fulfill their academic and career potential by participating in an exceptional support environment. Each participant is teamed with an academic counselor for one-on-one mentoring and advisement. The emphasis is on providing students with personal attention and access to support services that include academic advisement; tutoring (referrals for individual and group tutoring including review sessions in select courses and development of study group); co-curricular events; peer mentoring for first-time freshmen; workshops and study-skills courses in reading, writing, math and other subjects, as well as time management; counseling; and an introduction to campus resources.

ADMISSIONS

Students are admitted on an eligibility index based on high school GPA in college-prep courses and scores on ACT or SAT. Lower GPA requires higher scores on the test. Other factors such as impaction and residency status are also considered. The foreign language requirement may be waived in rare cases when supported by the testing data supporting a relevant learning disability. ACT or SAT Reasoning Test required. All applicants must have 2 social science, 4 English, 3 math, 2 science (science with a lab, 1 biological and 1 physical), and 2 foreign language. The GPA is calculated based on the college-prep courses completed in grades 10, 11, and if available, 12. Students must have at least a C in these courses. Grades of D or less cannot be validated by a higher second semester grade in any of the following disciplines: social science/history, English, laboratory science, visual/performing arts, and electives. Students must have C or higher in all semesters of English, other lab sciences than chemistry, social sciences/history, and visual/performing arts to have the course counted toward the required preparatory units. Applicants within the local area will be required to meet the minimum eligibility requirement of 2900 based on GPA and SAT result or a 694 based on GPA and ACT result. Students outside of the local area should not anticipate receiving an admissions decision until late January or February.

ADMISSIONS INFO FOR STUDENTS WITH LEARNING DIFFERENCES

SAT/ACT required: Yes
Interview required: No
Essay required: No
Additional application required: No
Documentation required for:
 LD: Psycho ed evaluation
 ADHD: Diagnosis based on DSM-V; history of behaviors impairing functioning in academic setting; diagnostic interview; history of symptoms; evidence of ongoing behaviors.
 ASD: Psycho ed evaluation
Documentation submitted to: Disabled Student Services
Special Ed. HS course work accepted: No
Separate application required for Programs/Services: No
Contact Information
Name of program or department: Disabled Student Services
Telephone: 657-278-3112
Email: tomthompson@fullerton.edu

California State University, Fullerton

Additional Information
The Intensive Learning Experience (ILE) program is designed to monitor the progress of any students fulfilling remedial compliance requirements and help students make successful progress in fulfilling the graduation requirements. ILE staff helps students on class planning, study skills, transfer work, campus resources, time management, and campus organizations. If not exempt from the English Placement Test (EPT) and Entry Level Mathematics (ELM), freshman must pass the EPT and/or ELM to move into the GE-level mathematics and English courses. If students do not pass they must take a developmental English and/or math course to fulfill the remedial compliance requirements. ILE provides students with an accommodation letter for professors each semester.

GENERAL ADMISSIONS
Very important factors considered include: academic GPA, standardized test scores, geographical residence, state residency. *Freshman Admission Requirements:* High school diploma is required and GED is accepted. *Academic units required:* 4 English, 3 math, 2 science, 2 science labs, 2 foreign language, 1 social studies, 1 history, 1 academic elective, 1 visual/performing arts. *Academic units recommended:* 4 English, 3 math, 2 science, 2 science labs, 3 foreign language, 1 social studies, 1 history, 1 academic elective, 1 visual/performing arts.

ACCOMMODATIONS OR SERVICES
Accommodations are decided upon an individual basis after a thorough review of appropriate, current documentation. The accommodations requests must be supported through the documentation provided and must be logically linked to the current impact of the condition on academic functioning.

FINANCIAL AID
Students should submit: FAFSA. The Princeton Review suggests that all financial aid forms be submitted as soon as possible after October 1. *Need-based scholarships/grants offered:* College/university scholarship or grant aid from institutional funds; Federal Nursing Scholarships; Federal Pell; Private scholarships; SEOG; State scholarships/grants. *Loan aid offered:* Direct PLUS loans; Direct Subsidized Stafford Loans; Direct Unsubsidized Stafford Loans. Federal Work-Study Program available. Institutional employment available.

CAMPUS LIFE
Activities: Choral groups; Concert band; Dance; Drama/theater; International Student Organization; Jazz band; Model UN; Music ensembles; Musical theater; Radio station; Student government; Student newspaper; Symphony orchestra.. **Organizations: Athletics (Intercollegiate):** *Men:* baseball, basketball, cross-country, fencing, soccer, track/field (outdoor), wrestling. *Women:* basketball, cross-country, fencing, gymnastics, soccer, softball, tennis, track/field (outdoor), volleyball. **On-Campus Highlights:** Student Recreation Center, Titan Student Union, Mihaylo Hall, Fullerton Arboretum, 5 Starbucks Coffee Shops.

ACCOMMODATIONS

Allowed in exams:	
Calculators	Yes
Dictionary	Yes
Computer	Yes
Spell-checker	Yes
Extended test time	Yes
Scribe	Yes
Proctors	Yes
Oral exams	Yes
Note-takers	Yes
Support services for students with	
LD	No
ADHD	No
ASD	No
Distraction-reduced environment	Yes
Recording of lecture allowed	Yes
Reading technology:	Yes
Audio books	Yes
Other assistive technology	Yes
Priority registration	Yes
Added costs for services:	
For LD:	No
For ADHD:	No
For ASD:	No
LD specialists	Yes
ADHD & ASD coaching	No
ASD specialists	No
Professional tutors	No
Peer tutors	Yes
Max. hours/week for services	Varies
How professors are notified of student approved accommodations	Student

COLLEGE GRADUATION REQUIREMENTS

Course waivers allowed	No
Course substitutions allowed	No

California State University–Long Beach

1250 BELLFLOWER BOULEVARD, LONG BEACH, CA 90840 • ADMISSIONS: 562-985-5471 • FAX: 562-985-4973

CAMPUS

Type of school	Public
Environment	Urban
Support	CS

STUDENTS

Undergrad enrollment	32,079
% male/female	44/56
% from out of state	1
% frosh live on campus	36

FINANCIAL FACTS

Annual in-state tuition	$5,742
Annual out-of-state tuition	$15,144
Room and board	$12,382
Required fees	$980

GENERAL ADMISSIONS INFO

Regular application deadline 11/30
Nonfall registration accepted.

Range SAT EBRW	460–570
Range SAT Math	470–600
Range ACT Composite	20–26

ACADEMICS

Student/faculty ratio 24:1
% students returning for sophomore year 91
Most classes have 20–29 students.
Most lab/discussion sessions have 10–19 students.

PROGRAMS/SERVICES FOR STUDENTS WITH LEARNING DIFFERENCES

The mission of the Disabled Student Services is to assist students with disabilities as they secure their university degrees at California State University, Long Beach. The Disabled Student Services Support Services and Advising Program provides accommodations for students with disabilities. Students who need accommodations must provide adequate medical verification of their disability and contact the office to receive services.

ADMISSIONS

Special Admission Information: The Special Admission process is a means by which applicants, who may not meet the California State University Long Beach (CSULB) admission requirements due to a disability, but who are "otherwise qualified," may request special consideration for admission. The DSS Special Admissions Committee facilitates this process by consulting with Enrollment Services while providing additional information about each applicant's special circumstances. It is the committee's function to evaluate disability documentation using guidelines established by the California State University (CSU) system. All applicants are reviewed on a case-by-case basis.

Additional Information

The Stephen Benson Program for Students with Learning Disabilities (SBP) was created to serve the needs of CSULB students who have a diagnosed learning disability. The program was established in 1980 and continues to be one of the most recognized post-secondary LD programs in the state. Typically, the SBP serves approximately 500 students with learning disabilities each semester. A learning disability can interfere with a student's ability to assimilate or process information in several ways. The purpose of the SBP is to provide students, with documented learning disabilities, a support system to assist them in attaining their academic goals.

ADMISSIONS INFO FOR STUDENTS WITH LEARNING DIFFERENCES

SAT/ACT required: Yes
Interview required: No
Essay required: Yes
Additional application required: No
Documentation required for:
  LD: Acceptable documentation should consist of a psycho-educational report and/or other professional verification. Documentation should be dated within the last 3 years from time of application. Note: Individual Educational Plans (IEP's) are not generally an acceptable form of verification for the California State University (CSU) system.
  ADHD: A psychoeducational report and/or other professional verification from an appropriately licensed professional with a DSM-5 diagnosis and/or medical verification.
  ASD: www.csulb.edu/autism
Documentation submitted to: Both support services and admission
Special Ed. HS course work accepted: N/A
Separate application required for Programs/Services: No
Contact Information
Name of program or department: Stephen Benson Learning Disability Program
Telephone: (562) 985-4430
Fax: (562) 985-4529
Email: dss@csulb.edu

California State University–Long Beach

GENERAL ADMISSIONS

Very important factors considered include: academic GPA, standardized test scores, geographical residence, state residency. *Important factors considered include:* talent/ability. *Other factors considered include:* rigor of secondary school record, application essay, recommendation(s), extracurricular activities, character/personal qualities, volunteer work, work experience. *Freshman Admission Requirements:* High school diploma is required and GED is accepted. *Academic units required:* 4 English, 3 math, 2 science, 2 science labs, 2 foreign language, 1 social studies, 1 history, 1 academic elective, and 1 unit from above areas or other academic areas.

ACCOMMODATIONS OR SERVICES

Accommodations are decided upon an individual basis after a thorough review of appropriate, current documentation. The accommodations requests must be supported through the documentation provided and must be logically linked to the current impact of the condition on academic functioning.

FINANCIAL AID

Students should submit: FAFSA. Applicants will be notified of awards on a rolling basis beginning 3/25. The Princeton Review suggests that all financial aid forms be submitted as soon as possible after October 1. *Need-based scholarships/grants offered:* College/university scholarship or grant aid from institutional funds; Federal Pell; Private scholarships; SEOG; State scholarships/grants. *Loan aid offered:* Direct PLUS loans; Direct Subsidized Stafford Loans; Direct Unsubsidized Stafford Loans. Federal Work-Study Program available. Institutional employment available.

CAMPUS LIFE

Activities: Choral groups; Concert band; Dance; Drama/theater; Jazz band; Literary magazine; Music ensembles; Musical theater; Opera; Radio station; Student government; Student newspaper; Student-run film society; Symphony orchestra; Television station; Yearbook.. **Organizations:** 300 registered organizations, 25 honor societies, 20 religious organizations, 16 fraternities, 15 sororities. **Athletics (Intercollegiate):** *Men:* baseball, basketball, cross-country, golf, track/field (outdoor), volleyball, water polo. *Women:* basketball, cross-country, golf, soccer, softball, tennis, track/field (outdoor), volleyball, water polo.

ACCOMMODATIONS

Allowed in exams:	
Calculators	Yes
Dictionary	Yes
Computer	Yes
Spell-checker	Yes
Extended test time	Yes
Scribe	Yes
Proctors	Yes
Oral exams	Yes
Note-takers	Yes
Support services for students with	
LD	Yes
ADHD	Yes
ASD	Yes
Distraction-reduced environment	Yes
Recording of lecture allowed	Yes
Reading technology:	Yes
Audio books	Yes
Other assistive technology	Yes
Priority registration	Yes
Added costs for services:	
For LD:	No
For ADHD:	No
For ASD:	No
LD specialists	Yes
ADHD & ASD coaching	Yes
ASD specialists	Yes
Professional tutors	No
Peer tutors	Yes
Max. hours/week for services	NR
How professors are notified of student approved accommodations	Student

COLLEGE GRADUATION REQUIREMENTS

Course waivers allowed	Varies
Course substitutions allowed	Yes
In what courses	

Math, Other General Education courses as needed; on a case-by-case basis by way of an appeal through Academic Affairs.

California State University, Northridge

18111 Nordhoff Street, Northridge, CA 91330-8207 • Admissions: 818-677-3700 • Fax: 818-677-3766

CAMPUS
Type of school	Public
Environment	City
Support	CS

STUDENTS
Undergrad enrollment	36,917
% male/female	46/54
% from out of state	1

FINANCIAL FACTS
Annual in-state tuition	$5,742
Annual out-of-state tuition	$0
Room and board	$9,962
Required fees	

GENERAL ADMISSIONS INFO
Application fee	$55

Nonfall registration accepted.

Range SAT EBRW	400–510
Range SAT Math	400–520
Range ACT Composite	60–120

ACADEMICS
Student/faculty ratio	NR
% students returning for sophomore year	78

Most classes have 10–19 students.
Most lab/discussion sessions have 10–19 students.

PROGRAMS/SERVICES FOR STUDENTS WITH LEARNING DIFFERENCES

Disability Resources and Educational Services (DRES) recognizes that students with disabilities can be quite successful in the university setting if appropriate educational support services are offered to them. In an effort to assist students with disabilities in reaching their full potential, the program offers a comprehensive and well-coordinated system of educational support services that allow students to be judged on the basis of their ability rather than disability. In order to accommodate different needs DRES has developed an individualized learning plan called "journey to success". Students must register with DRES to be eligible.

ADMISSIONS

There is no special admission process. However, if a student applies to the university and is rejected, they may appeal the descision. Students must get a C or better in: 4 years English, 3 years math, 1 year U.S. history, 1 year science, 2 years foreign language, 1 year visual/performing arts, and 3 years of electives. An eligibility index combining GPA and ACT or SAT is used.

Additional Information

During the Transition years students can expect staff to assist them in: managing workloads, developing compensatory strategies for life-long learning, learning self-advocacy skills, and learning how to access services. In the Foundation years students can expect staff to continue with a mentor relationship, map out career strategies, encourage the student to join co-curricular activities that contribute to personal and social growth and continuing relationship-building with faculty. Assistance in developing appropriate learning strategies is provided on an individual basis.

ADMISSIONS INFO FOR STUDENTS WITH LEARNING DIFFERENCES

SAT/ACT required: Yes
Interview required: Yes
Essay required: No
Additional application required: No
Documentation required for:
  LD: Must contain a specific diagnosis, indicating whether the disability is temporary or permanent, and a concise description of the functional limitations imposed by the disability. Copies of the assessment containing the results of a diagnostic interview, an assessment of aptitude, academic achievement, and information processing as well as a diagnosis with functional limitations are recommended.
  ADHD: Neuropsychological assessment signed by physician, other licensed health care professional, or rehabilitation counselor. The report should contain a specific diagnosis, indicating whether the disability is temporary or permanent, and a concise description of the functional limitations.
  ASD: Psycho ed evaluation
Documentation submitted to: Disability Resources and Educational Services
Special Ed. HS course work accepted: yes
Separate application required for Programs/Services: yes
Contact Information
Name of program or department: Disability Resources and Educational Services
Telephone: 818-677-2684
Fax: 818-677-4932
Email: dres@csun.edu

California State University, Northridge

GENERAL ADMISSIONS
Very important factors considered include: standardized test scores. *Freshman Admission Requirements:* High school diploma is required and GED is accepted; High school diploma is required and GED is not accepted. *Academic units required:* 4 English, 3 math, 1 science, 2 science labs, 2 foreign language, 2 history, 1 academic elective, and 1 unit from above areas or other academic areas.

ACCOMMODATIONS OR SERVICES
Accommodations are decided upon an individual basis after a thorough review of appropriate, current documentation. The accommodations requests must be supported through the documentation provided and must be logically linked to the current impact of the condition on academic functioning.

FINANCIAL AID
Students should submit: FAFSA. The Princeton Review suggests that all financial aid forms be submitted as soon as possible after October 1. *Need-based scholarships/grants offered:* College/university scholarship or grant aid from institutional funds; Federal Nursing Scholarships; Federal Pell; Private scholarships; SEOG; State scholarships/grants. *Loan aid offered:* Federal Work-Study Program available. Institutional employment available.

CAMPUS LIFE
Activities: Choral groups; Concert band; Dance; Drama/theater; International Student Organization; Jazz band; Literary magazine; Marching band; Music ensembles; Musical theater; Radio station; Student government; Student newspaper; Yearbook.. **Organizations:** 267 registered organizations, 18 honor societies, 13 religious organizations. 24 fraternities, 12 sororities. **Athletics (Intercollegiate):** *Men:* baseball, basketball, cross-country, diving, football, golf, soccer, swimming, track/field (outdoor), track/field (indoor), volleyball. *Women:* basketball, cross-country, diving, football, golf, soccer, softball, swimming, tennis, track/field (outdoor), track/field (indoor), volleyball. Valley Performing Arts Center, Student Recreation Center, Oviatt Library, Matador Book Store.

ACCOMMODATIONS
Allowed in exams:

Calculators	Yes
Dictionary	Yes
Computer	Yes
Spell-checker	Yes
Extended test time	Yes
Scribe	Yes
Proctors	Yes
Oral exams	Yes
Note-takers	Yes

Support services for students with

LD	Yes
ADHD	Yes
ASD	Yes
Distraction-reduced environment	Yes
Recording of lecture allowed	Yes
Reading technology:	Yes
Audio books	Yes
Other assistive technology	Yes
Priority registration	Yes

Added costs for services:

For LD:	No
For ADHD:	No
For ASD:	No
LD specialists	Yes
ADHD & ASD coaching	No
ASD specialists	No
Professional tutors	No
Peer tutors	Yes
Max. hours/week for services	2
How professors are notified of student approved accommodations	Student

COLLEGE GRADUATION REQUIREMENTS

Course waivers allowed	No
Course substitutions allowed	No

California State University–San Bernardino

5500 UNIVERSITY PARKWAY, SAN BERNARDINO, CA 92407-2397 • ADMISSIONS: 909-537-5188 • FAX: 909-537-7034

CAMPUS
Type of school	Public
Environment	City
Support	CS

STUDENTS
Undergrad enrollment	18,453
% male/female	40/60
% from out of state	1
% frosh live on campus	16

FINANCIAL FACTS
Annual in-state tuition	$5,742
Annual out-of-state tuition	$11,880
Room and board	$12,711
Required fees	$1,184

GENERAL ADMISSIONS INFO
Application fee	$55
Priority deadline	11/30

Nonfall registration accepted.

Range SAT EBRW	390–490
Range SAT Math	390–490
Range ACT Composite	16–20

ACADEMICS
Student/faculty ratio	28:1
% students returning for sophomore year	85

Most classes have 10–19 students.

PROGRAMS/SERVICES FOR STUDENTS WITH LEARNING DIFFERENCES

The Learning Disability Program is dedicated to assuring each student an opportunity to experience equity in education. Each student must complete an assessment, and then the staff helps to develop compensatory methods for handling assignments and classroom projects. Careful attention is paid to helping the student acquire learning skills and formulating and implementing specific strategies for note-taking and management of written materials. Recommendations are designed for each student as a result of a psychometric assessment, personal interview, and academic requirements. The emphasis of the plan is to assist the students with a learning disability in finding techniques to deal with it in college and in the job market. http://ssd.csusb.edu/index.html

ADMISSIONS

Entrance requires a minimum 15-unit pattern of courses for admission as a first-time freshman. Each unit is equal to a year of study in a subject area. A grade of C (GPA 2.0) or better is required for each course you use to meet any subject requirement. History/social science. Two years, including one year of world history, cultures and historical geography and one year of U.S. history, or one-half year of U.S. history and one-half year of American government or civics. English–Four years of college preparatory English that integrates reading of classic and modern literature, frequent and regular writing, and practice listening and speaking. Mathematics– Three years of collegepreparatory mathematics that include or integrate the topics covered in elementary and advanced algebra and two- and three-dimensional geometry. Laboratory science– Two years of laboratory science providing fundamental knowledge in at least two of the three disciplines of biology, chemistry and physics. Language other than English– Two years of the same language other than English or equivalent to the second level of high school instruction.

ADMISSIONS INFO FOR STUDENTS WITH LEARNING DIFFERENCES

SAT/ACT required: Yes

Interview required: No

Essay required: No

Additional application required: Yes

Documentation required for:

 LD: Psycho ed evaluation

 ADHD: Diagnosis based DSM-IV or-V; history of behaviors impairing functioning in academic setting; diagnostic interview; history of symptoms; evidence of ongoing behaviors.

 ASD: Diagnosis based on DSM-IV or -V; history of behaviors impairing functioning in academic setting; diagnostic interview; history of symptoms; evidence of ongoing behaviors.

Documentation submitted to: Support Program/Services

Special Ed. HS course work accepted: No

Separate application required for Programs/Services: No

Contact Information

Name of program or department: Services to Students with Disabilities

Telephone: 909-537-5238

Fax: 909-537-7090

Email: SSD@csusb.edu

California State University–San Bernardino

Additional Information

Services and accommodations for students with appropriate documentation could include the following: the use of calculators, dictionaries, computers, or spellchecker during exams; extended time on tests; distraction-free testing environments; oral exams; note-takers; proctors; scribes; tape recorders in class; books on tape; assisting technology; and priority registration. Specific services include assessment counseling and testing accommodations. Students on academic probation have two quarters to raise their GPA to a 2.0. The LD Program provides continual academic support.

GENERAL ADMISSIONS

Very important factors considered include: academic GPA, standardized test scores. *Important factors considered include:* geographical residence. *Freshman Admission Requirements:* High school diploma is required and GED is accepted. *Academic units required:* 4 English, 3 math, 2 science, 2 science labs, 2 foreign language, 1 social studies, 1 history, 1 academic elective, 1 visual/performing arts.

ACCOMMODATIONS OR SERVICES

Accommodations are decided upon an individual basis after a thorough review of appropriate, current documentation. The accommodations requests must be supported through the documentation provided and must be logically linked to the current impact of the condition on academic functioning.

FINANCIAL AID

Students should submit: FAFSA; State aid form. Applicants will be notified of awards on a rolling basis beginning 4/1. The Princeton Review suggests that all financial aid forms be submitted as soon as possible after October 1. *Need-based scholarships/grants offered:* College/university scholarship or grant aid from institutional funds; Federal Pell; Private scholarships; SEOG; State scholarships/grants. *Loan aid offered:* Direct PLUS loans; Direct Subsidized Stafford Loans; Direct Unsubsidized Stafford Loans. Federal Work-Study Program available. Institutional employment available.

CAMPUS LIFE

Activities: Campus Ministries; Choral groups; Dance; Drama/theater; International Student Organization; Jazz band; Model UN; Music ensembles; Musical theater; Radio station; Student government; Student newspaper; Television station.. **Organizations:** 97 registered organizations, 3 religious organizations. 9 fraternities, 6 sororities. **Athletics (Intercollegiate):** *Men:* baseball, basketball, golf, soccer, swimming, water polo. *Women:* basketball, cross-country, soccer, softball, swimming, tennis, volleyball, water polo. **On-Campus Highlights:** Coussoulis Arena, Robert and Frances Fullerton Museum of Art, Santos Manuel Student Union, John M. Pfau Library, Student Recreation & Fitness Center Facilities.

ACCOMMODATIONS

Allowed in exams:

Calculators	Yes
Dictionary	Yes
Computer	Yes
Spell-checker	Yes
Extended test time	Yes
Scribe	Yes
Proctors	Yes
Oral exams	Yes
Note-takers	Yes

Support services for students with

LD	Yes
ADHD	Yes
ASD	Yes
Distraction-reduced environment	Yes
Recording of lecture allowed	Y/N
Reading technology:	Yes
Audio books	Yes

Other assistive technology   audio-recording of lectures (not video) permitted

Priority registration	Yes

Added costs for services:

For LD:	No
For ADHD:	No
For ASD:	No
LD specialists	Yes
ADHD & ASD coaching	No
ASD specialists	No
Professional tutors	Yes
Peer tutors	Yes
Max. hours/week for services	Varies

How professors are notified of student approved accomodations

Director and Student

COLLEGE GRADUATION REQUIREMENTS

Course waivers allowed	No
Course substitutions allowed	Yes

In what courses

For general ed math for verified dyscalculia only

Loyola Marymount University

1 LMU Drive, Los Angeles, CA 90045-8350 • Admissions: 310-338-2750 • Fax: 310-338-2797

CAMPUS
Type of school	Private (nonprofit)
Environment	Town
Support	S

STUDENTS
Undergrad enrollment	6,257
% male/female	44/56
% from out of state	29
% frosh live on campus	95

FINANCIAL FACTS
Annual Tuition	$47,470
Room and board	$15,185
Required fees	$702

GENERAL ADMISSIONS INFO
Application fee	$60
Regular application deadline	1/15

Nonfall registration accepted. Admission may be deferred for a maximum of 1 year.

Range SAT EBRW	600–680
Range SAT Math	580–680
Range ACT Composite	26–31

ACADEMICS
Student/faculty ratio	NR
% students returning for sophomore year	91
% students graduating within 4 years	70
% students graduating within 6 years	79

PROGRAMS/SERVICES FOR STUDENTS WITH LEARNING DIFFERENCES

The Office of Disability Support Services (DSS) provides specialized assistance and resources that enable students with physical, perceptual, emotional, and learning disabilities to achieve maximum independence while they pursue their educational goals. Assisted by staff specialists from all areas of the university, the DSS Office works to eliminate physical and attitudinal barriers. To be eligible for services, students must provide documentation of the disability from a licensed professional. At the Learning Resource Center students can receive tutoring in over 250 LMU classes, attend workshops, and access assistance in writing, reading, and math with LRC specialists.

ADMISSIONS

There is no special admissions process for students with disabilities. The admission decision will be based upon the student's grade point average, SAT/ACT scores, strength of curriculum, the application essay, letters of recommendation, and extracurricular activities. Enrolled students have an average GPA of 3.75. Students are encouraged to have completed 4 years English, 3 years social sciences, 3 years foreign language, 3 years math (4 years for engineering and science), and 1 year elective.

Additional Information

There is an Academic Resource Center where all students can find specialists and tutors. There is course-specific tutoring, study skills programs (which include learning time management, overcoming test anxiety, conquering math word problems, mastering the textbook, preparing for exams, and studying efficiently), and other academic support programs with full-time professional staff members prepared to assist with writing, reading, math, ESL, and Disability Support Services. Logging in to DSS Online Services website students can select classes that they want to use their accomodations in as well as what accommodations they will need in that class. Specific accommodations for LD students with appropriate documentation could include: priority registration, notetakers, readers, transcribers, alternate testing conditions, taped books, and advocacy.

ADMISSIONS INFO FOR STUDENTS WITH LEARNING DIFFERENCES

SAT/ACT required: Yes
Interview required: No
Essay required: No
Additional application required: No
Documentation required for:
 LD: Most current psychoeducational evaluation, transcripts, accommodations in high school, SAT/ACT scores/accommodations, IEP or 504 if attended public school, medical documents if on medication
 ADHD: psychoeducational evaluation, transcripts, accommodations in high school, SAT/ACT scores/accommodations, IEP/504 if attended public high school
 ASD: Psycho ed evaluation
Documentation submitted to: Support program/services
Special Ed. HS course work accepted: No
Separate application required for Programs/Services: Yes
Contact Information
Name of program or department: Office of Disability Support Services (DSS)
Telephone: 310-338-4216
Fax: 310-338-5344

Loyola Marymount University

GENERAL ADMISSIONS
Very important factors considered include: academic GPA. *Important factors considered include:* rigor of secondary school record, application essay, standardized test scores, talent/ability, character/personal qualities. *Other factors considered include:* class rank, recommendation(s), extracurricular activities, first generation, alumni/ae relation, volunteer work, work experience. *Freshman Admission Requirements:* High school diploma is required and GED is accepted. *Academic units recommended:* 4 English, 3 math, 2 science, 2 science labs, 3 foreign language, 3 social studies, 1 academic elective.

ACCOMMODATIONS OR SERVICES
Accommodations are decided upon an individual basis after a thorough review of appropriate, current documentation. The accommodations requests must be supported through the documentation provided and must be logically linked to the current impact of the condition on academic functioning.

FINANCIAL AID
Students should submit: FAFSA. The Princeton Review suggests that all financial aid forms be submitted as soon as possible after October 1. *Need-based scholarships/grants offered:* College/university scholarship or grant aid from institutional funds; Federal Pell; Private scholarships; SEOG; State scholarships/grants. *Loan aid offered:* Direct PLUS loans; Direct Subsidized Stafford Loans; Direct Unsubsidized Stafford Loans. Federal Work-Study Program available. Institutional employment available.

CAMPUS LIFE
Activities: Campus Ministries; Choral groups; Dance; Drama/theater; International Student Organization; Literary magazine; Model UN; Music ensembles; Opera; Pep band; Radio station; Student government; Student newspaper; Student-run film society; Television station; Yearbook. **Organizations:** 120 registered organizations, 12 honor societies, 2 religious organizations. 6 fraternities, 8 sororities. **Athletics (Intercollegiate):** *Men:* baseball, basketball, crew/rowing, cross-country, golf, soccer, tennis, water polo. *Women:* basketball, crew/rowing, cross-country, soccer, softball, swimming, tennis, volleyball, water polo. Wm. H. Hannon Library, Malone Student Center, Burns Recreation Center, Lion's Den and Living Room, Life Sciences Building.

ACCOMMODATIONS

Allowed in exams:	
Calculators	Yes
Dictionary	Yes
Computer	Yes
Spell-checker	Yes
Extended test time	Yes
Scribe	Yes
Proctors	Yes
Oral exams	Yes
Note-takers	Yes
Support services for students with	
LD	Yes
ADHD	Yes
ASD	Yes
Distraction-reduced environment	Yes
Recording of lecture allowed	Yes
Reading technology:	Yes
Audio books	Yes
Other assistive technology	Yes
Priority registration	Yes
Added costs for services:	
For LD:	No
For ADHD:	No
For ASD:	No
LD specialists	Yes
ADHD & ASD coaching	No
ASD specialists	No
Professional tutors	No
Peer tutors	Yes
Max. hours/week for services	1 ea. subj.
How professors are notified of student approved accommodations	Student

COLLEGE GRADUATION REQUIREMENTS

Course waivers allowed	No
Course substitutions allowed	No

Menlo College

1000 El Camino Real, Atherton, CA 94027 • Admissions: 650-543-3753 • Fax: 650-543-4103

PROGRAMS/SERVICES FOR STUDENTS WITH LEARNING DIFFERENCES

The Menlo College Academic Success Center (ASC) welcomes all students including those with learning, psychological, and attention challenges. In its new configuration with the Bowman Library, now the Learning Community Commons, services have broadened to include library staff and resources. Students who present proper documentation of a disability may qualify for accommodations. All students are welcome to utilize the services of the Academic Success Center.

ADMISSIONS

Students are admitted to Menlo College on their own merits, without regard to disability. If students choose to self-disclose their learning challenges, they are encouraged to meet with the Academic Success Center in advance of their arrival to arrange for early set-up of accommodations. Menlo values the individual strengths and diversity that students bring to Menlo, so we choose not to follow a specific formula when making our admission decisions. Each applicant is reviewed individually, and the acceptance decisions are based on many factors including the strength of your course curriculum, the school you attend(ed), and your grades and test scores. In addition, we consider your extracurricular activities, community involvement, employment, and leadership roles. Menlo College is most interested in the quality of students' activities, rather than the quantity. Essay required regarding either 1) Academic strengths or weaknesses, or 2) Reasons for seeking college education, or 3) Learning experiences you hope to have, or 4) Why Menlo Counselor teacher recommendation, ACT/SAT.

Additional Information

The Academic Success Center provides a 'one-stop' center for information and resources that are key to academic and career success. The services include: advising, advocacy, assistive technology, note takers, books on tape, tutoring lab and writing center, testing and tutoring, documentation analysis and faculty liaison for Students with Disabilities. The Academic Success Center will help students improve test performance, obtain or update their Degree Check Sheet(s), understand why they may attend class regularly, but feel like they're missing important points or having trouble completing tests in the allotted time, feel like they don't have enough time to get everything done, not sure how to take notes, need a tutor or study group, or want information on meeting with your academic advisor.

Menlo College

GENERAL ADMISSIONS

Very important factors considered include: rigor of secondary school record, academic GPA, standardized test scores. *Important factors considered include:* class rank, application essay, recommendation(s), character/personal qualities, volunteer work. *Other factors considered include:* interview, alumni/ae relation, work experience, level of applicant's interest. *Freshman Admission Requirements:* High school diploma is required and GED is accepted. *Academic units recommended:* 4 English, 3 math, 3 science, 2 foreign language, 3 social studies.

ACCOMMODATIONS OR SERVICES

Accommodations are decided upon an individual basis after a thorough review of appropriate, current documentation. The accommodations requests must be supported through the documentation provided and must be logically linked to the current impact of the condition on academic functioning.

FINANCIAL AID

Students should submit: FAFSA; State aid form. Applicants will be notified of awards on a rolling basis beginning 12/15. The Princeton Review suggests that all financial aid forms be submitted as soon as possible after October 1. *Need-based scholarships/grants offered:* College/university scholarship or grant aid from institutional funds; Federal Pell; SEOG; State scholarships/grants. *Loan aid offered:* Direct PLUS loans; Direct Subsidized Stafford Loans; Direct Unsubsidized Stafford Loans. Federal Work-Study Program available. Institutional employment available.

CAMPUS LIFE

Activities: Dance; International Student Organization; Student government; Student newspaper; Student-run film society. **Organizations:** 30 registered organizations, 2 honor societies, **Athletics (Intercollegiate):** *Men:* baseball, basketball, cross-country, football, golf, soccer, wrestling. *Women:* basketball, cross-country, soccer, softball, volleyball, wrestling. **On-Campus Highlights:** Brawner Hall, Library, Student Union, Dining commons.

ACCOMMODATIONS

Allowed in exams:	
Calculators	Yes
Dictionary	Yes
Computer	Yes
Spell-checker	Yes
Extended test time	Yes
Scribe	Yes
Proctors	Yes
Oral exams	Yes
Note-takers	Yes
Support services for students with	
LD	Yes
ADHD	Yes
ASD	Yes
Distraction-reduced environment	Yes
Recording of lecture allowed	Yes
Reading technology:	Yes
Audio books	Yes
Other assistive technology	Kurzweil 3000
Dragon Naturally Speaking	
Priority registration	No
Added costs for services:	
For LD:	No
For ADHD:	No
For ASD:	No
LD specialists	Yes
ADHD & ASD coaching	No
ASD specialists	No
Professional tutors	Yes
Peer tutors	Yes
Max. hours/week for services	Varies
How professors are notified of student approved accommodations	
Director and Student	

COLLEGE GRADUATION REQUIREMENTS

Course waivers allowed	Yes
In what courses	
Foreign Language and Math (for some majors)	
Course substitutions allowed	Yes
In what courses	F
oreign Language and Math (for some majors)	

Occidental College

1600 CAMPUS ROAD, LOS ANGELES, CA 90041-3314 • ADMISSIONS: 800-825-5262 • FAX: 323-341-4875

CAMPUS
Type of school	Private (nonprofit)
Environment	Metropolis
Support	S

STUDENTS
Undergrad enrollment	2,041
% male/female	42/58
% from out of state	51
% frosh live on campus	100

FINANCIAL FACTS
Annual tuition	$52,260
Room and board	$14,968
Required fees	$578

GENERAL ADMISSIONS INFO
Application fee	$65
Regular application deadline	1/15

Nonfall registration accepted. Admission may be deferred for a maximum of 1 year.

Range SAT EBRW	650–720
Range SAT Math	630–720
Range ACT Composite	27–32

ACADEMICS
Student/faculty ratio	9:1
% students returning for sophomore year	91
% students graduating within 4 years	80
% students graduating within 6 years	84

Most classes have 10–19 students. Most lab/discussion sessions have 10–19 students.

PROGRAMS/SERVICES FOR STUDENTS WITH LEARNING DIFFERENCES

Through providing reasonable and appropriate accommodations, assisting students with self-advocacy, providing academic support and counseling, and ensuring adherence to state and federal disability laws, the Office of Disability Services is committed to enhancing students' academic development and independence. By working closely with faculty, staff, and administrators, our goal is to create a supportive community that promotes awareness, sensitivity and understanding of students with disabilities. Documentation must be provided by health care or mental health professionals appropriately licensed to diagnose medical, psychological and/or learning disorders (i.e. physicians, psychiatrists, school psychologists, and psychologists). Documentation must be printed on professional letterhead, include the contact information and license number of the professional, and be signed by the clinician performing the evaluation.

ADMISSIONS

Occidental utilizes a comprehensive review process when considering students for admission. The college values academic performance, extracurricular achievement and personal attributes when evaluating first-year and transfer applications. In the review of an academic record, Occidental places the most emphasis on course rigor and classroom performance. Because Occidental receives applications from students at a wide variety of schools across the United States and around the world, Oxy utilizes standardized test scores to give additional context to classroom performance. All applicants are required to submit either the SAT or ACT. . SAT Subject tests are not required for admission, but will consider those scores in the review process. The essay portion is recommended but not required. The admission committee will always look at you "on your best day," meaning they will always look at the best scores on each section of these exams. The median unweighted GPA is 3.7; the median SAT is 1350 combined (EBRW-680, M-680) and the median ACT is 30.

ADMISSIONS INFO FOR STUDENTS WITH LEARNING DIFFERENCES
SAT/ACT required: Yes
Interview required: No
Essay required: Not Applicable
Additional application required: Yes
Documentation required for:
 LD: Psycho-educational evaluation/assessment
 ADHD: Psycho-educational evaluation/assessment
 ASD: Psycho-educational evaluation/assessment
Documentation submitted to: Support Program/Services
Special Ed. HS course work accepted: Not Applicable
Separate application required for Programs/Services: No
Contact Information
Name of program or department: Disability Services
Telephone: 323-259-2969
Fax: 323-341-4927
Email: accessibility@oxy.edu

Occidental College

Additional Information
A staff member will help determine which accommodations students are eligible to receive based on disability-related functional limitations. In this intake meeting, all accommodation policies and procedures pertaining to the student accommodation plan will be reviewed and made available. Once admitted, students make a request for accommodations, provide documentation, and meet with a Disability Services coordinator to determine appropriate accommodations and go over all policies and procedures. Typical accommodations if appropriate include: Extended testing time, use of computer or assistive technology, reduced distraction testing environment, use of a calculator or spell checker, notetaker-recorder during lectures, or reduced course load

GENERAL ADMISSIONS
Very important factors considered include: rigor of secondary school record, academic GPA, application essay. *Important factors considered include:* class rank, standardized test scores, recommendation(s), extracurricular activities, character/personal qualities, volunteer work, work experience. *Other factors considered include:* interview, talent/ability, first generation, alumni/ae relation, geographical residence, racial/ethnic status, level of applicant's interest. *Freshman Admission Requirements:* High school diploma is required and GED is accepted. *Academic units recommended:* 4 English, 3 math, 3 science, 3 foreign language, 2 social studies, 3 history.

ACCOMMODATIONS OR SERVICES
Accommodations are decided upon an individual basis after a thorough review of appropriate, current documentation. The accommodations requests must be supported through the documentation provided and must be logically linked to the current impact of the condition on academic functioning.

FINANCIAL AID
Students should submit: CSS/Financial Aid PROFILE; FAFSA; Noncustodial PROFILE; State aid form. Applicants will be notified of awards on or about 3/25. The Princeton Review suggests that all financial aid forms be submitted as soon as possible after October 1. *Need-based scholarships/grants offered:* College/university scholarship or grant aid from institutional funds; Federal Pell; Private scholarships; SEOG; State scholarships/grants. *Loan aid offered:* Direct PLUS loans; Direct Subsidized Stafford Loans; Direct Unsubsidized Stafford Loans. Federal Work-Study Program available. Institutional employment available.

CAMPUS LIFE
Activities: Campus Ministries; Choral groups; Concert band; Dance; Drama/theater; International Student Organization; Jazz band; Literary magazine; Music ensembles; Pep band; Student government; Student newspaper; Yearbook. **Organizations:** 8 honor societies, 5 religious organizations. 4 fraternities, 4 sororities. **Athletics (Intercollegiate):** *Men:* baseball, basketball, cross-country, diving, football, golf, soccer, swimming, tennis, track/field (outdoor), water polo. *Women:* basketball, cross-country, diving, golf, lacrosse, soccer, softball, swimming, tennis, track/field (outdoor), volleyball, water polo. **On-Campus Highlights:** Green Bean Coffee Lounge, Clapp Library, Samuelson Pavilion (The Cooler), The Quad, Alumni Gymnasium Fitness Center.

ACCOMMODATIONS

Allowed in exams:	
Calculators	Yes
Dictionary	Yes
Computer	Yes
Spell-checker	Yes
Extended test time	Yes
Scribe	Yes
Proctors	Yes
Oral exams	Yes
Note-takers	Yes
Support services for students with	
LD	Yes
ADHD	Yes
ASD	Yes
Distraction-reduced environment	Yes
Recording of lecture allowed	Yes
Reading technology:	Yes
Audio books	Yes
Other assistive technology	Speech-to-text software Text-to-speech applications
Priority registration	Yes
Added costs for services:	
For LD:	No
For ADHD:	No
For ASD:	No
LD specialists	Yes
ADHD & ASD coaching	Yes
ASD specialists	Yes
Professional tutors	Yes
Peer tutors	Yes
Max. hours/week for services	Varies
How professors are notified of student approved accommodations	Student

COLLEGE GRADUATION REQUIREMENTS

Course waivers allowed	No
In what courses	
No waiver, but can substitute Foreign Language, Math	
Course substitutions allowed	Yes
In what courses	Math, Foreign Languages

San Diego State University

5500 CAMPANILE DRIVE, SAN DIEGO, CA 92182-7455 • ADMISSIONS: 619-594-6336 • FAX:

PROGRAMS/SERVICES FOR STUDENTS WITH LEARNING DIFFERENCES

The Student Ability Success Center(SASC) at San Diego State University (SASC) is the campus office responsible for determining and providing academic accommodations for students with documented disabilities. Support services are available to students with certified visual limitations, hearing and communication impairments, learning disabilities, and mobility and other functional limitations. The program currently serves over 1500 students, which includes undergraduate and graduate students. Student Disability Services' mission is to provide qualified students with disabilities equal access to higher education through academic support services, technology, and advocacy in order to promote their retention and graduation. To further this mission, SDS is committed to the following:
• Minimizing academic and physical barriers for students with disabilities.
• Promoting self-advocacy within students with disabilities.
• Working collaboratively with SDSU faculty, staff, and the campus community to increase disability awareness.

ADMISSIONS

All applicants must meet the admission criteria for California State University and San Diego State University. Under exceptional circumstances, students who are denied admission may appeal the decision. If the circumstances involve disability, contact Student Disability Services.

Additional Information

Students are encouraged to get volunteer note-takers from among other students enrolled in the class. Limited tutoring is available based on documented functional limitations related to subject matter. Tutoring, when authorized, is available at no charge. Students with learning disabilities may request permission to tape a lecture. Students will also need permission from the professor to use a calculator, dictionary, computer, or spellchecker in exams. High Tech Center is an assistive technology center available to students with disabilities. Services and accommodations are available for undergraduates and graduate students.

San Diego State University

General Admissions

Very important factors considered include: rigor of secondary school record, academic GPA, standardized test scores. *Important factors considered include:* geographical residence, state residency. *Freshman Admission Requirements:* High school diploma is required and GED is accepted. *Academic units required:* 4 English, 3 math, 2 science, 2 science labs, 2 foreign language, 1 social studies, 1 history, 1 academic elective, 1 visual/performing arts. *Academic units recommended:* 4 math.

Accommodations or Services

Accommodations are decided upon an individual basis after a thorough review of appropriate, current documentation. The accommodations requests must be supported through the documentation provided and must be logically linked to the current impact of the condition on academic functioning.

Financial Aid

Students should submit: FAFSA; State aid form. Applicants will be notified of awards on a rolling basis beginning 3/15. The Princeton Review suggests that all financial aid forms be submitted as soon as possible after October 1. *Need-based scholarships/grants offered:* College/university scholarship or grant aid from institutional funds; Federal Pell; Private scholarships; SEOG; State scholarships/grants. *Loan aid offered:* Direct PLUS loans; Direct Subsidized Stafford Loans; Direct Unsubsidized Stafford Loans. Federal Work-Study Program available. Institutional employment available.

Campus Life

Activities: Campus Ministries; Choral groups; Concert band; Dance; Drama/theater; International Student Organization; Jazz band; Literary magazine; Marching band; Music ensembles; Musical theater; Opera; Pep band; Radio station; Student government; Student newspaper; Student-run film society; Symphony orchestra; Television station. **Organizations:** 264 registered organizations, 6 honor societies, 14 religious organizations. 21 fraternities, 23 sororities. **Athletics (Intercollegiate):** *Men:* baseball, basketball, football, golf, soccer, tennis. *Women:* basketball, crew/rowing, cross-country, diving, golf, soccer, softball, swimming, tennis, track/field (outdoor), track/field (indoor), volleyball, water polo. Aztec Student Union, Aztec Recreation Center & Aquaplex, SDSU Library, Open Air Theatre and Viejas Arena, Starbucks.

ACCOMMODATIONS

Allowed in exams:	
Calculators	Yes
Dictionary	Yes
Computer	Yes
Spell-checker	Yes
Extended test time	Yes
Scribe	Yes
Proctors	Yes
Oral exams	Yes
Note-takers	Yes
Support services for students with	
LD	Yes
ADHD	Yes
ASD	Yes
Distraction-reduced environment	Yes
Recording of lecture allowed	Yes
Reading technology:	Yes
Audio books	Yes
Other assistive technologySmart Pen; Digital recorder; comprehensive software and hardware options.	
Priority registration	Yes
Added costs for services:	
For LD:	Not Applicable
For ADHD:	Not Applicable
For ASD:	Not Applicable
LD specialists	Yes
ADHD & ASD coaching	No
ASD specialists	No
Professional tutors	Yes
Peer tutors	Yes
Max. hours/week for services	Varies
How professors are notified of student approved accommodations	Student

COLLEGE GRADUATION REQUIREMENTS

Course waivers allowed	No
Course substitutions allowed	Yes
In what courses	
Mathematics; Foreign Language	

San Francisco State University

1600 HOLLOWAY AVENUE, SAN FRANCISCO, CA 93132 • ADMISSIONS: 415-338-6486 • FAX: 415-338-3880

CAMPUS

Type of school	Public
Environment	Metropolis
Support	CS

STUDENTS

Undergrad enrollment	25,903
% male/female	44/56
% from out of state	1
% frosh live on campus	62

FINANCIAL FACTS

Annual in-state tuition	$5,472
Annual out-of-state tuition	$16,632
Room and board	NR
Required fees	$1,012

GENERAL ADMISSIONS INFO

Application fee	$55
Priority deadline	10/1
Regular application deadline	11/30

Nonfall registration accepted.

Range SAT EBRW	430–540
Range SAT Math	430–550
Range ACT Composite	18–24

ACADEMICS

Student/faculty ratio	23:1
% students returning for sophomore year	79

Most classes have 10–19 students.
Most lab/discussion sessions have 20–29 students.

PROGRAMS/SERVICES FOR STUDENTS WITH LEARNING DIFFERENCES

The Disability Program and Resource Center (DPRC) is available to promote and provide equal access to the classroom and campus-related activities. A full range of support services is provided so that students may define and achieve personal autonomy at SFSU. The staff is sensitive to the diversity of disabilities, including those only recently recognized as disabilities requiring reasonable accommodations. Confidential support services are available. All students registered with DPRC are eligible for disability management advising. This consists of helping students access services from DPRC; manage DPRC services and school in general; problem-solve conflicts/concerns that are disability-related with individuals, programs, and services on campus; and understand "reasonable accommodation" under the law.

ADMISSIONS

Students with LD apply to the university through the regular application process. If the student is not eligible for regular admission for a disability-related reason, DPRC can provide special admissions assistance. To obtain special admissions assistance, students need to register with the DPRC office, provide verification of the disability, and notify the Admissions Office that the DPRC has the appropriate verification. When these steps have been taken, the Admissions Office will consult with the DPRC before making a decision. The admissions contact person can request substitutions of high school courses in math, foreign language, and science. Students with LD who are judged unable to fulfill specific requirements may take course substitutions. Substitutions are authorized on an individual basis after review and recommendation by the high school or community college counselor.

ADMISSIONS INFO FOR STUDENTS WITH LEARNING DIFFERENCES

SAT/ACT required: Yes
Interview required: Yes
Essay required: Yes
Additional application required: No
Documentation required for:
 LD: Psycho ed evaluation
 ADHD: Diagnosis based on DSM-V; history of behaviors impairing functioning in academic setting; diagnostic interview; history of symptoms; evidence of ongoing behaviors.
 ASD: Diagnosis based on DSM-V; history of behaviors impairing functioning in academic setting; diagnostic interview; history of symptom; evidence of ongoing behaviors; psycho ed evaluation.
Documentation submitted to: Disability Programs and Resource Center
Special Ed. HS course work accepted: Yes
Separate application required for Program/Services: Yes
Contact Information
Name of program or department: Disability Programs and Resource Center
Telephone: 415-338-2472
Fax: 415-338-1041

San Francisco State University

Additional Information

The DPRC offers a drop-in center with available tutorial services. The DPRC can also arrange for test accommodations and note-takers and will advocate for the student. The staff is very involved and offers comprehensive services through a team approach. There are no developmental courses offered at the university. However, there are skills classes. Students with documented LD may request assistance in locating tutors. Other services may include registration assistance, campus orientation, note-takers, readers, test-taking assistance, tutoring, disability-related counseling, and referral information. Go to the DPRC website for information on how to register with the department at http://www.sfsu.edu/~dprc/registering.html

GENERAL ADMISSIONS

Very important factors considered include: rigor of secondary school record, academic GPA, standardized test scores. *Important factors considered include:* state residency. *Other factors considered include:* geographical residence. *Freshman Admission Requirements:* High school diploma is required and GED is accepted. *Academic units required:* 4 English, 3 math, 2 science, 2 science labs, 2 foreign language, 1 social studies, 1 history, 1 academic elective, 1 visual/performing arts. *Academic units recommended:* 4 English, 4 math, 2 science, 2 science labs, 2 foreign language, 1 social studies, 1 history, 1 academic elective, 1 visual/performing arts.

ACCOMMODATIONS OR SERVICES

Accommodations are decided upon an individual basis after a thorough review of appropriate, current documentation. The accommodations requests must be supported through the documentation provided and must be logically linked to the current impact of the condition on academic functioning.

FINANCIAL AID

Students should submit: FAFSA. Applicants will be notified of awards on a rolling basis beginning 4/15. The Princeton Review suggests that all financial aid forms be submitted as soon as possible after October 1. *Need-based scholarships/grants offered:* College/university scholarship or grant aid from institutional funds; Federal Pell; Private scholarships; SEOG; State scholarships/grants. *Loan aid offered:* Direct PLUS loans; Direct Subsidized Stafford Loans; Direct Unsubsidized Stafford Loans. Federal Work-Study Program available. Institutional employment available.

CAMPUS LIFE

Activities: Choral groups; Concert band; Dance; Drama/theater; International Student Organization; Jazz band; Literary magazine; Marching band; Music ensembles; Musical theater; Opera; Radio station; Student government; Student newspaper; Student-run film society; Symphony orchestra; Television station. **Organizations:** 213 registered organizations, 6 honor societies, 13 religious organizations. 3 fraternities, 4 sororities. **Athletics (Intercollegiate):** *Men:* baseball, basketball, cross-country, soccer, wrestling. *Women:* basketball, cross-country, soccer, softball, track/field (outdoor), track/field (indoor), volleyball. **On-Campus Highlights:** J. Paul Leonard Library, Cesar Chavez Student Center, Cox Stadium, Residential Theme Communities, SFSU Fine Arts Gallery.

ACCOMMODATIONS

Allowed in exams:

Calculators	Yes
Dictionary	Yes
Computer	Yes
Spell-checker	Yes
Extended test time	Yes
Scribe	Yes
Proctors	Yes
Oral exams	No
Note-takers	Yes

Support services for students with

LD	Yes
ADHD	Yes
ASD	Yes
Distraction-reduced environment	Yes
Recording of lecture allowed	Yes
Reading technology:	Yes
Audio books	Yes
Other assistive technology	Yes
Priority registration	Yes

Added costs for services:

For LD:	Yes
For ADHD:	Yes
For ASD:	Yes
LD specialists	Yes
ADHD & ASD coaching	No
ASD specialists	No
Professional tutors	Yes
Peer tutors	Yes
Max. hours/week for services	Varies
How professors are notified of student approved accommodations	Student

COLLEGE GRADUATION REQUIREMENTS

Course waivers allowed	Yes
In what courses	Case by case
Course substitutions allowed	Yes
In what courses	Case by case

San Jose State University

ONE WASHINGTON SQUARE, SAN JOSE, CA 95192-0016 • ADMISSIONS: 408-283-7500 • FAX: 408-924-2050

CAMPUS
Type of school	Public
Environment	Metropolis
Support	CS

STUDENTS
Undergrad enrollment	27,778
% male/female	52/48
% from out of state	1
% frosh live on campus	54

FINANCIAL FACTS
Annual in-state tuition	$5,472
Annual out-of-state tuition	$14,976
Room and board	$16,250
Required fees	$1,979

GENERAL ADMISSIONS INFO
Application fee	$55
Regular application deadline	11/30

Nonfall registration accepted.

Range SAT EBRW	510–610
Range SAT Math	520–620
Range ACT Composite	19–26

ACADEMICS
Student/faculty ratio	26:1
% students returning for sophomore year	87
% students graduating within 4 years	10
% students graduating within 6 years	57

Most classes have 10–19 students.
Most lab/discussion sessions have 10–19 students.

PROGRAMS/SERVICES FOR STUDENTS WITH LEARNING DIFFERENCES

SJSU takes great pride in their tradition of being uncompromising cn their ommitment to offer access to higher education to all persons who meet the criteria for admission, yielding a stimulating mix of age groups, cultures, and economic backgrounds for teaching, learning, and research. SJSU takes pride in and is firmly committed to teaching and learning, with a faculty that is active in scholarship, research, technological innovation, community service, and the arts. The accessible education center presents its vision of redefining ability by providing the following: MyAEC Student Portal, MyAEC Notetaker Portal and MyAEC Faculty Portal.

ADMISSIONS

Pre-Admission Counseling—the following are services provided to prospective students: Application Workshops are conducted at local high school and community colleges by an SJSU representative to help you understand how CSUmentor and additional online resources can assist you. Pre-admission counseling is offered in the Student Services Center for prospective students. Pre-admission counseling is an important step in preparing for college as an undergraduate student. An Admission Counselor will review the following information: CSU & EOP application process, the online application process, pre-admissions undergraduate advising, admission requirements for first time freshmen and transfer students, A-G subject requirements, testing, and GPA requirements for first time freshmen, the Four Basic Skill requirements for transfer students.

Additional Information

The Accessible Education Center (AEC) strives to provide an array of academically related services for students with learning disabilities. Accommodations for curriculum requirements are determined on a case-by-case basis and provided specifically for coursework in which learning disability impacts curriculum requirements. Students can be self

ADMISSIONS INFO FOR STUDENTS WITH LEARNING DIFFERENCES

SAT/ACT required: Yes
Interview required: No
Essay required: No
Additional application required: No
Documentation required for:
  LD: WJ and WAIS. DRC will accept the WIAT test results—standard scores are required for all assessments. AEC will accept historical documentation for consideration of services and accommodations.
  ADHD: Documentation from a licensed professional trained/specializing in AD/HD and licensed to use the DSM IV/V criteria for AD/HD diagnosis
  ASD: Differential diagnosis of autism—the following professionals would generally be considered qualified to evaluate and diagnose autism spectrum disorders provided they have comprehensive training in the Spectrum Disorders and direct experience with an adolescent or adult autism population: clinical psychologists, neuropsychologists, psychiatrists, and other relevantly trained medical doctors. It is in the student's best interest to provide recent and appropriate documentation; however the AEC will accept historical documentation for consideration of services and accommodations.
Documentation submitted to: Support program/services
Special Ed. HS course work accepted: N/A
Separate application required for Programs/Services: No
Contact Information
Name of program or department: Accessible Education Center
Telephone: 408-924-6000
Fax: 408-924-5999
Email: aec-info@sjsu.edu

San Jose State University

identified or referred to the AEC. All students are encouraged to meet with professional staff well in advance of the start of classes to discuss their academic needs and to set up appropriate services. An Educational Assistant is employed by the Accessible Education Center (AEC_ to work on a one-to-one basis with a student registered with the AEC, whose disability impairment(s) prevents the student from meeting curriculum requirements. Eligibility for an Educational Assistant is determined by the AEC's Director or Counselors and is determined on a case-by-case basis. Students must meet with the AEC Director or a Coordinator each semester the service is needed.

GENERAL ADMISSIONS

Very important factors considered include: rigor of secondary school record, academic GPA, standardized test scores. *Important factors considered include:* geographical residence, state residency. *Freshman Admission Requirements:* High school diploma is required and GED is accepted. *Academic units required:* 4 English, 3 math, 2 science, 2 science labs, 2 foreign language, 1 social studies, 1 history, 1 academic elective, 1 visual/performing arts. *Academic units recommended:* 4 math, 3 science, 3 science labs.

ACCOMMODATIONS OR SERVICES

Accommodations are decided upon an individual basis after a thorough review of appropriate, current documentation. The accommodations requests must be supported through the documentation provided and must be logically linked to the current impact of the condition on academic functioning.

FINANCIAL AID

Students should submit: FAFSA; State aid form. Applicants will be notified of awards on a rolling basis beginning 3/1. The Princeton Review suggests that all financial aid forms be submitted as soon as possible after October 1. *Need-based scholarships/grants offered:* College/university scholarship or grant aid from institutional funds; Federal Pell; Private scholarships; SEOG; State scholarships/grants. *Loan aid offered:* Direct PLUS loans; Direct Subsidized Stafford Loans; Direct Unsubsidized Stafford Loans. Federal Work-Study Program available. Institutional employment available.

CAMPUS LIFE

Activities: Campus Ministries; Choral groups; Concert band; Dance; Drama/theater; International Student Organization; Jazz band; Literary magazine; Marching band; Model UN; Music ensembles; Musical theater; Opera; Pep band; Radio station; Student government; Student newspaper; Student-run film society; Symphony orchestra. **Organizations:** 283 registered organizations, 13 honor societies, 20 religious organizations. 20 fraternities, 15 sororities. **Athletics (Intercollegiate):** *Men:* baseball, basketball, cheerleading, cross-country, diving, football, golf, soccer, softball, swimming, volleyball, water polo. *Women:* basketball, cheerleading, cross-country, diving, golf, gymnastics, soccer, softball, swimming, tennis, volleyball, water polo. **On-Campus Highlights:** Martin Luther King, Jr. Library, Student Union, Event Center, Tower Hall, Student Health Center.

ACCOMMODATIONS

Allowed in exams:	
Calculators	Yes
Dictionary	Yes
Computer	Yes
Spell-checker	Yes
Extended test time	Yes
Scribe	Yes
Proctors	Yes
Oral exams	Yes
Note-takers	Yes
Support services for students with	
LD	Yes
ADHD	Yes
ASD	Yes
Distraction-reduced environment	Yes
Recording of lecture allowed	Yes
Reading technology:	Yes
Audio books	Yes
Other assistive technology	Yes
Priority registration	Yes
Added costs for services:	
For LD:	No
For ADHD:	No
For ASD:	No
LD specialists	Yes
ADHD & ASD coaching	No
ASD specialists	No
Professional tutors	No
Peer tutors	Yes
Max. hours/week for services	Varies
How professors are notified of student approved accommodations	Student

COLLEGE GRADUATION REQUIREMENTS

Course waivers allowed	No
Course substitutions allowed	Yes
In what courses	

General education quantitative reasoning substitutions made on case-by-case basis, must be disability related.

Santa Clara University

500 EL CAMINO REAL, SANTA CLARA, CA 95053 • ADMISSIONS: 408-554-4700 • FAX: 408-554-5255

CAMPUS

Type of school	Private (nonprofit)
Environment	City
Support	CS

STUDENTS

Undergrad enrollment	5,481
% male/female	50/50
% from out of state	29
% frosh live on campus	96

FINANCIAL FACTS

Annual Tuition	$51,081
Room and board	$14,910
Required fees	$630

GENERAL ADMISSIONS INFO

Application fee	$60
Regular application deadline	1/7

Nonfall registration accepted. Admission may be deferred for a maximum of One year, unless serving required military service or mission work.

Range SAT EBRW	630–710
Range SAT Math	640–730
Range ACT Composite	28–32

ACADEMICS

Student/faculty ratio	11:1
% students returning for sophomore year	94
% students graduating within 4 years	85
% students graduating within 6 years	90

Most classes have 10–19 students.
Most lab/discussion sessions have 10–19 students.

PROGRAMS/SERVICES FOR STUDENTS WITH LEARNING DIFFERENCES

The primary mission of Disabilities Resources is to enhance academic progress, promote social involvement, and build bridges connecting the various services of the university for all students. This goal is met by providing: academic intervention programs, opportunities to increase students' personal understanding of their disability, role models, and community outreach. Disabilities Resources is a resource area within the Drahmann Center that helps to ensure equal access to all academic and programmatic activities for students with disabilities. This goal is met through the provision of Academic Support Services, contact with other university offices, educational programming on disability issues for the university, and, most importantly, assistance in teaching students effective self-advocacy skills under the student development model. Students must submit proper documentation to obtain services through the Office of Disability Resources.

ADMISSIONS

Students should meet the minimum high school course requirements: History and Social Science: 3 years English: 4 years, Mathematics: 3 years required; 4 years recommended Laboratory Science: 2 years required; 3 years recommended, Language Other Than English: 2 years required; 3 years recommended; 4 years preferred, Visual and Performing Arts: 1 year recommended. Applicants select one of the academic schools/ colleges: the College of Arts and Sciences, the Leavey School of Business, or the School of Engineering. While the selectivity between schools and programs does not vary greatly, academic readiness for the program of interest will be gauged based on a student's expressed interest.

Additional Information

The disabilities resources staff meets individually with students. Some of the academic accommodations provided by DSR include notetaking, library assistance, and test accommodations. Other support services include priority registration; tutoring or academic counseling: and workshops on legal issues and self-advocacy. The DR is in the process of purchasing computer-aided technology to assist the students. Graduate students with learning disabilities are offered the same services and accommodations as those provided for undergraduate students. Students can be better served if the professional documentation they submit specifically identifies the accommodations needed for the student to be successful in college.

ADMISSIONS INFO FOR STUDENTS WITH LEARNING DIFFERENCES

SAT/ACT required: Yes
Interview required: No
Essay required: Not Applicable
Additional application required: Yes
Documentation required for:
 LD: Psycho ed evaluation
 ADHD: Documentation must be done by professional
 ASD: Documentation by a qualified professional
Documentation submitted to: Disabilities Resources
Special Ed. HS course work accepted: Not Applicable
Separate application required for Programs/Services: No
Contact Information
Name of program or department: Disabilities Resources
Telephone: 408-554-4109
Email: disabilitiesresources@scu.edu

Santa Clara University

GENERAL ADMISSIONS

Very important factors considered include: rigor of secondary school record, academic GPA, application essay. *Important factors considered include:* class rank, standardized test scores, recommendation(s), extracurricular activities, talent/ability, character/personal qualities, first generation, alumni/ae relation, racial/ethnic status, volunteer work. *Other factors considered include:* geographical residence, state residency, religious affiliation/commitment, work experience, level of applicant's interest. *Freshman Admission Requirements:* High school diploma is required and GED is accepted. *Academic units required:* 4 English, 3 math, 2 science, 2 science labs, 2 foreign language, 3 social studies, 1 academic elective, 1 visual/performing arts. *Academic units recommended:* 4 English, 4 math, 3 science, 3 science labs, 3 foreign language, 3 social studies, 2 academic electives, 2 visual/performing arts.

ACCOMMODATION OR SERVICES

Accommodations are decided upon an individual basis after a thorough review of appropriate, current documentation. The accommodations requests must be supported through the documentation provided and must be logically linked to the current impact of the condition on academic functioning.

FINANCIAL AID

Students should submit: CSS/Financial Aid PROFILE; FAFSA. Applicants will be notified of awards on or about 4/1. The Princeton Review suggests that all financial aid forms be submitted as soon as possible after October 1. *Need-based scholarships/grants offered:* College/university scholarship or grant aid from institutional funds; Federal Pell; Private scholarships; SEOG; State scholarships/grants. *Loan aid offered:* Direct PLUS loans; Direct Subsidized Stafford Loans; Direct Unsubsidized Stafford Loans. Federal Work-Study Program available. Institutional employment available.

CAMPUS LIFE

Activities: Campus Ministries; Choral groups; Dance; Drama/theater; International Student Organization; Jazz band; Literary magazine; Marching band; Model UN; Music ensembles; Musical theater; Opera; Pep band; Radio station; Student government; Student newspaper; Symphony orchestra; Yearbook. **Organizations:** 86 registered organizations, 25 honor societies, 5 religious organizations. **Athletics (Intercollegiate):** *Men:* baseball, basketball, crew/rowing, cross-country, golf, soccer, tennis, track/field (outdoor), water polo. *Women:* basketball, crew/rowing, cross-country, golf, soccer, softball, tennis, track/field (outdoor), volleyball, water polo. **On-Campus Highlights:** Historic Mission Church; Mission Gardens, Pat Malley Fitness Center, Harrington Learning Commons and Library, Benson Memorial Student Center, Patricia A. and Stephen C. Schott Admission & Enrollment Services Building.

ACCOMMODATIONS

Allowed in exams:	
Calculators	Yes
Dictionary	Not Applicable
Computer	Yes
Spell-checker	Not Applicable
Extended test time	Yes
Scribe	Yes
Proctors	Yes
Oral exams	Not Applicable
Note-takers	Yes
Support services for students with	
LD	Yes
ADHD	Yes
ASD	Yes
Distraction-reduced environment	Not Applicable
Recording of lecture allowed	Yes
Reading technology:	Yes
Audio books	Yes
Other assistive technology	Yes
Priority registration	Yes
Added costs for services:	
For LD:	No
For ADHD:	No
For ASD:	No
LD specialists	No
ADHD & ASD coaching	No
ASD specialists	Yes
Professional tutors	Yes
Peer tutors	Yes
Max. hours/week for services	Varies
How professors are notified of student approved accommodations	Director and Student

COLLEGE GRADUATION REQUIREMENTS

Course waivers allowed	No
In what courses	Varies
Course substitutions allowed	Yes
In what courses	Case by case

Sonoma State University

1801 East Cotati Avenue, Rohnert Park, CA 94928 • Admissions: 707-664-2778 • Fax: 707-664-2060

CAMPUS

Type of school	Public
Environment	Town
Support	S

STUDENTS

Undergrad enrollment	8,517
% male/female	38/62
% from out of state	NR
% frosh live on campus	88

FINANCIAL FACTS

Annual in-state tuition	$5,742
Annual out-of-state tuition	$17,622
Room and board	$13,554
Required fees	$1,982

GENERAL ADMISSIONS INFO

Application fee	$55.
Priority deadline	3/1
Regular application deadline	11/30
Nonfall registration accepted.	

Range SAT EBRW	500–590
Range SAT Math	480–580
Range ACT Composite	19–24

ACADEMICS

Student/faculty ratio	23:1
% students returning for sophomore year	77
% students graduating within 4 years	29
% students graduating within 6 years	58
Most classes have 10–19 students.	

PROGRAMS/SERVICES FOR STUDENTS WITH LEARNING DIFFERENCES

Disability Services for Students ensures that people with disabilities receive equal access to higher education. We work to protect and promote the civil rights of students with disabilities. We challenge and support students to develop selfdetermination and independence as people with disabilities. In reaching its determinations about appropriate accommodations, DSS considers factors such as the documentation from professionals specializing in the area of the student's diagnosed disability, the student's functional limitations, and the student's input and accommodation history in regard to particular needs and limitations. DSS works with the student and relevant faculty and staff through an interactive process designed to achieve an accommodation that meets the needs of all parties.

ADMISSIONS

Admission to Sonoma State University is competitive since we receive more applications than we can accommodate. Under special provisions approved by the California State University, Sonoma State University utilizes a combination of the undergraduate admissions requirements outlined in the Basic California State University Admissions Requirements. Supplementary admissions criteria for first-time freshmen include, but are not limited to, high school grade point averages, test scores (SAT I or ACT), and high school course preparation. In order to be considered for admission, you must file a complete undergraduate application at CSU Mentor. Sonoma State University is a selective admissions campus. Therefore it is important to apply during the designated applications periods. Wherever possible, we admit students on a rolling basis upon completion of an admissions file. So early application and prompt response to requests for application support documents will speed your admissions notification. Determination and Notification of Admission: After applications for admission have been received in the Office of Admissions and Records, they are processed and matched with required transcripts and test scores. Evaluation of the records is made to determine whether applicants meet the admissions requirements.

ADMISSIONS INFO FOR STUDENTS WITH LEARNING DIFFERENCES

SAT/ACT required: Yes
Interview required: No
Essay required: No
Additional application required: No
Documentation required for:
  LD: http://www.sonoma.edu/dss/media/print/ld_guidelines.pdf
  ADHD: http://www.sonoma.edu/dss/media/print/certification_adhd.pdf
  ASD: Psycho ed evaluation
Documentation submitted to: Disability Support Services
Special Ed. HS course work accepted: No
Separate application required for Programs/Services: Yes
Contact Information
Name of program or department: Sonoma State University
Telephone: 707-664-2677
Fax: 707-664-3330

Sonoma State University

Additional Information

The Disability Services for Students office (DSS) welcomes Sonoma State University students who are interested in receiving accommodation services related to their disability. The Learning Center provides academic support services including tutorial services for students with learning differences(no fee). The Learning Skills Service Program provides individualized instruction, computer based learning, learning plans based on learning strengths and multiple intelligences, mentoring with PALs, study skills workshops, and small group tutoring. The Tutorial Center provides individual and small group learning assistance in a broad range of academic subjects.

GENERAL ADMISSIONS

Very important factors considered include: academic GPA, standardized test scores. *Other factors considered include:* geographical residence. *Freshman Admission Requirements:* High school diploma is required and GED is accepted. *Academic units required:* 4 English, 3 math, 2 science, 1 science lab, 2 foreign language, 2 history, 1 academic elective, 1 visual/performing arts, and 1 unit from above areas or other academic areas.

ACCOMMODATIONS OR SERVICES

Accommodations are decided upon an individual basis after a thorough review of appropriate, current documentation. The accommodations requests must be supported through the documentation provided and must be logically linked to the current impact of the condition on academic functioning.

FINANCIAL AID

Students should submit: FAFSA; State aid form. Applicants will be notified of awards on a rolling basis beginning 3/25. The Princeton Review suggests that all financial aid forms be submitted as soon as possible after October 1. *Need-based scholarships/grants offered:* College/university scholarship or grant aid from institutional funds; Federal Pell; Private scholarships; SEOG; State scholarships/grants. *Loan aid offered:* Direct PLUS loans; Direct Subsidized Stafford Loans; Direct Unsubsidized Stafford Loans. Federal Work-Study Program available. Institutional employment available.

CAMPUS LIFE

Activities: Choral groups; Dance; Drama/theater; Jazz band; Literary magazine; Music ensembles; Musical theater; Opera; Pep band; Radio station; Student government; Student newspaper; Symphony orchestra. **Organizations:** 109 registered organizations, 2 honor societies, 4 religious organizations. 5 fraternities, 9 sororities. **Athletics (Intercollegiate):** *Men:* baseball, basketball, soccer, tennis. *Women:* basketball, cross-country, soccer, softball, tennis, track/field (outdoor), volleyball. **On-Campus Highlights:** Schultz Information Center, Environmental Technology Center, Charlie Brown's (coffee shop), Observatory, University Recreation Center.

ACCOMMODATIONS

Allowed in exams:	
Calculators	Yes
Dictionary	Yes
Computer	Yes
Spell-checker	Yes
Extended test time	Yes
Scribe	Yes
Proctors	Yes
Oral exams	Yes
Note-takers	Yes
Support services for students with	
LD	Yes
ADHD	Yes
ASD	Yes
Distraction-reduced environment	Yes
Recording of lecture allowed	Yes
Reading technology:	Yes
Audio books	Yes
Other assistive technology	Yes
Priority registration	Yes
Added costs for services:	
For LD:	No
For ADHD:	No
For ASD:	No
LD specialists	No
ADHD & ASD coaching	No
ASD specialists	No
Professional tutors	No
Peer tutors	Yes
Max. hours/week for services	Varies
How professors are notified of student approved accommodations	Student

COLLEGE GRADUATION REQUIREMENTS

Course waivers allowed	No
Course substitutions allowed	Yes
In what courses	case-by-case basis

Stanford University

450 Serra Mall, Stanford, CA 94305-6106 • Admissions: 650-723-2091 • Fax: 650-723-6050

CAMPUS

Type of school	Private (nonprofit)
Environment	City
Support	CS

STUDENTS

Undergrad enrollment	7,056
% male/female	50/50
% from out of state	59
% frosh live on campus	100

FINANCIAL FACTS

Annual tuition	$48,987
Room and board	$15,112
Required fees	$630

GENERAL ADMISSIONS INFO

Application fee	$90
Regular application deadline	1/2

Nonfall registration accepted. Admission may be deferred for a maximum of 2 years.

Range SAT EBRW	690–760
Range SAT Math	700–780
Range ACT Composite	32–35

ACADEMICS

Student/faculty ratio	4:1
% students returning for sophomore year	98
% students graduating within 4 years	75
% students graduating within 6 years	1

Most classes have 10–19 students.
Most lab/discussion sessions have 10–19 students.

PROGRAMS/SERVICES FOR STUDENTS WITH LEARNING DIFFERENCES

Stanford University has an institutional commitment to providing equal educational opportunities for qualified students with disabilities. Stanford University has a strong commitment to maintaining a diverse and stimulating academic community, representing a broad spectrum of talents and experiences. Students with disabilities, actively participating in the various aspects of life at Stanford, are an essential part of that diversity.

ADMISSIONS

All students at Stanford meet the same admission requirements. Stanford seeks to enroll students with excellent academic records who show evidence of their personal achievement outside the class room and who have used the resources available to them to their fullest potential. The policy on the admissions of students with learning disabilities makes clear there is no separate academic program. Students should take a strong college-preparatory curriculum, including honors and Advanced Placement courses.

ADMISSIONS INFO FOR STUDENTS WITH LEARNING DIFFERENCES

SAT/ACT required: Yes
Interview required: No
Essay required: Not Applicable
Additional application required:
Documentation required for:
  LD: Documentation from students with a Learning Disability attending Stanford University must demonstrate the current functional impact of the disability on one or more major life activities (e.g., reading, learning, concentrating, thinking, working etc.) and provide current evidence to support the requested academic or other disability related accommodations. Visit the website for more: https://oae.stanford.edu/students/registering-oae
  ADHD: Documentation from students with Attention-Deficit Hyperactivity/Disorder (ADHD) attending Stanford University must demonstrate the current functional impact of the disability on one or more major life activities (e.g., concentrating, learning, thinking, sleeping, etc.) and provide current evidence to support the requested academic or other disability-related accommodations. Visit the website for more: https://oae.stanford.edu/students/registering-oae
  ASD: Psycho ed evaluation
Documentation submitted to: Support Program/Services
Special Ed. HS course work accepted: No
Separate application required for Program/Services: No
Contact Information
Name of program or department: Office of Accessible Education
Telephone: 650-723-1066
Email: oae-contactus@stanford.edu

Stanford University

Additional Information

The Office of Accessible Education at Stanford is committed to helping students take full advantage of all the educational opportunities at Standford. A student with a documented disability may request a modification of certain generally applicable requirements. The request is made in writing to the OAE and should be accompanied by documentation of the disability. Among the factors relevant in determining appropriate modifications of academic requirements for students are: the nature of the student's disability and its nexus to the requested modification; whether the requested modification of the academic requirement will provide the student an equal educational opportunity; and whether the requested modification of the academic requirement would alter the essential requirements or standards, or would change the fundamental nature of an educational program.

GENERAL ADMISSIONS

Very important factors considered include: rigor of secondary school record, class rank, academic GPA, application essay, standardized test scores, recommendation(s), extracurricular activities, talent/ability, character/personal qualities. *Other factors considered include:* interview, first generation, alumni/ae relation, geographical residence, racial/ethnic status, volunteer work, work experience. *Freshman Admission Requirements:* High school diploma is required and GED is accepted. *Academic units recommended:* 4 English, 4 math, 3 science, 3 science labs, 3 foreign language, 3 social studies,

ACCOMMODATIONS OR SERVICES

Accommodations are decided upon an individual basis after a thorough review of appropriate, current documentation. The accommodations requests must be supported through the documentation provided and must be logically linked to the current impact of the condition on academic functioning.

FINANCIAL AID

Students should submit: CSS/Financial Aid PROFILE; FAFSA; Noncustodial PROFILE. Applicants will be notified of awards on a rolling basis beginning 4/1. The Princeton Review suggests that all financial aid forms be submitted as soon as possible after October 1. *Need-based scholarships/grants offered:* College/university scholarship or grant aid from institutional funds; Federal Pell; Private scholarships; SEOG; State scholarships/grants. *Loan aid offered:* Direct PLUS loans; Direct Subsidized Stafford Loans; Direct Unsubsidized Stafford Loans. Federal Work-Study Program available. Institutional employment available.

CAMPUS LIFE

Activities: Campus Ministries; Choral groups; Concert band; Dance; Drama/theater; International Student Organization; Jazz band; Literary magazine; Marching band; Model UN; Music ensembles; Musical theater; Opera; Pep band; Radio station; Student government; Student newspaper; Student-run film society; Symphony orchestra; Television station; Yearbook. **Organizations:** 600 registered organizations, 40 religious organizations. 17 fraternities, 11 sororities. **Athletics (Intercollegiate):** *Men:* baseball, basketball, crew/rowing, cross-country, diving, fencing, football, golf, gymnastics, sailing, soccer, swimming, tennis, track/field (outdoor), volleyball, water polo, wrestling. *Women:* basketball, crew/rowing, cross-country, diving, fencing, field hockey, golf, gymnastics, lacrosse, sailing, soccer, softball, squash, swimming, synchronized swimming, tennis, track/field (outdoor), volleyball, water polo. **On-Campus Highlights:** Cantor Center for the Visual Arts, The Anderson Collection at Stanford University, Memorial Church, Tresidder Memorial Union, Bing Concert Hall.

ACCOMMODATIONS

Allowed in exams:

Calculators	Yes
Dictionary	Yes
Computer	Yes
Spell-checker	Yes
Extended test time	Yes
Scribe	Yes
Proctors	No
Oral exams	No
Note-takers	Yes

Support services for students with

LD	Yes
ADHD	Yes
ASD	Yes
Distraction-reduced environment	Yes
Recording of lecture allowed	Yes
Reading technology:	Yes
Audio books	Yes

Other assistive technology   The Stanford Converter into Braille & E-Text (SCRIBE) is an online document conversion system supporting the transformation of text and image-based file types into different formats.

Priority registration	No

Added costs for services:

For LD:	No
For ADHD:	No
For ASD:	No
LD specialists	Yes
ADHD & ASD coaching	No
ASD specialists	Yes
Professional tutors	Yes
Peer tutors	Yes
Max. hours/week for services	10

How professors are notified of student
approved accommodations   Student

COLLEGE GRADUATION REQUIREMENTS

Course waivers allowed	No
Course substitutions allowed	Yes
In what courses	Case by case

University of California–Berkeley

110 Sproul Hall, Berkeley, CA 94720-5800 • Admissions: • Fax:

CAMPUS

Type of school	Public
Environment	City
Support	CS

STUDENTS

Undergrad enrollment	27,496
% male/female	48/52
% from out of state	15
% frosh live on campus	95

FINANCIAL FACTS

Annual in-state tuition	$11,442
Annual out-of-state tuition	$40,434
Room and board	$16,160
Required fees	$2,742

GENERAL ADMISSIONS INFO

Application fee	$70
Regular application deadline	11/30
Nonfall registration accepted.	
Range SAT EBRW	610–730
Range SAT Math	640–770
Range ACT Composite	29–34

ACADEMICS

Student/faculty ratio	17:1
% students returning for sophomore year	97

Most classes have 20–29 students.
Most lab/discussion sessions have 20–29 students.

PROGRAMS/SERVICES FOR STUDENTS WITH LEARNING DIFFERENCES

The Disabled Student Program (DSP) works to sustain a supportive environment that provides appropriate and necessary disability-related accommodations, enables students to demonstrate their knowledge and skills, facilitates students' success in academic pursuits, and promotes independence.. SP's services assist students as they develop their skills and the qualities needed to meet their educational, personal, and professional goals. Students with ADHD must submit a letter from a qualified professional who has an expertise in diagnosing ADHD in adults.

ADMISSIONS

An An LD and admission specialist are available to meet applicants with LD interested in UC Berkeley. Specialists will review the transcript and give advice on how to proceed with the application. DSP works closely with admissions. There are two tiers for admission: Tier I is an automatic admission; Tier II applicants may need other criteria to be admitted. The impact of a disability could be a factor in an admission for a Tier II applicant. When an applicant self-discloses a disability, DSP requests documentation, and a statement about the impact of the disability. DSP uses this information to answer questions about the applicant from the Admissions Office.

Additional Information

DSP provides academic accommodations; consulting with instructors about accommodations; academic strategies and study skills; academic advising, adaptive technology, support groups, and a course "Facilitating Success" for students with LD/ADHD that centers on understanding learning differences, maximizing strengths, academic planning, research, writing, exam preparation, and using university resources; priority registration; specialists to help in problem-solving strategies and solutions to difficult problems; informational workshops on topics like understanding disabilities and individual learning styles; reading, writing, and research efficiency; memory strategies, self-advocacy; computer applications that facilitate learning; and career or graduate school planning.

ADMISSIONS INFO FOR STUDENTS WITH LEARNING DIFFERENCES

SAT/ACT required: Yes
Interview required: No
Essay required: Yes
Additional application required: No
Documentation required for:
 LD: Psycho ed evaluation
 ADHD: Diagnosis based on DSM-V; history of behaviors impairing functioning in academic setting; diagnostic interview; history of symptoms; evidence of ongoing behaviors.
 ASD: Psycho ed evaluation
Documentation submitted to: Disabled Student Program
Special Ed. HS course work accepted: No
Separate application required for Programs/Services: Yes
Contact Information
Name of program or department: Disabled Students' Program
Telephone: 510-642-0518
Fax: 510-643-9686

University of California–Berkeley

GENERAL ADMISSIONS

Very important factors considered include: rigor of secondary school record, academic GPA, application essay, standardized test scores. *Important factors considered include:* extracurricular activities, character/personal qualities, volunteer work, work experience. *Other factors considered include:* first generation, state residency. *Freshman Admission Requirements:* High school diploma is required and GED is accepted. *Academic units required:* 4 English, 3 math, 2 science, 2 science labs, 2 foreign language, 2 history, 1 academic elective, 1 visual/performing arts. *Academic units recommended:* 4 English, 4 math, 3 science, 3 science labs, 3 foreign language, 2 history, 1 academic elective, 1 visual/performing arts.

ACCOMMODATIONS OR SERVICES

Accommodations are decided upon an individual basis after a thorough review of appropriate, current documentation. The accommodations requests must be supported through the documentation provided and must be logically linked to the current impact of the condition on academic functioning.

FINANCIAL AID

Students should submit: FAFSA; State aid form. Applicants will be notified of awards on or about 3/31. The Princeton Review suggests that all financial aid forms be submitted as soon as possible after October 1. *Need-based scholarships/grants offered:* College/university scholarship or grant aid from institutional funds; Federal Pell; Private scholarships; SEOG; State scholarships/grants. *Loan aid offered:* Direct PLUS loans; Direct Subsidized Stafford Loans; Direct Unsubsidized Stafford Loans. Federal Work-Study Program available. Institutional employment available.

CAMPUS LIFE

Activities: Campus Ministries; Choral groups; Concert band; Dance; Drama/theater; International Student Organization; Jazz band; Literary magazine; Marching band; Model UN; Music ensembles; Musical theater; Pep band; Radio station; Student government; Student newspaper; Student-run film society; Symphony orchestra; Television station; Yearbook. **Organizations:** 300 registered organizations, 6 honor societies, 28 religious organizations. 38 fraternities, 19 sororities. **Athletics (Intercollegiate):** *Men:* baseball, basketball, crew/rowing, cross-country, diving, football, golf, gymnastics, rugby, sailing, soccer, swimming, tennis, track/field (outdoor), water polo. *Women:* basketball, crew/rowing, cross-country, diving, field hockey, golf, gymnastics, lacrosse, sailing, soccer, softball, swimming, tennis, track/field (outdoor), volleyball, water polo. **On-Campus Highlights:** Botanical Gardens, Lawrence Hall of Science, Museum of Anthropology, Museum of Art.

ACCOMMODATIONS

Allowed in exams:

Calculators	Yes
Dictionary	Yes
Computer	Yes
Spell-checker	Yes
Extended test time	Yes
Scribe	Yes
Proctors	Yes
Oral exams	No
Note-takers	Yes

Support services for students with

LD	Yes
ADHD	Yes
ASD	Yes
Distraction-reduced environment	Yes
Recording of lecture allowed	Yes
Reading technology:	Yes
Audio books	Yes
Other assistive technology	Yes
Priority registration	Yes

Added costs for services:

For LD:	No
For ADHD:	No
For ASD:	No
LD specialists	Yes
ADHD & ASD coaching	No
ASD specialists	No
Professional tutors	No

Peer tutors   Some individual tutoring is available through the TRIO grant.

Max. hours/week for services	Varies

How professors are notified of student approved accommodations   Student

COLLEGE GRADUATION REQUIREMENTS

Course waivers allowed	Yes

In what courses
Math waivers are considered on a case-by-case basis

Course substitutions allowed	Yes

In what courses
      Foreign language requirement can be substituted with cultural courses on a case-by-case basis.

University of California, Los Angeles

405 Hilgard Avenue, Los Angeles, CA 90095-1436 • Admissions: 310-825-3101 • Fax: 310-206-1206

CAMPUS

Type of school	Public
Environment	Metropolis
Support	CS

STUDENTS

Undergrad enrollment	30,990
% male/female	43/57
% from out of state	12
% frosh live on campus	0

FINANCIAL FACTS

Annual in-state tuition	$11,502
Anual out-of-state tuition	$39,516
Room and board	$15,991
Required fees	$1,778

GENERAL ADMISSIONS INFO

Application fee	$70
Regular application deadline	11/30

Nonfall registration accepted.

Range SAT EBRW	630–730
Range SAT Math	610–760
Range ACT Composite	27–33

ACADEMICS

Student/faculty ratio	17:1
% students returning for sophomore year	97
% students graduating within 4 years	75
% students graduating within 6 years	91

Most classes have 10–19 students.

PROGRAMS/SERVICES FOR STUDENTS WITH LEARNING DIFFERENCES

UCLA complies with state, federal, and university guidelines that mandate full access for students with disabilities, including learning disabilities. UCLA complies with the requirement to provide reasonable accommodations for documented students to allow them to participate in their academic program to the greatest extent possible. Students with other documented types of learning disabilities, including attention deficit hyperactive disorder and traumatic brain injury, are also served by the LD program. The UCLA LD program is coordinated by a full-time learning disabilities specialist and offers a full range of accommodations and services. Services are individually designed and include counseling, special test arrangements, note-taker services, readers, priority enrollment, adaptive technology, and individual tutoring. An active support group provides opportunities for students to discuss mutual concerns and enhance learning strategies. Workshops and speakers address skill development and topics of interest. In the Peer Mentor Program, continuing students with learning disabilities serve as resources to entering students.

ADMISSIONS

There are no special admissions criteria for students with learning disabilities. In an academic review, the university will assess and balance a variety of academic factors to determine the overall scholastic strength of each applicant. UCLA does not use a formula. The comprehensive review includes the remainder of the freshman applicants after the academic review. While commitment to intellectual development and academic progress continues to be of primary importance, the personal statement also forms an integral part of this review.

Additional Information

Pathway at UCLA Extension is a sequential program for students with intellectual and other developmental disabilities, offering a blend of educational, social, and vocational experiences, taught and supervised by experienced instructors sensitive to the individual needs of our students. Pathway students attend classes and participate with UCLA students in the many social, recreational, and cultural activities .

ADMISSIONS INFO FOR STUDENTS WITH LEARNING DIFFERENCES

SAT/ACT required: Yes
Interview required: No
Essay required: Yes
Additional application required: No
Documentation required for:
 LD: Psycho ed evaluation
 ADHD: Diagnosis based on DSM-V; history of behaviors impairing functioning in academic setting; diagnostic interview; history of symptoms; evidence of ongoing behaviors.
 ASD: Psycho ed evaluation
Documentation submitted to: Office for Students with Disabilities
Special Ed. HS course work accepted: No
Separate application required for Programs/Services: No
Contact Information
Name of program or department: Center for Accessible Education
Telephone: 310-825-1501
Fax: 310-825-9656

University of California, Los Angeles

GENERAL ADMISSIONS

Very important factors considered include: rigor of secondary school record, academic GPA, application essay, standardized test scores. *Important factors considered include:* extracurricular activities, talent/ability, volunteer work, work experience. *Other factors considered include:* character/personal qualities, first generation, geographical residence. *Freshman Admission Requirements:* High school diploma is required and GED is accepted. *Academic units required:* 4 English, 3 math, 2 science, 2 science labs, 2 foreign language, 2 history, 1 academic elective, 1 visual/performing arts. *Academic units recommended:* 4 English, 4 math, 3 science, 3 science labs, 3 foreign language, 2 history, 1 academic elective, 1 visual/performing arts.

ACCOMMODATIONS OR SERVICES

Accommodations are decided upon an individual basis after a thorough review of appropriate, current documentation. The accommodations requests must be supported through the documentation provided and must be logically linked to the current impact of the condition on academic functioning.

FINANCIAL AID

Students should submit: FAFSA. Applicants will be notified of awards on a rolling basis beginning 3/15. The Princeton Review suggests that all financial aid forms be submitted as soon as possible after October 1. *Need-based scholarships/grants offered:* College/university scholarship or grant aid from institutional funds; Federal Nursing Scholarships; Federal Pell; Private scholarships; SEOG; State scholarships/grants; United Negro College Fund. *Loan aid offered:* Direct PLUS loans; Direct Subsidized Stafford Loans. Federal Work-Study Program available. Institutional employment available.

CAMPUS LIFE

Activities: Campus Ministries; Choral groups; Concert band; Dance; Drama/theater; International Student Organization; Jazz band; Literary magazine; Marching band; Model UN; Music ensembles; Musical theater; Opera; Pep band; Radio station; Student government; Student newspaper; Student-run film society; Symphony orchestra; Television station; Yearbook. **Organizations:** 870 registered organizations, 21 honor societies, 38 religious organizations. 36 fraternities, 28 sororities. **Athletics (Intercollegiate):** *Men:* baseball, basketball, cross-country, football, golf, soccer, tennis, track/field (outdoor), track/field (indoor), volleyball, water polo. *Women:* basketball, crew/rowing, cross-country, diving, golf, gymnastics, soccer, softball, swimming, tennis, track/field (outdoor), track/field (indoor), volleyball, water polo. **On-Campus Highlights:** The UCLA Library, UCLA Fowler Museum of Cultural History, UCLA Book Store, DeNeve Plaza, Pauley Pavilion—Sports Hall of Fame.

ACCOMODATIONS

Allowed in exams:

Calculators	Yes
Dictionary	Yes
Computer	Yes
Spell-checker	Yes
Extended test time	Yes
Scribe	Yes
Proctors	Yes
Oral exams	No
Note-takers	Yes

Support services for students with

LD	Yes
ADHD	Yes
ASD	Yes
Distraction-reduced environment	Yes
Recording of lecture allowed	Yes
Reading technology:	Yes
Audio books	No
Other assistive technology	Yes
Priority registration	Yes

Added costs for services:

For LD:	No
For ADHD:	No
For ASD:	No
LD specialists	Yes
ADHD & ASD coaching	No
ASD specialists	No
Professional tutors	No
Peer tutors	Yes
Max. hours/week for services	Unlimited
How professors are notified of student approved accommodations	Student and Director

COLLEGE GRADUATION REQUIREMENTS

Course waivers allowed	No
Course substitutions allowed	Yes
In what courses	

Foreign Language and math as appropriate based on documentation, history, and recommendation.

University of California–San Diego

9500 Gilman Drive, La Jolla, CA 92093-0021 • Admissions: 858-534-4831 • Fax: 858-534-5723

CAMPUS
Type of school	Public
Environment	Metropolis
Support	CS

STUDENTS
Undergrad enrollment	9,892
% male/female	3/97
% from out of state	6
% frosh live on campus	95

FINANCIAL FACTS
Annual in-state tuition	$12,630
Annual out-of-state tuition	$40,644
Room and board	$13,733
Required fees	$1,643

GENERAL ADMISSIONS INFO
Application fee	$70
Regular application deadline	11/30
Range SAT EBRW	550–660
Range SAT Math	590–720
Range ACT Composite	26–32

ACADEMICS
Student/faculty ratio	19:1
% students returning for sophomore year	94
% students graduating within 4 years	55
% students graduating within 6 years	84

Most classes have 10–19 students.
Most lab/discussion sessions have 10–19 students.

PROGRAMS/SERVICES FOR STUDENTS WITH LEARNING DIFFERENCES

The Office for Students with Disabilities (OSD) at UC San Diego works with undergraduate, graduates with documented disabilities, reviewing documentation and, through an interactive process with the student, determining reasonable accommodations.. The OSD serves as a resource to UC San Diego faculty and staff who are providing accommodations to students in classrooms and labs across campus, and have developed working relationships with other offices on campus to streamline services to students with disabilities.. The OSD recognizes the unique challenges that some students with disabilities face, Students must provide a comprehensive written evaluation that meets the following requirements: Assessment, including test scores and sub-tests. Testing must be current, and a narrative report needs to be included that discusses the needs of the student.

ADMISSIONS

There is no special admissions process for students with learning disabilities. All applicants must meet the same admission criteria. Students must satisfy subject, GPA, and examination requirements. 15 units of high school courses must be completed to fulfill the subject requirements. At least 7 of those 15 units must be taken in the last 2 years of high school and a grade of "C" or greater must be earned: History (2 years), English (4 years), Math (3 years, although 4 years are recommended), Lab science (2 years, although 3 years are recommended), Language other than English (2 years although 3 years are recommended), Visual and Performing Arts (1 year), College Prep Electives (1 year). Students need to earn a minimum GPA based on "a-g" courses taken in the 10th and 11th grades.

Additional Information

Depending upon the current functional limitations imposed by the diagnosed disability, accommodations may include the following: extended test time, note-taking, permission to tape record lectures, priority registration, calculators, etc.

ADMISSIONS INFO FOR STUDENTS WITH LEARNING DIFFERENCES

SAT/ACT required: Yes
Interview required: Not Applicable
Essay required: No
Additional application required: Not Applicable
Documentation required for:
  LD: https://disabilities.ucsd.edu/students/docguidelines.html
  ADHD: https://disabilities.ucsd.edu/students/docguidelines.html
  ASD: https://disabilities.ucsd.edu/students/docguidelines.html
Documentation submitted to: Support Program/Services
Special Ed. HS course work accepted: Not Applicable
Separate application required for Programs/Services: Not Applicable
Contact Information
Name of program or department: Office of Students with Disabilities
Telephone: (858) 534-4382
Fax: (858) 534-4650
Email: osd@ucsd.edu

University of California–San Diego

GENERAL ADMISSIONS

Very important factors considered include: rigor of secondary school record, academic GPA, application essay, standardized test scores. *Important factors considered include:* extracurricular activities, talent/ability, character/personal qualities, state residency, volunteer work. *Other factors considered include:* first generation, geographical residence, work experience. *Freshman Admission Requirements:* High school diploma is required and GED is accepted. *Academic units required:* 4 English, 3 math, 2 science, 2 science labs, 2 foreign language, 2 history, 1 academic elective, 1 visual/performing arts. *Academic units recommended:* 4 English, 4 math, 3 science, 3 science labs, 3 foreign language, 2 history, 1 academic elective, 1 visual/performing arts.

ACCOMMODATIONS OR SERVICES

Accommodations are decided upon an individual basis after a thorough review of appropriate, current documentation. The accommodations requests must be supported through the documentation provided and must be logically linked to the current impact of the condition on academic functioning.

FINANCIAL AID

Students should submit: FAFSA; State aid form. Applicants will be notified of awards on a rolling basis beginning 3/15. The Princeton Review suggests that all financial aid forms be submitted as soon as possible after October 1. *Need-based scholarships/grants offered:* College/university scholarship or grant aid from institutional funds; Federal Pell; Private scholarships; SEOG; State scholarships/grants. *Loan aid offered:* Direct PLUS loans; Direct Subsidized Stafford Loans; Direct Unsubsidized Stafford Loans. Federal Work-Study Program available. Institutional employment available.

CAMPUS LIFE

Activities: Campus Ministries; Choral groups; Concert band; Dance; Drama/theater; International Student Organization; Jazz band; Literary magazine; Marching band; Model UN; Music ensembles; Musical theater; Opera; Pep band; Radio station; Student government; Student newspaper; Student-run film society; Symphony orchestra; Television station; Yearbook. **Organizations:** 406 registered organizations, 5 honor societies, 46 religious organizations. 19 fraternities, 14 sororities. **Athletics (Intercollegiate):** *Men:* baseball, basketball, crew/rowing, cross-country, diving, fencing, golf, soccer, swimming, tennis, track/field (outdoor), volleyball, water polo. *Women:* basketball, crew/rowing, cross-country, diving, fencing, soccer, softball, swimming, tennis, track/field (outdoor), volleyball, water polo. **On-Campus Highlights:** Geisel Library, Stuart Art (sculpture) Gallery, Sun God Statue, Ocean Cliffs-Torrey Pines State Reserve, Stephen Birch Aquarium and Museum.

ACCOMMODATIONS

Allowed in exams:

Calculators	Yes
Dictionary	Yes
Computer	Yes
Spell-checker	Yes
Extended test time	Yes
Scribe	Yes
Proctors	Yes
Oral exams	Yes
Note-takers	Yes

Support services for students with

LD	No
ADHD	Yes
ASD	No
Distraction-reduced environment	Yes
Recording of lecture allowed	Yes
Reading technology:	Yes
Audio books	Yes
Other assistive technology	Yes
Priority registration	Yes

Added costs for services:

For LD:	No
For ADHD:	No
For ASD:	No
LD specialists	Yes
ADHD & ASD coaching	Yes
ASD specialists	No
Professional tutors	Yes
Peer tutors	Yes
Max. hours/week for services	Varies
How professors are notified of student approved accommodations	Student

COLLEGE GRADUATION REQUIREMENTS

Course waivers allowed	Not Applicable
Course substitutions allowed	Not Applicable

University of California–Santa Barbara

552 University Road, Santa Barbara, CA 93106-2014 • Admissions: 805-893-2881 • Fax: 805-893-2676

PROGRAMS/SERVICES FOR STUDENTS WITH LEARNING DIFFERENCES

The Disabled Student Program (DSP) is a department within the Division of Student Affairs that works to increase the retention and graduation ratio of students with temporary and permanent disabilities, assure equal access to all educational and academic programs, and foster student independence. The university is strongly committed to maintaining an environment that guarantees students with disabilities full access to educational programs and activities. The DSP office serves as a campus liaison regarding issues and regulations related to students with disabilities. DSP provides reasonable accommodations to students with disabilities; specific accommodations are determined on an individual basis. Admitted students should upload documentation to the DSP online system following the completion of an online application. The online system can be accessed at http://dsp.sa.ucsb.edu. Students enter the program via the DSP portal using their NetID and password following admission to the university. When students are set to a status of 'Ready for Meeting' they should schedule an appointment with a disabilities specialist. Accommodations and academically related services are not designed to provide remediation, but to accommodate a disorder that impairs the student's ability to acquire, process, or communicate information. Each accommodation will be made available to the extent that it does not compromise the academic integrity of the student's academic program.

ADMISSIONS

All students must meet the university requirements for admissions. Students may self-disclose their disability in their personal statement. Each essay is reviewed by three readers who assign a score to the application. The university seeks high achieving students who have made the most of their circumstances and are involved in a variety of activities. For California students applying as freshman must have a minimum 3.0 weighted GPA in 10th and 11th grade classes and be enrolled in college prep classes. The average weighted GPA for freshman admitted is 4.15. For out of state freshman the minimum required GPA is 3.43. The SAT or ACT with writing is required. For transfer students 60 semester or 90 quarter transferable units are required. Once a student is admitted to the university, they may apply to the Disabled Students Program.

University of California–Santa Barbara

Additional Information

Students with disabilities submit an on-line application for academic accommodations using the DSP website http://dsp.sa.ucsb.edu Documentation of incoming students for the fall quarter is reviewed by the Documentation Review Committee beginning the third week of June each year. Students receive an email regarding their DSP status. Students are invited to a fall DSP orientation program and meet with their disabilities specialist. Non-remedial drop in, group and individualized tutoring, as well as study skills workshops, are offered through the campus tutoring center, Campus Learning Assistance Services (CLAS) for all university students.

GENERAL ADMISSIONS

Very important factors considered include: academic GPA, application essay, standardized test scores. *Important factors considered include:* rigor of secondary school record. *Other factors considered include:* extracurricular activities, talent/ability, character/personal qualities, first generation, geographical residence, state residency, volunteer work, work experience. *Freshman Admission Requirements:* High school diploma is required and GED is accepted. *Academic units required:* 4 English, 3 math, 2 science, 2 science labs, 2 foreign language, 2 history, 1 academic elective, 1 visual/ performing arts. *Academic units recommended:* 4 English, 4 math, 3 science, 3 science labs, 3 foreign language, 2 history, 1 academic elective, 1 visual/performing arts.

ACCOMMODATIONS OR SERVICES

Accommodations are decided upon an individual basis after a thorough review of appropriate, current documentation. The accommodations requests must be supported through the documentation provided and must be logically linked to the current impact of the condition on academic functioning.

FINANCIAL AID

Students should submit: FAFSA. The Princeton Review suggests that all financial aid forms be submitted as soon as possible after October 1. *Need-based scholarships/grants offered:* College/university scholarship or grant aid from institutional funds; Federal Pell; SEOG; State scholarships/ grants. *Loan aid offered:* Direct PLUS loans; Direct Subsidized Stafford Loans; Direct Unsubsidized Stafford Loans. Federal Work-Study Program available. Institutional employment available.

CAMPUS LIFE

Activities: Campus Ministries; Choral groups; Concert band; Dance; Drama/theater; International Student Organization; Jazz band; Literary magazine; Model UN; Music ensembles; Musical theater; Opera; Pep band; Radio station; Student government; Student newspaper; Student-run film society; Symphony orchestra; Television station; Yearbook. **Organizations:** 508 registered organizations, 5 honor societies, 19 religious organizations. 17 fraternities, 18 sororities. **Athletics (Intercollegiate):** *Men:* baseball, basketball, cross-country, diving, golf, gymnastics, soccer, swimming, tennis, track/field (outdoor), volleyball, water polo. *Women:* basketball, cross-country, diving, gymnastics, soccer, softball, swimming, tennis, track/field (outdoor), volleyball, water polo. **On-Campus Highlights:** Storke Tower Plaza/University Center, University Art Museum, UCSB Davidson Library, Recreation Center, Career and Counseling Services Center.

ACCOMMODATIONS

Allowed in exams:

Calculators	Yes
Dictionary	Yes
Computer	Yes
Spell-checker	Yes
Extended test time	Yes
Scribe	Yes
Proctors	Yes
Oral exams	Yes
Note-takers	Yes

Support services for students with

LD	Yes
ADHD	Yes
ASD	Yes
Distraction-reduced environment	Yes
Recording of lecture allowed	Yes
Reading technology:	Yes
Audio books	Yes
Other assistive technology	Yes
Priority registration	Yes

Added costs for services:

For LD:	No
For ADHD:	No
For ASD:	No
LD specialists	No
ADHD & ASD coaching	No
ASD specialists	No
Professional tutors	No
Peer tutors	Yes
Max. hours/week for services	No
How professors are notified of student approved accommodations	
Student and DSP	

COLLEGE GRADUATION REQUIREMENTS

Course waivers allowed	No
Course substitutions allowed	No

University of San Francisco

2130 FULTON STREET, SAN FRANCISCO, CA 94117 • ADMISSIONS: 415-422-6563 • FAX: 415-422-2217

CAMPUS
Type of school	Private (nonprofit)
Environment	Metropolis
Support	CS

STUDENTS
Undergrad enrollment	6,664
% male/female	38/62
% from out of state	23
% frosh live on campus	91

FINANCIAL FACTS
Annual tuition	$47,550
Room and board	$14,830
Required fees	$516

GENERAL ADMISSIONS INFO
Application fee	$65
Regular application deadline	1/15

Nonfall registration accepted. Admission may be deferred for a maximum of 1 semester.

Range SAT EBRW	510–620
Range SAT Math	520–630
Range ACT Composite	23–28

ACADEMICS
% students returning for sophomore year 86
Most classes have 10–19 students.
Most lab/discussion sessions have fewer than 10 students.

PROGRAMS/SERVICES FOR STUDENTS WITH LEARNING DIFFERENCES
The mission of Student Disability Services, (SDS) is to help USF students with disabilities serve as fully contributing and actively participating members of the University community while acquiring and developing the knowledge, skills, values, and sensitivity to become women and men for others. Toward that end, SDS promotes a fully integrated University experience for students with disabilities by ensuring that students have equal access to all areas of student life and receive appropriate educational support and services to foster their academic and personal success.

ADMISSIONS
The average GPA was a 3.56, mid-50% SAT range 1140-1310 and mid-50% ACT range 23-29. USF does not use formulas to make admission decisions.

Additional Information
Students need to register with SDS using an online application and submit documentation. Every student will meet with a Disability Specialist to have a conversation about their experience and discuss appropriate accommodations and academic adjustments.

ADMISSIONS INFO FOR STUDENTS WITH LEARNING DIFFERENCES
SAT/ACT required: Yes
Interview required: No
Essay required: Not Applicable
Additional application required: Yes
Documentation required for:
 ASD: Psycho ed evaluation
Documentation submitted to: SDS
Special Ed. HS course work accepted: Not Applicable
Separate application required for Program/Services: No
Contact Information
Name of program or department: Student Disability Services
Telephone: (415) 422-2613
Fax: (415) 422-5906
Email: sds@usfca.edu

University of San Francisco

General Admissions

Very important factors considered include: rigor of secondary school record, academic GPA, application essay, standardized test scores. *Important factors considered include:* class rank, recommendation(s), extracurricular activities, character/personal qualities, volunteer work. *Other factors considered include:* interview, talent/ability, first generation, alumni/ae relation, racial/ethnic status, work experience. *Freshman Admission Requirements:* High school diploma is required and GED is accepted. *Academic units required:* 4 English, 3 math, 2 science, 2 foreign language, 3 social studies, 6 academic electives, and 2 units from above areas or other academic areas.

Accommodations or Services

Accommodations are decided upon an individual basis after a thorough review of appropriate, current documentation. The accommodations requests must be supported through the documentation provided and must be logically linked to the current impact of the condition on academic functioning.

Financial Aid

Students should submit: CSS/Financial Aid PROFILE; FAFSA. Applicants will be notified of awards on a rolling basis beginning 4/1. The Princeton Review suggests that all financial aid forms be submitted as soon as possible after October 1. *Need-based scholarships/grants offered:* College/university scholarship or grant aid from institutional funds; Federal Nursing Scholarships; Federal Pell; Private scholarships; SEOG; State scholarships/grants. *Loan aid offered:* Direct PLUS loans; Direct Subsidized Stafford Loans; Direct Unsubsidized Stafford Loans. Federal Work-Study Program available. Institutional employment available.

Campus Life

Activities: Campus Ministries; Choral groups; Dance; Drama/theater; International Student Organization; Jazz band; Literary magazine; Marching band; Music ensembles; Musical theater; Pep band; Radio station; Student government; Student newspaper; Television station; Yearbook. **Organizations:** 90 registered organizations, 14 honor societies, 4 fraternities, 4 sororities. **Athletics (Intercollegiate):** *Men:* baseball, basketball, cross-country, golf, riflery, soccer, tennis, track/field (outdoor). *Women:* basketball, cross-country, golf, riflery, soccer, tennis, track/field (outdoor), volleyball. **On-Campus Highlights:** Koret Health and Recreation Center, War Memorial Gym, St. Ignatius Church, Harney Science Center, Lone Mountain Campus.

ACCOMMODATIONS

Allowed in exams:

Calculators	Yes
Dictionary	Yes
Computer	Yes
Spell-checker	Yes
Extended test time	Yes
Scribe	Yes
Proctors	Yes
Oral exams	Yes
Note-takers	Yes

Support services for students with

LD	Yes
ADHD	Yes
ASD	Yes
Distraction-reduced environment	Yes
Recording of lecture allowed	Yes
Reading technology:	Yes
Audio books	Yes
Other assistive technology	Any

accommodations are determined and administered on a case-by-case basis.

Priority registration	Yes

Added costs for services:

For LD:	No
For ADHD:	No
For ASD:	No
LD specialists	Yes
ADHD & ASD coaching	Yes
ASD specialists	Yes
Professional tutors	Yes
Peer tutors	Yes
Max. hours/week for services	Varies

How professors are notified of student approved accommodations

Director and Student

COLLEGE GRADUATION REQUIREMENTS

Course waivers allowed	No
Course substitutions allowed	Yes

In what courses

This is all done on a case-by-case basis.

University of Southern California

UNIVERSITY PARK, LOS ANGELES, CA 90089-0911 • ADMISSIONS: 213-740-1111 • FAX: 213-821-0200

CAMPUS

Type of school	Private (nonprofit)
Environment	Metropolis
Support	CS

STUDENTS

Undergrad enrollment	19,059
% male/female	49/51
% from out of state	35
% frosh live on campus	98

FINANCIAL FACTS

Annual tuition	$55,320
Room and board	$15,395
Required fees	$905

GENERAL ADMISSIONS INFO

Application fee	$85
Priority deadline	12/1
Regular application deadline	1/15

Nonfall registration accepted. Admission may be deferred for a maximum of one year.

Range SAT EBRW	650–730
Range SAT Math	650–770
Range ACT Composite	30–34

ACADEMICS

Student/faculty ratio	8:1
% students returning for sophomore year	96
% students graduating within 4 years	77
% students graduating within 6 years	92

Most classes have 10–19 students.
Most lab/discussion sessions have 10–19 students.

PROGRAMS/SERVICES FOR STUDENTS WITH LEARNING DIFFERENCES

Disability Services and Programs is responsible for delivery of services to students with learning disabilities. It offers a comprehensive support program in the areas of educational therapy, content area tutoring, study skills instruction, special exam administration, liaison with textbook-taping services, advocacy, and network referral system. The learning specialists, graduate assistants, and learning assistants are available to students for academic therapy. A computer lab is available for computer-assisted learning and for word processing when working with a staff person. After admission, students with LD are counseled by advisors who dialogue with the learning specialist and who are sensitive to special needs. Educational counseling is done by the learning specialist. Off-campus referrals are made to students desiring comprehensive diagnostic testing. The support structure for students with documented learning disabilities is one that is totally individualized; there is no special program per se. Support is given at the request of the student. The learning disabilities specialist and/or grad assistants at USC are prepared to act as advocates when appropriate for any student experiencing academic problems that are related to the learning disability. USC aims to assure close, personal attention to its students even though it is a large campus.

ADMISSIONS

There are no special admissions for students with learning disabilities. Course requirements include 4 years of English, 3 years of math, 2 years of natural science, 2 years of social studies, 2 years of a foreign language, and 4 year-long electives. (The foreign language requirement is not waived in the admission process). It is helpful for comparison purposes to have both timed and untimed SAT or ACT test results. Transfer students are admitted on the basis of their college course work as well as the high school record. It is the student's responsibility to provide recent educational evaluations for documentation as part of the admissions application process. Testing must be current within 3 years, or 5 years for transfer or returning students.

ADMISSIONS INFO FOR STUDENTS WITH LEARNING DIFFERENCES

SAT/ACT required: Yes
Interview required: No
Essay required: Yes
Additional application required: No
Documentation required for:
 LD: Psycho ed evaluation
 ADHD: Diagnosis basedon DSM; history of behaviors impairing functioning in academic setting; diagnostic interview; history of symptoms; evidence of ongoing behaviors.
 ASD: Psycho ed evaluation
Documentation submitted to: Disability Services and Programs
Special Ed. HS course work accepted: Yes
Separate application required for Programs/Services: Yes
Contact Information
Name of program or department: USC Kortschak Center for Learning and Creativity
Telephone: 213-740-7884
Email: kortschakcenter@usc.edu

University of Southern California

Additional Information
The services provided are modifications that are determined to be appropriate for students with LD. During the first 3 weeks of each semester, students are seen on a walk-in basis by the staff in the LD Support Services. Students requesting assistance must have a planning appointment with an LD specialist or grad assistant; provide a copy of the current class schedule; and be sure that eligibility has been determined by documenting specific learning disabilities. Learning assistance most often involves one-on-one attention for academic planning, scheduling, organization, and methods of compensation. Students may have standing appointments with learning assistants and subject tutors. After one "no-show" or three canceled appointments, standing appointments will be canceled. Course accommodations could include taping of lectures, note-taking, extended time for tests, use of word processor, proofreader, limiting scheduling of consecutive exams, and advocacy. Other services include support groups, counseling, and coaching.

GENERAL ADMISSIONS
Very important factors considered include: rigor of secondary school record, academic GPA, application essay, standardized test scores, recommendation(s). *Important factors considered include:* extracurricular activities, talent/ability, character/personal qualities. *Other factors considered include:* class rank, interview, first generation, alumni/ae relation, racial/ethnic status, volunteer work, work experience. *Freshman Admission Requirements:* High school diploma is required and GED is not accepted. *Academic units required:* 4 English, 3 math, 2 science, 2 science labs, 2 foreign language, 2 social studies, 3 academic electives. *Academic units recommended:* 4 English, 4 math, 3 science, 3 science labs, 3 foreign language, 3 social studies, 3 academic electives.

ACCOMMODATIONS OR SERVICES
Accommodations are decided upon an individual basis after a thorough review of appropriate, current documentation. The accommodations requests must be supported through the documentation provided and must be logically linked to the current impact of the condition on academic functioning.

FINANCIAL AID
Students should submit: Business/Farm Supplement; CSS/Financial Aid PROFILE; FAFSA; Noncustodial PROFILE. Applicants will be notified of awards on or about 4/1. The Princeton Review suggests that all financial aid forms be submitted as soon as possible after October 1. *Need-based scholarships/grants offered:* College/university scholarship or grant aid from institutional funds; Federal Pell; Private scholarships; SEOG; State scholarships/grants. *Loan aid offered:* Direct PLUS loans; Direct Subsidized Stafford Loans; Direct Unsubsidized Stafford Loans. Federal Work-Study Program available. Institutional employment available.

CAMPUS LIFE
Activities: Campus Ministries; Choral groups; Concert band; Dance; Drama/theater; International Student Organization; Jazz band; Literary magazine; Marching band; Model UN; Music ensembles; Musical theater; Opera; Pep band; Radio station; Student government; Student newspaper; Student-run film society; Symphony orchestra; Television station; Yearbook. **Organizations:** 676 registered organizations, 49 honor societies, 74 religious organizations. 41 fraternities, 23 sororities. **Athletics (Intercollegiate):** *Men:* baseball, basketball, diving, football, golf, swimming, tennis, track/field (outdoor), volleyball, water polo. *Women:* basketball, crew/rowing, cross-country, diving, golf, soccer, swimming, tennis, track/field (outdoor), volleyball, water polo. **On-Campus Highlights:** Tutor Campus Center, Galen Center (event & training pavilion), Leavey Library (open 24 hours), Heritage Hall (athletic awards), Fisher Museum of Art.

ACCOMMODATIONS
Allowed in exams:

Calculators	Not Applicable
Dictionary	Not Applicable
Computer	Yes
Spell-checker	Not Applicable
Extended test time	Yes
Scribe	Yes
Proctors	Yes
Oral exams	Not Applicable
Note-takers	Yes

Support services for students with

LD	Yes
ADHD	Yes
ASD	Not Applicable
Distraction-reduced environment	Yes
Recording of lecture allowed	Yes
Reading technology:	Not Applicable
Audio books	Yes
Other assistive technology	Yes
Priority registration	Yes

Added costs for services:

For LD:	No
For ADHD:	No
For ASD:	No
LD specialists	No
ADHD & ASD coaching	No
ASD specialists	No
Professional tutors	No
Peer tutors	Yes
Max. hours/week for services	Varies
How professors are notified of student approved accommodations	Student

COLLEGE GRADUATION REQUIREMENTS

Course waivers allowed	No
Course substitutions allowed	No

University of the Pacific

3601 PACIFIC AVENUE, STOCKTON, CA 95211 • ADMISSIONS: 209-946-2211 • FAX: 209-946-4213

PROGRAMS/SERVICES FOR STUDENTS WITH LEARNING DIFFERENCES

There is no special program for students with learning disabilities, but the university does have a Learning Disabilities Support Program. This program offers assistance through tutoring, study skills classes, support groups, and testing accommodations. Documentation for LD must include psychoeducational evaluations from a professional. The documentation for ADHD must be from a medical doctor. Documentation should be sent to the Director of the Office of Services for Students with Disabilities. Students register for services after admission by contacting the Office of Services for Students with Disabilities. Student confidentiality is protected. The ultimate goal is for the student to earn a degree that is unmodified and unflagged. Faculty and staff are dedicated to providing students with learning disabilities all reasonable accommodations so that they may enjoy academic success. The LD Support Program helps keep University of the Pacific in compliance with the Americans with Disabilities Act and Section 504 of the Rehabilitation Act. Compliance is accomplished without compromising University of the Pacific standards, placing undue financial or administrative burden on the university, fundamentally altering the nature of programs, or extending unreasonable accommodations.

ADMISSIONS

UOP welcomes students with learning disabilities. Although there is no special admission procedure, students are given special consideration. There is no minimum ACT/SAT requirement. There are two alternative methods for admissions: (1) probationary admissions for the marginal student—C/D average with no special requirements, but the university advisor is notified of status; no required test score; and no quota regarding the number of students admitted; and (2) special admissions—students who begin college courses in the summer prior to freshman year and receive at least a C average in two courses and one study skills class (can take those courses at any local community college).

Additional Information

All admitted students are eligible for LD services with the appropriate assessment documentation. Academic Support Services offers services to improve learning opportunities for students with LD and are provided within reasonable limits. These services could include diagnostic assessment, accommodations for academic needs, electronic books and alternate formatting, readers, tutorials for academic courses, and referrals to appropriate resources. Skills courses for credit are available in reading, study skills, writing, and math. Services and accommodations are available for undergraduate and graduate students.

University of the Pacific

General Admissions

Very important factors considered include: rigor of secondary school record. *Important factors considered include:* academic GPA, standardized test scores, extracurricular activities, first generation. *Other factors considered include:* class rank, application essay, recommendation(s), talent/ability, character/personal qualities, alumni/ae relation, geographical residence, racial/ethnic status, volunteer work, work experience. *Freshman Admission Requirements:* High school diploma is required and GED is accepted. *Academic units recommended:* 4 English, 4 math, 3 science labs, 2 foreign language, 2 social studies, 1 history, 1 academic elective, 1 visual/performing arts.

Accommodations or Services

Accommodations are decided upon an individual basis after a thorough review of appropriate, current documentation. The accommodations requests must be supported through the documentation provided and must be logically linked to the current impact of the condition on academic functioning.

Financial Aid

Students should submit: FAFSA. Applicants will be notified of awards on a rolling basis beginning 3/1. The Princeton Review suggests that all financial aid forms be submitted as soon as possible after October 1. *Need-based scholarships/grants offered:* College/university scholarship or grant aid from institutional funds; Federal Pell; Private scholarships; SEOG; State scholarships/grants. *Loan aid offered:* Direct PLUS loans; Direct Subsidized Stafford Loans; Direct Unsubsidized Stafford Loans

Campus Life

Activities: Campus Ministries; Choral groups; Concert band; Dance; Drama/theater; International Student Organization; Jazz band; Literary magazine; Model UN; Music ensembles; Musical theater; Opera; Pep band; Radio station; Student government; Student newspaper; Student-run film society; Yearbook. **Organizations:** 100 registered organizations, 14 honor societies, 10 religious organizations. 8 fraternities, 7 sororities. **Athletics (Intercollegiate):** *Men:* baseball, basketball, golf, swimming, tennis, volleyball, water polo. *Women:* basketball, cross-country, field hockey, soccer, softball, swimming, tennis, volleyball, water polo. **On-Campus Highlights:** Brubeck Istitute for Jazz Studies, John Muir Collection and Center, Alex Spanos Center, Reynolds Art Gallery, Pharmacy and Health Sciences Bldg.

ACCOMMODATIONS

Allowed in exams:	
Calculators	Yes
Dictionary	Yes
Computer	Yes
Spell-checker	Yes
Extended test time	Yes
Scribe	Yes
Proctors	Yes
Oral exams	Yes
Note-takers	Yes
Support services for students with	
LD	Yes
ADHD	Yes
ASD	Yes
Distraction-reduced environment	Yes
Recording of lecture allowed	Yes
Reading technology:	Yes
Audio books	Yes
Other assistive technology	smart pens, Kurzweil
Priority registration	Yes
Added costs for services:	
For LD:	No
For ADHD:	No
For ASD:	No
LD specialists	No
ADHD & ASD coaching	Yes
ASD specialists	Yes
Professional tutors	Yes
Peer tutors	Yes
Max. hours/week for services	Varies
How professors are notified of student approved accommodations	Director

COLLEGE GRADUATION REQUIREMENTS

Course waivers allowed	No
Course substitutions allowed	Yes
In what courses	

Math fundamental skills and foreign language.

Whittier College

13406 PHILADELPHIA STREET, WHITTIER, CA 90608 • ADMISSIONS: 562-907-4238 • FAX: 562-907-4870

CAMPUS
Type of school	Private (nonprofit)
Environment	City
Support	S

STUDENTS
Undergrad enrollment	1,664
% male/female	44/56
% from out of state	16
% frosh live on campus	75

FINANCIAL FACTS
Annual tuition	$45,730
Room and board	$13,310
Required fees	$390

GENERAL ADMISSIONS INFO
Application fee	$50
Priority deadline	2/1

Nonfall registration accepted. Admission may be deferred for a maximum of 1 year.

Range SAT EBRW	510–620
Range SAT Math	500–600
Range ACT Composite	21–27

ACADEMICS
Student/faculty ratio	12:1
% students returning for sophomore year	78
% students graduating within 4 years	62
% students graduating within 6 years	69

Most classes have 10–19 students.
Most lab/discussion sessions have 10–19 students.

PROGRAMS/SERVICES FOR STUDENTS WITH LEARNING DIFFERENCES
The director of The Office of Disability Services provides assistance to students with documented disabilities. Accommodation requests are made through the director's office. Students with disabilities must make their needs known to the director of Disability Services to receive accommodations. To arrange for services, students must selfdisclose the disability and make an individual appointment to discuss their accommodation requests with the director. Learning Support Services offers additional services: peer tutoring, workshops on study skills, and basic English and math skills assistance. These services are provided at no cost.

ADMISSIONS
There is no special admissions process for students with disabilities. All applicants are expected to meet the same admission criteria. Students must submit the ACT or SAT Reasoning and have a minimum of a 2.0 GPA; the recommended courses include 4 years of English, 3–4 years of math, 2–3 years of a foreign language, 2–3 years of social studies, and 2–3 years of science labs.

Additional Information
The use of calculators, dictionaries, computers, or spellcheckers in exams would be considered on a case-by-case basis, depending on appropriate documentation and student needs. Students with appropriate documentation will have access to note-takers, readers, extended exam times, alternative exam locations, proctors, scribes, oral exams, books on tape, and priority registration. All students have access to a Math Lab, a Writing Center, a Learning Lab, and academic counseling. The Office of Disability Services also assists students with Self Advocacy Academic Support and Counseling Supportive Education Services Case Management Services (SES) helps students learn to cope with symptoms that can affect their college experience. Such symptoms can include problems with concentration, learning difficulties, test anxiety, trouble with organization, and understanding individual strengths and weaknesses.

ADMISSIONS INFO FOR STUDENTS WITH LEARNING DIFFERENCES
SAT/ACT required: Yes
Interview required: No
Essay required: No
Additional application required: No
Documentation required for:
 LD: Psycho ed evaluation
 ADHD: Diagnosis based on DSM-V; history of behaviors impairing functioning in academic setting; diagnostic interview; history of symptoms; evidence of ongoing behaviors.
 ASD: Psycho ed evaluation
Documentation submitted to: Disability Services
Special Ed. HS course work accepted: No
Separate application required for Programs/Services: Yes
Contact Information
Name of program or department: Student Disability Services
Telephone: 562-907-4825
Fax: 562-907-4827

Whittier College

GENERAL ADMISSIONS

Very important factors considered include: rigor of secondary school record, academic GPA, application essay, recommendation(s), character/personal qualities. *Important factors considered include:* interview, extracurricular activities, talent/ability, volunteer work. *Other factors considered include:* class rank, standardized test scores, first generation, alumni/ae relation, geographical residence, state residency, racial/ethnic status, work experience. *Freshman Admission Requirements:* High school diploma is required and GED is accepted. *Academic units required:* 3 English, 2 math, 1 science, 1 science lab, 2 foreign language, 1 social studies. *Academic units recommended:* 4 English, 3 math, 2 science, 3 foreign language, 2 social studies.

ACCOMMODATIONS OR SERVICES

Accommodations are decided upon an individual basis after a thorough review of appropriate, current documentation. The accommodations requests must be supported through the documentation provided and must be logically linked to the current impact of the condition on academic functioning.

FINANCIAL AID

Students should submit: FAFSA. Applicants will be notified of awards on a rolling basis beginning 2/15. The Princeton Review suggests that all financial aid forms be submitted as soon as possible after October 1. *Need-based scholarships/grants offered:* College/university scholarship or grant aid from institutional funds; Federal Pell; Private scholarships; SEOG; State scholarships/grants. *Loan aid offered:* Direct PLUS loans; Direct Subsidized Stafford Loans; Direct Unsubsidized Stafford Loans. Federal Work-Study Program available.

CAMPUS LIFE

Activities: Campus Ministries; Choral groups; Dance; Drama/theater; International Student Organization; Jazz band; Literary magazine; Model UN; Music ensembles; Radio station; Student government; Student newspaper; Student-run film society; Television station; Yearbook. **Organizations:** 60 registered organizations, 17 honor societies, 6 religious organizations. 4 fraternities, 5 sororities. **Athletics (Intercollegiate):** *Men:* baseball, basketball, cross-country, diving, football, golf, lacrosse, soccer, swimming, tennis, track/field (outdoor), water polo. *Women:* basketball, cross-country, diving, lacrosse, soccer, softball, swimming, tennis, track/field (outdoor), volleyball, water polo. **On-Campus Highlights:** The Campus Center, Bonnie Bell Wardman Library, Donald Graham Athletics Center, Ruth B. Shannon Center for the Performing Arts, the Rock (campus icon).

ACCOMMODATIONS

Allowed in exams:

Calculators	Yes
Dictionary	Yes
Computer	Yes
Spell-checker	Yes
Extended test time	Yes
Scribe	Yes
Proctors	Yes
Oral exams	No
Note-takers	Yes

Support services for students with

LD	Yes
ADHD	Yes
ASD	Yes
Distraction-reduced environment	Yes
Recording of lecture allowed	Yes
Reading technology:	Yes
Audio books	Yes
Other assistive technology	Yes
Priority registration	Yes

Added costs for services:

For LD:	No
For ADHD:	No
For ASD:	No
LD specialists	No
ADHD & ASD coaching	No
ASD specialists	No
Professional tutors	No
Peer tutors	Yes
Max. hours/week for services	Unlimited
How professors are notified of student approved accommodations	Student and Director

COLLEGE GRADUATION REQUIREMENTS

Course waivers allowed	Yes
In what courses	Foreign Language, Math
Course substitutions allowed	Yes
In what courses	
Foreign Language as an admissions requirement	

Colorado State University—Pueblo

2200 Bonforte Boulevard, Pueblo, CO 81001 • Admissions: 719-549-2461 • Fax: 719-549-2419

CAMPUS
Type of school	Public
Environment	City
Support	S

STUDENTS
Undergrad enrollment	3,947
% male/female	43/57
% from out of state	7
% frosh live on campus	90

FINANCIAL FACTS
Annual in-state tuition	$3,422
Annual out-of-state tuition	$13,543
Room and board	$6,300
Required fees	$996

GENERAL ADMISSIONS INFO
Application fee	$25
Regular application deadline	8/1

Nonfall registration accepted. Admission may be deferred for a maximum of 1 semester.

Range SAT EBRW	420–530
Range SAT Math	420–550
Range ACT Composite	18–22

ACADEMICS
Student/faculty ratio	17:1
% students returning for sophomore year	63

Most classes have 10–19 students.
Most lab/discussion sessions have 10–19 students.

PROGRAMS/SERVICES FOR STUDENTS WITH LEARNING DIFFERENCES
The Mission of the Disability Resource Office at Colorado State University—Pueblo is to ensure provision of reasonable academic accommodations and support, designed to enhance academic effectiveness and promote independence in students with documented disabilities.

ADMISSIONS
Colorado State University—Pueblo's admission process is designed to promote diversity within the student population and to assure equal access to qualified applicants. The final admission decision is based on the applicant's potential for attaining a degree at the university. All first-time freshmen must submit their high school transcripts with GPA and ACT/SAT scores along with CSU—Pueblo's application. Applicants who do not meet admission standards are encouraged to submit personal statements explaining their circumstances and to show academic progress throughout high school.

Additional Information
Skills classes are offered in note-taking strategies, study skills, and textbook-reading strategies. The request for the use of a dictionary, computer, or spellchecker during exams will depend on the student's documented needs and permission from the professor. Students with specific needs are encouraged to provide documentation that specifically identifies the disability and the accommodations needed. Tutoring is available through Student and Academic Services. The Academic Improvement Program helps students who are on GPA alerts or academic probation develop an Academic Improvement Plan to promote success. The writing room offers one-on-one writing assistance. The staff of Student Academic Services is committed to assisting all students in their academic lives. Students registered with the Disability Resource & Support Center at Colorado State University-Pueblo are provided with access to the University's self service Assistive Technology Lab. The lab has the following assistive technology software programs available for students to utilize: JAWS; Zoom Text; Dragon Naturally Speaking; Kurzweil 1000; Kurzweil 3000.

ADMISSIONS INFO FOR STUDENTS WITH LEARNING DIFFERENCES
SAT/ACT required: Yes
Interview required: No
Essay required: No
Additional application required: No
Documentation required for:
 LD: Psycho ed evaluation
 ADHD: Diagnosis based on DSM-V; history of behaviors impairing functioning in academic setting; diagnostic interview; history of symptoms; evidence of ongoing behaviors.
 ASD: Diagnosis based on DSM-V; history of behaviors impairing functioning in academic setting; list of current medications.
Documentation submitted to: Disability Resource Office
Special Ed. HS course work accepted: No
Separate application required for Programs/Services: No
Contact Information
Name of program or department: Disability Resource and Support Center
Telephone: 719-549-2648
Email: DRO@csupueblo.edu

Colorado State University—Pueblo

GENERAL ADMISSIONS

Very important factors considered include: rigor of secondary school record, academic GPA, standardized test scores. *Important factors considered include:* class rank. *Other factors considered include:* application essay, recommendation(s), interview, talent/ability, character/personal qualities, volunteer work, work experience, level of applicant's interest. *Freshman Admission Requirements:* High school diploma is required and GED is accepted. *Academic units required:* 4 English, 3 math, 3 science, 2 science labs, 2 foreign language, 2 social studies, 1 history. *Academic units recommended:* 4 English, 3 math, 3 science, 2 science labs, 2 foreign language, 2 social studies, 1 history.

ACCOMMODATIONS OR SERVICES

Accommodations are decided upon an individual basis after a thorough review of appropriate, current documentation. The accommodations requests must be supported through the documentation provided and must be logically linked to the current impact of the condition on academic functioning.

FINANCIAL AID

Students should submit: FAFSA; Institution's own financial aid form. Applicants will be notified of awards on a rolling basis beginning 3/15. The Princeton Review suggests that all financial aid forms be submitted as soon as possible after October 1. *Need-based scholarships/grants offered:* College/university scholarship or grant aid from institutional funds; Federal Pell; Private scholarships; SEOG; State scholarships/grants.

CAMPUS LIFE

Activities: Choral groups; Concert band; Dance; Jazz band; Literary magazine; Music ensembles; Pep band; Student government; Student newspaper; Symphony orchestra; Television station. **Organizations:** 24 registered organizations, 6 honor societies, 4 religious organizations. 2 fraternities, 1 sorority. **Athletics (Intercollegiate):** *Men:* baseball, basketball, golf, soccer, tennis. *Women:* basketball, cross-country, golf, soccer, softball, tennis, volleyball. **On-Campus Highlights:** University Library, Occhiato University Center - La Cantina, Occhiato University Center - The Underground, The Pavillion, The Wall.

ACCOMMODATIONS

Allowed in exams:	
Calculators	Yes
Dictionary	Yes
Computer	Yes
Spell-checker	Yes
Extended test time	Yes
Scribe	Yes
Proctors	Yes
Oral exams	Yes
Note-takers	Yes
Support services for students with	
LD	Yes
ADHD	No
ASD	No
Distraction-reduced environment	Yes
Recording of lecture allowed	Yes
Reading technology:	Yes
Audio books	No
Other assistive technology	Yes
Priority registration	No
Added costs for services:	
For LD:	No
For ADHD:	No
For ASD:	No
LD specialists	No
ADHD & ASD coaching	No
ASD specialists	No
Professional tutors	No
Peer tutors	Yes
Max. hours/week for services	As needed
How professors are notified of student approved accommodations	
Student	

COLLEGE GRADUATION REQUIREMENTS

Course waivers allowed	No
Course substitutions allowed	Yes
In what courses	Varies case by case

Regis University

3333 REGIS BOULEVARD, DENVER, CO 80221-1099 • ADMISSIONS: 303-458-4900 • FAX: 303-964-5534

CAMPUS

Type of school	Private (nonprofit)
Environment	Metropolis
Support	CS

STUDENTS

Undergrad enrollment	3,972
% male/female	39/61
% from out of state	38
% frosh live on campus	NR

FINANCIAL FACTS

Annual tuition	$34,100
Room and board	$10,420
Required fees	$350

GENERAL ADMISSIONS INFO

Priority deadline 4/15

Regular application deadline	8/1

Nonfall registration accepted. Admission may be deferred for a maximum of 1 year.

Range SAT EBRW	480–600
Range SAT Math	470–570
Range ACT Composite	22–26

ACADEMICS

Student/faculty ratio	14:1
% students returning for sophomore year	80

Most classes have 10–19 students.

PROGRAMS/SERVICES FOR STUDENTS WITH LEARNING DIFFERENCES

The Commitment Program, created in 1976, provides learning support courses, peer mentoring, study groups, and priority advising and registration for approximately 50 freshmen who are provisionally admitted to the university. Commitment students may not participate in varsity sports or off-campus employment during their freshman year, and are obliged to make regular use of academic support provided by the Program. Two Commitment study rooms are available all day every day, and weekly Forum meetings offer career counseling, study skills, time management, and other first-year enrichment services. LS courses (including critical reading and writing, and math and science learning strategies) apply toward elective credit. The director of the program works closely with the Office of Disability Services to support students in need of specific accommodations. In keeping with the Jesuit mission of "educating men and women in the service others," Commitment students work throughout the academic year in a variety of Father Woody Service Projects.

ADMISSIONS

There is no special admission for students with LD. Interview not required. Minimum GPA 2.56, SAT of 930, or ACT of 20 and 15 academic units. Students may be considered with 17 ACT or 810 SAT and 2.3 GPA. Students need to show sufficient evidence of motivation and ability to succeed in college, even though they may not have the required GPA or test scores. Recommendations and extracurricular activities will be considered. Students admitted on probation typically have stronger test scores and lower GPAs and are admitted on one semester probation. They need a 2.0 GPA to return the second semester. Other students may be admitted into the Freshman Commitment Program. These students usually have lower test scores and a C-plus average. Probationary admission is for two semesters.

ADMISSIONS INFO FOR STUDENTS WITH LEARNING DIFFERENCES

SAT/ACT required: Yes

Interview required: No

Essay required: No

Additional application required: No

Documentation required for:

LD: Psycho ed evaluation

ADHD: Diagnosis based on DSM-V; history of behaviors impairing functioning in academic setting; diagnostic interview; history of symptoms; evidence of ongoing behaviors.

ASD: Evaluations must be conducted by a qualified impartial professional. Eval to include: letterhead, diagnosis based on DSM-V criteria, history, comprehensive testing, comprehensive standardized IQ test (including cognitive/achievement scores), communication assessment, ADOS, ADI-R, GARS, GADS, AAA, impact of current medication to meet the demands of post-secondary environment, current functional limitations.

Documentation submitted to: Disability Services

Special Ed. HS course work accepted: No

Separate application required for Programs/Services: No

Contact Information

Name of program or department: Student Disability Services

Telephone: 303-458-4941

Fax: 303-964-6595

Email: disability@regis.edu

Regis University

Additional Information

Disability Services provides self-advocacy training; test-taking and learning strategies assistance; academic monitoring; note-takers; readers; scribes; extended testing time; and course substitutions. Students in the Commitment Program remain for one year and, with successful completion, are officially admitted to the college. They must pass all required commitment courses with a C or better, not fall below a 2.0 GPA in non-Commitment courses, and agree not to participate in varsity sports or other activities that interfere with class attendance while in the program. There are learning support courses, study groups, and tutorials. Tutors available and all students must pass 3 hours of math. There is a math learning support course or a remedial math class available prior to taking the regular college algebra class.

GENERAL ADMISSIONS

Very important factors considered include: rigor of secondary school record, academic GPA, standardized test scores, character/personal qualities. *Other factors considered include:* class rank, application essay, recommendation(s), interview, extracurricular activities, talent/ability, first generation, alumni/ae relation, racial/ethnic status, work experience, level of applicant's interest. *Freshman Admission Requirements:* High school diploma is required and GED is accepted. *Academic units recommended:* 4 English, 3 math, 2 science, 1 science lab, 2 foreign language, 2 social studies, 1 academic elective.

ACCOMMODATIONS OR SERVICES

Accommodations are decided upon an individual basis after a thorough review of appropriate, current documentation. The accommodations requests must be supported through the documentation provided and must be logically linked to the current impact of the condition on academic functioning.

FINANCIAL AID

Students should submit: FAFSA. Applicants will be notified of awards on a rolling basis beginning 3/15. The Princeton Review suggests that all financial aid forms be submitted as soon as possible after October 1. *Need-based scholarships/grants offered:* College/university scholarship or grant aid from institutional funds; Federal Pell; Private scholarships; SEOG; State scholarships/grants. *Loan aid offered:* Direct PLUS loans; Direct Subsidized Stafford Loans; Direct Unsubsidized Stafford Loans. Federal Work-Study Program available. Institutional employment available.

CAMPUS LIFE

Activities: Campus Ministries; Choral groups; Concert band; Dance; Drama/theater; International Student Organization; Jazz band; Literary magazine; Music ensembles; Musical theater; Radio station; Student government; Student newspaper; Yearbook. **Organizations:** 40 registered organizations, 1 honor society, 1 religious organization. **Athletics (Intercollegiate):** *Men:* baseball, basketball, cross-country, golf, soccer *Women:* basketball, cross-country, lacrosse, soccer, softball, volleyball. Residence Halls, Student Center, Science Building, Chapel, Arboretum.

ACCOMMODATIONS

Allowed in exams:	
Calculators	Yes
Dictionary	Yes
Computer	Yes
Spell-checker	Yes
Extended test time	Yes
Scribe	Yes
Proctors	Yes
Oral exams	Yes
Note-takers	Yes
Support services for students with	
LD	Yes
ADHD	Yes
ASD	Yes
Distraction-reduced environment	Yes
Recording of lecture allowed	Yes
Reading technology:	Yes
Audio books	Yes
Other assistive technology	Yes
Priority registration	Yes
Added costs for services:	
For LD:	No
For ADHD:	No
For ASD:	No
LD specialists	No
ADHD & ASD coaching	No
ASD specialists	No
Professional tutors	No
Peer tutors	Varies
Max. hours/week for services	Unlimited
How professors are notified of student approved accommodations	Student

COLLEGE GRADUATION REQUIREMENTS

Course waivers allowed	Yes
In what courses	

All students must take three hours of math. Foreign culture courses are substituted for foreign language if the documentation verifies a disability.

Course substitutions allowed	Yes
In what courses	

All students must take three hours of math. Foreign culture courses are substituted for foreign language if the documentation verifies a disability.

University of Colorado Boulder

OFFICE OF ADMISSIONS, BOULDER, CO 80309-0552 • ADMISSIONS: 303-492-6301 • FAX: 303-735-2501

CAMPUS

Type of school	Public
Environment	City
Support	CS

STUDENTS

Undergrad enrollment	28,667
% male/female	56/44
% from out of state	42
% frosh live on campus	94

FINANCIAL FACTS

Annual in-state tuition	$10,728
Annual out-of-state tuition	$35,482
Room and board	$14,418
Required fees	$1,804

GENERAL ADMISSIONS INFO

Application fee	$50
Priority deadline	11/15
Regular application deadline	1/15

Nonfall registration accepted. Admission may be deferred for a maximum of 1 year.

Range SAT EBRW	580–665
Range SAT Math	570–680
Range ACT Composite	25–30

ACADEMICS

Student/faculty ratio	NR
% students returning for sophomore year	88
% students graduating within 4 years	45
% students graduating within 6 years	69

Most classes have 10–19 students.

PROGRAMS/SERVICES FOR STUDENTS WITH LEARNING DIFFERENCES

The mission of Disability Services ensures that students with disabilities receive reasonable accommodations and services to participate fully in the academic environment. Vision: We envision a fully accessible, integrated, and universally designed campus community. Students with disabilities are one of the many groups that make up our campus community and a diverse comunity broadens our understanding and appreciation for the contributions of each individual. Philosophy: Disability Services provides leadership and guidance regarding accommodations and universal access.

ADMISSIONS

There is not a special admission process for students with disabilities. All students are considered under the same competitive admissions criteria. All application information should be submitted to admissions, but documentation should be submitted directly to Disability Services.

Additional Information

Services provided through Disability Services include an opportunity to meet with a disability specialist to identify appropriate accommodations, campus resources, advocacy, and short-term academics strategies. The Disability Specialist provides individualized support to students with all kinds of disabilities. This support can take many forms including informal academic advising, advocacy, and letters to professors designating reasonable accommodation, if appropriate. Disability Specialists assist students in developing strategies for time management, organization, study skills, test preparation, and transition to and beyond life at the university. Additionally, first year students who live in residence halls can access free tutoring through Housing and Dining Services' Academic Support .Assistance Program. For the most accurate information, students wishing to request services should access our website at http://colorado.edu/disabilityservices

ADMISSIONS INFO FOR STUDENTS WITH LEARNING DIFFERENCES

SAT/ACT required: Yes
Interview required: No
Essay required: Not Applicable
Additional application required: Yes
Documentation required for:
  LD: Specific Documentation Guidelines may be found at the following website: https://www.colorado.edu/disabilityservices/students/register-disability-services/documentation-guidelines
  ADHD: Specific Documentation Guidelines may be found at the following website: https://www.colorado.edu/disabilityservices/students/register-disability-services/documentation-guidelines
  ASD: Specific Documentation Guidelines may be found at the following website: https://www.colorado.edu/disabilityservices/students/register-disability-services/documentation-guidelines
Documentation submitted to: Support Program/Services
Special Ed. HS course work accepted: Not Applicable
Separate application required for Programs/Services: Not for LD, ADHD, or ASD.
Contact Information
Name of program or department: Disability Services
Telephone: 303-492-8671
Fax: 303-492-8671
Email: dsinfo@colorado.edu

University of Colorado Boulder

GENERAL ADMISSIONS

Very important factors considered include: rigor of secondary school record, class rank, academic GPA, standardized test scores. *Important factors considered include:* application essay, recommendation(s), extracurricular activities, talent/ability, character/personal qualities, first generation. *Other factors considered include:* alumni/ae relation, geographical residence, state residency, racial/ethnic status, volunteer work, work experience, level of applicant's interest. *Freshman Admission Requirements:* High school diploma is required and GED is accepted. *Academic units required:* 4 English, 4 math, 3 science, 2 science labs, 3 foreign language, 3 social studies, 1 history, and 1 unit from above areas or other academic areas.

ACCOMMODATIONS OR SERVICES

Accommodations are decided upon an individual basis after a thorough review of appropriate, current documentation. The accommodations requests must be supported through the documentation provided and must be logically linked to the current impact of the condition on academic functioning.

FINANCIAL AID

Students should submit: FAFSA. Applicants will be notified of awards on a rolling basis beginning 3/15. The Princeton Review suggests that all financial aid forms be submitted as soon as possible after October 1. *Need-based scholarships/grants offered:* College/university scholarship or grant aid from institutional funds; Federal Pell; Private scholarships; SEOG; State scholarships/grants. *Loan aid offered:* Direct PLUS loans; Direct Subsidized Stafford Loans; Direct Unsubsidized Stafford Loans. Federal Work-Study Program available. Institutional employment available.

CAMPUS LIFE

Activities: Campus Ministries; Choral groups; Concert band; Dance; Drama/theater; International Student Organization; Jazz band; Literary magazine; Marching band; Model UN; Music ensembles; Musical theater; Opera; Pep band; Radio station; Student government; Student newspaper; Student-run film society; Symphony orchestra. **Organizations:** 300 registered organizations, 26 honor societies, 35 religious organizations. 20 fraternities, 19 sororities. **Athletics (Intercollegiate):** *Men:* basketball, cross-country, football, golf, skiing (downhill/alpine), skiing (nordic/cross-country), track/field (outdoor), track/field (indoor). *Women:* basketball, cross-country, golf, skiing (downhill/alpine), skiing (nordic/cross-country), soccer, tennis, track/field (outdoor), track/field (indoor), volleyball. **On-Campus Highlights:** Center for Community, University Memorial Center (UMC), Student Recreation Center, Norlin Library, Farrand Field.

ACCOMMODATIONS

Allowed in exams:	
Calculators	Yes
Dictionary	Yes
Computer	Yes
Spell-checker	Yes
Extended test time	Yes
Scribe	Yes
Proctors	Yes
Oral exams	Yes
Note-takers	Yes
Support services for students with	
LD	Yes
ADHD	Yes
ASD	Yes
Distraction-reduced environment	Yes
Recording of lecture allowed	Yes
Reading technology:	Yes
Audio books	Yes
Other assistive technology	Yes
Priority registration	Yes
Added costs for services:	
For LD:	No
For ADHD:	No
For ASD:	No
LD specialists	No
ADHD & ASD coaching	No
ASD specialists	No
Professional tutors	No
Peer tutors	Yes
Max. hours/week for services	Varies
How professors are notified of student approved accommodations	Student

COLLEGE GRADUATION REQUIREMENTS

Course waivers allowed	No
Course substitutions allowed	No

University of Colorado at Colorado Springs

1420 Austin Bluffs Parkway, Colorado Springs, CO 80918 • Admissions: 719-255-3084 • Fax:

CAMPUS
Type of school	Public
Environment	Metropolis
Support	CS

STUDENTS
Undergrad enrollment	8,868
% male/female	47/53
% from out of state	11
% frosh live on campus	48

FINANCIAL FACTS
Annual in-state tuition	$9,630
Annual out-of-state tuition	$24,270
Room and board	$10,100
Required fees	$1,613

GENERAL ADMISSIONS INFO
Application fee	$50

Nonfall registration accepted. Admission may be deferred for a maximum of 3 terms.

Range SAT EBRW	470–590
Range SAT Math	472–600
Range ACT Composite	21–25

ACADEMICS
Student/faculty ratio	17:1
% students returning for sophomore year	71

Most classes have 10–19 students.
Most lab/discussion sessions have 10–19 students.

PROGRAMS/SERVICES FOR STUDENTS WITH LEARNING DIFFERENCES

University of Colorado—Colorado Springs is committed to providing equal educational opportunity for all students who meet the academic admission requirements. The purpose of Disability Services is to provide comprehensive support to meet the individual needs of students with disabilities. Students are expected to utilize the resources of Disability Services to the degree they determine necessary.

ADMISSIONS

An applicant's learning disability is not considered in an admission decision. All applicants are required to meet the Minimum Academic Preparation Standards (MAPS), including 4 years of English, 3 years of math (4 years for engineering and business), 3 years of natural science, 2 years of social science, 2 years of a foreign language, and 1 year of an elective; fine and performing arts are encouraged. Courses taken before 9th grade are accepted as long as the documentation provided shows that the courses were completed. American Sign Language is a qualified substitute for a foreign language. Successfully completing 2 years of a foreign language will satisfy the foreign language requirement regardless of whether the courses were taken before the 9th grade. Students with deficiencies may be admitted to the university provided they meet the other admission standards of test scores, rank in class, and GPA (minimum of 2.8), provided they make up any deficiencies in the MAPS prior to graduation.

Additional Information

Students with learning disabilities receive information in their acceptance letter about contacting Disability Services if they wish to request accommodations or services. Students must request services and submit appropriate documentation. Students must meet with Disability Services to discuss support services and/or accommodations that are appropriate. Strategy development is offered in study skills, reading, test performance, stress reduction, time management, and writing skills. Disability Services offers the use of volunteers who use carbonless paper provided by the support services. Services and accommodations are available for undergraduate and graduate students with learning disabilities. Tutors are available for all university students in labs; tutors are also provided for students with disabilities.

ADMISSIONS INFO FOR STUDENTS WITH LEARNING DIFFERENCES

SAT/ACT required: Yes
Interview required: No
Essay required: No
Additional application required: No
Documentation required for:
 LD: Psycho ed evaluation
 ADHD: Diagnosis based on DSM-V; history of behaviors impairing functioning in academic setting; diagnostic interview; history of symptoms; evidence of ongoing behaviors.
 ASD: Psycho ed evaluation
Documentation submitted to: Disability Services
Special Ed. HS course work accepted: No
Separate application required for Programs/Services: No
Contact Information
Name of program or department: Disability Services
Telephone: (719)255-3354
Fax: (719)255-3195
Email: dservice@uccs.edu

University of Colorado at Colorado Springs

GENERAL ADMISSIONS

Very important factors considered include: rigor of secondary school record, class rank, academic GPA, standardized test scores. *Other factors considered include:* application essay, recommendation(s). *Freshman Admission Requirements:* High school diploma is required and GED is accepted. *Academic units required:* 4 English, 4 math, 3 science, 2 science labs, 1 foreign language, 3 social studies, 1 history, 2 academic electives. *Academic units recommended:* 4 English, 4 math, 3 science, 2 science labs, 1 foreign language, 3 social studies, 1 history, 2 academic electives.

ACCOMMODATIONS OR SERVICES

Accommodations are decided upon an individual basis after a thorough review of appropriate, current documentation. The accommodations requests must be supported through the documentation provided and must be logically linked to the current impact of the condition on academic functioning.

FINANCIAL AID

Students should submit: FAFSA. Applicants will be notified of awards on a rolling basis beginning 4/15. The Princeton Review suggests that all financial aid forms be submitted as soon as possible after October 1. *Need-based scholarships/grants offered:* College/university scholarship or grant aid from institutional funds; Federal Pell; Private scholarships; SEOG; State scholarships/grants. *Loan aid offered:* Direct PLUS loans; Direct Subsidized Stafford Loans; Direct Unsubsidized Stafford Loans.

CAMPUS LIFE

Activities: Choral groups; Dance; Drama/theater; International Student Organization; Literary magazine; Pep band; Radio station; Student government; Student newspaper; Television station. **Organizations:** 55 registered organizations, 7 religious organizations. 1 sorority. **Athletics (Intercollegiate):** *Men:* basketball, cross-country, golf, soccer, tennis, track/field (outdoor). *Women:* basketball, cross-country, softball, tennis, track/field (outdoor), volleyball. **On-Campus Highlights:** Kraemer Family Library, University Center, Recreation Center, Osborne Center for Science & Engineering, Columbine Hall.

ACCOMMODATIONS

Allowed in exams:	
Calculators	Yes
Dictionary	Yes
Computer	Yes
Spell-checker	Yes
Extended test time	Yes
Scribe	Yes
Proctors	Yes
Oral exams	Yes
Note-takers	No
Support services for students with	
LD	Yes
ADHD	Yes
ASD	Yes
Distraction-reduced environment	Yes
Recording of lecture allowed	Yes
Reading technology:	Yes
Audio books	Yes
Other assistive technology	Yes
Priority registration	No
Added costs for services:	
For LD:	No
For ADHD:	No
For ASD:	No
LD specialists	Yes
ADHD & ASD coaching	No
ASD specialists	No
Professional tutors	No
Peer tutors	No
Max. hours/week for services	N/A
How professors are notified of student approved accommodations	Student

COLLEGE GRADUATION REQUIREMENTS

Course waivers allowed	No
In what courses	N/A
Course substitutions allowed	Yes
In what courses	

American Sign Language is accepted as a foreign language.

University of Denver

2199 South University Boulevard, Denver, CO 80208 • Admissions: (303) 871-2036 • Fax: 303-871-3301

CAMPUS

Type of school	Private
(nonprofit) Environment	Metropolis
Support	SP

STUDENTS

Undergrad enrollment	5,753
% male/female	47/53
% from out of state	62
% frosh live on campus	93

FINANCIAL FACTS

Annual tuition	$49,392
Room and board	$13,005
Required fees	$1,164

GENERAL ADMISSIONS INFO

Application fee	$65
Regular application deadline	1/15

Nonfall registration accepted. Admission may be deferred for a maximum of 1 year.

Range SAT EBRW	590–680
Range SAT Math	570–670
Range ACT Composite	25–30

ACADEMICS

Student/faculty ratio	11:1
% students returning for sophomore year	87
% students graduating within 4 years	65
% students graduating within 6 years	75

Most classes have fewer than 10 students. Most lab/discussion sessions have 10–19 students.

PROGRAMS/SERVICES FOR STUDENTS WITH LEARNING DIFFERENCES

The Learning Effectiveness Program (LEP) was founded in 1982 as an academic support program for University students with learning disabilities. Since then we have developed some of the most comprehensive and innovative learning disability (LD) and Attention Deficit Hyperactivity Disorder (ADHD) support services provided at the post-secondary level. Our nationally recognized program serves over 200 students each year.

ADMISSIONS

Admission to the university is distinct from enrollment in the LEP. All potential DU candidates must submit a general admissions application, essay, recommendations, activity sheet, high school transcript, and ACT/SAT scores. Students applying to LEP must be accepted by DU and make separate application to the LEP, as well as provide documentation of LD/ADHD through recent diagnostic tests. Strengths, weaknesses, maturity level, ability to handle frustration, and feelings about limitations should also be included in documentation sent to the LEP. A campus visit and interview with LEP is recommended after submission of all documentation and testing. Interviews should be scheduled as far in advance as possible. DU looks for students who have challenged themselves academically and recommend 4 years English, 3-4 years math, 3-4 years social studies, 3-4 years science and 3-4 foreign languages. The middle 50% GPA ranges from 3.51-4.0 The ACT or SAT is required and Denver will "super score" either the ACT or SAT to determine the highest composite score on either test. Extra-curricular activities are important as are the teacher/counselor recommendations.

Additional Information

LEP services are only available to students who are enrolled in the LEP program. The LEP is a fee-for-service, $1,200 per quarter program that provides services beyond the mandated accommodations provided under Section 504. There is an additional fee per year for this program. The director is an LD specialist and the staff is composed of professionals in a variety of academic disciplines and have been trained to work with students with learning differences. Professional tutoring is also available to students enrolled in this program. Students who feel that they need only basic accommodations and do not wish to participate in the comprehensive program should contact Disability Services Program at 303-871-2372 to make those arrangements. Learning disability assessments are available on campus through the Counseling Center. Connect to DSP and LEP through the website or connect in person to initiate services.

ADMISSIONS INFO FOR STUDENTS WITH LEARNING DIFFERENCES

SAT/ACT required:
Interview required: No
Essay required: Not Applicable
Additional application required: Yes
Documentation required for:
 LD: Psycho ed evaluation
 ADHD: Psycho ed evaluation
 ASD: documentation from a professional indicating the diagnosis and how the diagnosis affects the student.
Documentation submitted to: LEP
Special Ed. HS course work accepted: Not Applicable
Separate application required for Programs/Services: Yes
Contact Information
Name of program or department: Learning Effectiveness Program
Telephone: 303-871-2372
Email: dsp@du.edu

University of Denver

General Admissions

Very important factors considered include: rigor of secondary school record, academic GPA, standardized test scores. *Important factors considered include:* application essay, recommendation(s), extracurricular activities, talent/ability, character/personal qualities. *Other factors considered include:* first generation, alumni/ae relation, geographical residence, racial/ethnic status, volunteer work, work experience, level of applicant's interest. *Freshman Admission Requirements:* High school diploma is required and GED is accepted. *Academic units recommended:* 4 English, 3 math, 3 science, 2 science labs, 2 foreign language, 3 social studies.

Accommodations or Services

Accommodations are decided upon an individual basis after a thorough review of appropriate, current documentation. The accommodations requests must be supported through the documentation provided and must be logically linked to the current impact of the condition on academic functioning.

Financial Aid

Students should submit: CSS/Financial Aid PROFILE; FAFSA; Noncustodial PROFILE. Applicants will be notified of awards on or about 3/1. The Princeton Review suggests that all financial aid forms be submitted as soon as possible after October 1. *Need-based scholarships/grants offered:* College/university scholarship or grant aid from institutional funds; Federal Pell; Private scholarships; SEOG; State scholarships/grants. *Loan aid offered:* Direct PLUS loans; Direct Subsidized Stafford Loans; Direct Unsubsidized Stafford Loans. Federal Work-Study Program available. Institutional employment available.

Campus Life

Activities: Campus Ministries; Choral groups; Concert band; Dance; Drama/theater; International Student Organization; Jazz band; Literary magazine; Marching band; Model UN; Music ensembles; Musical theater; Opera; Pep band; Radio station; Student government; Student newspaper; Student-run film society; Symphony orchestra. **Organizations:** 160 registered organizations, 19 honor societies, 14 religious organizations. 9 fraternities, 6 sororities. **Athletics (Intercollegiate):** *Men:* basketball, diving, golf, ice hockey, lacrosse, skiing (downhill/alpine), skiing (nordic/cross-country), soccer, swimming, tennis. *Women:* basketball, diving, golf, gymnastics, lacrosse, skiing (downhill/alpine), skiing (nordic/cross-country), soccer, swimming, tennis, volleyball. **On-Campus Highlights:** Campus Green (Driscoll Lawn), Ritchie Center (athletic facility), Anderson Academic Commons (library), Newman Center (performing arts), Beans Cafe (inside Joy Burns Center).

ACCOMMODATIONS

Allowed in exams:

Calculators	Yes
Dictionary	Yes
Computer	Yes
Spell-checker	Yes
Extended test time	Yes
Scribe	Yes
Proctors	Yes
Oral exams	Yes
Note-takers	Yes

Support services for students with

LD	Yes
ADHD	Yes
ASD	Yes
Distraction-reduced environment	Yes
Recording of lecture allowed	Yes
Reading technology:	Yes
Audio books	Yes

Other assistive technology accommodations are available with appropriate documentation to meet the student's learning need.

Priority registration	Yes

Added costs for services:

For LD:	Yes
For ADHD:	Yes
For ASD:	Yes
LD specialists	Yes
ADHD & ASD coaching	No
ASD specialists	Yes
Professional tutors	Yes
Peer tutors	No
Max. hours/week for services	Varies
How professors are notified of student approved accommodations	Student

COLLEGE GRADUATION REQUIREMENTS

Course waivers allowed	No
Course substitutions allowed	Yes
In what courses	Foreign Language

University of Northern Colorado

501 20TH STREET, GREELEY, CO 80639 • ADMISSIONS: 970-351-2881 • FAX: 970-351-2984

CAMPUS

Type of school	Public
Environment	City
Support	S

STUDENTS

Undergrad enrollment	9,100
% male/female	35/65
% from out of state	16
% frosh live on campus	89

FINANCIAL FACTS

Annual in-state tuition	$7,374
Annual out-of-state tuition	$18,960
Room and board	$10,982
Required fees	$2,171

GENERAL ADMISSIONS INFO

Application fee	$45
Priority deadline	3/1
Regular application deadline	8/1

Nonfall registration accepted. Admission may be deferred for a maximum of 1 year.

Range SAT EBRW	510–620
Range SAT Math	490–610
Range ACT Composite	19–25

ACADEMICS

Student/faculty ratio	18:1
% students returning for sophomore year	71
% students graduating within 4 years	28
% students graduating within 6 years	48

Most classes have 10–19 students.
Most lab/discussion sessions have 10–19 students.

PROGRAMS/SERVICES FOR STUDENTS WITH LEARNING DIFFERENCES

Although the university does not offer a formal LD program, individual assistance is provided whenever possible. The Disability Support Services (DSS) provides access, accommodations, and advocacy for UNC students who have documented disabilities. Academic needs are determined by the documentation and a student interview. Students with disabilities have an equal opportunity to pursue their educational goals. DSS provides test accommodations, adaptive hardware and software, learning strategies, organizational skills, and a reader program. Students with ADHD must provide a medical or clinical diagnosis from a developmental pediatrician, neurologist, and psychiatrist, licensed clinical or educational psychologist, family physician, or a combination of such professionals.

ADMISSIONS

There is no special admission process for students with learning disabilities. All students with disabilities are admitted to UNC under the standard admission requirements of the university. Applicants are expected to have a minimum 2.5 GPA. ACT or SAT are required. Writing Section is not required.

Additional Information

Services for individuals with LD/ADHD includes learning strategies, organizational skills, and advocacy skills; reader program; test accommodations; assistance in arranging for note-takers; and assistive technology, including voice synthesizers, screen readers, screen enlargers, scanners, voice-recognition computer systems, large monitors, and word processing with spellchecker. Workshops are offered in student skills, organizational skills, study strategies, and time management. These workshops are electives and are not for credit. Services and accommodations are available for undergraduate and graduate students.

ADMISSIONS INFO FOR STUDENTS WITH LEARNING DIFFERENCES

SAT/ACT required: Yes
Interview required: Recommended
Essay required: No
Additional application required: No
Documentation required for:
 LD: Psycho ed evaluation
 ADHD: Diagnosis basedon DSM-V; history of behaviors impairing functioning in academic setting; diagnostic interview; history of symptoms;evidence of ongoing behaviors.
 ASD: Psycho ed evaluation
Documentation submitted to: Disability Support Services (DSS)
Special Ed. HS course work accepted: Yes
Separate application required for Programs/Services: No
Contact Information Name of program or department: Disability Support Services (DSS)
Telephone: 970-351-2289
Fax: 970-351-4166
Email: lorraine.harris@unco.edu

University of Northern Colorado

GENERAL ADMISSIONS

Very important factors considered include: class rank, academic GPA, standardized test scores. *Other factors considered include:* rigor of secondary school record, application essay, recommendation(s), interview, extracurricular activities, talent/ability, character/personal qualities, first generation, alumni/ae relation, geographical residence, state residency, volunteer work. *Freshman Admission Requirements:* High school diploma is required and GED is accepted. *Academic units recommended:* 4 English, 4 math, 3 science, 2 science labs, 1 foreign language, 2 social studies, 1 history, 2 academic electives.

ACCOMMODATIONS OR SERVICES

Accommodations are decided upon an individual basis after a thorough review of appropriate, current documentation. The accommodations requests must be supported through the documentation provided and must be logically linked to the current impact of the condition on academic functioning.

FINANCIAL AID

Students should submit: FAFSA. Applicants will be notified of awards on a rolling basis beginning 3/1. The Princeton Review suggests that all financial aid forms be submitted as soon as possible after October 1. *Need-based scholarships/grants offered:* College/university scholarship or grant aid from institutional funds; Federal Pell; Private scholarships; SEOG; State scholarships/grants. *Loan aid offered:* Direct PLUS loans; Direct Subsidized Stafford Loans; Direct Unsubsidized Stafford Loans. Federal Work-Study Program available. Institutional employment available.

CAMPUS LIFE

Activities: Campus Ministries; Choral groups; Concert band; Dance; Drama/theater; International Student Organization; Jazz band; Literary magazine; Marching band; Music ensembles; Musical theater; Opera; Student government; Student newspaper; Student-run film society; Symphony orchestra; Television station. **Organizations:** 137 registered organizations, 9 honor societies, 18 religious organizations. 9 fraternities, 8 sororities. **Athletics (Intercollegiate):** *Men:* baseball, basketball, football, golf, tennis, track/field (outdoor), wrestling. *Women:* basketball, cross-country, diving, golf, soccer, softball, swimming, tennis, track/field (outdoor), volleyball. **On-Campus Highlights:** University Center, James Michener Library, Recreation Center, Cultural & Resource Centers.

ACCOMMODATIONS	
Allowed in exams:	
Calculators	Yes
Dictionary	Yes
Computer	Yes
Spell-checker	Yes
Extended test time	Yes
Scribe	Yes
Proctors	Yes
Oral exams	Yes
Note-takers	Yes
Support services for students with	
LD	No
ADHD	No
ASD	No
Distraction-reduced environment	Yes
Recording of lecture allowed	Yes
Reading technology:	Yes
Audio books	Yes
Other assistive technology	Yes
Priority registration	Yes
Added costs for services:	
For LD:	No
For ADHD:	No
For ASD:	No
LD specialists	No
ADHD & ASD coaching	No
ASD specialists	No
Professional tutors	No
Peer tutors	Yes
Max. hours/week for services	Varies
How professors are notified of student approved accommodations	Student

COLLEGE GRADUATION REQUIREMENTS	
Course waivers allowed	No
Course substitutions allowed	No

Western Colorado University

600 N. Adams St., Gunnison, CO 81231 • Admissions: • Fax: (970) 943-2363

CAMPUS

Type of school	Public
Environment	Rural
Support	S

STUDENTS

Undergrad enrollment	1,899
% male/female	59/41
% from out of state	70
% frosh live on campus	89

FINANCIAL FACTS

Annual in-state tuition	$6,624
Annual out-of-state tuition	$18,096
Room and board	NR
Required fees	$3,490

GENERAL ADMISSIONS INFO

Application fee	$30.
Priority deadline	6/1
Nonfall registration accepted.	

Range SAT EBRW	500–590
Range SAT Math	500–590
Range ACT Composite	20–25

ACADEMICS

Student/faculty ratio	18:1
% students returning for sophomore year	64
% students graduating within 4 years	21
% students graduating within 6 years	41

Most classes have 10–19 students.
Most lab/discussion sessions have 10–19 students.

PROGRAMS/SERVICES FOR STUDENTS WITH LEARNING DIFFERENCES

Disability Services, located in Western's Academic Resource Center, coordinates support services for all qualified students with disabilities. We offer a variety of resources and accommodations to assist students as they pursue their academic and career goals. While providing a supportive environment, we encourage students to develop independence and take responsibility for their academic experiences. Personal consultation and workshops are available to help students improve learning, problem-solving, and self-advocacy skills.

ADMISSIONS

Admission to Western depends on academic performance and background, standardized test scores, and personal attributes. In addition to general admissions requirements, Western State recommends a personal essay and recommendations from teachers, counselors, or others who know the student's academic ability. The college tries to admit those students who have demonstrated their ability to succeed. Normally, students are admitted if they meet the following criteria: graduate from an accredited high school; have a cumulative GPA of 2.5 or better (on a 4.0 scale of college-prep courses) and/or rank in the upper two-thirds of the student's graduating class; and score 20 or higher on the ACT or 950 on the SAT. Western recommends 4 years of English, 3 years of mathematics to include algebra II, 2 years of natural science, and 2 years of social science. Modern language and computer science units are also important.

Additional Information

Students who choose to register for Learning Disability Program/Services typically do so soon after acceptance to Western. All accepted students will receive information regarding the Academic Resource Center, including Disability Services and the registration link (www.western.edu/dsinfo). Once registered, all students will go through an intake session with Disability Services staff to review policies, procedures, resources, and accommodations. Some of the services used by students include, but are not limited to, test accommodations, taped textbooks, readers, scribes, notetakers, and assistance with academic advising and course registration. Individual learning skills assistance is availalble through appointments and workshops, our staff works with students to help them develop effective learning skills and study strategies in areas such as reading, memory, test taking, note-taking, organization, and time management. We encourage

ADMISSIONS INFO FOR STUDENTS WITH LEARNING DIFFERENCES

SAT/ACT required: Yes
Interview required: No
Essay required: No
Additional application required: No
Documentation required for:
  LD: Psycho ed evaluation
  ADHD: Diagnosis based on DSM-V; history of behaviors impairing functioning in academic setting; diagnostic interview; history of symptoms; evidence of ongoing behaviors.
  ASD: Psycho ed evaluation
Documentation submitted to: Disability Services
Special Ed. HS course work accepted: Yes
Separate application required for Programs/Services: Yes
Contact Information
Name of program or department: Disability Services
Telephone: 970-943-7056
Fax: 970-943-3409

Western Colorado University

students who wish to enhance motivation, develop an understanding of individual learning styles, and improve academic performance to use the Academic Resource Center's resources.

GENERAL ADMISSIONS

Very important factors considered include: rigor of secondary school record, class rank, academic GPA, standardized test scores. *Important factors considered include:* application essay, recommendation(s). *Other factors considered include:* interview, extracurricular activities, talent/ability, character/personal qualities, first generation, alumni/ae relation, volunteer work, work experience. *Freshman Admission Requirements:* High school diploma is required and GED is accepted.

ACCOMMODATIONS OR SERVICES

Accommodations are decided upon an individual basis after a thorough review of appropriate, current documentation. The accommodations requests must be supported through the documentation provided and must be logically linked to the current impact of the condition on academic functioning.

FINANCIAL AID

Students should submit: FAFSA. Applicants will be notified of awards on a rolling basis beginning 3/15. The Princeton Review suggests that all financial aid forms be submitted as soon as possible after October 1. *Need-based scholarships/grants offered:* College/university scholarship or grant aid from institutional funds; Federal Pell; Private scholarships; SEOG; State scholarships/grants. *Loan aid offered:* Direct PLUS loans; Direct Subsidized Stafford Loans; Direct Unsubsidized Stafford Loans. Federal Work-Study Program available. Institutional employment available.

CAMPUS LIFE

Activities: Campus Ministries; Choral groups; Concert band; Dance; Drama/theater; International Student Organization; Jazz band; Literary magazine; Music ensembles; Pep band; Radio station; Student government; Student newspaper; Symphony orchestra; Television station. **Organizations:** 60 registered organizations, 8 honor societies, 5 religious organizations. **Athletics (Intercollegiate):** *Men:* basketball, cross-country, football, track/field (outdoor), track/field (indoor), wrestling. *Women:* basketball, cross-country, track/field (outdoor), track/field (indoor), volleyball. **On-Campus Highlights:** Unviersity Center–new student center, Hurst Hall—renovated science building, Kelley Hall–renovated social sciences, Mountaineer Field House—Highest Elevation NCAA basketball Court, Borick Business–new business building.

ACCOMMODATIONS

Allowed in exams:	
Calculators	Yes
Dictionary	No
Computer	Yes
Spell-checker	Yes
Extended test time	Yes
Scribe	Yes
Proctors	Yes
Oral exams	Yes
Note-takers	Yes
Support services for students with	
LD	Yes
ADHD	Yes
ASD	Yes
Distraction-reduced environment	Yes
Recording of lecture allowed	Yes
Reading technology:	Yes
Audio books	Yes
Other assistive technology	Yes
Priority registration	Yes
Added costs for services:	
For LD:	No
For ADHD:	No
For ASD:	No
LD specialists	No
ADHD & ASD coaching	No
ASD specialists	No
Professional tutors	No
Peer tutors	Yes
Max. hours/week for services	Varies
How professors are notified of student approved accommodations	Student

COLLEGE GRADUATION REQUIREMENTS

Course waivers allowed	No
Course substitutions allowed	Yes
In what courses	

Math substitutions may be approved for students with documented math learning disabilities, when appropriate.

Fairfield University

1073 NORTH BENSON ROAD, FAIRFIELD, CT 06824 • ADMISSIONS: 203-254-4100 • FAX: 203-254-4199

CAMPUS

Type of school	Private (nonprofit)
Environment	Town
Support	CS

STUDENTS

Undergrad enrollment	4,023
% male/female	40/60
% from out of state	71
% frosh live on campus	94

FINANCIAL FACTS

Annual tuition	$47,650
Room and board	$14,710
Required fees	$700

GENERAL ADMISSIONS INFO

Application fee	$60
Regular application deadline	1/15

Nonfall registration accepted. Admission may be deferred for a maximum of 1 year.

Range SAT EBRW	590–660
Range SAT Math	590–660
Range ACT Composite	25–29

ACADEMICS

Student/faculty ratio	12:1
% students returning for sophomore year	90
% students graduating within 4 years	79
% students graduating within 6 years	81

Most classes have 10–19 students.

PROGRAMS/SERVICES FOR STUDENTS WITH LEARNING DIFFERENCES

In line with our Jesuit mission, Fairfield University supports students with disabilities in obtaining the necessary accommodations to provide them with equal access to all aspects of campus life. Documentation that is required needs to be within the last three years and must be from a qualified and licensed professional that can attest to the student's disability and the related accommodations that are needed due to the student's disability.

ADMISSIONS

There is no special admissions process for students with learning disabilities. Admission criteria include ranking in top 40 percent of graduating class or better; maintaining a B average; scoring 25 ACT, although submitting ACT/SAT is optional; counselor recommendations; and college-prep courses.

Additional Information

Fairfield University is committed to providing qualified students who have disabilities an equal opportunity to access the benefits, rights and privileges of its services, programs, and activities in an accessible setting. Skills courses are offered in study skills, note-taking strategies, time management skills, and strategies for success. These skills courses are not for credit. Students are offered meetings with a professional who has a background in teaching students with disabilities. Letters are sent to professors on students' request. All students have access to content tutoring and a Writing Center. Services and accommodations are available for undergraduate and graduate students.

ADMISSIONS INFO FOR STUDENTS WITH LEARNING DIFFERENCES

SAT/ACT required: No
Interview required: Recommended
Essay required: No
Additional application required: No
Documentation required for:
 LD: Psycho ed evaluation
 ADHD: Psycho ed evaluation
 ASD: Psycho ed evaluation
Documentation submitted to: Accessibility
Special Ed. HS course work accepted: No
Separate application required for Programs/Services: No
Contact Information
Name of program or department: Accessibility
Telephone: 203-254-4081
Fax: 203-254-4314
Email: acdc@fairfield.edu

Fairfield University

GENERAL ADMISSIONS

Very important factors considered include: rigor of secondary school record, academic GPA, application essay, recommendation(s). *Important factors considered include:* interview, extracurricular activities, talent/ability, character/personal qualities, first generation, volunteer work, work experience, level of applicant's interest. *Other factors considered include:* class rank, standardized test scores, alumni/ae relation, geographical residence, racial/ethnic status. *Freshman Admission Requirements:* High school diploma is required and GED is accepted. *Academic units required:* 4 English, 3 math, 3 science, 2 science labs, 2 foreign language, 2 social studies, 2 history. *Academic units recommended:* 4 English, 4 math, 4 science, 4 foreign language, 2 social studies, 2 history.

ACCOMMODATIONS OR SERVICES

Accommodations are decided upon an individual basis after a thorough review of appropriate, current documentation. The accommodations requests must be supported through the documentation provided and must be logically linked to the current impact of the condition on academic functioning.

FINANCIAL AID

Students should submit: Business/Farm Supplement; CSS/Financial Aid PROFILE; FAFSA; Noncustodial PROFILE. Applicants will be notified of awards on or about 4/1. The Princeton Review suggests that all financial aid forms be submitted as soon as possible after October 1. *Need-based scholarships/grants offered:* College/university scholarship or grant aid from institutional funds; Federal Nursing Scholarships; Federal Pell; Private scholarships; SEOG; State scholarships/grants. *Loan aid offered:* Direct PLUS loans; Direct Subsidized Stafford Loans; Direct Unsubsidized Stafford Loans. Federal Work-Study Program available. Institutional employment available.

CAMPUS LIFE

Activities: Campus Ministries; Choral groups; Dance; Drama/theater; International Student Organization; Jazz band; Literary magazine; Model UN; Music ensembles; Musical theater; Pep band; Radio station; Student government; Student newspaper; Student-run film society; Symphony orchestra; Television station; Yearbook. **Organizations:** 110 registered organizations, 21 honor societies, 3 religious organizations. **Athletics (Intercollegiate):** *Men:* baseball, basketball, crew/rowing, cross-country, diving, golf, lacrosse, soccer, swimming, tennis. *Women:* basketball, crew/rowing, cross-country, diving, field hockey, golf, lacrosse, soccer, softball, swimming, tennis, volleyball. **On-Campus Highlights:** Bellarmine Hall, Barone Campus Center, Leslie C. Quick, Jr. Recreation Complex, DiMenna-Nyselius Library, Regina A. Quick Center for the Arts.

ACCOMMODATIONS

Allowed in exams:

Calculators	Yes
Dictionary	No
Computer	Yes
Spell-checker	Yes
Extended test time	Yes
Scribe	Yes
Proctors	Yes
Oral exams	Yes
Note-takers	Yes

Support services for students with

LD	Yes
ADHD	Yes
ASD	Yes
Distraction-reduced environment	Yes
Recording of lecture allowed	Yes
Reading technology:	Yes
Audio books	Yes

Other assistive technology   speech to text, magnifers, text to speech, and FM system

Priority registration	Yes

Added costs for services:

For LD:	No
For ADHD:	No
For ASD:	No
LD specialists	No
ADHD & ASD coaching	No
ASD specialists	Yes
Professional tutors	Yes
Peer tutors	Yes
Max. hours/week for services	4

How professors are notified of student
approved accommodations   Student

COLLEGE GRADUATION REQUIREMENTS

Course waivers allowed	Yes
In what courses	
Foreign Language and Math	
Course substitutions allowed	
Not Applicable	

Mitchell College

437 Pequot Ave., New London, CT 06320 • Admissions: 860-701-5011 • Fax: 860-444-1209

CAMPUS
Type of school	Private (nonprofit)
Environment	Town
Support	SP

STUDENTS
Undergrad enrollment	785
% male/female	53/47
% from out of state	42
% frosh live on campus	80

FINANCIAL FACTS
Annual tuition	$26,774
Room and board	$12,492
Required fees	$1,720

GENERAL ADMISSIONS INFO
Application fee	$30
Priority deadline	4/1

Nonfall registration accepted. Admission may be deferred for a maximum of 1 year.

Range SAT EBRW	NR
Range SAT Math	NR
Range ACT Composite	NR

ACADEMICS
Student/faculty ratio	14:1
% students returning for sophomore year	57

Most classes have 20–29 students. Most lab/discussion sessions have 10–19 students.

PROGRAMS/SERVICES FOR STUDENTS WITH LEARNING DIFFERENCES

Mitchell College is dedicated to providing a student-centered, supportive learning environment that addresses the educational needs of all students, including those with disabilities. The Duques Academic Success Center offers academic and other supports through five functions—the Tutoring Center offers professional tutoring to all students; the Career Center helps students investigate and pursue career options; the Academic Advising Center offers professional academic advising; Disability Student Services (DSS) determines eligibility for services and arranges accommodations; and the Bentsen Learning Resource Center (LRC) for students with documented learning disabilities and ADHD. The LRC offers three levels of academic support. Students participating at Level 1 work with a LRC Specialist 3 times a week. An individualized program of support is developed based on a student's learning strengths, challenges, and goals. Close individual attention, frequent contact, and structured follow up are the main components of the fee-based program. Level 2 is an enhanced support program offering less-involved and less-directed assistance on an individual and/or small group basis, with up to 2 scheduled appointments a week. Level 3 is appropriate for students who can apply a variety of learning strategies across the curriculum, but who may still benefit from limited support and one weekly meeting with a learning specialist.

ADMISSIONS

Students must first apply and be accepted into Mitchell College. Application requirements are listed on www.mitchell.edu and include the application itself, transcripts, at least one recommendation, a written personal statement, as well as an interview. Standardized tests are currently optional. A high school diploma or GED is required for admission. Applicants are evaluated holistically and admitted based on their potential. Generally, students who complete a college preparatory curriculum with a GPA of 2.0 or higher are admitted. Approximately 95 percent of those who are admitted receive financial aid, which can be applied to supplemental fees for services offered by the LRC. Students who are interested in participating in the LRC program need to complete a Request for Services Application. In addition, students need to submit documentation of a learning disability and or AD/HD to Disability Student Services.

ADMISSIONS INFO FOR STUDENTS WITH LEARNING DIFFERENCES

SAT/ACT required: No
Interview required: Yes
Essay required: Yes
Additional application required: No
Documentation required for:
 LD: Psycho ed evaluation
 ADHD: Diagnosis based on DSM-V; history of behaviors impairing functioning in academic setting; diagnostic interview; history of symptoms; evidence of ongoing behaviors.
 ASD: Psycho ed evaluation
Documentation submitted to: DSS
Special Ed. HS course work accepted: No
Separate application required for Programs/Services: No
Contact Information
Name of program or department: Bentsen Learning Resource Center
Telephone: 860-701-5145
Fax: 860-701-5090

Additional Information

Mitchell College also has the "Thames Academy," a post-grad (PG) or pre-college transitional experience. It is a year of academic preparation that students take between the end of their high school education and the start of their college studies. Unlike traditional post-grad programs at prep schools, Thames Academy at Mitchell College provides college-level courses for credit. Located on Mitchell College Campus, the Academy provides a structured residential program within a collegiate environment and co-curricular interaction with two- and four-year students.

GENERAL ADMISSIONS

Very important factors considered include: academic GPA, interview. *Important factors considered include:* rigor of secondary school record, application essay, recommendation(s), extracurricular activities, character/personal qualities, volunteer work.level of applicant's interest. *Other factors considered include:* standardized test scores, talent/ability, alumni/ae relation, work experience. *Freshman Admission Requirements:* High school diploma is required and GED is accepted. *Academic units recommended:* 4 English, 3 math, 3 science, 2 social studies, 2 history, 2 academic electives.

ACCOMMODATIONS OR SERVICES

Accommodations are decided upon an individual basis after a thorough review of appropriate, current documentation. The accommodations requests must be supported through the documentation provided and must be logically linked to the current impact of the condition on academic functioning.

FINANCIAL AID

Students should submit: FAFSA. Applicants will be notified of awards on a rolling basis beginning 3/1. The Princeton Review suggests that all financial aid forms be submitted as soon as possible after October 1. *Need-based scholarships/grants offered:* College/university scholarship or grant aid from institutional funds; Federal Pell; Private scholarships; SEOG; State scholarships/grants. *Loan aid offered:* Direct PLUS loans; Direct Subsidized Stafford Loans; Direct Unsubsidized Stafford Loans. Federal Work-Study Program available. Institutional employment available.

CAMPUS LIFE

Activities: Dance; Drama/theater; Radio station; Student government. **Organizations:** 30 registered organizations, 2 honor societies, 2 religious organizations. **Athletics (Intercollegiate):** *Men:* baseball, basketball, cross-country, golf, lacrosse, soccer, tennis. *Women:* basketball, cross-country, golf, soccer, softball, tennis, volleyball.

ACCOMMODATIONS

Allowed in exams:

Calculators	Yes
Dictionary	Yes
Computer	Yes
Spell-checker	Yes
Extended test time	Yes
Scribe	Yes
Proctors	Yes
Oral exams	Yes
Note-takers	Yes

Support services for students with

LD	Yes
ADHD	Yes
ASD	Yes
Distraction-reduced environment	Yes
Recording of lecture allowed	Yes
Reading technology:	Yes
Audio books	Yes
Other assistive technology	Yes
Priority registration	N/A

Added costs for services:

For LD:	Yes
For ADHD:	Yes
For ASD:	Yes
LD specialists	Yes
ADHD & ASD coaching	No
ASD specialists	No
Professional tutors	Yes
Peer tutors	No
Max. hours/week for services	4
How professors are notified of student approved accommodations	Student

COLLEGE GRADUATION REQUIREMENTS

Course waivers allowed	No
Course substitutions allowed	Yes

In what courses

Varies based on the student's history with the subject area and the school policies and procedures.

Southern Connecticut State University

501 CRESCENT STREET, NEW HAVEN, CT 06515-1202 • ADMISSIONS: 203-392-5644 • FAX: 203-392-5727

CAMPUS
Type of school	Public
Environment	Village
Support	CS

STUDENTS
Undergrad enrollment	8,525
% male/female	40/60
% from out of state	4
% frosh live on campus	62

FINANCIAL FACTS
Annual in-state tuition	$4,285
Annual out-of-state tuition	$15,137
Room and board	$10,687
Required fees	$4,256

GENERAL ADMISSIONS INFO
Application fee	$50
Regular application deadline	4/1

Nonfall registration accepted. Admission may be deferred for a maximum of 2 years.

Range SAT EBRW	420–520
Range SAT Math	410–530
Range ACT Composite	17–22

ACADEMICS
Student/faculty ratio	17:1

Most classes have 10–19 students.
Most lab/discussion sessions have 10–19 students.

PROGRAMS/SERVICES FOR STUDENTS WITH LEARNING DIFFERENCES
The mission of the DRC is to ensure educational equity for students with disabilities. The DRC assists students in arranging for individualized accommodations and support services. The Center of Excellence on ASD is a resource on campus as well as to the surrounding community.

ADMISSIONS
There is no special admissions process for students with learning disabilities. All applicants must meet the same criteria. Course requirements include 4 years of English, 3 years of math, 2 years of science, 2 years of a foreign language, 2 years of social studies, and 2 years of history.

Additional Information
Qualified students are invited to contact the DRC and schedule an in-take appointment to discuss their needs. The DRC also supports Outreach Unlimited, which is a student organization primarily made-up of students with disabilities. The DRC provides assistance with developing compensatory strategies such as time management, study skills, and identifying strengths and weaknesses. The DRC also helps with course selection, promotion of self determination in areas of self advocacy, goal setting, and career development. DRC Specialists offer weekly appointments of a first come first serve basis. Students can make an appointment at any point during the semester.

ADMISSIONS INFO FOR STUDENTS WITH LEARNING DIFFERENCES
SAT/ACT required: Yes
Interview required: No
Essay required: No
Additional application required: No
Documentation required for:
  LD: There is a wide variety of tests we review, there's no single test in particular. We usually follow the current industry standard tests administered by psychologists. Please go to www. southernct.edu/DRC for more information on our Doc policy
  ADHD: There is a wide variety of tests we review, there's no single test in particular. We usually follow the current industry standard tests administered by psychologists. Please go to www. southernct.edu/DRC for more information on our Doc policy
  ASD: There is a wide variety of tests we review, there's no single test in particular. We usually follow the current industry standard tests administered by psychologists. Please go to www. southernct.edu/DRC for more information on our Doc policy.
Documentation submitted to: Support program/services
Special Ed. HS course work accepted: N/A
Separate application required for Programs/Services: No
Contact Information
Name of program or department: Disability Resource Center (DRC)
Telephone: 203-392-6828
Fax: 203-392-6829
Email: DRC@southernct.edu

Southern Connecticut State University

GENERAL ADMISSIONS

Very important factors considered include: rigor of secondary school record, academic GPA. *Important factors considered include:* class rank, application essay, standardized test scores, recommendation(s). *Other factors considered include:* extracurricular activities, talent/ability, character/personal qualities, first generation, volunteer work, work experience. *Freshman Admission Requirements:* High school diploma is required and GED is accepted. *Academic units required:* 4 English, 3 math, 2 science, 1 science lab, 2 foreign language, 2 social studies, 2 history. *Academic units recommended:* 4 English, 4 math, 3 science, 4 foreign language, 3 social studies, 3 history.

ACCOMMODATIONS OR SERVICES

Accommodations are decided upon an individual basis after a thorough review of appropriate, current documentation. The accommodations requests must be supported through the documentation provided and must be logically linked to the current impact of the condition on academic functioning.

FINANCIAL AID

Students should submit: FAFSA. The Princeton Review suggests that all financial aid forms be submitted as soon as possible after October 1. *Need-based scholarships/grants offered:* College/university scholarship or grant aid from institutional funds; Federal Pell; SEOG; State scholarships/grants. *Loan aid offered:* Federal Work-Study Program available. Institutional employment available.

CAMPUS LIFE

Activities: Campus Ministries; Choral groups; Dance; Drama/theater; International Student Organization; Literary magazine; Music ensembles; Musical theater; Pep band; Radio station; Student government; Student newspaper; Television station; Yearbook. **Organizations:** 63 registered organizations, 3 religious organizations. 2 fraternities, 4 sororities. **Athletics (Intercollegiate):** *Men:* baseball, basketball, cross-country, football, golf, gymnastics, ice hockey, rugby, soccer, softball, swimming, track/field (outdoor), track/field (indoor), volleyball, wrestling. *Women:* basketball, cheerleading, cross-country, field hockey, golf, gymnastics, rugby, soccer, softball, swimming, track/field (outdoor), track/field (indoor), volleyball.

ACCOMMODATIONS

Allowed in exams:	
Calculators	Yes
Dictionary	Yes
Computer	Yes
Spell-checker	Yes
Extended test time	Yes
Scribe	Yes
Proctors	Yes
Oral exams	Yes
Note-takers	Yes
Support services for students with	
LD	Yes
ADHD	Yes
ASD	Yes
Distraction-reduced environment	Yes
Recording of lecture allowed	Yes
Reading technology:	Yes
Audio books	Yes
Other assistive technology	Yes
Priority registration	Yes
Added costs for services:	
For LD:	No
For ADHD:	No
For ASD:	No
LD specialists	Yes
ADHD & ASD coaching	No
ASD specialists	No
Professional tutors	Yes
Peer tutors	No
Max. hours/week for services	Varies
How professors are notified of student approved accommodations	Student

COLLEGE GRADUATION REQUIREMENTS

Course waivers allowed	No
In what courses	N/A
Course substitutions allowed	Yes
In what courses	Foreign Language

University of Connecticut

2131 HILLSIDE ROAD, STORRS, CT 06268-3088 • ADMISSIONS: 860-486-3137 • FAX: 860-486-1476

CAMPUS

Type of school	Public
Environment	Town
Support	CS

STUDENTS

Undergrad enrollment	19,030
% male/female	50/50
% from out of state	22
% frosh live on campus	97

FINANCIAL FACTS

Annual in-state tuition	$12,848
Annual out-of-state tuition	$35,216
Room and board	$13,452
Required fees	$2,882

GENERAL ADMISSIONS INFO

Application fee	$80
Regular application deadline	1/15

Nonfall registration accepted. Admission may be deferred for a maximum of 1 semester.

Range SAT EBRW	600–680
Range SAT Math	610–710
Range ACT Composite	26–31

ACADEMICS

Student/faculty ratio	16:1
% students returning for sophomore year	92
% students graduating within 4 years	70
% students graduating within 6 years	82

Most classes have 10–19 students.
Most lab/discussion sessions have fewer than 10 students.

PROGRAMS/SERVICES FOR STUDENTS WITH LEARNING DIFFERENCES

All students enrolled at UConn are eligible to apply to the Center for Students with Disabilities. The CSD engages in an interactive and individualized process with each student in order to determine reasonable and appropriate accommodations. The goal of the Center is to ensure a comprehensively accessible University experience where individuals with disabilities have the same access to programs, opportunities and activities as all others. Students are elibile for accomodations such as extended time on exams, notetaking assistance, alternate media for printed materials, foreign language and math substitutions, and assistive and learning technologies. In addition to accommodation, the center also offers an enhanced fee-for-service program, referred to as Beyond Access, which provides students with an opportunity to work one-on-one with a trained strategy instructor to work on developing skills such as: time management and organization, study skills, stress management, self-advocacy, memory and concentration, social skills, career preparation, health and wellness, and reading and writing strategies.

ADMISSIONS

There is no separate application or application process for students with LD seeking accomodations and/or disability services through the CSD. Students must meet regular admissions requirements for admissions into UConn.

Additional Information

Students enrolled in Beyond Access work closely with a trained Strategy Instructor (SI) to design and customize their program based on their individual goals and learning profile. Students can chose to meet with their SI for three hours a week (Track I) or one hour per week (Track II) to work on developing skills such as: time management and organization, study skills, stress management, self-advocacy, memory and concentration, social skills, career preparation, health and wellness, and reading and writing strategies. As this program goes beyond the legislative mandates, in order to provide the necessary materials and resources, participation in this program includes a rate of $3,600 per semester for Track I and $1,800, per semester for Track II. Goals of Beyond Access helps students identify strengths and challenges in both their academic and personal life;

ADMISSIONS INFO FOR STUDENTS WITH LEARNING DIFFERENCES

SAT/ACT required: Yes
Interview required: Recommended
Essay required: Yes
Additional application required: No
Documentation required for:
 LD: Please refer to the CSD website at http://www.csd.uconn.edu/documentation_guidelines.html
 ADHD: Please refer to the CSD website at http://www.csd.uconn.edu/documentation_guidelines.html
 ASD: Please refer to the CSD website at http://www.csd.uconn.edu/documentation_guidelines.html
Documentation submitted to: CSD
Special Ed. HS course work accepted: N/A
Separate application required for Programs/Services: Yes
Contact Information
Name of program or department: Center for Students with Disabilities
Telephone: 860-486-2020
Email: csd@uconn.edu

University of Connecticut

increase awareness of strategies, skills, and technologies for application in and out of the classroom; create a positive learning environment through active networking and communication amongst students, staff, faculty and parents and family members; and to help students build the self-determination needed to advocate for themselves on campus.

GENERAL ADMISSIONS

Very important factors considered include: rigor of secondary school record, class rank, academic GPA, standardized test scores. *Important factors considered include:* application essay, recommendation(s), extracurricular activities, talent/ability, character/personal qualities, first generation, volunteer work. *Other factors considered include:* alumni/ae relation, geographical residence, state residency, racial/ethnic status, work experience, level of applicant's interest. *Freshman Admission Requirements:* High school diploma is required and GED is accepted. *Academic units required:* 4 English, 3 math, 2 science, 2 science labs, 2 foreign language, 2 social studies, 3 academic electives. *Academic units recommended:* 3 foreign language.

ACCOMMODATIONS OR SERVICES

Accommodations are decided upon an individual basis after a thorough review of appropriate, current documentation. The accommodations requests must be supported through the documentation provided and must be logically linked to the current impact of the condition on academic functioning.

FINANCIAL AID

Students should submit: FAFSA. Applicants will be notified of awards on a rolling basis beginning 3/1. The Princeton Review suggests that all financial aid forms be submitted as soon as possible after October 1. *Need-based scholarships/grants offered:* College/university scholarship or grant aid from institutional funds; Federal Pell; Private scholarships; SEOG; State scholarships/grants. *Loan aid offered:* Direct PLUS loans; Direct Subsidized Stafford Loans; Direct Unsubsidized Stafford Loans. Federal Work-Study Program available. Institutional employment available.

CAMPUS LIFE

Activities: Campus Ministries; Choral groups; Concert band; Dance; Drama/theater; International Student Organization; Jazz band; Literary magazine; Marching band; Model UN; Music ensembles; Musical theater; Opera; Pep band; Radio station; Student government; Student newspaper; Student-run film society; Symphony orchestra; Television station; Yearbook. **Organizations:** 303 registered organizations, 29 honor societies, 17 religious organizations. 14 fraternities, 12 sororities. **Athletics (Intercollegiate):** *Men:* baseball, basketball, cross-country, diving, football, golf, ice hockey, soccer, swimming, tennis, track/field (outdoor), track/field (indoor). *Women:* basketball, crew/rowing, cross-country, diving, field hockey, ice hockey, lacrosse, soccer, softball, swimming, tennis, track/field (outdoor), track/field (indoor), volleyball. **On-Campus Highlights:** William Benton Museum of Art, UConn Dairy Bar, Puppetry Museum, J. Robert Donnelly Husky Heritage Sports Museum, Jorgensen Auditorium and Connecticut Repertory Theater.

ACCOMMODATIONS

Allowed in exams:	
Calculators	Yes
Dictionary	Yes
Computer	Yes
Spell-checker	Yes
Extended test time	Yes
Scribe	Yes
Proctors	Yes
Oral exams	Yes
Note-takers	Yes
Support services for students with	
LD	Yes
ADHD	Yes
ASD	Yes
Distraction-reduced environment	Yes
Recording of lecture allowed	Yes
Reading technology:	Yes
Audio books	Yes
Other assistive technology	Yes
Priority registration	Yes
Added costs for services:	
For LD:	No
For ADHD:	No
For ASD:	No
LD specialists	Yes
ADHD & ASD coaching	No
ASD specialists	No
Professional tutors	No
Peer tutors	Yes
Max. hours/week for services	1
How professors are notified of student approved accommodations	
Student and Director	

COLLEGE GRADUATION REQUIREMENTS

Course waivers allowed	No
Course substitutions allowed	Yes
In what courses	

Based on documented evidence of significant impairment, some students qualify for course substitutions in foreign language or math courses.

University of Hartford

200 BLOOMFIELD AVENUE, WEST HARTFORD, CT 06117 • ADMISSIONS: 860-768-4296 • FAX: 860-768-4961

CAMPUS
Type of school	Private (nonprofit)
Environment	Metropolis
Support	CS

STUDENTS
Undergrad enrollment	4,924
% male/female	49/51
% from out of state	51
% frosh live on campus	87

FINANCIAL FACTS
Annual tuition	$36,088
Room and board	$12,346
Required fees	$2,822

GENERAL ADMISSIONS INFO
Application fee	$35

Nonfall registration accepted. Admission may be deferred for a maximum of 1 year.

Range SAT EBRW	460–580
Range SAT Math	460–580
Range ACT Composite	20–26

ACADEMICS
Student/faculty ratio	9:1
% students returning for sophomore year	75

Most classes have 20–29 students. Most lab/discussion sessions have 10–19 students.

PROGRAMS/SERVICES FOR STUDENTS WITH LEARNING DIFFERENCES

The Access-Ability Services program is designed to meet the unique educational needs of students with documented disabilities such as learning disabilities, AD/HD, and Autism Spectrum Disorder. The mission is to facilitate equal opportunities and break down barriers for students with documented disabilities at the University of Hartford in order to assist students in reaching their academic potential. The aim is to help students learn how to manage their disabilities instead of being managed by them, by promoting self-advocacy and independence in a supportive environment.Admissions Students with learning disabilities do not apply to the Access-Ability Services, but do apply directly to one of the nine schools and colleges within the university. If admitted, students with learning disabilities may then elect to receive the support services offered. The Admissions Committee pays particular attention to the student's individual talents and aspirations, especially as they relate to programs available at the university. Some borderline applicants may be admitted as a summer admission. Course requirements include 4 years English, 3-3.5 years math, 2 years science, 2 years social studies, plus electives. Substitutions are allowed on rare occasions and depend on disability and major. Students may also apply to Hillyer College, which is a 2-year program with more flexible admission criteria. This is a developmental program, with flexible admission standards, offering many services. Hillyer provides students with the opportunity to be in a college atmosphere and, if successful, transfer into the 4-year program.

ADMISSIONS

Students with learning disabilities do not apply to the Access-Ability Services, but do apply directly to one of the nine schools and colleges within the university. If admitted, students with learning disabilities may then elect to receive the support services offered. The Admissions Committee pays particular attention to the student's individual talents and aspirations, especially as they relate to programs available at the university. Some borderline applicants may be admitted as a summer admission. Course requirements include 4 years English, 3-3.5 years math, 2 years science, 2 years social studies, plus electives. Substitutions are allowed on rare occasions and depend on disability and major. Students may also apply to Hillyer College, which is a 2-year program with more flexible admission criteria. This is a developmental program, with flexible admission standards, offering many services. Hillyer provides students with the opportunity to be in a college atmosphere and, if successful, transfer into the 4-year program.

ADMISSIONS INFO FOR STUDENTS WITH LEARNING DIFFERENCES

SAT/ACT required: Yes
Interview required: No
Essay required: No
Additional application required: No
Documentation required for:
  LD: WAIS and achievement testing
  ADHD: WAIS and achievement testing
  ASD: Psycho ed evaluation
Documentation submitted to: Access-Ability Services
Special Ed. HS course work accepted: Yes
Separate application required for Programs/Services: No
Contact Information
Name of program or department: ACCESS-ABILITY SERVICES
Telephone: 860-768-4312
Fax: 860-768-4183

University of Hartford

Additional Information

Professional Academic Coaches are available to meet one-on-one with students for academic strategies. The availability of appointments: appointments are scheduled on a first come, first served basis. A First-Year student may meet once per week for 30-45 minutes and sophomores may meet biweekly based on availability of appointments. Upperclassmen may access "Drop-In" appointments. Academic Coaches may work with students on topics including: Adjusting to college, Time Management, Organization, Stress management, Note taking and test preparation, and self advocacy.

GENERAL ADMISSIONS

Very important factors considered include: rigor of secondary school record. *Important factors considered include:* class rank, academic GPA, standardized test scores. *Other factors considered include:* application essay, recommendation(s), interview, extracurricular activities, talent/ability, character/personal qualities. *Freshman Admission Requirements:* High school diploma is required and GED is accepted. *Academic units required:* 4 English, 2 math, 2 science, 2 social studies, 2 history, 4 academic electives. *Academic units recommended:* 3 math, 3 science, 2 foreign language.

ACCOMOMDATIONS OR SERVICES

Accommodations are decided upon an individual basis after a thorough review of appropriate, current documentation. The accommodations requests must be supported through the documentation provided and must be logically linked to the current impact of the condition on academic functioning.

FINANCIAL AID

Students should submit: FAFSA. Applicants will be notified of awards on a rolling basis beginning 3/1. The Princeton Review suggests that all financial aid forms be submitted as soon as possible after October 1. *Need-based scholarships/grants offered:* College/university scholarship or grant aid from institutional funds; Federal Pell; Private scholarships; SEOG; State scholarships/grants. *Loan aid offered:* Direct PLUS loans; Direct Subsidized Stafford Loans; Direct Unsubsidized Stafford Loans.

CAMPUS LIFE

Activities: Campus Ministries; Choral groups; Concert band; Dance; Drama/theater; International Student Organization; Jazz band; Literary magazine; Music ensembles; Musical theater; Opera; Pep band; Radio station; Student government; Student newspaper.

ACCOMMODATIONS

Allowed in exams:	
Calculators	Yes
Dictionary	Yes
Computer	Yes
Spell-checker	Yes
Extended test time	Yes
Scribe	Yes
Proctors	Yes
Oral exams	Yes
Note-takers	Yes
Support services for students with	
LD	Yes
ADHD	Yes
ASD	Yes
Distraction-reduced environment	Yes
Recording of lecture allowed	Yes
Reading technology:	Yes
Audio books	No
Other assistive technology	Yes
Priority registration	Yes
Added costs for services:	
For LD:	No
For ADHD:	No
For ASD:	No
LD specialists	Yes
ADHD & ASD coaching	No
ASD specialists	No
Professional tutors	No
Peer tutors	Yes
Max. hours/week for services	Varies
How professors are notified of student approved accommodations	Student and Director

COLLEGE GRADUATION REQUIREMENTS

Course waivers allowed	Yes
Course substitutions allowed	Yes
In what courses	Math and Foreign Language

University of New Haven

300 BOSTON POST ROAD, WEST HAVEN, CT 06516 • ADMISSIONS: • FAX: 203-931-6093

CAMPUS

Type of school	Private (nonprofit)
Environment	Town
Support	S

STUDENTS

Undergrad enrollment	5,147
% male/female	47/53
% from out of state	56
% frosh live on campus	79

FINANCIAL FACTS

Annual tuition	$37,870
Room and board	$15,900
Required fees	$1,400

GENERAL ADMISSIONS INFO

Application fee	$50
Priority deadline	3/1
Nonfall registration accepted.	

Range SAT EBRW	510–610
Range SAT Math	500–600
Range ACT Composite	21–27

ACADEMICS

Student/faculty ratio	16:1
% students returning for sophomore year	79
% students graduating within 4 years	52
% students graduating within 6 years	60

Most classes have 20–29 students. Most lab/discussion sessions have fewer than 10 students.

PROGRAMS/SERVICES FOR STUDENTS WITH LEARNING DIFFERENCES

The primary responsibility of Accessibility Resources Center (ARC) is to provide services and support that promote access to the university's educational programs and services for students with disabilities. Students must self-identify and submit documentation of a disability and the need for accommodations. Documentation should be submitted once the student is accepted to the university along with a signed DSR Intake form to request accommodations. Students must also follow the established policies and procedures for making arrangements for accommodations each semester. Staff members act as advocates, liaisons, planners, and troubleshooters. Staff is responsible for assuring access, but at the same time, they avoid creating an artificial atmosphere of dependence on services that cannot reasonably be expected after graduation. The Center for Learning Resources (CLR) offers free tutoring for all students, including students with disabilities. The Office of Academic Services offers academic assistance to all students. Academic skills counselors work one-on-one with students to strengthen their abilities and develop individualized study strategies, which focus on reading, note-taking, time management, learning/memory, and test-taking skills.

ADMISSIONS

All applicants must meet the same admission requirements. SAT or ACT required. Students must submit a personal essay, and letter of recommendation. Foreign language is not required for admission. Students with learning disabilities may self-disclose if they feel that it would positively affect the admissions decision. Students admitted as a conditional admit are limited to four classes for the first semester.

Additional Information

ARC provides services that include the coordination of classroom accommodations, such as extended time for exams; use of a tape recorder, calculator, note-takers, and so on; access to readers, scribes, or books on tape; assistance during the course registration process; proctoring of tests when accommodations cannot be arranged for in the classroom; proctoring of English course post-tests and the Writing Proficiency Exam; and training in time management, organization, and test anxiety management. The office includes testing rooms and a mini computer

ADMISSIONS INFO FOR STUDENTS WITH LEARNING DIFFERENCES

SAT/ACT required: Yes
Interview required: No
Essay required: No
Additional application required: No
Documentation required for:
  LD: Psycho ed evaluation
  ADHD: Diagnosis based on DSM-V; history of behaviors impairing functioning in academic setting; diagnostic interview; history of symptoms; evidence of ongoing behaviors.
  ASD: Psycho ed evaluation
Documentation submitted to: Accessibility Resources Center
Special Ed. HS course work accepted: Yes
Separate application required for Programs/Services: No
Contact Information
Name of program or department: Accessibility Resources Center
Telephone: 203-932-7331
Fax: 203-931-6082
Email: LCopneyOkeke@newhaven.edu

University of New Haven

lab with some adaptive software. The Center for Learning Resources has a Math Lab, Writing Lab, and Computer Lab. The CLR presents free workshops on preparing resumes and preparing for the Writing Proficiency Exam. The Office of Academic Services presents free workshops on improving study skills, such as getting organized, textbook and lecture note-taking techniques, and test preparation and strategies.

GENERAL ADMISSIONS

versity scholarship or grant aid from institutional funds; Federal Pell; Private scholarships; SEOG; State scholarships/grants. *Loan aid offered:* Direct PLUS loans; Direct Subsidized Stafford Loans; Direct Unsubsidized Stafford Loans. Federal Work-Study Program available. Institutional employment available.

ACCOMMODATIONS OR SERVICES

Accommodations are decided upon an individual basis after a thorough review of appropriate, current documentation. The accommodations requests must be supported through the documentation provided and must be logically linked to the current impact of the condition on academic functioning.

FINANCIAL AID

Students should submit: FAFSA. Applicants will be notified of awards on a rolling basis beginning 3/1. The Princeton Review suggests that all financial aid forms be submitted as soon as possible after October 1. *Need-based scholarships/grants offered:* College/university scholarship or grant aid from institutional funds; Federal Pell; Private scholarships; SEOG; State scholarships/grants. *Loan aid offered:* Direct PLUS loans; Direct Subsidized Stafford Loans; Direct Unsubsidized Stafford Loans.

CAMPUS LIFE

Activities: Campus Ministries; Dance; Drama/theater; International Student Organization; Marching band; Model UN; Music ensembles; Pep band; Radio station; Student government; Student newspaper; Yearbook. **Organizations:** 50 registered organizations, 5 honor societies, 1 religious organization. 2 fraternities, 3 sororities. **Athletics (Intercollegiate):** *Men:* baseball, basketball, cross-country, golf, lacrosse, soccer, track/field (outdoor), track/field (indoor), volleyball. *Women:* basketball, cheerleading, cross-country, lacrosse, soccer, softball, tennis, volleyball.

ACCOMMODATIONS

Allowed in exams:

Calculators	Yes
Dictionary	Yes
Computer	Yes
Spell-checker	Yes
Extended test time	Yes
Scribe	Yes
Proctors	Yes
Oral exams	No
Note-takers	Yes

Support services for students with

LD	Yes
ADHD	Yes
ASD	Yes
Distraction-reduced environment	Yes
Recording of lecture allowed	Yes
Reading technology:	Yes
Audio books	No
Other assistive technology	Yes
Priority registration	No

Added costs for services:

For LD:	No
For ADHD:	No
For ASD:	No
LD specialists	No
ADHD & ASD coaching	No
ASD specialists	No
Professional tutors	No
Peer tutors	N/A
Max. hours/week for services	Unlimited

How professors are notified of student approved accommodations — Student

COLLEGE GRADUATION REQUIREMENTS

Course waivers allowed	No
Course substitutions allowed	Yes

In what courses
Courses that are not essential to the student's program of study

Western Connecticut State University

181 WHITE STREET, DANBURY, CT 06810-6855 • ADMISSIONS: 203-837-9000 • FAX: 203-837-8338

CAMPUS

Type of school	Public
Environment	City
Support	CS

STUDENTS

Undergrad enrollment	4,890
% male/female	48/52
% from out of state	9
% frosh live on campus	66

FINANCIAL FACTS

Annual in-state tuition	$5,424
Annual out-of-state tuition	$16,882
Room and board	$12,622
Required fees	$4,994

GENERAL ADMISSIONS INFO

Application fee	$50

Nonfall registration accepted. Admission may be deferred for a maximum of 1 year.

Range SAT EBRW	500–590
Range SAT Math	490–590
Range ACT Composite	NR

ACADEMICS

Student/faculty ratio	13:1
% students returning for sophomore year	74
% students graduating within 4 years	20
% students graduating within 6 years	44

Most classes have 10–19 students.
Most lab/discussion sessions have 10–19 students.

PROGRAMS/SERVICES FOR STUDENTS WITH LEARNING DIFFERENCES

The primary purpose of Accessibility Services is to provide the educational development of students in need of support due to a documented disability.. Students with learning disabilities will be assisted in receiving the services necessary to achieve their goals. Western Connecticut recognizes your right to reasonable accommodations and necessary services as a student qualified to be enrolled at this university. The Office of Accessibility Services directs and coordinates such services for students with disabilities that impact their educational experience. We provide advocacy, early registration, confidential counseling, empowerment counseling, complaint processing, accommodation planning, accommodation referrals, referrals to other university services, exam proctoring, accessibility, and other important services that are of value and consequence to students.

ADMISSIONS

Students with learning disabilities submit the general application form. No alternative admission policies are offered. Students should have a 2.5 GPA (C-plus or better), with the average SAT of 894 (ACT may be substituted). Courses required include 4 years of English, 3 years of math, 2 years of science, 2 science labs, 2 years of a foreign language (3 years of a foreign language recommended), 1 year of social studies, 1 year of history, and 3 years of electives. Students are encouraged to self-disclose their disability on the application and submit documentation to be used after admission to determine services and accommodations.

Additional Information

Services include priority registration, tutoring, testing accommodations, and advocacy and counseling. The university does not offer any skills classes. The university offers a special summer program for precollege freshmen with learning disabilities. Services and accommodations are available for undergraduate and graduate students.

ADMISSIONS INFO FOR STUDENTS WITH LEARNING DIFFERENCES

SAT/ACT required: Yes
Interview required: No
Essay required: No
Additional application required: No
Documentation required for:
 LD: Psycho ed evaluation
 ADHD: Diagnosis based on DSM-V; history of behaviors impairing functioning in academic setting; diagnostic interview; history of symptoms; evidence of ongoing behaviors.
 ASD: Psycho ed evaluation
Documentation submitted to: Accessibility Services
Special Ed. HS course work accepted: Yes
Separate application required for Programs/Services: No
Contact Information
Name of program or department: Accessibility Services
Telephone: 203-837-3235
Fax: 203-837-8225
Email: aas@wcsu.edu

Western Connecticut State University

GENERAL ADMISSIONS

Very important factors considered include: rigor of secondary school record, standardized test scores, talent/ability. *Important factors considered include:* class rank, academic GPA, extracurricular activities, level of applicant's interest. *Other factors considered include:* application essay, recommendation(s), interview, character/personal qualities, alumni/ae relation, state residency, racial/ethnic status, volunteer work, work experience. *Freshman Admission Requirements:* High school diploma is required and GED is accepted. *Academic units required:* 4 English, 3 math, 2 science, 2 science labs, 2 foreign language, 1 social studies, 1 history.

ACCOMMODATIONS OR SERVICES

Accommodations are decided upon an individual basis after a thorough review of appropriate, current documentation. The accommodations requests must be supported through the documentation provided and must be logically linked to the current impact of the condition on academic functioning.

FINANCIAL AID

Students should submit: FAFSA; Institution's own financial aid form. Applicants will be notified of awards on a rolling basis beginning 4/15. The Princeton Review suggests that all financial aid forms be submitted as soon as possible after October 1. *Need-based scholarships/grants offered:* College/university scholarship or grant aid from institutional funds; Federal Pell; Private scholarships; SEOG; State scholarships/grants. *Loan aid offered:* Direct PLUS loans; Direct Subsidized Stafford Loans; Direct Unsubsidized Stafford Loans. Federal Work-Study Program available. Institutional employment available.

CAMPUS LIFE

Activities: Campus Ministries; Choral groups; Concert band; Dance; Drama/theater; International Student Organization; Jazz band; Literary magazine; Music ensembles; Musical theater; Opera; Pep band; Radio station; Student government; Student newspaper; Symphony orchestra. **Organizations:** 40 registered organizations, 8 honor societies, 3 religious organizations. 3 fraternities, 4 sororities. **Athletics (Intercollegiate):** *Men:* baseball, basketball, football, lacrosse, soccer, tennis. *Women:* basketball, field hockey, lacrosse, soccer, softball, swimming, tennis, volleyball. **On-Campus Highlights:** Student Centers (Midtown and Westside), O'Neill Center, Science Building, White Hall, Ancell Classroom Building.

ACCOMMODATIONS

Allowed in exams:

Calculators	Yes
Dictionary	No
Computer	Yes
Spell-checker	Yes
Extended test time	Yes
Scribe	Yes
Proctors	Yes
Oral exams	Yes
Note-takers	Yes

Support services for students with

LD	Yes
ADHD	Yes
ASD	Yes
Distraction-reduced environment	Yes
Recording of lecture allowed	Yes
Reading technology:	Yes
Audio books	Yes
Other assistive technology	Yes
Priority registration	Yes

Added costs for services:

For LD:	No
For ADHD:	No
For ASD:	No
LD specialists	Yes
ADHD & ASD coaching	No
ASD specialists	No
Professional tutors	Yes
Peer tutors	N/A
Max. hours/week for services	N/A
How professors are notified of student approved accommodations	
Student and Director	

COLLEGE GRADUATION REQUIREMENTS

Course waivers allowed	Yes
In what courses	
As required depending on the student's ability	
Course substitutions allowed	Yes
In what courses	
As required depending on the student's ability	

University of Delaware

210 South College Ave., Newark, DE 19716 • Admissions: 302-831-8123 • Fax: 302-831-6905

CAMPUS

Type of school	Public
Environment	Town
Support	CS

STUDENTS

Undergrad enrollment	17,669
% male/female	42/58
% from out of state	62
% frosh live on campus	93

FINANCIAL FACTS

Annual in-state tuition	$12250
Annual out-of-state tuition	$32,880
Room and board	$12,862
Required fees	$1,430

GENERAL ADMISSIONS INFO

Application fee	$75
Regular application deadline	1/15

Nonfall registration accepted. Admission may be deferred for a maximum of 1 year.

Range SAT EBRW	540–650
Range SAT Math	550–650
Range ACT Composite	23–29

ACADEMICS

Student/faculty ratio	13:1
% students returning for sophomore year	92

Most classes have 10–19 students.
Most lab/discussion sessions have 10–19 students.

PROGRAMS/SERVICES FOR STUDENTS WITH LEARNING DIFFERENCES

Eligibility for reasonable accommodations is determined on a case-by-case basis upon receipt of appropriate documentation in order to determine that a disability exists and results in a functional limitation. Requested accommodations must be supported by the documentation and be logically linked to the current impact of the disability. Accommodations are provided in order to provide equal access to university course work, activities and programs. Accommodations may not interfere with or alter the essential skills of course curriculum.

ADMISSIONS

Students must be otherwise qualified to admissions. Applicants are typically admitted to their first choice major if admitted to the university. Only list a second major if there is active interest. Courses required include 4 English, 3 math, 3 science, 4 social studies, 2 foreign language, and 2 electives. Foreign language taken prior to 9th grade is not counted. The university looks for academic rigor; grades in college prep classes, and highly recommends that applicants be enrolled in 5 academic core courses each semester. Essays are important and students must submit at least one recommendation from an academic source. Most students submit more recommendations. ACT with writing or SAT required and they will super score. Once admitted and committed to attending the university, students are encouraged to self-disclose their disability to the Office of Disability Support Services (DSS).

Additional Information

CLSC stands for Career and Life Studies Certificate. CLSC is a two-year, residential certificate program at the University of Delaware for students with intellectual disabilities (ID). CLSC provides integrated academic, career/technical, and independent living instruction in preparation for gainful employment. CLSC students attend classes, participate in internships and work experiences, and engage in all aspects of campus life. All applicants' materials will be reviewed by an admissions committee to determine if (1) they meet federal eligibility requirements; and (2) their goals and background make them a good fit for the CLSC program. After applications are reviewed, eligible and qualified applicants are invited for an on-campus interview and offered the opportunity to observe a class. 12 students are admitted to the program.

ADMISSIONS INFO FOR STUDENTS WITH LEARNING DIFFERENCES

SAT/ACT required: Yes
Interview required: No
Essay required: Yes
Additional application required: No
Documentation required for:
 LD: Yes, after admission
 ADHD: Yes, after admission
 ASD: Yes, after admission
Documentation submitted to: Academic Success Services
Special Ed. HS course work accepted: No
Separate application required for Programs/Services: No
Contact Information
Name of program or department: Office of Disability Support Services
Telephone: 302-831-4643
Fax: 302-831-3261
Email: dssoffice@udel.edu

University of Delaware

GENERAL ADMISSIONS

Very important factors considered include: rigor of secondary school record, academic GPA, state residency. *Important factors considered include:* application essay, standardized test scores, recommendation(s), extracurricular activities, talent/ability, character/personal qualities, volunteer work, work experience. *Other factors considered include:* class rank, interview, first generation, alumni/ae relation, geographical residence, racial/ethnic status, level of applicant's interest. *Freshman Admission Requirements:* High school diploma is required and GED is accepted. *Academic units required:* 4 English, 3 math, 3 science, 2 science labs, 2 foreign language, 2 social studies, 2 history, 2 academic electives. *Academic units recommended:* 4 English, 4 math, 4 science, 3 science labs, 4 foreign language, 2 social studies, 2 history, 2 academic electives.

ACCOMMODATIONS OR SERVICES

Accommodations are decided upon an individual basis after a thorough review of appropriate, current documentation. The accommodations requests must be supported through the documentation provided and must be logically linked to the current impact of the condition on academic functioning.

FINANCIAL AID

Students should submit: FAFSA. Applicants will be notified of awards on a rolling basis beginning 3/15. The Princeton Review suggests that all financial aid forms be submitted as soon as possible after October 1. *Need-based scholarships/grants offered:* College/university scholarship or grant aid from institutional funds; Federal Pell; Private scholarships; SEOG; State scholarships/grants. *Loan aid offered:* Direct PLUS loans; Direct Subsidized Stafford Loans; Direct Unsubsidized Stafford Loans. Federal Work-Study Program available. Institutional employment available.

CAMPUS LIFE

Activities: Campus Ministries; Choral groups; Concert band; Dance; Drama/theater; International Student Organization; Jazz band; Literary magazine; Marching band; Model UN; Music ensembles; Musical theater; Opera; Pep band; Radio station; Student government; Student newspaper; Student-run film society; Symphony orchestra; Television station. **Organizations:** 250 registered organizations, 23 honor societies, 24 religious organizations. 22 fraternities, 15 sororities. **Athletics (Intercollegiate):** *Men:* baseball, basketball, cross-country, diving, football, golf, lacrosse, soccer, swimming, tennis, track/field (outdoor). *Women:* basketball, crew/rowing, cross-country, diving, field hockey, lacrosse, soccer, softball, swimming, tennis, track/field (outdoor), track/field (indoor), volleyball. **On-Campus Highlights:** Interdisciplinary Science Engineering Lab, Trabant University Center, Memorial Hall, Carpenter Sports Building, Perkins Student Center.

ACCOMMODATIONS

Allowed in exams:	
Calculators	Yes
Dictionary	No
Computer	Yes
Spell-checker	Yes
Extended test time	Yes
Scribe	Yes
Proctors	Yes
Oral exams	No
Note-takers	Yes
Support services for students with	
LD	Yes
ADHD	Yes
ASD	Yes
Distraction-reduced environment	Yes
Recording of lecture allowed	Yes
Reading technology:	Yes
Audio books	Yes
Other assistive technology	Yes
Priority registration	Yes
Added costs for services:	
For LD:	No
For ADHD:	No
For ASD:	No
LD specialists	Yes
ADHD & ASD coaching	No
ASD specialists	No
Professional tutors	No
Peer tutors	Yes
Max. hours/week for services	N/A
How professors are notified of student approved accommodations	
Student and DSS	

COLLEGE GRADUATION REQUIREMENTS

Course waivers allowed	No
Course substitutions allowed	Yes
In what courses	

Math and foreign language course substitution decisions are made on a case-by-case basis. Students are asked to attempt the class and work closely with a tutor before submitting a petition for a substitution.

American University

4400 MASSACHUSETTS AVE., NW, WASHINGTON, DC 20016-8001 • ADMISSIONS: 202-885-6000 • FAX: 202-885-1025

CAMPUS
Type of school	Private (nonprofit)
Environment	Metropolis
Support	SP

STUDENTS
Undergrad enrollment	7,433
% male/female	37/63
% from out of state	82
% frosh live on campus	NR

FINANCIAL FACTS
Annual tuition	$47,640
Room and board	$14,880
Required fees	$819

GENERAL ADMISSIONS INFO
Application fee	$70
Regular application deadline	1/15

Nonfall registration accepted. Admission may be deferred for a maximum of 1 year.

Range SAT EBRW	610–690
Range SAT Math	570–660
Range ACT Composite	26–30

ACADEMICS
Student/faculty ratio	11:1
% students returning for sophomore year	90
% students graduating within 4 years	76
% students graduating within 6 years	79

Most classes have fewer than 10 students.

PROGRAMS/SERVICES FOR STUDENTS WITH LEARNING DIFFERENCES

The Academic Support Center (ASC) provides extensive support for students with documented learning disabilities and ADHD. Any student whose documentation meets university guidelines can access approved accommodations, work with a learning specialist, meet with the assistive technology specialist, use the Writing Lab, request peer tutors, and take advantage of group workshops. The Learning Services Program (LSP), within the ASC, is a mainstream freshman transition program offering additional support for students who apply to the program with learning disabilities that impact writing. There is a one-time fee for this program, and students must apply at the time they apply to the university. Disability services continue to be available until graduation.

ADMISSIONS

Students with LD must be admitted to the university and then to the Learning Services Program. Students who wish to have program staff consult with the Admissions Office about their LD during the admissions process must submit a supplemental application to the Learning Services Program that requires documentation of the LD. Students should indicate interest in the program on their application. Special education courses taken in high school may be accepted if they meet the criteria for the Carnegie Units. The academic credentials of successful applicants with LD fall within the range of regular admissions criteria: the mean GPA is 2.9 for LD admits and 3.2 for regularly admitted students; ACT ranges from 24–29 for regular admits and 24–28 for LD admits or SAT 1110–1270 for regular admits and 1131 for LD admits. American Sign Language is an acceptable substitution for foreign language. The admission decision is made by a special Admissions Committee and is based on the high school record, recommendations, and all pertinent diagnostic reports.

Additional Information

All students work with an academic advisor in their school or college; students in the Learning Services Program have an advisor who consults on their learning disability. Students in the program meet weekly with a learning specialist for individual sessions that help them further develop college-level reading, writing, and study strategies—and with a writing tutor. Peer tutors assist with course content tutoring. Accommodations are based on diagnostic testing. Students are held to the same academic

ADMISSIONS INFO FOR STUDENTS WITH LEARNING DIFFERENCES

SAT/ACT required: Test flexible
Interview required: No
Essay required: Required
Additional application required: Yes
Documentation required for:
  LD: Please visit http://www.american.edu/ocl/asac/index.cfm for more details and consult with ASAC staff.
  ADHD: Please visit http://www.american.edu/ocl/asac/index.cfm for more details and consult with ASAC staff.
  ASD: Please visit http://www.american.edu/ocl/asac/index.cfm for more details and consult with ASAC staff.
Documentation submitted to: Support Program/Services
Separate application required for Programs/Services: No
Contact Information
Name of program or department: Learning Services Program
Telephone: 202-885-3360
Fax: 202-885-1042
Email: asac@american.edu

American University

standards as all students but may meet these standards through nontraditional means.

GENERAL ADMISSIONS

Very important factors considered include: rigor of secondary school record, academic GPA, level of applicant's interest. *Important factors considered include:* application essay, recommendation(s), extracurricular activities, talent/ability, character/personal qualities, volunteer work. *Other factors considered include:* standardized test scores, first generation, alumni/ae relation, geographical residence, racial/ethnic status, work experience. *Freshman Admission Requirements:* High school diploma is required and GED is accepted. *Academic units required:* 4 English, 3 math, 3 science, 2 science labs, 2 foreign language, 2 social studies, 3 academic electives. *Academic units recommended:* 4 English, 4 math, 4 science, 3 foreign language, 4 social studies, 4 academic electives.

ACCOMMODATIONS OR SERVICES

Accommodations are decided upon an individual basis after a thorough review of appropriate, current documentation. The accommodations requests must be supported through the documentation provided and must be logically linked to the current impact of the condition on academic functioning.

FINANCIAL AID

Students should submit: CSS/Financial Aid PROFILE; FAFSA. Applicants will be notified of awards on or about 4/1. The Princeton Review suggests that all financial aid forms be submitted as soon as possible after October 1. *Need-based scholarships/grants offered:* College/university scholarship or grant aid from institutional funds; Federal Pell; Private scholarships; SEOG *Loan aid offered:* Direct PLUS loans; Direct Subsidized Stafford Loans; Direct Unsubsidized Stafford Loans. Federal Work-Study Program available. Institutional employment available.

CAMPUS LIFE

Activities: Campus Ministries; Choral groups; Concert band; Dance; Drama/theater; International Student Organization; Jazz band; Literary magazine; Model UN; Music ensembles; Musical theater; Opera; Pep band; Radio station; Student government; Student newspaper; Student-run film society; Symphony orchestra; Television station; Yearbook. **Organizations:** 180 registered organizations, 15 honor societies, 15 religious organizations. 11 fraternities, 12 sororities. **Athletics (Intercollegiate):** *Men:* basketball, cross-country, diving, soccer, swimming, track/field (outdoor), track/field (indoor), wrestling. *Women:* basketball, cross-country, diving, field hockey, lacrosse, soccer, swimming, track/field (outdoor), track/field (indoor), volleyball. **On-Campus Highlights:** Mary Graydon Center (student activties hub and dining venues), Sports Center Complex and Jacobs Fitness Center, Katzen Arts Center, The Quad (large grassy area in the middle campus), Davenport Lounge (student-operated coffee shop and lounge).

ACCOMMODATIONS

Allowed in exams:

Calculators	Yes
Dictionary	Yes
Computer	Yes
Spell-checker	Yes
Extended test time	Yes
Scribe	Yes
Proctors	Yes
Oral exams	N/A
Note-takers	Yes

Support services for students with

LD	Yes
ADHD	Yes
ASD	Yes
Distraction-reduced environment	Yes
Recording of lecture allowed	Yes
Reading technology:	Yes
Audio books	Yes
Other assistive technology	Yes
Priority registration	Yes

Added costs for services:

For LD:	Yes
For ADHD:	Yes
For ASD:	Yes
LD specialists	No
ADHD & ASD coaching	No
ASD specialists	No
Professional tutors	No
Peer tutors	Yes
Max. hours/week for services	Varies
How professors are notified of student approved accommodations	Student

COLLEGE GRADUATION REQUIREMENTS

Course waivers allowed	No
Course substitutions allowed	No

The Catholic University of America

CARDINAL STATION, WASHINGTON, DC 20064 • ADMISSIONS: 202-319-5305 • FAX: 202-319-6533

CAMPUS
Type of school	Private (nonprofit)
Environment	Metropolis
Support	CS

STUDENTS
Undergrad enrollment	3,283
% male/female	46/54
% from out of state	97
% frosh live on campus	92

FINANCIAL FACTS
Annual tuition	$43,300
Room and board	$14,316
Required fees	$760

GENERAL ADMISSIONS INFO
Application fee	$55
Regular application deadline	1/15

Nonfall registration accepted. Admission may be deferred for a maximum of 1 year.

Range SAT EBRW	570–670
Range SAT Math	550–650
Range ACT Composite	23–29

ACADEMICS
Student/faculty ratio	7:1
% students returning for sophomore year	86
% students graduating within 4 years	66
% students graduating within 6 years	74

PROGRAMS/SERVICES FOR STUDENTS WITH LEARNING DIFFERENCES
All prospective or current students with a diagnosed disability are encouraged to make contact with DSS in the early stages of their college planning or as soon as they identify a need for accommodations. DSS will send information about our services and documentation requirements to help the student prepare. DSS staff are also available to meet with the student at any time. DSS does not recommend that prospective students submit their documentation to Admissions. It is advisable to send documentation directly to DSS, after you have been admitted. Your eligibility for services/accommodations from DSS is a separate process and is done independently of the Office of Admissions. After documentation and the DSS Registration forms are reviewed, DSS will send an email notification to the student acknowledging receipt of the documentation and eligibility status. At any time during the Admissions process, students are welcome to meet with disability counselors to provide information about eligibility for academic support services and accommodations, appropriate documentation of disability, housing considerations, and transition issues.

ADMISSIONS
Documentation of your disability should not be sent with your application. Prospective students with disabilities are encouraged to write an additional personal statement. Once enrolled at the university, students with a learning disability that impairs the ability to acquire a foreign language may apply to substitute for the graduation language requirement.

Additional Information
Once students have been admitted they should contact DSS and request an Intake Packet. DSS will review the application and documentation and determine accommodations and services. Students must complete a request form each semester to obtain an accommodation letter to give to professors. The Learning Specialist is available to meet one-on-one with students who are registered with DSS. The Learning Specialist helps students improve their learning.

ADMISSIONS INFO FOR STUDENTS WITH LEARNING DIFFERENCES
SAT/ACT required: Y/N depends if test optional
Interview required: No
Essay required: Recommended
Additional application required: Yes
Documentation required for:
  LD: DSS Registration Form as well as sufficient documentation related to their specific diagnosis. In the case of an LD diagnosis, a recent neuropsychological or psychoeducational evaluation is required
  ADHD: DSS Registration Form as well as sufficient documentation related to their specific diagnosis. In the case of an ADHD/ADD diagnosis, a recent neuropsychological or psychoeducational evaluation is required
  ASD: DSS Registration Form as well as sufficient documentation related to their specific diagnosis. In the case of an Autism Spectrum Disorder, a recent neuropsychological or psychoeducational evaluation is required
Documentation submitted to: Support Program/Services
Special Ed. HS course work accepted: No
Separate application required for Programs/Services: No
Contact Information
Name of program or department: Smart Start
Telephone: 202-319-5211
Fax: 202-319-5126
Email: Kunkes@cua.edu

The Catholic University of America

GENERAL ADMISSIONS

Very important factors considered include: rigor of secondary school record, academic GPA, recommendation(s), character/personal qualities. *Important factors considered include:* application essay, extracurricular activities, first generation. *Other factors considered include:* class rank, standardized test scores, interview, talent/ability, alumni/ae relation, geographical residence, racial/ethnic status, volunteer work, work experience, level of applicant's interest. *Freshman Admission Requirements:* High school diploma is required and GED is accepted. *Academic units recommended:* 4 English, 4 math, 3 science, 2 science labs, 3 foreign language, 4 social studies.

ACCOMMODATIONS OR SERVICES

Accommodations are decided upon an individual basis after a thorough review of appropriate, current documentation. The accommodations requests must be supported through the documentation provided and must be logically linked to the current impact of the condition on academic functioning.

FINANCIAL AID

Students should submit: CSS/Financial Aid PROFILE; FAFSA; Noncustodial PROFILE. Applicants will be notified of awards on a rolling basis beginning 3/20. The Princeton Review suggests that all financial aid forms be submitted as soon as possible after October 1. *Need-based scholarships/grants offered:* College/university scholarship or grant aid from institutional funds; Federal Pell; Private scholarships; SEOG; State scholarships/grants. *Loan aid offered:* Direct PLUS loans; Direct Subsidized Stafford Loans; Direct Unsubsidized Stafford Loans. Federal Work-Study Program available. Institutional employment available.

CAMPUS LIFE

Activities: Campus Ministries; Choral groups; Concert band; Dance; Drama/theater; International Student Organization; Jazz band; Literary magazine; Model UN; Music ensembles; Musical theater; Opera; Radio station; Student government; Student newspaper; Student-run film society; Symphony orchestra; Yearbook. **Organizations:** 87 registered organizations, 16 honor societies, 4 religious organizations. 1 fraternity, 1 sorority. **Athletics (Intercollegiate):** *Men:* baseball, basketball, cross-country, football, lacrosse, soccer, swimming, tennis, track/field (outdoor), track/field (indoor). *Women:* basketball, cross-country, field hockey, lacrosse, soccer, softball, swimming, tennis, track/field (outdoor), track/field (indoor), volleyball. **On-Campus Highlights:** Edward J. Pryzbyla University Center, Eugene I. Kane Fitness Center, St. Vincent de Paul Chapel, Raymond A. DuFour Athletic Center, John K. Mullen of Denver Memorial Library.

ACCOMMODATIONS

Allowed in exams:	
Calculators	Yes
Dictionary	Yes
Computer	Yes
Spell-checker	Yes
Extended test time	Yes
Scribe	Yes
Proctors	Yes
Oral exams	Yes
Note-takers	Yes
Support services for students with	
LD	Yes
ADHD	Yes
ASD	Yes
Distraction-reduced environment	Yes
Recording of lecture allowed	Yes
Reading technology:	Yes
Audio books	Yes
Other assistive technology	A blanket list of services are not provided based on an individual's disability. Accommodations and services are determined on a case-by-case basis and determined through a comprehensive review of a student's documentation, academic history and individu
Priority registration	Yes
Added costs for services:	
For LD:	No
For ADHD:	No
For ASD:	No
LD specialists	Yes
ADHD & ASD coaching	Yes
ASD specialists	Yes
Professional tutors	Yes
Peer tutors	Yes
Max. hours/week for services	Varies
How professors are notified of student approved accommodations	Student

COLLEGE GRADUATION REQUIREMENTS

Course waivers allowed	No
Once a student has officially registered with DSS, they can apply for a Foreign Language or Math substitution. These are not exemptions and the university determines replacement courses the student will need to complete prior to graduation.	
Course substitutions allowed	Yes
In what courses	Math and Foreign Language

The George Washington University

2121 Eye Street, NW, Washington, DC 20052 • Admissions: 202-994-6040 • Fax: 202-994-0325

CAMPUS
Type of school	Private (nonprofit)
Environment	Metropolis
Support	CS

STUDENTS
Undergrad enrollment	11,244
% male/female	43/57
% from out of state	97
% frosh live on campus	98

FINANCIAL FACTS
Annual tuition	$55,140
Room and board	$16,565
Required fees	$79

GENERAL ADMISSIONS INFO
Application fee	$75
Priority deadline	11/1
Regular application deadline	1/1

Nonfall registration accepted. Admission may be deferred.

Range SAT EBRW	580–690
Range SAT Math	600–700
Range ACT Composite	27–32

ACADEMICS
Student/faculty ratio	13:1
% students returning for sophomore year	90

Most classes have 10–19 students.
Most lab/discussion sessions have 10–19 students.

PROGRAMS/SERVICES FOR STUDENTS WITH LEARNING DIFFERENCES

Disability Support Services (DSS) provides support to learning disabled students so that they can participate fully in university life, derive the greatest benefit from their educational experiences, and achieve maximum personal success. Students with LD/ADHD are served through DSS. The staff is committed to providing student-centered services that meet the individual needs of each student. The ultimate goal of DSS is to assist students with disabilities as they gain knowledge to recognize strengths, accommodate differences, and become strong self-advocates. Staff are available to discuss issues such as course load, learning strategies, academic accommodations, and petitions for course waivers or substitutions. DSS offers individual assistance in addressing needs not provided through routine services.

ADMISSIONS

GW is test-optional, meaning students applying for freshman or transfer admission are not required to submit standardized test scores (SAT or ACT), except in the following select circumstances: Applicants applying to the accelerated Seven-Year B.A./M.D. Program; Applicants who are homeschooled or who attend an online high school; Applicants who attend secondary schools that provide only narrative evaluations rather than some form of grading scale; Recruited NCAA Division I athletesGW takes a holistic approach to the application review process, and has no minimum GPA or SAT/ACT requirements for admission. However, admission to GW is competitive and admitted students are typically strong academic students in their high school graduating class.

Additional Information

To be eligible, a student must provide to DSS documentation that substantiates the need for such services in compliance with Section 504 of the Rehabilitation Act and the Americans with Disabilities Act (ADA). Services provided without charge to students may include registration assistance, reading services, assistive technology, learning specialist services, notetaking assistance, test accommodations, and referrals. DSS does not provide content tutoring, although it is available on a fee basis from other campus resources.

ADMISSIONS INFO FOR STUDENTS WITH LEARNING DIFFERENCES

SAT/ACT required: Yes
Interview required: No
Essay required: N/A
Additional application required: No
Documentation required for:
  LD: Psycho ed evaluation
  ADHD: Diagnosis based on DSM-V; history of behaviors impairing functioning in academic setting; diagnostic interview; history of symptoms; evidence of ongoing behaviors.
  ASD: Psycho ed evaluation
Documentation submitted to: Disability Support Services
Special Ed. HS course work accepted: No
Separate application required for Programs/Services: No
Contact Information
Name of program or department: Disability Support Services
Telephone: 202-994-8250
Fax: 202-994-7610
Email: dss@gwu.edu

The George Washington University

GENERAL ADMISSIONS

Very important factors considered include: rigor of secondary school record, academic GPA. *Important factors considered include:* application essay, recommendation(s), extracurricular activities, talent/ability, volunteer work. *Other factors considered include:* standardized test scores, character/personal qualities, first generation, alumni/ae relation, geographical residence, racial/ethnic status, work experience, level of applicant's interest. *Freshman Admission Requirements:* High school diploma is required and GED is accepted. *Academic units required:* 4 English, 2 math, 2 science, 1 science lab, 2 foreign language, 2 social studies. *Academic units recommended:* 4 English, 4 math, 4 science, 4 foreign language, 4 social studies.

ACCOMMODATIONS OR SERVICES

Accommodations are decided upon an individual basis after a thorough review of appropriate, current documentation. The accommodations requests must be supported through the documentation provided and must be logically linked to the current impact of the condition on academic functioning.

FINANCIAL AID

Students should submit: CSS/Financial Aid PROFILE; FAFSA; Noncustodial PROFILE. Applicants will be notified of awards on a rolling basis beginning 3/24. The Princeton Review suggests that all financial aid forms be submitted as soon as possible after October 1. *Need-based scholarships/grants offered:* College/university scholarship or grant aid from institutional funds; Federal Pell; SEOG; State scholarships/grants. *Loan aid offered:* Direct PLUS loans; Direct Subsidized Stafford Loans; Direct Unsubsidized Stafford Loans. Federal Work-Study Program available. Institutional employment available.

CAMPUS LIFE

Activities: Choral groups; Concert band; Dance; Drama/theater; International Student Organization; Jazz band; Literary magazine; Marching band; Model UN; Music ensembles; Musical theater; Pep band; Radio station; Student government; Student newspaper; Student-run film society; Symphony orchestra; Television station; Yearbook. **Organizations:** 220 registered organizations, 3 honor societies, 5 religious organizations. 12 fraternities, 9 sororities. **Athletics (Intercollegiate):** *Men:* baseball, basketball, crew/rowing, cross-country, diving, fencing, golf, rugby, soccer, squash, swimming, tennis, water polo. *Women:* basketball, crew/rowing, cross-country, fencing, gymnastics, soccer, swimming, tennis, volleyball. **On-Campus Highlights:** The Smith Center, The Hippo, Media and Public Affairs Building, Kogan Plaza, Gelman Library.

ACCOMMODATIONS

Allowed in exams:	
Calculators	Yes
Dictionary	Yes
Computer	Yes
Spell-checker	Yes
Extended test time	Yes
Scribe	Yes
Proctors	Yes
Oral exams	Yes
Note-takers	Yes
Support services for students with	
LD	Yes
ADHD	Yes
ASD	Yes
Distraction-reduced environment	Yes
Recording of lecture allowed	Yes
Reading technology:	Yes
Audio books	Yes
Other assistive technology	Yes
Priority registration	Yes
Added costs for services:	
For LD:	No
For ADHD:	No
For ASD:	No
LD specialists	Yes
ADHD & ASD coaching	No
ASD specialists	No
Professional tutors	No
Peer tutors	No
Max. hours/week for services	Varies
How professors are notified of student approved accommodations	Student

COLLEGE GRADUATION REQUIREMENTS

Course waivers allowed	No
Course substitutions allowed	Yes
In what courses	

Determination is made on a case-by-case basis, primarily in the areas of math and foreign language.

Barry University

11300 NE 2ND AVENUE, MIAMI SHORES, FL 33161-6695 • ADMISSIONS: 305-899-3100 • FAX: 305-899-2971

CAMPUS

Type of school	Private (nonprofit)
Environment	Metropolis
Support	SP

STUDENTS

Undergrad enrollment	3,459
% male/female	40/60
% from out of state	20
% frosh live on campus	67

FINANCIAL FACTS

Annual tuition	$29,700
Room and board	$11,100
Required fees	$150

GENERAL ADMISSIONS INFO

Nonfall registration accepted. Admission may be deferred for a maximum of 1 year.

Range SAT EBRW	410–440
Range SAT Math	500–520
Range ACT Composite	17–20

ACADEMICS

Student/faculty ratio	13:1
% students returning for sophomore year	61
% students graduating within 6 years	35

Most classes have 50-99 students.

PROGRAMS/SERVICES FOR STUDENTS WITH LEARNING DIFFERENCES

Barry University offers a fee-for-service support program for students with LD. The Center for Advanced Learning (CAL) Program is a comprehensive, intensive, structured, and individualized approach to assisting students with LD throughout their college careers. It is designed to move students gradually toward increasing self-direction in academic, personal, and career activities. This program affirms Barry University's commitment to expand college opportunities to students with LD and provide the specialized services that can enhance college success. CAL program objectives: That all students have a right to fair and accessible education regardless of their challenges and learning differences; That with the right level of support, students can succeed; That individualized and specialized tutoring, mentoring, and advising services by compassionate, experienced professional staff; That CAL is dedicated to helping our students achieve their educational goals.

ADMISSIONS

Students with learning disabilities/ADHD must meet the regular admission criteria for the university, which includes 2.0 GPA, ACT of 17 or above, or SAT of 800 or above, and 4 years of English, 3–4 years of math, 3 years of natural science, and 3–4 years of social science. There is a process of individual review by learning disability professionals for those students who have a diagnosed disability and who do not meet the general admission criteria. These students must provide appropriate and current LD/ADHD documentation and be interviewed by the Director of the CAL Program. Students admitted are expected to meet all requirements established for them and those of the specific university program in which they enroll.

Additional Information

The CAL Program includes a full range of professionally managed and intensive support services that includes the following: Review of diagnostic information allowing for development of a personalized educational plan; individual and small-group subject-area tutoring; instruction in learning and study strategies; academic advising; assistance in developing interpersonal skills; individual and small-group personal, academic, and career counseling; assistance in obtaining study aids and training in the use of assistive technology; computer access; special test administration services; and advocacy with faculty. Additionally, all students have access to a math lab, reading and writing centers, and selected educational seminars. All instructional staff hold advanced degrees in their area of specialization, no peer tutors are used.

ADMISSIONS INFO FOR STUDENTS WITH LEARNING DIFFERENCES

SAT/ACT required: Yes
Interview required: No
Essay required: No
Additional application required: No
Documentation required for:
 LD: No
 ADHD: No
 ASD: No
Documentation submitted to: CAL
Special Ed. HS course work accepted: No
Separate application required for Programs/Services: Yes, Intake form
Contact Information
Name of program or department: Office of Disability Services
Telephone: 305-899-3488
Email: disabilityservices@barry.edu

Barry University

GENERAL ADMISSIONS

Very important factors considered include: academic GPA, standardized test scores. *Important factors considered include:* talent/ability, character/personal qualities. *Other factors considered include:* rigor of secondary school record, class rank, recommendation(s), extracurricular activities, first generation, volunteer work, level of applicant's interest. *Freshman Admission Requirements:* High school diploma is required and GED is accepted. *Academic units recommended:* 4 English, 3 math, 3 science, 3 social studies.

ACCOMMODATIONS OR SERVICES

Accommodations are decided upon an individual basis after a thorough review of appropriate, current documentation. The accommodations requests must be supported through the documentation provided and must be logically linked to the current impact of the condition on academic functioning.

FINANCIAL AID

Students should submit: FAFSA. Applicants will be notified of awards on or about 10/15. The Princeton Review suggests that all financial aid forms be submitted as soon as possible after October 1. *Need-based scholarships/grants offered:* College/university scholarship or grant aid from institutional funds; Federal Nursing Scholarships; Federal Pell; Private scholarships; SEOG; State scholarships/grants. *Loan aid offered:* Direct PLUS loans; Direct Subsidized Stafford Loans; Direct Unsubsidized Stafford Loans. Federal Work-Study Program available. Institutional employment available.

CAMPUS LIFE

Activities: Campus Ministries; Dance; Drama/theater; International Student Organization; Literary magazine; Music ensembles; Musical theater; Opera; Radio station; Student government; Student newspaper; Yearbook. **Organizations:** 67 registered organizations, 20 honor societies, 5 religious organizations. 2 fraternities, 2 sororities. **Athletics (Intercollegiate):** *Men:* baseball, basketball, golf, soccer, tennis. *Women:* basketball, crew/rowing, golf, soccer, softball, tennis, volleyball. **On-Campus Highlights:** R. Kirk Landon Student Union, Health and Sports Center, Penaport Pool, Residence Halls, Shepard and Ruth K. Broad Center for the Performing Arts.

ACCOMMODATIONS

Allowed in exams:	
Calculators	Yes
Dictionary	Yes
Computer	Yes
Spell-checker	Yes
Extended test time	Yes
Scribe	Yes
Proctors	Yes
Oral exams	Yes
Note-takers	Yes
Support services for students with	
LD	Yes
ADHD	Yes
ASD	Yes
Distraction-reduced environment	Yes
Recording of lecture allowed	Yes
Reading technology:	Yes
Audio books	Yes
Other assistive technology	Yes
Priority registration	No
Added costs for services:	
For LD:	Yes
For ADHD:	Yes
For ASD:	Yes
LD specialists	Yes
ADHD & ASD coaching	No
ASD specialists	No
Professional tutors	Yes
Peer tutors	No
Max. hours/week for services	Unlimited
How professors are notified of student approved accommodations	Student and Director

COLLEGE GRADUATION REQUIREMENTS

Course waivers allowed	No
Course substitutions allowed	Yes
In what courses:	

Must submit request and be approved by the specific department

Beacon College

105 E. Main Street, Leesburg, FL 34748 • Admissions: 352-638-9731 • Fax: 352-787-0721

CAMPUS
Type of school	Private (nonprofit)
Environment	Village
Support	SP

STUDENTS
Undergrad enrollment	128
% male/female	63/38
% from out of state	80
% frosh live on campus	99

FINANCIAL FACTS
Annual tuition	$27,000
Room and board	$8,150
Required fees	$700

GENERAL ADMISSIONS INFO
Application fee	$50.
Priority deadline	6/1
Regular application deadline	8/1
Nonfall registration accepted.	

Range SAT EBRW	NR
Range SAT Math	NR
Range ACT Composite	NR

ACADEMICS
Student/faculty ratio
% students returning for sophomore year 73
Most classes have 20–29 students. Most lab/discussion sessions have 20–29 students.

PROGRAMS/SERVICES FOR STUDENTS WITH LEARNING DIFFERENCES
Beacon College was founded to award bachelor degrees to students with learning disabilities, ADHD and other learning differences. The College is committed to student success, offering academic and personal support services that help each student achieve his or her goals. The four-year graduation rate of 83.3% far surpasses the national average for students with learning disabilities, proving the effectiveness of the teaching model founded at the College. Every Beacon student leaves the College with stronger critical thinking skills and, due to a strong four-year Career Development program, professional skills designed to help each student understand his or her specific skill set and goals. Career Development courses, along with professional internships, help insure each student embarks on the appropriate career path after leaving Beacon. The fact that 83.3% of graduating students either obtain a job or continue in their education after leaving Beacon demonstrates the success of this program.

ADMISSIONS
In order to be considered for admissions to Beacon College, an applicant must submit: a completed application, nonrefundable $50.00 application fee, and psychoeducational evaluation (completed within three years) that documents a learning disability, or AD/HD. The evaluation must include a complete WAIS with sub-test scores and assessments in reading and math. Official high school transcripts showing successful completion of a standard high school diploma or GED is also required. Beacon College does not place heavy emphasis on SAT/ACT scores. Interviews are preferred and provide a better understanding of the applicant.

Additional Information
The cornerstone of educational support services at Beacon College is our Academic Mentoring Program. In order to foster success, each student receives one-to-one academic mentoring services, which are designed to enhance academic performance and develop skills for life-long learning. The Field Placement Program allows students to complete supervised hours in the workplace to enhance their resumes and further their employment skills. The Cultural Studies Abroad Program gives students the opportunity to experience the life, history, culture, cuisine,

---

ADMISSIONS INFO FOR STUDENTS WITH LEARNING DIFFERENCES
SAT/ACT required: No
Interview required: No
Essay required: No
Additional application required: No
Documentation required for:
 LD: Psycho ed evaluation
 ADHD: Diagnosis based on DSM-V; history of behaviors impairing functioning in academic setting; diagnostic interview; history of symptoms; evidence of ongoing behaviors.
 ASD: Psycho ed evaluation
Documentation submitted to: Admissions
Special Ed. HS course work accepted: Yes
Separate application required for Programs/Services: Standard high school diploma
Contact Information
Name of program or department: Office of Admissions
Telephone: 855-220-5376
Fax: 352-787-0796
Email: admissions@beaconcollege.edu

Beacon College

architecture, music, and literature of exotic places. During the past ten years, students and professors have traveled to Italy, Greece, France, Spain, Australia, Russia, Sweden, Austria, England, and Ireland.

GENERAL ADMISSIONS

Very important factors considered include: recommendation(s). *Important factors considered include:* rigor of secondary school record, application essay, standardized test scores, talent/ability, character/personal qualities. *Other factors considered include:* class rank, academic GPA, interview, extracurricular activities, volunteer work, work experience. *Freshman Admission Requirements:* High school diploma is required and GED is accepted. *Academic units required:* 4 English, 1 math, 1 science, 1 social studies, 2 history, 3 academic electives.

ACCOMMODATIONS OR SERVICES

Accommodations are decided upon an individual basis after a thorough review of appropriate, current documentation. The accommodations requests must be supported through the documentation provided and must be logically linked to the current impact of the condition on academic functioning.

FINANCIAL AID

Students should submit: FAFSA; Institution's own financial aid form; State aid form. Applicants will be notified of awards on or about 2/1. The Princeton Review suggests that all financial aid forms be submitted as soon as possible after October 1. *Need-based scholarships/grants offered:* College/university scholarship or grant aid from institutional funds; Federal Pell; Private scholarships; SEOG; State scholarships/grants. *Loan aid offered:* Federal Work-Study Program available.

CAMPUS LIFE

Activities: Choral groups; Drama/theater; Literary magazine; Student government; Student newspaper; Yearbook. **Organizations:** 13 registered organizations, 1 honor society, 1 fraternity, 1 sorority. **On-Campus Highlights:** New Resident Apartment Complex, Student Center, Stoer Building–Office of Student Services, Beacon College Library, Administration Building.

ACCOMMODATIONS

Allowed in exams:	
Calculators	Yes
Dictionary	Yes
Computer	Yes
Spell-checker	Yes
Extended test time	Yes
Scribe	Yes
Proctors	Yes
Oral exams	Yes
Note-takers	Yes
Support services for students with	
LD	Yes
ADHD	Yes
ASD	Yes
Distraction-reduced environment	Yes
Recording of lecture allowed	Yes
Reading technology:	Yes
Audio books	Yes
Other assistive technology	Yes
Priority registration	N/A
Added costs for services:	
For LD:	No
For ADHD:	No
For ASD:	No
LD specialists	Yes
ADHD & ASD coaching	Yes
ASD specialists	Yes
Professional tutors	Yes
Peer tutors	Yes
Max. hours/week for services	Based on need
How professors are notifed of student approved accommodations	
Student and Director	

COLLEGE GRADUATION REQUIREMENTS

Course waivers allowed	Yes
In what courses	Math
Course substitutions allowed	Yes
In what courses	Math

Flagler College

74 King Street, St. Augustine, FL 32085-1027 • Admissions: 904-819-6220 • Fax: 904-819-6466

CAMPUS

Type of school	Private (nonprofit)
Environment	Village
Support	CS

STUDENTS

Undergrad enrollment	2,676
% male/female	35/65
% from out of state	43
% frosh live on campus	94

FINANCIAL FACTS

Annual tuition	$18,850
Room and board	$11,244
Required fees	$100

GENERAL ADMISSIONS INFO

Application fee	$50
Regular application deadline	3/1

Nonfall registration accepted. Admission may be deferred for a maximum of 1 year.

Range SAT EBRW	520 –610
Range SAT Math	430 –550
Range ACT Composite	21 –26

ACADEMICS

Student/faculty ratio	16:1.
% students returning for sophomore year	72
% students graduating within 4 years	43
% students graduating within 6 years	55

Most classes have 10-19 students.
Most lab/discussion sessions have 10-19 students.

PROGRAMS/SERVICES FOR STUDENTS WITH LEARNING DIFFERENCES

The office of Services for Students with Disabilities (OSSD) exists to support Flagler College's mission of a supportive and challenging environment in which students acquire knowledge and adhere to high ethical standards which is accomplished by providing students who qualify with appropriate and reasonable academic accommodations and support services while upholding integrity and rigor required of all Flagler College students. We are committed to providing students with disabilities equal access to the services, programs, and activities as intended by Section 504 of the Rehabilitation Act and the Americans with Disabilities Act.

ADMISSIONS

Flagler College is Test optional and ACT/SAT scores are not required. Applicants can use the Common Application or the Flagler College Application. The essay prompts are different in each of these applications. The average GPA is about 3.5. Flagler College allows applicants to self-report their grades and courses. Students requiring accommodations to complete the admission application procedures should contact the Office of Services for Students with Disabilities. However, no disclosure need be made unless accommodations are needed although students can disclose a learning disability in the application if a student feels this would better describe a challenge. Once a student has been admitted to the Flagler College, he or she is given the opportunity to declare a disability and to request academic accommodations.

Additional Information

The Office of Services for Students with Disabilities is available to provide learning strategies and time management advice as well as reasonable modifications and academic adjustments if the student avails themselves of the service. Otherwise the student is expected to be responsible to manage their own assignments. The Academic Success Lab helps students with effective test-taking skills, content reading, time management, speaking and listening strategies. Help with critical thinking skills and memorization techniques are also available.

ADMISSIONS INFO FOR STUDENTS WITH LEARNING DIFFERENCES

SAT/ACT required: No
Interview required: No
Essay required: Yes
Additional application required: No
Documentation required for:
 LD: Psychoeducational based on DSM standards, to include IQ and achievement standard test scores.
 ADHD: Psychoeducational based on DSM standards, to include IQ and achievement and behavioral checklist scores.
 ASD: Neuropsychological and/or psychoeducational evaluation based on DSM standards.
Documentation submitted to: Support Program/ServicesSpecial Ed.
Special Ed. HS course work accepted: Yes
Separate application required for Programs/Services: N/A
Contact Information
Name of program or department: Office of Services for Students with Disabilities
Telephone: 904 819-6460
Email: efrancisco@flagler.edu

GENERAL ADMISSIONS

Very important factors considered include: academic GPA, standardized test scores. *Important factors considered include:* rigor of secondary school record, application essay, recommendation(s), first generation, geographical residence. *Other factors considered include:* extracurricular activities, character/personal qualities, alumni/ae relation, volunteer work, work experience, level of applicant's interest. *Freshman Admission Requirements:* High school diploma is required and GED is accepted *Academic units recommended:* 4 English, 4 math, 3 science, 1 science labs, 2 foreign language, 1 social studies, 3 history,

ACCOMMODATION OR SERVICES

Accommodations are decided upon an individual basis after a thorough review of appropriate, current documentation. The accommodations requests must be supported through the documentation provided and must be logically linked to the current impact of the condition on academic functioning.

FINANCIAL AID

Students should submit: FAFSA; State aid form. Applicants will be notified of awards on a rolling basis beginning 11/1. The Princeton Review suggests that all financial aid forms be submitted as soon as possible after October 1. *Need-based scholarships/grants offered:* College/university scholarship or grant aid from institutional funds; Federal Pell; Private scholarships; SEOG; State scholarships/grants. *Loan aid offered:* Direct PLUS loans; Direct Subsidized Stafford Loans; Direct Unsubsidized Stafford Loans Federal Work-Study Program available. Institutional employment available.

CAMPUS LIFE

Activities: Campus Ministries; Choral groups; Dance ; Drama/theater; International Student Organization; Literary magazine; Model UN; Musical theater; Radio station ; Student government; Student newspaper; Student-run film society Organizations: 7 honor societies, 3 religious organizations. **Athletics (Intercollegiate):** *Men:* baseball, basketball, cross-country, golf, soccer, tennis *Women:* basketball, cross-country, golf, soccer, softball, tennis, volleyball. **On-Campus Highlights:** Ringhaver Student Center, Proctor Library, Campus Courtyard, Dining Hall, Flagler College Sports Complex.

ACCOMMODATIONS

Allowed in exams:

Calculators	Yes
Dictionary	Yes
Computer	Yes
Spell-checker	Yes
Extended test time	Yes
Scribe	Yes
Proctors	Yes
Oral exams	Yes
Note-takers	Yes

Support services for students with

LD	Yes
ADHD	Yes
ASD	Yes
Distraction-reduced environment	Yes
Recording of lecture allowed	Yes
Reading technology:	Yes
Audio books	Yes

Other assistive technology

JAWS is on all computers in the Library that students use, we braille our own documents and tests, etc., we use text to speech Kindles when appropriate, and various software programs as appropriate.

Priority registration	Yes

Added costs for services:

For LD:	No
For ADHD:	No
For ASD:	No
LD specialists	Yes
ADHD & ASD coaching	Yes
ASD specialists	Yes
Professional tutors	Yes
Peer tutors	Yes
Max. hours/week for services	Varies

How professors are notified of student approved accommodations Student

COLLEGE GRADUATION REQUIREMENTS

Course waivers allowed	No
Course substitutions allowed	Yes

In what courses

It's individual to the student's needs and appropriate documentation and handled on a case by case basis.

Florida Agriculture and Mechanical Universit

Lee Hall, Tallahassee, FL 32307-3200 • Admissions: 850-599-3796 • Fax: 850-599-3069

CAMPUS

Type of school	Public
Environment	City
Support	SP

STUDENTS

Undergrad enrollment	7,365
% male/female	35/65
% from out of state	13
% frosh live on campus	81

FINANCIAL FACTS

Annual in-state tuition	$5,645
Annual out-of-state tuition	$17,585
Room and board	$10,058
Required fees	$140

GENERAL ADMISSIONS INFO

Application fee	$30
Regular application deadline	5/15

Nonfall registration accepted.

Range SAT EBRW	460–550
Range SAT Math	440–530
Range ACT Composite	19–24

ACADEMICS

Student/faculty ratio	15:1
% students returning for sophomore year	83

Most classes have 10–19 students.
Most lab/discussion sessions have 10–19 students.

PROGRAMS/SERVICES FOR STUDENTS WITH LEARNING DIFFERENCES

The Center for Disability Access and Resources (CeDAR) at Florida A & M University provides comprehensive services and accommodations to FAMU students with disabilities. As an advocate for students with disabilities, the CeDAR collaborates with faculty, staff, and community partners to provide accommodations for the unique needs of students both in and out of the classroom. The mission is to provide enriching support programs, services, and reasonable accommodations. CeDAR hopes to foster a sense of empowerment in students with disabilities by educating them about their legal rights and responsibilities so that they can make informed choices, be critical thinkers, and self advocates. The goal is to ensure students with disabilities have access to the same programs, opportunities, and activities available to all FAMU students. The team works to celebrate and reward the unique backgrounds, viewpoints, skills, and talents of all CeDAR students.

ADMISSIONS

CeDAR helps applicants who do not meet standard admission criteria to be admitted to FAMU under alternate criteria when appropriate based on the applicant's disability. Students are reviewed under alternate criteria. In implementing this procedure, the CeDAR shall not compromise academic or admission standards in any way. Students requesting an alternate review must request this review in writing and provide documentation certifying the existence of a disability; and verifying functional limitations imposed. These applicants are forwarded to CeDAR by admissions and a review confirms that the applicant's disability necessitates using alternate criteria. CeDAR will make a recommendation to admissions.

Additional Information

The CeDAR offers a six-week summer transition program (CSSI; required attendance for some incoming students with a disability who request special admissions consideration) to students who will be graduating or have graduated from high school. This program provides students a chance to focus on remediation of skill deficits, technology, and researching their area of disability. There are no fees for services provided. Enrollment in the CeDAR ART Program comes with a recommendation for provisional admission to the university for the preceding summer term. Enrollees are required to attend and successfully complete the College Study Skills Institute (CSSI) held during the summer before a final recommendation for continued enrollment will be offered. The CeDAR ART Program is

ADMISSIONS INFO FOR STUDENTS WITH LEARNING DIFFERENCES

SAT/ACT required: Yes
Interview required: No
Essay required: Required
Additional application required: Yes
Documentation required for:
  LD: High School IEP form, Psychological Disability Verification Form
  ADHD: Certification of Attention-Deficit Disorder/Hyperactivity Disorder
  ASD: Psychological Disability Verification Form
Documentation submitted to: Support Program/Services
Special Ed. HS course work accepted: Not Applicable
Separate application required for Programs/Services: No
Contact Information
Name of program or department: CeDAR ART Program
Telephone: (850) 599-3180
Fax: (850) 561-2513
Email: cedar@famu.edu

Florida Agriculture and Mechanical University

a two year commitment to the institution as a stipulation for a student's continued enrollment at FAMU.

GENERAL ADMISSIONS

Very important factors considered include: rigor of secondary school record, academic GPA, application essay, standardized test scores, recommendation(s), first generation. *Important factors considered include:* extracurricular activities, talent/ability, character/personal qualities, state residency. *Other factors considered include:* alumni/ae relation, volunteer work, work experience. *Freshman Admission Requirements:* High school diploma is required and GED is accepted. *Academic units required:* 4 English, 4 math, 3 science, 2 science labs, 2 foreign language, 3 social studies, 2 academic electives.

ACCOMMODATIONS OR SERVICES

Accommodations are decided upon an individual basis after a thorough review of appropriate, current documentation. The accommodations requests must be supported through the documentation provided and must be logically linked to the current impact of the condition on academic functioning.

FINANCIAL AID

Students should submit: FAFSA. Applicants will be notified of awards on a rolling basis beginning 4/15. The Princeton Review suggests that all financial aid forms be submitted as soon as possible after October 1. *Need-based scholarships/grants offered:* College/university scholarship or grant aid from institutional funds; Federal Pell; Private scholarships; SEOG; State scholarships/grants; United Negro College Fund. *Loan aid offered:* Direct PLUS loans; Direct Subsidized Stafford Loans; Direct Unsubsidized Stafford Loans. Federal Work-Study Program available. Institutional employment available.

CAMPUS LIFE

Activities: Campus Ministries; Choral groups; Concert band; Dance; Drama/theater; International Student Organization; Jazz band; Literary magazine; Marching band; Music ensembles; Musical theater; Pep band; Radio station; Student government; Student newspaper; Symphony orchestra; Television station; Yearbook. **Organizations:** 145 registered organizations, 16 honor societies, 11 religious organizations. 4 fraternities, 4 sororities. **Athletics (Intercollegiate):** *Men:* baseball, basketball, cheerleading, cross-country, football, golf, swimming, tennis, track/field (outdoor), track/field (indoor). *Women:* basketball, bowling, cheerleading, cross-country, golf, softball, swimming, tennis, track/field (outdoor), track/field (indoor), volleyball. **On-Campus Highlights:** The Black Archives, FAMU/FSU College of Engineering, Athletic Department, Army/Navy ROTC, Alfred Lawson Jr. Multipurpose Center and Teaching Gymnasium.

ACCOMMODATIONS

Allowed in exams:	
Calculators	Yes
Dictionary	Yes
Computer	Yes
Spell-checker	Yes
Extended test time	Yes
Scribe	Yes
Proctors	Yes
Oral exams	Yes
Note-takers	Yes
Support services for students with	
LD	Yes
ADHD	Yes
ASD	Yes
Distraction-reduced environment	Yes
Recording of lecture allowed	Yes
Reading technology:	Yes
Audio books	Yes
Other assistive technology	Yes
Priority registration	No
Added costs for services:	
For LD:	No
For ADHD:	No
For ASD:	No
LD specialists	Yes
ADHD & ASD coaching	No
ASD specialists	No
Professional tutors	No
Peer tutors	Yes
Max. hours/week for services	Varies
How professors are notified of student approved accommodations	Student

COLLEGE GRADUATION REQUIREMENTS

Course waivers allowed	Yes
In what courses	
Depending on the course and program of study	
Course substitutions allowed	Yes
In what courses	
Depending on the course and program of study	

Florida Atlantic University

777 GLADES ROAD, BOCA RATON, FL 33431-0991 • ADMISSIONS: 561-297-3040 • FAX: 561-297-2758

PROGRAMS/SERVICES FOR STUDENTS WITH LEARNING DIFFERENCES

Student Accessibility Services (SAS) provides Comprehensive academic support services include advocacy, academic accommodations, Assistive Technology equipment/software training, Assistive Technology Computer Lab, Learning Strategies training, and an active student organization. SAS has offices across three of FAU's campuses – Boca Raton, Davie, and Jupiter; however, accessibility services are available for students attending any of the six FAU campuses.

ADMISSIONS

FSU has minimum scores and GPA for automatic admission which are 3.3 GPA and ACT of 22 or SAT equivalent. The mid 50% GPA is 3.8-4.5 and ACT 23-27 or SAT 1110-1240. No essay is required unless applying to the Honors College. Course required include 4 English, 4 math, 3 natural sciences, 3 social sciences, 2 foreign language and 2 electives. Some colleges require additional courses including an audition for music majors. There is no special application process for students with LD/ADHD/ASD.

Additional Information

The FAU Academy for Community Inclusion is a college program for high school graduates who have been diagnosed with intellectual and developmental disabilities. The program allows students to earn certificates in supported employment, supported community access, and supported community living. These certificates are offered in an inclusive college environment on the FAU Jupiter campus. The program allows students to participate in college activities, clubs, organizations, that are available to all FAU students.

ADMISSIONS INFO FOR STUDENTS WITH LEARNING DIFFERENCES

SAT/ACT required: Yes
Interview required: No
Essay required: No
Additional application required: No
Documentation required for:
  LD: The documentation must address of the student's functional limitations within the academic setting, as well as suggestions for accommodating the student: 1. Aptitude: WAIS and the Woodcock Johnson Test of Cognitive Ability 2. Achievement: Current levels of academic functioning in all aspects of reading, mathematics, and written language are required. 3. Information processing: Information processing should be addressed.
  ADHD: The documentation must address of the student's functional limitations within the academic setting, as well as suggestions for accommodating the student: 1. Interview: Clinical interview with the diagnostician; 2. Assessment: A standardized assessment of attention (e.g., Continuous Performance Test. ADHD should be clearly diagnosed utilizing DSM codes.
  ASD: Psycho ed evaluation
Documentation submitted to: SAS
Special Ed. HS course work accepted: No
Separate application required for Programs/Services: Yes
Contact Information
Name of program or department: Office for Students with Disabilities (OSD)
Telephone: 561-297-3880
Fax: Same as above

Florida Atlantic University

General Admissions

Very important factors considered include: academic GPA, standardized test scores. *Important factors considered include:* rigor of secondary school record, class rank. *Other factors considered include:* application essay, recommendation(s), extracurricular activities, talent/ability, character/personal qualities, first generation, alumni/ae relation, volunteer work, level of applicant's interest. *Freshman Admission Requirements:* High school diploma is required and GED is accepted. *Academic units required:* 4 English, 4 math, 3 science, 2 science labs, 2 foreign language, 3 social studies, 3 academic electives. *Academic units recommended:* 4 English, 4 math, 3 science, 2 science labs, 2 foreign language, 3 social studies, 3 academic electives.

Accommodations or Services

Accommodations are decided upon an individual basis after a thorough review of appropriate, current documentation. The accommodations requests must be supported through the documentation provided and must be logically linked to the current impact of the condition on academic functioning.

Financial Aid

Students should submit: FAFSA. Applicants will be notified of awards on a rolling basis beginning 5/1. The Princeton Review suggests that all financial aid forms be submitted as soon as possible after October 1. *Need-based scholarships/grants offered:* College/university scholarship or grant aid from institutional funds; Federal Nursing Scholarships; Federal Pell; Private scholarships; SEOG; State scholarships/grants. *Loan aid offered:* Federal Work-Study Program available. Institutional employment available.

Campus Life

Activities: Campus Ministries; Choral groups; Concert band; Dance; Drama/theater; International Student Organization; Jazz band; Literary magazine; Marching band; Model UN; Music ensembles; Musical theater; Opera; Pep band; Radio station; Student government; Student newspaper; Student-run film society; Symphony orchestra; Television station. **Organizations:** 150 registered organizations, 11 honor societies, 6 religious organizations. 9 fraternities, 4 sororities. **Athletics (Intercollegiate):** *Men:* baseball, basketball, cheerleading, cross-country, diving, football, golf, soccer, swimming, tennis. *Women:* basketball, cheerleading, cross-country, diving, golf, soccer, softball, swimming, tennis, track/field (outdoor), volleyball. **On-Campus Highlights:** Student Services Building, Student Union, Dining Hall, Breezeway, Residence Halls.

ACCOMMODATIONS

Allowed in exams:	
Calculators	Yes
Dictionary	Yes
Computer	Yes
Spell-checker	Yes
Extended test time	Yes
Scribe	Yes
Proctors	Yes
Oral exams	Yes
Note-takers	Yes
Support services for students with	
LD	Yes
ADHD	Yes
ASD	Yes
Distraction-reduced environment	Yes
Recording of lecture allowed	Yes
Reading technology:	Yes
Audio books	Yes
Other assistive technology	Yes
Priority registration	No
Added costs for services:	
For LD:	No
For ADHD:	No
For ASD:	No
LD specialists	Yes
ADHD & ASD coaching	No
ASD specialists	No
Professional tutors	No
Peer tutors	Yes
Max. hours/week for services	Varies
How professors are notified of student approved accommodations	Student

COLLEGE GRADUATION REQUIREMENTS

Course waivers allowed	Yes
Course substitutions allowed	Yes
In what courses	

Varies; it depends on the major requirements and the disability. Substitutions used rather than waivers.

Florida State University

PO Box 3062400, Tallahassee, FL 32306-2400 • Admissions: 850-644-6200 • Fax: 850-644-0197

CAMPUS

Type of school	Public
Environment	City
Support	CS

STUDENTS

Undergrad enrollment	32,699
% male/female	44/56
% from out of state	11
% frosh live on campus	81

FINANCIAL FACTS

Annual in-state tuition	$4,640
Annual out-of-state tuition	$19,806
Room and board	$10,666
Required fees	$1,877

GENERAL ADMISSIONS INFO

Application fee	$30
Regular application deadline	2/7
Nonfall registration accepted.	

Range SAT EBRW	600–670
Range SAT Math	590–660
Range ACT Composite	26–30

ACADEMICS

Student/faculty ratio	22:1
% students returning for sophomore year	94
% students graduating within 4 years	63
% students graduating within 6 years	80

Most classes have 10–19 students.
Most lab/discussion sessions have 20–29 students.

PROGRAMS/SERVICES FOR STUDENTS WITH LEARNING DIFFERENCES

The Student Disability Resource Center (SDRC) was established to serve as an advocate for Florida State students with disabilities and ensure that reasonable accommodations are provided. Florida State University is committed to providing a quality education to all qualified students and does not discriminate on the basis of race, creed, color, sex, religion, national origin, age, disability, genetic information, veterans' status, marital status, sexual orientation, gender identity, gender expression or any other legally protected group status. Providing services to more than 2,100 students, the Student Disability Resource Center is committed to ensuring the success of each Florida State University student. Through the provision of academic accommodations, testing support, assistive technologies, coaching and a space for students to feel part of the FSU community the SDRC creates an environment of success.

ADMISSIONS

Florida State University receives over 30,000 freshman applications each year. Because of the high number of applications the university receives, satisfying minimum requirements does not guarantee admission. The academic profile of the middle 50 percent of freshmen accepted in 2013 was: 3.9-4.7 weighted GPA; 26-30 ACT composite; 1730-1960 SAT total. In addition to the academic profile, a variety of other factors are also considered in the review process. These include the written essay, the rigor and quality of courses and curriculum, grade trends, class rank, strength of senior schedule in academic subjects, math level in the senior year, and number of years in a sequential foreign language. Applicants who bring other important attributes to the university community may also receive additional consideration. These applicants include students applying to the CARE Summer Bridge Program, visual and performing artists, and skilled athletes. Letters of recommendation are not required.

Additional Information

Students who choose to disclose their disability to receive accommodations must complete a Request for Services form provided by the SDRC. For an LD, documentation must be current (normed to the adult population) and provided by a qualified professional (Licensed psychologist.) Staff

---

ADMISSIONS INFO FOR STUDENTS WITH LEARNING DIFFERENCES

SAT/ACT required: Yes
Interview required: No
Essay required: Yes
Additional application required: No
Documentation required for:
 LD: Psychoeducational assessment or supporting documentation with history of diagnosis and accommodations
 ADHD: Psychoeducational assessment or supporting documentation with history of diagnosis and accommodations
 ASD: Psychoeducational assessment or supporting documentation with history of diagnosis and accommodations
Documentation submitted to: Student Disability Resource Center
Special Ed. HS course work accepted: No
Separate application required for Programs/Services: No
Contact Information
Name of program or department: Student Disability Resource Center
Telephone: 850-644-9566
Fax: 850-645-1852
Email: sdrc@fsu.edu

members assist students in exploring their needs and determining the necessary services and accommodations. Academic accommodations include alternate text formats, alternative testing location, extended time, reader and/or scribe, and inclass note-takers. Staff members meet individually with students with LD/ADHD. Services include teaching study skills, memory enhancement techniques, organizational skills, test-taking strategies, stress management techniques, ways to structure tutoring for best results, and skills for negotiating accommodations with instructors. Student Disability Union (SDU) act as a support group for students with disabilities.

GENERAL ADMISSIONS

Very important factors considered include: rigor of secondary school record. *Important factors considered include:* academic GPA, standardized test scores, talent/ability, state residency. *Other factors considered include:* class rank, application essay, extracurricular activities, character/personal qualities, first generation, geographical residence, volunteer work, work experience. *Freshman Admission Requirements:* High school diploma is required and GED is accepted. *Academic units required:* 4 English, 4 math, 3 science, 2 science labs, 2 foreign language, 1 social studies, 2 history, 3 academic electives. *Academic units recommended:* 4 English, 4 math, 4 science, 2 science labs, 4 foreign language, 2 social studies, 2 history, 3 academic electives,

ACCOMMODATIONS OR SERVICES

Accommodations are decided upon an individual basis after a thorough review of appropriate, current documentation. The accommodations requests must be supported through the documentation provided and must be logically linked to the current impact of the condition on academic functioning.

FINANCIAL AID

Students should submit: FAFSA; State aid form. Applicants will be notified of awards on a rolling basis beginning 4/5. The Princeton Review suggests that all financial aid forms be submitted as soon as possible after October 1. *Need-based scholarships/grants offered:* College/university scholarship or grant aid from institutional funds; Federal Pell; Private scholarships; SEOG; State scholarships/grants; United Negro College Fund. *Loan aid offered:* Direct PLUS loans; Direct Subsidized Stafford Loans; Direct Unsubsidized Stafford Loans. Federal Work-Study Program available. Institutional employment available.

CAMPUS LIFE

Activities: Campus Ministries; Choral groups; Concert band; Dance; Drama/theater; International Student Organization; Jazz band; Literary magazine; Marching band; Model UN; Music ensembles; Musical theater; Opera; Pep band; Radio station; Student government; Student newspaper; Student-run film society; Symphony orchestra; Television station; Yearbook. **Organizations:** 520 registered organizations, 23 honor societies, 30 religious organizations. 32 fraternities, 28 sororities. **Athletics (Intercollegiate):** *Men:* baseball, basketball, cheerleading, cross-country, diving, football, golf, swimming, tennis, track/field (outdoor), track/field (indoor). *Women:* basketball, cheerleading, cross-country, diving, golf, soccer, softball, swimming, tennis, track/field (outdoor), track/field (indoor), volleyball. **On-Campus Highlights:** Suwannee Dining Hall, Bobby E. Leach Student Recreation Center, Bobby Bowden Field at Doak Campbell Stadium, National High Magnetic Field Laboratory, FSU Reservation.

ACCOMMODATIONS

Allowed in exams:	
Calculators	Yes
Dictionary	Yes
Computer	Yes
Spell-checker	Yes
Extended test time	Yes
Scribe	Yes
Proctors	Yes
Oral exams	Yes
Note-takers	Yes
Support services for students with	
LD	Yes
ADHD	Yes
ASD	Yes
Distraction-reduced environment	Yes
Recording of lecture allowed	Yes
Reading technology:	Yes
Audio books	Yes
Other assistive technology	CCTV, Zoom Text, JAWS, Magic, Braille
Priority registration	Yes
Added costs for services:	
For LD:	No
For ADHD:	No
For ASD:	No
LD specialists	No
ADHD & ASD coaching	No
ASD specialists	Yes
Professional tutors	No
Peer tutors	Yes
Max. hours/week for services	Varies
How professors are notified of student approved accommodations	Student

COLLEGE GRADUATION REQUIREMENTS

Course waivers allowed	No
Course substitutions allowed	Yes
In what courses	Math and Foreign Language

Lynn University

3601 NORTH MILITARY TRAIL, BOCA RATON, FL 33431-5598 • ADMISSIONS: 561-237-7900 • FAX: 561-237-7100

CAMPUS

Type of school	Private (nonprofit)
Environment	City
Support	SP

STUDENTS

Undergrad enrollment	2,182
% male/female	52/48
% from out of state	41
% frosh live on campus	83

FINANCIAL FACTS

Annual tuition	$35,960
Room and board	$12,170
Required fees	$2,250

GENERAL ADMISSIONS INFO

Application fee	$45.
Priority deadline	3/1
Regular application deadline	8/1

Nonfall registration accepted. Admission may be deferred.

Range SAT EBRW	NR
Range SAT Math	NR
Range ACT Composite	19–24

ACADEMICS

Student/faculty ratio	17:1
% students returning for sophomore year	69
% students graduating within 4 years	44
% students graduating within 6 years	51

Most classes have 10–19 students.
Most lab/discussion sessions have 10–19 students.

PROGRAMS/SERVICES FOR STUDENTS WITH LEARNING DIFFERENCES

The comprehensive support program offered through The Institute for Achievement and Learning employs experts in the field of learning differences. This program includes group and individual tutoring, testing accommodations, an alternative testing environment, specialized classes, expert instructors who teach in a multimodality instruction and assessment format, workshops on anxiety and testing, progress updates, mid-term grades, and more. The coaching component of the program uses a diagnostic coaching model to addresses specific executive functioning issues such as organizational skills, procrastination, impulsivity, focus and attention, and study skills, etc.

ADMISSIONS

Students should submit the general application to Lynn University. Admissions criteria are dependent on the level of services required. Students needing the least restrictive services should have taken college-prep high school courses. Some students may be admitted provisionally after submitting official information. Typically, these students have an ACT of 18 or lower or an SAT of 850 or lower and 2.5 GPA.

Additional Information

The IAL (Institute for Achievement and Learning) program features include: individual and group tutoring; study strategy sessions to enhance study and organizational skills; test anxiety sessions; faculty progress reports; extended time exams and alternative testing procedures; academic coaching and schedule planning; selected core courses offered through

ADMISSIONS INFO FOR STUDENTS WITH LEARNING DIFFERENCES

SAT/ACT required: No
Interview required: No
Essay required: Yes
Additional application required: No
Documentation required for:
  LD: Neuropsychological testing or psychological educational testing that includes achievement, aptitude, tests of cognitive potential, tests of focus and attention, BASC, includes diagnosis and recommendations to make one's education accessible
  ADHD: Neuropsychological testing or psychological educational testing that includes achievement, aptitude, tests of cognitive potential, tests of focus and attention, BASC, includes diagnosis and recommendations to make one's education accessible
  ASD: Neuropsychological testing or psychological educational testing that includes achievement, aptitude, tests of cognitive potential, tests of focus and attention, BASC, includes diagnosis and recommendations to make one's education accessible
Documentation submitted to: IAL
Special Ed. HS course work accepted: Yes
Separate application required for Programs/Services: Not for LD, ADHD, or ASD.
Contact Information
Name of program or department: Institute for Achievement and Learning
Telephone: (561) 237-7064
Fax: (561) 237-7107
Email: admissions@lynn.edu

Lynn University

IAL trained faculty who teach students in a multimodality style in order to meet students' individual needs; communicative intervention with faculty and thematic instruction. The program uses a diagnostic coaching model to address behavioral issues such as organization skills, prioritizing of assignments and daily activities, strategies for procrastination, time management skills, coping with impulsivity, strategies to aid with focus and attention in and out of the classroom and study skills. Students should apply to Lynn University through the admission department. When filling out their application, if they are seeking additional support services, they should check the box stating they "would like to be considered for additional academic support".

GENERAL ADMISSIONS

Very important factors considered include: rigor of secondary school record, academic GPA, application essay. *Important factors considered include:* class rank, standardized test scores, recommendation(s), interview, extracurricular activities, character/personal qualities, volunteer work, work experience. *Other factors considered include:* level of applicant's interest. *Freshman Admission Requirements:* High school diploma is required and GED is accepted. *Academic units recommended:* 4 English, 4 math, 4 science, 2 social studies, 2 history.

ACCOMMODATIONS OR SERVICES

Accommodations are decided upon an individual basis after a thorough review of appropriate, current documentation. The accommodations requests must be supported through the documentation provided and must be logically linked to the current impact of the condition on academic functioning.

FINANCIAL AID

Students should submit: FAFSA. Applicants will be notified of awards on a rolling basis beginning 11/1. The Princeton Review suggests that all financial aid forms be submitted as soon as possible after October 1. *Need-based scholarships/grants offered:* College/university scholarship or grant aid from institutional funds; Federal Pell; Private scholarships; SEOG; State scholarships/grants. *Loan aid offered:* Direct PLUS loans; Direct Subsidized Stafford Loans; Direct Unsubsidized Stafford Loans. Federal Work-Study Program available. Institutional employment available.

CAMPUS LIFE

Activities: Campus Ministries; Dance; Drama/theater; International Student Organization; Literary magazine; Model UN; Music ensembles; Musical theater; Radio station; Student government; Student newspaper; Student-run film society; Symphony orchestra; Television station. **Organizations:** 25 registered organizations, 4 honor societies, 4 religious organizations. 2 fraternities, 1 sorority. **Athletics (Intercollegiate):** *Men:* baseball, basketball, golf, soccer, tennis. *Women:* basketball, golf, soccer, softball, tennis, volleyball. **On-Campus Highlights:** The International Business Center, The Wold Performing Arts Center, The Eugene M. and Christine E. Lynn Library, Elmore Dining Commons, Bobby Campbell Stadium.

ACCOMMODATIONS

Allowed in exams:	
Calculators	Yes
Dictionary	No
Computer	Yes
Spell-checker	Yes
Extended test time	Yes
Scribe	Yes
Proctors	Yes
Oral exams	Yes
Note-takers	No
Support services for students with	
LD	Yes
ADHD	Yes
ASD	Yes
Distraction-reduced environment	Yes
Recording of lecture allowed	Yes
Reading technology:	Yes
Audio books	Yes
Other assistive technology	iPad
Priority registration	No
Added costs for services:	
For LD:	No
For ADHD:	No
For ASD:	No
LD specialists	Yes
ADHD & ASD coaching	Yes
ASD specialists	No
Professional tutors	Yes
Peer tutors	No
Max. hours/week for services	Varies
How professors are notified of student approved accommodations	Student

COLLEGE GRADUATION REQUIREMENTS

Course waivers allowed	No
Course substitutions allowed	No

New College of Florida

5800 BAY SHORE RD, SARASOTA, FL 34243-2109 • ADMISSIONS: 941-487-5000 • FAX: 941-487-5001

CAMPUS
Type of school	Public
Environment	Town
Support	S

STUDENTS
Undergrad enrollment	835
% male/female	37/63
% from out of state	18
% frosh live on campus	95

FINANCIAL FACTS
Annual in-state tuition	$6,916
Annual out-of-state tuition	$29,944
Room and board	$9,370
Required fees	NR

GENERAL ADMISSIONS INFO
Application fee $30. Priority deadline 11/1. Regular application deadline   4/15 Nonfall registration accepted. Admission may be deferred for a maximum of 1 year.

Range SAT EBRW	620 –710
Range SAT Math	570 –670
Range ACT Composite	25 –30

ACADEMICS
Student/faculty ratio	10:1.
% students returning for sophomore year	79
students graduating within 4 years	57
students graduating within 6 years	65

Most classes have 10-19 students. Most lab/discussion sessions have fewer than 10 students.

PROGRAMS/SERVICES FOR STUDENTS WITH LEARNING DIFFERENCES
Disability Services, through the Office of Student Affairs, is a service for currently registered New College students. It is the mission of Student Disability Services (SDS) to create and maintain an environment on the New College campus that recognizes and supports students with disabilities by assuring them equal access to all educational opportunities. There is a legal imperative for this mission, embodied in Section 504 of the Rehabilitation Act of 1973, the Americans with Disabilities Act of 1990, and the ADA Amendments Act of 2008. SDS offers a range of services to students including reasonable accommodations, referrals to campus and community services, advocacy and auxiliary aids. These services are designed to support the students' participation in all programs and activities offered at New College. Services are individually designed and based on the specific needs of each student as identified and documented by SDS. In order to be eligible for disability related services, students are required to register and provide documentation of their disability through the SDS. If special accommodations are necessary, the student will be assisted in the development and implementation of the plan. The process is intended to coordinate efforts with faculty members and college staff while maintaining privacy for the student.

ADMISSIONS
The College will grant reasonable substitution or modification of any admission requirement based on evidence submitted by the applicant and through consultation with the College's Disabilities Services Coordinator, that the failure of the applicant to meet the requirement is due to his or her disability, and does not constitute a fundamental alteration in the nature of the College's academic program. ACT/SAT can be self reported. Factors used in admission are Level of difficulty of course work, Grades, essay, SAT or ACT scores. Letter of recommendation and Activities. Mid 50% weighted GPA 3.71-4/31, SAT 1200-1360 or ACT 25-30. Course requirements include: 4 English, 4 math , 3 science, 3 social science, 2 foreign language, and 2 additional academic electives.

ADMISSIONS INFO FOR STUDENTS WITH LEARNING DIFFERENCES
SAT/ACT required: Yes
Interview required: Not Applicable
Essay required: Not Applicable
Additional application required: No
Documentation required for:
 LD: Psycho ed evaluation
 ADHD: Psycho ed evaluation
 ASD: Psycho ed evaluation
Documentation submitted to: SDS
Special Ed. HS course work accepted: Not Applicable
Separate application required for program services: No
Contact Information
Name of program or department: Student Disability Services
Telephone: 941-487-4496
Email: disabilityservices@ncf.edu

New College of Florida

Additional Information

Testing Accommodations include extended time for exams (1.5 to 2x normal time allowed); alternate location/decreased distraction for exams; ability to request alternate exam date or time; use of computer for exams; and a reader for exam. Classroom Accommodations could include:: note-taking services; enlarged course material; permission to record lectures; computer in class to take notes; assistive listening devices; speech-to-text service; and textbooks in alternate format.

General Admissions

Very important factors considered include: rigor of secondary school record, academic GPA, application essay. *Important factors considered include:* class rank, standardized test scores, recommendation(s), extracurricular activities, character/personal qualities, volunteer work, work experience, level of applicant's interest. *Other factors considered include:* talent/ability, first generation, alumni/ae relation, geographical residence, state residency. *Freshman Admission Requirements:* High school diploma is required and GED is accepted *Academic units required:* 4 English, 4 math, 3 science, 2 science labs, 2 foreign language, 3 social studies, 2 academic electives, *Academic units recommended:* 4 English, 4 math, 4 science, 2 science labs, 4 foreign language, 4 social studies, 4 academic electives,

Accommodation or Services

Accommodations are decided upon an individual basis after a thorough review of appropriate, current documentation. The accommodations requests must be supported through the documentation provided and must be logically linked to the current impact of the condition on academic functioning.

Financial Aid

Students should submit: FAFSA. Applicants will be notified of awards on a rolling basis beginning 2/1.. The Princeton Review suggests that all financial aid forms be submitted as soon as possible after October 1. *Need-based scholarships/grants offered:* College/university scholarship or grant aid from institutional funds; Federal Pell; Private scholarships; SEOG; State scholarships/grants *Loan aid offered:* Direct PLUS loans; Direct Subsidized Stafford Loans; Direct Unsubsidized Stafford Loans Federal Work-Study Program available. Institutional employment available.

Campus Life

Activities: Campus Ministries; Choral groups; Dance ; Drama/theater; International Student Organization; Jazz band; Literary magazine; Music ensembles; Musical theater; Radio station ; Student government; Student newspaper; Student-run film society Organizations: 90 registered organizations, 5 religious organizations. **Athletics (Intercollegiate):** *Men:* sailing *Women:* sailing. **On-Campus Highlights:** Pritzker Marine Biology Research Center, Four Winds Cafe - student-run vegetarian coffeehouse, College Hall (Charles Ringling's mansion- visit center), Bayfront behind College Hall - sunset watching, Caples Fine Arts Complex - concerts and exhibits.

ACCOMMODATIONS

Allowed in exams:

Calculators	Yes
Dictionary	Yes
Computer	Yes
Spell-checker	Yes
Extended test time	Yes
Scribe	Yes
Proctors	Yes
Oral exams	Yes
Note-takers	Yes

Support services for students with

LD	Yes
ADHD	Yes
ASD	Yes
Distraction-reduced environment	Yes
Recording of lecture allowed	Yes
Reading technology:	Yes
Audio books	Yes
Other assistive technology	Varies based on the disability and specific needs.
Priority registration	Not Applicable

Added costs for services:

For LD:	No
For ADHD:	No
For ASD:	No
LD specialists	No
ADHD & ASD coaching	Yes
ASD specialists	Yes
Professional tutors	No
Peer tutors	Yes
Max. hours/week for services	
How professors are notified of student approved accommodations	Both

COLLEGE GRADUATION REQUIREMENTS

Course waivers allowed	No
Course substitutions allowed	Not Applicable

Stetson University

421 NORTH WOODLAND BOULEVARD, DELAND, FL 32723 • ADMISSIONS: 386-822-7100 • FAX: 386-822-7112

CAMPUS

Type of school	Private (nonprofit)
Environment	Town
Support	CS

STUDENTS

Undergrad enrollment	3,047
% male/female	43/57
% from out of state	27
% frosh live on campus	86

FINANCIAL FACTS

Annual tuition	$45,670
Room and board	$13,052
Required fees	$360

GENERAL ADMISSIONS INFO

Application fee	$50
Priority deadline	12/1

Nonfall registration accepted. Admission may be deferred.

Range SAT EBRW	570–650
Range SAT Math	540–640
Range ACT Composite	23–29

ACADEMICS

Student/faculty ratio	13:1
% students returning for sophomore year	78
% students graduating within 4 years	55
% students graduating within 6 years	62

Most classes have 10–19 students.
Most lab/discussion sessions have 10–19 students.

PROGRAMS/SERVICES FOR STUDENTS WITH LEARNING DIFFERENCES

Academic Success works to ensure equal access to the learning opportunities offered at Stetson University for all students. This is accomplished through reasonable accommodations for the classroom, as well as, education for the campus community around principles of universal design and inclusion. For students interested in establishing accommodations, there are two pieces of documentation needed. The first is an Accommodations Profile where a student can share their prior academic experience including strengths as a student and the barriers encountered in the learning environment. The second is supporting documentation. Guidelines for this supporting documentation can be found at www.stetson.edu/accessibility.

ADMISSIONS

Average GPA is 3.8. ACT/SAT is optional. Courses required include: English 4 years, Mathematics 3 years, Science 3 years, Foreign Language 2 years, Social Studies 3 years.

Additional Information

There is a three step process to establish accommodations. First, students complete an Accommodations Profile. Next students must provide appropriate documentation. Lastly the student will meet with the Academic Success team member.

ADMISSIONS INFO FOR STUDENTS WITH LEARNING DIFFERENCES

SAT/ACT required: No
Interview required: No
Essay required: Recommended
Additional application required: No
Documentation required for:
  LD: Documentation from a professional in the field that provides a diagnosis, explanation of how diagnosis impacts the student, and recommendations for potential accommodations. This documentation can be in the form of a letter, Psychoeducational evaluation, IEP, 504 plan, etc.
  ADHD: Documentation from a professional in the field that provides a diagnosis, explanation of how diagnosis impacts the student, and recommendations for potential accommodations. This documentation can be in the form of a letter, Psychoeducational evaluation, IEP, 504 plan, etc.
  ASD: Documentation from a professional in the field that provides a diagnosis, explanation of how diagnosis impacts the student, and recommendations for potential accommodations. This documentation can be in the form of a letter, Psychoeducational evaluation, IEP, 504 plan, etc.
Documentation submitted to: Support Program/Services
Special Ed. HS course work accepted: No
Contact Information
Name of program or department: Academic Success
Telephone: 386-822-7127
Fax: 386-822-7322
Email: asc@stetson.edu

Stetson University

GENERAL ADMISSIONS

Very important factors considered include: rigor of secondary school record, academic GPA. *Important factors considered include:* class rank, application essay, standardized test scores, recommendation(s), interview, extracurricular activities, talent/ability, character/personal qualities, volunteer work, work experience. *Other factors considered include:* alumni/ae relation, geographical residence, state residency, racial/ethnic status. *Freshman Admission Requirements:* High school diploma is required and GED is accepted. *Academic units required:* 4 English, 3 math, 3 science, 2 foreign language, 2 social studies.

ACCOMMODATIONS OR SERVICES

Accommodations are decided upon an individual basis after a thorough review of appropriate, current documentation. The accommodations requests must be supported through the documentation provided and must be logically linked to the current impact of the condition on academic functioning.

FINANCIAL AID

Students should submit: FAFSA. Applicants will be notified of awards on a rolling basis beginning 3/1. The Princeton Review suggests that all financial aid forms be submitted as soon as possible after October 1. *Need-based scholarships/grants offered:* College/university scholarship or grant aid from institutional funds; Federal Pell; Private scholarships; SEOG; State scholarships/grants. *Loan aid offered:* Direct PLUS loans; Direct Subsidized Stafford Loans; Direct Unsubsidized Stafford Loans. Federal Work-Study Program available. Institutional employment available.

CAMPUS LIFE

Activities: Campus Ministries; Choral groups; Concert band; Dance; Drama/theater; International Student Organization; Jazz band; Literary magazine; Marching band; Music ensembles; Musical theater; Opera; Pep band; Radio station; Student government; Student newspaper; Student-run film society; Symphony orchestra. **Organizations:** 125 registered organizations, 24 honor societies, 8 religious organizations. 6 fraternities, 5 sororities. **Athletics (Intercollegiate):** *Men:* baseball, basketball, crew/rowing, cross-country, golf, soccer, tennis. *Women:* basketball, crew/rowing, cross-country, golf, soccer, softball, tennis, volleyball. **On-Campus Highlights:** Palm Court, Stetson Coffee Shop, Hollis Center, DuPont-Ball Library/Student Success Center, Lynn Business Center.

ACCOMMODATIONS

Allowed in exams:

Calculators	Yes
Dictionary	Not Applicable
Computer	Yes
Spell-checker	Yes
Extended test time	Yes
Scribe	Yes
Proctors	Yes
Oral exams	Not Applicable
Note-takers	Yes

Support services for students with

LD	Yes
ADHD	Yes
ASD	Yes
Distraction-reduced environment	Yes
Recording of lecture allowed	Yes
Reading technology:	Yes
Audio books	Yes
Other assistive technology	Audio recording devices, Livescribe Smart Pens
Priority registration	Yes

Added costs for services:

For LD:	No
For ADHD:	No
For ASD:	No
LD specialists	No
ADHD & ASD coaching	Yes
ASD specialists	No
Professional tutors	Yes
Peer tutors	Yes
Max. hours/week for services	Varies
How professors are notified of student approved accommodations	Director

COLLEGE GRADUATION REQUIREMENTS

Course waivers allowed	No
Course substitutions allowed	Yes
In what courses	Foreign Language

University of Central Florida

4000 CENTRAL FLORIDA BLVD, ORLANDO, FL 32816-0111 • ADMISSIONS: 407-823-3000 • FAX: 407-823-5625

CAMPUS

Type of school	Public
Environment	City
Support	CS

STUDENTS

Undergrad enrollment	56,697
% male/female	46/54
% from out of state	6
% frosh live on campus	68

FINANCIAL FACTS

Annual in-state tuition	$6,368
Annual out-of-state tuition	$22,467
Room and board	$9,617
Required fees	NR

GENERAL ADMISSIONS INFO

Application fee	$30.
Priority deadline	1/1
Regular application deadline	5/1
Nonfall registration accepted.	

Range SAT EBRW	580–660
Range SAT Math	570–660
Range ACT Composite	24–29

ACADEMICS

Student/faculty ratio	30:1
% students returning for sophomore year	90
% students graduating within 4 years	40
% students graduating within 6 years	70
Most classes have 20–29 students.	

PROGRAMS/SERVICES FOR STUDENTS WITH LEARNING DIFFERENCES

The Student Accessibility Services provides information and individualized services consistent with the student's documented disability. To be eligible for disability-related services, individuals must have a documented disability as defined by applicable federal and state laws. Individuals seeking services are required to provide recent documentation from an appropriate health care provider or professional. See www.sds.ucf.edu for specific documentation required.

ADMISSIONS

Admission to the University of Central Florida requires graduation from an accredited high school with certain high school academic units, a cumulative high school GPA in those academic units, and SAT or ACT test scores. Course requirements include 4 years of English (at least 3 with substantial writing requirements); 3 years of mathematics (Algebra I and above); 3 years of natural science (at least 2 with labs); 3 years of social science; 2 sequential years of the same foreign language; 3 elective years (preferably from English, mathematics, natural science, social science, or foreign language areas). Students with disabilities who have not taken a foreign language in high school must submit, along with appropriate documentation, a letter from a school official verifying that not taking a foreign language was an accommodation for the disability. If a student needs special admission consideration based on a disability, the student should send the requested appropriate documentation to the Undergraduate Admissions Office. Satisfying minimum requirements does not guarantee admission to UCF since preference will be given to those students whose credentials indicate the greatest promise of academic success.

Additional Information

The University Writing Center (UWC) provides free writing support to all undergraduates and graduates at the University of Central Florida. The Student Accessibility Service program provides high-quality academic support programs, including tutoring and supplemental instruction, retention programs, academic advising programs, and various other academic programs and services. The Math Lab provides tutoring for students enrolled in mathematics courses.

ADMISSIONS INFO FOR STUDENTS WITH LEARNING DIFFERENCES

SAT/ACT required: Yes
Interview required: Yes
Essay required: Yes
Additional application required: No
Documentation required for:
 LD: Psycho ed evaluation
 ADHD: Diagnosis based on DSM-V; history of behaviors impairing functioning in academic setting; diagnostic interview; history of symptoms;evidence of ongoing behaviors.
 ASD: Students make an appointment with SDS Accessibility Consultant.
Accommodations are based on student self-report and third party documentation (IEP, 504 Plan, evaluations, letter from treating professional provider, etc.)
Documentation submitted to: Student Accessibility Services
Special Ed. HS course work accepted: Yes
Separate application required for Programs/Services: Yes
Contact Information
Name of program or department: Student Accessibility Services
Telephone: 407-823-2371
Fax: 407-823-2372
Email: sas@ucf.edu

University of Central Florida

GENERAL ADMISSIONS

Very important factors considered include: rigor of secondary school record, academic GPA, standardized test scores. *Important factors considered include:* application essay. *Other factors considered include:* class rank, recommendation(s), extracurricular activities, talent/ability, character/personal qualities, first generation, alumni/ae relation, geographical residence, state residency, volunteer work, work experience, level of applicant's interest. *Freshman Admission Requirements:* High school diploma is required and GED is accepted. *Academic units required:* 4 English, 4 math, 3 science, 2 science labs, 2 foreign language, 3 social studies, 2 academic electives.

ACCOMMODATIONS OR SERVICES

Accommodations are decided upon an individual basis after a thorough review of appropriate, current documentation. The accommodations requests must be supported through the documentation provided and must be logically linked to the current impact of the condition on academic functioning.

FINANCIAL AID

Students should submit: FAFSA. Applicants will be notified of awards on a rolling basis beginning 3/15. The Princeton Review suggests that all financial aid forms be submitted as soon as possible after October 1. *Need-based scholarships/grants offered:* College/university scholarship or grant aid from institutional funds; Federal Pell; Private scholarships; SEOG; State scholarships/grants. *Loan aid offered:* Direct PLUS loans; Direct Subsidized Stafford Loans; Direct Unsubsidized Stafford Loans. Federal Work-Study Program available. Institutional employment available.

CAMPUS LIFE

Activities: Campus Ministries; Choral groups; Concert band; Drama/theater; International Student Organization; Jazz band; Literary magazine; Marching band; Model UN; Music ensembles; Musical theater; Pep band; Radio station; Student government; Student-run film society; Symphony orchestra; Television station. **Organizations:** 361 registered organizations, 36 honor societies, 29 religious organizations. 21 fraternities, 18 sororities. **Athletics (Intercollegiate):** *Men:* baseball, basketball, cheerleading, cross-country, football, golf, soccer, tennis. *Women:* basketball, cheerleading, crew/rowing, cross-country, golf, soccer, softball, tennis, track/field (outdoor), track/field (indoor), volleyball. **On-Campus Highlights:** Student Union, Recreation and Wellness Center, Bookstore (Starbucks cafe), Reflecting Pond, Spectrum Stadium & CFE Arena.

ACCOMMODATIONS

Allowed in exams:

Calculators	Yes
Dictionary	Yes
Computer	Yes
Spell-checker	Yes
Extended test time	Yes
Scribe	Yes
Proctors	Yes
Oral exams	No
Note-takers	Yes

Support services for students with

LD	Yes
ADHD	Yes
ASD	Yes
Distraction-reduced environment	Yes
Recording of lecture allowed	Yes
Reading technology:	Yes
Audio books	Yes
Other assistive technology	Yes
Priority registration	Yes

Added costs for services:

For LD:	No
For ADHD:	No
For ASD:	No
LD specialists	No
ADHD & ASD coaching	Not Applicable
ASD specialists	No
Professional tutors	No
Peer tutors	Not Applicable
Max. hours/week for services	Varies
How professors are notified of student approved accommodations	Director

COLLEGE GRADUATION REQUIREMENTS

Course waivers allowed	No
Course substitutions allowed	Yes
In what courses	Math, Foreign Language

University of Florida

201 Criser Hall, Gainesville, FL 32611-4000 • Admissions: 352-392-1365 • Fax: 352-392-2115

CAMPUS

Type of school	Public
Environment	City
Support	CS

STUDENTS

Undergrad enrollment	33,654
% male/female	44/56
% from out of state	6
% frosh live on campus	73

FINANCIAL FACTS

Annual in-state tuition	$6,381
Annual out-of-state tuition	$28,658
Room and board	$10,120
Required fees	NR

GENERAL ADMISSIONS INFO

Application fee	$30
Regular application deadline	11/1
Range SAT EBRW	620–700
Range SAT Math	620–710
Range ACT Composite	28–32

ACADEMICS

Student/faculty ratio	21:1
% students graduating within 4 years	67
% students graduating within 6 years	87

Most classes have 10–19 students.
Most lab/discussion sessions have 10–19 students.

PROGRAMS/SERVICES FOR STUDENTS WITH LEARNING DIFFERENCES

The Disability Resource Center celebrates disability identity as a valued aspect of diversity. We champion a universally accessible community that supports the holistic advancement of individuals with disabilities. The Disability Resource Center envisions a universally inclusive community where all individuals are seen as valued and contributing leaders of society.AdmissionsApplicants with learning disabilities apply to the University under the same guidelines as all other students. However, applicants with any disabilitycan request special consideration because of disability.Few students are admitted purely on academic merit. While the potential for academic success is a primary consideration, UF's comprehensive holistic application review also considers personal essays, academic awards, extracurricular activities, family background and home community. All information in the applicant's file, academic and non-academic, is considered in relation to the size and strength of the applicant pool.

ADMISSIONS

Applicants with learning disabilities apply to the University under the same guidelines as all other students. However, applicants with any disability can request special consideration because of disability. Process guidelines: http://www.admissions.ufl.edu/disability.html.

Additional Information

The Dean of Students Office sponsors "Preview," a mandatory registration and orientation program. The DRC offers several student groups that are open for all DRC students. Groups are held on a weekly, biweekly, or monthly basis, depending on the group. The Innovation Academy at UF is a groundbreaking living/learning community that enrolls unique students from more than 30 majors into a spring-summer schedule filled with energy, collisions that become ideas, and one common minor: Innovation. The fall term is left open for other adventures, such as study abroad programs and there is an additional short essay on the application for students interested in IA.

ADMISSIONS INFO FOR STUDENTS WITH LEARNING DIFFERENCES

SAT/ACT required: Yes
Interview required: No
Essay required: Not Applicable
Additional application required: Not Applicable
Documentation required for:
 LD: Psycho ed evaluation
 ADHD: Psycho ed evaluation
 ASD: Neuro-Psychological evaluation enccouraged
Documentation submitted to: DRC
Special Ed. HS course work accepted: Not Applicable
Separate application required for Programs/Services: No
Contact Information
Name of program or department: Disability Resource Center
Telephone: 352-392-1261
Fax: 352-392-8570
Email: GerardoA@ufsa.ufl.edu

University of Florida

GENERAL ADMISSIONS

Very important factors considered include: rigor of secondary school record, academic GPA, application essay, extracurricular activities, talent/ability, character/personal qualities, volunteer work. *Important factors considered include:* standardized test scores, first generation, geographical residence, work experience. *Other factors considered include:* class rank, alumni/ae relation, state residency, level of applicant's interest. *Freshman Admission Requirements:* High school diploma is required and GED is accepted. *Academic units required:* 4 English, 4 math, 3 science, 2 science labs, 2 foreign language, 3 social studies.

ACCOMMODATIONS OR SERVICES

Accommodations are decided upon an individual basis after a thorough review of appropriate, current documentation. The accommodations requests must be supported through the documentation provided and must be logically linked to the current impact of the condition on academic functioning.

FINANCIAL AID

Students should submit: FAFSA. Applicants will be notified of awards on a rolling basis beginning 4/2. The Princeton Review suggests that all financial aid forms be submitted as soon as possible after October 1. *Need-based scholarships/grants offered:* College/university scholarship or grant aid from institutional funds; Federal Pell; Private scholarships; SEOG; State scholarships/grants; United Negro College Fund. *Loan aid offered:* Direct PLUS loans; Direct Subsidized Stafford Loans; Direct Unsubsidized Stafford Loans. Federal Work-Study Program available. Institutional employment available.

CAMPUS LIFE

Activities: Campus Ministries; Choral groups; Concert band; Dance; Drama/theater; International Student Organization; Jazz band; Literary magazine; Marching band; Model UN; Music ensembles; Musical theater; Pep band; Radio station; Student government; Student newspaper; Student-run film society; Symphony orchestra; Television station; Yearbook. **Organizations:** 853 registered organizations, **Athletics (Intercollegiate):** *Men:* baseball, basketball, cross-country, diving, football, golf, swimming, tennis, track/field (outdoor), track/field (indoor). *Women:* basketball, cross-country, diving, golf, gymnastics, lacrosse, soccer, softball, swimming, tennis, track/field (outdoor), track/field (indoor), volleyball. **On-Campus Highlights:** Southwest Recreation Center, Plaza of Americas, Library West, Ben Hill Griffin Stadium, J. Wayne Reitz Student Union.

ACCOMMODATIONS

Allowed in exams:

Calculators	Yes
Dictionary	Yes
Computer	Yes
Spell-checker	Yes
Extended test time	Yes
Scribe	Yes
Proctors	Yes
Oral exams	Yes
Note-takers	Yes

Support services for students with

LD	Yes
ADHD	Yes
ASD	Yes
Distraction-reduced environment	Yes
Recording of lecture allowed	Yes
Reading technology:	Yes
Audio books	Yes
Other assistive technology	Dragon, JAWS, Kurzweil, MAGic
Priority registration	Yes

Added costs for services:

For LD:	No
For ADHD:	No
For ASD:	No
LD specialists	Yes
ADHD & ASD coaching	Yes
ASD specialists	Yes
Professional tutors	No
Peer tutors	Not Applicable
Max. hours/week for services	0
How professors are notified of student approved accommodations	Student

COLLEGE GRADUATION REQUIREMENTS

Course waivers allowed	No
Course substitutions allowed	Yes
In what courses	

Students may petition for foreign language and/or math course substitutions. The courses offered in substitution are decided on a by college and case-by-case basis.

Brenau University

500 Washington St. SE, Gainesville, GA 30501 • Admissions: 770-534-6100 • Fax: 770-538-4306

CAMPUS
Type of school	Private (nonprofit)
Environment	Town
Support	SP

STUDENTS
Undergrad enrollment	1,722
% male/female	9/91
% from out of state	7
% frosh live on campus	62

FINANCIAL FACTS
Annual tuition	$28,650
Room and board	$12,418
Required fees	$400

GENERAL ADMISSIONS INFO
Priority deadline	5/1

Nonfall registration accepted. Admission may be deferred for a maximum of 1 year.

Range SAT EBRW	440–560
Range SAT Math	420–530
Range ACT Composite	17–23

ACADEMICS
Student/faculty ratio	11:1
% students returning for sophomore year	65
% students graduating within 4 years	31
% students graduating within 6 years	42

Most classes have 10–19 students.
Most lab/discussion sessions have 10–19 students.

PROGRAMS/SERVICES FOR STUDENTS WITH LEARNING DIFFERENCES

Brenau University strives to embrace a culture of inclusion, diversity and values all kinds of minds and learning styles. We seek to support students who have learning differences and disabilities by going above and beyond federal requirements by offering free professional tutoring, professional counseling, academic coaching, as well as accommodations. Small class sizes and the smaller, safe campus with free city bus access for students is an ideal environment for many learners who have learning disabilities.

ADMISSIONS

There is no special admissions process for students with disabilities, it is general admission. However, students who have disabilities may find that the fact that no minimum ACT or SAT score is required to be beneficial.

Additional Information

Art therapy and other groups are offered by the university counselor. The Learning Center sponsors study skills and test-taking workshops each semester. It's also a resource for students with learning disabilities, such as attention deficit disorder. Learning Center students can register early and receive regular academic advising from the Director of the program. Study skills and computer skills courses are offered for credit. At all service levels students may take tests in an extended-time format where oral assistance is available. Learning Center students begin tutoring with professional tutors during the first week of the term and contract to regularly attend tutoring sessions throughout the semester. All LC students may receive one free hour of educational support per week in addition to scheduled tutoring. Students may be tutored in one to four academic classes per semester. LD services and accommodations are available for undergraduate and graduate student.

ADMISSIONS INFO FOR STUDENTS WITH LEARNING DIFFERENCES

Additional application required: No
Documentation required for:
 LD: Psychological evaluation and/or psycho-educational testing and/or IEP or 504 Plan.
 ADHD: A letter from the treating physician with diagnosis and recommendations and/or a psychological evaluation.
 ASD: Nothing is required for admission.
Documentation submitted to: Support Program/Services
Special Ed. HS course work accepted: No
Separate application required for Programs/Services: Not for LD, ADHD, or ASD.
Contact Information
Name of program or department: Learning Center
Telephone: 770-534-6133
Fax: 770-297-5883
Email: learningcenter@brenau.edu

Brenau University

General Admissions

Very important factors considered include: academic GPA. *Important factors considered include:* rigor of secondary school record. *Other factors considered include:* class rank, application essay, standardized test scores, recommendation(s), interview, extracurricular activities, talent/ability, character/personal qualities, first generation, alumni/ae relation, volunteer work, work experience. *Freshman Admission Requirements:* High school diploma is required and GED is accepted. *Academic units required:* 4 English, 4 math, 3 science, 2 foreign language, 3 social studies.

Accommodations or Services

Accommodations are decided upon an individual basis after a thorough review of appropriate, current documentation. The accommodations requests must be supported through the documentation provided and must be logically linked to the current impact of the condition on academic functioning.

Financial Aid

Students should submit: FAFSA; State aid form. Applicants will be notified of awards on a rolling basis beginning 3/1. The Princeton Review suggests that all financial aid forms be submitted as soon as possible after October 1. *Need-based scholarships/grants offered:* College/university scholarship or grant aid from institutional funds; Federal Pell; Private scholarships; SEOG; State scholarships/grants. *Loan aid offered:* Direct PLUS loans; Direct Subsidized Stafford Loans; Direct Unsubsidized Stafford Loans. Federal Work-Study Program available. Institutional employment available.

Campus Life

Activities: Choral groups; Concert band; Dance; Drama/theater; International Student Organization; Jazz band; Literary magazine; Music ensembles; Musical theater; Opera; Pep band; Radio station; Student government; Student newspaper; Yearbook. **Organizations:** 54 registered organizations, 12 honor societies, 2 religious organizations. 8 sororities. **Athletics (Intercollegiate):** *Women:* basketball, cross-country, soccer, softball, swimming, tennis, volleyball. **On-Campus Highlights:** Pearce Auditorium, Burd Center for Performing Arts, Fitness Center, Dining Hall and Tea Room, Northeast Georgia History Center.

ACCOMMODATIONS

Allowed in exams:

Calculators	Yes
Dictionary	Yes
Computer	Yes
Spell-checker	Yes
Extended test time	Yes
Scribe	Yes
Proctors	Yes
Oral exams	Yes
Note-takers	No

Support services for students with

LD	Yes
ADHD	Yes
ASD	Yes
Distraction-reduced environment	Yes
Recording of lecture allowed	Yes
Reading technology:	Yes
Audio books	Not Applicable

Other assistive technology We provide CPEN reader pen (for text to speech), HESI exams can be ordered in text to speech format, and we do provide noise cancelling headphones, Mindview mind mapping writing assistant software at the Learning Center.

Priority registration	Yes

Added costs for services:

For LD:	No
For ADHD:	No
For ASD:	No
LD specialists	Yes
ADHD & ASD coaching	Yes
ASD specialists	Yes
Professional tutors	Yes
Peer tutors	Yes
Max. hours/week for services	8

How professors are notified of student approved accommodations
Director and Student

COLLEGE GRADUATION REQUIREMENTS

Course waivers allowed	No
Course substitutions allowed	Yes

In what courses

Course recommended for substitution by a physician or mental health professional (letter or evaluation with recommendations required).

Emory University

201 Dowman Drive, Atlanta, GA 30322 • Admissions: 404-727-6036 • Fax: 404-727-4303

CAMPUS
Type of school	Private (nonprofit)
Environment	City
Support	CS

STUDENTS
Undergrad enrollment	6,776
% male/female	41/59
% from out of state	78
% frosh live on campus	100

FINANCIAL FACTS
Annual tuition	$50,590
Room and board	$14,456
Required fees	$716

GENERAL ADMISSIONS INFO
Application fee	$75
Regular application deadline	1/1

Nonfall registration accepted. Admission may be deferred for a maximum of 2 years.

Range SAT EBRW	670–740
Range SAT Math	680–780
Range ACT Composite	30–33

ACADEMICS
Student/faculty ratio	9:1
% students returning for sophomore year	93
% students graduating within 4 years	82
% students graduating within 6 years	91

Most classes have fewer than 10 students. Most lab/discussion sessions have 10–19 students.

PROGRAMS/SERVICES FOR STUDENTS WITH LEARNING DIFFERENCES

Access, Disability Services and Resources is committed to advancing an accessible and "barrier-free" environment for its students, faculty, staff, patients, guests and visitors by ensuring that the principles of access, equity, inclusion and learning are applied and realized. As the administrative office responsible for: managing access needs, providing ADA accommodations, ensuring compliance with local, state and federal civil rights regulations pertaining to disability law, and serving as a critical resources for the enterprise, it is our role to embody Emory's commitment to its mission "in work and deed." Learning specialists are available to assist students in developing skills and strategies to define learning goals and individualized plans to reach a student's academic potential.

ADMISSIONS

Students with learning disabilities are required to submit everything requested by Admissions for all admissions. Teacher and/or counselor recommendations may be weighted more heavily in the admissions process. All applicants are evaluated individually and admitted based on potential for success. All first-year freshman applicants to Emory University are required to submit scores from either the SAT or the ACT. Emory University does not require applicants to take the optional writing section of either the SAT or ACT. There is no preference given to one exam over the other. SAT and/or ACT scores are important but are not the deciding factors. Strong grades in rigorous courses may cause the committee to overlook below average standardized test scores, but high board scores will never make up for .an applicant's weak course selection or grades.

Additional Information

The needs of students with learning disabilities are met through academic accommodations and a variety of support services. Tutoring is offered by Emory College in most subjects on a one-on-one basis or in small groups. ADSR staff provides information for students about how to access specific accommodation needs once the student is accepted and begins his or her academic work. Information can be obtained about ADSR at www.ods.emory.edu.

ADMISSIONS INFO FOR STUDENTS WITH LEARNING DIFFERENCES

SAT/ACT required: Yes
Interview required: No
Essay required: No
Additional application required: No
Documentation required for:
 LD: Psycho ed evaluation
 ADHD: Psycho ed evaluation
 ASD: Psycho ed evaluation
Documentation submitted to: ADSR
Special Ed. HS course work accepted: No
Separate application required for Programs/Services: No
Contact Information
Name of program or department: Access, Disability Services and Resources
Telephone: 404-727-9877
Fax: 404-727-1126

Emory University

GENERAL ADMISSIONS

Very important factors considered include: rigor of secondary school record, academic GPA, recommendation(s), extracurricular activities, talent/ability, character/personal qualities. *Important factors considered include:* application essay, standardized test scores, volunteer work. *Other factors considered include:* class rank, interview, first generation, alumni/ae relation, geographical residence, state residency, racial/ethnic status, work experience. *Freshman Admission Requirements:* High school diploma is required and GED is not accepted. *Academic units recommended:* 4 English, 4 math, 4 science, 2 science labs, 4 foreign language, 2 social studies, 2 history, 1 computer science, 1 visual/performing arts.

ACCOMMODATIONS OR SERVICES

Accommodations are decided upon an individual basis after a thorough review of appropriate, current documentation. The accommodations requests must be supported through the documentation provided and must be logically linked to the current impact of the condition on academic functioning.

FINANCIAL AID

Students should submit: CSS/Financial Aid PROFILE; FAFSA; Noncustodial PROFILE. Applicants will be notified of awards on or about 4/1. The Princeton Review suggests that all financial aid forms be submitted as soon as possible after October 1. *Need-based scholarships/grants offered:* College/university scholarship or grant aid from institutional funds; Federal Pell; Private scholarships; SEOG *Loan aid offered:* Direct PLUS loans; Direct Subsidized Stafford Loans; Direct Unsubsidized Stafford Loans. Federal Work-Study Program available. Institutional employment available.

CAMPUS LIFE

Activities: Campus Ministries; Choral groups; Concert band; Dance; Drama/theater; International Student Organization; Jazz band; Literary magazine; Model UN; Music ensembles; Musical theater; Opera; Radio station; Student government; Student newspaper; Student-run film society; Symphony orchestra; Television station. **Organizations:** 51 registered organizations, 30 honor societies, 27 religious organizations. 14 fraternities, 12 sororities. **Athletics (Intercollegiate):** *Men:* baseball, basketball, cross-country, diving, golf, soccer, swimming, tennis, track/field (outdoor). *Women:* basketball, cross-country, diving, soccer, softball, swimming, tennis, track/field (outdoor), volleyball. **On-Campus Highlights:** Michael C. Carlos Museum, Lullwater Park, Clifton Health Sciences Corridor, 10th Floor of the Woodruff Library, Candler Library Reading Room.

ACCOMMODATIONS

Allowed in exams:	
Calculators	Yes
Dictionary	Yes
Computer	Yes
Spell-checker	Yes
Extended test time	Yes
Scribe	Yes
Proctors	Yes
Oral exams	Yes
Note-takers	Yes
Support services for students with	
LD	Yes
ADHD	Yes
ASD	Yes
Distraction-reduced environment	Yes
Recording of lecture allowed	Yes
Reading technology:	Yes
Audio books	Yes
Other assistive technology	Yes
Priority registration	Yes
Added costs for services:	
For LD:	No
For ADHD:	No
For ASD:	No
LD specialists	No
ADHD & ASD coaching	No
ASD specialists	No
Professional tutors	No
Peer tutors	Yes
Max. hours/week for services	2
How professors are notified of student approved accommodations	Student

COLLEGE GRADUATION REQUIREMENTS

Course waivers allowed	No
Course substitutions allowed	No
In what courses	
Decisions made on a case-by-case basis.	

Georgia Southern University

P.O. Box 8126, Statesboro, GA 30460 • Admissions: 912-478-5391 • Fax: 912-478-7240

CAMPUS
Type of school	Public
Environment	Town
Support	CS

STUDENTS
Undergrad enrollment	17,062
% male/female	50/50
% from out of state	5
% frosh live on campus	90

FINANCIAL FACTS
Annual in-state tuition	$5,330
Annual out-of-state tuition	$18,812
Room and board	$10,070
Required fees	$2,092

GENERAL ADMISSIONS INFO
Application fee	$30
Priority deadline	4/1
Regular application deadline	5/1

Nonfall registration accepted. Admission may be deferred.

Range SAT EBRW	560–630
Range SAT Math	540–600
Range ACT Composite	22–26

ACADEMICS
Student/faculty ratio	22:1
% students returning for sophomore year	80
% students graduating within 4 years	26
% students graduating within 6 years	50

Most classes have 10–19 students.
Most lab/discussion sessions have 10–19 students.

PROGRAMS/SERVICES FOR STUDENTS WITH LEARNING DIFFERENCES

Georgia Southern University wants all students to have a rewarding and pleasant college experience. The university offers a variety of services specifically tailored to afford students with learning disabilities an equal opportunity for success. These services are in addition to those provided to all students and to the access provided by campus facilities. Opportunities available through the Student Disability Resource Center, include special registration, which allows students to complete the course registration process without going through the standard procedure, and academic/personal assistance for students who are having difficulty with passing a class and need help with time management, note-taking skills, study strategies, and self-confidence. The university has a support group designed to help students with disabilitiesdeal with personal and academic problems related to their disability. http://students.georgiasouthern.edu/sdrc/

ADMISSIONS

There is no special admission procedure for students with LD. All applicants must meet the same minimum requirements of 2.5 GPA and 20 ACT or 1030 SAT. The Office of Admissions can admit new freshmen to the Liberty Campus as long as they have earned a high school diploma. However, if students are admitted without meeting the admission criteria listed above for the Statesboro and Liberty Campuses, they must complete thirty or more credit hours with a cumulative 2.0+ GPA and make up and Required High School Curriculum deficiencies before transitioning from Liberty to another Georgia Southern campus.

Additional Information

The Academic Success Center offers a variety of tutoring and workshop services. However, the professional staff members of the Student Accessibility Resource Center are available to meet with students individually to help ensure their specific needs/goals are being addressed.

ADMISSIONS INFO FOR STUDENTS WITH LEARNING DIFFERENCES

SAT/ACT required: Yes
Interview required: No
Essay required: Not Applicable
Additional application required: No
Documentation required for:
 LD: Psycho ed evaluation
 ADHD: Psycho ed evaluation
 ASD: Psycho ed evaluation
Documentation submitted to: SARC
Special Ed. HS course work accepted: No
Separate application required for Programs/Services: No
Contact Information
Name of program or department: Student Disability Resource Center
Telephone: 912-478-1566
Fax: 912-478-1419
Email: sarcboro@georgiasouthern.edu

Georgia Southern University

GENERAL ADMISSIONS

Very important factors considered include: rigor of secondary school record, academic GPA, standardized test scores. *Other factors considered include:* class rank. *Freshman Admission Requirements:* High school diploma is required and GED is not accepted. *Academic units required:* 4 English, 4 math, 4 science, 2 science labs, 2 foreign language, 3 social studies.

ACCOMMODATIONS OR SERVICES

Accommodations are decided upon an individual basis after a thorough review of appropriate, current documentation. The accommodations requests must be supported through the documentation provided and must be logically linked to the current impact of the condition on academic functioning.

FINANCIAL AID

Students should submit: FAFSA. Applicants will be notified of awards on a rolling basis beginning 4/20. The Princeton Review suggests that all financial aid forms be submitted as soon as possible after October 1. *Need-based scholarships/grants offered:* College/university scholarship or grant aid from institutional funds; Federal Pell; Private scholarships; SEOG; State scholarships/grants. *Loan aid offered:* Direct PLUS loans; Direct Subsidized Stafford Loans; Direct Unsubsidized Stafford Loans. Federal Work-Study Program available. Institutional employment available.

CAMPUS LIFE

Activities: Campus Ministries; Choral groups; Concert band; Dance; Drama/theater; International Student Organization; Jazz band; Literary magazine; Marching band; Music ensembles; Musical theater; Opera; Radio station; Student government; Student newspaper; Student-run film society; Symphony orchestra. **Organizations:** 235 registered organizations, 17 honor societies, 20 religious organizations. 20 fraternities, 9 sororities. **Athletics (Intercollegiate):** *Men:* baseball, basketball, cheerleading, football, golf, soccer, tennis. *Women:* basketball, cheerleading, cross-country, diving, soccer, softball, swimming, tennis, track/field (outdoor), volleyball. **On-Campus Highlights:** Russell Union, Recreation Activity Center, Center for Wildlife Education, Georgia Southern Museum, Paulson Stadium.

ACCOMMODATIONS

Allowed in exams:

Calculators	Yes
Dictionary	Yes
Computer	Yes
Spell-checker	Yes
Extended test time	Yes
Scribe	Yes
Proctors	Yes
Oral exams	Yes
Note-takers	Yes

Support services for students with

LD	Yes
ADHD	Yes
ASD	Yes
Distraction-reduced environment	Yes
Recording of lecture allowed	Yes
Reading technology:	Yes
Audio books	No
Other assistive technology Support provided for numerous assistive technology needs.	
Priority registration	Yes

Added costs for services:

For LD:	No
For ADHD:	No
For ASD:	No
LD specialists	Yes
ADHD & ASD coaching	Yes
ASD specialists	Yes
Professional tutors	Yes
Peer tutors	No
Max. hours/week for services	Varies
How professors are notified of student approved accommodations	Student

COLLEGE GRADUATION REQUIREMENTS

Course waivers allowed	Yes
In what courses	
Foreign Language and math	
Course substitutions allowed	Yes
In what courses	
Foreign Language and math	

Georgia State University

P.O BOX 3965, ATLANTA, GA 30302-4009 • ADMISSIONS: 404-413-2500 • FAX: 404-413-2002

CAMPUS

Type of school	Public
Environment	Metropolis
Support	CS

STUDENTS

Undergrad enrollment	25,070
% male/female	41/59
% from out of state	4
% frosh live on campus	58

FINANCIAL FACTS

Annual in-state tuition	$8,730
Annual out-of-state tuition	$27,304
Room and board	$14,392
Required fees	$2,128

GENERAL ADMISSIONS INFO

Application fee	$60
Regular application deadline	3/1

Nonfall registration accepted. Admission may be deferred for a maximum of 2 terms.

Range SAT EBRW	500–580
Range SAT Math	470–590
Range ACT Composite	20–26

ACADEMICS

Student/faculty ratio	23:1
% students returning for sophomore year	77
% students graduating within 4 years	23
% students graduating within 6 years	54

Most classes have 10–19 students.

PROGRAMS/SERVICES FOR STUDENTS WITH LEARNING DIFFERENCES

Georgia State University is committed to helping each student, including those students with disabilities; realize his or her full potential. This commitment is fulfilled through the provision of reasonable accommodations to ensure equitable access to its programs and services for all qualified students with disabilities. In general, the university will provide accommodations for students with disabilities on an individualized and flexible basis. It is the student's responsibility to seek available assistance and make his or her needs known. All students are encouraged to contact the Office of Disability Services and/or Student Support Services in the early stages of their college planning. The pre-admission services include information regarding admission requirements and academic support services. Students should register with both services before classes begin. This will assure that appropriate services are in place prior to the first day of classes. As a rule, the university does not waive academic requirements because of any disability. Therefore, the student should carefully evaluate degree requirements early in his or her studies. The only exception to this policy is if there is a documented learning disability that would hinder the learning of a foreign language, in which case a student may petition for a substitution in the foreign language requirement.

ADMISSIONS

Students with LD must meet the same admission criteria as all other applicants. The university uses a predicted GPA of 2.1 for admission to a degree program or a GPA of 1.8 for admission to Learning Support Systems. This is determined by the ACT/SAT score and the high school GPA. The higher the GPA, the lower the ACT/SAT can be and vice versa. Course requirements include 4 years of English, 3 years of science, 3 years of math, 3 years of social science, and 2 years of a foreign language. (Substitutions are allowed for foreign language if the student has documentation that supports the substitution). Students may appeal an admission decision if they are denied and could be offered a probationary admission.

Additional Information

To receive LD services, students must submit documentation that evaluates intelligence; academic achievement in reading, math, and written language; auditory/phonological processing; language skills; visual-

ADMISSIONS INFO FOR STUDENTS WITH LEARNING DIFFERENCES

SAT/ACT required: Yes

Interview required: No

Essay required: No

Additional application required: No

Documentation required for:

 LD: Psycho ed evaluation

 ADHD: Diagnosis based on DSM-V; history of behaviors impairing functioning in academic setting; diagnostic interview; history of symptoms; evidence of ongoing behaviors.

 ASD: Psycho ed evaluation

Documentation submitted to: Margaret A. Station Office of Disability Services

Special Ed. HS course work accepted: No

Separate application required for Programs/Services: No

Contact Information

Name of program or department: Margaret A. Staton Office of Disabiltiy Services

Telephone: 404-413-1560

Email: twarren8@gsu.edu

Georgia State University

perceptual-spatial-constructural capabilities; attention; memory; executive function; motor skills; and social-emotional behavior. Student Support Services provides individual and group counseling, tutoring, advocacy, taped texts, advising, readers, learning lab, computer training, and referral for diagnosis of LD. The University Counseling Center provides study skills training; test-taking strategies; notetaking skills; textbook-reading skills; test anxiety and stress management, time management, and organizational techniques; thesis and dissertation writing; and personal counseling. Passport is a special section of the Personal and Academic Development Seminar Class offered through the Learning Support Program and is specifically designed for students with LD.

General Admissions

Very important factors considered include: rigor of secondary school record, academic GPA, standardized test scores. *Other factors considered include:* application essay, recommendation(s), talent/ability. *Freshman Admission Requirements:* High school diploma is required and GED is not accepted. *Academic units required:* 4 English, 4 math, 4 science, 2 science labs, 2 foreign language, 3 social studies. *Academic units recommended:* 4 English, 4 math, 4 science, 2 science labs, 2 foreign language, 3 social studies.

Accommodations or Services

Accommodations are decided upon an individual basis after a thorough review of appropriate, current documentation. The accommodations requests must be supported through the documentation provided and must be logically linked to the current impact of the condition on academic functioning.

Financial Aid

Students should submit: FAFSA. Applicants will be notified of awards on a rolling basis beginning 3/1. The Princeton Review suggests that all financial aid forms be submitted as soon as possible after October 1. *Need-based scholarships/grants offered:* College/university scholarship or grant aid from institutional funds; Federal Pell; Private scholarships; SEOG; State scholarships/grants; United Negro College Fund. *Loan aid offered:* Direct PLUS loans; Direct Subsidized Stafford Loans; Direct Unsubsidized Stafford Loans. Federal Work-Study Program available. Institutional employment available.

Campus Life

Activities: Campus Ministries; Choral groups; Concert band; Dance; Drama/theater; International Student Organization; Jazz band; Literary magazine; Marching band; Model UN; Music ensembles; Musical theater; Opera; Pep band; Radio station; Student government; Student newspaper; Student-run film society; Symphony orchestra; Television station. **Organizations:** 201 registered organizations, 19 honor societies, 21 religious organizations. 9 fraternities, 15 sororities. **Athletics (Intercollegiate):** *Men:* baseball, basketball, cross-country, golf, soccer, tennis, track/field (outdoor), volleyball. *Women:* basketball, cross-country, golf, soccer, softball, tennis, track/field (outdoor), volleyball. **On-Campus Highlights:** Recreation Center, Student Housing, Aderhold Learning Center, The Rialto Center for the Performing Arts, The Student Center.

ACCOMMODATIONS

Allowed in exams:

Calculators	Yes
Dictionary	Yes
Computer	Yes
Spell-checker	Yes
Extended test time	Yes
Scribe	No
Proctors	Yes
Oral exams	Yes
Note-takers	Yes

Support services for students with

LD	Yes
ADHD	Yes
ASD	No
Distraction-reduced environment	Yes
Recording of lecture allowed	Yes
Reading technology:	Yes
Audio books	Yes
Other assistive technology	Yes
Priority registration	Yes

Added costs for services:

For LD:	No
For ADHD:	No
For ASD:	No
LD specialists	No
ADHD & ASD coaching	No
ASD specialists	No
Professional tutors	No
Peer tutors	Yes
Max. hours/week for services	Varies
How professors are notified of student approved accommodations	Student

COLLEGE GRADUATION REQUIREMENTS

Course waivers allowed	No
Course substitutions allowed	No

Kennesaw State University

1000 CHASTAIN ROAD, KENNESAW, GA 30144-5591 • ADMISSIONS: 770-423-6300 • FAX: 470-578-9169

CAMPUS
Type of school	Public
Environment	Town
Support	S

STUDENTS
Undergrad enrollment	32,312
% male/female	53/47
% from out of state	12
% frosh live on campus	53

FINANCIAL FACTS
Annual in-state tuition	$5,426
Annual out-of-state tuition	$19,152
Room and board	$11,467
Required fees	$2,006

GENERAL ADMISSIONS INFO
Application fee	$40
Priority deadline	11/1
Regular application deadline	4/1
Nonfall registration accepted.	

Range SAT EBRW	550 –630
Range SAT Math	530 –610
Range ACT Composite	21 –26

ACADEMICS
Student/faculty ratio	20:1.
% students returning for sophomore year	78
% students graduating within 4 years	12
% students graduating within 6 years	42

Most classes have fewer than 10 students. Most lab/discussion sessions have 10-19 students.

PROGRAMS/SERVICES FOR STUDENTS WITH LEARNING DIFFERENCES

Goals in Support of the Mission Statement To provide a contact point for students with disabilities to identify themselves, provide appropriate documentation, determine approved accommodations, and coordinate necessary academic accommodations and services.   To encourage student success and persistence by providing individual and group support services such as academic advising, academic skills development, coordination with other campus departments, advocacy, and mentoring. To communicate with the University community in multiple modes to disseminate information regarding policies and procedures, awareness and sensitivity, appropriate accommodations, and other issues necessary to maintain compliance with federal and state mandates.   To maintain current knowledge and information regarding the University's many programs, services, activities, technology, and facilities, as well as future plans for program and facilities expansion, and to recommend adjustments and improvements as needed in order to assure compliance with ADA accessibility requirements.   To utilize all available technologies and resources to facilitate planning, communication and student learning. To utilize appropriate assessment measures to evaluate the quality and effectiveness of programs and services offered to students.   To encourage students' personal development through participation in University programs and activities that develop leadership, interdependence, respect for all human beings, and service to the community.

ADMISSIONS

Applicants should have a 2.5 GPA in 17 units of required high school courses. and either SAT of 1030 or ACT composite of 20 and an English subscore of 18 and math subscore of 18.

Additional Information
http://sds.kennesaw.edu/resources.php SDS emails individual Course Accessibility Letters directly to faculty and the student. The letter will outline the accommodations approved for that student by SDS. The additional comments regarding the deficits of the specific disabilities along with instructional tips provided in the letter, allow instructors to have a better picture of what barriers to instruction students with disabilities may face in a classroom. The instructional tips suggested are generally at the discretion of the instructor and are meant to give you greater insight into what is helpful. Additional information is also provided in the letter to provide faculty with helpful information in regards to reasonable implementation of accommodations.

ADMISSIONS INFO FOR STUDENTS WITH LEARNING DIFFERENCES
SAT/ACT required: Yes
Interview required: No
Essay required: No
Additional application required: Not Applicable
Documentation required for:
 LD: Psycho educational evaluation
 ADHD: Psycho educational evaluation
 ASD: Psycho educational evaluation
Documentation submitted to: SDS
Special Ed. HS course work accepted: Not Applicable
Separate application required for Programs/Services: No
Contact Information
Name of program or department: Student Disability Services
Telephone: 470-578-2666
Fax: 470-578-9164
Email: palmond@kennesaw.edu

Kennesaw State University

GENERAL ADMISSIONS

Very important factors considered include: academic GPA, standardized test scores. *Freshman Admission Requirements:* High school diploma is required and GED is not accepted *Academic units required:* 4 English, 4 math, 4 science, 2 science labs, 2 foreign language, 1 social studies, 2 history, *Academic units recommended:* 4 English, 4 math, 4 science, 2 science labs, 2 foreign language, 1 social studies, 2 history,

ACCOMMODATIONS OR SERVICES

Accommodations are decided upon an individual basis after a thorough review of appropriate, current documentation. The accommodations requests must be supported through the documentation provided and must be logically linked to the current impact of the condition on academic functioning.

FINANCIAL AID

Students should submit: . . The Princeton Review suggests that all financial aid forms be submitted as soon as possible after October 1. *Need-based scholarships/grants offered: Loan aid offered:* Federal Work-Study Program available. Institutional employment available.

CAMPUS LIFE

Activities: Campus Ministries; Choral groups; Concert band ; Dance ; Drama/theater; International Student Organization; Jazz band; Literary magazine; Marching band; Music ensembles; Musical theater; Opera; Pep band; Radio station ; Student government; Student newspaper; Symphony orchestra Organizations: 151 registered organizations, 20 honor societies, 18 religious organizations. 10 fraternities, 8 sororities, **Athletics (Intercollegiate):** *Men:* baseball, basketball, cross-country, golf, tennis, track/field (outdoor), track/field (indoor) *Women:* basketball, cheerleading, cross-country, golf, soccer, softball, tennis, track/field (outdoor), track/field (indoor), volleyball. **On-Campus Highlights:** The Commons (Student Culinary Center), Housing, Brand New Academic Buildings; Nursing, Social Sciences, and Business, Student Recreation and Wellness Center, Campus Green.

ACCOMMODATIONS

Allowed in exams:

Calculators	Yes
Dictionary	Yes
Computer	Yes
Spell-checker	Yes
Extended test time	Yes
Scribe	Yes
Proctors	Yes
Oral exams	Yes
Note-takers	Yes

Support services for students with

LD	Yes
ADHD	Yes
ASD	Yes
Distraction-reduced environment	Yes
Recording of lecture allowed	Yes
Reading technology:	Yes
Audio books	Yes

Other assistive technology

Livescribe Smart Pens, Assistive Listening Devices, JAWS, ClaroRead, and Kurzweil

Priority registration	Yes

Added costs for services:

For LD:	No
For ADHD:	No
For ASD:	No
LD specialists	Yes
ADHD & ASD coaching	Yes
ASD specialists	No
Professional tutors	Yes
Peer tutors	Yes
Max. hours/week for services	Varies

How professors are notified of student approved accommodations

Letter from SDS

COLLEGE GRADUATION REQUIREMENTS

Course waivers allowed	No
Course substitutions allowed	Yes

In what courses

Math and Foreign Language, if approved by the Board of Regents. Approval is based on standardized assessments documenting specific deficits in cognitive and academic achievement scores, as well as documented history of difficulties during K-12 education in either math or foreign language.

Reinhardt University

University Admissions Center, Waleska, GA 30183 • Admissions: 770-720-5526 • Fax: 770-720-5899

CAMPUS
Type of school	Private (nonprofit)
Environment	Rural
Support	SP

STUDENTS
Undergrad enrollment	980
% male/female	45/55
% from out of state	27
% frosh live on campus	62

FINANCIAL FACTS
Annual tuition	$22,400
Room and board	$10,200
Required fees	$800

GENERAL ADMISSIONS INFO
Application fee	$25

Nonfall registration accepted. Admission may be deferred.

Range SAT EBRW	410–540
Range SAT Math	430–530
Range ACT Composite	17–22

ACADEMICS
Student/faculty ratio	12:1
% students returning for sophomore year	56

Most classes have 10–19 students.

PROGRAMS/SERVICES FOR STUDENTS WITH LEARNING DIFFERENCES

The Academic Support Office (ASO) provides assistance to students with specific learning abilities or attention deficit disorders. Students are enrolled in regular college courses. The program focuses on compensatory skills and provides special services in academic advising, group tutoring, assistance in writing assignments, note-taking, testing accommodations, and coordination of assistive learning technologies. Reinhardt's ASO was established in 1982 to provide assistance to students with learning disabilities who meet regular college entrance requirements, have a diagnosed LD, and may or may not have received any LD services in the past due to ineligibility for high school services, or a recent diagnosis.

ADMISSIONS

Applicants with learning disabilities should request an ASO admission packet from Admissions; if they choose to selfdisclose upon application, they should complete the regular application; note an interest in Academic Support; fill out the supplemental form from ASO; provide IEPs from as many years of high school, psychological evaluations documenting the disability, and three references addressing aptitude, motivation, ability to set realistic goals, interpersonal skills, and readiness for college; and submit SAT/ACT scores. Students applying to the ASO program may be asked to interview with the ASO faculty. Admission decisions are made by the Admission Office. Students choosing not to self-disclose upon application should request information from the ASO Director.

Additional Information

ASO Tutorial: This is a paid tutorial program in which a student works one-on-one with a paid tutor in a specific subject in which the student needs more support. The paid tutors are seasoned faculty members who are proficient in working with students with learning disabilities and/or differing learning styles. They are also proficient in the use of special software program which they also incorporate into their tutorials. In addition,

ADMISSIONS INFO FOR STUDENTS WITH LEARNING DIFFERENCES

SAT/ACT required: Yes
Interview required: Yes
Essay required: N/A
Additional application required: No
Documentation required for:
 LD: Psycho ed evaluation
 ADHD: Diagnosis based on DSM-V; history of behaviors impairing functioning in academic setting; diagnostic interview; history of symptoms; evidence of ongoing behaviors.
 ASD: Psycho ed evaluation
Documentation submitted to: ASO
Special Ed. HS course work accepted: No
Separate application required for Programs/Services: Yes
Contact Information
Name of program or department: Academic Support Office (ASO)
Telephone: 770-720-5567
Fax: 770-720-5602
Email: AAA@reinhardt.edu

they are also trained academic coaches. Academic Coaching: Academic Coaching is a collaborative program between a coach and a student which helps students develop skills, strategies, structure,, support , self-reliance, self-awareness and responsibility. Coaching is an individualized process that facilitates goal clarification and academic achievement, which also stimulates and motivates students toward reaching their scholastic goals through structure, support and feedback. B.O.L.D: Building Opportunities for Students with Learning Disabilities (B.O.L.D.) The B.O.L.D program is built around the concept of universal design (UDI), which means we proactively seek to build learning opportunities and a support environment that anticipate the needs of students with leaning disabilities. The B.O.L.D program offers services that are individualized and go above and beyond standard accommodation. S.E.A.D: Strategic Education for Students With Autism Spectrum Disorders. By participating in the SEAD program, student should be able to achieve the following: have a smooth transition into the college atmosphere, increase awareness of strategies and skills for application in the social college atmosphere, and make connections with students and staff to maintain support throughout their college experience.

GENERAL ADMISSIONS

Very important factors considered include: academic GPA, standardized test scores. *Important factors considered include:* rigor of secondary school record, class rank. *Freshman Admission Requirements:* High school diploma is required and GED is accepted. *Academic units required:* 4 English, 4 math, 3 science, 3 social studies. *Academic units recommended:* 2 foreign language.

ACCOMMODATIONS OR SERVICES

Accommodations are decided upon an individual basis after a thorough review of appropriate, current documentation. The accommodations requests must be supported through the documentation provided and must be logically linked to the current impact of the condition on academic functioning.

FINANCIAL AID

Students should submit: FAFSA; State aid form. Applicants will be notified of awards on a rolling basis beginning 1/1. The Princeton Review suggests that all financial aid forms be submitted as soon as possible after October 1. *Need-based scholarships/grants offered:* College/university scholarship or grant aid from institutional funds; Federal Pell; Private scholarships; SEOG; State scholarships/grants. *Loan aid offered:* Direct PLUS loans; Direct Subsidized Stafford Loans; Direct Unsubsidized Stafford Loans. Federal Work-Study Program available.

CAMPUS LIFE

Activities: Campus Ministries; Choral groups; Concert band; Drama/theater; International Student Organization; Jazz band; Literary magazine; Music ensembles; Musical theater; Student government; Student newspaper; Student-run film society; Symphony orchestra; Television station; Yearbook. **Organizations:** 40 registered organizations, 6 honor societies, 5 religious organizations. **Athletics (Intercollegiate):** *Men:* baseball, basketball, cheerleading, cross-country, golf, soccer, tennis. *Women:* basketball, cheerleading, cross-country, golf, soccer, softball, tennis, volleyball. **On-Campus Highlights:** Falany Performing Arts Center, Funk Heritage Center, Gordy Center, Library, Class room building.

ACCOMMODATIONS

Allowed in exams:	
Calculators	Yes
Dictionary	No
Computer	Yes
Spell-checker	Yes
Extended test time	Yes
Scribe	Yes
Proctors	Yes
Oral exams	Yes
Note-takers	Yes
Support services for students with	
LD	Yes
ADHD	Yes
ASD	Yes
Distraction-reduced environment	Yes
Recording of lecture allowed	Yes
Reading technology:	Yes
Audio books	Yes
Other assistive technology	Yes
Priority registration	Yes
Added costs for services:	
For LD:	Yes
For ADHD:	Yes
For ASD:	Yes
LD specialists	Yes
ADHD & ASD coaching	Yes
ASD specialists	No
Professional tutors	Yes
Peer tutors	No
Max. hours/week for services	Unlimited
How professors are notified of student approved accommodations	Student and Director

COLLEGE GRADUATION REQUIREMENTS

Course waivers allowed	No
Course substitutions allowed	No

Savannah College of Art and Design

P.O. Box 3146, Savannah, GA 31402-3146 • Admissions: 912-525-5100 * Fax: 912-525-5986

CAMPUS
Type of school	Private (nonprofit)
Environment	City
Support	S

STUDENTS
Undergrad enrollment	10,483
% male/female	33/67
% from out of state	79
% frosh live on campus	84

FINANCIAL FACTS
Annual tuition	$35,190
Room and board	$13,905
Required fees	NR

GENERAL ADMISSIONS INFO
Application fee	$40

Nonfall registration accepted. Admission may be deferred for a maximum of 2 consec qtr.

Range SAT EBRW	490–610
Range SAT Math	460–580
Range ACT Composite	21–27

ACADEMICS
Student/faculty ratio	19:1
% students returning for sophomore year	85

Most classes have 10-19 students.

PROGRAMS/SERVICES FOR STUDENTS WITH LEARNING DIFFERENCES

All reasonable accommodations are determined for students on an individual basis. In order to receive academic adjustments and/or reasonable accommodations, students must make an appointment with their accommodation specialist each term to make their specific accommodation requests known.

ADMISSIONS

Applicants who do not meet the standard criteria for admission are encouraged to submit supplementary materials. Application materials cannot be returned. Exceptions to the general rules of admission may be made for applicants with exceptional drive and passion for the arts. Supplementary materials may include one or all of the following: One to three recommendations may be submitted by a teacher, counselor or community leader with whom the applicant has had immediate contact. Recommendations should address the applicant's level of commitment, as well as attributes such as creativity, initiative, motivation, character and academic achievement, to aid in assessing the applicant's reasonable potential for success as a student at SCAD.; A Statement of Purpose should be no more than 500 words in length and should give an overview of the applicant's academic and personal experience, describing preparation for and commitment to further study at SCAD, as well as educational and professional goals and aspirations; Students who submit portfolio, audition, riding or writing submission will have it scored according to a rubric relevant to the type of submission; Résumé/list of achievements and awards; and a personal or telephone interview which may be scheduled by contacting the admission department.

Additional Information

The The office of counseling and student support services invites all students with a diagnosed disability and their parent or guardian to attend Jump Start, a special expanded orientation in Savannah, Georgia, held before the general SCAD orientation begins. Jump Start is designed to increase awareness of the services and resources available to students with disabilities, ease the transition to college and provide strategies for success at SCAD. In addition to excellent professor instruction, state-of-the-art specialized equipment and cutting-edge technology, SCAD students have access to a wealth of learning resources outside the classroom. SCAD offers a variety of supplemental

APPLICATION REQUIREMENTS FOR SERVICES

SAT/ACT required: Yes
Interview required: No
Essay required: No
Additional application required: No
Documentation required for:
  LD: Psycho ed evaluation
  ADHD: Psycho ed evaluation
  ASD: Psycho ed evaluation
Documentation submitted to: Disability Services
Special Ed. HS course work accepted: No
Separate application required for Programs/Services: No
Contact Information
Name of program or department: SCAD Counseling and Student Support Services
Telephone: 912-525-6971
Email: counseling@scad.edu

Savannah College of Art and Design

programs designed to provide students with individual attention focused on their specific academic needs. Learning assistance is designated by subject or class and is provided to students free of charge. On-site peer tutors are available. Numerous academic and skill-based workshops take place to supplement in-class instruction.

GENERAL ADMISSIONS

Very important factors considered include: academic GPA. Important factors considered include: rigor of secondary school record, standardized test scores, level of applicant's interest. Other factors considered include: class rank, application essay, recommendation(s), interview, extracurricular activities, talent/ability, character/personal qualities. Freshman Admission Requirements: High school diploma is required and GED is accepted

ACCOMMODATIONS OR SERVICES

Accommodations are decided upon an individual basis after a thorough review of appropriate, current documentation. The accommodations requests must be supported through the documentation provided and must be logically linked to the current impact of the condition on academic functioning.

FINANCIAL AID

Students should submit: FAFSA; State aid form. Applicants will be notified of awards on a rolling basis beginning 3/1.. The Princeton Review suggests that all financial aid forms be submitted as soon as possible after October 1. Need-based scholarships/grants offered: College/university scholarship or grant aid from institutional funds; Federal Pell; Private scholarships; SEOG; State scholarships/grants; United Negro College Fund Loan aid offered: Direct PLUS loans; Direct Subsidized Stafford Loans; Direct Unsubsidized Stafford Loans Federal Work-Study Program available. Institutional employment available.

CAMPUS LIFE

Activities: Campus Ministries; Choral groups; Dance ; Drama/theater; International Student Organization; Literary magazine; Music ensembles; Musical theater; Radio station ; Student newspaper; Television station Organizations: 68 registered organizations, 2 honor societies, 3 religious organizations. Athletics (Intercollegiate): Men: baseball, basketball, cross-country, equestrian sports, golf, lacrosse, soccer, swimming, tennis Women: basketball, cross-country, equestrian sports, golf, lacrosse, soccer, softball, swimming, tennis, volleyball. On-Campus Highlights: SCAD Museum of Art, Club SCAD, Jen Library, Cafe SCAD, Trustees Theatre.

ACCOMMODATIONS

Allowed in exams:	
Calculators	Yes
Dictionary	Yes
Computer	Yes
Spell-checker	Yes
Extended test time	Yes
Scribe	Yes
Proctors	Yes
Oral exams	Yes
Note-takers	Yes
Support services for students with	
LD	Yes
ADHD	Yes
ASD	Yes
Distraction-reduced environment	Yes
Recording of lecture alowed	Yes
Reading technology:	Yes
Audio books	Yes
Other assistive technology	Kurzweil 3000, Dragon Naturally Speaking, and Inspiration
Priority registration	Yes
Added costs of services:	
For LD:	No
For ADHD:	No
For ASD:	No
LD specialists	Yes
ADHD & ASD coaching	Yes
ASD specialists	No
Professional tutors	Yes
Peer tutors	Yes
Max. hours/week for services	8
How professors are notified of student approved accommodations	Student

COLLEGE GRADUATION REQUIREMENTS

Course waivers allowed	Yes
In what courses	Math, Foreign Languages
Course substitutions allowed	Yes
In what courses	Math, Foreign Languages

University of Georgia

ADMINISTRATION BUILDING, ATHENS, GA 30602-1633 • ADMISSIONS: 706-542-8776 • FAX:

CAMPUS
Type of school	Public
Environment	City
Support	CS

STUDENTS
Undergrad enrollment	22,919
% male/female	44/56
% from out of state	11
% frosh live on campus	98

FINANCIAL FACTS
Annual tuition	$28,126
Room and board	$10,038
Required fees	$2,278

GENERAL ADMISSIONS INFO
Application fee	$60
Priority deadline	10/15
Regular application deadline	1/1

Nonfall registration accepted. Admission may be deferred for a maximum of one academic year.

Range SAT EBRW	610–690
Range SAT Math	590–680
Range ACT Composite	26–31

ACADEMICS
Student/faculty ratio	17:1
% students returning for sophomore year	96
% students graduating within 4 years	63
% students graduating within 6 years	85

Most classes have 10–19 students. Most lab/discussion sessions have fewer than 10 students.

PROGRAMS/SERVICES FOR STUDENTS WITH LEARNING DIFFERENCES
The Disability Resource Center (DRC) assists the University in fulfilling its commitment to educate and serve students with disabilities who qualify for admissions. The DRC coordinates and provides a variety of academic and support services to students, including students with Learning Disabilities (LDs), Attention Deficit Hyperactivity Disorder (ADHD), and Asperger Syndrome (AS). Our mission is to promote equal educational opportunities and a welcoming environment for students with disabilities at the University of Georgia. DRC staff members are dedicated professionals with a wide range of expertise in disability related issues. These encompass disability specific accommodations, universal design, program access, assistive technology, alternative text, architectural access, and disability law. Staff can hold regular meetings with students to discuss and monitor academic progress, assist students in understanding their disability, make referrals to other campus and community resources, and consult with faculty as needed. Documentation guidelines can be found on the DRC's website at <https://drc.uga.edu/students/documentation-guidelines>.

ADMISSIONS
There are no special admission criteria for students with disabilities. All students must meet the admission criteria set by the University. However, a student with a disability may disclose his/her diagnosis in a personal statement/essay to further explain test scores and/or grades received.

Additional Information
DRC staff refer students to campus resources as requested/necessary. The Academic Resource Center located in Milledge Hall provides a variety of academic assistance for all students on campus. The ARC has a peer-based tutor program that includes drop-in labs for chemistry, math, and physics, as well as appointment-based tutoring for more than 60 courses. The ARC also has a Writing Center which is staffed with specialists who are experts in their field. Every fall, academic success workshops are offered on issues such as time management, stress management, and preparing for final exams.

ADMISSIONS INFO FOR STUDENTS WITH LEARNING DIFFERENCES
SAT/ACT required: Yes
Interview required: No
Essay required: Not Applicable
Additional application required: Yes
Documentation required for:
  LD: See <https://drc.uga.edu/students/documentation-guidelines/eligibility-LD> for documentation guidelines for LDs.
  ADHD: See <https://drc.uga.edu/students/documentation-guidelines/ADHD> for documentation guidelines for ADHD.
  ASD: See <https://drc.uga.edu/students/documentation-guidelines/eligibility-AS> for documentation guidelines for ASDs.
Documentation submitted to: Support Program/Services
Special Ed. HS course work accepted: No
Separate application required for Programs/Services: No
Contact Information
Name of program or department: Disability Resource Center
Telephone: 706-542-8719
Fax: 706-542-7719
Email: DSINFO@uga.edu

University of Georgia

GENERAL ADMISSIONS

Very important factors considered include: rigor of secondary school record, academic GPA. *Important factors considered include:* standardized test scores. *Other factors considered include:* application essay, recommendation(s), extracurricular activities, talent/ability, character/personal qualities, first generation, volunteer work, work experience. *Freshman Admission Requirements:* High school diploma is required and GED is accepted. *Academic units required:* 4 English, 4 math, 4 science, 2 science labs, 2 foreign language, 3 social studies. *Academic units recommended:* 4 English, 4 math, 4 science, 2 science labs, 3 foreign language, 3 social studies, 1 academic elective.

ACCOMMODATIONS OR SERVICES

Accommodations are decided upon an individual basis after a thorough review of appropriate, current documentation. The accommodations requests must be supported through the documentation provided and must be logically linked to the current impact of the condition on academic functioning.

FINANCIAL AID

Students should submit: FAFSA. Applicants will be notified of awards on a rolling basis beginning 5/1. The Princeton Review suggests that all financial aid forms be submitted as soon as possible after October 1. *Need-based scholarships/grants offered:* College/university scholarship or grant aid from institutional funds; Federal Pell; Private scholarships; SEOG; State scholarships/grants. *Loan aid offered:* Direct PLUS loans; Direct Subsidized Stafford Loans; Direct Unsubsidized Stafford Loans. Federal Work-Study Program available. Institutional employment available.

CAMPUS LIFE

Activities: Campus Ministries; Choral groups; Concert band; Dance; Drama/theater; International Student Organization; Jazz band; Literary magazine; Marching band; Model UN; Music ensembles; Musical theater; Opera; Pep band; Radio station; Student government; Student newspaper; Student-run film society; Symphony orchestra; Yearbook. **Organizations:** 597 registered organizations, 22 honor societies, 35 religious organizations. 34 fraternities, 25 sororities. **Athletics (Intercollegiate):** *Men:* baseball, basketball, cross-country, diving, football, golf, swimming, tennis, track/field (outdoor), track/field (indoor). *Women:* basketball, cross-country, diving, equestrian sports, golf, gymnastics, soccer, softball, swimming, tennis, track/field (outdoor), track/field (indoor), volleyball. **On-Campus Highlights:** Zell B. Miller Learning Center, Sanford Stadium, Ramsey Student Center for Physical Activ, Performing and Visual Arts Complex, Tate Student Center.

ACCOMMODATIONS

Allowed in exams:	
Calculators	Yes
Dictionary	No
Computer	Yes
Spell-checker	Yes
Extended test time	Yes
Scribe	Yes
Proctors	Yes
Oral exams	Yes
Note-takers	Yes
Support services for students with	
LD	Yes
ADHD	Yes
ASD	Yes
Distraction-reduced environment	Yes
Recording of lecture allowed	Yes
Reading technology:	Yes
Audio books	Yes
Other assistive technology	Mindjet; Dragon Naturally Speaking; CLARO Reader; Learning Ally; Read and Write Gold; provision of white noise
Priority registration	Yes
Added costs for services:	
For LD:	No
For ADHD:	No
For ASD:	No
LD specialists	Yes
ADHD & ASD coaching	No
ASD specialists	No
Professional tutors	No
Peer tutors	No
Max. hours/week for services	Varies
How professors are notified of student approved accommodations	Student

COLLEGE GRADUATION REQUIREMENTS

Course waivers allowed	No
Course substitutions allowed	Yes
In what courses	Foreign Language; Math

Bradley University

1501 W. BRADLEY AVENUE, PEORIA, IL 61625 • ADMISSIONS: 309-677-1000 • FAX: 309-677-2797

CAMPUS

Type of school	Private (nonprofit)
Environment	City
Support	S

STUDENTS

Undergrad enrollment	4,643
% male/female	49/51
% from out of state	18
% frosh live on campus	93

FINANCIAL FACTS

Annual tuition	$33,360
Room and board	$10,620
Required fees	$400

GENERAL ADMISSIONS INFO

Application fee	$35
Priority deadline	2/1
Regular application deadline	5/1

Nonfall registration accepted. Admission may be deferred for a maximum of 1 year.

Range SAT EBRW	550–640
Range SAT Math	530–650
Range ACT Composite	22–28

ACADEMICS

Student/faculty ratio	12:1
% students returning for sophomore year	87
% students graduating within 4 years	51
% students graduating within 6 years	72

Most classes have fewer than 10 students. Most lab/discussion sessions have fewer than 10 students.

PROGRAMS/SERVICES FOR STUDENTS WITH LEARNING DIFFERENCES

The Office of Student Access Services (SAS) is committed to the fulfillment of equal educational opportunity, academic freedom and human dignity for students with disabilities. The SAS exists to provide reasonable and appropriate accommodations for qualified students with documented disabilities, to assist students in self-advocacy, to educate the Bradley community about disabilities, and ensure compliance with federal and state law.

ADMISSIONS

Students with learning disabilities must meet the same admission requirements as all applicants. ACT or SAT score is required. Mid 50% SAT 1040-1310 or ACT 22-28. and an average GPA of 3.6.

Additional Information

The most common test accommodations include extended time, testing in a distraction-reduced environment, tests in alternative formats, interpreted tests, and the use of adaptive equipment. Students are responsible for arranging testing accommodations with their professor and/or Student Access Services. Students need to schedule exams with the SAS and the instructor at least three days prior to the testing date to arrange for accommodations. It may sometimes be necessary for a student with certain limitations to substitute one course for another in order to meet specific graduation requirements. This substitution request is normally first discussed with the student's academic advisor and then with our office before an approval can be granted and the necessary arrangements can be made. Even if students are provided with a note taker, they are expected to take some notes to assist them in focusing their attention during the class. The note taker is not to assist with out-of-class assignments, homework or alternative testing arrangements.

ADMISSIONS INFO FOR STUDENTS WITH LEARNING DIFFERENCES

SAT/ACT required: Yes
Interview required: No
Essay required: Yes
Additional application required: No
Documentation required for:
  LD: Yes
  ADHD: Yes
  ASD: Yes
Documentation submitted to: Support Program/Services
Special Ed. HS course work accepted: Yes
Separate application required for Programs/Services: No
Contact Information
Name of program or department: Student Access Services
Telephone: 309-677-3654
Fax: 309-677-3685
Email: eagorman@bradley.edu

Bradley University

GENERAL ADMISSIONS

Very important factors considered include: rigor of secondary school record, academic GPA. *Important factors considered include:* class rank, standardized test scores. *Other factors considered include:* application essay, recommendation(s), interview, extracurricular activities, talent/ability, character/personal qualities, first generation, alumni/ae relation, geographical residence, racial/ethnic status, volunteer work, work experience, level of applicant's interest. *Freshman Admission Requirements:* High school diploma is required and GED is accepted *Academic units required:* 4 English, 3 math, 2 science, 2 science labs, 2 social studies, *Academic units recommended:* 5 English, 4 math, 3 science, 3 science labs, 2 foreign language, 3 social studies, 2 history,

ACCOMMODATIONS OR SERVICES

Accommodations are decided upon an individual basis after a thorough review of appropriate, current documentation. The accommodations requests must be supported through the documentation provided and must be logically linked to the current impact of the condition on academic functioning.

FINANCIAL AID

Students should submit: FAFSA. Applicants will be notified of awards on a rolling basis beginning 9/1.. The Princeton Review suggests that all financial aid forms be submitted as soon as possible after October 1. *Need-based scholarships/grants offered:* College/university scholarship or grant aid from institutional funds; Federal Pell; Private scholarships; SEOG; State scholarships/grants; United Negro College Fund *Loan aid offered:* Direct PLUS loans; Direct Subsidized Stafford Loans; Direct Unsubsidized Stafford Loans Federal Work-Study Program available. Institutional employment available.

CAMPUS LIFE

Activities: Campus Ministries; Choral groups; Concert band ; Dance ; Drama/theater; International Student Organization; Jazz band; Literary magazine; Music ensembles; Musical theater; Pep band; Radio station ; Student government; Student newspaper; Student-run film society; Symphony orchestra ; Television station Organizations: 220 registered organizations, 31 honor societies, 17 religious organizations. 16 fraternities, 11 sororities, **Athletics (Intercollegiate):** *Men:* baseball, basketball, cross-country, golf, soccer, tennis *Women:* basketball, cross-country, golf, softball, tennis, track/field (outdoor), track/field (indoor), volleyball. **On-Campus Highlights:** Markin Family Student Recreation Center, Caterpillar Global Communications Center, Olin Hall of Science, Michel Student Center, Renaissance Coliseum.

ACCOMMODATIONS

Allowed in exams:

Calculators	Yes
Dictionary	Yes
Computer	Yes
Spell-checker	Yes
Extended test time	Yes
Scribe	Yes
Proctors	Yes
Oral exams	Yes
Note-takers	Yes

Support services for students with

LD	No
ADHD	No
ASD	No
Distraction-reduced environment	Yes
Recording of lecture allowed	Yes
Reading technology:	Yes
Audio books	Yes
Other assistive technology	Audio Text,

ZoomText, Screen readers, magnifiers, Kurzwiel3000, others based on needs

Priority registration	Yes

Added costs for services:

For LD:	No
For ADHD:	No
For ASD:	No
LD specialists	No
ADHD & ASD coaching	Yes
ASD specialists	Yes
Professional tutors	Yes
Peer tutors	Yes
Max. hours/week for services	Varies
How professors are notified of student approved accommodations	Both

COLLEGE GRADUATION REQUIREMENTS

Course waivers allowed	Yes

In what courses

Dependent upon documentation, major and licensure/accreditation requirements.

Course substitutions allowed	Yes

In what courses

Dependent upon documentation, major and licensure/accreditation requirements.

DePaul University

1 East Jackson Boulevard, Chicago, IL 60604-2287 • Admissions: 312-362-8300 • Fax: 312-362-5749

CAMPUS

Type of school	Private (nonprofit)
Environment	Metropolis
Support	CS

STUDENTS

Undergrad enrollment	14,591
% male/female	47/53
% from out of state	24
% frosh live on campus	68

FINANCIAL FACTS

Annual tuition	$39,369
Room and board	$14,325
Required fees	$606

GENERAL ADMISSIONS INFO

Priority deadline	11/15
Regular application deadline	2/1

Nonfall registration accepted. Admission may be deferred for a maximum of 1 year.

Range SAT EBRW	550–670
Range SAT Math	530–640
Range ACT Composite	22–28

ACADEMICS

Student/faculty ratio	16:1
% students returning for sophomore year	84
% students graduating within 4 years	59
% students graduating within 6 years	71

Most classes have 10–19 students. Most lab/discussion sessions have 10–19 students.

PROGRAMS/SERVICES FOR STUDENTS WITH LEARNING DIFFERENCES

The Center for Students with Disabilities (CSD) is designed to service and support students with learning disabilities, attention deficit hyperactivity disorder, and all other disabilities. The immediate goals are to provide learning strategies based on students' strengths and weaknesses to assist students in the completion of course work. The ultimate goal is to impart academic and study skills that will enable the students to function independently in the academic environment and competitive job market. CSD provides intensive help on a one-on-one basis. It is designed to assist with regular college courses, improve learning deficits, and help the student learn compensatory skills. Students can choose to work with learning disability specialists with whom they can meet for up to 2 hours per week.

ADMISSIONS

There is no separate process for students with learning disabilities who wish to be considered for admission to the university. Students with earning disabilities must be first accepted to DePaul University before they can be accepted to the Center for Students with Disabilities (CSD). DePaul is Test Optinal and ACT or SAT is not required for admission

Additional Information

DePaul's Center for Students with Disabilities (CSD) coordinates DePaul University's provision of accommodations and other services to students pursuant to the Americans with Disabilities Act and Section 504 of the Rehabilitation Act of 1973. CSD provides support services for all enrolled students at DePaul; part-time and full-time, undergraduate and graduate, and across all Schools/Colleges within DePaul for all campuses. Recommendations for accommodations are determined by CSD staff after reviewing the documentation provided and an interview with the student. CSD follows the guidelines of the newly updated Americans with Disabilities Act (ADA) and related legislation to determine the most appropriate accommodations for the students. CSD provides appropriate accommodations and services for studentsrelated to the nature of their disability.

ADMISSIONS INFO FOR STUDENTS WITH LEARNING DIFFERENCES

SAT/ACT required: Yes
Interview required: Yes
Essay required: No
Additional application required: No
Documentation required for:
  LD: Psycho ed evaluation
  ADHD: Diagnosis based on DSM-V; history of behaviors impairing functioning in academic setting; diagnostic interview; history of symptoms; evidence of ongoing behaviors.
  ASD: Psycho ed evaluation
Documentation submitted to: Center for Students with Disabilities (CSD)
Special Ed. HS course work accepted: Yes
Separate application required for Programs/Services: Yes
Contact Information
Name of program or department: Center for Students with Disabilities
Telephone: 773-325-1677
Fax: 773-325-3720

DePaul University

GENERAL ADMISSIONS

Very important factors considered include: rigor of secondary school record, academic GPA, standardized test scores. *Important factors considered include:* class rank, recommendation(s), extracurricular activities, talent/ability, character/personal qualities, volunteer work, work experience, level of applicant's interest. *Other factors considered include:* application essay, interview, first generation, alumni/ae relation, geographical residence, state residency, religious affiliation/commitment, racial/ethnic status. *Freshman Admission Requirements:* High school diploma is required and GED is accepted. *Academic units required:* 4 English, 3 math, 3 science, 2 science labs, and 2 units from above areas or other academic areas. *Academic units recommended:* 4 English, 3 math, 3 science, 2 science labs, 2 foreign language, 2 units from above areas or other academic areas.

ACCOMMODATIONS OR SERVICES

Accommodations are decided upon an individual basis after a thorough review of appropriate, current documentation. The accommodations requests must be supported through the documentation provided and must be logically linked to the current impact of the condition on academic functioning.

FINANCIAL AID

Students should submit: FAFSA. Applicants will be notified of awards on a rolling basis beginning 12/15. The Princeton Review suggests that all financial aid forms be submitted as soon as possible after October 1. *Need-based scholarships/grants offered:* College/university scholarship or grant aid from institutional funds; Federal Pell; Private scholarships; SEOG; State scholarships/grants. *Loan aid offered:* Direct PLUS loans; Direct Subsidized Stafford Loans; Direct Unsubsidized Stafford Loans. Federal Work-Study Program available. Institutional employment available.

CAMPUS LIFE

Activities: Campus Ministries; Choral groups; Concert band; Dance; Drama/theater; International Student Organization; Jazz band; Literary magazine; Model UN; Music ensembles; Musical theater; Opera; Pep band; Radio station; Student government; Student newspaper; Student-run film society; Symphony orchestra. **Organizations:** 311 registered organizations, 9 honor societies, 19 religious organizations. 9 fraternities, 13 sororities. **Athletics (Intercollegiate):** *Men:* basketball, cross-country, golf, soccer, tennis, track/field (outdoor), track/field (indoor). *Women:* basketball, cross-country, soccer, softball, tennis, track/field (outdoor), track/field (indoor), volleyball. **On-Campus Highlights:** Student Center, Lincoln Park Campus, Ray Meyer Fitness Center, The Pit, in Schmitt Academic Center (SAC), 11th floor, DePaul Center, Loop Campus, The Bean Cafe in the SAC.

ACCOMMODATIONS

Allowed in exams:	
Calculators	Yes
Dictionary	Yes
Computer	Yes
Spell-checker	Yes
Extended test time	Yes
Scribe	Yes
Proctors	Yes
Oral exams	Yes
Note-takers	No
Support services for students with	
LD	Yes
ADHD	Yes
ASD	Yes
Distraction-reduced environment	Yes
Recording of lecture allowed	Yes
Reading technology:	Yes
Audio books	Yes
Other assistive technology	Yes
Priority registration	Yes
Added costs for services:	
For LD:	No
For ADHD:	No
For ASD:	No
LD specialists	Yes
ADHD & ASD coaching	No
ASD specialists	No
Professional tutors	No
Peer tutors	No
Max. hours/week for services	2
How professors are notified of student approved accommodations	Student

COLLEGE GRADUATION REQUIREMENTS

Course waivers allowed	Yes
In what courses	
Foreign Language (LD and ADHD)	
Course substitutions allowed	Yes
In what courses	
Foreign Language (LD and ADHD)	

Eastern Illinois University

600 LINCOLN AVENUE, CHARLESTON, IL 61920 • ADMISSIONS: 217-581-2223 • FAX: 217-581-7060

CAMPUS

Type of school	Public
Environment	Village
Support	S

STUDENTS

Undergrad enrollment	5,750
% male/female	40/60
% from out of state	6
% frosh live on campus	94

FINANCIAL FACTS

Annual in-state tuition	$8,670
Annual out-of-state tuition	$10,830
Room and board	$9,546
Required fees	$2,910

GENERAL ADMISSIONS INFO

Application fee	$30
Regular application deadline	8/15

Nonfall registration accepted. Admission may be deferred for a maximum of 1 year.

Range ACT Composite	18–24

ACADEMICS

Student/faculty ratio	14:1
% students returning for sophomore year	71
% students graduating within 4 years	33
% students graduating withing 6 years	56

Most classes have 10–19 students. Most lab/discussion sessions have 20–29 students.

PROGRAMS/SERVICES FOR STUDENTS WITH LEARNING DIFFERENCES

The Office of Disability Services provides support to students with LD/ADHD as appropriate with documentation. Eastern Illinois University's Students with Autism Transitional Education Program focuses on providing enhanced support in three main skill set areas. A solid foundation of Academic, Social , and Daily-living (ASD) skill sets is crucial for the success of post-secondary students.

ADMISSIONS

Applicants must have a high school grade-point average (GPA) of 2.5 on a 4.0 (unweighted scale) and SAT: 960 or ACT: 18. The Writing Section is not required. Any student who falls slightly below the criteria listed above, or had a noticeable decrease in semester GPA, is strongly encouraged to include a personal statement and letter of recommendation. The student should use the statement to provide more information as EIU reviews the application. Additional materials may be requested and used in the decision process.

Additional Information

Contact Disability Services or Admissions. STEP provides enhanced training at EIU on Academic, Social, and Daily-living skills (ASD) to allow students the opportunity to navigate their college experience successfully. In order to directly address these areas, the Transition Program provides opportunities for growth through: Individualized peer mentorships that work to develop ASD skill sets, Personalized campus tours focused on the individual's schedule/routine each semester, Social skills groups that focus on utilizing interpersonal skills in the classroom and throughout the campus community, A positive educational work environment through regularly scheduled academic study tables, Social events tailored to interests of the participants of the program to enhance the opportunity for friendships, active involvement on campus , and vocational skill development, Physical fitness programs personalized to individual needs and abilities, Residential support through trained residence assistants, Single-room option for an additional fee that supports the opportunity to decompress and regulate (based on availability), Early move-in date that allows for a calmer transition from the home to residence hall life, Regular daily-living skill trainings to ensure that students adequately adjust to

ADMISSIONS INFO FOR STUDENTS WITH LEARNING DIFFERENCES

SAT/ACT required: Yes
Interview required: Yes
Essay required: Not Applicable
Additional application required: No
Documentation required for:
  LD: Diagnosis, functional limitations, how it impacts student in educational setting.
  ADHD: Diagnosis from a licensed practitioner stating diagnosis and how it affects the student with recommendation.
  ASD: same as above
Documentation submitted to: Support Program/Services
Special Ed. HS course work accepted: Not Applicable
Separate application required for Programs/Services: Yes
Contact Information
Name of program or department: Student Disability Services
Telephone: 217-581-6583
Fax: 217-581-7208
Email: jwalters@eiu.edu

daily-living skill trainings to ensure that students adequately adjust to adulthood, and Option for parental involvement to allow for optimum teamwork between the individual, campus supports, and the family. There is a fee of $3,000 per semester.

GENERAL ADMISSIONS

Very important factors considered include: rigor of secondary school record, academic GPA, standardized test scores. *Other factors considered include:* class rank, application essay, recommendation(s), talent/ability, character/personal qualities. *Freshman Admission Requirements:* High school diploma is required and GED is accepted. *Academic units required:* 4 English, 3 math, 3 science, 3 science labs, 3 social studies, 2 academic electives. *Academic units recommended:* 2 foreign language.

ACCOMMODATIONS OR SERVICES

Accommodations are decided upon an individual basis after a thorough review of appropriate, current documentation. The accommodations requests must be supported through the documentation provided and must be logically linked to the current impact of the condition on academic functioning.

FINANCIAL AID

Students should submit: FAFSA. Applicants will be notified of awards on a rolling basis beginning 3/1. The Princeton Review suggests that all financial aid forms be submitted as soon as possible after October 1. *Need-based scholarships/grants offered:* College/university scholarship or grant aid from institutional funds; Federal Pell; Private scholarships; SEOG; State scholarships/grants. *Loan aid offered:* Direct PLUS loans; Direct Subsidized Stafford Loans; Direct Unsubsidized Stafford Loans. Federal Work-Study Program available. Institutional employment available.

CAMPUS LIFE

Activities: Campus Ministries; Choral groups; Concert band; Dance; Drama/theater; International Student Organization; Jazz band; Literary magazine; Marching band; Music ensembles; Musical theater; Pep band; Radio station; Student government; Student newspaper; Student-run film society; Symphony orchestra; Television station; Yearbook. **Organizations:** 232 registered organizations, 19 honor societies, 16 religious organizations. 15 fraternities, 11 sororities. **Athletics (Intercollegiate):** *Men:* baseball, basketball, cross-country, football, golf, soccer, swimming, tennis, track/field (outdoor), track/field (indoor). *Women:* basketball, cross-country, golf, rugby, soccer, softball, swimming, tennis, track/field (outdoor), track/field (indoor), volleyball. **On-Campus Highlights:** Doudna Fine Arts Center, Old Main, Martin Luther King Jr. University Union, Booth Library, Student Recreation Center.

ACCOMMODATIONS

Allowed in exams:	
Calculators	Yes
Dictionary	Yes
Computer	Yes
Spell-checker	Yes
Extended test time	Yes
Scribe	No
Proctors	Yes
Oral exams	Yes
Note-takers	Yes
Support services for students with	
LD	Yes
ADHD	Yes
ASD	Yes
Distraction-reduced environment	Yes
Recording of lecture allowed	Yes
Reading technology:	Yes
Audio books	Yes
Other assistive technology	Inspiration,
Kuzweil, Read and Write Gold	Yes
Priority registration	Yes
Added costs for services:	Yes, for STEP
For LD:	No
For ADHD:	No
For ASD:	No
LD specialists	Yes
ADHD & ASD coaching	Yes
ASD specialists	Yes
Professional tutors	Yes
Peer tutors	Yes
Max. hours/week for services	Varies
How professors are notified of student approved accommodations	Student

COLLEGE GRADUATION REQUIREMENTS

Course waivers allowed	No
Course substitutions allowed	No

Illinois State University

ADMISSIONS, NORMAL, IL 61790-2200 • ADMISSIONS: 309-438-2181 • FAX: 309-438-3932

CAMPUS

Type of school	Public
Environment	City
Support	CS

STUDENTS

Undergrad enrollment	18,571
% male/female	45/55
% from out of state	2
% FROSH LIVE ON CAMPUS	**98**

FINANCIAL FACTS

Annual in-state tuition	$11,108
Annual out-of-state tuition	$22,215
Room and board	$9,948
Required fees	$2,953

GENERAL ADMISSIONS INFO

Application fee	$50.
Priority deadline	11/15
Regular application deadline	4/1

Nonfall registration accepted.
  Admission may be deferred for a maximum
  of 2 semesters.

Range SAT EBRW	NR
Range SAT Math	NR
Range ACT Composite	21–26

ACADEMICS

Student/faculty ratio	18:1
% students returning for sophomore year	81

Most classes have 10–19 students.
Most lab/discussion sessions have 10–19
students.

PROGRAMS/SERVICES FOR STUDENTS WITH LEARNING DIFFERENCES

Illinois State University is dedicated to the principles of equal opportunity in education and accepts diversity as an affirmation of individual identity within a welcoming community. Student Access and Accommodation Services (SAAS) embraces the richness and value that disability brings to our campus community as it strengthens our learning, attitudes, and respect for each other. SAAS accomplished this through: 1. Individual accommodation(s) to facilitate and support an accessible educational environment through inclusion of students with disabilities by removing or reducing barriers in the university setting. 2. Collaborative partnerships with students, faculty, staff, members of the campus community, and university stakeholders to make Illinois State University accessible to everyone.

ADMISSIONS

Middle 50% ranges for 2018. The middle 50% ranges for admitted students are GPA: 3.07–3.83 on a 4.0 scale, SAT: 1020–1200, or ACT: 21–26. For students whose applications require further review, an optional academic personal statement may help Admissions come to the right decision. If a student chooses to submit a statement, it will be considered along with the transcript and test score information to determine eligibility for admission. If a student chooses to submit a statement, it should be approximately 500 words and address the following: State why you feel Illinois State University is a good fit for your educational goals; Identify and explain your academic strengths and weaknesses; Explain any circumstances which affected your high school academic performance, if applicable. It may be in the student's best interest to complete the optional statement if the student falls below or in the lower end of one or all of the middle 50 percent ranges for admitted students.

Additional Information

The following are options for accommodations based on appropriate documentation and needs: notetaker; readers; e-text; scribes; computer; testing accommodations; conference with LD/ADHD specialist; and quiet study rooms. Skills courses are offered to all.

ADMISSIONS INFO FOR STUDENTS WITH LEARNING DIFFERENCES

SAT/ACT required: Yes
Interview required: No
Essay required: Not Applicable
Additional application required: No
Documentation required for:
 LD: Psycho ed evaluation
 ADHD: Psycho ed evaluation
 ASD: Psycho ed evaluation
Documentation submitted to: SASS
Special Ed. HS course work accepted: Yes
Separate application required for Programs/Services: No
Contact Information
Name of program or department: Student Access and Accommodation Services
Telephone: 309-438-5853
Fax: 309-438-7713
Email: ableisu@ilstu.edu

Illinois State University

General Admissions

Very important factors considered include: academic GPA, standardized test scores. *Other factors considered include:* rigor of secondary school record, application essay, talent/ability. *Freshman Admission Requirements:* High school diploma is required and GED is accepted. *Academic units required:* 4 English, 3 math, 2 science, 2 science labs, 2 foreign language, 2 social studies, 2 academic electives.

Accommodations or Services

Accommodations are decided upon an individual basis after a thorough review of appropriate, current documentation. The accommodations requests must be supported through the documentation provided and must be logically linked to the current impact of the condition on academic functioning.

Financial Aid

Students should submit: FAFSA. Applicants will be notified of awards on a rolling basis beginning 4/1. The Princeton Review suggests that all financial aid forms be submitted as soon as possible after October 1. *Need-based scholarships/grants offered:* College/university scholarship or grant aid from institutional funds; Federal Nursing Scholarships; Federal Pell; Private scholarships; SEOG; State scholarships/grants. *Loan aid offered:* Direct PLUS loans; Direct Subsidized Stafford Loans; Direct Unsubsidized Stafford Loans. Federal Work-Study Program available. Institutional employment available.

Campus Life

Activities: Campus Ministries; Choral groups; Concert band; Dance; Drama/theater; International Student Organization; Jazz band; Literary magazine; Marching band; Model UN; Music ensembles; Musical theater; Opera; Pep band; Radio station; Student government; Student newspaper; Student-run film society; Symphony orchestra; Television station. **Organizations:** 270 registered organizations, 23 honor societies, 22 religious organizations. 21 fraternities, 17 sororities. **Athletics (Intercollegiate):** *Men:* baseball, basketball, cheerleading, cross-country, football, golf, tennis, track/field (outdoor), track/field (indoor). *Women:* basketball, cheerleading, cross-country, diving, golf, gymnastics, soccer, softball, swimming, tennis, track/field (outdoor), track/field (indoor), volleyball. **On-Campus Highlights:** Student Fitness Center, Hancock Stadium, Bone Student Center, Redbird Arena, State Farm Hall of Business.

ACCOMMODATIONS

Allowed in exams:

Calculators	Yes
Dictionary	No
Computer	Yes
Spell-checker	Yes
Extended test time	Yes
Scribe	Yes
Proctors	Yes
Oral exams	Yes
Note-takers	Yes

Support services for students with

LD	Yes
ADHD	Yes
ASD	Yes
Distraction-reduced environment	Yes
Recording of lecture allowed	Yes
Reading technology:	Yes
Audio books	Yes

Other assistive technology Electronic text is available to students who qualify. Electronic text is used in place of books on tape.

Priority registration	Yes

Added costs for services:

For LD:	No
For ADHD:	No
For ASD:	No
LD specialists	Yes
ADHD & ASD coaching	No
ASD specialists	No
Professional tutors	Yes
Peer tutors	Not Applicable
Max. hours/week for services	Varies

How professors are notified of student approved accommodations   Student

COLLEGE GRADUATION REQUIREMENTS

Course waivers allowed	No
Course substitutions allowed	Yes

In what courses
Determined on an individual basis.

Loyola University of Chicago

1032 W. Sheridan Rd., Chicago, IL 60611 • Admissions: 312-915-6500 • Fax: 312-915-7216

CAMPUS
Type of school	Private (nonprofit)
Environment	Metropolis
Support	CS

STUDENTS
Undergrad enrollment	11,193
% male/female	34/66
% from out of state	35
% frosh live on campus	84

FINANCIAL FACTS
Annual tuition	$42,720
Room and board	$14,480
Required fees	$1,358

GENERAL ADMISSIONS INFO
Priority deadline	12/1

Nonfall registration accepted.

Range SAT EBRW	570–660
Range SAT Math	550–650
Range ACT Composite	24–29

ACADEMICS
Student/faculty ratio	14:1
% students returning for sophomore year	83
% students graduating within 4 years	69
% students graduating within 6 years	77

PROGRAMS/SERVICES FOR STUDENTS WITH LEARNING DIFFERENCES
Any student with a documented disability is encouraged to register with the services for Students with Disabilities office (SSWD). Students are required to provide Documentation from a medical provider, therapist, psychiatrist, etc. that clearly states their diagnosis. Additional information about symptoms and how their diagnosis impacts their college career is encouraged; supplemental documentation (IEP, 504 plans, documents from previous universities, etc.) are all accepted forms of supplemental documentation after an intake appointment to determine accommodations, students are registered with our office and work 1:1 as needed with a case manager.

ADMISSIONS
There is no separate application process for students with learning disabilities. All applicants must meet the same admission criteria. The average GPA is 3.6 and the mid 50% SAT is 1110-1320 or ACT 24-29.

Additional Information
Students are encouraged to meet with a staff member in the Services for Students with Disabilities office early on to determine accommodations and services for the upcoming semester. Documentation should provide a clear description of the recommended accommodations, connect these to the impact of the condition, provide possible alternatives to the recommended accommodations, and include a statement regarding the level of need for accommodations.

ADMISSIONS INFO FOR STUDENTS WITH LEARNING DIFFERENCES
SAT/ACT required: Y/N depends if Test Optional
Interview required: No
Essay required: Not Applicable
Additional application required: Yes
Documentation required for:
  LD: Psycho ed evaluation
  ADHD: Psycho ed evaluation
  ASD: Psycho ed evaluation
Documentation submitted to: SSWD
Special Ed. HS course work accepted: Yes
Separate application required for Programs/Services: Not for LD, ADHD, or ASD.
Contact Information
Name of program or department: Services for Students with Disabilities
Telephone: 773-508-3700
Fax: 773-508-3810
Email: ssw@luc.edu

Loyola University of Chicago

GENERAL ADMISSIONS

Very important factors considered include: rigor of secondary school record, academic GPA, standardized test scores. *Important factors considered include:* application essay, recommendation(s), extracurricular activities, character/personal qualities, volunteer work. level of applicant's interest. *Other factors considered include:* class rank, interview, talent/ability, first generation, alumni/ae relation, geographical residence, state residency, work experience. *Freshman Admission Requirements:* High school diploma is required and GED is accepted. *Academic units required:* 4 English, 3 math, 3 science, 2 foreign language, 2 social studies, 1 history. *Academic units recommended:* 4 English, 4 math, 3 science, 2 foreign language, 2 social studies, 2 history, 3 academic electives.

ACCOMMODATIONS OR SERVICES

Accommodations are decided upon an individual basis after a thorough review of appropriate, current documentation. The accommodations requests must be supported through the documentation provided and must be logically linked to the current impact of the condition on academic functioning.

FINANCIAL AID

Students should submit: FAFSA. Applicants will be notified of awards on a rolling basis beginning 2/15. The Princeton Review suggests that all financial aid forms be submitted as soon as possible after October 1. *Need-based scholarships/grants offered:* College/university scholarship or grant aid from institutional funds; Federal Pell; Private scholarships; SEOG; State scholarships/grants. *Loan aid offered:* Direct PLUS loans; Direct Subsidized Stafford Loans; Direct Unsubsidized Stafford Loans Institutional employment available.

CAMPUS LIFE

Activities: Campus Ministries; Choral groups; Concert band; Dance; Drama/theater; International Student Organization; Jazz band; Literary magazine; Model UN; Music ensembles; Musical theater; Pep band; Radio station; Student government; Student newspaper; Student-run film society; Television station. **Organizations:** 185 registered organizations, 11 honor societies, 9 religious organizations. 6 fraternities, 9 sororities. **Athletics (Intercollegiate):** *Men:* basketball, cheerleading, cross-country, golf, soccer, track/field (outdoor), track/field (indoor), volleyball. *Women:* basketball, cheerleading, cross-country, golf, soccer, softball, track/field (outdoor), track/field (indoor), volleyball. **On-Campus Highlights:** Damen Student center, Klarchek Information Commons, Institute of Environmental Sustainability, Halas Recreation Center, Madonna della Strada Chapel.

ACCOMMODATIONS

Allowed in exams:

Calculators	Yes
Dictionary	No
Computer	Yes
Spell-checker	Yes
Extended test time	Yes
Scribe	Yes
Proctors	Yes
Oral exams	Yes
Note-takers	Yes

Support services for students with

LD	Yes
ADHD	Yes
ASD	Yes
Distraction-reduced environment	Yes
Recording of lecture allowed	Yes
Reading technology:	Yes
Audio books	Yes
Other assistive technology	Kurzweil; JAWS, Dragon Dictation
Priority registration	Yes

Added costs for services:

For LD:	No
For ADHD:	No
For ASD:	No
LD specialists	Yes
ADHD & ASD coaching	Yes
ASD specialists	Yes
Professional tutors	Yes
Peer tutors	Yes
Max. hours/week for services	Varies
How professors are notified of student approved accommodations	Student

COLLEGE GRADUATION REQUIREMENTS

Course waivers allowed	No
In what courses	

They can receive substitutions (foreign language requirement substituted with foreign literature courses), but they cannot be exempted entirely

Course substitutions allowed	Yes
In what courses	

Foreign language; math; course substitutions are considered on an individual basis

Northern Illinois University

1425 W. Lincoln Hwy. DeKalb, IL 60115-2828 • Admissions: 815-753-0446:

CAMPUS

Type of school	Public
Environment	Village
Support	CS

STUDENTS

Undergrad enrollment	14,036
% male/female	51/49
% from out of state	3
% frosh live on campus	91

FINANCIAL FACTS

Room and board	$9,670
Required fees	$2,758

GENERAL ADMISSIONS INFO

Application fee	$40
Priority deadline	3/1
Regular application deadline	8/1
Nonfall registration accepted.	
Range ACT Composite	19–25

ACADEMICS

Student/faculty ratio	15:1
% students returning for sophomore year	73
% students graduating within 4 years	21
% students graduating withing 6 years	45

Most classes have 20–29 students. Most lab/discussion sessions have 10–19 students.

PROGRAMS/SERVICES FOR STUDENTS WITH LEARNING DIFFERENCES

The Disability Resource Center (DRC) offers guidance, services and resources to help you succeed at NIU. We will work with you to determine your needs and develop a plan to meet them. Come prepared to discuss issues related to accessibility that may impact your success at NIU. Our office works to provide reasonable and appropriate accommodations for students and the campus community. Exam accommodations, classroom accommodations, reformatting of course materials and adaptive technology are a few of the accommodations we offer. Promoting self-advocacy and communication skills, we focus on helping students create collaborative relationships with faculty and staff. Faculty are integral to supporting students who are eligible for accommodations in the classroom. We work with faculty and department staff so accommodations are understood and implemented for student access and success.

ADMISSIONS

NIU's DRC does not have a program, therefore there is not a separate admissions process. All new students seeking access/ accommodations participate in an initial interview then develop an Accommodation Plan. General admission requires 4 years English, 2 years math, 2 years science, and 2 years social studies. The Chance Program is only available to Illinois residents from targeted schools or who participate in certain academic preparatory programs. The ACT or SAT is required for admission but the Writing Section is not required.

ADMISSIONS INFO FOR STUDENTS WITH LEARNING DIFFERENCES

SAT/ACT required: Y/N depends if Test Optional
Interview required: No
Essay required: Not Applicable
Additional application required: No
Documentation required for:
  LD: Letter from medical or counseling professional and/or I.E.P. from High School; and/or documentation from previous institution.
  ADHD: Letter from medical or counseling professional and/or I.E.P. from High School; and/or documentation from previous institution.
  ASD: Letter from medical or counseling professional and/or I.E.P. from High School; and/or documentation from previous institution.
Documentation submitted to: DRC
Special Ed. HS course work accepted: No
Separate application required for Programs/Services: No
Contact Information
Name of program or department: Disability Resource Center
Telephone: 815- 753-1303
Fax: 815-753-9570
Email: drc@niu.edu

Northern Illinois University

Additional Information

A student's Letter of Accommodation has a list of all approved accommodations, though some may require additional dialogue with faculty, i.e. providing support in situations that include clinical, field, or internship experiences. Accommodations are individualized for students and sometimes for specific courses. The guiding mission of the CHANCE Program is to identify, recruit, admit, and assist otherwise capable students whose pre-college education has not fully enabled them to take maximum advantage of their potential and the opportunities of higher education at NIU. CHANCE services include: individual and group academic, personal and career counseling, academic monitoring and follow-up throughout the student's undergraduate career, tutorial assistance for courses, academic skills-enhancement courses, introductory university transition skills-building course taught by a counselor and peer mentoring for freshmen and transfer students.

GENERAL ADMISSIONS

Very important factors considered include: rigor of secondary school record, class rank, standardized test scores. *Other factors considered include:* application essay, recommendation(s), interview, extracurricular activities, talent/ability, racial/ethnic status. *Freshman Admission Requirements:* High school diploma is required and GED is accepted. *Academic units required:* 4 English, 2 math, 2 science, 1 science lab, 1 foreign language, 2 social studies, 1 history. *Academic units recommended:* 4 math, 4 science, 2 science labs, 2 foreign language, 3 social studies.

ACCOMMODATIONS OR SERVICES

Accommodations are decided upon an individual basis after a thorough review of appropriate, current documentation. The accommodations requests must be supported through the documentation provided and must be logically linked to the current impact of the condition on academic functioning.

FINANCIAL AID

Students should submit: FAFSA; Institution's own financial aid form; Noncustodial PROFILE. Applicants will be notified of awards on a rolling basis beginning 3/1. The Princeton Review suggests that all financial aid forms be submitted as soon as possible after October 1. *Need-based scholarships/grants offered:* College/university scholarship or grant aid from institutional funds; Federal Nursing Scholarships; Federal Pell; Private scholarships; SEOG; State scholarships/grants. *Loan aid offered:* Federal Work-Study Program available. Institutional employment available.

CAMPUS LIFE

Activities: Campus Ministries; Choral groups; Concert band; Dance; Drama/theater; International Student Organization; Jazz band; Marching band; Model UN; Music ensembles; Musical theater; Opera; Pep band; Radio station; Student government; Student newspaper; Student-run film society; Symphony orchestra; Television station. **Organizations:** 200 registered organizations, 13 religious organizations. 22 fraternities, 14 sororities. **Athletics (Intercollegiate):** *Men:* baseball, basketball, diving, football, golf, soccer, swimming, tennis, wrestling. *Women:* basketball, cross-country, golf, gymnastics, soccer, softball, swimming, tennis, volleyball. **On-Campus Highlights:** Barsema Hall, Convocation Center, Holmes Student Center, Campus Life Building, Recreation Center.

ACCOMMODATIONS

Allowed in exams:	
Calculators	Yes
Dictionary	Yes
Computer	Yes
Spell-checker	Yes
Extended test time	Yes
Scribe	Yes
Proctors	Yes
Oral exams	Yes
Note-takers	Yes
Support services for students with	
LD	Yes
ADHD	Yes
ASD	Yes
Distraction-reduced environment	Yes
Recording of lecture allowed	Yes
Reading technology:	Yes
Audio books	Yes
Other assistive technology	Yes
Priority registration	Yes
Added costs for services:	
For LD:	No
For ADHD:	No
For ASD:	No
LD specialists	No
ADHD & ASD coaching	Yes
ASD specialists	Yes
Professional tutors	Yes
Peer tutors	Yes
Max. hours/week for services	Varies
How professors are notified of student approved accommodations	Student

COLLEGE GRADUATION REQUIREMENTS

Course waivers allowed	Yes
In what courses	Course substitutions
waiver rarely granted, depends on specific circumstance.	
Course substitutions allowed	Yes

Northwestern University

633 Clark Street, Evanston, IL 60204 • Admissions: 847-491-7271

CAMPUS

Type of school	Private (nonprofit)
Environment	City
Support	CS

STUDENTS

Undergrad enrollment	8,271
% male/female	50/50
% from out of state	68
% frosh live on campus	100

FINANCIAL FACTS

Annual tuition	$50,424
Room and board	$15,489
Required fees	$431

GENERAL ADMISSIONS INFO

Application fee	$75
Regular application deadline	1/1

Nonfall registration accepted. Admission may be deferred for a maximum of 1 year.

Range SAT EBRW	680–760
Range SAT Math	710–800
Range ACT Composite	32–34

ACADEMICS

Student/faculty ratio	6:1
% students returning for sophomore year	98
% students graduating within 4 years	84
% students graduating within 6 years	94

Most classes have 10–19 students. Most lab/discussion sessions have 20–29 students.

PROGRAMS/SERVICES FOR STUDENTS WITH LEARNING DIFFERENCES

AccessibleNU is the campus resource that provides students with LD, ADHD and all other disabilities the tools, reasonable accommodations and support services needed to participate fully in the university Environment. A wide range of services are provided to students with disabilities enrolled in undergraduate, graduate, or professional schools, allowing them full access to programs and activities at Northwestern University. It is the responsibility of the student to provide documentation of disability, to inform the AccessibleNU office and to request accommodations and services if needed. A student who has a disability but has not registered with AccessibleNU is not entitled to services or accommodations.

ADMISSIONS

There is no special admissions procedure for students with learning disabilities or ADHD. All applicants must meet the general admission criteria. Most students have taken AP and honors courses in high school and been very successful in these competitive college-prep courses. ACT/SAT tests are required, and SAT Subject Tests are recommended. Foreign-language substitutions may be allowed and are decided on a case-by-case basis.

Additional Information

Some students who received disability-related services in high school may decide to try taking their Northwestern courses without any accommodations or services. AccessibleNU recommends that those students nonetheless provide documentation of their disability. In this way, the AccessibleNU office can easily serve the student if they later find that accommodations are needed. AccessibleNU maintains confidentiality of information, meaning that records contained in AccessibleNU files are housed only in the AccessibleNU office and are not part of the student's academic file. Support services may include testing accommodations, such as extended time and alternative test environment, note-taking services, materials in e-text and audio format, access to adaptive equipment and software, scribe, study strategy assistance, access to a computer to type exam responses, sign language interpreter, C-Print and assistance in activity relocation.

ADMISSIONS INFO FOR STUDENTS WITH LEARNING DIFFERENCES

SAT/ACT required: Yes
Interview required: No
Essay required: Yes
Additional application required: No
Documentation required for:
 LD: Psycho ed evaluation
 ADHD: Diagnosis based on DSM-V; history of behaviors impairing functioning in academic setting; diagnostic interview; history of symptoms; evidence of ongoing behaviors.
 ASD: Psycho ed evaluation
Documentation submitted to: AccessibleNU
Special Ed. HS course work accepted: No
Separate application required for Programs/Services: No
Contact Information
Name of program or department: AccessibleNU
Telephone: 847-467-5530
Fax: 847-467-5531
Email: accessiblenu@northwestern.edu

Northwestern University

General Admissions

Very important factors considered include: rigor of secondary school record, class rank, academic GPA, standardized test scores. *Important factors considered include:* application essay, recommendation(s), extracurricular activities, talent/ability, character/personal qualities. *Other factors considered include:* interview, first generation, alumni/ae relation, racial/ethnic status, volunteer work, work experience, level of applicant's interest. *Freshman Admission Requirements:* High school diploma is required and GED is accepted. *Academic units recommended:* 4 English, 3 math, 2 science, 2 science labs, 2 foreign language, 2 social studies, 2 history, 1 academic elective.

Accommodations or Services

Accommodations are decided upon an individual basis after a thorough review of appropriate, current documentation. The accommodations requests must be supported through the documentation provided and must be logically linked to the current impact of the condition on academic functioning.

Financial Aid

Students should submit: CSS/Financial Aid PROFILE; FAFSA; Noncustodial PROFILE. Applicants will be notified of awards on or about 4/15. The Princeton Review suggests that all financial aid forms be submitted as soon as possible after October 1. *Need-based scholarships/grants offered:* College/university scholarship or grant aid from institutional funds; Federal Pell; SEOG; State scholarships/grants. *Loan aid offered:* Direct PLUS loans; Direct Subsidized Stafford Loans; Direct Unsubsidized Stafford Loans. Federal Work-Study Program available. Institutional employment available.

Campus Life

Activities: Campus Ministries; Choral groups; Concert band; Dance; Drama/theater; International Student Organization; Jazz band; Literary magazine; Marching band; Model UN; Music ensembles; Musical theater; Opera; Pep band; Radio station; Student government; Student newspaper; Student-run film society; Symphony orchestra; Television station; Yearbook. **Organizations:** 415 registered organizations, 23 honor societies, 29 religious organizations. 17 fraternities, 19 sororities. **Athletics (Intercollegiate):** *Men:* baseball, basketball, cheerleading, diving, football, golf, soccer, swimming, tennis, wrestling. *Women:* basketball, cheerleading, cross-country, diving, fencing, field hockey, golf, lacrosse, soccer, softball, swimming, tennis, volleyball. **On-Campus Highlights:** Shakespeare Garden, Dearborn Observatory, Norris Student Center, Henry Crown Sports Pavilion and Acquatic Center, The lakefill on Lake Michigan.

ACCOMMODATIONS

Allowed in exams:	
Calculators	Yes
Dictionary	Yes
Computer	Yes
Spell-checker	Yes
Extended test time	Yes
Scribe	Yes
Proctors	Yes
Oral exams	Yes
Note-takers	Yes
Support services for students with	
LD	Yes
ADHD	Yes
ASD	Yes
Distraction-reduced environment	Yes
Recording of lecture allowed	Yes
Reading technology:	Yes
Audio books	Yes
Other assistive technology	Yes
Priority registration	Yes
Added costs for services:	
For LD:	No
For ADHD:	No
For ASD:	No
LD specialists	Yes
ADHD & ASD coaching	No
ASD specialists	No
Professional tutors	No
Peer tutors	No
Max. hours/week for services	Usually one hour
How professors are notified of student approved accommodations	Student

COLLEGE GRADUATION REQUIREMENTS

Course waivers allowed	No
Course substitutions allowed	Yes
In what courses	On a case-by-case basis

Roosevelt University

430 SOUTH MICHIGAN AVENUE, CHICAGO, IL 60605 • ADMISSIONS: 877-277-5978 • FAX: 847-619-4216

CAMPUS
Type of school	Private (nonprofit)
Environment	Metropolis
Support	CS

STUDENTS
Undergrad enrollment	2,710
% male/female	36/64
% from out of state	15
% frosh live on campus	71

FINANCIAL FACTS
Annual tuition	$28,963
Room and board	NR
Required fees	NR

GENERAL ADMISSIONS INFO
Application fee	$25
Priority deadline	8/15

Nonfall registration accepted. Admission may be deferred for a maximum of 1 year.

Range SAT EBRW	455–595
Range SAT Math	450–550
Range ACT Composite	19–24

ACADEMICS
Student/faculty ratio	11:1
% students returning for sophomore year	65

Most classes have 20–29 students. Most lab/discussion sessions have 20–29 students.

PROGRAMS/SERVICES FOR STUDENTS WITH LEARNING DIFFERENCES

The Learning and Support Services Program (LSSP) is designed to assist students with learning differences in their pursuit of a college education. Individualized tutoring is provided. A fee is included. Students with Learning Differences, not participating in the LSSP, often utilize Disability Services, under the same office as the LSSP.

ADMISSIONS

Applicants can self report GPA and ACT or SAT. The Writing section is not required. There is no separate admissions process for students with learning disabilities. Though not initially required, a personal statement, essay, letters of recommendation, and/or official transcripts may be requested after initial review of your application.

Additional Information

The Learning and Support Services Program is available to students with learning disabilities, attention disorders, traumatic brain injury, and any other condition that presents learning disorders. Assistance is available in course selection, required course readings, assignments, and more. Depending on individual needs, tutoring assistance may include course-related training, time management, organizational skills, to name a few. Students are highly encouraged to utilize other appropriate resources, such as counseling, career development, campus life and tutoring center. Services and accommodations are available to undergraduate and graduate students.

ADMISSIONS INFO FOR STUDENTS WITH LEARNING DIFFERENCES

SAT/ACT required: Yes
Interview required: Yes
Essay required: Yes
Additional application required: No
Documentation required for:
 LD: Psycho ed evaluation
 ADHD: Diagnosis based on DSM-V; history of behaviors impairing functioning in academic setting; diagnostic interview; history of symptoms; evidence of ongoing behaviors
 ASD: Diagnosis based on DSM-V; history of behaviors impairing functioning in academic setting; diagnostic interview; history of symptoms; evidence of ongoing behaviors.
Documentation submitted to: Academic Success Center
Special Ed. HS course work accepted: Yes
Separate application required for Programs/Services: Yes
Contact Information
Name of program or department: Academic Success Center
Telephone: 312-341-3811
Fax: 312-341-2471
Email: academicsuccess@roosevelt.edu

Roosevelt University

GENERAL ADMISSIONS

Very important factors considered include: academic GPA, standardized test scores. *Other factors considered include:* rigor of secondary school record, class rank, application essay, recommendation(s), interview, extracurricular activities, talent/ability, character/personal qualities, first generation, alumni/ae relation, level of applicant's interest. *Freshman Admission Requirements:* High school diploma is required and GED is accepted. *Academic units required:* 4 English, 3 math, 2 science, 2 science labs, 2 social studies. *Academic units recommended:* 4 English, 4 math, 3 science, 3 science labs, 2 foreign language, 3 social studies, 2 history, 2 academic electives.

ACCOMMODATIONS OR SERVICES

Accommodations are decided upon an individual basis after a thorough review of appropriate, current documentation. The accommodations requests must be supported through the documentation provided and must be logically linked to the current impact of the condition on academic functioning.

FINANCIAL AID

Students should submit: FAFSA; Institution's own financial aid form. Applicants will be notified of awards on a rolling basis beginning 2/1. The Princeton Review suggests that all financial aid forms be submitted as soon as possible after October 1. *Need-based scholarships/grants offered:* College/university scholarship or grant aid from institutional funds; Federal Pell; Private scholarships; SEOG; State scholarships/grants. *Loan aid offered:* Direct PLUS loans; Direct Subsidized Stafford Loans; Direct Unsubsidized Stafford Loans. Federal Work-Study Program available. Institutional employment available.

CAMPUS LIFE

Activities: Choral groups; Concert band; Dance; Drama/theater; International Student Organization; Jazz band; Literary magazine; Music ensembles; Musical theater; Opera; Pep band; Radio station; Student government; Student newspaper; Symphony orchestra. **Organizations:** 48 registered organizations, 3 honor societies, 4 religious organizations. 1 fraternity, 2 sororities. Vertical Campus: 32-story building downtown Chicago, Auditorium Building: national historic landmark, University Center: largest multi-college residence hall in the US, Gage Building: historic classroom building overlooking Millennium Park, Schaumburg Cam.

ACCOMMODATIONS

Allowed in exams:

Calculators	Yes
Dictionary	Not Applicable
Computer	Yes
Spell-checker	Yes
Extended test time	Yes
Scribe	Yes
Proctors	Yes
Oral exams	Not Applicable
Note-takers	Yes

Support services for students with

LD	Yes
ADHD	Yes
ASD	Yes
Distraction-reduced environment	Yes
Recording of lecture allowed	Yes
Reading technology:	Yes
Audio books	Yes
Other assistive technology	enlarged type, visual enhancements, readers
Priority registration	Yes

Added costs for services:

For LD:	No
For ADHD:	No
For ASD:	No
LD specialists	No
ADHD & ASD coaching	Yes
ASD specialists	No
Professional tutors	Yes
Peer tutors	Yes
Max. hours/week for services	No
How professors are notified of student approved accommodations	Student and Director

COLLEGE GRADUATION REQUIREMENTS

Course waivers allowed	No
Course substitutions allowed	No

Southern Illinois University Carbondale

Undergraduate Admissions, Mailcode 4710, Carbondale, IL 62901 • Admissions: 618-536-4405 • Fax: 618-453-4609

CAMPUS

Type of school	Public
Environment	Town
Support	SP

STUDENTS

Undergrad enrollment	10,896
% male/female	54/46
% from out of state	17
% frosh live on campus	91

FINANCIAL FACTS

Annual tuition	$9,638
Room and board	$10,622
Required fees	$4,961

GENERAL ADMISSIONS INFO

Application fee	$40
Regular application deadline	5/1

Nonfall registration accepted.
  Admission may be deferred.

Range SAT EBRW	440–530
Range SAT Math	480–600
Range ACT Composite	20–26

ACADEMICS

Student/faculty ratio	14:1
% students returning for sophomore year	68
% students graduating within 4 years	23
% students graduating within 6 years	40

Most classes have 10–19 students.
Most lab/discussion sessions have 10–19 students.

PROGRAMS/SERVICES FOR STUDENTS WITH LEARNING DIFFERENCES

Southern Illinois University provides students with disabilities equal opportunity and access to seek their educational goals through the Disability Support Services office. In addition, SIU offers the Achieve Program, a comprehensive program of support for students with LD, ADHD, ASD, and other learning differences. Documentation requirements for the Disability Support Services office can be found here: http://disabilityservices.siu.edu/ Documentation and application materials for the Achieve Program can be found here: http://achieve. siu.edu/

ADMISSIONS

SIU freshman admissions criteria: 1. Have graduated from high school before beginning classes at SIU. Exceptions are made for students participating in our High School Concurrent Enrollment program and for those who have earned the G.E.D. 2. Meet high school course pattern requirements. 3. Meet certain criteria based primarily on high school core grade point average, ACT or SAT score and course subject pattern. (The holistic review process also considers ACT or SAT subscores, high school rank, improvements in high school GPA from year to year, letters of recommendation, participation in service or extracurricular activities and extenuating circumstances.)

ADMISSIONS INFO FOR STUDENTS WITH LEARNING DIFFERENCES

SAT/ACT required: Yes
Interview required: Yes
Essay required: Required
Additional application required: Yes
Documentation required for:
  LD: Achieve requires as much comprehensive diagnostic and psychoeducational evaluations and records as can be provided. Achieve wants to see records across the lifespan, if possible. Measures of cognitive ability, academic ability, and social and emotional abilities are highly useful in Achieve's evaluation process. Achieve also wants to see current IEP's, SOP's, and/or 504 plan accommodations.
  ADHD: Achieve requires as much comprehensive diagnostic and psychoeducational evaluations and records as can be provided. Achieve wants to see records across the lifespan, if possible. Measures of cognitive ability, academic ability, and social and emotional abilities are highly useful in Achieve's evaluation process. Achieve also wants to see current IEP's, SOP's, and/or 504 plan accommodations.
  ASD: No specific diagnostic tool, rating scale, or professional statements are required, but clear and specific diagnostic materials which identify the disorder must be present.
Documentation submitted to: Achieve Program
Special Ed. HS course work accepted: Yes
Separate application required for Programs/Services: Yes
Contact Information
Name of program or department: The Achieve Program
Telephone: 618-453-6155
Fax: 618-453-3711
Email: achieve@siu.edu

Southern Illinois University Carbondale

Additional Information
Achieve Program admissions process: Meet criteria for Achieve admission 1) Primary diagnosis of a learning disability, attention deficit disorder, or other learning difference 2) IQ commensurate with college achievement 3) Age appropriate social and emotional maturity Complete Achieve Program application available at achieve.siu.edu. Submit all required documentation and paperwork. The Achieve Program reviews and makes an initial decision about a candidate. If the candidate is a good fit, the candidate is invited to complete a staff interview. At the conclusion of the interview, staff will make a decision about acceptance into the Achieve Program.

GENERAL ADMISSIONS
Very important factors considered include: rigor of secondary school record, class rank, academic GPA, standardized test scores. *Important factors considered include:* talent/ability. *Other factors considered include:* application essay, recommendation(s), interview, extracurricular activities, character/personal qualities, volunteer work, work experience. *Freshman Admission Requirements:* High school diploma is required and GED is accepted. *Academic units required:* 4 English, 3 math, 3 science, 3 science labs, 3 social studies, 2 academic electives. *Academic units recommended:* 4 English, 4 math, 3 science, 3 science labs, 3 social studies, 2 academic electives.

ACCOMMODATIONS OR SERVICES
Accommodations are decided upon an individual basis after a thorough review of appropriate, current documentation. The accommodations requests must be supported through the documentation provided and must be logically linked to the current impact of the condition on academic functioning.

FINANCIAL AID
Students should submit: FAFSA. Applicants will be notified of awards on or about 3/15. The Princeton Review suggests that all financial aid forms be submitted as soon as possible after October 1. *Need-based scholarships/grants offered:* College/university scholarship or grant aid from institutional funds; Federal Pell; Private scholarships; SEOG; State scholarships/grants. *Loan aid offered:* Direct PLUS loans; Direct Subsidized Stafford Loans; Direct Unsubsidized Stafford Loans. Federal Work-Study Program available. Institutional employment available.

CAMPUS LIFE
Activities: Campus Ministries; Choral groups; Concert band; Dance; Drama/theater; International Student Organization; Jazz band; Literary magazine; Marching band; Model UN; Music ensembles; Musical theater; Opera; Pep band; Radio station; Student government; Student newspaper; Student-run film society; Symphony orchestra; Television station. **Organizations:** 408 registered organizations, 26 honor societies, 25 religious organizations. 20 fraternities, 8 sororities. **Athletics (Intercollegiate):** *Men:* baseball, basketball, cheerleading, cross-country, diving, football, golf, swimming, tennis, track/field (outdoor), track/field (indoor). *Women:* basketball, cheerleading, cross-country, diving, golf, softball, swimming, tennis, track/field (outdoor), track/field (indoor), volleyball. **On-Campus Highlights:** Morris Library, Student Center, Recreation Center, Saluki Stadium and SIU Arena, Campus Lake.

ACCOMMODATIONS
Allowed in exams:

Calculators	Yes
Dictionary	Yes
Computer	Yes
Spell-checker	Yes
Extended test time	Yes
Scribe	Yes
Proctors	Yes
Oral exams	Yes
Note-takers	Yes

Support services for students with

LD	Yes
ADHD	Yes
ASD	Yes
Distraction-reduced environment	Yes
Recording of lecture allowed	Yes
Reading technology:	Yes
Audio books	Yes

Other assistive technology   A wide array of different technologies are available to all students on campus, and many specialized pieces of hardware and software are available to students with disabilities.

Priority registration	Yes

Added costs for services:

For LD:	Yes, in Achieve Program
For ADHD:	Yes, in Achieve Program
For ASD:	Yes, in Achieve Program
LD specialists	Yes
ADHD & ASD coaching	Yes
ASD specialists	Yes
Professional tutors	Yes
Peer tutors	Yes

Max. hours/week for services
How professors are notified of
  student approved accommodations
Director and Student

COLLEGE GRADUATION REQUIREMENTS

Course waivers allowed	Yes

 In what courses
 There is a process through which some waivers can be granted. The University offers many options for students to meet curriculum demands without a waiver.

Course substitutions allowed	Yes

 In what courses
 The University offers many options for students to substitute courses to meet their graduation requirements.

Southern Illinois University—Edwardsville

Box 1027, Edwardsville, IL 62026-1047 • Admissions: 618-650-3705 • Fax: 618-650-5013

CAMPUS

Type of school	Public
Environment	Town
Support	CS

STUDENTS

Undergrad enrollment	11,339
% male/female	47/53
% from out of state	12
% frosh live on campus	72

FINANCIAL FACTS

Annual in-state tuition	$8,770
Annual out-of-state tuition	$21,930
Room and board	$9,481
Required fees	$2,721

GENERAL ADMISSIONS INFO

Application fee	$40
Priority deadline	12/1

Regular application deadline   7/19. Nonfall registration accepted. Admission may be deferred.

Range SAT EBRW	485–625
Range SAT Math	495–600
Range ACT Composite	20–26

ACADEMICS

Student/faculty ratio	20:1
% students returning for sophomore year	73
% students graduating within 4 years	27
% students graduating within 6 years	48

Most classes have fewer than 10 students. Most lab/discussion sessions have 20–29 students.

PROGRAMS/SERVICES FOR STUDENTS WITH LEARNING DIFFERENCES

Disability Support Services provides reasonable accommodations to ensure that students with disabilities have access to the University and its programs through intentional interventions, programs, and services in order to meet federal guidelines, encourage personal growth, and increase effective communication.

ADMISSIONS

Students with learning disabilities are required to submit the same general application form as all other students. Students should submit documentation of their learning disability in order to receive services once enrolled. This documentation should be sent to DSS. Regular admissions criteria recommended: 4 years of English, 3 years of math, 3 years of science, 3 years of social science, 2 years of a foreign language or electives (students with deficiencies need to check with the Office of Admissions); grade point average of 2.5/4.0 and an ACT minimum of 18 (the average is 22.4) or SAT of 860-890. Students not meeting this criteria are encouraged to apply and may be subject to additional review; Students denied admission may appeal the decision.

Additional Information

The Learning Support Service is available to help students with disabilities improve their time management skills and develop effective study strategies. Current resources include advocacy, priority registration, books in alternate format,extended time testing (double time), assistance in writing/ready exams, and volunteer note takers. In addition, the DSSstaff members act as liaisons with faculty and staff regarding learning disabilities and accommodations needed by students. Services and accommodations are available for undergraduate and graduate students.

ADMISSIONS INFO FOR STUDENTS WITH LEARNING DIFFERENCES

SAT/ACT required: Yes
Interview required: No
Essay required: Not Applicable
Additional application required: Yes
Documentation required for:
  LD: Adult intelligence and achievement testing
  ADHD: Specialist in the field must submit a completed outline of documentation to establish disability
  ASD: Psycho ed evaluation
Documentation submitted to: Disability Support
Special Ed. HS course work accepted: No
Separate application required for Programs/Services: No
Contact Information
Name of program or department: Disability Support Services
Telephone: 618-650-3726
Fax: 618-650-5691
Email: DisabilitySupport@siue.edu

Southern Illinois University—Edwardsville

General Admissions

Very important factors considered include: academic GPA, standardized test scores. *Important factors considered include:* rigor of secondary school record, class rank. *Freshman Admission Requirements:* High school diploma is required and GED is accepted. *Academic units required:* 4 English, 3 math, 3 science, 3 science labs, 3 social studies, 2 academic electives. *Academic units recommended:* 2 foreign language.

Accommodations or Services

Accommodations are decided upon an individual basis after a thorough review of appropriate, current documentation. The accommodations requests must be supported through the documentation provided and must be logically linked to the current impact of the condition on academic functioning.

Financial Aid

Students should submit: FAFSA. Applicants will be notified of awards on a rolling basis beginning 12/15. The Princeton Review suggests that all financial aid forms be submitted as soon as possible after October 1. *Need-based scholarships/grants offered:* College/university scholarship or grant aid from institutional funds; Federal Nursing Scholarships; Federal Pell; Private scholarships; SEOG; State scholarships/grants. *Loan aid offered:* Direct PLUS loans; Direct Subsidized Stafford Loans; Direct Unsubsidized Stafford Loans. Federal Work-Study Program available. Institutional employment available.

Campus Life

Activities: Campus Ministries; Choral groups; Concert band; Dance; Drama/theater; International Student Organization; Jazz band; Literary magazine; Music ensembles; Musical theater; Opera; Pep band; Radio station; Student government; Student newspaper; Symphony orchestra. **Organizations:** 140 registered organizations, 15 honor societies, 9 religious organizations. 10 fraternities, 7 sororities. **Athletics (Intercollegiate):** *Men:* baseball, basketball, cross-country, golf, soccer, tennis, track/field (outdoor), track/field (indoor), wrestling. *Women:* basketball, cross-country, golf, soccer, softball, tennis, track/field (outdoor), track/field (indoor), volleyball. **On-Campus Highlights:** Morris University Center, Student Success Center, Starbucks/Kaldis Coffee, Residence Halls, Vadalebene Center - Student Fitness Center.

ACCOMMODATIONS

Allowed in exams:

Calculators	Yes
Dictionary	Yes
Computer	Yes
Spell-checker	No
Extended test time	Yes
Scribe	Yes
Proctors	Yes
Oral exams	Yes
Note-takers	Yes

Support services for students with

LD	Yes
ADHD	Yes
ASD	Yes
Distraction-reduced environment	Yes
Recording of lecture allowed	Yes
Reading technology:	Yes
Audio books	Yes

Other assistive technology Dragon Naturally Speaking, Jaws, Open Book Unbound, Text-a-loud, Kurzweil 3000

Priority registration	Yes

Added costs for services:

For LD:	No
For ADHD:	No
For ASD:	No
LD specialists	Yes
ADHD & ASD coaching	No
ASD specialists	Yes
Professional tutors	No
Peer tutors	No
Max. hours/week for services	Varies

How professors are notified of student approved accommodations   Student

COLLEGE GRADUATION REQUIREMENTS

Course waivers allowed	No
Course substitutions allowed	Yes
In what courses	Math, Foreign Language

University of Illinois Springfield

ONE UNIVERSITY PLAZA, SPRINGFIELD, IL 62703-5407 • ADMISSIONS: 217-206-4847 • FAX: 217-206-6620

CAMPUS
Type of school	Public
Environment	City
Support	S

STUDENTS
Undergrad enrollment	2,833
% male/female	51/49
% from out of state	14
% frosh live on campus	87

FINANCIAL FACTS
Annual in-state tuition	$9,405
Annual out-of-state tuition	$18,930
Room and board	$11,660
Required fees	$2,008

GENERAL ADMISSIONS INFO
Application fee	$50

Nonfall registration accepted. Admission may be deferred for a maximum of 1 term.

Range SAT EBRW	NR
Range SAT Math	NR
Range ACT Composite	20–27

ACADEMICS
Student/faculty ratio	13:1
% students returning for sophomore year	78
% students graduating within 4 years	36
% students graduating within 6 years	50

Most classes have fewer than 10 students. Most lab/discussion sessions have 10–19 students.

PROGRAMS/SERVICES FOR STUDENTS WITH LEARNING DIFFERENCES
The Office of Disability Sevices is the central services that provides students with accomodations. The Center for Acdemic Success is designed to be a one-stop academic support place for students. The Learning Hub under the Center offers free academic support services. Through a peer tutoring program they offer one-to-one appointments. in writing, math, accounting,economics,science and academic skills.

ADMISSIONS
In addition to the transcript and ACT or SAT (Writing section not required) applicants submit the personal and academic statement which are viewed as an applicant's opportunity to speak on his or her own behalf. The statement should address any circumstances (positive or negative) that may have affected the applicant's high school experience and that are not readily apparent from academic records or standardized test scores. The middle 50% SAT is 950-1220 or ACT 20-26 and the average GPA is 3.44. Admissions is based on core courses, GPA and test scores. Students also submit a personal and academic statement which is viewed as an applicant's opportunity to speak on his or her own behalf. The statementshould address any circumstances (positive or negative) that may have affected the applicant's high school experience and that are not readily apparent from academic records or standardized test scores. Students wishing to appeal their admission decision must submit a letter of appeal to the attention of the Director of Admissions, chair of the Appeals Committee, detailing the reason they believe the decision should be overturned and providing any supporting documents. The Appeals Committee will determine by vote whether or not to overturn the admissions decision. Students whose previous denial decision is overturned upon appeal may be subject to conditions placed upon their admission to UIS.

Additional Information
The Learning Hub is part of the Center for Academic Success. The writing resources provide academic assistance for the writing of effective essays and research papers and serve students at every level through one-to-one tutoring, workshops, and requested presentations where students learn together outside of formal classes. They will not simply proofread a paper for grammatical or citation mistakes. Rather, tutors will walk students through primary concerns such as argument, logic, organization, clarity,

ADMISSIONS INFO FOR STUDENTS WITH LEARNING DIFFERENCES
SAT/ACT required: Not Applicable
Interview required: No
Essay required: Not Applicable
Additional application required: No
Documentation required for:
 LD: Psycho ed evaluation
 ADHD: Psycho ed evaluation
 ASD: Psycho ed evaluation
Documentation submitted to: Center for Academic Success
Special Ed. HS course work accepted: Not Applicable
Contact Information
Name of program or department: The Office of Disability Services (ODS)
Telephone: 217-206-6666
Fax: 217-206-7154
Email: sweav3@uis.edu

University of Illinois Springfield

and flow, before then working on secondary concerns including grammar and mechanics. Services are free but students are limited in the number of hours per week they can ask for tutoring in specific courses. There are 30 state of the art testing stations available to proctor make-up exams, exam re-takes, online student exams and certification exams.

GENERAL ADMISSIONS

Very important factors considered include: academic GPA, standardized test scores. *Important factors considered include:* rigor of secondary school record, class rank. *Other factors considered include:* application essay, recommendation(s). *Freshman Admission Requirements:* High school diploma is required and GED is accepted. *Academic units required:* 4 English, 3 math, 3 science, 2 science labs, 2 foreign language, 3 social studies.

ACCOMMODATIONS OR SERVICES

Accommodations are decided upon an individual basis after a thorough review of appropriate, current documentation. The accommodations requests must be supported through the documentation provided and must be logically linked to the current impact of the condition on academic functioning.

FINANCIAL AID

Students should submit: FAFSA. Applicants will be notified of awards on a rolling basis beginning 1/1. The Princeton Review suggests that all financial aid forms be submitted as soon as possible after October 1. *Need-based scholarships/grants offered:* College/university scholarship or grant aid from institutional funds; Federal Pell; Private scholarships; SEOG; State scholarships/grants. *Loan aid offered:* Direct PLUS loans; Direct Subsidized Stafford Loans; Direct Unsubsidized Stafford Loans. Federal Work-Study Program available. Institutional employment available.

CAMPUS LIFE

Activities: Campus Ministries; Choral groups; Concert band; Dance; Drama/theater; International Student Organization; Jazz band; Model UN; Music ensembles; Pep band; Radio station; Student government; Student newspaper; Student-run film society. **Organizations:** 76 registered organizations, **Athletics (Intercollegiate):** *Men:* basketball, golf, soccer, tennis. *Women:* basketball, cheerleading, golf, soccer, softball, tennis, volleyball. **On-Campus Highlights:** Student Union, University Hall, Recreation and Athletic Center, Public Affairs Center.

ACCOMMODATIONS

Allowed in exams:	
Calculators	Yes
Dictionary	Yes
Computer	Yes
Spell-checker	Yes
Extended test time	Yes
Scribe	Yes
Proctors	Yes
Oral exams	Yes
Note-takers	Yes
Support services for students with	
LD	Yes
ADHD	Yes
ASD	Yes
Distraction-reduced environment	Yes
Recording of lecture allowed	Yes
Reading technology:	Yes
Audio books	Yes
Other assistive technology	JAWS Zoomtest
Priority registration	Yes
Added costs for services:	
For LD:	No
For ADHD:	No
For ASD:	No
LD specialists	Yes
ADHD & ASD coaching	No
ASD specialists	Yes
Professional tutors	Not Applicable
Peer tutors	Not Applicable
Max. hours/week for services	Varies
How professors are notified of student approved accommodations	Student

COLLEGE GRADUATION REQUIREMENTS

Course waivers allowed	Yes
In what courses	
Math and foreign language. Depends upon individual circumstances	
Course substitutions allowed	Yes
In what courses	
Math and foreign language. Depends upon individual circumstances	

University of Illinois at Urbana-Champaign

601 E. JOHN ST., CHAMPAIGN, IL 61801-3028 • ADMISSIONS: 217-333-0302 • FAX: 217-244-4614

CAMPUS

Type of school	Public
Environment	City
Support	CS

STUDENTS

Undergrad enrollment	32,752
% male/female	55/45
% from out of state	14
% frosh live on campus	99

FINANCIAL FACTS

Annual in-state tuition	$12,036
Annual out-of-state tuition	$28,156
Room and board	$11,308
Required fees	$3,832

GENERAL ADMISSIONS INFO

Application fee	$50
Priority deadline	11/1
Regular application deadline	12/1

Nonfall registration accepted. Admission may be deferred for a maximum of 1 year.

Range SAT EBRW	580–690
Range SAT Math	700–790
Range ACT Composite	26–32

ACADEMICS

Student/faculty ratio
% students returning for sophomore year 94
Most classes have 10–19 students.
Most lab/discussion sessions have 10–19 students.

PROGRAMS/SERVICES FOR STUDENTS WITH LEARNING DIFFERENCES

While DRES has a longstanding reputation for providing accommodation and an accessible campus for students with visible disabilities, we have also been providing outstanding services to students with non visible disabilitiesr for more than 25 years. This includes: Having a learning disability specialist on staff who works with students on compensatory strategies in test preparation, test taking, reading comprehension, and written expression; and four licensed clinical psychologists and other mental health professionals who are on staff to provide supports and services given the large growth in the number of students with ADHD, acquired brain injury, autism spectrum disorders, and psychiatric disabilities. DRES provides students with academic accommodations and access.

ADMISSIONS

Students self report their GPA and ACT/SAT and the Writing Section is not required. Student select which College they are applying to in the university and the admission criteria will vary by college. Applicants with LD/ADHD are expected to meet the same criteria as all other applicants. However applicants can self-disclose challenges or obstacles faced that may have had an impact on their academic record.

Additional Information

In addition most DRES students contact professors and set up their own accommodations; however, with many of our students with autism, we may email their professors for them, role-play to practice talking to instructors, or meet with the student and their professors to discuss accommodations. DRES will check in with their professors on a regular basis to be proactive about solving problems and serve as consultants with faculty, departments, and housing to provide recommendations for accommodations for unique classroom requirements or problem behaviors. Graduation rate for students on the autism spectrum is 85%, which is consistent with the University of Illinois graduation rate. Most of these students are employed or go on to graduate school.

ADMISSIONS INFO FOR STUDENTS WITH LEARNING DIFFERENCES

SAT/ACT required: Yes
Interview required: Not Applicable
Essay required: Not Applicable
Additional application required: Yes
Documentation required for:
 LD: Psycho ed evaluation
 ADHD: Psycho ed evaluation
 ASD: Psycho ed evaluation
Documentation submitted to: DRES
Special Ed. HS course work accepted: Not Applicable
Separate application required for Programs/Services: No
Contact Information
Name of program or department: Disability Resources and Educational Services (DRES)
Telephone: 217-333-4603
Fax: 217-244-0014
Email: disability@illinois.edu

University of Illinois at Urbana-Champaign

GENERAL ADMISSIONS

Very important factors considered include: rigor of secondary school record, academic GPA. *Important factors considered include:* application essay, standardized test scores, extracurricular activities, talent/ability. *Other factors considered include:* class rank, character/personal qualities, first generation, geographical residence, state residency, racial/ethnic status, volunteer work, work experience. *Freshman Admission Requirements:* High school diploma is required and GED is accepted. *Academic units required:* 4 English, 3 math, 2 science, 2 science labs, 2 foreign language, 2 social studies, 2 academic electives. *Academic units recommended:* 4 English, 4 math, 4 science, 4 science labs, 4 foreign language, 4 social studies, 4 academic electives.

ACCOMMODATIONS OR SERVICES

Accommodations are decided upon an individual basis after a thorough review of appropriate, current documentation. The accommodations requests must be supported through the documentation provided and must be logically linked to the current impact of the condition on academic functioning.

FINANCIAL AID

Students should submit: FAFSA. Applicants will be notified of awards on a rolling basis beginning 3/10. The Princeton Review suggests that all financial aid forms be submitted as soon as possible after October 1. *Need-based scholarships/grants offered:* College/university scholarship or grant aid from institutional funds; Federal Pell; Private scholarships; SEOG; State scholarships/grants; United Negro College Fund. *Loan aid offered:* Direct PLUS loans; Direct Subsidized Stafford Loans; Direct Unsubsidized Stafford Loans. Federal Work-Study Program available. Institutional employment available.

CAMPUS LIFE

Activities: Choral groups; Concert band; Dance; Drama/theater; International Student Organization; Jazz band; Literary magazine; Marching band; Music ensembles; Musical theater; Opera; Pep band; Radio station; Student government; Student newspaper; Student-run film society; Symphony orchestra; Television station; Yearbook. **Organizations:** 1000 registered organizations, 30 honor societies, 95 religious organizations. 60 fraternities, 36 sororities. **Athletics (Intercollegiate):** *Men:* baseball, basketball, cheerleading, cross-country, football, golf, gymnastics, tennis, track/field (outdoor), wrestling. *Women:* basketball, cheerleading, cross-country, diving, golf, gymnastics, soccer, softball, swimming, tennis, track/field (outdoor), volleyball.

ACCOMMODATIONS

Allowed in exams:	
Calculators	Yes
Dictionary	Yes
Computer	Yes
Spell-checker	Yes
Extended test time	Yes
Scribe	Yes
Proctors	Yes
Oral exams	Yes
Note-takers	Yes
Support services for students with	
LD	Yes
ADHD	Yes
ASD	Yes
Distraction-reduced environment	Yes
Recording of lecture allowed	Yes
Reading technology:	Yes
Audio books	Yes
Other assistive technology	Wide range
depending on disability and needs of student to include: word prediction, dragon naturally speaking, text to speech, various apps to facilitate time management, organization, etc.	
Priority registration	Yes
Added costs for services:	
For LD:	No
For ADHD:	No
For ASD:	No
LD specialists	Yes
ADIID & ASD coaching	Yes
ASD specialists	Yes
Professional tutors	Yes
Peer tutors	Yes
Max. hours/week for services	Varies
How professors are notified of student approved accommodations	Student

COLLEGE GRADUATION REQUIREMENTS

Course waivers allowed	No
Course substitutions allowed	Yes

University of St. Francis

500 WILCOX STREET, JOLIET, IL 60435 • ADMISSIONS: 815-740-2270 • FAX: 815-740-5078

CAMPUS

Type of school	Private (nonprofit)
Environment	City
Support	S

STUDENTS

Undergrad enrollment	1,329
% male/female	37/63
% from out of state	5
% frosh live on campus	45

FINANCIAL FACTS

Annual tuition	$32,000
Room and board	$9,544
Required fees	$320

GENERAL ADMISSIONS INFO

Application fee	$30
Regular application deadline	8/1

Nonfall registration accepted. Admission may be deferred for a maximum of 1 year.

Range SAT EBRW	490–630
Range SAT Math	540–610
Range ACT Composite	20–25

ACADEMICS

Student/faculty ratio	12:1
% students returning for sophomore year	80
% students graduating within 4 years	41
% students graduating within 6 years	63

Most classes have 20–29 students.
Most lab/discussion sessions have fewer than 10 students.

PROGRAMS/SERVICES FOR STUDENTS WITH LEARNING DIFFERENCES

The Office of Disability Services is commuted to ensuring equal access by fostering an accessible learning environment. The Censer for Academic Success provides a successful advising center.

ADMISSIONS

Freshmen Criteria 2.5 GPA/4.0 scale top 50% of class 20 ACT or 1390 SAT 4 yrs. English 3 yrs. math including Alg I, Geometry, Alg.II or higher 2 yrs. social studies 2 yrs. science including 1 with lab, 3 yrs fine arts, computers, or for. lang. 3 yrs. of electives   Transfer Criteria 2.5 transfer GPA for most majors.

Additional Information

Oasis is a program designed for first-year students who, upon applying for admission, have demonstrated a need for academic support and whose secondary school records indicate potential for college success. Students in the program receive extra support for their academic and social transition to college. The program teaches and reinforces important academic skills, while also introducing them to services across campus that will help them succeed..

ADMISSIONS INFO FOR STUDENTS WITH LEARNING DIFFERENCES

SAT/ACT required: Yes
Interview required: No
Essay required: Not Applicable
Additional application required: Yes
Documentation required for:
 LD: Psycho ed evaluation
 ADHD: Psycho ed evaluation
 ASD: Psycho ed evaluation
Documentation submitted to: ODS
Special Ed. HS course work accepted: Yes
Separate application required for Programs/Services: No
Contact Information
Name of program or department: Office of Disability Services
Telephone: 815-740-3204
Fax: 815-740-3726
Email: CAS@francis.edu

University of St. Francis

GENERAL ADMISSIONS

Very important factors considered include: rigor of secondary school record, class rank, academic GPA, standardized test scores. *Other factors considered include:* application essay, recommendation(s), interview. *Freshman Admission Requirements:* High school diploma is required and GED is accepted. *Academic units required:* 4 English, 3 math, 2 science, 1 science lab, 2 social studies, 3 academic electives, and 3 units from above areas or other academic areas.

ACCOMMODATIONS OR SERVICES

Accommodations are decided upon an individual basis after a thorough review of appropriate, current documentation. The accommodations requests must be supported through the documentation provided and must be logically linked to the current impact of the condition on academic functioning.

FINANCIAL AID

Students should submit: FAFSA; Institution's own financial aid form. Applicants will be notified of awards on a rolling basis beginning 10/15. The Princeton Review suggests that all financial aid forms be submitted as soon as possible after October 1. *Need-based scholarships/grants offered:* College/university scholarship or grant aid from institutional funds; Federal Pell; Private scholarships; SEOG; State scholarships/grants. *Loan aid offered:* Direct PLUS loans; Direct Subsidized Stafford Loans; Direct Unsubsidized Stafford Loans. Federal Work-Study Program available. Institutional employment available.

CAMPUS LIFE

Activities: Campus Ministries; Choral groups; Dance; Drama/theater; International Student Organization; Music ensembles; Musical theater; Opera; Radio station; Student government; Student newspaper; Symphony orchestra; Television station. **Organizations:** 29 registered organizations, 13 honor societies, 1 religious organization. **Athletics (Intercollegiate):** *Men:* baseball, basketball, cross-country, football, golf, soccer, tennis, track/field (outdoor), track/field (indoor). *Women:* basketball, cheerleading, cross-country, golf, soccer, softball, tennis, track/field (outdoor), track/field (indoor), volleyball. **On-Campus Highlights:** Bistro, Fireside Lounge in Motherhouse, The Abbey, Bernie's Pub, The Quad.

ACCOMMODATIONS

Allowed in exams:	
Calculators	Yes
Dictionary	Yes
Computer	Yes
Spell-checker	Yes
Extended test time	Yes
Scribe	Yes
Proctors	Yes
Oral exams	Yes
Note-takers	Yes
Support services for students with	
LD	Yes
ADHD	Yes
ASD	Yes
Distraction-reduced environment	Yes
Recording of lecture allowed	Yes
Reading technology:	Yes
Audio books	Yes
Other assistive technology	Technology for vision and hearing impairments
Priority registration	Yes
Added costs for services:	
For LD:	No
For ADHD:	No
For ASD:	No
LD specialists	No
ADHD & ASD coaching	No
ASD specialists	No
Professional tutors	Yes
Peer tutors	Yes
Max. hours/week for services	Varies
How professors are notified of student approved accommodations	Student

COLLEGE GRADUATION REQUIREMENTS

Course waivers allowed	Yes
In what courses	
Decided case by case and with approval of dean	
Course substitutions allowed	Yes
In what courses	
Decided case by case and with approval of dean	

Western Illinois University

1 UNIVERSITY CIRCLE, MACOMB, IL 61455-1390 • ADMISSIONS: 309-298-3157 • FAX: 309-298-3111

CAMPUS
Type of school	Public
Environment	Village
Support	CS

STUDENTS
Undergrad enrollment	7,599
% male/female	49/51
% from out of state	10
% frosh live on campus	91

FINANCIAL FACTS
Annual tuition	$8,541
Room and board	$9,630
Required fees	NR

GENERAL ADMISSIONS INFO
Application fee	$30

Nonfall registration accepted. Admission may be deferred.

Range SAT EBRW	NR
Range SAT Math	NR
Range ACT Composite	18–23

ACADEMICS
Student/faculty ratio	14:1
% students returning for sophomore year	68
% students graduating within 4 years	30
% students graduating within 6 years	50

Most classes have 10–19 students.
Most lab/discussion sessions have 20–29 students.

PROGRAMS/SERVICES FOR STUDENTS WITH LEARNING DIFFERENCES
DRC Core Beliefs Human variation is natural and vital in the development of dynamic communities. Disability is a social/political category that includes people with a variety of conditions who are bound together by common experiences. Inclusion and full participation are a matter of social justice. Design is powerful and profoundly influences our daily lives. Good design is essential for achieving inclusion and full participation. Creating usable, equitable, sustainable, and inclusive environments is a shared responsibility. http://www.wiu.edu/student_services/disability_resource_center/students/documentationGuidelines.php

ADMISSIONS
The average ACT is 21 or SAT 1060. The ACT middle 50% is 18–23 or SAT 940–1150. The average GPA is 3.15 and the middle 50% is 2.72-3.52 Applicants whose ACT/SAT score or GPA falls below the middle 50% range of this profile are encouraged to submit a personal statement which addresses their academic goals and how they plan to realize those goals at WIU. The statement may also explain any extenuating circumstances that may have affected their academic performance in high school. Letters of support will also be considered. Students may also be admitted through the Office for Academic Services. Students must have a minimum ACT of 16 or a minimum SAT score of 880 (with a GPA equal to or greater than 2.0/4.0 scale) to beeligible. Admission requirements for the Office of Academic Services are on a sliding scale: lower ACT orSAT scores require a greater GPA, higher ACT or SAT scores allow for a somewhat lower GPA, with a 2.0minimum. We strongly recommend that all students who fall below the profile of 18-23 ACT or 940-1130SAT and 2.6-3.3 cumulative grade point average submit personal statements and letters of support. Admittance with an ACT score less than 16 or an SAT score less than 880 is dependent upon anappeal to the Committee on Admission and Graduation Standards.Additional InformationStudents admitted through the Office of Academic Services remain in the program until they complete a minimum of 27 semester hours at Western, earn a cumulative grade point average of at least a 2.00 and declare a major course of study. Some majors have a higher GPA threshold; therefore, students have to stay in OAS until they reach the minimum required for that major. There are many resources, services, and programs designed specifically to assist students in realizing their academic potential. Academic advising, career exploration and development, and tutoring are only a few of the services available. Students can also obtain individual assistance with test taking, preparing for finals, textbook comprehension, note-taking, test

ADMISSIONS INFO FOR STUDENTS WITH LEARNING DIFFERENCES
SAT/ACT required: Yes
Interview required: No
Essay required: No
Additional application required: No
Documentation required for:
 LD/ADHD: Psycho ed evaluation
 ASD: Psycho ed evaluation
Documentation submitted to: DRC
Special Ed. HS course work accepted: N/A
Separate application required for Programs/Services: No
Contact Information
Name of program or department: same as above
Telephone: 309-298-2512
Fax: 309-298-2361
Email: disability@wiu.edu

Western Illinois University

anxiety, time management, and more. Study skills seminars are conducted throughout the year, and address important topics such as testtaking, textbook comprehension, note-taking, test anxiety, time management, and preparing for finals.

Additional Information

The purpose of the DRC exam service is to modify aspects of the testing environment in a manner that allows for accurate assessment of achievement. Exam accommodations include but are not limited to extended time, a reduceddistraction test environment, readers, scribes, and a computer for essay and short answer exams. While instructors may provide these accommodations to students if they wish, DRC offers an exam service for faculty who do not have the resources to provided necessary modifications within their respective departments. Students who plan to take exams using the DRC exam service, will meet with a DRC staff member to schedule exams. The university may allow course substitutions for students receiving DRC services, based on strong documentation of a weakness in a specific area. A student must write a letter of appeal to the Council on Admission, Graduation and Academic Standards (CAGAS). The student should send a copy of the appeal letter to Disability Resource Center. http://www.wiu.edu/student_services/disability_resource_center/

GENERAL ADMISSIONS

Very important factors considered include: academic GPA, standardized test scores. *Other factors considered include:* rigor of secondary school record. *Freshman Admission Requirements:* High school diploma is required and GED is accepted. *Academic units required:* 4 English, 3 math, 3 science, 3 social studies, 2 academic electives.

ACCOMMODATIONS OR SERVICES

Accommodations are decided upon an individual basis after a thorough review of appropriate, current documentation. The accommodations requests must be supported through the documentation provided and must be logically linked to the current impact of the condition on academic functioning.

FINANCIAL AID

Students should submit: FAFSA. Applicants will be notified of awards on a rolling basis beginning 1/15. The Princeton Review suggests that all financial aid forms be submitted as soon as possible after October 1. *Need-based scholarships/grants offered:* College/university scholarship or grant aid from institutional funds; Federal Pell; Private scholarships; SEOG; State scholarships/grants. *Loan aid offered:* Direct PLUS loans; Direct Subsidized Stafford Loans; Direct Unsubsidized Stafford Loans. Federal Work-Study Program available. Institutional employment available.

CAMPUS LIFE

Activities: Campus Ministries; Choral groups; Concert band; Dance; Drama/theater; International Student Organization; Jazz band; Literary magazine; Marching band; Model UN; Music ensembles; Musical theater; Opera; Pep band; Radio station; Student government; Student newspaper; Student-run film society; Symphony orchestra; Television station. **Organizations:** 200 registered organizations, 25 honor societies, 12 religious organizations. 14 fraternities, 11 sororities. **Athletics (Intercollegiate):** *Men:* baseball, basketball, cross-country, diving, football, golf, soccer, swimming, tennis, track/field (outdoor), track/field (indoor). *Women:* basketball, cheerleading, cross-country, diving, golf, soccer, softball, swimming, tennis, track/field (outdoor), track/field (indoor), volleyball. **On-Campus Highlights:** University Union, Student Recreation Center, Leslie Malpass Library, Hanson Field, Multicultural Center.

ACCOMMODATIONS

Allowed in exams:

Calculators	Yes
Dictionary	Yes
Computer	Yes
Spell-checker	Yes
Extended test time	Yes
Scribe	Yes
Proctors	Yes
Oral exams	Yes
Note-takers	Yes

Support services for students with

LD	Yes
ADHD	Yes
ASD	Yes
Distraction-reduced environment	Yes
Recording of lecture allowed	Yes
Reading technology:	Yes
Audio books	Not Applicable
Other assistive technology	Audio Note

Taking Software by Sonocent, allows students to record and annotate lectures in real time. Mobile app also included.

Priority registration	Yes

Added costs for services:

For LD:	No
For ADHD:	No
For ASD:	No
LD specialists	Yes
ADHD & ASD coaching	No
ASD specialists	No
Professional tutors	Yes
Peer tutors	Yes
Max. hours/week for services	Varies

How professors are notified of student approved accommodations   Director and Student

COLLEGE GRADUATION REQUIREMENTS

Course waivers allowed	No
Course substitutions allowed	Yes

Wheaton College (IL)

501 COLLEGE AVENUE, WHEATON, IL 60187 • ADMISSIONS: 630-752-5011 • FAX: 630-752-5285

CAMPUS
Type of school	Private (nonprofit)
Environment	Town
Support	S

STUDENTS
Undergrad enrollment	2,356
% male/female	45/55
% from out of state	72
% frosh live on campus	99

FINANCIAL FACTS
Annual tuition	$36,420
Room and board	$10,180
Required fees	NR

GENERAL ADMISSIONS INFO
Application fee	$50
Regular application deadline	1/10

Nonfall registration accepted. Admission may be deferred for a maximum of 1 year.

Range SAT EBRW	630–720
Range SAT Math	600–690
Range ACT Composite	27–32

ACADEMICS
Student/faculty ratio	11:1
% students returning for sophomore year	93
% students graduating within 4 years	80
% students graduating within 6 years	89

Most classes have 20–29 students. Most lab/discussion sessions have fewer than 10 students.

PROGRAMS/SERVICES FOR STUDENTS WITH LEARNING DIFFERENCES

Academic Disability Services enhances and enriches the way you learn and approach classes and also have resources if you have a learning, physical, or mental health need that impacts academics or campus life. Through one-on-one strategic meetings and academic workshops/seminars you have the opportunity to develop new strategies, build existing skills, and figure out how you are uniquely wired in order to maximize your learning experience. A series of workshops are offered each year that cover topics that are relevant to you- like time management, strategies for reading and note-taking, paper-writing and research, how to get the most out of your test preparation, overcoming procrastination and perfectionism and more!

ADMISSIONS

The average GPA is 3.7.. The mid 50% SAT is 1240-1550 or ACT 27-32. Applicants with LD must meet the same admission requirements as all applicants.

Additional Information

Through one-on-one counseling and academic workshops, students are offered the opportunity to improve existing skills, to develop new strategies, and to maximize their learning experience. A series of workshops are offered each year in the areas of time management, college reading and note-taking, college writing and research, exam preparation, procrastination and perfectionism. Individual meetings are available by appointment to offer accountability, coaching and accommodation advocacy. Academic counseling is available for all students. Accommodation approval and services for students with documented learning including assessment screening for potential learning challenges are available and can include: learning style assessment, academic coaching and accountability, and strategic learning improvement information.

ADMISSIONS INFO FOR STUDENTS WITH LEARNING DIFFERENCES
SAT/ACT required: Yes
Interview required: No
Essay required: Not Applicable
Additional application required: No
Documentation required for:
  LD: Psychoeducational evaluation completed by a licensed psychologist or psychiatrist.
  ADHD: Evaluation from a licensed psychologist or form completed by physician that includes diagnosis, impact/functional limitations, previous accommodations, specific recommendations.
  ASD: A letter or evaluation from a physician, licensed psychologist or psychiatrist that includes diagnosis, impact/functional limitations, previous accommodations, specific recommendations.
Documentation submitted to: Academic and Disability Services
Special Ed. HS course work accepted: Not Applicable
Separate application required for Programs/Services: Not for LD, ADHD, or ASD.
Contact Information
Name of program or department: Academic and Disability Services
Telephone: 630-752-5674
Fax: 630-752-7226
Email: academic.disability.services@wheaton.edu

Wheaton College (IL)

GENERAL ADMISSIONS

Very important factors considered include: rigor of secondary school record, academic GPA, application essay, standardized test scores, recommendation(s), character/personal qualities, religious affiliation/commitment. *Important factors considered include:* interview, extracurricular activities, talent/ability, volunteer work. *Other factors considered include:* class rank, first generation, alumni/ae relation, geographical residence, state residency, racial/ethnic status, work experience, level of applicant's interest. *Freshman Admission Requirements:* High school diploma is required and GED is accepted. *Academic units required:* 4 English, 3 math, 3 science, 2 foreign language, 3 social studies. *Academic units recommended:* 4 English, 4 math, 4 science, 3 foreign language, 4 social studies.

ACCOMMODATIONS OR SERVICES

Accommodations are decided upon an individual basis after a thorough review of appropriate, current documentation. The accommodations requests must be supported through the documentation provided and must be logically linked to the current impact of the condition on academic functioning.

FINANCIAL AID

Students should submit: FAFSA. Applicants will be notified of awards on a rolling basis beginning 12/31. The Princeton Review suggests that all financial aid forms be submitted as soon as possible after October 1. *Need-based scholarships/grants offered:* College/university scholarship or grant aid from institutional funds; Federal Pell; Private scholarships; SEOG; State scholarships/grants. *Loan aid offered:* Direct PLUS loans; Direct Subsidized Stafford Loans; Direct Unsubsidized Stafford Loans. Federal Work-Study Program available. Institutional employment available.

CAMPUS LIFE

Activities: Campus Ministries; Choral groups; Concert band; Dance; Drama/theater; International Student Organization; Jazz band; Literary magazine; Model UN; Music ensembles; Musical theater; Opera; Pep band; Student government; Student newspaper; Student-run film society; Symphony orchestra. **Organizations:** 85 registered organizations, 13 honor societies, 12 religious organizations. **Athletics (Intercollegiate):** *Men:* baseball, basketball, cross-country, football, golf, soccer, swimming, tennis, track/field (outdoor), track/field (indoor), wrestling. *Women:* basketball, cross-country, golf, soccer, softball, swimming, tennis, track/field (outdoor), track/field (indoor), volleyball, water polo. **On-Campus Highlights:** "The Stupe" grill in the Beamer Student Center, C.S. Lewis reading room in the Wade Center, Rock climbing wall in the Student Recreation Complex, Perry Mastodon exhibit in the Meyer Science Center, Billy Graham Center museum.

ACCOMMODATIONS

Allowed in exams:	
Calculators	Yes
Dictionary	Yes
Computer	Yes
Spell-checker	Not Applicable
Extended test time	Yes
Scribe	Yes
Proctors	Yes
Oral exams	Yes
Note-takers	Yes
Support services for students with	
LD	Yes
ADHD	Yes
ASD	Yes
Distraction-reduced environment	Yes
Recording of lecture allowed	Yes
Reading technology:	Yes
Audio books	Yes
Other assistive technology	Zoomtext, OCR
Priority registration	No
Added costs for services:	
For LD:	No
For ADHD:	No
For ASD:	No
LD specialists	No
ADHD & ASD coaching	Yes
ASD specialists	Yes
Professional tutors	Yes
Peer tutors	Yes
Max. hours/week for services	Varies
How professors are notified of student approved accommodations	Director and Student

COLLEGE GRADUATION REQUIREMENTS

Course waivers allowed	Yes
In what courses	
Foreign Language substitution but no waivers	
Course substitutions allowed	Yes
In what courses	
Foreign Language, in rare cases public speaking	

Anderson University (IN)

1100 East Fifth Street, Anderson, IN 46012-3495 • Admissions: 765-641-4080 • Fax: 765-641-4091

CAMPUS
Type of school	Private (nonprofit)
Environment	Town
Support	CS

STUDENTS
Undergrad enrollment	1,506
% male/female	41/59
% from out of state	24
% frosh live on campus	87

FINANCIAL FACTS
Annual tuition	$29,950
Room and board	$9,740
Required fees	$500

GENERAL ADMISSIONS INFO
Application fee	$25
Priority deadline	1/1
Regular application deadline	7/1

Nonfall registration accepted. Admission may be deferred for a maximum of 1 year.

Range SAT EBRW	450–550
Range SAT Math	460–560
Range ACT Composite	19–25

ACADEMICS
Student/faculty ratio	10:1
% students returning for sophomore year	73
% students graduating within 4 years	48
% students graduating within 6 years	57

PROGRAMS/SERVICES FOR STUDENTS WITH LEARNING DIFFERENCES
The Office of Disability Services provides individualized support for students diagnosed with Specific Learning Disabilities or for those with Other Disabilities who meet 504 Guidelines. To secure support services, students must notify the office of Disability Services for Students (DSS) of the disability, provide appropriate documentation of the disability, and request specific accommodations.

ADMISSIONS
Students with specific learning disabilities who apply to Anderson do so through the regular admission channels. The university recommends that students have the following courses in their high school background: 4 years of English, 3 years of mathematics, 2 years of a foreign language, 3 years of science, and 3 years of social studies. Also considered in the evaluation of each application is the student's seriousness of purpose; personality and character; expressed willingness to live within the standards of the Anderson University community; and service to school, church, and community. Documentation of a specific learning disability must be included with the application. We encourage students to self-disclose because they may qualify for special consideration and be admitted through the LD program. Failure to disclose could result in nonacceptance based on standardized class scores, GPA, etc. Upon request for consideration for the program, prospective students are expected to make an on-campus visit, at which time a personal interview is arranged with the program director. All applicants are considered on an individual basis.

Additional Information
The Bridges program helps students with specific learning disabilities and/or ADHD achieve their educational goals. The Bridges program provides these students an extra layer of support during the transition from high school to college. During their first semester, students who are accepted into the Bridges program must take a two-credit-hour college survival skills/study skills course that is taught by a DSS staff member/ members. Freshmen enrolled in the program are typically limited to a lighter course load during their first semester. Students are fully integrated into the university and follow the regular curriculum and requirements for graduation. Students who wish to apply to the Bridges program must

ADMISSIONS INFO FOR STUDENTS WITH LEARNING DIFFERENCES
SAT/ACT required: Yes
Interview required: No
Essay required: Recommended
Additional application required: No
Documentation required for:
 LD: If the student seeks accommodations, documentation of the disability and need for accommodations is required.
 ADHD: If the student seeks accommodations, documentation of the disability and need for accommodations is required.
 ASD: If the student seeks accommodations, documentation of the disability and need for accommodations is required.
Documentation submitted to: Office of Disability Services
Special Ed. HS course work accepted: No
Separate application required for Programs/Services: No
Contact Information
Name of program or department: Bridges
Telephone: 765 6414223
Fax: 765 6413851
Email: tjcoplin@anderson.edu

notify the DSS director. Documentation of a specific learning disability and/or ADHD must be provided. Students applying for the program are required to have a personal interview with the program director.

GENERAL ADMISSIONS

Very important factors considered include: rigor of secondary school record, recommendation(s), religious affiliation/commitment. *Important factors considered include:* class rank, academic GPA, standardized test scores, interview, extracurricular activities, character/personal qualities, volunteer work. *Other factors considered include:* application essay, talent/ability, first generation, alumni/ae relation, racial/ethnic status, level of applicant's interest. *Freshman Admission Requirements:* High school diploma is required and GED is accepted. *Academic units required:* 4 English, 3 math, 3 science, 3 science labs, 2 foreign language, 1 social studies, 1 history. *Academic units recommended:* 4 English, 4 math, 4 science, 4 science labs, 3 foreign language, 2 social studies, 2 history, 5 academic electives, 1 computer science, 1 visual/performing arts.

ACCOMMODATIONS OR SERVICES

Accommodations are decided upon an individual basis after a thorough review of appropriate, current documentation. The accommodations requests must be supported through the documentation provided and must be logically linked to the current impact of the condition on academic functioning.

FINANCIAL AID

Students should submit: FAFSA. Applicants will be notified of awards on a rolling basis beginning 2/15. The Princeton Review suggests that all financial aid forms be submitted as soon as possible after October 1. *Need-based scholarships/grants offered:* College/university scholarship or grant aid from institutional funds; Federal Pell; Private scholarships; SEOG; State scholarships/grants. *Loan aid offered:* Federal Work-Study Program available.

CAMPUS LIFE

Activities: Campus Ministries; Choral groups; Concert band; Dance; Drama/theater; International Student Organization; Jazz band; Literary magazine; Model UN; Music ensembles; Musical theater; Opera; Pep band; Radio station; Student government; Student newspaper; Symphony orchestra; Yearbook. **Organizations:** 33 registered organizations, 12 honor societies, 15 religious organizations. **Athletics (Intercollegiate):** *Men:* baseball, basketball, cheerleading, cross-country, football, golf, soccer, tennis, track/field (outdoor). *Women:* basketball, cheerleading, cross-country, golf, soccer, softball, tennis, track/field (outdoor), volleyball. **On-Campus Highlights:** Kardatzke Wellness Center, Mocha Joe's in the Olt Student Center, Decker Commons and Create, Reardon Auditorium, York Performance Hall.

ACCOMMODATIONS

Allowed in exams:	
Calculators	Yes
Dictionary	No
Computer	Yes
Spell-checker	Yes
Extended test time	Yes
Scribe	Yes
Proctors	Yes
Oral exams	No
Note-takers	Yes
Support services for students with	
LD	Yes
ADHD	Yes
ASD	Yes
Distraction-reduced environment	Yes
Recording of lecture allowed	Yes
Reading technology:	Yes
Audio books	Yes
Other assistive technology	Yes
Priority registration	No
Added costs for services:	
For LD:	No
For ADHD:	No
For ASD:	No
LD specialists	Yes
ADHD & ASD coaching	No
ASD specialists	No
Professional tutors	Yes
Peer tutors	Yes
Max. hours/week for services	Varies
How professors are notified of student approved accommodations	Student

COLLEGE GRADUATION REQUIREMENTS

Course waivers allowed	No
Course substitutions allowed	Yes
In what courses	Case by case decision.

Indiana University Bloomington

107 SOUTH INDIANA AVENUE, BLOOMINGTON, IN 47405-1106 • ADMISSIONS: 812-855-0661 • FAX: 812-855-5102

CAMPUS
Type of school	Public
Environment	City
Support	CS

STUDENTS
Undergrad enrollment	33,104
% male/female	51/49
% from out of state	34
% frosh live on campus	90

FINANCIAL FACTS
Annual in-state tuition	$9,342
Annual out-of-state tuition	$34,117
Room and board	$10,465
Required fees	$1,339

GENERAL ADMISSIONS INFO
Application fee	$65
Priority deadline	2/1

Nonfall registration accepted. Admission may be deferred for a maximum of 1 year.

Range SAT EBRW	570–670
Range SAT Math	570–680
Range ACT Composite	25–31

ACADEMICS
Student/faculty ratio	17:1
% students returning for sophomore year	91
% students graduating within 4 years	60
% students graduating within 6 years	76

Most classes have 10–19 students.
Most lab/discussion sessions have 10–19 students.

PROGRAMS/SERVICES FOR STUDENTS WITH LEARNING DIFFERENCES

The Office of Disability Services for Students (DSS) specializes in assisting students with various disabilities including physical, psychological, learning, neurological, medical, vision, hearing, and temporary impairments to achieve their academic goals. We work with you and your instructors to facilitate accommodations and to link you to resources – tutoring, mentoring and internship programs, housing and transportation service, community – essential to success.

ADMISSIONS

The middle 50% range for GPA for admitted freshmen is 3.57–4.00. The cumulative GPA, as well as the grades earned in the 34 courses required for admission, will be an important part of the application review process. If a high school computes a weighted GPA and includes this GPA on a transcript, IU will consider it for both the admission and scholarship processes. The middle 50 % range of SAT scores is 1180–1370. The middle 50 % range for the ACT composite is 25–31.

Additional Information

Accommodations can be made to provide: test modifications, referrals to tutors, peer note-takers, books on tape, adaptive technology, and priority registration for students needing books on tape. Students must provide appropriate documentation and submit request for services. Students need to request a letter from DSS to give to their professors. No course requirements are waived automatically. Students who have difficulty with math or foreign language should discuss with DSS. The Student Academic Center offers workshops, courses for credit, and individualized academic assesments. No fees.

ADMISSIONS INFO FOR STUDENTS WITH LEARNING DIFFERENCES
SAT/ACT required: Yes
Interview required: No
Essay required: Yes
Additional application required: No
Documentation required for:
 LD: Psycho ed evaluation
 ADHD: Psycho ed evaluation
 ASD: Psycho ed evaluation
Documentation submitted to: Office of Disability Services
Special Ed. HS course work accepted: No
Separate application required for Programs/Services: No
Contact Information
Name of program or department: Disability Services for Students
Telephone: (812) 855-7578
Fax: (812) 855-7650
Email: iubdss@indiana.edu

Indiana University Bloomington

GENERAL ADMISSIONS

Very important factors considered include: rigor of secondary school record, class rank, academic GPA, standardized test scores. *Important factors considered include:* application essay. *Other factors considered include:* recommendation(s), interview, extracurricular activities, talent/ability, character/personal qualities, first generation, alumni/ae relation, geographical residence, state residency, racial/ethnic status, volunteer work, work experience. *Freshman Admission Requirements:* High school diploma is required and GED is accepted. *Academic units required:* 4 English, 3.5 math, 3 science, 2 science labs, 2 foreign language, 3 social studies, 1.5 academic electives.

ACCOMMODATIONS OR SERVICES

Accommodations are decided upon an individual basis after a thorough review of appropriate, current documentation. The accommodations requests must be supported through the documentation provided and must be logically linked to the current impact of the condition on academic functioning.

FINANCIAL AID

Students should submit: FAFSA. Applicants will be notified of awards on a rolling basis beginning 2/15. The Princeton Review suggests that all financial aid forms be submitted as soon as possible after October 1. *Need-based scholarships/grants offered:* College/university scholarship or grant aid from institutional funds; Federal Pell; Private scholarships; SEOG; State scholarships/grants. *Loan aid offered:* Direct PLUS loans; Direct Subsidized Stafford Loans; Direct Unsubsidized Stafford Loans. Federal Work-Study Program available. Institutional employment available.

CAMPUS LIFE

Activities: Campus Ministries; Choral groups; Concert band; Dance; Drama/theater; International Student Organization; Jazz band; Literary magazine; Marching band; Music ensembles; Musical theater; Opera; Pep band; Radio station; Student government; Student newspaper; Symphony orchestra; Television station; Yearbook. **Organizations:** 9 religious organizations. **Athletics (Intercollegiate):** *Men:* baseball, basketball, cheerleading, cross-country, diving, football, golf, soccer, swimming, tennis, track/field (outdoor), wrestling. *Women:* basketball, cheerleading, cross-country, diving, field hockey, golf, soccer, softball, swimming, tennis, track/field (outdoor), volleyball, water polo. **On-Campus Highlights:** Indiana Memorial Union, Art Museum, Lilly Library, Assembly Hall, Student Recreational Sports Center.

ACCOMMODATIONS

Allowed in exams:	
Calculators	Yes
Dictionary	Yes
Computer	Yes
Spell-checker	Yes
Extended test time	Yes
Scribe	Yes
Proctors	Yes
Oral exams	Yes
Note-takers	Yes
Support services for students with	
LD	Yes
ADHD	Yes
ASD	Yes
Distraction-reduced environment	Yes
Recording of lecture allowed	Yes
Reading technology:	Yes
Audio books	Yes
Other assistive technology	Yes
Priority registration	Yes
Added costs for services:	
For LD:	No
For ADHD:	No
For ASD:	No
LD specialists	Yes
ADHD & ASD coaching	No
ASD specialists	No
Professional tutors	Yes
Peer tutors	Yes
Max. hours/week for services	Varies
How professors are notified of student approved accommodations	Student

COLLEGE GRADUATION REQUIREMENTS

Course waivers allowed	No
Course substitutions allowed	No

Indiana University—Purdue University Indianapolis

420 University Boulevard, Indianapolis, IN 46202 • Admissions: 317-274-4591 • Fax: 317-278-1862

CAMPUS

Type of school	Public
Environment	Metropolis
Support	S

STUDENTS

Undergrad enrollment	20,870
% male/female	44/56
% from out of state	4
% frosh live on campus	37

FINANCIAL FACTS

Annual in-state tuition	$8,371
Annual out-of-state tuition	$28,727
Room and board	$8,924
Required fees	$1,094

GENERAL ADMISSIONS INFO

Application fee	$65
Regular application deadline	5/1

Nonfall registration accepted.

Range SAT EBRW	500 –600
Range SAT Math	500 –590
Range ACT Composite	19 –26

ACADEMICS

Student/faculty ratio	17:1
% students returning for sophomore year	75
% students graduating within 4 years	19
% students graduating within 6 years	47

Most classes have 10-19 students.

PROGRAMS/SERVICES FOR STUDENTS WITH LEARNING DIFFERENCES

AES Mission AES is the IUPUI office dedicated to working with students with documented disabilities to ensure that these students receive the appropriate accommodations so they have an equal opportunity to be successful at higher education. AES Goals AES receives students' documentation of disabilities, evaluates it in order to determine the correct accommodations and services students are entitled to receive. AES provides some accommodations for students and directs them to other campus or off-campus groups that can provide other assistance. AES works to educate the IUPUI staff and faculty both in Indianapolis and at Columbus regarding the university's and its employees' legal responsibilities regarding students with disabilities. AES works with academic units to provide academic substitutions and waivers for students with disabilities which do not fundamentally alter those programs' standards. AES serves as an advocate for students with disabilities, working as a mediator with faculty over classroom issues, with administrators regarding campus policies, and encouraging the university to expand its vision and policies regarding persons with disabilities.

ADMISSIONS

http://aes.iupui.edu/apply.html. Students with learning disabilities must meet the same admission criteria as all applicants. Most applicants are expected to have a B average. ACT or SAT test score is required for admission. The Mid 50% SAT 970-1200 or ACT 19-26.

ADMISSIONS INFO FOR STUDENTS WITH LEARNING DIFFERENCES

SAT/ACT required: Yes
Interview required: No
Essay required: No
Additional application required: No
Documentation required for:
  LD: Psycho educational evaluation. http://aes.iupui.edu/apply.html
  ADHD: Psycho educational evaluation. http://aes.iupui.edu/apply.html
  ASD: Psycho educational evaluation. http://aes.iupui.edu/apply.html
Documentation submitted to: AES
Special Ed. HS course work accepted: No
Separate application required for Programs/Services: No
Contact Information
Name of program or department: Adaptive Educational Services
Telephone: (317) 274-3241
Fax: (317) 278-2051
Email: aes@iupui.edu

Indiana University—Purdue University Indianapolis

Additional Information
http://aes.iupui.edu/services.html   http://aes.iupui.edu/resources.html. AES provides some accommodations for students and directs them to other campus or off-campus groups that can provide other assistance. AES works to educate the IUPUI staff regarding the university's and its employees' legal responsibilities regarding students with disabilities. AES works with academic units to provide academic substitutions and waivers for students with disabilities which do not fundamentally alter those programs' standards. AES serves as an advocate for students with disabilities, working as a mediator with faculty over classroom issues, with administrators regarding campus policies, and encouraging the university to expand its vision and policies regarding persons with disabilities.

GENERAL ADMISSIONS
Very important factors considered include: rigor of secondary school record, academic GPA, standardized test scores. *Other factors considered include:* class rank, application essay, character/personal qualities, first generation, volunteer work, work experience. *Freshman Admission Requirements:* High school diploma is required and GED is accepted *Academic units required:* 4 English, 3 math, 3 science, 3 science labs, 3 social studies, 7 academic electives,

ACCOMMODATIONS OR SERVICES
Accommodations are decided upon an individual basis after a thorough review of appropriate, current documentation. The accommodations requests must be supported through the documentation provided and must be logically linked to the current impact of the condition on academic functioning.

FINANCIAL AID
Students should submit: FAFSA. Applicants will be notified of awards on a rolling basis beginning 4/1.. The Princeton Review suggests that all financial aid forms be submitted as soon as possible after October 1. *Need-based scholarships/grants offered:* College/university scholarship or grant aid from institutional funds; Federal Pell; Private scholarships; SEOG; State scholarships/grants *Loan aid offered:* Direct PLUS loans; Direct Subsidized Stafford Loans; Direct Unsubsidized Stafford Loans Federal Work-Study Program available. Institutional employment available.

CAMPUS LIFE
Activities: Campus Ministries; Choral groups; Dance ; Drama/theater; International Student Organization; Jazz band; Literary magazine; Model UN; Music ensembles; Pep band; Student government; Student newspaper; Student-run film society Organizations: 154 registered organizations, 9 honor societies, 10 religious organizations. 2 fraternities, 1 sororities, **Athletics (Intercollegiate):** *Men:* basketball, cross-country, diving, golf, soccer, swimming, tennis *Women:* basketball, cross-country, diving, golf, soccer, softball, swimming, tennis, volleyball. **On-Campus Highlights:** IUPUI Sport Complex, University College, Cavanaugh Hall, University Library, Eskenazi Hall.

ACCOMMODATIONS
Allowed in exams:

Calculators	Yes
Dictionary	Yes
Computer	Yes
Spell-checker	Yes
Extended test time	Yes
Scribe	Yes
Proctors	Yes
Oral exams	Yes
Note-takers	Yes

Support services for students with

LD	Yes
ADHD	Yes
ASD	Yes
Distraction-reduced environment	Yes
Recording of lecture allowed	Yes
Reading technology:	Yes
Audio books	No
Other assistive technology	Yes
Priority registration	Yes

Added costs for services:

For LD:	No
For ADHD:	No
For ASD:	No
LD specialists	Yes
ADHD & ASD coaching	No
ASD specialists	No
Professional tutors	Yes
Peer tutors	Yes
Max. hours/week for services	Varies by college
How professors are notified of student approved accommodations	Student and Director

COLLEGE GRADUATION REQUIREMENTS

Course waivers allowed	No
Course substitutions allowed	No

Manchester University

604 E. COLLEGE AVENUE, NORTH MANCHESTER, IN 46962 • ADMISSIONS: 260-982-5055 • FAX: 260-982-5239

CAMPUS

Type of school	Private (nonprofit)
Environment	Rural
Support	CS

STUDENTS

Undergrad enrollment	1,254
% male/female	48/52
% from out of state	12
% frosh live on campus	94

FINANCIAL FACTS

Annual tuition	$31,500
Room and board	$9,500
Required fees	$1,258

GENERAL ADMISSIONS INFO

Application fee	$25
Priority deadline	12/31

Nonfall registration accepted. Admission may be deferred for a maximum of 1 year.

Range SAT EBRW	430–540
Range SAT Math	435–550
Range ACT Composite	18–30

ACADEMICS

Student/faculty ratio	14:1
% students returning for sophomore year	69

Most classes have fewer than 10 students.

PROGRAMS/SERVICES FOR STUDENTS WITH LEARNING DIFFERENCES

Manchester University does not have a specific program for students with learning disabilities. The college is, however, very sensitive to all students. The key word at Manchester University is "success," which means graduating in 4 years. The college wants all students to be able to complete their degree in 4 years. The college does provide support services to students identified as disabled to allow them to be successful. The goal is to assist students in their individual needs.

ADMISSIONS

Students with learning disabilities submit the regular application form, and are required to meet the same admission criteria as all other applicants. Course requirements include 4 years of English, 2 years of math (3 years recommended), 2 years of science (3 years recommended), 2 years of science labs (3 years of science labs recommended), 2 years of a foreign language required, 2 years of social studies, 1 year of history (2 years recommended), and 1 year of an elective (2 years recommended). Average ACT is 22 or SAT Reasoning 990. Students are admitted to the college and use the support services as they choose. If special consideration for admission is requested, it is done individually, based on potential for graduation from the college. Manchester considers a wide range of information in making individual admission decisions. Students are encouraged to provide information beyond what is required on the application form if they believe it will strengthen their application or help the college to understand the students' performance or potential. Students who self-disclose the existence of a learning disability and are denied can ask to appeal the decision and have their application reviewed in a "different" way. The key question that will be asked is if the student can graduate in 4 years or, at the most, 5 years.

ADMISSIONS INFO FOR STUDENTS WITH LEARNING DIFFERENCES

SAT/ACT required: Yes
Interview required: Yes
Essay required: No
Additional application required: No
Documentation required for:
 LD: Psycho ed evaluation
 ADHD: Diagnosis based on DSM-V; history of behaviors impairing functioning in academic setting; diagnostic interview; history of symptoms; evidence of ongoing behaviors.
 ASD: Psycho ed evaluation
Documentation submitted to: Learning Support Services
Special Ed. HS course work accepted: Yes
Separate application required for Programs/Services: Yes
Contact Information
Name of program or department: Academic Success
Telephone: 260-982-5076
Fax: 260-982-5888

Manchester University

Additional Information

The Success Center provides tutoring for all students at the college. A course is offered presenting college level study skills with opportunities for students to apply these skills in their current course texts. Specific topics include time management, note-taking, vocabulary, text study techniques, test-taking, and memory strategies. Other topics include: college expectations, learning styles and assessments, self-management, and educational and career planning.

GENERAL ADMISSIONS

Very important factors considered include: rigor of secondary school record, class rank, academic GPA, recommendation(s). *Important factors considered include:* extracurricular activities, talent/ability, character/ personal qualities. *Other factors considered include:* application essay, standardized test scores, interview, alumni/ae relation, volunteer work, work experience, level of applicant's interest. *Freshman Admission Requirements:* High school diploma is required and GED is accepted. *Academic units required:* 4 English, 2 math, 2 science, 2 science labs, 1 social studies, 1 history, 2 academic electives. *Academic units recommended:* 4 English, 3 math, 3 science, 2 science labs, 2 foreign language, 2 social studies, 2 history, 2 academic electives, 1 computer science, 1 visual/ performing arts.

ACCOMMODATIONS OR SERVICES

Accommodations are decided upon an individual basis after a thorough review of appropriate, current documentation. The accommodations requests must be supported through the documentation provided and must be logically linked to the current impact of the condition on academic functioning.

FINANCIAL AID

Students should submit: FAFSA. Applicants will be notified of awards on a rolling basis beginning 3/18. The Princeton Review suggests that all financial aid forms be submitted as soon as possible after October 1. *Need-based scholarships/grants offered:* College/university scholarship or grant aid from institutional funds; Federal Pell; Private scholarships; SEOG; State scholarships/grants. *Loan aid offered:* Direct PLUS loans; Direct Subsidized Stafford Loans; Direct Unsubsidized Stafford Loans. Federal Work-Study Program available. Institutional employment available.

CAMPUS LIFE

Activities: Campus Ministries; Choral groups; Concert band; Dance; Drama/theater; International Student Organization; Jazz band; Literary magazine; Model UN; Music ensembles; Opera; Pep band; Radio station; Student government; Student newspaper; Symphony orchestra; Yearbook. **Organizations:** 47 registered organizations, 3 honor societies, 5 religious organizations. **Athletics (Intercollegiate):** *Men:* baseball, basketball, cheerleading, cross-country, football, golf, soccer, tennis, track/field (outdoor), wrestling. *Women:* basketball, cheerleading, cross-country, golf, soccer, softball, tennis, track/field (outdoor), volleyball. **On-Campus Highlights:** Athletic Facilities, Residence Halls, College Union, Petersime Chapel, Science Center.

ACCOMMODATIONS

Allowed in exams:

Calculators	Yes
Dictionary	No
Computer	Yes
Spell-checker	Yes
Extended test time	Yes
Scribe	Yes
Proctors	Yes
Oral exams	Yes
Note-takers	Yes

Support services for students with

LD	Yes
ADHD	Yes
ASD	Yes
Distraction-reduced environment	Yes
Recording of lecture allowed	Yes
Reading technology:	Yes
Audio books	No
Other assistive technology	Yes
Priority registration	No

Added costs for services:

For LD:	No
For ADHD:	No
For ASD:	No
LD specialists	Yes
ADHD & ASD coaching	No
ASD specialists	No
Professional tutors	No
Peer tutors	Yes
Max. hours/week for services	Unlimited
How professors are notified of student approved accommodations	Student and Director

COLLEGE GRADUATION REQUIREMENTS

Course waivers allowed	No
Course substitutions allowed	No

University of Indianapolis

1400 East Hanna Avenue, Indianapolis, IN 46227-3697 • Admissions: 317-788-3216 • Fax: 317-788-3300

PROGRAMS/SERVICES FOR STUDENTS WITH LEARNING DIFFERENCES

The University of Indianapolis offers a full support system for students with learning disabilities called BUILD (Baccalaureate for University of Indianapolis Learning Disabled). The goal of this program is to help students with learning disabilities reach their academic potential. This program is designed for students who are diagnosed with a disability such as a specific learning disability, attention deficit/hyperactivity disorder, mental health issues or autism spectrum disorder. All students with disabilities at the university have reasonable modifications available to them at no extra charge. The BUILD program offers accommodations significantly more in depth than just minimal requirements. Services are comprehensive, and the staff is knowledgeable about learning disabilities. The basic tenets of this collaboration include: Commitment to an understanding of one's strengths and difficulties, Honesty in academic endeavors, Dedication to one's own academic and personal growth, careful organization of time and information, personal accountability, persistence and hard work towards achieving goals, and utilization of all support offered at the University.

ADMISSIONS

Admission to the BUILD program occurs after a student has been accepted to the university. Students with LD must meet the university admissions requirements. However, consideration is given for individual strengths and weaknesses. The student must submit the following to the Office of Admissions: university application for admission, high school transcript, SAT or ACT scores. The student must submit the following to the BUILD Program: current documentation regarding I.Q. scores, reading and math proficiency level, primary learning style, and major learning difficulty. After BUILD reviews the information, interviews will be arranged for those applicants being considered for final selection into the BUILD Program. Acceptance into BUILD is determined by the program director.

University of Indianapolis

Additional Information

All students and staff of the BUILD program are members of a unique educational community whose goal is to access each student's potential for success. Such a goal requires tremendous individual and cooperative effort on the part of each member of this community. The BUILD program supports self-advocacy. Students are expected to function independently as mature, responsible adults in fulfilling academic requirements and attaining their scholastic and personal goals. Students are expected to attend all class sessions and interact with professors. BUILD tutorial sessions are to support student academic endeavors. However, tutors will assist students, review class information, discern main concepts, set goals and recommend skills to reach goals. Students are expected to attend each tutorial session having already attempted homework and reading assignments. Tutors will be available to help explain unclear concepts; however, students are encouraged to meet frequently with professors.

GENERAL ADMISSIONS

Very important factors considered include: rigor of secondary school record, academic GPA. *Important factors considered include:* standardized test scores. *Other factors considered include:* class rank, recommendation(s), interview, talent/ability. *Freshman Admission Requirements:* High school diploma is required and GED is accepted. *Academic units required:* 4 English, 3 math, 2 science, 1 science lab, 2 foreign language, 2 social studies, 1 history, 3 academic electives, 1 computer science, 2 visual/performing arts. *Academic units recommended:* 4 English, 3 math, 3 science, 2 science labs, 3 foreign language, 2 social studies, 1 history, 3 academic electives, 1 computer science, 2 visual/performing arts.

ACCOMMODATIONS OR SERVICES

Accommodations are decided upon an individual basis after a thorough review of appropriate, current documentation. The accommodations requests must be supported through the documentation provided and must be logically linked to the current impact of the condition on academic functioning.

FINANCIAL AID

Students should submit: FAFSA; Institution's own financial aid form. Applicants will be notified of awards on a rolling basis beginning 3/1. The Princeton Review suggests that all financial aid forms be submitted as soon as possible after October 1. *Need-based scholarships/grants offered:* College/university scholarship or grant aid from institutional funds; Federal Pell; Private scholarships; SEOG; State scholarships/grants. *Loan aid offered:* Direct PLUS loans; Direct Subsidized Stafford Loans; Direct Unsubsidized Stafford Loans. Federal Work-Study Program available. Institutional employment available.

CAMPUS LIFE

Activities: Campus Ministries; Choral groups; Concert band; Dance; Drama/theater; International Student Organization; Jazz band; Literary magazine; Music ensembles; Musical theater; Opera; Pep band; Radio station; Student government; Student newspaper; Television station; Yearbook. **Organizations:** 53 registered organizations, 14 honor societies, 4 religious organizations. **Athletics (Intercollegiate):** *Men:* baseball, basketball, cross-country, diving, football, golf, soccer, swimming, tennis, track/field (outdoor), wrestling. *Women:* basketball, cross-country, diving, golf, soccer, softball, swimming, tennis, track/field (outdoor), volleyball. **On-Campus Highlights:** Ruth Lilly Fitness Center, Schwitzer Center, Krannert Memorial Library, Christel Dehaan Fine Arts Center, Martin Hall.

ACCOMMODATIONS

Allowed in exams:	
Calculators	Yes
Dictionary	Yes
Computer	Yes
Spell-checker	Yes
Extended test time	Yes
Scribe	Yes
Proctors	Yes
Oral exams	Yes
Note-takers	Yes
Support services for students with	
LD	Yes
ADHD	Yes
ASD	Yes
Distraction-reduced environment	Yes
Recording of lecture allowed	Yes
Reading technology:	Yes
Audio books	Yes
Other assistive technology	Yes
Priority registration	Yes
Added costs for services:	
For LD:	Yes, for BUILD
For ADHD:	Yes, for BUILD
For ASD:	Yes, for BUILD
LD specialists	Yes
ADHD & ASD coaching	No
ASD specialists	No
Professional tutors	No
Peer tutors	Yes
Max. hours/week for services	Varies
How professors are notified of student approved accommodations	Student

COLLEGE GRADUATION REQUIREMENTS

Course waivers allowed	No
Course substitutions allowed	No

University of Notre Dame

220 MAIN BUILDING, NOTRE DAME, IN 46556 • ADMISSIONS: 574-631-7505 • FAX: 574-631-8865

CAMPUS
Type of school	Private (nonprofit)
Environment	City
Support	S

STUDENTS
Undergrad enrollment	8,527
% male/female	53/47
% from out of state	92
% frosh live on campus	100

FINANCIAL FACTS
Annual tuition	$52,884
Room and board	$15,410
Required fees	$507

GENERAL ADMISSIONS INFO
Application fee	$75
Regular application deadline	1/1

Nonfall registration accepted. Admission may be deferred for a maximum of 1 year.

Range SAT EBRW	680–750
Range SAT Math	690–770
Range ACT Composite	32–34

ACADEMICS
Student/faculty ratio	10:1
% students returning for sophomore year	98
% students graduating within 4 years	92
% students graduating within 6 years	95

Most classes have 10–19 students.

PROGRAMS/SERVICES FOR STUDENTS WITH LEARNING DIFFERENCES

It is the mission of Disability Services to ensure that Notre Dame students with disabilities have access to the programs and facilities of the university. Disability Services is committed to forming partnerships with students to share the responsibility of meeting individual needs. At the University of Notre Dame, students with disabilities may use a variety of services intended to reduce the effects that a disability may have on their educational experience. Services do not lower course standards or alter essential degree requirements, but instead give students an equal opportunity to demonstrate their academic abilities. Students can initiate a request for services by registering with Disability Services and providing information that documents the disability. Individual assistance is provided in selecting the services that will provide access to the academic programs and facilities of the university.

ADMISSIONS

Notre Dame will use the highest ACT composite score from a single testing date. The writing portion of the ACT is not required. Both the previous SAT and redesigned SAT are acceptable. The essay portion of the redesigned SAT is not required, and UND will superscore the SAT. The university will not superscore sub-scores from the current SAT with the redesigned SAT. Essays are the most enjoyable part of the application reading process that helps UND learn about important decisions you've made, adventures you've survived, lessons you've learned, family traditions you've experienced, challenges you've faced, embarrassing moments you've overcome. Interviews are not offered.

Additional Information

Services for students with learning disabilities or Attention Deficit Disorder include taped textbooks, note-takers, exam modifications, assistance with developing time management skills and learning strategies, and screening and referral for diagnostic testing. Students may substitute American Sign Language for Foreign Language requirement. Tutors are available for all students from other resources. There is also a Writing Center for all students. meets the academic requirements of a course or academic program.

ADMISSIONS INFO FOR STUDENTS WITH LEARNING DIFFERENCES
SAT/ACT required: Yes
Interview required: No
Essay required: Yes
Additional application required: No
Documentation required for:
  LD: Psycho ed evaluation
  ADHD: Psycho ed evaluation
  ASD: Psycho ed evaluation
Documentation submitted to: Disability Services
Special Ed. HS course work accepted: No
Separate application required for Programs/Services: No
Contact Information
Name of program or department: Sara Bea Disability Services
Telephone: 574-631-7141
Email: showland@nd.edu

University of Notre Dame

GENERAL ADMISSIONS

Very important factors considered include: rigor of secondary school record. *Important factors considered include:* class rank, academic GPA, application essay, standardized test scores, recommendation(s), extracurricular activities, talent/ability, character/personal qualities, alumni/ae relation, volunteer work. *Other factors considered include:* first generation, religious affiliation/commitment, racial/ethnic status, work experience, level of applicant's interest. *Freshman Admission Requirements:* High school diploma is required and GED is not accepted. *Academic units required:* 4 English, 3 math, 2 science, 2 science labs, 2 foreign language, 2 history, 3 academic electives. *Academic units recommended:* 4 English, 4 math, 4 science, 2 science labs, 4 foreign language, 4 history.

ACCOMMODATIONS OR SERVICES

Accommodations are decided upon an individual basis after a thorough review of appropriate, current documentation. The accommodations requests must be supported through the documentation provided and must be logically linked to the current impact of the condition on academic functioning.

FINANCIAL AID

Students should submit: Business/Farm Supplement; CSS/Financial Aid PROFILE; FAFSA. Applicants will be notified of awards on a rolling basis beginning 2/15. The Princeton Review suggests that all financial aid forms be submitted as soon as possible after October 1. *Need-based scholarships/grants offered:* College/university scholarship or grant aid from institutional funds; Federal Pell; Private scholarships; SEOG; State scholarships/grants. *Loan aid offered:* Direct PLUS loans; Direct Subsidized Stafford Loans; Direct Unsubsidized Stafford Loans. Federal Work-Study Program available. Institutional employment available.

CAMPUS LIFE

Activities: Campus Ministries; Choral groups; Concert band; Dance; Drama/theater; Jazz band; Literary magazine; Marching band; Model UN; Music ensembles; Musical theater; Opera; Pep band; Radio station; Student government; Student newspaper; Student-run film society; Symphony orchestra; Television station; Yearbook. **Organizations:** 299 registered organizations, 10 honor societies, 11 religious organizations. **Athletics (Intercollegiate):** *Men:* baseball, basketball, cross-country, diving, fencing, football, golf, ice hockey, lacrosse, soccer, swimming, tennis, track/field (outdoor). *Women:* basketball, crew/rowing, cross-country, diving, fencing, golf, lacrosse, soccer, softball, swimming, tennis, track/field (outdoor), volleyball. **On-Campus Highlights:** Grotto, The Golden Dome (Main Building), Basilica of the Sacred Heart, Notre Dame Stadium, Eck Center.

ACCOMMODATIONS

Allowed in exams:	
Calculators	Yes
Dictionary	Yes
Computer	No
Spell-checker	Yes
Extended test time	Yes
Scribe	Yes
Proctors	Yes
Oral exams	Yes
Note-takers	Yes
Support services for students with	
LD	Yes
ADHD	Yes
ASD	Yes
Distraction-reduced environment	Yes
Recording of lecture allowed	Yes
Reading technology:	Yes
Audio books	Yes
Other assistive technology	Yes
Priority registration	Yes
Added costs for services:	
For LD:	No
For ADHD:	No
For ASD:	No
LD specialists	Yes
ADHD & ASD coaching	No
ASD specialists	No
Professional tutors	No
Peer tutors	Yes
Max. hours/week for services	Varies
How professors are notified of student approved accommodations	Student

COLLEGE GRADUATION REQUIREMENTS

Course waivers allowed	No
Course substitutions allowed	No

University of Saint Francis

2701 SPRING STREET, FORT WAYNE, IN 46808 • ADMISSIONS: 260-399-8000 • FAX: 260-399-8152

CAMPUS

Type of school	Private (nonprofit)
Environment	City
Support	CS

STUDENTS

Undergrad enrollment	1,840
% male/female	29/71
% from out of state	10
% frosh live on campus	48

FINANCIAL FACTS

Annual tuition	$29,360
Room and board	$9,840
Required fees	$1,070

GENERAL ADMISSIONS INFO

Nonfall registration accepted. Admission may be deferred for a maximum of one semester.

Range SAT EBRW	480–580
Range SAT Math	480–560
Range ACT Composite	19–24

ACADEMICS

Student/faculty ratio	10:1
% students returning for sophomore year	72
% students graduating within 4 years	39
% students graduating within 6 years	56

Most classes have 10–19 students.

PROGRAMS/SERVICES FOR STUDENTS WITH LEARNING DIFFERENCES

Students with documented disabilities enjoy access to all university educational programs and activities through accommodations, adjustments and coordinated services. The Student Disability Services office works collaboratively with students with documented disabilities to ensure equal access.

ADMISSIONS

For admission to the University of Saint Francis, incoming students should meet the following requirements for automatic admission: rank in the upper 1/2 of the class; have a 2.3 GPA; SAT of 1000 or ACT of 21. Candidates who do not meet the criteria for automatic admission may still apply for admissions. These applications will be reviewed by the Academic Review Committee.

Additional Information

The Academic Resource Center (ARC) offers a variety of opportunities and academic support services to help students to reach their potential and achieve their goals In the center, students will find computers, study aids, study tables, comfortable spots for reading and friendly people to offer individualized help. Tutoring in a variety of subjects is available from students, faculty members or professional staff. Support for USF distance education students is happily provided by telephone and e-mail. ARC offers students: New techniques for learning; Exam preparation assistance; Study aid; Test preparation Workshops on time management, note-taking, learning styles, dosage calculations and memory techniques; Learning Strategies in reading, study habits, test taking and test anxiety. Students may receive one-on-one assessment of learning strategies and coaching in study skills by making an appointment.

ADMISSIONS INFO FOR STUDENTS WITH LEARNING DIFFERENCES

SAT/ACT required: Yes
Interview required: No
Essay required: Not Applicable
Additional application required: Yes
Documentation required for:
  LD: Statement by qualified professional giving diagnosis, functional limitations and impact in learning environment.
  ADHD: Diagnosis by qualified professional.
  ASD: Diagnosis by qualified professional.
Documentation submitted to: SDS
Special Ed. HS course work accepted: Yes
Separate application required for Programs/Services: No
Contact Information
Name of program or department: Student Disability Services
Telephone: 260-399-8065
Fax: 260-399-8161
Email: gburgess@sf.edu

University of Saint Francis

GENERAL ADMISSIONS

Very important factors considered include: rigor of secondary school record, academic GPA, standardized test scores. *Important factors considered include:* class rank. *Other factors considered include:* application essay, recommendation(s), interview, extracurricular activities, volunteer work, work experience, level of applicant's interest. *Freshman Admission Requirements:* High school diploma is required and GED is accepted. *Academic units required:* 4 English, 3 math, 2 science, 2 social studies, 1 history, 1 academic elective. *Academic units recommended:* 4 English, 4 math, 3 science, 3 social studies, 1 history, 4 academic electives.

ACCOMMODATIONS OR SERVICES

Accommodations are decided upon an individual basis after a thorough review of appropriate, current documentation. The accommodations requests must be supported through the documentation provided and must be logically linked to the current impact of the condition on academic functioning.

FINANCIAL AID

Students should submit: FAFSA. Applicants will be notified of awards on a rolling basis beginning 12/1. The Princeton Review suggests that all financial aid forms be submitted as soon as possible after October 1. *Need-based scholarships/grants offered:* College/university scholarship or grant aid from institutional funds; Federal Pell; Private scholarships; SEOG; State scholarships/grants. *Loan aid offered:* Direct PLUS loans; Direct Subsidized Stafford Loans; Direct Unsubsidized Stafford Loans. Federal Work-Study Program available. Institutional employment available.

CAMPUS LIFE

Activities: Campus Ministries; Choral groups; Dance; Drama/theater; Jazz band; Literary magazine; Marching band; Music ensembles; Musical theater; Pep band; Student government; Student newspaper; Student-run film society. **On-Campus Highlights:** Pope John Paul II Center - Library, Collaboratory, Campus Shoppe, Lounges, Cyber Fresh Cafe, Hutzell Fitness Center, Business Center—Cougar Cafe and Study Spaces, Residence Hall Lounges.

ACCOMMODATIONS

Allowed in exams:

Calculators	Yes
Dictionary	Yes
Computer	Yes
Spell-checker	Yes
Extended test time	Yes
Scribe	Yes
Proctors	Yes
Oral exams	Yes
Note-takers	Yes

Support services for students with

LD	Yes
ADHD	Yes
ASD	Yes
Distraction-reduced environment	Yes
Recording of lecture allowed	Yes
Reading technology:	Yes
Audio books	Yes

Other assistive technology Kurtzweil, Dragon Naturally Speaking, Zoom Text, Chemsketch II, Smartpen Echo, Desktop Magnifier

Priority registration	Yes

Added costs for services:

For LD:	No
For ADHD:	No
For ASD:	No
LD specialists	No
ADHD & ASD coaching	No
ASD specialists	Yes
Professional tutors	Yes
Peer tutors	Yes
Max. hours/week for services	Varies
How professors are notified of student approved accommodations	Student

COLLEGE GRADUATION REQUIREMENTS

Course waivers allowed	No
Course substitutions allowed	Yes
In what courses	Math and Foreign Language

University of Southern Indiana

8600 University Boulevard, Evansville, IN 47712 • Admissions: 812-464-1765 • Fax: 812-465-7154

CAMPUS

Type of school	Public
Environment	City
Support	S

STUDENTS

Undergrad enrollment	7,662
% male/female	38/62
% from out of state	13
% frosh live on campus	67

FINANCIAL FACTS

Annual in-state tuition	$7,460
Annual out-of-state tuition	$18,116
Room and board	$8,838
Required fees	$510

GENERAL ADMISSIONS INFO

Application fee	$40
Regular application deadline	8/15

Nonfall registration accepted.
  Admission may be deferred for a maximum of 1 semester.

Range SAT EBRW	490–590
Range SAT Math	480–580
Range ACT Composite	19–25

ACADEMICS

Student/faculty ratio	17:1
% students returning for sophomore year	71
% students graduating within 4 years	21
% students graduating within 6 years	40

Most classes have 20–29 students.
Most lab/discussion sessions have 20–29 students.

PROGRAMS/SERVICES FOR STUDENTS WITH LEARNING DIFFERENCES

USI Disability Resources (DR) coordinates services and academic acommodations for USI students with disabilities to ensure equal access. DR reviews documentation for eligibility,collaborate with students to determine appropriate acommodations, and assists with implementing acommodations.

ADMISSIONS

Admissions criteria are the same for all students; however, the admissions office will always work with students on an individual basis if needed. In general, students with a 3.6 GPA or higher are admitted with honors. Students with a 2.0–3.5 GPA are admitted in good standing, and students with a GPA below a 2.0 are accepted conditionally. The conditional admissions procedure is for new freshmen who earned below a 2.0 in English, math, science, and social studies. The following are required for those admitted conditionally: freshman seminar; 2.0 GPA; registration through the University Division rather than a specific major; enrollment in no more than 12 credit hours. ACT/SAT scores are used for placement purposes.

Additional Information

In order to use resources for a disability, professional documentation of a disability attached to the university's Verification of Disability form must be provided by the student. Skills classes are offered in basic grammar, algebra review, reading, and study skills. Credit is given for the hours, but the grades are Pass/No Pass. There are no paid note-takers, but special supplies and copy services are provided at no charge to allow the students to get copies of other students'notes. Other services include: assistance obtaining alternative format textbooks; test accommodations; and advocacy and counseling. Services and accommodations are available for undergraduate and graduate students.

ADMISSIONS INFO FOR STUDENTS WITH LEARNING DIFFERENCES

SAT/ACT required: Yes
Interview required: Not Applicable
Essay required: Not Applicable
Additional application required: Not Applicable
Documentation required for:
  LD: Psycho ed evaluation
  ADHD: Psycho ed evaluation
  ASD: Psycho ed evaluation
Documentation submitted to: DR
Special Ed. HS course work accepted: No
Separate application required for Programs/Services: Not for LD, ADHD, or ASD.
Contact Information
Name of program or department: Disability Resources
Telephone: 812-464-1961
Fax: 812-464-1935
Email: rfstone@usi.edu

University of Southern Indiana

GENERAL ADMISSIONS

Very important factors considered include: academic GPA, standardized test scores. *Important factors considered include:* class rank. *Other factors considered include:* rigor of secondary school record, application essay, recommendation(s), interview, extracurricular activities, talent/ability, character/personal qualities, volunteer work. *Freshman Admission Requirements:* High school diploma is required and GED is accepted. *Academic units recommended:* 4 English, 4 math, 2 science, 2 foreign language, 2 social studies, 2 history, 2 academic electives.

ACCOMMODATIONS OR SERVICES

Accommodations are decided upon an individual basis after a thorough review of appropriate, current documentation. The accommodations requests must be supported through the documentation provided and must be logically linked to the current impact of the condition on academic functioning.

FINANCIAL AID

Students should submit: FAFSA. Applicants will be notified of awards on a rolling basis beginning 4/1. The Princeton Review suggests that all financial aid forms be submitted as soon as possible after October 1. *Need-based scholarships/grants offered:* College/university scholarship or grant aid from institutional funds; Federal Nursing Scholarships; Federal Pell; Private scholarships; SEOG; State scholarships/grants; United Negro College Fund. *Loan aid offered:* Direct PLUS loans; Direct Subsidized Stafford Loans; Direct Unsubsidized Stafford Loans. Federal Work-Study Program available. Institutional employment available.

CAMPUS LIFE

Activities: Campus Ministries; Choral groups; Dance; Drama/theater; International Student Organization; Jazz band; Literary magazine; Pep band; Radio station; Student government; Student newspaper; Television station. **Organizations:** 102 registered organizations, 6 honor societies, 7 religious organizations. 7 fraternities, 4 sororities. **Athletics (Intercollegiate):** *Men:* baseball, basketball, cross-country, golf, soccer, tennis, track/field (outdoor), track/field (indoor). *Women:* basketball, cross-country, golf, soccer, softball, tennis, track/field (outdoor), track/field (indoor), volleyball. **On-Campus Highlights:** University Center, Recreation, Fitness, and Wellness Center, Rice Library, USI Performance Center (Teaching Theatre), USI-Burdette Trail.

ACCOMMODATIONS

Allowed in exams:

Calculators	Yes
Dictionary	Yes
Computer	Yes
Spell-checker	Yes
Extended test time	Yes
Scribe	Yes
Proctors	Yes
Oral exams	Yes
Note-takers	Yes

Support services for students with

LD	Yes
ADHD	Yes
ASD	Yes
Distraction-reduced environment	Yes
Recording of lecture allowed	Yes
Reading technology:	Yes
Audio books	Yes

Other assistive technology Accommodations are determined on an individual basis with the goal of assuring access to all programs and services.

Priority registration	Yes

Added costs for services:

For LD:	No
For ADHD:	No
For ASD:	No
LD specialists	Yes
ADHD & ASD coaching	No
ASD specialists	No
Professional tutors	Yes
Peer tutors	Yes
Max. hours/week for services	Varies
How professors are notified of student approved accommodations	Student

COLLEGE GRADUATION REQUIREMENTS

Course waivers allowed	No

In what courses

Substitutions are sometimes approved.

Course substitutions allowed	Yes

In what courses

Substitutions are only granted after committee review.

Wabash College

P.O. Box 352, Crawfordsville, IN 47933 • Admissions: 765-361-6225 • Fax: 765-361-6437

CAMPUS

Type of school	Private (nonprofit)
Environment	Village
Support	S

STUDENTS

Undergrad enrollment	861
% male/female	100/0
% from out of state	22
% frosh live on campus	100

FINANCIAL FACTS

Annual tuition	$42,800
Room and board	$9,800
Required fees	$850

GENERAL ADMISSIONS INFO

Application fee	$50
Priority deadline	10/15
Regular application deadline	1/15

Nonfall registration accepted. Admission may be deferred for a maximum of 1 year.

Range SAT EBRW	530–630
Range SAT Math	540–650
Range ACT Composite	23–28

ACADEMICS

Student/faculty ratio	10:1
% students returning for sophomore year	87
% students graduating within 4 years	72
% students graduating within 6 years	77

Most classes have 10-19 students.
Most lab/discussion sessions have 10-19 students.

PROGRAMS/SERVICES FOR STUDENTS WITH LEARNING DIFFERENCES

Disability Services is the most helpful to students with special needs when students identify their needs before they begin classes. Once the student is on campus, the coordinator is available to work with him at any point in the academic year. Students vary in their need for consultation and guidance by the coordinator. Wabash, like all colleges and universities, requires documentation of a disability if a student is to receive accommodation for his disability. The documentation is kept on file in the office of Disability Services and is confidential. It is the decision of the student whether or not to request accommodation, and it is his responsibility to provide acceptable documentation and notify the relevant staff members of his condition and of his desire for accommodation(s).

ADMISSIONS

Admissions requires students to submit an ACT or SAT score. Mid 50% SAT 1100-1300 or ACT 23-28. Most admitted students have a B+ GPA and those below a 3.25 GPA are less likely to be admitted.

Additional Information

Wabash does not have any special programs for students with disabilities and do not have a separate office of any kind. Wabash has students with hidden disabilities (ADHD, language –processing difficulties, dyscalculia, psychological challenges (autism, depression, social anxiety, obsessive-compulsive disorder) and fewer with physical challenges: mobility, hearing impairment, for example. Most students who self disclose provide documentation of ADHD. The director of academic support services provides study skills guidance to any Wabash student in time management, test-taking, note-taking, reading, and other academic skills usually grouped under this heading.

ADMISSIONS INFO FOR STUDENTS WITH LEARNING DIFFERENCES

SAT/ACT required: Yes
Interview required: No
Essay required: No
Additional application required: No
Documentation required for:
 LD: Psycho ed evaluation
 ADHD: Psycho ed evaluation
 ASD: Psycho ed evaluation
Documentation submitted to: Disability Services
Special Ed. HS course work accepted: No
Separate application required for Programs/Services: No
Contact Information
Name of program or department: Disability Services
Telephone: 765-361-6347
Fax: 765-361-6432
Email: thrushh@wabash.edu

Wabash College

GENERAL ADMISSIONS

Very important factors considered include: rigor of secondary school record, class rank, academic GPA, level of applicant's interest. *Important factors considered include:* standardized test scores, interview, extracurricular activities, talent/ability. *Other factors considered include:* application essay, recommendation(s), character/personal qualities, first generation, alumni/ae relation, geographical residence, racial/ethnic status, volunteer work, work experience. *Freshman Admission Requirements:* High school diploma is required and GED is accepted *Academic units recommended:* 4 English, 4 math, 2 science, 2 science labs, 2 foreign language, 2 social studies, 2 history, 2 academic electives,

ACCOMMODATIONS OR SERVICES

Accommodations are decided upon an individual basis after a thorough review of appropriate, current documentation. The accommodations requests must be supported through the documentation provided and must be logically linked to the current impact of the condition on academic functioning.

FINANCIAL AID

Students should submit: FAFSA. Applicants will be notified of awards on a rolling basis beginning 12/15.. The Princeton Review suggests that all financial aid forms be submitted as soon as possible after October 1. *Need-based scholarships/grants offered:* College/university scholarship or grant aid from institutional funds; Federal Pell; Private scholarships; SEOG; State scholarships/grants; United Negro College Fund *Loan aid offered:* Direct PLUS loans; Direct Subsidized Stafford Loans; Direct Unsubsidized Stafford Loans Federal Work-Study Program available. Institutional employment available.

CAMPUS LIFE

Activities: Campus Ministries; Choral groups; Concert band ; Dance ; Drama/theater; International Student Organization; Jazz band; Literary magazine; Music ensembles; Musical theater; Pep band; Radio station ; Student government; Student newspaper; Student-run film society; Symphony orchestra ; Yearbook Organizations: 65 registered organizations, 7 honor societies, 5 religious organizations. 9 fraternities, **Athletics (Intercollegiate):** *Men:* baseball, basketball, cross-country, diving, football, golf, soccer, swimming, tennis, track/field (outdoor), track/field (indoor), wrestling . **On-Campus Highlights:** Allen Athletics and Recreation Center, Wabash Chapel, Fine Arts Center, Sparks Student Center, 1832 Brew Coffee Shop.

ACCOMMODATIONS

Allowed in exams:	
Calculators	Yes
Dictionary	Yes
Computer	Yes
Spell-checker	Yes
Extended test time	Yes
Scribe	Yes
Proctors	Yes
Oral exams	Yes
Note-takers	Yes
Support services for students with	
LD	No
ADHD	No
ASD	No
Distraction-reduced environment	Yes
Recording of lecture allowed	With permission
Reading technology:	Yes
Audio books	Yes
Other assistive technology	Yes
Priority registration	No
Added costs for services:	
For LD:	No
For ADHD:	No
For ASD:	No
LD specialists	No
ADHD & ASD coaching	No
ASD specialists	No
Professional tutors	Yes
Peer tutors	Yes
Max. hours/week for services	Varies
How professors are notified of student approved accommodations	Both

COLLEGE GRADUATION REQUIREMENTS

Course waivers allowed	No
Course substitutions allowed	No

Cornell College

600 First Street SW, Mount Vernon, IA 52314-1098 • Admissions: 319-895-4161 • Fax: 319-895-4451

CAMPUS

Type of school	Private (nonprofit)
Environment	Rural
Support	S

STUDENTS

Undergrad enrollment	1,003
% male/female	51/49
% from out of state	81
% frosh live on campus	98

FINANCIAL FACTS

Annual tuition	$41,874
Room and board	$9,384
Required fees	$425

GENERAL ADMISSIONS INFO

Application fee	$30
Priority deadline	12/1

Nonfall registration accepted. Admission may be deferred for a maximum of 1 year.

Range SAT EBRW	550 –675
Range SAT Math	550 –665
Range ACT Composite	23 –29

ACADEMICS

Student/faculty ratio	11:1
% students returning for sophomore year	81
% students graduating within 4 years	65
% students graduating within 6 years	71

Most classes have 10-19 students. Most lab/discussion sessions have 10-19 students.

PROGRAMS/SERVICES FOR STUDENTS WITH LEARNING DIFFERENCES

Cornell College is committed to being an exciting place of learning and discovery for all of its students and strives to provide equal educational opportunities to students with disabilities. Students are encouraged to contact the disabilities services coordinator with any questions or concerns. Cornell College offers a variety of services and resources to help students succeed. Cornell faculty and staff members work closely with students who have documented disabilities requiring accommodation to ensure access to the College's programs, activities and services. The Coordinator of Academic Support and Advising is the designated office at Cornell College that maintains disability-related documents, certifies eligibility for services, and determines reasonable accommodations for students with disabilities.

ADMISSIONS

Students with a disability, can contact Academic Support and Advising early in the admission process so have questions answered. Students can apply with no ACT/SAT test and should choose the "No Test" option and be prepared to answer additional questions. Students also have the option to submit a portfolio instead of test scores or in addition to your test scores to showcase skills, talents, and why they will flourish at Cornell. Students can use the portfolio to show us what they do to excel—maybe it's a photo journal of a community project you led, a portfolio of paintings or drawings, a recording of performing on stage, or something so creative the college does not even know it exists.

ADMISSIONS INFO FOR STUDENTS WITH LEARNING DIFFERENCES

SAT/ACT required: Yes
Interview required: No
Essay required: Yes
Additional application required: No
Documentation required for:
 LD: Psycho ed evaluation
 ADHD: Psycho ed evaluation
 ASD: Psycho ed evaluation
Documentation submitted to: Academic Support and Advising
Special Ed. HS course work accepted: No
Separate application required for Programs/Services: No
Contact Information
Name of program or department: Academic Support and Advising
Telephone: (319) 895-4382
Fax: (319) 895-5187
Email: Bpaulsen@cornellcollege.edu

Cornell College

Additional Information

Quick Start is a one-day program designed specifically for incoming students who are concerned about easing the transition to college and may have been diagnosed with Autism Spectrum Disorder or a high level of anxiety when dealing with new situations. QuickStart Early Orientation takes place during the day before all other new students arrive on campus.. Support and Advising for an intake meeting to finalized accommodations. Academic Support and Advising coordinates content tutors, workshops on study skills, and teaches an adjunct course each spring called the Academic Performance Tutorial, where students can hone their academic skills needed for success on the block plan.

General Admissions

Very important factors considered include: rigor of secondary school record, academic GPA, character/personal qualities. *Important factors considered include:* class rank, application essay, recommendation(s), extracurricular activities, talent/ability, volunteer work, work experience. *Other factors considered include:* standardized test scores, interview, first generation, alumni/ae relation, geographical residence, state residency, racial/ethnic status, level of applicant's interest. *Freshman Admission Requirements:* High school diploma is required and GED is accepted *Academic units recommended:* 4 English, 3 math, 3 science, 2 foreign language, 3 social studies, 1 academic electives,

Accommodations or Services

Accommodations are decided upon an individual basis after a thorough review of appropriate, current documentation. The accommodations requests must be supported through the documentation provided and must be logically linked to the current impact of the condition on academic functioning.

Financial Aid

Students should submit: FAFSA. Applicants will be notified of awards on a rolling basis beginning 3/1.. The Princeton Review suggests that all financial aid forms be submitted as soon as possible after October 1. *Need-based scholarships/grants offered:* College/university scholarship or grant aid from institutional funds; Federal Pell; SEOG; State scholarships/grants *Loan aid offered:* Direct PLUS loans; Direct Subsidized Stafford Loans; Direct Unsubsidized Stafford Loans Federal Work-Study Program available. Institutional employment available.

Campus Life

Activities: Campus Ministries; Choral groups; Concert band ; Dance ; Drama/theater; International Student Organization; Jazz band; Literary magazine; Music ensembles; Musical theater; Radio station ; Student government; Student newspaper; Student-run film society; Symphony orchestra ; Yearbook Organizations: 90 registered organizations, 11 honor societies, 11 religious organizations. 8 fraternities, 7 sororities, **Athletics (Intercollegiate):** *Men:* baseball, basketball, cross-country, football, golf, soccer, tennis, track/field (outdoor), track/field (indoor), wrestling *Women:* basketball, cross-country, golf, soccer, softball, tennis, track/field (outdoor), track/field (indoor), volleyball. **On-Campus Highlights:** Thomas Commons - Orange Carpet - student center, Cole Library, Small Multi-Sports Center, Kimmel Theatre - state of the art theatre, McWethy Hall.

ACCOMMODATIONS

Allowed in exams:

Calculators	Yes
Dictionary	Yes
Computer	Yes
Spell-checker	Yes
Extended test time	Yes
Scribe	Yes
Proctors	Yes
Oral exams	Yes
Note-takers	Yes

Support services for students with

LD	Yes
ADHD	Yes
ASD	Yes
Distraction-reduced environment	Yes
Recording of lecture allowed	Yes
Reading technology:	Yes
Audio books	Yes
Other assistive technology	Yes
Priority registration	No

Added costs for services:

For LD:	No
For ADHD:	No
For ASD:	No
LD specialists	No
ADHD & ASD coaching	No
ASD specialists	No
Professional tutors	Yes
Peer tutors	Yes
Max. hours/week for services	Varies
How professors are notified of student approved accommodations	Director

COLLEGE GRADUATION REQUIREMENTS

Course waivers allowed	No
Course substitutions allowed	Yes
In what courses	Foreign language

Drake University

2507 University Avenue, Des Moines, IA 50311-4505 • Admissions: 515-271-3181 • Fax: 515-271-2831

CAMPUS

Type of school	Private (nonprofit)
Environment	Metropolis
Support	S

STUDENTS

Undergrad enrollment	3,038
% male/female	43/57
% from out of state	69
% frosh live on campus	98

FINANCIAL FACTS

Annual tuition	$41,250
Room and board	$10,528
Required fees	$146

GENERAL ADMISSIONS INFO

Priority deadline	3/1

Nonfall registration accepted. Admission may be deferred for a maximum of 1 year.

Range SAT EBRW	540–660
Range SAT Math	560–690
Range ACT Composite	24–30

ACADEMICS

Student/faculty ratio	11:1
% students returning for sophomore year	87
% students graduating within 4 years	73
% students graduating within 6 years	79

Most classes have 10–19 students.
Most lab/discussion sessions have 20–29 students.

PROGRAMS/SERVICES FOR STUDENTS WITH LEARNING DIFFERENCES

The Student Disability Services' purpose is to facilitate and enhance the opportunity for students with any type of disability to successfully complete their postsecondary education. The SDS is committed to enriching the academic experience of Drake students with disabilities through individualized assessment of accommodations and resource needs. It is the students' responsibility to self-identify a learning disability; to provide documentation of their disability; and to request the accommodations that they need.

ADMISSIONS

There is no special admission process for students with learning disabilities. All applicants are expected to meet the same admission criteria.. Students must be admitted and enrolled in the university prior to seeking accommodations or services for a learning disability. Admissions reviews each application for admission individually, there is no single, inflexible set of standards—such as GPA or test score. Instead, first-year students can choose the Standard Application or Test-Flexible Application. The Standard Application path provides a holistic admission review of the traditional admission measurements: transcript, ACT or SAT score, essay, and the other parts of your application. The Test-Flexible Application path requires an interview in lieu of an ACT or SAT; first-year students can only choose this path if they have a cumulative GPA of 3.0 or higher (on a weighted or unweighted scale) and are not pursuing per-pharmacy. per-athletic training, per-occupational therapy, or the National Alumni Scholarship.

Additional Information

The SDS can offer students appointments at the pre-admission and pre-enrollment stages; review of Drake's policies and procedures regarding students with disabilities; identification and coordination of classroom accommodations; assessment of service needs; note-takers, scribes, and readers; referral to appropriate campus resources; advocacy and liaison with the university community; and training on the use of assistive technology. Services provided by the SDS do not lower any course standards or change any requirements of a particular degree.

ADMISSIONS INFO FOR STUDENTS WITH LEARNING DIFFERENCES

SAT/ACT required: Yes
Interview required: No
Essay required: No
Additional application required: No
Documentation required for:
  LD: Psycho ed evaluation
  ADHD: Psycho ed evaluation
  ASD: Psycho ed evaluation
Documentation submitted to: Student Disability Services
Special Ed. HS course work accepted: Yes
Separate application required for Programs/Services: No
Contact Information
Name of program or department: Student Disability Services
Telephone: 515-271-1835
Email: michelle.laughlin@drake.edu

Drake University

GENERAL ADMISSIONS

Very important factors considered include: academic GPA, application essay, standardized test scores. *Important factors considered include:* rigor of secondary school record, recommendation(s), interview. *Other factors considered include:* class rank, extracurricular activities, talent/ability, character/personal qualities, volunteer work, work experience. *Freshman Admission Requirements:* High school diploma is required and GED is accepted. *Academic units recommended:* 4 English, 3 math, 2 science, 1 science lab, 2 foreign language, 4 social studies.

ACCOMMODATIONS OR SERVICES

Accommodations are decided upon an individual basis after a thorough review of appropriate, current documentation. The accommodations requests must be supported through the documentation provided and must be logically linked to the current impact of the condition on academic functioning.

FINANCIAL AID

Students should submit: FAFSA. Applicants will be notified of awards on a rolling basis beginning 1/1. The Princeton Review suggests that all financial aid forms be submitted as soon as possible after October 1. *Need-based scholarships/grants offered:* College/university scholarship or grant aid from institutional funds; Federal Pell; Private scholarships; SEOG; State scholarships/grants. *Loan aid offered:* Direct PLUS loans; Direct Subsidized Stafford Loans; Direct Unsubsidized Stafford Loans. Federal Work-Study Program available. Institutional employment available.

CAMPUS LIFE

Activities: Choral groups; Concert band; Dance; Drama/theater; International Student Organization; Jazz band; Literary magazine; Marching band; Model UN; Music ensembles; Musical theater; Pep band; Radio station; Student government; Student newspaper; Symphony orchestra. **Organizations:** 160 registered organizations, 24 honor societies, 10 religious organizations. 7 fraternities, 6 sororities. **Athletics (Intercollegiate):** *Men:* basketball, cheerleading, cross-country, football, golf, soccer, tennis, track/field (outdoor), track/field (indoor). *Women:* basketball, cheerleading, crew/rowing, cross-country, golf, soccer, softball, tennis, track/field (outdoor), track/field (indoor), volleyball. **On-Campus Highlights:** Athletic Facilities, Olmsted Center, Anderson Gallery, Helmick Commons, Residence Halls / Residence Life.

ACCOMMODATIONS

Allowed in exams:	
Calculators	Yes
Dictionary	Yes
Computer	Yes
Spell-checker	Yes
Extended test time	Yes
Scribe	Yes
Proctors	Yes
Oral exams	Yes
Note-takers	Yes
Support services for students with	
LD	Yes
ADHD	Yes
ASD	Yes
Distraction-reduced environment	Yes
Recording of lecture allowed	Yes
Reading technology:	Yes
Audio books	Yes
Other assistive technology	Yes
Priority registration	No
Added costs for services:	
For LD:	No
For ADHD:	No
For ASD:	No
LD specialists	No
ADHD & ASD coaching	No
ASD specialists	No
Professional tutors	No
Peer tutors	Yes
Max. hours/week for services	Unlimited
How professors are notified of student approved accommodations	Student

COLLEGE GRADUATION REQUIREMENTS

Course waivers allowed	No
Course substitutions allowed	No

Grand View University

1200 GRANDVIEW AVENUE, DES MOINES, IA 50316-1599 • ADMISSIONS: 515-263-2810 • FAX: 515-263-2974

CAMPUS
Type of school	Private (nonprofit)
Environment	
Support	CS

STUDENTS
Undergrad enrollment	2,079
% male/female	42/58
% from out of state	13
% frosh live on campus	85

FINANCIAL FACTS
Annual tuition	$22,986
Room and board	$7,554
Required fees	$530

GENERAL ADMISSIONS INFO
Regular application deadline	8/15

Nonfall registration accepted. Admission may be deferred for a maximum of 1 semester.

Range SAT EBRW	380–450
Range SAT Math	400–480
Range ACT Composite	19–23

ACADEMICS
Student/faculty ratio	13:1
% students returning for sophomore year	69

Most classes have 20–29 students.
Most lab/discussion sessions have 20–29 students.

PROGRAMS/SERVICES FOR STUDENTS WITH LEARNING DIFFERENCES
Accommodations are decided upon an individual basis after a thorough review of appropriate, current documentation. The accommodations requests must be supported through the documentation provided and must be logically linked to the current impact of the condition on academic functioning.

ADMISSIONS
There is no special admissions process for students with LD and ADHD. There is a freshman academy for students who do not have sufficient preparation to undertake college work but show potential for success in college. Grand View has a personalized admission and enrollment policy. Consideration may be given to: class rank and test scores; quality of high school curriculum completed; co-curricular achievement; and maturity and seriousness of purpose as displayed through church, community, school, work, and family activities. Students planning to attend Grand View University are encouraged to pursue a college-preparatory course of study in high school. It is recommended that students complete: Four years of English, three years of math, three years of science, three years of social science and two years of foreign language. Admission to a particular program or major may be governed by different standards.

Additional Information
Academic Enrichment Center provides resources which complement classroom instruction enabling students to optimize their academic experience. Students can receive help with reading comprehension, study skills, organizational skills, developing a personal management plan, test-taking strategies, writing skills, personalized instruction in math, and peer tutoring. The Career Center provides services, resources, and educational opportunities by assisting students in developing, evaluating, initiating, and implementing personal career and life plans. Faculty members serve as academic advisors. Core courses can have substitutions options. Other services or accommodations offered for students with appropriate documentation include the use of calculators, computers, or spellcheckers; extended testing time; scribes; proctors; oral exams; note-takers; a distraction-free environment for taking tests; tape-recording of lectures; and services for students with ADHD.

ADMISSIONS INFO FOR STUDENTS WITH LEARNING DIFFERENCES
SAT/ACT required: Yes
Interview required: No
Essay required: No
Additional application required: No
Documentation required for:
  LD: Psycho ed evaluation
  ADHD: Psycho ed evaluation
  ASD: Psycho ed evaluation
Documentation submitted to: Academic Success
Special Ed. HS course work accepted: Yes
Separate application required for Programs/Services: No
Contact Information
Name of program or department: Academic Enrichment Center
Telephone: 515-263-2971
Fax: 515-263-2824

Grand View University

GENERAL ADMISSIONS

Very important factors considered include: rigor of secondary school record, class rank, academic GPA, character/personal qualities. *Important factors considered include:* standardized test scores. *Other factors considered include:* extracurricular activities, talent/ability, alumni/ae relation, volunteer work, work experience. *Freshman Admission Requirements:* High school diploma is required and GED is accepted. *Academic units recommended:* 4 English, 3 math, 3 science, 2 foreign language, 3 social studies.

ACCOMMODATIONS OR SERVICES

Accommodations are decided upon an individual basis after a thorough review of appropriate, current documentation. The accommodations requests must be supported through the documentation provided and must be logically linked to the current impact of the condition on academic functioning.

FINANCIAL AID

Students should submit: FAFSA. Applicants will be notified of awards on a rolling basis beginning 3/1. The Princeton Review suggests that all financial aid forms be submitted as soon as possible after October 1. *Need-based scholarships/grants offered:* College/university scholarship or grant aid from institutional funds; Federal Pell; Private scholarships; SEOG; State scholarships/grants. *Loan aid offered:* Federal Work-Study Program available. Institutional employment available.

CAMPUS LIFE

Activities: Campus Ministries; Choral groups; Concert band; Dance; Drama/theater; International Student Organization; Jazz band; Literary magazine; Music ensembles; Pep band; Radio station; Student government; Student newspaper; Television station. **Organizations:** 28 registered organizations, 1 religious organization. **Athletics (Intercollegiate):** *Men:* baseball, basketball, cross-country, golf, soccer *Women:* basketball, cross-country, golf, soccer, softball, volleyball.

ACCOMMODATIONS

Allowed in exams:

Calculators	Yes
Dictionary	Yes
Computer	Yes
Spell-checker	Yes
Extended test time	Yes
Scribe	Yes
Proctors	Yes
Oral exams	Yes
Note-takers	Yes

Support services for students with

LD	Yes
ADHD	Yes
ASD	Yes
Distraction-reduced environment	Yes
Recording of lecture allowed	Yes
Reading technology:	Yes
Audio books	Yes
Other assistive technology	Yes
Priority registration	Yes

Added costs for services:

For LD:	No
For ADHD:	No
For ASD:	No
LD specialists	Yes
ADHD & ASD coaching	No
ASD specialists	No
Professional tutors	No
Peer tutors	Yes
Max. hours/week for services	Unlimited
How professors are notified of student approved accommodations	Student in collaboration with the director

COLLEGE GRADUATION REQUIREMENTS

Course waivers allowed	No
Course substitutions allowed	Yes
In what courses	Substitutions/options vary and must qualify

Grinnell College

1103 Park Street, Grinnell, IA 50112-1690 • Admissions: 641-269-3600 • Fax: 641-269-4800

CAMPUS

Type of school	Private (nonprofit)
Environment	Village
Support	S

STUDENTS

Undergrad enrollment	1,660
% male/female	46/54
% from out of state	92
% frosh live on campus	100

FINANCIAL FACTS

Annual tuition	$51,924
Room and board	$12,810
Required fees	$468

GENERAL ADMISSIONS INFO

Regular application deadline 1/15
Nonfall registration accepted. Admission may be deferred for a maximum of 1 year.

Range SAT EBRW	640–740
Range SAT Math	670–770
Range ACT Composite	30–34

ACADEMICS

Student/faculty ratio	9:1
% students returning for sophomore year	96
% students graduating within 4 years	84
% students graduating within 6 years	87

PROGRAMS/SERVICES FOR STUDENTS WITH LEARNING DIFFERENCES

A Commitment to Inclusion Grinnell College's commitment to creating a diverse, multicultural campus community includes many students, faculty, and staff with disabilities. Our goal is an environment that allows people of all abilities do their best work. Using universal design principals, we try to remove as many barriers as possible, and make accommodations for disabilities when needed. We provide accommodations and support for Grinnellians with disabilities such as learning, psychiatric, physical, or sensory disabilities. We offer many services to all students that can be of help to those with disabilities, including mentoring, technology, academic skills training, and career services. Grinnellians — whether they are students, faculty, or staff — continue to share and learn from each other and the latest research about the different abilities each of us bring, and how we can create an accessible, supportive environment for everyone. Students have the responsibiity to make their needs known. The most important factors for success are seeking help early and learning to be a self-advocate.

ADMISSIONS

Admission Criteria is the same for all students. Admission to Grinnell is highly selective, and while there is no single factor that guarantees admission, it helps to have taken a challenging, balanced high school curriculum. The recommended secondary school program is: 4 years of English, 4 years of mathematics (at least through pre-calculus), 3 years of social studies, 3 years of lab science, and 3 years of a foreign language. First-year applicants may interview beginning in February of their junior years and until mid-December of their senior years. Interviews are not required for admission, and applicants may only interview once. ACT/ SAT required.

Additional Information

The Academic Advising office staff will work with you on nearly any academic concern. You can come to the office for instruction on study skills and time management, to receive peer tutoring, to get support for managing your academic obligations while dealing with a personal or medical concern, or to apply for a leave of absence.

ADMISSIONS INFO FOR STUDENTS WITH LEARNING DIFFERENCES

SAT/ACT required: Yes
Interview required: No
Essay required: Yes
Additional application required: No
Documentation required for:
 LD: Psycho ed evaluation
 ADHD: Psycho ed evaluation
 ASD: Psycho ed evaluation
Documentation submitted to: Accessibility and Disability Services
Special Ed. HS course work accepted: No
Separate application required for Programs/Services: No
Contact Information
Name of program or department: Accessibility and Disability Services
Telephone: (641) 269-3702
Email: wilkeaut@grinnell.edu

GENERAL ADMISSIONS

Very important factors considered include: rigor of secondary school record, class rank, academic GPA, recommendation(s). *Important factors considered include:* application essay, standardized test scores, extracurricular activities, talent/ability. *Other factors considered include:* interview, character/personal qualities, first generation, alumni/ae relation, geographical residence, state residency, racial/ethnic status, volunteer work, work experience, level of applicant's interest. *Freshman Admission Requirements:* High school diploma is required and GED is accepted. *Academic units recommended:* 4 English, 4 math, 3 science, 3 science labs, 3 foreign language, 3 social studies, 3 history.

ACCOMMODATIONS OR SERVICES

Accommodations are decided upon an individual basis after a thorough review of appropriate, current documentation. The accommodations requests must be supported through the documentation provided and must be logically linked to the current impact of the condition on academic functioning.

FINANCIAL AID

Students should submit: CSS/Financial Aid PROFILE; FAFSA; Noncustodial PROFILE. Applicants will be notified of awards on or about 4/1. The Princeton Review suggests that all financial aid forms be submitted as soon as possible after October 1. *Need-based scholarships/grants offered:* College/university scholarship or grant aid from institutional funds; Federal Pell; Private scholarships; SEOG; State scholarships/grants. *Loan aid offered:* Direct PLUS loans; Direct Subsidized Stafford Loans; Direct Unsubsidized Stafford Loans. Federal Work-Study Program available. Institutional employment available.

CAMPUS LIFE

Activities: Campus Ministries; Choral groups; Concert band; Dance; Drama/theater; International Student Organization; Jazz band; Literary magazine; Model UN; Music ensembles; Musical theater; Pep band; Radio station; Student government; Student newspaper; Student-run film society; Symphony orchestra; Yearbook. **Organizations:** 240 registered organizations, 2 honor societies, 12 religious organizations. **Athletics (Intercollegiate):** *Men:* baseball, basketball, cross-country, diving, football, golf, soccer, swimming, tennis, track/field (outdoor), track/field (indoor). *Women:* basketball, cross-country, diving, golf, soccer, softball, swimming, tennis, track/field (outdoor), track/field (indoor), volleyball. **On-Campus Highlights:** Two building on campus are listed on the National Register of Historic Places: Mears Cottage and Goodnow Hall, Faulconer Gallery, Joe Rosenfield '25 Center, Bucksbaum Center for the Arts, Charles Benson Bear '39 Recreation and Athletic Center.

ACCOMMODATIONS

Allowed in exams:	
Calculators	Yes
Dictionary	Yes
Computer	Yes
Spell-checker	Yes
Extended test time	Yes
Scribe	Yes
Proctors	Yes
Oral exams	Yes
Note-takers	Yes
Support services for students with	
LD	Yes
ADHD	Yes
ASD	Yes
Distraction-reduced environment	Yes
Recording of lecture allowed	Yes
Reading technology:	Yes
Audio books	Yes
Other assistive technology	Wide range
including speech to text, text to speech, Braille, tactile graphics, etc. All students receive Read & Write Gold.	
Priority registration	Yes
Added costs for services:	
For LD:	No
For ADHD:	No
For ASD:	No
LD specialists	Yes
ADHD & ASD coaching	Yes
ASD specialists	No
Professional tutors	Yes
Peer tutors	Yes
Max. hours/week for services	Unlimited
How professors are notified of student approved accommodations	
Director and Student	

COLLEGE GRADUATION REQUIREMENTS

Course waivers allowed	No
Course substitutions allowed	No

Iowa State University

100 Enrollment Services Center, Ames, IA 50011-2011 • Admissions: 515-294-5836 • Fax: 515-294-2592

CAMPUS

Type of school	Public
Environment	Town
Support	CS

STUDENTS

Undergrad enrollment	29,957
% male/female	58/42
% from out of state	35
% frosh live on campus	93

FINANCIAL FACTS

Annual in-state tuition	$7,456
Annual out-of-state tuition	$21,292
Room and board	$8,546
Required fees	$1,180

GENERAL ADMISSIONS INFO

Application fee	$40

Nonfall registration accepted. Admission may be deferred for a maximum of 1 year.

Range SAT EBRW	NR
Range SAT Math	545–680
Range ACT Composite	22–28

ACADEMICS

Student/faculty ratio	19:1
% students returning for sophomore year	88
% students graduating within 4 years	45
% students graduating within 6 years	73

Most classes have 20–29 students.
Most lab/discussion sessions have 10–19 students.

PROGRAMS/SERVICES FOR STUDENTS WITH LEARNING DIFFERENCES

ISU is committed to providing equal opportunities and facilitating the personal growth and development of all students. Staff from the Student Disability Resources Office assists students with issues relating to the documented disability. A thorough review of most current LD evaluation and documentation is completed to determine the possible accommodations needed. SDR staff also offers assistance in articulating needs to faculty and staff, and may serve as a liaison in student/staff negotiations. Documentation should include current diagnosis, functional limitations, and relevant information about the student and examiner's qualifications; behavioral observation of the way students present themselves, verbal andnonverbal communication, interpersonal skills and behavior during testing; a narrative describing developmental and educational history; a description of the effect of the disability on learning is required. Recommendations concerning possible accommodations is welcomed.

ADMISSIONS

Students are admitted directly if they meet the Regent Admission Index (RAI) score. There are two mathematical formulas for computing student's RAI scores, the primary RAI formula (for students whose high school provides class rank) and the Alternative RAI formula (for students whose high school does not provide class rank. Students with LD who feel their academic record does not reflect their ability to succeed may request to considered on an individual basis. These students should submit a letter requesting special consideration and provide a description of how the disability impacts academic performance., services used in high school and documentation of the disability.

Additional Information

The Academic Learning Lab is a "learning-how-to-learn" center designed to help all students. Counselors work one-on-one to evaluate and identify problem study habits and devise strategies to improve them. The Learning Lab and Tutoring and Student Support Services are in one area called the Academic Success Center (ASC). ASC coordinates services including counseling, teaching reading, and study skills, and provides a list of tutors. The Writing Center is available to all students. The LD specialist provides

ADMISSIONS INFO FOR STUDENTS WITH LEARNING DIFFERENCES

SAT/ACT required: Yes
Interview required: No
Essay required: No
Additional application required: Yes
Documentation required for:
 LD: Psycho ed evaluation
 ADHD: Psycho ed evaluation
 ASD: Psycho ed evaluation
Documentation submitted to: SDR
Special Ed. HS course work accepted: No
Separate application required for Programs/Services: No
Contact Information
Name of program or department: Student Disability Resources
Telephone: (515) 294-7220
Email: smoats@iastate.edu

information about readers, note-takers, and scribes. Peer Supplemental Instruction (SI) is an academic assistance program attached to very difficult courses. SI leaders attend classes and conduct biweekly sessions to help students learn and study the course material. Student Support Services is a federally funded program for students with LD and others qualified to receive academic support in the form of free tutoring and skill-building workshops.

GENERAL ADMISSIONS

Very important factors considered include: rigor of secondary school record, class rank, academic GPA, standardized test scores. *Other factors considered include:* application essay, recommendation(s), interview, extracurricular activities, talent/ability, character/personal qualities, geographical residence, state residency, volunteer work, work experience. *Freshman Admission Requirements:* High school diploma is required and GED is accepted. *Academic units required:* 4 English, 3 math, 3 science, 2 science labs, 2 foreign language, 2 social studies. *Academic units recommended:* 4 English, 4 math, 4 science, 3 science labs, 3 foreign language, 4 social studies.

ACCOMMODATIONS OR SERVICES

Accommodations are decided upon an individual basis after a thorough review of appropriate, current documentation. The accommodations requests must be supported through the documentation provided and must be logically linked to the current impact of the condition on academic functioning.

FINANCIAL AID

Students should submit: FAFSA. Applicants will be notified of awards on a rolling basis beginning 1/30. The Princeton Review suggests that all financial aid forms be submitted as soon as possible after October 1. *Need-based scholarships/grants offered:* College/university scholarship or grant aid from institutional funds; Federal Pell; SEOG; State scholarships/grants. *Loan aid offered:* Direct PLUS loans; Direct Subsidized Stafford Loans; Direct Unsubsidized Stafford Loans. Federal Work-Study Program available. Institutional employment available.

CAMPUS LIFE

Activities: Campus Ministries; Choral groups; Concert band; Dance; Drama/theater; International Student Organization; Jazz band; Literary magazine; Marching band; Model UN; Music ensembles; Musical theater; Pep band; Radio station; Student government; Student newspaper; Student-run film society; Symphony orchestra; Television station. **Organizations:** 799 registered organizations, 43 honor societies, 34 religious organizations. 34 fraternities, 19 sororities. **Athletics (Intercollegiate):** *Men:* basketball, cross-country, football, golf, track/field (outdoor), track/field (indoor), wrestling. *Women:* basketball, cross-country, diving, golf, gymnastics, soccer, softball, swimming, tennis, track/field (outdoor), track/field (indoor), volleyball. **On-Campus Highlights:** Union Drive Community Center (dining center), Reiman Gardens, Lied Recreation Center, Memorial Union, Virtual Reality Lab (available to visitors also).

ACCOMMODATIONS

Allowed in exams:	
Calculators	Yes
Dictionary	Yes
Computer	Yes
Spell-checker	Yes
Extended test time	Yes
Scribe	Yes
Proctors	Yes
Oral exams	No
Note-takers	Yes
Support services for students with	
LD	Yes
ADHD	Yes
ASD	Yes
Distraction-reduced environment	Yes
Recording of lecture allowed	Yes
Reading technology:	Yes
Audio books	Yes
Other assistive technology .	Yes
Priority registration	Yes
Added costs for services:	
For LD:	No
For ADHD:	No
For ASD:	No
LD specialists	Yes
ADHD & ASD coaching	No
ASD specialists	No
Professional tutors	Yes
Peer tutors	Yes
Max. hours/week for services	Varies
How professors are notified of student approved accommodations	Student

COLLEGE GRADUATION REQUIREMENTS

Course waivers allowed	No
Course substitutions allowed	No

Loras College

1450 Alta Vista, Dubuque, IA 52001 • Admissions: 563-588-7236 • Fax: 563-588-7119

CAMPUS
Type of school	Private (nonprofit)
Environment	Town
Support	SP

STUDENTS
Undergrad enrollment	1,362
% male/female	52/48
% from out of state	58
% frosh live on campus	96

FINANCIAL FACTS
Annual tuition	$32,524
Room and board	$8,275
Required fees	$1,660

GENERAL ADMISSIONS INFO
Nonfall registration accepted. Admission may be deferred for a maximum of 1 year.

Range SAT EBRW	515–575
Range SAT Math	530–605
Range ACT Composite	20–26

ACADEMICS
Student/faculty ratio	12:1
% students returning for sophomore year	76
% students graduating within 4 years	57
% students graduating within 6 years	68

Most classes have 20–29 students.

PROGRAMS/SERVICES FOR STUDENTS WITH LEARNING DIFFERENCES

Loras College provides a supportive, comprehensive program for the motivated individual with a learning disability or AD/HD. Students can be successful in Loras' competitive environment if they have had adequate preparation, are willing to work with program staff, and take responsibility for their own learning. The Enhanced Program staff has three specialists to serve as guides and advocates, encouraging and supporting students to become independent learners. Students with LD or ADHD who are enrolled in college-preparatory courses in high school are the most appropriate candidates for the Loras program.

ADMISSIONS

Students interested in the Enhanced Program should apply simultaneously to the College and the Enhanced Program. The Enhanced Program Application and current documentation should be submitted to the Lynch Learning Center. After the materials are reviewed, appropriate candidates will be invited for an official interview with a Lynch Learning Center staff member. All application materials for the Enhanced Program must be received by December 15, the priority application date. Students are encouraged to apply early in their senior year.

Additional Information

The Autism Specific Program ARCH is designed to help students with ASD thrive emotionally, academically and socially. Through the four-year program, students work directly with Certified Autism Specialists. Students meet weekly with their coach and attend weekly study table sessions and bi-monthly mentoring meetings.

ADMISSIONS INFO FOR STUDENTS WITH LEARNING DIFFERENCES
SAT/ACT required: Yes
Interview required: Yes
Essay required: Not Applicable
Additional application required: Yes
Documentation required for:
  LD: Any documentation that provides diagnosis
  ADHD: Any documentation that provides diagnosis
  ASD: Any documentation that provides diagnosis
Documentation submitted to: Lynch Learning Center
Special Ed. HS course work accepted: Yes for ARCH
Separate application required for Programs/Services: No
Contact Information
Name of program or department: ARCH Program & Enhanced Program
Telephone: 563-588-7921
Email: lynn.gallagher@loras.edu

Loras College

GENERAL ADMISSIONS

Very important factors considered include: rigor of secondary school record, academic GPA, standardized test scores. *Other factors considered include:* class rank, application essay, recommendation(s), interview, extracurricular activities, character/personal qualities, racial/ethnic status, volunteer work, work experience, level of applicant's interest. *Freshman Admission Requirements:* High school diploma is required and GED is accepted. *Academic units recommended:* 4 English, 4 math, 3 science, 2 science labs, 3 social studies, 2 academic electives.

ACCOMMODATIONS OR SERVICES

Accommodations are decided upon an individual basis after a thorough review of appropriate, current documentation. The accommodations requests must be supported through the documentation provided and must be logically linked to the current impact of the condition on academic functioning.

FINANCIAL AID

Students should submit: FAFSA. The Princeton Review suggests that all financial aid forms be submitted as soon as possible after October 1. *Need-based scholarships/grants offered:* College/university scholarship or grant aid from institutional funds; Federal Pell; Private scholarships; SEOG; State scholarships/grants. *Loan aid offered:* Direct PLUS loans; Direct Subsidized Stafford Loans; Direct Unsubsidized Stafford Loans. Federal Work-Study Program available. Institutional employment available.

CAMPUS LIFE

Activities: Campus Ministries; Choral groups; Concert band; Dance; Drama/theater; International Student Organization; Jazz band; Literary magazine; Music ensembles; Pep band; Radio station; Student government; Student newspaper; Television station; Yearbook. **Organizations:** 71 registered organizations, 710 honor societies, 5 religious organizations. 2 fraternities, 2 sororities. **Athletics (Intercollegiate):** *Men:* baseball, basketball, cross-country, diving, football, golf, soccer, swimming, tennis, track/field (outdoor), track/field (indoor), wrestling. *Women:* basketball, cross-country, diving, golf, soccer, softball, swimming, tennis, track/field (outdoor), track/field (indoor), volleyball. **On-Campus Highlights:** Academic Resource Center, Alumni Campus Center, Rock Bowl Stadium, Athletic and Wellness Center, Center for Dubuque History.

ACCOMMODATIONS

Allowed in exams:

Calculators	Yes
Dictionary	Yes
Computer	Yes
Spell-checker	Yes
Extended test time	Yes
Scribe	Yes
Proctors	Yes
Oral exams	Yes
Note-takers	Yes

Support services for students with

LD	Yes
ADHD	Yes
ASD	Yes
Distraction-reduced environment	Yes
Recording of lecture allowed	Yes
Reading technology:	Yes
Audio books	Yes
Other assistive technology	Smart pen
Speech to text software	
Priority registration	Yes

Added costs for services:

For LD:	Yes, ARCH and Enhanced
For ADHD:	Yes, ARCH and Enhanced
For ASD:	Yes, ARCH and Enhanced
LD specialists	Yes
ADHD & ASD coaching	Yes
ASD specialists	Yes
Professional tutors	Yes
Peer tutors	Yes
Max. hours/week for services	Varies
How professors are notified of student approved accommodations	Student

COLLEGE GRADUATION REQUIREMENTS

Course waivers allowed	Yes
In what courses	Varies
Course substitutions allowed	No

Morningside College

1501 MORNINGSIDE AVENUE, SIOUX CITY, IA 51106-1751 • ADMISSIONS: 712-274-5511 • FAX: 712-274-5101

CAMPUS
Type of school	Private (nonprofit)
Environment	City
Support	CS

STUDENTS
Undergrad enrollment	1,180
% male/female	46/54
% from out of state	32
% frosh live on campus	94

FINANCIAL FACTS
Annual tuition	$21,116
Room and board	$6,729
Required fees	$1,130

GENERAL ADMISSIONS INFO
Application fee	$25
Priority deadline	8/15

Nonfall registration accepted. Admission may be deferred.

Range SAT EBRW	NR
Range SAT Math	NR
Range ACT Composite	20–25

ACADEMICS
Student/faculty ratio	17:1
% students returning for sophomore year	70

Most classes have 20–29 students.
Most lab/discussion sessions have 20–29 students.

PROGRAMS/SERVICES FOR STUDENTS WITH LEARNING DIFFERENCES

Students with learning disabilities can and do succeed in college. However, students with different learning styles may need assistance in order to be truly successful students. Morningside College will require supportive data to verify that a disability exists. These may include, but are not necessarily limited to, the following: high school records; specific plans recommended by qualified professionals and/or consultants; and satisfactory medical determination as required.

ADMISSIONS

Morningside's selective admissions program is based on the following criteria: class rank, college preparatory course work, GPA, ACT or SAT, essay participation recommended but not required, character, and personal abilities. Students with ACT of 20 or SAT of 1410, and either ranked in the top half of their class or have achieved a high school GPA of 2.5 meet the academic standards for admissions. First-year students who have been out of high school more than 5 years are not required to submit ACT or SAT test scores but are required to take math and/or English placement assessments. Students who have not completed high school may be admitted on the basis of a GED score.

Additional Information

Reasonable accommodations for students might include the following: note-taking, copies of instructor's notes, taperecording of class, reasonable equipment modification, preferential seating, books on tape, test-taking accommodations, word processor adaptations, and reader service. The Academic Support Center is open to all students. Academic Support Center staff helps students improve or strengthen their academics by providing free assistance in writing techniques. Writing specialists are available to help students with the basics as well as help proficient writers who want assistance for particular writing assignments or projects.. Staff and student tutors are available in the Academic Support Center for students who want help in areas such as accounting, biology, chemistry, economics, history, math, science, religion, and sociology. The Krone Advising Center houses a team of full-time, professional, first-year advisers.

ADMISSIONS INFO FOR STUDENTS WITH LEARNING DIFFERENCES

SAT/ACT required: Yes
Interview required: Yes
Essay required: Yes
Additional application required: No
Documentation required for:
  LD: Psycho ed evaluation
  ADHD: Diagnosis based on DSM-V; history of behaviors impairing functioning in academic setting; diagnostic interview; history of symptoms; evidence of ongoing behaviors.
  ASD: Psycho ed evaluation
Documentation submitted to: Associate Dean for Academic Affairs
Special Ed. HS course work accepted: N/A
Separate application required for Programs/Services: Yes
Contact Information
Name of program or department: Academic Support Center
Telephone: 800-831-0806, ext- 5388
Fax: 712-274-5358

Morningside College

General Admissions

Very important factors considered include: rigor of secondary school record, class rank, academic GPA, standardized test scores, recommendation(s). *Important factors considered include:* interview, extracurricular activities, talent/ability. *Other factors considered include:* application essay. *Freshman Admission Requirements:* High school diploma is required and GED is accepted. *Academic units recommended:* 3 English, 2 math, 2 science, 3 social studies.

Accommodations or Services

Accommodations are decided upon an individual basis after a thorough review of appropriate, current documentation. The accommodations requests must be supported through the documentation provided and must be logically linked to the current impact of the condition on academic functioning.

Financial Aid

Students should submit: FAFSA. Applicants will be notified of awards on a rolling basis beginning 3/31. The Princeton Review suggests that all financial aid forms be submitted as soon as possible after October 1. *Need-based scholarships/grants offered:* College/university scholarship or grant aid from institutional funds; Federal Pell; Private scholarships; SEOG; State scholarships/grants. *Loan aid offered:* Federal Work-Study Program available. Institutional employment available.

Campus Life

Activities: Campus Ministries; Choral groups; Concert band; Dance; Drama/theater; International Student Organization; Jazz band; Literary magazine; Marching band; Music ensembles; Musical theater; Pep band; Radio station; Student government; Student newspaper; Television station; Yearbook. **Organizations:** 40 registered organizations, 15 honor societies, 10 religious organizations. 2 fraternities, 1 sorority. **Athletics (Intercollegiate):** *Men:* baseball, basketball, cheerleading, cross-country, football, golf, soccer, swimming, tennis, track/field (outdoor), track/field (indoor), wrestling. *Women:* basketball, cheerleading, cross-country, golf, soccer, softball, swimming, tennis, track/field (outdoor), track/field (indoor), volleyball. **On-Campus Highlights:** New Student Apartments, Health-Fitness Center, Eppley Auditorium, Olsen Student Center, Walker Science Center.

ACCOMMODATIONS

Allowed in exams:

Calculators	Yes
Dictionary	Yes
Computer	Yes
Spell-checker	Yes
Extended test time	Yes
Scribe	Yes
Proctors	Yes
Oral exams	Yes
Note-takers	Yes

Support services for students with

LD	Yes
ADHD	Yes
ASD	Yes
Distraction-reduced environment	Yes
Recording of lecture allowed	Yes
Reading technology:	No
Audio books	Yes
Other assistive technology	No
Priority registration	No

Added costs for services:

For LD:	No
For ADHD:	No
For ASD:	No
LD specialists	No
ADHD & ASD coaching	No
ASD specialists	No
Professional tutors	Yes
Peer tutors	Yes
Max. hours/week for services	Unlimited
How professors are notified of student approved accommodations	Associate Dean

COLLEGE GRADUATION REQUIREMENTS

Course waivers allowed	No
Course substitutions allowed	No

St. Ambrose University

518 W. Locust Street, Davenport, IA 52803-2898 • Admissions: 563-333-6300 • Fax: 563-333-6038

CAMPUS

Type of school	Private (nonprofit)
Environment	City
Support	CS

STUDENTS

Undergrad enrollment	2,381
% male/female	43/57
% from out of state	60
% frosh live on campus	90

FINANCIAL FACTS

Annual tuition	$29,736
Room and board	$10,164
Required fees	$280

GENERAL ADMISSIONS INFO

Nonfall registration accepted. Admission may be deferred.

Range SAT EBRW	NR
Range SAT Math	NR
Range ACT Composite	20–25

ACADEMICS

Student/faculty ratio	12:1
% students returning for sophomore year	77

Most classes have 20–29 students.
Most lab/discussion sessions have 20–29 students.

PROGRAMS/SERVICES FOR STUDENTS WITH LEARNING DIFFERENCES

At SAU, all students get the chance to demonstrate their academic abilities. The Accessibility Resource Center does not lower course standards or alter degree requirements. It does offer services and reasonable accommodations intended to reduce the effects a disability may have on your performance in a traditional academic setting.

ADMISSIONS

Applicants can be admitted with a cumulative grade point average of 2.5 or above (on a 4.0 unweighted scale) from an accredited high school and have an ACT of 20 or above or a 1020 or above on the SAT. Students who graduated from high school five or more years ago do not need to supply ACT or SAT scores. The writing portion of the ACT is optional for admission to St. Ambrose University.If applicants can't satisfy both of the requirements above, they may qualify for Conditional Admission. Minimum requirements for Conditional/Provisional status are GPA: 2.0 cumulative GPA (on a 4.0 unweighted scale) and 18 on the ACT or 940 on the SAT.. These students will have their academic progress monitored each semester by the SAU Board of Studies, which is comprised of SAU faculty.Additional InformationThe learning disability specialist or SDS director acts as academic advisor for students with disabilities during their first year. SDS staff assists students in selecting courses while taking into consideration their disability. Students receive support in practicing self-advocacy with faculty and others when identifying and requesting appropriate accommodations.

Additional Information

Through Student Disability Services students may have access to the following services: academic advising; advocacy; alternate exam arrangements including extended time, large print, separate testing room, readers, scribes, or use of a computer; books in alternative format; assitive technology; equipment loans; LD specialist to provide one-to-one learning skills instruction; liaison with outside agencies; screening and referral for diagnosis of learning disabilities; and other accommodations to meet appropriate needs. A four-week Summer Transition Program is available for collegebound students with learning disabilities, Asperger's and/or ADHD who have completed their junior year in high school. Students do not have to be admitted to St. Ambrose to participate in this program, and completion of the program does not guarantee admission to St. Ambrose University. Students take either Intro to Psychology or Intro to Sociology, and engage in sessions where they receive instruction on study skills, note-taking, textbook reading, memorization strategies,

ADMISSIONS INFO FOR STUDENTS WITH LEARNING DIFFERENCES

SAT/ACT required: Yes
Interview required: No
Essay required: Not Applicable
Additional application required: Yes
Documentation required for:
 LD: Psycho ed evaluation
 ADHD: Psycho ed evaluation
 ASD: Psycho ed evaluation
Documentation submitted to: Accessibility Resource Center
Special Ed. HS course work accepted: Yes
Separate application required for Programs/Services: No
Contact Information
Name of program or department: Accessibility Resource Center
Telephone: 563-333-6275
Email: SaddlerRyanC@sau.edu

and test preparation. Additional sessions are also required where students are engaged in informal discussion groups on topics such as rights and responsibilities of students with disabilities, selecting accommodations, understanding their disability, and self-advocacy. Learning disability specialists attend the psych class and assist students in applying learning skills to their course work.

GENERAL ADMISSIONS

Very important factors considered include: rigor of secondary school record, class rank, academic GPA, standardized test scores. *Other factors considered include:* application essay, recommendation(s), interview, extracurricular activities, talent/ability, character/personal qualities, first generation, alumni/ae relation, racial/ethnic status, volunteer work. *Freshman Admission Requirements:* High school diploma is required and GED is accepted. *Academic units recommended:* 4 English, 3 math, 2 science, 2 science labs, 1 foreign language, 1 social studies, 1 history, 4 academic electives. Accomodation or Services Accommodations are decided upon an individual basis after a thorough review of appropriate, current documentation. The accommodations requests must be supported through the documentation provided and must be logically linked to the current impact of the condition on academic functioning.

ACCOMMODATIONS OR SERVICES

Accommodations are decided upon an individual basis after a thorough review of appropriate, current documentation. The accommodations requests must be supported through the documentation provided and must be logically linked to the current impact of the condition on academic functioning.

FINANCIAL AID

Students should submit: FAFSA. Applicants will be notified of awards on a rolling basis beginning 2/1. The Princeton Review suggests that all financial aid forms be submitted as soon as possible after October 1. *Need-based scholarships/grants offered:* College/university scholarship or grant aid from institutional funds; Federal Pell; Private scholarships; SEOG; State scholarships/grants. *Loan aid offered:* Direct PLUS loans; Direct Subsidized Stafford Loans; Direct Unsubsidized Stafford Loans. Federal Work-Study Program available. Institutional employment available.

CAMPUS LIFE

Activities: Campus Ministries; Choral groups; Concert band; Dance; Drama/theater; International Student Organization; Jazz band; Literary magazine; Marching band; Model UN; Music ensembles; Pep band; Radio station; Student government; Student newspaper; Symphony orchestra; Television station. **Organizations:** 26 registered organizations, 12 honor societies, 3 religious organizations. **Athletics (Intercollegiate):** *Men:* baseball, basketball, bowling, cheerleading, cross-country, football, golf, soccer, tennis, track/field (outdoor), track/field (indoor), volleyball. *Women:* basketball, bowling, cheerleading, cross-country, golf, soccer, softball, tennis, track/field (outdoor), track/field (indoor), volleyball. **On-Campus Highlights:** Rogalski Center (Student Union), Wellness Center, St. Vincent Fields, Chapel, Galvin Fine Arts Building.

ACCOMMODATIONS

Allowed in exams:	
Calculators	Yes
Dictionary	Yes
Computer	Yes
Spell-checker	Yes
Extended test time	Yes
Scribe	Yes
Proctors	Yes
Oral exams	Yes
Note-takers	Yes
Support services for students with	
LD	Yes
ADHD	Yes
ASD	Yes
Distraction-reduced environment	Yes
Recording of lecture allowed	Yes
Reading technology:	Yes
Audio books	Yes
Other assistive technology	Determined
based on needs of student	
Priority registration	No
Added costs for services:	
For LD:	No
For ADHD:	No
For ASD:	No
LD specialists	Yes
ADHD & ASD coaching	Yes
ASD specialists	No
Professional tutors	Yes
Peer tutors	Yes
Max. hours/week for services	Varies
How professors are notified of student	
approved accommodations	Student

COLLEGE GRADUATION REQUIREMENTS

Course waivers allowed	No
Course substitutions allowed	Yes
In what courses	Foreign Language

University of Iowa

101 Jessup Hall, Iowa City, IA 52242 • Admissions: 319-335-3847 • Fax: 319-333-1535

CAMPUS

Type of school	Public
Environment	City
Support	CS

STUDENTS

Undergrad enrollment	23,349
% male/female	47/53
% from out of state	37
% frosh live on campus	92

FINANCIAL FACTS

Annual in-state tuition	$7,486
Annual out-of-state tuition	$29,130
Room and board	$10,450
Required fees	$1,479

GENERAL ADMISSIONS INFO

Application fee	$40
Regular application deadline	5/1

Nonfall registration accepted. Admission may be deferred.

Range SAT EBRW	570–680
Range SAT Math	570–690
Range ACT Composite	23–28

ACADEMICS

Student/faculty ratio	16:1
% students returning for sophomore year	87
% students graduating within 4 years	54
% students graduating within 6 years	1

Most classes have fewer than 10 students. Most lab/discussion sessions have 10–19 students.

PROGRAMS/SERVICES FOR STUDENTS WITH LEARNING DIFFERENCES

The mission of LD/ADHD Services in the University of Iowa's Student Disability Services (SDS) is to facilitate individualized academic accommodations for eligible students. Each student has an assigned staff adviser who assists the student in identifying appropriate course accommodations, commumincating classroom needs to faculty, accessing other related services and resources. Students with LD/ADHD who need disability servcies are encouraged to register with SDS as soon as possible. Students are encouraged to schedule an on-campus interview with the LD/ADHD coordinator to learn more about disability services for students with LD-ADHD and about the university. The University of Iowa also offers the REACH Program. This is a transition certificate program for college students with disabilities, such as autism, intellectual disabilities, and learning disabilities. UI REACH provides a Big Ten college experience and empowers young adults to become independent members of the community. Coursework, campus life, and career experiences prepare students to reach their full potential.

ADMISSIONS

Students are admitted directly if they meet the Regent Admission Index (RAI) score. There are two mathematical formulas for computing student's RAI scores, the primary RAI formula (for students whose high school class rank) and the Alternative RAI formula (for students whose high school does not provide class rank. Students with LD who feel their academic record does not reflect their ability to succeed may request to considered on an individual basis. These students should submit a letter requesting special consideration and provide a description of how the disability impacts academic performance., services used in high school and documentation of the disability. UI REACH recognizes the unique attributes of each applicant and seeks to identify those students who are most likely to benefit from the UI REACH experience. The application and interview process are designed to determine the compatibility of an applicant's learning performance, current life skills, motivation, and job interests with the program goals.

Additional Information

Students requesting disability-related services from Student Disability Services are required to provide satisfactory evidence of their eligibility for services. Services are determined on a case-by-case basis. They include priority registration for courses, assistance in communicating with faculty and administrators, facilitation of classroom accomodations, alternative

ADMISSIONS INFO FOR STUDENTS WITH LEARNING DIFFERENCES

SAT/ACT required: Yes
Interview required: No
Essay required: No
Additional application required: No
Documentation required for:
 LD: Psycho ed evaluation
 ADHD: Psycho ed evaluation
 ASD: Psycho ed evaluation
Documentation submitted to: Student Disability Services
Special Ed. HS course work accepted: No
Separate application required for Programs/Services: No
Contact Information
Name of program or department: Student Disability Services
Telephone: 319-335-1462
Fax: 319-335-3973
Email: sds-info@uiowa.edu

examination services, text-to-audio services, counseling referrals, and tutoring referrals.

GENERAL ADMISSIONS

Very important factors considered include: rigor of secondary school record, class rank, academic GPA, standardized test scores. *Other factors considered include:* recommendation(s), talent/ability, character/personal qualities, state residency. *Freshman Admission Requirements:* High school diploma is required and GED is accepted. *Academic units required:* 4 English, 3 math, 3 science, 2 foreign language, 3 social studies. *Academic units recommended:* 4 math.

ACCOMMODATIONS OR SERVICES

Accommodations are decided upon an individual basis after a thorough review of appropriate, current documentation. The accommodations requests must be supported through the documentation provided and must be logically linked to the current impact of the condition on academic functioning.

FINANCIAL AID

Students should submit: FAFSA. Applicants will be notified of awards on a rolling basis beginning 11/15. The Princeton Review suggests that all financial aid forms be submitted as soon as possible after October 1. *Need-based scholarships/grants offered:* College/university scholarship or grant aid from institutional funds; Federal Pell; Private scholarships; SEOG; State scholarships/grants. *Loan aid offered:* Direct PLUS loans; Direct Subsidized Stafford Loans; Direct Unsubsidized Stafford Loans. Federal Work-Study Program available. Institutional employment available.

CAMPUS LIFE

Activities: Campus Ministries; Choral groups; Concert band; Dance; Drama/theater; International Student Organization; Jazz band; Literary magazine; Marching band; Model UN; Music ensembles; Musical theater; Opera; Pep band; Radio station; Student government; Student newspaper; Student run film society; Symphony orchestra; Television station. **Organizations:** 488 registered organizations, 21 honor societies, 24 religious organizations. 18 fraternities, 18 sororities. **Athletics (Intercollegiate):** *Men:* baseball, basketball, cheerleading, cross-country, diving, football, golf, gymnastics, swimming, tennis, track/field (outdoor), track/field (indoor), wrestling. *Women:* basketball, cheerleading, crew/rowing, cross-country, diving, field hockey, golf, gymnastics, soccer, softball, swimming, tennis, track/field (outdoor), track/field (indoor), volleyball. **On-Campus Highlights:** Kinnick Stadium/Carver Hawkeye Arena, Campus Recreation and Wellness Center, Finkbine Golf Course, Pentacrest/Old Capitol, UI Main Library.

ACCOMMODATIONS

Allowed in exams:

Calculators	Yes
Dictionary	No
Computer	Yes
Spell-checker	Yes
Extended test time	Yes
Scribe	Yes
Proctors	Yes
Oral exams	No
Note-takers	Yes

Support services for students with

LD	Yes
ADHD	Yes
ASD	Yes
Distraction-reduced environment	Yes
Recording of lecture allowed	Yes
Reading technology:	Yes
Audio books	Yes
Other assistive technology systems.	Jaws, FM
Priority registration	Yes

Added costs for services:

For LD:	No
For ADHD:	No
For ASD:	No
LD specialists	Yes
ADHD & ASD coaching	No
ASD specialists	No
Professional tutors	Yes
Peer tutors	Yes
Max. hours/week for services	Varies
How professors are notified of student approved accommodations	Student

COLLEGE GRADUATION REQUIREMENTS

Course waivers allowed	No
Course substitutions allowed	Yes
In what courses	World Language

University of Northern Iowa

1227 West 27th Street, Cedar Falls, IA 50614-0018 • Admissions: 319-273-2281 • Fax: 319-273-2885

CAMPUS

Type of school	Public
Environment	Town
Support	S

STUDENTS

Undergrad enrollment	9,836
% male/female	43/57
% from out of state	6
% frosh live on campus	92

FINANCIAL FACTS

Annual in-state tuition	$7,665
Annual out-of-state tuition	$18,207
Room and board	$8,948
Required fees	$1,273

GENERAL ADMISSIONS INFO

Application fee	$40

Nonfall registration accepted. Admission may be deferred.

Range SAT EBRW	NR
Range SAT Math	NR
Range ACT Composite	24–21

ACADEMICS

Student/faculty ratio	18:1
% students returning for sophomore year	81
% students graduating within 4 years	40
% students graduating within 6 years	67

Most classes have 20–29 students.
Most lab/discussion sessions have 10–19 students.

PROGRAMS/SERVICES FOR STUDENTS WITH LEARNING DIFFERENCES

Student Disability Services' mission is to provide services and promote an accessible environment which allows people with disabilities an equal opportunity for participation in educational and other campus activities. The office is responsible for determining eligibility for academic and residence hall accommodations.

ADMISSIONS

Students are admitted directly if they meet the Regent Admission Index (RAI) score. There are two mathematical formulas for computing student's RAI scores, the primary RAI formula (for students whose high school class rank) and the Alternative RAI formula (for students whose high school does not provide class rank. Students with LD who feel their academic record does not reflect their ability to succeed may request to considered on an individual basis. These students should submit a letter requesting special consideration and provide a description of how the disability impacts academic performance., services used in high school and documentation of the disability.

Additional Information

Students with disabilities requiring services should register with office of Student Disability Services (SDS) in order to determine eligibility for academic accommodations. Accommodations for students are determined by SDS staff on a case-by-case basis.

ADMISSIONS INFO FOR STUDENTS WITH LEARNING DIFFERENCES

SAT/ACT required: Yes
Interview required: No
Essay required: Not Applicable
Additional application required: Yes
Documentation required for:
  LD: Students are encouraged to submit a recent psychoeducational evaluation for documentation. If such documentation does not exist, they can submit their most recent IEP/504 Plan.
  ADHD: Students are encouraged to submit a recent psychoeducational evaluation for documentation. If such documentation does not exist, they can submit a letter from their treating physician/psychologist or their most recent IEP/504 Plan.
  ASD: A letter from a mental health provider (i.e. psychologist, therapist, counselor), an IEP or 504 plan, or a psychoeducational evaluation.
Documentation submitted to: Student Disability Services
Special Ed. HS course work accepted: No
Separate application required for Programs/Services: No
Contact Information
Name of program or department: Student Disability Services
Telephone: 319-273-2677
Fax: 319-273-7576
Email: disabilityservices@uni.edu

University of Northern Iowa

GENERAL ADMISSIONS

Very important factors considered include: rigor of secondary school record, class rank, academic GPA, standardized test scores. *Other factors considered include:* application essay, recommendation(s), interview, talent/ability, first generation. *Freshman Admission Requirements:* High school diploma is required and GED is accepted. *Academic units required:* 4 English, 3 math, 3 science, 3 social studies, 2 academic electives. *Academic units recommended:* 1 science labs, 2 foreign language.

ACCOMMODATIONS OR SERVICES

Accommodations are decided upon an individual basis after a thorough review of appropriate, current documentation. The accommodations requests must be supported through the documentation provided and must be logically linked to the current impact of the condition on academic functioning.

FINANCIAL AID

Students should submit: FAFSA. Applicants will be notified of awards on a rolling basis beginning 1/15. The Princeton Review suggests that all financial aid forms be submitted as soon as possible after October 1. *Need-based scholarships/grants offered:* College/university scholarship or grant aid from institutional funds; Federal Pell; Private scholarships; SEOG; State scholarships/grants. *Loan aid offered:* Direct PLUS loans; Direct Subsidized Stafford Loans; Direct Unsubsidized Stafford Loans. Federal Work-Study Program available. Institutional employment available.

CAMPUS LIFE

Activities: Campus Ministries; Choral groups; Concert band; Dance; Drama/theater; International Student Organization; Jazz band; Literary magazine; Marching band; Model UN; Music ensembles; Musical theater; Opera; Pep band; Radio station; Student government; Student newspaper; Symphony orchestra; Yearbook. **Organizations:** 278 registered organizations, 18 honor societies, 21 religious organizations. 5 fraternities, 4 sororities. **Athletics (Intercollegiate):** *Men:* basketball, cross-country, football, golf, track/field (outdoor), track/field (indoor), wrestling. *Women:* basketball, cross-country, diving, golf, soccer, softball, swimming, tennis, track/field (outdoor), track/field (indoor), volleyball. **On-Campus Highlights:** Wellness Recreation Center, Gallagher-Bluedorn Performing Arts Center, Piazza and Rialto Dining Centers, Maucker University Union, UNI-DOME and McLeod Center.

ACCOMMODATIONS

Allowed in exams:

Calculators	Yes
Dictionary	No
Computer	Yes
Spell-checker	Yes
Extended test time	Yes
Scribe	Yes
Proctors	Yes
Oral exams	Yes
Note-takers	Yes

Support services for students with

LD	Yes
ADHD	Yes
ASD	Yes
Distraction-reduced environment	Yes
Recording of lecture allowed	Yes
Reading technology:	Yes
Audio books	Yes

Other assistive technology Read&Write Gold, JAWS, ZoomText, Dragon Naturally Speaking.

Priority registration	Yes

Added costs for services:

For LD:	No
For ADHD:	No
For ASD:	No
LD specialists	No
ADHD & ASD coaching	Yes
ASD specialists	Yes
Professional tutors	Yes
Peer tutors	Yes
Max. hours/week for services	2
How professors are notified of student approved accommodations	Student

COLLEGE GRADUATION REQUIREMENTS

Course waivers allowed	No
Course substitutions allowed	Yes
In what courses	
Depending on individual student need	

Kansas State University

110 Anderson Hall, Manhattan, KS 66506 • Admissions: 785-532-6250 • Fax: 785-532-6393

CAMPUS
Type of school	Public
Environment	Town
Support	CS

STUDENTS
Undergrad enrollment	18,171
% male/female	53/47
% from out of state	18
% frosh live on campus	75

FINANCIAL FACTS
Annual in-state tuition	$8,750
Annual out-of-state tuition	$23,220
Room and board	$8,970
Required fees	$888

GENERAL ADMISSIONS INFO
Application fee	$40

Nonfall registration accepted.

Range SAT EBRW	NR
Range SAT Math	NR
Range ACT Composite	22–28

ACADEMICS
Student/faculty ratio	18:1
% students returning for sophomore year	84
% students graduating within 4 years	33
% students graduating within 6 years	63

Most classes have 20–29 students.
Most lab/discussion sessions have 10–19 students.

PROGRAMS/SERVICES FOR STUDENTS WITH LEARNING DIFFERENCES

Student Access Center appreciates disability as an integral part of the K-State University experience. We are committed to providing equal access and opportunity to all campus programs and services for students with disabilities. Through collaboration and support of the entire campus community, the Access Center promotes disability pride, self-determination of the student, and universally accessible design principles, so that everyone has full access to university life.

ADMISSIONS

Complete the pre-college curriculum with at least a 2.5 grade point average on a 4.0 scale. Achieve a 2.0 GPA on all attempted college work. Students can be admitted with an ACT minimum composite of 21, a minimum SAT 980.

Additional Information

The Academic assistance Center provides a variety of academic support services, including learning skills instruction, computer-assisted mathematics practice, academic counseling, credit by examination, entrance and professional examinations, and tutoring in a variety of K-State courses. Students experiencing academic difficulties are aided directly by a member of the Academic Assistance Center staff.

ADMISSIONS INFO FOR STUDENTS WITH LEARNING DIFFERENCES

SAT/ACT required: Yes
Interview required: Not Applicable
Essay required: Not Applicable
Additional application required: Yes
Documentation required for:
  LD: Demonstrate current, functional limitations in the learning environment. Verification of history for receiving specific accommodations is strongly considered.
  ADHD: Demonstrate current, functional limitations in the learning environment. Verification of history for receiving specific accommodations is strongly considered.
  ASD: Demonstrate current, functional limitations in the learning environment. Verification of history for receiving specific accommodations is strongly considered.
Documentation submitted to: Student Access Center
Special Ed. HS course work accepted: Not Applicable
Contact Information
Name of program or department: Student Access Center
Telephone: 785-532-6441
Fax: 785-532-6457
Email: accesscenter@ksu.edu

Kansas State University

GENERAL ADMISSIONS
Very important factors considered include: rigor of secondary school record, class rank, academic GPA, standardized test scores. *Important factors considered include:* level of applicant's interest. *Other factors considered include:* recommendation(s). *Freshman Admission Requirements:* High school diploma is required and GED is accepted. *Academic units required:* 4 English, 3 math, 3 science, 3 social studies, 3 academic electives.

ACCOMMODATIONS OR SERVICES
Accommodations are decided upon an individual basis after a thorough review of appropriate, current documentation. The accommodations requests must be supported through the documentation provided and must be logically linked to the current impact of the condition on academic functioning.

FINANCIAL AID
Students should submit: FAFSA. Applicants will be notified of awards on a rolling basis beginning 4/1. The Princeton Review suggests that all financial aid forms be submitted as soon as possible after October 1. *Need-based scholarships/grants offered:* College/university scholarship or grant aid from institutional funds; Federal Pell; Private scholarships; SEOG; State scholarships/grants. *Loan aid offered:* Direct PLUS loans; Direct Subsidized Stafford Loans; Direct Unsubsidized Stafford Loans. Federal Work-Study Program available. Institutional employment available.

CAMPUS LIFE
Activities: Campus Ministries; Choral groups; Concert band; Dance; Drama/theater; International Student Organization; Jazz band; Marching band; Music ensembles; Musical theater; Pep band; Radio station; Student government; Student newspaper; Symphony orchestra; Television station; Yearbook. **Organizations:** 594 registered organizations, 36 honor societies, 37 religious organizations. 28 fraternities, 16 sororities. **Athletics (Intercollegiate):** *Men:* baseball, basketball, cheerleading, cross-country, football, golf, track/field (outdoor), track/field (indoor). *Women:* basketball, cheerleading, crew/rowing, cross-country, equestrian sports, golf, tennis, track/field (outdoor), track/field (indoor), volleyball. **On-Campus Highlights:** Peters Recreation Complex, Sports Complexes: Wagner Field, Bramlage Coliseum, K-State Student Union, Ahearn Fieldhouse, Beach Museum of Art.

ACCOMMODATIONS
Allowed in exams:

Calculators	Yes
Dictionary	Yes
Computer	Yes
Spell-checker	Yes
Extended test time	Yes
Scribe	Yes
Proctors	Yes
Oral exams	Yes
Note-takers	Yes

Support services for students with

LD	Yes
ADHD	Yes
ASD	Yes
Distraction-reduced environment	Yes
Recording of lecture allowed	Yes
Reading technology:	Yes
Audio books	Yes
Other assistive technology	Writing Pens, Zoom Text, Read and Write Software, Dictation Software
Priority registration	Yes

Added costs for services:

For LD:	No
For ADHD:	No
For ASD:	No
LD specialists	Yes
ADHD & ASD coaching	Yes
ASD specialists	No
Professional tutors	Yes
Peer tutors	Not Applicable
Max. hours/week for services	2
How professors are notified of student approved accommodations	Director and Student

COLLEGE GRADUATION REQUIREMENTS

Course waivers allowed	Yes
In what courses	Math, Foreign Language
Course substitutions allowed	Yes
In what courses	Math, Foreign Language

Pittsburg State University

1701 SOUTH BROADWAY, PITTSBURG, KS 66762 • ADMISSIONS: 620-235-4251 • FAX: 620-235-6003

CAMPUS

Type of school	Public
Environment	Village
Support	CS

STUDENTS

Undergrad enrollment	5,536
% male/female	53/47
% from out of state	30
% frosh live on campus	74

FINANCIAL FACTS

Annual in-state tuition	$6,508
Annual out-of-state tuition	$16,978
Room and board	$6,734
Required fees	$1,196

GENERAL ADMISSIONS INFO

Application fee	$30

Nonfall registration accepted. Admission may be deferred for a maximum of 3 semesters.

Range SAT EBRW	NR
Range SAT Math	NR
Range ACT Composite	19–24

ACADEMICS

Student/faculty ratio	17:1
% students returning for sophomore year	74

Most classes have 10–19 students.

PROGRAMS/SERVICES FOR STUDENTS WITH LEARNING DIFFERENCES

The Center for Student Accommodations (CSA) provides support services to currently enrolled reasonable accommodations depend upon the nature and degree of severity of the documented disability. While the Americans with Disabilities Act of 1990 requires that priority consideration be given to the specific methods requested by the student, it does not imply that a particular accommodation must be granted if it is deemed not reasonable and other suitable techniques are available.

ADMISSIONS

Admission is the same for all applicants.. Applicants should complete the pre-college curriculum with at least a 2.0 GPA (2.5 for non-residents) on a 4.0 scale) and have either an ACT of 21 or higher or rank in the top 1/3 of the high school graduating class.

Additional Information

The Center for Student Accommodation provides services determined on an individual basis. They match the student with the appropriate service. Reasonable accommodations are typically categorized on the basis of: (a) mode of presentation (e.g., note-taker for class lectures, reader for exams); (b) mode of expression (e.g., use of a computer for written exams), (c) location and setting (e.g., distraction reduced testing location), and (d) time (e.g., extra time for tests). The Center for Student Accommodations can also provide study skill strategies and direct students to other appropriate university support services.

ADMISSIONS INFO FOR STUDENTS WITH LEARNING DIFFERENCES

SAT/ACT required:
Interview required: No
Essay required: No
Additional application required: Yes
Documentation required for:
  LD: Recent assessments or psychological reports with test analysis and interpretation of learning disability. Needs to be within 3 years.
  ADHD: Recent assessments or medical report from physician or psychiatrist of ADHD diagnosis. (Within 3 years)
  ASD: Recent (within 3 years) assessment/medical reports/psych reports from licensed health care professional or psychologist of diagnosis.
Documentation submitted to: Center for Student Accommodations
Special Ed. HS course work accepted: No
Separate application required for Programs/Services: No
Contact Information
Name of program or department: Center for Student Accommodations
Telephone: 620-235-4309
Fax: 620-235-4190
Email: csa@pittstate.edu

Pittsburg State University

GENERAL ADMISSIONS
Very important factors considered include: rigor of secondary school record, class rank, academic GPA, standardized test scores. *Freshman Admission Requirements:* High school diploma is required and GED is accepted. *Academic units required:* 4 English, 4 math, 3 science, 3 social studies, 3 academic electives.

ACCOMMODATIONS OR SERVICES
Accommodations are decided upon an individual basis after a thorough review of appropriate, current documentation. The accommodations requests must be supported through the documentation provided and must be logically linked to the current impact of the condition on academic functioning.

FINANCIAL AID
Students should submit: FAFSA; State aid form. Applicants will be notified of awards on a rolling basis beginning 3/1. The Princeton Review suggests that all financial aid forms be submitted as soon as possible after October 1. *Need-based scholarships/grants offered:* College/university scholarship or grant aid from institutional funds; Federal Pell; Private scholarships; SEOG; State scholarships/grants. *Loan aid offered:* Direct PLUS loans; Direct Subsidized Stafford Loans; Direct Unsubsidized Stafford Loans. Federal Work-Study Program available. Institutional employment available.

CAMPUS LIFE
Activities: Campus Ministries; Choral groups; Concert band; Drama/theater; International Student Organization; Jazz band; Literary magazine; Marching band; Music ensembles; Opera; Radio station; Student government; Student newspaper; Television station; Yearbook. **Organizations:** 150 registered organizations, 8 fraternities, 3 sororities. **Athletics (Intercollegiate):** *Men:* baseball, basketball, cheerleading, cross-country, football, golf, track/field (outdoor), track/field (indoor). *Women:* basketball, cheerleading, cross-country, softball, track/field (outdoor), track/field (indoor), volleyball. **On-Campus Highlights:** Planetarium, Veterans Memorial Amphitheater, Gorilla Village, Brandenburg Field/Carnie Smith Stadium, Timmons Chapel.

ACCOMMODATIONS
Allowed in exams:

Calculators	Yes
Dictionary	Yes
Computer	Yes
Spell-checker	Yes
Extended test time	Yes
Scribe	Yes
Proctors	Yes
Oral exams	Yes
Note-takers	Yes
Support services for students with	
LD	Yes
ADHD	Yes
ASD	Yes
Distraction-reduced environment	Yes
Recording of lecture allowed	Yes
Reading technology:	Yes
Audio books	Yes
Other assistive technology	Yes
Priority registration	No
Added costs for services:	
For LD:	No
For ADHD:	No
For ASD:	No
LD specialists	Yes
ADHD & ASD coaching	Yes
ASD specialists	No
Professional tutors	No
Peer tutors	Yes
Max. hours/week for services	Varies
How professors are notified of student approved accommodations	Director

COLLEGE GRADUATION REQUIREMENTS

Course waivers allowed	No
Course substitutions allowed	No

University of Kansas

OFFICE OF ADMISSIONS, LAWRENCE, KS 66045-7576 • ADMISSIONS: 785-864-3911 • FAX: 785-864-5017

CAMPUS

Type of school	Public
Environment	City
Support	CS

STUDENTS

Undergrad enrollment	18,903
% male/female	49/51
% from out of state	28
% frosh live on campus	66

FINANCIAL FACTS

Annual in-state tuition	$10,092
Annual out-of-state tuition	$26,302
Room and board	$10,350
Required fees	$1,056

GENERAL ADMISSIONS INFO

Application fee	$40
Priority deadline	11/1

Nonfall registration accepted.

Range SAT EBRW	NR
Range SAT Math	NR
Range ACT Composite	23–28

ACADEMICS

Student/faculty ratio	17:1
% students returning for sophomore year	83
% students graduating within 4 years	42
% students graduating within 6 years	63

Most classes have fewer than 10 students. Most lab/discussion sessions have 10–19 students.

PROGRAMS/SERVICES FOR STUDENTS WITH LEARNING DIFFERENCES

The Academic Achievement and Access Center (AAAC) facilitates appropriate academic accommodations and auxiliary aids and services that are necessary to afford an individual with a disability an equal opportunity to participate in the University's programs and activities. Specifically, students must provide written documentation from a qualified professional on the nature and impact of the disability. The student and the AAAC will then engage in an interactive process to determine what, if any, accommodations are appropriate based on the student's disability and individual needs.

ADMISSIONS

All applications are welcomed; assured admission is just one way to become a Jayhawk, and our individual review takes more into account. We encourage all students interested in the University of Kansas to complete an application, which will be reviewed individually by KU's admissions staff. Our review covers these factors: cumulative high school GPA, ACT or SAT scores, GPA in the core curriculum, and strength of courses. Students who don't meet the assured admissions requirements (below) will be asked to answer two to four short questions on the application, and responses will be included in the individual review.

Additional Information

Skill workshops are available in study skills, time management, stress management, and preparing for exams. Disability Resources also serves as an advocate or liaison for students. Tutoring services for students who meet qualifications are available through Supportive Educational Services at no cost. Tutoring Services offered through the Academic Achievement and Access Center are also available in most challenging entry level courses for a fee. Services and accommodations are available for undergraduate and graduate students.

ADMISSIONS INFO FOR STUDENTS WITH LEARNING DIFFERENCES

SAT/ACT required: Yes
Interview required: No
Essay required: Recommended
Additional application required: Not Applicable
Documentation required for:
Documentation submitted to: Support Program/Services
Special Ed. HS course work accepted: Not Applicable
Separate application required for Programs/Services: Not for LD, ADHD, or ASD.
Contact Information
Name of program or department: Academic Achievement and Access Center
Telephone: 785-864-4064
Fax: 785-864-2817
Email: achieve@ku.edu

University of Kansas

GENERAL ADMISSIONS

Very important factors considered include: academic GPA, standardized test scores. *Freshman Admission Requirements:* High school diploma is required and GED is accepted. *Academic units required:* 4 English, 3 math, 3 science, 1 science lab, 3 social studies, 3 academic electives. *Academic units recommended:* 4 English, 4 math, 3 science, 3 social studies, 3 academic electives.

ACCOMMODATIONS OR SERVICES

Accommodations are decided upon an individual basis after a thorough review of appropriate, current documentation. The accommodations requests must be supported through the documentation provided and must be logically linked to the current impact of the condition on academic functioning.

FINANCIAL AID

Students should submit: FAFSA. Applicants will be notified of awards on a rolling basis beginning 4/1. The Princeton Review suggests that all financial aid forms be submitted as soon as possible after October 1. *Need-based scholarships/grants offered:* College/university scholarship or grant aid from institutional funds; Federal Pell; Private scholarships; SEOG; State scholarships/grants. *Loan aid offered:* Direct PLUS loans; Direct Subsidized Stafford Loans; Direct Unsubsidized Stafford Loans. Federal Work-Study Program available. Institutional employment available.

CAMPUS LIFE

Activities: Choral groups; Concert band; Dance; Drama/theater; International Student Organization; Jazz band; Literary magazine; Marching band; Model UN; Music ensembles; Musical theater; Opera; Pep band; Radio station; Student government; Student newspaper; Symphony orchestra; Television station. **Organizations:** 476 registered organizations, 14 honor societies, 39 religious organizations. 27 fraternities, 16 sororities. **Athletics (Intercollegiate):** *Men:* baseball, basketball, cross-country, football, golf, track/field (outdoor), track/field (indoor). *Women:* basketball, crew/rowing, cross-country, diving, golf, soccer, softball, swimming, tennis, track/field (outdoor), track/field (indoor), volleyball. **On-Campus Highlights:** Spencer Museum of Art, Kansas Union and Bookstore, Natural History Museum, Booth Hall of Athletics, DeBruce Center, and Allen Fieldhouse, Robert J. Dole Institute of Politics.

ACCOMMODATIONS

Allowed in exams:	
Calculators	Yes
Dictionary	Yes
Computer	Yes
Spell-checker	Yes
Extended test time	Yes
Scribe	Yes
Proctors	Yes
Oral exams	Yes
Note-takers	Yes
Support services for students with	
LD	Yes
ADHD	Yes
ASD	Yes
Distraction-reduced environment	Yes
Recording of lecture allowed	Yes
Reading technology:	Yes
Audio books	Yes
Other assistive technology	We are a Read and Write Campus. All students have access to Read and Write software
Priority registration	Yes
Added costs for services:	
For LD:	No
For ADHD:	No
For ASD:	No
LD specialists	Yes
ADHD & ASD coaching	No
ASD specialists	No
Professional tutors	Yes
Peer tutors	Yes
Max. hours/week for services	Varies
How professors are notified of student approved accommodations	Student

COLLEGE GRADUATION REQUIREMENTS

Course waivers allowed	No
Course substitutions allowed	Yes
In what courses	college algebra only

Eastern Kentucky University

521 LANCASTER AVENUE, RICHMOND, KY 40475 • ADMISSIONS: 859-622-2106 • FAX: 859-622-8024

CAMPUS

Type of school	Public
Environment	Town
Support	CS

STUDENTS

Undergrad enrollment	13,333
% male/female	44/56
% from out of state	13
% frosh live on campus	74

FINANCIAL FACTS

Annual in-state tuition	$8,188
Annual out-of-state tuition	$17,640
Room and board	$8,188

GENERAL ADMISSIONS INFO

Application fee	$35
Regular application deadline	8/1

Nonfall registration accepted.
  Admission may be deferred for a maximum
  of 1 semester.

Range SAT EBRW	NR
Range SAT Math	NR
Range ACT Composite	19–24

ACADEMICS

Student/faculty ratio	16:1
% students returning for sophomore year	68

Most classes have 20–29 students.
Most lab/discussion sessions have 10–19
students.

PROGRAMS/SERVICES FOR STUDENTS WITH LEARNING DIFFERENCES

The mission of Project SUCCESS is to respond effectively and efficiently to the individual educational needs of eligible university students with learning disabilities through a cost-effective, flexible program of peer tutors, academic coaching, focus groups, and assistive technology. Upon admittance Project SUCCESS develops an individualized program of services that serve to enhance the academic success of each student. The services a student utilizes will be determined in a conference between the student and the program director. At the core of our program is Academic Coaching and individualized tutoring services.

ADMISSIONS

Students who meet the following criteria will be granted full admission to the University: Have graduated from an accredited high school earning a minimum cumulative high school grade point average of 2.5 on a 4.0 scale; OR have submitted a minimum ACT composite score of 20 or SAT combined verbal/critical reading score of 950 or higher AND meet the Kentucky Pre-College Curriculum ANDhave submitted an official six-semester high school transcript, or a General Equivalency Diploma (GED), or documentation indicating completion of an EKU approved home-school or distance learning high school program.

Additional Information

Project SUCCESS services provided include academic coaching, one-on-one tutoring, note-taking services, e-texts, test accommodations, advocacy, weekly seminars. Skills classes are offered in study skills, reading skills, weekly workshops in transition, time management, learning and study strategies, test-taking skills, developmental math, developmental reading, and developmental writing. "Planning to Win" is a summer transitions program specifically designed for high school junior and graduating seniors with learning disabilities, attention deficit disorder and other cognitive disorders. The program is geared towards high school students who are planning to attend college in the fall as well as those who are only exploring post-secondary educational options at any college. Students attend three days of educational and inspiring workshops, fellowship with current college students and spend two nights in an EKU residence hall. The Planning to Win Program is focused on students; however parents and interested educators are also welcome.

ADMISSIONS INFO FOR STUDENTS WITH LEARNING DIFFERENCES

SAT/ACT required: Yes
Interview required: Yes
Essay required: No
Additional application required: No
Documentation required for:
  LD: Psycho ed evaluation
  ADHD: Diagnosis based on DSM-V; history of behaviors impairing functioning in academic setting; diagnostic interview; history of symptoms; evidence of ongoing behaviors.
  ASD: Psycho ed evaluation
Documentation submitted to: OSID
Special Ed. HS course work accepted: Yes
Separate application required for Programs/Services: Yes
Contact Information
Name of program or department: Office of Services for Individuals with Disabilities
Telephone: 859-622-2933
Fax: 859-622-6794

Eastern Kentucky University

GENERAL ADMISSIONS

Very important factors considered include: rigor of secondary school record, academic GPA, standardized test scores. *Freshman Admission Requirements:* High school diploma is required and GED is accepted. *Academic units required:* 4 English, 3 math, 3 science, 1 science lab, 2 foreign language, 3 social studies, 7 academic electives, and 2 units from above areas or other academic areas.

ACCOMMODATIONS OR SERVICES

Accommodations are decided upon an individual basis after a thorough review of appropriate, current documentation. The accommodations requests must be supported through the documentation provided and must be logically linked to the current impact of the condition on academic functioning.

FINANCIAL AID

Students should submit: FAFSA. Applicants will be notified of awards on a rolling basis beginning 4/1. The Princeton Review suggests that all financial aid forms be submitted as soon as possible after October 1. *Need-based scholarships/grants offered:* College/university scholarship or grant aid from institutional funds; Federal Pell; Private scholarships; SEOG; State scholarships/grants. *Loan aid offered:* Direct PLUS loans; Direct Subsidized Stafford Loans; Direct Unsubsidized Stafford Loans. Federal Work-Study Program available. Institutional employment available.

CAMPUS LIFE

Activities: Campus Ministries; Choral groups; Concert band; Dance; Drama/theater; International Student Organization; Jazz band; Literary magazine; Marching band; Music ensembles; Musical theater; Pep band; Radio station; Student government; Student newspaper; Student-run film society; Symphony orchestra; Yearbook. **Organizations:** 178 registered organizations, 30 honor societies, 11 religious organizations. 16 fraternities, 13 sororities. **Athletics (Intercollegiate):** *Men:* baseball, basketball, cheerleading, cross-country, football, golf, tennis, track/field (outdoor), track/field (indoor). *Women:* basketball, cheerleading, cross-country, golf, soccer, softball, tennis, track/field (outdoor), track/field (indoor), volleyball. **On-Campus Highlights:** Student Wellness Center (New), Library Cafe (New), Student Services Building (New), First Weekend Events.

ACCOMMODATIONS

Allowed in exams:

Calculators	Yes
Dictionary	Yes
Computer	Yes
Spell-checker	Yes
Extended test time	Yes
Scribe	Yes
Proctors	Yes
Oral exams	Possibly
Note-takers	Yes

Support services for students with

LD	Yes
ADHD	Yes
ASD	Yes
Distraction-reduced environment	Yes
Recording of lecture allowed	Yes
Reading technology:	Yes
Audio books	Yes
Other assistive technology	Yes
Priority registration	Yes

Added costs for services:

For LD:	Yes
For ADHD:	Yes
For ASD:	Yes
LD specialists	Yes
ADHD & ASD coaching	No
ASD specialists	No
Professional tutors	No
Peer tutors	Yes
Max. hours/week for services	6
How professors are notified of student approved accommodations	Student

COLLEGE GRADUATION REQUIREMENTS

Course waivers allowed	Yes
In what courses	
Waivers and substitutions are determined on a case-by-case basis	
Course substitutions allowed	Yes
In what courses	
Waivers and substitutions are determined on a case-by-case basis	

Thomas More College

CAMPUS
Type of school	Private (nonprofit)
Environment	Village
Support	SP

STUDENTS
Undergrad enrollment	1,399
% male/female	51/49
% from out of state	47
% frosh live on campus	54

FINANCIAL FACTS
Annual tuition	$28,850
Room and board	$7,592
Required fees	$1,420

GENERAL ADMISSIONS INFO
Priority deadline	3/15

Nonfall registration accepted.

Range SAT EBRW	450–580
Range SAT Math	460–580
Range ACT Composite	19–24

ACADEMICS
Student/faculty ratio	16:1
% students returning for sophomore year	67
% students graduating within 4 years	34
% students graduating withing 6 years	44

Most classes have 10–19 students.

PROGRAMS/SERVICES FOR STUDENTS WITH LEARNING DIFFERENCES

Thomas More College's Student Support Services program is committed to the individual academic, personal, cultural/social, and financial needs of the student. It is committed to promoting sensitivity and cultural awareness of the population served and to promoting varied on/off campus services and events that enhance the student's educational opportunities. A variety of support services are offered, including developmental courses, peer tutoring, and individual counseling. Students with deficits in speech/language, study skills, written expression, ongoing additional skills, perceptual skills, reading, speaking, math, fine motor, and ADHD with or without LD are admissible.

ADMISSIONS

For admission to Thomas More College, first-year students must earn: 20 ACT composite score or 940 SAT combined Critical Reading + Mathematics score; 18 ACT English subscore or 450 SAT Critical Reading sub score; 2.5/4.0 GPA (80% or better/C+ average). The following high school credits are required for entrance: English: 4 credits, Foreign Language: 2 credits, Social Science: 3 credits, Mathematics: 3 credits, Science: 3 credits., Arts Appreciation: 1 credit, and Computer Literacy: 1 credit. Applicants lacking some of these units may be admitted at the discretion of the Admissions Committee. The ILD helps students develop and IEP plan and the strategic learning specialists can then provide students with the tools needed to meet the academic demands of college. While the program is designed for students who have a primary diagnosis of ADHD, language-based learning disability, or ASD yet have otherwise normal intellectual ability it may serve other qualified students. Services may include:Strategic Learning Specialist, Individualized Learning Plan, Executive Function Skills Development, Academic Support Services/Professional Tutoring, Social Skills Development, Self-Advocacy Coaching, Educational Assistive Technology Workshops, Life Skills Development, Learning Communities, and Academic Monitoring/Early Intervention System, Services are fee-based and contingent upon enrollment into the program. Accommodations with the compliance of section 504 of the Rehabilitation act are offered to all qualified students at no additional charge.

ADMISSIONS INFO FOR STUDENTS WITH LEARNING DIFFERENCES

SAT/ACT required: Yes
Interview required: Yes, for ILD Program
Essay required: Yes, for ILD Program
Additional application required: Yes, for ILD Program
Documentation required for:
 LD: Psycho ed evaluation
 ADHD: Psycho ed evaluation
 ASD: Psycho ed evaluation
Documentation submitted to: Disability Services for traditional accommodations; submitted to ILD for fee based services
Special Ed. HS course work accepted: Yes
Separate application required for Programs/Services: Yes, for ILD
Contact Information
Name of program or department: Institute for Learning Differences
Telephone: 859-344-3582
Fax: 859-344-3609
Email: ild@thomasmore.edu

Thomas More College

Additional Information

The Institute for Learning Differences, a division of the Thomas More Success Center, offers a comprehensive fee based program designed to support students with documented learning differences on their journey to achieve a college education. The Institute for Learning Differences (ILD) is designed for students with a diagnosed learning difference who have at least average intellectual learning abilities. This fee-based program provides best practices and researched-based approaches to best support those students striving for college success. To ensure our team is fully prepared to best serve the students in the program, the applications are carefully evaluated to identify whose needs best match the services offered by the ILD. All applicants must submit supporting documents as well as an application for admissions to Thomas More College. Accommodations in compliance with section 504 of the Rehabilitation Act of 1973 are offered to the student at no charge through Disability Services.

GENERAL ADMISSIONS

Very important factors considered include: academic GPA, standardized test scores. *Important factors considered include:* rigor of secondary school record. *Other factors considered include:* class rank, application essay, recommendation(s), interview, extracurricular activities, talent/ability, character/personal qualities, volunteer work. *Freshman Admission Requirements:* High school diploma is required and GED is accepted. *Academic units required:* 4 English, 3 math, 3 science, 1 science lab, 2 foreign language, 3 social studies. *Academic units recommended:* 2 visual/performing arts.

ACCOMMODATIONS OR SERVICES

Accommodations are decided upon an individual basis after a thorough review of appropriate, current documentation. The accommodations requests must be supported through the documentation provided and must be logically linked to the current impact of the condition on academic functioning.

FINANCIAL AID

Students should submit: FAFSA; Institution's own financial aid form. Applicants will be notified of awards on a rolling basis beginning 3/1. The Princeton Review suggests that all financial aid forms be submitted as soon as possible after October 1. *Need-based scholarships/grants offered:* College/university scholarship or grant aid from institutional funds; Federal Pell; Private scholarships; SEOG; United Negro College Fund. *Loan aid offered:*

CAMPUS LIFE

Activities: Campus Ministries; Choral groups; Dance; Drama/theater; International Student Organization; Literary magazine; Marching band; Music ensembles; Student government.

ACCOMMODATIONS

Allowed in exams:

Calculators	Per accommodations
Dictionary	Yes
Computer	Per accommodations
Spell-checker	No
Extended test time	Yes
Scribe	Yes
Proctors	Yes
Oral exams	Yes
Note-takers	Yes

Support services for students with

LD	Yes
ADHD	Yes
ASD	Yes
Distraction-reduced environment	Yes
Recording of lecture allowed	Yes
Reading technology:	Yes
Audio books	Yes
Other assistive technology	Per accommodations
Priority registration	No

Added costs for services:

For LD:	No
For ADHD:	No
For ASD:	No
LD specialists	No
ADHD & ASD coaching	Yes, ILD
ASD specialists	Yes, ILD
Professional tutors	Yes
Peer tutors	Yes
Max. hours/week for services	Unlimited
How professors are notified of student approved accommodations	Student

COLLEGE GRADUATION REQUIREMENTS

Course waivers allowed	Yes
In what courses	Foreign Language and Math
Course substitutions allowed	No

University of Kentucky

101 MAIN BUILDING, LEXINGTON, KY 40506 • ADMISSIONS: 859-257-2000 • FAX: (859) 257-3823

CAMPUS
Type of school	Public
Environment	City
Support	CS

STUDENTS
Undergrad enrollment	22,078
% male/female	45/55
% from out of state	31
% frosh live on campus	90

FINANCIAL FACTS
Annual in-state tuition	$10,896
Annual out-of-state tuition	$27,553
Room and board	$12,982
Required fees	$1,349

GENERAL ADMISSIONS INFO
Application fee	$50
Priority deadline	2/15
Regular application deadline	2/15

Nonfall registration accepted. Admission may be deferred for a maximum of 1 year.

Range SAT EBRW	550–660
Range SAT Math	490–630
Range ACT Composite	22–28

ACADEMICS
Student/faculty ratio	17:1
% students returning for sophomore year	83
% students graduating within 4 years	40
% students graduating within 6 years	61

Most classes have 10–19 students.
Most lab/discussion sessions have 20–29 students.

PROGRAMS/SERVICES FOR STUDENTS WITH LEARNING DIFFERENCES
The mission of the Testing and Disability Services is to facilitate equal access to KSU's campus, programs, activities, and services, in accordance with federal and state regulations and University policies. We support this mission by applying eligibility guidelines and coordinating the delivery of appropriate accommodations so that students with disabilities can pursue their educational goals. Additionally, we promote greater disability awareness campus-wide.

ADMISSIONS
Admission for freshman applicants is based on a holistic review including high school grades, national college admission test results, successful completion of the pre-college curriculum, essay and academic letter of recommendation. Most undergraduate majors at UK permit a student to be directly admitted to their program (or with a pre-major designation) as part of the general undergraduate admission process. However, some colleges and programs at UK require an admission process separate from general undergraduate admission to the University.

Additional Information
The DRC consultants will meet with students one-on-one to discuss needs and how to be successful at UK. Documentation of a disability is not provided by:IEP, 504 plans or Transition Plans. These documents, however, are useful for documenting a history of accommodation and effective interventions for an individual with a disability.. Providing this information and having a history of the disability in elementary or secondary school does not automatically guarantee that one will receive the requested services.

ADMISSIONS INFO FOR STUDENTS WITH LEARNING DIFFERENCES
SAT/ACT required: Yes
Interview required: No
Essay required: Not Applicable
Additional application required: Yes
Documentation required for:
 LD: Psycho ed evaluation
 ADHD: Psycho ed evaluation
 ASD: Psycho ed evaluation
Documentation submitted to: DRC
Special Ed. HS course work accepted: No
Separate application required for Programs/Services: No
Contact Information
Name of program or department: Disability Resource Center
Telephone: (859) 257-2754
Fax: (859) 257-1980
Email: dtbeac1@uky.edu

University of Kentucky

GENERAL ADMISSIONS

Very important factors considered include: rigor of secondary school record, academic GPA, standardized test scores. *Important factors considered include:* application essay, recommendation(s). *Other factors considered include:* class rank, interview, extracurricular activities, talent/ability, character/personal qualities, alumni/ae relation, geographical residence, state residency, volunteer work. *Freshman Admission Requirements:* High school diploma is required and GED is accepted. *Academic units required:* 4 English, 3 math, 3 science, 1 science lab, 3 foreign language, 3 social studies, 7 academic electives, 1 visual/performing arts, and 1 unit from above areas or other academic areas.

ACCOMMODATIONS OR SERVICES

Accommodations are decided upon an individual basis after a thorough review of appropriate, current documentation. The accommodations requests must be supported through the documentation provided and must be logically linked to the current impact of the condition on academic functioning.

FINANCIAL AID

Students should submit: FAFSA. Applicants will be notified of awards on a rolling basis beginning 3/15. The Princeton Review suggests that all financial aid forms be submitted as soon as possible after October 1. *Need-based scholarships/grants offered:* College/university scholarship or grant aid from institutional funds; Federal Pell; Private scholarships; SEOG; State scholarships/grants. *Loan aid offered:* Direct PLUS loans; Direct Subsidized Stafford Loans; Direct Unsubsidized Stafford Loans. Federal Work-Study Program available.

CAMPUS LIFE

Activities: Campus Ministries; Choral groups; Concert band; Dance; Drama/theater; International Student Organization; Jazz band; Literary magazine; Marching band; Model UN; Music ensembles; Musical theater; Opera; Pep band; Radio station; Student government; Student newspaper; Symphony orchestra; Television station; Yearbook. **Organizations:** 348 registered organizations, 28 honor societies, 20 religious organizations, 19 fraternities, 16 sororities. **Athletics (Intercollegiate):** *Men:* baseball, basketball, cheerleading, cross-country, diving, football, golf, riflery, soccer, swimming, tennis, track/field (outdoor), track/field (indoor). *Women:* basketball, cheerleading, cross-country, diving, golf, gymnastics, riflery, soccer, softball, swimming, tennis, track/field (outdoor), track/field (indoor), volleyball. **On-Campus Highlights:** W.T. Young Library, Johnson Fitness Center, Memorial Coliseum, Arboretum, Memorial Hall.

ACCOMMODATIONS

Allowed in exams:	
Calculators	No
Dictionary	No
Computer	Yes
Spell-checker	No
Extended test time	Yes
Scribe	Yes
Proctors	Yes
Oral exams	Yes
Note-takers	No
Support services for students with	
LD	Yes
ADHD	Yes
ASD	Yes
Distraction-reduced environment	Yes
Recording of lecture allowed	Yes
Reading technology:	Yes
Audio books	Yes
Other assistive technology	Software

programs that read aloud, dictate and write, and enlarge text are available. All accommodations are determined based on individual documentation and need.

Priority registration	Yes
Added costs for services:	
For LD:	No
For ADHD:	No
For ASD:	No
LD specialists	Yes
ADHD & ASD coaching	No
ASD specialists	No
Professional tutors	Yes
Peer tutors	Not Applicable
Max. hours/week for services	Varies
How professors are notified of student approved accommodations	Student

COLLEGE GRADUATION REQUIREMENTS

Course waivers allowed	No
Course substitutions allowed	Yes
In what courses	

Possibly in math, statistics, foreign language, depending on the student's degree program and documentation of need.

Western Kentucky University

1906 College Heights Blvd., Bowling Green, KY 42101-1020 • Admissions: 270-745-2551 • Fax: 270-745-6133

CAMPUS

Type of school	Public
Environment	Town
Support	CS

STUDENTS

Undergrad enrollment	14,529
% male/female	43/57
% from out of state	21
% frosh live on campus	83

FINANCIAL FACTS

Annual in-state tuition	$10,202
Annual out-of-state tuition	$25,512
Room and board	$8,350

GENERAL ADMISSIONS INFO

Application fee	$45.
Regular application deadline	8/1

Nonfall registration accepted. Admission may be deferred.

Range SAT EBRW	500–600
Range SAT Math	470–580
Range ACT Composite	19–27

ACADEMICS

Student/faculty ratio	18:1
% students returning for sophomore year	70
% students graduating within 4 years	28
% students graduating within 6 years	51

Most classes have fewer than 10 students. Most lab/discussion sessions have greater than 100 students.

PROGRAMS/SERVICES FOR STUDENTS WITH LEARNING DIFFERENCES

The purpose of SARC is to coordinate services and accommodations for studnts with documented disabilities.There is an online system for managing accommodations and services..This system is used to receive Faculty Notification Letters and coordinate notetaking services.

ADMISSIONS

Students admitted to WKU may be placed in an appropriate academic support program based on academic needs at the time of admission. Students will be notified regarding any academic placement by the appropriate office. ACT/SAT required but essay scores for the ACT and SAT are not evaluated for admission, scholarship, or placement purposes.

Additional Information

Testing accommodations, such as extended time, quiet room and use of computer assistive technology are provided . There are strict guidelines that need to be followed in order to schedule exam accommodations. For students registered for note taking accommodations they can use the recording devices, note taker applications for each class or request a notetaker for each class. The student is responsible for working in partnership with potential classmates, course instructors and the SARC to secure a classroom Notetaker.

ADMISSIONS INFO FOR STUDENTS WITH LEARNING DIFFERENCES

SAT/ACT required: Yes
Interview required: Yes
Essay required: N/A
Additional application required: No
Documentation required for:
 LD: Psycho ed evaluation
 ADHD: Diagnosis based on DSM-V; history of behaviors impairing functioning in academic setting; diagnostic interview; history of symptoms; evidence of ongoing behaviors.
 ASD: Psycho ed evaluation
Documentation submitted to: Support Program/Services
Special Ed. HS course work accepted: Yes
Separate application required for Programs/Services: No
Contact Information
Name of program or department: Student Accessibility Resource Center
Telephone: (270) 745-3095
Email: robert.unseld@wku.edu

Western Kentucky University

GENERAL ADMISSIONS

Very important factors considered include: academic GPA, standardized test scores. *Freshman Admission Requirements:* High school diploma is required and GED is accepted. *Academic units required:* 4 English, 3 math, 3 science, 1 science lab, 2 foreign language, 3 social studies, 1 history, 5 academic electives, and 1 unit from above areas or other academic areas.

ACCOMMODATIONS OR SERVICES

Accommodations are decided upon an individual basis after a thorough review of appropriate, current documentation. The accommodations requests must be supported through the documentation provided and must be logically linked to the current impact of the condition on academic functioning.

FINANCIAL AID

Students should submit: FAFSA. Applicants will be notified of awards on a rolling basis beginning 3/1. The Princeton Review suggests that all financial aid forms be submitted as soon as possible after October 1. *Need-based scholarships/grants offered:* College/university scholarship or grant aid from institutional funds; Federal Pell; Private scholarships; SEOG; State scholarships/grants; United Negro College Fund. *Loan aid offered:* Direct PLUS loans; Direct Subsidized Stafford Loans; Direct Unsubsidized Stafford Loans. Federal Work-Study Program available. Institutional employment available.

CAMPUS LIFE

Activities: Campus Ministries; Choral groups; Concert band; Dance; Drama/theater; International Student Organization; Jazz band; Literary magazine; Marching band; Model UN; Music ensembles; Musical theater; Opera; Pep band; Radio station; Student government; Student newspaper; Student-run film society; Symphony orchestra; Television station; Yearbook. **Organizations:** 360 registered organizations, 28 honor societies, 23 religious organizations. 18 fraternities, 13 sororities. **Athletics (Intercollegiate):** *Men:* baseball, basketball, cross-country, diving, football, golf, riflery, swimming, tennis, track/field (outdoor), track/field (indoor). *Women:* basketball, cross-country, diving, golf, riflery, soccer, swimming, tennis, track/field (outdoor), track/field (indoor), volleyball. **On-Campus Highlights:** Downing Student Union, Preston Health and Activities Center, E.A. Diddle Arena, Houchens Industries-L.T. Smith Stadium, Jody Richards Hall (Mass Media and Technology).

ACCOMMODATIONS

Allowed in exams:

Calculators	Yes
Dictionary	Yes
Computer	Yes
Spell-checker	Yes
Extended test time	Yes
Scribe	Yes
Proctors	Yes
Oral exams	Yes
Note-takers	Yes

Support services for students with

LD	Yes
ADHD	Yes
ASD	Yes
Distraction-reduced environment	Yes
Recording of lecture allowed	Yes
Reading technology:	Yes
Audio books	Yes
Other assistive technology	Video Relay, Video Phone, Captioned Phone, JAWS, Read Write Gold, Dragon Naturally Speaking, Talking Calculator, Intellikeys Adaptive Keyboard, Orbit Trackball Mouse, Zoom Text Screen Magnifier
Priority registration	Yes

Added costs for services:

For LD:	Yes
For ADHD:	Yes
For ASD:	Yes
LD specialists	Yes
ADHD & ASD coaching	Yes
ASD specialists	Yes
Professional tutors	Yes
Peer tutors	Yes
Max. hours/week for services	20
How professors are notified of student approved accommodations	Student and Director

COLLEGE GRADUATION REQUIREMENTS

Course waivers allowed	Yes
In what courses	
Courses that can be substituted are handled on a case-by-case basis	
Course substitutions allowed	Yes

Louisiana College

1140 College Drive, Pineville, LA 71359-0566 • Admissions: 318-487-7259 • Fax:

Programs/Services for Students with Learning Differences

Students who have diagnosed disabilities as identified under the Americans with Disabilities Act or Section 504 of the Rehabilitation Act of 1973, and who choose to identify their disabilities are provided with accommodations.

Admissions

Prospective students with learning differences would benefit greatly from contacting the Student Success Center and speaking personally with the Director.

Additional Information

Tutoring sessions are conducted in most subjects taken by Level I students. Additional tutorial help is available at the higher levels as needed. The PASS staff will carefully work with individual professors and the student's academic advisor to coordinate and accommodate the student's learning needs. Students admitted to PASS will remain in the program as long as they are at Louisiana College. Noncompliance with any component of the program may result in a student's dismissal from the program. Skills classes are offered in study techniques, test-taking strategies, and time management through orientation, and private tutoring from a PASS staff member. Incoming freshmen are encouraged to attend one summer session (5 weeks) to become familiar with the campus and college life. There is an additional fee for the PASS program that ranges from $450-$850 per semester, depending on the level of support provided.

Louisiana College

GENERAL ADMISSIONS
Very important factors considered include: academic GPA, standardized test scores. *Other factors considered include:* rigor of secondary school record, application essay, extracurricular activities, talent/ability, character/personal qualities, religious affiliation/commitment. *Freshman Admission Requirements:* High school diploma is required and GED is accepted. *Academic units required:* 4 English, 4 math, 3 science, 2 science labs, 3 social studies, and 8 units from above areas or other academic areas.

ACCOMMODATIONS OR SERVICES
Accommodations are decided upon an individual basis after a thorough review of appropriate, current documentation. The accommodations requests must be supported through the documentation provided and must be logically linked to the current impact of the condition on academic functioning.

FINANCIAL AID
Students should submit: FAFSA; Institution's own financial aid form. Applicants will be notified of awards on a rolling basis beginning 1/1. The Princeton Review suggests that all financial aid forms be submitted as soon as possible after October 1. *Need-based scholarships/grants offered:* College/university scholarship or grant aid from institutional funds; Federal Pell; SEOG; State scholarships/grants. *Loan aid offered:* Direct PLUS loans; Direct Subsidized Stafford Loans; Direct Unsubsidized Stafford Loans. Federal Work-Study Program available. Institutional employment available.

CAMPUS LIFE
Activities: Campus Ministries; Choral groups; Concert band; Drama/theater; International Student Organization; Jazz band; Marching band; Music ensembles; Musical theater; Opera; Pep band; Radio station; Student government; Symphony orchestra; Yearbook. **Organizations:** Healthplex/Wellness Center, Hixon Student Center/Granberry, Martin Performing Arts Center, Weathersby Fine Arts Building, Alexandria Hall.

ACCOMMODATIONS

Allowed in exams:

Calculators	Yes
Dictionary	Not Applicable
Computer	Not Applicable
Spell-checker	Not Applicable
Extended test time	Yes
Scribe	Yes
Proctors	Yes
Oral exams	Yes
Note-takers	Yes

Support services for students with

LD	Yes
ADHD	Yes
ASD	Yes
Distraction-reduced environment	Yes
Recording of lecture allowed	Yes
Reading technology:	Yes
Audio books	Yes
Other assistive technology	We use any available technology to assist students.
Priority registration	No

Added costs for services:

For LD:	No
For ADHD:	Not Applicable
For ASD:	Not Applicable
LD specialists	Yes
ADHD & ASD coaching	Yes
ASD specialists	No
Professional tutors	Yes
Peer tutors	Yes
Max. hours/week for services	Varies
How professors are notified of student approved accommodations	Director and Student

COLLEGE GRADUATION REQUIREMENTS

Course waivers allowed	No
Course substitutions allowed	No

Louisiana State University

1146 PLEASANT HALL, BATON ROUGE, LA 70803 • ADMISSIONS: 225-578-1175 • FAX: 225-578-4433

CAMPUS

Type of school	Public
Environment	City
Support	CS

STUDENTS

Undergrad enrollment	24,904
% male/female	48/52
% from out of state	17
% frosh live on campus	66

FINANCIAL FACTS

Annual in-state tuition	$8,038
Annual out-of-state tuition	$24,715
Room and board	$11,750
Required fees	$3,336

GENERAL ADMISSIONS INFO

Application fee	$40
Priority deadline	11/15
Regular application deadline	4/15

Nonfall registration accepted. Admission may be deferred for a maximum of 1 academic year.

Range SAT EBRW	510–620
Range SAT Math	510–640
Range ACT Composite	23–28

ACADEMICS

Student/faculty ratio	23:1
% students returning for sophomore year	85

Most classes have 20–29 students.

PROGRAMS/SERVICES FOR STUDENTS WITH LEARNING DIFFERENCES

The purpose of Disability Services (DS) is to assist any student who finds his or her disability to be a barrier to achieving educational and/or personal goals. The office provides support services to students with learning disabilities. These services are provided to encourage students with LD/ADHD to achieve success in college. The consequences of a disability may include specialized requirements; therefore, the particular needs of each student are considered on an individual basis. DS dedicates its efforts to meeting both the needs of students with disabilities and the interests of faculty, staff, and the university as a whole. It is the practice of DS that issues concerning accommodations of students with disabilities in academic and other programs and activities be resolved between the student requesting the accommodation and the university employee representing the department within which the academic program or service is located. After intervention, if the student does not find the provision of an accommodation satisfactory, the student may file a formal grievance.

ADMISSIONS

Students interested in Ogden Honors College consideration and top scholarships should complete the writing section. Students who are borderline to meeting admission requirements are still encouraged to apply. Other factors considered for admission may include choice of degree program, rank in class, credit in advanced placement or honors courses, rigor of the high school curriculum, and grade trends.

Additional Information

Specialized support services are based on individual disability-based needs. Services available include disability management counseling; adaptive equipment loan; note-takers; referral for tutoring; assistance with enrollment and registration; liaison assistance and referral to on-campus and off-campus resources; supplemental orientation to the campus; and advocacy on behalf of students with campus faculty, staff, and students. Learning Assistance Center is open to all students on campus.

ADMISSIONS INFO FOR STUDENTS WITH LEARNING DIFFERENCES

SAT/ACT required: Yes
Interview required: Not Applicable
Essay required: Not Applicable
Additional application required: Not Applicable
Documentation required for:
　LD: Full psychoeducational evaluation
　ADHD: Form from Disability Services website www.lsu.edu/disability
　ASD: Full psychoeducational evaluation
Documentation submitted to: Support Program/Services
Special Ed. HS course work accepted: Not Applicable
Separate application required for Programs/Services: No
Contact Information
Name of program or department: Disability Services
Telephone: 225-578-5919
Fax: 225-578-4560
Email: bjcornw@lsu.edu

Louisiana State University

GENERAL ADMISSIONS

Very important factors considered include: rigor of secondary school record, academic GPA, standardized test scores. *Important factors considered include:* talent/ability. *Other factors considered include:* class rank, application essay, recommendation(s), interview, extracurricular activities, first generation, alumni/ae relation, level of applicant's interest. *Freshman Admission Requirements:* High school diploma is required and GED is accepted. *Academic units required:* 4 English, 4 math, 4 science, 2 foreign language, 3 social studies, 1 history, 1 visual/performing arts.

ACCOMMODATIONS OR SERVICES

Accommodations are decided upon an individual basis after a thorough review of appropriate, current documentation. The accommodations requests must be supported through the documentation provided and must be logically linked to the current impact of the condition on academic functioning.

FINANCIAL AID

Students should submit: FAFSA; Institution's own financial aid form. Applicants will be notified of awards on a rolling basis beginning 11/15. The Princeton Review suggests that all financial aid forms be submitted as soon as possible after October 1. *Need-based scholarships/grants offered:* College/university scholarship or grant aid from institutional funds; Federal Pell; Private scholarships; SEOG; State scholarships/grants. *Loan aid offered:* Direct PLUS loans; Direct Subsidized Stafford Loans; Direct Unsubsidized Stafford Loans. Federal Work-Study Program available. Institutional employment available.

CAMPUS LIFE

Activities: Campus Ministrics; Choral groups; Concert band; Dance; Drama/theater; International Student Organization; Jazz band; Literary magazine; Marching band; Music ensembles; Musical theater; Opera; Pep band; Radio station; Student government; Student newspaper; Student-run film society; Symphony orchestra; Television station; Yearbook. **Organizations:** 300 registered organizations, 32 honor societies, 25 religious organizations. 23 fraternities, 15 sororities. **Athletics (Intercollegiate):** *Men:* baseball, basketball, cheerleading, cross-country, diving, football, golf, swimming, tennis, track/field (outdoor), track/field (indoor). *Women:* basketball, cheerleading, cross-country, diving, golf, gymnastics, soccer, softball, swimming, tennis, track/field (outdoor), track/field (indoor), volleyball. **On-Campus Highlights:** LSU Student Union, Mike VI Tiger Habitat, Parade Grounds, Tiger Stadium, Alex Box Stadium.

ACCOMMODATIONS

Allowed in exams:

Calculators	Yes
Dictionary	No
Computer	Yes
Spell-checker	Yes
Extended test time	Yes
Scribe	Yes
Proctors	Yes
Oral exams	Yes
Note-takers	Yes

Support services for students with

LD	Yes
ADHD	Yes
ASD	Yes
Distraction-reduced environment	Yes
Recording of lecture allowed	Yes
Reading technology:	Yes
Audio books	Yes
Other assistive technology	Yes
Priority registration	No

Added costs for services:

For LD:	No
For ADHD:	No
For ASD:	No
LD specialists	No
ADHD & ASD coaching	No
ASD specialists	Yes
Professional tutors	Not Applicable
Peer tutors	Yes
Max. hours/week for services	Varies
How professors are notified of student approved accommodations	Student

COLLEGE GRADUATION REQUIREMENTS

Course waivers allowed	Yes
In what courses	Foreign Languages
Course substitutions allowed	No

Nicholls State University

P.O.Box 2009 Univ. Station, Thibodaux, LA 70310 • Admissions: 985-448-4507 • Fax: 985-448-4929

Programs/Services for Students with Learning Differences

Bridge to Independence – Degree program is designed to provide add-on services to help students with ASD successfully transition to college life and further develop their social skills and campus friendships. To qualify for the program, students will first need to apply and be accepted to Nicholls based on admission requirements (such as GPA, ACT scores and high school curriculum).Degree program students who participate in the Bridge program will: Attend weekly social skill seminars, receive systematic monitoring of their academic, behavioral and social performance, be provided with academic coaches and peer mentors to help them successfully progress toward earning their college degree, receive liaison services between the Bridge program and their faculty members, participate in campus activities and organizations, receive assistance coordinating any necessary student or academic services such as counseling or tutoring.

Admissions

Applications will be reviewed on an individual basis and an admissions decision will be made considering each applicant's potential for success and will include factors such as ACT score, special talents, and the University's commitment to a demographically diverse student population. Students who receive their GED or graduate from Non-Accredited Home School Programs who are under the age of 25 must submit ACT scores with a minimum 23 Composite score in order to be admitted and demonstrate no need for remedial coursework.

Additional Information

The Dyslexia Center provides a support system; equipment; remediation; academic planning; resources; and assistance. Accommodation forms with appropriate classroom and testing accommodations are given to professors. Typical accommodations may include but are not limited to extended time; use of an electronic dictionary; oral reader; or use of a computer. Students are enrolled in regular college classes. Other campus services for students with disabilities include the Office for Students with Disabilities; the Testing Center for special testing accommodations such as extended time or a quiet room; the Tutorial and Academic Enhancement Center for tutoring assistance; the university Counseling Center, which provides counseling directed at self-encouragement, self-esteem, assertiveness,

Nicholls State University

stress management, and test anxiety; and the computer lab for assistance with written assignments. Assessment is available for a fee for students applying to the university.

GENERAL ADMISSIONS
Very important factors considered include: rigor of secondary school record. *Important factors considered include:* standardized test scores. *Other factors considered include:* class rank, academic GPA, talent/ability. *Freshman Admission Requirements:* High school diploma is required and GED is accepted. *Academic units required:* 4 English, 3 math, 3 science, 2 foreign language, 1 social studies, 2 history, 2 academic electives.

ACCOMMODATIONS OR SERVICES
Accommodations are decided upon an individual basis after a thorough review of appropriate, current documentation. The accommodations requests must be supported through the documentation provided and must be logically linked to the current impact of the condition on academic functioning.

FINANCIAL AID
Students should submit: FAFSA; Institution's own financial aid form; Noncustodial PROFILE; State aid form. The Princeton Review suggests that all financial aid forms be submitted as soon as possible after October 1. *Need-based scholarships/grants offered:* College/university scholarship or grant aid from institutional funds; Federal Pell; Private scholarships; SEOG; State scholarships/grants. *Loan aid offered:* Federal Work-Study Program available. Institutional employment available.

CAMPUS LIFE
Activities: Choral groups; Concert band; Dance; Drama/theater; Jazz band; Literary magazine; Marching band; Music ensembles; Musical theater; Radio station; Student government; Student newspaper; Student-run film society; Television station; Yearbook. **Organizations:** 121 registered organizations, 24 honor societies, 6 religious organizations. 10 fraternities, 5 sororities. **Athletics (Intercollegiate):** *Men:* baseball, basketball, cross-country, football, golf, tennis. *Women:* basketball, cross-country, golf, soccer, softball, tennis, track/field (outdoor), track/field (indoor), volleyball. **On-Campus Highlights:** Admissions Office, Student Union, Ellender Memorial Library, Guidry Stadium.

ACCOMMODATIONS
Allowed in exams:

Calculators	Yes
Dictionary	Yes
Computer	Yes
Spell-checker	Yes
Extended test time	Yes
Scribe	Yes
Proctors	Yes
Oral exams	Yes
Note-takers	Yes
Support services for students with	
LD	Yes
ADHD	Yes
ASD	Yes
Distraction-reduced environment	Yes
Recording of lecture allowed	Yes
Reading technology:	Yes
Audio books	Yes
Other assistive technology	Yes
Priority registration	Yes
Added costs for services:	
For LD:	No
For ADHD:	No
For ASD:	No
LD specialists	No
ADHD & ASD coaching	No
ASD specialists	No
Professional tutors	No
Peer tutors	No
Max. hours/week for services	N/A
How professors are notified of student approved accommodations	Student

COLLEGE GRADUATION REQUIREMENTS

Course waivers allowed	No
Course substitutions allowed	No

Tulane University

6823 St. Charles Avenue, New Orleans, LA 70118 • Admissions: 504-865-5731 • Fax: 504-862-8715

CAMPUS
Type of school	Private (nonprofit)
Environment	Metropolis
Support	S

STUDENTS
Undergrad enrollment	6,571
% male/female	41/59
% from out of state	77
% frosh live on campus	98

FINANCIAL FACTS
Annual tuition	$50,780
Room and board	$15,190
Required fees	$4,040

GENERAL ADMISSIONS INFO
Priority deadline 11/1.

Regular application deadline	11/15

Nonfall registration accepted. Admission may be deferred for a maximum of 1 year.

Range SAT EBRW	670–740
Range SAT Math	660–750
Range ACT Composite	30–33

ACADEMICS
Student/faculty ratio	8:1
% students returning for sophomore year	93
% students graduating within 4 years	73
% students graduating within 6 years	83

Most classes have 10–19 students.

PROGRAMS/SERVICES FOR STUDENTS WITH LEARNING DIFFERENCES
The Goldman Office of Disability Services (ODS) is committed to providing equal access and a friendly environment for all who study and work at Tulane University. We offer accommodations and modifications of the academic or work environment to students and employees with psychological, medical/physical, and learning/developmental disabilities. Our staff members focus on "leveling the playing field", and work directly with students, faculty and staff to accomplish this objective. When necessary, reasonable accommodations can be implemented to modify the academic environment to meet the needs of our students. Because no two students are alike, our staff members work collaboratively to develop an individualized plan which gives each student the same opportunity for success as their peers.

ADMISSIONS
SAT (pre-2016) composite 1950-2150 or ACT composite 30-33. Course requirements include 4 English, 3 math, 3 science, 3 social studies and 2 foreign language.

Additional Information
1. Complete Request for Accommodation form 2. Submit supporting documentation 3. Meet with ODS staff discuss approved accommodations and implementation of those accommodations. 4. Meet with ODs staff as needed for ongoing support.

ADMISSIONS INFO FOR STUDENTS WITH LEARNING DIFFERENCES
SAT/ACT required: Yes
Interview required: No
Essay required: Not Applicable
Additional application required: No
Documentation required for:
  LD: Psycho ed evaluation
  ADHD: Diagnosis based on DSM-V; history of behaviors impairing functioning in academic setting; diagnostic interview; history of symptoms, evidence of ongoing behaviors
Documentation submitted to: Goldman Office of Disability Services
Special Ed. HS course work accepted: No
Separate application required for Programs/Services: No
Contact Information
Name of program or department: Goldman Office of Disability Services
Telephone: 504-862-8433
Fax: 504-862-8435
Email: ods@tulane.edu

Tulane University

GENERAL ADMISSIONS

Very important factors considered include: rigor of secondary school record, class rank, academic GPA, standardized test scores. *Important factors considered include:* application essay, recommendation(s), character/personal qualities. *Other factors considered include:* interview, extracurricular activities, talent/ability, first generation, alumni/ae relation, volunteer work, work experience, level of applicant's interest. *Freshman Admission Requirements:* High school diploma is required and GED is accepted. *Academic units recommended:* 4 English, 3 math, 3 science, 3 science labs, 3 foreign language, 3 social studies.

ACCOMMODATIONS OR SERVICES

Accommodations are decided upon an individual basis after a thorough review of appropriate, current documentation. The accommodations requests must be supported through the documentation provided and must be logically linked to the current impact of the condition on academic functioning.

FINANCIAL AID

Students should submit: Business/Farm Supplement; CSS/Financial Aid PROFILE; FAFSA; Noncustodial PROFILE. Applicants will be notified of awards on a rolling basis beginning 3/15. The Princeton Review suggests that all financial aid forms be submitted as soon as possible after October 1. *Need-based scholarships/grants offered:* College/university scholarship or grant aid from institutional funds; Federal Pell; Private scholarships; SEOG; State scholarships/grants. *Loan aid offered:* Direct PLUS loans; Direct Subsidized Stafford Loans; Direct Unsubsidized Stafford Loans. Federal Work-Study Program available. Institutional employment available.

CAMPUS LIFE

Activities: Campus Ministries; Choral groups; Concert band; Dance; Drama/theater; International Student Organization; Jazz band; Literary magazine; Marching band; Music ensembles; Musical theater; Pep band; Radio station; Student government; Student newspaper; Student-run film society; Symphony orchestra; Television station; Yearbook. **Organizations:** 250 registered organizations, 43 honor societies, 16 religious organizations. 15 fraternities, 11 sororities. **Athletics (Intercollegiate):** *Men:* baseball, basketball, cross-country, football, tennis, track/field (outdoor). *Women:* basketball, cross-country, diving, golf, swimming, tennis, track/field (outdoor), track/field (indoor), volleyball. **On-Campus Highlights:** Amistad Research Center, Newcomb Art Gallery, Reily Recreation Center, Howard Tilton Memorial Library, Yulman Stadium.

ACCOMMODATIONS

Allowed in exams:	
Calculators	Yes
Dictionary	No
Computer	Yes
Spell-checker	No
Extended test time	Yes
Scribe	Yes
Proctors	Yes
Oral exams	Yes
Note-takers	Yes
Support services for students with	
LD	Yes
ADHD	Yes
ASD	Yes
Distraction-reduced environment	Yes
Recording of lecture allowed	Yes
Reading technology:	Yes
Audio books	Yes
Other assistive technology	Closed Captioning
Services for students with hearing impairment	
Priority registration	No
Added costs for services:	
For LD:	No
For ADHD:	No
For ASD:	No
LD specialists	No
ADHD & ASD coaching	No
ASD specialists	Yes
Professional tutors	Yes
Peer tutors	Yes
Max. hours/week for services	Varies
How professors are notified of student approved accommodations	Student

COLLEGE GRADUATION REQUIREMENTS

Course waivers allowed	Yes
In what courses	Foreign Language
Course substitutions allowed	Yes
In what courses	Foreign Language

University of New Orleans

2000 LAKESHORE DR., NEW ORLEANS, LA 70148 • ADMISSIONS: 504-280-6595 • FAX: 504-280-3973

CAMPUS
Type of school	Public
Environment	Metropolis
Support	S

STUDENTS
Undergrad enrollment	5,917
% male/female	51/49
% from out of state	NR
% frosh live on campus	0

FINANCIAL FACTS
Annual in-state tuition	$6,090
Annual out-of-state tuition	$10,926
Room and board	$10,575
Required fees	$2,394

GENERAL ADMISSIONS INFO
Application fee	$25
Priority deadline	12/15
Regular application deadline	7/15
Nonfall registration accepted.	

Range SAT EBRW	520–640
Range SAT Math	510–610
Range ACT Composite	20–25

ACADEMICS
Student/faculty ratio	22:1
% students returning for sophomore year	62
% students graduating within 4 years	14
% students graduating within 6 years	32

PROGRAMS/SERVICES FOR STUDENTS WITH LEARNING DIFFERENCES
The University of New Orleans is committed to providing all students with equal opportunities for academic and extracurricular success. The Office of Disability Services (ODS) coordinates all services and programs. In addition to serving its primary function as a liaison between the student and the university, the office provides a limited number of direct services to students with all kinds of permanent and temporary disabilities. Services begin when a student registered with the university contacts the ODS office, provides documentation of the disability, and requests assistance. ODS encourages student independence, program accessibility, and a psychologically supportive environment, so students may achieve their educational objectives. ODS also seeks to educate the campus community about disability issues.

ADMISSIONS
Students with LD should submit the general application form and are expected to meet the same admission standards as all other applicants.

Additional Information
Privateer Pathways is designed for students who, because of their ACT or SAT scores, need additional support in mathematics and/or English. Skills will be developed through the strategic delivery of academic support to students. The programs cover aspects such as time management, academic honesty, and financial aid. Bi-weekly Success Coaching is also available to first-year students. Each student will be individually evaluated for program eligibility based on high school transcripts and test scores. Participants will receive academic advising on courses required as part of the Pathways program.

ADMISSIONS INFO FOR STUDENTS WITH LEARNING DIFFERENCES
SAT/ACT required: Yes
Interview required: No
Essay required: No
Additional application required: No
Documentation required for:
  LD: Psycho ed evaluation
  ADHD: Diagnosis based on DSM-V; history of behaviors impairing functioning in academic setting; diagnostic interview; history of symptoms; evidence of ongoing behaviors.
  ASD: Psycho ed evaluation
Documentation submitted to: Office of Student Accountability, Advocacy and Disability Services
Special Ed. HS course work accepted: Yes
Separate application required for Programs/Services: Yes
Contact Information
Name of program or department: Office of Student Accountability, Advocacy and Disability Services
Telephone: 504-280-6222
Fax: 504-280-3975
Email: aaking@uno.edu

University of New Orleans

GENERAL ADMISSIONS

Very important factors considered include: academic GPA, standardized test scores. *Freshman Admission Requirements:* High school diploma is required and GED is accepted. *Academic units required:* 4 English, 4 math, 4 science, 2 foreign language, 4 social studies, 1 visual/performing arts.

ACCOMMODATIONS OR SERVICES

Accommodations are decided upon an individual basis after a thorough review of appropriate, current documentation. The accommodations requests must be supported through the documentation provided and must be logically linked to the current impact of the condition on academic functioning.

FINANCIAL AID

Students should submit: FAFSA; Institution's own financial aid form. Applicants will be notified of awards on or about 1/15. The Princeton Review suggests that all financial aid forms be submitted as soon as possible after October 1. *Need-based scholarships/grants offered:* College/university scholarship or grant aid from institutional funds; Federal Pell; Private scholarships; SEOG; State scholarships/grants. *Loan aid offered:* Direct PLUS loans; Direct Subsidized Stafford Loans; Direct Unsubsidized Stafford Loans. Federal Work-Study Program available. Institutional employment available.

CAMPUS LIFE

Activities: Campus Ministries; Choral groups; Concert band; Dance; Drama/theater; International Student Organization; Jazz band; Literary magazine; Model UN; Music ensembles; Musical theater; Pep band; Radio station; Student government; Student newspaper; Student-run film society. **Organizations:** 120 registered organizations, 7 religious organizations. 9 fraternities, 8 sororities. **Athletics (Intercollegiate): Men:** baseball, basketball, diving, golf, swimming, tennis. *Women:* basketball, diving, swimming, tennis, volleyball. **On-Campus Highlights:** Recreation and Fitness Center, The University Center, Ponchartrain Hall, Earl K. Long Library, The Cove.

ACCOMMODATIONS

Allowed in exams:	
Calculators	Yes
Dictionary	Yes
Computer	Yes
Spell-checker	Yes
Extended test time	Yes
Scribe	Yes
Proctors	Yes
Oral exams	Yes
Note-takers	Yes
Support services for students with	
LD	Yes
ADHD	Yes
ASD	Yes
Distraction-reduced environment	Yes
Recording of lecture allowed	Yes
Reading technology:	No
Audio books	No
Other assistive technology	Yes
Priority registration	No
Added costs for services:	
For LD:	No
For ADHD:	No
For ASD:	No
LD specialists	No
ADHD & ASD coaching	No
ASD specialists	No
Professional tutors	Yes
Peer tutors	Yes
Max. hours/week for services	Varies
How professors are notified of student approved accommodations	Student

COLLEGE GRADUATION REQUIREMENTS

Course waivers allowed	No
Course substitutions allowed	Not Applicable

Southern Maine Community College

2 Fort Road, South Portland, ME 04106 • Admissions: (207) 741-5800 • Fax: 207-741-5760

CAMPUS

Type of school	Public
Environment	Town
Support	S

STUDENTS

Undergrad enrollment	4,962
% male/female	46/54
% from out of state	NR
% frosh live on campus	NR

FINANCIAL FACTS

Annual in-state tuition	$2,820
Annual out-of-state tuition	$5,640
Room and board	$9,488
Required fees	$1,000

GENERAL ADMISSIONS INFO

Application fee	$20

Nonfall registration accepted. Admission may be deferred.

Range SAT EBRW	NR
Range SAT Math	NR
Range ACT Composite	NR

ACADEMICS

Student/faculty ratio	18:1

Most classes have 10–19 students.

PROGRAMS/SERVICES FOR STUDENTS WITH LEARNING DIFFERENCES

The Disability Services program is designed to offer academic support to students through various individualized services. Students can get professional faculty tutoring in their most difficult courses; learn about their specific learning style; improve concentration and memory; study more efficiently for tests; learn how to better manage their time; learn the basic skills that are the foundation of their specific technology; and use a computer toward processing, Internet research, and other computer applications.

ADMISSIONS

All students must meet the same admission criteria. There is no special admissions process for students with learning disabilities. All students have access to disability services, including those with a diagnosed learning disability. Some students are required to take the Accuplacer tests for placement into many courses. Students are exempt from the English portion with an SAT Critical Reading score of 450+ or ACT of 21. Students are exempt from Math portion of Accuplacer with SAT 490 Math or ACT 21.

Additional Information

TRIO Student Support Services are available to eligible students. As a TRIO SSS participant, students receive one-on-one support from their own dedicated Success Coach. Each semester, students regularly meet with their TRIO Coach to: develop your college success plan; set academic and other goals; address any challenges; provide students with the skills and resources needed to succeed. TRIO Coaches collaborate with SMCC staff and faculty advisors to ensure student success. Students must complete a separate application for TRIO SSS.

ADMISSIONS INFO FOR STUDENTS WITH LEARNING DIFFERENCES
SAT/ACT required: Yes
Interview required: No
Essay required: Not Applicable
Additional application required: No
Documentation required for:
  LD: Psycho ed evaluation
  ADHD: Diagnosis based on DSM-V; history of behaviors impairing functioning in academic setting; diagnostic interview; history of symptoms; evidence of ongoing behaviors.
  ASD: Psycho ed evaluation
Documentation submitted to: Counseling and Disability Services
Special Ed. HS course work accepted: Yes
Separate application required for Programs/Services: No
Levels of services available for ASD students: No
Contact Information
Name of program or department: Counseling and Disability Services
Telephone: 207-741-5923

Southern Maine Community College

GENERAL ADMISSIONS

Other factors considered include: state residency. *Freshman Admission Requirements:* High school diploma is required and GED is accepted

ACCOMMODATIONS OR SERVICES

Accommodations are decided upon an individual basis after a thorough review of appropriate, current documentation. The accommodations requests must be supported through the documentation provided and must be logically linked to the current impact of the condition on academic functioning.

FINANCIAL AID

Students should submit: FAFSA. The Princeton Review suggests that all financial aid forms be submitted as soon as possible after October 1. *Need-based scholarships/grants offered:* College/university scholarship or grant aid from institutional funds; Federal Pell; Private scholarships; State scholarships/grants. *Loan aid offered:* Direct PLUS loans; Direct Subsidized Stafford Loans; Direct Unsubsidized Stafford Loans

CAMPUS LIFE

Activities: Choral groups; Drama/theater; Literary magazine; Student government; Student newspaper. **On-Campus Highlights:** Campus Center (offices, coffee shop, library, tutoring center).

ACCOMMODATIONS
Allowed in exams:	
Calculators	Yes
Dictionary	Yes
Computer	Yes
Spell-checker	Yes
Extended test time	Yes
Scribe	Yes
Proctors	Yes
Oral exams	Yes
Note-takers	Yes
Support services for students with	
LD	Yes
ADHD	Yes
ASD	Yes
Distraction-reduced environment	Yes
Recording of lecture allowed	Yes
Reading technology:	Yes
Audio books	Yes
Other assistive technology	Yes
Priority registration	Yes
Added costs for services:	
For LD:	No
For ADHD:	No
For ASD:	No
LD specialists	No
ADHD & ASD coaching	Yes - TRIO Program
ASD specialists	No
Professional tutors	Yes
Peer tutors	Yes
Max. hours/week for services	3
How professors are notified of student approved accommodations	Director and Student

COLLEGE GRADUATION REQUIREMENTS
Course waivers allowed	Yes
In what courses	Limited
Course substitutions allowed	Yes
In what courses	Limited

University of Maine

168 College Ave, Orono, ME 04469-5713 • Admissions: 207-581-1561 • Fax: 207-581-1213

CAMPUS
Type of school	Public
Environment	Village
Support	S

STUDENTS
Undergrad enrollment	8,836
% male/female	53/47
% from out of state	35
% frosh live on campus	92

FINANCIAL FACTS
Annual in-state tuition	$8,580
Annual out-of-state tuition	$27,960
Room and board	$10,136
Required fees	$2,322

GENERAL ADMISSIONS INFO
Application fee	$40
Priority deadline	2/1
Regular application deadline	2/1

Nonfall registration accepted. Admission may be deferred for a maximum of 2 semesters.

Range SAT EBRW	530–630
Range SAT Math	520–620
Range ACT Composite	22–27

ACADEMICS
Student/faculty ratio	16:1.
% students returning for sophomore year	75
% students graduating within 4 years	38
% students graduating within 6 years	58

Most classes have fewer than 10 students. Most lab/discussion sessions have 10-19 students.

PROGRAMS/SERVICES FOR STUDENTS WITH LEARNING DIFFERENCES

The primary goal of the University of Maine Disability Support Services (DSS) is to create educational access for students with disabilities at UMaine by providing or coordinating disability accommodations, giving information about the University and available resources to students and families and educating the campus community. Some of the services provided or coordinated for students with disabilities include testing accommodations, note takers, ordering alternate format texts, classroom relocation, advisement on disability issues, and housing related accommodations. The staff of DSS promotes self-determination and personal responsibility for students with disabilities by educating them about their rights and responsibilities so that they can make informed choices in order to meet or exceed the standards expected of all students at the University of Maine.

ADMISSIONS

All students applying to the University of Maine have the same admissions process.

Additional Information

DSS does not provide tutoring as an accommodation. Students are referred to the UMaine Tutoring Center. This program provides small

ADMISSIONS INFO FOR STUDENTS WITH LEARNING DIFFERENCES

SAT/ACT required: Yes

Interview required: No

Essay required: Recommended

Additional application required: No

Documentation required for:

ASD: Please provide the following information under separate cover and on practice letterhead. The authorized release of information is to include but not be limited to the following: 1. Presenting diagnosis(es) utilizing diagnostic categorization or classification of the ICD or DSM IV. Diagnoses should indicate primary, secondary, etc., and significant findings, particularly in respect to presenting problems. 2.Date the examination/assessment/evaluation was performed for the presenting diagnosis, or if following the student for an extended time, date of onset and date of an evaluation of the condition that is recent enough to demonstrate the student's current level of functioning. 3.Tests, methodology used to determine disability.PLEASE do not send copies of the student's medical records. 4. Identify the current functional impact on the student's physical, perceptual and cognitive performance in activities such as mobility, self -care, note taking, laboratory assignment, testing/examinations, housing conditions/arrangements. Is this condition temporary? If temporary, what is the expected length of time to recovery? 5.Describe any treatments, medications, assistive devices/services the student is currently using. Note their effectiveness and any side effects that may impact the student's physical, perceptual or cognitive performance. 6. Recommendations for accommodations. Explain the relationship between the student's functional limitations and the recommendations. 7. Credentials (certification, licensure and/or training) of the diagnosing professional(s).

Documentation submitted to: Student Accessibility Services

Special Ed. HS course work accepted: No

Separate application required for Programs/Services: No

Contact Information

Name of program or department: Student Accessibility Services

Telephone: 207-581-2319

Fax: 207-581-9420

Email: shenry@maine.edu

group tutoring for 100 and 200 level courses. These tutorials are study skills based and do not reteach the classroom material. Currently, students are only assigned a tutor for one class each semester. Students who want one on one tutoring have the option to recruit and hire tutors on their own. Additionaly, UMaine has both a Math Lab and a Writing Center that are open to all students. They are staffed by upper-class students in math and English. The Math Lab is open on a drop-in basis whereas the Writing Center is available both for drop-ins and by appointment. These services are held in different locations on campus and thus a student with a disability must be highly motivated and independent enough to follow through with using these resources.

GENERAL ADMISSIONS

Very important factors considered include: rigor of secondary school record, class rank, academic GPA, standardized test scores. *Important factors considered include:* application essay, recommendation(s). *Other factors considered include:* interview, extracurricular activities, talent/ability, character/personal qualities, volunteer work, work experience. *Freshman Admission Requirements:* High school diploma is required and GED is accepted *Academic units required:* 4 English, 3 math, 2 science, 2 science labs, 2 social studies, 4 academic electives, *Academic units recommended:* 4 English, 4 math, 4 science, 3 science labs, 2 foreign language, 2 social studies, 1 history, 4 academic electives,

ACCOMMODATIONS OR SERVICES

Accommodations are decided upon an individual basis after a thorough review of appropriate, current documentation. The accommodations requests must be supported through the documentation provided and must be logically linked to the current impact of the condition on academic functioning.

FINANCIAL AID

Students should submit: FAFSA. Applicants will be notified of awards on a rolling basis beginning 1/1.. The Princeton Review suggests that all financial aid forms be submitted as soon as possible after October 1. *Need-based scholarships/grants offered:* College/university scholarship or grant aid from institutional funds; Federal Pell; Private scholarships; SEOG; State scholarships/grants *Loan aid offered:* Direct PLUS loans; Direct Subsidized Stafford Loans; Direct Unsubsidized Stafford Loans Federal Work-Study Program available. Institutional employment available.

CAMPUS LIFE

Activities: Campus Ministries; Choral groups; Concert band ; Dance ; Drama/theater; International Student Organization; Jazz band; Literary magazine; Marching band; Music ensembles; Musical theater; Opera; Pep band; Radio station ; Student government; Student newspaper; Student-run film society; Symphony orchestra Organizations: 224 registered organizations, 42 honor societies, 7 religious organizations. 13 fraternities, 6 sororities, **Athletics (Intercollegiate):** *Men:* baseball, basketball, cross-country, diving, football, ice hockey, soccer, swimming, track/field (outdoor), track/field (indoor) *Women:* basketball, cross-country, diving, field hockey, ice hockey, soccer, softball, swimming, track/field (outdoor), track/field (indoor), volleyball. **On-Campus Highlights:** New Balance Student Recreation Center, Alfond Arena, Bear's Den, Collins Center for the Arts, The Mall (grass quad central to campus).

ACCOMMODATIONS

Allowed in exams:

Calculators	Yes
Dictionary	No
Computer	Yes
Spell-checker	Yes
Extended test time	Yes
Scribe	Yes
Proctors	Yes
Oral exams	Yes
Note-takers	Yes

Support services for students with

LD	Yes
ADHD	Yes
ASD	Yes
Distraction-reduced environment	Yes
Recording of lecture allowed	Yes
Reading technology:	Yes
Audio books	Yes
Other assistive technology	Dragon

NaturallySpeaking, Natural Reader, LiveScribe Pens, Digital Recorders

Priority registration	No

Added costs for services:

For LD:	Not Applicable
For ADHD:	Not Applicable
For ASD:	Not Applicable
LD specialists	No
ADHD & ASD coaching	No
ASD specialists	No
Professional tutors	Yes
Peer tutors	Yes
Max. hours/week for services	Varies
How professors are notified of student approved accommodations	Student

COLLEGE GRADUATION REQUIREMENTS

Course waivers allowed	Yes

In what courses Decisions about course waivers are made through an individualized process in collaboration with faculty from the department and Student Accessibility Services at UMaine.

Course substitutions allowed	Yes

In what courses Decisions about course substitutions are made through an individualized process in collaboration with faculty from the department and Student Accessibility Services at UMaine.

University of New England

11 Hills Beach Road, Biddeford, ME 04005-9599 • Admissions: 207-602-2297 • Fax: 207-602-5900

CAMPUS

Type of school	Private (nonprofit)
Environment	Town
Support	S

STUDENTS

Undergrad enrollment	2,360
% male/female	30/70
% from out of state	70
% frosh live on campus	94

FINANCIAL FACTS

Annual tuition	$36,300
Room and board	$14,790
Required fees	$1,320

GENERAL ADMISSIONS INFO

Application fee	$40
Priority deadline	12/1

Nonfall registration accepted. Admission may be deferred for a maximum of 1 year.

Range SAT EBRW	520–610
Range SAT Math	510–600
Range ACT Composite	21–26

ACADEMICS

Student/faculty ratio	13:1
% students returning for sophomore year	78
% students graduating within 4 years	54
% students graduating within 6 years	60

Most classes have 10–19 students.

PROGRAMS/SERVICES FOR STUDENTS WITH LEARNING DIFFERENCES

The Student Access Center (formerly Disability Services) works to ensure that the University promotes respect for individual differences and that no person who meets the academic and technical standards needed for admission and continued enrollment at UNE is denied benefits or subjected to discrimination due to a disability. Toward this end, and in conjunction with federal and state laws, the University provides reasonable accommodations for qualified students.

ADMISSIONS

Admission process is the same for all applicants.

Additional Information

The Student Academic Success Center (SASC) provides a comprehensive array of academic support services including placement testing, courses, workshops, and tutoring. The mission of the Student Academic Success Center is to assist students to become independent learners so that they are able to meet the University's academic standards and attain their personal educational goals. In the Student Academic Success Center, professional staff members help students develop and maintain the skills they need to meed the challenges of undergraduate and graduate study. This is accomplished through individual consultations, workshops, and classroom presentations. The SASC Learning Specialist's time is spent working with students to assess progress and effectiveness in implementing practices designed to enable success. SASC provides a staff of peer, graduate, and professional tutors to support a wide selection of undergraduate courses.

ADMISSIONS INFO FOR STUDENTS WITH LEARNING DIFFERENCES

SAT/ACT required: No
Interview required: No
Essay required: Not Applicable
Additional application required: Not Applicable
Documentation required for:
  LD: guidelines listed on our website
  ADHD: guidelines listed on our website
Documentation submitted to: Student Access Center
Special Ed. HS course work accepted: Not Applicable
Separate application required for Programs/Services: No
Contact Information
Name of program or department: Student Access Center
Telephone: 207-221-4418
Email: hpatterson@une.edu

University of New England

GENERAL ADMISSIONS

Very important factors considered include: rigor of secondary school record, academic GPA. *Important factors considered include:* class rank. *Other factors considered include:* application essay, standardized test scores, recommendation(s), extracurricular activities, talent/ability, character/personal qualities, alumni/ae relation, geographical residence, volunteer work, work experience, level of applicant's interest. *Freshman Admission Requirements:* High school diploma is required and GED is accepted. *Academic units required:* 4 English, 3 math, 3 science, 2 science labs, 2 social studies, 2 history. *Academic units recommended:* 4 math, 4 science, 3 science labs, 2 foreign language, 4 social studies, 4 history, 4 academic electives.

ACCOMMODATIONS OR SERVICES

Accommodations are decided upon an individual basis after a thorough review of appropriate, current documentation. The accommodations requests must be supported through the documentation provided and must be logically linked to the current impact of the condition on academic functioning.

FINANCIAL AID

The Princeton Review suggests that all financial aid forms be submitted as soon as possible after October 1. *Need-based scholarships/grants offered: Loan aid offered:* Federal Work-Study Program available. Institutional employment available.

CAMPUS LIFE

Activities: Choral groups; Dance; Drama/theater; International Student Organization; Jazz band; Literary magazine; Model UN; Music ensembles; Musical theater; Pep band; Radio station; Student government; Student newspaper; Yearbook. **Organizations:** 36 registered organizations, 3 honor societies, 1 religious organization. **Athletics (Intercollegiate):** *Men:* basketball, cross-country, golf, lacrosse, soccer *Women:* basketball, cross-country, field hockey, golf, lacrosse, soccer, softball, swimming, volleyball. **On-Campus Highlights:** Marine Science Center, Alfond Health Science Center, UNE Beach (on Atlantic Ocean and Saco River), Danielle N. Ripich Commons, Harold Alfond Forum (Athletics).

ACCOMMODATIONS

Allowed in exams:	
Calculators	Yes
Dictionary	Yes
Computer	Yes
Spell-checker	Yes
Extended test time	Yes
Scribe	Yes
Proctors	Yes
Oral exams	No
Note-takers	Yes
Support services for students with	
LD	Yes
ADHD	Yes
ASD	Yes
Distraction-reduced environment	Yes
Recording of lecture allowed	Yes
Reading technology:	Yes
Audio books	Yes
Other assistive technology	smart pens for note taking assistance
Priority registration	Yes
Added costs for services:	
For LD:	No
For ADHD:	No
For ASD:	No
LD specialists	No
ADHD & ASD coaching	No
ASD specialists	No
Professional tutors	No
Peer tutors	Yes
Max. hours/week for services	Varies
How professors are notified of student approved accommodations	Student

COLLEGE GRADUATION REQUIREMENTS

Course waivers allowed	No
Course substitutions allowed	No

Frostburg State University

101 BRADDOCK RD., FROSTBURG, MD 21532 • ADMISSIONS: 301-687-4201 • FAX: 301-687-7074

CAMPUS
Type of school	Public
Environment	Village
Support	S

STUDENTS
Undergrad enrollment	4,486
% male/female	48/52
% from out of state	7
% frosh live on campus	72

FINANCIAL FACTS
Annual in-state tuition	$6,468
Annual out-of-state tuition	$19,816
Room and board	$9,210
Required fees	$2,446

GENERAL ADMISSIONS INFO
Application fee	$45
Priority deadline	6/1

Nonfall registration accepted.

Range SAT EBRW	470–560
Range SAT Math	450–550
Range ACT Composite	17–23

ACADEMICS
Student/faculty ratio	15:1
% students returning for sophomore year	74
% students graduating within 4 years	25
% students graduating within 6 years	47

Most classes have 20–29 students.
Most lab/discussion sessions have 10–19 students.

PROGRAMS/SERVICES FOR STUDENTS WITH LEARNING DIFFERENCES

Frostburg State University provides comprehensive support services for students with disabilities to assist them in achieving their potential. To be eligible for the services, admitted students must provide recent and appropriate documentation relating to their disability. Some of the services provided are extended time for testing, note takers, advocacy, electronic texts, priority registration, readers and scribes, and assistive technology. The goal of the program is to provide appropriate support services to enhance learning and to strive for student self-advocacy and understanding of and independence in their learning styles.

ADMISSIONS

There is no special admission procedure for students with learning disabilities. All students must complete the mainstream program in high school and meet all of the requirements for the university and the state. There is a Student Support Services/Disabled Student Services information form that must be completed by students to enroll in these programs. Admission to FSU is determined by the Admissions Office, which assesses an applicant's likelihood of success in a regular college program with support service assistance.

Additional Information

Student Support Services (SSS), TRiO program, is an educational opportunity project which helps students with disabilities achieve their academic and personal goals. SSS acts as an advocate for qualified students, plans and coordinates services and provides programs which help students develop the academic, interpersonal and social skills they need for success at Frostburg.

ADMISSIONS INFO FOR STUDENTS WITH LEARNING DIFFERENCES

SAT/ACT required: Yes
Interview required: No
Essay required: No
Additional application required: No
Documentation required for:
  LD: Psycho ed evaluation
  ADHD: Diagnosis based on DSM-V; history of behaviors impairing functioning in academic setting; diagnostic interview; history of symptoms; evidence of ongoing behaviors.
  ASD: Statement of diagnosis from a qualified professional with recommendations for accomodations; statement of limitation and how the disability may affect the student; any assessment that were completed. ASD documentation not required with general application.
Documentation submitted to: Disability Support Services
Special Ed. HS course work accepted: Yes
Separate application required for Programs/Services: No
Contact Information
Name of program or department: Disability Support Services
Telephone: 301-687-4483
Email: hhveith@frostburg.edu

Frostburg State University

GENERAL ADMISSIONS

Very important factors considered include: rigor of secondary school record, academic GPA, standardized test scores. *Important factors considered include:* recommendation(s), interview. *Other factors considered include:* extracurricular activities, talent/ability, character/personal qualities, alumni/ae relation. *Freshman Admission Requirements:* High school diploma is required and GED is accepted. *Academic units required:* 4 English, 3 math, 3 science, 2 science labs, 2 foreign language, 3 history.

ACCOMMODATIONS OR SERVICES

Accommodations are decided upon an individual basis after a thorough review of appropriate, current documentation. The accommodations requests must be supported through the documentation provided and must be logically linked to the current impact of the condition on academic functioning.

FINANCIAL AID

Students should submit: FAFSA. Applicants will be notified of awards on a rolling basis beginning 3/15. The Princeton Review suggests that all financial aid forms be submitted as soon as possible after October 1. *Need-based scholarships/grants offered:* College/university scholarship or grant aid from institutional funds; Federal Pell; Private scholarships; SEOG; State scholarships/grants. *Loan aid offered:* Direct PLUS loans; Direct Subsidized Stafford Loans; Direct Unsubsidized Stafford Loans. Federal Work-Study Program available. Institutional employment available.

CAMPUS LIFE

Activities: Campus Ministries; Choral groups; Dance; Drama/theater; International Student Organization; Jazz band; Literary magazine; Marching band; Model UN; Music ensembles; Pep band; Radio station; Student government; Student newspaper; Television station; Yearbook. **Organizations:** 95 registered organizations, 18 honor societies, 6 religious organizations. 9 fraternities, 6 sororities. **Athletics (Intercollegiate):** *Men:* baseball, basketball, cross-country, diving, football, golf, soccer, swimming, tennis, track/field (outdoor), track/field (indoor). *Women:* basketball, cross-country, diving, field hockey, lacrosse, soccer, softball, swimming, tennis, track/field (outdoor), track/field (indoor), volleyball. **On-Campus Highlights:** Lane University Center, Game Room & Loft, Cordts PE Center, Performing Arts Center, Compton Science Center.

ACCOMMODATIONS

Allowed in exams:	
Calculators	Yes
Dictionary	Yes
Computer	Yes
Spell-checker	Yes
Extended test time	Yes
Scribe	Yes
Proctors	Yes
Oral exams	Yes
Note-takers	Yes
Support services for students with	
LD	Yes
ADHD	Yes
ASD	Yes
Distraction-reduced environment	Yes
Recording of lecture allowed	Yes
Reading technology:	Yes
Audio books Not through the school but the student can get a student membership.	
Other assistive technology	Yes
Priority registration	Yes
Added costs for services:	
For LD:	No
For ADHD:	No
For ASD:	No
LD specialists	No
ADHD & ASD coaching We have someone that can work with students on time management, test taking skills, notetaking, etc.	
ASD specialists	No
Professional tutors	Yes
Peer tutors	Yes
Max. hours/week for services	Varies
How professors are notified of student approved accommodations	Student

COLLEGE GRADUATION REQUIREMENTS

Course waivers allowed	No
Course substitutions allowed	Yes
In what courses	
Students may appeal for any course to be substituted. Appeals are determined on a case-by-case basis.	

McDaniel College

2 COLLEGE HILL, WESTMINSTER, MD 21157 • ADMISSIONS: 410-857-2230 • FAX:

CAMPUS
Type of school	Private (nonprofit)
Environment	Town
Support	CS

STUDENTS
Undergrad enrollment	1,549
% male/female	49/51
% from out of state	34
% frosh live on campus	95

FINANCIAL FACTS
Annual tuition	$43,260
Room and board	$11,430
Required fees	NR

GENERAL ADMISSIONS INFO
Application fee	$50
Priority deadline	2/1
Regular application deadline	4/1

Nonfall registration accepted. Admission may be deferred for a maximum of 1 year.

Range SAT EBRW	540–620
Range SAT Math	520–610
Range ACT Composite	21–28

ACADEMICS
Student/faculty ratio	11:1
% students returning for sophomore year	81
% students graduating within 4 years	59
% students graduating within 6 years	68

PROGRAMS/SERVICES FOR STUDENTS WITH LEARNING DIFFERENCES

Student Academic Support Services (SASS) ensures that all students with documented disabilities receive appropriate academic accommodations. The Mentorship Advantage Program (MAP) offers interactive workshops on topics such as socialization, organization, assistive technology, time management, resume writing and interviewing. The Providing Academic Support for Success (PASS) program offers students the opportunity to learn alongside their peers and supported by Graduate Assistants three evenings a week. The Academic Skills Program (ASP), a fee-based opportunity ($3,150 annual fee), provides students with weekly consultation with an Academic Counselor, academic skills tutoring with a SASS graduate assistant, use of supervised study/computer lab, learning style and priority registration.

ADMISSIONS

The admission process is the same for all applicants. General admission criteria include a minimum 2.75 GPA in core academic courses including 4 years English, 3 years math, 3 years science, 3 years social studies and 3 years of a foreign language (substitutions are allowed in foreign language if appropriate). Students with a 3.5 GPA do not have to submit an ACT or SAT. The average ACT is 21 and average SAT is 1000. Any documentation for LD or ADHD should be sent to ASC to be used after a student is admitted and enrolled.

Additional Information

McDaniel "Step Ahead" is an optional 5-day summer bridge opportunity offered for first-year students with disabilities. Intensive workshops, team-building activities and field trips are available for students to familiarize themselves with the resources, staff and peers who comprise and utilize McDaniel's SASS. Each participant is matched with a peer mentor. Some typical accommodations offered by the SASS include: note takers, alternative testing arrangements such as extra time, books on tape, computer with speech input, separate testing room, tape recorder, foreign language substitution and math substitution.

ADMISSIONS INFO FOR STUDENTS WITH LEARNING DIFFERENCES

SAT/ACT required: Yes
Interview required: No
Essay required: Yes
Additional application required: No
Documentation required for:
 LD: Psycho ed evaluation
 ADHD: Diagnosis based on DSM-V; history of behaviors impairing functioning in academic setting; diagnostic interview; history of symptoms; evidence of ongoing behaviors.
 ASD: Psycho ed evaluation
Documentation submitted to: Academic Skills Center
Special Ed. HS course work accepted: No
Separate application required for Programs/Services: Yes
Contact Information
Name of program or department: Student Academic Support Services
Telephone: 410-857-2504
Fax: 410-386-4617
Email: sass@mcdaniel.edu

McDaniel College

GENERAL ADMISSIONS

Very important factors considered include: rigor of secondary school record, academic GPA. *Important factors considered include:* application essay, standardized test scores, recommendation(s). *Other factors considered include:* class rank, interview, extracurricular activities, talent/ability, character/personal qualities, first generation, alumni/ae relation, volunteer work, work experience, level of applicant's interest. *Freshman Admission Requirements:* High school diploma is required and GED is accepted. *Academic units required:* 4 English, 3 math, 3 science, 3 science labs, 3 foreign language, 3 social studies. *Academic units recommended:* 4 English, 4 math, 4 science, 4 foreign language, 3 social studies.

ACCOMMODATIONS OR SERVICES

Accommodations are decided upon an individual basis after a thorough review of appropriate, current documentation. The accommodations requests must be supported through the documentation provided and must be logically linked to the current impact of the condition on academic functioning.

FINANCIAL AID

Students should submit: FAFSA. Applicants will be notified of awards on a rolling basis beginning 3/15. The Princeton Review suggests that all financial aid forms be submitted as soon as possible after October 1. *Need-based scholarships/grants offered:* College/university scholarship or grant aid from institutional funds; Federal Pell; Private scholarships; SEOG; State scholarships/grants. *Loan aid offered:* Direct PLUS loans; Direct Subsidized Stafford Loans; Direct Unsubsidized Stafford Loans. Federal Work-Study Program available. Institutional employment available.

CAMPUS LIFE

Activities: Campus Ministries; Choral groups; Concert band; Dance; Drama/theater; International Student Organization; Jazz band; Literary magazine; Model UN; Music ensembles; Musical theater; Pep band; Radio station; Student government; Student newspaper; Student-run film society; Television station; Yearbook. **Organizations:** 136 registered organizations, 22 honor societies, 5 religious organizations. 6 fraternities, 4 sororities. **Athletics (Intercollegiate):** *Men:* baseball, basketball, cross-country, football, golf, lacrosse, soccer, swimming, tennis, track/field (outdoor), track/field (indoor), volleyball, wrestling. *Women:* basketball, cross-country, field hockey, golf, lacrosse, soccer, softball, swimming, tennis, track/field (outdoor), track/field (indoor), volleyball. **On-Campus Highlights:** The Hoover Library & Caseys' Corner, Merritt Fitness Center, Decker College Center, Gill Stadium, Golf Course.

ACCOMMODATIONS

Allowed in exams:	
Calculators	Yes
Dictionary	Yes
Computer	Yes
Spell-checker	Yes
Extended test time	Yes
Scribe	Yes
Proctors	Yes
Oral exams	Yes
Note-takers	Yes
Support services for students with	
LD	Yes
ADHD	Yes
ASD	Yes
Distraction-reduced environment	Yes
Recording of lecture allowed	Yes
Reading technology:	Yes
Audio books	Yes
Other assistive technology	Yes
Priority registration	Yes
Added costs for services:	
For LD:	Yes
For ADHD:	Yes
For ASD:	Yes
LD specialists	Yes
ADHD & ASD coaching	No
ASD specialists	No
Professional tutors	Yes
Peer tutors	Yes
Max. hours/week for services	Unlimited
How professors are notified of student approved accommodations	Student

COLLEGE GRADUATION REQUIREMENTS

Course waivers allowed	Yes
In what courses	Foreign Language
Course substitutions allowed	Yes
In what courses	Foreign Language

Salisbury University

1101 Camden Avenue, Salisbury, MD 21801 • Admissions: 410-543-6161 • Fax: 410-546-6016

CAMPUS
Type of school	Public
Environment	Town
Support	S

STUDENTS
Undergrad enrollment	7,552
% male/female	44/56
% from out of state	13
% frosh live on campus	88

FINANCIAL FACTS
Annual in-state tuition	$7,122
Annual out-of-state tuition	$16,824
Room and board	$11,950
Required fees	$2,702

GENERAL ADMISSIONS INFO
Application fee	$50
Regular application deadline	1/15

Nonfall registration accepted. Admission may be deferred for a maximum of 1 year.

Range SAT EBRW	560–630
Range SAT Math	540–630
Range ACT Composite	20–25

ACADEMICS
Student/faculty ratio	16:1
% students returning for sophomore year	83
% students graduating within 4 years	48
% students graduating within 6 years	70

Most classes have 20–29 students.
Most lab/discussion sessions have 10–19 students.

PROGRAMS/SERVICES FOR STUDENTS WITH LEARNING DIFFERENCES
The Disabilities Resource Center (DRC) aims to inform educate and support students with disabilities in ways in which allow them to achieve their educational, career, and life goals on the basis of their personal skills, abilities, interests, and values. Equity in access, rights of privacy, and the integrity of academic programs, policies, and practices are emphasized by the DRC.

ADMISSIONS
Applicants must submit the completed application for admission, official high school transcripts, essay, and letter(s) of recommendation. Standardized SAT or ACT test scores are required for applicants with a weighted grade point average of 3.50 or less on a 4.0 scale. Applicants choosing to exclude standardized test scores should provide evidence of individual achievements and/or experiences which would not be evident from a review of the official high school transcripts. Leadership qualities, community service, artistic talent, athletic talent and diversity of background, including cultural, experiential and geographic, are additional factors used in the holistic review of each applicant.

Additional Information
Once the DRC has evaluated the submitted disability documentation, confirmed that documentation meets the necessary criteria for receiving reasonable accommodations, and received the students' completed intake form, the student should contact the DRC in order to schedule an Intake Conference. At this meeting, the student and DRC staff member will discuss the students accommodation plans, strategies for a successful academic career, and campus resources and services, among other topics. All documentation submitted should contain a comprehensive written evaluation, prepared by a qualified professional, and should include a statement of diagnosis of a disability, a description of that disability and a description of the nature and severity of the students disability. Please see: http://www.salisbury.edu/students/dss.

ADMISSIONS INFO FOR STUDENTS WITH LEARNING DIFFERENCES
SAT/ACT required: No
Interview required: No
Essay required: Not Applicable
Additional application required: Yes
Documentation required for:
 LD: Psycho ed evaluation
 ADHD: Psycho ed evaluation
 ASD: Psycho-educational Education
Documentation submitted to: Support Program/Services
Special Ed. HS course work accepted: No
Separate application required for Programs/Services: No
Contact Information
Name of program or department: Office of Student Disability Support Services
Telephone: 410-677-6536
Fax: 410-548-4052
Email: disabilitysupport@salisbury.edu

Salisbury University

GENERAL ADMISSIONS

Very important factors considered include: rigor of secondary school record, academic GPA. *Important factors considered include:* class rank, standardized test scores. *Other factors considered include:* application essay, recommendation(s), extracurricular activities, talent/ability, character/personal qualities, first generation, alumni/ae relation, geographical residence, state residency, racial/ethnic status, volunteer work, work experience, level of *Freshman Admission Requirements:* High school diploma is required and GED is accepted. *Academic units required:* 4 English, 4 math, 3 science, 2 science labs, 2 foreign language, 3 social studies. *Academic units recommended:* 4 English, 4 math, 4 science, 3 science labs, 3 foreign language, 3 social studies, 3 academic electives.

ACCOMMODATIONS OR SERVICES

Accommodations are decided upon an individual basis after a thorough review of appropriate, current documentation. The accommodations requests must be supported through the documentation provided and must be logically linked to the current impact of the condition on academic functioning.

FINANCIAL AID

Students should submit: FAFSA. Applicants will be notified of awards on or about 3/15. The Princeton Review suggests that all financial aid forms be submitted as soon as possible after October 1. *Need-based scholarships/grants offered:* College/university scholarship or grant aid from institutional funds; Federal Pell; Private scholarships; SEOG; State scholarships/grants. *Loan aid offered:* Direct PLUS loans; Direct Subsidized Stafford Loans; Direct Unsubsidized Stafford Loans. Federal Work-Study Program available. Institutional employment available.

CAMPUS LIFE

Activities: Campus Ministries; Choral groups; Concert band; Dance; Drama/theater; International Student Organization; Jazz band; Literary magazine; Model UN; Music ensembles; Musical theater; Opera; Pep band; Radio station; Student government; Student newspaper; Student-run film society; Symphony orchestra; Television station. **Organizations:** 126 registered organizations, 23 honor societies, 8 religious organizations. 8 fraternities, 4 sororities. **Athletics (Intercollegiate):** *Men:* baseball, basketball, cross-country, football, lacrosse, soccer, swimming, tennis, track/field (outdoor). *Women:* basketball, cross-country, field hockey, lacrosse, soccer, softball, swimming, tennis, track/field (outdoor), volleyball. **On-Campus Highlights:** Guerrieri Academic Commons, The Commons (houses Bookstore and Dining Hall), Cool Beans Cyber Cafe, Maggs Gym / University Fitness Center, Red Square.

ACCOMMODATIONS

Allowed in exams:	
Calculators	Yes
Dictionary	Yes
Computer	Yes
Spell-checker	Yes
Extended test time	Yes
Scribe	Yes
Proctors	Yes
Oral exams	Yes
Note-takers	Yes
Support services for students with	
LD	Yes
ADHD	Yes
ASD	Yes
Distraction-reduced environment	Yes
Recording of lecture allowed	Yes
Reading technology:	Yes
Audio books	Yes
Other assistive technology	
Priority registration	Yes
Added costs for services:	
For LD:	No
For ADHD:	No
For ASD:	No
LD specialists	No
ADHD & ASD coaching	Yes
ASD specialists	Yes
Professional tutors	Yes
Peer tutors	Yes
Max. hours/week for services	Varies
How professors are notified of student approved accommodations	Student

COLLEGE GRADUATION REQUIREMENTS

Course waivers allowed	Yes
In what courses - Requests are evaluated on a case-by-case basis.	
Course substitutions allowed	Yes
In what courses - Requests are evaluated on a case-by-case basis.	

Towson University

8000 YORK ROAD, TOWSON, MD 21252-0001 • ADMISSIONS: 410-704-2113 • FAX: 410-704-3030

CAMPUS
Type of school	Public
Environment	Metropolis
Support	CS

STUDENTS
Undergrad enrollment	19,367
% male/female	40/60
% from out of state	14
% frosh live on campus	84

FINANCIAL FACTS
Annual in-state tuition	$6,826
Annual out-of-state tuition	$20,094
Room and board	$13,034
Required fees	$3,114

GENERAL ADMISSIONS INFO
Application fee	$45
Priority deadline	12/1
Regular application deadline	1/17

Nonfall registration accepted. Admission may be deferred for a maximum of 1 year.

Range SAT EBRW	535–610
Range SAT Math	520–600
Range ACT Composite	21–25

ACADEMICS
Student/faculty ratio	17:1
% students returning for sophomore year	85
% students graduating within 4 years	47
% students graduating within 6 years	72

Most classes have 20–29 students. Most lab/discussion sessions have 10–19 students.

PROGRAMS/SERVICES FOR STUDENTS WITH LEARNING DIFFERENCES

Disability is an aspect of diversity that is integral to our society and to the Towson University community. Disability Support Services' (DSS) mission is to provide leadership in promoting equal access to educational opportunities to students with disabilities. DSS collaborates with students, faculty, and staff to identify and remove barriers to foster an all-inclusive campus. The office provides individual services and facilitates accommodations to students with disabilities, and offers institution-wide guidance, consultation, and training on disability-related topics. Disability Support Services at Towson University provides accommodations and services to students with various disabilities and some temporary impairments that substantially limit one or more major life activities. The DSS staff is available to answer questions concerning accommodations and services as well as to provide information about other resources on and off campus. DSS works with students with disabilities such as: • Learning disabilities • Attention-deficit/hyperactivity disorder • Mental health disabilities • Autism spectrum disorder • Brain injuries • Physical/mobility and medical disabilities • Vision and hearing impairments DSS works with students to determine and facilitate reasonable accommodations based on documentation and a personal interview. Students are encouraged to register with DSS as soon as possible after admission to the university to ensure timely provision of services. DSS encourages new students to maintain regular contact with our office, especially during their first year. This contact provides the opportunity for DSS staff to guide students and to work with them proactively to address any issues that may arise. Eligibility for accommodations is established through a variety of information sources, including the student's self-report, observation and interaction with the student, previous accommodations received and the particular accommodations requested, the unique characteristics of a course or program, as well as documentation from external sources, such as psychologists, educational professionals and health care providers.

ADMISSIONS INFO FOR STUDENTS WITH LEARNING DIFFERENCES
SAT/ACT required: Y/N depends if Test Optional
Interview required: No
Essay required: Recommended
Additional application required: Yes
Documentation required for:
LD: Current psycho-educational evaluation which includes assessments of cognitive skills and academic performance.
ADHD: Documentation provided by a licensed mental health provider stating the diagnosis, severity of the diagnosis, educational impact and recommended accommodations.
ASD: Documentation provided by a licensed mental health provider stating the diagnosis, severity of the diagnosis, educational impact and recommended accommodations.
Documentation submitted to: Disability Support Services
Special Ed. HS course work accepted: Yes
Separate application required for Programs/Services: For LD, ADHD, or ASD.
Contact Information
Name of program or department: Disability Support Services
Telephone: (410) 704-2638
Fax: (410) 704-4247
Email: swillemin@towson.edu

Towson University

ADMISSIONS
The Admissions Committee reviews each applicant holistically using the Towson University Online Application, essay, official transcript and test scores from SAT and/or ACT. The essay allows you to show us what makes you exceptional. We enjoy reading ess

Additional Information
See the DSS website for additional information at www.towson.edu/dss. The College Orientation & Life Activities Program (COLA) is a fee based program designed for TU students with autism who would like support in adjusting to college life. The COLA program focuses on supporting students in addressing challenges, developing strengths, exploring opportunities, and planning for success as a TU student. Support is tailored to each COLA student's self-determined goals in independent living, social experiences, academic success, and work exploration. Two levels of services are offered: COLA Regular, $4,000/semester and COLA Lite, $2,200/semester.

GENERAL ADMISSIONS
Very important factors considered include: academic GPA. *Important factors considered include:* rigor of secondary school record, standardized test scores. *Other factors considered include:* class rank, application essay, recommendation(s), talent/ability, first generation. *Freshman Admission Requirements:* High school diploma is required and GED is accepted. *Academic units required:* 4 English, 4 math, 3 science, 2 science labs, 2 foreign language, 3 social studies, 6 academic electives.

ACCOMMODATIONS OR SERVICES
Accommodations are decided upon an individual basis after a thorough review of appropriate, current documentation. The accommodations requests must be supported through the documentation provided and must be logically linked to the current impact of the condition on academic functioning.

FINANCIAL AID
Students should submit: FAFSA;; State aid form. Applicants will be notified of awards on a rolling basis beginning 3/15. The Princeton Review suggests that all financial aid forms be submitted as soon as possible after October 1. *Need-based scholarships/grants offered:* College/university scholarship or grant aid from institutional funds; Federal Pell; Private scholarships; SEOG; State scholarships/grants. *Loan aid offered:* Direct PLUS loans; Direct Subsidized Stafford Loans; Direct Unsubsidized Stafford Loans. Federal Work-Study Program available. Institutional employment available.

CAMPUS LIFE
Activities: Campus Ministries; Choral groups; Concert band; Dance; Drama/theater; International Student Organization; Jazz band; Literary magazine; Marching band; Model UN; Music ensembles; Musical theater; Opera; Pep band; Radio station; Student government; Student newspaper; Student-run film society; Symphony orchestra; Television station. **Organizations:** 198 registered organizations, 15 honor societies, 12 religious organizations. 12 fraternities, 10 sororities. **Athletics (Intercollegiate):** *Men:* baseball, basketball, cheerleading, cross-country, diving, football, golf, lacrosse, soccer, swimming, tennis. *Women:* basketball, cheerleading, cross-country, diving, field hockey, gymnastics, lacrosse, soccer, softball, swimming, tennis, track/field (outdoor), volleyball. **On-Campus Highlights:** Johnny Unitas Stadium/SECU Arena, University Union, Burdick Hall-athletic facilities, West Village Commons, College of Liberal Arts Building.

ACCOMMODATIONS

Allowed in exams:	
Calculators	Yes
Dictionary	No
Computer	Yes
Spell-checker	Yes
Extended test time	Yes
Scribe	Yes
Proctors	Yes
Oral exams	Yes
Note-takers	Yes
Support services for students with	
LD	Yes
ADHD	Yes
ASD	Yes
Distraction-reduced environment	Yes
Recording of lecture allowed	Yes
Reading technology:	Yes
Audio books	Yes
Other assistive technology	Yes
Priority registration	Yes
Added costs for services:	
For LD:	Not Applicable
For ADHD:	Not Applicable
For ASD:	Not Applicable
LD specialists	Yes
ADHD & ASD coaching	Yes
ASD specialists	Yes
Professional tutors	No
Peer tutors	Yes
Max. hours/week for services	Varies
How professors are notified of student approved accommodations	Student

COLLEGE GRADUATION REQUIREMENTS

Course waivers allowed	No
Course substitutions allowed	Yes
In what courses	

Chiefly math. Foreign language is not required for most majors.

University of Maryland, College Park

MITCHELL BUILDING, COLLEGE PARK, MD 20742-5235 • ADMISSIONS: 301-314-8385 • FAX: 301-314-9693

CAMPUS

Type of school	Public
Environment	Metropolis
Support	CS

STUDENTS

Undergrad enrollment	29,273
% male/female	53/47
% from out of state	22
% frosh live on campus	92

FINANCIAL FACTS

Annual in-state tuition	$8,651
Annual out-of-state tuition	$33,272
Room and board	$12,429
Required fees	$1,944

GENERAL ADMISSIONS INFO

Application fee	$75
Priority deadline	11/1
Regular application deadline	1/20

Nonfall registration accepted. Admission may be deferred for a maximum of 1 year.

Range SAT EBRW	640–720
Range SAT Math	650–750
Range ACT Composite	29–33

ACADEMICS

Student/faculty ratio	18:1
% students returning for sophomore year	96
% students graduating within 4 years	67
% students graduating within 6 years	85

Most classes have 20–29 students.

PROGRAMS/SERVICES FOR STUDENTS WITH LEARNING DIFFERENCES

The goal of the Disability Support Service is coordinate services which ensure individuvals with disabilities equal access to University programs. This goal is accomplished by: 1) providing and coordinating individually tailored direct services to students, faculty and staff, and campus visitors who have disabilities; 2) providing consultation to university staff regarding the Adaptive Technology needs of students and staff who have disabilities; 3) providing support and information to students and staff which promotes the development of advocacy and negotiation skills.

ADMISSIONS

Applicants must use the Coalition Application for Access and Affordability and Success to apply. Academic merit is assessed on the basis of each applicant's achievements and potential in a broad range of academic categories, as influenced by the opportunities and challenges faced by the applicant. These categories include: Educational Performance, Potential for College Success, Potential to Promote Beneficial Educational Outcomes and to Contribute to Campus and Community Life, Students' Persistence and Commitment to Educational Success. The review process considers more than 26 factors.

Additional Information

Learning Assistance Service (LAS) is the academic support unit of the University Counseling Center. LAS exists to help students achieve their academic goals by providing a range of services. LAS also provides Academic Success Workshop series to help students become successful, active learners. Workshops focus on helping students manage their time and improve their approach to studying and learning at UM. LAS offers learning strategy courses to help develop college level learning strategies.

ADMISSIONS INFO FOR STUDENTS WITH LEARNING DIFFERENCES

SAT/ACT required: Yes
Interview required: No
Essay required: Yes
Additional application required: No
Documentation required for:
  LD: Psycho-educational or neuropsychological evaluation (including Apititude and achievement testing). We will review IEP's for specificity and if specific enough, they may suffice as adequate documentation.
  ADHD: Neuropsychological or Psycho-educational evaluation (including Apititude and achievement testing) or a comprehensive letter from a licensed counselor or psychologist, or a psychiatrist.
  ASD: Psycho ed evaluation
Documentation submitted to: DSS
Special Ed. HS course work accepted: Yes
Separate application required for Programs/Services: No
Contact Information
Name of program or department: Disability Support Service (DSS)
Telephone: 301-314-7682
Fax: 301-405-0813

University of Maryland, College Park

GENERAL ADMISSIONS

Very important factors considered include: rigor of secondary school record, academic GPA, standardized test scores. *Important factors considered include:* class rank, application essay, recommendation(s), talent/ability, first generation, state residency. *Other factors considered include:* extracurricular activities, character/personal qualities, alumni/ae relation, geographical residence, racial/ethnic status, volunteer work, work experience. *Freshman Admission Requirements:* High school diploma is required and GED is accepted. *Academic units required:* 4 English, 4 math, 3 science, 2 science labs, 2 foreign language, 3 social studies. *Academic units recommended:* 4 English, 4 math, 3 science, 2 science labs, 2 foreign language, 3 social studies.

ACCOMMODATIONS OR SERVICES

Accommodations are decided upon an individual basis after a thorough review of appropriate, current documentation. The accommodations requests must be supported through the documentation provided and must be logically linked to the current impact of the condition on academic functioning.

FINANCIAL AID

Students should submit: FAFSA. Applicants will be notified of awards on a rolling basis beginning 4/1. The Princeton Review suggests that all financial aid forms be submitted as soon as possible after October 1. *Need-based scholarships/grants offered:* College/university scholarship or grant aid from institutional funds; Federal Pell; Private scholarships; SEOG; State scholarships/grants. *Loan aid offered:* Direct PLUS loans; Direct Subsidized Stafford Loans; Direct Unsubsidized Stafford Loans. Federal Work-Study Program available. Institutional employment available.

CAMPUS LIFE

Activities: Campus Ministries; Choral groups; Concert band; Dance; Drama/theater; International Student Organization; Jazz band; Literary magazine; Marching band; Model UN; Music ensembles; Musical theater; Opera; Pep band; Radio station; Student government; Student newspaper; Student-run film society; Symphony orchestra; Television station; Yearbook. **Organizations:** 574 registered organizations, 53 honor societies, 55 religious organizations. 36 fraternities, 27 sororities. **Athletics (Intercollegiate):** *Men:* baseball, basketball, cross-country, football, golf, lacrosse, soccer, swimming, tennis, track/field (outdoor), track/field (indoor), wrestling. *Women:* basketball, cheerleading, cross-country, field hockey, golf, gymnastics, lacrosse, soccer, softball, swimming, tennis, track/field (outdoor), track/field (indoor), volleyball, water polo. **On-Campus Highlights:** Clarice Smith Performing Arts Center, Adele H. Stamp Student Union, Eppley Recreation Center, Chevy Chase Bank Field at Byrd Stadium, Comcast Center.

ACCOMMODATIONS

Allowed in exams:	
Calculators	Yes
Dictionary	Yes
Computer	Yes
Spell-checker	Yes
Extended test time	Yes
Scribe	Yes
Proctors	Yes
Oral exams	Yes
Note-takers	Yes
Support services for students with	
LD	Yes
ADHD	Yes
ASD	Yes
Distraction-reduced environment	Yes
Recording of lecture allowed	Yes
Reading technology:	Yes
Audio books	Yes
Other assistive technology	Yes
Priority registration	Yes
Added costs for services:	
For LD:	No
For ADHD:	No
For ASD:	No
LD specialists	Yes
ADHD & ASD coaching	No
ASD specialists	No
Professional tutors	No
Peer tutors	Yes
Max. hours/week for services	Varies
How professors are notified of student approved accommodations	Student

COLLEGE GRADUATION REQUIREMENTS

Course waivers allowed	No
Course substitutions allowed	Yes
In what courses	Math, Foreign Language

American International College

1000 STATE STREET, SPRINGFIELD, MA 01109-3184 • ADMISSIONS: 413-205-3201 • FAX: 413-205-3051

CAMPUS

Type of school	Private (nonprofit)
Environment	City
Support	SP

STUDENTS

Undergrad enrollment	1,478
% male/female	40/60
% from out of state	39
% frosh live on campus	80

FINANCIAL FACTS

Annual tuition	$33,140
Room and board	$13,590
Required fees	$60

GENERAL ADMISSIONS INFO

Nonfall registration accepted. Admission may be deferred for a maximum of 1 year.

Range SAT EBRW	390–480
Range SAT Math	400–500
Range ACT Composite	16–23

ACADEMICS

Student/faculty ratio	14:1
% students returning for sophomore year	72

Most classes have 10–19 students.
Most lab/discussion sessions have 10–19 students.

PROGRAMS/SERVICES FOR STUDENTS WITH LEARNING DIFFERENCES

Supportive Learning Services (SLS) has been an integral part of the American International College campus since 1977. The staff recognizes that everyone learns differently and serves students as individuals with customized approaches and plans specific to their learning styles. AIC values their students' individual strengths above all things and truly believes they can achieve their dreams if given the right tools. This fee-based program provides the required tools, along with ongoing support and encouragement in the form of regular, individualized professional tutoring and academic coaching, group study sessions facilitated by professional educators, and skill-based workshops. SLS tutors work closely with college faculty and staff using a proactive advising model to support students. Assistance is available to each student in the program for the duration of his or her college career.

ADMISSIONS

In addition to the standard AIC application, applicants to SLSP need to provide a recently administered Wechsler Adult Intelligence Scale, relevant diagnostic material, any supportive assistance they've received in the past and ACT or SAT scores. AIC evaluates high school coursework, grades and standardized test scores. However, they are equally interested in student activities, personal statement, and letters of recommendations.

Additional Information

Their expert staff reviews each student's documentation and gets to know them through a personal interview. Tutors then work creatively to find the best way to help them improve vital academic skills like: Goal setting, Organization and planning, Note taking, Time management, and Study skills, like volume reading and writing and Test taking. In addition to helping build academic skills, SLS staff can help students develop and practice self-advocacy skills and explore technologies that support academic success. Collegiate Disability Services (CDS), housed with SLS,

ADMISSIONS INFO FOR STUDENTS WITH LEARNING DIFFERENCES

SAT/ACT required: Yes
Interview required: Yes
Essay required: No
Additional application required: No
Documentation required for:
  LD: Psycho ed evaluation
  ADHD: Diagnosis based on DSM-V; history of behaviors impairing functioning in academic setting; diagnostic interview; history of symptoms; evidence of ongoing behaviors.
  ASD: Psycho ed evaluation
Documentation submitted to: Supportive Learning Services Program
Special Ed. HS course work accepted: No
Separate application required for Programs/Services: Yes
Contact Information
Name of program or department: Supportive Learning Services Program
Telephone: 413-205-3426
Fax: 413-205-3908

American International College

ensures that all qualified students with disabilities receive accommodations & services that support an accessible, equitable, and inclusive learning and living environment at American International College. CDS staff works closely with Academics and Student Life to reduce or eliminate any disadvantages that may occur as a result of an individual's disability.

GENERAL ADMISSIONS

Very important factors considered include: academic GPA, standardized test scores. *Important factors considered include:* rigor of secondary school record. *Other factors considered include:* application essay, recommendation(s), extracurricular activities, talent/ability, character/personal qualities, first generation, alumni/ae relation, volunteer work, work experience, level of applicant's interest. *Freshman Admission Requirements:* High school diploma is required and GED is accepted. *Academic units recommended:* 4 English, 3 math, 2 science, 2 science labs, 1 foreign language, 2 social studies, 4 academic electives.

ACCOMMODATIONS OR SERVICES

Accommodations are decided upon an individual basis after a thorough review of appropriate, current documentation. The accommodations requests must be supported through the documentation provided and must be logically linked to the current impact of the condition on academic functioning.

FINANCIAL AID

Students should submit: FAFSA. Applicants will be notified of awards on a rolling basis beginning 3/1. The Princeton Review suggests that all financial aid forms be submitted as soon as possible after October 1. *Need-based scholarships/grants offered:* College/university scholarship or grant aid from institutional funds; Federal Nursing Scholarships; Federal Pell; Private scholarships; SEOG; State scholarships/grants. *Loan aid offered:* Direct PLUS loans; Direct Subsidized Stafford Loans; Direct Unsubsidized Stafford Loans. Federal Work-Study Program available. Institutional employment available.

CAMPUS LIFE

Activities: Campus Ministries; Dance; Drama/theater; International Student Organization; Literary magazine; Model UN; Pep band; Student government; Student newspaper; Yearbook. **Organizations:** 45 registered organizations, 5 honor societies, 3 religious organizations. 4 fraternities, 5 sororities. **Athletics (Intercollegiate):** *Men:* baseball, basketball, cheerleading, cross-country, football, golf, ice hockey, lacrosse, soccer, tennis, track/field (outdoor), track/field (indoor), wrestling. *Women:* basketball, cheerleading, cross-country, field hockey, lacrosse, soccer, softball, tennis, track/field (outdoor), track/field (indoor), volleyball. **On-Campus Highlights:** Courniotes Hall - Health Sciences, Karen Sprague Cultural Arts Center, Butova & Metcalf Gymnasiums, Dining Commons, The Stinger.

ACCOMMODATIONS

Allowed in exams:	
Calculators	Yes
Dictionary	No
Computer	Yes
Spell-checker	Yes
Extended test time	Yes
Scribe	Yes
Proctors	Yes
Oral exams	Yes
Note-takers	No
Support services for students with	
LD	Yes
ADHD	Yes
ASD	Yes
Distraction-reduced environment	Yes
Recording of lecture allowed	Yes
Reading technology:	Yes
Audio books	Yes
Other assistive technology	Yes
Priority registration	Yes
Added costs for services:	
For LD:	Yes
For ADHD:	Yes
For ASD:	Yes
LD specialists	Yes
ADHD & ASD coaching	Yes
ASD specialists	No
Professional tutors	Yes
Peer tutors	No
Max. hours/week for services	5
How professors are notified of student approved accommodations	Student and Director

COLLEGE GRADUATION REQUIREMENTS

Course waivers allowed	No
Course substitutions allowed	No

Boston College

140 Commonwealth Avenue, Chestnut Hill, MA 02467-3809 • Admissions: 617-552-3100 • Fax: 617-552-0798

CAMPUS
Type of school	Private (nonprofit)
Environment	City
Support	CS

STUDENTS
Undergrad enrollment	9,358
% male/female	47/53
% from out of state	74
% frosh live on campus	100

FINANCIAL FACTS
Annual tuition	$54,600
Room and board	$14,478
Required fees	$864

GENERAL ADMISSIONS INFO
Application fee	$80.
Regular application deadline	1/1

Nonfall registration accepted. Admission may be deferred for a maximum of 2 years.

Range SAT EBRW	660–760
Range SAT Math	660–730
Range ACT Composite	31–33

ACADEMICS
Student/faculty ratio	12:1
% students returning for sophomore year	95
% students graduating within 6 years	93

Most classes have 20–29 students.
Most lab/discussion sessions have 20–29 students.

PROGRAMS/SERVICES FOR STUDENTS WITH LEARNING DIFFERENCES
Complete guidelines to document a dissability can be found here http://www.bc.edu/libraries/help/tutoring/specialservices/docinfo.html#spec

ADMISSIONS
Complete Admissions information for students with learning disabilities can be found here http://www.bc.edu/libraries/help/tutoring/specialservices/docinfo.html#admin

Additional Information
Additional information about all services available via the Connors Family Learning Center can be found here http://www.bc.edu/libraries/help/tutoring/specialservices.html

ADMISSIONS INFO FOR STUDENTS WITH LEARNING DIFFERENCES
SAT/ACT required: Yes
Interview required: Not Applicable
Essay required: Not Applicable
Additional application required: No
Documentation required for:
  ADHD: Documentation for ADHD must be no older than four years and provide information regarding the onset, longevity, and severity of the symptoms, as well as the specifics of describing how it has interfered with educational achievement. It must include an in-depth evaluation including both cognitive and achievement data from the psychiatrist/psychologist/physician who made the diagnosis, as well as specific educational recommendations. Information regarding suggested pharmacological interventions should be made as well. Please submit additional documentation(s) if applicable: Proof of high school accommodation(s): 504 / IEP / Other, and proof of standardized testing accommodation(s): College Board / ACT.
  ASD: Psycho ed evaluation
Documentation submitted to: The Connors Family Learning Center
Special Ed. HS course work accepted: Not Applicable
Separate application required for Programs/Services: Not Applicable
Contact Information
Name of program or department: The Connors Family Learning Center
Telephone: 617-552-8055
Email: dugganka@bc.edu

Boston College

GENERAL ADMISSIONS

Very important factors considered include: rigor of secondary school record, academic GPA, standardized test scores. *Important factors considered include:* class rank, application essay, recommendation(s), extracurricular activities, talent/ability, character/personal qualities, alumni/ae relation, religious affiliation/commitment, volunteer work. *Other factors considered include:* first generation, racial/ethnic status, work experience. *Freshman Admission Requirements:* High school diploma is required and GED is accepted. *Academic units recommended:* 4 English, 4 math, 4 science, 4 science labs, 4 foreign language, 4 social studies, 4 history.

ACCOMMODATIONS OR SERVICES

Accommodations are decided upon an individual basis after a thorough review of appropriate, current documentation. The accommodations requests must be supported through the documentation provided and must be logically linked to the current impact of the condition on academic functioning.

FINANCIAL AID

Students should submit: Business/Farm Supplement; CSS/Financial Aid PROFILE; FAFSA; Noncustodial PROFILE. Applicants will be notified of awards on or about 4/1. The Princeton Review suggests that all financial aid forms be submitted as soon as possible after October 1. *Need-based scholarships/grants offered:* College/university scholarship or grant aid from institutional funds; Federal Pell; Private scholarships; SEOG; State scholarships/grants. *Loan aid offered:* Direct PLUS loans; Direct Subsidized Stafford Loans; Direct Unsubsidized Stafford Loans. Federal Work-Study Program available. Institutional employment available.

CAMPUS LIFE

Activities: Campus Ministries; Choral groups; Concert band; Dance; Drama/theater; International Student Organization; Jazz band; Literary magazine; Marching band; Music ensembles; Musical theater; Pep band; Radio station; Student government; Student newspaper; Student-run film society; Symphony orchestra; Television station; Yearbook. **Organizations:** 225 registered organizations, 12 honor societies, 14 religious organizations. **Athletics (Intercollegiate):** *Men:* baseball, basketball, cross-country, diving, fencing, football, golf, ice hockey, lacrosse, sailing, skiing (downhill/alpine), soccer, swimming, tennis, track/field (outdoor), track/field (indoor). *Women:* basketball, crew/rowing, cross-country, diving, fencing, field hockey, golf, ice hockey, lacrosse, sailing, skiing (downhill/alpine), soccer, softball, swimming, tennis, track/field (outdoor), track/field (indoor), volleyball. **On-Campus Highlights:** McMullen Museum of Art, Alumni Stadium/Conte Forum, Robsham Theater, Bapst Library, McElroy Commons/Bookstore.

ACCOMMODATIONS

Allowed in exams:	
Calculators	Yes
Dictionary	No
Computer	Yes
Spell-checker	Yes
Extended test time	Yes
Scribe	Yes
Proctors	Yes
Oral exams	Yes
Note-takers	Yes
Support services for students with	
LD	No
ADHD	No
ASD	No
Distraction-reduced environment	Yes
Recording of lecture allowed	No
Reading technology:	No
Audio books	Yes
Other assistive technology	Yes
Priority registration	Yes
Added costs for services:	
For LD:	No
For ADHD:	No
For ASD:	Not Applicable
LD specialists	Yes
ADHD & ASD coaching	No
ASD specialists	No
Professional tutors	Yes
Peer tutors	Yes
Max. hours/week for services	3
How professors are notified of student approved accommodations	Director and Student

COLLEGE GRADUATION REQUIREMENTS

Course waivers allowed	No
Course substitutions allowed	Yes
In what courses	Foreign Language

Boston University

ONE SILBER WAY, BOSTON, MA 02215 • ADMISSIONS: 617-353-2300 • FAX: 617-353-9695

CAMPUS

Type of school	Private (nonprofit)
Environment	Metropolis
Support	CS

STUDENTS

Undergrad enrollment	16,716
% male/female	39/61
% from out of state	80
% frosh live on campus	99

FINANCIAL FACTS

Annual tuition	$52,816
Room and board	$15,720
Required fees	$1,132

GENERAL ADMISSIONS INFO

Application fee	$80
Priority deadline	11/1.
Regular application deadline	1/2

Nonfall registration accepted. Admission may be deferred for a maximum of 1 year.

Range SAT EBRW	640–720
Range SAT Math	660–760
Range ACT Composite	29–32

ACADEMICS

Student/faculty ratio	10:1
% students returning for sophomore year	93
% students graduating within 4 years	81
% students graduating within 6 years	87

Most classes have 10–19 students.
Most lab/discussion sessions have 10–19 students.

PROGRAMS/SERVICES FOR STUDENTS WITH LEARNING DIFFERENCES

Boston University recognizes that many students with a learning disability, attention deficit hyperactivity disorder, or psychiatry disability (including autism spectrum diagnoses) can succeed in a university if they are provided with support services and appropriate accommodations. The Office of Disability Services (ODS) is committed to assisting individuals with disabilities in achieving fulfillment and success in all aspects of university life. The primary objective of ODS is to foster academic excellence, personal responsibility, and leadership growth in students with disabilities through vigorous programming and the provision of reasonable accommodations. We further this commitment through the promotion of independence and self-advocacy in students with LD, ADHD, or other disabilities. The university does not waive program requirements or permit substitutions for required courses. Several degree programs have foreign language or mathematics requirements. The university considers these degree requirements essential to its programs.

ADMISSIONS

The Office of Admissions makes all admissions decisions on an individual basis. BU expects that students with disabilities, including those with LD, will meet the same competitive admissions criteria as their peers without disabilities. Thus, there are no special admissions procedures for applicants with LD. ODS does not participate in any way in the application process or in admissions decisions. Admission is based on the strength of a student's secondary school record.

Additional Information

The Office of Disability Services ("Disability Services") provides academic accommodations and services to students with learning and attentional disabilities. Disability Services arranges for academic accommodations for students with learning differences. Such accommodations may include the use of a note taker, course materials in alternative formats, reduced course load, or possibly examination-related accommodations such as extended time or a distraction-reduced environment. Students seeking accommodations must provide appropriate medical documentation of their disability so that Disability Services can determine the student's eligibility for accommodations; and if the student is eligible, determine appropriate academic accommodations.

ADMISSIONS INFO FOR STUDENTS WITH LEARNING DIFFERENCES

SAT/ACT required: Yes
Interview required: No
Essay required: No
Additional application required: No
Documentation required for:
  LD: Psycho ed evaluation
  ADHD: Diagnosis based on DSM-V; history of behaviors impairing functioning in academic setting; diagnostic interview; history of symptoms; evidence of ongoing behaviors.
  ASD: Psycho ed evaluation
Documentation submitted to: Office of Disability Services
Special Ed. HS course work accepted: No
Separate application required for Programs/Services: No
Contact Information
Name of program or department: Office of Disability Services
Telephone: 617-353-3658
Fax: 617-353-9646

Boston University

GENERAL ADMISSIONS

Very important factors considered include: rigor of secondary school record. *Important factors considered include:* class rank, academic GPA, application essay, standardized test scores, recommendation(s), extracurricular activities, character/personal qualities, alumni/ae relation, level of applicant's interest. *Other factors considered include:* first generation, geographical residence, state residency, racial/ethnic status, volunteer work, work experience. *Freshman Admission Requirements:* High school diploma is required and GED is accepted. *Academic units required:* 4 English, 3 math, 3 science, 3 science labs, 2 foreign language, 3 social studies, 3 history. *Academic units recommended:* 4 English, 4 math, 4 science, 4 science labs, 4 foreign language, 4 social studies, 4 history.

ACCOMMODATIONS OR SERVICES

Accommodations are decided upon an individual basis after a thorough review of appropriate, current documentation. The accommodations requests must be supported through the documentation provided and must be logically linked to the current impact of the condition on academic functioning.

FINANCIAL AID

Students should submit: CSS/Financial Aid PROFILE; FAFSA; Noncustodial PROFILE. Applicants will be notified of awards on a rolling basis beginning 4/1. The Princeton Review suggests that all financial aid forms be submitted as soon as possible after October 1. *Need-based scholarships/grants offered:* College/university scholarship or grant aid from institutional funds; Federal Pell; Private scholarships; SEOG; State scholarships/grants. *Loan aid offered:* Direct PLUS loans; Direct Subsidized Stafford Loans; Direct Unsubsidized Stafford Loans. Federal Work-Study Program available. Institutional employment available.

CAMPUS LIFE

Activities: Campus Ministries; Choral groups; Concert band; Dance; Drama/theater; International Student Organization; Jazz band; Literary magazine; Marching band; Model UN; Music ensembles; Musical theater; Opera; Pep band; Radio station; Student government; Student newspaper; Student-run film society; Symphony orchestra; Television station; Yearbook. **Organizations:** 400 registered organizations, 11 honor societies, 26 religious organizations. 9 fraternities, 9 sororities. **Athletics (Intercollegiate):** *Men:* basketball, crew/rowing, cross-country, diving, golf, ice hockey, soccer, swimming, tennis, track/field (outdoor), track/field (indoor), wrestling. *Women:* basketball, crew/rowing, cross-country, diving, field hockey, golf, ice hockey, lacrosse, soccer, softball, swimming, tennis, track/field (outdoor), track/field (indoor). **On-Campus Highlights:** George Sherman Student Union, Yawkey Center for Student Services, Build Lab Student Innovation Center, Joan & Edgar Booth Theatre & BU Production Center, Fitness and Recreation Center.

ACCOMMODATIONS

Allowed in exams:

Calculators	No
Dictionary	No
Computer	Yes
Spell-checker	Yes
Extended test time	Yes
Scribe	Yes
Proctors	Yes
Oral exams	Yes
Note-takers	Yes

Support services for students with

LD	Yes
ADHD	Yes
ASD	Yes
Distraction-reduced environment	Yes
Recording of lecture allowed	Yes
Reading technology:	No
Audio books	Yes
Other assistive technology	Yes
Priority registration	No

Added costs for services:

For LD:	Yes
For ADHD:	Yes
For ASD:	Yes
LD specialists	Yes
ADHD & ASD coaching	No
ASD specialists	No
Professional tutors	No
Peer tutors	No
Max. hours/week for services	N/A
How professors are notified of student approved accommodations	Student

COLLEGE GRADUATION REQUIREMENTS

Course waivers allowed	No
Course substitutions allowed	No

Clark University

950 Main Street, Worcester, MA 01610-1477 • Admissions: 508-793-7431 • Fax: 508-793-8821

CAMPUS

Type of school	Private (nonprofit)
Environment	City
Support	CS

STUDENTS

Undergrad enrollment	2,204
% male/female	39/61
% from out of state	62
% frosh live on campus	98

FINANCIAL FACTS

Annual tuition	$44,050
Room and board	$8,860
Required fees	$350

GENERAL ADMISSIONS INFO

Application fee	$60
Regular application deadline	1/15

Nonfall registration accepted. Admission may be deferred for a maximum of 1 year.

Range SAT EBRW	600–700
Range SAT Math	580–680
Range ACT Composite	27–31

ACADEMICS

Student/faculty ratio	10:1
% students returning for sophomore year	85
% students graduating within 4 years	77
% students graduating within 6 years	83

Most classes have 10–19 students.

PROGRAMS/SERVICES FOR STUDENTS WITH LEARNING DIFFERENCES

Clark University is committed to providing equal access to otherwise qualified students with disabilities who are able to effectively function in a rigorous, campus-based, liberal-arts environment. Although Clark does not offer a specialized program, or a learning center for students with disabilities, the University does provide a support service for qualified students who register with Student Accessibility Services. The director of Student Accessibility Services works with students to coordinate academic accommodations and services on campus. Student Accessibility Services is located in the Goddard Library, Room 430. This office is the point of contact for any student seeking accommodations.

ADMISSIONS

Students with disabilities should self-advocate for their needs and self-identify during the admissions process. By doing so admissions can help applicants get connected with appropriate resources on campus.

Additional Information

An early orientation program 2 days prior to general orientation is designed to meet the needs of entering students with LD. This program is highly recommended as it provides intensive exposure to academic services on campus. Students take a reading comprehension and writing exam, and results are used to match students to the most appropriate academic program. Graduate students work with students on time management and organizational skills. Although note-takers are available, Special Services supplements this accommodation with the taping of lectures and highly recommends that students use a cassette recorder with a count.

ADMISSIONS INFO FOR STUDENTS WITH LEARNING DIFFERENCES

SAT/ACT required: No
Interview required: No
Essay required: Not Applicable
Additional application required: No
Documentation required for:
LD: Typically students provide a Neuropsychological Evaluation, Psychoeducational Evaluation, or other learning evaluation. Please see our website for more info.
ADHD: Official documentation of disability from an appropriately licensed professional, typically a psychoeducational evaluation. Please see our website for more info.
ASD: Official documentation of disability from an appropriately licensed professional. Please see our website for more info.
Documentation submitted to: Support Program/Services
Special Ed. HS course work accepted: No
Separate application required for Programs/Services: Not for LD, ADHD, or ASD.
Contact Information
Name of program or department: Student Accessibility Services
Telephone: 508-798-4368
Fax: 508-421-3700
Email: acurran@clarku.edu

Clark University

GENERAL ADMISSIONS

Very important factors considered include: rigor of secondary school record, academic GPA, recommendation(s). *Important factors considered include:* application essay, extracurricular activities, talent/ability, character/personal qualities, volunteer work. *Other factors considered include:* class rank, standardized test scores, interview, first generation, alumni/ae relation, geographical residence, racial/ethnic status, work experience, level of applicant's interest. *Freshman Admission Requirements:* High school diploma is required and GED is accepted. *Academic units recommended:* 4 English, 3 math, 3 science, 2 science labs, 2 foreign language, 2 social studies, 2 history.

ACCOMMODATIONS OR SERVICES

Accommodations are decided upon an individual basis after a thorough review of appropriate, current documentation. The accommodations requests must be supported through the documentation provided and must be logically linked to the current impact of the condition on academic functioning.

FINANCIAL AID

Students should submit: CSS/Financial Aid PROFILE; FAFSA; Noncustodial PROFILE. Applicants will be notified of awards on or about 3/31. The Princeton Review suggests that all financial aid forms be submitted as soon as possible after October 1. *Need-based scholarships/grants offered:* College/university scholarship or grant aid from institutional funds; Federal Pell; SEOG; State scholarships/grants. *Loan aid offered:* Direct PLUS loans; Direct Subsidized Stafford Loans; Direct Unsubsidized Stafford Loans. Federal Work-Study Program available. Institutional employment available.

CAMPUS LIFE

Activities: Campus Ministries; Choral groups; Concert band; Dance; Drama/theater; International Student Organization; Jazz band; Literary magazine; Marching band; Model UN; Music ensembles; Musical theater; Pep band; Radio station; Student government; Student newspaper; Student-run film society; Symphony orchestra; Television station; Yearbook. **Organizations:** 110 registered organizations, 10 honor societies, 7 religious organizations. **Athletics (Intercollegiate):** *Men:* baseball, basketball, crew/rowing, cross-country, diving, lacrosse, soccer, swimming, tennis. *Women:* basketball, crew/rowing, cross-country, diving, field hockey, soccer, softball, swimming, tennis, volleyball. **On-Campus Highlights:** Academic Commons at Goddard Library, Campus Green (in warmer months), The Bistro in the University Center, Alumni Student Engagement Center, Larger-than-life statue of Sigmund Freud in Red Square.

ACCOMMODATIONS

Allowed in exams:

Calculators	Yes
Dictionary	Yes
Computer	Yes
Spell-checker	Yes
Extended test time	Yes
Scribe	Yes
Proctors	Yes
Oral exams	Yes
Note-takers	Yes

Support services for students with

LD	Yes
ADHD	Yes
ASD	Yes
Distraction-reduced environment	Yes
Recording of lecture allowed	Yes
Reading technology:	Yes
Audio books	Yes
Other assistive technology	We provide appropriate assistive technology on a case by case as needed basis.
Priority registration	Yes

Added costs for services:

For LD:	No
For ADHD:	No
For ASD:	No
LD specialists	Yes
ADHD & ASD coaching	Yes
ASD specialists	Yes
Professional tutors	Yes
Peer tutors	Not Applicable
Max. hours/week for services	Varies
How professors are notified of student approved accommodations	Director and Student

COLLEGE GRADUATION REQUIREMENTS

Course waivers allowed	Yes

In what courses
All students must complete graduation requirements. These requirements are waived/replaced in only exceptional circumstances and all cases are considered on an individual basis based on documentation of disability.

Course substitutions allowed	Yes

In what courses
All students must complete graduation requirements. These requirements are waived/replaced in only exceptional circumstances and all cases are considered on an individual basis based on documentation of disability.

Curry College

1071 Blue Hill Avenue, Milton, MA 02186 • Admissions: 617-333-2210 • Fax: 617-333-2114

CAMPUS

Type of school	Private (nonprofit)
Environment	Village
Support	SP

STUDENTS

Undergrad enrollment	2,843
% male/female	37/63
% from out of state	22
% frosh live on campus	89

FINANCIAL FACTS

Annual tuition	$34,730
Room and board	$13,900
Required fees	$1,715

GENERAL ADMISSIONS INFO

Application fee	$50
Priority deadline	4/1

Nonfall registration accepted. Admission may be deferred.

Range SAT EBRW	420–520
Range SAT Math	430–520
Range ACT Composite	18–21

ACADEMICS

Student/faculty ratio	11:1
% students returning for sophomore year	71

Most classes have 10–19 students. Most lab/discussion sessions have fewer than 10 students.

PROGRAMS/SERVICES FOR STUDENTS WITH LEARNING DIFFERENCES

The Program for Advancement of Learning (PAL) at Curry College is a comprehensive individualized program for students with specific learning disabilities and ADHD. Students in PAL participate fully in Curry College course work and extracurricular activities. The goal of PAL is to facilitate students' understanding of their individual learning styles and help them achieve independence as learners. Students' empowerment is developed via intensive study of their own strengths, needs, and learning styles. PAL is a place where students are honored for the strengths and talents they bring to the learning process and are given the chance to demonstrate their abilities. PAL students are leaders on campus. The PAL summer program is a 3-week course that is strongly recommended for new students to ease the transition to college and provide excellent preparation.

ADMISSIONS

Courses required for general admission include 4 English, 3 math, 2 science, 2 science lab, 1 social studies, 1 history, and 5 electives. For admission into the Program of the Advancement of Learning, applicants must submit a recent diagnostic evaluation describing a Specific Learning Disability and/or ADHD. Diagnostic evaluations must be less than three years old and contain the results of cognitive and achievement tests. In addition, an IEP or its equivalent is requested, if available. On-campus interviews are strongly recommended and may be required of some applicants. Space is limited for the program. Students applying to PAL are not required to submit SAT or ACT. Students may also respond to an "Optional" Supplement. Admission decisions are made jointly by PAL and the Office of Admissions.

Additional Information

PAL students must commit to the program for at least 1 year and have the option to continue with full or partial support beyond the first year. A 3-week 3-credit summer PAL summer session is strongly recommended. Students meet regularly with their own PAL instructor who is a learning specialist. The focus is on using the student's strengths to improve skills in areas such as listening, speaking, reading, writing, organization and time management, note-taking, and test-taking. Students also receive help with readings, papers, and assignments for classes as the basis for learning about their unique learning style. The specialist reviews diagnostic testing to help the student understand the profile of strengths and needs. Students earn

ADMISSIONS INFO FOR STUDENTS WITH LEARNING DIFFERENCES

SAT/ACT required: No
Interview required: No, but strongly recommend
Essay required: Yes
Additional application required: No
Documentation required for:
 LD: Psycho ed evaluation
 ADHD: Diagnosis based on DSM-V; history of behaviors impairing functioning in academic setting; diagnostic interview; history of symptoms; evidence of ongoing behaviors.
 ASD: Psycho ed evaluation
Documentation submitted to: Program for the Advancement of Learning (PAL)
Special Ed. HS course work accepted: Yes
Separate application required for Programs/Services: Yes
Contact Information
Name of program or department: Program for Advancement of Learning (PAL)
Telephone: 617-333-2250
Fax: 617-333-2018

Curry College

three credits toward graduation for the first year. Skills classes, for credit, are offered through the Academic Enrichment Center in developmental reading, writing, and math. Another special offering is diagnostic testing, which available through the Educational Diagnostic Center at PAL at 617-333-2314.

GENERAL ADMISSIONS

Very important factors considered include: rigor of secondary school record. *Important factors considered include:* academic GPA, application essay, standardized test scores, recommendation(s), interview, extracurricular activities, character/personal qualities. *Other factors considered include:* class rank, talent/ability, alumni/ae relation, volunteer work, work experience, level of applicant's interest. *Freshman Admission Requirements:* High school diploma is required and GED is accepted. *Academic units required:* 4 English, 3 math. *Academic units recommended:* 2 science, 1 science lab, 2 foreign language, 2 social studies, 2 history.

ACCOMMODATIONS OR SERVICES

Accommodations are decided upon an individual basis after a thorough review of appropriate, current documentation. The accommodations requests must be supported through the documentation provided and must be logically linked to the current impact of the condition on academic functioning.

FINANCIAL AID

Students should submit: FAFSA. Applicants will be notified of awards on a rolling basis beginning 3/1. The Princeton Review suggests that all financial aid forms be submitted as soon as possible after October 1. *Need-based scholarships/grants offered:* College/university scholarship or grant aid from institutional funds; Federal Pell; Private scholarships; SEOG; State scholarships/grants. *Loan aid offered:* Direct PLUS loans; Direct Subsidized Stafford Loans; Direct Unsubsidized Stafford Loans

CAMPUS LIFE

Activities: Campus Ministries; Choral groups; Dance; Drama/theater; International Student Organization; Literary magazine; Music ensembles; Radio station; Student government; Student newspaper; Student-run film society; Television station; Yearbook. **Organizations:** 1 honor society, 2 religious organizations. **Athletics (Intercollegiate):** *Men:* baseball, basketball, cheerleading, football, ice hockey, lacrosse, soccer, tennis. *Women:* basketball, cheerleading, cross-country, lacrosse, soccer, softball, tennis. **On-Campus Highlights:** Drapkin Student Center, Levin Library, WMLN Campus Radio Station, The Suites- New Residence Hall, Hafer Academic Center.

ACCOMMODATIONS

Allowed in exams:	
Calculators	Yes
Dictionary	Yes
Computer	Yes
Spell-checker	Yes
Extended test time	Yes
Scribe	Yes
Proctors	Yes
Oral exams	Yes
Note-takers	Yes
Support services for students with	
LD	Yes
ADHD	Yes
ASD	Yes
Distraction-reduced environment	Yes
Recording of lecture allowed	Yes
Reading technology:	Yes
Audio books	Yes
Other assistive technology	Yes
Priority registration	No
Added costs for services:	
For LD:	Yes
For ADHD:	Yes
For ASD:	Yes
LD specialists	Yes
ADHD & ASD coaching	No
ASD specialists	No
Professional tutors	Yes
Peer tutors	Yes
Max. hours/week for services	2.5
How professors are notified of student approved accommodations	Student

COLLEGE GRADUATION REQUIREMENTS

Course waivers allowed	No
Course substitutions allowed	Yes
In what courses	Varies

Emerson College

120 BOYLSTON STREET, BOSTON, MA 02116-4624 • ADMISSIONS: 617-824-8600 • FAX: 617-824-8609

CAMPUS

Type of school	Private (nonprofit)
Environment	Metropolis
Support	CS

STUDENTS

Undergrad enrollment	3,799
% male/female	41/59
% from out of state	79
% frosh live on campus	99

FINANCIAL FACTS

Annual tuition	$46,016
Room and board	$17,690
Required fees	$836

GENERAL ADMISSIONS INFO

Application fee	$65.
Regular application deadline	1/15

Nonfall registration accepted. Admission may be deferred for a maximum of 1 year.

Range SAT EBRW	620–700
Range SAT Math	580–660
Range ACT Composite	26–30

ACADEMICS

Student/faculty ratio	13:1
% students returning for sophomore year	88
% students graduating within 4 years	77
% students graduating within 6 years	81

Most classes have 10–19 students.
Most lab/discussion sessions have 10–19 students.

PROGRAMS/SERVICES FOR STUDENTS WITH LEARNING DIFFERENCES

Emerson College is committed to providing equal access to its academic programs and social activities for all qualified students with disabilities. While upholding this commitment, we maintain the high standards of achievement that are essential to the integrity of the college's programs and services. One of the primary goals of the Student Accessibility Services (SAS) is to foster a welcoming and accessible environment for students across the campus. The school's philosophy is that students are independent and self-determined, and that students with disabilities—just like all students—have control over their lives at Emerson and they are ultimately responsible for making their own decisions. Emerson's SAS offers academic accommodations and related services to qualified students with documented physical, medical, visual, hearing, learning, and psychological disabilities. Students with disabilities are not required to register with the SAS, but in order to receive accommodations they must self-identify to the SAS and request accommodations.

ADMISSIONS

Emerson College accepts the Common Application with a required Supplement. Admission is competitive. In choosing candidates for the entering class, we look for students who present academic promise in their secondary school record, recommendations, and writing competency, as well as personal qualities as seen in extracurricular activities, community involvement, and demonstrated leadership. There is no separate application for students with learning disabilities.

Additional Information

Emerson College offers academic support services, free of charge, to all undergraduate and graduate Emerson students. The College's Writing & Academic Resource Center (WARC) consists of three full-time professionals, graduate assistant writing tutors, and peer tutors. The professional staff provides academic counseling and support with study strategies and time management to individuals seeking academic support.

ADMISSIONS INFO FOR STUDENTS WITH LEARNING DIFFERENCES

SAT/ACT required: Yes
Interview required: No
Essay required: Yes
Additional application required: No
Documentation required for:
  LD: Psycho ed evaluation
  ADHD: Psycho ed evaluation
  ASD: Psycho ed evaluation
Documentation submitted to: Student Accessibility Services
Special Ed. HS course work accepted: No
Separate application required for Programs/Services: No
Contact Information
Name of program or department: Student Accessibility Services
Telephone: (617) 824-8592
Fax: (617) 824-8941
Email: sas@emerson.edu

Emerson College

GENERAL ADMISSIONS

Very important factors considered include: academic GPA, application essay. *Important factors considered include:* rigor of secondary school record, class rank, recommendation(s), extracurricular activities, talent/ability, character/personal qualities. *Other factors considered include:* standardized test scores, first generation, alumni/ae relation, geographical residence, racial/ethnic status, volunteer work, work experience. *Freshman Admission Requirements:* High school diploma is required and GED is accepted. *Academic units required:* 4 English, 3 math, 3 science, 3 foreign language, 3 social studies. *Academic units recommended:* 4 English, 3 math, 3 science, 3 foreign language, 3 social studies, 4 academic electives.

ACCOMMODATIONS OR SERVICES

Accommodations are decided upon an individual basis after a thorough review of appropriate, current documentation. The accommodations requests must be supported through the documentation provided and must be logically linked to the current impact of the condition on academic functioning.

FINANCIAL AID

Students should submit: Business/Farm Supplement; CSS/Financial Aid PROFILE; FAFSA; Noncustodial PROFILE. Applicants will be notified of awards on or about 4/1. The Princeton Review suggests that all financial aid forms be submitted as soon as possible after October 1. *Need-based scholarships/grants offered:* College/university scholarship or grant aid from institutional funds; Federal Pell; Private scholarships; SEOG; State scholarships/grants. *Loan aid offered:* Direct PLUS loans; Direct Subsidized Stafford Loans; Direct Unsubsidized Stafford Loans. Federal Work-Study Program available. Institutional employment available.

CAMPUS LIFE

Activities: Campus Ministries; Choral groups; Dance; Drama/theater; International Student Organization; Literary magazine; Model UN; Music ensembles; Musical theater; Radio station; Student government; Student newspaper; Student-run film society; Television station; Yearbook. **Organizations:** 60 registered organizations, 4 honor societies, 4 religious organizations. 4 fraternities, 3 sororities. **Athletics (Intercollegiate):** *Men:* baseball, basketball, cross-country, golf, lacrosse, soccer, tennis, track/field (indoor), volleyball. *Women:* basketball, cross-country, golf, lacrosse, soccer, softball, tennis, track/field (indoor), volleyball. **On-Campus Highlights:** WERS-FM (Boston's oldest public radio), Historic Cutler Majestic Theatre, Tufte Performance and Production Center, Journalism's Integrated Digital Newsroom, Piano Row Residence Hall/College Center.

ACCOMMODATIONS

Allowed in exams:	
Calculators	Yes
Dictionary	Yes
Computer	Yes
Spell-checker	Yes
Extended test time	Yes
Scribe	Yes
Proctors	Yes
Oral exams	No
Note-takers	Yes
Support services for students with	
LD	Yes
ADHD	Yes
ASD	No
Distraction-reduced environment	Yes
Recording of lecture allowed	Yes
Reading technology:	Yes
Audio books	No
Other assistive technology	Yes
Priority registration	N/A
Added costs for services:	
For LD:	No
For ADHD:	No
For ASD:	No
LD specialists	Yes
ADHD & ASD coaching	No
ASD specialists	No
Professional tutors	No
Peer tutors	Yes
Max. hours/week for services	4
How professors are notified of student approved accommodations	Student

COLLEGE GRADUATION REQUIREMENTS

Course waivers allowed	Yes
In what courses	
Quantitative reasoning (math), world languages	
Course substitutions allowed	Yes
In what courses	
Students can choose to take American Sign Language to fulfill the World Language requirement.	

Fitchburg State University

160 Pearl Street, Fitchburg, MA 01420-2697 • Admissions: 978-665-3144 • Fax: 978-665-4540

CAMPUS
Type of school	Public
Environment	Town
Support	S

STUDENTS
Undergrad enrollment	3,958
% male/female	46/54
% from out of state	8
% frosh live on campus	70

FINANCIAL FACTS
Annual in-state tuition	$970
Annual out-of-state tuition	$7,050
Room and board	$8,256
Required fees	$7,330

GENERAL ADMISSIONS INFO
Application fee	$25

Nonfall registration accepted. Admission may be deferred for a maximum of 1 year.

Range SAT EBRW	450–560
Range SAT Math	460–560
Range ACT Composite	19–23

ACADEMICS
Student/faculty ratio	16:1
% students returning for sophomore year	73
% students graduating within 4 years	36
% students graduating withing 6 years	60

Most classes have 20–29 students.
Most lab/discussion sessions have 20–29 students.

Programs/Services for Students with Learning Differences
The Disability Services Office provides support services and programs for students with disabilities. Disability Services empowers eligible students to succeed by striving to assure equal access and opportunity of curricular and extracurricular activities. Student autonomy is encouraged through the provision of reasonable accommodations, services, training in the use of assistive technology and self-advocacy. Disability Services will verify student eligibility for accommodations and for coordinating accommodations across campus. Students must request services themselves and must provide appropriate documentation to support the need for such services. Once students have obtained copies of their disability documentation from their high school or medical provider, to support the need for such services, they should meet with staff in the Disability Services office to register for services. Documentation must clearly state the diagnosis, describe the symptoms that impact the student's ability to function in the educational environment and provide specific recommendations for accommodations.

Admissions
Students requesting a waiver of ACT/SAT or foreign language requirement must submit the psycho-educational testing (within 3 years) with 504 Plan or IEP. Office of Admissions forwards testing to the Office of Disability Services for review who informs Admissions if a student meets the criteria for the waiver(s). If so applicants do not need to submit ACT/SAT or proof of completion of foreign language. (Must complete two additional college prep electives to substitute for the foreign language. General admission includes: 4 English, 3 math, 3 science (2 lab science), 2 social science, 2 foreign language, and 2 electives. GPA is based on all college-prep courses and weighs Honors and Advanced Placement courses. The university wants a weighted GPA of 3.0, however considers GPAs between 2.0-2.99 if students submit SAT/ACT scores meeting the sliding scale requirements. Applicants not meeting the sliding scale requirements will be considered on an individual basis for a limited number of admission exceptions. Applicants who meet the 3.0 GPA requirements do not have to use the sliding scale for admission, but still must submit competitive SAT/ACT scores if they are applying within 3 years of high school graduation.

ADMISSIONS INFO FOR STUDENTS WITH LEARNING DIFFERENCES
SAT/ACT required: Yes
Interview required: No
Essay required: Yes
Additional application required: No
Documentation required for:
  LD: Psycho ed evaluation
  ADHD: Diagnosis based on DSM-V; history of behaviors impairing functioning in academic setting; diagnostic interview; history of symptoms; evidence of ongoing behaviors.
  ASD: Psych-Educational Evaluation within the last 3 years and IEP if available
Documentation submitted to: Disability Services Office
Special Ed. HS course work accepted: No
Separate application required for Programs/Services: Yes
Contact Information
Name of program or department: Disability Services
Telephone: 978-665-4020
Fax: 978-665-4786

Fitchburg State University

Additional Information

The Office of Disability Services provides support services, programs and academic accommodations for students with documented disabilities. Some examples of academic accommodations include: testing accommodations, materials in an alternate format, adaptive software and computer equipment, assistive listening devices, sign language interpreters, reduced course load waiver (below 12 credits), academic skill building workshops, support with the development of leadership, self-advocacy and self-determination skills. To be eligible for academic accommodations, students must request services themselves and must provide appropriate documentation to support the need for such services. Requests for accommodations must be made in a timely manner and must be reasonable given the nature of the disability.

GENERAL ADMISSIONS

Very important factors considered include: rigor of secondary school record. *Important factors considered include:* academic GPA, application essay, standardized test scores. *Other factors considered include:* recommendation(s), extracurricular activities, talent/ability, character/personal qualities, alumni/ae relation, volunteer work, work experience, level of applicant's interest. *Freshman Admission Requirements:* High school diploma is required and GED is accepted. *Academic units required:* 4 English, 3 math, 3 science, 2 science labs, 2 foreign language, 1 social studies, 1 history, 2 academic electives.

ACCOMMODATIONS OR SERVICES

Accommodations are decided upon an individual basis after a thorough review of appropriate, current documentation. The accommodations requests must be supported through the documentation provided and must be logically linked to the current impact of the condition on academic functioning.

FINANCIAL AID

Students should submit: FAFSA. Applicants will be notified of awards on a rolling basis beginning 3/15. The Princeton Review suggests that all financial aid forms be submitted as soon as possible after October 1. *Need-based scholarships/grants offered:* College/university scholarship or grant aid from institutional funds; Federal Pell; Private scholarships; SEOG; State scholarships/grants. *Loan aid offered:* Direct PLUS loans; Direct Subsidized Stafford Loans; Direct Unsubsidized Stafford Loans. Federal Work-Study Program available. Institutional employment available.

CAMPUS LIFE

Activities: Choral groups; Concert band; Dance; Drama/theater; Jazz band; Literary magazine; Model UN; Radio station; Student government; Student newspaper; Student-run film society. **Organizations:** 60 registered organizations, 8 honor societies, 1 religious organization. 2 fraternities, 3 sororities. **Athletics (Intercollegiate):** *Men:* baseball, basketball, cross-country, football, ice hockey, soccer, track/field (outdoor), track/field (indoor). *Women:* basketball, cross-country, field hockey, lacrosse, soccer, softball, track/field (outdoor), track/field (indoor). **On-Campus Highlights:** Campus Recreation Center, Student Center Lounge, Campus Dining Hall, Commuter Cafe, Computer Labs.

ACCOMMODATIONS

Allowed in exams:

Calculators	Yes
Dictionary	Yes
Computer	Yes
Spell-checker	Yes
Extended test time	Yes
Scribe	Yes
Proctors	Yes
Oral exams	Yes
Note-takers	Yes

Support services for students with

LD	Yes
ADHD	Yes
ASD	Yes
Distraction-reduced environment	Yes
Recording of lecture allowed	Yes
Reading technology:	Yes
Audio books	No
Other assistive technology	Yes
Priority registration	No

Added costs for services:

For LD:	No
For ADHD:	No
For ASD:	No
LD specialists	No
ADHD & ASD coaching	No
ASD specialists	No
Professional tutors	Yes
Peer tutors	Yes
Max. hours/week for services	Unspecified
How professors are notified of student approved accommodations	Student

COLLEGE GRADUATION REQUIREMENTS

Course waivers allowed	No
In what courses	Varies
Course substitutions allowed	Yes
In what courses	Varies

Northeastern University

360 Huntington Avenue, Boston, MA 02115 • Admissions: 617-373-2200 • Fax: 617-373-8780

CAMPUS

Type of school	Private (nonprofit)
Environment	Metropolis
Support	SP

STUDENTS

Undergrad enrollment	18,109
% male/female	49/51
% from out of state	73
% frosh live on campus	99

FINANCIAL FACTS

Annual tuition	$48,560
Room and board	$16,240
Required fees	$937

GENERAL ADMISSIONS INFO

Application fee	$75.
Regular application deadline	1/1

Nonfall registration accepted. Admission may be deferred.

Range SAT EBRW	680–750
Range SAT Math	690–770
Range ACT Composite	32–34

ACADEMICS

Student/faculty ratio	14:1
% students returning for sophomore year	97

Most classes have 10–19 students.

PROGRAMS/SERVICES FOR STUDENTS WITH LEARNING DIFFERENCES

For students with documented learning disabilities and/or ADHD, Northeastern offers both a comprehensive program and basic support services. The Learning Disabilities Program (LDP) is a comprehensive academic support program for students with LD and/or ADHD. Students meet with an LDP specialist for two regularly-scheduled, one-hour appointments each week. Content for meetings includes time management, organization, reading and writing strategies, exam preparation and metacognitive skills. The LDP is a fee-based service and requires an additional application and interview. The Disability Resource Center (DRC) offers accommodations to students with disabilities, including exam accommodations, note-taking services, and alternate format text. Students registered with the DRC may also meet with a disability specialist for support in using accommodations and other disability-related needs. There is no charge for basic support services.

ADMISSIONS

There is no separate or different admissions process for students with disabilities. However, students who are interested in the Learning Disabilities Program (LDP) must apply to the LDP as well as the University. Students are encouraged to submit an application to the LDP immediately upon their decision to attend the university. The LDP also requires an interview for admission to the program. LDP application and additional information about the program are available at www.northeastern.edu/uhcs/idp.

Additional Information

Students who are interested in basic services, including accommodations, are encouraged to provide documentation to the Disability Resource Center (DRC) while their applications are being reviewed by the Admissions Office..

ADMISSIONS INFO FOR STUDENTS WITH LEARNING DIFFERENCES

SAT/ACT required: Yes
Interview required: Yes
Essay required: Not Applicable
Additional application required: Yes
Documentation required for:
  LD: Please see website for detailed information: www.northeastern.edu/drc
  ADHD: Please see website for detailed information: www.northeastern.edu/drc
  ASD: Please see website for detailed information: www.northeastern.edu/drc
Documentation submitted to: Learning Disabilities Program
Special Ed. HS course work accepted: Yes
Separate application required for Programs/Services: No
Contact Information
Name of program or department: Learning Disabilities Program
Telephone: 617-373-4526
Fax: 617-373-4142
Email: j.newton@northeastern.edu

Northeastern University

GENERAL ADMISSIONS

Very important factors considered include: rigor of secondary school record, academic GPA, application essay, standardized test scores, recommendation(s). *Important factors considered include:* extracurricular activities, talent/ability, character/personal qualities, volunteer work, work experience. *Other factors considered include:* class rank, first generation, geographical residence, racial/ethnic status, level of applicant's interest. *Freshman Admission Requirements:* High school diploma is required and GED is accepted. *Academic units required:* 4 English, 3 math, 3 science, 2 science labs, 2 foreign language, 3 social studies, 2 history. *Academic units recommended:* 4 math, 4 science.

ACCOMMODATIONS OR SERVICES

Accommodations are decided upon an individual basis after a thorough review of appropriate, current documentation. The accommodations requests must be supported through the documentation provided and must be logically linked to the current impact of the condition on academic functioning.

FINANCIAL AID

Students should submit: CSS/Financial Aid PROFILE; FAFSA; Noncustodial PROFILE. Applicants will be notified of awards on or about 4/1. The Princeton Review suggests that all financial aid forms be submitted as soon as possible after October 1. *Need-based scholarships/grants offered:* College/university scholarship or grant aid from institutional funds; Federal Pell; Private scholarships; SEOG; State scholarships/grants. *Loan aid offered:* Direct PLUS loans; Direct Subsidized Stafford Loans; Direct Unsubsidized Stafford Loans. Federal Work-Study Program available. Institutional employment available.

CAMPUS LIFE

Activities: Choral groups; Concert band; Dance; Drama/theater; International Student Organization; Jazz band; Literary magazine; Model UN; Music ensembles; Musical theater; Pep band; Radio station; Student government; Student newspaper; Student-run film society; Symphony orchestra; Television station; Yearbook. **Organizations:** 225 registered organizations, 15 honor societies, 20 religious organizations. 9 fraternities, 8 sororities. **Athletics (Intercollegiate):** *Men:* baseball, basketball, crew/rowing, cross-country, ice hockey, soccer, track/field (outdoor), track/field (indoor). *Women:* basketball, crew/rowing, cross-country, diving, field hockey, ice hockey, soccer, swimming, track/field (outdoor), track/field (indoor), volleyball. **On-Campus Highlights:** Curry Student Center, Marino Health and Fitness Center, Cyber Cafe, International Village, Levine Marketplace.

ACCOMMODATIONS

Allowed in exams:	
Calculators	Yes
Dictionary	Yes
Computer	Yes
Spell-checker	Yes
Extended test time	Yes
Scribe	Yes
Proctors	Yes
Oral exams	Yes
Note-takers	Yes
Support services for students with	
LD	Yes
ADHD	Yes
ASD	Yes
Distraction-reduced environment	Yes
Recording of lecture allowed	Yes
Reading technology:	Yes
Audio books	Yes
Other assistive technology	Read and Write Gold, ZoomText
Priority registration	Not Applicable
Added costs for services:	
For LD:	Yes
For ADHD:	Yes
For ASD:	Yes
LD specialists	Yes
ADHD & ASD coaching	No
ASD specialists	No
Professional tutors	Yes
Peer tutors	Yes
Max. hours/week for services	Varies
How professors are notified of student approved accommodations	Student

COLLEGE GRADUATION REQUIREMENTS

Course waivers allowed	No
Course substitutions allowed	Yes
In what courses	

Foreign language course substitutions available for eligible students.

Smith College

ELM ST., NORTHAMPTON, MA 01063 • ADMISSIONS: 413-585-2500 • FAX: 415-585-4498

PROGRAMS/SERVICES FOR STUDENTS WITH LEARNING DIFFERENCES

Smith College does not have a formal LD program. However, the college is both philosophically committed and legally required to enable students with documented disabilities to participate in college programs by providing reasonable accommodations for them. The Office of Disabilities Services (ODS) facilitates the provision of services and offers services aimed to eliminate barriers through modification of the program when necessary. A student may voluntarily register with ODS by completing a disability identification form and providing documentation of the disability, after which proper accommodations will be determined. Students with disabilities who need academic services are asked to make their needs known and file timely request forms for accommodations in course work each semester with ODS. Students are encouraged to tell professors about the accommodations needed. The college is responsible for providing that, within certain limits, students are not denied the opportunity to participate in college programs on the basis of a disability. The college will provide support services to students with appropriate evaluations and documentation. Students should contact the ODS for consultation and advice. Through the ODS office there are Peer Mentors.

ADMISSIONS

There is no special admissions procedure for students with learning disabilities. ACT/SAT are optional. Students may release scores at their discretion. Leniency may be granted in regard to a high school's waiving of foreign language requirements due to a learning disability. High school courses recommended are 4 years of English composition and literature, 3 years of a foreign language (or 2 years in each of 2 languages), 3 years of math, 2 years of science, and 2 years of history. Essays are required and help them understand how the student thinks, writes and what they are about. Recommendations are required. Interviews are highly recommended.

ADMISSIONS INFO FOR STUDENTS WITH LEARNING DIFFERENCES

SAT/ACT required: Yes
Interview required: Yes
Essay required: Yes
Additional application required: No
Documentation required for:
 LD: Psycho ed evaluation
 ADHD: Diagnosis based on DSM-V; history of behaviors impairing functioning in academic setting; diagnostic interview; history of symptoms; evidence of ongoing behaviors.
 ASD: Psycho ed evaluation
Documentation submitted to: Office of Disability Services
Special Ed. HS course work accepted: No
Separate application required for Programs/Services: No
Contact Information
Name of program or department: Office of Disability Services (ODS)
Telephone: 413-585-2071
Fax: 413-585-4498

Additional Information

The support services assist students to meet their requirements through modifications to programs when necessary. Courses are available in quantitative skills, study skills, and time management skills. The Special Needs Action Group for Support is a cross-disability, student-led group that meets regularly to provide support and peer mentoring and plan activities. Support services include readers, note-takers, scribes, assistive listening devices, typists, computing software and hardware, books on tape, writing counseling, peer tutoring, and time management/study skills training. If peer tutors are not available, other tutorial services may be sought.

GENERAL ADMISSIONS

Very important factors considered include: rigor of secondary school record, academic GPA, application essay, recommendation(s), character/personal qualities. *Important factors considered include:* class rank, interview, extracurricular activities, talent/ability. *Other factors considered include:* standardized test scores, first generation, alumni/ae relation, racial/ethnic status, volunteer work, work experience. *Freshman Admission Requirements:* High school diploma or equivalent is not required *Academic units recommended:* 4 English, 3 math, 3 science, 3 science labs, 3 foreign language, 2 history, 1 academic elective.

ACCOMMODATIONS OR SERVICES

Accommodations are decided upon an individual basis after a thorough review of appropriate, current documentation. The accommodations requests must be supported through the documentation provided and must be logically linked to the current impact of the condition on academic functioning.

FINANCIAL AID

Students should submit: CSS/Financial Aid PROFILE; FAFSA; Institution's own financial aid form; Noncustodial PROFILE. Applicants will be notified of awards on or about 4/1. The Princeton Review suggests that all financial aid forms be submitted as soon as possible after October 1. *Need-based scholarships/grants offered:* College/university scholarship or grant aid from institutional funds; Federal Pell; Private scholarships; SEOG; State scholarships/grants. *Loan aid offered:* Direct PLUS loans; Direct Subsidized Stafford Loans; Direct Unsubsidized Stafford Loans. Federal Work-Study Program available. Institutional employment available.

CAMPUS LIFE

Activities: Campus Ministries; Choral groups; Concert band; Dance; Drama/theater; International Student Organization; Jazz band; Literary magazine; Model UN; Music ensembles; Musical theater; Radio station; Student government; Student newspaper; Television station; Yearbook. **Organizations:** 133 registered organizations, 3 honor societies, 9 religious organizations. **Athletics (Intercollegiate):** *Women:* basketball, crew/rowing, cross-country, diving, equestrian sports, field hockey, lacrosse, skiing (downhill/alpine), soccer, softball, squash, swimming, tennis, track/field (outdoor), track/field (indoor), volleyball. **On-Campus Highlights:** Smith Art Museum, The Botanical Gardens, Campus Center, Mendenhall Center for Performing Arts, Ford Hall (Engineering, science).

ACCOMMODATIONS

Allowed in exams:	
Calculators	Yes
Dictionary	No
Computer	Yes
Spell-checker	Yes
Extended test time	Yes
Scribe	Yes
Proctors	No
Oral exams	Yes
Note-takers	Yes
Support services for students with	
LD	Yes
ADHD	Yes
ASD	Yes
Distraction-reduced environment	Yes
Recording of lecture allowed	Yes
Reading technology:	Yes
Audio books	Yes
Other assistive technology	Yes
Priority registration	Yes
Added costs for services:	
For LD:	No
For ADHD:	No
For ASD:	No
LD specialists	No
ADHD & ASD coaching	No
ASD specialists	No
Professional tutors	Yes
Peer tutors	Yes
Max. hours/week for services	Unlimited
How professors are notified of student approved accommodations	Student and Director

COLLEGE GRADUATION REQUIREMENTS

Course waivers allowed	No
Course substitutions allowed	Yes
In what courses	Foreign Language

University of Massachusetts Amherst

UNIVERSITY ADMISSIONS CENTER, AMHERST, MA 01003 • ADMISSIONS: 413-545-0222 • FAX: 413-545-4312

CAMPUS

Type of school	Public
Environment	Town
Support	CS

STUDENTS

Undergrad enrollment	23,010
% male/female	50/50
% from out of state	18
% frosh live on campus	99

FINANCIAL FACTS

Annual in-state tuition	$15,406
Annual out-of-state tuition	$34,089
Room and board	$13,202
Required fees	$481

GENERAL ADMISSIONS INFO

Application fee	$80.
Regular application deadline	1/15

Nonfall registration accepted. Admission may be deferred.

Range SAT EBRW	590–670
Range SAT Math	590–690
Range ACT Composite	26–31

ACADEMICS

Student/faculty ratio	17:1
% students returning for sophomore year	91
% students graduating within 4 years	67
% students graduating within 6 years	77

Most classes have 10–19 students.
Most lab/discussion sessions have 10–19 students.

PROGRAMS/SERVICES FOR STUDENTS WITH LEARNING DIFFERENCES

Disability Services' philosophy is one of inclusion and diversity. We understand that disability as an identity is experienced differently by each person and henceforth value the information that students share with us regarding their disability and accommodation needs in addition to the diagnostic documentation they provide. Students struggling academically who think they may need testing for a learning disability can apply for a scholarship through our department to cover some or all of their testing costs. Disability Services works closely with all departments on campus to ensure accessibility compliance.

ADMISSIONS

It is at the student's discretion whether or not they disclose as a person with a disability when they apply for admission. Students who are MA residents can provide documentation to obtain permission not to provide their SAT scores for review.

Additional Information

Students with a disability are encouraged to register with Disability Services upon their decision to attend the university. Disability Services provides a Spring Orientation for parents and accepted students who have identified themselves as people with learning disabilities. The Massachusetts Inclusive Concurrent Enrollment Initiative (MAICEI) provides high school students aged 18-21 with significant (typically autism or intellectual) disabilities the opportunity to have a college experience alongside their non-disabled peers. MAICEI students are supported by the MAICEI Program Coordinator, Educational Coaches and Peer Mentors. The goal of the University of Massachusetts Amherst MAICEI Program is to enhance the academic success, career development and independence skills of its participants.

ADMISSIONS INFO FOR STUDENTS WITH LEARNING DIFFERENCES

SAT/ACT required: Not Applicable
Interview required: No
Essay required: Not Applicable
Additional application required: Yes
Documentation required for:
LD: Diagnosis of LD is expected. It is preferable to provide a neuropsychological evaluation or testing results specifically, but not required.
ADHD: Diagnosis of ADHD is expected. It is preferable to provide a neuropsychological evaluation but not required.
Documentation submitted to: Disability Services
Special Ed. HS course work accepted: Not Applicable
Separate application required for Programs/Services: For ASD.
Contact Information
Name of program or department: Disability Services
Telephone: (413) 545-0892
Fax: (413) 577-0122

University of Massachusetts Amherst

GENERAL ADMISSIONS

Very important factors considered include: rigor of secondary school record, academic GPA, standardized test scores. *Important factors considered include:* class rank, application essay, recommendation(s), extracurricular activities, talent/ability, character/personal qualities, first generation, work experience, level of applicant's interest. *Other factors considered include:* alumni/ae relation, geographical residence, state residency, racial/ethnic status, volunteer work. *Freshman Admission Requirements:* High school diploma is required and GED is accepted. *Academic units required:* 4 English, 4 math, 3 science, 2 science labs, 2 foreign language, 2 social studies, 2 academic electives.

ACCOMMODATIONS OR SERVICES

Accommodations are decided upon an individual basis after a thorough review of appropriate, current documentation. The accommodations requests must be supported through the documentation provided and must be logically linked to the current impact of the condition on academic functioning.

FINANCIAL AID

Students should submit: FAFSA. Applicants will be notified of awards on a rolling basis beginning 12/15. The Princeton Review suggests that all financial aid forms be submitted as soon as possible after October 1. *Need-based scholarships/grants offered:* College/university scholarship or grant aid from institutional funds; Federal Pell; Private scholarships; SEOG; State scholarships/grants. *Loan aid offered:* Direct PLUS loans; Direct Subsidized Stafford Loans; Direct Unsubsidized Stafford Loans. Federal Work-Study Program available. Institutional employment available.

CAMPUS LIFE

Activities: Campus Ministries; Choral groups; Concert band; Dance; Drama/theater; International Student Organization; Jazz band; Literary magazine; Marching band; Model UN; Music ensembles; Musical theater; Opera; Pep band; Radio station; Student government; Student newspaper; Student-run film society; Symphony orchestra; Television station; Yearbook. **Organizations:** 291 registered organizations, 30 honor societies, 14 religious organizations. 21 fraternities, 15 sororities. **Athletics (Intercollegiate):** *Men:* baseball, basketball, cross-country, diving, football, ice hockey, lacrosse, soccer, swimming, track/field (outdoor), track/field (indoor). *Women:* basketball, crew/rowing, cross-country, diving, field hockey, lacrosse, soccer, softball, swimming, tennis, track/field (outdoor), track/field (indoor). **On-Campus Highlights:** The Campus Center & Student Union, The Learning Commons, The Recreation Center, The Mullins Center, The Fine Arts Center.

ACCOMMODATIONS

Allowed in exams:	
Calculators	Yes
Dictionary	Yes
Computer	Yes
Spell-checker	Yes
Extended test time	Yes
Scribe	Yes
Proctors	Yes
Oral exams	Yes
Note-takers	Yes
Support services for students with	
LD	Yes
ADHD	Yes
ASD	Yes
Distraction-reduced environment	Yes
Recording of lecture allowed	Yes
Reading technology:	Yes
Audio books	Yes
Other assistive technology	Yes
Priority registration	Yes
Added costs for services:	
For LD:	No
For ADHD:	No
For ASD:	No
LD specialists	Yes
ADHD & ASD coaching	No
ASD specialists	No
Professional tutors	Yes
Peer tutors	Not Applicable
Max. hours/week for services	Varies
How professors are notified of student approved accommodations	Director

COLLEGE GRADUATION REQUIREMENTS

Course waivers allowed	No
Course substitutions allowed	Yes
In what courses	
Math, Analytical Reasoning, and Foreign Language	

Wheaton College (MA)

26 East Main Street, Norton, MA 02766 • Admissions: 508-286-8251 • Fax: 508-286-8271

CAMPUS
Type of school	Private (nonprofit)
Environment	Village
Support	S

STUDENTS
Undergrad enrollment	1,677
% male/female	39/61
% from out of state	63
% frosh live on campus	98

FINANCIAL FACTS
Annual tuition	$52,288
Room and board	$13,424
Required fees	$338

GENERAL ADMISSIONS INFO
Application fee	$60
Regular application deadline	1/1

Nonfall registration accepted. Admission may be deferred for a maximum of 1 year.

Range SAT EBRW	590–680
Range SAT Math	560–670
Range ACT Composite	26–30

ACADEMICS
Student/faculty ratio	10:1
% students returning for sophomore year	88
% students graduating within 4 years	74
% students graduating within 6 years	78

Most classes have 20–29 students.
Most lab/discussion sessions have 20–29 students.

PROGRAMS/SERVICES FOR STUDENTS WITH LEARNING DIFFERENCES

Wheaton College encourages life-long learning by assisting students to become self-advocates and independent learners. The college does not have a special program for students with LD. The Assistant Dean for College Skills serves as the 504/ADA coordinator. Students with LD can access services through the dean. The Academic Advising Center houses the Dean of Academic Advising who holds drop-in office hours and assists students with petitions to the Committee on Admissions and Academic Standing, Orientation, and Probation; general advising; and incomplete grade resolution. The advising staff can assist with pressing advising questions. Students also have access to tutors, peer advisors, and preceptors who offer assistance with study strategies. All students have access to these services.

ADMISSIONS

All applicants must meet the same admission standards. Students with LD may choose to meet with the Assistant Dean for College Skills. It is strongly suggested that students take 4 years of English, 3–4 years of math, 3–4 years of a foreign language, 2 years of social studies, and 3–4 years of science. Students are encouraged to take AP and honors courses and courses in visual/performing arts. Wheaton will accept courses taken in the special education department. Students with LD are encouraged to self-disclose and provide current documentation. All LD testing information should be sent to both admissions and support services.

Additional Information

Contact: Accessibility Services Abigail Cohen. Abilities 1st! is pre-orientation gives students the opportunity to to move into their dorm two days before the rest of the class, learn about the Writing Center, Library Information Services and Assistive Technology, and First Year Seminar (FYS).

ADMISSIONS INFO FOR STUDENTS WITH LEARNING DIFFERENCES

SAT/ACT required: No
Interview required: No
Essay required: Not Applicable
Additional application required: No
Documentation required for:
 LD: Psycho ed evaluation
 ADHD: Psycho ed evaluation
 ASD: Psycho ed evaluation
Documentation submitted to: Accessibility Services
Special Ed. HS course work accepted: No
Separate application required for Programs/Services: Not for LD, ADHD, or ASD.
Contact Information
Name of program or department: Accessibility Services
Telephone: (508) 286-8215
Fax: (508) 286-5621

Wheaton College (MA)

General Admissions

Very important factors considered include: rigor of secondary school record, academic GPA, application essay, recommendation(s), character/personal qualities. *Important factors considered include:* extracurricular activities, talent/ability, alumni/ae relation, level of applicant's interest. *Other factors considered include:* class rank, standardized test scores, interview, first generation, geographical residence, state residency, racial/ethnic status, volunteer work, work experience. *Freshman Admission Requirements:* High school diploma is required and GED is accepted. *Academic units required:* 4 English. *Academic units recommended:* 4 math, 4 science, 4 foreign language, 4 social studies, 4 history.

Accommodations or Services

Accommodations are decided upon an individual basis after a thorough review of appropriate, current documentation. The accommodations requests must be supported through the documentation provided and must be logically linked to the current impact of the condition on academic functioning.

Financial Aid

Students should submit: Business/Farm Supplement; CSS/Financial Aid PROFILE; FAFSA; Noncustodial PROFILE. Applicants will be notified of awards on or about 3/15. The Princeton Review suggests that all financial aid forms be submitted as soon as possible after October 1. *Need-based scholarships/grants offered:* College/university scholarship or grant aid from institutional funds; Federal Pell; Private scholarships; SEOG; State scholarships/grants. *Loan aid offered:* Direct PLUS loans; Direct Subsidized Stafford Loans; Direct Unsubsidized Stafford Loans. Federal Work-Study Program available. Institutional employment available.

Campus Life

Activities: Campus Ministries; Choral groups; Dance; Drama/theater; International Student Organization; Jazz band; Literary magazine; Model UN; Music ensembles; Musical theater; Radio station; Student government; Student newspaper; Student-run film society; Symphony orchestra; Yearbook. **Organizations:** 60 registered organizations, 8 honor societies, 4 religious organizations. **Athletics (Intercollegiate):** *Men:* baseball, basketball, cross-country, diving, lacrosse, soccer, swimming, tennis, track/field (outdoor), track/field (indoor). *Women:* basketball, cross-country, diving, field hockey, lacrosse, soccer, softball, swimming, synchronized swimming, tennis, track/field (outdoor), track/field (indoor), volleyball. **On-Campus Highlights:** Mars Center for Science and Technology, Mars Arts and Humanities Arts facility, Haas Athletic Center, Mary Lyon Hall (Wheaton's oldest building), Balfour-Hood Campus Center.

ACCOMMODATIONS

Allowed in exams:	
Calculators	Yes
Dictionary	No
Computer	Yes
Spell-checker	No
Extended test time	Yes
Scribe	Yes
Proctors	Not Applicable
Oral exams	Not Applicable
Note-takers	Yes
Support services for students with	
LD	Yes
ADHD	Yes
ASD	Yes
Distraction-reduced environment	Yes
Recording of lecture allowed	Yes
Reading technology:	Yes
Audio books	Yes
Other assistive technology	Screen reader (i.e. JAWS or Voiceover) for quizzes, exams, in-class assignments; Assistive listening devices; Communication Access Realtime Translation; Text to speech software; specialized magnifiers; tactile boards
Priority registration	Yes
Added costs for services:	
For LD:	No
For ADHD:	No
For ASD:	No
LD specialists	No
ADHD & ASD coaching	No
ASD specialists	No
Professional tutors	Yes
Peer tutors	Yes
Max. hours/week for services	Varies
How professors are notified of student approved accommodations	Student

COLLEGE GRADUATION REQUIREMENTS

Course waivers allowed	No
Course substitutions allowed	Yes
In what courses	Foreign Language

Adrian College

110 South Madison Street, Adrian, MI 49221 • Admissions: 517-265-5161 • Fax: 517-264-3331

CAMPUS
Type of school	Private (nonprofit)
Environment	Town
Support	CS

STUDENTS
Undergrad enrollment	1,308
% male/female	53/47
% from out of state	24
% frosh live on campus	85

FINANCIAL FACTS
Annual tuition	$23,090
Room and board	$7,600
Required fees	$300

GENERAL ADMISSIONS INFO
Priority deadline 3/15.
Nonfall registration accepted. Admission may be deferred for a maximum of 1 year.

Range SAT EBRW	430–515
Range SAT Math	410–535
Range ACT Composite	20–25

ACADEMICS
Student/faculty ratio	12:1
% students returning for sophomore year	73

Programs/Services for Students with Learning Differences
Adrian College has extensive academic support services for all students with disabilities. The more the students are mainstreamed in high school, the greater their chances of success at Adrian. There is no special or separate curriculum for students with learning disabilities.

Admissions
Students with learning disabilities must meet regular admission criteria. Students should demonstrate the ability to do college-level work through an acceptable GPA in college-preparatory classes (average 3.22) including four years English, three years math, social studies, science and language, ACT (average 19–24) or SAT. Furthermore, by their senior year in high school, students should, for the most part, be mainstreamed. Courses taken in special education will be considered for admission. The applications of students who self-disclose are reviewed by Academic Services staff, not to determine admissions, but to start a documentation file. There is a special admissions program designed for students who demonstrate academic potential. This Adrian College Enrichment Program (ACE) requires students to sign a contract and maintain a certain GPA each of the first two semesters.

Additional Information
Academic Services Department offers a wide variety of services. Staff members help identify alternative study strategies and develop time management plans. Strategies for more effective reading, note-taking, and test-taking are also offered. The staff teaches a number of skills courses. Course adaptations help to make courses more understandable. Skills classes are available in reading, math, study skills and research paper writing, and students are granted credit toward their GPA. Tutorial assistance is available for all students. P.R.I.D.E. (Promoting the Rights of Individuals Everywhere) communicates information about the difficulties and accomplishments of people with disabilities.

ADMISSIONS INFO FOR STUDENTS WITH LEARNING DIFFERENCES
SAT/ACT required: Yes
Interview required: No
Essay required: N/A
Additional application required: No
Documentation required for:
  LD: Psycho ed evaluation
  ADHD: Diagnosis based on DSM-V; history of behaviors impairing functioning in academic setting; diagnostic interview; history of symptoms; evidence of ongoing behaviors.
  ASD: Psycho ed evaluation
Documentation submitted to: ACCESS, Academic Services
Special Ed. HS course work accepted: Yes
Separate application required for Programs/Services: No
Contact Information
Name of program or department: ACCESS, Academic Services
Telephone: 517-265-5161, ext- 4093
Fax: 517-264-3331

Adrian College

General Admissions

Very important factors considered include: rigor of secondary school record, class rank. *Important factors considered include:* academic GPA, standardized test scores, talent/ability. *Other factors considered include:* interview, extracurricular activities, character/personal qualities, alumni/ae relation, volunteer work, work experience, level of applicant's interest. *Freshman Admission Requirements:* High school diploma is required and GED is accepted. *Academic units recommended:* 4 English, 3 math, 2 science, 1 science lab, 2 foreign language, 1 social studies, 1 history, 2 academic electives.

Accommodations or Services

Accommodations are decided upon an individual basis after a thorough review of appropriate, current documentation. The accommodations requests must be supported through the documentation provided and must be logically linked to the current impact of the condition on academic functioning.

Financial Aid

Students should submit: FAFSA. Applicants will be notified of awards on a rolling basis beginning 3/15. The Princeton Review suggests that all financial aid forms be submitted as soon as possible after October 1. *Need-based scholarships/grants offered:* College/university scholarship or grant aid from institutional funds; Federal Pell; Private scholarships; SEOG; State scholarships/grants. *Loan aid offered:* Federal Work-Study Program available. Institutional employment available.

Campus Life

Activities: Campus Ministries; Choral groups; Concert band; Dance; Drama/theater; International Student Organization; Jazz band; Literary magazine; Marching band; Music ensembles; Musical theater; Pep band; Radio station; Student government; Student newspaper; Symphony orchestra; Yearbook. **Organizations:** 68 registered organizations, 13 honor societies, 8 religious organizations. 4 fraternities, 3 sororities. **Athletics (Intercollegiate):** *Men:* baseball, basketball, cross-country, football, golf, ice hockey, lacrosse, soccer, tennis, track/field (outdoor). *Women:* basketball, bowling, cross-country, golf, ice hockey, lacrosse, soccer, softball, tennis, track/field (outdoor), volleyball. **On-Campus Highlights:** Caine Student Center, Shipman Library, Merillat Sport and Fitness Center.

ACCOMMODATIONS

Allowed in exams:

Calculators	No
Dictionary	Yes
Computer	Yes
Spell-checker	Yes
Extended test time	Yes
Scribe	Yes
Proctors	Yes
Oral exams	Yes
Note-takers	Yes

Support services for students with

LD	Yes
ADHD	Yes
ASD	Yes
Distraction-reduced environment	Yes
Recording of lecture allowed	Yes
Reading technology:	Yes
Audio books	Yes
Other assistive technology	Yes
Priority registration	No

Added costs for services:

For LD:	No
For ADHD:	No
For ASD:	No
LD specialists	Yes
ADHD & ASD coaching	No
ASD specialists	No
Professional tutors	No
Peer tutors	Yes
Max. hours/week for services	Varies
How professors are notified of student approved accommodations	Student and Director

COLLEGE GRADUATION REQUIREMENTS

Course waivers allowed	No
Course substitutions allowed	No

Calvin College

3201 Burton Street S.E., Grand Rapids, MI 49546 • Admissions: 616-526-6106 • Fax: 616-526-6777

CAMPUS
Type of school	Private (nonprofit)
Environment	Metropolis
Support	CS

STUDENTS
Undergrad enrollment	3,656
% male/female	47/53
% from out of state	42
% frosh live on campus	95

FINANCIAL FACTS
Annual tuition	$33,100
Room and board	$9,990
Required fees	NR

GENERAL ADMISSIONS INFO
Application fee	$35.
Regular application deadline	8/15

Nonfall registration accepted. Admission may be deferred for a maximum of 1 year.

Range SAT EBRW	560–660
Range SAT Math	540–670
Range ACT Composite	23–30

ACADEMICS
Student/faculty ratio	13:1
% students returning for sophomore year	87
% students graduating within 4 years	59
% students graduating within 6 years	72

Most classes have 20–29 students.
Most lab/discussion sessions have fewer than 10 students.

PROGRAMS/SERVICES FOR STUDENTS WITH LEARNING DIFFERENCES
We are committed to serving students with disabilities and our goal is to ensure that every student who has a disability is provided with access to the needed services that will ensure equity of opportunity. Because each person's situation is unique, we ask any interested student to meet with us. In accordance with the spirit of the legislative updates to the ADA, documentation requirements vary by situation.

ADMISSIONS
There are no special admissions criteria for students with LD. Applicants are expected to have an ACT of 20 (19 English and 20 Math) or SAT of 940 (470 Critical Reading and 470 Math). The mid 50 percent for ACT is 23–25, and for SAT, it is 1090–1320. Courses required include: 3 English, 1 algebra, 1 geometry, and a minimum of 2 in any two of the following fields: social science, language, or natural science; one of the foreign language, math, social science, and natural science fields must include at least 3 years of study. The mid 50 percent GPA is 3.3–3.9. The Access Program provides an alternate entry track for first-time students who show promise of being successful at Calvin, but who cannot meet all of the admissions standards. The students are provided with placement testing in math and/or English, special advising, and enrollment in a college thinking and learning course during their first semester at Calvin. Depending on the outcome of the placement testing, additional developmental courses may be required as a condition of admission. The Access Program helps students develop new approaches, methods, and skills for learning by means of placement testing, academic advising, Academic Services Courses (ASC), and consultation with students' professors.

Additional Information
We provide assistance to all students that have disclosed a disability, chronic health impairment, or a visual, mobility or hearing impairment. Please contact a Disability Coordinator to get started, 616-526-6155.

ADMISSIONS INFO FOR STUDENTS WITH LEARNING DIFFERENCES
SAT/ACT required: Yes
Interview required: No
Essay required: Not Applicable
Additional application required: No
Documentation required for:
LD: Please see our documentation requirements here: www.calvin.edu/academic/services/disability/documentation.html
ADHD: Please see our documentation requirements here: www.calvin.edu/academic/services/disability/documentation.html
ASD: Please see our documentation requirements here: www.calvin.edu/academic/services/disability/documentation.html
Documentation submitted to: Disability Services
Special Ed. HS course work accepted: No
Separate application required for Programs/Services: No
Contact Information
Name of program or department: Disability Services
Telephone: 616-526-6155
Fax: 616-526-7066
Email: successcenter@calvin.edu

Calvin College

GENERAL ADMISSIONS

Very important factors considered include: rigor of secondary school record, academic GPA, standardized test scores, religious affiliation/commitment. *Important factors considered include:* application essay, recommendation(s), extracurricular activities, character/personal qualities. *Other factors considered include:* class rank, volunteer work, work experience, level of applicant's interest. *Freshman Admission Requirements:* High school diploma is required and GED is accepted. *Academic units required:* 3 English, 3 math, 2 science, 2 social studies, 3 academic electives. *Academic units recommended:* 4 English, 3 math, 2 science, 1 science lab, 2 foreign language, 3 social studies, 3 academic electives.

ACCOMMODATIONS OR SERVICES

Accommodations are decided upon an individual basis after a thorough review of appropriate, current documentation. The accommodations requests must be supported through the documentation provided and must be logically linked to the current impact of the condition on academic functioning.

FINANCIAL AID

Students should submit: FAFSA. Applicants will be notified of awards on a rolling basis beginning 12/15. The Princeton Review suggests that all financial aid forms be submitted as soon as possible after October 1. *Need-based scholarships/grants offered:* College/university scholarship or grant aid from institutional funds; Federal Pell; Private scholarships; SEOG; State scholarships/grants. *Loan aid offered:* Direct PLUS loans; Direct Subsidized Stafford Loans; Direct Unsubsidized Stafford Loans. Federal Work-Study Program available. Institutional employment available.

CAMPUS LIFE

Activities: Campus Ministries; Choral groups; Concert band; Dance; Drama/theater; International Student Organization; Jazz band; Literary magazine; Music ensembles; Pep band; Student government; Student newspaper; Student-run film society; Symphony orchestra; Yearbook. **Organizations:** 60 registered organizations, 6 honor societies, 5 religious organizations. **Athletics (Intercollegiate):** *Men:* baseball, basketball, cross-country, diving, golf, soccer, swimming, tennis, track/field (outdoor). *Women:* basketball, cross-country, diving, golf, soccer, softball, swimming, tennis, track/field (outdoor), volleyball. **On-Campus Highlights:** Spoelhof Fieldhouse Complex, Johnny's Cafe, Hekman Library, DeVos Communications Building, Covenant Fine Arts Center.

ACCOMMODATIONS

Allowed in exams:	
Calculators	Yes
Dictionary	Yes
Computer	Yes
Spell-checker	Yes
Extended test time	Yes
Scribe	Yes
Proctors	Yes
Oral exams	Yes
Note-takers	Yes
Support services for students with	
LD	Yes
ADHD	Yes
ASD	Yes
Distraction-reduced environment	Yes
Recording of lecture allowed	Yes
Reading technology:	Yes
Audio books	Yes
Other assistive technology	Yes
Priority registration	Yes
Added costs for services:	
For LD:	No
For ADHD:	No
For ASD:	No
LD specialists	No
ADHD & ASD coaching	Yes
ASD specialists	Yes
Professional tutors	Yes
Peer tutors	Yes
Max. hours/week for services	1
How professors are notified of student approved accommodations	Student

COLLEGE GRADUATION REQUIREMENTS

Course waivers allowed	No
In what courses	Students may be eligible for course substitutions.
Course substitutions allowed	Yes
In what courses	Foreign Language

Ferris State University

1201 S. STATE STREET, BIG RAPIDS, MI 49307 • ADMISSIONS: 231-591-2100 • FAX: 231-591-3944

CAMPUS
Type of school	Public
Environment	Village
Support	CS

STUDENTS
Undergrad enrollment	12,550
% male/female	49/51
% from out of state	7
% frosh live on campus	77

FINANCIAL FACTS
Annual in-state tuition	$11,760
Annual out-of-state tuition	$17,640
Room and board	$9,652
Required fees	

GENERAL ADMISSIONS INFO
Regular application deadline	8/1
Nonfall registration accepted.	

Range SAT EBRW	NR
Range SAT Math	NR
Range ACT Composite	19–25

ACADEMICS
Student/faculty ratio	16:1
% students returning for sophomore year	75

Most classes have 10–19 students.
Most lab/discussion sessions have 20–29 students.

PROGRAMS/SERVICES FOR STUDENTS WITH LEARNING DIFFERENCES

Ferris State University is committed to a policy of equal opportunity for qualified students. The mission of Disabilities Services is to serve and advocate for students with disabilities, empowering them for self-reliance and independence. Ferris State does not have a program for students with learning disabilities, but does provide a variety of support services and accommodations for students with documented learning disabilities that interfere with the learning process. Ferris State does not, however, attempt to rehabilitate learning disabilities. To obtain support services, students need to meet with a counselor in the Educational Counseling and Disability Services. Students will complete a request for services application and a copy of the documentation of the disability. Documentation for LD/ADHD must be current and be submitted by a qualified professional. Professional development is offered to faculty and staff.

ADMISSIONS

Students with learning disabilities must submit the general application form and should meet the same entrance criteria as all students. Qualified persons with disabilities may not be denied or subjected to discrimination in admission. There is no limit on the number of students admitted with disabilities. ACT scores are used for placement only and may not have an adverse effect on applicants with disabilities. No pre-admission inquiry regarding a possible disability can be made. Therefore, students with LD/ADHD are encouraged to self-disclose and provide information as to the extent of the disability. Sometimes a pre-admission interview is required if the GPA is questionable. In general, students should have a 2.0 GPA, but some programs require a higher GPA and specific courses. Diverse curricula offerings and a flexible admissions policy allow for the admission of most high school graduates and transfer students. Some programs are selective in nature and require the completion of specific courses and/or a minimum GPA.

Additional Information

Disability Services provides services and accommodations to students with LD or ADHD with appropriate documentation. These could include the Kurzweil Reading System; calculators for exams; Dragon Naturally Speaking extended testing times; electronic text; spellchecker for essay tests or exams; note-takers; word processing for essay tests; use of student

---

ADMISSIONS INFO FOR STUDENTS WITH LEARNING DIFFERENCES

SAT/ACT required: Yes
Interview required: Yes
Essay required: Not Applicable
Additional application required: No
Documentation required for:
 LD: Psycho ed evaluation
 ADHD: Psycho ed evaluation
 ASD: Psycho ed evaluation
Documentation submitted to: Educational Counseling & Disabilities Services
Special Ed. HS course work accepted: No
Separate application required for Programs/Services: No
Contact Information
Name of program or department: Educational Counseling & Disabilities Services
Telephone: 231-591-3057
Fax: 231-591-3939
Email: ecds@ferris.edu

Ferris State University

supplied recording device in class; quiet areas for testing; educational counseling; and JAWS. The Academic Support Center offers tutoring for most courses.

GENERAL ADMISSIONS

Very important factors considered include: rigor of secondary school record. *Important factors considered include:* academic GPA, standardized test scores, character/personal qualities. *Other factors considered include:* class rank, first generation, alumni/ae relation, geographical residence, volunteer work, work experience. *Freshman Admission Requirements:* High school diploma is required and GED is accepted. *Academic units recommended:* 4 English, 4 math, 3 science, 2 foreign language, 3 social studies, 1 academic elective, 1 visual/performing arts.

ACCOMMODATIONS OR SERVICES

Accommodations are decided upon an individual basis after a thorough review of appropriate, current documentation. The accommodations requests must be supported through the documentation provided and must be logically linked to the current impact of the condition on academic functioning.

FINANCIAL AID

Students should submit: FAFSA. Applicants will be notified of awards on a rolling basis beginning 12/9. The Princeton Review suggests that all financial aid forms be submitted as soon as possible after October 1. *Need-based scholarships/grants offered:* College/university scholarship or grant aid from institutional funds; Federal Pell; Private scholarships; SEOG; State scholarships/grants. *Loan aid offered:* Direct PLUS loans; Direct Subsidized Stafford Loans; Direct Unsubsidized Stafford Loans. Federal Work-Study Program available. Institutional employment available.

CAMPUS LIFE

Activities: Campus Ministries; Choral groups; Concert band; Dance; Drama/theater; International Student Organization; Jazz band; Model UN; Music ensembles; Musical theater; Pep band; Student government; Student newspaper. **Organizations:** 180 registered organizations, 11 honor societies, 14 religious organizations. 8 fraternities, 6 sororities. **Athletics (Intercollegiate):** *Men:* basketball, cheerleading, cross-country, football, golf, ice hockey, tennis, track/field (outdoor). *Women:* basketball, cheerleading, cross-country, golf, soccer, softball, tennis, track/field (outdoor), volleyball. **On-Campus Highlights:** University Center, Student Recreation Center, FLITE Library, Card Wildlife Center, Ewigleben Ice Arena.

ACCOMMODATIONS

Allowed in exams:

Calculators	Yes
Dictionary	Yes
Computer	Yes
Spell-checker	Yes
Extended test time	Yes
Scribe	Yes
Proctors	No
Oral exams	Yes
Note-takers	Yes

Support services for students with

LD	Yes
ADHD	Yes
ASD	Yes
Distraction-reduced environment	Yes
Recording of lecture allowed	Yes
Reading technology:	No
Audio books	Yes
Other assistive technology software.	Text to talk
Priority registration	Yes

Added costs for services:

For LD:	No
For ADHD:	No
For ASD:	No
LD specialists	No
ADHD & ASD coaching	Yes
ASD specialists	No
Professional tutors	Yes
Peer tutors	Yes
Max. hours/week for services	Varies
How professors are notified of student approved accommodations	
Director and Student	

COLLEGE GRADUATION REQUIREMENTS

Course waivers allowed	No
Course substitutions allowed	No

Grand Valley State University

1 CAMPUS DRIVE, ALLENDALE, MI 49401 • ADMISSIONS: 616-331-2025 • FAX: 616-331-2000

CAMPUS
Type of school	Public
Environment	City
Support	S

STUDENTS
Undergrad enrollment	21,824
% male/female	41/59
% from out of state	7
% frosh live on campus	87

FINANCIAL FACTS
Annual in-state tuition	$12,484
Annual out-of-state tuition	$17,762
Room and board	$8,690
Required fees	NR

GENERAL ADMISSIONS INFO
Application fee	$30
Priority deadline	5/1

Nonfall registration accepted.

Range SAT EBRW	530–620
Range SAT Math	530–610
Range ACT Composite	21–26

ACADEMICS
Student/faculty ratio	17:1
% students returning for sophomore year	83
% students graduating within 4 years	34
% students graduating within 6 years	66

Most classes have 10–19 students.
Most lab/discussion sessions have 10–19 students.

PROGRAMS/SERVICES FOR STUDENTS WITH LEARNING DIFFERENCES
We strive to provide persons with disabilities with the resources needed to be successful as a student through innovative approaches and effective collaboration. Skills assistance provides students with strategies for collegiate success through individual preparation and guidance with a learning skills curriculum specialist. This program is designed for students in DSR who have a desire to improve academic performance or be more successful. This service is provided to identify and explore the unique learning characteristics of students who feel that their own study efforts are not reflected in the academic performance. The goal of Learning Skills assistance is to help students get the most out of their learning experiences as motivated and organized learners at Grand Valley State University. Students may meet with the learning skills curriculum specialist throughout the academic year.

ADMISSIONS
Follow the admissions guidelines per the admission website.

Additional Information
Please schedule a visit to our office to hear of the resources available in DSR.

ADMISSIONS INFO FOR STUDENTS WITH LEARNING DIFFERENCES
SAT/ACT required: Y/N depends if Test Optional
Interview required: No
Essay required: Recommended
Additional application required: Yes
Documentation required for:
LD: Documentation that states a disability, an impairment that limits a major life activity and supports the needs for academic accommodations. Documentation no older than 5 years.
ADHD: Documentation that states a disability, an impairment that limits a major life activity and supports the needs for academic accommodations. Documentation no older than 5 years.
ASD: Documentation that states a disability, an impairment that limits a major life activity and supports the needs for academic accommodations. Documentation no older than 5 years.
Documentation submitted to: Campus Links Red and Blue Program for Students with ASD
Special Ed. HS course work accepted: No
Separate application required for Programs/Services: For LD.
Contact Information
Name of program or department: Campus Links Red and Blue Program for Students with ASD
Telephone: 616-331-2490
Fax: 616-331-3880
Email: dsr@gvsu.edu

Grand Valley State University

GENERAL ADMISSIONS

Very important factors considered include: rigor of secondary school record, academic GPA. *Important factors considered include:* standardized test scores. *Other factors considered include:* class rank, application essay, recommendation(s), extracurricular activities, talent/ability, first generation, alumni/ae relation, volunteer work, work experience. *Freshman Admission Requirements:* High school diploma is required and GED is accepted. *Academic units required:* 4 English, 3 math, 3 science, 2 science labs, 2 foreign language, 3 social studies.

ACCOMMODATIONS OR SERVICES

Accommodations are decided upon an individual basis after a thorough review of appropriate, current documentation. The accommodations requests must be supported through the documentation provided and must be logically linked to the current impact of the condition on academic functioning.

FINANCIAL AID

Students should submit: FAFSA. Applicants will be notified of awards on a rolling basis beginning 1/16. The Princeton Review suggests that all financial aid forms be submitted as soon as possible after October 1. *Need-based scholarships/grants offered:* College/university scholarship or grant aid from institutional funds; Federal Pell; Private scholarships; SEOG; State scholarships/grants. *Loan aid offered:* Direct PLUS loans; Direct Subsidized Stafford Loans; Direct Unsubsidized Stafford Loans. Federal Work-Study Program available. Institutional employment available.

CAMPUS LIFE

Activities: Campus Ministries; Choral groups; Concert band; Dance; Drama/theater; International Student Organization; Jazz band; Literary magazine; Marching band; Music ensembles; Musical theater; Pep band; Radio station; Student government; Student newspaper; Symphony orchestra; Television station. **Organizations:** 301 registered organizations, 20 honor societies, 20 religious organizations. 11 fraternities, 11 sororities. **Athletics (Intercollegiate):** *Men:* baseball, basketball, cross-country, diving, football, golf, swimming, tennis, track/field (outdoor), track/field (indoor). *Women:* basketball, cross-country, diving, golf, soccer, softball, swimming, tennis, track/field (outdoor), track/field (indoor), volleyball. **On-Campus Highlights:** Living Centers, Cook DeVos Center for Health Sciences, Recreation Center and Fieldhouse, Laker Turf Building, Kirkhof Center.

ACCOMMODATIONS

Allowed in exams:

Calculators	Yes
Dictionary	Yes
Computer	Yes
Spell-checker	Yes
Extended test time	Yes
Scribe	Yes
Proctors	Yes
Oral exams	Yes
Note-takers	Yes

Support services for students with

LD	Yes
ADHD	Yes
ASD	Yes
Distraction-reduced environment	Yes
Recording of lecture allowed	Yes
Reading technology:	Yes
Audio books	Yes

Other assistive technology   We attempt to assist all students to be successful. Some resources offered within DSR may go above the federal requirements to meet the needs of students.

Priority registration	Yes

Added costs for services:

For LD:	No
For ADHD:	No
For ASD:	No
LD specialists	Yes
ADHD & ASD coaching	Yes
ASD specialists	Yes
Professional tutors	Yes
Peer tutors	Yes
Max. hours/week for services	1
How professors are notified of student approved accommodations	Student

COLLEGE GRADUATION REQUIREMENTS

Course waivers allowed	No
Course substitutions allowed	No

Lake Superior State University

650 WEST EASTERDAY AVENUE, SAULT STE. MARIE, MI 49783-1699 • ADMISSIONS: 906-635-2231 • FAX: 906-635-6669

CAMPUS

Type of school	Public
Environment	City
Support	S

STUDENTS

Undergrad enrollment	2,440
% male/female	50/50
% from out of state	5
% frosh live on campus	69

FINANCIAL FACTS

Annual in-state tuition	$9,540
Annual out-of-state tuition	$14,410
Room and board	$8,481
Required fees	$100

GENERAL ADMISSIONS INFO

Application fee	$35
Priority deadline	3/1

Nonfall registration accepted. Admission may be deferred for a maximum of 1 year.

Range SAT EBRW	NR
Range SAT Math	NR
Range ACT Composite	20–25

ACADEMICS

Student/faculty ratio	17:1.
% students returning for sophomore year	70

Most classes have 10-19 students. Most lab/discussion sessions have 10-19 students.

PROGRAMS/SERVICES FOR STUDENTS WITH LEARNING DIFFERENCE

Lake Superior State University is committed to providing a welcoming and inclusive campus environment for people of all abilities. The Accessibility Services (AS) office is committed to helping students with disabilities participate as fully as possible in the university's programs, services and activities. It is the policy of the university that persons with disabilities have access to any program, service, or activity offered by the university that is comparable to the access received by persons without disabilities, unless such access would place an undue burden upon the university. If technologies or other products are needed to provide access to university programs, services, or activities, AS will make every reasonable effort to purchase such products; if these products cannot be purchased, AS will make provisions for effective alternatives that meet the accessibility requirements.

ADMISSIONS

Lake Superior College is an open admission policy institution and has few admission thresholds admits all applicants so long as certain minimum requirements are met. ACT or SAT is not required for admission.

Additional Information

Services provided include small group tutoring; a Writing Center available for students to have drop in sessions or appointments for longer assignments, a Math Center for tutoring, the LSSU Mentoring that connects students with mentors, and Supplemental Instruction courses for historically challenging courses and the Aleks Math Program that provides two options for satisfying beginning math and pre requisites.

APPLICATION REQUIREMENTS FOR SERVICES

SAT/ACT required: No
Interview required: No
Essay required: No
Additional application required: No
Documentation required for:
  LD: Yes, Psycho Educational Evaluation
  ADHD: Yes, Psycho Educational Evaluation
  ASD: Yes, Psycho Educational Evaluation
Documentation submitted to: AS
Special Ed. HS course work accepted: Yes
Separate application required for Programs/Services: No
Contact Information
Name of program or department: Accessibility Services and Students with Disabilities.
Telephone: 906-635-2355
Email: accessibility@lssu.edu

Lake Superior State University

GENERAL ADMISSIONS

Very important factors considered include: rigor of secondary school record, academic GPA, standardized test scores. Other factors considered include: class rank, recommendation(s), interview, geographical residence. Freshman Admission Requirements: High school diploma is required and GED is accepted   Academic units recommended: 4 English, 3 math, 3 science, 3 science labs, 2 foreign language, 2 social studies, 1 history,

ACCOMMODATIONS OR SERVICES

Accommodations are decided upon an individual basis after a thorough review of appropriate, current documentation. The accommodations requests must be supported through the documentation provided and must be logically linked to the current impact of the condition on academic functioning.

FINANCIAL AID

Students should submit: FAFSA. Applicants will be notified of awards on a rolling basis beginning 10/11. The Princeton Review suggests that all financial aid forms be submitted as soon as possible after October 1. Need-based scholarships/grants offered: College/university scholarship or grant aid from institutional funds; Federal Nursing Scholarships; Federal Pell; Private scholarships; SEOG; State scholarships/grants Loan aid offered: Direct PLUS loans; Direct Subsidized Stafford Loans; Direct Unsubsidized Stafford Loans

CAMPUS LIFE

Activities: Campus Ministries; Choral groups; Dance; Drama/theater; International Student Organization; Literary magazine; Model UN; Pep band; Radio station; Student government; Student newspaper Organizations: 60 registered organizations, 4 fraternities, 4 sororities, Athletics (Intercollegiate): Men: basketball, cross-country, ice hockey, tennis, track/field (outdoor), track/field (indoor) Women: basketball, cross-country, softball, tennis, track/field (outdoor), track/field (indoor), volleyball.

ACCOMMODATIONS

Allowed in exams:	
Calculators	Yes
Dictionary	Yes
Computer	Yes
Spell-checker	Yes
Extended test time	Yes
Scribe	Yes
Proctors	Yes
Oral exams	Yes
Note-takers	Yes
Support services for students with	
LD	Yes
ADHD	Yes
ASD	Yes
Distraction-reduced environment	Yes
Recording of lecture allowed	Yes
Reading technology:	Yes
Audio books	Yes
Other assistive technology	Yes
Priority registration	Yes
Added costs of services:	
For LD:	No
For ADHD:	No
For ASD:	No
LD specialists	No
ADHD & ASD coaching	No
ASD specialists	No
Professional tutors	Yes
Peer tutors	Yes
Max. hours/week for services	Varies
How professors are notified of student approved accommodations	Student

COLLEGE GRADUATION REQUIREMENTS

Course waivers allowed	No
Course substitutions allowed	No

Michigan State University

426 Auditorium Rd., East Lansing, MI 48824 • Admissions: 517-355-8332 • Fax: 517-353-1647

CAMPUS
Type of school	Public
Environment	City
Support	CS

STUDENTS
Undergrad enrollment	38,770
% male/female	49/51
% from out of state	13
% frosh live on campus	95

FINANCIAL FACTS
Annual in-state tuition	$14,460
Annual out-of-state tuition	$39,765
Room and board	$9,976
Required fees	NR

GENERAL ADMISSIONS INFO
Application fee	$65
Priority deadline	11/1

Nonfall registration accepted.
Admission may be deferred for a maximum of 1 semester.

Range SAT EBRW	550–650
Range SAT Math	550–670
Range ACT Composite	23–28

ACADEMICS
Student/faculty ratio	16:1
% students returning for sophomore year	91
% students graduating within 4 years	52
% students graduating within 6 years	79

Most classes have 20–29 students.
Most lab/discussion sessions have 20–29 students.

PROGRAMS/SERVICES FOR STUDENTS WITH LEARNING DIFFERENCES

Disabilities need not preclude the achievement of goals and dreams. Rather, they mandate a greater level of creativity, commitment and a repertoire of compensatory techniques. The team of professionals at the RCPD is ready to assist students, employees and visitors with resources that create an environment of opportunity. We value full integration of persons with disabilities throughout the university mission, programs and services. We believe that persons with disabilities at MSU are as much in control of their educational/work experience as a person without a disability. Under the Americans with Disabilities Act and Section 504 of the Rehabilitation Act of 1973, individuals with disabilities are guaranteed certain protections and rights of equal access to programs and services. Documentation establishing the presence of a disability and explaining the nature and degree to which the disability affects major life activities including learning is essential for RCPD staff to accurately assess a condition and determine what accommodations would most effectively facilitate full participation at MSU. Students with disabilities must therefore provide medical/psychological documentation indicating the presence of a disability that substantially limits a major life activity. To aid the documentation process, RCPD offers guidelines and fillable forms below to facilitate provision of needed clarity and detail from treating professionals. Submission of these fillable forms or equivalent will speed the registration process.

ADMISSIONS

Freshman admission is based on: Academic performance in high school Strength and quality of curriculum Recent trends in academic performance Class rank Standardized test results English language proficiency for non-U.S. citizens or permanent resident

Additional Information

MSU Counseling Center offers free support groups and group counseling options for both undergraduate and graduate students: http:// counseling.msu.edu/student_services/group-counseling/

ADMISSIONS INFO FOR STUDENTS WITH LEARNING DIFFERENCES
SAT/ACT required: Yes
Interview required: No
Essay required: Not Applicable
Additional application required: Yes
Documentation required for:
 ASD: https://www.rcpd.msu.edu/services/asd Documentation of a disability must appear on official letterhead from a licensed medical or diagnostic professional and include a diagnosis, scope or degree of involvement, and summary of related functional limitations. RCPD provides a downloadable Autism Spectrum Disorders form that may be used by medical providers to document conditions.
Documentation submitted to: Support Program/Services
Special Ed. HS course work accepted: No
Separate application required for Programs/Services: No
Contact Information
Name of program or department: Resource Center for Persons with Disabilities
Telephone: 517-884-1900
Fax: 517-432-3191
Email: mjh@msu.edu

Michigan State University

GENERAL ADMISSIONS

Very important factors considered include: academic GPA, application essay, standardized test scores. *Important factors considered include:* rigor of secondary school record, level of applicant's interest. *Other factors considered include:* class rank, extracurricular activities, talent/ability, character/personal qualities, first generation, geographical residence, state residency, volunteer work. *Freshman Admission Requirements:* High school diploma is required and GED is accepted. *Academic units required:* 4 English, 3 math, 3 science, 1 science lab, 2 foreign language, 3 social studies. *Academic units recommended:* 4 English, 4 math, 3 science, 1 science lab, 2 foreign language, 3 social studies.

ACCOMMODATIONS OR SERVICES

Accommodations are decided upon an individual basis after a thorough review of appropriate, current documentation. The accommodations requests must be supported through the documentation provided and must be logically linked to the current impact of the condition on academic functioning.

FINANCIAL AID

Students should submit: FAFSA. Applicants will be notified of awards on a rolling basis beginning 1/1. The Princeton Review suggests that all financial aid forms be submitted as soon as possible after October 1. *Need-based scholarships/grants offered:* College/university scholarship or grant aid from institutional funds; Federal Pell; Private scholarships; SEOG; State scholarships/grants; United Negro College Fund. *Loan aid offered:* Direct PLUS loans; Direct Subsidized Stafford Loans; Direct Unsubsidized Stafford Loans. Federal Work-Study Program available. Institutional employment available.

CAMPUS LIFE

Activities: Campus Ministries; Choral groups; Concert band; Dance; Drama/theater; International Student Organization; Jazz band; Literary magazine; Marching band; Model UN; Music ensembles; Musical theater; Opera; Pep band; Radio station; Student government; Student newspaper; Student-run film society; Symphony orchestra; Television station; Yearbook. **Organizations:** 500 registered organizations, 47 honor societies, 50 religious organizations. 31 fraternities, 19 sororities. **Athletics (Intercollegiate):** *Men:* baseball, basketball, cheerleading, cross-country, diving, football, golf, ice hockey, soccer, swimming, tennis, track/field (outdoor), track/field (indoor), wrestling. *Women:* basketball, cheerleading, crew/rowing, cross-country, diving, field hockey, golf, gymnastics, soccer, softball, swimming, tennis, track/field (outdoor), track/field (indoor), volleyball. **On-Campus Highlights:** MSU Student Union, Jack Breslin Student Events Center, MSU Main Library and Cyber Cafe, International Center, Wharton Center for the Performing Arts.

ACCOMMODATIONS

Allowed in exams:	
Calculators	Yes
Dictionary	No
Computer	Yes
Spell-checker	Yes
Extended test time	Yes
Scribe	Yes
Proctors	Yes
Oral exams	Yes
Note-takers	Yes
Support services for students with	
LD	Yes
ADHD	Yes
ASD	Yes
Distraction-reduced environment	Yes
Recording of lecture allowed	Yes
Reading technology:	Yes
Audio books	Yes

Other assistive technologyhttps://www.rcpd. msu.edu/programs/learningtech: Technology and training in technology covers the following areas and more: Text-readers, use of electronic text (in-house e-book production), support with downloading both free and commercial text readers fo

Priority registration	Yes
Added costs for services:	
For LD:	No
For ADHD:	No
For ASD:	No
LD specialists	Yes
ADHD & ASD coaching	Yes
ASD specialists	Yes
Professional tutors	Yes
Peer tutors	Yes
Max. hours/week for services	2
How professors are notified of student approved accommodations	Student

COLLEGE GRADUATION REQUIREMENTS

Course waivers allowed	No
Course substitutions allowed	Yes

In what courses

In very rare cirucmstances, MSU will offer a course substitution process for a student with a disability who has repeatedly been unable to meet a math-related university requirement.

Michigan Technological University

1400 TOWNSEND DRIVE, HOUGHTON, MI 49931 • ADMISSIONS: 906-487-2335 • FAX: 906-487-2125

CAMPUS
Type of school	Public
Environment	Village
Support	CS

STUDENTS
Undergrad enrollment	5,854
% male/female	73/27
% from out of state	22
% frosh live on campus	93

FINANCIAL FACTS
Annual in-state tuition	$15,346
Annual out-of-state tuition	$33,426
Room and board	$10,756
Required fees	$300

GENERAL ADMISSIONS INFO
Priority deadline	1/15

Nonfall registration accepted. Admission may be deferred for a maximum of 1 year.

Range SAT EBRW	570–660
Range SAT Math	590–680
Range ACT Composite	25–30

ACADEMICS
Student/faculty ratio	12:1
% students returning for sophomore year	83
% students graduating within 4 years	28
% students graduating within 6 years	67

Most classes have 10–19 students.
Most lab/discussion sessions have fewer than 10 students.

PROGRAMS/SERVICES FOR STUDENTS WITH LEARNING DIFFERENCES

Accommodations are decided on an individual basis. Discussion with the student and a review of documentation are both part of the process that identifies the supports that are appropriate for the individual.

ADMISSIONS

Student Disability Services will work with any student who believes that their learning style, personal habits, or preparation are impacting their success. We are an academic, as well as a disability, support area.

Additional Information

Counseling Services offers support groups dependent on student interests and participation. Students run their own Autism Support group, The Spectrum Connection. Career Services works with Spectrum students on transitioning to careers.

ADMISSIONS INFO FOR STUDENTS WITH LEARNING DIFFERENCES

SAT/ACT required: Yes
Interview required: No
Essay required: Not Applicable
Additional application required: Not Applicable
Documentation required for:
  LD: We prefer current documentation prepared by a specialist qualified to make the diagnosis, with suggestions for appropriate academic supports.
  ADHD: We prefer current documentation prepared by a specialist qualified to make the diagnosis, with suggestions for appropriate academic supports.
  ASD: We prefer current documentation prepared by a specialist qualified to make the diagnosis, with suggestions for appropriate academic supports.
Documentation submitted to: Student Disability Services
Special Ed. HS course work accepted: Not Applicable
Separate application required for Programs/Services: No
Contact Information
Name of program or department: Student Disability Services
Telephone: 906-487-2212
Fax: 906-487-3060
Email: deanofstudents@mtu.edu

Michigan Technological University

GENERAL ADMISSIONS

Very important factors considered include: academic GPA, standardized test scores. *Important factors considered include:* rigor of secondary school record. *Other factors considered include:* class rank, application essay, recommendation(s), extracurricular activities, talent/ability, character/ personal qualities, volunteer work. *Freshman Admission Requirements:* High school diploma is required and GED is accepted. *Academic units required:* 3 English, 3 math, 2 science. *Academic units recommended:* 4 English, 4 math, 3 science, 2 foreign language, 3 social studies, 2 academic electives, 1 computer science.

ACCOMMODATIONS OR SERVICES

Accommodations are decided upon an individual basis after a thorough review of appropriate, current documentation. The accommodations requests must be supported through the documentation provided and must be logically linked to the current impact of the condition on academic functioning.

FINANCIAL AID

Students should submit: FAFSA. Applicants will be notified of awards on a rolling basis beginning 2/1. The Princeton Review suggests that all financial aid forms be submitted as soon as possible after October 1. *Need-based scholarships/grants offered:* College/university scholarship or grant aid from institutional funds; Federal Pell; Private scholarships; SEOG; State scholarships/grants. *Loan aid offered:* Direct PLUS loans; Direct Subsidized Stafford Loans; Direct Unsubsidized Stafford Loans. Federal Work-Study Program available. Institutional employment available.

CAMPUS LIFE

Activities: Campus Ministries; Choral groups; Concert band; Dance; Drama/theater; International Student Organization; Jazz band; Literary magazine; Music ensembles; Musical theater; Pep band; Radio station; Student government; Student newspaper; Student-run film society; Symphony orchestra. **Organizations:** 210 registered organizations, 16 honor societies, 16 religious organizations. 13 fraternities, 8 sororities. **Athletics (Intercollegiate):** *Men:* basketball, cross-country, football, ice hockey, skiing (nordic/cross-country), tennis, track/field (outdoor). *Women:* basketball, cross-country, skiing (nordic/cross-country), tennis, track/field (outdoor), volleyball. **On-Campus Highlights:** Student Development Complex, Rozsa Center for the Performing Arts, Mont Ripley Ski Hill, Portage Lake Golf Course, Van Pelt and Opie Library.

ACCOMMODATIONS

Allowed in exams:

Calculators	Yes
Dictionary	Not Applicable
Computer	Yes
Spell-checker	Not Applicable
Extended test time	Yes
Scribe	Yes
Proctors	Yes
Oral exams	Not Applicable
Note-takers	Yes

Support services for students with

LD	Yes
ADHD	Yes
ASD	Yes
Distraction-reduced environment	Yes
Recording of lecture allowed	Yes
Reading technology:	Yes
Audio books	Yes

Other assistive technology: We have provided personal FM hearing loop units, Pulse Pens, duplicate note-taking books, and other supports as appropriate.

Priority registration	Yes

Added costs for services:

For LD:	No
For ADHD:	No
For ASD:	No
LD specialists	Yes
ADHD & ASD coaching	Yes
ASD specialists	Yes
Professional tutors	Yes
Peer tutors	Yes
Max. hours/week for services	Varies

How professors are notified of student approved accommodations
Director and Student

COLLEGE GRADUATION REQUIREMENTS

Course waivers allowed	No
Course substitutions allowed	No

Northern Michigan University

1401 Presque Isle Avenue, Marquette, MI 49855 • Admissions: 906-227-2650 • Fax: 906-227-1747

CAMPUS
Type of school	Public
Environment	Village
Support	S

STUDENTS
Undergrad enrollment	6,618
% male/female	46/54
% from out of state	19
% frosh live on campus	81

FINANCIAL FACTS
Annual in-state tuition	$9,528
Annual out-of-state tuition	$15,024
Room and board	$10,328
Required fees	$712

GENERAL ADMISSIONS INFO
Application fee	$35

Nonfall registration accepted. Admission may be deferred for a maximum of 1 year.

Range SAT EBRW	480–590
Range SAT Math	460–560
Range ACT Composite	20–26

ACADEMICS
Student/faculty ratio	20:1
% students returning for sophomore year	78
% students graduating within 4 years	27
% students graduating within 6 years	53

Most classes have 10–19 students.

PROGRAMS/SERVICES FOR STUDENTS WITH LEARNING DIFFERENCES

Disability Services (DS) provides services and accommodations to all students with disabilities. The goal of DS is to meet the individual needs of students. Student Support Services is a multifaceted educational support project designed to assist students in completing their academic programs at NMU. The Student Support Services professional staff, peer tutors, mentors, and peer advisors provide program participants with individualized attention. Disability Services provides assistance and accommodations to students who have documented disabilities. Accommodation request are reviewed on an individual basis. Student are required to complete the Application for DS; provide appropriate documentation, which includes a diagnosis, symptoms of the disability, test scores and data that support the diagnosis, and recommendations regarding classroom accommodations; and schedule an appointment with the Disability Coordinator. Students with ADHD must provide appropriate documentation through a written report submitted by a medical doctor, psychiatrist, psychologist, counselor, or school psychologist to receive appropriate accommodations.

ADMISSIONS

There are no special admissions for students with learning disabilities. All students submit the same general application and are expected to have an ACT of 19 or higher and a high school GPA of at least 2.25. There are no specific high school courses required for admissions, though the university recommends 4 years English, 4 years math, 3 years history/social studies, 3 years science, 3 years foreign language, 2 years fine or performing arts, and 1 year computer instruction. Applicants not meeting all of the criteria will be fully considered by the Admission Review Committee. Applicants may be asked to take a preadmission test or supply further information.

ADMISSIONS INFO FOR STUDENTS WITH LEARNING DIFFERENCES

SAT/ACT required: No
Interview required: No
Essay required: No
Additional application required: No
Documentation required for:
  LD: Psycho ed evaluation
  ADHD: Diagnosis based on DSM-V; history of behaviors impairing functioning in academic setting; diagnostic interview; history of symptoms; evidence of ongoing behaviors.
  ASD: Psycho ed evaluation
Documentation submitted to: Disability Services
Special Ed. HS course work accepted: Yes
Separate application required for Programs/Services: No
Contact Information
Name of program or department: Disability Services
Telephone: 906-227-1700
Fax: 906-227-1714

Northern Michigan University

Additional Information

The coordinator of DS works one-on-one with students as needed, and will also meet with students who do not have specific documentation if they request assistance. Skill classes are offered in reading, writing, math, study skills, sociocultural development, and interpersonal growth. No course waivers are granted for graduation requirements from NMU. Substitutions, however, are granted when appropriate. Student Support Services provides each student with an individual program of educational support services, including academic advising; basic skill building in reading, math, and writing; counseling; career advisement; developmental skill building; mentoring; support groups and study groups; tutoring from paraprofessionals; specialized tutors; group tutoring or supplemental instruction; and workshops on personal development and study skills improvement.

General Admissions

Very important factors considered include: academic GPA, standardized test scores. *Freshman Admission Requirements:* High school diploma is required and GED is accepted. *Academic units recommended:* 4 English, 4 math, 4 science, 2 foreign language, 4 social studies.

Accommodations or Services

Accommodations are decided upon an individual basis after a thorough review of appropriate, current documentation. The accommodations requests must be supported through the documentation provided and must be logically linked to the current impact of the condition on academic functioning.

Financial Aid

Students should submit: FAFSA. Applicants will be notified of awards on a rolling basis beginning 12/15. The Princeton Review suggests that all financial aid forms be submitted as soon as possible after October 1. *Need-based scholarships/grants offered:* College/university scholarship or grant aid from institutional funds; Federal Pell; Private scholarships; SEOG; State scholarships/grants. *Loan aid offered:* Direct PLUS loans; Direct Subsidized Stafford Loans; Direct Unsubsidized Stafford Loans. Federal Work-Study Program available. Institutional employment available.

Campus Life

Activities: Campus Ministries; Choral groups; Concert band; Dance; Drama/theater; International Student Organization; Jazz band; Literary magazine; Marching band; Model UN; Music ensembles; Musical theater; Opera; Pep band; Radio station; Student government; Student newspaper; Student-run film society; Symphony orchestra; Television station. **Organizations:** 308 registered organizations, 11 honor societies, 19 religious organizations. 3 fraternities, 4 sororities. **Athletics (Intercollegiate):** *Men:* basketball, football, golf, ice hockey, skiing (nordic/cross-country) *Women:* basketball, cross-country, diving, skiing (nordic/cross-country), soccer, swimming, track/field (outdoor), track/field (indoor), volleyball. **On-Campus Highlights:** Hedgcock Student Service Center, Superior Dome, New Science Facility, Market Place Dining Facility, De Vos Art Galleries.

ACCOMMODATIONS

Allowed in exams:	
Calculators	Yes
Dictionary	Yes
Computer	Yes
Spell-checker	Yes
Extended test time	Yes
Scribe	Yes
Proctors	Yes
Oral exams	Yes
Note-takers	Yes
Support services for students with	
LD	Yes
ADHD	Yes
ASD	Yes
Distraction-reduced environment	Yes
Recording of lecture allowed	Yes
Reading technology:	No
Audio books	Yes
Other assistive technology	Yes
Priority registration	No
Added costs for services:	
For LD:	No
For ADHD:	No
For ASD:	No
LD specialists	No
ADHD & ASD coaching	No
ASD specialists	No
Professional tutors	No
Peer tutors	Yes
Max. hours/week for services	2-4
How professors are notified of student approved accommodations	Student

COLLEGE GRADUATION REQUIREMENTS

Course waivers allowed	No
Course substitutions allowed	Yes
In what courses	

Substitutions permitted to fulfill graduation requirements with appropriate documentation.

University of Michigan—Ann Arbor

500 S. State St., Ann Arbor, MI 48109-1316 • Admissions: 734-764-7433 • Fax: 734-936-0740

CAMPUS

Type of school	Public
Environment	City
Support	CS

STUDENTS

Undergrad enrollment	29,550
% male/female	50/50
% from out of state	41
% frosh live on campus	98

FINANCIAL FACTS

Annual in-state tuition	$14,934
Annual out-of-state tuition	$49,022
Room and board	$11,534
Required fees	$328

GENERAL ADMISSIONS INFO

Application fee	$75
Priority deadline	11/1
Regular application deadline	2/1

Nonfall registration accepted. Admission may be deferred for a maximum of 1 year.

Range SAT EBRW	660–730
Range SAT Math	670–770
Range ACT Composite	30–33

ACADEMICS

Student/faculty ratio	15:1
% students returning for sophomore year	97
% students graduating within 4 years	77
% students graduating within 6 years	92

Most classes have 10–19 students. Most lab/discussion sessions have 10–19 students.

PROGRAMS/SERVICES FOR STUDENTS WITH LEARNING DIFFERENCES

The philosophy of Services for Students with Disabilities (SSD) is based on the legal actions described in Section 504 of the Rehabilitation Act of 1973. SSD services are dependent on self-advocacy of the students and are "non-intrusive," giving the students the responsibility to seek out assistance. SSD offers selected student services that are not provided by other University of Michigan offices or outside organizations. SSD assists students in negotiating disability-related barriers to the pursuit of their education; strives to improve access to university programs, activities, and facilities; and promotes increased awareness of disability issues on campus. SSD encourages inquiries for information and will confidentially discuss concerns.

ADMISSIONS

Students with learning disabilities are expected to meet the same admission requirements as their peers. There is no set minimum GPA as it is contingent on several other factors. For students with learning disabilities, the admissions office will accept letters of recommendation from LD specialists. When applying for admission to the University of Michigan, students with learning disabilities are encouraged to self-identify on the application form or by writing a cover letter.

Additional Information

Academic Coaching is available to students with learning disabilities through SSD. Academic Coaching is a working partnership that focuses on the 'process of learning.' Together with a professional coach, students examine their learning styles, habits of working, and current difficulties or barriers to success. Then together this team (coach and student) works to create and put in place more effective strategies than are the norm. The aim is to heighten awareness of what it takes to achieve academic success and anchor this with new strategies, a supportive relationship, and personal accountability.

ADMISSIONS INFO FOR STUDENTS WITH LEARNING DIFFERENCES

SAT/ACT required: Yes
Interview required: No
Essay required: Not Applicable
Additional application required: No
Documentation required for:
  LD: Psycho ed evaluation
  ADHD: Psycho ed evaluation
  ASD: Psycho ed evaluation
Documentation submitted to: Services for Students with Disabilities
Special Ed. HS course work accepted: No
Separate application required for Programs/Services: No
Contact Information
Name of program or department: Services for Students with Disabilities
Telephone: 734-763-3000
Fax: 734-936-3947
Email: sssegal@umich.edu

University of Michigan–Ann Arbor

GENERAL ADMISSIONS

Very important factors considered include: rigor of secondary school record, academic GPA. *Important factors considered include:* application essay, standardized test scores, recommendation(s), character/personal qualities, first generation. *Other factors considered include:* extracurricular activities, talent/ability, alumni/ae relation, geographical residence, state residency, volunteer work, work experience, level of applicant's interest. *Freshman Admission Requirements:* High school diploma is required and GED is accepted. *Academic units required:* 4 English, 3 math, 3 science, 1 science lab, 2 foreign language, 1 social studies, 3 history. *Academic units recommended:* 4 English, 4 math, 4 science, 1 science lab, 4 foreign language, 1 social studies, 3 history, 1 computer science, 2 visual/performing arts.

ACCOMMODATIONS OR SERVICES

Accommodations are decided upon an individual basis after a thorough review of appropriate, current documentation. The accommodations requests must be supported through the documentation provided and must be logically linked to the current impact of the condition on academic functioning.

FINANCIAL AID

Students should submit: CSS/Financial Aid PROFILE; FAFSA. Applicants will be notified of awards on a rolling basis beginning 3/15. The Princeton Review suggests that all financial aid forms be submitted as soon as possible after October 1. *Need-based scholarships/grants offered:* College/university scholarship or grant aid from institutional funds; Federal Pell; Private scholarships; SEOG; State scholarships/grants. *Loan aid offered:* Direct PLUS loans; Direct Subsidized Stafford Loans; Direct Unsubsidized Stafford Loans. Federal Work-Study Program available. Institutional employment available.

CAMPUS LIFE

Activities: Campus Ministries; Choral groups; Concert band; Dance; Drama/theater; International Student Organization; Jazz band; Literary magazine; Marching band; Model UN; Music ensembles; Musical theater; Opera; Pep band; Radio station; Student government; Student newspaper; Student-run film society; Symphony orchestra; Television station; Yearbook. **Organizations:** 1000 registered organizations, 13 honor societies, 67 religious organizations. 39 fraternities, 27 sororities. **Athletics (Intercollegiate):** *Men:* baseball, basketball, cheerleading, cross-country, diving, football, golf, gymnastics, ice hockey, swimming, tennis, track/field (outdoor), track/field (indoor), wrestling. *Women:* basketball, cheerleading, crew/rowing, cross-country, diving, field hockey, golf, gymnastics, soccer, softball, swimming, tennis, track/field (outdoor), track/field (indoor), volleyball, water polo. **On-Campus Highlights:** Michigan Stadium, Michigan Union, Diag, Campus Recreation Buildings, Wave Field.

ACCOMMODATIONS

Allowed in exams:

Calculators	Yes
Dictionary	Yes
Computer	Yes
Spell-checker	Yes
Extended test time	Yes
Scribe	Yes
Proctors	No
Oral exams	No
Note-takers	Yes

Support services for students with

LD	Yes
ADHD	Yes
ASD	Yes
Distraction-reduced environment	Yes
Recording of lecture allowed	Yes
Reading technology:	Yes
Audio books	No
Other assistive technology	Yes
Priority registration	No

Added costs for services:

For LD:	No
For ADHD:	No
For ASD:	No
LD specialists	Yes
ADHD & ASD coaching	No
ASD specialists	No
Professional tutors	Yes
Peer tutors	Yes
Max. hours/week for services	Varies
How professors are notified of student approved accommodations	Student

COLLEGE GRADUATION REQUIREMENTS

Course waivers allowed	No
Course substitutions allowed	No

Augsburg College

2211 Riverside Avenue, Minneapolis, MN 55454 • Admissions: 612-330-1001 • Fax: 612-330-1590

CAMPUS
Type of school	Private (nonprofit)
Environment	Metropolis
Support	SP

STUDENTS
Undergrad enrollment	3,014
% male/female	45/55
% from out of state	13
% frosh live on campus	82

FINANCIAL FACTS
Annual tuition	$29,794
Room and board	$8,072
Required fees	$624

GENERAL ADMISSIONS INFO
Application fee	$25
Priority deadline	5/1
Regular application deadline	8/15

Nonfall registration accepted. Admission may be deferred for a maximum of 2 years.

Range SAT EBRW	510–640
Range SAT Math	500–640
Range ACT Composite	19–25

ACADEMICS
Student/faculty ratio	16:1
% students returning for sophomore year	83

Most classes have 10–19 students.

PROGRAMS/SERVICES FOR STUDENTS WITH LEARNING DIFFERENCES

CLASS illustrates its commitment to student success at Augsburg College by providing those academic services needed to accommodate individuals with learning, attentional, psychiatric or other cognitive-based disabilities, as well as students with physical disabilities and other health concerns including temporary disabilities. The foundation of CLASS, however, is deeply rooted in the promotion of student independence and the personal realization of one's full potential. Augsburg students who are eligible to receive CLASS services, once admitted, will work one-on-one with a CLASS Disability Specialist. The Specialist will work to provide academic guidance and service-related assistance whenever appropriate. No additional or supplemental fee is required for CLASS services.

ADMISSIONS

Students with disabilities are evaluated for admission to Augsburg College according to the same criteria and standards as other applicants. Once admitted to the college, students with disabilities complete the same General Education Core Curriculum and must meet the same essential course requirements (with or without reasonable academic accommodations) as students without disabilities. Students do not need to disclose their learning difference to Admissions, and it is not taken into consideration in admission decisions. Any documentation of a learning disability should be sent directly to CLASS and not included with the application to the college.

Additional Information

To establish eligibility for services students must submit appropriate documentation for a cognitive-related disability that usually includes a current psychological, psycho-educational or neuro-psychological evaluation. In some cases, they may ask for a treating clinician to complete and return the Verification of Disability form as a supplement to other documentation. If a student has an Autism Spectrum Disorder they should fill out and return the PDD questionnaire in an effort to identify how the

ADMISSIONS INFO FOR STUDENTS WITH LEARNING DIFFERENCES

SAT/ACT required: Yes
Interview required: Yes
Essay required: N/A
Additional application required: No
Documentation required for:
 LD: Psycho ed evaluation
 ADHD: Diagnosis based on DSM-V; history of behaviors impairing functioning in academic setting; diagnostic interview; history of symptoms; evidence of ongoing behaviors.
 ASD: Psycho ed evaluation
Documentation submitted to: CLASS
Special Ed. HS course work accepted: N/A
Separate application required for Programs/Services: Yes
Contact Information
Name of program or department: Center for Learning and Adaptive Student Services (CLASS)
Telephone: 612-330-1053
Fax: 612-330-1137

Augsburg College

Pervasive Developmental Disorder diagnosis is currently and uniquely impacting the student. Students do not need to wait until they have been accepted to the college before determining their eligibility for CLASS services. They will review documentation for any prospective student who has applied for admission to Augsburg and will contact students about their eligibility once they have reviewed the documentation.

GENERAL ADMISSIONS

Very important factors considered include: rigor of secondary school record, class rank, academic GPA, application essay, recommendation(s). *Important factors considered include:* standardized test scores, extracurricular activities, alumni/ae relation, level of applicant's interest. *Other factors considered include:* interview, talent/ability, first generation, volunteer work, work experience. *Freshman Admission Requirements:* High school diploma is required and GED is accepted. *Academic units required:* 4 English, 3 math, 3 science, 2 foreign language, 2 social studies. *Academic units recommended:* 4 social studies, 2 history.

ACCOMMODATIONS OR SERVICES

Accommodations are decided upon an individual basis after a thorough review of appropriate, current documentation. The accommodations requests must be supported through the documentation provided and must be logically linked to the current impact of the condition on academic functioning.

FINANCIAL AID

Students should submit: FAFSA. Applicants will be notified of awards on a rolling basis beginning 3/1. The Princeton Review suggests that all financial aid forms be submitted as soon as possible after October 1. *Need-based scholarships/grants offered:* College/university scholarship or grant aid from institutional funds; Federal Pell; Private scholarships; SEOG; State scholarships/grants. *Loan aid offered:* Direct PLUS loans; Direct Subsidized Stafford Loans; Direct Unsubsidized Stafford Loans

CAMPUS LIFE

Activities: Campus Ministries; Choral groups; Concert band; Dance; Drama/theater; International Student Organization; Jazz band; Literary magazine; Music ensembles; Opera; Radio station; Student government; Student newspaper; Yearbook. **Organizations:** 35 registered organizations, 1 honor society, 1 religious organization. **Athletics (Intercollegiate):** *Men:* baseball, basketball, cross-country, football, golf, ice hockey, soccer, tennis, track/field (outdoor), track/field (indoor), wrestling. *Women:* basketball, cheerleading, cross-country, golf, ice hockey, soccer, softball, swimming, tennis, track/field (outdoor), track/field (indoor), volleyball. **On-Campus Highlights:** Christensen Center/Starbucks Coffee Shop, Si Melby Athletic Fieldhouse, Lindell Library, Foss Center/Atrium, Gateway Center.

ACCOMMODATIONS

Allowed in exams:	
Calculators	Yes
Dictionary	Yes
Computer	Yes
Spell-checker	Yes
Extended test time	Yes
Scribe	Yes
Proctors	Yes
Oral exams	Yes
Note-takers	Yes
Support services for students with	
LD	Yes
ADHD	Yes
ASD	Yes
Distraction-reduced environment	Yes
Recording of lecture allowed	Yes
Reading technology:	Yes
Audio books	Some available
Other assistive technology	Yes
Priority registration	No
Added costs for services:	
For LD:	No
For ADHD:	No
For ASD:	No
LD specialists	Yes
ADHD & ASD coaching	No
ASD specialists	No
Professional tutors	No
Peer tutors	Yes
Max. hours/week for services	Varies
How professors are notified of student approved accommodations	Student

COLLEGE GRADUATION REQUIREMENTS

Course waivers allowed	No
Course substitutions allowed	Yes
In what courses	Foreign Language

Minnesota State University Moorhead

1104 SEVENTH AVENUE SOUTH, MOORHEAD, MN 56563 • ADMISSIONS: 218-477-2161 • FAX: 218-477-4374

CAMPUS
Type of school	Public
Environment	City
Support	S

STUDENTS
Undergrad enrollment	5,025
% male/female	40/60
% from out of state	33
% frosh live on campus	91

FINANCIAL FACTS
Annual in-state tuition	$7,410
Annual out-of-state tuition	$14,820
Room and board	$9,280
Required fees	$1,086

GENERAL ADMISSIONS INFO
Application fee	$20.
Regular application deadline	6/15

Nonfall registration accepted. Admission may be deferred for a maximum of one semester.

Range SAT EBRW	445–520
Range SAT Math	480–570
Range ACT Composite	20–25

ACADEMICS
Student/faculty ratio	17:1
% students returning for sophomore year	73

Most classes have 10–19 students.
Most lab/discussion sessions have 20–29 students.

PROGRAMS/SERVICES FOR STUDENTS WITH LEARNING DIFFERENCES
The university is committed to ensuring that all students have equal access to programs and services. The Disability Resource Center (DRC) addresses the needs of students who have disabilities. The purpose of the DRC is to provide services and accommodations to students with documented disabilities, work closely with faculty and staff in an advisory capacity, assist in the development of reasonable accommodations for students, and provide equal access for otherwise qualified individuals with disabilities. A student with a documented learning disability may be eligible for services. DRC will assist in the development of reasonable accommodations for students with disabilities. To be eligible to receive services, students must provide appropriate documentation. This documentation should identify the nature and extent of the disability and provide information on the functional limitations as related to the academic environment. The documentation should provide recommended reasonable accommodations. Requests that would alter the academic standards are not granted. Students are responsible for monitoring their progress with faculty, requesting assistance, and meeting university standards.

ADMISSIONS
To be automatically admitted to Minnesota State University Moorhead, you must have graduated from high school or earned a GED and meet the following requirements: An ACT (preferred) composite score of 21 or SAT score of 1000 or above in Critical Reading and Math SAT admissions tests, or rank in the top 50% of your high school graduating class AND achieve a minimum score of 17 on the ACT or 830 on the SAT (Critical Reading and Math). If you are interested in MSU Moorhead and do not meet the above requirements, you are still encouraged to apply. Applications are reviewed based on such factors as strength of college preparation coursework, grade point average, academic progression, class rank, test scores, and probability of success. Additional information may be requested to help facilitate an admission decision. Visit msum.com for more information.

ADMISSIONS INFO FOR STUDENTS WITH LEARNING DIFFERENCES
SAT/ACT required: Yes
Interview required: No
Essay required: No
Additional application required: No
Documentation required for:
 LD: Psycho ed evaluation
 ADHD: Diagnosis based on DSM-V; history of behaviors impairing functioning in academic setting; diagnostic interview; history of symptoms; evidence of ongoing behaviors.
 ASD: Psycho ed evaluation
Documentation submitted to: Director, Disability Services
Special Ed. HS course work accepted: Yes
Separate application required for Programs/Services: Yes
Contact Information
Name of program or department: Disability Services
Telephone: 218-477-4318
Fax: 218-477-2420

Minnesota State University Moorhead

Additional Information

Examples of general accommodations or services include the following: extended test times, reduced distraction testing environments, taped texts, note-taking, assistive technology, scribes, readers, tape-recording lectures, faculty liaisons, strategy development, priority registration, and individual support. Study skills courses are offered and students may earn credits for these courses. Services and accommodations are available for undergraduate and graduate students.

GENERAL ADMISSIONS

Very important factors considered include: class rank, academic GPA, standardized test scores. *Other factors considered include:* rigor of secondary school record, application essay, recommendation(s). *Freshman Admission Requirements:* High school diploma is required and GED is accepted. *Academic units required:* 4 English, 3 math, 3 science, 1 science lab, 2 foreign language, 3 social studies, and 1 unit from above areas or other academic areas.

ACCOMMODATIONS OR SERVICES

Accommodations are decided upon an individual basis after a thorough review of appropriate, current documentation. The accommodations requests must be supported through the documentation provided and must be logically linked to the current impact of the condition on academic functioning.

FINANCIAL AID

Students should submit: FAFSA; State aid form. The Princeton Review suggests that all financial aid forms be submitted as soon as possible after October 1. *Need-based scholarships/grants offered:* College/university scholarship or grant aid from institutional funds; Private scholarships; State scholarships/grants. *Loan aid offered:* Direct PLUS loans; Direct Subsidized Stafford Loans; Direct Unsubsidized Stafford Loans. Federal Work-Study Program available. Institutional employment available.

CAMPUS LIFE

Activities: Campus Ministries; Choral groups; Concert band; Dance; Drama/theater; International Student Organization; Jazz band; Literary magazine; Model UN; Music ensembles; Musical theater; Pep band; Radio station; Student government; Student newspaper; Student-run film society; Television station. **Organizations:** 109 registered organizations, 6 honor societies, 11 religious organizations. 2 sororities. **Athletics (Intercollegiate):** *Men:* basketball, cross-country, football, track/field (outdoor), track/field (indoor), wrestling. *Women:* basketball, cross-country, golf, soccer, softball, swimming, tennis, track/field (outdoor), track/field (indoor), volleyball. **On-Campus Highlights:** Underground Night Club, Comstock Memorial Student Union, Regional Science Center, Nemzek Athletic Complex, Planetarium.

ACCOMMODATIONS

Allowed in exams:	
Calculators	Yes
Dictionary	Yes
Computer	Yes
Spell-checker	Yes
Extended test time	Yes
Scribe	Yes
Proctors	Yes
Oral exams	Yes
Note-takers	Yes
Support services for students with	
LD	Yes
ADHD	Yes
ASD	Yes
Distraction-reduced environment	Yes
Recording of lecture allowed	Yes
Reading technology:	Yes
Audio books	Yes
Other assistive technology	Yes
Priority registration	Yes
Added costs for services:	
For LD:	No
For ADHD:	No
For ASD:	No
LD specialists	No
ADHD & ASD coaching	No
ASD specialists	No
Professional tutors	No
Peer tutors	Yes
Max. hours/week for services	1
How professors are notified of student approved accommodations	Student and Director

COLLEGE GRADUATION REQUIREMENTS

Course waivers allowed	Yes
In what courses	
Depends on the disability and requirements of the student's major	
Course substitutions allowed	Yes
In what courses	
Depends on the disability and requirements of the student's major	

St. Catherine University

2004 RANDOLPH AVENUE, SAINT PAUL, MN 55105 • ADMISSIONS: • FAX: 651-690-8868

CAMPUS
Type of school	Private (nonprofit)
Environment	Metropolis
Support	CS

STUDENTS
Undergrad enrollment	3,100
% male/female	3/97
% from out of state	12
% frosh live on campus	69

FINANCIAL FACTS
Annual tuition	$41,504
Room and board	$9,260
Required fees	$759

GENERAL ADMISSIONS INFO
Priority deadline	4/15

Nonfall registration accepted. Admission may be deferred for a maximum of 1 year.

Range SAT EBRW	530–665
Range SAT Math	510–645
Range ACT Composite	21–26

ACADEMICS
Student/faculty ratio	10:1
% students returning for sophomore year	81
% students graduating within 4 years	37
% students graduating within 6 years	58

Most classes have 20–29 students.

PROGRAMS/SERVICES FOR STUDENTS WITH LEARNING DIFFERENCES

St. Catherine University has two campuses where learning support is available. The Academic Success Center (Minneapolis Campus) provides a wide range of academic support. They offer individual and group tutoring, both online and in person with peer tutors and professional staff. The O'Neill Center for Academic Development (St. Paul campus) provides individual academic support through the Writing/Reading Center, the Math/Science Center, the Disability Resources Center and Student Mentors.

ADMISSIONS

There is no special admission procedure for students with learning disabilities, though the college tends to give special consideration if students self-disclose this information. Disclosure can help explain test scores, difficulties with certain course work, and so on. Saint Catherine University does not discriminate on the basis of disability in admission. A student may be accepted on a conditional basis, to a program which provides special advising, limited course lad and a course in strategies for success.

Additional Information

To access services, the student and Access Consultant discuss the anticipated demands of the courses for which the student is registered and develop accommodation letters. The letters identify the learning strategies and accommodations that will be used. For example, texts in alternative formats, testing accommodations, and note-takers are some of the more frequently offered accommodations. The specific nature of the disability is not addressed the student delivers the accommodation letters to her professors. Some students meet with Access Consultants on a weekly basis for timemanagement and study strategies. Within the O'Neill Center, a student may access assistance in writing, math and science courses.

ADMISSIONS INFO FOR STUDENTS WITH LEARNING DIFFERENCES

SAT/ACT required: Yes
Interview required: No
Essay required: Yes
Additional application required: No
Documentation required for:
  LD: Psycho ed evaluation
  ADHD: Diagnosis based on DSM-V; history of behaviors impairing functioning in academic setting; diagnostic interview; history of symptoms; evidence of ongoing behaviors.
  ASD: Psycho ed evaluation
Documentation submitted to: O'Neill Learning Center
Special Ed. HS course work accepted: Yes
Separate application required for Programs/Services: No
Contact Information
Name of program or department: O'Neill Learning Center
Telephone: 651-590-6563
Fax: 651-690-6718

St. Catherine University

GENERAL ADMISSIONS

Very important factors considered include: rigor of secondary school record. *Important factors considered include:* class rank, academic GPA, application essay, standardized test scores, recommendation(s). *Other factors considered include:* interview, first generation, level of applicant's interest. *Freshman Admission Requirements:* High school diploma is required and GED is accepted. *Academic units recommended:* 4 English, 3 math, 2 science, 4 foreign language, 2 social studies.

ACCOMMODATIONS OR SERVICES

Accommodations are decided upon an individual basis after a thorough review of appropriate, current documentation. The accommodations requests must be supported through the documentation provided and must be logically linked to the current impact of the condition on academic functioning.

FINANCIAL AID

Students should submit: FAFSA; Institution's own financial aid form. The Princeton Review suggests that all financial aid forms be submitted as soon as possible after October 1. *Need-based scholarships/grants offered:* College/university scholarship or grant aid from institutional funds; Federal Nursing Scholarships; Federal Pell; Private scholarships; SEOG; State scholarships/grants. *Loan aid offered:* Direct PLUS loans; Direct Subsidized Stafford Loans; Direct Unsubsidized Stafford Loans. Federal Work-Study Program available. Institutional employment available.

CAMPUS LIFE

Activities: Campus Ministries; Choral groups; Dance; Drama/theater; International Student Organization; Literary magazine; Music ensembles; Musical theater; Radio station; Student government; Student newspaper. **Organizations:** 40 registered organizations, 24 honor societies, 4 religious organizations. 1 sorority. **Athletics (Intercollegiate):** *Women:* basketball, cross-country, diving, ice hockey, soccer, softball, swimming, tennis, track/field (outdoor), track/field (indoor), volleyball. **On-Campus Highlights:** Coeur de Catherine, English garden, Butler Center, Dew Drop Pond, Art Gallery.

ACCOMMODATIONS

Allowed in exams:	
Calculators	Yes
Dictionary	Yes
Computer	Yes
Spell-checker	Yes
Extended test time	Yes
Scribe	Yes
Proctors	Yes
Oral exams	Rarely
Note-takers	Yes
Support services for students with	
LD	Yes
ADHD	Yes
ASD	Yes
Distraction-reduced environment	Yes
Recording of lecture allowed	Yes
Reading technology:	Yes
Audio books	Yes
Other assistive technology	Yes
Priority registration	Yes
Added costs for services:	
For LD:	No
For ADHD:	No
For ASD:	No
LD specialists	Yes
ADHD & ASD coaching	No
ASD specialists	No
Professional tutors	No
Peer tutors	Yes
Max. hours/week for services	Unlimited
How professors are notified of student approved accommodations	Student and Director

COLLEGE GRADUATION REQUIREMENTS

Course waivers allowed	No
Course substitutions allowed	Yes
In what courses	Math, Foreign Language

St. Olaf College

1520 St. Olaf Avenue, Northfield, MN 55057 • Admissions: 507-786-3025 • Fax: 507-786-3832

CAMPUS

Type of school	Private (nonprofit)
Environment	Village
Support	S

STUDENTS

Undergrad enrollment	3,004
% male/female	42/58
% from out of state	53
% frosh live on campus	100

FINANCIAL FACTS

Annual tuition	$47,840
Room and board	$10,430
Required fees	NR

GENERAL ADMISSIONS INFO

Regular application deadline	1/15

Nonfall registration accepted. Admission may be deferred for a maximum of 1 year.

Range SAT EBRW	580–690
Range SAT Math	570–700
Range ACT Composite	25–31

ACADEMICS

Student/faculty ratio	12:1
% students returning for sophomore year	92
% students graduating within 4 years	85
% students graduating within 6 years	88

Most classes have 10–19 students.
Most lab/discussion sessions have 10–19 students.

PROGRAMS/SERVICES FOR STUDENTS WITH LEARNING DIFFERENCES

The goal of the services at St. Olaf is to provide equal access to a St. Olaf education for all students with disabilities. The purpose is to create and maintain an environment in which students may achieve their fullest potential, limited to the least extent possible by individual disabilities. All faculty, staff, and students of the college are expected to adhere to this philosophy of equal access to educational opportunity and assume broad responsibility for its implementation. In order to receive services through Student Disability Services, students must provide a clear statement of diagnosed disability.

ADMISSIONS

All applicants must meet the same competitive admission criteria. There is no separate application process for students with learning disabilities or attention deficit disorder. It's recommended that students have a strong academic curriculum. Once admitted, students with documented disabilities should have their current documentation sent to the Student Disability Services Office.

Additional Information

Academic Coaching is available and offered free of charge for students who wish to learn more about managing time, learning styles and strategies, study skills or strategies, accountability, test-taking strategies, test-taking anxiety, note taking strategies, and more.

ADMISSIONS INFO FOR STUDENTS WITH LEARNING DIFFERENCES

SAT/ACT required: Yes
Interview required: N/A
Essay required: N/A
Additional application required: No
Documentation required for:
  LD: Clear statement of diagnosed disability with results from appropriate assessment instruments. Student Disability Services will work individually with students to determine whether documentation presented is sufficient.
  ADHD: Same documentation required for LD.
  ASD: Psycho ed evaluation
Documentation submitted to: Academic Support Center: Disability and Access
Special Ed. HS course work accepted: N/A
Separate application required for Programs/Services: No
Contact Information
Name of program or department: Academic Support Center: Disability and Access
Telephone: 507-786-3385
Email: glampe@stolaf.edu

St. Olaf College

GENERAL ADMISSIONS
Very important factors considered include: rigor of secondary school record, academic GPA, application essay. *Important factors considered include:* class rank, standardized test scores, recommendation(s), interview, extracurricular activities, talent/ability, character/personal qualities. *Other factors considered include:* first generation, alumni/ae relation, geographical residence, state residency, religious affiliation/commitment, racial/ethnic status, volunteer work, work experience, level of applicant's interest. *Freshman Admission Requirements:* High school diploma is required and GED is accepted. *Academic units recommended:* 4 English, 4 math, 4 science, 2 science labs, 4 foreign language, 4 social studies.

ACCOMMODATIONS OR SERVICES
Accommodations are decided upon an individual basis after a thorough review of appropriate, current documentation. The accommodations requests must be supported through the documentation provided and must be logically linked to the current impact of the condition on academic functioning.

FINANCIAL AID
Students should submit: CSS/Financial Aid PROFILE; FAFSA; Noncustodial PROFILE. Applicants will be notified of awards on or about 4/1. The Princeton Review suggests that all financial aid forms be submitted as soon as possible after October 1. *Need-based scholarships/grants offered:* College/university scholarship or grant aid from institutional funds; Federal Pell; Private scholarships; SEOG; State scholarships/grants. *Loan aid offered:* Direct PLUS loans; Direct Subsidized Stafford Loans; Direct Unsubsidized Stafford Loans. Federal Work-Study Program available. Institutional employment available.

CAMPUS LIFE
Activities: Campus Ministries; Choral groups; Concert band; Dance; Drama/theater; International Student Organization; Jazz band; Literary magazine; Model UN; Music ensembles; Musical theater; Opera; Pep band; Radio station; Student government; Student newspaper; Student-run film society; Symphony orchestra. **Organizations:** 193 registered organizations, 18 honor societies, 16 religious organizations. **Athletics (Intercollegiate):** *Men:* baseball, basketball, cross-country, diving, football, golf, ice hockey, skiing (downhill/alpine), skiing (nordic/cross-country), soccer, swimming, tennis, track/field (outdoor), track/field (indoor), wrestling. *Women:* basketball, cross-country, diving, golf, ice hockey, skiing (downhill/alpine), skiing (nordic/cross-country), soccer, softball, swimming, tennis, track/field (outdoor), track/field (indoor), volleyball. **On-Campus Highlights:** Fireside Lounge, Buntrock Commons, The Lion's Pause (student-run nightclub), Tostrud Recreation Center.

ACCOMMODATIONS

Allowed in exams:	
Calculators	Yes
Dictionary	Yes
Computer	Yes
Spell-checker	Yes
Extended test time	Yes
Scribe	Yes
Proctors	N/A
Oral exams	Yes
Note-takers	Yes
Support services for students with	
LD	Yes
ADHD	Yes
ASD	Yes
Distraction-reduced environment	Yes
Recording of lecture allowed	Yes
Reading technology:	Yes
Audio books	Yes
Other assistive technology	Yes
Priority registration	Yes
Added costs for services:	
For LD:	No
For ADHD:	No
For ASD:	No
LD specialists	No
ADHD & ASD coaching	No
ASD specialists	No
Professional tutors	No
Peer tutors	Yes
Max. hours/week for services	none
How professors are notified of student approved accommodations	Student

COLLEGE GRADUATION REQUIREMENTS

Course waivers allowed	No
Course substitutions allowed	Yes
In what courses	

Alternatives are rarely considered. A subcommittee must recommend substitutions and a faculty committee makes the decision. Most often a student is required to try a language with support from department, tutors, labs and study groups first.

University of Minnesota, Morris

600 E 4TH ST, MORRIS, MN 56267 • ADMISSIONS: 320-589-6035 • FAX: 320-589-6051

CAMPUS

Type of school	Public
Environment	Rural
Support	S

STUDENTS

Undergrad enrollment	1,552
% male/female	44/56
% from out of state	17
% frosh live on campus	95

FINANCIAL FACTS

Annual in-state tuition	$12,142
Annual out-of-state tuition	$14,170
Room and board	$8,342
Required fees	$1,172

GENERAL ADMISSIONS INFO

Application fee	$35
Priority deadline	12/15
Regular application deadline	3/15

Nonfall registration accepted. Admission may be deferred for a maximum of 1 year.

Range SAT EBRW	560–680
Range SAT Math	590–710
Range ACT Composite	22–28

ACADEMICS

Student/faculty ratio	11:1
% students returning for sophomore year	80
% students graduating within 4 years	50
% students graduating within 6 years	59

Most classes have 10–19 students.
Most lab/discussion sessions have 10–19 students.

PROGRAMS/SERVICES FOR STUDENTS WITH LEARNING DIFFERENCES

The Disability Resource Center (DRC) promotes access and equity for all students, faculty, staff, and guests of the University of Minnesota Morris. Our mission is Facilitating Access, and our goal is to maintain an environment where everyone is treated in a respectful manner. Documentation is confidential information from an appropriately qualified health or other service professional who is knowledgeable about the student's condition. This professional might be a therapist, doctor, rehabilitation counselor, audiologist, nurse practitioner, or mobility specialist. Documentation can vary in length and format, but should focus on the ways the condition currently affects the student, especially in an academic environment. The DRC Coordinator uses documentation to better understand a student's experience of their condition, identify impacts in an academic setting, and make informed decisions to determine reasonable and appropriate accommodations. When additional information is needed to determine accommodations, the DRC Coordinator can help the student obtain what is necessary, which may require the student to sign a release of information for current providers. If the student is not working with a provider, the Coordinator can provide referral information to the student. Students are responsible for the cost of assessments and appointments with providers.

ADMISSIONS

ACT/SAT writing test results, recommendations, interview, evidence of exceptional achievement, aptitude, or personal accomplishment not reflected in the academic record or standardized test scores, evidence of exceptional talent or ability in artistic, scholarly, leadership, or athletic performance, evidence that enrollment would enhance the cultural, gender, age, economic, racial, or geographic diversity of the student body, evidence of exceptional motivation, maturity, or responsibility, community involvement, work, or overcome barriers.

ADMISSIONS INFO FOR STUDENTS WITH LEARNING DIFFERENCES

SAT/ACT required: Yes
Interview required: No
Essay required: Not Applicable
Additional application required: Yes
Documentation required for:
  LD: N/A
  ADHD: N/A
  ASD: N/A
Documentation submitted to: Disability Resource Center
Special Ed. HS course work accepted: Yes
Separate application required for Programs/Services: For ASD.
Contact Information
Name of program or department: Disability Resource Center
Telephone: 320-589-6163
Fax: 320-589-6473
Email: hoekstra@morris.umn.edu

University of Minnesota, Morris

Additional Information

Students are encouraged to contact the DRC as early as possible to discuss reasonable accommodations or services. The DRC Coordinator and students will discuss how the disability impacts academics and student life. Academic coaching offers students the opportunity to sit down one-on-one with a professional who specializes in helping students improve their academic performance. Services range from a one-time visit focusing on a specific study skill to ongoing meetings focusing on the creation and maintenance of an academic success plan.

General Admissions

Very important factors considered include: rigor of secondary school record, class rank, academic GPA, standardized test scores. *Important factors considered include:* extracurricular activities, talent/ability, character/personal qualities, volunteer work, work experience. *Other factors considered include:* application essay, recommendation(s), interview, first generation. *Freshman Admission Requirements:* High school diploma is required and GED is accepted. *Academic units required:* 4 English, 4 math, 3 science, 2 foreign language, 3 social studies.

Accommodations or Services

Accommodations are decided upon an individual basis after a thorough review of appropriate, current documentation. The accommodations requests must be supported through the documentation provided and must be logically linked to the current impact of the condition on academic functioning.

Financial Aid

Students should submit: FAFSA. Applicants will be notified of awards on a rolling basis beginning 4/1. The Princeton Review suggests that all financial aid forms be submitted as soon as possible after October 1. *Need-based scholarships/grants offered:* College/university scholarship or grant aid from institutional funds; Federal Pell; Private scholarships; SEOG; State scholarships/grants. *Loan aid offered:* Direct PLUS loans; Direct Subsidized Stafford Loans; Direct Unsubsidized Stafford Loans. Federal Work-Study Program available. Institutional employment available.

Campus Life

Activities: Campus Ministries; Choral groups; Concert band; Dance; Drama/theater; International Student Organization; Jazz band; Literary magazine; Music ensembles; Musical theater; Radio station; Student government; Student newspaper; Symphony orchestra. **Organizations:** 90 registered organizations, 5 honor societies, 12 religious organizations. **Athletics (Intercollegiate):** *Men:* baseball, basketball, football, golf, tennis, track/field (outdoor), track/field (indoor). *Women:* basketball, cross-country, diving, golf, soccer, softball, swimming, tennis, track/field (outdoor), track/field (indoor), volleyball. **On-Campus Highlights:** Student Center—KUMM, Turtle Mountain cafe', Regional Fitness Center—Indoor/Outdoor Center, pools, Science Center, Humanities Fine Arts Center—gallery, concerts, recitals, The Mall—outdoor grass/recreation area.

ACCOMMODATIONS

Allowed in exams:

Calculators	Yes
Dictionary	Yes
Computer	Yes
Spell-checker	Yes
Extended test time	Yes
Scribe	Yes
Proctors	Yes
Oral exams	Yes
Note-takers	Yes

Support services for students with

LD	Yes
ADHD	Yes
ASD	Yes
Distraction-reduced environment	Yes
Recording of lecture allowed	Yes
Reading technology:	Yes
Audio books	Yes
Other assistive technology	
Priority registration	Yes

Added costs for services:

For LD:	No
For ADHD:	No
For ASD:	No
LD specialists	No
ADHD & ASD coaching	Yes
ASD specialists	Yes
Professional tutors	Yes
Peer tutors	Yes
Max. hours/week for services	Varies
How professors are notified of student approved accommodations	
Director and Student	

COLLEGE GRADUATION REQUIREMENTS

Course waivers allowed	Yes

In what courses
Students may submit a petition for a waiver to be determined by a committee

Course substitutions allowed	Yes

In what courses
Students may submit a petition for a substitution to be determined by a committee

Winona State University

P.O. Box 5838, Winona, MN 55987 • Admissions: 507-457-5100 • Fax: 507-457-5620

CAMPUS
Type of school	Public
Environment	Town
Support	S

STUDENTS
Undergrad enrollment	7,280
% male/female	36/64
% from out of state	28
% frosh live on campus	92

FINANCIAL FACTS
Annual in-state tuition	$7,377
Annual out-of-state tuition	$13,298
Room and board	$8,066
Required fees	$2,004

GENERAL ADMISSIONS INFO
Application fee	$20.
Regular application deadline	7/1

Nonfall registration accepted. Admission may be deferred for a maximum of 1 year.

Range SAT EBRW	NR
Range SAT Math	NR
Range ACT Composite	20–25

ACADEMICS
Student/faculty ratio	18:1
% students returning for sophomore year	78
% students graduating within 4 years	38
% students graduating within 6 years	61

Most classes have 10–19 students.

PROGRAMS/SERVICES FOR STUDENTS WITH LEARNING DIFFERENCES
"Helping Students Succeed" is the motto of WSU's Access Services. Many academic resources are offered free of charge to qualified students. Examples of academic accommodations include but are not limited to extended time on exams, low distraction test environment and alternate format textbooks.

ADMISSIONS
Winona State University Admissions requirements: ACT score of 21 or better with class rank in top 2/3 of high school class or Top 50 percent of graduating class with an ACT score of 18, 19, or 20. Course requirements include: 4 years English, 3 years math, 3 years science, 3 years social studies, 2 years foreign language (American Sign Language is accepted), and 1 additional year of an elective. The student's academic transcript will be reviewed to see that they have completed the Minnesota State University Preparation Requirements. Admissions decisions are processed in 15 to 20 days.

Additional Information
More information about services available at "Getting Started" website at http://www.winona.edu/accessservices/gettingstarted.asp.

ADMISSIONS INFO FOR STUDENTS WITH LEARNING DIFFERENCES
SAT/ACT required: Yes
Interview required: Not Applicable
Essay required: Not Applicable
Additional application required: Yes
Documentation required for:
 LD: All students requesting academic accommodations are required to submit: 1) statement of the disability on the letterhead of a qualified professional; 2) statement of how the disability functionally limits him/her in the academic environment; 3) recommendations for specific accommodations and rationale for those recommendations
 ADHD: All students requesting academic accommodations are required to submit: 1) statement of the disability on the letterhead of a qualified professional; 2) statement of how the disability functionally limits him/her in the academic environment; 3) recommendations for specific accommodations and rationale for those recommendations
 ASD: All students requesting academic accommodations are required to submit: 1) statement of the disability on the letterhead of a qualified professional; 2) statement of how the disability functionally limits him/her in the academic environment; 3) recommendations for specific accommodations and rationale for those recommendations
Documentation submitted to: Access Services for Students with Disabilities
Special Ed. HS course work accepted: Not Applicable
Separate application required for Programs/Services: No
Contact Information
Name of program or department: Access Services for Students with Diabilities
Telephone: 507-457-5878
Fax: 507-457-2957
Email: access@winona.edu

Winona State University

GENERAL ADMISSIONS

Very important factors considered include: rigor of secondary school record, class rank, academic GPA, standardized test scores. *Freshman Admission Requirements:* High school diploma is required and GED is accepted. *Academic units required:* 4 English, 3 math, 3 science, 3 science labs, 2 foreign language, 2 social studies, 1 history, 1 academic elective.

ACCOMMODATIONS OR SERVICES

Accommodations are decided upon an individual basis after a thorough review of appropriate, current documentation. The accommodations requests must be supported through the documentation provided and must be logically linked to the current impact of the condition on academic functioning.

FINANCIAL AID

Students should submit: FAFSA. Applicants will be notified of awards on a rolling basis beginning 12/1. The Princeton Review suggests that all financial aid forms be submitted as soon as possible after October 1. *Need-based scholarships/grants offered:* College/university scholarship or grant aid from institutional funds; Federal Pell; Private scholarships; SEOG; State scholarships/grants. *Loan aid offered:* Direct PLUS loans; Direct Subsidized Stafford Loans; Direct Unsubsidized Stafford Loans. Federal Work-Study Program available. Institutional employment available.

CAMPUS LIFE

Activities: Campus Ministries; Choral groups; Concert band; Dance; Drama/theater; International Student Organization; Jazz band; Literary magazine; Model UN; Music ensembles; Musical theater; Pep band; Radio station; Student government; Student newspaper; Symphony orchestra. **Organizations:** 208 registered organizations, 14 honor societies, 10 religious organizations. 2 fraternities, 3 sororities. **Athletics (Intercollegiate):** *Men:* baseball, basketball, cross-country, football, golf *Women:* basketball, cross country, golf, gymnastics, soccer, softball, tennis, track/field (outdoor), track/field (indoor), volleyball. **On-Campus Highlights:** The Library, Lourdes Hall - Residential College, Central Courtyard/Clock Tower/Gazebo, The Smaug - Kryzsko Commons, Integrated Wellness Complex.

ACCOMMODATIONS

Allowed in exams:

Calculators	Yes
Dictionary	No
Computer	Yes
Spell-checker	Yes
Extended test time	Yes
Scribe	Yes
Proctors	Yes
Oral exams	Yes
Note-takers	Yes

Support services for students with

LD	Yes
ADHD	Yes
ASD	Yes
Distraction-reduced environment	Yes
Recording of lecture allowed	Yes
Reading technology:	Yes
Audio books	Yes
Other assistive technology	Natural Reader, SmartPens, Mac Reader
Priority registration	Yes

Added costs for services:

For LD:	No
For ADHD:	No
For ASD:	No
LD specialists	No
ADHD & ASD coaching	No
ASD specialists	No
Professional tutors	Yes
Peer tutors	Yes
Max. hours/week for services	1
How professors are notified of student approved accommodations	Director and Student

COLLEGE GRADUATION REQUIREMENTS

Course waivers allowed	No
Course substitutions allowed	Yes
In what courses	

Substitution only available for courses that do not fundamentally alter the nature of the program or degree

Saint Louis University

1 N. Grand Blvd., St. Louis, MO 63103 • Admissions: 314-977-2500 • phone: 800-758-3678

CAMPUS
Type of school	Private (nonprofit)
Environment	Metropolis
Support	S

STUDENTS
Undergrad enrollment	7,209
% male/female	40/60
% from out of state	59
% frosh live on campus	92

FINANCIAL FACTS
Annual Tuition	$43,160
Room and board	$12,290
Required fees	$724

GENERAL ADMISSIONS INFO
Priority deadline	12/1
Regular application deadline	8/15

Nonfall registration accepted. Admission may be deferred for a maximum of 1 year.

Range SAT EBRW	590–690
Range SAT Math	580–700
Range ACT Composite	25–31

ACADEMICS
Student/faculty ratio	9:1
% students returning for sophomore year	90
% students graduating within 4 years	68
% students graduating within 6 years	76

Most classes have 20-29 students.

PROGRAMS/SERVICES FOR STUDENTS WITH LEARNING DIFFERENCES

We partner with students, faculty, academic departments and service providers to facilitate equal access to and opportunity to participate in all University programs, services and experiences. We coordinate aids and services to meet the needs of students with disabilities to create a safe and supportive campus community for everyone.

ADMISSIONS

All applicants must meet the same admission requirements to SLU. ACT OR SAT score is required for admission. Students applying to major in music must audition or applying to art must submit a portfolio. Prospective students are also strongly encouraged to present five academic courses for each of their four years of high school, including: Four years each of English and mathematics and three years each of foreign language, natural sciences, social sciences and academic electives.

Additional Information

Students with LD are responsible for contacting Disability Services in order to learn about the accommodation process on campus and to receive academic accommodations within the classroom. Student Support Services (SSS) works with students throughout their time at SLU, from assisting with their transition to college to planning for what

APPLICATION REQUIREMENTS FOR SERVICES

SAT/ACT required: Yes
Interview required: No
Essay required: Not Applicable
Additional application required: No
Documentation required for:
LD: Documentation should be from a medical provider and should confirm the diagnosis, indicate how the condition impacts the student, list any ongoing treatment, and include any history. It should be as current as possible and be typed on the medical provider's letterhead. See Disability Services Website: http://www.slu.edu/retention-and-academic-success/disability-services
ADHD: Documentation should be from a medical provider and should confirm the diagnosis, indicate how the condition impacts the student, list any ongoing treatment, and include any history. It should be as current as possible and be typed on the medical provider's letterhead. See Disability Services Website: http://www.slu.edu/retention-and-academic-success/disability-services
ASD: Documentation should be from a medical provider and should confirm the diagnosis, indicate how the condition impacts the student, list any ongoing treatment, and include any history. It should be as current as possible and be typed on the medical provider's letterhead. See Disability Services Website: http://www.slu.edu/retention-and-academic-success/disability-services
Documentation submitted to: Disability Services in the Student Success Center
Special Ed. HS course work accepted: Not Applicable
Separate application required for Programs/Services: No
Contact Information
Name of program or department: Disability Services in the Student Success Center
Telephone: (314) 977-3484
Fax: (314) 977-3486
Email: disability_services@slu.edu

Saint Louis University

comes after their bachelor's degree is in hand. They do this in a variety of ways and strive to provide the students with quality programming and support during their journey. Some of our goals for our students include: Successful transition; Academic success; and Developing a sense of self. You will have both a primary advisor in your college and a SSS advisor. Students are expected to meet with advisers at least once each semester. Standing tutoring appointments allow students to meet with the same tutor at the same day and time each week for the entire semester. SSS also has its own writing consultant to help students with papers and to grow skills in the writing process.

GENERAL ADMISSIONS

Very important factors considered include: academic GPA, application essay, standardized test scores. Important factors considered include: rigor of secondary school record, interview, extracurricular activities, talent/ability, character/personal qualities, volunteer work. Other factors considered include: recommendation(s), first generation, alumni/ae relation, work experience, level of applicant's interest. Freshman Admission Requirements: High school diploma is required and GED is accepted Academic units required: 4 English, 4 math, 3 science, 3 foreign language, 3 social studies, 3 academic electives, Academic units recommended: 4 English, 4 math, 3 science, 3 foreign language, 3 social studies, 3 academic electives,

ACCOMMODATIONS OR SERVICES

Accommodations are decided upon an individual basis after a thorough review of appropriate, current documentation. The accommodations requests must be supported through the documentation provided and must be logically linked to the current impact of the condition on academic functioning.

FINANCIAL AID

Students should submit: FAFSA. Applicants will be notified of awards on a rolling basis beginning 2/1.. The Princeton Review suggests that all financial aid forms be submitted as soon as possible after October 1. Need-based scholarships/grants offered: College/university scholarship or grant aid from institutional funds; Federal Nursing Scholarships; Federal Pell; Private scholarships; SEOG; State scholarships/grants Loan aid offered: Direct PLUS loans; Direct Subsidized Stafford Loans; Direct Unsubsidized Stafford Loans Federal Work-Study Program available. Institutional employment available.

CAMPUS LIFE

Activities: Campus Ministries; Choral groups; Dance ; Drama/theater; International Student Organization; Jazz band; Literary magazine; Model UN; Music ensembles; Musical theater; Pep band; Radio station ; Student government; Student newspaper; Symphony orchestra ; Television station Organizations: 170 registered organizations, 25 honor societies, 36 religious organizations. 11 fraternities, 6 sororities, Athletics (Intercollegiate): Men: baseball, basketball, cross-country, diving, soccer, swimming, tennis, track/field (outdoor), track/field (indoor) Women: basketball, cross-country, diving, field hockey, soccer, softball, swimming, tennis, track/field (outdoor), track/field (indoor), volleyball. On-Campus Highlights: St. Francis Xavier Church, Busch Student Center, Pius Library, Simon Recreation Center, Chaifetz Arena.

ACCOMMODATIONS

Allowed in exams:	
Calculators	Yes
Dictionary	Yes
Computer	Yes
Spell-checker	Yes
Extended test time	Yes
Scribe	Yes
Proctors	Yes
Oral exams	Yes
Note-takers	Yes
Support services for students with	
LD	No
ADHD	No
ASD	No
Distraction-reduced environment	Yes
Recording of lecture allowed	Yes
Reading technology:	Yes
Audio books	No
Other assistive technology	Yes
Audio books	Yes
Priority registration	Yes
Added costs of services:	
For LD:	Not Applicable
For ADHD:	No
For ASD:	Not Applicable
LD specialists	No
ADHD & ASD coaching	Yes
ASD specialists	No
Professional tutors	Yes
Peer tutors	Not Applicable
Max. hours/week for services	Varies
How professors are notified of student	
approved accommodations	Both

COLLEGE GRADUATION REQUIREMENTS

Course waivers allowed	Yes
In what courses	Varies
Course substitutions allowed	Yes
In what courses	Varies

University of Missouri

230 JESSE HALL, COLUMBIA, MO 65211 • ADMISSIONS: 573-882-7786 • FAX: 573-882-7887

CAMPUS

Type of school	Public
Environment	City
Support	CS

STUDENTS

Undergrad enrollment	23,455
% male/female	48/52
% from out of state	21
% frosh live on campus	87

FINANCIAL FACTS

Annual in-state tuition	$8,460
Annual out-of-state tuition	$25,179
Room and board	$10,676
Required fees	$1,327

GENERAL ADMISSIONS INFO

Application fee	$60
Priority deadline	5/1

Nonfall registration accepted. Admission may be deferred.

Range SAT EBRW	570–680
Range SAT Math	550–670
Range ACT Composite	23–29

ACADEMICS

Student/faculty ratio	18:1
% students returning for sophomore year	87
% students graduating within 6 years	68

Most classes have 20–29 students. Most lab/discussion sessions have 20–29 students.

PROGRAMS/SERVICES FOR STUDENTS WITH LEARNING DIFFERENCES

Reasonable accommodations, auxiliary aids, and support services are provided by the Office of Disability Services (ODS) to ensure that any student with a disability will have equal access to the educational programs and activities at the university. MU does not have a stand-alone program oriented to students with specific learning disabilities; all students with disabilities are supported through ODS. Students with disabilities (including specific learning disabilities or ADD/ADHD) are required to adhere to the same academic standards as other students at the university. As in any higher education setting, students with disabilities have the responsibility to self-identify and are encouraged to request accommodations through ODS as early as possible.

ADMISSIONS

There are no special admissions for students with learning disabilities. General admission is based on high school curriculum, ACT scores, and class rank.

Additional Information

Auxiliary aids and classroom accommodations include note-takers, lab assistants, readers, and assistive technology. Testing accommodations include time extensions, distraction-reduced environments, readers, scribes, or adaptive equipment. Coordinators can offer support and counseling in the areas of time management, study skills, learning styles, and other academic and social issues. Group support is also available. The Learning Center works cooperatively with ODS to provide individual tutoring free of charge. Other services include writing assistance, math assistance, test reviews, help with reading comprehension, and study skills training.

ADMISSIONS INFO FOR STUDENTS WITH LEARNING DIFFERENCES

SAT/ACT required: Yes
Interview required: No
Essay required: No
Additional application required: No
Documentation required for:
  LD: Psycho ed evaluation to include: relevant historical info, instructional interventions, related services, age diagnosed, objective data (aptitude, achievement, info processing), test scores (standard, percentile and grade equivalents) and describe functional limitations.
  ADHD: Diagnosis based on DSM-V; history of behaviors impairing functioning in academic setting; diagnostic interview; history of symptoms; evidence of ongoing behaviors.
  ASD: Psycho ed evaluation
Documentation submitted to: Office of Disability Services
Special Ed. HS course work accepted: Yes
Separate application required for Programs/Services: No
Contact Information
Name of program or department: Disability Center
Telephone: 573-882-4696
Fax: 573-884-5002
Email: disabilitycenter@missouri.edu

University of Missouri

General Admissions

Very important factors considered include: academic GPA, standardized test scores. *Important factors considered include:* rigor of secondary school record, class rank. *Other factors considered include:* application essay, recommendation(s), talent/ability, first generation, racial/ethnic status, volunteer work, work experience, level of applicant's interest. *Freshman Admission Requirements:* High school diploma is required and GED is accepted. *Academic units required:* 4 English, 4 math, 3 science, 1 science lab, 2 foreign language, 3 social studies, and 1 unit from above areas or other academic areas.

Accommodations or Services

Accommodations are decided upon an individual basis after a thorough review of appropriate, current documentation. The accommodations requests must be supported through the documentation provided and must be logically linked to the current impact of the condition on academic functioning.

Financial Aid

Students should submit: FAFSA. Applicants will be notified of awards on a rolling basis beginning 12/15. The Princeton Review suggests that all financial aid forms be submitted as soon as possible after October 1. *Need-based scholarships/grants offered:* College/university scholarship or grant aid from institutional funds; Federal Nursing Scholarships; Federal Pell; Private scholarships; SEOG; State scholarships/grants. *Loan aid offered:* Direct PLUS loans; Direct Subsidized Stafford Loans; Direct Unsubsidized Stafford Loans. Federal Work-Study Program available. Institutional employment available.

Campus Life

Activities: Campus Ministries; Choral groups; Concert band; Dance; Drama/theater; International Student Organization; Jazz band; Literary magazine; Marching band; Model UN; Music ensembles; Musical theater; Opera; Pep band; Radio station; Student government; Student newspaper; Student-run film society; Symphony orchestra; Television station; Yearbook. **Organizations:** 598 registered organizations, 25 honor societies, 47 religious organizations. 32 fraternities, 19 sororities. **Athletics (Intercollegiate):** *Men:* baseball, basketball, cross-country, diving, football, golf, swimming, track/field (outdoor), track/field (indoor), wrestling. *Women:* basketball, cheerleading, cross-country, diving, golf, gymnastics, soccer, softball, swimming, tennis, track/field (outdoor), track/field (indoor), volleyball. **On-Campus Highlights:** Student Recreation Center - expanded & renovated in 2005, Mizzou Arena - home of Tiger Basketball, Memorial Stadium - home of Tiger Football, Jesse Hall - administration; concert hall, Life Sciences Center - interdisciplinary research facility.

ACCOMMODATIONS

Allowed in exams:	
Calculators	Yes
Dictionary	Yes
Computer	Yes
Spell-checker	Yes
Extended test time	Yes
Scribe	Yes
Proctors	Yes
Oral exams	Yes
Note-takers	Yes
Support services for students with	
LD	Yes
ADHD	Yes
ASD	Yes
Distraction-reduced environment	Yes
Recording of lecture allowed	Yes
Reading technology:	Yes
Audio books	Yes
Other assistive technology	Yes
Priority registration	Yes
Added costs for services:	
For LD:	No
For ADHD:	No
For ASD:	No
LD specialists	Yes
ADHD & ASD coaching	Yes
ASD specialists	No
Professional tutors	Yes
Peer tutors	Yes
Max. hours/week for services	Unlimited
How professors are notified of student approved accommodations	Student

COLLEGE GRADUATION REQUIREMENTS

Course waivers allowed	No
Course substitutions allowed	Yes
In what courses	Varies

University of Missouri–Kansas City

5100 ROCKHILL ROAD, KANSAS CITY, MO 64114 • ADMISSIONS: 816-235-1111 • FAX: 816-235-5544

CAMPUS

Type of school	Public
Environment	Metropolis
Support	S

STUDENTS

Undergrad enrollment	7,872
% male/female	43/57
% from out of state	20
% frosh live on campus	57

FINANCIAL FACTS

Annual in-state tuition	$9,884
Annual out-of-state tuition	$25,010
Room and board	$10,334
Required fees	$1,384

GENERAL ADMISSIONS INFO

Application fee	$45
Priority deadline	4/1

Nonfall registration accepted.
  Admission may be deferred for a maximum of 2 semesters.

Range SAT EBRW	NR
Range SAT Math	NR
Range ACT Composite	21–28

ACADEMICS

Student/faculty ratio	14:1
% students returning for sophomore year	74
% students graduating within 4 years	26
% students graduating within 6 years	48

Most classes have fewer than 10 students.
Most lab/discussion sessions have 10–19 students.

PROGRAMS/SERVICES FOR STUDENTS WITH LEARNING DIFFERENCES

The Office of Services for Students with Disabilities' mission is to educate and support the UMKC community to understand the unique challenges, myths and stereotypes faced by people with disabilities; recognize the unique contributions that people with disabilities make to society; and accept and engage people with disabilities in the daily flow of life. We are also here to provide reasonable accommodations to help students demonstrate their abilities, knowledge and skills.

ADMISSIONS

Same as any other student

Additional Information

Contact the Office at 816-235-5696 and schedule an appointment. We will need documentation of your disability.

ADMISSIONS INFO FOR STUDENTS WITH LEARNING DIFFERENCES

SAT/ACT required: Not Applicable
Interview required: Not Applicable
Essay required: Not Applicable
Additional application required: Not Applicable
Documentation required for:
  LD: We look for a wide range of testing that substantiate the diagnosis. Typically a WAIS and other work up.
  ADHD: A letter from a qualified medical professional describing the condition and a description of its impact.
  ASD: A letter from a qualified medical professional describing the condition and a description of its impact.
Documentation submitted to: Office of Services for Students with Disabilities
Special Ed. HS course work accepted: Not Applicable
Separate application required for Programs/Services: No
Contact Information
Name of program or department: Office of Services for Students with Disabilities
Telephone: 816-235-5696
Fax: 816-235-6363
Email: laurentr@umkc.edu

University of Missouri–Kansas City

GENERAL ADMISSIONS
Very important factors considered include: rigor of secondary school record, class rank, academic GPA, standardized test scores. *Other factors considered include:* application essay, recommendation(s), interview, extracurricular activities, talent/ability, character/personal qualities, first generation, volunteer work, work experience. *Freshman Admission Requirements:* High school diploma is required and GED is accepted. *Academic units required:* 4 English, 4 math, 3 science, 1 science lab, 2 foreign language, 3 social studies, 1 visual/performing arts.

ACCOMMODATIONS OR SERVICES
Accommodations are decided upon an individual basis after a thorough review of appropriate, current documentation. The accommodations requests must be supported through the documentation provided and must be logically linked to the current impact of the condition on academic functioning.

FINANCIAL AID
Students should submit: FAFSA. Applicants will be notified of awards on a rolling basis beginning 4/15. The Princeton Review suggests that all financial aid forms be submitted as soon as possible after October 1. *Need-based scholarships/grants offered:* College/university scholarship or grant aid from institutional funds; Federal Nursing Scholarships; Federal Pell; Private scholarships; SEOG; State scholarships/grants; United Negro College Fund. *Loan aid offered:* Direct PLUS loans; Direct Subsidized Stafford Loans; Direct Unsubsidized Stafford Loans. Federal Work-Study Program available. Institutional employment available.

CAMPUS LIFE
Activities: Campus Ministries; Choral groups; Concert band; Dance; Drama/theater; International Student Organization; Jazz band; Literary magazine; Model UN; Music ensembles; Musical theater; Opera; Pep band; Radio station; Student government; Student newspaper; Student-run film society; Symphony orchestra. **Organizations:** 200 registered organizations, 32 honor societies, 13 religious organizations. 6 fraternities, 7 sororities. **Athletics (Intercollegiate):** *Men:* basketball, cheerleading, cross-country, golf, riflery, soccer, tennis, track/field (outdoor). *Women:* basketball, cheerleading, cross-country, golf, riflery, softball, tennis, track/field (outdoor), volleyball. **On-Campus Highlights:** UMKC Student Union, Swinney Recreation Center, Robot Cafe at Miller-Nichols Library, Warkoczewski Public Observatory, Minsky's Pizza.

ACCOMMODATIONS
Allowed in exams:

Calculators	Yes
Dictionary	Yes
Computer	Yes
Spell-checker	Yes
Extended test time	Yes
Scribe	Yes
Proctors	Yes
Oral exams	Yes
Note-takers	Yes

Support services for students with

LD	Yes
ADHD	Yes
ASD	Yes
Distraction-reduced environment	Yes
Recording of lecture allowed	Yes
Reading technology:	Yes
Audio books	Yes
Other assistive technology	Braille embosser, JAWS, ZoomText
Priority registration	Yes

Added costs for services:

For LD:	No
For ADHD:	No
For ASD:	No
LD specialists	No
ADHD & ASD coaching	Yes
ASD specialists	Yes
Professional tutors	Yes
Peer tutors	Not Applicable
Max. hours/week for services	Varies
How professors are notified of student approved accommodations	Student

COLLEGE GRADUATION REQUIREMENTS

Course waivers allowed	No
Course substitutions allowed	Yes
In what courses	Math, Foreign Language

Washington University in St. Louis

Campus Box 1089, St. Louis, MO 63130-4899 • Admissions: 314-935-6000 • Fax: 314-935-4290

CAMPUS

Type of school	Private (nonprofit)
Environment	City
Support	CS

STUDENTS

Undergrad enrollment	7,253
% male/female	47/53
% from out of state	91
% frosh live on campus	100

FINANCIAL FACTS

Annual tuition	$52,400
Room and board	$16,440
Required fees	$999

GENERAL ADMISSIONS INFO

Application fee	$75.
Regular application deadline	1/2

Nonfall registration accepted. Admission may be deferred for a maximum of 2 years.

Range SAT EBRW	720–770
Range SAT Math	750–800
Range ACT Composite	32–34

ACADEMICS

Student/faculty ratio	8:1
% students returning for sophomore year	97
% students graduating within 4 years	88
% students graduating within 6 years	94

Most classes have 10–19 students. Most lab/discussion sessions have 20–29 students.

PROGRAMS/SERVICES FOR STUDENTS WITH LEARNING DIFFERENCES

Disability Resources assists students with disabilities by providing guidance and accommodations to ensure equal access to our campus, both physically and academically. In accordance with the ADA Amendments Act (ADAAA) and University policy, students must provide appropriate documentation to the Disability Resources (DR) office in a timely manner before they can be considered for accommodations. Students must submit a request for accommodation, including documentation of the disability, to Disability Resources. Disability Resources will then determine eligibility and work with each individual student to implement accommodations.

ADMISSIONS

Washington University gives full consideration to all applicants for admission. There is no special admissions process for students with learning disabilities. Students may choose to voluntarily identify themselves as learning disabled in the admissions process. If they chose to self-identify, details of the history and treatment of their disability, of how they have met different academic requirements in light of the disability, and the relationship between the disability and the students' academic record help the university to understand more fully the applicants' profiles. This information can be helpful in the application process to explain, for example, lower grades in certain subjects.

Additional Information

The Center for Advanced Learning provides support services to help the students to succeed academically. These include: essential study and test-taking skills, access to peer mentors, executive functioning, and time management and study techniques, etc.

ADMISSIONS INFO FOR STUDENTS WITH LEARNING DIFFERENCES

SAT/ACT required: Yes
Interview required: No
Essay required: Recommended
Additional application required: No
Documentation required for:

LD: Please visit our "Documentation Guidelines" listed specifically for students with Learning Disabilities on the Disability Resources website at: cornerstone.wustl.edu/disability-resources/request-and-use-accommodations/documentation-guidelines/

ADHD: Please visit our "Documentation Guidelines" listed specifically for students with ADHD on the Disability Resources website at: cornerstone.wustl.edu/disability-resources/request-and-use-accommodations/documentation-guidelines/

ASD: Please visit our "Documentation Guidelines" listed specifically for students with ASD on the Disability Resources website at: cornerstone.wustl.edu/disability-resources/request-and-use-accommodations/documentation-guidelines/

Documentation submitted to: Disability Resources
Special Ed. HS course work accepted: No
Separate application required for Programs/Services: No
Contact Information
Name of program or department: Disability Resources
Telephone: 314-935-5970
Fax: 314-935-7559
Email: disabilityresources@wustl.edu

Washington University in St. Louis

GENERAL ADMISSIONS

Very important factors considered include: rigor of secondary school record, class rank, academic GPA, application essay, standardized test scores, recommendation(s), extracurricular activities, talent/ability, character/personal qualities, volunteer work, work experience. *Important factors considered include:* level of applicant's interest. *Other factors considered include:* interview, first generation, alumni/ae relation, geographical residence, racial/ethnic status. *Freshman Admission Requirements:* High school diploma is required and GED is accepted. *Academic units required:* 4 English, 3 math, 3 science, 2 science labs, 2 foreign language, 2 social studies, 2 history. *Academic units recommended:* 4 English, 4 math, 4 science, 4 science labs, 4 foreign language, 4 social studies, 4 history.

ACCOMMODATIONS OR SERVICES

Accommodations are decided upon an individual basis after a thorough review of appropriate, current documentation. The accommodations requests must be supported through the documentation provided and must be logically linked to the current impact of the condition on academic functioning.

FINANCIAL AID

Students should submit: CSS/Financial Aid PROFILE; FAFSA; Noncustodial PROFILE. Applicants will be notified of awards on or about 4/1. The Princeton Review suggests that all financial aid forms be submitted as soon as possible after October 1. *Need-based scholarships/grants offered:* College/university scholarship or grant aid from institutional funds; Federal Pell; Private scholarships; SEOG; State scholarships/grants; United Negro College Fund. *Loan aid offered:* Direct PLUS loans; Direct Subsidized Stafford Loans; Direct Unsubsidized Stafford Loans. Federal Work-Study Program available. Institutional employment available.

CAMPUS LIFE

Activities: Campus Ministries; Choral groups; Concert band; Dance; Drama/theater; International Student Organization; Jazz band; Literary magazine; Model UN; Music ensembles; Musical theater; Opera; Pep band; Radio station; Student government; Student newspaper; Student-run film society; Symphony orchestra; Television station. **Organizations:** 200 registered organizations, 18 honor societies, 19 religious organizations. 12 fraternities, 6 sororities. **Athletics (Intercollegiate):** *Men:* baseball, basketball, cross-country, diving, football, soccer, swimming, tennis, track/field (outdoor), track/field (indoor). *Women:* basketball, cross-country, diving, golf, soccer, softball, swimming, tennis, track/field (outdoor), track/field (indoor), volleyball. **On-Campus Highlights:** Art Museum, Whispers Cafe in Olin Library, Danforth University Center, Brookings Quadrangle, South 40 Residential Area.

ACCOMMODATIONS

Allowed in exams:	
Calculators	Yes
Dictionary	Yes
Computer	Yes
Spell-checker	Yes
Extended test time	Yes
Scribe	Yes
Proctors	Yes
Oral exams	Yes
Note-takers	Yes
Support services for students with	
LD	Yes
ADHD	Yes
ASD	Yes
Distraction-reduced environment	Yes
Recording of lecture allowed	Yes
Reading technology:	Yes
Audio books	Yes
Other assistive technology	Kurzweil, Dragon naturally speaking, Inspiration, Sonocent, Smart Pen
Priority registration	Yes
Added costs for services:	
For LD:	No
For ADHD:	No
For ASD:	No
LD specialists	No
ADHD & ASD coaching	Yes
ASD specialists	Yes
Professional tutors	Yes
Peer tutors	Yes
Max. hours/week for services	Varies
How professors are notified of student approved accommodations	Student

COLLEGE GRADUATION REQUIREMENTS

Course waivers allowed	No
Course substitutions allowed	No

Westminster College (MO)

501 WESTMINSTER AVENUE, FULTON, MO 65251 • ADMISSIONS: 573-592-5251 • FAX: 573-592-5255

CAMPUS

Type of school	Private (nonprofit)
Environment	Village
Support	SP

STUDENTS

Undergrad enrollment	764
% male/female	56/44
% from out of state	19
% frosh live on campus	94

FINANCIAL FACTS

Annual tuition	$25,700
Room and board	$10,140
Required fees	$1,900

GENERAL ADMISSIONS INFO

Nonfall registration accepted. Admission may be deferred for a maximum of 1 year.

Range SAT EBRW	500–600
Range SAT Math	515–575
Range ACT Composite	21–26

ACADEMICS

Student/faculty ratio	11:1
% students returning for sophomore year	73

PROGRAMS/SERVICES FOR STUDENTS WITH LEARNING DIFFERENCES

The Learning Differences Program (LDP) provides the encouragement and support that students diagnosed with neurodevelopmental disorders need to be successful learners in the academic environment they share with regularly admitted students. The LDP's services are tailored to meet the specific needs of students with professionally diagnosed neurodevelopmental disorders.

ADMISSIONS

There is a special application and admissions procedure for students with learning disabilities. Students submit a completed Westminster College application form and a separate application form for the LD program; results of an eye and hearing exam, WAIS, WJ, and achievement tests; SAT scores of 900-plus or ACT scores of 19-plus; two copies of their high school transcript; recent reports from school counselors, learning specialists, psychologists, or physicians who have diagnosed the disability; four recommendations from counselors or teachers familiar with their performance; and an evaluation from an educational specialist. An on-campus interview is required.

Additional Information

The College Transition Program (CTP) provides the support that students diagnosed with Autism Spectrum Disorder need to be successful learners in the academic environment they share with regularly admitted students. Services are tailored to meet the specific needs of students with Autism Spectrum Disorder, many of whom also have Attention Deficit/Hyperactivity Disorder: one-on-one academic advising; enrollment in supplemental courses designed to encourage and support academic success in the Humanities, Natural and Mathematical Sciences, and Social Sciences; extended-time testing; class notes; dictation; access to a quiet and/or supportive study environment. Students who are admitted to and enroll in the CTP pay an additional fee for each semester they are in the program. For more information on the current fee schedule, contact the Office of Enrollment Services at 1-800-475-3361.

ADMISSIONS INFO FOR STUDENTS WITH LEARNING DIFFERENCES

SAT/ACT required: Yes
Interview required: Yes
Essay required: Recommended
Additional application required: No
Documentation required for:
  LD: WAIS-R; (WISC III or IV) and written evaluation within 2 years; Woodcock-Johnson or WAIS
  ADHD: Connors Parent/Teacher Rating Scale; various behavioral assessments
  ASD: Psycho ed evaluation
Documentation submitted to: Learning Opportunity Center
Special Ed. HS course work accepted: Yes
Separate application required for Programs/Services: Yes
Contact Information
Name of program or department: Learning Opportunity Center
Telephone: 573-592-5304
Fax: 573-592-5191

Westminster College (MO)

GENERAL ADMISSIONS

Very important factors considered include: rigor of secondary school record, standardized test scores, character/personal qualities. *Important factors considered include:* class rank, academic GPA, recommendation(s), extracurricular activities, volunteer work. *Other factors considered include:* application essay, interview, talent/ability, alumni/ae relation, work experience. *Freshman Admission Requirements:* High school diploma is required and GED is accepted. *Academic units required:* 4 English, 3 math, 2 science, 2 science labs. *Academic units recommended:* 2 foreign language, 2 social studies, 2 academic electives.

ACCOMMODATIONS OR SERVICES

Accommodations are decided upon an individual basis after a thorough review of appropriate, current documentation. The accommodations requests must be supported through the documentation provided and must be logically linked to the current impact of the condition on academic functioning.

FINANCIAL AID

Students should submit: FAFSA. Applicants will be notified of awards on a rolling basis beginning 3/15. The Princeton Review suggests that all financial aid forms be submitted as soon as possible after October 1. *Need-based scholarships/grants offered:* College/university scholarship or grant aid from institutional funds; Federal Pell; Private scholarships; SEOG; State scholarships/grants. *Loan aid offered:* Direct PLUS loans; Direct Subsidized Stafford Loans; Direct Unsubsidized Stafford Loans. Federal Work-Study Program available. Institutional employment available.

CAMPUS LIFE

Activities: Campus Ministries; Choral groups; Dance; Drama/theater; International Student Organization; Jazz band; Literary magazine; Model UN; Music ensembles; Pep band; Student government; Student newspaper. **Organizations:** 49 registered organizations, 15 honor societies, 2 religious organizations. 6 fraternities, 3 sororities. **Athletics (Intercollegiate):** *Men:* baseball, basketball, cheerleading, cross-country, football, golf, soccer, tennis, track/field (outdoor). *Women:* basketball, cheerleading, cross-country, golf, soccer, softball, tennis, track/field (outdoor), volleyball. **On-Campus Highlights:** Coulter Science Center, Johnson College Inn (student center), Hunter Activity Center, Library, Wetterau Athletic Facility.

ACCOMMODATIONS

Allowed in exams:	
Calculators	Yes
Dictionary	Yes
Computer	Yes
Spell-checker	Yes
Extended test time	Yes
Scribe	Yes
Proctors	Yes
Oral exams	Yes
Note-takers	Yes
Support services for students with	
LD	Yes
ADHD	Yes
ASD	Yes
Distraction-reduced environment	Yes
Recording of lecture allowed	Yes
Reading technology:	Yes
Audio books	Yes
Other assistive technology	Yes
Priority registration	No
Added costs for services:	
For LD:	No
For ADHD:	No
For ASD:	No
LD specialists	Yes
ADHD & ASD coaching	No
ASD specialists	No
Professional tutors	No
Peer tutors	Yes
Max. hours/week for services	Varies
How professors are notified of student approved accommodations	
Student and Director	

COLLEGE GRADUATION REQUIREMENTS

Course waivers allowed	No
Course substitutions allowed	Yes
In what courses	

Students can petition the academic dean for substitute courses in any area.

Montana State University Billings

1500 UNIVERSITY DRIVE, BILLINGS, MT 59101 • ADMISSIONS: 406-657-2158 • FAX: 406-657-2302

CAMPUS
Type of school	Public
Environment	City
Support	S

STUDENTS
Undergrad enrollment	3,570
% male/female	39/61
% from out of state	9
% frosh live on campus	33

FINANCIAL FACTS
Annual in-state tuition	$4,397
Annual out-of-state tuition	$16,662
Room and board	$7,510
Required fees	$1,429

GENERAL ADMISSIONS INFO
Application fee	$30
Priority deadline	3/1

Nonfall registration accepted.

Range SAT EBRW	430–520
Range SAT Math	420–500
Range ACT Composite	18–22

ACADEMICS
Student/faculty ratio	17:1
% students returning for sophomore year	55

Most classes have fewer than 10 students.

PROGRAMS/SERVICES FOR STUDENTS WITH LEARNING DIFFERENCES
The DSS mission statement is: Disability Support Services assists in creating an accessible university community where students with documented disabilities have an equal opportunity to fully participate in all aspects of the educational environment. We coordinate the provision of reasonable accommodations, advocate for an accessible and amenable learning environment, and promote self-determination for the students we serve.

ADMISSIONS
There is no special admission process for students with learning disabilities. All students must meet the same admission criteria. Freshmen applicants must meet one of the following conditions: ACT of 22 or SAT of 920, a 2.5 GPA; or rank in the top half of the class.

Additional Information
Students must request services, provide documentation specifying a learning disability or ADHD, make an appointment for an intake with DSS, meet with professors at the beginning of each semester, and work closely with DSS. DSS must keep documentation and intake on file, make a determination of accommodations, issue identification cards to qualified students, and serve as a resource and a support system. Services include course and testing accommodations, alternative testing, priority scheduling, technical assistance, liaison and referral services, taped textbooks, and career, academic, and counseling referrals. The use of a computer, calculator, dictionary, or spellchecker is at the discretion of the individual professor and based on the documented needs of the student. Services and accommodations are available for undergraduate and graduate students.

ADMISSIONS INFO FOR STUDENTS WITH LEARNING DIFFERENCES
SAT/ACT required: Yes
Interview required: No
Essay required: Recommended
Additional application required: Yes
Documentation required for:
 LD: educational testing
 ADHD: doctor's statement
 ASD: doctor's statement
Documentation submitted to: Disability Support Services
Special Ed. HS course work accepted: No
Separate application required for Programs/Services: No
Contact Information
Name of program or department: Disability Support Services
Telephone: 406-657-2283
Fax: 406-657-1658
Email: tcarey@msubillings.edu

Montana State University Billings

GENERAL ADMISSIONS

Very important factors considered include: rigor of secondary school record, class rank, academic GPA, standardized test scores. *Other factors considered include:* character/personal qualities, work experience. *Freshman Admission Requirements:* High school diploma is required and GED is accepted. *Academic units required:* 4 English, 3 math, 2 science, 2 science labs, 3 social studies, and 2 units from above areas or other academic areas.

ACCOMMODATIONS OR SERVICES

Accommodations are decided upon an individual basis after a thorough review of appropriate, current documentation. The accommodations requests must be supported through the documentation provided and must be logically linked to the current impact of the condition on academic functioning.

FINANCIAL AID

Students should submit: FAFSA. Applicants will be notified of awards on a rolling basis beginning 3/1. The Princeton Review suggests that all financial aid forms be submitted as soon as possible after October 1. *Need-based scholarships/grants offered:* College/university scholarship or grant aid from institutional funds; Federal Pell; Private scholarships; SEOG; State scholarships/grants. *Loan aid offered:* Direct PLUS loans; Direct Subsidized Stafford Loans; Direct Unsubsidized Stafford Loans. Federal Work-Study Program available. Institutional employment available.

CAMPUS LIFE

Activities: Campus Ministries; Choral groups; Concert band; Drama/theater; International Student Organization; Jazz band; Literary magazine; Music ensembles; Musical theater; Pep band; Radio station; Student government; Student newspaper; Symphony orchestra. **Organizations:** 53 registered organizations, 10 honor societies, 8 religious organizations. **Athletics (Intercollegiate):** *Men:* baseball, basketball, cross-country, golf, soccer, tennis, track/field (outdoor), track/field (indoor). *Women:* basketball, cross-country, golf, soccer, softball, tennis, track/field (outdoor), track/field (indoor), volleyball. **On-Campus Highlights:** Alterowitz Gym, Stingers Bistro, SUB Coffee Shop, Liberal Arts Coffee Shop, Library.

ACCOMMODATIONS

Allowed in exams:	
Calculators	Yes
Dictionary	Yes
Computer	Yes
Spell-checker	Yes
Extended test time	Yes
Scribe	Yes
Proctors	Yes
Oral exams	Yes
Note-takers	Yes
Support services for students with	
LD	Yes
ADHD	Yes
ASD	Yes
Distraction-reduced environment	Yes
Recording of lecture allowed	Yes
Reading technology:	Yes
Audio books	Yes
Other assistive technology	Zoomtext Jaws CCTV Dragon
Priority registration	Yes
Added costs for services:	
For LD:	No
For ADHD:	No
For ASD:	No
LD specialists	No
ADHD & ASD coaching	No
ASD specialists	No
Professional tutors	Yes
Peer tutors	Yes
Max. hours/week for services	Varies
How professors are notified of student approved accommodations	Director and Student

COLLEGE GRADUATION REQUIREMENTS

Course waivers allowed	No
Course substitutions allowed	Not Applicable

Montana Tech of the University of Montana

1300 West Park Street, Butte, MT 59701 • Admissions: 406-496-4256 • Fax: 406-496-4710

CAMPUS
Type of school	Public
Environment	Town
Support	CS

STUDENTS
Undergrad enrollment	2,096
% male/female	64/36
% from out of state	14
% frosh live on campus	54

FINANCIAL FACTS
Annual in-state tuition	$7,411
Annual out-of-state tuition	$22,575
Room and board	$9,828
Required fees	NR

GENERAL ADMISSIONS INFO
Application fee	$30.

Nonfall registration accepted. Admission may be deferred for a maximum of 1 semester.

Range SAT EBRW	540–630
Range SAT Math	575–670
Range ACT Composite	22–27

ACADEMICS
Student/faculty ratio	13:1
% students returning for sophomore year	77
% students graduating within 6 years	44

Most classes have 20–29 students. Most lab/discussion sessions have 10–19 students.

PROGRAMS/SERVICES FOR STUDENTS WITH LEARNING DIFFERENCES
All persons with disabilities have the right to participate fully and equally in the programs and services of Montana Tech. Tech is committed to making the appropriate accommodations. Montana Tech's student life counselors are resources for students with disabilities. The counselors are a general resource for all students who may need assistance. Availability of services from Disability Services is subject to a student's eligibility for these and any other services. Students must provide appropriate and current documentation prior to requesting and receiving services or accommodations. All faculty and staff at the college are responsible for assuring access by providing reasonable accommodations. The Montana Tech Learning Center offers a variety of services to help students achieve their full academic potential. Tutors are available to help all students with course work in an assortment of subject areas. The Learning Center addresses the importance of developing basic college success skills.

ADMISSIONS
There is no special admission process for students with LD or ADHD. Applicants must have a 22 ACT or 1540 SAT Reasoning, or be in the upper 50 percent of their high school class, or have a 2.5 GPA. The GED is accepted. Students must have 14 academic high school credits, including 4 years of English, 2 years of science, 3 years of math, 3 years of social studies, and 2 years from other academic areas, including foreign language, computer science, visual/performing arts, and vocational education. Interviews are not required, and special education courses in high school are not accepted. Students who do not meet any of the general admission criteria may ask to be evaluated considering other factors. Students with LD/ADHD are encouraged to self-disclose in the admissions process.

ADMISSIONS INFO FOR STUDENTS WITH LEARNING DIFFERENCES
SAT/ACT required: Yes
Interview required: No
Essay required: No
Additional application required: No
Documentation required for:
  LD: Psycho ed evaluation to include: relevant historical info, instructional interventions, related services, age diagnosed, objective data (aptitude, achievement, info processing), test scores (standard, percentile and grade equivalents) and describe functional limitations.
  ADHD: Diagnosis based on DSM-V; history of behaviors impairing functioning in academic setting; diagnostic interview; history of symptoms; evidence of ongoing behaviors.
  ASD: Psycho ed evaluation
Documentation submitted to: Disability Services
Special Ed. HS course work accepted: No
Separate application required for Programs/Services: No
Contact Information
Name of program or department: Disability Services
Telephone: 406-496-4129
Fax: 406-496-4757

Montana Tech of the University of Montana

Additional Information
The following types of services are offered to students with disabilities: responses to requests for accommodation, assistance in working with faculty members, text accommodation in concert with instructors, access to assistive technology, note-taking, and career services. Documentation to receive services should be sent directly to Disability Services. Montana Tech offers compensatory classes for students with LD in both math and English. Services and accommodations are available for undergraduate and graduate students.

GENERAL ADMISSIONS
Very important factors considered include: class rank, academic GPA, standardized test scores. *Freshman Admission Requirements:* High school diploma is required and GED is accepted. *Academic units required:* 4 English, 3 math, 2 science, 2 science labs, 3 social studies, and 2 units from above areas or other academic areas. *Academic units recommended:* 4 math.

ACCOMMODATIONS OR SERVICES
Accommodations are decided upon an individual basis after a thorough review of appropriate, current documentation. The accommodations requests must be supported through the documentation provided and must be logically linked to the current impact of the condition on academic functioning.

FINANCIAL AID
Students should submit: FAFSA. Applicants will be notified of awards on a rolling basis beginning 3/15. The Princeton Review suggests that all financial aid forms be submitted as soon as possible after October 1. *Need-based scholarships/grants offered:* College/university scholarship or grant aid from institutional funds; Federal Pell; Private scholarships; SEOG; State scholarships/grants. *Loan aid offered:* Direct PLUS loans; Direct Subsidized Stafford Loans; Direct Unsubsidized Stafford Loans. Federal Work-Study Program available. Institutional employment available.

CAMPUS LIFE
Activities: Campus Ministries; Choral groups; International Student Organization; Pep band; Radio station; Student government; Student newspaper. **Organizations:** 58 registered organizations, 2 honor societies, 3 religious organizations. **Athletics (Intercollegiate):** *Men:* basketball, football, golf *Women:* basketball, golf, volleyball. **On-Campus Highlights:** Mineral Museum, Mill Building (student lounge & activity area), HPER (athletic facility), Student Union, Mall area (outdoor center of campus).

ACCOMMODATIONS

Allowed in exams:	
Calculators	Yes
Dictionary	Yes
Computer	Yes
Spell-checker	Yes
Extended test time	Yes
Scribe	Yes
Proctors	Yes
Oral exams	Yes
Note-takers	Yes
Support services for students with	
LD	Yes
ADHD	Yes
ASD	Yes
Distraction-reduced environment	Yes
Recording of lecture allowed	Yes
Reading technology:	Yes
Audio books	Yes
Other assistive technology	Yes
Priority registration	Yes
Added costs for services:	
For LD:	No
For ADHD:	No
For ASD:	No
LD specialists	Yes
ADHD & ASD coaching	No
ASD specialists	No
Professional tutors	No
Peer tutors	0-12
Max. hours/week for services	Unlimited
How professors are notified of student approved accommodations	
By both student and counselors	

COLLEGE GRADUATION REQUIREMENTS

Course waivers allowed	No
Course substitutions allowed	No

Rocky Mountain College

1511 POLY DRIVE, BILLINGS, MT 59102-1796 • ADMISSIONS: 406-657-1026 • FAX: 406-657-1189

CAMPUS
Type of school	Private (nonprofit)
Environment	City
Support	CS

STUDENTS
Undergrad enrollment	984
% male/female	51/49
% from out of state	44
% frosh live on campus	82

FINANCIAL FACTS
Annual tuition	$22,442
Room and board	$7,160
Required fees	$450

GENERAL ADMISSIONS INFO
Application fee	$35
Priority deadline	3/1

Nonfall registration accepted. Admission may be deferred for a maximum of 1 year.

Range SAT EBRW	440–540
Range SAT Math	450–550
Range ACT Composite	20–25

ACADEMICS
Student/faculty ratio	12:1
% students returning for sophomore year	67

Most classes have 10–19 students.
Most lab/discussion sessions have 10–19 students.

PROGRAMS/SERVICES FOR STUDENTS WITH LEARNING DIFFERENCES

Rocky Mountain College is committed to providing courses, programs, and services for students with disabilities. Services for Academic Success (SAS) provides a comprehensive support program for students with LD. To be eligible, participants must meet one of the primary criteria: come from a low-income family, be a first-generation college student, or have a physical or learning disability. Participants must also be U.S. citizens and have an academic need for the program. Students are responsible for identifying themselves, providing appropriate documentation, and requesting reasonable accommodations. The program tailors services to meet the needs of the individuals. SAS welcomes applications from students who are committed to learning and who are excited about meeting the challenges of college with the support provided by the SAS staff. The SAS program is supported by a grant from the U.S. Department of Education and funds from Rocky Mountain College. The small size of the college, together with the caring attitude of the faculty and an excellent support program, make Rocky a learning disability-friendly college.

ADMISSIONS

There is no special admissions application for students with learning disabilities. All applicants must meet the same criteria, which include an ACT of 21 or SAT of 1000, a GPA of 2.5, and courses in English, math, science, and social studies. There is the opportunity to be considered for a conditional admission if scores or grades are below the cutoffs. To identify and provide necessary support services as soon as possible, students with disabilities are encouraged to complete a Services for Academic Success application when they are accepted. All documentation is confidential. Recommended courses for admissions include 4 years of English, 3 years of math, 3 years of social science, 2 years of science lab, and 2 years of a foreign language.

ADMISSIONS INFO FOR STUDENTS WITH LEARNING DIFFERENCES

SAT/ACT required: Yes
Interview required: No
Essay required: No
Additional application required: No
Documentation required for:
  LD: Psycho ed evaluation
  ADHD: Diagnosis based on DSM-V; history of behaviors impairing functioning in academic setting; diagnostic interview; history of symptoms; evidence of ongoing behaviors.
  ASD: Psycho ed evaluation
Documentation submitted to: Services for Academic Success
Special Ed. HS course work accepted: No
Separate application required for Programs/Services: Yes
Contact Information
Name of program or department: Services for Academic Success (SAS)
Telephone: 406-657-1128
Fax: 406-259-9751

Rocky Mountain College

Additional Information
SAS provides a variety of services tailored to meet a student's individual needs. Services are free to participants and include developmental course work in reading, writing, and mathematics, study skills classes, tutoring in all subjects, academic, career, and personal counseling, graduate school counseling, accommodations for students with learning disabilities, alternative testing arrangements, taping of lectures or textbooks, cultural and academic enrichment opportunities, and advocacy. SAS staff meets with each student to talk about the supportive services the student needs and then develop a semester plan. Skills classes for college credit are offered in math, English, and studying techniques.

General Admissions
Very important factors considered include: academic GPA, standardized test scores, level of applicant's interest. *Important factors considered include:* rigor of secondary school record, application essay, recommendation(s). *Other factors considered include:* class rank, interview, extracurricular activities, talent/ability, character/personal qualities, first generation, alumni/ae relation, work experience. *Freshman Admission Requirements:* High school diploma is required and GED is accepted. *Academic units required:* 4 English, 4 math, 3 science, 3 social studies, 2 history, 3 academic electives.

Accommodations or Services
Accommodations are decided upon an individual basis after a thorough review of appropriate, current documentation. The accommodations requests must be supported through the documentation provided and must be logically linked to the current impact of the condition on academic functioning.

Financial Aid
Students should submit: FAFSA. Applicants will be notified of awards on a rolling basis beginning 2/15. The Princeton Review suggests that all financial aid forms be submitted as soon as possible after October 1. *Need-based scholarships/grants offered:* College/university scholarship or grant aid from institutional funds; Federal Pell; Private scholarships; SEOG; State scholarships/grants. *Loan aid offered:* Direct PLUS loans; Direct Subsidized Stafford Loans; Direct Unsubsidized Stafford Loans. Federal Work-Study Program available. Institutional employment available.

Campus Life
Activities: Campus Ministries; Choral groups; Concert band; Drama/theater; International Student Organization; Jazz band; Music ensembles; Musical theater; Pep band; Student government; Student newspaper; Yearbook. **Organizations:** 28 registered organizations, 1 honor society, 4 religious organizations. **Athletics (Intercollegiate):** *Men:* basketball, cheerleading, football, golf, skiing (downhill/alpine) *Women:* basketball, cheerleading, golf, skiing (downhill/alpine), soccer, volleyball. **On-Campus Highlights:** Prescott Hall, Morledge-Kimball Hall, Herb Klindt Field-Football Stadium, Fortin Athletic Center, Losekamp Hall-Music Theatre.

ACCOMMODATIONS

Allowed in exams:

Calculators	Yes
Dictionary	Yes
Computer	Yes
Spell-checker	Yes
Extended test time	Yes
Scribe	Yes
Proctors	Yes
Oral exams	Yes
Note-takers	Yes

Support services for students with

LD	Yes
ADHD	Yes
ASD	Yes
Distraction-reduced environment	Yes
Recording of lecture allowed	Yes
Reading technology:	Yes
Audio books	Yes
Other assistive technology	Yes
Priority registration	No

Added costs for services:

For LD:	No
For ADHD:	No
For ASD:	No
LD specialists	Yes
ADHD & ASD coaching	No
ASD specialists	No
Professional tutors	Yes
Peer tutors	Yes
Max. hours/week for services	Unlimited
How professors are notified of student approved accommodations	Student and Director

COLLEGE GRADUATION REQUIREMENTS

Course waivers allowed	No
Course substitutions allowed	Yes
In what courses	Varies

The University of Montana

32 CAMPUS DRIVE, MISSOULA, MT 59812 • ADMISSIONS: 243-6266 • FAX: 406-243-5711

CAMPUS

Type of school	Public
Environment	City
Support	S

STUDENTS

Undergrad enrollment	8,958
% male/female	45/55
% from out of state	28
% frosh live on campus	72

FINANCIAL FACTS

Annual in-state tuition	$5,182
Annual out-of-state tuition	$23,062
Room and board	$9,178
Required fees	$1,881

GENERAL ADMISSIONS INFO

Application fee	$30
Priority deadline	3/1

Nonfall registration accepted. Admission may be deferred for a maximum of 1 year.

Range SAT EBRW	540–650
Range SAT Math	520–620
Range ACT Composite	21–26

ACADEMICS

Student/faculty ratio	17:1
% students returning for sophomore year	69
% students graduating within 4 years	25
% students graduating within 6 years	49

Most classes have 20–29 students.
Most lab/discussion sessions have 20–29 students.

PROGRAMS/SERVICES FOR STUDENTS WITH LEARNING DIFFERENCES

Disability Services for Students ensures that programs of the University of Montana are as accessible to and usable by students with disabilities as they are for any student. We determine the student's eligibility to request reasonable modifications and coordinate modifications for those who are registered with our office. Disability Services assigns a coordinator to each student. The Coordinator and the student collaborate to address barriers in the university program that may deny or limit full and equal program access. Students are encouraged to secure their rights through the student-coordinator relationship.

ADMISSIONS

To register with Disability Services, students contact the office, meet with a coordinator, provide disability documentation, and choose the modifications that best apply in the student's academic study.

Additional Information

The University of Montana offers a wide variety of support services to all students including students with disabilities. Examples include math lab, writing center, library assistance, health services including medical, counseling,dental, and pharmacy, tutoring services, study groups, academic and career advising, study skill courses, financial aid, housing, leadership development programs.

ADMISSIONS INFO FOR STUDENTS WITH LEARNING DIFFERENCES

SAT/ACT required: Y/N depends if Test Optional
Interview required: No
Essay required: Not Applicable
Additional application required: Yes
Documentation required for:
  ASD: To register with Disability Services, medical records, psycho-educational testing, or school records are recommended as helpful documentation. We suggest that the documentation includes the following information: Credentials and contact information of the evaluator(s) including the professional's name, title, certification/license, mailing address, telephone number and signature. Diagnostic statement identifying the disability with the date of diagnosis. Description of the current impact and functional limitations caused by the student's disability. Severity of the disability: mild, moderate, or severe. Approximate duration and prognosis of the disability. History of clinical contact with student including the date of the last clinical contact. Statement of how treatment such as medication impacts the student's functioning in an academic, workplace, and/or residential setting. Recommendations for modifications in order to equalize the student's educational opportunities at the university. (e.g., test taking, note taking, comprehension, and/or class attendance).
Documentation submitted to: Disability Services for Students
Special Ed. HS course work accepted: No
Separate application required for Programs/Services: No
Contact Information
Name of program or department: Disability Services for Students
Telephone: 406-243-2243
Fax: 406-243-5330
Email: dss@umontana.edu

The University of Montana

GENERAL ADMISSIONS

Very important factors considered include: rigor of secondary school record, class rank, academic GPA, standardized test scores. *Important factors considered include:* extracurricular activities, talent/ability. *Other factors considered include:* application essay, recommendation(s). *Freshman Admission Requirements:* High school diploma is required and GED is accepted. *Academic units required:* 4 English, 3 math, 2 science, 2 science labs, 3 social studies, 2 history. *Academic units recommended:* 2 foreign language, 2 computer science, 2 visual/performing arts, 2 units from above areas or other academic areas.

ACCOMMODATIONS OR SERVICES

Accommodations are decided upon an individual basis after a thorough review of appropriate, current documentation. The accommodations requests must be supported through the documentation provided and must be logically linked to the current impact of the condition on academic functioning.

FINANCIAL AID

Students should submit: FAFSA. Applicants will be notified of awards on a rolling basis beginning 3/16. The Princeton Review suggests that all financial aid forms be submitted as soon as possible after October 1. *Need-based scholarships/grants offered:* College/university scholarship or grant aid from institutional funds; Federal Pell; Private scholarships; SEOG; State scholarships/grants. *Loan aid offered:* Direct PLUS loans; Direct Subsidized Stafford Loans; Direct Unsubsidized Stafford Loans. Federal Work-Study Program available. Institutional employment available.

CAMPUS LIFE

Activities: Campus Ministries; Choral groups; Concert band; Dance; Drama/theater; International Student Organization; Jazz band; Literary magazine; Marching band; Model UN; Music ensembles; Musical theater; Opera; Pep band; Radio station; Student government; Student newspaper; Symphony orchestra; Television station. **Organizations:** 150 registered organizations, 5 fraternities, 4 sororities. **Athletics (Intercollegiate):** *Men:* basketball, cheerleading, cross-country, football, tennis, track/field (outdoor), track/field (indoor). *Women:* basketball, cheerleading, cross-country, golf, soccer, tennis, track/field (outdoor), track/field (indoor), volleyball. **On-Campus Highlights:** Adams Event Center (sports, entertainment, etc.), Washington-Grizzly Stadium (football, other), Campus Recreation Center (student recreation), University Center (student center, movie theater), Performing Arts-RadioTV Center (public radio-TV).

ACCOMMODATIONS

Allowed in exams:	
Calculators	Yes
Dictionary	No
Computer	Yes
Spell-checker	Yes
Extended test time	Yes
Scribe	Yes
Proctors	Yes
Oral exams	No
Note-takers	Yes
Support services for students with	
LD	Yes
ADHD	Yes
ASD	Yes
Distraction-reduced environment	Yes
Recording of lecture allowed	Yes
Reading technology:	Yes
Audio books	Yes
Other assistive technology Read&Write Gold, JAWS (screen reader), Dragon Naturally Speaking (voice recognition), Smart Pens, Olympus audio recorders.	
Priority registration	Yes
Added costs for services:	
For LD:	No
For ADHD:	No
For ASD:	No
LD specialists	Not Applicable
ADHD & ASD coaching	No
ASD specialists	No
Professional tutors	No
Peer tutors	Not Applicable
Max. hours/week for services	Varies
How professors are notified of student approved accommodations	Student

COLLEGE GRADUATION REQUIREMENTS

Course waivers allowed	No
Course substitutions allowed	Yes
In what courses	

Students can receive assistance with course substitution petition from Disability Services.

The University of Montana—Western

710 South Atlantic, Dillon, MT 59725 • Admissions: 406-683-7331 • Fax: 406-683-7493

CAMPUS

Type of school	Public
Environment	Rural
Support	S

STUDENTS

Undergrad enrollment	1,467
% male/female	39/61
% from out of state	24
% frosh live on campus	72

FINANCIAL FACTS

Annual in-state tuition	$5,347
Annual out-of-state tuition	$23,062
Room and board	$9,178
Required fees	$1,897

GENERAL ADMISSIONS INFO

Application fee	$30
Priority deadline	7/1

Nonfall registration accepted. Admission may be deferred for a maximum of 1 year.

Range SAT EBRW	430–540
Range SAT Math	420–530
Range ACT Composite	17–22

ACADEMICS

Student/faculty ratio	19:1
% students returning for sophomore year	68

Most classes have fewer than 10 students.

PROGRAMS/SERVICES FOR STUDENTS WITH LEARNING DIFFERENCES

The U of Montana, Western strives to accommodate all students with special needs. These needs may be physical, social, and/or academic. Almost all services are free to the student. Both the Dean of Students and the Student Affairs Offices are in charge of making special accommodations available to students with learning disabilities. If an applicant has a documented learning disability and requests special accommodations for a class, he or she must contact the Associate Dean of Students so that arrangements can be made. The professor of the class, the Associate Dean, and the student will meet to set up an IEP for that class, and documentation will be kept on file in the Student Life Office.

ADMISSIONS

The college has no special requirements other than those outlined by the state Board of Regents: a valid high school diploma or GED. Criteria for general admission includes 4 years of English, 3 years of math, 3 years of science, 3 years of social studies, and 2 years from foreign language, computer science, visual/performing arts, or vocational education; a 2.5 GPA (minimum 2.0 for students with learning disabilities); a 20 ACT or 960 SAT; and ranking within the top 50 percent of the applicant's class. Students with documented learning disabilities may request waivers or substitutions in courses affected by the disability. Because Western Montana is a small university, each individual can set up an admissions plan. There is a 15 percent window of exemption for some students who do not meet admission requirements. These students can be admitted provisionally if they provide satisfactory evidence that they are prepared to pursue successfully the special courses required.

Additional Information

Students who present appropriate documentation may be eligible for some of the following services or accommodations: the use of calculators, dictionaries, computers, or spellcheckers during tests; extended time on tests; distractionfree environments for tests; proctors; scribes; oral exams; note-takers; tape recorders in class; books on tape; and priority registration. The Learning Center offers skill-building classes in reading, writing, and math. These classes do not count toward a student's GPA, but they do for athletic eligibility. Students whose ACT or entrance tests show that they would profit from such instruction will be placed in courses that will best meet their needs and ensure a successful college career. Free tutoring is available in most areas on a drop-in basis and/or at prescribed

ADMISSIONS INFO FOR STUDENTS WITH LEARNING DIFFERENCES

SAT/ACT required: Yes
Interview required: No
Essay required: No
Additional application required: No
Documentation required for:
 LD: Psycho ed evaluation
 ADHD: Diagnosis based on DSM-V; history of behaviors impairing functioning in academic setting; diagnostic interview; history of symptoms; evidence of ongoing behaviors.
 ASD: Psycho ed evaluation
Documentation submitted to: Disability Services
Special Ed. HS course work accepted: Yes
Separate application required for Programs/Services: Yes
Contact Information
Name of program or department: Disability Services
Telephone: 406-683-7565
Fax: 406-683-7570

The University of Montana—Western

times. Services and accommodations are available for undergraduate and graduate students.

GENERAL ADMISSIONS

Very important factors considered include: rigor of secondary school record, class rank, academic GPA, standardized test scores. *Freshman Admission Requirements:* High school diploma is required and GED is accepted. *Academic units required:* 4 English, 3 math, 2 science, 2 science labs, 2 social studies, 1 history, 2 academic electives. *Academic units recommended:* 4 English, 4 math, 3 science, 2 science labs, 2 social studies, 1 history, 3 academic electives.

ACCOMMODATIONS OR SERVICES

Accommodations are decided upon an individual basis after a thorough review of appropriate, current documentation. The accommodations requests must be supported through the documentation provided and must be logically linked to the current impact of the condition on academic functioning.

FINANCIAL AID

Students should submit: FAFSA. Applicants will be notified of awards on a rolling basis beginning 3/1. The Princeton Review suggests that all financial aid forms be submitted as soon as possible after October 1. *Need-based scholarships/grants offered:* College/university scholarship or grant aid from institutional funds; Federal Pell; Private scholarships; SEOG; State scholarships/grants. *Loan aid offered:* Direct PLUS loans; Direct Subsidized Stafford Loans; Direct Unsubsidized Stafford Loans. Federal Work-Study Program available. Institutional employment available.

CAMPUS LIFE

Activities: Campus Ministries; Choral groups; Drama/theater; Music ensembles; Musical theater; Radio station; Student government. **Organizations:** 25 registered organizations, 2 honor societies, 2 religious organizations. **Athletics (Intercollegiate):** *Men:* basketball, cheerleading, football, golf, rodeo *Women:* basketball, cheerleading, golf, rodeo, volleyball. **On-Campus Highlights:** SUB (Sudent Union Building), Straugh Arena, The Cup, STC Tech Building, Bark'n Bite.

ACCOMMODATIONS

Allowed in exams:

Calculators	Yes
Dictionary	Yes
Computer	Yes
Spell-checker	Yes
Extended test time	Yes
Scribe	Yes
Proctors	Yes
Oral exams	Yes
Note-takers	Yes

Support services for students with

LD	Yes
ADHD	Yes
ASD	Yes
Distraction-reduced environment	Yes
Recording of lecture allowed	Yes
Reading technology:	Yes
Audio books	Yes
Other assistive technology	Yes
Priority registration	Yes

Added costs for services:

For LD:	No
For ADHD:	No
For ASD:	No
LD specialists	No
ADHD & ASD coaching	No
ASD specialists	No
Professional tutors	Yes
Peer tutors	Yes
Max. hours/week for services	Unlimited

How professors are notified of student approved accommodations
Student and Director

COLLEGE GRADUATION REQUIREMENTS

Course waivers allowed	Yes
In what coursesGeneral education courses	
Course substitutions allowed	Yes
In what coursesGeneral education courses	

University of Nebraska–Lincoln

1400 R St, Lincoln, NE 68588-0417 • Admissions: 402-472-2023 • Fax: 402-472-0670

CAMPUS
Type of school	Public
Environment	City
Support	S

STUDENTS
Undergrad enrollment	20,954
% male/female	52/48
% from out of state	23
% frosh live on campus	87

FINANCIAL FACTS
Annual in-state tuition	$7,350
Annual out-of-state tuition	$23,145
Room and board	$10,930
Required fees	$1,804

GENERAL ADMISSIONS INFO
Application fee	$45
Priority deadline	3/1
Regular application deadline	5/1

Nonfall registration accepted.

Range SAT EBRW	550–680
Range SAT Math	550–700
Range ACT Composite	22–29

ACADEMICS
Student/faculty ratio	21:1
% students returning for sophomore year	83
% students graduating within 4 years	39
% students graduating within 6 years	68

Most classes have fewer than 10 students. Most lab/discussion sessions have fewer than 10 students.

PROGRAMS/SERVICES FOR STUDENTS WITH LEARNING DIFFERENCES

The mission of SSD is to facilitate equal and integrated access to the academic, social, cultural and recreational programs offered at the University of Nebraska-Lincoln and to foster independent decision making skills necessary to achieve personal and academic success. The University's policy is that no qualified student with a disability will be excluded from participating in any university program or activity, denied the benefits of any university program or activity, or otherwise subjected to discrimination with regard to any university program or activity. Services are designed to meet the unique educational needs of enrolled students with documented disabilities. SSD assists students in realizing their academic potential and facilitates the elimination of physical, programmatic, and attitudinal barriers. Students are encouraged to assess their needs realistically, to take advantage of appropriate support, and to be clear and proactive about gaining assistance. Any student who needs a reasonable accommodation based on a qualified disability is required to register with the SSD office for assistance. The Office of Services for Students with Disabilities also serves as a resource to UNL's administrative units and academic departments that have responsibility to accommodate faculty, staff and campus visitors with disabilities. The University of Nebraska Building Accepting Campus Communities (BACC) program offers a 3 credit course for students registered with the SSD. This course provides instruction in test taking strategies, note taking skills, how to write college research papers, and time management strategies. Students learn self-advocacy skills, and receive individualized instruction on study strategies specific to their needs and the courses they are taking.

ADMISSIONS

Students with disabilities are considered for admission on the same basis as all other applicants and must meet the same academic standards.

Additional Information

The objectives of the UNL Disability Club are academics, advocacy, service opportunities and social opportunities.

ADMISSIONS INFO FOR STUDENTS WITH LEARNING DIFFERENCES

SAT/ACT required: Yes
Interview required: No
Essay required: Not Applicable
Additional application required: Yes
Documentation required for:
 LD: No required documentation
 ADHD: No required documentation
 ASD: No required documentation
Documentation submitted to: Services for Students with Disabilities
Special Ed. HS course work accepted: No
Separate application required for Programs/Services: No
Contact Information
Name of program or department: Services for Students with Disabilities
Telephone: 402-472-3787
Fax: 402-472-0080
Email: acontreras3@unl.edu

University of Nebraska–Lincoln

GENERAL ADMISSIONS
Very important factors considered include: class rank, standardized test scores. *Important factors considered include:* rigor of secondary school record. *Other factors considered include:* academic GPA. *Freshman Admission Requirements:* High school diploma is required and GED is accepted. *Academic units required:* 4 English, 4 math, 3 science, 1 science lab, 2 foreign language, 1 social studies, 2 history.

ACCOMMODATIONS OR SERVICES
Accommodations are decided upon an individual basis after a thorough review of appropriate, current documentation. The accommodations requests must be supported through the documentation provided and must be logically linked to the current impact of the condition on academic functioning.

FINANCIAL AID
Students should submit: FAFSA. Applicants will be notified of awards on a rolling basis beginning 4/1. The Princeton Review suggests that all financial aid forms be submitted as soon as possible after October 1. *Need-based scholarships/grants offered:* College/university scholarship or grant aid from institutional funds; Federal Pell; Private scholarships; SEOG; State scholarships/grants. *Loan aid offered:* Direct PLUS loans; Direct Subsidized Stafford Loans; Direct Unsubsidized Stafford Loans. Federal Work-Study Program available. Institutional employment available.

CAMPUS LIFE
Activities: Campus Ministries; Choral groups; Concert band; Dance; Drama/theater; International Student Organization; Jazz band; Literary magazine; Marching band; Model UN; Music ensembles; Musical theater; Opera; Pep band; Radio station; Student government; Student newspaper; Student-run film society; Symphony orchestra; Television station. **Organizations:** 335 registered organizations, 57 honor societies, 25 religious organizations. 27 fraternities, 18 sororities. **Athletics (Intercollegiate):** *Men:* baseball, basketball, cross-country, football, golf, gymnastics, rodeo, tennis, track/field (outdoor), track/field (indoor), wrestling. *Women:* basketball, bowling, cross-country, diving, golf, gymnastics, riflery, rodeo, soccer, softball, swimming, tennis, track/field (outdoor), track/field (indoor), volleyball. **On-Campus Highlights:** Student Union, Campus Recreation Center, Arboretum and Sculpture Garden, Memorial Stadium and Hewitt Center, Adele Coryell Hall Learning Commons.

ACCOMMODATIONS

Allowed in exams:

Calculators	Yes
Dictionary	Yes
Computer	Yes
Spell-checker	Yes
Extended test time	Yes
Scribe	Yes
Proctors	No
Oral exams	Yes
Note-takers	Yes

Support services for students with

LD	Yes
ADHD	Yes
ASD	Yes
Distraction-reduced environment	Yes
Recording of lecture allowed	Yes
Reading technology:	Yes
Audio books	Yes
Other assistive technology	JAWS, Dragon, Optelec Reader, Zoomtext
Priority registration	Yes

Added costs for services:

For LD:	No
For ADHD:	No
For ASD:	No
LD specialists	No
ADHD & ASD coaching	No
ASD specialists	Yes
Professional tutors	No
Peer tutors	Yes
Max. hours/week for services	Varies
How professors are notified of student approved accommodations	Director and Student

COLLEGE GRADUATION REQUIREMENTS

Course waivers allowed	No
Course substitutions allowed	Yes
In what courses	Foreign Language

Wayne State College

1111 MAIN STREET, WAYNE, NE 68787 • ADMISSIONS: 402-375-7234 • FAX: 402-375-7204

CAMPUS
Type of school	Public
Environment	Rural
Support	S

STUDENTS
Undergrad enrollment	2,610
% male/female	43/57
% from out of state	15
% frosh live on campus	95

FINANCIAL FACTS
Annual in-state tuition	$5,310
Annual out-of-state tuition	$10,620
Room and board	$6,928
Required fees	$1,679

GENERAL ADMISSIONS INFO
Priority deadline	12/1
Regular application deadline	8/21

Nonfall registration accepted. Admission may be deferred.

Range SAT EBRW	NR
Range SAT Math	NR
Range ACT Composite	18–25

ACADEMICS
Student/faculty ratio	19:1
% students returning for sophomore year	69
% students graduating within 4 years	25
% students graduating within 6 years	48

Most classes have 10–19 students.
Most lab/discussion sessions have 10–19 students.

PROGRAMS/SERVICES FOR STUDENTS WITH LEARNING DIFFERENCES

The Disability Services Program provides services for students with disabilities at Wayne State College. Disability services are offered through the Holland Academic Success Center and include determination of eligibility for services, referral to appropriate resources and responses to requests for accommodations. Accommodations can include exam accommodations, recorded books and campus reader service, learning strategies, support/discussion groups, and screening and referral for evaluation. The TRiO Student Support Services mission is to empower students with disabilities to lead healthy and enriched lives. TRiO works collaboratively with the Disability Services Office on campus to ensure equal learning opportunities for students with disabilities.

ADMISSIONS

Admission to Wayne State College is open to all high school graduates or students with a GED or equivalent. High school special education courses are accepted.

Additional Information

Holland Academic Success Center coaches create a personal and confidential relationship with students to focus on academic goals. Specific plans for these goals are structured in weekly individual meetings throughout the semester. Academic Coaching: motivates students to take ownership of their academic success; focuses students on their academic goals and helps them identify the steps to reach them; develops time management skills; encourages use of all available campus resources; does not take the place of program advisors.

ADMISSIONS INFO FOR STUDENTS WITH LEARNING DIFFERENCES

SAT/ACT required: Yes
Interview required: No
Essay required: N/A
Additional application required: No
Documentation required for:
  LD: Psycho ed evaluation to include: relevant historical info, instructional interventions, related services, age diagnosed, objective data (aptitude, achievement, info processing), test scores (standard, percentile and grade equivalents) and describe functional limitations.
  ADHD: Diagnosis based on DSM-V; history of behaviors impairing functioning in academic setting; diagnostic interview; history of symptoms; evidence of ongoing behaviors.
  ASD: Psycho ed evaluation
Documentation submitted to: Counseling Center
Special Ed. HS course work accepted: Yes
Separate application required for Programs/Services: No
Contact Information
Name of program or department: Counseling Center
Telephone: 402-375-7496
Email: jubose1@wsc.edu

Wayne State College

GENERAL ADMISSIONS

Freshman Admission Requirements: High school diploma is required and GED is accepted. *Academic units recommended:* 4 English, 3 math, 2 science, 2 foreign language, 3 social studies, 2 computer science, 2 visual/performing arts.

ACCOMMODATIONS OR SERVICES

Accommodations are decided upon an individual basis after a thorough review of appropriate, current documentation. The accommodations requests must be supported through the documentation provided and must be logically linked to the current impact of the condition on academic functioning.

FINANCIAL AID

Students should submit: FAFSA. Applicants will be notified of awards on a rolling basis beginning 4/1. The Princeton Review suggests that all financial aid forms be submitted as soon as possible after October 1. *Need-based scholarships/grants offered:* College/university scholarship or grant aid from institutional funds; Federal Pell; Private scholarships; SEOG; State scholarships/grants. *Loan aid offered:* Direct PLUS loans; Direct Subsidized Stafford Loans; Direct Unsubsidized Stafford Loans. Federal Work-Study Program available. Institutional employment available.

CAMPUS LIFE

Activities: Campus Ministries; Choral groups; Concert band; Dance; Drama/theater; International Student Organization; Jazz band; Literary magazine; Marching band; Music ensembles; Musical theater; Pep band; Radio station; Student government; Student newspaper; Television station. **Organizations:** 96 registered organizations, 18 honor societies, 7 religious organizations. 2 fraternities, 3 sororities. **Athletics (Intercollegiate):** *Men:* baseball, basketball, cross-country, football, golf, track/field (outdoor), track/field (indoor). *Women:* basketball, cross-country, golf, soccer, softball, track/field (outdoor), track/field (indoor), volleyball.

ACCOMMODATIONS

Allowed in exams:	
Calculators	Yes
Dictionary	Yes
Computer	Yes
Spell-checker	Yes
Extended test time	Yes
Scribe	Yes
Proctors	Yes
Oral exams	Yes
Note-takers	Yes
Support services for students with	
LD	Yes
ADHD	Yes
ASD	Yes
Distraction-reduced environment	Yes
Recording of lecture allowed	Yes
Reading technology:	Yes
Audio books	Yes
Other assistive technology	Kurzweil Program
Priority registration	Yes
Added costs for services:	
For LD:	No
For ADHD:	No
For ASD:	No
LD specialists	No
ADHD & ASD coaching	No
ASD specialists	No
Professional tutors	No
Peer tutors	Yes
Max. hours/week for services	Unlimited
How professors are notified of student approved accommodations	Student

COLLEGE GRADUATION REQUIREMENTS

Course waivers allowed	No
Course substitutions allowed	No

University of Nevada, Las Vegas

4505 S. Maryland Parkway, Las Vegas, NV 89154-1021 • Admissions: 702-774-8658 • Fax: 702-774-8008

CAMPUS
Type of school	Public
Environment	Metropolis
Support	CS

STUDENTS
Undergrad enrollment	23,329
% male/female	44/56
% from out of state	11
% frosh live on campus	24

FINANCIAL FACTS
Annual in-state tuition	$6,764
Annual out-of-state tuition	$20,952
Room and board	$10,806
Required fees	$546

GENERAL ADMISSIONS INFO
Application fee	$60
Priority deadline	2/1
Regular application deadline	7/1

Nonfall registration accepted. Admission may be deferred for a maximum of 1 year.

Range SAT EBRW	440–560
Range SAT Math	450–560
Range ACT Composite	18–25

ACADEMICS
Student/faculty ratio	20:1
% students returning for sophomore year	74

Most classes have 20–29 students.
Most lab/discussion sessions have 20–29 students.

PROGRAMS/SERVICES FOR STUDENTS WITH LEARNING DIFFERENCES

The Disability Resource Center (DRC) provides academic accommodations for students with documented disabilities who are otherwise qualified for university programs. Compliance with Section 504 requires that reasonable academic accommodations be made for students with disabilities. These accommodations might include note-taking, testing accommodations, books on tape, readers, assistive technology, housing adjustments and dietary adjustments. To establish services, students will need to provide DRC with appropriate documentation of their disability. Appropriate accommodations will be determined after both a review of the reporting student's documentation of a disability as well as a discussion with that student to clarify his or her disability related needs.

ADMISSIONS

All applicants are expected to meet the same admission criteria. Freshmen applicants should have a weighted 3.0 grade point average (GPA) in the following high school academic courses: 4 years English, 3 years math, 3 years social science, and 3 years natural science with a total of 13 units. If a student has completed the 13 core high school courses but does not have a 3.0 GPA the student may fulfill any of the following admission requirements to be admissible to UNLV: Have a combined score from the SAT Critical Reading and Math sections of at least 1040, or an ACT composite score of at least 22, or a Nevada Advanced High School Diploma. If the applicant does not satisfy the minimum admission requirements the student may still be eligible for admission.

Additional Information

The Disability Resource Center offers help to all students on campus who have a diagnosed disability. Following their evaluation students meet with DRC specialists to develop a plan for services. Psychological services are available through the Counseling and Psychological Services Office. Assistance is provided year round to active students. Students remain active by requesting service each semester. Services are available to undergraduate, graduate, and continuing education students.

ADMISSIONS INFO FOR STUDENTS WITH LEARNING DIFFERENCES
SAT/ACT required: No
Interview required: No
Essay required: N/A
Additional application required: No
Documentation required for:
 LD: Psycho ed evaluation
 ADHD: Psycho ed evaluation
 ASD: Psycho ed evaluation
Documentation submitted to:DRC
Special Ed. HS course work accepted: No
Separate application required for Programs/Services: No
Contact Information
Name of program or department: Disability Resource Center (DRC)
Telephone: 702-895-0866
Fax: 702-895-0651

University of Nevada, Las Vegas

GENERAL ADMISSIONS

Very important factors considered include: rigor of secondary school record, academic GPA. *Important factors considered include:* standardized test scores. *Freshman Admission Requirements:* High school diploma is required and GED is not accepted. *Academic units required:* 4 English, 3 math, 3 science, 2 science labs, 3 social studies,

ACCOMMODATIONS OR SERVICES

Accommodations are decided upon an individual basis after a thorough review of appropriate, current documentation. The accommodations requests must be supported through the documentation provided and must be logically linked to the current impact of the condition on academic functioning.

FINANCIAL AID

Students should submit: FAFSA. The Princeton Review suggests that all financial aid forms be submitted as soon as possible after October 1. *Need-based scholarships/grants offered:* College/university scholarship or grant aid from institutional funds; Federal Pell; Private scholarships; SEOG; State scholarships/grants. *Loan aid offered:* Direct PLUS loans; Direct Subsidized Stafford Loans; Direct Unsubsidized Stafford Loans. Federal Work-Study Program available. Institutional employment available.

CAMPUS LIFE

Activities: Campus Ministries; Choral groups; Concert band; Dance; Drama/theater; International Student Organization; Jazz band; Literary magazine; Marching band; Model UN; Music ensembles; Musical theater; Opera; Pep band; Radio station; Student government; Student newspaper; Student-run film society; Symphony orchestra; Television station; Yearbook. **Organizations:** 24 honor societies, 14 religious organizations. 8 fraternities, 6 sororities. **Athletics (Intercollegiate):** *Men:* baseball, basketball, football, golf, soccer, swimming, tennis. *Women:* basketball, cross-country, equestrian sports, golf, soccer, softball, swimming, tennis, track/field (outdoor), volleyball. **On-Campus Highlights:** Lied Library, Artemus W. Ham Concert Hall, Moyer Student Union, Judy Bailey Theatre, Student Services Complex.

ACCOMMODATIONS

Allowed in exams:	
Calculators	Yes
Dictionary	Yes
Computer	Yes
Spell-checker	Yes
Extended test time	Yes
Scribe	Yes
Proctors	Yes
Oral exams	Yes
Note-takers	Yes
Support services for students with	
LD	Yes
ADHD	Yes
ASD	Yes
Distraction-reduced environment	Yes
Recording of lecture allowed	Yes
Reading technology:	Yes
Audio books	Yes
Other assistive technology	Yes
Priority registration	Yes
Added costs for services:	
For LD:	No
For ADHD:	No
For ASD:	No
LD specialists	Yes
ADHD & ASD coaching	No
ASD specialists	No
Professional tutors	No
Peer tutors	No
Max. hours/week for services	N/A
How professors are notified of student approved accommodations	Student

COLLEGE GRADUATION REQUIREMENTS

Course waivers allowed	No
Course substitutions allowed	Yes
In what courses	

Foreign language is only required for English majors; substitutions are available. Math is required for graduation. All requests go to Academic Standards Committee after initial approval from the College Advisor, Chair of the Department, and Dean.

Colby-Sawyer College

541 MAIN STREET, NEW LONDON, NH 03257-7835 • ADMISSIONS: 603-526-3700 • FAX: 603-526-3452

CAMPUS

Type of school	Private (nonprofit)
Environment	Rural
Support	CS

STUDENTS

Undergrad enrollment	942
% male/female	35/65
% from out of state	68
% frosh live on campus	98

FINANCIAL FACTS

Annual tuition	$29,620
Room and board	$10,340
Required fees	NR

GENERAL ADMISSIONS INFO

Application fee	$45
Regular application deadline	4/1

Nonfall registration accepted. Admission may be deferred for a maximum of 1 year.

Range SAT EBRW	440–540
Range SAT Math	440–530
Range ACT Composite	18–22

ACADEMICS

Student/faculty ratio	11:1
% students returning for sophomore year	71

Most classes have 20–29 students.
Most lab/discussion sessions have 20–29 students.

PROGRAMS/SERVICES FOR STUDENTS WITH LEARNING DIFFERENCES

Students at Colby-Sawyer College are at the center of everything the college does, and the college excels at providing an individualized learning experience. Opportunities for faculty contact and academic support services are plentiful and initiated by the student. The curriculum at Colby-Sawyer College is writing intensive, requires critical reading and thinking skills and quantitative literacy abilities. Students are required to complete an internship related to their major. Colby- Sawyer College does not offer specialized programs for students with learning or any other disabilities. Through Access Resources (AR) Colby-Sawyer has Learning Specialists who provide services to students with documented disabilities. These specialists ensure that students have equal access to the curriculum.

ADMISSIONS

There is no special admissions process for students with learning disabilities. Access Resources (AR) does not accept disability documentation prior to the student receiving an acceptance to the college and submitting an enrollment deposit. During the application process students do not disclose disability information, however, parents and students may schedule to meet with AR and bring documentation for review prior to acceptance.

Additional Information

ADA Accommodations for students with documented disabilities are offered on an individualized basis. These include half-hour weekly meeting with a learning specialist for academic coaching, Live Scribe Echo Pens on loan, access to Kurzweil, and Dragon Naturally Speaking at the Academic Development Center and accommodations for testing. Professors are not required to modify curricular expectations (late submissions of work, modified assignments or exams, use of word banks-if not offered to entire class, etc.) Students need to have good self-advocacy and communication skills, the ability to analyze and synthesize information using college level material, the willingness to attend classes regularly.

ADMISSIONS INFO FOR STUDENTS WITH LEARNING DIFFERENCES

SAT/ACT required: Optional
Interview required: No
Essay required: Yes
Additional application required: No
Documentation required for:
  LD: Psychoeducational evaluation—aptitude and achievement results
  ADHD: Diagnostic interview and substantiation and statement of diagnosis
  ASD: Psycho ed evaluation
Documentation submitted to: Academic Development Center
Special Ed. HS course work accepted: Yes
Separate application required for Programs/Services: No
Contact Information
Name of program or department: Academic Development Center
Telephone: 603-526-3711
Fax: 603-526-3115

Colby-Sawyer College

GENERAL ADMISSIONS

Very important factors considered include: rigor of secondary school record, academic GPA, interview. *Important factors considered include:* class rank, application essay, standardized test scores, recommendation(s), extracurricular activities, talent/ability, alumni/ae relation, volunteer work, work experience, level of applicant's interest. *Other factors considered include:* first generation, geographical residence, state residency. *Freshman Admission Requirements:* High school diploma is required and GED is accepted. *Academic units recommended:* 4 English, 3 math, 3 science, 3 science labs, 2 foreign language, 3 social studies.

ACCOMMODATIONS OR SERVICES

Accommodations are decided upon an individual basis after a thorough review of appropriate, current documentation. The accommodations requests must be supported through the documentation provided and must be logically linked to the current impact of the condition on academic functioning.

FINANCIAL AID

Students should submit: FAFSA. Applicants will be notified of awards on a rolling basis beginning 3/1. The Princeton Review suggests that all financial aid forms be submitted as soon as possible after October 1. *Need-based scholarships/grants offered:* College/university scholarship or grant aid from institutional funds; Federal Pell; Private scholarships; SEOG; State scholarships/grants. *Loan aid offered:* Federal Work-Study Program available. Institutional employment available.

CAMPUS LIFE

Activities: Choral groups; Dance; Drama/theater; Literary magazine; Musical theater; Radio station; Student government; Student newspaper; Yearbook. **Organizations:** 40 registered organizations, 5 honor societies, 1 religious organization. **Athletics (Intercollegiate):** *Men:* baseball, basketball, diving, equestrian sports, skiing (downhill/alpine), soccer, swimming, tennis, track/field (outdoor). *Women:* basketball, diving, equestrian sports, lacrosse, skiing (downhill/alpine), soccer, swimming, tennis, track/field (outdoor), volleyball. **On-Campus Highlights:** Dan and Kathleen Hogan Sports Center, Susan Colgate Cleveland Library/Learning Center, Lethbridge Lodge, Thornton Livingroom, Rooke Hall.

ACCOMMODATIONS

Allowed in exams:	
Calculators	Yes
Dictionary	Yes
Computer	Yes
Spell-checker	Yes
Extended test time	Yes
Scribe	Yes
Proctors	Yes
Oral exams	No
Note-takers	Yes
Support services for students with	
LD	Yes
ADHD	Yes
ASD	Yes
Distraction-reduced environment	Yes
Recording of lecture allowed	Yes
Reading technology:	Yes
Audio books	Yes
Other assistive technology	Yes
Priority registration	No
Added costs for services:	
For LD:	No
For ADHD:	No
For ASD:	No
LD specialists	Yes
ADHD & ASD coaching	Yes
ASD specialists	Yes
Professional tutors	Yes
Peer tutors	Yes
Max. hours/week for services	1 hour per class per week plus 3 writing consultations per paper
How professors are notified of student approved accommodations	Student

COLLEGE GRADUATION REQUIREMENTS

Course waivers allowed	No
Course substitutions allowed	No

New England College

15 Main Street, Henniker, NH 03242 • Admissions: 603-428-2223 • Fax: 603-428-3155

CAMPUS

Type of school	Private (nonprofit)
Environment	Rural
Support	CS

STUDENTS

Undergrad enrollment	1,816
% male/female	40/60
% from out of state	80
% frosh live on campus	73

FINANCIAL FACTS

Annual tuition	$35,858
Room and board	$12,550
Required fees	$1,096

GENERAL ADMISSIONS INFO

Application fee	$30

Nonfall registration accepted. Admission may be deferred for a maximum of 1 year.

Range SAT EBRW	430–550
Range SAT Math	420–530
Range ACT Composite	0–0

ACADEMICS

Student/faculty ratio	13:1
% students returning for sophomore year	51
% students graduating within 4 years	35
% students graduating within 6 years	45

Most classes have fewer than 10 students. Most lab/discussion sessions have 10–19 students.

PROGRAMS/SERVICES FOR STUDENTS WITH LEARNING DIFFERENCES

Pathways Services provides services for all students in a welcoming and supportive environment. Students come to the center with a variety of academic needs. Some want help writing term papers. Some feel they read too slowly. Others are confused and anxious about their ability to perform as college students. Some students may have learning disabilities. The center provides individual or small group tutoring, academic counseling, and referral services. Tutoring is available in most subject areas. The center focuses primarily on helping students make a successful transition to New England College while supporting all students in their effort to become independent and successful learners. The support services meet the needs of students who do not require a formal, structured program, but who can find success when offered support and advocacy by a trained and experienced staff in conjunction with small classes and personal attention by faculty. Typically, these students have done well in mainstream programs in high school when given assistance. Students with learning disabilities are encouraged to visit NEC and Pathways Services to determine whether the support services will adequately meet their academic needs.

ADMISSIONS

Students with learning disabilities submit the general New England College application. Students should have a 2.0 GPA. SAT/ACT results are optional. Course requirements include 4 years of English, 2 years of math, 2 years of science, and 2 years of social studies. Documentation of the learning disability should be submitted. An interview is recommended. Successful applicants have typically done well in mainstream programs in high school when given tutorial and study skills assistance.

Additional Information

Students may elect to use the Pathways Services with regular appointments or only occasionally in response to particular or difficult assignments. The center provides tutoring in content areas; computer facilities; study skills instruction; time management strategies; writing support in planning, editing, and proofreading; referrals to other college services; and one-on-one writing support for first-year students taking WR 101–102.

ADMISSIONS INFO FOR STUDENTS WITH LEARNING DIFFERENCES

SAT/ACT required: No
Interview required: As requested
Essay required: Required
Additional application required: No
Documentation required for:
 LD: Psycho ed evaluation
 ADHD: Diagnosis based on DSM-V; history of behaviors impairing functioning in academic setting; diagnostic interview; history of symptoms; evidence of ongoing behaviors.
 ASD: Psycho ed evaluation
Documentation submitted to: Disability Services
Special Ed. HS course work accepted: College prep courses
Separate application required for Programs/Services: No
Contact Information
Name of program or department: Disability Services Office
Telephone: 603-428-2218
Fax: 603-428-2433

New England College

Students are encouraged to use the word processors to generate writing assignments and to use the tutors to help plan and revise papers. The writing faculty works closely with the center to provide coordinated and supportive learning for all students. Professional tutors work with students individually and in small groups. These services are provided in a secure and accepting atmosphere. Currently, 20 percent of the student body has a diagnosed LD, and 10 percent have a diagnosed ADHD.

GENERAL ADMISSIONS

Very important factors considered include: academic GPA. *Important factors considered include:* volunteer work, work experience, level of applicant's interest. *Other factors considered include:* rigor of secondary school record, class rank, application essay, recommendation(s), extracurricular activities, talent/ability, character/personal qualities, alumni/ae relation. *Freshman Admission Requirements:* High school diploma is required and GED is accepted. *Academic units required: Academic units recommended:* 4 English, 3 math, 3 science, 1 science lab, 3 social studies.

ACCOMMODATIONS OR SERVICES

Accommodations are decided upon an individual basis after a thorough review of appropriate, current documentation. The accommodations requests must be supported through the documentation provided and must be logically linked to the current impact of the condition on academic functioning.

FINANCIAL AID

Students should submit: CSS/Financial Aid PROFILE; FAFSA. Applicants will be notified of awards on a rolling basis beginning 2/1. The Princeton Review suggests that all financial aid forms be submitted as soon as possible after October 1. *Need-based scholarships/grants offered:* College/university scholarship or grant aid from institutional funds; Federal Pell; Private scholarships; SEOG; State scholarships/grants. *Loan aid offered:* Direct PLUS loans; Direct Subsidized Stafford Loans; Direct Unsubsidized Stafford Loans. Federal Work-Study Program available. Institutional employment available.

CAMPUS LIFE

Activities: Drama/theater; International Student Organization; Literary magazine; Radio station; Student government; Student newspaper. **Organizations:** 26 registered organizations, 2 honor societies, 1 religious organization. 2 fraternities, 2 sororities. **Athletics (Intercollegiate):** *Men:* baseball, basketball, cross-country, ice hockey, lacrosse, soccer *Women:* basketball, cheerleading, cross-country, field hockey, ice hockey, lacrosse, soccer, softball. **On-Campus Highlights:** Simon Center (Student Center), Center of Education Innovation, Fitness Center, Gilmore Dining Hall, Coffee House.

ACCOMMODATIONS

Allowed in exams:	
Calculators	Yes
Dictionary	No
Computer	Yes
Spell-checker	Yes
Extended test time	Yes
Scribe	Yes
Proctors	Yes
Oral exams	Yes
Note-takers	Lecture notes
Support services for students with	
LD	Yes
ADHD	Yes
ASD	Yes
Distraction-reduced environment	Yes
Recording of lecture allowed	Yes
Reading technology:	No
Audio books	Yes
Other assistive technology	No
Priority registration	No
Added costs for services:	
For LD:	No
For ADHD:	No
For ASD:	No
LD specialists	Yes
ADHD & ASD coaching	No
ASD specialists	No
Professional tutors	Yes
Peer tutors	Yes
Max. hours/week for services	3
How professors are notified of student approved accommodations	Student provides professor with form.

COLLEGE GRADUATION REQUIREMENTS

Course waivers allowed	No
Course substitutions allowed	No

Rivier University

420 South Main Street, Nashua, NH 03060 • Admissions: 603-897-8219 • Fax: 603-891-1799

CAMPUS
Type of school	Private (nonprofit)
Environment	City
Support	S

STUDENTS
Undergrad enrollment	1,370
% male/female	15/85
% from out of state	38
% frosh live on campus	65

FINANCIAL FACTS
Annual tuition	$25,410
Room and board	$9,798
Required fees	$600

GENERAL ADMISSIONS INFO
Application fee	$25

Nonfall registration accepted. Admission may be deferred for a maximum of 1 year.

Range SAT EBRW	410–510
Range SAT Math	410–510
Range ACT Composite	17–21

ACADEMICS
Student/faculty ratio	17:1
% students returning for sophomore year	78
% students graduating within 4 years	34
% students graduating withing 6 years	54

Most classes have 20–29 students.
Most lab/discussion sessions have 20–29 students.

PROGRAMS/SERVICES FOR STUDENTS WITH LEARNING DIFFERENCES

Rivier University recognizes that learning styles differ from person to person. The college is committed to providing supports that allow all otherwise qualified individuals with disabilities an equal educational opportunity. Disability Services provides the opportunity for all individuals who meet academic requirements to be provided auxiliary services, facilitating their earning of a college education. To be eligible for support services, students are required to provide appropriate documentation of their disabilities to the coordinator of Disability Services. This documentation shall be provided from a professional in the field of psychoeducational testing or a physician and shall be current (completed within the past 3 to 5 years). This information will be confidential and is kept in the coordinator's office for the purpose of planning appropriate support services. To access services, students must contact the coordinator of Disability Services before the start of each semester to schedule an appointment and provide documentation; together the coordinator and the student will discuss and arrange for support services specifically related to the disability.

ADMISSIONS

There is no special admissions process for students with LD. All applicants must meet the same criteria. Students should have a combined SAT of 820, a GPA in the top 80 percent of their graduating class, and take college-prep courses in high school. Courses required include 4 years of English, 2 years of a foreign language (though this may be substituted), 1 year of science, 3 years of math, 2 years of social science, and 4 years of academic electives. Applicants not meeting the general admission requirements may inquire about alternative admissions. The college offers a probational admit option that requires students to maintain a minimum 2.0 GPA their first semester.

ADMISSIONS INFO FOR STUDENTS WITH LEARNING DIFFERENCES

SAT/ACT required: Yes
Interview required: No
Essay required: Yes
Additional application required: No
Documentation required for:
 LD: Psycho ed evaluation
 ADHD: Diagnosis based on DSM-V; history of behaviors impairing functioning in academic setting; diagnostic interview; history of symptoms; evidence of ongoing behaviors.
 ASD: Psycho ed evaluation
Documentation submitted to: Disability Services
Special Ed. HS course work accepted: No
Separate application required for Programs/Services: No
Contact Information
Name of program or department: Disability Services
Telephone: 603-897-8497
Fax: 603-897-8887

Rivier University

Additional Information

Services available include academic, career, and personal counseling; preferential registration; classroom accommodations including tape recording of lectures, extended times for test completion, testing free from distractions, and note-takers; student advocacy; a writing center for individualized instruction in writing; and individualized accommodations as developed by the coordinator of Disability Services with the student. Services and accommodations are available for undergraduate and graduate students.

General Admissions

Very important factors considered include: rigor of secondary school record, academic GPA. *Important factors considered include:* class rank, application essay, standardized test scores, extracurricular activities, talent/ability, volunteer work, work experience. *Other factors considered include:* recommendation(s), interview, character/personal qualities. *Freshman Admission Requirements:* High school diploma is required and GED is accepted. *Academic units recommended:* 4 English, 3 math, 1 science, 1 science lab, 2 foreign language, 2 social studies, 1 history, 3 academic electives.

Accommodations or Services

Accommodations are decided upon an individual basis after a thorough review of appropriate, current documentation. The accommodations requests must be supported through the documentation provided and must be logically linked to the current impact of the condition on academic functioning.

Financial Aid

Students should submit: FAFSA. Applicants will be notified of awards on a rolling basis beginning 3/1. The Princeton Review suggests that all financial aid forms be submitted as soon as possible after October 1. *Need-based scholarships/grants offered:* College/university scholarship or grant aid from institutional funds; Federal Pell; Private scholarships; SEOG; State scholarships/grants. *Loan aid offered:* Direct PLUS loans; Direct Subsidized Stafford Loans; Direct Unsubsidized Stafford Loans. Federal Work-Study Program available. Institutional employment available.

Campus Life

Activities: Campus Ministries; Choral groups; Dance; Drama/theater; International Student Organization; Model UN; Music ensembles; Student government; Television station; Yearbook. **Organizations:** 30 registered organizations, 2 honor societies, 2 religious organizations. **Athletics (Intercollegiate):** *Men:* baseball, basketball, cross-country, soccer, volleyball. *Women:* basketball, cross-country, soccer, softball, volleyball. Regina Library, Muldoon Fitness Center, Dion Student Center.

ACCOMMODATIONS

Allowed in exams:

Calculators	Yes/No
Dictionary	No
Computer	Yes
Spell-checker	Yes/No
Extended test time	Yes
Scribe	Yes
Proctors	Yes
Oral exams	Yes
Note-takers	Yes

Support services for students with

LD	Yes
ADHD	Yes
ASD	Yes
Distraction-reduced environment	Yes
Recording of lecture allowed	Yes
Reading technology:	Yes
Audio books	Yes
Other assistive technology	Yes
Priority registration	Yes

Added costs for services:

For LD:	No
For ADHD:	No
For ASD:	No
LD specialists	No
ADHD & ASD coaching	No
ASD specialists	No
Professional tutors	No
Peer tutors	Yes
Max. hours/week for services	N/A
How professors are notified of student approved accommodations	Student and Director

COLLEGE GRADUATION REQUIREMENTS

Course waivers allowed	No
Course substitutions allowed	Yes
In what courses	

Each course substitution is looked at individually.

University of New Hampshire

105 Main Street, Durham, NH 03824 • Admissions: 603-862-1360 • Fax: 603-862-0077

CAMPUS
Type of school	Public
Environment	Village
Support	CS

STUDENTS
Undergrad enrollment	12,847
% male/female	45/55
% from out of state	53
% frosh live on campus	95

FINANCIAL FACTS
Annual in-state tuition	$15,140
Annual out-of-state tuition	$30,520
Room and board	$11,266
Required fees	$3,359

GENERAL ADMISSIONS INFO
Application fee	$50
Regular application deadline	2/1

Nonfall registration accepted. Admission may be deferred for a maximum of 1 year.

Range SAT EBRW	550–630
Range SAT Math	530–630
Range ACT Composite	23–28

ACADEMICS
Student/faculty ratio	18:1
% students returning for sophomore year	86
% students graduating within 4 years	68
% students graduating within 6 years	77

Most classes have 10–19 students.

PROGRAMS/SERVICES FOR STUDENTS WITH LEARNING DIFFERENCES

The University of New Hampshire andStudent Accessibility Services (SAS) take great pride in promoting the development of student self-reliance and the personal independence necessary to succeed in a university climate. SAS seeks to create a comprehensively accessible environment where students are viewed on a basis of ability, not disability. The University of New Hampshire believes that students have the right and also the responsibility to determine whether or not to use support services. In keeping with this objective, students are expected and encouraged to utilize the resources of SAS to the degree they determine necessary. Therefore, it is the prerogative of the student to disclose or not disclose their disability to the university. There is not a specific LD program at this time. Services and accommodations are based on student self-disclosure and providing documentation as appropriate to the student's disability. Documentation guidelines can be viewed at http://www.unh.edu/disabilityservices/unh-guidelines. Student Accessibility Services (SAS) is where students with documented disabilities can receive those accommodations and academic services that offer them equal access to the classroom. All students with LD/ADHD must provide current and appropriate documentation to qualify for services. Through one to one meetings with SAS staff or a variety of workshops provided across campus, students can learn and further develop their self-advocacy skills, notetaking skills, exam preparation skills, organization and time management. SAS recently added a new Assistive Technology (AT) Lab. Students with LD/ADHD may benefit from using some of the AT available. Trainings are available for students who have had no prior experience with a particular piece of AT.

ADMISSIONS
Same as for all students.

Additional Information
Self-referral.

ADMISSIONS INFO FOR STUDENTS WITH LEARNING DIFFERENCES
SAT/ACT required: Yes
Interview required: No
Essay required: Not Applicable
Additional application required: Yes
Documentation required for:
  LD: A neuropsychological evaluation or other comprehensive tool to identify impact & needs.
  ADHD: A neuropsychological evaluation or other comprehensive tool to identify impact & needs.
  ASD: Best practices within the field
Documentation submitted to: Student Accessibility Services
Special Ed. HS course work accepted: No
Separate application required for Programs/Services: No
Contact Information
Name of program or department: Student Accessibility Services
Telephone: 603-862-2607
Fax: 603-862-4043
Email: disability.office@unh.edu

University of New Hampshire

GENERAL ADMISSIONS

Very important factors considered include: rigor of secondary school record, class rank, academic GPA. *Important factors considered include:* recommendation(s). *Other factors considered include:* application essay, standardized test scores, extracurricular activities, talent/ability, character/personal qualities, first generation, alumni/ae relation, geographical residence, state residency, racial/ethnic status, volunteer work, work experience. *Freshman Admission Requirements:* High school diploma is required and GED is accepted. *Academic units required:* 4 English, 3 math, 3 science, 2 science labs, 2 foreign language, 3 social studies. *Academic units recommended:* 4 English, 4 math, 4 science, 3 science labs, 3 foreign language, 3 social studies, 1 visual/performing arts.

ACCOMMODATIONS OR SERVICES

Accommodations are decided upon an individual basis after a thorough review of appropriate, current documentation. The accommodations requests must be supported through the documentation provided and must be logically linked to the current impact of the condition on academic functioning.

FINANCIAL AID

Students should submit: FAFSA. Applicants will be notified of awards on a rolling basis beginning 12/1. The Princeton Review suggests that all financial aid forms be submitted as soon as possible after October 1. *Need-based scholarships/grants offered:* College/university scholarship or grant aid from institutional funds; Federal Pell; Private scholarships; SEOG; State scholarships/grants. *Loan aid offered:* Direct PLUS loans; Direct Subsidized Stafford Loans; Direct Unsubsidized Stafford Loans. Federal Work-Study Program available. Institutional employment available.

CAMPUS LIFE

Activities: Campus Ministries; Choral groups; Concert band; Dance; Drama/theater; International Student Organization; Jazz band; Literary magazine; Marching band; Model UN; Music ensembles; Musical theater; Opera; Pep band; Radio station; Student government; Student newspaper; Student-run film society; Symphony orchestra; Yearbook. **Organizations:** 187 registered organizations, 18 honor societies, 10 religious organizations. 10 fraternities, 7 sororities. **Athletics (Intercollegiate):** *Men:* basketball, cross-country, football, ice hockey, skiing (downhill/alpine), skiing (nordic/cross-country), soccer, track/field (outdoor), track/field (indoor). *Women:* basketball, cross-country, diving, field hockey, gymnastics, ice hockey, lacrosse, skiing (downhill/alpine), skiing (nordic/cross-country), soccer, swimming, track/field (outdoor), track/field (indoor), volleyball. **On-Campus Highlights:** Dimond Library, Whittemore Center, Hamel Recreation Center, Student Union/Holloway Commons, College Woods.

ACCOMMODATIONS

Allowed in exams:	
Calculators	Yes
Dictionary	Yes
Computer	Yes
Spell-checker	Yes
Extended test time	Yes
Scribe	Yes
Proctors	Yes
Oral exams	Yes
Note-takers	Yes
Support services for students with	
LD	Yes
ADHD	Yes
ASD	Yes
Distraction-reduced environment	Yes
Recording of lecture allowed	Yes
Reading technology:	Yes
Audio books	Yes
Other assistive technology	Yes
Priority registration	Yes
Added costs for services:	
For LD:	No
For ADHD:	No
For ASD:	No
LD specialists	Not Applicable
ADHD & ASD coaching	Yes
ASD specialists	Yes
Professional tutors	Yes
Peer tutors	Yes
Max. hours/week for services	Varies
How professors are notified of student approved accommodations	Director

COLLEGE GRADUATION REQUIREMENTS

Course waivers allowed	No
Course substitutions allowed	Yes
In what courses	

May be substitution of courses for a foreign language requirement.

Fairleigh Dickinson University, College at Florham

285 Madison Avenue, Madison, NJ 07940 • Admissions: 800-338-8803 • Fax: 973-443-8088

CAMPUS
Type of school	Private (nonprofit)
Environment	Village
Support	SP

STUDENTS
Undergrad enrollment	2,356
% male/female	45/55
% from out of state	16
% frosh live on campus	79

FINANCIAL FACTS
Annual tuition	$36,386
Room and board	$12,294
Required fees	$958

GENERAL ADMISSIONS INFO
Application fee	$40
Priority deadline	1/15

Nonfall registration accepted.

Range SAT EBRW	450–560
Range SAT Math	460–570
Range ACT Composite	NR

ACADEMICS
Student/faculty ratio	12:1
% students returning for sophomore year	76

Most classes have 10–19 students.
Most lab/discussion sessions have 10–19 students.

PROGRAMS/SERVICES FOR STUDENTS WITH LEARNING DIFFERENCES

The Regional Center for College Students with Learning Disabilities offers a structured plan of intensive advisement, academic support, and counseling services that is tailored to the unique needs of students with LD. The goal is to provide a framework within which college students identified with "Specific Learning Disabilities" will develop the confidence to succeed in their studies and the independence to do their best. Planning, learning strategies, professional tutors, counseling, and accommodations are the cornerstones of the Regional Center. Staffed by professionals with services at both the Metropolitan Campus and the Campus of Florham, the LD program and special services are free of charge. Assistance to students is intensive and the program is fully integrated into the coursework. Students are in touch with faculty on a regular basis. The program encourages involvement in the community, particularly service-type activities relevant to the students with LD. Performance data are routinely reviewed to identify students in need of more intensive help. Upon admission students are invited to attend a summer orientation session. During this time, students meet with center staff to develop an Individual Academic Plan in order to develop a class schedule with the right balance. For more information, visit www.fdu.edu/rcsld

ADMISSIONS

Admissions decisions are made independently by FDU Admissions and the LD Program Admissions Directors. Students must be admitted to the university before applications can be reviewed by the Regional Center. Criteria include documentation of a primary diagnosis of a language based learning disability made by licensed professionals dated within 24 months of the application; evidence of adequate performance in mainstream college-prep high school courses; and evidence of motivation as reflected in recommendations. Students enrolled solely in special education high school classes are usually not admissible.

Additional Information

COMPASS at FDU is an individually tailored, comprehensive, academic and social support program for a very limited number of college students with high functioning Autism Spectrum Disorder or Asperger's Syndrome. COMPASS is offered separately on each of FDU's two New Jersey campuses. The goals of this two year program are to help each student recognize and make use of existing academic and social strengths,

ADMISSIONS INFO FOR STUDENTS WITH LEARNING DIFFERENCES

SAT/ACT required: Yes
Interview required: No
Essay required: Recommended
Additional application required: No
Documentation required for:
  LD: Psycho educational Evaluation
  ADHD: N/A to Regional Center Program
  ASD: Psyco ed Evaluation
Documentation submitted to: COMPASS
Special Ed. HS course work accepted: Yes
Separate application required for Programs/Services: Yes
Contact Information
Name of program or department: Office of Disability Support Services/COMPASS
Telephone: 973-443-8079
Fax: 201-692-2813

Fairleigh Dickinson University, College at Florham

to aid in the development of new abilities, and to promote progress toward a higher level of independent functioning. Students interested in COMPASS must first apply and be accepted to Fairleigh Dickinson University through the general application process at one of FDU's New Jersey campuses. Fee for COMPASS, $6520 per semester.

GENERAL ADMISSIONS

Very important factors considered include: academic GPA, standardized test scores. *Important factors considered include:* rigor of secondary school record, recommendation(s). *Other factors considered include:* class rank, application essay, interview, extracurricular activities, talent/ability, character/personal qualities, alumni/ae relation, volunteer work, level of applicant's interest. *Freshman Admission Requirements:* High school diploma is required and GED is accepted. *Academic units required:* 4 English, 3 math, 2 science, 2 science labs, 2 history, 3 academic electives. *Academic units recommended:* 4 English, 3 math, 3 science, 2 science labs, 2 foreign language, 2 history, 4 academic electives.

ACCOMMODATIONS OR SERVICES

Accommodations are decided upon an individual basis after a thorough review of appropriate, current documentation. The accommodations requests must be supported through the documentation provided and must be logically linked to the current impact of the condition on academic functioning.

FINANCIAL AID

Students should submit:. The Princeton Review suggests that all financial aid forms be submitted as soon as possible after October 1. *Need-based scholarships/grants offered: Loan aid offered:* Federal Work-Study Program available. Institutional employment available.

CAMPUS LIFE

Activities: Campus Ministries; Choral groups; Dance; Drama/theater; International Student Organization; Literary magazine; Musical theater; Radio station; Student government; Student newspaper; Student-run film society. **Organizations:** 44 registered organizations, 9 honor societies, 3 religious organizations. 6 fraternities, 4 sororities. **Athletics (Intercollegiate):** *Men:* baseball, basketball, cross-country, football, golf, lacrosse, soccer, swimming, tennis. *Women:* basketball, cross-country, field hockey, lacrosse, soccer, softball, swimming, tennis, volleyball. **On-Campus Highlights:** Recreation Center, Bottle Hill Pub, Florham Perks, L'Orangerie of Library, Mansion gardens.

ACCOMMODATIONS

Allowed in exams:

Calculators	Yes
Dictionary	Yes
Computer	Yes
Spell-checker	Yes
Extended test time	Yes
Scribe	No
Proctors	Yes
Oral exams	Yes
Note-takers	No

Support services for students with

LD	Yes
ADHD	No
ASD	Yes
Distraction-reduced environment	Yes
Recording of lecture allowed	Yes
Reading technology:	Yes
Audio books	Yes
Other assistive technology	Yes
Priority registration	Yes

Added costs for services:

For LD:	No
For ADHD:	No
For ASD:	No
LD specialists	Yes
ADHD & ASD coaching	No
ASD specialists	Yes - COMPASS
Professional tutors	Yes
Peer tutors	No
Max. hours/week for services	4

How professors are notified of student approved accommodations
Student and Director

COLLEGE GRADUATION REQUIREMENTS

Course waivers allowed	No
Course substitutions allowed	Yes

In what courses
Mathematics and foreign language substitutions are available if appropriate to students with LD enrolled in the Center.

Fairleigh Dickinson University, Metropolitan Campus

1000 RIVER ROAD, TEANECK, NJ 07666-1966 • ADMISSIONS: 201-692-2553 • FAX: 201-692-7319

CAMPUS
Type of school	Private (nonprofit)
Environment	Town
Support	SP

STUDENTS
Undergrad enrollment	4,101
% male/female	43/57
% from out of state	14
% frosh live on campus	41

FINANCIAL FACTS
Annual tuition	$33,920
Room and board	$12,742
Required fees	$958

GENERAL ADMISSIONS INFO
Application fee	$40
Priority deadline	1/15

Nonfall registration accepted.

Range SAT EBRW	440–530
Range SAT Math	450–550
Range ACT Composite	NR

ACADEMICS
Student/faculty ratio	15:1
% students returning for sophomore year	70

Most classes have 10–19 students.

PROGRAMS/SERVICES FOR STUDENTS WITH LEARNING DIFFERENCES

The Regional Center for College Students with LD offers a structured plan of intensive advisement, academic support, and counseling services tailored to the unique needs of students with language-based disabilities. The goal is to provide a framework within which college students identified with "Specific Learning Disabilities" will develop the confidence to succeed in their studies and the independence to do their best. Planning, learning strategies, professional tutors, counseling, and accommodations are the cornerstones of the Regional Center. Staffed by professionals at the Metropolitan Campus and the Campus of Florham, the LD program and special services are free. Assistance is intensive and the program fully integrated into the course work. Performance data is routinely reviewed to identify students in need of more intensive help. Upon admission students are invited to attend a summer orientation session.

ADMISSIONS

Admissions decisions are made independently by FDU Admissions and the LD Program Admissions Directors. Students must be admitted to the university before applications can be reviewed by the Regional Center. Criteria include documentation of a primary diagnosis of a language-based learning disability made by licensed professionals dated within 24 months of the application; evidence of adequate performance in mainstream college-prep high school courses; and evidence of motivation as reflected in recommendations. Students enrolled solely in special education high school classes are usually not admissible.

Additional Information

Students with a language-based learning disability enrolled at both the Metropolitan and Florham campuses during their undergraduate career are provided comprehensive professional support free of charge. Students are provided with structured plans of intensive academic support and counseling services specific to the unique learning needs of each student. Freshman can receive up to four support sessions a week per semester, sophomores three supports a semester, juniors and seniors one or two supports per semester.

ADMISSIONS INFO FOR STUDENTS WITH LEARNING DIFFERENCES

SAT/ACT required: Yes
Interview required: No
Essay required: Recommended
Additional application required: No
Documentation required for:
 LD: Psycho ed evaluation
 ADHD: Diagnosis based on DSM-V; history of behaviors impairing functioning in academic setting; diagnostic interview; history of symptoms; evidence of ongoing behaviors.
 ASD: Psycho ed evaluation
Documentation submitted to: COMPASS
Special Ed. HS course work accepted: yes
Separate application required for Programs/Services: Yes
Contact Information
Name of program or department: Office of the Provost / COMPASS
Telephone: 201-692-2460
Email: mourton@fdu.edu

Fairleigh Dickinson University, Metropolitan Campus

GENERAL ADMISSIONS

Very important factors considered include: academic GPA, standardized test scores. *Important factors considered include:* rigor of secondary school record, recommendation(s). *Other factors considered include:* class rank, application essay, interview, extracurricular activities, talent/ability, character/personal qualities, alumni/ae relation, volunteer work, level of applicant's interest. *Freshman Admission Requirements:* High school diploma is required and GED is accepted. *Academic units required:* 4 English, 3 math, 2 science, 2 science labs, 2 history, 3 academic electives. *Academic units recommended:* 4 English, 3 math, 3 science, 2 science labs, 2 foreign language, 2 history, 4 academic electives.

ACCOMMODATIONS OR SERVICES

Accommodations are decided upon an individual basis after a thorough review of appropriate, current documentation. The accommodations requests must be supported through the documentation provided and must be logically linked to the current impact of the condition on academic functioning.

FINANCIAL AID

Students should submit:. The Princeton Review suggests that all financial aid forms be submitted as soon as possible after October 1. *Need-based scholarships/grants offered: Loan aid offered:* Federal Work-Study Program available.

CAMPUS LIFE

Activities: Campus Ministries; Choral groups; Dance; Drama/theater; International Student Organization; Literary magazine; Music ensembles; Musical theater; Radio station; Student government; Student newspaper; Student-run film society. **Organizations:** 72 registered organizations, 10 honor societies, 4 religious organizations. 5 fraternities, 7 sororities. **Athletics (Intercollegiate):** *Men:* baseball, basketball, cross-country, golf, soccer, tennis, track/field (indoor). *Women:* basketball, bowling, cross-country, fencing, golf, soccer, softball, tennis, track/field (indoor), volleyball. **On-Campus Highlights:** Weiner Library, Fitness Center, Jeepers (Wireless Cafe), Knight Club, Hackensack River.

ACCOMMODATIONS

Allowed in exams:	
Calculators	Yes
Dictionary	No
Computer	Yes
Spell-checker	Yes
Extended test time	Yes
Scribe	No
Proctors	Yes
Oral exams	Yes
Note-takers	No
Support services for students with	
LD	Yes
ADHD	No
ASD	Yes
Distraction-reduced environment	Yes
Recording of lecture allowed	Yes
Reading technology:	Yes
Audio books	Yes
Other assistive technology	Yes
Priority registration	N/A
Added costs for services:	
For LD:	No
For ADHD:	No
For ASD:	No
LD specialists	Yes
ADHD & ASD coaching	No
ASD specialists	Yes - COMPASS
Professional tutors	Yes
Peer tutors	No
Max. hours/week for services	8
How professors are notified of student approved accommodations	
Letter from Regional Center and student	

COLLEGE GRADUATION REQUIREMENTS

Course waivers allowed	No
Course substitutions allowed	Yes
In what courses	Math

Georgian Court University

900 Lakewood Avenue, Lakewood, NJ 08701-2697 • Admissions: 732-987-2700 • Fax: 732-987-2000

CAMPUS

Type of school	Private (nonprofit)
Environment	Town
Support	SP

STUDENTS

Undergrad enrollment	1,447
% male/female	26/74
% from out of state	6
% frosh live on campus	62

FINANCIAL FACTS

Annual tuition	$30,800
Room and board	$10,808
Required fees	$1,460

GENERAL ADMISSIONS INFO

Application fee	$40
Regular application deadline	8/1

Nonfall registration accepted. Admission may be deferred for a maximum of 1 year.

Range SAT EBRW	460–570
Range SAT Math	450–550
Range ACT Composite	17–22

ACADEMICS

Student/faculty ratio	12:1
% students returning for sophomore year	72
% students graduating within 4 years	28
% students graduating within 6 years	48

PROGRAMS/SERVICES FOR STUDENTS WITH LEARNING DIFFERENCES

The Learning Center (TLC) is an assistance program designed to provide an environment for students with mild to moderate learning disabilities who desire a college education. The program is not one of remediation, but it is an individualized support program to assist candidates in becoming successful college students. Emphasis is placed on developing self-help strategies and study techniques.

ADMISSIONS

The class rank and transcript should give evidence of the ability to succeed in college. Students must submit SAT scores. Conditional admission may be offered to some applicants. The Associate Director of Admissions is the liaison between the admissions staff and the TLC.

Additional Information

College graduation requirements are not waived for TLC students. Reduced course load is recommended for students with learning disabilities, and program completion may take longer than 4 years. The program offers individuals one-onone support with a professional staff member known as an Academic Development Specialist.

ADMISSIONS INFO FOR STUDENTS WITH LEARNING DIFFERENCES

SAT/ACT required: Y/N depends if Test Optional
Interview required: Yes
Essay required: No
Additional application required: No
Documentation required for:
  LD: Psycho ed evaluation to include: relevant historical info, instructional interventions, related services, age diagnosed, objective data (aptitude, achievement, info processing), test scores (standard, percentile and grade equivalents) and describe functional limitations.
  ADHD: Diagnosis based on DSM-V; history of behaviors impairing functioning in academic setting; diagnostic interview; history of symptoms; evidence of ongoing behaviors.
  ASD: Psycho ed evaluation
With general application:
Documentation submitted to: The Learning Connection
Special Ed. HS course work accepted: No
Separate application required for Programs/Services: No
Contact Information
Name of program or department: The Learning Connection
Telephone: 732-987-2646
Fax: 732-987-2026
Email: lfahr@georgian.edu

Georgian Court University

GENERAL ADMISSIONS

Very important factors considered include: rigor of secondary school record, academic GPA. *Important factors considered include:* standardized test scores. *Other factors considered include:* class rank, application essay, recommendation(s), interview, extracurricular activities, talent/ability, character/personal qualities, first generation, alumni/ae relation, volunteer work, work experience, level of applicant's interest. *Freshman Admission Requirements:* High school diploma is required and GED is accepted. *Academic units required:* 4 English, 2 math, 1 science, 1 science lab, 2 foreign language, 1 history, 6 academic electives.

ACCOMMODATIONS OR SERVICES

Accommodations are decided upon an individual basis after a thorough review of appropriate, current documentation. The accommodations requests must be supported through the documentation provided and must be logically linked to the current impact of the condition on academic functioning.

FINANCIAL AID

Students should submit: FAFSA. Applicants will be notified of awards on a rolling basis beginning 12/1. The Princeton Review suggests that all financial aid forms be submitted as soon as possible after October 1. *Need-based scholarships/grants offered:* College/university scholarship or grant aid from institutional funds; Federal Pell; Private scholarships; SEOG; State scholarships/grants. *Loan aid offered:* Direct PLUS loans; Direct Subsidized Stafford Loans; Direct Unsubsidized Stafford Loans. Federal Work-Study Program available. Institutional employment available.

CAMPUS LIFE

Activities: Campus Ministries; Choral groups; Concert band; Dance; Drama/theater; International Student Organization; Jazz band; Literary magazine; Model UN; Music ensembles; Student government; Student newspaper. **Organizations:** 48 registered organizations, 18 honor societies, 1 religious organization. **Athletics (Intercollegiate):** *Women:* basketball, cross-country, lacrosse, soccer, softball, tennis, track/field (outdoor), volleyball. **On-Campus Highlights:** Arboretum, Wellness Center, Art Gallery, Library, NASA Educational Resource Center.

ACCOMMODATIONS

Allowed in exams:	
Calculators	Yes
Dictionary	Yes
Computer	Yes
Spell-checker	Yes
Extended test time	Yes
Scribe	Yes
Proctors	Yes
Oral exams	Yes
Note-takers	Yes
Support services for students with	
LD	Yes
ADHD	Yes
ASD	Yes
Distraction-reduced environment	Yes
Recording of lecture allowed	Yes
Reading technology:	Yes
Audio books	Yes
Other assistive technology	Yes
Priority registration	Yes
Added costs for services:	
For LD:	No
For ADHD:	No
For ASD:	No
LD specialists	Yes
ADHD & ASD coaching	No
ASD specialists	No
Professional tutors	Yes
Peer tutors	No
Max. hours/week for services	Varies
How professors are notified of student approved accommodations	
By both student and director	

COLLEGE GRADUATION REQUIREMENTS

Course waivers allowed	No
Course substitutions allowed	Yes
In what courses	Foreign Language, if applicable

Kean University

1000 Morris Ave, PO Box 411, Union, NJ 07083-0411 • Admissions: 908-737-7100 • Fax: 908-737-7105

CAMPUS

Type of school	Public
Environment	City
Support	CS

STUDENTS

Undergrad enrollment	11,761
% male/female	40/60
% from out of state	2
% frosh live on campus	41

FINANCIAL FACTS

Annual in-state tuition	$9,740
Annual out-of-state tuition	$16,775
Room and board	$14,470
Required fees	$2,608

GENERAL ADMISSIONS INFO

Application fee	$75
Priority deadline	4/30
Regular application deadline	8/15

Nonfall registration accepted.
   Admission may be deferred for a maximum
   of 1 semester.

Range SAT EBRW	440–540
Range SAT Math	440–530
Range ACT Composite	16–22

ACADEMICS

Student/faculty ratio	17:1
% students returning for sophomore year	76
% students graduating within 4 years	21
% students graduating within 6 years	50

Most classes have 10–19 students.

PROGRAMS/SERVICES FOR STUDENTS WITH LEARNING DIFFERENCES

Disability Services provides support, accommodations, educational programs and activities to ensure that all students have the maximum possible opportunity to equal access to all areas of University life. Students with disabilities must provide current documentation that shows the functional limitations of their disability. Accommodations for classrooms, testing and residence life are provided to create equal access on campus. Services include accommodations, assistive technology training, alternate testing room, and a mentoring program.

ADMISSIONS

There is no special admissions process for students with LD. All applicants must meet the same admission criteria. Courses taken in special education may be considered. SAT/ACT results are required. The minimum GPA is 2.8 and the average GPA is 3.0. Kean requires two recommendations and a personal essay. Although students are asked to write about their educational and career objectives, they can also share noteworthy accomplishments in their lives or discuss something or someone who helped them become the person they are today. The student must be highly motivated, able to do college work, be of at least average intelligence, have a documented learning disability, have areas of academic strength, and make a commitment to work responsibly and attend classes, tutoring, workshops, and counseling sessions. Students are encouraged to apply by early March.

Additional Information

Students requesting services must submit documentation and make an appointment with Disability Services for an Intake Interview before accommodations or other services can be provided.

ADMISSIONS INFO FOR STUDENTS WITH LEARNING DIFFERENCES

SAT/ACT required: Yes
Interview required: Yes
Essay required: Not Applicable
Additional application required: No
Documentation required for:
   LD: Educational and Psychological evaluations
   ADHD: Educational and Psychological evaluations as well as Medical Verification
   ASD: Educational and Psychological evaluations
Documentation submitted to: Office of Disability Services
Special Ed. HS course work accepted: No
Separate application required for Programs/Services: No
Contact Information
Name of program or department: Office of Disability Services
Telephone: 908-737-4910
Fax: 908-737-4865
Email: disabilityservices@kean.edu

Kean University

GENERAL ADMISSIONS

Very important factors considered include: rigor of secondary school record, academic GPA. *Important factors considered include:* standardized test scores. *Other factors considered include:* application essay, recommendation(s), interview, extracurricular activities, talent/ability, character/personal qualities, alumni/ae relation, volunteer work, work experience. *Freshman Admission Requirements:* High school diploma is required and GED is accepted. *Academic units required:* 4 English, 3 math, 2 science, 2 science labs, 2 history, 5 academic electives. *Academic units recommended:* 4 English, 3 math, 2 science, 2 science labs, 2 foreign language, 2 social studies, 2 history, 5 academic electives.

ACCOMMODATIONS OR SERVICES

Accommodations are decided upon an individual basis after a thorough review of appropriate, current documentation. The accommodations requests must be supported through the documentation provided and must be logically linked to the current impact of the condition on academic functioning.

FINANCIAL AID

Students should submit: FAFSA. Applicants will be notified of awards on a rolling basis beginning 11/1. The Princeton Review suggests that all financial aid forms be submitted as soon as possible after October 1. *Need-based scholarships/grants offered:* College/university scholarship or grant aid from institutional funds; Federal Pell; Private scholarships; SEOG; State scholarships/grants. *Loan aid offered:* Direct PLUS loans; Direct Subsidized Stafford Loans; Direct Unsubsidized Stafford Loans. Federal Work-Study Program available. Institutional employment available.

CAMPUS LIFE

Activities: Campus Ministries; Choral groups; Concert band; Dance; Drama/theater; International Student Organization; Jazz band; Literary magazine; Music ensembles; Musical theater; Pep band; Radio station; Student government; Student newspaper; Student-run film society; Symphony orchestra; Television station; Yearbook. **Organizations:** 143 registered organizations, 23 honor societies, 6 religious organizations. 16 fraternities, 17 sororities. **Athletics (Intercollegiate):** *Men:* baseball, basketball, football, lacrosse, soccer, track/field (outdoor). *Women:* basketball, field hockey, lacrosse, soccer, softball, tennis, track/field (outdoor), volleyball. **On-Campus Highlights:** University (Student) Center, Harwood Arena Sports Complex, Green Lane Academic Bldg, New Jersey Center for Science, Technology & Mathematics, Maxine and Jack Lane Center for Academic Success (CAS).

ACCOMMODATIONS

Allowed in exams:	
Calculators	Yes
Dictionary	Yes
Computer	Yes
Spell-checker	Yes
Extended test time	Yes
Scribe	Yes
Proctors	Yes
Oral exams	Yes
Note-takers	Yes
Support services for students with	
LD	Yes
ADHD	Yes
ASD	Yes
Distraction-reduced environment	Yes
Recording of lecture allowed	Yes
Reading technology:	Yes
Audio books	Yes
Other assistive technology smart pens, Read and Write software, speech to text software, ebooks	
Priority registration	Yes
Added costs for services:	
For LD:	No
For ADHD:	No
For ASD:	No
LD specialists	Yes
ADHD & ASD coaching	Yes
ASD specialists	Yes
Professional tutors	Yes
Peer tutors	Yes
Max. hours/week for services	5
How professors are notified of student approved accommodations	Student

COLLEGE GRADUATION REQUIREMENTS

Course waivers allowed	No
Course substitutions allowed	Yes
In what courses	
Depends on documentation and major	

Monmouth University (NJ)

400 CEDAR AVENUE, WEST LONG BRANCH, NJ 07764-1898 • ADMISSIONS: 732-571-3456 • FAX: 732-263-5166

CAMPUS
Type of school	Private (nonprofit)
Environment	Village
Support	CS

STUDENTS
Undergrad enrollment	4,683
% male/female	42/58
% from out of state	16
% frosh live on campus	86

FINANCIAL FACTS
Annual tuition	$37,438
Room and board	$13,981
Required fees	$700

GENERAL ADMISSIONS INFO
Application fee	$50
Priority deadline	12/1
Regular application deadline	3/1

Nonfall registration accepted.
  Admission may be deferred for a maximum of 2 semesters.

Range SAT EBRW	490–600
Range SAT Math	480–590
Range ACT Composite	19–26

ACADEMICS
Student/faculty ratio	13:1
% students returning for sophomore year	79
% students graduating within 4 years	57
% students graduating within 6 years	70

Most classes have 10–19 students.
Most lab/discussion sessions have 20–29 students.

PROGRAMS/SERVICES FOR STUDENTS WITH LEARNING DIFFERENCES

Monmouth University recognizes the special needs of students with disabilities who are capable, with appropriate assistance, of excelling in a demanding university environment. Reasonable support services and a nurturing environment contribute to their success. Monmouth's commitment is to provide a learning process and atmosphere that allows students to pursue their educational goals, realize their full potential, contribute actively to their community and society, and determine the direction of their lives. Students are enrolled in regular courses and are not isolated from the rest of the student body in any manner. Students with documented disabilities may request reasonable accommodations and/or auxiliary aids. It is important that students disclose their disability and provide the required documentation to Department of Disability Services for Students. Much of their success has to do with individual recognition of their specific learning needs, and a willingness to self-advocate in a student-driven program.

ADMISSIONS

There is no special admissions process for students with diagnosed disabilities.

Additional Information

Monmouth University offers one course that is designed for students with disabilities. Transition to College is a onecredit elective course geared toward incoming freshmen with disabilities. The course attempts to assist students in their transition by presenting material that will help them become independent learners. Topics include: learning styles, self-advocacy, organizational methods, and time management study skills.

ADMISSIONS INFO FOR STUDENTS WITH LEARNING DIFFERENCES
SAT/ACT required: Yes
Interview required: N/A
Essay required: No
Additional application required: No
Documentation required for:
  LD: Copy of grade 12 IEP; and copies of most recent CST testing (psychoeducational evaluation, including WAIS-R and WJ3 results).
  ADHD: Copy of high school IEP or 504 Plan; copy of educational and/or psychological test results; Monmouth University Disability Provider Form (if student is under the care of a treating physician and is prescribed medication).
  ASD: Determined on a case-by-case basis.
Documentation submitted to: Department of Disability Services for Students
Special Ed. HS course work accepted: Yes
Separate application required for Programs/Services: Yes
Contact Information
Name of program or department: Department of Disability Services for Students
Telephone: 732-571-3460
Fax: 732-263-5126

Monmouth University (NJ)

General Admissions

Very important factors considered include: rigor of secondary school record, academic GPA, standardized test scores. *Important factors considered include:* application essay, recommendation(s), extracurricular activities, volunteer work, work experience. *Other factors considered include:* character/personal qualities, alumni/ae relation. *Freshman Admission Requirements:* High school diploma is required and GED is accepted. *Academic units required:* 4 English, 3 math, 2 science, 1 science lab, 2 history, 5 academic electives. *Academic units recommended:* 2 foreign language, 2 social studies.

Accommodations or Services

Accommodations are decided upon an individual basis after a thorough review of appropriate, current documentation. The accommodations requests must be supported through the documentation provided and must be logically linked to the current impact of the condition on academic functioning.

Financial Aid

Students should submit: FAFSA. Applicants will be notified of awards on a rolling basis beginning 12/22. The Princeton Review suggests that all financial aid forms be submitted as soon as possible after October 1. *Need-based scholarships/grants offered:* College/university scholarship or grant aid from institutional funds; Federal Pell; Private scholarships; SEOG; State scholarships/grants. *Loan aid offered:* Direct PLUS loans; Direct Subsidized Stafford Loans; Direct Unsubsidized Stafford Loans. Federal Work-Study Program available. Institutional employment available.

Campus Life

Activities: Campus Ministries; Choral groups; Concert band; Dance; Drama/theater; International Student Organization; Jazz band; Literary magazine; Model UN; Music ensembles; Musical theater; Pep band; Radio station; Student government; Student newspaper; Television station; Yearbook. **Organizations:** 67 registered organizations, 19 honor societies, 3 religious organizations. 7 fraternities, 6 sororities. **Athletics (Intercollegiate):** *Men:* baseball, basketball, cross-country, football, golf, soccer, tennis, track/field (outdoor), track/field (indoor). *Women:* basketball, cross-country, field hockey, golf, lacrosse, soccer, softball, tennis, track/field (outdoor), track/field (indoor). **On-Campus Highlights:** Rebecca Stafford Student Center, OceanFirst Bank Center, Magill Commons residential restuarant, Pollak Theatre, Dunkin' Donuts.

ACCOMMODATIONS

Allowed in exams:	
Calculators	Yes
Dictionary	Yes
Computer	Yes
Spell-checker	Yes
Extended test time	Yes
Scribe	Yes
Proctors	Yes
Oral exams	No
Note-takers	Yes
Support services for students with	
LD	Yes
ADHD	Yes
ASD	Yes
Distraction-reduced environment	Yes
Recording of lecture allowed	Yes
Reading technology:	Yes
Audio books	Yes
Other assistive technology	Yes
Priority registration	No
Added costs for services:	
For LD:	No
For ADHD:	No
For ASD:	No
LD specialists	Yes
ADHD & ASD coaching	No
ASD specialists	No
Professional tutors	Yes
Peer tutors	Yes
Max. hours/week for services	Varies
How professors are notified of student approved accommodations	Student

COLLEGE GRADUATION REQUIREMENTS

Course waivers allowed	No
Course substitutions allowed	No

Montclair State University

One Normal Avenue, Montclair, NJ 07043-1624 • Admissions: 973-655-4444 • Fax: 973-655-7700

CAMPUS

Type of school	Public
Environment	Town
Support	S

STUDENTS

Undergrad enrollment	16,673
% male/female	39/61
% from out of state	3
% frosh live on campus	51

FINANCIAL FACTS

Annual in-state tuition	$10,808
Annual out-of-state tuition	$18,920
Room and board	$13,466
Required fees	$1,647

GENERAL ADMISSIONS INFO

Application fee	$65
Priority deadline	12/15
Regular application deadline	3/1

Nonfall registration accepted. Admission may be deferred for a maximum of 1 semester.

Range SAT EBRW	500–580
Range SAT Math	490–570
Range ACT Composite	NR

ACADEMICS

Student/faculty ratio	17:1
% students returning for sophomore year	81
% students graduating within 4 years	42
% students graduating within 6 years	65

PROGRAMS/SERVICES FOR STUDENTS WITH LEARNING DIFFERENCES

Montclair State University is committed to the full inclusion of students with disabilities in all curricular and co-curricular activities as mandated by Section 504 of the Rehabilitation Act of 1973. The Disability Resource Center (DRC) will assist you in receiving the accommodations and services necessary to equalize access. The DRC provides assistance to students with physical, sensory, learning, psychological, neurological, and chronic medical disabilities.

ADMISSIONS

Same as for all applicants

Additional Information

The DRC provides accommodations and services (Appropriate academic accommodations are determined on a case-by-case basis and must be supported by documentation). Academic Accomodations are note takers, readers, scribes, extended testing, textbooks on CD ,equipment loans and adaptive technology.

ADMISSIONS INFO FOR STUDENTS WITH LEARNING DIFFERENCES

SAT/ACT required: No
Interview required: No
Essay required: Not Applicable
Additional application required: No
Documentation required for:
Documentation submitted to: Disability Resource Center
Special Ed. HS course work accepted: Yes
Separate application required for Programs/Services: No
Contact Information
Name of program or department: Disability Resource Center
Telephone: 973-655-5431
Fax: 973-655-5308
Email: drc@mail.montclair.edu

Montclair State University

GENERAL ADMISSIONS

Very important factors considered include: rigor of secondary school record, academic GPA, recommendation(s). *Important factors considered include:* application essay. *Other factors considered include:* class rank, standardized test scores, extracurricular activities, talent/ability, character/personal qualities, religious affiliation/commitment, work experience. *Freshman Admission Requirements:* High school diploma is required and GED is accepted. *Academic units required:* 4 English, 3 math, 2 science, 2 science labs, 2 foreign language, 2 social studies, 3 academic electives.

ACCOMODATION OR SERVICES

Accommodations are decided upon an individual basis after a thorough review of appropriate, current documentation. The accommodations requests must be supported through the documentation provided and must be logically linked to the current impact of the condition on academic functioning.

FINANCIAL AID

Students should submit: FAFSA; State aid form. Applicants will be notified of awards on a rolling basis beginning 2/15. The Princeton Review suggests that all financial aid forms be submitted as soon as possible after October 1. *Need-based scholarships/grants offered:* College/university scholarship or grant aid from institutional funds; Federal Pell; Private scholarships; SEOG; State scholarships/grants. *Loan aid offered:* Direct PLUS loans; Direct Subsidized Stafford Loans; Direct Unsubsidized Stafford Loans. Federal Work-Study Program available. Institutional employment available.

CAMPUS LIFE

Activities: Campus Ministries; Choral groups; Concert band; Dance; Drama/theater; International Student Organization; Jazz band; Literary magazine; Marching band; Music ensembles; Musical theater; Opera; Pep band; Radio station; Student government; Student newspaper; Student-run film society; Symphony orchestra; Television station; Yearbook. **Organizations:** 121 registered organizations, 28 honor societies, 8 religious organizations. 13 fraternities, 16 sororities. **Athletics (Intercollegiate):** *Men:* baseball, basketball, diving, football, lacrosse, soccer, swimming, track/field (outdoor). *Women:* basketball, diving, field hockey, lacrosse, soccer, softball, swimming, track/field (outdoor), volleyball. **On-Campus Highlights:** Living Communities, The Heights, John J. Cali School of Music, CELS, Kasser Theater.

ACCOMMODATIONS

Allowed in exams:	
Calculators	Yes
Dictionary	Yes
Computer	Yes
Spell-checker	Yes
Extended test time	Yes
Scribe	Yes
Proctors	Yes
Oral exams	Yes
Note-takers	Yes
Support services for students with	
LD	Yes
ADHD	Yes
ASD	Yes
Distraction-reduced environment	Yes
Recording of lecture allowed	Yes
Reading technology:	Yes
Audio books	Yes
Other assistive technology	JAWS, Dragon Dictate, ZoomText, Kurtzweil
Priority registration	Yes
Added costs for services:	
For LD:	No
For ADHD:	No
For ASD:	No
LD specialists	Yes
ADHD & ASD coaching	Yes
ASD specialists	Yes
Professional tutors	No
Peer tutors	Yes
Max. hours/week for services	Varies
How professors are notified of student approved accommodations	Student

COLLEGE GRADUATION REQUIREMENTS

Course waivers allowed	No
Course substitutions allowed	Yes
In what courses	
Foreign Language, Physical Education, Public Speaking	

New Jersey City University

2039 KENNEDY BOULEVARD, JERSEY CITY, NJ 07305 • ADMISSIONS: 888-441-6528 • FAX: 201-200-2044

CAMPUS

Type of school	Public
Environment	City
Support	SP

STUDENTS

Undergrad enrollment	6,357
% male/female	41/59
% from out of state	9
% frosh live on campus	20

FINANCIAL FACTS

Annual in-state tuition	$8,114
Annual out-of-state tuition	$17,142
Room and board	$12,805
Required fees	$3,315

GENERAL ADMISSIONS INFO

Application fee	$50

Nonfall registration accepted. Admission may be deferred.

Range SAT EBRW	430–540
Range SAT Math	440–540

ACADEMICS

Student/faculty ratio	15:1
% students returning for sophomore year	77
% students graduating within 4 years	13
% students graduating withing 6 years	33

Most classes have fewer than 10 students. Most lab/discussion sessions have 10–19 students.

PROGRAMS/SERVICES FOR STUDENTS WITH LEARNING DIFFERENCES

Students with Disabilities are served by the Office of Specialized Services for Student with Disabilities at New Jersey City University. The Office of Specialized Services (OSS) provides NJCU students with disabilities equal access to college programs. The OSS serves as a resource for students with mobility, vision, hearing, learning, and other disabilities that are in need of campus accommodations. The OSS assists students, on an individual basis, in securing reasonable accommodations, including, but not limited to alternate testing arrangements, adaptive technology, and assistance in arranging other support services (e.g., sign language interpreters, books on tape, and note-taking support) supported by documentation. It is the student's responsibility to self-identify and request services. Students requesting academic adjustments are required to submit appropriate and recent documentation of their disability. Students wishing to obtain accommodations may do so by contacting the OSS Director.

ADMISSIONS

There is no separate application for students with disabilities. All applicants are expected to meet the same admission standards. Applicants must submit 2 letters of recommendations. Students may also write an essay to describe aspirations and motivations. ACT or SAT required.

Additional Information

The Center for Student Success (CSS) offers access to peer and professional tutoring services and academic resources, enabling all NJCU students to attain the necessary skills, strategies, and behaviors necessary to improve their academic standing and to identify appropriate career objectives. The CSS provides: individual and small group peer tutoring in basic English and math; study halls in basic English and math; workshops on study skills, learning styles, information literacy, financial literacy, and success strategies; Access to computer-based learning skills materials and resources; referrals to on-campus academic and personal assistance programs; co-curricular transcript application; learning and study skills strategies; and exposure to leadership opportunities.

ADMISSIONS INFO FOR STUDENTS WITH LEARNING DIFFERENCES

SAT/ACT required: Yes
Interview required: No
Essay required: No
Additional application required: No
Documentation required for:
  LD: Yes if requesting accommodations
  ADHD: Yes if requesting accommodations
  ASD: Yes if requesting accommodations
Documentation submitted to: ODS
Special Ed. HS course work accepted: Yes
Separate application required for Programs/Services: No
Contact Information
Name of program or department: Disability Resource Center
Telephone: 201-200-2000

New Jersey City University

GENERAL ADMISSIONS

Very important factors considered include: rigor of secondary school record, academic GPA, standardized test scores. *Important factors considered include:* class rank. *Other factors considered include:* application essay, recommendation(s), interview, extracurricular activities, talent/ability, character/personal qualities, volunteer work, level of applicant's interest. *Freshman Admission Requirements:* High school diploma is required and GED is accepted. *Academic units required:* 4 English, 4 math, 4 science, 2 science labs, 4 social studies. *Academic units recommended:* 4 English, 4 math, 4 science, 3 science labs, 2 foreign language, 4 social studies.

ACCOMMODATIONS OR SERVICES

Accommodations are decided upon an individual basis after a thorough review of appropriate, current documentation. The accommodations requests must be supported through the documentation provided and must be logically linked to the current impact of the condition on academic functioning.

FINANCIAL AID

Students should submit: FAFSA. Applicants will be notified of awards on or about 5/15. The Princeton Review suggests that all financial aid forms be submitted as soon as possible after October 1. *Need-based scholarships/grants offered:* College/university scholarship or grant aid from institutional funds; Federal Pell; SEOG; State scholarships/grants. *Loan aid offered:* Direct PLUS loans; Direct Subsidized Stafford Loans; Direct Unsubsidized Stafford Loans. Federal Work-Study Program available. Institutional employment available.

CAMPUS LIFE

Activities: Campus Ministries; Choral groups; Concert band; Dance; Drama/theater; Jazz band; Literary magazine; Music ensembles; Musical theater; Opera; Radio station; Student government; Student newspaper; Symphony orchestra; Yearbook. **Organizations:** 50 registered organizations, 2 religious organizations. 7 fraternities, 5 sororities. **Athletics (Intercollegiate):** *Men:* baseball, basketball, cross-country, soccer, track/field (outdoor), track/field (indoor), volleyball. *Women:* basketball, bowling, cross-country, soccer, softball, track/field (outdoor), track/field (indoor), volleyball. **On-Campus Highlights:** Student Union Building, Physical fitness center, Library, Cafeteria, Dunkin' Donuts.

ACCOMMODATIONS

Allowed in exams:	
Calculators	Yes
Dictionary	Yes
Computer	Yes
Spell-checker	Yes
Extended test time	Yes
Scribe	Yes
Proctors	Yes
Oral exams	Yes
Note-takers	Yes
Support services for students with	
LD	Yes
ADHD	Yes
ASD	Yes
Distraction-reduced environment	Yes
Recording of lecture allowed	Yes
Reading technology:	Yes
Audio books	Yes
Other assistive technology	Yes
Priority registration	Yes
Added costs for services:	
For LD:	No
For ADHD:	No
For ASD:	No
LD specialists	Yes
ADHD & ASD coaching	Yes
ASD specialists	No
Professional tutors	No
Peer tutors	Yes
Max. hours/week for services	Unlimited
How professors are notified of student approved accommodations	
By both student and director	

COLLEGE GRADUATION REQUIREMENTS

Course waivers allowed	No
Course substitutions allowed	Yes
In what courses	
Each case is reviewed on an individual basis.	

Rider University

2083 LAWRENCEVILLE ROAD, LAWRENCEVILLE, NJ 08648-3099 • ADMISSIONS: 609-896-5042 • FAX: 609-895-6645

PROGRAMS/SERVICES FOR STUDENTS WITH LEARNING DIFFERENCES

Rider University, through complying with all applicable non-discrimination laws, wishes to enable every Rider student with a disability to enjoy an equal opportunity to achieve her/his full potential while attending the university.

ADMISSIONS

Admissions performs a holistic review of an application. Please refer to the average GPA since many factors go into the decisions that are made for a student.

Additional Information

Students are encouraged to self-identify and meet with a professional in the Services for Students with Disabilities office, so that they can become aware of the accommodations and support services specifically available to them. Prospective students and families are encouraged to call the office to receive information.

Rider University

General Admissions

Very important factors considered include: rigor of secondary school record, academic GPA, application essay, standardized test scores, recommendation(s). *Other factors considered include:* class rank, interview, extracurricular activities, talent/ability, character/personal qualities, alumni/ae relation, geographical residence, state residency, volunteer work, work experience, level of applicant's interest. *Freshman Admission Requirements:* High school diploma is required and GED is accepted. *Academic units required:* 4 English, 3 math. *Academic units recommended:* 4 math, 4 science, 2 science labs, 2 foreign language, 2 social studies, 2 history.

Accommodations or Services

Accommodations are decided upon an individual basis after a thorough review of appropriate, current documentation. The accommodations requests must be supported through the documentation provided and must be logically linked to the current impact of the condition on academic functioning.

Financial Aid

Students should submit: FAFSA. Applicants will be notified of awards on a rolling basis beginning 2/1. The Princeton Review suggests that all financial aid forms be submitted as soon as possible after October 1. *Need-based scholarships/grants offered:* College/university scholarship or grant aid from institutional funds; Federal Pell; Private scholarships; SEOG; State scholarships/grants. *Loan aid offered:* Direct PLUS loans; Direct Subsidized Stafford Loans; Direct Unsubsidized Stafford Loans. Federal Work-Study Program available. Institutional employment available.

Campus Life

Activities: Campus Ministries; Choral groups; Concert band; Dance; Drama/theater; International Student Organization; Literary magazine; Model UN; Music ensembles; Musical theater; Opera; Pep band; Radio station; Student government; Student newspaper; Student-run film society; Television station; Yearbook. **Organizations:** 84 registered organizations, 24 honor societies, 6 religious organizations. 4 fraternities, 8 sororities. **Athletics (Intercollegiate):** *Men:* baseball, basketball, cheerleading, cross-country, diving, golf, soccer, swimming, tennis, track/field (outdoor), wrestling. *Women:* basketball, cheerleading, cross-country, diving, field hockey, soccer, softball, swimming, tennis, track/field (outdoor), volleyball. **On-Campus Highlights:** Residence Hall Quad, Alumni Gym, Student Recreation Center, Daly's Dining Hall/Cranberry Cafe, Academic Quad.

ACCOMMODATIONS

Allowed in exams:

Calculators	Yes
Dictionary	Yes
Computer	Yes
Spell-checker	Yes
Extended test time	Yes
Scribe	Yes
Proctors	Yes
Oral exams	Yes
Note-takers	Not Applicable

Support services for students with

LD	Yes
ADHD	Yes
ASD	Yes
Distraction-reduced environment	Yes
Recording of lecture allowed	Yes
Reading technology:	Yes
Audio books	Yes

Other assistive technology Kurzweil, Dragon Naturally Speaking, Livescribe pens, hand-held digital recorders, Reading Pens, assistance with using appropriate applications on laptops or Ipads.

Priority registration	Yes

Added costs for services:

For LD:	No
For ADHD:	No
For ASD:	No
LD specialists	Yes
ADHD & ASD coaching	Yes
ASD specialists	No
Professional tutors	Yes
Peer tutors	Yes
Max. hours/week for services	Varies
How professors are notified of student approved accommodations	Student

COLLEGE GRADUATION REQUIREMENTS

Course waivers allowed	No
Course substitutions allowed	Yes

In what courses

With appropriate documentation foreign language and math courses may be substituted, except if they are essential to the student's major.

Seton Hall University

400 SOUTH ORANGE AVENUE, SOUTH ORANGE, NJ 07079 • ADMISSIONS: (800) THE HALL • FAX: 973-275-2339

CAMPUS

Type of school	Private (nonprofit)
Environment	Village
Support	CS

STUDENTS

Undergrad enrollment	5,295
% male/female	41/59
% from out of state	22
% frosh live on campus	74

FINANCIAL FACTS

Annual tuition	$35,940
Room and board	$11,522
Required fees	$1,782

GENERAL ADMISSIONS INFO

Application fee	$55
Priority deadline	3/1

Nonfall registration accepted. Admission may be deferred for a maximum of 1 year.

Range SAT EBRW	490–590
Range SAT Math	510–610
Range ACT Composite	22–27

ACADEMICS

Student/faculty ratio	NR
% students returning for sophomore year	85

PROGRAMS/SERVICES FOR STUDENTS WITH LEARNING DIFFERENCES

The mission of Disability Support Services (DSS) is to provide students with disabilities equal access to all university programs and activities, while raising campus-wide awareness of issues impacting this student population. DSS works collaboratively with academic departments and student affairs offices to engage and support the intellectual and social development of students with disabilities. To this end, DSS employs policies and programming to promote academic excellence, the development of self-advocacy skills, and increased student leadership opportunities. Accommodations are provided based on submission of appropriate documentation, which is reviewed by DSS staff in compliance with university policy, Section 504 of the Rehabilitation Act, the Americans with Disabilities Act (ADA), and the New Jersey Law against Discrimination (NJLAD).

ADMISSIONS

There is no special admission process for students with learning disabilities, and all applicants must meet the same admission criteria.

Additional Information

In coordinating its activities with other departments of the university (such as Residence Life and Academic Services), Student Support Services works to assure that the university remains in compliance with all federal laws and regulations. The DSS office provides the following services to individuals with LD (with appropriate documentation): reduced course load, extended time to complete assignments, tape recorders, note-taking, taped texts, readers, extended time for in class assignments, assistive technology (calculator, word processor, etc.), extended time for testing, and a distractionreduced environment. The recommendation from DSS is that students meed with their instructor at least one week before each scheduled exam to determine how exam accommodations will be implemented.

ADMISSIONS INFO FOR STUDENTS WITH LEARNING DIFFERENCES

SAT/ACT required: Yes
Interview required: No
Essay required: N/A
Additional application required: No
Documentation required for:
  LD: Psycoeducational evaluation
  ADHD: Psycho ed evaluation
  ASD: Psycho ed evaluation
Documentation submitted to: Disability Support Services
Special Ed. HS course work accepted: No
Separate application required for Programs/Services: Yes
Contact Information
Name of program or department: Disability Support Services (DSS)
Telephone: 973-313-6003
Fax: 973-761-9185

Seton Hall University

GENERAL ADMISSIONS

Freshman Admission Requirements: High school diploma is required and GED is accepted. *Academic units required:* 4 English, 3 math, 1 science, 1 science lab, 2 foreign language, 2 social studies, 4 academic electives.

ACCOMMODATIONS OR SERVICES

Accommodations are decided upon an individual basis after a thorough review of appropriate, current documentation. The accommodations requests must be supported through the documentation provided and must be logically linked to the current impact of the condition on academic functioning.

FINANCIAL AID

Students should submit: FAFSA. The Princeton Review suggests that all financial aid forms be submitted as soon as possible after October 1. *Need-based scholarships/grants offered: Loan aid offered:* Federal Work-Study Program available. Institutional employment available.

CAMPUS LIFE

Activities:. **Organizations:** 100 registered organizations, 13 honor societies, 3 religious organizations. **Athletics (Intercollegiate):** *Men:* baseball, basketball, cross-country, diving, golf, soccer, swimming, track/field (outdoor). *Women:* basketball, cross-country, diving, soccer, softball, swimming, tennis, track/field (outdoor). **On-Campus Highlights:** University Center, Recreation Center, Walsh Library, Dunkin Donuts, Chapel of the Immaculate Conception.

ACCOMMODATIONS

Allowed in exams:

Calculators	Yes
Dictionary	Yes
Computer	Yes
Spell-checker	Yes
Extended test time	Yes
Scribe	Yes
Proctors	Yes
Oral exams	Yes
Note-takers	Yes

Support services for students with

LD	Yes
ADHD	Yes
ASD	Yes
Distraction-reduced environment	Yes
Recording of lecture allowed	Yes
Reading technology:	Yes
Audio books	Yes
Other assistive technology	Yes
Priority registration	No

Added costs for services:

For LD:	No
For ADHD:	No
For ASD:	No
LD specialists	Yes
ADHD & ASD coaching	No
ASD specialists	No
Professional tutors	Yes
Peer tutors	Yes
Max. hours/week for services	Varies

How professors are notified of student approved accommodations — Student

COLLEGE GRADUATION REQUIREMENTS

Course waivers allowed	Yes

In what courses
Course substitutions for mathematics and world languages are available as long as they are not core courses required for the student's major. These determinations are based on documented need.

Course substitutions allowed	Yes

In what courses
Students may request course substitutions through the DSS office for mathematics and world languages. DSS's recommendation is then submitted to the dean of each school or college for review and approval.

New Mexico Institute of Mining and Technology

Campus Station, Socorro, NM 87801 • Admissions: 575-835-5424 • Fax: 575-835-5989

CAMPUS
Type of school	Public
Environment	Village
Support	S

STUDENTS
Undergrad enrollment	1,358
% male/female	73/27
% from out of state	11
% frosh live on campus	89

FINANCIAL FACTS
Annual in-state tuition	$6,133
Annual out-of-state tuition	$19,941
Room and board	$8,202
Required fees	$1,050

GENERAL ADMISSIONS INFO
Application fee	$15
Priority deadline	3/1
Regular application deadline	8/1

Nonfall registration accepted. Admission may be deferred for a maximum of 1 year.

Range SAT EBRW	610–780
Range SAT Math	550–690
Range ACT Composite	23–29

ACADEMICS
Student/faculty ratio	11:1
% students returning for sophomore year	74

Most classes have 10–19 students. Most lab/discussion sessions have fewer than 10 students.

PROGRAMS/SERVICES FOR STUDENTS WITH LEARNING DIFFERENCES

New Mexico Tech does not have a specific program for students with LD. Services for students with disabilities are available in the Counseling and Student Health Center. Students must present recent documentation completed within the previous 3 years. The documentation should be sent to the Office for Counseling and Disability Services. New Mexico Tech sends a letter to all admitted students asking those with disabilities to contact the Office for Counseling and Disability Services. There is a special application required after admission and enrollment to receive services or accommodations. The counseling staff works with students with disabilities on an individual basis to accommodate their special needs. Students may also use the counseling service to reduce their stress, think through problems or difficulties, clarify options, and express and explore feelings.

ADMISSIONS

There is no special admission process for students with LD. The minimum GPA is a 2.5. The college requires an ACT composite score of 21 or higher or an SAT score of 970 or higher. The college will accept the SAT, but prefers the ACT. The GED is accepted with a score of 50 or higher. High school course requirements include 4 years of English, 2 years of science (including biology, physics, chemistry, and earth science), 3 years of math, and 3 years of social science, of which one must be history. Students are encouraged to self-disclose their disability during the admission process.

Additional Information

Students will work with staff to determine appropriate accommodations or services. These services may include coordinating academic accommodations, extended time for tests, calculators in exams, skills classes in study strategies and time management, and tutorial services available for all students on campus.

ADMISSIONS INFO FOR STUDENTS WITH LEARNING DIFFERENCES

SAT/ACT required: Yes
Interview required: No
Essay required: No
Additional application required: No
Documentation required for:
 LD: Psycho ed evaluation
 ADHD: Diagnosis based on DSM-V; history of behaviors impairing functioning in academic setting; diagnostic interview; history of symptoms; evidence of ongoing behaviors.
 ASD: Psycho ed evaluation
Documentation submitted to: Office for Counseling and Disability Services
Special Ed. HS course work accepted: Yes
Separate application required for Programs/Services: Yes
Contact Information
Name of program or department: Office of Counseling and Disability Services
Telephone: 575-835-6619
Fax: 575-835-5959

New Mexico Institute of Mining and Technology

GENERAL ADMISSIONS

Very important factors considered include: rigor of secondary school record, academic GPA, standardized test scores. *Other factors considered include:* class rank, extracurricular activities, talent/ability. *Freshman Admission Requirements:* High school diploma is required and GED is accepted. *Academic units required:* 4 English, 3 math, 2 science, 2 science labs, 2 social studies, 1 history, 3 academic electives. *Academic units recommended:* 4 English, 4 math, 4 science, 3 science labs, 2 foreign language, 3 social studies, 1 history.

ACCOMMODATIONS OR SERVICES

Accommodations are decided upon an individual basis after a thorough review of appropriate, current documentation. The accommodations requests must be supported through the documentation provided and must be logically linked to the current impact of the condition on academic functioning.

FINANCIAL AID

Students should submit: FAFSA. Applicants will be notified of awards on a rolling basis beginning 5/1. The Princeton Review suggests that all financial aid forms be submitted as soon as possible after October 1. *Need-based scholarships/grants offered:* College/university scholarship or grant aid from institutional funds; Federal Pell; Private scholarships; SEOG; State scholarships/grants. *Loan aid offered:* Direct PLUS loans; Direct Subsidized Stafford Loans; Direct Unsubsidized Stafford Loans. Federal Work-Study Program available. Institutional employment available.

CAMPUS LIFE

Activities: Choral groups; Concert band; Dance; Drama/theater; International Student Organization; Jazz band; Music ensembles; Musical theater; Radio station; Student government; Student newspaper. **Organizations:** 60 registered organizations, 7 honor societies, 3 religious organizations. **On-Campus Highlights:** Fidel Student Center, Skeen Library, Workman Center.

ACCOMMODATIONS

Allowed in exams:

Calculators	Yes
Dictionary	No
Computer	Yes
Spell-checker	Yes
Extended test time	Yes
Scribe	Yes
Proctors	Yes
Oral exams	Yes
Note-takers	Yes

Support services for students with

LD	Yes
ADHD	Yes
ASD	Yes
Distraction-reduced environment	Yes
Recording of lecture allowed	Yes
Reading technology:	Yes
Audio books	Yes
Other assistive technology	Yes
Priority registration	Yes

Added costs for services:

For LD:	No
For ADHD:	No
For ASD:	No
LD specialists	No
ADHD & ASD coaching	No
ASD specialists	No
Professional tutors	No
Peer tutors	Yes
Max. hours/week for services	Unlimited
How professors are notified of student approved accommodations	Student and Director

COLLEGE GRADUATION REQUIREMENTS

Course waivers allowed	No
Course substitutions allowed	No

New Mexico State University

PO Box 30001, Las Cruces, NM 88003-8001 • Admissions: 575-646-3121 • Fax: 575-646-6330

CAMPUS

Type of school	Public
Environment	City
Support	S

STUDENTS

Undergrad enrollment	11,173
% male/female	46/54
% from out of state	26
% frosh live on campus	62

FINANCIAL FACTS

Annual in-state tuition	$7,368
Annual out-of-state tuition	$23,508
Room and board	$9,252
Required fees	NR

GENERAL ADMISSIONS INFO

Application fee	$20

Nonfall registration accepted.

Range SAT EBRW	450–580
Range SAT Math	460–580
Range ACT Composite	18–23

ACADEMICS

Student/faculty ratio	16:1
% students returning for sophomore year	74
% students graduating within 4 years	18
% students graduating within 6 years	46

Most classes have fewer than 10 students.
Most lab/discussion sessions have fewer than 10 students.

PROGRAMS/SERVICES FOR STUDENTS WITH LEARNING DIFFERENCES

Students need to provide documentation of a diagnosis of a disability to the Student Accessibility Services office. The functional limitations identified need to support the request for accommodations. All students participate in an interactive meeting with Student Accessibility Services staff to discuss the requests.

ADMISSIONS

There is no special admissions criteria for students with disabilities. All prospective students need to comply with the university admissions criteria that includes high school transcripts or GED, GPA, ACT/SAT scores, etc. Please visit admissions.nmsu.edu.

Additional Information

Over 200 student groups, clubs, and organizations along with intramural sports, Greek life and recreational programs help NMSU student to discover their interests, leadership skills, and make lifelong friends. Academic advisors are available to assist students.

ADMISSIONS INFO FOR STUDENTS WITH LEARNING DIFFERENCES

SAT/ACT required: Yes
Interview required: No
Essay required: Recommended
Additional application required: Yes
Documentation required for:
  LD: Once admitted, new students with disabilities are encouraged to schedule an appointment with the Director of Student Accessibility Services and provide appropriate documentation of diagnosis of their disability. Please visit sas.nmsu.edu/new-students/ for more information.
  ADHD: Once admitted, new students with disabilities are encouraged to schedule an appointment with the Director of Student Accessibility Services and provide appropriate documentation of diagnosis of their disability. Please visit sas.nmsu.edu/new-students/ for more information.
  ASD: Once admitted, new students with disabilities are encouraged to schedule an appointment with the Director of Student Accessibility Services and provide appropriate documentation of diagnosis of their disability. Please visit sas.nmsu.edu/new-students/ for more information.
Documentation submitted to: Student Accessibility Services
Special Ed. HS course work accepted: Yes
Separate application required for Programs/Services: No
Contact Information
Name of program or department: Student Accessibility Services
Telephone: 575-646-6840
Email: tlukin@nmsu.edu

New Mexico State University

GENERAL ADMISSIONS

Very important factors considered include: academic GPA, standardized test scores. *Other factors considered include:* rigor of secondary school record, class rank. *Freshman Admission Requirements:* High school diploma is required and GED is accepted. *Academic units required:* 4 English, 4 math, 2 science, 2 science labs, 1 foreign language.

ACCOMMODATIONS OR SERVICES

Accommodations are decided upon an individual basis after a thorough review of appropriate, current documentation. The accommodations requests must be supported through the documentation provided and must be logically linked to the current impact of the condition on academic functioning.

FINANCIAL AID

Students should submit: FAFSA. Applicants will be notified of awards on a rolling basis beginning 1/1. The Princeton Review suggests that all financial aid forms be submitted as soon as possible after October 1. *Need-based scholarships/grants offered:* College/university scholarship or grant aid from institutional funds; Federal Pell; Private scholarships; SEOG; State scholarships/grants. *Loan aid offered:* Direct PLUS loans; Direct Subsidized Stafford Loans; Direct Unsubsidized Stafford Loans. Federal Work-Study Program available. Institutional employment available.

CAMPUS LIFE

Activities: Campus Ministries; Choral groups; Concert band; Dance; Drama/theater; International Student Organization; Jazz band; Literary magazine; Marching band; Model UN; Music ensembles; Musical theater; Opera; Pep band; Radio station; Student government; Student newspaper; Symphony orchestra; Television station. **Organizations:** 263 registered organizations, 24 honor societies, 23 religious organizations. 14 fraternities, 5 sororities. **Athletics (Intercollegiate):** *Men:* baseball, basketball, cross-country, football, golf, tennis. *Women:* basketball, cross-country, golf, softball, swimming, tennis, track/field (outdoor), volleyball. Corbett Center Student Union, Zhul Library, Barnes and Noble, Activity Center, Frenger Food Court.

ACCOMMODATIONS

Allowed in exams:

Calculators	Yes
Dictionary	No
Computer	Yes
Spell-checker	No
Extended test time	Yes
Scribe	Yes
Proctors	Yes
Oral exams	Yes
Note-takers	Yes

Support services for students with

LD	Yes
ADHD	Yes
ASD	Yes
Distraction-reduced environment	Yes
Recording of lecture allowed	Yes
Reading technology:	Yes
Audio books	Yes
Other assistive technology	Yes
Priority registration	Yes

Added costs for services:

For LD:	No
For ADHD:	No
For ASD:	No
LD specialists	No
ADHD & ASD coaching	No
ASD specialists	No
Professional tutors	Yes
Peer tutors	Yes
Max. hours/week for services	Unlimited
How professors are notified of student approved accommodations	Student

COLLEGE GRADUATION REQUIREMENTS

Course waivers allowed	No
Course substitutions allowed	Yes
In what courses	

Communications and Foreign Language courses

Adelphi University

1 SOUTH AVENUE, GARDEN CITY, NY 11530 • ADMISSIONS: 516-877-3050 • FAX: 516-877-3039

CAMPUS

Type of school	Private (nonprofit)
Environment	Metropolis
Support	SP

STUDENTS

Undergrad enrollment	5,162
% male/female	31/69
% from out of state	6
% frosh live on campus	37

FINANCIAL FACTS

Annual tuition	$36,920
Room and board	$16,030
Required fees	$1,740

GENERAL ADMISSIONS INFO

Application fee	$40
Priority deadline	3/1

Nonfall registration accepted. Admission may be deferred.

Range SAT EBRW	530--600
Range SAT Math	530--620
Range ACT Composite	22--27

ACADEMICS

Student/faculty ratio	12:1
% students returning for sophomore year	80
% students graduating within 4 years	1
% students graduating within 6 years	68

Most classes have 20-29 students.

PROGRAMS/SERVICES FOR STUDENTS WITH LEARNING DIFFERENCES

The Learning Resource Program provides support services to students with learning disabilities. The mission of the program is to encourage independence, assist students in realizing their academic potential, and to facilitate the elimination of barriers. The program focuses on an individualized approach to each student.

ADMISSIONS

Applicants submit a separate application to the Learning Resource Program, along with documentation and recommendations. If a match is determined, applicants are invited for a personal interview. Students may be considered for admission to the Learning Resources Program whether or not they meet the traditional criteria for enrollment in the University.

Additional Information

In the Learning Resource Program students receive intensive academic tutoring and individual counseling. Course content and requirements are never compromised for students with LD but program procedures do help to ease the way in the classroom. BAP staff consists almost exclusively of Adelphi graduate students who are studying psychology, social work, education, or communication disorders. Each student is assigned at least two staff members to work with them a minimum of four times per week on academic issues. These meetings focus on executive functioning strategies to help the student remain aware of, and plan for, upcoming assignments, exams and meetings; and assignment completion, exam preparation, and research.

ADMISSIONS INFO FOR STUDENTS WITH LEARNING DIFFERENCES

SAT/ACT required: Yes
Interview required: Yes
Essay required: Recommended
Additional application required: Yes
Documentation required for:
  LD: Recent (within 3 years) psycho-educational evaluation that includes cognitive and achievement testing. WAIS or Woodcock-Johnson. WIAT for achievement.
  ADHD: Recent psycho-educational evaluation and ADHD Certification form.
ASD: There is no documentation needed to enroll in the Bridges to Adelphi Program. There is no separate application to the Bridges to Adelphi Program. Students who apply to the university, and are accepted, may choose to enroll in the Bridges to Adelphi Program.
Documentation submitted to: Student Access Office
Special Ed. HS course work accepted: Adelphi University
Separate application required for Programs/Services: LD, ADHD
Contact Information
Name of program or department: Student Access Office
Telephone: 516-877-4710
Fax: 516-877-4711
Email: lrp@adelphi.edu

Adelphi University

GENERAL ADMISSIONS

Very important factors considered include: rigor of secondary school record. *Important factors considered include:* class rank, academic GPA, application essay, standardized test scores, recommendation(s), extracurricular activities, talent/ability, character/personal qualities, volunteer work. *Other factors considered include:* interview, first generation, alumni/ae relation, work experience, level of applicant's interest. *Freshman Admission Requirements:* High school diploma is required and GED is accepted *Academic units recommended:* 4 English, 3 math, 3 science, 2 foreign language, 4 units from above areas or other academic areas.

ACCOMMODATIONS OR SERVICES

Accommodations are decided upon an individual basis after a thorough review of appropriate, current documentation. The accommodations requests must be supported through the documentation provided and must be logically linked to the current impact of the condition on academic functioning.

FINANCIAL AID

Students should submit: FAFSA; State aid form. Applicants will be notified of awards on a rolling basis beginning 12/15. The Princeton Review suggests that all financial aid forms be submitted as soon as possible after October 1. *Need-based scholarships/grants offered:* College/university scholarship or grant aid from institutional funds; Federal Pell; Private scholarships; SEOG; State scholarships/grants; United Negro College Fund *Loan aid offered:* Direct PLUS loans; Direct Subsidized Stafford Loans; Direct Unsubsidized Stafford Loans Federal Work-Study Program available. Institutional employment available.

CAMPUS LIFE

Activities: 0 **Organizations:** 80 registered organizations, 21 honor societies, 5 religious organizations. 3 fraternities, 7 sororities, **Athletics (Intercollegiate):** *Men:* baseball, basketball, cross-country, golf, lacrosse, soccer, swimming, tennis, track/field (outdoor), track/field (indoor) *Women:* basketball, bowling, cross-country, field hockey, lacrosse, soccer, softball, swimming, tennis, track/field (outdoor), track/field (indoor), volleyball. **On-Campus Highlights:** Ruth S. Harley University Center, Underground Café, Swirbul Library, Nexus Building, Center for Recreation and Sports.

ACCOMMODATIONS

Allowed in exams:	
Calculators	Yes
Dictionary	Yes
Computer	Yes
Spell-checker	Yes
Extended test time	Yes
Scribe	Yes
Proctors	Yes
Oral exams	No
Note-takers	Yes

Support services for students with	
LD	Yes
ADHD	Yes
ASD	Yes
Distraction-reduced environment	Yes
Recording of lecture allowed	Yes
Reading technology:	Yes
Audio books	Yes

Other assistive technology We have a limited number of Live Scribe Smart pens for students to borrow each semester, we offer text to speech software programs, CART services, adaptable art and science lab tools and equipment, FM systems, hand held CCTV, desktop CCTV, talking calculators, and dragon naturally speaking device with software.

Priority registration	Yes

Added costs for services:	
For LD:	Not Applicable
For ADHD:	No
For ASD:	No
LD specialists	Yes
ADHD & ASD coaching	Yes
ASD specialists	Yes
Professional tutors	Yes
Peer tutors	Yes
Max. hours/week for services	Varies
How professors are notified of student approved accommodations	Student

COLLEGE GRADUATION REQUIREMENTS

Course waivers allowed	No
Course substitutions allowed	Yes
In what courses	Math, Foreign Language

Barnard College

3009 BROADWAY, NEW YORK, NY 10027 • ADMISSIONS: 212-854-2014 • FAX: 212-280-8797

CAMPUS

Type of school	Private (nonprofit)
Environment	Metropolis
Support	S

STUDENTS

Undergrad enrollment	2,600
% male/female	0/100
% from out of state	73
% frosh live on campus	99

FINANCIAL FACTS

Tuition	$53,252
Room and board	$17,525
Required fees	$1,780

GENERAL ADMISSIONS INFO

Application fee	$75
Regular application deadline	1/1

Nonfall registration accepted. Admission may be deferred for a maximum of 1 year.

Range SAT EBRW	660–760
Range SAT Math	650–740
Range ACT Composite	30–33

ACADEMICS

Student/faculty ratio	10:1
% students returning for sophomore year	95
% students graduating within 4 years	87
% students graduating within 6 years	93

Most classes have fewer than 10 students. Most lab/discussion sessions have 10–19 students.

PROGRAMS/SERVICES FOR STUDENTS WITH LEARNING DIFFERENCES

The Office of Disability Services' mission is to provide support services to students, faculty and staff which encourage Barnard students with disabilities to become self-sufficient in managing their own accommodations. In 1978, Barnard established a program to provide services for students with disabilities which enhance their educational, pre-professional and personal development. The Office of Disability Services (ODS) serves students with visual, mobility and hearing disabilities and students with invisible disabilities such as chronic medical conditions, learning disabilities/ADD, psychiatric disabilities and substance use/recovery. ODS works with and empowers students with disabilities in order to coordinate support services that enable equal access to education and college life. Barnard has a tradition of meeting the needs of individual students, and in 1978 this long-standing commitment was formalized with the establishment of the Office of Disability Services (ODS). Responding to the mandate of Section 504 of the Rehabilitation Act of 1973, and with contributions from public, private and College resources, the campus has become increasingly accessible. The Office of Disability Services works to ensure that reasonable accommodations are made to provide programmatic and physical access.

ADMISSIONS

Students are held to the same admissions criteria as students without any needs for accommodations.

Additional Information

To register with ODS, you will need to have an intake session with our director or accommodations coordinator. Call the office at 212-854-4634 to set up an appointment time. Accommodations are not retroactive, so we can only set up accommodations for you.

ADMISSIONS INFO FOR STUDENTS WITH LEARNING DIFFERENCES

SAT/ACT required: Yes
Interview required: Not Applicable
Essay required: Not Applicable
Additional application required: Not Applicable
Documentation required for:
  LD: N/A
  ADHD: N/A
  ASD: N/A
Documentation submitted to: Office of Disability Services
Special Ed. HS course work accepted: Yes
Separate application required for Programs/Services: No
Contact Information
Name of program or department: Office of Disability Services
Telephone: 212-854-4634
Fax: 212-854-6275
Email: ods@barnard.edu

Barnard College

GENERAL ADMISSIONS

Very important factors considered include: rigor of secondary school record, academic GPA, application essay, recommendation(s), character/personal qualities. *Important factors considered include:* class rank, standardized test scores, extracurricular activities, talent/ability, volunteer work, work experience. *Other factors considered include:* interview, first generation, alumni/ae relation, geographical residence, racial/ethnic status, level of applicant's interest. *Freshman Admission Requirements:* High school diploma is required and GED is accepted. *Academic units recommended:* 4 English, 3 math, 3 science, 3 foreign language, 3 history.

ACCOMMODATIONS OR SERVICES

Accommodations are decided upon an individual basis after a thorough review of appropriate, current documentation. The accommodations requests must be supported through the documentation provided and must be logically linked to the current impact of the condition on academic functioning.

FINANCIAL AID

Students should submit: CSS/Financial Aid PROFILE; FAFSA; Noncustodial PROFILE;; State aid form. Applicants will be notified of awards on or about 3/31. The Princeton Review suggests that all financial aid forms be submitted as soon as possible after October 1. *Need-based scholarships/grants offered:* College/university scholarship or grant aid from institutional funds; Federal Pell; Private scholarships; SEOG; State scholarships/grants. *Loan aid offered:* Direct PLUS loans; Direct Subsidized Stafford Loans; Direct Unsubsidized Stafford Loans. Federal Work-Study Program available. Institutional employment available.

CAMPUS LIFE

Activities: Campus Ministries; Choral groups; Concert band; Dance; Drama/theater; International Student Organization; Jazz band; Literary magazine; Marching band; Model UN; Music ensembles; Musical theater; Opera; Pep band; Radio station; Student government; Student newspaper; Student-run film society; Symphony orchestra; Yearbook. **Organizations:** 100 registered organizations, 1 honor society, **Athletics (Intercollegiate):** *Women:* archery, basketball, crew/rowing, cross-country, diving, fencing, field hockey, golf, lacrosse, soccer, softball, swimming, tennis, track/field (outdoor), volleyball. **On-Campus Highlights:** Milstein Center (opening late summer 2018), Diana Center, The Quad, Lefrak Center, Liz's Place Cafe.

ACCOMMODATIONS	
Allowed in exams:	
Calculators	Yes
Dictionary	Yes
Computer	Yes
Spell-checker	Yes
Extended test time	Yes
Scribe	Yes
Proctors	Yes
Oral exams	No
Note-takers	Yes
Support services for students with	
LD	Yes
ADHD	Yes
ASD	Yes
Distraction-reduced environment	Yes
Recording of lecture allowed	Yes
Reading technology:	No
Audio books	Yes
Other assistive technology	Yes
Priority registration	No
Added costs for services:	
For LD:	No
For ADHD:	No
For ASD:	No
LD specialists	No
ADHD & ASD coaching	Yes
ASD specialists	No
Professional tutors	Yes
Peer tutors	Yes
Max. hours/week for services	Varies
How professors are notified of student approved accommodations	Director and Student

COLLEGE GRADUATION REQUIREMENTS	
Course waivers allowed	No
Course substitutions allowed	No

Canisius College

2001 MAIN STREET, BUFFALO, NY 14208 • ADMISSIONS: 716-888-2200 • FAX: 716-888-3230

CAMPUS

Type of school	Private (nonprofit)
Environment	Metropolis
Support	S

STUDENTS

Undergrad enrollment	2,325
% male/female	50/50
% from out of state	11
% frosh live on campus	62

FINANCIAL FACTS

Annual tuition	$27,000
Room and board	$11,300
Required fees	$1,488

GENERAL ADMISSIONS INFO

Nonfall registration accepted. Admission may be deferred for a maximum of 1 year.

Range SAT EBRW	520-630
Range SAT Math	520-630
Range ACT Composite	22-28

ACADEMICS

Student/faculty ratio	11:1
% students returning for sophomore year	83
% % students graduating within 4 years	62
% % students graduating within 6 years	69
Most classes have 20–29 students.	

PROGRAMS/SERVICES FOR STUDENTS WITH LEARNING DIFFERENCES

Academic Mentor Program (OM 317) — offers assistance to students with a variety of issues that may arise through their academic career. Academic Mentors meet regularly with students and assist with better time management, handling of courses, study skills, etc., to help achieve academic success. Accessibility Support (OM 317) — is committed to creating equal access for all Canisius students with disabilities. It is our goal to help meet the needs of individuals registered and documented through the office, whether the disability is permanent or temporary.

ADMISSIONS

There is no special admissions criteria for students with learning disabilities. When reviewing the application for admission, the Admissions Committee looks for students with at least a solid B average in a college preparatory program of study. Rigor of curriculum, including the types of courses being taken in the senior year, is considered the most important factor in the admissions decision.

Additional Information

Students must self-identify with the GRIFF Center for Academic Engagement , complete the Accessibility Support intake form, and provide current documentation. The student then meets with a professional in AS to discuss the accommodations, and to become familiar with the procedures. Students can receive alternative texts, note takers, readers, talking calculators, and assistive listening devices . The Griff Center Proctor Site is a designated area for students that need testing accommodations due to a disability or to make up a missed exam. Test accommodations are determined on a case-by-case basis.

ADMISSIONS INFO FOR STUDENTS WITH LEARNING DIFFERENCES

SAT/ACT required: Yes
Interview required: No
Essay required: Not Applicable
Additional application required: Not Applicable
Documentation required for:
  LD: Written confirmation supplied by a Medical Provider
  ADHD: Written confirmation supplied by a Medical Provider
  ASD: Written confirmation Supplied by a Medical Provider
Documentation submitted to: Support Program/Services
Special Ed. HS course work accepted: Not Applicable
Separate application required for program services: No
Contact Information
Name of program or department: Accessibility Support Services
Telephone: 716-888-2476
Fax: 716-888-3212

Canisius College

GENERAL ADMISSIONS

Very important factors considered include: rigor of secondary school record, academic GPA, standardized test scores. *Important factors considered include:* application essay, recommendation(s), extracurricular activities, volunteer work. *Other factors considered include:* class rank, interview, talent/ability, character/personal qualities, first generation, alumni/ae relation, work experience, level of applicant's interest. *Freshman Admission Requirements:* High school diploma is required and GED is accepted. *Academic units required:* 4 English, 3 math, 3 science, 2 science labs, 2 foreign language, 4 social studies. *Academic units recommended:* 4 English, 4 math, 4 science, 2 science labs, 4 foreign language, 4 social studies, 4 academic electives.

ACCOMMODATION OR SERVICES

Accommodations are decided upon an individual basis after a thorough review of appropriate, current documentation. The accommodations requests must be supported through the documentation provided and must be logically linked to the current impact of the condition on academic functioning.

FINANCIAL AID

Students should submit: FAFSA; State aid form. Applicants will be notified of awards on a rolling basis beginning 12/20. The Princeton Review suggests that all financial aid forms be submitted as soon as possible after October 1. *Need-based scholarships/grants offered:* College/university scholarship or grant aid from institutional funds; Federal Pell; Private scholarships; SEOG; State scholarships/grants; United Negro College Fund. *Loan aid offered:* Direct PLUS loans; Direct Subsidized Stafford Loans; Direct Unsubsidized Stafford Loans. Federal Work-Study Program available. Institutional employment available.

CAMPUS LIFE

Activities: Campus Ministries; Choral groups; Concert band; Dance; Drama/theater; International Student Organization; Jazz band; Literary magazine; Marching band; Model UN; Music ensembles; Musical theater; Pep band; Radio station; Student government; Student newspaper; Student-run film society; Symphony orchestra; Television station; Yearbook. **Organizations:** 102 registered organizations, 16 honor societies, 2 religious organizations. 1 fraternity, 1 sorority. **Athletics (Intercollegiate):** *Men:* baseball, basketball, cross-country, diving, golf, ice hockey, lacrosse, soccer, swimming *Women:* basketball, cross-country, diving, lacrosse, soccer, softball, swimming, synchronized swimming, volleyball. **On-Campus Highlights:** Montante Cultural Center, Village Townhouses, Palisano Pavillion, Koessler Athletic Center, Richard E. Winter Student Center.

ACCOMMODATIONS

Allowed in exams:	
Calculators	Yes
Dictionary	Yes
Computer	Yes
Spell-checker	Yes
Extended test time	Yes
Scribe	Yes
Proctors	Yes
Oral exams	Yes
Note-takers	Yes
Support services for students with	
LD	Yes
ADHD	Yes
ASD	Yes
Distraction-reduced environment	Yes
Recording of lecture allowed	Yes
Reading technology:	Yes
Audio books	Yes
Other assistive technology	Device that reads books aloud to students
Priority registration	No
Added costs for services:	
For LD:	
For ADHD:	
For ASD:	
LD specialists	Yes
ADHD & ASD coaching	Yes
ASD specialists	Yes
Professional tutors	Yes
Peer tutors	No
Max. hours/week for services	47
How professors are notified of student approved accommodations	Director

COLLEGE GRADUATION REQUIREMENTS

Course waivers allowed	Yes
In what courses	
Based on applicable documentation mainly math and foreign language	
Course substitutions allowed	Yes
In what courses	
Primarily Math and Foreign Language	

Clarkson University

8 Clarkson Avenue, Potsdam, NY 13699 • Admissions: 315-268-6480 • Fax: 315-268-7647

CAMPUS

Type of school	Private (nonprofit)
Environment	Village
Support	S

STUDENTS

Undergrad enrollment	2,991
% male/female	70/30
% from out of state	27
% frosh live on campus	98

FINANCIAL FACTS

Annual tuition	$48,194
Room and board	$15,222
Required fees	$1,250

GENERAL ADMISSIONS INFO

Application fee	$50
Regular application deadline	1/15

Nonfall registration accepted. Admission may be deferred for a maximum of 1 year.

Range SAT EBRW	563–650
Range SAT Math	580–680
Range ACT Composite	24–29

ACADEMICS

Student/faculty ratio	14:1
% students returning for sophomore year	87
% students graduating within 4 years	58
% students graduating within 6 years	74

Most classes have 10–19 students.

PROGRAMS/SERVICES FOR STUDENTS WITH LEARNING DIFFERENCES

For AccessABILITY Services to determine if a student's condition meets the standard defined by the law, an evaluative intake interview will be conducted with the student and any additional documentation supplied will be reviewed. All decisions are made on a case-by-case basis and any additional information requested following the intake interview will be used to determine the current functional limitations caused by the disability and reasonable modifications in an academic or residential setting. Decisions made by the Office of AccessABILITY Services may not translate to other institutions or be applicable for high-stakes exams such as the GRE, FE, MCAT, etc. For more information, visit http://www.clarkson.edu/accessability-services/student-resources-and-expectations

ADMISSIONS

The admission process and The admission process and criteria are the same for all students applying to Clarkson. Disability status will not be a consideration in admission decisions. Documentation should be submitted to the Office of Accommodative Services only after the student has been admitted. Students or their counselor can submit unofficial test scores but should not super score. Students should provide the individual section scores and the date of the test administration. Clarkson reserves the right to withdraw the offer of admission if there is a discrepancy in self-reported scores versus official scores. Upon enrollment, students will be asked to submit official scores from the SAT or ACT. Students are not required to take the Writing Section of ACT/SAT. Business or Humanities majors should take at least four years English, three years math, and one year of science. Engineering, Engineering & Management, or the Sciences majors should take four years English, four years math, and three or four years of science, including chemistry and physics.

Additional Information

Students with disabilities and/or medical conditions who require a specific type of housing to ensure good health or equal access to education may request a housing accommodation through the Office of AccessABILITY Services. Students will need to participate in an evaluative intake process, which may also include representatives of the Campus Health Center, Campus Dining Services and the Counseling Center, as deemed

ADMISSIONS INFO FOR STUDENTS WITH LEARNING DIFFERENCES

SAT/ACT required: Yes
Interview required: No
Essay required: Not Applicable
Additional application required: No
Documentation required for:
  LD: Psycho ed evaluation
  ADHD: Psycho ed evaluation
  ASD: Psycho ed evaluation
Documentation submitted to: Office of Accommodative Services
Special Ed. HS course work accepted: Not Applicable
Separate application required for program services: No
# of students last year receiving services/accommodations for:
  LD: 190
Contact Information
Name of program or department: Office of AccessABILITY Services
Telephone: 315-268-7643
Fax: 315-268-2400
Email: oas@clarkson.edu

Clarkson University

appropriate by the Director of the Office of AccessABILITY Services. A representative from Residence Life will join with the other representatives for the review of requests. Requests for special housing consideration for students with disabilities will be evaluated and prioritized based on need. Factors to be considered include severity of the condition, timing of the request, feasibility and availability. There is no guarantee that on campus housing will be available. Incoming freshman will be notified of the determination early in July and current students will be notified prior to the Housing Lottery. Approximately one in ten Clarkson students has registered with OAS for assistance with a disability. Clarkson students affiliated with OAS have the same academic success (based on grade point averages) as their peers.

GENERAL ADMISSIONS

Very important factors considered include: rigor of secondary school record, academic GPA. *Important factors considered include:* class rank, standardized test scores, recommendation(s), extracurricular activities, volunteer work. *Other factors considered include:* application essay, talent/ability, character/personal qualities, first generation, alumni/ae relation, work experience, level of applicant's interest. *Freshman Admission Requirements:* High school diploma is required and GED is accepted. *Academic units required:* 4 English, 3 math, 1 science, and 4 units from above areas or other academic areas. *Academic units recommended:* 4 math, 4 science.

ACCOMMODATION OR SERVICES

Accommodations are decided upon an individual basis after a thorough review of appropriate, current documentation. The accommodations requests must be supported through the documentation provided and must be logically linked to the current impact of the condition on academic functioning.

FINANCIAL AID

Students should submit: FAFSA; State aid form. Applicants will be notified of awards on a rolling basis beginning 2/17. The Princeton Review suggests that all financial aid forms be submitted as soon as possible after October 1. *Need-based scholarships/grants offered:* College/university scholarship or grant aid from institutional funds; Federal Pell; Private scholarships; SEOG; State scholarships/grants. *Loan aid offered:* Direct PLUS loans; Direct Subsidized Stafford Loans; Direct Unsubsidized Stafford Loans. Federal Work-Study Program available. Institutional employment available.

CAMPUS LIFE

Activities: Choral groups; Dance; Drama/theater; International Student Organization; Jazz band; Model UN; Musical theater; Pep band; Radio station; Student government; Student newspaper; Symphony orchestra; Television station; Yearbook. **Organizations:** 117 registered organizations, 7 honor societies, 3 religious organizations. 11 fraternities, 3 sororities. **Athletics (Intercollegiate):** *Men:* baseball, basketball, cross-country, diving, golf, ice hockey, lacrosse, skiing (downhill/alpine), skiing (nordic/cross-country), soccer, swimming *Women:* basketball, cross-country, diving, ice hockey, lacrosse, skiing (downhill/alpine), skiing (nordic/cross-country), soccer, swimming, volleyball. **On-Campus Highlights:** Student Center Forum & Java City, Wooded Recreational Trails, Cheel Campus Center & Arena, Adirondack Lodge, Residence Hall Rooms.

ACCOMMODATIONS	
Allowed in exams:	
Calculators	Yes
Dictionary	Yes
Computer	Yes
Spell-checker	Yes
Extended test time	Yes
Scribe	Yes
Proctors	Yes
Oral exams	Yes
Note-takers	Yes
Support services for students with	
LD	Yes
ADHD	Yes
ASD	Yes
Distraction-reduced environment	Yes
Recording of lecture allowed	Yes
Reading technology:	Yes
Audio books	Yes
Other assistive technology listening devices, magnification devices, FM systems, voice recorders, LiveScribe pens, speech-to-text, screen readers	
Priority registration	Yes
Added costs for services:	
For LD:	No
For ADHD:	No
For ASD:	No
LD specialists	Yes
ADHD & ASD coaching	Yes
ASD specialists	Yes
Professional tutors	Yes
Peer tutors	Yes
Max. hours/week for services	
How professors are notified of student approved accommodations	
	Director and student

COLLEGE GRADUATION REQUIREMENTS	
Course waivers allowed	Yes
In what courses	on a case-by-case basis
Course substitutions allowed	Yes
In what courses	on a case-by-case basis

Colgate University

13 Oak Drive, Hamilton, NY 13346 • Admissions: 315-228-7401 • Fax: 315-228-7524

CAMPUS

Type of school	Private (nonprofit)
Environment	Rural
Support	CS

STUDENTS

Undergrad enrollment	2,852
% male/female	45/55
% from out of state	74
% frosh live on campus	100

FINANCIAL FACTS

Annual tuition	$53,650
Room and board	$13,520
Required fees	$330

GENERAL ADMISSIONS INFO

Application fee	$60
Regular application deadline	1/15

Nonfall registration accepted. Admission may be deferred for a maximum of 1 year.

Range SAT EBRW	660–730
Range SAT Math	650–770
Range ACT Composite	31–33

ACADEMICS

Student/faculty ratio	9:1
% students returning for sophomore year	94
% students graduating within 4 years	88
% students graduating within 6 years	91

Most classes have 10–19 students. Most lab/discussion sessions have 10–19 students.

Programs/Services for Students with Learning Differences

Colgate provides for a small student body a liberal arts education that will expand individual potential and ability to participate effectively in society's affairs. There are many resources available for all students. Colgate's goal is to offer resources and services within the campus-wide support system that are responsive to the various talents, needs, and preferences of students with disabilities. For the university to understand and prepare for the accommodations that may be requested, students are asked to complete a confidential self-assessment questionnaire and provide appropriate documentation about their disability. The Director of Academic Support and Disability Services works with students and faculty to assure that the needs of students with disabilities are met, serves as clearinghouse for information about disabilities, provides training and individual consultation for all members of the Colgate community, and provides academic counseling and individualized instruction. Seeking help early and learning to be a self-advocate are essential to college success.

Admissions

There is no special admission process for students with learning disabilities. The Office of Admissions reviews the applications of all candidates for admission. The admissions staff looks for evidence of substantial achievement in a rigorous secondary school curriculum, one counselor recommendation, standardized testing, a personalized essay, and extracurricular involvement. Also valued are qualities such as curiosity, originality, thoughtfulness, and persistence. Admission is very competitive. Criteria include 16 courses in a college-preparatory program (20 recommended): 4 years of English, 3–4 years of math, 3–4 years of science, 3–4 years of social studies, and 3 years of a foreign language. The ACT average is 29 or the SAT Reasoning Test average is 1348. Three SAT Subject Tests of the applicant's choice are required if the applicant submits the SAT Reasoning Test. However, SAT Subject Tests are not required if the applicant submits the ACT.

ADMISSIONS INFO FOR STUDENTS WITH LEARNING DIFFERENCES

SAT/ACT required: Yes
Interview required: No
Essay required: No
Additional application required: No
Documentation required for:
 LD: Psycho ed evaluation to include: relevant historical info, instructional interventions, related services, age diagnosed, objective data (aptitude, achievement, info processing), test scores (standard, percentile and grade equivalents) and describe functional limitations.
 ADHD: Diagnosis based on DSM-V; history of behaviors impairing functioning in academic setting; diagnostic interview; history of symptoms; evidence of ongoing behaviors.
 ASD: Psycho ed evaluation
Documentation submitted to: Academic Support
Special Ed. HS course work accepted: No
Separate application required for program services: No
Contact Information
Name of program or department: Academic Program Support and Disability Services
Telephone: 315-228-7375
Fax: 315-228-7831

Colgate University

Additional Information

Students are encouraged to seek help early; meet with professors at the beginning of each semester to discuss approaches and accommodations that will meet their needs; and seek assistance from the Director of Academic Support and Disability Services, administrative advisor, and faculty advisor. Modifications in the curriculum are made on an individual basis. Colgate provides services in support of academic work on an as-needed basis, such as assistance with note-takers, tape-recorded lectures, tutors, readers, and assistive technology. There is a Writing and Speaking Center and tutoring, and skills help is available in writing, reading, and study strategies. Services and accommodations are available for undergraduate and graduate students. Students must complete a Special Needs Identification Form.

GENERAL ADMISSIONS

Very important factors considered include: rigor of secondary school record, class rank, academic GPA. *Important factors considered include:* application essay, standardized test scores, recommendation(s), extracurricular activities, talent/ability, character/personal qualities. *Other factors considered include:* first generation, alumni/ae relation, geographical residence, racial/ethnic status, volunteer work, work experience. *Freshman Admission Requirements:* High school diploma is required and GED is accepted. *Academic units required:* 4 English, 3 math, 3 science, 2 science labs, 3 foreign language, 3 social studies. *Academic units recommended:* 4 English, 4 math, 4 science, 4 science labs, 4 foreign language, 4 social studies.

ACCOMMODATION OR SERVICES

Accommodations are decided upon an individual basis after a thorough review of appropriate, current documentation. The accommodations requests must be supported through the documentation provided and must be logically linked to the current impact of the condition on academic functioning.

FINANCIAL AID

Students should submit: CSS/Financial Aid PROFILE; FAFSA; Noncustodial PROFILE. Applicants will be notified of awards on or about 3/20. The Princeton Review suggests that all financial aid forms be submitted as soon as possible after October 1. *Need-based scholarships/grants offered:* College/university scholarship or grant aid from institutional funds; Federal Pell; SEOG *Loan aid offered:* Direct PLUS loans; Direct Subsidized Stafford Loans; Direct Unsubsidized Stafford Loans. Federal Work-Study Program available. Institutional employment available.

CAMPUS LIFE

Activities: Campus Ministries; Choral groups; Concert band; Dance; Drama/theater; International Student Organization; Jazz band; Literary magazine; Model UN; Music ensembles; Musical theater; Opera; Pep band; Radio station; Student government; Student newspaper; Symphony orchestra; Yearbook. **Organizations:** 160 registered organizations, 4 honor societies, 8 religious organizations. 6 fraternities, 3 sororities. **Athletics (Intercollegiate):** *Men:* basketball, crew/rowing, cross-country, diving, football, golf, ice hockey, lacrosse, soccer, swimming, tennis, track/field (outdoor). *Women:* basketball, crew/rowing, cross-country, diving, field hockey, ice hockey, lacrosse, soccer, softball, swimming, tennis, track/field (outdoor), volleyball. **On-Campus Highlights:** O'Connor Campus Center, Hieber Cafe in Case-Geyer Library, ALANA Cultural Center, Ho Tung Visualization Lab, Trudy Fitness Center.

ACCOMMODATIONS

Allowed in exams:

Calculators	Yes
Dictionary	Yes
Computer	Yes
Spell-checker	Yes
Extended test time	Yes
Scribe	Yes
Proctors	Yes
Oral exams	Yes
Note-takers	Yes

Support services for students with

LD	Yes
ADHD	Yes
ASD	Yes
Distraction-reduced environment	Yes
Recording of lecture allowed	Yes
Reading technology:	Yes
Audio books	No
Other assistive technology	Yes
Priority registration	Yes

Added costs for services:

For LD:	No
For ADHD:	No
For ASD:	No
LD specialists	Yes
ADHD & ASD coaching	No
ASD specialists	No
Professional tutors	No
Peer tutors	Yes
Max. hours/week for services	Unlimited
How professors are notified of student approved accommodations	Student

COLLEGE GRADUATION REQUIREMENTS

Course waivers allowed	Yes
In what courses	Varies
Course substitutions allowed	Yes
In what courses	Foreign Language- all

requests are considered case-by-case.

Concordia College (NY)

171 White Plains Road, Bronxville, NY 10708 • Admissions: 914-337-9300 • Fax: 914-395-4636

CAMPUS
Type of school	Private (nonprofit)
Environment	Village
Support	CS

STUDENTS
Undergrad enrollment	1,466
% male/female	32/68
% from out of state	27
% frosh live on campus	72

FINANCIAL FACTS
Annual tuition	$27,740
Room and board	$10,265
Required fees	$1,030

GENERAL ADMISSIONS INFO
Application fee	$50
Priority deadline	3/15
Regular application deadline	3/15

Nonfall registration accepted. Admission may be deferred.

Range SAT EBRW	420–500
Range SAT Math	415–505
Range ACT Composite	16–20

ACADEMICS
Student/faculty ratio	12:1
% students returning for sophomore year	69

Most classes have fewer than 10 students. Most lab/discussion sessions have 10–19 students.

PROGRAMS/SERVICES FOR STUDENTS WITH LEARNING DIFFERENCES

Concordia Connection is a program for students with LD who have demonstrated the potential to earn a college degree. Their commitment is to provide an intimate, supportive, and caring environment where students with special learning needs can experience college as a successful and rewarding endeavor. This is a mainstream program. Students are fully integrated into the college. During the fall and spring semesters, students are registered for four or five classes. Additionally, students are registered for a one-credit independent study, which incorporates a weekly, 1-hour group session with the director and staff that focuses on the development of individualized learning strategies. Progress is monitored, and an assessment of learning potential and academic levels is provided. The program's director coordinates support services and works with the assigned freshman advisor to assure an optimal course plan each semester. A one summer orientation and academic seminar is required for all new Concordia Connection students.

ADMISSIONS

Students wishing to apply should submit the following documents to the Admissions Office: a Concordia application and the student's current transcript; SAT/ACT scores; documentation of LD, which must minimally include a WAIS–IV profile with subtest scores that was completed within the past year and the student's most recent IEP; recommendations from an LD specialist and a guidance counselor; and an essay describing the nature of the LD, the effect on learning patterns, and the student's reason for pursuing college. Visits are encouraged. Applicants must be high school graduates, have a diagnosed LD, have college-prep courses, and be committed to being successful. General admissions criteria include a B average, ACT/SAT scores (used to assess strengths and weaknesses rather than for acceptance or denial), and college-preparatory courses in high school (foreign language is recommended but not required). Students with LD who self-disclose and provide documentation will be reviewed by the Admissions Office and the director of Concordia Connection.

ADMISSIONS INFO FOR STUDENTS WITH LEARNING DIFFERENCES

SAT/ACT required: Yes
Interview required: No
Essay required: Yes
Additional application required: No
Documentation required for:
  LD: Psycho ed evaluation to include: relevant historical info, instructional interventions, related services, age diagnosed, objective data (aptitude, achievement, info processing), test scores (standard, percentile and grade equivalents) and describe functional limitations.
  ADHD: Diagnosis based on DSM-V; history of behaviors impairing functioning in academic setting; diagnostic interview; history of symptoms; evidence of ongoing behaviors.
  ASD: Psycho ed evaluation
Documentation submitted to: Admissions
Special Ed. HS course work accepted: No
Separate application required for program services: No
# of students last year receiving services/accommodations for:
  LD: 32-50
Contact Information
Name of program or department: The Concordia Connection Program
Telephone: 914-337-9300, ext- 2361
Fax: 914-395-4500

Concordia College (NY)

Additional Information

The Concordia Connection provides services to all students. These include test-taking modifications, taped text books, computer access, and tutoring. Although there are no charges for students requesting peer tutoring, there is a $6,000 charge for program services. Skills courses for credit are offered in time management, organizational skills, and study skills. The 1-day summer orientation helps students get acquainted with support services, get exposure to academic expectations, review components and requirements of the freshman year, develop group cohesion, and explore individualized needs and strategies for seeking assistance.

GENERAL ADMISSIONS

Very important factors considered include: rigor of secondary school record. *Important factors considered include:* class rank, standardized test scores, interview, character/personal qualities. *Other factors considered include:* application essay, recommendation(s), extracurricular activities, talent/ability, alumni/ae relation, religious affiliation/commitment, volunteer work, work experience. *Freshman Admission Requirements:* High school diploma is required and GED is accepted.

ACCOMMODATION OR SERVICES

Accommodations are decided upon an individual basis after a thorough review of appropriate, current documentation. The accommodations requests must be supported through the documentation provided and must be logically linked to the current impact of the condition on academic functioning.

FINANCIAL AID

Students should submit:. The Princeton Review suggests that all financial aid forms be submitted as soon as possible after October 1. *Need-based scholarships/grants offered: Loan aid offered:* Federal Work-Study Program available. Institutional employment available.

CAMPUS LIFE

Activities: Choral groups; Concert band; Dance; Drama/theater; International Student Organization; Jazz band; Literary magazine; Music ensembles; Musical theater; Student government; Student newspaper; Yearbook. **Organizations:** 35 registered organizations, 1 honor society, 3 religious organizations. **Athletics (Intercollegiate):** *Men:* baseball, basketball, soccer, tennis, volleyball. *Women:* basketball, soccer, softball, tennis, volleyball.

ACCOMMODATIONS

Allowed in exams:

Calculators	Yes
Dictionary	Yes
Computer	Yes
Spell-checker	Yes
Extended test time	Yes
Scribe	Yes
Proctors	Yes
Oral exams	Yes
Note-takers	Yes

Support services for students with

LD	Yes
ADHD	Yes
ASD	Yes
Distraction-reduced environment	Yes
Recording of lecture allowed	Yes
Reading technology:	Yes
Audio books	No
Other assistive technology	No
Priority registration	Yes

Added costs for services:

For LD:	No
For ADHD:	No
For ASD:	No
LD specialists	Yes
ADHD & ASD coaching	No
ASD specialists	No
Professional tutors	Yes
Peer tutors	Yes
Max. hours/week for services	10

How professors are notified of student approved accommodations   Student and director

COLLEGE GRADUATION REQUIREMENTS

Course waivers allowed	No
Course substitutions allowed	Yes

In what courses   Substitution of American Sign Language for Foreign Language

Cornell University

410 THURSTON AVENUE, ITHACA, NY 14850 • ADMISSIONS: 607-255-5241 • FAX: 607-255-0659

CAMPUS
Type of school	Private (nonprofit)
Environment	Town
Support	S

STUDENTS
Undergrad enrollment	14,815
% male/female	48/52
% from out of state	59
% frosh live on campus	100

FINANCIAL FACTS
Annual tuition	$54,584
Room and board	$14,816
Required fees	$604

GENERAL ADMISSIONS INFO
Application fee	$80
Regular application deadline	1/2

Nonfall registration accepted. Admission may be deferred.

Range SAT EBRW	690–760
Range SAT Math	700–790
Range ACT Composite	31–34

ACADEMICS
Student/faculty ratio	9:1
% students returning for sophomore year	97
% students graduating within 4 years	85
% students graduating within 6 years	93

Most classes have 10–19 students.
Most lab/discussion sessions have 10–19 students.

PROGRAMS/SERVICES FOR STUDENTS WITH LEARNING DIFFERENCES
Cornell University strives to be an accessible community where students with disabilities have an equitable opportunity to fully participate in all aspects of university life. Students with disabilities must submit requests for disability services to the Student Disability Services (SDS) office. The SDS staff is responsible for determining appropriate and effective federally mandated support services for eligible students. The university provides support services for a broad range of disabilities. There is not a specific program designed for students with learning disabilities. Once a student has been approved for disability services, many units across campus are responsible for fulfilling access needs. Students are directly involved in the process of arranging accommodations with instructors and for following established procedures for using disability services.

ADMISSIONS
Cornell does not have a special admissions process for students with learning disabilities. All students applying to Cornell are expected to meet admissions criteria. General admission requirements include 16 units of English, math, science, social studies, and foreign language. Each of the seven undergraduate colleges has its own specific requirements. Admission is very competitive and most of the admitted students rank in the top 10 percent of the class, at least, and have taken AP and honors courses in high school. Disability documentation should not be sent along with the admissions application, but should be sent directly to Student Disability Services after acceptance to Cornell.

Additional Information
Student Disability Services (SDS) staff will work with students on an individual basis to determine reasonable accommodations that facilitate access to learning, living, and other experiences. The information

ADMISSIONS INFO FOR STUDENTS WITH LEARNING DIFFERENCES
SAT/ACT required: No
Interview required: No
Essay required: No
Additional application required: No
Documentation required for:
  LD: Guidelines for documentation are available at https://sds.cornell.edu/get-started/documentation-guidelines
  ADHD: Guidelines for documentation are available at https://sds.cornell.edu/get-started/documentation-guidelines
  ASD: Guidelines for documentation are available at https://sds.cornell.edu/get-started/documentation-guidelines
Documentation submitted to: Student Disability Services
Special Ed. HS course work accepted: No
Separate application required for program services: No
Contact Information
Name of program or department: Student Disability Services
Telephone: 607-254-4545
Fax: 607-255-1562
Email: sds_cu@cornell.edu

Cornell University

students provide is an essential component in the determination of reasonable accommodations and services. SDS staff determine approved accommodations after reviewing requests for support services, past use of accommodations, and the likely impact of the disability on a student's educational experiences at Cornell. Examples of frequently used accommodations include: exam modifications (e.g., extended time, reduced-distraction location, use of a computer), and assistive technology. The procedure for using most academic accommodation requires requesting an accommodation letter for course(s) through SDS Online Services and giving the letter to your instructor or designated course administrator in a timely manner.

General Admissions

Very important factors considered include: rigor of secondary school record, academic GPA, application essay, standardized test scores, recommendation(s), extracurricular activities, talent/ability, character/personal qualities. *Important factors considered include:* class rank. *Other factors considered include:* interview, first generation, alumni/ae relation, geographical residence, state residency, racial/ethnic status, volunteer work, work experience. *Freshman Admission Requirements:* High school diploma or equivalent is not required *Academic units required:* 4 English, 3 math. *Academic units recommended:* 3 science, 3 science labs, 3 foreign language, 3 social studies, 3 history.

Accommodation or Services

Accommodations are decided upon an individual basis after a thorough review of appropriate, current documentation. The accommodations requests must be supported through the documentation provided and must be logically linked to the current impact of the condition on academic functioning.

Financial Aid

Students should submit: CSS/Financial Aid PROFILE; FAFSA; Noncustodial PROFILE. Applicants will be notified of awards on or about 4/1. The Princeton Review suggests that all financial aid forms be submitted as soon as possible after October 1. *Need-based scholarships/grants offered:* College/university scholarship or grant aid from institutional funds; Federal Pell; Private scholarships; SEOG; State scholarships/grants. *Loan aid offered:* Direct PLUS loans; Direct Subsidized Stafford Loans; Direct Unsubsidized Stafford Loans. Federal Work-Study Program available. Institutional employment available.

Campus Life

Activities: Campus Ministries; Choral groups; Concert band; Dance; Drama/theater; International Student Organization; Jazz band; Literary magazine; Marching band; Model UN; Music ensembles; Musical theater; Pep band; Radio station; Student government; Student newspaper; Student-run film society; Symphony orchestra; Television station; Yearbook. **Organizations:** 841 registered organizations, 22 honor societies, 61 religious organizations. 50 fraternities, 19 sororities. **Athletics (Intercollegiate):** *Men:* baseball, basketball, crew/rowing, cross-country, diving, football, golf, ice hockey, lacrosse, polo, soccer, squash, swimming, tennis, track/field (outdoor), track/field (indoor), wrestling. *Women:* basketball, crew/rowing, cross-country, diving, equestrian sports, fencing, field hockey, gymnastics, ice hockey, lacrosse, polo, soccer, softball, squash, swimming, tennis, track/field (outdoor), track/field (indoor), volleyball. **On-Campus Highlights:** Lynah Rink, The Trillium, The Lindseth Climbing Wall, Ho Plaza, Willard Straight Hall.

ACCOMMODATIONS

Allowed in exams:

Calculators	Yes
Dictionary	Yes
Computer	Yes
Spell-checker	Yes
Extended test time	Yes
Scribe	Yes
Proctors	Yes
Oral exams	Yes
Note-takers	Yes

Support services for students with

LD	Yes
ADHD	Yes
ASD	Yes
Distraction-reduced environment	Yes
Recording of lecture allowed	Yes
Reading technology:	Yes
Audio books	Yes
Other assistive technology	
Priority registration	Not Applicable

Added costs for services:

For LD:	No
For ADHD:	No
For ASD:	No
LD specialists	No
ADHD & ASD coaching	No
ASD specialists	No
Professional tutors	No
Peer tutors	Yes
Max. hours/week for services	Varies

How professors are notified of student approved accommodations
Student

COLLEGE GRADUATION REQUIREMENTS

Course waivers allowed	No
Course substitutions allowed	No

Hobart and William Smith Colleges

300 Pulteney Street, Geneva, NY 14456 • Admissions: 315-781-3622 • Fax: 315-781-3914

CAMPUS
Type of school	Private (nonprofit)
Environment	Village
Support	S

STUDENTS
Undergrad enrollment	2,220
% male/female	49/51
% from out of state	60
% frosh live on campus	100

FINANCIAL FACTS
Annual tuition	$52,345
Room and board	$13,525
Required fees	$1,180

GENERAL ADMISSIONS INFO

Regular application deadline 2/1
Nonfall registration accepted. Admission may be deferred for a maximum of 1 year.

Range SAT EBRW	610 –680
Range SAT Math	600 –680
Range ACT Composite	27 –31

ACADEMICS
Student/faculty ratio	10:1
% students returning for sophomore year	86
students graduating within 4 years	75
students graduating within 6 years	81

Most classes have 10-19 students.
Most lab/discussion sessions have 20-29 students.

PROGRAMS/SERVICES FOR STUDENTS WITH LEARNING DIFFERENCES

The Office of Disability Services seeks to promote academic achievement, extracurricular involvement, and help students with disabilities take full advantage of the academic and extracurricular opportunities available at HWS. The Coordinator of Disability Services works independently and in cooperation with other administrative offices and academic departments to: Identify and implement individualized accommodations while fostering the academic and personal development of students; The Center for Teaching and Learning offers weekly Learning Tips for First-Year students. The series is designed to provide first-year students with study and learning strategies. Additionaly students may meet with a tutor,either idividually or in small groups.

ADMISSIONS

The admissions process for students with learning differences is the same. Students are welcome to disclose their LD/ADHD/ASD status, but it is not required.

Additional Information

Hobart and William Smith Colleges welcome students with learning differences and disabilities. Our admissions process is centered upon getting to know students as individuals. We welcome the opportunity to learn from students about their accomplishments, challenges they have faced and how they have succeeded. An admissions interview is the perfect format to share that information.

ADMISSIONS INFO FOR STUDENTS WITH LEARNING DIFFERENCES

SAT/ACT required: No
Interview required: No
Essay required: Not Applicable
Additional application required: No
Documentation required for:
  LD: Documentation and guidelines are available online: http://www.hws.edu/academics/ctl/disability_services.aspx
  ADHD: Documentation and guidelines are available online: http://www.hws.edu/academics/ctl/disability_services.aspx
  ASD: Documentation and guidelines are available online: http://www.hws.edu/academics/ctl/disability_services.aspx
Documentation submitted to: Support Program/Services
Special Ed. HS course work accepted: Not Applicable
Separate application required for program services: No
# of students last year receiving services/accommodations for:
  LD: 149
  ADHD: 141
Contact Information
Name of program or department: Disability Services
Telephone: 315-781-3351
Fax: 315-781-3862
Email: ctl@hws.edu

Hobart and William Smith Colleges

GENERAL ADMISSIONS

Very important factors considered include: rigor of secondary school record, academic GPA. *Important factors considered include:* application essay, recommendation(s), interview, extracurricular activities, character/personal qualities, volunteer work, work experience. *Other factors considered include:* class rank, standardized test scores, talent/ability, first generation, alumni/ae relation, geographical residence, state residency, racial/ethnic status, level of applicant's interest. *Freshman Admission Requirements:* High school diploma is required and GED is accepted *Academic units required:* 4 English, 3 math, 3 science, 2 science labs, 2 foreign language, 2 social studies, 2 academic electives, *Academic units recommended:* 3 foreign language, 3 social studies, 4 academic electives,

ACCOMMODATION OR SERVICES

Accommodations are decided upon an individual basis after a thorough review of appropriate, current documentation. The accommodations requests must be supported through the documentation provided and must be logically linked to the current impact of the condition on academic functioning.

FINANCIAL AID

Students should submit: CSS/Financial Aid PROFILE; FAFSA; Noncustodial PROFILE; State aid form. Applicants will be notified of awards on or about 4/1.. The Princeton Review suggests that all financial aid forms be submitted as soon as possible after October 1. *Need-based scholarships/grants offered:* College/university scholarship or grant aid from institutional funds; Federal Pell; Private scholarships; SEOG; State scholarships/grants *Loan aid offered:* Direct PLUS loans; Direct Subsidized Stafford Loans; Direct Unsubsidized Stafford Loans Federal Work-Study Program available. Institutional employment available.

CAMPUS LIFE

Activities: Campus Ministries; Choral groups; Concert band ; Dance ; Drama/theater; International Student Organization; Jazz band; Literary magazine; Music ensembles; Radio station ; Student government; Student newspaper; Student-run film society; Yearbook Organizations: 77 registered organizations, 12 honor societies, 4 religious organizations. 5 fraternities, **Athletics (Intercollegiate):** *Men:* basketball, crew/rowing, cross-country, football, golf, ice hockey, lacrosse, sailing, soccer, squash, tennis *Women:* basketball, crew/rowing, cross-country, diving, field hockey, golf, lacrosse, sailing, soccer, squash, swimming, tennis. **On-Campus Highlights:** Scandling Campus Center, The Katherine D. Elliott Studio Arts Center, Stern Hall, Caird Center for Sports and Recreation, Rosensweig Learning Commons.

ACCOMMODATIONS

Allowed in exams:

Calculators	Yes
Dictionary	Yes
Computer	Yes
Spell-checker	Yes
Extended test time	Yes
Scribe	Yes
Proctors	Yes
Oral exams	Yes
Note-takers	Yes

Support services for students with

LD	Yes
ADHD	Yes
ASD	Yes
Distraction-reduced environment	Yes
Recording of lecture allowed	Yes
Reading technology:	Yes
Audio books	Yes
Other assistive technology	voice-to-text, smart pens, electronic note-taking, etc.
Priority registration	No

Added costs for services:

For LD:	No
For ADHD:	No
For ASD:	No
LD specialists	Yes
ADHD & ASD coaching	No
ASD specialists	Yes
Professional tutors	Yes
Peer tutors	Yes
Max. hours/week for services	Varies
How professors are notified of student approved accommodations	Both Student and Director

COLLEGE GRADUATION REQUIREMENTS

Course waivers allowed	Yes
In what courses	Foreign Language
Course substitutions allowed	Yes
In what courses	Foreign Language

Hofstra University

100 HOFSTRA UNIVERSITY, HEMPSTEAD, NY 11549 • ADMISSIONS: 516-463-6700 • FAX: 516-463-5100

CAMPUS

Type of school	Private (nonprofit)
Environment	City
Support	SP

STUDENTS

Undergrad enrollment	6,783
% male/female	45/55
% from out of state	38
% frosh live on campus	68

FINANCIAL FACTS

Annual tuition	$44,640
Room and board	$15,708
Required fees	$1,060

GENERAL ADMISSIONS INFO

Application fee	$70

Nonfall registration accepted. Admission may be deferred for a maximum of 1 year.

Range SAT EBRW	570–660
Range SAT Math	560–650
Range ACT Composite	24–29

ACADEMICS

Student/faculty ratio	13:1
% students returning for sophomore year	81
% students graduating within 4 years	53
% students graduating within 6 years	63

Most classes have 10–19 students. Most lab/discussion sessions have fewer than 10 students.

PROGRAMS/SERVICES FOR STUDENTS WITH LEARNING DIFFERENCES

Students will be held to the same admissions standards as their non-disabled peers. The mission of Student Access Services is to provide disability related education, services, and resources to the Hofstra Community. SAS ensures equal access to education for all Hofstra students, regardless of disability, in compliance with federal law and in keeping with Hofstra's long standing commitment to equality and access in its programs and services. We respectfully serve our students by facilitating barrier free educational opportunities and assisting them in becoming independent, self-advocating learners. Students who are applying to the fee based PALS program may be asked to provide documentation and come to campus for a personal interview to determine if the PALS program is the right fit.

ADMISSIONS

Students will be held to the same admission criteria as any other student who is looking for admission to the University. Students may be required to interview with the admission staff and /or the disabilities staff to asses a fit for the University. Hofstra is test optional for ACT/SAT. Hofstra offers a student the option to decide for themselves how to present their academic strengths, talents and abilities to the admission committee. This enables each individual student to decide whether or not their standardized test results accurately reflect his or her academic ability and potential. Students are admitted to PALS through a deliberative and separate process involving Hofstra's Office of Admission and Student Access Services. Students complete the undergraduate admission application, and indicate on the application that they are interested in applying for PALS enrollment. In addition to the required admission materials, students submit comprehensive documentation of their specific disability Documentation must be in the form of a current (within two years of application to Hofstra) psycho educational evaluation. A decision to both the University and PALS are generally made two weeks after interview (if required). If no interview is required, decisions will be mailed three weeks after the application is complete with testing results.

ADMISSIONS INFO FOR STUDENTS WITH LEARNING DIFFERENCES

SAT/ACT required: No
Interview required: No
Essay required: Recommended
Additional application required: No
Documentation required for:
  LD: Psychoeducational or neuropsychological exam.
  ADHD: Psychoeducational or neuropsychological exam.
  ASD: Psychoeducational or neuropsychological exam.
Documentation submitted to: Support Program/Services
Special Ed. HS course work accepted: Yes
Separate application required for program services: No
# of students last year receiving services/accommodations for:
  LD: 239
  ADHD: 231
  ASD: 45
Contact Information
Name of program or department: Progam for Academic Learning Skills (PALS)
Telephone: 516-463-7075
Fax: 516-463-7070
Email: SAS@hofstra.edu

Hofstra University

Additional Information

Enrollment in PALS is a two-semester (one-year) commitment. Students enrolled in PALS are billed a one-time, $13,000 charge during their first year at Hofstra. However, this one-time fee entitles the student to continue meeting with a learning specialist for the duration of his or her academic program at Hofstra. PALS students are also eligible for reasonable accommodations through SAS. Reasonable accommodations are adjustments to Hofstra University programs, policies and practices that "level the playing field" for students with disabilities. Reasonable accommodations may include extended time on examinations; testing in a smaller, proctored environment; and supplemental note-taking services. As with learning strategies, accommodations are based on each student's disability-related needs and careful review of comprehensive disability documentation.

General Admissions

Very important factors considered include: rigor of secondary school record, class rank, academic GPA, application essay, recommendation(s). *Important factors considered include:* interview, extracurricular activities, talent/ability, character/personal qualities. *Other factors considered include:* standardized test scores, first generation, alumni/ae relation, geographical residence, racial/ethnic status, volunteer work, work experience, level of applicant's interest. *Freshman Admission Requirements:* High school diploma is required and GED is accepted. *Academic units required:* 4 English, 3 math, 3 science, 1 science lab, 2 foreign language, 3 social studies. *Academic units recommended:* 4 math, 4 science, 2 science labs, 3 foreign language, 4 social studies.

Accommodation or Services

Accommodations are decided upon an individual basis after a thorough review of appropriate, current documentation. The accommodations requests must be supported through the documentation provided and must be logically linked to the current impact of the condition on academic functioning.

Financial Aid

Students should submit: FAFSA; State aid form. Applicants will be notified of awards on a rolling basis beginning 1/15. The Princeton Review suggests that all financial aid forms be submitted as soon as possible after October 1. *Need-based scholarships/grants offered:* College/university scholarship or grant aid from institutional funds; Federal Pell; Private scholarships; SEOG; State scholarships/grants; United Negro College Fund. *Loan aid offered:* Direct PLUS loans; Direct Subsidized Stafford Loans; Direct Unsubsidized Stafford Loans. Federal Work-Study Program available. Institutional employment available.

Campus Life

Activities: Campus Ministries; Choral groups; Concert band; Dance; Drama/theater; International Student Organization; Jazz band; Literary magazine; Model UN; Music ensembles; Musical theater; Opera; Pep band; Radio station; Student government; Student newspaper; Student-run film society; Symphony orchestra; Television station; Yearbook. **Organizations:** 135 registered organizations, 32 honor societies, 9 religious organizations. 13 fraternities, 12 sororities. **Athletics (Intercollegiate):** *Men:* baseball, basketball, cross-country, golf, lacrosse, soccer, tennis, wrestling. *Women:* basketball, cross-country, field hockey, golf, lacrosse, soccer, softball, tennis, volleyball. 1. Mack Student Center—home of the newly renovated Commuter Lounge and Pride Den (the campus living room), is the focal point of campus community life where students meet for meals, socializing, club and organizational events, a large game room, the boo.

ACCOMMODATIONS	
Allowed in exams:	
Calculators	Yes
Dictionary	Yes
Computer	Yes
Spell-checker	Yes
Extended test time	Yes
Scribe	Yes
Proctors	Yes
Oral exams	Yes
Note-takers	Yes
Support services for students with	
LD	Yes
ADHD	Yes
ASD	Yes
Distraction-reduced environment	Yes
Recording of lecture allowed	Yes
Reading technology:	Yes
Audio books	Yes
Other assistive technology	Note-taking
technology and dictation software.	
Priority registration	No
Added costs for services:	
For LD:	Yes
For ADHD:	Yes
For ASD:	Yes
LD specialists	Yes
ADHD & ASD coaching	Yes
ASD specialists	Yes
Professional tutors	Yes
Peer tutors	Yes
Max. hours/week for services	4.5
How professors are notified of student approved accommodations	Student

COLLEGE GRADUATION REQUIREMENTS	
Course waivers allowed	No
Course substitutions allowed	Yes
In what courses	Foreign Language

Iona College

715 North Avenue, New Rochelle, NY 10801 • Admissions: 914-633-2502 • Fax: 914-633-2182

CAMPUS

Type of school	Private (nonprofit)
Environment	City
Support	SP

STUDENTS

Undergrad enrollment	2,989
% male/female	49/51
% from out of state	24
% frosh live on campus	63

FINANCIAL FACTS

Annual tuition	$36,612
Room and board	$15,278
Required fees	$2,200

GENERAL ADMISSIONS INFO

Application fee	$50
Priority deadline	2/15
Regular application deadline	2/15

Nonfall registration accepted. Admission may be deferred for a maximum of 1 year.

Range SAT EBRW	500–590
Range SAT Math	480–590
Range ACT Composite	20–25

ACADEMICS

Student/faculty ratio	15:1
% students returning for sophomore year	75
% students graduating within 4 years	59
% students graduating within 6 years	64

Most classes have fewer than 10 students. Most lab/discussion sessions have fewer than 10 students.

PROGRAMS/SERVICES FOR STUDENTS WITH LEARNING DIFFERENCES

The College Assistance Program (CAP) of Iona College is an optional, fee-based program that offers comprehensive support and services for students with learning disabilities, AD/HD, traumatic brain injuries or are on the autism spectrum. In addition to encouraging success by providing instruction tailored to individual strengths and needs, the program emphasizes broadly applicable strategies that cross academic disciplines. The team of professional learning specialists who work with CAP students is devoted to the support and guidance of each student. They train students to incorporate appropriate skills-based strategies which cross the disciplines. The goal is for students to gradually practice these skills until they are able to master them independently. With success comes self-confidence and a greater ability to plan and achieve academic, personal and career goals. Additionally, the CAP counselor assists students with academic coaching, stress management, and career and internship planning. Students take the standard full-time course requirements for baccalaureate degree programs.

ADMISSIONS

To be a realistic candidate for admission, an applicant should have taken: 4 years English, 2 years Foreign Language, 4 years Math, 3 years Natural Science (including two laboratory sciences) and 3 years Social Studies. Iona College prefers to see students who have maintained at least a solid B/B+ (85-89) average in high school and earned an SAT around 1000 or 19 ACT. The type and level of courses taken, is reviewed, and is part of a holistic review, and a complement to the GPA and test scores themselves. Iona does not require the writing section of the SAT or ACT.

Additional Information

In addition to tuition, CAP students are required to pay separate program fees. The current fee per semester is $1,770. During the early part of the summer, all entering CAP freshmen participate in this transition program where a number of skills are addressed. The aim is to provide students with a solid foundation from which the college experience can begin with confidence. The fee is $1375.

An experienced staff instructs and guides students in intensive writing instruction, study skills, organizational and time management skills. Individual learning styles are explored and opportunities are provided to

ADMISSIONS INFO FOR STUDENTS WITH LEARNING DIFFERENCES

SAT/ACT required: Yes
Interview required: Yes
Essay required: Required
Additional application required: No
Documentation required for:
  LD: 1.A Psychoeducational Report or Neuropsychological Report 2.Cognitive Testing: The Wechsler Adult Intelligence Scale, Fourth Edition (WAIS-IV) is the most acceptable form of testing. 3.A full scale IQ Report with scores and interpretation
  ADHD: ADHD Verification Form
  ASD: Psycho ed evaluation
Documentation submitted to: College Assistance Program
Special Ed. HS course work accepted: No
Separate application required for program services: LD, ADHD, For ASD.
Contact Information
Name of program or department: College Assistance Program
Telephone: 914-633-2159
Email: CAPInformation@iona.edu

practice self-advocacy. In addition, several workshops are offered in areas that meet the students' specific needs. CAP works with each student to create an individual schedule that blends both interests and abilities with Iona's Core Curriculum. Consideration is given to matching the student's learning strengths with a professor's teaching style. Both students and staff agree that the summer transition program facilitates a successful transition from high school to college. Students engage in an average two hours per week of skills-based tutoring with a learning specialist. Students are also encouraged to participate in weekly group tutoring. Students who are enrolled in CAP register early and receive help with course selection and registration. The CAP counselor offers academic coaching, time management, and stress management strategies, based on the individual needs of each student. Students are encouraged to meet with the counselor on a regular basis until they are able to manage these strategies on their own. CAP arranges for students to study in groups for many of the core classes.

GENERAL ADMISSIONS

Very important factors considered include: rigor of secondary school record, academic GPA. *Important factors considered include:* application essay, standardized test scores, character/personal qualities, level of applicant's interest. *Other factors considered include:* class rank, recommendation(s), interview, extracurricular activities, talent/ability, first generation, alumni/ae relation, geographical residence, volunteer work, work experience. *Freshman Admission Requirements:* High school diploma is required and GED is accepted. *Academic units required:* 4 English, 3 math, 3 science, 2 science labs, 2 foreign language, 2 social studies, 1 history, 1 academic elective. *Academic units recommended:* 4 math, 2 history, 3 academic electives.

ACCOMMODATION OR SERVICES

Accommodations are decided upon an individual basis after a thorough review of appropriate, current documentation. The accommodations requests must be supported through the documentation provided and must be logically linked to the current impact of the condition on academic functioning.

FINANCIAL AID

Students should submit: FAFSA; State aid form. Applicants will be notified of awards on a rolling basis beginning 1/1. The Princeton Review suggests that all financial aid forms be submitted as soon as possible after October 1. *Need-based scholarships/grants offered:* College/university scholarship or grant aid from institutional funds; Federal Pell; Private scholarships; SEOG; State scholarships/grants. *Loan aid offered:* Direct PLUS loans; Direct Subsidized Stafford Loans; Direct Unsubsidized Stafford Loans. Federal Work-Study Program available. Institutional employment available.

CAMPUS LIFE

Activities: Campus Ministries; Choral groups; Concert band; Dance; Drama/theater; International Student Organization; Literary magazine; Model UN; Music ensembles; Musical theater; Pep band; Radio station; Student government; Student newspaper; Student-run film society; Television station; Yearbook. **Organizations:** 65 registered organizations, 9 honor societies, 4 religious organizations. 4 fraternities, 6 sororities. **Athletics (Intercollegiate):** *Men:* baseball, basketball, crew/rowing, cross-country, diving, golf, soccer, swimming, track/field (outdoor), track/field (indoor), water polo. *Women:* basketball, crew/rowing, cross-country, diving, lacrosse, soccer, softball, swimming, track/field (outdoor), track/field (indoor), volleyball, water polo. **On-Campus Highlights:** Lapenta Student Union, Hynes Athletics Center, Ryan Library, Residence Halls, Starbucks.

ACCOMMODATIONS	
Allowed in exams:	
Calculators	Yes
Dictionary	Yes
Computer	Yes
Spell-checker	Yes
Extended test time	Yes
Scribe	Yes
Proctors	Yes
Oral exams	Yes
Note-takers	Yes
Support services for students with	
LD	Yes
ADHD	Yes
ASD	Yes
Distraction-reduced environment	Yes
Recording of lecture allowed	Yes
Reading technology:	Yes
Audio books	Yes
Other assistive technology	Yes
Priority registration	Yes
Added costs for services:	
For LD:	No
For ADHD:	No
For ASD:	No
CAP fee:	Yes
LD specialists	Yes
ADHD & ASD coaching	Yes
ASD specialists	Yes
Professional tutors	Yes
Peer tutors	No
Max. hours/week for services	Unlimited
How professors are notified of student approved accommodations	Student

COLLEGE GRADUATION REQUIREMENTS	
Course waivers allowed	Yes
In what courses	Foreign Language if documented in student's evaluation.
Course substitutions allowed	Yes
In what courses	Foreign Language if documented in student's evaluation.

Le Moyne College

1419 Salt Springs Rd., Syracuse, NY 13214-1301 • Admissions: 315-445-4300 • Fax: 315-445-4711

CAMPUS
Type of school	Private (nonprofit)
Environment	City
Support	S

STUDENTS
Undergrad enrollment	2,676
% male/female	40/60
% from out of state	6
% frosh live on campus	80

FINANCIAL FACTS
Annual tuition	$33,560
Room and board	$13,780
Required fees	$1,065

GENERAL ADMISSIONS INFO
Priority deadline 2/1.
Nonfall registration accepted. Admission may be deferred for a maximum of 1 year.

Range SAT EBRW	540–620
Range SAT Math	540–620
Range ACT Composite	22–27

ACADEMICS
Student/faculty ratio	12:1
% students returning for sophomore year	84
% students graduating within 4 years	64
% students graduating within 6 years	74

Most classes have 10–19 students.
Most lab/discussion sessions have 10–19 students.

PROGRAMS/SERVICES FOR STUDENTS WITH LEARNING DIFFERENCES

Le Moyne College welcomes people with disabilities and, in compliance with Section 504 of the Rehabilitation Act of 1973, as amended, and the Americans with Disabilities Act of 1990, supports students' entitlements and does not discriminate on the basis of disability. Academic support services for students with disabilities are coordinated by the Director of Disability Support Services in the Academic Support Center. Students with Special Needs have access to the same support services provided to all students--individual sessions with professionals in the Academic Support Center (ASC) regarding study skills and learning strategies, ASC Workshops provided each fall semester, and individual and small- group tutoring in writing, mathematics, foreign languages, economics, and the natural sciences. In addition, students with disabilities receive individualized services through the ASC. Our goal is to create collaborative partnerships that put students in the driver's seat of their education to enhance their chances for academic success.

ADMISSIONS

Le Moyne College is a test-optional school. Suggested courses for admission include 4 years English, 3-4 years Foreign Language, 3-4 years Math, 3-4 years Social Studies and 3-4 Natural Sciences. Students are encouraged to complete a four unit sequence of college preparatory mathematics courses, including, at a minimum, Algebra I, geometry and Algebra II. Students failing to achieve the minimum standard may be accepted at the discretion of the Admission Committee, but these students will be required to successfully complete a non-credit intermediate algebra course in the first year and prior to any credit bearing mathematics course. Students planning to major in biological sciences, natural systems science, chemistry, mathematics or physics should make plans to complete four years of college preparatory mathematics prior to enrollment as freshmen. Applicants will typically be expected to have achieved at least an 80-percent average in academic subjects and to rank in the upper half of their class. Strength of the academic program (both the level and the courses taken) is the single most important factor in the admission decision.

Additional Information

Upon receiving a student's documentation, a file is set up in DSS and students meet with the Director to do a formal intake and find out which accommodations fit the student's needs. Each semester, the Director meets with all students with disabilities in order to set up their academic

ADMISSIONS INFO FOR STUDENTS WITH LEARNING DIFFERENCES
SAT/ACT required: No
Interview required: No
Essay required: Required
Additional application required: No
Documentation required for:
  LD: Psycho education evaluation
  ADHD: Psycho education evaluation
  ASD: Psycho education evaluation
Documentation submitted to: Disability Support Services
Special Ed. HS course work accepted: No
Separate application required for program services: No
Contact Information
Name of program or department: Disability Support Services
Telephone: 315-445-4118
Fax: 315-445-6014
Email: dss@lemoyne.edu

Le Moyne College

accommodations for the semester, as they relate to their particular courses. Accessibility and Disability Support can arrange academic accommodations for students with learning disabilities, review previously administered diagnostic tests, make referrals to appropriate diagnosticians, provide supplemental academic advising, assist students in developing self-advocacy skills, provide liaison and advocacy measures between students and faculty or staff. Accommodations could include: Note Taker Services, ETexts/Digital texts time extensions for quizzes , tests, and exams, alternate testing locations, alternative exam formats, and preferential seating,

GENERAL ADMISSIONS

Very important factors considered include: rigor of secondary school record, academic GPA. *Important factors considered include:* class rank, application essay, recommendation(s), interview, extracurricular activities, talent/ability, work experience. *Other factors considered include:* standardized test scores, character/personal qualities, alumni/ae relation, geographical residence, state residency, volunteer work, level of applicant's interest. *Freshman Admission Requirements:* High school diploma is required and GED is accepted. *Academic units required:* 4 English, 3 math, 3 science, 3 foreign language, 4 social studies. *Academic units recommended:* 4 math, 4 science, 3 science labs.

ACCOMMODATION OR SERVICES

Accommodations are decided upon an individual basis after a thorough review of appropriate, current documentation. The accommodations requests must be supported through the documentation provided and must be logically linked to the current impact of the condition on academic functioning.

FINANCIAL AID

Students should submit: FAFSA; State aid form. Applicants will be notified of awards on or about 2/15. The Princeton Review suggests that all financial aid forms be submitted as soon as possible after October 1. *Need-based scholarships/grants offered:* College/university scholarship or grant aid from institutional funds; Federal Pell; Private scholarships; SEOG; State scholarships/grants. *Loan aid offered:* Direct PLUS loans; Direct Subsidized Stafford Loans; Direct Unsubsidized Stafford Loans. Federal Work-Study Program available. Institutional employment available.

CAMPUS LIFE

Activities: Campus Ministries; Choral groups; Concert band; Dance; Drama/theater; International Student Organization; Jazz band; Literary magazine; Model UN; Music ensembles; Musical theater; Radio station; Student government; Student newspaper; Student-run film society; Symphony orchestra; Television station; Yearbook. **Organizations:** 70 registered organizations, 14 honor societies, 11 religious organizations. **Athletics (Intercollegiate):** *Men:* baseball, basketball, cross-country, diving, golf, lacrosse, soccer, swimming, tennis. *Women:* basketball, cross-country, diving, golf, lacrosse, soccer, softball, swimming, tennis, volleyball. **On-Campus Highlights:** The Thomas J. Niland Athletic Complex, Campus Center, The W.Carroll Coyne Center for the Performing Arts, Panasci Family Chapel, Noreen Reale Falcone Library.

ACCOMMODATIONS

Allowed in exams:

Calculators	Yes
Dictionary	Yes
Computer	Yes
Spell-checker	Yes
Extended test time	Yes
Scribe	Not Applicable
Proctors	Yes
Oral exams	Not Applicable
Note-takers	Yes

Support services for students with

LD	Yes
ADHD	Yes
ASD	Yes
Distraction-reduced environment	Yes
Recording of lecture allowed	Yes
Reading technology:	Yes
Audio books	Yes
Other assistive technology	ADAPTIVE

TECHNOLOGY AVAILABLE: CCTV; Co:Writer; Dragon Naturally Speaking; Duxbury Braille Translation; Eclipse Reader; Inspiration; Jaws; Kurzweil 1000; Kurzweil 3000; OmniPage; Word Processing; ZoomText Extra; Premier Accessiblity Suite.

Priority registration	Yes

Added costs for services:

For LD:	No
For ADHD:	No
For ASD:	No
LD specialists	No
ADHD & ASD coaching	No
ASD specialists	No
Professional tutors	Yes
Peer tutors	Yes
Max. hours/week for services	Varies
How professors are notified of student approved accommodations	Student

COLLEGE GRADUATION REQUIREMENTS

Course waivers allowed	No
Course substitutions allowed	Yes

In what courses

Course substitutions are provided on a case-by-case basis. American Sign Language may be accepted by some majors.

Long Island University Post

720 Northern Blvd., Brookville, NY 11548 • Admissions: 516-299-2900 • Fax: 516-299-2137

CAMPUS
Type of school	Private (nonprofit)
Environment	Metropolis
Support	SP

STUDENTS
Undergrad enrollment	3,133
% male/female	39/61
% from out of state	9
% frosh live on campus	47

FINANCIAL FACTS
Annual tuition	$35,038
Room and board	$13,720
Required fees	$1,940

GENERAL ADMISSIONS INFO
Application fee	$50
Priority deadline	12/1

Nonfall registration accepted. Admission may be deferred for a maximum of one semester.

Range SAT EBRW	530–620
Range SAT Math	525–620
Range ACT Composite	21–26

ACADEMICS
Student/faculty ratio	14:1
% students returning for sophomore year	78
% students graduating within 4 years	29
% students graduating within 6 years	48

Most classes have 10–19 students.
Most lab/discussion sessions have 10–19 students.

PROGRAMS/SERVICES FOR STUDENTS WITH LEARNING DIFFERENCES

The Academic Resource Program (ARP), is housed in our Learning Support Center, is a comprehensive, structured, fee- for-service support program designed to meet the needs of students certified as having a LD and/or ADHD. Students are provided with one-on-one sessions with a trained learning assistant; an up-to-date computer lab with assistive technology; weekly meetings with an ARP administrator; and as needed, sessions with our social worker, time management counselor, and/or Bridges to Post counselor. The staff is committed to working with each individual student enrolled in the program to help students learn the strategies and skills needed to transition and succeed in college. The staff provides each student with the opportunity, structure, and support necessary to help him or her develop the academic, social, problem-solving, and strategic skills to achieve goals. This is accomplished through a structured program and an approach that is designed to assist the individual student. The key ingredient is, of course, the student and the student's desire to succeed and willingness to be actively involved in the program.

ADMISSIONS

Admission to the ARP is separate and distinct from admission to the university. Upon receipt of an acceptance letter from the Office of Admissions, prospective students should contact the Learning Support Center at 516-299-3057 to request an application for the Academic Resource Program. The student must submit the completed Academic Resource Program application, together with

ADMISSIONS INFO FOR STUDENTS WITH LEARNING DIFFERENCES
SAT/ACT required: Yes
Interview required: Yes
Essay required: Required
Additional application required: Yes
Documentation required for:
  LD: WAIS-IV with sub-test scores, scaled scores, verbal performance, full-scale IQ, general ability index, and statement of diagnosis and the academic limitations resulting from the disability. Current levels of functioning in reading, math, and written language are required. Acceptable instruments include the Woodcock-Johnson Psycho-educational Battery and the Wechsler Individual Achievement Test (WIAT).
  ADHD: Students with a primary diagnosis of ADHD must also provide a copy of a diagnostic report within the last three years, which states the DSM diagnosis, symptoms, and functional limitations; the testing methods used to make the diagnosis; and the dosage, type, and frequency of medication.
  ASD: Documentation should be current and relevant, and include the diagnosis and date of diagnosis; the testing and results that explain the functional limitations and behavioral manifestations; how it currently impacts the student academically or otherwise; and suggestions of accommodations that might work for the student.
Documentation submitted to: Support Program/Services
Special Ed. HS course work accepted: Yes
Separate application required for program services: LD, ADHD, ASD.
# of students last year receiving services/accommodations for:
  LD: 65-75
Contact Information
Name of program or department: Academic Resource Program
Telephone: 516-299-3057
Fax: 516-299-2126

Long Island University Post

the required essay, and a Diagnostic Evaluation conducted within the past three years. Upon receipt of the completed application essay, and required psychological-educational evaluations, the staff will contact eligible candidates to schedule a personal interview, which is an integral part of the admission to ARP process. Students who do not meet LIU Post's admissions requirements but demonstrate potential for academic success, may be eligible for the P.A.S. Program. Through this one-year academic program, a limited number of freshman enroll as matriculated students with restrictions and benefit from a unique support network component that includes a full-time modified course load, smaller class sizes, academic support services, tutoring and continuous guidance throughout the freshman year. The goal of this support program is to help freshman students become matriculated without restriction by their sophomore year. For general admission LIU Post recommends 4 years English, 3 years Math, 3 years Science (2 years must be a laboratory science), 3 years Social Studies, and 2 years Foreign Language. The mid 50% SAT score is 105-1230 the mid-50% ACT score is 21-26. The Writing section of ACT/SAT is not required.

Additional Information

The fee for the Academic Resource Program is $2,000.00 per semester, which is in addition to the cost for tuition, room and board, and books.. Learning assistants help freshmen make the transition from high school to college. They assist all Academic Resource Program students in time management, organizational skills, note-taking techniques, study skills, and other necessary learning strategies. Each student is responsible for his or her attendance and participation in these sessions. Freshmen and sophomores meet with a learning assistant for two hours per week. Students are welcome to schedule more hours if necessary. Juniors and seniors are given the opportunity to schedule and contract more flexible hours with the ARP staff. Auxiliary aids and ancillary services are provided at no charge.

GENERAL ADMISSIONS

Very important factors considered include: rigor of secondary school record, academic GPA, standardized test scores. *Important factors considered include:* application essay, recommendation(s), extracurricular activities, talent/ability, character/personal qualities, first generation, volunteer work, work experience, level of applicant's interest. *Other factors considered include:* class rank, interview, alumni/ae relation. *Freshman Admission Requirements:* High school diploma is required and GED is accepted. *Academic units recommended:* 4 English, 3 math, 3 science, 3 science labs, 2 foreign language, 4 social studies.

ACCOMMODATION OR SERVICES

Accommodations are decided upon an individual basis after a thorough review of appropriate, current documentation. The accommodations requests must be supported through the documentation provided and must be logically linked to the current impact of the condition on academic functioning.

FINANCIAL AID

Students should submit: FAFSA; State aid form. Applicants will be notified of awards on a rolling basis beginning 12/20. The Princeton Review suggests that all financial aid forms be submitted as soon as possible after October 1. *Need-based scholarships/grants offered:* College/university scholarship or grant aid from institutional funds; Federal Pell; Private scholarships; SEOG; State scholarships/grants; United Negro College Fund. *Loan aid offered:* Direct PLUS loans; Direct Subsidized Stafford Loans; Direct Unsubsidized Stafford Loans. Federal Work-Study Program available. Institutional employment available.

ACCOMMODATIONS

Allowed in exams:

Calculators	Yes
Dictionary	No
Computer	Yes
Spell-checker	Yes
Extended test time	Yes
Scribe	Yes
Proctors	Yes
Oral exams	Yes
Note-takers	Yes

Support services for students with

LD	Yes
ADHD	Yes
ASD	Yes
Distraction-reduced environment	Yes
Recording of lecture allowed	Yes
Reading technology:	Yes
Audio books	No

Other assistive technology   Most students who require assistive technology have their own software programs on personal laptops.

Priority registration	No

Added costs for services: There is a fee for the ARP program.

For LD:	No
For ADHD:	No
For ASD:	No
LD specialists	Yes
ADHD & ASD coaching	Yes
ASD specialists	No
Professional tutors	Yes
Peer tutors	Not Applicable
Max. hours/week for services	Unlimited

How professors are notified of student approved accommodations   Student with Accommodations form

COLLEGE GRADUATION REQUIREMENTS

Course waivers allowed	No
Course substitutions allowed	Yes

In what courses   Math and Foreign Language, if supported by documentation.

Manhattanville College

2900 PURCHASE STREET, PURCHASE, NY 10577 • ADMISSIONS: 914-323-5464 • FAX: 914-694-1732

CAMPUS

Type of school	Private (nonprofit)
Environment	Town
Support	SP

STUDENTS

Undergrad enrollment	1,674
% male/female	37/63
% from out of state	27
% frosh live on campus	71

FINANCIAL FACTS

Annual tuition	$37,370
Room and board	$14,520
Required fees	$1,450

GENERAL ADMISSIONS INFO

Application fee	$50
Priority deadline	3/1

Nonfall registration accepted. Admission may be deferred for a maximum of 1 year.

Range SAT Math	430–625
Range ACT Composite	17–27

ACADEMICS

Student/faculty ratio	11:1
% students returning for sophomore year	74
% students graduating within 4 years	49
% students graduating within 6 years	55

Most classes have 10–19 students.

PROGRAMS/SERVICES FOR STUDENTS WITH LEARNING DIFFERENCES

Manhattanville College has two fee-based programs designed to support students who are independent, college-ready, self-motivating individuals. The Valiant Learning Support Program (VLSP) is a fee-based program that serves as a center of support for students with documented learning disabilities. It is designed to assist college-ready students to navigate the academic challenges of the college curriculum. This program offers students customized learning strategy sessions with highly trained, professional Learning Specialists. The Pathways and Connections Program(PAC) is an innovative and comprehensive fee based program designed to assist college-ready students on the Autism Spectrum and individuals with related diagnoses. The program focuses on executive functioning skills in the social realm and supports students with transitional skills and integration into the campus community. Students are encouraged to participate in all components of the program in order to enhance the overall college experience. Students may enroll in VLSP and/or PAC after they have been accepted by the College and have registered with the Center for Student Accommodations.

ADMISSIONS

Students enroll in VLSP and/or PAC after college acceptance by the College. For general admissions the average GPA is 89 (3.4), Admissions considers more than GPA when evaluating an application. Writing section used for placement.

Additional Information

Learning Specialists in the VLSP provide each student enrolled in the program with 3 hours of 1:1 academic support on a weekly basis which may include working with students on writing skills, reading comprehension skills, executive functioning skills such as time management and prioritization, and study skills. Learning Specialists use the student's own course work to support students in their efforts to take ownership of their own learning and partner with students to promote self-advocacy and self-determination. The PAC program is an innovative and comprehensive fee based program designed to assist college-ready students on the Autism Spectrum and individuals with related diagnoses. The program focuses on executive functioning skills in the social realm and supports students with

ADMISSIONS INFO FOR STUDENTS WITH LEARNING DIFFERENCES

SAT/ACT required: Yes
Interview required: No
Essay required: Yes
Additional application required: For VLSP and PAC
Documentation required for:
 LD: Psycho Educational Evaluation
 ADHD: Psycho Educational Evaluation
 ASD: The evaluations should include a diagnostic statement including a description of the diagnostic criteria, evaluation methods, procedures, tests and dates of administration, and clinical narrative, observation, and specific results.
Documentation submitted to: Center for Student Accommodations
Special Ed. HS course work accepted: Yes
# of students last year receiving services/accommodations for:
 LD: 325
 ADHD: 27
 ASD: 34
Contact Information
Name of program or department: Valiant Learning Support Program
Telephone: (914) 323-7129

Manhattanville College

transitional skills and integration into the campus community. Students are encouraged to participate in all components of the program in order to enhance the overall college experience. The PAC Program components include Individual, customized weekly meetings with PAC Coordinator, weekly group sessions with topics based on the needs and interests of program participants, optional peer mentoring, and social events on and off-campus. There is limited space in either program and is filled on a first come first serve basis. Documentation is time stamped when received by the Center for Student Accommodations and students are notified on a rolling basis. The Center for Student Accommodations also provides federally mandated reasonable accommodations and support services to students with documented disabilities.

GENERAL ADMISSIONS

Very important factors considered include: academic GPA, application essay, recommendation(s), extracurricular activities, talent/ability, character/personal qualities, alumni/ae relation. *Important factors considered include:* rigor of secondary school record, standardized test scores, interview, first generation, geographical residence, volunteer work.level of applicant's interest. *Other factors considered include:* class rank, state residency, work experience. *Freshman Admission Requirements:* High school diploma is required and GED is accepted. *Academic units required:* 4 English, 3 math, 2 science, 2 social studies, 5 academic electives.

ACCOMMODATION OR SERVICES

Accommodations are decided upon an individual basis after a thorough review of appropriate, current documentation. The accommodations requests must be supported through the documentation provided and must be logically linked to the current impact of the condition on academic functioning.

FINANCIAL AID

Students should submit: FAFSA; State aid form. Applicants will be notified of awards on a rolling basis beginning 1/1. The Princeton Review suggests that all financial aid forms be submitted as soon as possible after October 1. *Need-based scholarships/grants offered:* College/university scholarship or grant aid from institutional funds; Federal Pell; Private scholarships; SEOG; State scholarships/grants. *Loan aid offered:* Direct PLUS loans; Direct Subsidized Stafford Loans; Direct Unsubsidized Stafford Loans. Federal Work-Study Program available. Institutional employment available.

CAMPUS LIFE

Activities: Campus Ministries; Choral groups; Concert band; Dance; Drama/theater; International Student Organization; Jazz band; Literary magazine; Model UN; Music ensembles; Musical theater; Opera; Radio station; Student government; Student newspaper; Student-run film society. **Organizations:** 46 registered organizations, 2 honor societies, 5 religious organizations. **Athletics (Intercollegiate):** *Men:* baseball, basketball, golf, ice hockey, lacrosse, soccer, tennis. *Women:* basketball, cheerleading, field hockey, ice hockey, lacrosse, soccer, softball, tennis, volleyball. **On-Campus Highlights:** The Castle, Library Cafe, Richard Berman Student Center, Kennedy Gymnasium, Quad.

ACCOMMODATIONS

Allowed in exams:	
Calculators	Yes
Dictionary	Yes
Computer	Yes
Spell-checker	Yes
Extended test time	Yes
Scribe	Yes
Proctors	Yes
Oral exams	Yes
Note-takers	Yes
Support services for students with	
LD	Yes
ADHD	Yes
ASD	Yes
Distraction-reduced environment	Yes
Recording of lecture allowed	Yes
Reading technology:	Yes
Audio books	Yes
Other assistive technology	
Priority registration	No
Added costs for services:	
For LD:	Yes
For ADHD:	Yes
For ASD:	Yes
LD specialists	Yes
ADHD & ASD coaching	Yes
ASD specialists	Yes
Professional tutors	Yes
Peer tutors	Not Applicable
Max. hours/week for services	4
How professors are notified of student approved accommodations	Student

COLLEGE GRADUATION REQUIREMENTS

Course waivers allowed	No
Course substitutions allowed	Yes

Marist College

3399 North Road, Poughkeepsie, NY 12601-1387 • Admissions: 845-575-3226 • Fax: 845-575-3215

PROGRAMS/SERVICES FOR STUDENTS WITH LEARNING DIFFERENCES

The Learning Support Program provides a complement of academic services that are designed to meet the individual needs of students. The Program focuses on the development and use of strategies that will promote independence and personal success. Students are expected to serve as their own advocates in a continually increasing fashion. Students are enrolled in credit-bearing courses and completes degree requirements required by all students. Learning Disability Specialists work closely with faculty and administration to assist the students. Each individual is encouraged to openly discuss his or her learning needs with appropriate faculty at the start of the semester. Specialists frequently assist students in preparation for this meeting. Participation in the Program is available to students on a continual basis for as long as the Specialist and student mutually agree is necessary. Students are expected to assume increasingly higher levels of responsibility for their academic success and to function independently as soon as possible beyond the freshman year. The Learning Support Program is a fee-based program.

ADMISSIONS

No ACT/SAT is required. Students wishing to participate in the Learning Support Program must apply to Marist College by submitting a regular application to the Undergraduate Admissions Office. Applicants to the Learning Support Program should have a documented learning disability /ADD/ADHD, aptitude solidly in the average range, a college preparatory course of study, and a commitment to work with a Learning Specialist. Applicants admitted demonstrate a need for the service and determination, skill and maturity required to manage the demands of college. Marist places a strong emphasis on a student's strengths and abilities.

Additional Information

The Program emphasizes the development of compensatory strategies. Each student is assigned to work one-on-one with a Learning Specialist. Freshmen meet with the Specialist twice a week. The goals of each session are individualized and typical sessions concentrate on Improving skills in writing, note taking, organization, time management and test-taking strategies, The Specialist establishes a plan for necessary and appropriate academic accommodations. Students who are a good fit for the Program typically possess a knowledge and acceptance of their learning disability, ADD or ADHD, a willingness to accept assistance and access support, an ability to independently implement strategies taught in sessions, self-motivation a desire to participate in the Program and sound study skills and work habits. There is a fee for the program. There is no charge for students with documentation who are not in the program and are just requesting reasonable accommodations.

GENERAL ADMISSIONS

Very important factors considered include: rigor of secondary school record, academic GPA. *Important factors considered include:* class rank, application essay, recommendation(s), extracurricular activities, talent/ability, character/personal qualities, geographical residence, state residency, volunteer work, work experience. *Other factors considered include:* standardized test scores, first generation, alumni/ae relation, racial/ethnic status, level of applicant's interest. *Freshman Admission Requirements:* High school diploma is required and GED is accepted. *Academic units required:* 4 English, 3 math, 3 science, 2 science labs, 2 foreign language, 2 social studies, 1 history, 2 academic electives. *Academic units recommended:* 4 math, 4 science, 3 science labs, 3 foreign language.

ACCOMMODATION OR SERVICES

Accommodations are decided upon an individual basis after a thorough review of appropriate, current documentation. The accommodations requests must be supported through the documentation provided and must be logically linked to the current impact of the condition on academic functioning.

FINANCIAL AID

Students should submit: FAFSA. Applicants will be notified of awards on or about 3/31. The Princeton Review suggests that all financial aid forms be submitted as soon as possible after October 1. *Need-based scholarships/grants offered:* College/university scholarship or grant aid from institutional funds; Federal Pell; Private scholarships; SEOG; State scholarships/grants. *Loan aid offered:* Direct PLUS loans; Direct Subsidized Stafford Loans; Direct Unsubsidized Stafford Loans. Federal Work-Study Program available. Institutional employment available.

CAMPUS LIFE

Activities: Campus Ministries; Choral groups; Concert band; Dance; Drama/theater; International Student Organization; Jazz band; Literary magazine; Marching band; Model UN; Music ensembles; Musical theater; Pep band; Radio station; Student government; Student newspaper; Symphony orchestra; Television station. **Organizations:** 86 registered organizations, 16 honor societies, 6 religious organizations. 3 fraternities, 4 sororities. **Athletics (Intercollegiate):** *Men:* baseball, basketball, crew/rowing, cross-country, diving, football, lacrosse, soccer, swimming, tennis, track/field (outdoor). *Women:* basketball, crew/rowing, cross-country, diving, lacrosse, soccer, softball, swimming, tennis, track/field (outdoor), volleyball, water polo. **On-Campus Highlights:** James A Cannavino Library, James J McCann Recreation Center, Hancock Center, Murray Student Center and Dining Hall, Newly Built Music Department.

ACCOMMODATIONS

Allowed in exams:

Calculators	Yes
Dictionary	Not Applicable
Computer	Yes
Spell-checker	Not Applicable
Extended test time	Yes
Scribe	Yes
Proctors	Yes
Oral exams	Not Applicable
Note-takers	Yes

Support services for students with

LD	Yes
ADHD	Yes
ASD	NR
Distraction-reduced environment	Yes
Recording of lecture allowed	Yes
Reading technology:	Yes
Audio books	No
Other assistive technology	Read and Write Gold
Priority registration	No

Added costs for services:

For LD:	No
For ADHD:	No
For ASD:	No
LD specialists	Yes
ADHD & ASD coaching	No
ASD specialists	Yes
Professional tutors	Yes
Peer tutors	Yes
Max. hours/week for services	12
How professors are notified of student approved accommodations	Student

COLLEGE GRADUATION REQUIREMENTS

Course waivers allowed	No
Course substitutions allowed	No

Marymount Manhattan College

221 East 71st Street, New York, NY 10021 • Admissions: 212-517-0430 • Fax: 212-517-0448

CAMPUS

Type of school	Private (nonprofit)
Environment	Metropolis
Support	SP

STUDENTS

Undergrad enrollment	1,875
% male/female	23/77
% from out of state	59
% frosh live on campus	79

FINANCIAL FACTS

Annual tuition	$28,870
Room and board	$15,990
Required fees	$1,420

GENERAL ADMISSIONS INFO

Application fee	$60
Priority deadline	8/1

Nonfall registration accepted. Admission may be deferred.

Range SAT EBRW	470–590
Range SAT Math	440–550
Range ACT Composite	20–26

ACADEMICS

Student/faculty ratio	11:1
% students returning for sophomore year	74

Most classes have 20–29 students.
Most lab/discussion sessions have fewer than 10 students.

PROGRAMS/SERVICES FOR STUDENTS WITH LEARNING DIFFERENCES

Marymount Manhattan College's Program for Academic Access includes a full range of support services that center on academic and personal growth for students with learning disabilities. Students who have been admitted to the full-time program are required to demonstrate commitment to overcoming learning difficulties through regular attendance and tutoring. Academic advisement and counseling is provided to assist in developing a program plan suited to individual needs. The college is looking for highly motivated students with a commitment to compensate for their learning disabilities and to fully participate in the tutoring program. Once admitted into the program, students receive a program plan suited to their needs, based on a careful examination of the psycho-educational evaluations. Full time students sign a contract to regularly attend tutoring provided by professionals experienced within the field of LD. In addition to assisting students in the development of skills and strategies for their coursework, LD specialists coach participants in the attitudes and behavior necessary for college success. Professors assist learning specialists in carefully monitoring students' progress throughout the academic year and arranging for accommodations. Students must submit a current and complete Psycho ed evaluation that meets the documentation guidelines by giving clear and specific evidence of the disability and its limitations on academic functioning in the diagnosis summary statement. Students with ADD must have a licensed physician, psychiatrist or psychologist provide a complete and current (within the last 3 years) documentation of the disorder.

ADMISSIONS

Admission to Marymount Manhattan College's Program for Academic Access is based on a diagnosis of dyslexia, ADHD, or other primary learning disability; intellectual potential within the average to superior range; and a serious commitment in attitude and work habits to meeting the program and college academic requirements. Prospective students are required to submit the following: high school transcript or GED. Students are expected to have college prep courses in high school but foreign language is not required for admission; ACT or SAT are required; results of a recent complete Psycho ed evaluation (within one year); letters of recommendation from teachers, tutors, or counselors; and have a personal interview. Students may be admitted to the college through the Program for Academic Access. Students interested in being considered for admission through the program must self disclose

ADMISSIONS INFO FOR STUDENTS WITH LEARNING DIFFERENCES

SAT/ACT required: Yes
Interview required: Yes
Essay required: Yes
Additional application required: No
Documentation required for:
  LD: Psychoeducational evaluation within the last 3 years.
  ADHD: Signed letter from psychiatrist or psychologist with diagnostic code.
  ASD: Psycho ed evaluation
Documentation submitted to: Support program/services
Special Ed. HS course work accepted: No
Separate application required for program services: No
# of students last year receiving services/accommodations for:
  LD: 30
Contact Information
Name of program or department: Disability Services
Telephone: 212-774-0724
Fax: 212-774-4875

Marymount Manhattan College

their LD/ADHD in a personal statement with the application. There is no fixed deadline for the application, however there are a limited number of slots available. Completed files received by mid-January are at an advantage to be elligible for selection.

Additional Information
There are three LD professionals associated with the program. Students have access to two hours of tutoring per week with a learning specialist, drop-in tutoring and monthly parent meetings. Skills classes are offered in study skills, reading, vocabulary development and workshops in overcoming procrastination and study reading and effectiveness. The following services are offered to students with appropriate documentation: the use of calculators, computer and spell checker in exams; extended time on tests; proctors; oral exams; distraction-free testing environment; tape recorder in class; books on tape; Kurzweil software, note-takers, separate and alternative forms of testing; and priority registration.

GENERAL ADMISSIONS
Very important factors considered include: rigor of secondary school record, academic GPA, standardized test scores. *Important factors considered include:* application essay, recommendation(s), talent/ability, character/personal qualities, level of applicant's interest. *Other factors considered include:* interview, extracurricular activities, first generation, alumni/ae relation, geographical residence, state residency, volunteer work, work experience. *Freshman Admission Requirements:* High school diploma is required and GED is accepted. *Academic units required:* 4 English, 3 math, 3 science, 3 social studies, 4 academic electives. *Academic units recommended:* 2 science labs, 2 foreign language.

ACCOMMODATION OR SERVICES
Accommodations are decided upon an individual basis after a thorough review of appropriate, current documentation. The accommodations requests must be supported through the documentation provided and must be logically linked to the current impact of the condition on academic functioning.

FINANCIAL AID
Students should submit: FAFSA; State aid form. Applicants will be notified of awards on a rolling basis beginning 3/15. The Princeton Review suggests that all financial aid forms be submitted as soon as possible after October 1. *Need-based scholarships/grants offered:* College/university scholarship or grant aid from institutional funds; Federal Pell; Private scholarships; SEOG; State scholarships/grants. *Loan aid offered:* Direct PLUS loans; Direct Subsidized Stafford Loans; Direct Unsubsidized Stafford Loans. Federal Work-Study Program available. Institutional employment available.

CAMPUS LIFE
Activities: Campus Ministries; Choral groups; Dance; Drama/theater; International Student Organization; Musical theater; Radio station; Student government; Student newspaper; Yearbook. **Organizations:** 30 registered organizations, 7 honor societies, 2 religious organizations. **On-Campus Highlights:** Theresa Lang Theatre, Hewitt Gallery of Art, Science Laboratories, 55th Street Residence Hall, Shanahan Library.

ACCOMMODATIONS
Allowed in exams:

Calculators	Yes
Dictionary	Yes
Computer	Yes
Spell-checker	Yes
Extended test time	Yes
Scribe	Yes
Proctors	Yes
Oral exams	Yes
Note-takers	Yes
Support services for students with	
LD	Yes
ADHD	Yes
ASD	Yes
Distraction-reduced environment	Yes
Recording of lecture allowed	Yes
Reading technology:	Yes
Audio books	Yes
Other assistive technology	Yes
Priority registration	Yes
Added costs for services:	
For LD:	Yes
For ADHD:	No
For ASD:	No
LD specialists	Yes
ADHD & ASD coaching	Yes, through
Academic Access Program	
ASD specialists	No
Professional tutors	No
Peer tutors	No
Max. hours/week for services	2
How professors are notified of student approved accommodations	Student

COLLEGE GRADUATION REQUIREMENTS

Course waivers allowed	No
Course substitutions allowed	No

New York University

70 Washington Square South, New York, NY 10012 • Admissions: 212-998-4500 • Fax: 212-995-4902

CAMPUS
Type of school	Private (nonprofit)
Environment	Metropolis
Support	CS

STUDENTS
Undergrad enrollment	26,055
% male/female	43/57
% from out of state	66
% frosh live on campus	85

FINANCIAL FACTS
Annual tuition	$47,942
Room and board	$17,664
Required fees	$2,522

GENERAL ADMISSIONS INFO
Application fee	$80
Regular application deadline	1/1

Nonfall registration accepted. Admission may be deferred for a maximum of 1-2 years.

Range SAT EBRW	650–730
Range SAT Math	640–760
Range ACT Composite	29–33

ACADEMICS
Student/faculty ratio	10:1
% students returning for sophomore year	93
% students graduating within 4 years	82
% students graduating within 6 years	84

Most classes have 10–19 students.
Most lab/discussion sessions have 10–19 students.

PROGRAMS/SERVICES FOR STUDENTS WITH LEARNING DIFFERENCES
The Henry and Lucy Moses Center for Students with Disabilities (CSD) works with students with a documented disability or disabilities who register with the office to obtain appropriate accommodations and services. This process is designed to encourage independence, backed by a strong system of supports. Each student who is approved through CSD works with a staff specialist to develop an individualized and reasonable accommodation plan. Reasonable accommodations are adjustments to policy, practice, and programs that "level the playing field" for students with disabilities and provide equal access to NYU's programs and activities. Accommodation plans and other related services are based on each student's disability documentation and NYU program requirements and are therefore determined on a case-by-case basis.

ADMISSIONS
There is no special application process for students with disabilities applying to NYU, although a student may voluntarily disclose their disability during the admissions process. Disclosing a disability has no impact on the admissions decision. Applicants to programs in Steinhardt School of Culture, Education, and Human Development and our Tisch School of the Arts requiring an audition or portfolio are not required to submit ACT/SAT for consideration and doing so is entirely optional. For other programs NYU has a flexible testing policy and applicants can submit one of the following: SAT or ACT (no essay test required), 3 SAT Subject Tests, 3 AP exams, International Baccalaureate (IB) Diploma, 3 IB higher-level exam scores if not an IB Diploma candidate, or certain international qualifications showing completion of a secondary education.

ADMISSIONS INFO FOR STUDENTS WITH LEARNING DIFFERENCES
SAT/ACT required: No
Interview required: No
Essay required: Yes
Additional application required: No
Documentation required for:
  LD: Psycho ed evaluation to include: relevant historical info, instructional interventions, related services, age diagnosed, objective data (aptitude, achievement, info processing), test scores (standard, percentile and grade equivalents) and describe functional limitations. ADHD: Diagnosis based on DSM-V; history of behaviors impairing functioning in academic setting; diagnostic interview; history of symptoms; evidence of ongoing behaviors.
  ASD: Psycho ed evaluation
Documentation submitted to: Moses Center for Students with Disabilities
Special Ed. HS course work accepted: Yes
Separate application required for program services: Yes
Contact Information
Name of program or department: Henry and Lucy Moses Center for Students with Disabilities
Telephone: 212-998-4980
Fax: 212-995-4114

New York University

Additional Information

Once students submit an application for accommodations, they will be contacted by a Disability Specialist within 2-3 business days to set up a meeting to discuss appropriate and reasonable accommodations. The University Learning Centers provide free individual and group review sessions for specific courses as well as academic coaching and skills workshops, The Moses Center annually provides a limited number of tuition awards made possible by grant funding to registered students with disabilities based on applicant's financial need, severity of disability, and academic qualifications.

GENERAL ADMISSIONS

Very important factors considered include: rigor of secondary school record, class rank, academic GPA, standardized test scores, talent/ability. *Important factors considered include:* application essay, recommendation(s), extracurricular activities, character/personal qualities. *Other factors considered include:* interview, first generation, alumni/ae relation, geographical residence, racial/ethnic status, volunteer work, work experience, level of applicant's interest. *Freshman Admission Requirements:* High school diploma is required and GED is accepted. *Academic units required:* 4 English, 3 math, 3 science, 3 science labs, 3 foreign language, 3 social studies, 3 history. *Academic units recommended:* 4 English, 4 math, 4 science, 4 science labs, 4 foreign language, 4 social studies, 4 history.

ACCOMMODATION OR SERVICES

Accommodations are decided upon an individual basis after a thorough review of appropriate, current documentation. The accommodations requests must be supported through the documentation provided and must be logically linked to the current impact of the condition on academic functioning.

FINANCIAL AID

Students should submit: CSS/Financial Aid PROFILE; FAFSA; Noncustodial PROFILE. Applicants will be notified of awards on or about 4/1. The Princeton Review suggests that all financial aid forms be submitted as soon as possible after October 1. *Need-based scholarships/grants offered:* College/university scholarship or grant aid from institutional funds; Federal Nursing Scholarships; Federal Pell; Private scholarships; SEOG; State scholarships/grants. *Loan aid offered:* Direct PLUS loans; Direct Subsidized Stafford Loans; Direct Unsubsidized Stafford Loans. Federal Work-Study Program available. Institutional employment available.

CAMPUS LIFE

Activities: Campus Ministries; Choral groups; Concert band; Dance; Drama/theater; International Student Organization; Jazz band; Literary magazine; Model UN; Music ensembles; Musical theater; Opera; Pep band; Radio station; Student government; Student newspaper; Student-run film society; Symphony orchestra; Television station; Yearbook. **Organizations:** 407 registered organizations, 3 honor societies, 31 religious organizations. 14 fraternities, 10 sororities. **Athletics (Intercollegiate):** *Men:* basketball, cross-country, diving, fencing, golf, soccer, swimming, tennis, track/field (outdoor), track/field (indoor), volleyball, wrestling. *Women:* basketball, cross-country, diving, fencing, golf, soccer, swimming, tennis, track/field (outdoor), track/field (indoor), volleyball. **On-Campus Highlights:** Kimmel Center for Student Life, Coles Athletic Center, Palladium Athletic Facility, Skirball Center for the Performing Arts, Center for Spiritual Life.

ACCOMMODATIONS

Allowed in exams:

Calculators	Yes
Dictionary	Yes
Computer	Yes
Spell-checker	Yes
Extended test time	Yes
Scribe	Yes
Proctors	Yes
Oral exams	No
Note-takers	Yes

Support services for students with

LD	Yes
ADHD	Yes
ASD	Yes
Distraction-reduced environment	Yes
Recording of lecture allowed	Yes
Reading technology:	Yes
Audio books	No
Other assistive technology	Yes
Priority registration	Yes

Added costs for services:

For LD:	No
For ADHD:	No
For ASD:	No
LD specialists	Yes
ADHD & ASD coaching	No
ASD specialists	No

Professional tutors Yes (NYU Writing Center)
Peer tutors   Yes (University Learning Center)
Max. hours/week for services   One session for Writing Center; tutoring at College Learning Center variable.
How professors are notified of student approved accommodations   Student

COLLEGE GRADUATION REQUIREMENTS

Course waivers allowed	No
Course substitutions allowed	Yes

In what courses   Determined by the student's Office of the Dean on a case-by-case basis,

Pace University

1 PACE PLAZA, NEW YORK, NY 10038 • ADMISSIONS: 212-346-1323 • FAX: 212-346-1040

CAMPUS

Type of school	Private (nonprofit)
Environment	Metropolis
Support	S

STUDENTS

Undergrad enrollment	8,456
% male/female	39/61
% from out of state	41
% frosh live on campus	73

FINANCIAL FACTS

Annual tuition	$42,354
Room and board	$18,002
Required fees	$1,632

GENERAL ADMISSIONS INFO

Application fee	$50

Priority deadline 2/15
Nonfall registration accepted. Admission may be deferred for a maximum of 1 year.

Range SAT EBRW	530 –620
Range SAT Math	510 –600
Range ACT Composite	21 –27

ACADEMICS

Student/faculty ratio	14:1.
% students returning for sophomore year	80
students graduating within 4 years	39
students graduating within 6 years	54

Most classes have 10-19 students.
Most lab/discussion sessions have 10-19 students.

PROGRAMS/SERVICES FOR STUDENTS WITH LEARNING DIFFERENCES

Pace University is committed to providing equal access for students with disabilities to its facilities, educational programs, and activities. Pace prohibits discrimination on the basis of disability and makes assistance available to students through the Office of Disability Services, which provides reasonable accommodations to address the needs of students with disabilities. Accommodations are determined on a case-by-case basis according to a student's documented needs, guidelines suggested by federal and state law, and criteria developed by the University. Identifying and implementing a reasonable accommodation for a student with a disability is an interactive process that includes shared responsibility between the University and the student. It is the student's responsibility to request an accommodation. Before an accommodation will be provided, the student may be required to submit medical and/or other diagnostic information concerning the student's impairments and limitations. The documentation required varies depending on the disability; all documentation must be provided by an appropriately credentialed professional. Finally, the University is required to provide a reasonable accommodation; it is not required to provide the specific accommodation requested by the student. In providing accommodations, the University is not required to lower or effect substantial modifications to essential requirements or to make modifications that would fundamentally alter the nature of the service, program, or activity. Other resources available for students with documented disabilities include The OASIS Program, a comprehensive fee-for-service support program for students with autism, Asperger Syndrome, learning disabilities, nonverbal learning differences and related challenges.

ADMISSIONS INFO FOR STUDENTS WITH LEARNING DIFFERENCES

SAT/ACT required: Yes
Interview required: No
Essay required: Not Applicable
Additional application required: No
Documentation required for:
  LD: Determined on a case-by-case basis
  ADHD: An updated and current neuropsychological evaluation is generally recommended for students with ASD
  ASD: Determined on a case-by-case basis
Documentation submitted to: Office of Disability Services
Special Ed. HS course work accepted   : Yes
Separate application required for program services: No
Contact Information
Name of program or department: Office of Disability Services
Telephone: 212-346-1088
Fax: 914-773-3639

Pace University

ADMISSIONS

The same rigorous admission and academic standards apply to students with and without a disability.

Additional Information

To request an accommodation for a disability, a student must self-identify and register with the Office of Disability Services for his or her campus. The student will be responsible for providing documentation and meeting with a member of the Office of Disability Services staff to discuss their accommodation requests and be oriented to office policies and procedures for accessing accommodations. The OASIS program has a separate application process. Applicants for OASIS go through a special admissions process in which they are evaluated by the admissions team during a personal interview. All OASIS applicants must also submit a current (within 18 months) neuropsychological evaluation.

GENERAL ADMISSIONS

Very important factors considered include: rigor of secondary school record, application essay, standardized test scores. *Important factors considered include:* class rank, academic GPA, recommendation(s). *Other factors considered include:* interview, extracurricular activities, talent/ability, character/personal qualities, alumni/ae relation, volunteer work, work experience. *Freshman Admission Requirements:* High school diploma is required and GED is accepted *Academic units required:* 4 English, 3 math, 2 science labs, 2 foreign language, 3 history, 2 academic electives,

ACCOMMODATION OR SERVICES

Accommodations are decided upon an individual basis after a thorough review of appropriate, current documentation. The accommodations requests must be supported through the documentation provided and must be logically linked to the current impact of the condition on academic functioning.

FINANCIAL AID

Students should submit: FAFSA. Applicants will be notified of awards on a rolling basis beginning 12/1.. The Princeton Review suggests that all financial aid forms be submitted as soon as possible after October 1. *Need-based scholarships/grants offered:* College/university scholarship or grant aid from institutional funds; Federal Nursing Scholarships; Federal Pell; Private scholarships; SEOG; State scholarships/grants *Loan aid offered:* Direct PLUS loans; Direct Subsidized Stafford Loans; Direct Unsubsidized Stafford Loans Federal Work-Study Program available. Institutional employment available.

CAMPUS LIFE

Activities: Choral groups; Dance ; Drama/theater; International Student Organization; Literary magazine; Model UN; Musical theater; Radio station ; Student government; Student newspaper; Student-run film society; Television station; Yearbook Organizations: 79 registered organizations, 25 honor societies, 4 religious organizations. 11 fraternities, 9 sororities, **Athletics (Intercollegiate):** *Men:* baseball, basketball, cross-country, football, golf, lacrosse, swimming, tennis, track/field (outdoor), track/field (indoor) *Women:* basketball, cheerleading, cross-country, equestrian sports, soccer, softball, swimming, tennis, track/field (outdoor), track/field (indoor), volleyball. **On-Campus Highlights:** Student Union, Fitness Center, Theater, Library, Residence Halls.

ACCOMMODATIONS

Allowed in exams:	
Calculators	Yes
Dictionary	Yes
Computer	Yes
Spell-checker	Yes
Extended test time	Yes
Scribe	Yes
Proctors	Yes
Oral exams	Yes
Note-takers	Yes
Support services for students with	
LD	Yes
ADHD	Yes
ASD	Yes
Distraction-reduced environment	Yes
Recording of lecture allowed	Yes
Reading technology:	Yes
Audio books	Yes
Other assistive technology	Yes
Priority registration	Yes
Added costs for services:	
For LD:	No
For ADHD:	No
For ASD:	No
LD specialists	No
ADHD & ASD coaching	Yes
ASD specialists	Yes
Professional tutors	Yes
Peer tutors	Yes
Max. hours/week for services	Varies
How professors are notified of student approved accommodations	Student

COLLEGE GRADUATION REQUIREMENTS

Course waivers allowed	Yes
In what courses	Case-by-case basis
Course substitutions allowed	Yes
In what courses	Case-by-case basis

Rochester Institute of Technology

One Lomb Memorial Drive, Rochester, NY 14623-5604 • Admissions: 585-475-6631 • Fax: 585-475-7424

CAMPUS
Type of school	Private (nonprofit)
Environment	City
Support	SP

STUDENTS
Undergrad enrollment	12,858
% male/female	67/33
% from out of state	48
% frosh live on campus	96

FINANCIAL FACTS
Annual tuition	$43,546
Room and board	$13,046
Required fees	$584

GENERAL ADMISSIONS INFO
Application fee	$65
Priority deadline	1/15

Nonfall registration accepted. Admission may be deferred for a maximum of 1 year.

Range SAT EBRW	590–680
Range SAT Math	600–700
Range ACT Composite	26–32

ACADEMICS
Student/faculty ratio	13:1
% students returning for sophomore year	90
% students graduating within 4 years	28
% students graduating within 6 years	70

Most classes have 20–29 students.

PROGRAMS/SERVICES FOR STUDENTS WITH LEARNING DIFFERENCES

The Spectrum Support Program provides innovative supports that positively impact the college experience for RIT students, particularly those with autism spectrum disorders. RIT is committed to helping students build connections that will assist them in achieving academic, social and career success. The program seeks to create a campus culture of acceptance and support through collaboration, consultation, and training. Enrollment in the Spectrum Support Program has increased since its inception and averages 30 new incoming students each fall. The Program provides services to incoming freshmen and continues to provide support even as students transition out of RIT. In addition the RIT Disability Services Office provides reasonable accommodations to students with LD, ADHD and other health related disabilities.

ADMISSIONS

Most students applying to RIT choose a specific major as part of the admission process. In addition, all colleges offer undeclared options and the University Studies program is available to applicants with interests in two or more colleges. Admission requirements and entrance exam score ranges vary from one major to another. Applicants for the Spectrum Support Program (SSP) must meet all the academic requirements of admission to RIT and be matriculated into an undergraduate program. Deaf and hard-of-hearing students seeking admission to bachelor's degree programs should refer to the information for the appropriate college and apply for NTID support and access services during the application process. A Pre-baccalaureate Studies Option is also available for students who may need additional preparation before entering a bachelor's degree program.

Additional Information

SSP does not require specific documentation of an autism spectrum disorder as a condition of enrollment in SSP, however, students should identify as a member of the community of students on the autism spectrum at RIT. The Spectrum Support Program provides support in academic skills, social competence, self-care, self-advocacy, and executive functioning. Support is provided through one on one coaching, small group seminars, social events, and collaboration with cross-campus partners. There is a different fee structure for students who are entering freshmen and students continuing after freshmen year and depends on sessions once of twice a week or twice monthly. A pre-orientation program is offered three-days prior to fall New Student Orientation and assists program enrolled students in transitioning to RIT. Separate registration and fee applies.

ADMISSIONS INFO FOR STUDENTS WITH LEARNING DIFFERENCES

SAT/ACT required: Yes
Interview required: No
Essay required: Yes
Additional application required: No
Documentation required for:
 LD: Psycho ed evaluation
 ADHD: Psycho ed evaluation
 ASD: Psycho ed evaluation
Documentation submitted to: SSP or Disability Services Office
Special Ed. HS course work accepted: No
Separate application required for program services: No
Contact Information
Name of program or department: Disability Services Office
Telephone: 585-475-6988
Fax: 585-475-2915
Email: smacst@rit.edu

Rochester Institute of Technology

GENERAL ADMISSIONS
Very important factors considered include: rigor of secondary school record, academic GPA. *Important factors considered include:* class rank, standardized test scores. *Other factors considered include:* application essay, recommendation(s), interview, extracurricular activities, talent/ability, character/personal qualities, first generation, alumni/ae relation, geographical residence, racial/ethnic status, volunteer work, work experience, level of applic *Freshman Admission Requirements:* High school diploma is required and GED is accepted. *Academic units required:* 4 English, 2 math, 2 science, 1 science lab, 4 social studies, 10 academic electives. *Academic units recommended:* 4 English, 3 math, 3 science, 2 science labs, 3 foreign language, 4 social studies, 5 academic electives.

ACCOMMODATION OR SERVICES
Accommodations are decided upon an individual basis after a thorough review of appropriate, current documentation. The accommodations requests must be supported through the documentation provided and must be logically linked to the current impact of the condition on academic functioning.

FINANCIAL AID
Students should submit: FAFSA; State aid form. Applicants will be notified of awards on a rolling basis beginning 3/1. The Princeton Review suggests that all financial aid forms be submitted as soon as possible after October 1. *Need-based scholarships/grants offered:* College/university scholarship or grant aid from institutional funds; Federal Pell; Private scholarships; SEOG; State scholarships/grants. *Loan aid offered:* Direct PLUS loans; Direct Subsidized Stafford Loans; Direct Unsubsidized Stafford Loans. Federal Work-Study Program available. Institutional employment available.

CAMPUS LIFE
Activities: Campus Ministries; Choral groups; Concert band; Dance; Drama/theater; International Student Organization; Jazz band; Literary magazine; Music ensembles; Musical theater; Pep band; Radio station; Student government; Student newspaper; Student-run film society; Symphony orchestra; Yearbook. **Organizations:** 175 registered organizations, 9 honor societies, 5 religious organizations. 19 fraternities, 10 sororities. **Athletics (Intercollegiate):** *Men:* baseball, basketball, crew/rowing, cross-country, diving, ice hockey, lacrosse, soccer, swimming, tennis, track/field (outdoor), track/field (indoor), wrestling. *Women:* basketball, cheerleading, crew/rowing, cross-country, diving, ice hockey, lacrosse, soccer, softball, swimming, tennis, track/field (outdoor), track/field (indoor), volleyball. **On-Campus Highlights:** Java Wally's (Wallace Library coffee sho, Student Life Center/Field House/Ice Aren, ESPN Zone @ RIT Student Alumni Union, Ben and Jerry's (RIT Student Alumni Uni, The Cafe and Market at Crossroads.

ACCOMMODATIONS

Allowed in exams:	
Calculators	Yes
Dictionary	Yes
Computer	Yes
Spell-checker	Yes
Extended test time	Yes
Scribe	Yes
Proctors	Yes
Oral exams	Yes
Note-takers	Yes
Support services for students with	
LD	Yes
ADHD	Yes
ASD	Yes
Distraction-reduced environment	Yes
Recording of lecture allowed	Yes
Reading technology:	Yes
Audio books	Yes
Other assistive technology	Yes
Priority registration	Yes
Added costs for services:	
For LD:	No
For ADHD:	No
For ASD:	No
LD specialists	Yes
ADHD & ASD coaching	Yes
ASD specialists	Yes
Professional tutors	No
Peer tutors	Yes
Max. hours/week for services	Varies
How professors are notified of student approved accommodations	Director

COLLEGE GRADUATION REQUIREMENTS

Course waivers allowed	No
Course substitutions allowed	No
In what courses	
This is rarely requested but a discussion could be entertained.	

St. Bonaventure University

3261 WEST STATE ROAD, ST. BONAVENTURE, NY 14778 • ADMISSIONS: 716-375-2434 • FAX: 716-375-4005

CAMPUS
Type of school	Private (nonprofit)
Environment	Village
Support	S

STUDENTS
Undergrad enrollment	1,597
% male/female	52/48
% from out of state	32
% frosh live on campus	97

FINANCIAL FACTS
Annual tuition	$33,336
Room and board	$13,055
Required fees	$965

GENERAL ADMISSIONS INFO
Priority deadline	2/15
Regular application deadline	7/30

Nonfall registration accepted. Admission may be deferred for a maximum of 1 year.

Range SAT EBRW	510–610
Range SAT Math	510–610
Range ACT Composite	21–27

ACADEMICS
Student/faculty ratio	12:1
% students returning for sophomore year	84
% students graduating within 4 years	59
% students graduating within 6 years	69

Most classes have 20–29 students.
Most lab/discussion sessions have 10–19 students.

PROGRAMS/SERVICES FOR STUDENTS WITH LEARNING DIFFERENCES

St. Bonaventure University makes reasonable accommodations for otherwise qualified students with disabilities. Specific accommodations are arranged individually with each student depending upon the type and extent of the disability.. It is expected that a student with a disability, with appropriate accommodations, will be able to meet the basic requirements of a liberal arts education. The Coordinator of Disability Support Services (DSS) does not diagnose disabilities and students are required to provide appropriate documentation to be eligible for accommodations.. Students meet with the Coordinator of DSS to arrange accommodations each semester and students deliver accommodation letters to professors after accommodations have been arranged.

ADMISSIONS

St. Bonaventure University, has a rolling admissions policy and review applications throughout the year. SBU evaluates the highest sub scores for each test and uses highest test score for the admission. Other considerations include a personal essay and additional recommendations. There is not a formula to determine admissibility to St. Bonaventure University. The admission committee reviews each applicant's qualifications individually, considering a variety of characteristics that indicate academic preparation and potential for success. and look carefully at applicants who have achieved academic success in high school and those who have demonstrated significant promise but have yet to show the world their full potential. An average GPA is 90% and average ACT 25 or SAT 1135.

Additional Information

Students with LD may obtain assistance with assessing learning strengths and weaknesses and consult one-on-one or in groups to acquire a greater command of a subject, get help with a specific assignment, or discuss academic challenges. Services might include, but are not limited to: alternative testing arrangements, taped texts and classes, access to word processors/spellchecker, note-takers, tutors, peer mentors,

ADMISSIONS INFO FOR STUDENTS WITH LEARNING DIFFERENCES

SAT/ACT required: Yes
Interview required: No
Essay required: No
Additional application required: Not Applicable
Documentation required for:
  LD: Psycho ed evaluation to include: relevant historical info, instructional interventions, related services, age diagnosed, objective data (aptitude, achievement, info processing), test scores (standard, percentile and grade equivalents) and describe functional limitations
  ADHD: Diagnosis based on DSM-V; history of behaviors impairing functioning in academic setting; diagnostic interview; history of symptoms; evidence of ongoing behaviors.
  ASD: Psycho ed evaluation
Documentation submitted to: Disability Support Services
Special Ed. HS course work accepted: Yes
Separate application required for prográm services: No
# of students last year receiving services/accommodations for:
  LD: 50-100
Contact Information
Name of program or department: Disability Support Services
Telephone: 716-375-2065
Fax: 716-375-2071

time management and study skills training, and weekly individual appointments. Assistance can be offered in requesting books on tape. Tutoring services are available to all students and are not intended to be a substitute for independent study or preparation.

GENERAL ADMISSIONS

Very important factors considered include: rigor of secondary school record, academic GPA, recommendation(s), character/personal qualities. *Important factors considered include:* application essay, standardized test scores, extracurricular activities, talent/ability, volunteer work. *Other factors considered include:* class rank, interview, first generation, alumni/ae relation, geographical residence, state residency, work experience, level of applicant's interest. *Freshman Admission Requirements:* High school diploma is required and GED is accepted. *Academic units recommended:* 4 English, 3 math, 3 science, 3 science labs, 2 foreign language, 4 social studies.

ACCOMMODATION OR SERVICES

Accommodations are decided upon an individual basis after a thorough review of appropriate, current documentation. The accommodations requests must be supported through the documentation provided and must be logically linked to the current impact of the condition on academic functioning.

FINANCIAL AID

Students should submit: FAFSA; State aid form. Applicants will be notified of awards on a rolling basis beginning 3/1. The Princeton Review suggests that all financial aid forms be submitted as soon as possible after October 1. *Need-based scholarships/grants offered:* College/university scholarship or grant aid from institutional funds; Federal Pell; Private scholarships; SEOG; State scholarships/grants. *Loan aid offered:* Direct PLUS loans; Direct Subsidized Stafford Loans; Direct Unsubsidized Stafford Loans. Federal Work-Study Program available. Institutional employment available.

CAMPUS LIFE

Activities: Campus Ministries; Choral groups; Concert band; Dance; Drama/theater; International Student Organization; Jazz band; Literary magazine; Model UN; Music ensembles; Radio station; Student government; Student newspaper; Television station; Yearbook. **Organizations:** 47 registered organizations, 7 honor societies, 6 religious organizations. **Athletics (Intercollegiate):** *Men:* baseball, basketball, cross-country, diving, golf, soccer, swimming, tennis. *Women:* basketball, cross-country, diving, lacrosse, soccer, softball, swimming, tennis. **On-Campus Highlights:** Reilly Center, Richter Center, Quick Arts Center, Swan Business Center, Golf Course and Clubhouse.

ACCOMMODATIONS

Allowed in exams:	
Calculators	Yes
Dictionary	Yes
Computer	Yes
Spell-checker	Yes
Extended test time	Yes
Scribe	Yes
Proctors	Yes
Oral exams	Yes
Note-takers	Yes
Support services for students with	
LD	Yes
ADHD	Yes
ASD	Yes
Distraction-reduced environment	Yes
Recording of lecture allowed	Yes
Reading technology:	Yes
Audio books	Yes
Other assistive technology	Yes
Priority registration	No
Added costs for services:	
For LD:	No
For ADHD:	No
For ASD:	No
LD specialists	No
ADHD & ASD coaching	No
ASD specialists	No
Professional tutors	Yes
Peer tutors	Yes
Max. hours/week for services	Varies
How professors are notified of student approved accommodations	Student

COLLEGE GRADUATION REQUIREMENTS

Course waivers allowed	No
Course substitutions allowed	Yes
In what courses	Foreign Language

St. Lawrence University

23 ROMODA DRIVE, CANTON, NY 13617 • ADMISSIONS: 315-229-5261 • FAX: 315-229-5818

CAMPUS

Type of school	Private (nonprofit)
Environment	Village
Support	S

STUDENTS

Undergrad enrollment	2,373
% male/female	44/56
% from out of state	60
% frosh live on campus	100

FINANCIAL FACTS

Annual tuition	$50,830
Room and board	$13,190
Required fees	$370

GENERAL ADMISSIONS INFO

Application fee	$60
Regular application deadline	2/1

Nonfall registration accepted. Admission may be deferred for a maximum of 1 year.

Range SAT EBRW	590–680
Range SAT Math	580–675
Range ACT Composite	25–30

ACADEMICS

Student/faculty ratio	11:1
% students returning for sophomore year	92
% students graduating within 4 years	82
% students graduating within 6 years	85

Most classes have 10–19 students.
Most lab/discussion sessions have 10–19 students.

PROGRAMS/SERVICES FOR STUDENTS WITH LEARNING DIFFERENCES

The Disability and Accessibility Services Office provides information regarding support services at St. Lawrence University. Every effort is made to individually and appropriately serve students to enable them to attain success and reach their goals. The staff is made up of three professionals who provide a wide range of support services and accommodations for students with disabilities. Students must identify themselves as having a disability. Each student must provide appropriate documentation that clearly supports the disability and specifically recommends accommodations that relate specifically to the manifestations of the individual's condition. The accommodations assigned to each student are made on case-by-case basis.

ADMISSIONS

Students with disabilities operate through the same admissions process and criteria as the general applicant body. An interview is recommended and can be done off campus with an alumni representative. Counselor and 2 teacher recommendations.

Additional Information

Students need to be self-starters (to seek out the service early and follow through). As soon as possible, students should provide the official documents that describe the learning disability, the office helps develop the IEP—and notify the professors about the learning disability. Academic requirements required for graduation are waived. Services and accommodations are available for undergraduate and graduate students.

ADMISSIONS INFO FOR STUDENTS WITH LEARNING DIFFERENCES

SAT/ACT required: Optional
Interview required: Not Applicable
Essay required: Not Applicable
Additional application required: No
Documentation required for:
  LD: Documentation requirements to received accommodations from the Disability and Accessibility Services Office are made on a case-by-case basis.
  ADHD: Documentation requirements to received accommodations from the Disability and Accessibility Services Office are made on a case-by-case basis.
  ASD: Documentation requirements to received accommodations from the Disability and Accessibility Services Office are made on a case-by-case basis.
Documentation submitted to: Support Program/Services
Special Ed. HS course work accepted: Not Applicable
Separate application required for program services: No
Contact Information
Name of program or department: Disability and Accessibility Services
Telephone: 315-229-5678

St. Lawrence University

GENERAL ADMISSIONS
Very important factors considered include: rigor of secondary school record, academic GPA, application essay, recommendation(s), character/personal qualities. *Important factors considered include:* class rank, interview, extracurricular activities, racial/ethnic status. *Other factors considered include:* standardized test scores, talent/ability, first generation, alumni/ae relation, geographical residence, volunteer work, work experience, level of applicant's interest. *Freshman Admission Requirements:* High school diploma is required and GED is accepted. *Academic units recommended:* 4 English, 4 math, 4 science, 4 foreign language, 2 social studies, 2 history.

ACCOMMODATION OR SERVICES
Accommodations are decided upon an individual basis after a thorough review of appropriate, current documentation. The accommodations requests must be supported through the documentation provided and must be logically linked to the current impact of the condition on academic functioning.

FINANCIAL AID
Students should submit: FAFSA. The Princeton Review suggests that all financial aid forms be submitted as soon as possible after October 1. *Need-based scholarships/grants offered:* College/university scholarship or grant aid from institutional funds; Federal Pell; Private scholarships; SEOG; State scholarships/grants. *Loan aid offered:* Direct PLUS loans; Direct Subsidized Stafford Loans; Direct Unsubsidized Stafford Loans. Federal Work-Study Program available. Institutional employment available.

CAMPUS LIFE
Activities: Campus Ministries; Choral groups; Concert band; Dance; Drama/theater; International Student Organization; Jazz band; Literary magazine; Model UN; Music ensembles; Radio station; Student government; Student newspaper; Student-run film society; Yearbook. **Organizations:** 117 registered organizations, 22 honor societies, 4 religious organizations. 2 fraternities, 4 sororities. **Athletics (Intercollegiate):** *Men:* baseball, basketball, crew/rowing, cross-country, equestrian sports, football, golf, ice hockey, lacrosse, skiing (downhill/alpine), skiing (nordic/cross-country), soccer, squash, swimming, tennis, track/field (outdoor), track/field (indoor). *Women:* basketball, crew/rowing, cross-country, equestrian sports, field hockey, golf, ice hockey, lacrosse, skiing (downhill/alpine), skiing (nordic/cross-country), soccer, softball, squash, swimming, tennis, track/field (outdoor), track/field (indoor), volleyball. **On-Campus Highlights:** Newell Field House & Stafford Fitness Center, Brewer Bookstore, Johnson Hall of Science, Owen D. Young Library, Sullivan Student Center.

ACCOMMODATIONS

Allowed in exams:

Calculators	Yes
Dictionary	No
Computer	Yes
Spell-checker	Yes
Extended test time	Yes
Scribe	Yes
Proctors	Yes
Oral exams	Yes
Note-takers	Yes

Support services for students with

LD	Yes
ADHD	Yes
ASD	Yes
Distraction-reduced environment	Yes
Recording of lecture allowed	Yes
Reading technology:	Yes
Audio books	Yes
Other assistive technology	Yes
Priority registration	No

Added costs for services:

For LD:	No
For ADHD:	No
For ASD:	No
LD specialists	Yes
ADHD & ASD coaching	No
ASD specialists	No
Professional tutors	Yes
Peer tutors	Yes
Max. hours/week for services	Varies
How professors are notified of student approved accommodations	Student

COLLEGE GRADUATION REQUIREMENTS

Course waivers allowed	No
Course substitutions allowed	No

St. Thomas Aquinas College

125 Route 340, Sparkill, NY 10976 • Admissions: 845-398-4100 • Fax: 845-398-4372

CAMPUS

Type of school	Private (nonprofit)
Environment	Village
Support	SP

STUDENTS

Undergrad enrollment	1,114
% male/female	49/51
% from out of state	21
% frosh live on campus	73

FINANCIAL FACTS

Annual tuition	$29,950
Room and board	$12,750
Required fees	$800

GENERAL ADMISSIONS INFO

Application fee	$30

Nonfall registration accepted. Admission may be deferred for a maximum of one year.

Range SAT EBRW	440–560
Range SAT Math	440–550
Range ACT Composite	17–23

ACADEMICS

Student/faculty ratio	12:1
% students returning for sophomore year	74

Most classes have 10–19 students.
Most lab/discussion sessions have 10–19 students.

PROGRAMS/SERVICES FOR STUDENTS WITH LEARNING DIFFERENCES

The mission of Pathways is to facilitate the academic performance of bright college students with LD and ADHD so that they may demonstrate their knowledge and abilities. Pathways has an individualized and interpersonal emphasis, and program services are comprehensive and specialized. We focus on the development of effective learning strategies and attitudes by working with students and educating them about their specific needs and abilities. The aim is to break the pattern of helplessness often created in students with learning differences, foster a spirit of active learning, teach students to maximize strengths in order to compensate for weaknesses, and inspire self-confidence and self-efficacy. At the heart of the program are mentoring sessions. Students meet twice weekly with a professional mentor in one-to-one sessions tailored to meet specific needs. Mentors are not tutors, but guides who help students develop learning strategies, improve organizational and study skills, assist with editing, understand course concepts, and negotiate academic life.

ADMISSIONS

Applicants to Pathways must submit the general application to STAC and the Pathways application. If the College accepts the student into STAC then, the Pathways staff will formally review the application materials submitted directly to Pathways. If a student is eligible for admission to Pathways, a personal interview will be scheduled. typically in January through March. Within a week of the interview, a decision about admission to Pathways will be sent by mail. The Pathways Program is for students with select learning disabilities. ACT or SAT required. for admission plus one letter of recommendation and essay.

Additional Information

Students meet twice weekly with a Pathway professional mentor in one-to-one sessions tailored to meet specific needs. Mentors are not tutors, but guides who help students develop learning strategies, improve organizational and study skills, assist with editing, understand course concepts, and negotiate academic life. Pathways also provides seminars, workshops, and study groups tailored to meet students' needs, academic counseling, course advisement, and priority registration, and a specialized summer program prior to the first semester at STAC. Only those students who apply and have been accepted and

ADMISSIONS INFO FOR STUDENTS WITH LEARNING DIFFERENCES

SAT/ACT required: Yes
Interview required: Yes
Essay required: Yes
Additional application required: Yes for Pathways Program
Documentation required for:
  LD: Within three years: Adult intelligence test (WAIS-IV); full educational evaluation; report describing impact of disability on student's current functioning.
  ADHD: Same as LD documentation, plus documentation of ADHD by an appropriate professional
  ASD: Psycho ed evaluation
Documentation submitted to: Disability Services-Pathways
Special Ed. HS course work accepted: No
Contact Information
Name of program or department: Disability Services-Pathways
Telephone: 845-398-4230
Fax: 845-398-4229

St. Thomas Aquinas College

enroll in Pathways may access these services. Certain accommodations for students with ILD may be available through the college without charge through the Committee for Academic Accommodations of Disabilities.

General Admissions

Very important factors considered include: rigor of secondary school record. *Important factors considered include:* standardized test scores, recommendation(s), interview, extracurricular activities, talent/ability. *Other factors considered include:* academic GPA, application essay, alumni/ae relation, volunteer work, work experience, level of applicant's interest. *Freshman Admission Requirements:* High school diploma is required and GED is accepted. *Academic units required:* 4 English, 3 math, 3 science, 2 science labs, 3 foreign language, 4 social studies.

Accommodation or Services

Accommodations are decided upon an individual basis after a thorough review of appropriate, current documentation. The accommodations requests must be supported through the documentation provided and must be logically linked to the current impact of the condition on academic functioning.

Financial Aid

Students should submit: FAFSA. Applicants will be notified of awards on a rolling basis beginning 11/1. The Princeton Review suggests that all financial aid forms be submitted as soon as possible after October 1. *Need-based scholarships/grants offered:* College/university scholarship or grant aid from institutional funds; Federal Pell; Private scholarships; SEOG; State scholarships/grants. *Loan aid offered:* Direct PLUS loans; Direct Subsidized Stafford Loans; Direct Unsubsidized Stafford Loans. Federal Work-Study Program available. Institutional employment available.

Campus Life

Activities: Campus Ministries; Choral groups; Concert band; Dance; Drama/theater; Literary magazine; Music ensembles; Musical theater; Radio station; Student government; Student newspaper; Yearbook. **Organizations:** 35 registered organizations, 8 honor societies, 1 religious organization. **Athletics (Intercollegiate):** *Men:* baseball, basketball, cross-country, golf, soccer, tennis, track/field (outdoor), track/field (indoor). *Women:* basketball, cross-country, lacrosse, soccer, softball, tennis, track/field (outdoor). **On-Campus Highlights:** The College Commons, The Kraus Fitness Center, The Romano Alumni Center, The Art Gallery, The Techonology Corridor.

ACCOMMODATIONS

Allowed in exams:

Calculators	Yes
Dictionary	Not Applicable
Computer	Yes
Spell-checker	Yes
Extended test time	Yes
Scribe	Yes
Proctors	Yes
Oral exams	Not Applicable
Note-takers	Yes

Support services for students with

LD	Yes
ADHD	Yes
ASD	Yes
Distraction-reduced environment	Yes
Recording of lecture allowed	Yes
Reading technology:	Yes
Audio books	Yes
Other assistive technology	No
Priority registration	Yes

Added costs for services:

For LD:	No
For ADHD:	No
For ASD:	No
LD specialists	Yes
ADHD & ASD coaching	No
ASD specialists	Yes
Professional tutors	Yes
Peer tutors	No
Max. hours/week for services	Varies

How professors are notified of student approved accommodations   Student

COLLEGE GRADUATION REQUIREMENTS

Course waivers allowed	No
Course substitutions allowed	Yes

In what coursesForeign Language; Speech; Math (only when math is not a requirement of the major)

State University of New York at Binghamton

PO Box 6000, Binghamton, NY 13902-6001 • Admissions: 607-777-2171 • Fax: 607-777-4445

CAMPUS
Type of school	Public
Environment	City
Support	S

STUDENTS
Undergrad enrollment	13,693
% male/female	51/49
% from out of state	7
% frosh live on campus	98

FINANCIAL FACTS
Annual in-state tuition	$6,870
Annual out-of-state tuition	$21,550
Room and board	$15,058
Required fees	$2,938

GENERAL ADMISSIONS INFO
Application fee	$50
Priority deadline	1/15

Nonfall registration accepted. Admission may be deferred for a maximum of 1 year.

Range SAT EBRW	640–711
Range SAT Math	650–720
Range ACT Composite	28–31

ACADEMICS
Student/faculty ratio	19:1
% students returning for sophomore year	91
% students graduating within 4 years	73
% students graduating within 6 years	82

Most classes have 10–19 students.
Most lab/discussion sessions have 10–19 students.

PROGRAMS/SERVICES FOR STUDENTS WITH LEARNING DIFFERENCES

Services for Students with Disabilities (SSD) provides a wide range of assistance to enrolled students with learning or other disabilities. The office is part of the Division of Student Affairs and interfaces with offices and departments throughout the University. Students who register with the office interact with a dedicated staff who partner with them in the determination and arrangement of reasonable accommodations and support services designed to facilitate their university involvement and academic success. Student Support Services, promotes academic success and personal growth for students with disabilities. Through this innovative practices and programming, students are able to achieve their goals and enrich their college experiences.

ADMISSIONS

Binghamton University welcomes applications from all qualified individuals. While there are no special admissions procedures or academic programs expressly for students with disabilities, the Services for Students with Disabilities Office provides a wide range of support services to enrolled students. Diagnostic tests are not required for admissions, but students are encouraged to meet with the director of Services for Students with Disabilities and provide documentation to determine appropriate accommodations. Through nonmatriculated enrollment, students can take courses but are not enrolled in a degree program. If they do well, they may then apply for matriculation, using credits earned toward their degree. General admission criteria includes 4 years of English, 2.5 years of math, 2 years of social science, 2 years of science, and 2 years of 2 foreign languages or 3 years of 1 foreign language. The mid 50 percent score range on the SAT is 1100–1330.

Additional Information

Incoming Binghamton University students who have been invited to join Student Support Services are eligible to attend the summer program called S4P. This summer program is an opportunity for the university to welcome students to SSS and to help prepare for transition to Binghamton

ADMISSIONS INFO FOR STUDENTS WITH LEARNING DIFFERENCES

SAT/ACT required: Yes
Interview required: No
Essay required: Not Applicable
Additional application required: Yes
Documentation required for:
  LD: No documentation / diagnostic testing is required for admission to Binghamton University, however guidelines for LD admission are available at the SSD website http://binghamton.edu/ssd/new-students/disability-documentation-guidelines.html
  ADHD: No documentation is required for admission to Binghamton University, however guidelines for ADHD admission are available at the SSD websitehttp://binghamton.edu/ssd/new-students/disability-documentation-guidelines.html
  ASD: There are no requirements for documentation for ASD in order to be admitted to Binghamton University
Documentation submitted to: SSD
Special Ed. HS course work accepted: Not Applicable
Separate application required for program services: Yes
Contact Information
Name of program or department: SSD
Telephone: 607-777-2686
Fax: 607-777-6893
Email: ssd@binghamton.edu

State University of New York at Binghamton

University. S4P runs for four weeks in conjunction with Binghamton University's Summer Session Term II. Student Support Services provides free tutoring support for all of its program participants in a number of different subjects on a drop-in or appointment basis.

GENERAL ADMISSIONS

Very important factors considered include: rigor of secondary school record, academic GPA, standardized test scores. *Important factors considered include:* class rank, application essay, recommendation(s), extracurricular activities. *Other factors considered include:* talent/ability, character/personal qualities, first generation, alumni/ae relation, geographical residence, state residency, racial/ethnic status, volunteer work, work experience, level of applicant's interest. *Freshman Admission Requirements:* High school diploma is required and GED is accepted. *Academic units required:* 4 English, 3 math, 2 science, 3 foreign language, 2 social studies. *Academic units recommended:* 4 math, 4 science, 4 social studies, 4 history.

ACCOMMODATION OR SERVICES

Accommodations are decided upon an individual basis after a thorough review of appropriate, current documentation. The accommodations requests must be supported through the documentation provided and must be logically linked to the current impact of the condition on academic functioning.

FINANCIAL AID

Students should submit: FAFSA; State aid form. Applicants will be notified of awards on a rolling basis beginning 1/31. The Princeton Review suggests that all financial aid forms be submitted as soon as possible after October 1. *Need-based scholarships/grants offered:* College/university scholarship or grant aid from institutional funds; Federal Pell; Private scholarships; SEOG; State scholarships/grants. *Loan aid offered:* Direct PLUS loans; Direct Subsidized Stafford Loans; Direct Unsubsidized Stafford Loans. Federal Work-Study Program available. Institutional employment available.

CAMPUS LIFE

Activities: Campus Ministries; Choral groups; Concert band; Dance; Drama/theater; International Student Organization; Jazz band; Literary magazine; Model UN; Music ensembles; Musical theater; Opera; Radio station; Student government; Student newspaper; Student-run film society; Symphony orchestra; Television station; Yearbook. **Organizations:** 23 honor societies, 15 religious organizations. 23 fraternities, 23 sororities. **Athletics (Intercollegiate):** *Men:* baseball, basketball, cross-country, diving, golf, lacrosse, soccer, swimming, tennis, track/field (outdoor), track/field (indoor), wrestling. *Women:* basketball, cross-country, diving, lacrosse, soccer, softball, swimming, tennis, track/field (outdoor), track/field (indoor), volleyball. **On-Campus Highlights:** Union (The MarketPlace, Late Nite Binghamton, bookstore), FitSpace, Events Center (concerts, basketball, special events), Indoor/Outdoor Performing Arts Center, Nature Preserve.

ACCOMMODATIONS

Allowed in exams:	
Calculators	Yes
Dictionary	No
Computer	Yes
Spell-checker	No
Extended test time	Yes
Scribe	Yes
Proctors	Yes
Oral exams	Not Applicable
Note-takers	Yes
Support services for students with	
LD	Yes
ADHD	Yes
ASD	Yes
Distraction-reduced environment	Yes
Recording of lecture allowed	Yes
Reading technology:	Yes
Audio books	Yes
Other assistive technology	Yes
Priority registration	No
Added costs for services:	
For LD:	No
For ADHD:	No
For ASD:	No
LD specialists	Yes
ADHD & ASD coaching	No
ASD specialists	Yes
Professional tutors	No
Peer tutors	Not Applicable
Max. hours/week for services	Varies
How professors are notified of student approved accommodations	Student

COLLEGE GRADUATION REQUIREMENTS

Course waivers allowed	No
Course substitutions allowed	Yes
In what courses	
Foreign Language on a case by case basis	

Farmingdale State College

2350 Broadhollow Rd, Farmingdale, NY 11735 • Admissions: 631-420-2200 • Fax: 631-420-2633

CAMPUS

Type of school	Public
Environment	Village
Support	S

STUDENTS

Undergrad enrollment	9,005
% male/female	57/43
% from out of state	0
% frosh live on campus	15

FINANCIAL FACTS

Annual in-state tuition	$6,670
Annual out-of-state tuition	$16,320
Room and board	$12,892
Required fees	$1,406

GENERAL ADMISSIONS INFO

Application fee	$50
Priority deadline	1/1
Regular application deadline	5/1

Nonfall registration accepted. Admission may be deferred for a maximum of 1 year.

Range SAT EBRW	490–570
Range SAT Math	490–570
Range ACT Composite	19–23

ACADEMICS

Student/faculty ratio	20:1
% students returning for sophomore year	83
% students graduating within 4 years	29
% students graduating within 6 years	53

Most classes have 10–19 students.
Most lab/discussion sessions have 20–29 students.

PROGRAMS/SERVICES FOR STUDENTS WITH LEARNING DIFFERENCES

There is no learning disabilities program at the college, but the Disability Services Center is dedicated to the principle that equal opportunity to realize one's full potential should be available to all students. In keeping with this philosophy, the staff offers services to students with disabilities in accordance with their needs. Students may be able to meet individually with a learning disability specialist or in group meetings. Services include academic remediation with emphasis on compensatory strategies, study skills strategies training, test accommodations, time management instruction, tutoring, and self-understanding of disability. The services offered strive to instill independence, self-confidence, and self-advocacy skills.

ADMISSIONS

Typical applicants should have an 85% GPA (subject to change based on specific majors;) SAT: Combined score of 1010 between the Critical Reading and Math or ACT: Composite score of 21. Letters of recommendation, resumes and personal statements are not required, but are encouraged for admission.

Additional Information

Services and accommodations available with appropriate documentation may include extended testing times; distraction-free environments; use of calculators, computers, and spellchecker; note-takers; scribes; proctors; assistive technology; tutors; and recording in classes. ASD includes autism, Asperger Syndrome, and pervasive developmental disorder. Documentation must be within three years and appropriate to establishing eligibility for services to include:Written statement of diagnosis, names of the assessment instrument(s) used and scores, social and developmental history information,Information specifying current level of receptive, expressive and pragmatic communication skills, current medications, side effects and impact on academic performance, and any impact of executive functioning skills.

ADMISSIONS INFO FOR STUDENTS WITH LEARNING DIFFERENCES

SAT/ACT required: Yes
Interview required: Yes
Essay required: No
Additional application required: No
Documentation required for:
 LD: Psycho ed evaluation to include: relevant historical info, instructional interventions, related services, age diagnosed, objective data (aptitude, achievement, info processing), test scores (standard, percentile and grade equivalents) and describe functional limitations.
 ADHD: Diagnosis based on DSM-V; history of behaviors impairing functioning in academic setting; diagnostic interview; history of symptoms; evidence of ongoing behaviors.
 ASD: Psycho educational evaluation
Documentation submitted to: Disability Services Center (DSC)
Special Ed. HS course work accepted: Yes
Separate application required for program services: No
# of students last year receiving services/accommodations for:
 LD: 145-155
Contact Information
Name of program or department: Disability Services Center (DSC)
Telephone: 631-420-2411

Farmingdale State College

GENERAL ADMISSIONS

Very important factors considered include: academic GPA, standardized test scores. *Important factors considered include:* rigor of secondary school record, application essay, recommendation(s). *Other factors considered include:* interview, extracurricular activities, talent/ability, character/personal qualities, first generation, alumni/ae relation, volunteer work, work experience, level of applicant's interest. *Freshman Admission Requirements:* High school diploma is required and GED is accepted. *Academic units required:* 4 English, 3 math, 3 science, 4 social studies. *Academic units recommended:* 1 foreign language.

ACCOMMODATION OR SERVICES

Accommodations are decided upon an individual basis after a thorough review of appropriate, current documentation. The accommodations requests must be supported through the documentation provided and must be logically linked to the current impact of the condition on academic functioning.

FINANCIAL AID

Students should submit: FAFSA. Applicants will be notified of awards on a rolling basis beginning 3/1. The Princeton Review suggests that all financial aid forms be submitted as soon as possible after October 1. *Need-based scholarships/grants offered:* College/university scholarship or grant aid from institutional funds; Federal Pell; Private scholarships; SEOG; State scholarships/grants. *Loan aid offered:* Direct PLUS loans; Direct Subsidized Stafford Loans; Direct Unsubsidized Stafford Loans. Federal Work-Study Program available. Institutional employment available.

CAMPUS LIFE

Activities: Dance; Drama/theater; International Student Organization; Model UN; Musical theater; Radio station; Student government; Student newspaper; Yearbook. **Organizations: Athletics (Intercollegiate):** *Men:* baseball, basketball, cross-country, golf, lacrosse, soccer, track/field (outdoor), track/field (indoor). *Women:* basketball, cross-country, soccer, softball, track/field (outdoor), track/field (indoor), volleyball. Campus Center, Memorial Gallery Hale Hall, Ornamental Horticulture Teaching Gardens, Nold Hall Athletic Facility, Greenley Library.

ACCOMMODATIONS

Allowed in exams:	
Calculators	Yes
Dictionary	No
Computer	Yes
Spell-checker	Yes
Extended test time	Yes
Scribe	Yes
Proctors	Yes
Oral exams	Yes
Note-takers	Yes
Support services for students with	
LD	Yes
ADHD	Yes
ASD	Yes
Distraction-reduced environment	Yes
Recording of lecture allowed	Yes
Reading technology:	Yes
Audio books	Yes
Other assistive technology	Yes
Priority registration	No
Added costs for services:	
For LD:	No
For ADHD:	No
For ASD:	No
LD specialists	Yes
ADHD & ASD coaching	Yes
ASD specialists	No
Professional tutors	No
Peer tutors	Yes
Max. hours/week for services	Unlimited
How professors are notified of student approved accommodations	Student

COLLEGE GRADUATION REQUIREMENTS

Course waivers allowed	No
Course substitutions allowed	Yes
In what courses	Foreign language

State University of New York—Alfred State College

10 Upper College Drive, Alfred, NY 14802 • Admissions: 607-587-4215 • Fax: 607-587-4299

CAMPUS
Type of school	Public
Environment	Rural
Support	CS

STUDENTS
Undergrad enrollment	3,665
% male/female	64/36
% from out of state	4
% frosh live on campus	85

FINANCIAL FACTS
Annual in-state tuition	$6,670
Annual out-of-state tuition	$9,740
Room and board	$12,250
Required fees	$1,657

GENERAL ADMISSIONS INFO
Application fee	$50

Nonfall registration accepted. Admission may be deferred.

Range SAT EBRW	470–560
Range SAT Math	470–570
Range ACT Composite	19–25

ACADEMICS
Student/faculty ratio	18:1
% students returning for sophomore year	65
students graduating within 4 years	37
students graduating within 6 years	51

Most classes have fewer than 10 students. Most lab/discussion sessions have 20-29 students.

PROGRAMS/SERVICES FOR STUDENTS WITH LEARNING DIFFERENCES
Alfred State welcomes all students who meet our admissions criteria, regardless of disability status. When applying, the admissions staff do not include a disability status in the decision making. Students with documented disabilities are highly encouraged to to self disclose and submit appropriate documentation to the Student Disabilities Services office regardless of possible declassification during the K-12 process. Appropriate documentation includes Psychological Evaluations and/or medical documentation. IEP's are not accepted as a stand-alone document to determine eligibility for services. Appropriate accommodations are determined on an individual basis and are based upon the submitted documentation and subsequent discussion with the student.

ADMISSIONS
Admissions criteria do not vary regardless of a documented learning difference. Assistance is available for those students who need it, upon request.

Additional Information
The Educational Opportunity Program at Alfred State College offers opportunites to high school graduate or the equivalent who do not meet normally applied admission criteria but who have the potential for college success. The program features tutoring, counseling, and special grants in the service of retention and degree completion. There is also a Summer Prep Academy for incoming students allowing them to become acclimated to campus, set up their living arrangements, and structure their support resources and strategies without the stress of classes.

ADMISSIONS INFO FOR STUDENTS WITH LEARNING DIFFERENCES
SAT/ACT required: No
Interview required: No
Essay required: Recommended
Additional application required: No
Documentation required for:
  LD: Psychological evaluation
  ADHD: Psychological evaluation and/or medical documentation outlining functional limitations of student
  ASD: Psychological evaluation and/or medical documentation outlining functional limitations of student
Documentation submitted to: Office of Special Academic Services
Special Ed. HS course work accepted: Yes
Separate application required for program services: No
# of students last year receiving services/accommodations for:
  LD: 191
  ADHD: 70
  ASD: 26
Contact Information
Name of program or department: Office of Special Academic Services
Telephone: 607-587-4506

State University of New York—Alfred State College

GENERAL ADMISSIONS

Very important factors considered include: rigor of secondary school record, academic GPA, standardized test scores. *Other factors considered include:* application essay, recommendation(s), interview, extracurricular activities, talent/ability, character/personal qualities, volunteer work, work experience, level of applicant's interest. *Freshman Admission Requirements:* High school diploma is required and GED is accepted

ACCOMMODATION OR SERVICES

Accommodations are decided upon an individual basis after a thorough review of appropriate, current documentation. The accommodations requests must be supported through the documentation provided and must be logically linked to the current impact of the condition on academic functioning.

FINANCIAL AID

Students should submit: FAFSA; State aid form. . The Princeton Review suggests that all financial aid forms be submitted as soon as possible after October 1. *Need-based scholarships/grants offered:* College/university scholarship or grant aid from institutional funds; Federal Pell; Private scholarships; SEOG; State scholarships/grants *Loan aid offered:* Direct PLUS loans; Direct Subsidized Stafford Loans; Direct Unsubsidized Stafford Loans Federal Work-Study Program available. Institutional employment available.

CAMPUS LIFE

Activities: Campus Ministries; Choral groups; Concert band ; Dance ; Drama/theater; International Student Organization; Jazz band; Literary magazine; Music ensembles; Musical theater; Pep band; Radio station ; Student government; Student newspaper; Symphony orchestra ; Yearbook Organizations: 60 registered organizations, 4 honor societies, 3 fraternities, 2 sororities, **Athletics (Intercollegiate):** *Men:* baseball, basketball, cheerleading, cross-country, football, lacrosse, soccer, swimming, track/field (outdoor), wrestling *Women:* basketball, cheerleading, cross-country, soccer, softball, swimming, track/field (outdoor), volleyball. **On-Campus Highlights:** Student Leadership Center, Orvis (Athletic Center), Pioneer Center, Central Dining Hall, Upperclassmen Apartment Suite Complex.

ACCOMMODATIONS

Allowed in exams:	
Calculators	Yes
Dictionary	Yes
Computer	Yes
Spell-checker	Yes
Extended test time	Yes
Scribe	Yes
Proctors	Yes
Oral exams	Yes
Note-takers	Yes
Support services for students with	
LD	Yes
ADHD	Yes
ASD	Yes
Distraction-reduced environment	Yes
Recording of lecture allowed	Yes
Reading technology:	Yes
Audio books	Yes
Other assistive technology	
Priority registration	Yes
Added costs for services:	
For LD:	No
For ADHD:	No
For ASD:	No
LD specialists	No
ADHD & ASD coaching	Yes
ASD specialists	Yes
Professional tutors	Yes
Peer tutors	Yes
Max. hours/week for services	15
How professors are notified of student approved accommodations	Director

COLLEGE GRADUATION REQUIREMENTS

Course waivers allowed	Yes
Course substitutions allowed	Yes

State University of New York—Potsdam

44 Pierrepont Avenue, Potsdam, NY 13676 • Admissions: 315-267-2180 • Fax: 315-267-2163

CAMPUS	
Type of school	Public
Environment	Village
Support	S

STUDENTS	
Undergrad enrollment	3,296
% male/female	42/58
% from out of state	4
% frosh live on campus	92

FINANCIAL FACTS	
Annual in-state tuition	$6,870
Annual out-of-state tuition	$16,650
Room and board	$13,295
Required fees	$1,593

GENERAL ADMISSIONS INFO

Application fee	$50

Nonfall registration accepted. Admission may be deferred for a maximum of 1 year.

Range SAT EBRW	500–600
Range SAT Math	500–590
Range ACT Composite	20–26

ACADEMICS

Student/faculty ratio	11:1
% students returning for sophomore year	75
% students graduating within 4 years	34
% students graduating within 6 years	53

Most classes have 20–29 students.

PROGRAMS/SERVICES FOR STUDENTS WITH LEARNING DIFFERENCES

The State University of New York College—Potsdam is committed to the full inclusion of all individuals who can benefit from educational opportunities. Accommodative Services provides academic accommodations for all qualified students who have documented learning, emotional, and/or physical disabilities and a need for accommodations. The ultimate goal is to promote individuals' independence within the academic atmosphere of the university. Students are assisted in this process by the support services and programs available to all Potsdam students. Students must submit (written) documentation of the disability and the need for accommodations. After forwarding documentation, students are encouraged to make an appointment to meet with the coordinator to discuss accommodations. All accommodations are determined on an individual basis. Accommodative Services makes every effort to ensure access to academic accommodations.

ADMISSIONS

In most cases the minimum GPA requirement is an 80 on a 0-100 scale or a 2.5 on a 4.0 scale. The average GPA is 88.2. However, students falling below these figures should speak with an Admissions Counselor before ruling out Potsdam. Courses recommended include 4 years English, 3 years mathematics, 3 years science, 4 years social science, 4 years foreign language and 1 year of fine or performing arts. The ACT/SAT is not required and the majority of applicants will NOT submit a test score unless applying for Mount Emmons Scholarship. Minimum scores for scholarship consideration are a 1300 SAT or a 29 ACT.

Additional Information

Accommodations available through Accommodative Services include note-takers; test readers/books on tape; alternative testing such as extended time and/or distraction-reduced environment, exam readers/scribes, and use of word processor with spellchecker; and lending of some equipment. Additional services can include special registration and academic advising. Accommodative Services will assist students

ADMISSIONS INFO FOR STUDENTS WITH LEARNING DIFFERENCES

SAT/ACT required: No
Interview required: No
Essay required: No
Additional application required: No
Documentation required for:
  LD: Psycho ed evaluation to include: relevant historical info, instructional interventions, related services, age diagnosed, objective data (aptitude, achievement, info processing), test scores (standard, percentile and grade equivalents) and describe functional limitations.
  ADHD: Diagnosis based on DSM-V; history of behaviors impairing functioning in academic setting; diagnostic interview; history of symptoms; evidence of ongoing behaviors.
  ASD: Psycho ed evaluation
Documentation submitted to: Accommodative Services
Special Ed. HS course work accepted: No
Separate application required for program services: No
# of students last year receiving services/accommodations for:
  LD: 45-50
Contact Information
Name of program or department: Accommodative Services
Telephone: 315-267-3267
Fax: 315-267-3268

State University of New York—Potsdam

requesting non-academic auxiliary aids or services in locating the appropriate campus resources to address the request. The College Counseling Center provides psychological services. The early warning system asks each instructor to indicate at midpoint in each semester if a student is making unsatisfactory academic progress. Results of this inquiry are sent to the student and advisor. Student Support Services provides academic support, peer mentoring, and counseling. Tutoring is available for all students one-on-one or in small

General Admissions

Important factors considered include: rigor of secondary school record, academic GPA, application essay, recommendation(s). *Other factors considered include:* standardized test scores, interview, extracurricular activities, talent/ability, character/personal qualities, volunteer work, work experience, level of applicant's interest. *Freshman Admission Requirements:* High school diploma is required and GED is accepted. *Academic units required:* 4 English, 4 social studies. *Academic units recommended:* 4 English, 3 math, 3 science, 3 foreign language, 4 social studies, 1 visual/performing arts.

Accommodation or Services

Accommodations are decided upon an individual basis after a thorough review of appropriate, current documentation. The accommodations requests must be supported through the documentation provided and must be logically linked to the current impact of the condition on academic functioning.

Financial Aid

Students should submit: FAFSA; State aid form. Applicants will be notified of awards on a rolling basis beginning 1/1. The Princeton Review suggests that all financial aid forms be submitted as soon as possible after October 1. *Need-based scholarships/grants offered:* College/university scholarship or grant aid from institutional funds; Federal Pell; Private scholarships; SEOG; State scholarships/grants. *Loan aid offered:* Direct PLUS loans; Direct Subsidized Stafford Loans; Direct Unsubsidized Stafford Loans. Federal Work-Study Program available. Institutional employment available.

Campus Life

Activities: Campus Ministries; Choral groups; Concert band; Dance; Drama/theater; International Student Organization; Jazz band; Literary magazine; Music ensembles; Musical theater; Opera; Pep band; Radio station; Student government; Student newspaper; Symphony orchestra. **Organizations:** 100 registered organizations, 17 honor societies, 3 religious organizations. 4 fraternities, 7 sororities. **Athletics (Intercollegiate):** *Men:* basketball, cross-country, diving, equestrian sports, golf, ice hockey, lacrosse, soccer, swimming *Women:* basketball, cross-country, diving, equestrian sports, ice hockey, lacrosse, soccer, softball, swimming, tennis, volleyball. **On-Campus Highlights:** Performing Arts Center, Maxcy Hall Athletic Complex, Barrington Student Union, The Art Museum at SUNY Potsdam, The Crane School of Music.

ACCOMMODATIONS

Allowed in exams:

Calculators	Yes
Dictionary	Yes
Computer	Yes
Spell-checker	Yes
Extended test time	Yes
Scribe	Yes
Proctors	Yes
Oral exams	Yes
Note-takers	Yes

Support services for students with

LD	Yes
ADHD	Yes
ASD	Yes
Distraction-reduced environment	Yes
Recording of lecture allowed	Yes
Reading technology:	Yes
Audio books	Yes
Other assistive technology	
Priority registration	Yes

Added costs for services:

For LD:	No
For ADHD:	No
For ASD:	No
LD specialists	No
ADHD & ASD coaching	No
ASD specialists	Yes
Professional tutors	Yes
Peer tutors	Yes
Max. hours/week for services	
How professors are notified of student approved accommodations	Director and student

COLLEGE GRADUATION REQUIREMENTS

Course waivers allowed	Yes
In what courses	Individually assessed
Course substitutions allowed	Yes
In what courses	Individually assessed

State University of New York—Stony Brook University

OFFICE OF ADMISSIONS, STONY BROOK, NY 11794-1901 • ADMISSIONS: 631-632-6868 • FAX: 631-632-9898

CAMPUS

Type of school	Public
Environment	Town
Support	CS

STUDENTS

Undergrad enrollment	17,215
% male/female	53/47
% from out of state	6
% frosh live on campus	83

FINANCIAL FACTS

Annual in-state tuition	$6,870
Annual out-of-state tuition	$24,540
Room and board	$13,698
Required fees	$2,755

GENERAL ADMISSIONS INFO

Application fee	$50
Priority deadline	1/15

Nonfall registration accepted. Admission may be deferred for a maximum of 2 semesters.

Range SAT EBRW	590–680
Range SAT Math	620–730
Range ACT Composite	26–31

ACADEMICS

Student/faculty ratio	18:1
% students returning for sophomore year	90
% students graduating within 4 years	53
% students graduating within 6 years	72

Most classes have 20–29 students. Most lab/discussion sessions have 20–29 students.

PROGRAMS/SERVICES FOR STUDENTS WITH LEARNING DIFFERENCES

Disability Support Services (DSS) coordinates advocacy and support services for students with disabilities. These services assist integrating students' needs with the resources available at the university to eliminate physical or programmatic barriers and ensure an accessible academic environment. All information and documentation of student disabilities is confidential. Students are responsible for identifying and documenting their disabilities through the DSS office. Students receive assistance with special housing and transportation, recruitment of readers, interpreters, note-takers, test accommodations, and counseling. A learning disabilities specialist is available to refer students for diagnostic testing and educational programming, meet accommodation needs, and provide in-service training to the university community. A Supported Education Program offering individual counseling and group sessions is available for students with psychological disabilities. Students who anticipate requiring assistance should contact Disability Support Services as early as possible to allow time for implementing recommended services.

ADMISSIONS

Admissions looks for a strong high school academic program that includes: 4 years English, 4 years social studies, 3 years math (4 units required for engineering and applied sciences), 3 years science (4 units required for engineering and applied sciences), and 2-3 years foreign language. ACT/SAT required but students do not need to take the writing Section. Students who show evidence of leadership, special talents or interests, and other personal qualities through extracurricular activities, volunteer work, and other non-academic pursuits will receive special consideration. Freshman applicants admitted to the University but not initially accepted into their major of choice may apply for admission into the major after satisfying the requirements.

Additional Information

Every semester the student should go to the DSS to meet with a counselor and fill out an accommodation request form to generate a letter to each professor that explains the accommodations. Types of

ADMISSIONS INFO FOR STUDENTS WITH LEARNING DIFFERENCES

SAT/ACT required: Yes
Interview required: No
Essay required: No
Additional application required: No
Documentation required for:
  LD: : Psycho ed evaluation to include: relevant historical info, instructional interventions, related services, age diagnosed, objective data (aptitude, achievement, info processing), test scores (standard, percentile and grade equivalents) and describe functional limitations.
  ADHD: Diagnosis based on DSM-V; history of behaviors impairing functioning in academic setting; diagnostic interview; history of symptoms; evidence of ongoing behaviors.
  ASD: Psycho ed evaluation
Documentation submitted to: Disability Support Services
Special Ed. HS course work accepted: No
Separate application required for program services: No
# of students last year receiving services/accommodations for:
  LD: 165
Contact Information
Name of program or department: Disability Support Services
Telephone: 631-632-6748
Fax: 631-632-6747
Email: dss@stonybrook.edu

State University of New York—Stony Brook University

services and accommodations available are pre-registration advisement, liaising with faculty and staff, taped texts, learning strategies and time management training, assistance in locating tutors, assistance in arranging for note-takers and readers, tutorial computer programs, proctoring and/or modified administration of exams, support groups, referrals to appropriate campus resources, peer advising, and aid in vocational decision making. Services and accommodations are available to undergraduate and graduate students. No skills classes are offered.

GENERAL ADMISSIONS

Very important factors considered include: rigor of secondary school record, academic GPA, standardized test scores. *Important factors considered include:* application essay, recommendation(s). *Other factors considered include:* class rank, interview, extracurricular activities, talent/ability, character/personal qualities, first generation, alumni/ae relation, geographical residence, state residency, volunteer work, work experience, level of applicant's interest. *Freshman Admission Requirements:* High school diploma is required and GED is accepted. *Academic units required:* 4 English, 4 math, 4 science, 4 social studies. *Academic units recommended:* 4 English, 4 math, 4 science, 3 foreign language, 4 social studies.

ACCOMMODATION OR SERVICES

Accommodations are decided upon an individual basis after a thorough review of appropriate, current documentation. The accommodations requests must be supported through the documentation provided and must be logically linked to the current impact of the condition on academic functioning.

FINANCIAL AID

Students should submit: FAFSA;; State aid form. Applicants will be notified of awards on a rolling basis beginning 4/1. The Princeton Review suggests that all financial aid forms be submitted as soon as possible after October 1. *Need-based scholarships/grants offered:* College/university scholarship or grant aid from institutional funds; Federal Pell; Private scholarships; SEOG; State scholarships/grants. *Loan aid offered:* Direct PLUS loans; Direct Subsidized Stafford Loans; Direct Unsubsidized Stafford Loans. Federal Work-Study Program available. Institutional employment available.

CAMPUS LIFE

Activities: Campus Ministries; Choral groups; Concert band; Dance; Drama/theater; International Student Organization; Jazz band; Literary magazine; Marching band; Model UN; Music ensembles; Musical theater; Opera; Pep band; Radio station; Student government; Student newspaper; Student-run film society; Symphony orchestra; Television station. **Organizations:** 292 registered organizations, 6 honor societies, 25 religious organizations. 17 fraternities, 16 sororities. **Athletics (Intercollegiate):** *Men:* baseball, basketball, cross-country, diving, football, lacrosse, soccer, swimming, tennis, track/field (outdoor), track/field (indoor). *Women:* basketball, cross-country, diving, lacrosse, soccer, softball, swimming, tennis, track/field (outdoor), track/field (indoor), volleyball. **On-Campus Highlights:** Staller Center for the Arts, Sports Complex and Lavalle Stadium, Student Activities Center, Walter J. Hawrys Campus Recreation Center, The Charles B. Wang Center.

ACCOMMODATIONS

Allowed in exams:	
Calculators	Yes
Dictionary	No
Computer	Yes
Spell-checker	Yes
Extended test time	Yes
Scribe	Yes
Proctors	Yes
Oral exams	No
Note-takers	Yes
Support services for students with	
LD	Yes
ADHD	Yes
ASD	Yes
Distraction-reduced environment	Yes
Recording of lecture allowed	Yes
Reading technology:	Yes
Audio books	Yes
Other assistive technology	Yes
Priority registration	Yes
Added costs for services:	
For LD:	No
For ADHD:	No
For ASD:	No
LD specialists	No
ADHD & ASD coaching	No
ASD specialists	Yes
Professional tutors	No
Peer tutors	No
Max. hours/week for services	Varies
How professors are notified of student approved accommodations	Director and student

COLLEGE GRADUATION REQUIREMENTS

Course waivers allowed	Yes
In what courses	Case by case basis
Course substitutions allowed	Yes
In what courses	Case by case basis

University at Albany—SUNY

1400 WASHINGTON AVENUE, ALBANY, NY 12222 • ADMISSIONS: 518-442-5435 • FAX: 518-442-5383

CAMPUS
Type of school	Public
Environment	City
Support	S

STUDENTS
Undergrad enrollment	13,320
% male/female	49/51
% from out of state	5
% frosh live on campus	92

FINANCIAL FACTS
Annual in-state tuition	$6,870
Annual out-of-state tuition	$23,710
Room and board	$13,864
Required fees	$2,946

GENERAL ADMISSIONS INFO
Application fee	$50
Priority deadline	3/1
Regular application deadline	3/1

Nonfall registration accepted. Admission may be deferred for a maximum of 1 year.

Range SAT EBRW	500–600
Range SAT Math	500–590
Range ACT Composite	22–26

ACADEMICS
Student/faculty ratio	19:1
% students returning for sophomore year	83
% students graduating within 4 years	56
% students graduating within 6 years	65

Most classes have 20–29 students.
Most lab/discussion sessions have 10–19 students.

PROGRAMS/SERVICES FOR STUDENTS WITH LEARNING DIFFERENCES
Reasonable accommodations will be provided for students with documented disabilities through the Disability Resource Center. Students are responsible for providing the University with documentation of the disability. Do not send documentation with the general application for admission to the University. Documentation must be submitted to the DRC either via fax, email, "snail mail" or in person. The mission of the DRC is to empower individual students, using appropriate supportive services, as well as acting as an expert resource for the university community.

ADMISSIONS
The average GPA is 92.2 (3.6/4.0). The middle 50% were between 88% and 96% (3.2-3.8). Freshman applicants must take the SAT or ACT (Writing sections not required) and the middle 50% scored between 1150 and 1310 SAT and 23 to 27 on ACT. Academic performance is important but not the only factor used. Courses should include 4 years English, 3 years Math, including elementary algebra, geometry, and at least one additional academic unit of mathematics or the equivalent, 2 years laboratory science, 3 years social science including one of U.S. History, and At least 1 year of foreign language (two years or more is strongly encouraged.nAcademic performance in high school is considered to be the best predictor of academic success, but it is not the only factor that will play a role in a student's experience as an undergraduate. The admissions committee looks at the whole person, recognizing special talents and interests outside the classroom as well as in it.

ADMISSIONS INFO FOR STUDENTS WITH LEARNING DIFFERENCES
SAT/ACT required: Yes
Interview required: No
Essay required: No
Additional application required: No
Documentation required for:
  LD: Current psychological/educational evaluation (within the last 3 years). Documentation must state area of disability (state a diagnosis). Reasonable academic accommodations must be supported by documentation. Academic accommodations must not change the academic mission of the university nor may the accommodation decrease the academic standards of a course or plan of study. Foreign language is required for graduation. If the student had a foreign language exemption in high school, documentation must include what evaluation was used to support the exemption—NOT just a statement on the IEP that estudents disability adversely impact ability to learn a foreign language.
  ADHD: Medical documenation is sufficient for individual appointments. Psychological-Educational evaluation (completed within the last 3 years) will need to be submitted to support any academic accommodations that the student may seek. Academic accommodations must not change the academic mission of the university nor may the accommodation decrease the academic standards of a course or plan of study.
  ASD: Psycho ed evaluation
Documentation submitted to: Support program/services
Special Ed. HS course work accepted: Yes
Separate application required for program services: No
Contact Information
Name of program or department: Disability Resource Center
Telephone: 518-442-5490
Fax: 518-442-5400

Additional Information

Documentation may be from the high school including the most recent Psychological/Educational evaluation) or from the student's physician or a psychological professional. While an IEP or 504 plan is helpful in telling WHAT accommodations were received in high school, it generally does not tell WHY, and is not sufficient documentation on its own. The Center for Autism and Related Disabilities((CARD Albany) is a university - affiliated resource center that provides evidence-based training and support to families and professionals and contributes knowledge to the field of autism spectrum disorders.

GENERAL ADMISSIONS

Very important factors considered include: rigor of secondary school record, class rank, academic GPA, standardized test scores, recommendation(s), character/personal qualities. *Important factors considered include:* application essay. *Other factors considered include:* extracurricular activities, talent/ability, first generation, alumni/ae relation, geographical residence, volunteer work, work experience, level of applicant's interest. *Freshman Admission Requirements:* High school diploma is required and GED is accepted. *Academic units required:* 4 English, 2 math, 2 science, 2 science labs, 1 foreign language, 3 social studies, 2 history, 4 academic electives. *Academic units recommended:* 4 math, 3 science, 3 science labs, 3 foreign language.

ACCOMMODATION OR SERVICES

Accommodations are decided upon an individual basis after a thorough review of appropriate, current documentation. The accommodations requests must be supported through the documentation provided and must be logically linked to the current impact of the condition on academic functioning.

FINANCIAL AID

Students should submit: FAFSA. Applicants will be notified of awards on a rolling basis beginning 3/2. The Princeton Review suggests that all financial aid forms be submitted as soon as possible after October 1. *Need-based scholarships/grants offered:* College/university scholarship or grant aid from institutional funds; Federal Pell; Private scholarships; SEOG; State scholarships/grants. *Loan aid offered:* Direct PLUS loans; Direct Subsidized Stafford Loans; Direct Unsubsidized Stafford Loans. Federal Work-Study Program available. Institutional employment available.

CAMPUS LIFE

Activities: Campus Ministries; Choral groups; Concert band; Dance; Drama/theater; International Student Organization; Jazz band; Literary magazine; Model UN; Music ensembles; Musical theater; Pep band; Radio station; Student government; Student newspaper; Student-run film society; Symphony orchestra; Television station; Yearbook. **Organizations:** 200 registered organizations, 20 honor societies, 17 religious organizations. 11 fraternities, 18 sororities. **Athletics (Intercollegiate):** *Men:* baseball, basketball, cross-country, football, lacrosse, soccer, track/field (outdoor), track/field (indoor). *Women:* basketball, cross-country, field hockey, golf, lacrosse, soccer, softball, tennis, track/field (outdoor), track/field (indoor), volleyball. **On-Campus Highlights:** Campus Center with bookstore, cafes, and lounges, SEFCU Arena, Science Library /Main Library, Performing Arts Center, University Art Museum.

ACCOMMODATIONS

Allowed in exams:	
Calculators	Yes
Dictionary	Yes
Computer	Yes
Spell-checker	Yes
Extended test time	Yes
Scribe	Yes
Proctors	Yes
Oral exams	Yes
Note-takers	Yes
Support services for students with	
LD	Yes
ADHD	Yes
ASD	Yes
Distraction-reduced environment	Yes
Recording of lecture allowed	Yes
Reading technology:	Yes
Audio books	Yes
Other assistive technology	Yes
Priority registration	Yes
Added costs for services:	
For LD:	No
For ADHD:	No
For ASD:	No
LD specialists	Yes
ADHD & ASD coaching	No
ASD specialists	No
Professional tutors	No
Peer tutors	Yes
How professors are notified of student approved accommodations	Student

COLLEGE GRADUATION REQUIREMENTS

Course waivers allowed	No
Course substitutions allowed	Yes

In what courses Determined on a case-by-case basis with supporting documentation.

Syracuse University

900 South Crouse Ave., Syracuse, NY 13244-2130 • Admissions: 315-443-3611 • Fax: 315-443-4226

CAMPUS

Type of school	Private (nonprofit)
Environment	City
Support	CS

STUDENTS

Undergrad enrollment	14,788
% male/female	46/54
% from out of state	60
% frosh live on campus	99

FINANCIAL FACTS

Annual tuition	$50,230
Room and board	$15,910
Required fees	$1,623

GENERAL ADMISSIONS INFO

Application fee	$75
Priority deadline	11/15
Regular application deadline	1/1

Nonfall registration accepted. Admission may be deferred for a maximum of 1 year.

Range SAT EBRW	580–670
Range SAT Math	580–680
Range ACT Composite	25–30

ACADEMICS

Student/faculty ratio	15:1
% students returning for sophomore year	91
% students graduating within 4 years	70
% students graduating within 6 years	83

Most classes have 20–29 students.
Most lab/discussion sessions have 10–19 students.

PROGRAMS/SERVICES FOR STUDENTS WITH LEARNING DIFFERENCES

The Office of Disability Service's (ODS) mission is to engage the university community to empower students, enhance equity and provide a platform for innovation and inclusion. On Track at Syracuse University is a fee-based program providing enhanced academic support for students with Attention Deficit Hyperactivity Disorder (ADHD) and Learning Disabilities (LD). It is designed to meet the growing demand for individualized support among SU students and open the door for prospective students seeking that support in college. It will elevate the level of service options for ADHD and LD students at SU, aligning with the University's commitment to meet the unique needs of today's students. The goal of this program will be to address both academic and social-emotional readiness.

ADMISSIONS

All students must meet regular admission standards and submit the general application form. General admission criteria include 4 yearsEnglish, 3–4 years math, 3–4 years science, 3–4 years social studies, and 2 years foreign language. ACT or SAT required (Writing section not required). Many colleges within the university have their own college-specific admission requirements and typically the ACT or SAT is not required for theater or music applicants. Applicants apply to one of nine undergraduate colleges, depending upon the program of study of interest. interest.

Additional Information

Students in On Track meet regularly with a specially trained coach for monitoring or academic support, guidance in connecting with other university and community services, and counseling focused on building independence and executive function. The program will transition participants to standard University support systems by their second year, as they receive follow up support with "step down" services through the Office of Disability Services. The Learning Assessment Center provides consultant and diagnostic services to students who suspect they may have a learning disability. The Center for Learning and Student Success

ADMISSIONS INFO FOR STUDENTS WITH LEARNING DIFFERENCES

SAT/ACT required: Yes
Interview required: Yes
Essay required: Yes
Additional application required: Not Applicable
Documentation required for:
  LD: Psycho ed evaluation to include: relevant historical info, instructional interventions, related services, age diagnosed, objective data (aptitude, achievement, info processing), test scores (standard, percentile and grade equivalents) and describe functional limitations.
  ADHD: Diagnosis based on DSM-V; history of behaviors impairing functioning in academic setting; diagnostic interview; history of symptoms; evidence of ongoing behaviors.
  ASD: Psycho ed evaluation
Documentation submitted to: Office of Disability Services
Special Ed. HS course work accepted: No
Separate application required for program services: No
# of students last year receiving services/accommodations for:
  LD: 450
Contact Information
Name of program or department: Office of Disability Services
Telephone: 315-443-4498
Fax: 315-443-1312
Email: disabilityservices@syr.edu

(CLASS) provides and facilitates academic support services for students, including one-on-one tutoring, small-group tutoring and workshops, and academic integrity education and training. Through collaboration with academic departments and offices, the Center coordinates programs and disseminates information about campus-wide academic resources available to students. Students are assigned to work with an Access Counselor upon registration with OSD. These counselors work with students throughout their tenure at SU. The services provide the development and implementation of a comprehensive Disability Access Plan and acts as central point of contact for disability related issues.

GENERAL ADMISSIONS

Very important factors considered include: rigor of secondary school record, class rank, academic GPA, application essay, standardized test scores, recommendation(s), interview, extracurricular activities, talent/ability, character/personal qualities, volunteer work, level of applicant's interest. *Other factors considered include:* first generation, alumni/ae relation, geographical residence, state residency, racial/ethnic status, work experience. *Freshman Admission Requirements:* High school diploma is required and GED is accepted. *Academic units recommended:* 4 English, 4 math, 4 science, 4 science labs, 3 foreign language, 4 social studies, 4 history.

ACCOMMODATION OR SERVICES

Accommodations are decided upon an individual basis after a thorough review of appropriate, current documentation. The accommodations requests must be supported through the documentation provided and must be logically linked to the current impact of the condition on academic functioning.

FINANCIAL AID

Students should submit: CSS/Financial Aid PROFILE; FAFSA; Noncustodial PROFILE. Applicants will be notified of awards on or about 3/15. The Princeton Review suggests that all financial aid forms be submitted as soon as possible after October 1. *Need-based scholarships/grants offered:* College/university scholarship or grant aid from institutional funds; Federal Pell; Private scholarships; SEOG; State scholarships/grants. *Loan aid offered:* Direct PLUS loans; Direct Subsidized Stafford Loans; Direct Unsubsidized Stafford Loans. Federal Work-Study Program available. Institutional employment available.

CAMPUS LIFE

Activities: Campus Ministries; Choral groups; Concert band; Dance; Drama/theater; International Student Organization; Jazz band; Literary magazine; Marching band; Model UN; Music ensembles; Musical theater; Opera; Pep band; Radio station; Student government; Student newspaper; Student-run film society; Symphony orchestra; Television station; Yearbook. **Organizations:** 347 registered organizations, 43 honor societies, 30 religious organizations. 29 fraternities, 19 sororities. **Athletics (Intercollegiate):** *Men:* basketball, cheerleading, crew/rowing, cross-country, diving, football, lacrosse, soccer, swimming, track/field (outdoor). *Women:* basketball, cheerleading, crew/rowing, cross-country, diving, field hockey, ice hockey, lacrosse, soccer, softball, swimming, tennis, track/field (outdoor), volleyball. **On-Campus Highlights:** Schine Student Center, Carrier Dome, Bird Library, Einhorn Family Walk, Archbold Gymnasium.

ACCOMMODATIONS

Allowed in exams:	
Calculators	Yes
Dictionary	Yes
Computer	Yes
Spell-checker	Yes
Extended test time	Yes
Scribe	Yes
Proctors	Yes
Oral exams	Yes
Note-takers	Yes
Support services for students with	
LD	Yes
ADHD	Yes
ASD	Yes
Distraction-reduced environment	Yes
Recording of lecture allowed	Yes
Reading technology:	Yes
Audio books	Yes
Other assistive technology	Read & Write, Live Scribe Pen, Dragon Naturally Speaking, Zoom Text, JAWS, Adobe, recording devices, FM system and brailler
Priority registration	Yes
Added costs for services: For On Track	
For LD:	No
For ADHD:	No
For ASD:	No
LD specialists	Yes
ADHD & ASD coaching	Yes
ASD specialists	Yes
Professional tutors	Yes
Peer tutors	Yes
Max. hours/week for services	23
How professors are notified of student approved accommodations	Student

COLLEGE GRADUATION REQUIREMENTS

Course waivers allowed	Yes
In what courses	Math and Foreign Language, reviewed on a case by case basis.
Course substitutions allowed	Yes
In what courses	Math and Foreign Language

Utica College

1600 BURRSTONE ROAD, UTICA, NY 13502-4892 • ADMISSIONS: 315-792-3006 • FAX: 315-792-3003

CAMPUS

Type of school	Private (nonprofit)
Environment	City
Support	CS

STUDENTS

Undergrad enrollment	3,637
% male/female	40/60
% from out of state	19
% frosh live on campus	72

FINANCIAL FACTS

Annual tuition	$20,127
Room and board	$10,828
Required fees	$550

GENERAL ADMISSIONS INFO

Application fee	$40
Priority deadline	3/1

Nonfall registration accepted. Admission may be deferred for a maximum of one year.

Range SAT EBRW	500–590
Range SAT Math	480–590
Range ACT Composite	20–26

ACADEMICS

Student/faculty ratio	13:1
% students returning for sophomore year	76
% students graduating within 4 years	35
% students graduating within 6 years	49

Most classes have 10–19 students. Most lab/discussion sessions have fewer than 10 students.

PROGRAMS/SERVICES FOR STUDENTS WITH LEARNING DIFFERENCES

The Office of Learning Services provides academic support and advisement to students who identify themselves as disabled and who provide appropriate supporting documentation. Accommodations are determined on a case-by-case basis based on supportive documentation provided by the student. Students are responsible for initiating a request for accommodations; for providing documentation of a disability; and for contacting the Office of Learning Services as early as possible upon admission. The Office of Learning Services professional staff members determine eligibility for services based on documentation; consult with students about appropriate accommodations; assist students in selfmonitoring the effectiveness of the accommodations; coordinate auxiliary services; provide information regarding rights and responsibilities of students; provide individualized educational advising; and serve as advocates for the student.

ADMISSIONS

Utica College does not require the ACT or SAT except for specific programs. Students are evaluated on an individualized basis. Students should have four years of English, three years of social studies, three years of math, three years of science, and two years of foreign language. Documentation of a disability should be sent to the Office of Learning Services. Students are not required to self-disclose the disability during the admission process.

Additional Information

The Office of Learning Services provides accommodations to students with disabilities based on appropriate and current documentation. Documentation would be a written evaluation completed by an appropriate professional which states the specific disability, what functional limitations the student has because of the disability, and which offers recommendations for academic accommodations. Services may include priority registration, specific skill remediation, learning and

ADMISSIONS INFO FOR STUDENTS WITH LEARNING DIFFERENCES

SAT/ACT required: No
Interview required: No
Essay required: Required
Additional application required: No
Documentation required for:
  LD: Psycho ed evaluation to include: relevant historical info, instructional interventions, related services, age diagnosed, objective data (aptitude, achievement, info processing), test scores (standard, percentile and grade equivalents) and describe functional limitations.
  ADHD: Diagnosis based on DSM-V; history of behaviors impairing functioning in academic setting; diagnostic interview; history of symptoms; evidence of ongoing behaviors.
  ASD: Psycho educatinal evaluation
Documentation submitted to: Learning Services Office
Special Ed. HS course work accepted: Yes
Separate application required for program services: No
# of students last year receiving services/accommodations for:
  LD: 172
Contact Information
Name of program or department: Learning Services Office
Telephone: 315-792-3032

Utica College

study strategy development, referrals for diagnostic evaluation, time management strategies, professional tutoring. Accommodations may include such items as: use of a tape recorder; time extensions for tests and/or alternative testing methods; note-takers; and separate location for tests. An accommodation letter is generated for each student stating what accommmodations are appropriate in each individual case. It is the responsibility of the students to meet with their instructors to discuss their disability and their accommodations.

GENERAL ADMISSIONS

Very important factors considered include: rigor of secondary school record, academic GPA. *Important factors considered include:* application essay, standardized test scores, level of applicant's interest. *Other factors considered include:* class rank, recommendation(s), interview, extracurricular activities, talent/ability, character/personal qualities, first generation, alumni/ae relation, volunteer work, work experience. *Freshman Admission Requirements:* High school diploma is required and GED is accepted. *Academic units required:* 4 English, 3 math, 3 science, 1 foreign language, 4 social studies, 3.5 academic electives, 1 visual/performing arts, and 2.5 units from above areas or other academic areas.

ACCOMMODATION OR SERVICES

Accommodations are decided upon an individual basis after a thorough review of appropriate, current documentation. The accommodations requests must be supported through the documentation provided and must be logically linked to the current impact of the condition on academic functioning.

FINANCIAL AID

Students should submit: FAFSA; State aid form. Applicants will be notified of awards on a rolling basis beginning 2/1. The Princeton Review suggests that all financial aid forms be submitted as soon as possible after October 1. *Need-based scholarships/grants offered:* College/university scholarship or grant aid from institutional funds; Federal Pell; Private scholarships; SEOG; State scholarships/grants. *Loan aid offered:* Direct PLUS loans; Direct Subsidized Stafford Loans; Direct Unsubsidized Stafford Loans. Federal Work-Study Program available. Institutional employment available.

CAMPUS LIFE

Activities: Campus Ministries; Choral groups; Concert band; Dance; Drama/theater; International Student Organization; Jazz band; Literary magazine; Music ensembles; Radio station; Student government; Student newspaper; Television station; Yearbook. **Organizations:** 80 registered organizations, 8 honor societies, 4 religious organizations. 5 fraternities, 4 sororities. **Athletics (Intercollegiate):** *Men:* baseball, basketball, cross-country, diving, football, golf, ice hockey, lacrosse, soccer, swimming, tennis, track/field (outdoor). *Women:* basketball, cross-country, diving, field hockey, ice hockey, lacrosse, soccer, softball, swimming, tennis, track/field (outdoor), volleyball, water polo. **On-Campus Highlights:** Strebel Student Center and Lounge, Pioneer Cafe, Clark Athletic Center, Romano Hall Lounge, Library Cafe.

ACCOMMODATIONS

Allowed in exams:	
Calculators	Yes
Dictionary	Yes
Computer	Yes
Spell-checker	Yes
Extended test time	Yes
Scribe	Yes
Proctors	Yes
Oral exams	Yes
Note-takers	Yes
Support services for students with	
LD	Yes
ADHD	Yes
ASD	Yes
Distraction-reduced environment	Yes
Recording of lecture allowed	Yes
Reading technology:	Yes
Audio books	Yes
Other assistive technology	
Priority registration	Yes
Added costs for services:	
For LD:	No
For ADHD:	No
For ASD:	No
LD specialists	Yes
ADHD & ASD coaching	Yes
ASD specialists	Yes
Professional tutors	Yes
Peer tutors	Not Applicable
Max. hours/week for services	Varies
How professors are notified of student approved accommodations	Director and student

COLLEGE GRADUATION REQUIREMENTS

Course waivers allowed	Not Applicable
Course substitutions allowed	Yes
In what courses	Case by case basis

Appalachian State University

OFFICE OF ADMISSIONS, BOONE, NC 28608-2004 • ADMISSIONS: 828-262-2120 • FAX: 828-262-3296

CAMPUS

Type of school	Public
Environment	Village
Support	CS

STUDENTS

Undergrad enrollment	16,891
% male/female	45/55
% from out of state	8
% frosh live on campus	99

FINANCIAL FACTS

Annual in-state tuition	$4,242
Annual out-of-state tuition	$18,675
Room and board	$8,174
Required fees	$3,061

GENERAL ADMISSIONS INFO

Application fee	$65
Priority deadline	11/15
Regular application deadline	3/15

Nonfall registration accepted. Admission may be deferred for a maximum of 2 terms.

Range SAT EBRW	560–640
Range SAT Math	540–630
Range ACT Composite	23–27

ACADEMICS

Student/faculty ratio	16:1
% students returning for sophomore year	89
% students graduating within 4 years	51
% students graduating within 6 years	74

Most classes have 20–29 students. Most lab/discussion sessions have 20–29 students.

PROGRAMS/SERVICES FOR STUDENTS WITH LEARNING DIFFERENCES

The Office of Disability Services (ODS) and the Office of Equity, Diversity and Compliance strives to ensure that the dignity of students, employees and campus visitors is upheld when equal access to education and employment is guaranteed, respectful treatment is assured, and an appreciation of differences is fostered for all members of the university community. ODS works diligently to ensure that individuals with disabilities are provided equal access at ASU by broadening disability awareness, removing barriers and providing reasonable accommodations.

ADMISSIONS

Students must be admitted to through the regular admissions process in order to participate in As-U-R. The middle 50% of first-year admits have a weighted GPA of 3.94–4.48 SAT of 1120–1290, ACT 23–28. Course requirements include 4 English, 4 math , 3 science, 2 social studies and 2 foreign language . Letters of recommendations, resumes, interviews, essays or personal statements are not part of admission.. However, ASU encourages applicants to submit a personal statement.

Additional Information

As-U-R is an intensive student support program focused on supporting students with executive function challenges (EFCs) with challenges such as organization, planning and setting priorities, getting started and completing tasks, monitoring progress on tasks, and decision-making. As-U-R provides a variety of supports and resources for students including: strategic tutoring and peer mentoring, learning strategy instruction tailored to the needs of college students, drop-in assistance, quiet study rooms, specific training to address executive function challenges, access to assistive technology, transition assistance for incoming, as well as graduating students, and coordination of individualized services. Academic Strategy Instruction includes one-on-one appointments on study skills topics and are free to all students.

ADMISSIONS INFO FOR STUDENTS WITH LEARNING DIFFERENCES

SAT/ACT required: Yes

Interview required: No

Essay required: Not Applicable

Additional application required: Not Applicable

Documentation required for:

 LD: Psycho Educational Evaluation

 ADHD: Psycho Educational Evaluation

 ASD: Disability documentation are outlined at ods.appstate.edu and is required for students seeking accommodations. All services/programs through the Student Learning Center are at no cost and do not require disability documentation.

Documentation submitted to: Support Program/Services

Special Ed. HS course work accepted: No

Separate application required for program services: Not Applicable

# of students last year receiving services/accommodations for:

 LD: 150

 ADHD: 275

 ASD: 35

Contact Information

Name of program or department: Office of Disability Services

Telephone: 828-262-3056

Fax: 828-262-7904

Email: ods@appstate.edu

Appalachian State University

GENERAL ADMISSIONS

Very important factors considered include: rigor of secondary school record, class rank, academic GPA, standardized test scores. *Other factors considered include:* application essay, recommendation(s), extracurricular activities, talent/ability, character/personal qualities, first generation, alumni/ae relation, racial/ethnic status, volunteer work, work experience, level of applicant's interest. *Freshman Admission Requirements:* High school diploma is required and GED is accepted. *Academic units required:* 4 English, 4 math, 3 science, 1 science lab, 2 foreign language, 1 social studies, 1 history.

ACCOMMODATION OR SERVICES

Accommodations are decided upon an individual basis after a thorough review of appropriate, current documentation. The accommodations requests must be supported through the documentation provided and must be logically linked to the current impact of the condition on academic functioning.

FINANCIAL AID

Students should submit: FAFSA. Applicants will be notified of awards on a rolling basis beginning 3/15. The Princeton Review suggests that all financial aid forms be submitted as soon as possible after October 1. *Need-based scholarships/grants offered:* College/university scholarship or grant aid from institutional funds; Federal Pell; Private scholarships; SEOG; State scholarships/grants. *Loan aid offered:* Direct PLUS loans; Direct Subsidized Stafford Loans; Direct Unsubsidized Stafford Loans. Federal Work-Study Program available. Institutional employment available.

CAMPUS LIFE

Activities: Campus Ministries; Choral groups; Concert band; Dance; Drama/theater; International Student Organization; Jazz band; Literary magazine; Marching band; Model UN; Music ensembles; Musical theater; Opera; Pep band; Radio station; Student government; Student newspaper; Student-run film society; Symphony orchestra; Television station. **Organizations:** 270 registered organizations, 20 honor societies, 25 religious organizations. 18 fraternities, 11 sororities. **Athletics (Intercollegiate):** *Men:* baseball, basketball, cross-country, football, golf, soccer, tennis, track/field (outdoor), track/field (indoor), wrestling. *Women:* basketball, cross-country, field hockey, golf, soccer, softball, tennis, track/field (outdoor), track/field (indoor), volleyball. **On-Campus Highlights:** Plemmons Student Union, Roess Dining Hall, Kidd Brewer Stadium "The Rock", Student Recreation Center, Sanford Mall / Greenspace.

ACCOMMODATIONS

Allowed in exams:

Calculators	Yes
Dictionary	Yes
Computer	Yes
Spell-checker	Yes
Extended test time	Yes
Scribe	Yes
Proctors	Yes
Oral exams	Yes
Note-takers	Yes

Support services for students with

LD	Yes
ADHD	Yes
ASD	Yes
Distraction-reduced environment	Yes
Recording of lecture allowed	Yes
Reading technology:	Yes
Audio books	Yes
Other assistive technology	Yes
Priority registration	Yes

Added costs for services:

For LD:	No
For ADHD:	No
For ASD:	No
LD specialists	No
ADHD & ASD coaching	Yes
ASD specialists	No
Professional tutors	Yes
Peer tutors	Yes
Max. hours/week for services	Varies
How professors are notified of student approved accommodations	Student

COLLEGE GRADUATION REQUIREMENTS

Course waivers allowed	Yes

In what courses

These waivers are determined on a case-by-case basis

Course substitutions allowed	Yes

In what courses

Determined on a case-by-case basis, accommodations can not lower essential requirements of programs or degrees.

Brevard College

ONE BEAR PLACE #97056, BREVARD, NC 28712 • ADMISSIONS: 828-884-8300 • FAX: 828-884-3790

CAMPUS

Type of school	Private (nonprofit)
Environment	Village
Support	CS

STUDENTS

Undergrad enrollment	696
% male/female	58/42
% from out of state	42
% frosh live on campus	87

FINANCIAL FACTS

Annual tuition	$28,400
Room and board	$9,900
Required fees	$950

GENERAL ADMISSIONS INFO

Nonfall registration accepted. Admission may be deferred for a maximum of one semester.

Range SAT EBRW	420–520
Range SAT Math	420–530
Range ACT Composite	17–22

ACADEMICS

Student/faculty ratio	11:1
% students returning for sophomore year	59

Most classes have 10–19 students.

PROGRAMS/SERVICES FOR STUDENTS WITH LEARNING DIFFERENCES

Brevard College welcomes students who learn differently. Although the College does not offer a special program or curriculum for such students, the college has an excellent disabilities support service, as well as the Academic Enrichment Center, where any student can receive such services as counseling on academic matters, tutoring in a specific subject, advice on organizing work and/or managing time, assistance with reading skills, study skills, test taking skills, and arrange note-taking. The Director of the Office for Students with Special Needs and Disabilities reviews student documentation and identifies academic accommodations which are adjustments to course policies. The director works with students to determine what would be useful to use in a particular course, and what the student must do in order to obtain these accommodations. The director can also assist students with talking to their professors about the learning disability and accommodations.

ADMISSIONS

There is no special admission process for students with LD. Brevard asks for quite a bit of information from applicants and from those who know the applicants and their learning style. If applicants are aware of a learning disability, they are encouraged to provide the Office for Students with Special Needs & Disabilities with as much information as possible, for example, counseling testing and reports, recommendations, and assessments. Applicants must provide official transcripts, letters of recommendation from college counselor or dean, a teacher of English, and one other teacher or adult who has worked with the student and knows the student well. Brevard is Test-Optional and does not require students to submit the ACT or SAT. The average GPA is 3.07. Brevard looks for strong verbal ability as represented in an applicant's writing sample(s). This gives the college a chance to know what the student struggles with, what the student feels confident about, what the student wants to achieve by earning a degree. Conditional admission status is available for students who display some, but not all, of the indicators of success as a post-secondary liberal arts student.

ADMISSIONS INFO FOR STUDENTS WITH LEARNING DIFFERENCES

SAT/ACT required: No, Test Optional
Interview required: No
Essay required: No
Additional application required: No
Documentation required for:
  LD: Psycho ed evaluation to include: relevant historical info, instructional interventions, related services, age diagnosed, objective data (aptitude, achievement, info processing), test scores (standard, percentile and grade equivalents) and describe functional limitations.
  ADHD: Diagnosis based on DSM-V; history of behaviors impairing functioning in academic setting; diagnostic interview; history of symptoms; evidence of ongoing behaviors.
  ASD: Psycho ed evaluation
Documentation submitted to: Office for Students with Special Needs and Disabilities
Special Ed. HS course work accepted: No
Separate application required for program services: No
Contact Information
Name of program or department: Office for Students with Special Needs and Disabilities
Telephone: 828-884-8131
Fax: 828-884-8293

Brevard College

Additional Information

As the central academic resource and support center on campus, the Academic Enrichment Center is designed to enrich the academic life of all students by providing strong academic support services and enrichment programming. The AEC services are offered on the premise that all students who are successful in college are those who have learned to take charge of their own learning and to utilize available resources to attain their academic goals. Students can get support or develop skills by going to a career workshop, working on studying techniques, getting tutored by a fellow student, or meeting with professional staff for an individualized academic plan. Experiential Opportunities in the AEC include: one-on-one individualized attention from academic coordinators, student tutors, and even professors whenever students need it. The Writing or Math lab (staffed by both faculty and peer tutors) can provide help with a revision of a final paper or one-on-one help with algebra homework. There are also a variety of academic resource materials to prepare for graduate entrance exams, develop study strategies, and improve performance in current courses.

GENERAL ADMISSIONS

Very important factors considered include: rigor of secondary school record, academic GPA, level of applicant's interest. *Important factors considered include:* class rank, application essay, interview, extracurricular activities, talent/ability, character/personal qualities, volunteer work. *Other factors considered include:* standardized test scores, recommendation(s), alumni/ae relation, work experience. *Freshman Admission Requirements:* High school diploma is required and GED is accepted. *Academic units recommended:* 4 English, 3 math, 3 science, 1 science lab, 2 foreign language, 4 social studies, 1 history, 4 academic electives.

ACCOMMODATION OR SERVICES

Accommodations are decided upon an individual basis after a thorough review of appropriate, current documentation. The accommodations requests must be supported through the documentation provided and must be logically linked to the current impact of the condition on academic functioning.

FINANCIAL AID

Students should submit: FAFSA. Applicants will be notified of awards on a rolling basis beginning 2/1. The Princeton Review suggests that all financial aid forms be submitted as soon as possible after October 1. *Need-based scholarships/grants offered:* College/university scholarship or grant aid from institutional funds; Federal Pell; Private scholarships; SEOG; State scholarships/grants. *Loan aid offered:* Direct PLUS loans; Direct Subsidized Stafford Loans; Direct Unsubsidized Stafford Loans. Federal Work-Study Program available. Institutional employment available.

CAMPUS LIFE

Activities: Campus Ministries; Choral groups; Concert band; Dance; Drama/theater; Jazz band; Literary magazine; Music ensembles; Musical theater; Opera; Pep band; Student government; Student newspaper; Yearbook. **Organizations:** 32 registered organizations, 3 honor societies, 1 religious organization. **Athletics (Intercollegiate):** *Men:* baseball, basketball, cheerleading, cross-country, cycling, football, golf, soccer, tennis, track/field (outdoor). *Women:* basketball, cheerleading, cross-country, cycling, golf, soccer, softball, tennis, track/field (outdoor), volleyball. **On-Campus Highlights:** Food Court & Dining Hall, Porter Center for Performing Arts, Jones Library, MG Super Lab, Boshamer Gym.

ACCOMMODATIONS

Allowed in exams:	
Calculators	Yes
Dictionary	Yes
Computer	Yes
Spell-checker	Yes
Extended test time	Yes
Scribe	Yes
Proctors	Yes
Oral exams	Yes
Note-takers	Yes
Support services for students with	
LD	Yes
ADHD	Yes
ASD	Yes
Distraction-reduced environment	Yes
Recording of lecture allowed	Yes
Reading technology:	Yes
Audio books	Yes
Other assistive technology	Yes
Priority registration	Yes
Added costs for services:	
For LD:	No
For ADHD:	No
For ASD:	No
LD specialists	Yes
ADHD & ASD coaching	Yes
ASD specialists	No
Professional tutors	No
Peer tutors	Yes
Max. hours/week for services	Varies
How professors are notified of student approved accommodations	Student

COLLEGE GRADUATION REQUIREMENTS

Course waivers allowed	No
Course substitutions allowed	Yes

In what courses Substitutions are done on a case-by-case basis. Foreign Language is not required for graduation.

Davidson College

Box 5000, Davidson, NC 28035-7156 • Admissions: 704-894-2230 • Fax: 704-894-2016

CAMPUS
Type of school	Private (nonprofit)
Environment	Village
Support	CS

STUDENTS
Undergrad enrollment	1,800
% male/female	51/49
% from out of state	77
% frosh live on campus	100

FINANCIAL FACTS
Annual tuition	$49,454
Room and board	$13,954
Required fees	$495

GENERAL ADMISSIONS INFO
Application fee	$50
Regular application deadline	1/2

Nonfall registration accepted. Admission may be deferred for a maximum of 1 year.

Range SAT EBRW	660–740
Range SAT Math	650–730
Range ACT Composite	30–33

ACADEMICS
Student/faculty ratio	9:1
% students returning for sophomore year	95

Most classes have 10–19 students.
Most lab/discussion sessions have 10–19 students.

PROGRAMS/SERVICES FOR STUDENTS WITH LEARNING DIFFERENCES

Students enroll in Davidson with a proven record of academic achievement and the ability to utilize resources, persevere, and excel. The college provides services and accommodations to allow students an opportunity to continue to be successful. Special procedures have been developed for students handicapped by learning disabilities. Students who seek adapted instruction on the basis of a learning disability undergo an evaluation by college-designated learning specialists, usually at the student's expense. The results of the evaluation, made available to the college with the student's permission, may include recommendations for compensatory learning strategies to be used by the student and recommendations for services and accommodations to be provided by the college. Using these recommendations as a guide, the Student Learning Support Committee works with the student to develop a learning plan that enhances learning strengths and compensates for learning difficulties. If the learning plan recommends adjustment to academic requirements, the recommendation is considered by the Curriculum Requirements Committee and may result in the approval of the recommendation or the substitution of the academic requirement. All students seeking accommodations on the basis of an LD must provide recent documentation. The Dean of Students, with the student's permission, will notify professors of an individual student's need for adaptations. Accommodations are not universal in nature but are designed to meet the specific need of the individual to offset a specific disability.

ADMISSIONS

There is no special admission process for students with LD, though the Admissions Office may seek comments from support staff knowledgeable about LD. Students are encouraged to self-disclose their ADHD. The admission process is very competitive, and the disclosure can help the Admissions Office more fairly evaluate the transcript. This disclosure could address any specific academic issues related to the LD, such as no foreign language in high school because of the specific LD or lower grades in math as a result of a math disability. The GPA is recalculated to reflect rigor with 97 percent of the accepted students having a recalculated

ADMISSIONS INFO FOR STUDENTS WITH LEARNING DIFFERENCES

SAT/ACT required: Yes
Interview required: No
Essay required: No
Additional application required: No
Documentation required for:
  LD: Psycho ed evaluation to include: relevant historical info, instructional interventions, related services, age diagnosed, objective data (aptitude, achievement, info processing), test scores (standard, percentile and grade equivalents) and describe functional limitations.
  ADHD: Diagnosis based on DSM-V; history of behaviors impairing functioning in academic setting; diagnostic interview; history of symptoms; evidence of ongoing behaviors.
  ASD: Psycho ed evaluation.
Documentation submitted to: Dean of Students Office
Special Ed. HS course work accepted: No
Separate application required for program services: No
# of students last year receiving services/accommodations for:
  LD: 50
Contact Information
Name of program or department: Dean of Students Office
Telephone: 704-894-2225
Fax: 704-894-2849

Davidson College

GPA of 3.0. Students have completed at least 4 years of English, 3 years of math, 2 years of the same foreign language, 2 years of science, and 2 years of history/social studies. Courses taken in special education are not accepted. The mid 50 percent of students have an ACT between 28 and 31 or SAT between 1240 and 1420. Interviews are not required but are recommended.

Additional Information

Support services and accommodations available include, but are not limited to: referrals for appropriate diagnostic evaluation; individual coaching and instruction in compensatory strategies and study skills; consultation with faculty and staff; student support groups as requested; classroom accommodations such as extra test-taking time, taped texts, note-takers, use of tape recorders, use of computers with spellcheckers, and individual space for study or test-taking; reduced course loads; and course substitutions or waivers (rarely).

GENERAL ADMISSIONS

Very important factors considered include: rigor of secondary school record, recommendation(s), character/personal qualities, volunteer work. *Important factors considered include:* application essay, standardized test scores, extracurricular activities, talent/ability. *Other factors considered include:* class rank, academic GPA, alumni/ae relation. *Freshman Admission Requirements:* High school diploma is required and GED is not accepted. *Academic units required:* 4 English, 3 math, 2 science, 2 foreign language, and 2 units from above areas or other academic areas. *Academic units recommended:* 4 math, 4 science, 4 foreign language, 4 units from above areas or other academic areas.

ACCOMMODATION OR SERVICES

Accommodations are decided upon an individual basis after a thorough review of appropriate, current documentation. The accommodations requests must be supported through the documentation provided and must be logically linked to the current impact of the condition on academic functioning.

FINANCIAL AID

Students should submit: Business/Farm Supplement; CSS/Financial Aid PROFILE; FAFSA; Noncustodial PROFILE. Applicants will be notified of awards on or about 4/1. The Princeton Review suggests that all financial aid forms be submitted as soon as possible after October 1. *Need-based scholarships/grants offered:* College/university scholarship or grant aid from institutional funds; Federal Pell; Private scholarships; SEOG; State scholarships/grants. *Loan aid offered:* Direct PLUS loans; Direct Subsidized Stafford Loans; Direct Unsubsidized Stafford Loans. Federal Work-Study Program available. Institutional employment available.

CAMPUS LIFE

Activities: Campus Ministries; Choral groups; Dance; Drama/theater; International Student Organization; Jazz band; Literary magazine; Music ensembles; Musical theater; Pep band; Radio station; Student government; Student newspaper; Symphony orchestra; Yearbook. **Organizations:** 151 registered organizations, 15 honor societies, 16 religious organizations. 8 fraternities, **Athletics (Intercollegiate):** *Men:* baseball, basketball, cross-country, diving, football, golf, soccer, swimming, tennis, track/field (outdoor), wrestling. *Women:* basketball, cross-country, diving, field hockey, lacrosse, soccer, swimming, tennis, track/field (outdoor), volleyball. **On-Campus Highlights:** Belk Visual Arts Center, Baker-Watt Science Complex, Baker Sports Complex, Campus Center, Lake Campus.

ACCOMMODATIONS

Allowed in exams:	
Calculators	Yes
Dictionary	Yes
Computer	Yes
Spell-checker	Yes
Extended test time	Yes
Scribe	Yes
Proctors	Yes
Oral exams	No
Note-takers	Yes

Support services for students with	
LD	Yes
ADHD	Yes
ASD	Yes
Distraction-reduced environment	Yes
Recording of lecture allowed	Yes
Reading technology:	Yes
Audio books	No
Other assistive technology	Yes
Priority registration	No

Added costs for services:	
For LD:	No
For ADHD:	No
For ASD:	No
LD specialists	Yes
ADHD & ASD coaching	Limited to improving time management and academic study skills
ASD specialists	No
Professional tutors	No
Peer tutors	Yes
Max. hours/week for services	Unlimited
How professors are notified of student approved accommodations	Student and director

COLLEGE GRADUATION REQUIREMENTS

Course waivers allowed	No
Course substitutions allowed	Yes
In what courses	
Substitutions in any appropriate course	

Duke University

Chapel Drive, Durham, NC 27708-0586 • Admissions: 919-684-3214 • Fax: 919668-1661

CAMPUS
Type of school	Private (nonprofit)
Environment	City
Support	CS

STUDENTS
Undergrad enrollment	6,467
% male/female	51/49
% from out of state	85
% frosh live on campus	100

FINANCIAL FACTS
Annual tuition	$53,760
Room and board	$15,178
Required fees	$1,935

GENERAL ADMISSIONS INFO
Application fee	$85
Priority deadline	12/20
Regular application deadline	1/3

Nonfall registration accepted. Admission may be deferred for a maximum of 1 year.

Range SAT EBRW	680–770
Range SAT Math	700–800
Range ACT Composite	31–34

ACADEMICS
Student/faculty ratio	6:1

Most classes have 10–19 students.

PROGRAMS/SERVICES FOR STUDENTS WITH LEARNING DIFFERENCES

Duke University does not provide a formal, highly structured program for students with LD. The university does provide, however, significant academic support services for students through the Academic Resource Center (ARC). Students who submit appropriate documentation of their learning disability to the ARC clinical director are eligible for assistance in obtaining reasonable academic adjustments and auxiliary aids. In addition, the ARC clinical director and instructors can provide individualized instruction in academic skills and learning strategies, academic support counseling, and referrals for other services. Students with learning disabilities voluntarily access and use the services of the ARC, just as they might access and use other campus resources. Student interactions with the ARC staff are confidential. The goals of the support services for students with learning disabilities are in keeping with the goals of all services provided through the ARC: to help students achieve their academic potential within the context of a competitive university setting, promote a disciplined approach to study, and foster active, independent learners.

ADMISSIONS

There is no special admission process for students with LD. All applicants must meet the general Duke admission criteria. Most applicants are in the top 10% of their class and have completed a demanding curriculum including many AP and honors courses. The ACT with Writing or SAT Reasoning and 2 Subject tests are required. Duke considers the highest ACT composite score and highest sub scores on each section, regardless of test date, but will not recalculate the composite score. Students who take the ACT are not required to submit SAT or SAT Subject Tests. Duke uses the highest available SAT Critical Reading, Writing, and Math sub scores, plus the two highest subject test sub scores, regardless of the date those tests were taken. Students may elect "Score Choice" when releasing their SAT scores. Students must submit two teacher and one counselor recommendation. Applicants may also submit one optional personal recommendation from a coach, a director, a teacher from an elective

ADMISSIONS INFO FOR STUDENTS WITH LEARNING DIFFERENCES
SAT/ACT required: Yes
Interview required: No
Essay required: No
Additional application required: No
Documentation required for:
  LD: Psycho ed evaluation to include: relevant historical info, instructional interventions, related services, age diagnosed, objective data (aptitude, achievement, info processing), test scores (standard, percentile and grade equivalents) and describe functional limitations.
  ADHD: Diagnosis based on DSM-V; history of behaviors impairing functioning in academic setting; diagnostic interview; history of symptoms; evidence of ongoing behaviors.
  ASD: Psycho ed evaluation
Documentation submitted to: ARC
Special Ed. HS course work accepted: No
Separate application required for program services: No
# of students last year receiving services/accommodations for:
  LD: 40-60
Contact Information
Name of program or department: Student Disability Access Office/Academic Resource Center (ARC)
Telephone: 919-684-5917
Fax: 919-684-5917

Duke University

course, a family member, or anyone else who knows the student well and will. This optional information will be considered in understanding the student as a person, but will not be formally evaluated as part of the application. Some students choose to disclose a disability in their application because it is an important element of their experiences or to share how they dealt with an obstacle. Duke considers this information in understanding a student's achievements and evaluates accomplishments within the context of opportunities or challenges presented to that student. Duke does not use information to deny admission to a student.

Additional Information

The Student Disability Access Office (SDAO) explores possible coverage and reasonable accommodations for qualified undergraduate, graduate and professional students who are disabled in compliance with Section 504 of the Federal Rehabilitation Act of 1973, the Americans with Disabilities Act (ADA) of 1990 and the ADA Amendments Act of 2008. SDAO provides and coordinate accommodations, support services and programs that enable students with disabilities to have equal access to all Duke University programs and activities.

GENERAL ADMISSIONS

Very important factors considered include: rigor of secondary school record, academic GPA, application essay, standardized test scores, recommendation(s), extracurricular activities, talent/ability, character/ personal qualities. *Other factors considered include:* class rank, interview, first generation, alumni/ae relation, geographical residence, state residency, religious affiliation/commitment, racial/ethnic status, volunteer work, work experience, level of applicant's interest. *Freshman Admission Requirements:* High school diploma is required and GED is not accepted. *Academic units recommended:* 4 English, 3 math, 3 science, 3 foreign language, 3 social studies.

ACCOMMODATION OR SERVICES

Accommodations are decided upon an individual basis after a thorough review of appropriate, current documentation. The accommodations requests must be supported through the documentation provided and must be logically linked to the current impact of the condition on academic functioning.

FINANCIAL AID

Students should submit: Business/Farm Supplement; CSS/Financial Aid PROFILE; FAFSA; Noncustodial PROFILE. Applicants will be notified of awards on or about 4/1. The Princeton Review suggests that all financial aid forms be submitted as soon as possible after October 1. *Need-based scholarships/grants offered:* College/university scholarship or grant aid from institutional funds; Federal Pell; Private scholarships; SEOG; State scholarships/grants. *Loan aid offered:* Direct PLUS loans; Direct Subsidized Stafford Loans; Direct Unsubsidized Stafford Loans. Federal Work-Study Program available. Institutional employment available.

CAMPUS LIFE

Activities: Campus Ministries; Choral groups; Concert band; Dance; Drama/theater; International Student Organization; Jazz band; Literary magazine; Marching band; Model UN; Music ensembles; Musical theater; Opera; Pep band; Radio station; Student government; Student newspaper; Student-run film society; Symphony orchestra; Television station. **Organizations:** 200 registered organizations, 10 honor societies, 25 religious organizations. 21 fraternities, 14 sororities.

ACCOMMODATIONS

Allowed in exams:	
Calculators	Yes
Dictionary	Yes
Computer	Yes
Spell-checker	Yes
Extended test time	Yes
Scribe	Yes
Proctors	Yes
Oral exams	Yes
Note-takers	Yes
Support services for students with	
LD	Yes
ADHD	Yes
ASD	Yes
Distraction-reduced environment	Yes
Recording of lecture allowed	Yes
Reading technology:	Yes
Audio books	Yes
Other assistive technology	Yes
Priority registration	No
Added costs for services:	
For LD:	No
For ADHD:	No
For ASD:	No
LD specialists	Yes
ADHD & ASD coaching	Yes
ASD specialists	No
Professional tutors	No
Peer tutors	Yes
Max. hours/week for services	Unlimited
How professors are notified of student approved accommodations	
Student and director	

COLLEGE GRADUATION REQUIREMENTS

Course waivers allowed	No
Course substitutions allowed	No

East Carolina University

EAST 5TH STREET, GREENVILLE, NC 27858-4353 • ADMISSIONS: 252-328-6640 • FAX: 252-328-6945

CAMPUS

Type of school	Public
Environment	City
Support	CS

STUDENTS

Undergrad enrollment	22,598
% male/female	43/57
% from out of state	10
% frosh live on campus	97

FINANCIAL FACTS

Annual in-state tuition	$4,452
Annual out-of-state tuition	$20,729
Room and board	$10,354
Required fees	$2,736

GENERAL ADMISSIONS INFO

Application fee	$75
Regular application deadline	3/1

Nonfall registration accepted. Admission may be deferred for a maximum of 1 semester.

Range SAT EBRW	520–590
Range SAT Math	510–590
Range ACT Composite	20–24

ACADEMICS

Student/faculty ratio	19:1
% students returning for sophomore year	83
% students graduating within 4 years	36
% students graduating within 6 years	61

Most classes have 10–19 students.
Most lab/discussion sessions have 20–29 students.

PROGRAMS/SERVICES FOR STUDENTS WITH LEARNING DIFFERENCES

The STEPP Program's mission is to provide students with learning disabilities with access and comprehensive support throughout the university experience. STEPP fosters a network of opportunities and resources to empower and support students from admission to graduation. By providing access to college for a bright group of students, designing an integrated and collaborative system of support on a public university campus, STEPP pens the door to a college education for students with LD.

ADMISSIONS

Although the STEPP Program has some flexibility in alternate admissions criteria, students who fall short of requirements in multiple areas or who are significantly below standards in a requirement are generally less competitive candidates. In particular, it's important to ensure that applicants complete 2 years of the same foreign language and 4 years of math (Algebra 1, Geometry, Algebra 2, and an "advanced math" course that requires Algebra 2 as a prerequisite) before you graduate from high school. Students should begin their application to STEPP 19 months before enrolling.

Additional Information

STEPP provides incoming transition activities and support including: monthly transition mailings provide guided preparation in key areas of college readiness, individualized consultation targeting support to students, families, and schools as needed, and Boot Camp jump-starts the college experience for first-year students and parents with an intensive introduction to ECU held the week before the fall semester begins. Ongoing services and requirements during the college years include: required study hall hours enabling students to create a structured schedule, mentoring by ECU graduate students offering support and guidance as first-year students implement new skills and access campus resources, peer tutoring providing assistance in selected subjects during study hall hours, a parallel curriculum of five STEPP Program courses, taken in addition to ECU's academic requirements, developing skills and habits essential

ADMISSIONS INFO FOR STUDENTS WITH LEARNING DIFFERENCES

SAT/ACT required: Yes
Interview required: No
Essay required: No
Additional application required: No
Documentation required for:
  LD: Psycho ed evaluation to include: relevant historical info, instructional interventions, related services, age diagnosed, objective data (aptitude, achievement, info processing), test scores (standardm percentile, and grade equivalents) and describe functional limitations.
  ADHD: Diagnosis based on DSM-V; history of behaviors impairing functioning in academic setting; diagnostic interview; history of symptoms; evidence of ongoing behaviors.
  ASD: Psycho ed evaluation.
Documentation submitted to: Department for Disability Support Services
Special Ed. HS course work accepted: Yes
Separate application required for program services: No
# of students last year receiving services/accommodations for:
  LD: 100-150
Contact Information
Name of program or department: Department for Disability Support Services
Telephone: 252-737-1016
Email: dssdept@ecu.edu

tutoring providing assistance in selected subjects during study hall hours, a parallel curriculum of five STEPP Program courses, taken in addition to ECU's academic requirements, developing skills and habits essential to academic success,, assistive technology resources, ongoing advising (including goal setting, grade reporting, and consultation) tracking academic progress, a dual-advising model partners STEPP Program with advisors in each student's major, campus Living connections include residence hall placement within an ECU living-learning community for all first-year students, guidance in accessing Disability Support Services and other campus resources fosters establishing and maintaining connections with ECU. Outgoing transition activities and support internship facilitates the transition from college to career, and development of a professional portfolio identifies critical competencies within each student's field of study and showcases accomplishments. Students can access reasonable accommodations through the Department for Disability Support Services. Students show official verification of their disability and are assigned to academic advisors. Accommodations can include: alternative testing, accommodations, noise-free environment, reader-assisted test-taking, and other arrangements that satisfy the needs of the student. A maximum of double time can be allowed for students to complete a test or an exam. The university offers a modified language sequence for students enrolled in Spanish.

GENERAL ADMISSIONS

Very important factors considered include: rigor of secondary school record, academic GPA, standardized test scores, state residency. *Important factors considered include:* class rank. *Other factors considered include:* application essay, extracurricular activities, talent/ability, character/personal qualities, first generation, alumni/ae relation, volunteer work, work experience, level of applicant's interest. *Freshman Admission Requirements:* High school diploma is required and GED is accepted. *Academic units required:* 4 English, 4 math, 3 science, 1 science lab, 2 foreign language, 2 social studies, 1 history. *Academic units recommended:* 4 English, 4 math, 3 science, 1 science lab, 2 foreign language, 2 social studies, 1 history, 1 visual/performing arts.

ACCOMMODATION OR SERVICES

Accommodations are decided upon an individual basis after a thorough review of appropriate, current documentation. The accommodations requests must be supported through the documentation provided and must be logically linked to the current impact of the condition on academic functioning.

FINANCIAL AID

Students should submit: FAFSA. Applicants will be notified of awards on a rolling basis beginning 4/1. The Princeton Review suggests that all financial aid forms be submitted as soon as possible after October 1. *Need-based scholarships/grants offered:* College/university scholarship or grant aid from institutional funds; Federal Nursing Scholarships; Federal Pell; Private scholarships; SEOG; State scholarships/grants. *Loan aid offered:* Direct PLUS loans; Direct Subsidized Stafford Loans; Direct Unsubsidized Stafford Loans. Federal Work-Study Program available. Institutional employment available.

CAMPUS LIFE

Activities: Campus Ministries; Choral groups; Concert band; Dance; Drama/theater; International Student Organization; Jazz band; Literary magazine; Marching band; Model UN; Music ensembles; Musical theater; Opera; Pep band; Radio station; Student government; Student newspaper; Student-run film society; Symphony orchestra; Television

ACCOMMODATIONS

Allowed in exams:	
Calculators	Yes
Dictionary	Yes
Computer	Yes
Spell-checker	Yes
Extended test time	Yes
Scribe	Yes
Proctors	Yes
Oral exams	Yes
Note-takers	Yes
Support services for students with	
LD	Yes
ADHD	Yes
ASD	No
Distraction-reduced environment	Yes
Recording of lecture allowed	Yes
Reading technology:	Yes
Audio books	Yes
Other assistive technology	Yes
Priority registration	Yes
Added costs for services:	
For LD:	No
For ADHD:	No
For ASD:	No
LD specialists	Yes
ADHD & ASD coaching	No
ASD specialists	No
Professional tutors	Yes
eer tutors	No
Max. hours/week for services	Varies
How professors are notified of student approved accommodations	Student

COLLEGE GRADUATION REQUIREMENTS

Course waivers allowed	No
Course substitutions allowed	No

Elon University

100 Campus Drive, Elon, NC 27244-2010 • Admissions: 336-278-3566 • Fax: 336-278-7699

CAMPUS
Type of school	Private (nonprofit)
Environment	Town
Support	S

STUDENTS
Undergrad enrollment	6,045
% male/female	40/60
% from out of state	82
% frosh live on campus	99

FINANCIAL FACTS
Annual tuition	$35,319
Room and board	$12,230
Required fees	$444

GENERAL ADMISSIONS INFO
Application fee	$50
Priority deadline	11/10
Regular application deadline	1/10

Nonfall registration accepted. Admission may be deferred for a maximum of 1 year.

Range SAT EBRW	580–670
Range SAT Math	560–660
Range ACT Composite	25–29

ACADEMICS
Student/faculty ratio	12:1
% students returning for sophomore year	89
% students graduating within 4 years	78
% students graduating within 6 years	84

PROGRAMS/SERVICES FOR STUDENTS WITH LEARNING DIFFERENCES
Elon University is committed to the principle of equal opportunity. We assist students with disabilities in finding approaches and accommodations that provide them an opportunity to benefit from the many programs offered on campus. Faculty, staff, administrators, and students work together to find approaches and accommodations that enable students to benefit from the wide variety of programs and activities on campus.

ADMISSIONS
Students with disabilities must meet the same admissions criteria as other applicants. There is no special admission process. Most important factors in admissions are academic rigor, grades, ACT (with writing) or SAT and counselor recommendation, activities, involvement and essay. GPA is converted to 4.0 scale, and then Elon gives weight to honors, AP or IB courses. Courses required include 4 years English, 3 years math, 2 years foreign language, 3 years social studies, and 3 years science. Students may be admitted with one deficiency. Disclosing a disability is totally up to the applicant.

Additional Information
Students must provide current documentation to request accommodations. They are encouraged to be proactive and develop an ongoing conversation with their professors and service providers. Every student is assigned an advisor, a professor or an administrator who helps students get information regarding programs, tutors and special needs. All students have access to The Tutoring Center and Writing Center. Waivers for foreign language or math courses are never approved. However, students may request a foreign language substitution. Documentation is required that demonstrates the presence of deficits that make learning a foreign language extremely difficult, as well as, a history of poor grades in the subject. Students who have never taken such classes will be asked to enroll; performance will be evaluated before the end of the drop/add period and a decision will be made regarding the substitution.

ADMISSIONS INFO FOR STUDENTS WITH LEARNING DIFFERENCES
SAT/ACT required: Yes
Interview required: No
Essay required: No
Additional application required: No
Documentation required for:
  LD: Psycho ed evaluation to include: relevant historical info, instructional interventions, related services, age diagnosed, objective data (aptitude, achievement, info processing), test scores (standard, percentile and grade equivalents) and describe functional limitations.
  ADHD: Diagnosis based on DSM-V; history of behaviors impairing functioning in academic setting; diagnostic interview; history of symptoms; evidence of ongoing behaviors.
  ASD: Psycho ed evaluation
Documentation submitted to: The Office of Disabilities Resources
Special Ed. HS course work accepted: No
Separate application required for program services: No
Contact Information
Name of program or department: The Office of Disabilities Resources
Telephone: 336 278-6500

Elon University

GENERAL ADMISSIONS

Very important factors considered include: rigor of secondary school record, academic GPA, application essay, standardized test scores, recommendation(s). *Important factors considered include:* extracurricular activities, talent/ability, alumni/ae relation, volunteer work, work experience. *Other factors considered include:* class rank, character/personal qualities, first generation, geographical residence, state residency, racial/ethnic status, level of applicant's interest. *Freshman Admission Requirements:* High school diploma is required and GED is accepted. *Academic units required:* 4 English, 3 math, 3 science, 1 science lab, 2 foreign language, 2 social studies, 1 history. *Academic units recommended:* 4 English, 4 math, 3 science, 1 science lab, 3 foreign language, 2 social studies, 1 history.

ACCOMMODATION OR SERVICES

Accommodations are decided upon an individual basis after a thorough review of appropriate, current documentation. The accommodations requests must be supported through the documentation provided and must be logically linked to the current impact of the condition on academic functioning.

FINANCIAL AID

Students should submit: CSS/Financial Aid PROFILE; FAFSA. Applicants will be notified of awards on a rolling basis beginning 1/31. The Princeton Review suggests that all financial aid forms be submitted as soon as possible after October 1. *Need-based scholarships/grants offered:* College/university scholarship or grant aid from institutional funds; Federal Pell; Private scholarships; SEOG; State scholarships/grants; United Negro College Fund. *Loan aid offered:* Direct PLUS loans; Direct Subsidized Stafford Loans; Direct Unsubsidized Stafford Loans. Federal Work-Study Program available. Institutional employment available.

CAMPUS LIFE

Activities: Campus Ministries; Choral groups; Concert band; Dance; Drama/theater; International Student Organization; Jazz band; Literary magazine; Marching band; Model UN; Music ensembles; Musical theater; Pep band; Radio station; Student government; Student newspaper; Student-run film society; Symphony orchestra; Television station; Yearbook. **Organizations:** 150 registered organizations, 27 honor societies, 10 religious organizations. 11 fraternities, 12 sororities. **Athletics (Intercollegiate):** *Men:* baseball, basketball, cheerleading, cross-country, football, golf, soccer, tennis. *Women:* basketball, cheerleading, cross-country, golf, soccer, softball, tennis, track/field (outdoor), track/field (indoor), volleyball. **On-Campus Highlights:** Belk Library, Rhodes Football Stadium, Koury Business Center, Moseley Student Center, Koury Athletic Center.

ACCOMMODATIONS

Allowed in exams:	
Calculators	Yes
Dictionary	Yes
Computer	Yes
Spell-checker	Yes
Extended test time	Yes
Scribe	Yes
Proctors	Yes
Oral exams	No
Note-takers	Yes
Support services for students with	
LD	Yes
ADHD	Yes
ASD	Yes
Distraction-reduced environment	Yes
Recording of lecture allowed	Yes
Reading technology:	Yes
Audio books	No
Other assistive technology	Yes
Priority registration	Yes
Added costs for services:	
For LD:	No
For ADHD:	No
For ASD:	No
LD specialists	No
ADHD & ASD coaching	No
ASD specialists	No
Professional tutors	No
Peer tutors	Yes
Max. hours/week for services	Unlimited
How professors are notified of student approved accommodations	Director and student

COLLEGE GRADUATION REQUIREMENTS

Course waivers allowed	No
In what courses	
Course substitutions allowed	Yes
In what courses	
World Languages requirement or Math general education requirement	

Guilford College

5800 WEST FRIENDLY AVENUE, GREENSBORO, NC 27410 • ADMISSIONS: 336-316-2100 • FAX: 336-316-2954

CAMPUS
Type of school	Private (nonprofit)
Environment	City
Support	S

STUDENTS
Undergrad enrollment	1,493
% male/female	46/54
% from out of state	29
% frosh live on campus	89

FINANCIAL FACTS
Annual tuition	$36,460
Room and board	$11,200
Required fees	$660

GENERAL ADMISSIONS INFO
Priority deadline	11/15

Nonfall registration accepted. Admission may be deferred for a maximum of 1 year.

Range SAT EBRW	440–585
Range SAT Math	463–558
Range ACT Composite	19–25

ACADEMICS
Student/faculty ratio	12:1
% students returning for sophomore year	66
% students graduating within 4 years	45
% students graduating within 6 years	53

PROGRAMS/SERVICES FOR STUDENTS WITH LEARNING DIFFERENCES
The mission of the Accessibility Resource Center (ARC) is to assure that all students have equal access to and equal opportunity in all programs and services, and to empower students to become strong self-advocates. The ARC staff is committed to working with students to address individual needs and providing the necessary accommodations for academic success. The Learning Commons (LC) serves the learning needs of a diverse campus by providing professional and peer tutoring, workshops, advocacy, and realistic encouragement. The focus is on self-advocacy and the articulation of both strengths and weaknesses. Faculty tutors work one-on-one with students on time management, study skills, test-taking, reading, and writing. A large student tutoring service offers course-specific tutoring.

ADMISSIONS
Students with learning disabilities meet the same admission requirement as all students. Guilford is test optional and applicants do not have to submit either SAT or ACT. There is a required essay and applicants must submit recommendations. Course requirements include 4 years English, 3 years math, 3-4 natural sciences, 3 years social studies and 2 years foreign language. With appropriate documentation, applicants can request to substitute some high school courses in areas that impact their ability to learn.

Additional Information
The Learning Commons offer an academic coaching service that provides learning strategies, assignment and writing assistance for students, faculty, and staff. There is face-to-face consultations for writing and course specific assignments, as well as a collection of online resources for writers and educators. First Year Experience is a challenging and rewarding program designed to get students started on the right track. They receive academic and personal support while exploring fascinating topics and enhancing their communication, writing and critical thinking skills.

ADMISSIONS INFO FOR STUDENTS WITH LEARNING DIFFERENCES
SAT/ACT required: No
Interview required: No
Essay required: Yes
Additional application required: No
Documentation required for:
  LD: Psycho ed evaluation to include: relevant historical info, instructional interventions, related services, age diagnosed, objective data (aptitude, achievement, info processing), test scores (standard, percentile and grade equivalents) and describe functional limitations.
  ADHD: Diagnosis based on DSM-V; history of behaviors impairing functioning in academic setting; diagnostic interview; history of symptoms; evidence of ongoing behaviors.
  ASD: Psycho ed evaluation
Documentation submitted to: Accessibility Resource Center
Special Ed. HS course work accepted: Yes
Separate application required for program services: No
Contact Information
Name of program or department: Accessibility Resource Center
Telephone: 336-316-2837
Fax: 336-346-2946

Guilford College

GENERAL ADMISSIONS

Important factors considered include: rigor of secondary school record, class rank, academic GPA, application essay, standardized test scores, character/personal qualities, volunteer work.level of applicant's interest. *Other factors considered include:* recommendation(s), interview, extracurricular activities, talent/ability, first generation, alumni/ae relation, geographical residence, state residency, religious affiliation/commitment, racial/ethnic status, work experience. *Freshman Admission Requirements:* High school diploma is required and GED is accepted. *Academic units recommended:* 4 English, 3 math, 3 science, 2 foreign language, 3 social studies.

ACCOMMODATION OR SERVICES

Accommodations are decided upon an individual basis after a thorough review of appropriate, current documentation. The accommodations requests must be supported through the documentation provided and must be logically linked to the current impact of the condition on academic functioning.

FINANCIAL AID

Students should submit: FAFSA. Applicants will be notified of awards on a rolling basis beginning 3/1. The Princeton Review suggests that all financial aid forms be submitted as soon as possible after October 1. *Need-based scholarships/grants offered:* College/university scholarship or grant aid from institutional funds; Federal Pell; Private scholarships; SEOG; State scholarships/grants. *Loan aid offered:* Direct PLUS loans; Direct Subsidized Stafford Loans; Direct Unsubsidized Stafford Loans. Federal Work-Study Program available. Institutional employment available.

CAMPUS LIFE

Activities: Campus Ministries; Choral groups; Drama/theater; International Student Organization; Jazz band; Music ensembles; Pep band; Radio station; Student government; Student newspaper; Student-run film society; Yearbook. **Organizations:** 47 registered organizations, 1 honor society, 8 religious organizations. **Athletics (Intercollegiate):** *Men:* baseball, basketball, cross-country, football, golf, lacrosse, rugby, soccer, tennis. *Women:* basketball, cross-country, lacrosse, rugby, soccer, softball, swimming, tennis, volleyball. **On-Campus Highlights:** Hege Library and Art Gallery, Regan Brown Field House & Physical Education Center & Mary Ragsdale Fitness, Frank Family Science Center, Founders Student Center and the new Grill 155, The Greenleaf Cafe - coffee co-op or Community Center.

ACCOMMODATIONS

Allowed in exams:

Calculators	Yes
Dictionary	Yes
Computer	Yes
Spell-checker	Yes
Extended test time	Yes
Scribe	Yes
Proctors	No
Oral exams	Yes
Note-takers	Yes

Support services for students with

LD	Yes
ADHD	Yes
ASD	Yes
Distraction-reduced environment	Yes
Recording of lecture allowed	Yes
Reading technology:	Yes
Audio books	Yes
Other assistive technology	Yes
Priority registration	No

Added costs for services:

For LD:	No
For ADHD:	No
For ASD:	No
LD specialists	Yes
ADHD & ASD coaching	Yes
ASD specialists	No
Professional tutors	Yes
Peer tutors	Yes
Max. hours/week for services	Varies

How professors are notified of student approved accommodations
Director and student

COLLEGE GRADUATION REQUIREMENTS

Course waivers allowed	Yes
In what courses Math/Quantitative Literacy	
Course substitutions allowed	Yes
In what courses	Foreign Languages

Lenoir Rhyne University

635 NORTH 7TH AVENUE, HICKORY, NC 28603 • ADMISSIONS: 828.328.7300 • FAX:

CAMPUS

Type of school	Private (nonprofit)
Environment	Town
Support	S

STUDENTS

Undergrad enrollment	1,573
% male/female	40/60
% from out of state	19
% frosh live on campus	77

FINANCIAL FACTS

Annual tuition	$35,350
Room and board	$12,150

GENERAL ADMISSIONS INFO

Application fee	$35

Nonfall registration accepted. Admission may be deferred for a maximum of 1 year.

Range SAT EBRW	480–580
Range SAT Math	490–590

ACADEMICS

Student/faculty ratio	13:1
% students returning for sophomore year	73
% students graduating within 4 years	32
% students graduating within 6 years	43

Most classes have 10–19 students.
Most lab/discussion sessions have 10–19 students.

PROGRAMS/SERVICES FOR STUDENTS WITH LEARNING DIFFERENCES

The Lenoir-Rhyne College Disability Services Office strives to provide the highest quality service to each student with a disability through appropriate modification of college policies, practices and procedures. It is the mission of the office to ensure that every student with a disability has an equal chance to benefit from college programs. Furthermore, the office emphasizes personal independence and responsibility, on the part of the student, in the provision of services. The office will also serve as a campus and community resource for information about people with disabilities and the issues that affect them.

ADMISSIONS

There is no special admissions process for students with learning disabilities. All students are reviewed on an individual case-by-case basis. Basic admissions criteria include: 2.0 GPA, top 50% class rank, 850 SAT or 17 ACT, 4 years English, 3 years math, 1 year history, 2 years foreign language.

Additional Information

Advising and Academic Services Center offers a variety of services to help students achieve academic success through Group Peer Tutoring, Advising and Assessment, and Academic Skills Counseling. With appropriate documentation students with LD/ADD may be appropriate for some of the following services/accommodations: the use of calculators, dictionary, computer or spellcheck in exams; extended time on tests; distraction-free environment; scribe; proctor; oral exams; note taker; tape recorder in class; books on tape; and substitution of the foreign language requirement. (Extensive documentation is required for foreign language substitution). Services to students with disabilities varies depending on the type and nature of the disability. There is also the Lohr Learning Commons that provides assistance with writing, public speaking, course-specific tutoring, math tutoring lab, and general learning strategies. And a separate Writing Center to assist students in improving writing ability.

ADMISSIONS INFO FOR STUDENTS WITH LEARNING DIFFERENCES

SAT/ACT required: Yes
Interview required: No
Essay required: Yes
Additional application required: No
Documentation required for:
 LD: Full psychoeducational evaluation with IQ scores listed
 ADHD: Full psychoeducational evaluation with IQ scores listed
 ASD: Psych ed evaluation
Documentation submitted to: Support program/services
Special Ed. HS course work accepted: No
Separate application required for program services: No
Contact Information
Name of program or department: Disability Services Office
Telephone: 828-328-7296
Fax: 828-267-3441

Lenoir Rhyne University

GENERAL ADMISSIONS

Very important factors considered include: academic GPA, standardized test scores. *Important factors considered include:* rigor of secondary school record, class rank, application essay, recommendation(s), extracurricular activities, character/personal qualities, volunteer work, work experience. *Freshman Admission Requirements:* High school diploma is required and GED is accepted. *Academic units required:* 4 English, 3 math, 1 science, 1 science lab, 2 foreign language, 1 history. *Academic units recommended:* 4 English, 4 math, 2 science, 1 science lab, 3 foreign language, 2 history.

ACCOMMODATION OR SERVICES

Accommodations are decided upon an individual basis after a thorough review of appropriate, current documentation. The accommodations requests must be supported through the documentation provided and must be logically linked to the current impact of the condition on academic functioning.

FINANCIAL AID

Students should submit: FAFSA. The Princeton Review suggests that all financial aid forms be submitted as soon as possible after October 1. *Need-based scholarships/grants offered:* College/university scholarship or grant aid from institutional funds; Federal Pell; Private scholarships; SEOG; State scholarships/grants. *Loan aid offered:* Direct PLUS loans; Direct Subsidized Stafford Loans; Direct Unsubsidized Stafford Loans. Federal Work-Study Program available. Institutional employment available.

CAMPUS LIFE

Activities: Campus Ministries; Choral groups; Concert band; Dance; Drama/theater; International Student Organization; Jazz band; Literary magazine; Marching band; Model UN; Music ensembles; Musical theater; Pep band; Radio station; Student government; Student newspaper; Student-run film society; Symphony orchestra; Yearbook. **Organizations:** 54 registered organizations, 10 honor societies, 6 religious organizations. 4 fraternities, 4 sororities. **Athletics (Intercollegiate):** *Men:* baseball, basketball, cheerleading, cross-country, football, golf, soccer *Women:* basketball, cheerleading, cross-country, golf, soccer, softball, volleyball. **On-Campus Highlights:** McCrorie Center, Cromer College Center, Shuford Physical Education Complex, Alex and Lee George Hall, Grace Chapel.

ACCOMMODATIONS

Allowed in exams:	
Calculators	Yes
Dictionary	Yes
Computer	Yes
Spell-checker	Yes
Extended test time	Yes
Scribe	Yes
Proctors	Yes
Oral exams	Yes
Note-takers	Yes
Support services for students with	
LD	Yes
ADHD	Yes
ASD	Yes
Distraction-reduced environment	Yes
Recording of lecture allowed	Yes
Reading technology:	Yes
Audio books	Yes
Other assistive technology	Read & Write Gold Zoom Text
Priority registration	No
Added costs for services:	
For LD:	No
For ADHD:	No
For ASD:	No
LD specialists	No
ADHD & ASD coaching	No
ASD specialists	Not Applicable
Professional tutors	Yes
Peer tutors	No
Max. hours/week for services	35
How professors are notified of student approved accommodations	Director and student

COLLEGE GRADUATION REQUIREMENTS

Course waivers allowed	No
Course substitutions allowed	Yes
In what courses	Foreign Language if deemed appropriate

North Carolina State University

Box 7001, Raleigh, NC 27695 • Admissions: 919-515-2434 • Fax: 919-515-5039

CAMPUS

Type of school	Public
Environment	Metropolis
Support	CS

STUDENTS

Undergrad enrollment	22,755
% male/female	55/45
% from out of state	10
% frosh live on campus	93

FINANCIAL FACTS

Annual in-state tuition $6,535 Annual out-of-state tuition	$25,879
Room and board	$11,078
Required fees	$2,565

GENERAL ADMISSIONS INFO

Application fee	$85
Priority deadline	10/15
Regular application deadline	1/15

Nonfall registration accepted. Admission may be deferred for a maximum of 1 year.

Range SAT EBRW	610–680
Range SAT Math	620–710
Range ACT Composite	27–31

ACADEMICS

Student/faculty ratio	13:1
% students returning for sophomore year	94
% students graduating within 4 years	50
% students graduating within 6 years	79

Most classes have 10–19 students. Most lab/discussion sessions have 20–29 students.

PROGRAMS/SERVICES FOR STUDENTS WITH LEARNING DIFFERENCES

Essential to the larger mission of the institution, the Disability Services Office promotes universally designed environments and facilitates accommodations and services that promote independence and allow equal access to the North Carolina State University experience. Goals include: Promote an accessible campus environment where students are viewed on their ability, not disability; Establish and publicize clear guidelines and procedures to address the responsibilities of the University and student in compliance with Section 504 of the Rehabilitation Act of 1973 and the Americans with Disabilities Act of 1990 as amended 2008; Determine appropriate academic accommodations for students with disabilities to ensure equal access and promote the opportunity for academic success; Utilize the latest technology to enhance and support the educational experiences of students with disabilities; Provide students with disabilities the opportunity to develop and grow skills necessary to advocate for themselves within the campus community.

ADMISSIONS

All applicants must meet the same admission criteria. The mid 50% of the applicants have a 27-31 ACT or 1240-1370 Average SAT. The mid 50% unweighted GPA is 3.57-3.91. minimum course requirements include four years English, three years math (including algebra I, algebra II, and geometry), two years social studies (including U.S. History), three years science (including one life science, one physical science, and one laboratory science), and two years of the same foreign language.

Additional Information

All enrolled students may receive services and accommodations through the coordinator of learning disabilities of the DSO if they present appropriate documentation. The documentation should include a written report with a statement specifying areas of learning disabilities. Services and accommodations available with appropriate documentation include extended testing times for exams; reduced distraction testing environments; use of calculators, dictionaries, computers, or spellcheckers

ADMISSIONS INFO FOR STUDENTS WITH LEARNING DIFFERENCES

SAT/ACT required: Yes
Interview required: No
Essay required: No
Additional application required: No
Documentation required for:
  LD: Psycho ed evaluation to include: relevant historical info, instructional interventions, related services, age diagnosed, objective data (aptitude, achievement, info processing), test scores (standard, percentile and grade equivalents) and describe functional limitations.
  ADHD: Diagnosis based on DSM-V; history of behaviors impairing functioning in academic setting; diagnostic interview; history of symptoms; evidence of ongoing behaviors.
  ASD: Psycho ed evaluation
Documentation submitted to: Disability Services Office
Special Ed. HS course work accepted: No
Separate application required for program services: Yes
# of students last year receiving services/accommodations for:
  LD: 275
Contact Information
Name of program or department: Disability Services Office
Telephone: 919-515-7653
Fax: 919-513-2840
Email: disability@ncsu.edu

North Carolina State University

during exams; proctors; scribes; note-takers; audio format; assistive technology; and priority registration. If new needs are identified, services are modified or developed to accommodate them.

General Admissions

Very important factors considered include: rigor of secondary school record, class rank, academic GPA, standardized test scores. *Other factors considered include:* application essay, extracurricular activities, talent/ability, character/personal qualities, first generation, alumni/ae relation, geographical residence, state residency, racial/ethnic status, volunteer work, work experience. *Freshman Admission Requirements:* High school diploma is required and GED is accepted. *Academic units required:* 4 English, 4 math, 3 science, 1 science lab, 2 foreign language, 1 social studies, 1 history. *Academic units recommended:* 4 English, 4 math, 3 science, 1 science lab, 2 foreign language, 1 social studies, 1 history.

Accommodation or Services

Accommodations are decided upon an individual basis after a thorough review of appropriate, current documentation. The accommodations requests must be supported through the documentation provided and must be logically linked to the current impact of the condition on academic functioning.

Financial Aid

Students should submit: FAFSA. Applicants will be notified of awards on a rolling basis beginning 4/1. The Princeton Review suggests that all financial aid forms be submitted as soon as possible after October 1. *Need-based scholarships/grants offered:* College/university scholarship or grant aid from institutional funds; Federal Pell; Private scholarships; SEOG; State scholarships/grants; United Negro College Fund. *Loan aid offered:* Direct PLUS loans; Direct Subsidized Stafford Loans; Direct Unsubsidized Stafford Loans. Federal Work-Study Program available. Institutional employment available.

Campus Life

Activities: Campus Ministries; Choral groups; Concert band; Dance; Drama/theater; International Student Organization; Jazz band; Literary magazine; Marching band; Model UN; Music ensembles; Musical theater; Pep band; Radio station; Student government; Student newspaper; Student-run film society; Symphony orchestra; Yearbook. **Organizations:** 560 registered organizations, 26 honor societies, 25 religious organizations. 33 fraternities, 17 sororities. **Athletics (Intercollegiate):** *Men:* baseball, basketball, cheerleading, cross-country, diving, football, golf, riflery, soccer, swimming, tennis, track/field (outdoor), track/field (indoor), wrestling. *Women:* basketball, cheerleading, cross-country, diving, golf, gymnastics, riflery, soccer, softball, swimming, tennis, track/field (outdoor), track/field (indoor), volleyball. **On-Campus Highlights:** Hunt Library, Gregg Museum of Art and Design, Carter Finley Stadium / PNC Center, Talley Student Union, University Theatre.

ACCOMMODATIONS

Allowed in exams:	
Calculators	Yes
Dictionary	Yes
Computer	Yes
Spell-checker	Yes
Extended test time	Yes
Scribe	Yes
Proctors	Yes
Oral exams	Yes
Note-takers	Yes
Support services for students with	
LD	Yes
ADHD	Yes
ASD	Yes
Distraction-reduced environment	Yes
Recording of lecture allowed	Yes
Reading technology:	Yes
Audio books	Yes
Other assistive technology	Yes
Priority registration	Yes
Added costs for services:	
For LD:	No
For ADHD:	No
For ASD:	No
LD specialists	Yes
ADHD & ASD coaching	No
ASD specialists	Yes
Professional tutors	Yes
Peer tutors	No
Max. hours/week for services	Varies
How professors are notified of student approved accommodations	Director

COLLEGE GRADUATION REQUIREMENTS

Course waivers allowed	No

St. Andrews University

1700 Dogwood Mile, Laurinburg, NC 28352 • Admissions: 910-277-5555 • Fax: 910-277-5020

CAMPUS

Type of school	Private (nonprofit)
Environment	Rural
Support	CS

STUDENTS

Undergrad enrollment	601
% male/female	46/54
% from out of state	59
% frosh live on campus	99

FINANCIAL FACTS

Annual tuition	$25,874
Room and board	$10,396

GENERAL ADMISSIONS INFO

Application fee	$35

Nonfall registration accepted.

Range SAT EBRW	430-610
Range SAT Math	355–605
Range ACT Composite	16-23

ACADEMICS

Student/faculty ratio	15:1
% students returning for sophomore year	59
% students graduating within 4 years	27
% students graduating within 6 years	33

PROGRAMS/SERVICES FOR STUDENTS WITH LEARNING DIFFERENCES

St. Andrews University, a branch of Webber International University, acknowledges its responsibility, both legally and educationally, to serve students with learning disabilities by providing reasonable accommodations. These services do not guarantee success, but endeavor to assist students in pursuing a quality postsecondary education. The Office of Disability Services and The Center for Academic Success at St. Andrews offer a range of support services for students with disabilities. These services are meant to help students devise strategies for meeting college demands and to foster independence, responsibility, and self-advocacy. The Office of Disability Services responds to each request for services and helps students develop a viable plan for personal success. The Office of Disability Services at St. Andrews University is committed to ensuring that all student information remains confidential. Students may begin the process for requesting accommodations, by visiting this site: https://www.sa.edu/student-life/disability-accommodations.

ADMISSIONS

Each application is reviewed on an individual basis. Factors considered are an SAT minimum of 800 or ACT minimum of 17 and students' high school profiles and courses attempted, as well as a minimum GPA of 2.5; an essay and counselor and/ or teacher recommendations are optional but strongly recommended. Courses recommended include 3 credits of college prep English, 3 credits of math including Algebra II and Geometry, 3 credits of science, 3 credits of social studies, and 1 year of a foreign language. Prospective students are strongly encouraged to visit the campus. Students with learning disabilities complete the regular admissions application. Students with a diagnosis of attention deficit hyperactivity disorder are required to show achievement and ability testing (adult version) that validates the DSM–IV diagnosis. All students must meet the same admissions criteria. For the Admissions Committee to make the most informed decision, students are encouraged to self-disclose the existence of a learning disability in their personal statement. Any other personal information indicating the student's ability to

ADMISSIONS INFO FOR STUDENTS WITH LEARNING DIFFERENCES

SAT/ACT required: Yes
Interview required: No
Essay required: No
Additional application required: No
Documentation required for:
  LD: Psycho ed evaluation to include: relevant historical info, instructional interventions, related services, age diagnosed, objective data (aptitude, achievement, info processing), test scores (standard, percentile and grade equivalents) and describe functional limitations.
  ADHD: Diagnosis based on DSM-V; history of behaviors impairing functioning in academic setting; diagnostic interview; history of symptoms; evidence of ongoing behaviors.
  ASD: Psycho ed evaluation
Documentation submitted to: Office of Disability Services
Special Ed. HS course work accepted: Only as accepted for regular college entrance
Separate application required for program services: Yes
Contact Information
Name of program or department: Office of Disability Services and Center for Academic Success
Telephone: 910-277-5667
Fax: 910-277-5746

succeed in college should also be included with the application. All documentation of a specific learning disability should be sent separately with an application for services to the Office of Disability Services at St. Andrews. Application forms for disability services are on the college website.

Additional Information

All accommodations are based on the submitted current documentation. Each case is reviewed individually. Disability Services reserves the right to determine eligibility for services based on the quality of the submitted documentation. The services and accommodations include note-taking, extended time on tests, alternative test formats, separate locations for tests, books on tape through Recordings for the Blind and Dyslexic or from readers, and content tutoring through individual departments. Franklin Language Masters and audiotape equipment are available for loan. All computers in computer labs are equipped with spellchecker and there are two Kurzweil Readers in the Center for Academic Success.

GENERAL ADMISSIONS

Important factors considered include: academic GPA, standardized test scores, extracurricular activities, character/personal qualities. *Other factors considered include:* rigor of secondary school record, class rank, application essay, recommendation(s), interview, talent/ability, first generation, volunteer work, work experience. *Freshman Admission Requirements:* High school diploma is required and GED is accepted. *Academic units required:* 3 English, 3 math, 3 science, 1 foreign language, 3 social studies.

ACCOMMODATION OR SERVICES

Accommodations are decided upon an individual basis after a thorough review of appropriate, current documentation. The accommodations requests must be supported through the documentation provided and must be logically linked to the current impact of the condition on academic functioning.

FINANCIAL AID

Students should submit:. The Princeton Review suggests that all financial aid forms be submitted as soon as possible after October 1. *Need-based scholarships/grants offered:* College/university scholarship or grant aid from institutional funds; Federal Pell; Private scholarships; SEOG; State scholarships/grants. *Loan aid offered:* Direct PLUS loans; Direct Subsidized Stafford Loans; Direct Unsubsidized Stafford Loans. Federal Work-Study Program available. Institutional employment available.

CAMPUS LIFE

Activities:. **Organizations:** 30 registered organizations, 3 honor societies, 1 religious organization. **Athletics (Intercollegiate):** *Men:* baseball, basketball, cross-country, equestrian sports, golf, horseback riding, lacrosse, soccer, track/field (outdoor), wrestling. *Women:* basketball, cross-country, equestrian sports, horseback riding, lacrosse, soccer, softball, track/field (outdoor), volleyball, wrestling. **On-Campus Highlights:** Equesterian Center, Morgan Jones Science Labs, Electronic and Fine Arts Center, Athletic Facilities, Art Studios.

ACCOMMODATIONS

Allowed in exams:	
Calculators	Yes
Dictionary	Yes
Computer	Yes
Spell-checker	Yes
Extended test time	Yes
Scribe	Yes
Proctors	Yes
Oral exams	Yes
Note-takers	Yes
Support services for students with	
LD	Yes
ADHD	Yes
ASD	Yes
Distraction-reduced environment	Yes
Recording of lecture allowed	Yes
Reading technology:	Yes
Audio books	Yes
Other assistive technology	Yes
Priority registration	No
Added costs for services:	
For LD:	No
For ADHD:	No
For ASD:	No
LD specialists	Yes
ADHD & ASD coaching	No
ASD specialists	No
Professional tutors	No
Peer tutors	Yes
Max. hours/week for services	As needed
How professors are notified of student approved accommodations	Student

COLLEGE GRADUATION REQUIREMENTS

Course waivers allowed	No
Course substitutions allowed	Yes
In what courses	Foreign Language

University of North Carolina at Asheville

One University Heights, Asheville, NC 28804-8502 • Admissions: 828-251-6481 • Fax: 828-251-6482

CAMPUS

Type of school	Public
Environment	Town
Support	S

STUDENTS

Undergrad enrollment	3,497
% male/female	43/57
% from out of state	11
% frosh live on campus	94

FINANCIAL FACTS

Annual in-state tuition	$4,122
Annual out-of-state tuition	$20,845
Room and board	$9,106
Required fees	$3,023

GENERAL ADMISSIONS INFO

Application fee	$75
Priority deadline	11/15
Regular application deadline	2/15

Nonfall registration accepted. Admission may be deferred for a maximum of One year.

Range SAT EBRW	550–650
Range SAT Math	530–610
Range ACT Composite	22–27

ACADEMICS

Student/faculty ratio	13:1
% students returning for sophomore year	75
% students graduating within 4 years	42
% students graduating within 6 years	62

Most classes have 10–19 students.

PROGRAMS/SERVICES FOR STUDENTS WITH LEARNING DIFFERENCES

The Office of Academic Accessibility works collaboratively with students, faculty, and staff to ensure that all aspects of campus life - learning, working, and living - are universally accessible. The Office provides the University community with resources, education, innovative programming, and direct services in order that people with disabilities may have a greater opportunity to achieve social justice and equity.

ADMISSIONS

Admissions criteria and procedures for the university are the same for students with and without disabilities.

Additional Information

Through Academic Accessibility, the university seeks to meed individual needs. In order to get accommodations students submit a Voluntary Disclosure of Disability Form and describe classroom curriculum accommodations needed to participate in the classroom setting; and describe the history of accommodations listing any accommodations used in the past.

ADMISSIONS INFO FOR STUDENTS WITH LEARNING DIFFERENCES

SAT/ACT required: Yes
Interview required: No
Essay required: Not Applicable
Additional application required: Yes
Documentation required for:
  LD: Diagnostic statement identifying the disability including ICD or DSM classification. Description of the current functional impact to student's experiences. Assessment method(s) used and assessment score reports used in the determination of the diagnosis, when applicable.
  ADHD: Diagnostic statement identifying the disability including ICD or DSM classification. Description of the current functional impact to student's experiences. Assessment method(s) used and assessment score reports used in the determination of the diagnosis, when applicable.
  ASD: Diagnostic statement identifying the disability including ICD or DSM classification. Description of the current functional impact to student's experiences. Assessment method(s) used and assessment score reports used in the determination of the diagnosis, when applicable.
Documentation submitted to: Office of Academic Accessibility
Special Ed. HS course work accepted: Not Applicable
Separate application required for program services: No
Contact Information
Name of program or department: Office of Academic Accessibility
Telephone: 828-250-3979
Fax: 828-251-6492
Email: academicaccess@unca.edu

University of North Carolina at Asheville

GENERAL ADMISSIONS

Very important factors considered include: rigor of secondary school record, class rank, academic GPA. *Important factors considered include:* application essay, standardized test scores, recommendation(s), talent/ability, character/personal qualities, level of applicant's interest. *Other factors considered include:* interview, extracurricular activities, first generation, alumni/ae relation, geographical residence, state residency, racial/ethnic status, volunteer work, work experience. *Freshman Admission Requirements:* High school diploma is required and GED is not accepted. *Academic units required:* 4 English, 4 math, 3 science, 1 science lab, 2 foreign language, 1 social studies, 1 history. *Academic units recommended:* 4 academic electives.

ACCOMMODATION OR SERVICES

Accommodations are decided upon an individual basis after a thorough review of appropriate, current documentation. The accommodations requests must be supported through the documentation provided and must be logically linked to the current impact of the condition on academic functioning.

FINANCIAL AID

Students should submit: FAFSA. Applicants will be notified of awards on a rolling basis beginning 3/15. The Princeton Review suggests that all financial aid forms be submitted as soon as possible after October 1. *Need-based scholarships/grants offered:* College/university scholarship or grant aid from institutional funds; Federal Pell; Private scholarships; SEOG; State scholarships/grants. *Loan aid offered:* Direct PLUS loans; Direct Subsidized Stafford Loans; Direct Unsubsidized Stafford Loans. Federal Work-Study Program available. Institutional employment available.

CAMPUS LIFE

Activities: Campus Ministries; Choral groups; Concert band; Dance; Drama/theater; International Student Organization; Jazz band; Literary magazine; Model UN; Music ensembles; Musical theater; Pep band; Radio station; Student government; Student newspaper; Student-run film society. **Organizations:** 82 registered organizations, 14 honor societies, 10 religious organizations. 1 fraternity, 2 sororities. **Athletics (Intercollegiate):** *Men:* baseball, basketball, cheerleading, cross-country, soccer, tennis, track/field (outdoor). *Women:* basketball, cheerleading, cross-country, soccer, tennis, track/field (outdoor), volleyball. **On-Campus Highlights:** Sherrill Center for Health and Wellness, Main Campus Quadrangle, Highsmith Union, Asheville Botanical Gardens, Argo Tea in Ramsey Library.

ACCOMMODATIONS

Allowed in exams:	
Calculators	Yes
Dictionary	Yes
Computer	Yes
Spell-checker	Yes
Extended test time	Yes
Scribe	Yes
Proctors	Yes
Oral exams	Yes
Note-takers	Yes
Support services for students with	
LD	Yes
ADHD	Yes
ASD	Yes
Distraction-reduced environment	Yes
Recording of lecture allowed	Yes
Reading technology:	Yes
Audio books	Yes
Other assistive technology	JAWS, Read & Write, LiveScribe pens, Zoomtext
Priority registration	Yes
Added costs for services:	
For LD:	No
For ADHD:	No
For ASD:	No
LD specialists	No
ADHD & ASD coaching	Yes
ASD specialists	No
Professional tutors	Yes
Peer tutors	Yes
Max. hours/week for services	4
How professors are notified of student approved accommodations	Student

COLLEGE GRADUATION REQUIREMENTS

Course waivers allowed	Yes
In what courses Math, Foreign Language, and others on an individual basis.	
Course substitutions allowed	Yes
In what courses Math, Foreign Language, and others on an individual basis.	

The University of North Carolina at Chapel Hill

103 SOUTH BUILDING, CHAPEL HILL, NC 27599-2200 • ADMISSIONS: 919-966-3621 • FAX: 919-962-3045

CAMPUS

Type of school	Public
Environment	Town
Support	CS

STUDENTS

Undergrad enrollment	18,683
% male/female	41/59
% from out of state	16
% frosh live on campus	100

FINANCIAL FACTS

Annual in-state tuition	$7,019
Annual out-of-state tuition	$32,602
Room and board	$11,556
Required fees	$1,986

GENERAL ADMISSIONS INFO

Application fee	$80
Regular application deadline	10/15

Nonfall registration accepted. Admission may be deferred for a maximum of 1 year.

Range SAT EBRW	640–720
Range SAT Math	620–720
Range ACT Composite	27–32

ACADEMICS

Student/faculty ratio	13:1
% students returning for sophomore year	97
% students graduating within 4 years	84
% students graduating within 6 years	91

Most classes have 10–19 students.
Most lab/discussion sessions have 20–29 students.

PROGRAMS/SERVICES FOR STUDENTS WITH LEARNING DIFFERENCES

The Academic Success Program, or ASP (www.unc.edu/asp), is one of the many programs within the Learning Center. We provide accommodations and services for undergraduate, professional and graduate students who have a documented learning disability and/or attention-deficit/hyperactivity disorder (AD/HD). The staff determines legally mandated accommodations and collaborates with the Department of Disability Services in providing them. The staff also provides a variety of services to eligible students, including learning strategy sessions and coaching.

ADMISSIONS

All applicants must meet the same admission criteria. Teacher recommendation and counselor statement are required. Students must submit either the SAT or ACT (Writing not required). . There is one long and one short essay required. UNC does notuse formulas or cutoffs for admission. They look for and celebrate diversity of interests, backgrounds,

ADMISSIONS INFO FOR STUDENTS WITH LEARNING DIFFERENCES

SAT/ACT required: Yes
Interview required: No
Essay required: Not Applicable
Additional application required: Yes
Documentation required for:
  LD: Psycho ed evaluation to include: relevant historical info, instructional interventions, related services, age diagnosed, objective data (aptitude, achievement, info processing), test scores (standard, percentile and grade equivalents) and describe functional limitations.
  ADHD: Requested documentation is not based on type of disability but rather related to functional limitations and the requested accommodations as a result of the identified functional limitation. The following information is generally requested from all students identifying in the Accessibility Resource and Service department: (1) Self-Identification Form, to be completed by person requesting registration with ARS and accommodations; (2) Current documentation prepared by a professional relevant to the requested accommodations; and/or (3) If applicable / available, historical use of accommodations via IEPs, SOPs, 504s or other accommodation approvals.
  ASD: Requested documentation is not based on type of disability but rather related to functional limitations and the requested accommodations as a result of the identified functional limitation. The following information is generally requested from all students identifying in the Accessibility Resource and Service department: (1) Self-Identification Form, to be completed by person requesting registration with ARS and accommodations; (2) Current documentation prepared by a professional relevant to the requested accommodations; and/or (3) If applicable / available, historical use of accommodations via IEPs, SOPs, 504s or other accommodation approvals
Documentation submitted to: Learning Center - ADHD/LD Services
Special Ed. HS course work accepted: No
Separate application required for program services: Yes
# of students last year receiving services/accommodations for:
  LD: 276
  ADHD: 575
Contact Information
Name of program or department: Learning Center - ADHD/LD Services
Telephone: 919-962-3782
Email: learning_center@unc.edu

The University of North Carolina at Chapel Hill

and aspirations. UNC focuses first on academics using courses, GPA tests, recommendations, and essays. Rigor of courses is very important. Beyond academics they look at leadership and service, and character. Although it is not required, applicants may choose to disclose a disability when applying to the University. Disclosure will not impact the review process; each application is considered in competition with others. If an applicant believes the disability has impacted academic progress, the applicant should provide disability documentation and also write the optional essay in the application.

Additional Information

Accessibility Resources and Services meet the individual needs of applicants and current students with disabilities. Academic coaches help students succeed by giving the tools to properly balance academic demands and everything else. They work one-on-one to help students improve academic strategies, develop effective study habits, and find school/life balance. Peer tutoring is available on drop in basis or by appointment.

General Admissions

Very important factors considered include: rigor of secondary school record, application essay, standardized test scores, recommendation(s), extracurricular activities, talent/ability, character/personal qualities, state residency. *Important factors considered include:* class rank, academic GPA, volunteer work, work experience. *Other factors considered include:* first generation, alumni/ae relation, racial/ethnic status. *Freshman Admission Requirements:* High school diploma is required and GED is not accepted. *Academic units required:* 4 English, 4 math, 3 science, 1 science lab, 2 foreign language, 1 social studies, 1 history, 1 academic elective.

Accommodation or Services

Accommodations are decided upon an individual basis after a thorough review of appropriate, current documentation. The accommodations requests must be supported through the documentation provided and must be logically linked to the current impact of the condition on academic functioning.

Financial Aid

Students should submit: CSS/Financial Aid PROFILE; FAFSA. Applicants will be notified of awards on a rolling basis beginning 3/15. The Princeton Review suggests that all financial aid forms be submitted as soon as possible after October 1. *Need-based scholarships/grants offered:* College/university scholarship or grant aid from institutional funds; Federal Pell; Private scholarships; SEOG; State scholarships/grants. *Loan aid offered:* Direct PLUS loans; Direct Subsidized Stafford Loans; Direct Unsubsidized Stafford Loans. Federal Work-Study Program available. Institutional employment available.

Campus Life

Activities: Campus Ministries; Choral groups; Concert band; Dance; Drama/theater; International Student Organization; Jazz band; Literary magazine; Marching band; Model UN; Music ensembles; Musical theater; Opera; Pep band; Radio station; Student government; Student newspaper; Student-run film society; Symphony orchestra; Television station; Yearbook. **Organizations:** 635 registered organizations, 19 honor societies, 42 religious organizations. 35 fraternities, 23 sororities. **Athletics (Intercollegiate):** *Men:* baseball, basketball, cross-country, diving, fencing, football, golf, lacrosse, soccer, swimming, tennis, track/field (outdoor), track/field (indoor), wrestling. *Women:* basketball, crew/rowing, cross-country, diving, fencing, field hockey, golf, gymnastics, lacrosse, soccer, softball, swimming, tennis, track/field (outdoor), track/field (indoor), volleyball. **On-Campus Highlights:** The Pit, McCorkle Place, Polk Place, Dean Smith Center, Student Union.

ACCOMMODATIONS

Allowed in exams:

Calculators	Yes
Dictionary	Yes
Computer	Yes
Spell-checker	Yes
Extended test time	Yes
Scribe	Yes
Proctors	Yes
Oral exams	Yes
Note-takers	Yes

Support services for students with

LD	Yes
ADHD	Yes
ASD	Yes
Distraction-reduced environment	Yes
Recording of lecture allowed	Yes
Reading technology:	Yes
Audio books	Yes
Other assistive technology	Livescribe Pen
Priority registration	Yes

Added costs for services:

For LD:	No
For ADHD:	No
For ASD:	No
LD specialists	Yes
ADHD & ASD coaching	Yes
ASD specialists	No
Professional tutors	Yes
Peer tutors	Yes
Max. hours/week for services	Varies

How professors are notified of student approved accommodations
  Director and student

COLLEGE GRADUATION REQUIREMENTS

Course waivers allowed	No
In what courses	
Course substitutions allowed	Yes
In what courses	Math and Foreign

Language only; through a staff reviewed process students can apply to take an alternative course to fulfill the requirement.

University of North Carolina at Charlotte

9201 University City Boulevard, Charlotte, NC 28223-0001 • Admissions: 704-687-5507 • Fax: 704-687-6483

CAMPUS
Type of school	Public
Environment	Metropolis
Support	CS

STUDENTS
Undergrad enrollment	23,622
% male/female	53/47
% from out of state	4
% frosh live on campus	79

FINANCIAL FACTS
Annual in-state tuition	$3,812
Annual out-of-state tuition	$17,246
Room and board	$10,780
Required fees	$2,909

GENERAL ADMISSIONS INFO
Application fee	$60
Regular application deadline	6/1
Nonfall registration accepted.	
Range SAT EBRW	560–630
Range SAT Math	550–630
Range ACT Composite	22–26

ACADEMICS
Student/faculty ratio	19:1
% students returning for sophomore year	83
% students graduating within 4 years	29
% students graduating within 6 years	54

Most classes have 10–19 students.
Most lab/discussion sessions have 10–19 students.

PROGRAMS/SERVICES FOR STUDENTS WITH LEARNING DIFFERENCES

The mission of Disability Services reflects the university's commitment to diversity by ensuring access to educational opportunities for persons with disabilities. The professional staff in Disability Services assists students with disabilities, including learning disabilities, through an interactive process based on their individual needs.

ADMISSIONS

All applicants must meet the general admissions requirements.and any special requirements for a particular major. Students must be admitted and enrolled to request disability accommodations. Average GPA is 3.8-4.5 weighted or 3.2-3.7 unweighted. SAT mid 50% is 1130-1280 and will be super scored. The mid 50% for ACT is 22-27 and no super score. Writing Section of ACT or SAT not required. Courses include: 4 English, 4 Math, 2 Social Studies: (one must be US History), 3 Science, and 2 Foreign Language. Admission Decisions Are Based On the following: Academic courses in grades 9–11, GPA, courses selected for senior year, and SAT or ACT Scores. Business, Nursing, Computing & Informatics, and Engineering are the most competitive majors.

Additional Information

Services offered are based on the student's disability documentation, the functional impact of the disability upon the student and an interactive process between the student and the Disability Services counselor. UNC Charlotte has a Tutoring Center and a Writing Center available to all students. Academic Services at UNC Charlotte enriches the academic community by offering a broad range of initiatives promoting student success, ensuring access, and enhancing the educational experience of all students. Through transition programs, learning communities, support for student-athletes, academic advising, career services, experiential learning, university-wide honors programs, disability services, tutorial programs, and initiatives for underrepresented students, Academic Services cultivates life skills critical to successful graduation and global citizenship. Advocating for the needs of a diverse student population, Academic Services utilizes an integrated student-centered approach

ADMISSIONS INFO FOR STUDENTS WITH LEARNING DIFFERENCES
SAT/ACT required: Yes
Interview required: No
Essay required: Not Applicable
Additional application required: No
Documentation required for:
  LD: Psycho ed evaluation to include: relevant historical info, instructional interventions, related services, age diagnosed, objective data (aptitude, achievement, info processing), test scores (standard, percentile and grade equivalents) and describe functional limitations.
  ADHD: Diagnosis based on DSM-V; history of behaviors impairing functioning in academic setting; diagnostic interview; history of symptoms; evidence of ongoing behaviors.
  ASD: Psycho ed evaluation
Documentation submitted to: Office of Disability Services
Special Ed. HS course work accepted: Not Applicable
Separate application required for program services: No
# of students last year receiving services/accommodations for:
  LD: 83
Contact Information
Name of program or department: Office of Disability Services
Telephone: 704-687-0040
Fax: 704-687-1395
Email: disability@uncc.edu

University of North Carolina at Charlotte

that reinforces rigorous academic expectations and encourages student engagement from the time of enrollment through graduation.

GENERAL ADMISSIONS

Very important factors considered include: rigor of secondary school record, academic GPA, standardized test scores. *Other factors considered include:* extracurricular activities, talent/ability, character/personal qualities, geographical residence, state residency, work experience, level of applicant's interest. *Freshman Admission Requirements:* High school diploma is required and GED is accepted. *Academic units required:* 4 English, 4 math, 3 science, 1 science lab, 2 foreign language, 1 social studies, 1 history. *Academic units recommended:* 3 foreign language.

ACCOMMODATION OR SERVICES

Accommodations are decided upon an individual basis after a thorough review of appropriate, current documentation. The accommodations requests must be supported through the documentation provided and must be logically linked to the current impact of the condition on academic functioning.

FINANCIAL AID

Students should submit: FAFSA. Applicants will be notified of awards on or about 3/1. The Princeton Review suggests that all financial aid forms be submitted as soon as possible after October 1. *Need-based scholarships/grants offered:* College/university scholarship or grant aid from institutional funds; Federal Pell; Private scholarships; SEOG; State scholarships/grants; United Negro College Fund. *Loan aid offered:* Direct PLUS loans; Direct Subsidized Stafford Loans; Direct Unsubsidized Stafford Loans. Federal Work-Study Program available. Institutional employment available.

CAMPUS LIFE

Activities: Campus Ministries; Choral groups; Concert band; Dance; Drama/theater; International Student Organization; Jazz band; Literary magazine; Marching band; Model UN; Music ensembles; Musical theater; Opera; Pep band; Radio station; Student government; Student newspaper; Student-run film society; Symphony orchestra; Television station. **Organizations:** 222 registered organizations, 25 honor societies, 22 religious organizations. 14 fraternities, 10 sororities. **Athletics (Intercollegiate):** *Men:* baseball, basketball, cross-country, golf, soccer, tennis, track/field (outdoor). *Women:* basketball, cross-country, soccer, softball, tennis, track/field (outdoor), volleyball. **On-Campus Highlights:** Popp Martin Student Union, SoVi (South Village Dining Hall), Belk Gym, The Prospector, J Murrey Atkins Library.

ACCOMMODATIONS

Allowed in exams:

Calculators	Yes
Dictionary	Yes
Computer	Yes
Spell-checker	Yes
Extended test time	Yes
Scribe	No
Proctors	No
Oral exams	No
Note-takers	Yes

Support services for students with

LD	Yes
ADHD	Yes
ASD	Yes
Distraction-reduced environment	Yes
Recording of lecture allowed	Yes
Reading technology:	Yes
Audio books	Not Applicable
Other assistive technology	Read and Write Gold Dragon
Priority registration	Yes

Added costs for services:

For LD:	No
For ADHD:	No
For ASD:	No
LD specialists	Yes
ADHD & ASD coaching	Not Applicable
ASD specialists	No
Professional tutors	Yes
Peer tutors	Not Applicable
Max. hours/week for services	Varies
How professors are notified of student approved accommodations	Student

COLLEGE GRADUATION REQUIREMENTS

Course waivers allowed	No
Course substitutions allowed	No

The University of North Carolina at Greensboro

PO Box 26170, Greensboro, NC 27402-6170 • Admissions: 336-334-5243 • Fax: 336-334-4180

CAMPUS

Type of school	Public
Environment	City
Support	CS

STUDENTS

Undergrad enrollment	15,988
% male/female	34/66
% from out of state	5
% frosh live on campus	78

FINANCIAL FACTS

Annual in-state tuition	$4,422
Annual out-of-state tuition	$19,582
Room and board	$10,183
Required fees	$2,828

GENERAL ADMISSIONS INFO

Application fee	$65
Priority deadline	11/1
Regular application deadline	3/1
Nonfall registration accepted.	

Range SAT EBRW	520–600
Range SAT Math	510–580
Range ACT Composite	20–25

ACADEMICS

Student/faculty ratio	18:1
% students returning for sophomore year	76
% students graduating within 4 years	29
% students graduating within 6 years	53

Most classes have 10–19 students.
Most lab/discussion sessions have 10–19 students.

PROGRAMS/SERVICES FOR STUDENTS WITH LEARNING DIFFERENCES

The Office of Accessibility Resources and Services believes that every student has the capability to be successful. The students' understanding of their learning needs and learning styles is critical to their success in college. Specific accommodations are unique to every student. The office strives to assist every student in identifying and understanding his/her unique learning strengths. Staff is passionate about assisting students in their growth and development. It is our hope that through this learning experience students will be successful in advocating for themselves within the university and ultimately upon graduation.

ADMISSIONS

There is no special admissions process for students with learning disabilities. Admission is competitive and based on academic qualifications. No pre-admission inquiry regarding a learning disability is made. However, students may self-disclose a disability in the application for admission. ACT or SAT required (no writing Section required). The average GPA is 3.83 (weighted); SAT middle 50% ranges: 520-600 critical reading 510-580 math; and average ACT is 23. Courses required include 4 English, 4 math, 3 science, 2 social science, and 2 foreign language.

Additional Information

Trained staff members are available for counseling to assist students with academic and/or personal problems. Voluntary note-takers are solicited through OAR, and photocopying is available. Students will meet with their faculty advisor to discuss courses that need to be taken, and OAR will stamp the students' registration cards to verify that they are registered with OAR and warrant priority registration. Students are provided with information regarding campus tutorials and labs. Individual tutors are provided when it seems necessary. Students can receive help with study skills and time management techniques.

ADMISSIONS INFO FOR STUDENTS WITH LEARNING DIFFERENCES

SAT/ACT required: Yes
Interview required: No
Essay required: No
Additional application required: Yes
Documentation required for:
 LD: A student who has decided to attend UNCG should contact his/her doctor or diagnostician for a copy of their disability documentation.
 ADHD: A student who has decided to attend UNCG should contact his/her doctor or diagnostician for a copy of their disability documentation.
 ASD: A student who has decided to attend UNCG should contact his/her doctor or diagnostician for a copy of their disability documentation.
Documentation submitted to: Office of Accessibility Resources and Services
Special Ed. HS course work accepted: Not Applicable
Separate application required for program services: LD, ADHD, ASD
# of students last year receiving services/accommodations for:
 LD: 200
Contact Information
Name of program or department: Office of Accessibility Resources and Services
Telephone: 336-334-5440
Fax: 336-334-4415
Email: oars@uncg.edu

The University of North Carolina at Greensboro

General Admissions

Very important factors considered include: rigor of secondary school record, academic GPA. *Important factors considered include:* standardized test scores. *Other factors considered include:* class rank, application essay, recommendation(s), extracurricular activities, volunteer work. *Freshman Admission Requirements:* High school diploma is required and GED is accepted. *Academic units required:* 4 English, 4 math, 3 science, 1 science lab, 2 foreign language, 2 social studies.

Accommodation or Services

Accommodations are decided upon an individual basis after a thorough review of appropriate, current documentation. The accommodations requests must be supported through the documentation provided and must be logically linked to the current impact of the condition on academic functioning.

Financial Aid

Students should submit: FAFSA. Applicants will be notified of awards on a rolling basis beginning 3/15. The Princeton Review suggests that all financial aid forms be submitted as soon as possible after October 1. *Need-based scholarships/grants offered:* College/university scholarship or grant aid from institutional funds; Federal Pell; Private scholarships; SEOG; State scholarships/grants. *Loan aid offered:* Direct PLUS loans; Direct Subsidized Stafford Loans; Direct Unsubsidized Stafford Loans. Federal Work-Study Program available. Institutional employment available.

Campus Life

Activities: Campus Ministries; Choral groups; Concert band; Dance; Drama/theater; International Student Organization; Jazz band; Literary magazine; Marching band; Model UN; Music ensembles; Musical theater; Opera; Pep band; Radio station; Student government; Student newspaper; Student-run film society; Symphony orchestra. **Organizations:** 200 registered organizations, 23 honor societies, 13 religious organizations. 11 fraternities, 11 sororities. **Athletics (Intercollegiate):** *Men:* baseball, basketball, cross-country, golf, soccer, tennis, wrestling. *Women:* basketball, cross-country, golf, soccer, softball, tennis, volleyball. **On-Campus Highlights:** Kaplan Center for Wellness, Elliott University Center, Weatherspoon Art Museum, Peabody Park, UNCG Theatre.

ACCOMMODATIONS

Allowed in exams:

Calculators	Yes
Dictionary	Yes
Computer	Yes
Spell-checker	Yes
Extended test time	Yes
Scribe	Yes
Proctors	Yes
Oral exams	Yes
Note-takers	Yes

Support services for students with

LD	Yes
ADHD	Yes
ASD	Yes
Distraction-reduced environment	Yes
Recording of lecture allowed	Yes
Reading technology:	Yes
Audio books	Yes

Other assistive technologyMaterials allowed in lectures, labs, and/or exams are at the discretion of the faculty.

Priority registration	No

Added costs for services:

For LD:	No
For ADHD:	No
For ASD:	No
LD specialists	Yes
ADHD & ASD coaching	Yes
ASD specialists	No
Professional tutors	Yes
Peer tutors	Yes
Max. hours/week for services	3
How professors are notified of student approved accommodations	Student

COLLEGE GRADUATION REQUIREMENTS

Course waivers allowed	No

In what courses

If a student deems it necessary to request deviation from the prescribed course of study, the student should consult the dean of the college or school, or the chairperson of the department of the student's major.

Course substitutions allowed	Yes

In what courses

If a student deems it necessary to request deviation from the prescribed course of study, the student should consult the dean of the college or school, or the chairperson of the department of the student's major.

University of North Carolina—Wilmington

601 SOUTH COLLEGE RD, WILMINGTON, NC 28403-5904 • ADMISSIONS: 910-962-3243 • FAX: 910-962-3038

CAMPUS
Type of school	Public
Environment	City
Support	CS

STUDENTS
Undergrad enrollment	14,183
% male/female	38/62
% from out of state	12
% frosh live on campus	90

FINANCIAL FACTS
Annual in-state tuition	$4,443
Annual out-of-state tuition	$18,508
Room and board	$10,490
Required fees	$2,557

GENERAL ADMISSIONS INFO
Application fee	$80
Priority deadline	11/1
Regular application deadline	2/1

Nonfall registration accepted. Admission may be deferred for a maximum of 1 year.

Range SAT EBRW	600–660
Range SAT Math	580–650
Range ACT Composite	23–27

ACADEMICS
Student/faculty ratio	18:1
% students returning for sophomore year	87
% students graduating within 4 years	54
% students graduating within 6 years	72

PROGRAMS/SERVICES FOR STUDENTS WITH LEARNING DIFFERENCES

Students with Learning Disabilities are responsible for making a timely disclosure of their disability, ensuring that the university is aware of the disabilities that require accommodations. Students should contact the Disability Resource Center, as it is the only designated campus agency responsible for classroom accommodations. After providing appropriate documentation of the disability, the student must register with the Disability Resource Center and request accommodations each semester. Once students is register they contact faculty members in each course to provide a Faculty Accommodation Letter. This confidential form tells faculty members of the student's necessary and specific course accommodations. Students with disabilities are expected to maintain the same responsibility for their education as other students. This includes maintaining the same academic levels, attending class, maintaining appropriate behavior, and providing notification of any special needs. It is the student's responsibility to utilize the services and keep in close contact with the Disability Resource Center.

ADMISSIONS

Courses required include: 4 English, 4 math, 2 foreign language, 3 science, and 2 social studies. The middle 50% ACT composite is 24-28. Middle 50% SAT is 200-1310. UNCW will continue to "superscore" within the same SAT test version. The middle 50% weighted GPA is 3.80-4.43 (A/B average, with few, if any, C's and no D's or F's). The minimum GPA for the UNC System is a 2.5 but (unlikely to be admitted). A GPA will not be recalculated, however it is reviewed in the context of the student's high school's individual grading scale (regional college reps are familiar with high schools). Class rank will be considered, if provided. (not in classes less than 50 students) Internships and dual enrollment requiring early release from school are viewed as weakening an application.

ADMISSIONS INFO FOR STUDENTS WITH LEARNING DIFFERENCES
SAT/ACT required: Yes
Interview required: No
Essay required: Yes
Additional application required: Not Applicable
Documentation required for:
  LD: Psycho ed evaluation to include: relevant historical info, instructional interventions, related services, age diagnosed, objective data (aptitude, achievement, info processing), test scores (standard, percentile and grade equivalents) and describe functional limitations.
  ADHD: Diagnosis based on DSM-V; history of behaviors impairing functioning in academic setting; diagnostic interview; history of symptoms; evidence of ongoing behaviors.
  ASD: Psycho ed evaluation
Documentation submitted to: Disability Services
Special Ed. HS course work accepted: No
Separate application required for program services: No
# of students last year receiving services/accommodations for:
  LD: 250
Contact Information
Name of program or department: Disability Services (DS)
Telephone: 910-962-7555
Fax: 910-962-7556

University of North Carolina—Wilmington

Additional Information

Read&Write Gold "is a discrete, customizable toolbar that integrates reading, writing, studying, and research support tools with common applications." It reads text on the screen and is compatible with Adobe Acrobat/Reader, Daisy and Microsoft Word. DRC will provide RWG trainings, starting with basic download and installation instruction. Reasonable accommodations are provided based on individual need as assessed through documentation. It is the student's responsibility to provide DRC with appropriate documentation. DRC does not do any formal assessments but does have a referral list available. Students are not required to identify themselves as a student with a disability if they do not want services and accommodations.

GENERAL ADMISSIONS

Very important factors considered include: rigor of secondary school record, academic GPA, application essay, standardized test scores, recommendation(s). *Important factors considered include:* class rank. *Other factors considered include:* extracurricular activities, talent/ability, character/personal qualities, first generation, alumni/ae relation, geographical residence, state residency, racial/ethnic status, volunteer work, work experience, level of applicant's interest. *Freshman Admission Requirements:* High school diploma is required and GED is accepted. *Academic units required:* 4 English, 4 math, 3 science, 1 science lab, 2 foreign language, 1 social studies, 1 history.

ACCOMMODATION OR SERVICES

Accommodations are decided upon an individual basis after a thorough review of appropriate, current documentation. The accommodations requests must be supported through the documentation provided and must be logically linked to the current impact of the condition on academic functioning.

FINANCIAL AID

Students should submit: FAFSA; Institution's own financial aid form. Applicants will be notified of awards on or about 3/29. The Princeton Review suggests that all financial aid forms be submitted as soon as possible after October 1. *Need-based scholarships/grants offered:* College/university scholarship or grant aid from institutional funds; Federal Nursing Scholarships; Federal Pell; Private scholarships; SEOG; State scholarships/grants; United Negro College Fund. *Loan aid offered:* Direct PLUS loans; Direct Subsidized Stafford Loans; Direct Unsubsidized Stafford Loans. Federal Work-Study Program available. Institutional employment available.

CAMPUS LIFE

Activities: Campus Ministries; Choral groups; Concert band; Dance; Drama/theater; International Student Organization; Literary magazine; Model UN; Music ensembles; Pep band; Radio station; Student government; Student newspaper; Student-run film society; Television station. **Organizations:** 173 registered organizations, 8 honor societies, 14 religious organizations. 11 fraternities, 11 sororities. **Athletics (Intercollegiate):** *Men:* baseball, basketball, cheerleading, cross-country, diving, golf, soccer, swimming, tennis, track/field (outdoor). *Women:* basketball, cheerleading, cross-country, diving, golf, soccer, softball, swimming, tennis, track/field (outdoor), volleyball. **On-Campus Highlights:** Fisher Student Center, William Randall Library, UNCW Student Recreation Center, Trask Coliseum, Fisher University Union.

ACCOMMODATIONS

Allowed in exams:	
Calculators	Yes
Dictionary	No
Computer	Yes
Spell-checker	Yes
Extended test time	Yes
Scribe	Yes
Proctors	Yes
Oral exams	Yes
Note-takers	Yes
Support services for students with	
LD	Yes
ADHD	Yes
ASD	Yes
Distraction-reduced environment	Yes
Recording of lecture allowed	Yes
Reading technology:	Yes
Audio books	Yes
Other assistive technology	Yes
Priority registration	Yes
Added costs for services:	
For LD:	No
For ADHD:	No
For ASD:	No
LD specialists	Yes
ADHD & ASD coaching	Not Applicable
ASD specialists	Yes
Professional tutors	Yes
Peer tutors	Yes
Max. hours/week for services	Varies
How professors are notified of student approved accommodations	Director and student

COLLEGE GRADUATION REQUIREMENTS

Course waivers allowed	Not Applicable
Course substitutions allowed	Not Applicable

Wake Forest University

P.O. Box 7373 Reynolda Station, Winston Salem, NC 27109 • Admissions: 336-758-5201 • Fax: 336-758-4324

CAMPUS

Type of school	Private (nonprofit)
Environment	City
Support	CS

STUDENTS

Undergrad enrollment	5,101
% male/female	46/54
% from out of state	78
% frosh live on campus	98

FINANCIAL FACTS

Annual tuition	$52,348
Room and board	$16,032
Required fees	$974

GENERAL ADMISSIONS INFO

Application fee	$65.
Regular application deadline	1/1
Nonfall registration accepted.	

Range SAT EBRW	630–710
Range SAT Math	630–730
Range ACT Composite	28–32

ACADEMICS

Student/faculty ratio	11:1
% students returning for sophomore year	94
% students graduating within 4 years	84
% students graduating within 6 years	88

Most classes have 30–39 students. Most lab/discussion sessions have 30–39 students.

PROGRAMS/SERVICES FOR STUDENTS WITH LEARNING DIFFERENCES

The Learning Assistance Center (LAC) offers support for academic success. For students with documented disabilities, the program director will work with the student and members of the faculty to help implement any approved course accommodations. The students with learning disabilities have a series of conferences with staff members who specialize in academic skills and who help design an overall study plan to improve scholastic performance in those areas needing assistance. If special course accommodations are needed, the LAC staff will serve as an advocate for the students with members of the faculty.

ADMISSIONS

There are no special admissions procedures for students with learning disabilities. Students with LD submit the general Wake Forest University application and are expected to meet the same admission criteria as all applicants. Students should self-disclose to the Learning Assistance Center after admission. Services are available to all enrolled students with documentation on file. Students are encouraged to provide a recent psychoeducational evaluation.

Additional Information

The Learning Assistance Program staff will assist students with learning disabilities to learn new approaches to studying and methods for improving reading comprehension, note-taking, time management, study organization, memory, motivation, and self-modification. The LAC offers peer tutoring services. In addition to one-on-one tutoring in many academic subjects, the LAC provides collaborative learning groups comprised of two to five students. The LAC also assists students who present special academic needs. Accommodations are determined based on appropriate documentation. All students with or without learning disabilities are eligible for group or individual tutoring in basic academic subjects. The tutors are advanced undergraduates or graduate students who have demonstrated mastery of specific subject areas and are supervised by the LAC staff for their tutoring activities. The LAC also offers all students individual academic counseling to help

ADMISSIONS INFO FOR STUDENTS WITH LEARNING DIFFERENCES

SAT/ACT required: No
Interview required: No
Essay required: Yes
Additional application required: No
Documentation required for:
 LD: Psycho ed evaluation to include: relevant historical info, instructional interventions, related services, age diagnosed, objective data (aptitude, achievement, info processing), test scores (standard, percentile and grade equivalents) and describe functional limitations.
 ADHD: Diagnosis based on DSM-V; history of behaviors impairing functioning in academic setting; diagnostic interview; history of symptoms; evidence of ongoing behaviors.
 ASD: Psycho ed evaluation
Documentation submitted to: LAC
Special Ed. HS course work accepted: No
Separate application required for program services: No
# of students last year receiving services/accommodations for:
 LD: 221
Contact Information
Name of program or department: Learning Assistance Center (LAC)
Telephone: 336-758-5929
Fax: 336-758-1991

Wake Forest University

develop study, organization, and time management strategies that are important for successful college-level learning.

GENERAL ADMISSIONS

Very important factors considered include: rigor of secondary school record, class rank, academic GPA, application essay, character/personal qualities. *Important factors considered include:* recommendation(s), interview, extracurricular activities, talent/ability. *Other factors considered include:* standardized test scores, first generation, alumni/ae relation, geographical residence, state residency, religious affiliation/commitment, racial/ethnic status, volunteer work, level of applicant's interest. *Freshman Admission Requirements:* High school diploma is required and GED is accepted. *Academic units required:* 4 English, 3 math, 1 science, 2 foreign language, 2 social studies. *Academic units recommended:* 4 English, 4 math, 4 science, 4 foreign language, 4 social studies.

ACCOMMODATION OR SERVICES

Accommodations are decided upon an individual basis after a thorough review of appropriate, current documentation. The accommodations requests must be supported through the documentation provided and must be logically linked to the current impact of the condition on academic functioning.

FINANCIAL AID

Students should submit: CSS/Financial Aid PROFILE; FAFSA; Noncustodial PROFILE; State aid form. Applicants will be notified of awards on a rolling basis beginning 4/1. The Princeton Review suggests that all financial aid forms be submitted as soon as possible after October 1. *Need-based scholarships/grants offered:* College/university scholarship or grant aid from institutional funds; Federal Pell; Private scholarships; SEOG; State scholarships/grants; United Negro College Fund. *Loan aid offered:* Direct PLUS loans; Direct Subsidized Stafford Loans; Direct Unsubsidized Stafford Loans. Federal Work-Study Program available. Institutional employment available.

CAMPUS LIFE

Activities: Campus Ministries; Choral groups; Concert band; Dance; Drama/theater; International Student Organization; Jazz band; Literary magazine; Marching band; Model UN; Music ensembles; Musical theater; Pep band; Radio station; Student government; Student newspaper; Student-run film society; Symphony orchestra; Television station; Yearbook. **Organizations:** 168 registered organizations, 16 honor societies, 16 religious organizations. 14 fraternities, 9 sororities. **Athletics (Intercollegiate):** *Men:* baseball, basketball, cheerleading, cross-country, football, golf, soccer, tennis, track/field (outdoor), track/field (indoor). *Women:* basketball, cheerleading, cross-country, field hockey, golf, soccer, tennis, track/field (outdoor), track/field (indoor), volleyball. **On-Campus Highlights:** Charlotte and Philip Hanes Art Gallery, Museum of Anthropology, The Z. Smith Reynolds Library, Wait Chapel, Benson University Center.

ACCOMMODATIONS

Allowed in exams:

Calculators	No
Dictionary	Yes
Computer	Yes
Spell-checker	Yes
Extended test time	Yes
Scribe	No
Proctors	No
Oral exams	No
Note-takers	No

Support services for students with

LD	Yes
ADHD	Yes
ASD	Yes
Distraction-reduced environment	Yes
Recording of lecture allowed	Yes
Reading technology:	Yes
Audio books	No
Other assistive technology	No
Priority registration	No

Added costs for services:

For LD:	No
For ADHD:	No
For ASD:	No
LD specialists	Yes
ADHD & ASD coaching	No
ASD specialists	No
Professional tutors	No
Peer tutors	Yes
Max. hours/week for services	Varies
How professors are notified of student approved accommodations	Student and director

COLLEGE GRADUATION REQUIREMENTS

Course waivers allowed	No
Course substitutions allowed	Yes

In what courses Foreign Language only. If there is a documented language-based LD and a good faith effort has been made by the student to learn a foreign language without success, then two courses from an approved list of classics and humanities courses may be substituted.

Western Carolina University

102 CAMP BUILDING, CULLOWHEE, NC 28723 • ADMISSIONS: 828-227-7317 • FAX: 828-227-7319

CAMPUS

Type of school	Public
Environment	Rural
Support	CS

STUDENTS

Undergrad enrollment	9,234
% male/female	45/55
% from out of state	7
% frosh live on campus	97

FINANCIAL FACTS

Annual in-state tuition	$3,971
Annual out-of-state tuition	$14,364
Room and board	$9,553
Required fees	$3,220

GENERAL ADMISSIONS INFO

Application fee	$65
Priority deadline	11/15
Regular application deadline	3/1

Nonfall registration accepted.

Range SAT EBRW	510-610
Range SAT Math	510–590
Range ACT Composite	19–24

ACADEMICS

Student/faculty ratio	17:1
% students returning for sophomore year	79
% students graduating within 4 years	40
% students graduating within 6 years	59

Most classes have 20–29 students.
Most lab/discussion sessions have fewer than 10 students.

PROGRAMS/SERVICES FOR STUDENTS WITH LEARNING DIFFERENCES

The Office of Disability Services attempts to respond to the needs of students with learning disabilities by making services and assistive technologies available as needed.

ADMISSIONS

Students with learning disabilities are admitted under the same standards as students who do not have learning disabilities. WCU does not have a strict minimum GPA. Students not admissible through the regular admission process may be offered a probationary admission and must begin in the summer prior to freshman year. The admission decision is made by the Admissions Office.

Additional Information

To qualify for services, students must be enrolled at the university and have updated medical documentation. The following are examples of services or accommodations are available for students with appropriate documentation: the use of calculators, dictionaries, computers, or spellcheckers during exams; extended time on tests; quiet environments; scribes; proctors; oral exams; note-takers; tape recorders in class; text in alternate format; and priority registration. All students have access to tutoring, writing and math centers, a Technology Assistance Center, and counseling and psychological services. Admitted students should maintain good class attendance, strive for good grades, cooperate with counselors and advisors, set realistic career goals, and meet with the Office of Disability Services to arrange accommodations. Services and accommodations are available for all enrolled students.

ADMISSIONS INFO FOR STUDENTS WITH LEARNING DIFFERENCES

SAT/ACT required: Yes
Interview required: No
Essay required: No
Additional application required: Yes
Documentation required for:
  LD: Psycho ed evaluation to include: relevant historical info, instructional interventions, related services, age diagnosed, objective data (aptitude, achievement, info processing), test scores (standard, percentile and grade equivalents) and describe functional limitations.
  ADHD: Diagnosis based on DSM-V; history of behaviors impairing functioning in academic setting; diagnostic interview; history of symptoms; evidence of ongoing behaviors.
  ASD: Psycho ed evaluation
Documentation submitted to: Office of Disability Services(ODS)
Special Ed. HS course work accepted: No
Separate application required for program services: No
# of students last year receiving services/accommodations for:
  LD: 100-120
Contact Information
Name of program or department: Office of Disability Services (ODS)
Telephone: 828-227-3886
Fax: 828-227-7078
Email: disabilityservices@wcu.edu

Western Carolina University

GENERAL ADMISSIONS

Very important factors considered include: rigor of secondary school record, class rank, academic GPA, standardized test scores, level of applicant's interest. *Important factors considered include:* application essay, recommendation(s), extracurricular activities, talent/ability, character/personal qualities, work experience. *Other factors considered include:* interview, first generation, geographical residence, state residency. *Freshman Admission Requirements:* High school diploma is required and GED is accepted. *Academic units required:* 4 English, 4 math, 3 science, 3 science labs, 2 foreign language, 2 social studies, 1 history, 4 academic electives. *Academic units recommended:* 4 English, 4 math, 3 science, 3 science labs, 2 foreign language, 2 social studies, 1 history, 8 academic electives.

ACCOMMODATION OR SERVICES

Accommodations are decided upon an individual basis after a thorough review of appropriate, current documentation. The accommodations requests must be supported through the documentation provided and must be logically linked to the current impact of the condition on academic functioning.

FINANCIAL AID

Students should submit: FAFSA; Institution's own financial aid form. Applicants will be notified of awards on a rolling basis beginning 4/1. The Princeton Review suggests that all financial aid forms be submitted as soon as possible after October 1. *Need-based scholarships/grants offered:* College/university scholarship or grant aid from institutional funds; Federal Pell; Private scholarships; SEOG; State scholarships/grants. *Loan aid offered:* Direct PLUS loans; Direct Subsidized Stafford Loans; Direct Unsubsidized Stafford Loans. Federal Work-Study Program available. Institutional employment available.

CAMPUS LIFE

Activities: Campus Ministries; Choral groups; Concert band; Dance; Drama/theater; International Student Organization; Jazz band; Literary magazine; Marching band; Model UN; Music ensembles; Musical theater; Pep band; Radio station; Student government; Student newspaper; Student-run film society; Television station. **Organizations:** 103 registered organizations, 7 honor societies, 12 religious organizations. 11 fraternities, 8 sororities. **Athletics (Intercollegiate):** *Men:* baseball, basketball, cheerleading, cross-country, football, golf, track/field (outdoor), track/field (indoor). *Women:* basketball, cheerleading, cross-country, golf, soccer, softball, tennis, track/field (outdoor), track/field (indoor), volleyball. **On-Campus Highlights:** University Center, Campus Recreation Center, Hunter Library, Courtyard Dining Hall, Ramsey Regional Activity Center.

ACCOMMODATIONS

Allowed in exams:	
Calculators	Yes
Dictionary	Yes
Computer	Yes
Spell-checker	Yes
Extended test time	Yes
Scribe	Yes
Proctors	Yes
Oral exams	Yes
Note-takers	Yes
Support services for students with	
LD	Yes
ADHD	Yes
ASD	Yes
Distraction-reduced environment	Yes
Recording of lecture allowed	Yes
Reading technology:	Yes
Audio books	No
Other assistive technology	Yes
Priority registration	Yes
Added costs for services:	
For LD:	No
For ADHD:	No
For ASD:	No
LD specialists	Yes
ADHD & ASD coaching	No
ASD specialists	No
Professional tutors	Yes
Peer tutors	Yes
Max. hours/week for services	Varies
How professors are notified of student approved accommodations	Student

COLLEGE GRADUATION REQUIREMENTS

Course waivers allowed	Yes
In what courses	Individually considered
Course substitutions allowed	Yes
In what courses	Individually considered

North Dakota State University

PO Box 6050, Fargo, ND 58108 • Admissions: 701-231-8643 • Fax: 701-231-8802

CAMPUS

Type of school	Public
Environment	City
Support	S

STUDENTS

Undergrad enrollment	11,609
% male/female	55/45
% from out of state	57
% frosh live on campus	93

FINANCIAL FACTS

Annual in-state tuition	$6,762
Annual out-of-state tuition	$18,056
Room and board	$7,502
Required fees	$1,216

GENERAL ADMISSIONS INFO

Application fee	$35
Regular application deadline	8/1

Nonfall registration accepted. Admission may be deferred for a maximum of 3 years.

Range SAT EBRW	480–630
Range SAT Math	500–630
Range ACT Composite	21–26

ACADEMICS

Student/faculty ratio	17:1
% students returning for sophomore year	78
% students graduating within 4 years	32
% students graduating within 6 years	58

Most classes have 20–29 students.
Most lab/discussion sessions have 10–19 students.

PROGRAMS/SERVICES FOR STUDENTS WITH LEARNING DIFFERENCES

The mission of NDSU Disability Services is to ensure equal access to educational opportunities for students with disabilities to fully participate in the university environment. Disability Services (DS) assists both students with disabilities, and faculty and staff working with students with disabilities. DS staff members can provide individual consultation regarding the possible presence of a disability, making referrals when appropriate; determine eligibility for accommodations and services, explain how to access services, provide assistance when arranging accommodations; consult with students, faculty and staff and partner with NDSU personnel to implement appropriate accommodations; and make referrals to other available support services. Disability Services staff members work to promote equal access to academic programs, promote self-awareness and advocacy skill development, educate campus community about disability-related issues and collaborate with various support services.

ADMISSIONS

Students with learning disabilities submit the general application form and are expected to meet the same admission standards as all other applicants. Applicants are expected to have taken high school courses in math, including algebra; English; science labs; and social studies. Students with learning disabilities may include a self-disclosure or information explaining or documenting their disability.

Additional Information

Skills courses are offered. A technology lab/resource room is available for student use. Individual, career, and academic counseling along with support groups are available through the NDSU Counseling Center. TRIO-Student Support Services Program provides tutoring and small group instruction in study strategies, reading, computers, math, and science. The Academic Collegiate Experience (ACE) offers group tutoring. Individuals with learning disabilities or attention deficit hyperactive disorder may utilize these services. Students need to apply and qualify for TRIO-Student Support Services.

ADMISSIONS INFO FOR STUDENTS WITH LEARNING DIFFERENCES

SAT/ACT required: Yes
Interview required: No
Essay required: Recommended
Additional application required: No
Documentation required for:
  LD: Psycho ed evaluation to include: relevant historical info, instructional interventions, related services, age diagnosed, objective data (aptitude, achievement, info processing), test scores (standard, percentile and grade equivalents) and describe functional limitations.
  ADHD: Diagnosis based on DSM-V; history of behaviors impairing functioning in academic setting; diagnostic interview; history of symptoms; evidence of ongoing behaviors.
  ASD: Psycho ed evaluation
Documentation submitted to: Disability Services
Special Ed. HS course work accepted: No
Separate application required for program services: No
Contact Information
Name of program or department: Disability Services
Telephone: 701-231-8463
Fax: 701-231-5205
Email: ndsu.disability.services@ndsu.edu

North Dakota State University

General Admissions

Very important factors considered include: academic GPA, standardized test scores. *Freshman Admission Requirements:* High school diploma is required and GED is accepted. *Academic units required:* 4 English, 3 math, 3 science, 3 science labs, 3 social studies.

Accommodation or Services

Accommodations are decided upon an individual basis after a thorough review of appropriate, current documentation. The accommodations requests must be supported through the documentation provided and must be logically linked to the current impact of the condition on academic functioning.

Financial Aid

Students should submit: FAFSA. Applicants will be notified of awards on a rolling basis beginning 4/1. The Princeton Review suggests that all financial aid forms be submitted as soon as possible after October 1. *Need-based scholarships/grants offered:* College/university scholarship or grant aid from institutional funds; Federal Pell; Private scholarships; SEOG; State scholarships/grants. *Loan aid offered:* Direct PLUS loans; Direct Subsidized Stafford Loans; Direct Unsubsidized Stafford Loans. Federal Work-Study Program available. Institutional employment available.

Campus Life

Activities: Campus Ministries; Choral groups; Concert band; Dance; Drama/theater; International Student Organization; Jazz band; Marching band; Model UN; Music ensembles; Musical theater; Opera; Pep band; Radio station; Student government; Student newspaper; Symphony orchestra; Television station. **Organizations:** 218 registered organizations, 22 honor societies, 18 religious organizations. 10 fraternities, 5 sororities. **Athletics (Intercollegiate):** *Men:* baseball, basketball, cross-country, football, golf, track/field (outdoor), track/field (indoor), wrestling. *Women:* basketball, cross-country, golf, soccer, softball, track/field (outdoor), track/field (indoor), volleyball. **On-Campus Highlights:** Wellness Center, Memorial Union, Fargo Dome, STEM Classroom and Lab Building, Quentin Burdick Building.

ACCOMMODATIONS

Allowed in exams:	
Calculators	Yes
Dictionary	Yes
Computer	Yes
Spell-checker	Yes
Extended test time	Yes
Scribe	Yes
Proctors	Yes
Oral exams	Yes
Note-takers	Yes
Support services for students with	
LD	Yes
ADHD	Yes
ASD	Yes
Distraction-reduced environment	Yes
Recording of lecture allowed	Yes
Reading technology:	Yes
Audio books	No
Other assistive technology	Yes
Priority registration	Yes
Added costs for services:	
For LD:	No
For ADHD:	No
For ASD:	No
LD specialists	No
ADHD & ASD coaching	No
ASD specialists	No
Professional tutors	No
Peer tutors	Yes
Max. hours/week for services	Unlimted
How professors are notified of student approved accommodations	Student

COLLEGE GRADUATION REQUIREMENTS

Course waivers allowed	Yes
Course substitutions allowed	Yes

University of Jamestown

6000 College Lane, Jamestown, ND 58405-0001 • Admissions: 701-252-3467 • Fax: 701-253-4318

CAMPUS

Type of school	Private (nonprofit)
Environment	Village
Support	S

STUDENTS

Undergrad enrollment	892
% male/female	51/49
% from out of state	49
% frosh live on campus	95

FINANCIAL FACTS

Annual tuition	$21,196
Room and board	$7,886
Required fees	$780

GENERAL ADMISSIONS INFO

Priority deadline	5/1

Nonfall registration accepted. Admission may be deferred.

Range SAT EBRW	460–520
Range SAT Math	480–530
Range ACT Composite	19–24

ACADEMICS

Student/faculty ratio	12:1
% students returning for sophomore year	72
% students graduating within 4 years	40
% students graduating within 6 years	52

Most classes have 10–19 students. Most lab/discussion sessions have 10–19 students.

PROGRAMS/SERVICES FOR STUDENTS WITH LEARNING DIFFERENCES

The Student Success Center includes advising, tutor services, and disability services. To support University of Jamestown's dedication to the development of wholeness in our students, academic excellence, and growth of the individual, the university is committed to meeting the following goals: Provide accurate information regarding educational opportunities, requirements, policies and procedures to students and advisors; Identify and coordinate reasonable accommodations for qualified students with disabilities to ensure their access to the university curriculum; Support and educate faculty and staff regarding (a) the legal and moral issues of accommodating students with disabilities and (b) the implementation of reasonable accommodations for students with disabilities.Provide qualified and effective peer tutors.

ADMISSIONS

The University of Jamestown undergraduate admissions criteria is a GPA of 2.5 and a minimum ACT of 19. Each applicant is reviewed on an individual basis and decisions are made within two weeks of completion of a completed application received.

Additional Information

In addition to one-on-one tutoring, the Student Success Center offers several study sessions each semester. If more on-on-one attention is needed beyond a study group, students complete a tutor request form and the Center does their best to line up with a one-on-one tutor. The UJ Writing Center believe that writing is a process, from considering what needs to be written, who will be reading it, and how it can best be accomplished. This includes self-reflection, research, drafting, and revising. Writing consultants are experienced in navigating this process and provide support.

ADMISSIONS INFO FOR STUDENTS WITH LEARNING DIFFERENCES

SAT/ACT required: Yes
Interview required: No
Essay required: Not Applicable
Additional application required: Yes
Documentation required for:
  LD: Documentation that outlines diagnosis and functioning limitations of the disability
  ADHD: Documentation that outlines diagnosis and functioning limitations of the disability
  ASD: Documentation that outlines diagnosis and functioning limitations of the disability
Documentation submitted to: Office of Disability Services
Special Ed. HS course work accepted: Yes
Separate application required for program services: Yes
# of students last year receiving services/accommodations for:
  LD: 37
Contact Information
Name of program or department: Office of Disability Services
Telephone: (701) 252-3467
Fax: (701) 253-4318
Email: registrar@uj.edu

University of Jamestown

GENERAL ADMISSIONS

Very important factors considered include: academic GPA, standardized test scores. *Other factors considered include:* rigor of secondary school record, application essay, recommendation(s), interview, extracurricular activities, talent/ability, character/personal qualities, alumni/ae relation, level of applicant's interest. *Freshman Admission Requirements:* High school diploma is required and GED is accepted. *Academic units recommended:* 4 English, 3 math, 4 science, 2 foreign language, 3 social studies.

ACCOMMODATION OR SERVICES

Accommodations are decided upon an individual basis after a thorough review of appropriate, current documentation. The accommodations requests must be supported through the documentation provided and must be logically linked to the current impact of the condition on academic functioning.

FINANCIAL AID

Students should submit: FAFSA. Applicants will be notified of awards on a rolling basis beginning 10/15. The Princeton Review suggests that all financial aid forms be submitted as soon as possible after October 1. *Need-based scholarships/grants offered:* Federal Pell; Private scholarships; SEOG; State scholarships/grants. *Loan aid offered:* Direct PLUS loans; Direct Subsidized Stafford Loans; Direct Unsubsidized Stafford Loans. Federal Work-Study Program available. Institutional employment available.

CAMPUS LIFE

Activities: Campus Ministries; Choral groups; Concert band; Dance; Drama/theater; International Student Organization; Jazz band; Literary magazine; Music ensembles; Musical theater; Pep band; Student government; Student newspaper. **Organizations:** 35 registered organizations, 6 honor societies, 5 religious organizations. **Athletics (Intercollegiate):** *Men:* baseball, basketball, cross-country, football, golf, track/field (outdoor), track/field (indoor), wrestling. *Women:* basketball, cross-country, golf, soccer, softball, track/field (outdoor), track/field (indoor), volleyball, wrestling. **On-Campus Highlights:** Nafus Student Center - Java Hut, Jimmie Connection, Newman Center, Residence Hall lounges, Reiland Fine Arts Center.

ACCOMMODATIONS

Allowed in exams:	
Calculators	Yes
Dictionary	Yes
Computer	Yes
Spell-checker	Yes
Extended test time	Yes
Scribe	Not Applicable
Proctors	Yes
Oral exams	Yes
Note-takers	Yes
Support services for students with	
LD	Yes
ADHD	Yes
ASD	Yes
Distraction-reduced environment	Yes
Recording of lecture allowed	Yes
Reading technology:	Not Applicable
Audio books	Not Applicable
Other assistive technology	Yes
Priority registration	No
Added costs for services:	
For LD:	No
For ADHD:	No
For ASD:	No
LD specialists	Yes
ADHD & ASD coaching	No
ASD specialists	Yes
Professional tutors	Yes
Peer tutors	Yes
Max. hours/week for services	Varies
How professors are notified of student approved accommodations	Director and student

COLLEGE GRADUATION REQUIREMENTS

Course waivers allowed	Yes
In what courses	A petition process is in place for all students to petition a general education requirement.
Course substitutions allowed	Yes
In what courses	A petition process is in place for all students to petition a general education requirement.

Bowling Green State University

200 UNIVERSITY HALL, BOWLING GREEN, OH 43403-0085 • ADMISSIONS: 419-372-2478 • FAX: 419-372-6955

CAMPUS
Type of school	Public
Environment	Town
Support	S

STUDENTS
Undergrad enrollment	13,789
% male/female	44/56
% from out of state	12
% frosh live on campus	89

FINANCIAL FACTS
Annual in-state tuition	$9,096
Annual out-of-state tuition	$16,632
Room and board	$8,898
Required fees	$1,961

GENERAL ADMISSIONS INFO
Application fee	$45
Priority deadline	2/1
Regular application deadline	7/15

Nonfall registration accepted. Admission may be deferred.

Range SAT EBRW	510–610
Range SAT Math	510–610
Range ACT Composite	20–25

ACADEMICS
Student/faculty ratio	18:1
% students returning for sophomore year	77
% students graduating within 4 years	35
% students graduating within 6 years	52

Most classes have 10–19 students.
Most lab/discussion sessions have 10–19 students.

PROGRAMS/SERVICES FOR STUDENTS WITH LEARNING DIFFERENCES
The FLY (Falcon Learning Your Way) Program is a fee-based academic support program that provides a comprehensive range of enhanced services to Bowling Green State University students transitioning from high school to college who have learning and/or attention challenges. The range of services in the FLY Program facilitates student learning, self-advocacy, and independence. Students take ownership of their education through working with a Learning Specialist to create an individualized Falcon Learning Plan; engaging in strategies for time management, organization, reading and writing; utilizing tutoring by peer tutors who are internationally certified by the College Reading and Learning Association; and accessing assistive technology in the BGSU Learning Commons. Learning Commons is open to all BGSU students, and the extent of participation is determined by the student. The lab provides a tutorial service and additional support in the development of efficient techniques for studying, reading textbooks, taking notes, time management, and strategies for effective test-taking and text-preparation.

ADMISSIONS
Students must submit a general application to the University prior to submitting an application to the FLY Program. After students have been admitted, they may complete The FLY Program application located on the Admissions webpage. Students should submit documentation of their disability to Accessibility Services and to the FLY Program.

Additional Information
The FLY Program provides Learning Specialists who help students create an individualized Falcon Learning Plan and meet with students weekly. Students have access to one-to-one tutoring services in addition to accommodations granted by Accessibility Services. Workshops are offered in reading, writing, organization, time management, test preparation, and test-taking strategies. There is a special orientation for FLY Program participants before their freshman year. The fee for the FLY Program is $2500 per semester. General services include priority registration; advising

ADMISSIONS INFO FOR STUDENTS WITH LEARNING DIFFERENCES
SAT/ACT required: Yes
Interview required: No
Essay required: Not Applicable
Additional application required: No
Documentation required for:
  LD: Psychoeducational evaluation to include relevant historical info, instructional interventions, related services, age diagnosed, objective data (aptitude, achievement, info processing), test scores (standard, percentile and grade equivalents), describe functional limitations, and/or current ETR (Evaluation Team Report)/MFE (Multi-factor Evaluation).
  ADHD: Neuropsychological evaluation; developmental history; diagnosed based on DSM-V; history of behaviors impairing functioning in academic setting; diagnostic interview; history of symptoms; evidence of ongoing behaviors.
  ASD: Psychoeducational evaluation
Documentation submitted to: Fly Program and Accesibility Services
Special Ed. HS course work accepted: No
Separate application required for program services: Yes
Contact Information
Name of program or department: Fly Program/Accessibility Services
Telephone: 419-372-8495
Fax: 419-372-8496
Email: access@bgsu.edu

Bowling Green State University

by sharing information on instructors' teaching and testing styles; and free tutoring, academic coaching, study skills classes, math tutors, and writing consultants through The Learning Commons. All accommodations and services (such as testing accommodations, note-taker, scribe, reader, dictionary, calculator) are provided through Accessibility Services at no additional cost. To be eligible for accommodations, students are required to provide documentation that provides a clear indication/recommendation for the need requested.

GENERAL ADMISSIONS

Very important factors considered include: rigor of secondary school record, academic GPA, standardized test scores. *Important factors considered include:* class rank. *Other factors considered include:* application essay, recommendation(s), interview, extracurricular activities, talent/ability, character/personal qualities, first generation, alumni/ae relation, racial/ethnic status, volunteer work, work experience, level of applicant's interest. *Freshman Admission Requirements:* High school diploma is required and GED is accepted. *Academic units recommended:* 4 English, 4 math, 3 science, 2 science labs, 2 foreign language, 3 social studies, 1 visual/performing arts.

ACCOMMODATION OR SERVICES

Accommodations are decided upon an individual basis after a thorough review of appropriate, current documentation. The accommodations requests must be supported through the documentation provided and must be logically linked to the current impact of the condition on academic functioning.

FINANCIAL AID

Students should submit: FAFSA. Applicants will be notified of awards on a rolling basis beginning 2/1. The Princeton Review suggests that all financial aid forms be submitted as soon as possible after October 1. *Need-based scholarships/grants offered:* College/university scholarship or grant aid from institutional funds; Federal Pell; Private scholarships; SEOG; State scholarships/grants. *Loan aid offered:* Direct PLUS loans; Direct Subsidized Stafford Loans; Direct Unsubsidized Stafford Loans. Federal Work-Study Program available. Institutional employment available.

CAMPUS LIFE

Activities: Campus Ministries; Choral groups; Concert band; Dance; Drama/theater; International Student Organization; Jazz band; Literary magazine; Marching band; Model UN; Music ensembles; Musical theater; Opera; Pep band; Radio station; Student government; Student newspaper; Student-run film society; Symphony orchestra; Television station; Yearbook. **Organizations:** 20 honor societies, 24 fraternities, 19 sororities. **Athletics (Intercollegiate):** *Men:* baseball, basketball, cross-country, football, golf, ice hockey, soccer *Women:* basketball, cross-country, golf, gymnastics, soccer, softball, swimming, tennis, track/field (outdoor), track/field (indoor), volleyball. **On-Campus Highlights:** Bowen Thompson Student Union, Stroh Center, The Wolfe Center, College of Business Administration, New Residence Halls/ New Dining Halls.

ACCOMMODATIONS

Allowed in exams:	
Calculators	Yes
Dictionary	No
Computer	Yes
Spell-checker	Yes
Extended test time	Yes
Scribe	Yes
Proctors	Yes
Oral exams	Yes
Note-takers	Yes
Support services for students with	
LD	Yes
ADHD	Yes
ASD	Yes
Distraction-reduced environment	Yes
Recording of lecture allowed	Yes
Reading technology:	Yes
Audio books	Yes
Other assistive technology	Yes
Priority registration	Yes
Added costs for services:	
For LD:	No
For ADHD:	No
For ASD:	No
LD specialists	No
ADHD & ASD coaching	No
ASD specialists	No
Professional tutors	Yes
Peer tutors	No
Max. hours/week for services	Varies
How professors are notified of student approved accommodations	Student

COLLEGE GRADUATION REQUIREMENTS

Course waivers allowed	No
Course substitutions allowed	Yes
In what courses	Foreign Language

Case Western Reserve University

10900 EUCLID AVENUE, CLEVELAND, OH 44106-7055 • ADMISSIONS: 216-368-4450 • FAX: 216-368-5111

CAMPUS

Type of school	Private (nonprofit)
Environment	Metropolis
Support	S

STUDENTS

Undergrad enrollment	5,020
% male/female	56/44
% from out of state	72
% frosh live on campus	97

FINANCIAL FACTS

Annual tuition	$48,604
Room and board	$15,190
Required fees	$438

GENERAL ADMISSIONS INFO

Application fee	$70
Regular application deadline	1/15

Nonfall registration accepted. Admission may be deferred for a maximum of 1 year.

Range SAT EBRW	650–740
Range SAT Math	690–780
Range ACT Composite	30–33

ACADEMICS

Student/faculty ratio	11:1
% students returning for sophomore year	93
% students graduating within 4 years	66
% students graduating within 6 years	83

Most classes have 10–19 students.

PROGRAMS/SERVICES FOR STUDENTS WITH LEARNING DIFFERENCES

Students at CWRU are not required to disclose disability information to anyone. However, in order to use services and appropriate accommodations, students should notify Disability Resources so that staff members that are aware of a disability. Students decide who needs to know about their disability. Disability Resources is the only department that will determine eligibility. Disability Resources will work closely with students and design an individual plan for accommodations. Included in that plan are strategies for disclosure to professors as well as identifying specific accommodations that will be needed for each course.

ADMISSIONS

Admission counselors review academics, life experiences and interests. Applicants should complete a minimum of: 4 years English, 3 years math, 3 years science, 3 years social studies, and 2 years foreign language. Applicants considering engineering or the sciences should have d an additional year of math and laboratory science. Liberal arts majors should consider an additional year of social studies and foreign language. Applicants must submit either SAT or ACT, (Writing is optional). SAT Subject tests are not required. Students can submit self-reported scores by completing the form on their applicant portal. Enrolling students will confirm their testing with official score reports. CWRU "superscore" students' test results on SAT or ACT. Middle 50%) SAT is 1310–1470 or ACT 30–34.

Additional Information

Disability Resources and the Office of Accommodated Testing and Services (OATS) are committed to providing required course material in alternate formats for students with approved accommodations. Students who are denied eligibility or who are dissatisfied with an accommodation method may request that the Associate Director of Disability Resources reconsider the decision. Service learning integrates experiential learning and community service in an academic context. Through activities and

ADMISSIONS INFO FOR STUDENTS WITH LEARNING DIFFERENCES

SAT/ACT required: Yes
Interview required: No
Essay required: Not Applicable
Additional application required: No
Documentation required for:
  LD: We request a neuropsychological evaluation from a qualified specialist.
  ADHD: We request a neuropsychological evaluation or narrative from a qualified professional with a history with the student.
  ASD: We prefer a neuropsychological evaluation but will accept a narrative from any qualified specialist the student has worked with on an on-going basis.
Documentation submitted to: Disability Resources
Special Ed. HS course work accepted: Yes
Separate application required for program services: No
# of students last year receiving services/accommodations for:
  LD: 154
  ADHD: 302
  ASD: NR
Contact Information
Name of program or department: Disability Resources
Telephone: (216) 368-5230
Fax: (216) 368-8826

Case Western Reserve University

experiences mutually negotiated between academic and community partners, service learning addresses identified needs, enhances the curriculum, and fosters civic responsibility. Facilitated by the Center for Civic Engagement.

GENERAL ADMISSIONS

Very important factors considered include: rigor of secondary school record, class rank, academic GPA, standardized test scores, extracurricular activities. *Important factors considered include:* application essay, recommendation(s), interview, talent/ability, character/personal qualities, racial/ethnic status, volunteer work. *Other factors considered include:* first generation, alumni/ae relation, work experience, level of applicant's interest. *Freshman Admission Requirements:* High school diploma is required and GED is accepted. *Academic units required:* 4 English, 3 math, 3 science, 2 science labs, 2 foreign language, 3 social studies. *Academic units recommended:* 4 math, 3 science labs, 3 foreign language, 4 social studies.

ACCOMMODATION OR SERVICES

Accommodations are decided upon an individual basis after a thorough review of appropriate, current documentation. The accommodations requests must be supported through the documentation provided and must be logically linked to the current impact of the condition on academic functioning.

FINANCIAL AID

Students should submit: CSS/Financial Aid PROFILE; FAFSA; Institution's own financial aid form; Noncustodial PROFILE. Applicants will be notified of awards on a rolling basis beginning 3/20. The Princeton Review suggests that all financial aid forms be submitted as soon as possible after October 1. *Need-based scholarships/grants offered:* College/university scholarship or grant aid from institutional funds; Federal Pell; Private scholarships; SEOG; State scholarships/grants. *Loan aid offered:* Direct PLUS loans; Direct Subsidized Stafford Loans; Direct Unsubsidized Stafford Loans. Federal Work-Study Program available. Institutional employment available.

CAMPUS LIFE

Activities: Campus Ministries; Choral groups; Concert band; Dance; Drama/theater; International Student Organization; Jazz band; Literary magazine; Marching band; Model UN; Music ensembles; Musical theater; Pep band; Radio station; Student government; Student newspaper; Student-run film society; Symphony orchestra; Yearbook. **Organizations:** 150 registered organizations, 8 honor societies, 4 religious organizations. 16 fraternities, 8 sororities. **Athletics (Intercollegiate):** *Men:* baseball, basketball, cross-country, football, soccer, swimming, tennis, track/field (outdoor), track/field (indoor), wrestling. *Women:* basketball, cross-country, soccer, softball, swimming, tennis, track/field (outdoor), track/field (indoor), volleyball. **On-Campus Highlights:** Kelvin Smith Library, Thwing Center, Jolly Scholar, Starbucks, Biomedical Research Building Dining Commons.

ACCOMMODATIONS

Allowed in exams:	
Calculators	Yes
Dictionary	Yes
Computer	Yes
Spell-checker	Yes
Extended test time	Yes
Scribe	Yes
Proctors	Yes
Oral exams	Yes
Note-takers	Yes
Support services for students with	
LD	Yes
ADHD	Yes
ASD	Yes
Distraction-reduced environment	Yes
Recording of lecture allowed	Yes
Reading technology:	Yes
Audio books	Yes
Other assistive technology	Echo SmartPen, Read and Write Gold
Priority registration	Yes
Added costs for services:	
For LD:	No
For ADHD:	No
For ASD:	No
Fly Program:	$2500 per semester
LD specialists	Yes
ADHD & ASD coaching	Yes
ASD specialists	Yes
Professional tutors	Yes
Peer tutors	Yes
Max. hours/week for services	5
How professors are notified of student approved accommodations	Director and student

COLLEGE GRADUATION REQUIREMENTS

Course waivers allowed	No
Course substitutions allowed	Yes
In what courses	Math

Cedarville University

251 N Main Street, Cedarville, OH 45314 • Admissions: 937-766-7700 • Fax: 937-766-7575

CAMPUS

Type of school	Private (nonprofit)
Environment	Rural
Support	S

STUDENTS

Undergrad enrollment	3,132
% male/female	47/53
% from out of state	57
% frosh live on campus	96

FINANCIAL FACTS

Annual tuition	$30,070
Room and board	$7,360
Required fees	$200

GENERAL ADMISSIONS INFO

Application fee	$30
Priority deadline	11/1.
Regular application deadline	8/1

Nonfall registration accepted. Admission may be deferred for a maximum of 1 year.

Range SAT EBRW	580–680
Range SAT Math	550–670
Range ACT Composite	23–29

ACADEMICS

Student/faculty ratio	14:1
% students returning for sophomore year	84
% students graduating within 4 years	60
% students graduating within 6 years	72

Most classes have 10–19 students.
Most lab/discussion sessions have 10–19 students.

PROGRAMS/SERVICES FOR STUDENTS WITH LEARNING DIFFERENCES

Disability Services is part of the Academic Enrichment Center, also known as The Cove. The Cove provides academic resources and support to all students, while Disability Services exists to ensure that students who are impacted by a disability are provided the access that they need. Disability Services is the office designated by Cedarville University to evaluate accommodation requests related to the impact of a diagnosed disability, determine reasonable accommodations for qualified students with disabilities.

ADMISSIONS

Cedarville University seeks motivated student who know Christ personally and want to grow academically. Some academic departments require specific credentials, an interview, or audition for admission to their majors. Liberal arts majors are admitted provisionally with 27 ACT or 1280 SAT and a 3.5 high school GPA. However, they must maintain at least a 3.25 GPA and supply two faculty recommendations at the end of the freshman year in order to stay in the program. Nursing Majors need a24 ACT or 1170 SAT: 1170 and show a strong commitment to leading a godly lifestyle and a desire to use nursing as ministry for Chris. Engineering applicants need ACT Math sub-score of 25 or higher or an SAT Math sub-score of 620 or higher* to declare one of the engineering majors. Students not meeting this requirement but wishing to declare an engineering major will be identified simply as Engineering students until they have competed Calculus I and Digital Logic Design with a "C". Music and Worship majors must audition.

Additional Information

The Cove offers several options for students who need academic support. Students can customize learning experiences to fit needs. Academic Peer Coaches (APCs) are available 20 weekly sessions provided by Academic Peer Coaches (APCs). APCs are students who lead weekly review and drop-in sessions for a course, working closely with the professor. Students can attend one of the more than 10 tutoring hours in The Cove's tutoring lab each week for math and chemistry courses. There are also study groups and Individual tutoring. Students can apply for a tutor in a study group or individual setting for any course that does not have an APC or tutoring lab.

ADMISSIONS INFO FOR STUDENTS WITH LEARNING DIFFERENCES

SAT/ACT required: Yes
Interview required: No
Essay required: Not Applicable
Additional application required: No
Documentation required for:
  LD: Documentation is recommended. There is a process.
  ADHD: Documentation is recommended. There is a process.
  ASD: Documentation is recommended. There is a process.
Documentation submitted to: Disability Services at The Cove
Special Ed. HS course work accepted: Not Applicable
Separate application required for program services: No
# of students last year receiving services/accommodations for:
  LD: 50
Contact Information
Name of program or department: Disability Services at The Cove
Telephone: 937-766-7437
Fax: 937-766-7419
Email: disabilityservices@cedarville.edu

GENERAL ADMISSIONS

Very important factors considered include: rigor of secondary school record, academic GPA, standardized test scores, recommendation(s), character/personal qualities. *Important factors considered include:* class rank, application essay, alumni/ae relation, religious affiliation/commitment, racial/ethnic status, level of applicant's interest. *Other factors considered include:* extracurricular activities, talent/ability, first generation, geographical residence, state residency, volunteer work, work experience. *Freshman Admission Requirements:* High school diploma is required and GED is accepted. *Academic units recommended:* 4 English, 3 math, 3 science, 2 science labs, 3 foreign language, 2 social studies, 2 history.

ACCOMMODATION OR SERVICES

Accommodations are decided upon an individual basis after a thorough review of appropriate, current documentation. The accommodations requests must be supported through the documentation provided and must be logically linked to the current impact of the condition on academic functioning.

FINANCIAL AID

Students should submit: FAFSA. Applicants will be notified of awards on a rolling basis beginning 3/1. The Princeton Review suggests that all financial aid forms be submitted as soon as possible after October 1. *Need-based scholarships/grants offered:* College/university scholarship or grant aid from institutional funds; Federal Nursing Scholarships; Federal Pell; Private scholarships; SEOG; State scholarships/grants. *Loan aid offered:* Direct PLUS loans; Direct Subsidized Stafford Loans; Direct Unsubsidized Stafford Loans. Federal Work-Study Program available. Institutional employment available.

CAMPUS LIFE

Activities: Campus Ministries; Choral groups; Concert band; Dance; Drama/theater; International Student Organization; Jazz band; Model UN; Music ensembles; Musical theater; Pep band; Radio station; Student government; Student newspaper; Student-run film society; Symphony orchestra; Yearbook. **Organizations:** 74 registered organizations, 4 honor societies, **Athletics (Intercollegiate):** *Men:* baseball, basketball, cheerleading, cross-country, golf, soccer, tennis, track/field (outdoor), track/field (indoor). *Women:* basketball, cheerleading, cross-country, soccer, softball, tennis, track/field (outdoor), track/field (indoor), volleyball. **On-Campus Highlights:** Fitness and Recreation Center, Stingers/Rinnova - snack shop and coffee bar, Dixon Ministry Center - daily chapel and concerts, Chucks - student cafeteria (popular hangout), Center for Biblical and Theological Studies lobby.

ACCOMMODATIONS

Allowed in exams:	
Calculators	Yes
Dictionary	Yes
Computer	Yes
Spell-checker	Yes
Extended test time	Yes
Scribe	Yes
Proctors	Yes
Oral exams	Yes
Note-takers	Yes
Support services for students with	
LD	Yes
ADHD	Yes
ASD	Yes
Distraction-reduced environment	Yes
Recording of lecture allowed	Yes
Reading technology:	Yes
Audio books	Yes
Other assistive technology	Braille, Smart Pens, Recorders, etc.
Priority registration	Yes
Added costs for services:	
For LD:	No
For ADHD:	No
For ASD:	No
LD specialists	Yes
ADHD & ASD coaching	Yes
ASD specialists	Yes
Professional tutors	Yes
Peer tutors	Yes
Max. hours/week for services	2
How professors are notified of student approved accommodations	Director and student

COLLEGE GRADUATION REQUIREMENTS

Course waivers allowed	Yes
In what courses math, Foreign Language; if appropriate - case by case basis	
Course substitutions allowed	Yes
In what courses math, Foreign Language; if appropriate - case by case basis	

Central Ohio Technical College

1179 UNIVERSITY DRIVE, NEWARK, OH 43055 • ADMISSIONS: 740-366-9494 • FAX: 740-366-9290

CAMPUS
Type of school	Public
Environment	City
Support	CS

STUDENTS
Undergrad enrollment	3,513
% male/female	29/71
% from out of state	1
% frosh live on campus	1

FINANCIAL FACTS
Annual in-state tuition	$4,200
Annual out-of-state tuition	$6,960

GENERAL ADMISSIONS INFO
Application fee	$20

Nonfall registration accepted.

ACADEMICS
Student/faculty ratio	14:1
% students returning for sophomore year	53

Most classes have 10–19 students.

PROGRAMS/SERVICES FOR STUDENTS WITH LEARNING DIFFERENCES

Technical College and The Ohio State University at Newark ODS provides FREE programs and services designed to help students have full access to college life. All students are encouraged to contact the Office for Disability Services in the early stages of their college planning. Pre admission services include information about academic support services, specialized equipment, transition issues, admission requirements, and meetings with staff counselors.

ADMISSIONS

Admission is open to all applicants with a high school diploma or the GED, except in health programs. There are no specific course requirements. ACT/SAT tests are not required. The application process is the same for all students. There is no requirement to provide disability-related information to the Admissions Office. Documentation of your disability should be sent directly to DS. Eligibility for services/accommodations from DS is a separate process from admissions. All prospective students are encouraged to contact DS in the early stages of their college planning. Preadmission services include information about academic support services, transition issues, admission requirements, and appropriate documentation and meetings with staff disability professionals.

Additional Information

A degree modification, or course requirement substitution is permitted if the modification does not constitute a fundamental change in the degree and is supported by the student's documentation of a disability. In order to substitute a required class, the student files an appeal petition, discusses the academic difficulties with ODS and requests assistance from ODS in the petition process. Students meet with the advisor for the degree, and discusses the disability related needs and potential modifications. Once a substitution is determined, the student completes the course information on the Petition to Substitute Required Course form. Lastly, the student returns to the ODS and requests that the appropriate staff member help complete the "Academic Reason(s) Justification for the Request" section of the form. If the request is reasonable, the staff member advocates for the student throughout the process. The Tutoring Center and the Assistive Technology Lab are for students with learning disabilities and ADHD. All students are automatically eligible for services. The tutoring program includes peer tutoring in almost any course, scheduled at the student's convenience for 2 hours each week per course. The Assistive Technology

ADMISSIONS INFO FOR STUDENTS WITH LEARNING DIFFERENCES

SAT/ACT required: No
Interview required: No
Essay required: No
Additional application required: No
Documentation required for:
  LD: Psychological report, IEP, MFE/ETR, or other diagnostic assessments
  ADHD: Psychological report, IEP, MFE/ETR, or other diagnostic assessments
  ASD: Psycho educational evaluation
Documentation submitted to: Office for Disability Services
Special Ed. HS course work accepted: No
Separate application required for program services: No
Contact Information
Name of program or department: Office for Disability Services
Telephone: 740-366-9441
Fax: 740-364-9646

Central Ohio Technical College

Lab has resources to improve reading, math, and language skills; word processing; and study aids for some courses and national tests. The Study Skills Workshop Series provides assistance in improving study skills and 50-minute workshops on time management, learning styles/memory, test preparation and taking, reading textbooks effectively, and note taking. Students also have access to proctors, individualized instruction designed to meet special needs, advocacy assistance, coaching, and assistance with accommodations.

GENERAL ADMISSIONS

Freshman Admission Requirements: High school diploma is required and GED is accepted.

ACCOMMODATION OR SERVICES

Accommodations are decided upon an individual basis after a thorough review of appropriate, current documentation. The accommodations requests must be supported through the documentation provided and must be logically linked to the current impact of the condition on academic functioning.

FINANCIAL AID

Students should submit:. The Princeton Review suggests that all financial aid forms be submitted as soon as possible after October 1.

CAMPUS LIFE

Activities: Choral groups; Drama/theater; Music ensembles; Student government; Student newspaper.

ACCOMMODATIONS

Allowed in exams:

Calculators	Yes
Dictionary	No
Computer	Yes
Spell-checker	No
Extended test time	Yes
Scribe	Yes
Proctors	Yes
Oral exams	Yes
Note-takers	Yes

Support services for students with

LD	Yes
ADHD	Yes
ASD	Yes
Distraction-reduced environment	Yes
Recording of lecture allowed	Yes
Reading technology:	Yes
Audio books	Yes
Other assistive technology	Yes
Priority registration	No

Added costs for services:

For LD:	No
For ADHD:	No
For ASD:	No
LD specialists	Yes
ADHD & ASD coaching	No
ASD specialists	No
Professional tutors	Yes
Peer tutors	Yes
Max. hours/week for services	Varies

How professors are notified of student
approved accommodations — Student

COLLEGE GRADUATION REQUIREMENTS

Course waivers allowed	No
Course substitutions allowed	No

Mount St. Joseph University

5701 Delhi Road, Cincinnati, OH 45233 • Admissions: 513-244-4531 • Fax: 513-244-4629

CAMPUS

Type of school	Private (nonprofit)
Environment	Metropolis
Support	SP

STUDENTS

Undergrad enrollment	1,177
% male/female	43/57
% from out of state	81
% frosh live on campus	60

FINANCIAL FACTS

Annual tuition	$29,100
Room and board	$9,551
Required fees	$1,000

GENERAL ADMISSIONS INFO

Application fee	$25
Priority deadline	3/3
Regular application deadline	8/18

Nonfall registration accepted. Admission may be deferred for a maximum of 1 year.

Range SAT EBRW	490–578
Range SAT Math	490–578
Range ACT Composite	20–24

ACADEMICS

Student/faculty ratio	11:1
% students returning for sophomore year	72
% students graduating within 4 years	44
% students graduating within 6 years	61

Most classes have 20–29 students.
Most lab/discussion sessions have 20–29 students.

PROGRAMS/SERVICES FOR STUDENTS WITH LEARNING DIFFERENCES

Project EXCEL is a comprehensive academic support program for students with learning disabilities enrolled in the college. The program's goals are to assist students in the transition from a secondary program to a college curriculum and to promote the development of learning strategies and compensatory skills that will enable students to achieve success in a regular academic program. The structure of the program and supportive environment at the Mount give Project EXCEL its singular quality. Project EXCEL offers students individualized attention and a variety of support services to meet specific needs, including supervised tutoring by professional tutors; monitoring of student progress; instruction in learning strategies, time management, and coping skills; and academic advising with attention to the students' specific learning needs. Students admitted to the program must maintain a 2.25 overall GPA, and their progress is evaluated on an ongoing basis.

ADMISSIONS

Admission to Project EXCEL is multi-stepped, including: an interview with the program director; completed general admission application; completed Project EXCEL forms (general information, applicant goal and self-assessment, and educational data completed by high school); psycho-educational evaluation; transcript; ACT minimum of 15 or SAT of 700–740; and a recommendation. The application is reviewed by the Project EXCEL Director and Project EXCEL Admission Committee. The diagnostic evaluation must indicate the presence of specific LD and provide reasonable evidence that the student can successfully meet college academic requirements. Academic performance problems that exist concomitantly with a diagnosed ADD/ADHD will be considered in the review of the student's diagnostic profile. Students can be admitted to the college through Project EXCEL. Students not meeting all EXCEL admission requirements may be admitted part-time or on a probationary basis. Apply early. Other students not meeting admission requirements can take up to 6 hours per semester to a maximum of 13 hours. At that point, if they have a 2.0+ GPA they are admitted to the college.

ADMISSIONS INFO FOR STUDENTS WITH LEARNING DIFFERENCES

SAT/ACT required: Yes
Interview required: Yes
Essay required: Yes
Additional application required: Yes
Documentation required for:
  LD: Educational Evaluation including an Adult IQ Test and Educational testing as well as Executive Function Testing and a review of educational records.
  ADHD: Educational and Psychological Evaluation is preferred; however, our office has a Physician/Specialist Form available.
  ASD: A Psychological and Educational Evaluation including an Adult IQ Test, Educational Testing, Diagnostic Scale for ASD, Executive Function Testing, Clinical Interview
Documentation submitted to:Project EXCEL
Special Ed. HS course work accepted: Yes
Separate application required for program services: Yes
# of students last year receiving services/accommodations for:
  LD: 75
Contact Information
Name of program or department: Project EXCEL
Telephone: 513-244-4623
Fax: 513-244-4629

Mount St. Joseph University

Additional Information

Project EXCEL students are assisted with course and major selection. Students are offered individualized attention and a variety of support services to meet specific needs, including supervised tutoring, monitoring of student progress, writing lab, note takers, accommodated testing, instruction in learning strategies, time management, and coping skills; liaison with faculty and academic advising with attention to specific learning needs. Students enroll in regular classes and must fulfill the same course requirements as all Mount students. The curriculum is closely supervised, and specialized instruction is offered in writing, reading, and study skills to fit the individual needs of the students. The program director serves as student advisor.

GENERAL ADMISSIONS

Very important factors considered include: rigor of secondary school record, academic GPA, standardized test scores. *Important factors considered include:* extracurricular activities, volunteer work, work experience, level of applicant's interest. *Other factors considered include:* class rank, application essay, recommendation(s), interview, talent/ability, character/personal qualities. *Freshman Admission Requirements:* High school diploma is required and GED is accepted. *Academic units required:* 4 English, 3 math, 2 science, 2 science labs, 2 foreign language, 1 visual/performing arts. *Academic units recommended:* 3 social studies, 3 history.

ACCOMMODATION OR SERVICES

Accommodations are decided upon an individual basis after a thorough review of appropriate, current documentation. The accommodations requests must be supported through the documentation provided and must be logically linked to the current impact of the condition on academic functioning.

FINANCIAL AID

Students should submit: FAFSA. The Princeton Review suggests that all financial aid forms be submitted as soon as possible after October 1. *Need-based scholarships/grants offered:* College/university scholarship or grant aid from institutional funds; Federal Pell; Private scholarships; SEOG; State scholarships/grants. *Loan aid offered:* Direct PLUS loans; Direct Subsidized Stafford Loans; Direct Unsubsidized Stafford Loans. Federal Work-Study Program available. Institutional employment available.

CAMPUS LIFE

Activities: Campus Ministries; Choral groups; Concert band; Dance; Drama/theater; Jazz band; Literary magazine; Musical theater; Pep band; Student government; Student newspaper. **Organizations:** 35 registered organizations, 10 honor societies, 1 religious organization. **Athletics (Intercollegiate):** *Men:* baseball, basketball, cross-country, football, golf, lacrosse, soccer, tennis, track/field (outdoor), track/field (indoor), volleyball, wrestling. *Women:* basketball, cheerleading, cross-country, golf, lacrosse, soccer, softball, tennis, track/field (outdoor), track/field (indoor), volleyball. **On-Campus Highlights:** Harrington Student Center/Sports Complex, Food Court, Residential Suites, Computer Learning Center, Sports Complex / Schueler Field.

ACCOMMODATIONS

Allowed in exams:

Calculators	Yes
Dictionary	Not Applicable
Computer	Yes
Spell-checker	No
Extended test time	Yes
Scribe	Yes
Proctors	Yes
Oral exams	Yes
Note-takers	Yes

Support services for students with

LD	Yes
ADHD	Yes
ASD	Yes
Distraction-reduced environment	Yes
Recording of lecture allowed	Yes
Reading technology:	Yes
Audio books	Yes
Other assistive technology	All

accommodations decisions are based upon a student interview, a review of documentation and prior educational history.

Priority registration	No

Added costs for services:

For LD:	No
For ADHD:	No
For ASD:	No
Project EXCEL:	Yes
LD specialists	Yes
ADHD & ASD coaching	Yes
ASD specialists	Nu
Professional tutors	Yes
Peer tutors	No
Max. hours/week for services	Varies
How professors are notified of student approved accommodations	Student

COLLEGE GRADUATION REQUIREMENTS

Course waivers allowed	No

In what courses   Foreign language is not required for graduation.

Kent State University—Kent Campus

PO Box 5190, Kent, OH 44242-0001 • Admissions: 330-672-2444 • Fax: 330-672-2499

PROGRAMS/SERVICES FOR STUDENTS WITH LEARNING DIFFERENCES
The mission of Student Accessibility Services is to provide students with disabilities equal opportunity to participate in, contribute to, and benefit from all university programs, services and activities. Students are encouraged to take advantage of Accessibility Services (disability-related services), Academic Success Center (tutoring and Supplemental Instruction), Academic Advising (course planning and scheduling) and the Center for Student Involvement (student organizations and clubs),

ADMISSIONS
Students with LD must meet the same admission requirements as all applicants. The mean GPA is 3.4 and the mean ACT is 23 and SAT of 1130. Some academic programs have additional requirements. Core courses required are 4 English, 4 Math, 3 Science, 3 Social Studies, 2 Foreign Language, and 1 Art (or additional unit of foreign language). Admissions may defer students who do not meet admissions criteria but who demonstrate areas of promise for successful college study. Deferred applicants may begin their college coursework at one of seven Regional Campuses of Kent State University.

Additional Information
Career and Community Studies (CCS) is a college-based, transition, non-degree program to prepare students with intellectual and developmental disabilities for adult life through academic pursuits, peer socialization, and career discovery and preparation. The program integrates inclusive classes, a typical college experience, and a transition curriculum to assist students in achieving adult roles and a quality of life in a community of their choice. The CCS program is for students who have completed high

Kent State University—Kent Campus

school requirements and be at least 18 years of age. The first year of the program is designed as a foundation with courses covering disability issues, personal development, health and wellness, and preparing for a rigorous college experience. Year two allows students to extend their knowledge and skills in participating in college-level courses and other campus environments. The last two years focus on career-field specialization with courses in independent living, life-long learning competencies, and career development and employment, as well as internships in the community where students apply their learning in jobs of choice. The disHUBility provides students who have disabilities a space to relax and find camaraderie. The disHUBility was created by the student organization, Autism Connections Kent (ACK).

GENERAL ADMISSIONS

Very important factors considered include: academic GPA, standardized test scores. *Important factors considered include:* rigor of secondary school record. *Other factors considered include:* application essay, recommendation(s), interview, talent/ability, level of applicant's interest. *Freshman Admission Requirements:* High school diploma is required and GED is accepted. *Academic units recommended:* 4 English, 4 math, 3 science, 2 science labs, 2 foreign language, 3 social studies, 1 visual/performing arts.

ACCOMMODATION OR SERVICES

Accommodations are decided upon an individual basis after a thorough review of appropriate, current documentation. The accommodations requests must be supported through the documentation provided and must be logically linked to the current impact of the condition on academic functioning.

FINANCIAL AID

Students should submit: FAFSA. Applicants will be notified of awards on a rolling basis beginning 1/15. The Princeton Review suggests that all financial aid forms be submitted as soon as possible after October 1. *Need-based scholarships/grants offered:* College/university scholarship or grant aid from institutional funds; Federal Pell; Private scholarships; SEOG; State scholarships/grants. *Loan aid offered:* Direct PLUS loans; Direct Subsidized Stafford Loans; Direct Unsubsidized Stafford Loans. Federal Work-Study Program available. Institutional employment available.

CAMPUS LIFE

Activities: Campus Ministries; Choral groups; Concert band; Dance; Drama/theater; International Student Organization; Jazz band; Literary magazine; Marching band; Model UN; Music ensembles; Musical theater; Opera; Pep band; Radio station; Student government; Student newspaper; Symphony orchestra; Television station. **Organizations:** 214 registered organizations, 10 honor societies, 15 religious organizations. 17 fraternities, 6 sororities. **Athletics (Intercollegiate):** *Men:* baseball, basketball, cheerleading, cross-country, football, golf, track/field (outdoor), track/field (indoor), wrestling. *Women:* basketball, cheerleading, cross-country, field hockey, football, golf, gymnastics, soccer, softball, track/field (outdoor), track/field (indoor), volleyball. **On-Campus Highlights:** Student Recreation and Wellness Center, University Library, Kent Student Center and Plaza, New College of Architecture and Environmental Design, May 4 Visitors Center.

ACCOMMODATIONS

Allowed in exams:

Calculators	Yes
Dictionary	Yes
Computer	Yes
Spell-checker	Yes
Extended test time	Yes
Scribe	Yes
Proctors	Yes
Oral exams	Yes
Note-takers	Yes

Support services for students with

LD	Yes
ADHD	Yes
ASD	Yes
Distraction-reduced environment	Yes
Recording of lecture allowed	Yes
Reading technology:	Yes
Audio books	Yes
Other assistive technology	Dependent on student need
Priority registration	Yes

Added costs for services:

For LD:	No
For ADHD:	No
For ASD:	No
LD specialists	Yes
ADHD & ASD coaching	No
ASD specialists	No
Professional tutors	Yes
Peer tutors	Yes
Max. hours/week for services	Varies
How professors are notified of student approved accommodations	Student

COLLEGE GRADUATION REQUIREMENTS

Course waivers allowed	No
Course substitutions allowed	No

Miami University

501 E. High Street, Oxford, OH 45056 • Admissions: 513-529-2531 • Fax: 513-529-1550

CAMPUS
Type of school	Public
Environment	Village
Support	CS

STUDENTS
Undergrad enrollment	16,816
% male/female	50/50
% from out of state	36
% frosh live on campus	98

FINANCIAL FACTS
Annual in-state tuition	$14,315
Annual out-of-state tuition	$33,832
Room and board	$13,031
Required fees	$859

GENERAL ADMISSIONS INFO
Application fee	$50.
Regular application deadline	2/1

Nonfall registration accepted. Admission may be deferred.

Range SAT EBRW	580–670
Range SAT Math	610–710
Range ACT Composite	26–31

ACADEMICS
Student/faculty ratio	17:1
% students returning for sophomore year	91
% students graduating within 4 years	67
% students graduating within 6 years	79

Most classes have 20–29 students.

PROGRAMS/SERVICES FOR STUDENTS WITH LEARNING DIFFERENCES

The Student Disability Services staff coordinates university and community resources to meet the academic and personal needs of students with LD; assist faculty in understanding the characteristics and needs of these students; and provide services on an individual basis to students with appropriate documentation. Appropriate services and accommodations are determined through a flexible, interactive process that involves the student and the coordinator and are arranged through dialogue with faculty and staff responsible for implementing many of these services or accommodations. Decisions about services and accommodations for students with LD are made on the basis of the disability documentation and the functional limitations caused by the disability, as well as the current needs of the student. Students with ADHD must meet with the LD coordinator to initiate services after discussing disability-related needs and providing documentation of the disability and its impact on learning.

ADMISSIONS

Students with LD are admitted through the regular admission process; therefore, it is important to ensure that the information in the application accurately reflects a student's academic ability and potential. Students may self-disclose LD or ADHD on their application. The review process is comprehensive and individualized.considering many variables including (in alpha order): class rank, commitment to social service, demonstrated leadership, employment, extenuating circumstances, extra curricular, first-generation, GPA, grade trends, high school profile, legacy status, Letter(s) of recommendation, Life experiences, obstacles overcome, potential contributions to diversity, socioeconomic status, special abilities, talents, and achievements, standardized test scores, strength of curriculum, and writing ability.

Additional Information

Services for students with LD include priority registration; classroom accommodations such as test modifications, extended exam times, and so on; liaison with faculty; campus advocacy; counseling; and career awareness. In addition, students with LD can utilize services through the Rinella Learning Center, which works with students encountering academic difficulties. Its tutorial assistance program provides peer tutors. The Bernard B. Rinella Jr. Learning Center has special services designed to

ADMISSIONS INFO FOR STUDENTS WITH LEARNING DIFFERENCES

SAT/ACT required: Yes
Interview required: No
Essay required: Essay recommended
Additional application required: No
Documentation required for:
  LD: Psycho ed evaluation
  ADHD: Psycho ed evaluation
  ASD: Psycho ed evaluation
Documentation submitted to: Student Disability Services
Special Ed. HS course work accepted: No
Separate application required for program services: No
Contact Information
Name of program or department: Student Disability Services
Telephone: 513-529-1541
Fax: 513-529-8595
Email: SDS@miamioh.edu

help students experiencing academic problems. In meeting with a learning specialist, students' existing learning strategies will be assessed, and new effective strategies will be introduced. Topics of time management, note-taking, test-taking, writing, and organization will be covered. New study strategies will be reinforced through individual conferences with a learning specialist, peer mentoring, and/or tutoring.

GENERAL ADMISSIONS

Very important factors considered include: rigor of secondary school record, class rank, academic GPA, application essay, standardized test scores, recommendation(s), talent/ability, character/personal qualities. *Other factors considered include:* extracurricular activities, first generation, alumni/ae relation, geographical residence, state residency, volunteer work, work experience. *Freshman Admission Requirements:* High school diploma is required and GED is accepted. *Academic units recommended:* 4 English, 4 math, 3 science, 2 foreign language, 2 social studies, 1 history, 1 visual/performing arts.

ACCOMMODATION OR SERVICES

Accommodations are decided upon an individual basis after a thorough review of appropriate, current documentation. The accommodations requests must be supported through the documentation provided and must be logically linked to the current impact of the condition on academic functioning.

FINANCIAL AID

Students should submit: FAFSA. Applicants will be notified of awards on a rolling basis beginning 3/20. The Princeton Review suggests that all financial aid forms be submitted as soon as possible after October 1. *Need-based scholarships/grants offered:* College/university scholarship or grant aid from institutional funds; Federal Pell; Private scholarships; SEOG; State scholarships/grants. *Loan aid offered:* Direct PLUS loans; Direct Subsidized Stafford Loans; Direct Unsubsidized Stafford Loans. Federal Work-Study Program available. Institutional employment available.

CAMPUS LIFE

Activities: Campus Ministries; Choral groups; Concert band; Dance; Drama/theater; International Student Organization; Jazz band; Literary magazine; Marching band; Model UN; Music ensembles; Musical theater; Opera; Pep band; Radio station; Student government; Student newspaper; Student-run film society; Symphony orchestra; Television station; Yearbook. **Organizations:** 304 registered organizations, 38 honor societies, 22 religious organizations. 32 fraternities, 23 sororities. **Athletics (Intercollegiate):** *Men:* baseball, basketball, cross-country, diving, football, golf, ice hockey, swimming, track/field (outdoor). *Women:* basketball, cross-country, diving, field hockey, soccer, softball, swimming, tennis, track/field (outdoor), volleyball. **On-Campus Highlights:** Farmer School of Business, McGuffey Museum, Center for the Performing Arts, Recreational Sports Center, Peabody Hall (National Historical Landmark).

ACCOMMODATIONS

Allowed in exams:

Calculators	Yes
Dictionary	Yes
Computer	Yes
Spell-checker	Yes
Extended test time	Yes
Scribe	Yes
Proctors	Yes
Oral exams	Yes
Note-takers	Yes

Support services for students with

LD	Yes
ADHD	Yes
ASD	Yes
Distraction-reduced environment	Yes
Recording of lecture allowed	Yes
Reading technology:	Yes
Audio books	Yes

Other assistive technology JAWS, Zoomtext, Kurzweil, Read & Write Gold, Tactile Conversation hardware and software

Priority registration	Yes

Added costs for services:

For LD:	No
For ADHD:	No
For ASD:	No
LD specialists	Yes
ADHD & ASD coaching	Yes
ASD specialists	Yes
Professional tutors	No
Peer tutors	Yes
Max. hours/week for services	Varies

How professors are notified of student approved accommodations Director and student

COLLEGE GRADUATION REQUIREMENTS

Course waivers allowed	No
Course substitutions allowed	Yes
In what courses	Math and Foreign

Language substitutions available with supporting documentation.

Muskingum University

163 Stormont Street, New Concord, OH 43762 • Admissions: 740-826-8137 • Fax: 614-826-8100

CAMPUS

Type of school	Private (nonprofit)
Environment	Rural
Support	SP

STUDENTS

Undergrad enrollment	1,524
% male/female	44/56
% from out of state	8
% frosh live on campus	85

FINANCIAL FACTS

Annual tuition	$26,900
Room and board	$11,040
Required fees	$912

GENERAL ADMISSIONS INFO

Priority deadline 3/1.
Regular application deadline 8/1
Nonfall registration accepted. Admission may be deferred for a maximum of 1 year.

Range SAT EBRW	463–578
Range SAT Math	460–530
Range ACT Composite	18–24

ACADEMICS

Student/faculty ratio	14:1
% students returning for sophomore year	74
% students graduating within 4 years	34
% students graduating within 6 years	48

PROGRAMS/SERVICES FOR STUDENTS WITH LEARNING DIFFERENCES

The PLUS Program provides college students who have learning disorders with the opportunity to reach their academic potential. The program is built upon a proven model of Embedded Learning Strategies Instruction blended with a Learning Conversation approach. This model facilitates life-long learning, essential to success in college, work, and life pursuits. Through Learning Strategy Instruction, Learning Consultants assist students by providing systematic and explicit instruction in learning strategies that are embedded in course content. Learning strategy instruction areas include time and materials management, organization, test-taking, note-taking, reading, writing, memory and study skills, among others. Through Learning Conversations, Learning Consultants provide the context within which students may appreciate that they can succeed, recognize the factors that influence their success, develop a possibility perspective, improve self-confidence, and understand their unique learning profile and what it means for their learning. The success of students can be attributed in part to the highly qualified, professional adult Learning Consultants who engage students in academic support services. Students participating in the Full PLUS Program receive an average of one contact hour per week for each eligible course for an average total of 3-4 hours per week. Maintenance PLUS Program students receive one half hour of PLUS tutorial services per week for each eligible course. Both levels of service are provided with additional services, including a Primary Learning Consultant who acts as liaison to home, faculty, and others; guidance to promote favorable number of courses; optimal course selection and balanced course load; continuum of services to provide a range of individual support for short term needs.

ADMISSIONS

The PLUS Program reflects the university's commitment to the ultimate success of its students. Course and graduate requirements are not compromised for PLUS students. Each applicant is evaluated by a committee for the potential to complete degree requirements and succeed in the campus residential environment. Students should have a university

ADMISSIONS INFO FOR STUDENTS WITH LEARNING DIFFERENCES

SAT/ACT required: Yes
Interview required: Yes
Essay required: Yes
Additional application required: No
Documentation required for:
  LD: Psycho ed evaluation to include: relevant historical info, instructional interventions, related services, age diagnosed, objective data (aptitude, achievement, info processing), test scores (standard, percentile and grade equivalents) and describe functional limitations.
  ADHD: Diagnosis based on DSM-V; history of behaviors impairing functioning in academic setting; diagnostic interview; history of symptoms; evidence of ongoing behaviors.
  ASD: Psycho ed evaluation
Documentation submitted to: PLUS Program
Special Ed. HS course work accepted: Yes
Separate application required for program services: No
# of students last year receiving services/accommodations for:
  LD: 130-160
Contact Information
Name of program or department: PLUS Program, Center for Advancement of Learning or Disability Education Office
Telephone: 740-826-8284
Fax: 740-826-8285

Muskingum University

preparatory curriculum. Generally 4 years of English, Algebra I and II, and Geometry; at least 2 years of science with lab and social sciences are recommended for admissions. To apply to the PLUS Program, an applicant should complete all materials required for regular admission to the university. In addition, PLUS applicants should submit a recent comprehensive evaluation, which includes aptitude testing, achievement testing, and a diagnostic summary. Admission to the university and the PLUS Program are based upon application materials and a personal interview. Rolling admissions apply. Due to the great demand for the PLUS Program services, early application is strongly advised.

Additional Information
Muskingum University offers the First Step Transition Program, a two-week summer transition program to help bridge the gap between high school and university life.

GENERAL ADMISSIONS
Very important factors considered include: rigor of secondary school record, academic GPA. *Important factors considered include:* class rank, standardized test scores. *Other factors considered include:* application essay, recommendation(s), interview, extracurricular activities, talent/ability, character/personal qualities, alumni/ae relation, geographical residence, racial/ethnic status, work experience. *Freshman Admission Requirements:* High school diploma is required and GED is accepted. *Academic units required:* 4 English, 2 math, 2 science, 1 science lab, 2 foreign language, 2 social studies. *Academic units recommended:* 4 English, 3 math, 3 science, 2 science labs, 2 foreign language, 3 social studies.

ACCOMMODATION OR SERVICES
Accommodations are decided upon an individual basis after a thorough review of appropriate, current documentation. The accommodations requests must be supported through the documentation provided and must be logically linked to the current impact of the condition on academic functioning.

FINANCIAL AID
Students should submit: FAFSA. Applicants will be notified of awards on a rolling basis beginning 12/15. The Princeton Review suggests that all financial aid forms be submitted as soon as possible after October 1. *Need-based scholarships/grants offered:* College/university scholarship or grant aid from institutional funds; Federal Pell; Private scholarships; SEOG; State scholarships/grants. *Loan aid offered:* Direct PLUS loans; Direct Subsidized Stafford Loans; Direct Unsubsidized Stafford Loans. Federal Work-Study Program available. Institutional employment available.

CAMPUS LIFE
Activities: Campus Ministries; Choral groups; Concert band; Dance; Drama/theater; International Student Organization; Jazz band; Literary magazine; Marching band; Model UN; Music ensembles; Musical theater; Pep band; Radio station; Student government; Student newspaper; Symphony orchestra; Television station. **Organizations:** 95 registered organizations, 16 honor societies, 4 religious organizations. 5 fraternities, 5 sororities. **Athletics (Intercollegiate):** *Men:* baseball, basketball, cheerleading, cross-country, football, golf, soccer, tennis, track/field (outdoor), track/field (indoor), wrestling. *Women:* basketball, cheerleading, cross-country, golf, soccer, softball, tennis, track/field (outdoor), track/field (indoor), volleyball. **On-Campus Highlights:** Philip and Betsey Caldwell Hall, Boyd Science Center, Rec Center, Otto and Fran Walter Hall, Walter K. Chess Student Center.

ACCOMMODATIONS

Allowed in exams:	
Calculators	Yes
Dictionary	Yes
Computer	Yes
Spell-checker	Yes
Extended test time	Yes
Scribe	Yes
Proctors	Yes
Oral exams	Yes
Note-takers	Yes
Support services for students with	
LD	Yes
ADHD	Yes
ASD	Yes
Distraction-reduced environment	Yes
Recording of lecture allowed	Yes
Reading technology:	Yes
Audio books	No
Other assistive technology	Yes
Priority registration	Yes
Added costs for services: For PLUS Program	
For LD:	No
For ADHD:	No
For ASD:	No
LD specialists	Yes
ADHD & ASD coaching	No
ASD specialists	No
Professional tutors	Yes
Peer tutors	No
Max. hours/week for services	3-4
How professors are notified of student approved accommodations	
Student	

COLLEGE GRADUATION REQUIREMENTS

Course waivers allowed	No
Course substitutions allowed	No

Oberlin College

70 North Professor Street, Oberlin, OH 44074 • Admissions: 440-775-8411 • Fax: 440-775-6905

CAMPUS

Type of school	Private (nonprofit)
Environment	Village
Support	CS

STUDENTS

Undergrad enrollment	2,827
% male/female	42/58
% from out of state	94
% frosh live on campus	100

FINANCIAL FACTS

Annual tuition	$52,762
Room and board	$15,212
Required fees	$698

GENERAL ADMISSIONS INFO

Priority deadline	1/15
Regular application deadline	1/15

Nonfall registration accepted. Admission may be deferred for a maximum of 1 year.

Range SAT EBRW	650–720
Range SAT Math	630–730
Range ACT Composite	28–33

ACADEMICS

Student/faculty ratio	10:1
% students returning for sophomore year	91
% students graduating within 4 years	75
% students graduating within 6 years	86

Most classes have 10–19 students.

PROGRAMS/SERVICES FOR STUDENTS WITH LEARNING DIFFERENCES

Personnel from the Disability Resources at the Center for Student Success (DRCSS) provide services, as well as coordinate accommodations, to meet the needs of students who have disabilities. Their goal is to maximize the student's entire educational potential while helping him or her develop and maintain independence. The program philosophy is one that encourages self-advocacy. Students who are diagnosed by DRCSS personnel as having LD, as well as those who can provide documentation of a current diagnosis of LD, are eligible for services. To verify a previously diagnosed LD, a student must provide a psychological assessment, educational test results, and a recent copy of an IEP that specifies placement in a learning disabilities program. These documents will be reviewed by personnel from DRCSS to determine eligibility. Students requesting services are interviewed by a learning disability counselor before a service plan is developed or initiated.

ADMISSIONS

There is no special admissions procedure for students with LD. All applicants must meet the same admission requirements. Courses required include 4 years of English and math and at least 3 years of social science and science. The average GPA is typically a B average or better. ACT scores range between 25 and 30; SAT Reasoning test scores range between 1100 and 1320, and SAT Subject Test scores range between 560 and 680 on each Subject Test. Students who self-disclose and provide documentation may have their files read by DRCSS personnel, who will provide a recommendation to the Office of Admissions. Students who can provide valid and recent documentation of a psychoeducational diagnosis of LD may receive services. The report must include the name, title, and credentials of the professional. All letters must be typed on letterhead, signed, and dated. It would be useful if the report contains the following components: diagnosis and a description of the methodology used; previous history and prognosis of the disability; description of the current functional limitations and explanation of how the diagnosis substantially limits a major life activity; the severity of the condition; an

ADMISSIONS INFO FOR STUDENTS WITH LEARNING DIFFERENCES

SAT/ACT required: Yes
Interview required: No
Essay required: No
Additional application required: No
Documentation required for:
 LD: Psycho ed evaluation to include: relevant historical info, instructional interventions, related services, age diagnosed, objective data (aptitude, achievement, info processing), test scores (standard, percentile and grade equivalents) and describe functional limitations.
 ADHD: Diagnosis based on DSM-V; history of behaviors impairing functioning in academic setting; diagnostic interview; history of symptoms; evidence of ongoing behaviors.
 ASD: Psycho ed evaluation
Documentation submitted to: Disability Resources at the Center for Student Success
Special Ed. HS course work accepted: Yes
Separate application required for program services: No
# of students last year receiving services/accommodations for:
 LD: 200
Contact Information
Name of program or department: Disability Resources at the Center for Student Success
Telephone: 440-775-5588
Fax: 440-775-5589

Oberlin College

explanation of past services and accommodations; recommendations and rationale as to why the accommodations are requested.

Additional Information

A Learning Resource Center and an Adaptive Technology Center are available for all students. Skills classes are offered for college credit in reading, study skills, and writing. DRCSS can arrange one or all of the following services for students with learning disabilities: quiet space for exams; extended examination times, up to twice the time typically allotted, based on diagnosis; oral exams; scribes; individual academic, personal, and vocational counseling; computer resources for additional academic skill development and assistance; alternate text; priority academic scheduling; peer tutoring; new student orientation assistance; and faculty/staff consultation. In addition, DRCSS can provide information about other support services sponsored by the college.

GENERAL ADMISSIONS

Very important factors considered include: rigor of secondary school record, class rank, academic GPA, standardized test scores. *Important factors considered include:* extracurricular activities, talent/ability, character/personal qualities, first generation. *Other factors considered include:* application essay, recommendation(s), interview, alumni/ae relation, racial/ethnic status, volunteer work, work experience, level of applicant's interest. *Freshman Admission Requirements:* High school diploma is required and GED is not accepted. *Academic units required:* 4 English, 3 math, 3 science, 3 foreign language, 3 social studies. *Academic units recommended:* 4 science.

ACCOMMODATION OR SERVICES

Accommodations are decided upon an individual basis after a thorough review of appropriate, current documentation. The accommodations requests must be supported through the documentation provided and must be logically linked to the current impact of the condition on academic functioning.

FINANCIAL AID

Students should submit: Business/Farm Supplement; CSS/Financial Aid PROFILE; FAFSA; Institution's own financial aid form; Noncustodial PROFILE. Applicants will be notified of awards on or about 4/1. The Princeton Review suggests that all financial aid forms be submitted as soon as possible after October 1. *Need-based scholarships/grants offered:* College/university scholarship or grant aid from institutional funds; Federal Pell; Private scholarships; SEOG; State scholarships/grants. *Loan aid offered:* Direct PLUS loans; Direct Subsidized Stafford Loans; Direct Unsubsidized Stafford Loans. Federal Work-Study Program available. Institutional employment available.

CAMPUS LIFE

Activities: Campus Ministries; Choral groups; Concert band; Dance; Drama/theater; International Student Organization; Jazz band; Literary magazine; Marching band; Music ensembles; Musical theater; Opera; Pep band; Radio station; Student government; Student newspaper; Student-run film society; Symphony orchestra; Yearbook. **Organizations:** 125 registered organizations, 3 honor societies, 10 religious organizations. **Athletics (Intercollegiate):** *Men:* baseball, basketball, cross-country, diving, football, golf, lacrosse, soccer, swimming, tennis, track/field (outdoor), track/field (indoor). *Women:* basketball, cross-country, diving, field hockey, golf, lacrosse, soccer, softball, swimming, tennis, track/field (outdoor), track/field (indoor), volleyball. **On-Campus Highlights:** Allen Memorial Art Museum, Oberlin College Science Center, Adam Joseph Lewis Center for Environmental Studies, Arboretum, Jesse Philips Recreational Center.

ACCOMMODATIONS

Allowed in exams:

Calculators	Yes
Dictionary	Yes
Computer	Yes
Spell-checker	Yes
Extended test time	Yes
Scribe	Yes
Proctors	Yes
Oral exams	Yes
Note-takers	Yes

Support services for students with

LD	Yes
ADHD	Yes
ASD	Yes
Distraction-reduced environment	Yes
Recording of lecture allowed	Yes
Reading technology:	Yes
Audio books	Yes
Other assistive technology	Yes
Priority registration	Yes

Added costs for services:

For LD:	No
For ADHD:	No
For ASD:	No
LD specialists	Yes
ADHD & ASD coaching	No
ASD specialists	No
Professional tutors	No
Peer tutors	Yes
Max. hours/week for services	Unlimited

How professors are notified of student approved accommodations
Student and director

COLLEGE GRADUATION REQUIREMENTS

Course waivers allowed	No
Course substitutions allowed	Yes
In what courses	Case-by-case

The Ohio State University—Columbus

STUDENT ACADEMIC SERVICES BUILDING, COLUMBUS, OH 43210 • ADMISSIONS: 614-292-3980 • FAX: 614-292-3980

CAMPUS
Type of school	Public
Environment	Metropolis
Support	CS

STUDENTS
Undergrad enrollment	44,853
% male/female	52/48
% from out of state	19
% frosh live on campus	94

FINANCIAL FACTS
Annual in-state tuition	$10,591
Annual out-of-state tuition	$30,742
Room and board	$12,434

GENERAL ADMISSIONS INFO
Application fee	$60
Regular application deadline	2/1

Nonfall registration accepted. Admission may be deferred for a maximum of 1 year.

Range SAT EBRW	610–700
Range SAT Math	650–750
Range ACT Composite	27–31

ACADEMICS
Student/faculty ratio	19:1
% students returning for sophomore year	94
% students graduating within 4 years	59
% students graduating within 6 years	83

Most classes have fewer than 10 students. Most lab/discussion sessions have 10–19 students.

PROGRAMS/SERVICES FOR STUDENTS WITH LEARNING DIFFERENCES

The Office for Disability Services (ODS) at Ohio State University offers a variety of services for students with documented disabilities, including learning disabilities, hearing or visual impairments, attention deficit disorders, and psychiatric or medical disabilities. The mission of ODS is to provide and coordinate support services and programs that enable students with disabilities to maximize their educational potential. ODS serves as a resource to all members of the university community so that students with disabilities can freely and actively participate in all facets of university life.

ADMISSIONS

Students with LD are admitted under the same criteria as regular applicants. However, consideration can be given to students with LD with support from ODS in instances where the student's rank, GPA, or lack of courses, such as foreign language, have affected performance in high school. Applicants interested in services should submit a general application for admission; complete the section under optional personal statement that gives students the opportunity to provide information if they feel that their high school performance was adversely affected by special circumstances; and submit documentation of the disability to ODS, including the latest IEP and the results of the last psychoeducational testing. In some cases, ODS will be asked to consider supporting an appeal of an admissions decision. ODS will review the application, look at course work and deficiencies, review services received in high school and determine if the student's needs can be met at OSU if the student is not normally admissible, look at when a diagnosis was made and at the IEP, and make a recommendation to the Admissions Office. Students exceeding the minimum curriculum in math, natural resources, or foreign language will be given additional consideration. Other factors considered include the competitiveness of the high school, accelerated courses taken, if the applicant is a first-generation college student, or the student's cultural, economic, racial, or geographic diversity; outstanding talents; extracurricular activities; significant work experiences; or leadership positions.

ADMISSIONS INFO FOR STUDENTS WITH LEARNING DIFFERENCES
SAT/ACT required: Yes
Interview required: No
Essay required: Recommended
Additional application required: No
Documentation required for:
  LD: Results of psycho-edcuational, IEP, 504 plan, history of LD services are part of the process for review that also includes narative of educational impact. Eligibility determinations are case-by-case.
  ADHD: Results of psycho-edcuational, IEP, 504 plan, history of LD services are part of the process for review that also includes narative of educational impact. Eligibility determinations are case-by-case.
  ASD: Results of psycho-edcuational, IEP, 504 plan, history of LD services are part of the process for review that also includes narative of educational impact. Eligibility determinations are case-by-case.
Documentation submitted to: Support program/services
Special Ed. HS course work accepted: No
Separate application required for program services: No
# of students last year receiving services/accommodations for:
  LD: 278
Contact Information
Name of program or department: Student Life Disability Services
Telephone: 614-292-3307
Fax: 614-292-4190
Email: slds@osu.edu

The Ohio State University—Columbus

Additional Information

Transition. Success. Independence. (TOPS) offers students with developmental disabilities a unique opportunity to engage in OSU academic coursework and work experiences while developing independent living skills and participating in campus and community organizations, social activities, and events. Potential applicants are interested in lifelong learning and will benefit from experiences gained at OSU. Prerequisite criteria are: Graduate from high school with traditional diploma or certificate of completion. able to benefit from curricula to improve academic, employment, social and independent living outcomes. demonstrate functional communication skills, demonstrates a desire to continue learning. demonstrates good attendance, demonstrates functional academic skills in all areas. demonstrates the motivation to become a self-determined adult, demonstrates independent self-help skills. demonstrates the ability to maintain appropriate behavior in a variety of settings, demonstrates the ability to accept feedback and direction from others and modify performance accordingly.and demonstrates independent travel skills, passes criminal background check and drug test for employment. and demonstrates a desire to work competitively, and agrees in writing to abide by all university and program rules.

GENERAL ADMISSIONS

Very important factors considered include: rigor of secondary school record, class rank, academic GPA, standardized test scores. *Important factors considered include:* application essay, extracurricular activities, talent/ability, first generation, volunteer work, work experience. *Other factors considered include:* recommendation(s), character/personal qualities, geographical residence, state residency, racial/ethnic status. *Freshman Admission Requirements:* High school diploma is required and GED is accepted. *Academic units required:* 4 English, 3 math, 3 science, 3 science labs, 2 foreign language, 2 social studies, 1 academic elective, 1 visual/performing arts. *Academic units recommended:* 4 English, 4 math, 3 science, 3 science labs, 3 foreign language, 3 social studies, 1 academic elective, 1 visual/performing arts.

ACCOMMODATION OR SERVICES

Accommodations are decided upon an individual basis after a thorough review of appropriate, current documentation. The accommodations requests must be supported through the documentation provided and must be logically linked to the current impact of the condition on academic functioning.

FINANCIAL AID

Students should submit: FAFSA. The Princeton Review suggests that all financial aid forms be submitted as soon as possible after October 1. *Need-based scholarships/grants offered:* College/university scholarship or grant aid from institutional funds; Federal Pell; Private scholarships; SEOG; State scholarships/grants. *Loan aid offered:* Direct PLUS loans; Direct Subsidized Stafford Loans; Direct Unsubsidized Stafford Loans. Federal Work-Study Program available. Institutional employment available.

CAMPUS LIFE

Activities: Campus Ministries; Choral groups; Concert band; Dance; Drama/theater; International Student Organization; Jazz band; Literary magazine; Marching band; Model UN; Music ensembles; Musical theater; Opera; Pep band; Radio station; Student government; Student newspaper; Student-run film society; Symphony orchestra; Television station. **Organizations:** 950 registered organizations, 39 honor societies, 93 religious organizations. 42 fraternities, 25 sororities.

ACCOMMODATIONS

Allowed in exams:

Calculators	Yes
Dictionary	Yes
Computer	Yes
Spell-checker	Yes
Extended test time	Yes
Scribe	Yes
Proctors	Yes
Oral exams	Yes
Note-takers	Yes

Support services for students with

LD	Yes
ADHD	Yes
ASD	Yes
Distraction-reduced environment	Yes
Recording of lecture allowed	Yes
Reading technology:	Yes
Audio books	Yes

Other assistive technology   Read & Write Gold, Zoomtext, JAWS, Sonocent Audio Notetaker, Dragon.

Priority registration	Yes

Added costs for services:

For LD:	No
For ADHD:	No
For ASD:	No
LD specialists	Yes
ADHD & ASD coaching	No
ASD specialists	No
Professional tutors	No
Peer tutors	Yes
Max. hours/week for services	Varies

How professors are notified of student approved accommodations   Student

COLLEGE GRADUATION REQUIREMENTS

Course waivers allowed	Yes
In what courses	Varies
Course substitutions allowed	Yes

In what courses   On a case-by-case basis and with appropriate supporting disability documentation, some students can petition for a substitution of the foreign language if it is not essential for the major. Math substitutions are rare.

Ohio University—Athens

1 OHIO UNIVERSITY, ATHENS, OH 45701 • ADMISSIONS: 740-593-4100 • FAX: 740-593-0560

CAMPUS
Type of school	Public
Environment	Town
Support	S

STUDENTS
Undergrad enrollment	23,084
% male/female	40/60
% from out of state	15
% frosh live on campus	95

FINANCIAL FACTS
Annual in-state tuition	$10,602
Annual out-of-state tuition	$19,566
Room and board	$10,734

GENERAL ADMISSIONS INFO
Application fee	$50
Priority deadline	12/1
Regular application deadline	2/1

Nonfall registration accepted. Admission may be deferred for a maximum of 1 year.

Range SAT EBRW	550–640
Range SAT Math	530–620
Range ACT Composite	22–26

ACADEMICS
Student/faculty ratio	17:1
% students returning for sophomore year	80
% students graduating within 4 years	44
% students graduating within 6 years	64

Most classes have 10–19 students.

PROGRAMS/SERVICES FOR STUDENTS WITH LEARNING DIFFERENCES

Student Accessibility Services facilitates requests for accommodations in accordance with the Americans with Disabilities Act and Section 504 of the Rehabilitation Act. Students wishing to request accommodations should complete an application for accommodation and submit supporting documentation to SAS, preferably before you begin your first semester. Each eligible student will be assigned an Accessibility Coordinator who will assist the student in transition to college through determination of reasonable accommodations, referral to pertinent resources to support student success, assist students in developing self-advocacy skills, and to serve as a central point of contact for navigating the college experience. Accessibility Coordinators are available and willing to meet upon a student's request; however progress is not formally monitored by the SAS. There is not a separate support program to which a student applies for admission; rather all admitted students with a disability may request accommodation through the Student Accessibility Services.

ADMISSIONS

Applicants with LD meet the same admission criteria as all other applicants. General admission Students not meeting the admission criteria are encouraged to self-disclose by writing a narrative explaining the impact of the disability. The average ACT is 22-26 and SAT of 1090-1240. The average GPA is 3.54. Admissions considers curriculum, class rank, GPA, and ACT/SAT. Some programs have more selective criteria. Courses required are 4 English, 4 math, 3 science, 3 social studies, 2 foreign language, 1 visual or performing arts, and 4 additional electives.

Additional Information

SAS has coaching support for students on the autism spectrum. The program provides an additional layer of individualized support. Coaches work individually with students on five key competency areas to develop the skills and strategies necessary to succeed in college. As students progress, the program's focus shifts from adjustment to the college environment to the pursuit of optimal independence and the transition to the workforce. Coaches are experienced, upper class student-employees

ADMISSIONS INFO FOR STUDENTS WITH LEARNING DIFFERENCES

SAT/ACT required: Yes
Interview required: No
Essay required: Yes
Additional application required: No
Documentation required for:
  LD: Prefer a recent, full Psycho ed evaluation to include: relevant historical info, instructional interventions, related services, age diagnosed, objective data (aptitude, achievement, info processing), test scores (standard, percentile and grade equivalents) and describe functional limitations. Recommended to contact SAS and speak with an Accessibility Coordinator to discuss your specific situation.
  ADHD: Yes
  ASD: Psycho ed evaluation
Documentation submitted to: Student AccessibilityServices
Special Ed. HS course work accepted: Yes
Separate application required for program services: No
# of students last year receiving services/accommodations for:
  LD: 400
Contact Information
Name of program or department: Student Accessibility Services
Telephone: 740-593-2620
Fax: 740-593-0790
Email: disabilities@ohio.edu

trained to serve as an additional resource for students with ASD. Priority consideration is given to those who apply by May 15.

GENERAL ADMISSIONS

Very important factors considered include: rigor of secondary school record, academic GPA, standardized test scores. *Important factors considered include:* class rank, application essay, first generation. *Other factors considered include:* recommendation(s), interview, extracurricular activities, talent/ability, character/personal qualities, alumni/ae relation, geographical residence, state residency, volunteer work, work experience. *Freshman Admission Requirements:* High school diploma is required and GED is accepted. *Academic units required:* 4 English, 4 math, 3 science, 2 foreign language, 3 social studies, 4 academic electives, and 1 unit from above areas or other academic areas. *Academic units recommended:* 1 visual/performing arts.

ACCOMMODATION OR SERVICES

Accommodations are decided upon an individual basis after a thorough review of appropriate, current documentation. The accommodations requests must be supported through the documentation provided and must be logically linked to the current impact of the condition on academic functioning.

FINANCIAL AID

Students should submit: FAFSA. Applicants will be notified of awards on or about 2/1. The Princeton Review suggests that all financial aid forms be submitted as soon as possible after October 1. *Need-based scholarships/grants offered:* College/university scholarship or grant aid from institutional funds; Federal Pell; Private scholarships; SEOG; State scholarships/grants. *Loan aid offered:* Direct PLUS loans; Direct Subsidized Stafford Loans; Direct Unsubsidized Stafford Loans. Federal Work-Study Program available. Institutional employment available.

CAMPUS LIFE

Activities: Campus Ministries; Choral groups; Concert band; Dance; Drama/theater; International Student Organization; Jazz band; Literary magazine; Marching band; Music ensembles; Musical theater; Opera; Pep band; Radio station; Student government; Student newspaper; Student-run film society; Symphony orchestra; Television station; Yearbook. **Organizations:** 323 registered organizations, 16 honor societies, 27 religious organizations. 17 fraternities, 12 sororities. **Athletics (Intercollegiate):** *Men:* baseball, basketball, cheerleading, cross-country, football, golf, wrestling. *Women:* basketball, cheerleading, cross-country, diving, field hockey, golf, soccer, softball, swimming, track/field (outdoor), volleyball. **On-Campus Highlights:** Charles J. Ping Recreation Center, Kennedy Museum of Art, Templeton-Blackburn Memorial Auditorium, Convocation Center, Alden Library.

ACCOMMODATIONS

Allowed in exams:

Calculators	Yes
Dictionary	Yes
Computer	Yes
Spell-checker	Yes
Extended test time	Yes
Scribe	Yes
Proctors	Yes
Oral exams	Not Applicable
Note-takers	Yes

Support services for students with

LD	Yes
ADHD	Yes
ASD	Yes
Distraction-reduced environment	Yes
Recording of lecture allowed	Yes
Reading technology:	Yes
Audio books	Yes
Other assistive technology	Dragon Naturally Speaking
Priority registration	Yes

Added costs for services:

For LD:	No
For ADHD:	No
For ASD:	No
LD specialists	No
ADHD & ASD coaching	No
ASD specialists	No
Professional tutors	Yes
Peer tutors	No
Max. hours/week for services	Varies
How professors are notified of student approved accommodations	Student

COLLEGE GRADUATION REQUIREMENTS

Course waivers allowed	No
Course substitutions allowed	Yes
In what courses	Varies

University of Cincinnati

P.O. Box 210063, Cincinnati, OH 45221-0091 • Admissions: 513-556-1100 • Fax: 513-556-1105

CAMPUS

Type of school	Public
Environment	Metropolis
Support	CS

STUDENTS

Undergrad enrollment	25,573
% male/female	51/49
% from out of state	16
% frosh live on campus	80

FINANCIAL FACTS

Annual in-state tuition	$9,322
Annual out-of-state tuition	$24,656
Room and board	$11,118
Required fees	$1,678

GENERAL ADMISSIONS INFO

Application fee	$50
Priority deadline	12/1
Regular application deadline	3/1

Nonfall registration accepted. Admission may be deferred for a maximum of 1 year.

Range SAT EBRW	560–660
Range SAT Math	560–680
Range ACT Composite	23–28

ACADEMICS

Student/faculty ratio	17:1
% students returning for sophomore year	86
% students graduating within 4 years	34
% students graduating within 6 years	69

Most classes have 20–29 students.
Most lab/discussion sessions have fewer than 10 students.

Programs/Services for Students with Learning Differences

Accessibility Resources is dedicated to empowering students with disabilities through the delivery of reasonable accommodations and support services, and bridging post-secondary education with future real-world experiences. Students with disabilities who need academic accommodations or other specialized services while attending UC will receive reasonable accommodations to meet their individual needs as well as advocacy assistance on disability-related issues. The university is strongly committed to maintaining an environment that guarantees students with disabilities full access to educational programs, activities, and facilities.

Admissions

There is no special admission procedure for students with learning disabilities. All students submit the university's general application form. Requests for substitutions/waivers of admission requirements should be made to the admissions office. The University of Cincinnati expects all baccalaureate students to have completed the following articulation requirements: four units of college-prep English, three units of college-prep math, two units of science, two units of social science, two units of a single foreign language, one unit of fine arts, two additional units of any of these. ACT/SAT scores are also required for baccalaureate programs. Branch campuses require a high school diploma or GED for admission. ACT/SAT scores are recommended but not required.

Additional Information

TAP provides a four-year college experience for individuals with mild to moderate intellectual or developmental disabilities (ID/DD). Students live in the residence halls, attend classes, engage in vocational internships and participate in an active social life. TAP's mission is to enhance the quality of life of students through advocacy, access, and research. Applicants must have: a cognitive assessment with documented intellectual or developmental disability; a high school diploma and be age 18 or older; basic academic skills; the ability to learn and participate in inclusive classrooms and work settings; demonstrate interest and ability to pursue educational, employment, and life experiences through post-secondary education The cost of the program is approximately $30,000 per year.

ADMISSIONS INFO FOR STUDENTS WITH LEARNING DIFFERENCES

SAT/ACT required: Yes
Interview required:No
Essay required: No
Additional application required: No
Documentation required for:
  LD:Psycho ed evaluation to include: relevant historical info, instructional interventions, related services, age diagnosed, objective data (aptitude, achievement, info processing), test scores (standard, percentile and grade equivalents) and describe functional limitations.
  ADHD: Diagnosis based on DSM-V; history of behaviors impairing functioning in academic setting; diagnostic interview; history of symptoms; evidence of ongoing behaviors.
  ASD: Psycho ed evaluation
Documentation submitted to:Accessibility Resources
Special Ed. HS course work accepted: Yes
Separate application required for program services: No
Contact Information
Name of program or department: Accessibility Resources
Telephone: 513-556-6823
Fax: 513-556-1383
Email: disabisv@ucmail.uc.edu

University of Cincinnati

GENERAL ADMISSIONS

Very important factors considered include: rigor of secondary school record, academic GPA, standardized test scores. *Important factors considered include:* application essay, recommendation(s), talent/ability. *Other factors considered include:* class rank, extracurricular activities, character/personal qualities, volunteer work, work experience. *Freshman Admission Requirements:* High school diploma is required and GED is accepted. *Academic units required:* 4 English, 4 math, 3 science, 3 social studies, and 5 units from above areas or other academic areas. *Academic units recommended:* 2 foreign language.

ACCOMMODATION OR SERVICES

Accommodations are decided upon an individual basis after a thorough review of appropriate, current documentation. The accommodations requests must be supported through the documentation provided and must be logically linked to the current impact of the condition on academic functioning.

FINANCIAL AID

Students should submit: FAFSA. Applicants will be notified of awards on a rolling basis beginning 3/1. The Princeton Review suggests that all financial aid forms be submitted as soon as possible after October 1. *Need-based scholarships/grants offered:* College/university scholarship or grant aid from institutional funds; Federal Pell; Private scholarships; SEOG; State scholarships/grants; United Negro College Fund. *Loan aid offered:* Direct PLUS loans; Direct Subsidized Stafford Loans; Direct Unsubsidized Stafford Loans. Federal Work-Study Program available. Institutional employment available.

CAMPUS LIFE

Activities: Campus Ministries; Choral groups; Concert band; Dance; Drama/theater; International Student Organization; Jazz band; Marching band; Music ensembles; Musical theater; Opera; Pep band; Radio station; Student government; Student newspaper; Student-run film society; Symphony orchestra; Television station. **Organizations:** 250 registered organizations, 16 honor societies, 23 religious organizations. 23 fraternities, 10 sororities. **Athletics (Intercollegiate):** *Men:* baseball, basketball, cheerleading, cross-country, diving, football, golf, soccer, swimming, track/field (outdoor). *Women:* basketball, cheerleading, cross-country, diving, golf, lacrosse, soccer, swimming, tennis, track/field (outdoor), track/field (indoor), volleyball. Tangeman University Center (TUC), Campus Recreation Center (CRC), Nippert Stadium, Main Street, Sheakley Lawn.

ACCOMMODATIONS

Allowed in exams:	
Calculators	Yes
Dictionary	Yes
Computer	Yes
Spell-checker	Yes
Extended test time	Yes
Scribe	Yes
Proctors	Yes
Oral exams	No
Note-takers	Yes
Support services for students with	
LD	Yes
ADHD	Yes
ASD	Yes
Distraction-reduced environment	Yes
Recording of lecture allowed	Yes
Reading technology:	Yes
Audio books	Yes
Other assistive technology	Read and Write Gold
Priority registration	Yes
Added costs for services:Yes, for TAP	
For LD:	No
For ADHD:	No
For ASD:	No
LD specialists	No
ADHD & ASD coaching	No
ASD specialists	Yes
Professional tutors	Yes
Peer tutors	Yes
Max. hours/week for services	Varies
How professors are notified of student approved accommodations	Director and student

COLLEGE GRADUATION REQUIREMENTS

Course waivers allowed	No
Course substitutions allowed	Yes

In what courses

We will offer course substitutions in foreign language and in rare occasions, if given Departmental approval, mathematics. Most importantly is to ensure that the substitution does not create a fundamental alteration of the program.

University of Dayton

300 College Park, Dayton, OH 45469-1669 • Admissions: 937-229-4411 • Fax: 937-229-4729

CAMPUS

Type of school	Private (nonprofit)
Environment	City
Support	CS

STUDENTS

Undergrad enrollment	8,422
% male/female	52/48
% from out of state	52
% frosh live on campus	95

FINANCIAL FACTS

Annual tuition	$42,900
Room and board	$13,580

GENERAL ADMISSIONS INFO

Priority deadline	12/15
Regular application deadline	3/1

Nonfall registration accepted. Admission may be deferred.

Range SAT EBRW	550–650
Range SAT Math	550–660
Range ACT Composite	24–29

ACADEMICS

Student/faculty ratio	15:1
% students returning for sophomore year	90
% students graduating within 4 years	60
% students graduating within 6 years	79

Most classes have 20–29 students.
Most lab/discussion sessions have 20–29 students.

Programs/Services for Students with Learning Differences

The University of Dayton is: one of the nation's ten largest Catholic universities and Ohio's largest private university, with undergraduate and graduate programs; a university founded in 1850 by the Society of Mary (Marianists), a Roman Catholic teaching order of priests and brothers; a residential learning community with more than 70 academic programs in arts and sciences, business administration, education and allied professions, engineering and law; a diverse community committed to educating the whole person and to linking learning and scholarship with leadership and service; a vibrant living-learning environment, where modern campus housing blurs the line between living and learning. The LTC's Office of Learning Resources (OLR) focus is to provide all students with disabilities an equitable opportunity to participate freely and actively in all areas of university life.

Admissions

Applications for admission are reviewed for specific academic majors or, when applicable, for undeclared status in an academic division. Five factors are considered when we assess your preparation for a chosen field of study: your selection of courses in preparation for college, your grade record and pattern throughout high school, your class standing or ranking, results of either the SAT or ACT, and your character and record of leadership and service. Balanced consideration is given to all aspects of your college-preparation. While no minimum grade point average, class rank, or standardized test score is specified, these measures must provide evidence of your readiness for college studies in your chosen academic program.

Additional Information

Because the university recognizes that students have individually unique academic and personal strengths and weaknesses, the Office of Learning Resources (OLR) provides support services to students such as drop-in tutoring (peer-facilitated), with additional support models (Supplemental Instruction) linked to specific classes, and writing support across the curriculum. All OLR support services are provided free of charge. OLR services are most effective if the student takes advantage of them before he or she falls too far behind or receives too many low grades.

ADMISSIONS INFO FOR STUDENTS WITH LEARNING DIFFERENCES

SAT/ACT required: Yes
Interview required: No
Essay required: Not Applicable
Additional application required: Yes
Documentation required for:
  LD:Psycho ed evaluation to include: relevant historical info, instructional interventions, related services, age diagnosed, objective data (aptitude, achievement, info processing), test scores (standard, percentile and grade equivalents) and describe functional limitations.
  ADHD: Diagnosis based on DSM-V; history of behaviors impairing functioning in academic setting; diagnostic interview; history of symptoms; evidence of ongoing behaviors.
  ASD:Psycho ed evaluation
Documentation submitted to: Office of Learning Resources
Special Ed. HS course work accepted: No
Separate application required for program services: No
Contact Information
Name of program or department: Office of Learning Resources
Telephone: 937-229-2066
Fax: 937-229-3270
Email: disabilityservices@udayton.edu

University of Dayton

Every individual student with a disability is guaranteed equal access to all educational programs and services at the University of Dayton. OLR serves qualified students with disabilities after they have been accepted to the University of Dayton and registered with OLR. Students with disabilities must submit appropriate, current documentation of their disability (see website for specific requirements) and participate in the interactive process. There is no obligation for any student to identify a disability; however, students who wish to receive reasonable accommodations must submit proper documentation, participate in an interactive assessment interview with the OLR Disabilities Staff, request in writing the need for specific services following established published guidelines and deadlines. The Ryan C. Harris Adaptive Learning Lab is specifically designed with assistive technology for students with various physical and cognitive disabilities. Staff members provide technical assistance and proctored testing.

General Admissions

Very important factors considered include: rigor of secondary school record, class rank, academic GPA, application essay, standardized test scores. *Important factors considered include:* recommendation(s), extracurricular activities, character/personal qualities, alumni/ae relation, level of applicant's interest. *Other factors considered include:* talent/ability, first generation, racial/ethnic status, volunteer work, work experience. *Freshman Admission Requirements:* High school diploma is required and GED is accepted. *Academic units recommended:* 4 English, 4 math, 4 science, 1 science lab, 2 foreign language, 4 social studies, 4 history, 4 computer science, 4 visual/performing arts.

Accommodation or Services

Accommodations are decided upon an individual basis after a thorough review of appropriate, current documentation. The accommodations requests must be supported through the documentation provided and must be logically linked to the current impact of the condition on academic functioning.

Financial Aid

Students should submit: FAFSA. Applicants will be notified of awards on a rolling basis beginning 2/17. The Princeton Review suggests that all financial aid forms be submitted as soon as possible after October 1. *Need-based scholarships/grants offered:* College/university scholarship or grant aid from institutional funds; Federal Pell; Private scholarships; SEOG; State scholarships/grants. *Loan aid offered:* Direct PLUS loans; Direct Subsidized Stafford Loans; Direct Unsubsidized Stafford Loans. Federal Work-Study Program available. Institutional employment available.

Campus Life

Activities: Campus Ministries; Choral groups; Concert band; Dance; Drama/theater; International Student Organization; Jazz band; Literary magazine; Marching band; Model UN; Music ensembles; Musical theater; Opera; Pep band; Radio station; Student government; Student newspaper; Symphony orchestra; Television station; Yearbook. **Organizations:** 200 registered organizations, 14 honor societies, 30 religious organizations. 13 fraternities, 9 sororities. **Athletics (Intercollegiate):** *Men:* baseball, basketball, cheerleading, cross-country, football, golf, soccer, tennis. *Women:* basketball, cheerleading, crew/rowing, cross-country, golf, soccer, softball, tennis, track/field (outdoor), track/field (indoor), volleyball. **On-Campus Highlights:** John F. Kennedy Memorial Union, Ryan C. Harris Learning-Teaching Center, University of Dayton Arena, University of Dayton Science Center, Kettering Laboratories; UDRI.

ACCOMMODATIONS

Allowed in exams:

Calculators	Yes
Dictionary	Yes
Computer	Yes
Spell-checker	Yes
Extended test time	Yes
Scribe	Yes
Proctors	Yes
Oral exams	No
Note-takers	Yes

Support services for students with

LD	Yes
ADHD	Yes
ASD	Yes
Distraction-reduced environment	Yes
Recording of lecture allowed	Yes
Reading technology:	Yes
Audio books	Yes
Other assistive technology	Decisions on accommodation appropriateness are based upon disability and class information and determined on a case-by-case basis.
Priority registration	Yes

Added costs for services:

For LD:	No
For ADHD:	No
For ASD:	No
LD specialists	Yes
ADHD & ASD coaching	Yes
ASD specialists	No
Professional tutors	Yes
Peer tutors	Yes
Max. hours/week for services	Varies
How professors are notified of student approved accommodations	Student

COLLEGE GRADUATION REQUIREMENTS

Course waivers allowed	No
Course substitutions allowed	Yes
In what courses	

Courses specific to the disability that do not change the essential functions of the program on a case-by-case basis.

Ursuline College

2550 LANDER ROAD, PEPPER PIKE, OH 44124-4398 • ADMISSIONS: 440-449-4203 • FAX: 440-684-6138

CAMPUS

Type of school	Private (nonprofit)
Environment	City
Support	SP

STUDENTS

Undergrad enrollment	641
% male/female	7/93
% from out of state	8
% frosh live on campus	72

FINANCIAL FACTS

Annual tuition	$32,070
Room and board	$10,776
Required fees	$320

GENERAL ADMISSIONS INFO

Regular application deadline   2/1
Nonfall registration accepted. Admission may be deferred for a maximum of 1 year.

Range SAT EBRW	425–590
Range SAT Math	440–535
Range ACT Composite	19–24

ACADEMICS

Student/faculty ratio	7:1
% students returning for sophomore year	59
% students graduating within 4 years	31
% students graduating within 6 years	53

Most classes have 10–19 students.
Most lab/discussion sessions have fewer than 10 students.

PROGRAMS/SERVICES FOR STUDENTS WITH LEARNING DIFFERENCES

Ursuline College is a small Catholic college committed to helping students with learning disabilities succeed in their courses and become independent learners. The Program for Students with Learning Disabilities (FOCUS) is a voluntary, comprehensive fee-paid program. The goals of the FOCUS program include providing a smooth transition to college life, helping students learn to apply the most appropriate learning strategies in college courses, and teaching self-advocacy skills. To be eligible for FOCUS admission, a student must present documentation of an LD, which consists of a WAIS-R, the Woodcock-Johnson, and any other standardized measures of achievement. The psychoeducational evaluation must clearly indicate that the student has a specific learning disability and should have been conducted within the last 3 years. Students must have average to above-average intellectual ability and an appropriate academic foundation to succeed in a 4-year liberal arts college.

ADMISSIONS

To participate in the FOCUS program, students must first meet with the LD specialist to discuss whether the program is suitable for them. Students must then meet the requirements for clear or conditional admission to the college by applying to the admissions office and completing all regular admission procedures. Students with learning disabilities usually meet the same requirements for admission to the college as all other students. A student may receive a "conditional" admission if the GPA and ACT are lower. Students with conditional admission are limited to 12 credit hours per semester for the first year. The final admission decision is made by the Office of Admissions.

Additional Information

The fee based FOCUS program is offered in multiple phases to better meet individual students' needs. FOCUS STAGE 1: One guaranteed weekly meeting with a disability specialist to cover all areas of academic progress, co-advising on academic courses majors, mid-term progress monitoring and monthly communication with faculty and priority registration. FOCUS STAGE 2: Incoming special orientation with the disability specialist, two guaranteed weekly meetings with a disability specialist to

ADMISSIONS INFO FOR STUDENTS WITH LEARNING DIFFERENCES

SAT/ACT required: Yes
Interview required: No
Essay required: No
Additional application required: Yes
Documentation required for:
  LD: A diagnosis from a qualified professional which includes actual test scores.
  ADHD: A diagnosis from a qualified professional which includes any testing information and assessment the evaluator deems necessary and appropriate.
  ASD: A speech diagnosis of an ASD based on current DSM criteria from a qualified professional.
Documentation submitted to:Disabilities Services, FOCUS
Special Ed. HS course work accepted: No
Separate application required for program services: No
# of students last year receiving services/accommodations for:
  LD: 25
Contact Information
Name of program or department: FOCUS: for Students with LD
Telephone: 440-449-4026

Ursuline College

cover all areas of academic progress, co-advising on courses and majors, academic and social support, mid-term progress monitoring, biweekly communication with faculty and priority registration FOCUS STAGE 3: Students meet with the disability specialist a minimum of 3 times per week, bi-weekly monitoring and communication with faculty, co-advising on academic courses, majors and priority registration. Academic and social support are provided. FOCUS STAGE 4: For students who are transitioning out of college.

GENERAL ADMISSIONS

Very important factors considered include: academic GPA, standardized test scores. *Other factors considered include:* rigor of secondary school record, class rank, application essay, recommendation(s), interview, alumni/ae relation. *Freshman Admission Requirements:* High school diploma is required and GED is accepted. *Academic units recommended:* 4 English, 3 math, 3 science, 2 science labs, 2 foreign language, 3 social studies, 1 visual/performing arts, 1 unit from above areas or other academic areas.

ACCOMMODATION OR SERVICES

Accommodations are decided upon an individual basis after a thorough review of appropriate, current documentation. The accommodations requests must be supported through the documentation provided and must be logically linked to the current impact of the condition on academic functioning.

FINANCIAL AID

Students should submit: FAFSA. Applicants will be notified of awards on a rolling basis beginning 2/15. The Princeton Review suggests that all financial aid forms be submitted as soon as possible after October 1. *Need-based scholarships/grants offered:* College/university scholarship or grant aid from institutional funds; Federal Nursing Scholarships; Federal Pell; Private scholarships; SEOG; State scholarships/grants. *Loan aid offered:* Direct PLUS loans; Direct Subsidized Stafford Loans; Direct Unsubsidized Stafford Loans. Federal Work-Study Program available.

CAMPUS LIFE

Activities: Campus Ministries; Drama/theater; Literary magazine; Student government. **Organizations:** 21 registered organizations, 4 honor societies, **Athletics (Intercollegiate):** *Women:* basketball, bowling, cross-country, golf, soccer, softball, swimming, tennis, track/field (outdoor), volleyball. **On-Campus Highlights:** Bishop Anthony M. Pilla Student Learning Center, Florence O'Donnell Wasmer Gallery, Joseph J. Mullen Academic Center, Ralph M. Besse Library.

ACCOMMODATIONS

Allowed in exams:

Calculators	Yes
Dictionary	Yes
Computer	Yes
Spell-checker	Yes
Extended test time	Yes
Scribe	Yes
Proctors	Yes
Oral exams	Yes
Note-takers	Yes

Support services for students with

LD	Yes
ADHD	Yes
ASD	Yes
Distraction-reduced environment	Yes
Recording of lecture allowed	Yes
Reading technology:	Yes
Audio books	Yes
Other assistive technology	Yes
Priority registration	Yes

Added costs for services:

For LD:	No
For ADHD:	No
For ASD:	No
FOCUS:	Yes
LD specialists	Yes
ADHD & ASD coaching	Yes
ASD specialists	Yes
Professional tutors	Yes
Peer tutors	Yes
Max. hours/week for services	13
How professors are notified of student approved accommodations	Student

COLLEGE GRADUATION REQUIREMENTS

Course waivers allowed	No
In what courses	
Course substitutions allowed	Yes
In what courses	

This is evaluated according to the student's specific needs on a case by case basis

Wright State University

3640 Colonel Glenn Highway, Dayton, OH 45435 • Admissions: 937-775-5700 • Fax: 937-775-4410

CAMPUS
Type of school	Public
Environment	City
Support	CS

STUDENTS
Undergrad enrollment	11,251
% male/female	48/52
% from out of state	5
% frosh live on campus	49

FINANCIAL FACTS
Annual in-state tuition	$9,254
Annual out-of-state tuition	$18,398
Room and board	$11,832

GENERAL ADMISSIONS INFO
Application fee	$30
Regular application deadline	8/20

Nonfall registration accepted. Admission may be deferred for a maximum of One year.

Range SAT EBRW	490–640
Range SAT Math	490–630
Range ACT Composite	19–25

ACADEMICS
% students returning for sophomore year	63
% students graduating within 4 years	19
% students graduating within 6 years	36

Most classes have 10–19 students. Most lab/discussion sessions have 10–19 students.

PROGRAMS/SERVICES FOR STUDENTS WITH LEARNING DIFFERENCES
ODS staff members work with admitted Wright State students to ensure equal access to university programs and services. Whether they are making the transition from high school, community college, or another university, students should be aware of the process to request Accommodations and/or auxiliary aids on the basis of a disability or temporary health condition. Services are supportive in nature, designed to provide the academic support necessary for students to have an equal opportunity for a college education.

ADMISSIONS
High school graduates will be granted admission to Wright State University if they meet one of the following options: Option 1: Complete the Ohio Core curriculum and have a 2.0 GPA and have a 15 ACT or 830 SAT. Option 2: Complete the Ohio Core curriculum and have GPA of 2.5 and submit any score on ACT or SAT. Out-of-state students must complete an equivalent rigorous curriculum. Recommended courses are: 4 years English, 4 years Math 3 years Science, 3 years of Social Studies (including American History, American Government and Economics/Financial Literacy, integrated or stand alone), 2 years of the same foreign language, and 1 Fine Arts.

ADMISSIONS INFO FOR STUDENTS WITH LEARNING DIFFERENCES
SAT/ACT required: Yes
Interview required: Yes
Essay required: No
Additional application required: Not Applicable
Documentation required for:
  LD: Psycho-educational report including: diagnosis; summary of assessment findings; description of current substantial limitations; aptitude/cognitive test (e.g. WAIS-IV, WJ-Cog -III); academic achievement test (e.g. WIAT II, WJ-Ach-III, SATA); test data providing the student's processing ability (e.g. index scores from the WAIS-IV); and all standard test scores.
  ADHD: Psycho-educational report including: diagnosis; summary of assessment findings; description of current substantial limitations; rating Scales to supplement the DSM-5 diagnosis (e.g. Wender Connors Continuous Performance test Brwon Attention-Deficit Disorder Scale); aptitude/cognitive ability test (e.g. WAIS-IV, WJ-Cog-III); academic achievement test (e.g. WIAT II, WJ-Ach-III, SATA); test data providing processing ability (e.g. index scores from the WAIS-IV); and all standard test scores.
  ASD: Psycho-educational report including: diagnosis; summary of assessment findings; description of current substantial limitations; aptitude/cognitive test (e.g. WAIS-IV, WJ-Cog III); academic achievement test (e.g. WIAT II, WJ-Ach-III, SATA); test data providing the student's processing ability (e.g. index scores from the WAIS-IV); and all standard test scores.
Documentation submitted to: Office of Disability Services
Special Ed. HS course work accepted: No
Separate application required for program services: Yes
# of students last year receiving services/accommodations for:
  LD: 147
  ADHD: 163
  ASD: 78
Contact Information
Name of program or department: Office of Disability Services
Telephone: 937-775-5680
Fax: 937-775-5699
Email: disability_services@wright.edu

Wright State University

Additional Information

RASE Transition Coach Program is a fee based program which provides support to students on the Autism Spectrum. Students are assigned a transition coach to work with them, one-on-one, for up to 5 hours per week. The transition coaches are experienced undergraduate or graduate students who are available as a resource for students on the Autism Spectrum. Coaches work with students on transition competency areas to develop the structure and framework necessary to be successful in college. The coach's focus can include assisting the student with learning self-advocacy skills, accessing campus resources and services, and problem-solving. RASE program cost is $750 per semester for year one and $300 per semester for additional years. PreFlight is a residential bridge program that will supply a variety of benefits including: Early move-in, Writing Workshop: and Engagement in College Transition Success Programming.

GENERAL ADMISSIONS

Very important factors considered include: rigor of secondary school record, academic GPA, standardized test scores. *Important factors considered include:* class rank. *Other factors considered include:* recommendation(s), state residency. *Freshman Admission Requirements:* High school diploma is required and GED is accepted. *Academic units required:* 4 English, 4 math, 3 science, 3 science labs, 3 social studies. *Academic units recommended:* 2 foreign language, 1 visual/performing arts.

ACCOMMODATION OR SERVICES

Accommodations are decided upon an individual basis after a thorough review of appropriate, current documentation. The accommodations requests must be supported through the documentation provided and must be logically linked to the current impact of the condition on academic functioning.

FINANCIAL AID

Students should submit: FAFSA. Applicants will be notified of awards on or about 12/15. The Princeton Review suggests that all financial aid forms be submitted as soon as possible after October 1. *Need-based scholarships/grants offered:* College/university scholarship or grant aid from institutional funds; Federal Nursing Scholarships; Federal Pell; Private scholarships; SEOG; State scholarships/grants; United Negro College Fund. *Loan aid offered:* Direct PLUS loans; Direct Subsidized Stafford Loans; Direct Unsubsidized Stafford Loans. Federal Work-Study Program available. Institutional employment available.

CAMPUS LIFE

Activities: Campus Ministries; Choral groups; Concert band; Dance; Drama/theater; International Student Organization; Jazz band; Literary magazine; Model UN; Music ensembles; Musical theater; Opera; Pep band; Radio station; Student government; Student newspaper; Symphony orchestra; Television station. **Organizations:** 145 registered organizations, 22 honor societies, 9 religious organizations. 8 fraternities, 8 sororities. **Athletics (Intercollegiate):** *Men:* baseball, basketball, cheerleading, cross-country, diving, golf, soccer, swimming, tennis. *Women:* basketball, cheerleading, cross-country, diving, soccer, softball, swimming, tennis, track/field (outdoor), volleyball. **On-Campus Highlights:** Student Union, Creative Arts Center, Rec Center, Paul Laurence Dunbar Library, Nutter Center.

ACCOMMODATIONS

Allowed in exams:

Calculators	Yes
Dictionary	Yes
Computer	Yes
Spell-checker	Yes
Extended test time	Yes
Scribe	Yes
Proctors	Yes
Oral exams	Yes
Note-takers	Yes

Support services for students with

LD	Yes
ADHD	Yes
ASD	Yes
Distraction-reduced environment	Yes
Recording of lecture allowed	Yes
Reading technology:	Yes
Audio books	Yes

Other assistive technology   An adaptive computer lab with nine computer stations with various hardware and software accessibility programs such as Read and Write Gold, JAWS, OpenBook

Priority registration	No

Added costs for services: Yes, for RASE Program

For LD:	No
For ADHD:	No
For ASD:	No
LD specialists	Yes
ADHD & ASD coaching	Yes
ASD specialists	Yes
Professional tutors	Yes
Peer tutors	Yes
Max. hours/week for services	2

How professors are notified of student
approved accommodations   Student

COLLEGE GRADUATION REQUIREMENTS

Course waivers allowed	Yes

In what courses   Considered on a case by case basis, however waivers are traditionally not offered.

Course substitutions allowed	Yes

In what courses   Any course will be considered

Xavier University (OH)

3800 Victory Parkway, Cincinnati, OH 45207-5311 • Admissions: 513-745-3301 • Fax: 513-745-4319

CAMPUS

Type of school	Private (nonprofit)
Environment	Metropolis
Support	CS

STUDENTS

Undergrad enrollment	4,572
% male/female	46/54
% from out of state	53
% frosh live on campus	91

FINANCIAL FACTS

Annual tuition	$38,300
Room and board	$12,780
Required fees	$230

GENERAL ADMISSIONS INFO

Application fee	$35
Priority deadline	2/1

Nonfall registration accepted. Admission may be deferred for a maximum of 1 year.

Range SAT EBRW	540–620
Range SAT Math	520–620
Range ACT Composite	22–28

ACADEMICS

Student/faculty ratio	12:1
% students returning for sophomore year	84
% students graduating within 4 years	61
% students graduating within 6 years	69

Most classes have 20–29 students.
Most lab/discussion sessions have 20–29 students.

PROGRAMS/SERVICES FOR STUDENTS WITH LEARNING DIFFERENCES

Saint Xavier University is committed to providing equal access and reasonable accommodations to students with disabilities. The Office of disability Services provides academic accomodations and support services to provide equal access to educational oportunities. Formerly in partnership with the Learning Center/Writing Studio, the Center for Accessibility Resources is the heart of academic support. The Center for Accessibility Resources works closely with students and faculty, providing services and academic assistance to students with documented disabilities. The student has an obligation to self-identify that he or she has a disability and needs accommodations.

ADMISSIONS

The middle 50 percent GPA is 3.19–3.91; the middle 50 percent class rank is 62–89 percent; the middle 50 percent ACT score is 22–28; and the middle 50 percent SAT score is 1110–1290. Students applying to majors in nursing, biology, chemistry receive two admission decisions: one for undergraduate admission to Xavier and one for the selected major. Music applicants must submit a music audition application.

Additional Information

The X-Path Program is established to provide individualized support for students on the autism spectrum or with related disorders. Support and coaching is tailored to the needs of each participating student to promote the development of academic competence, social integration, and self-advocacy. The mission of the X-Path Program is to increase opportunities for success for students who have autism and related disorders. Each student will work directly with the Accommodation and Support Coordinator and will also be assigned to a Peer Coach. The X-Path Program is for students on the Autism Spectrum To be considered for this

ADMISSIONS INFO FOR STUDENTS WITH LEARNING DIFFERENCES

SAT/ACT required: Yes
Interview required: No
Essay required: Yes
Additional application required: Yes
Documentation required for:
  LD: Psycho ed evaluation to include: relevant historical info, instructional interventions, related services, age diagnosed, objective data (aptitude, achievement, info processing), test scores (standard, percentile and grade equivalents) and describe functional limitations.
  ADHD: Diagnosis based on DSM-V; history of behaviors impairing functioning in academic setting; diagnostic interview; history of symptoms; evidence of ongoing behaviors.
  ASD: Psycho ed evaluation
Documentation submitted to: Support Program/Services
Special Ed. HS course work accepted: No
Separate application required for program services: No
# of students last year receiving services/accommodations for:
  LD: 265
Contact Information
Name of program or department: Office of Disability Services
Telephone: 513-745-3280
Fax: 513-745-3387
Email: disabilityservices@xavier.edu

Xavier University (OH)

optional, fee-based program, applicants must meet the following criteria: Be admitted to Xavier University through the Office of Undergraduate Admissions; and be registered with the Office of Disability Services; Submit a completed online X-Path Program application. Applications will be reviewed to ensure that the program requirements above are met and to assess whether the X-Path Program would be an appropriate option for the applicant's specific needs. Applicants may be contacted by program staff for an in-person or phone interview. All applicants accepted to the X-Path Program will receive a contract for program participation. The fee for participation in the X-Path program is $1500 per semester. Applicants may apply for financial assistance. All financial aid decisions will be determined by Xavier's Office of Student Financial Assistance.

GENERAL ADMISSIONS
Very important factors considered include: rigor of secondary school record, academic GPA, standardized test scores. *Important factors considered include:* application essay, recommendation(s), extracurricular activities, character/personal qualities, volunteer work. *Other factors considered include:* class rank, talent/ability, first generation, alumni/ae relation, work experience, level of applicant's interest. *Freshman Admission Requirements:* High school diploma is required and GED is accepted. *Academic units recommended:* 4 English, 3 math, 3 science, 2 foreign language, 3 social studies, 5 academic electives, 1 unit from above areas or other academic areas.

ACCOMMODATION OR SERVICES
Accommodations are decided upon an individual basis after a thorough review of appropriate, current documentation. The accommodations requests must be supported through the documentation provided and must be logically linked to the current impact of the condition on academic functioning.

FINANCIAL AID
Students should submit: FAFSA. Applicants will be notified of awards on a rolling basis beginning 12/15. The Princeton Review suggests that all financial aid forms be submitted as soon as possible after October 1. *Need-based scholarships/grants offered:* College/university scholarship or grant aid from institutional funds; Federal Pell; Private scholarships; SEOG; State scholarships/grants; United Negro College Fund. *Loan aid offered:* Direct PLUS loans; Direct Subsidized Stafford Loans; Direct Unsubsidized Stafford Loans. Federal Work-Study Program available. Institutional employment available.

CAMPUS LIFE
Activities: Campus Ministries; Choral groups; Concert band; Dance; Drama/theater; International Student Organization; Literary magazine; Model UN; Music ensembles; Musical theater; Pep band; Student government; Student newspaper; Television station. **Organizations:** 124 registered organizations, 10 honor societies, 11 religious organizations. **Athletics (Intercollegiate):** *Men:* baseball, basketball, cheerleading, cross-country, golf, soccer, swimming, tennis, track/field (outdoor), track/field (indoor). *Women:* basketball, cheerleading, cross-country, golf, soccer, swimming, tennis, track/field (outdoor), track/field (indoor), volleyball.

ACCOMMODATIONS
Allowed in exams:

Calculators	Yes
Dictionary	Yes
Computer	Yes
Spell-checker	Yes
Extended test time	Yes
Scribe	Yes
Proctors	Yes
Oral exams	Yes
Note-takers	Yes

Support services for students with

LD	Yes
ADHD	Yes
ASD	Yes
Distraction-reduced environment	Yes
Recording of lecture allowed	Yes
Reading technology:	Yes
Audio books	Yes
Other assistive technology Dragon Naturally Speaking	
Priority registration	Yes
Added costs for services: Yes for X-Path program	
For LD:	No
For ADHD:	No
For ASD:	No
LD specialists	No
DHD & ASD coaching	Yes
ASD specialists	Yes
Professional tutors	Yes
Peer tutors	Yes
Max. hours/week for services	1
How professors are notified of student approved accommodations	Student

COLLEGE GRADUATION REQUIREMENTS

Course waivers allowed	No
Course substitutions allowed	Yes
In what courses	Foreign language

Oklahoma State University

219 Student Union, Stillwater, OK 74078 • Admissions: 405-744-5358 • Fax: 405-744-7092

CAMPUS

Type of school	Public
Environment	Town
Support	S

STUDENTS

Undergrad enrollment	20,736
% male/female	51/49
% from out of state	27
% frosh live on campus	94

FINANCIAL FACTS

Annual in-state tuition	$5,357
Annual out-of-state tuition	$20,877
Room and board	$8,996
Required fees	$3,662

GENERAL ADMISSIONS INFO

Application fee	$40.

Nonfall registration accepted. Admission may be deferred.

Range SAT EBRW	540–630
Range SAT Math	530–630
Range ACT Composite	22–28

ACADEMICS

Student/faculty ratio	20:1
% students returning for sophomore year	81
% students graduating within 4 years	39
% students graduating within 6 years	63

Most classes have 10–19 students.
Most lab/discussion sessions have 10–19 students.

PROGRAMS/SERVICES FOR STUDENTS WITH LEARNING DIFFERENCES

Oklahoma State University does not have a formal learning disabilities program but uses a service-based model to assist the students in obtaining the necessary accommodations for specific learning disabilities. Through the Disability Resource Center students with LD may request priority enrollment and a campus orientation to assist in scheduling classes. Other services developed in coordination with the faculty work to minimize the students' difficulties in relation to course work.

ADMISSIONS

There is no special admissions policy for students with LD. However, if ability to meet admission criteria was impacted by a disability (such as late identification, no accommodations, or high school courses waived), students should include a personal statement with their application and contact Disability Services. Course requirements include four units English, three units math, two units lab science, three units history & citizenship skills (economics, geography, government, or non-western culture), and three units from previous areas and/or computer science and/or foreign language. Students with appropriate documentation may be allowed to substitute courses for math or foreign language. Students not meeting admission requirements may qualify for admission through: (1) Alternative Admission for students whose high school achievement is slightly below the standards and/or deficient in no more than one curricular unit (2) Summer Provision Program for students who meet all the curricular requiremetns and have a GPA of 2.5 or above, or ACT of 18 or above or SAT of 870 or above. These students may enter in the summer on probation and may be required to take placement tests prior to a final acceptance.

ADMISSIONS INFO FOR STUDENTS WITH LEARNING DIFFERENCES

SAT/ACT required: Yes
Interview required: No
Essay required: No
Additional application required: No
Documentation required for:
  LD: Psycho ed evaluation to include: relevant historical info, instructional interventions, related services, age diagnosed, objective data (aptitude, achievement, info processing), test scores (standard, percentile and grade equivalents) and describe functional limitations.
  ADHD: Diagnosis based on DSM-V; history of behaviors impairing functioning in academic setting; diagnostic interview; history of symptoms; evidence of ongoing behaviors.
  ASD: Psycho ed evaluation
Documentation submitted to: Student Disability Services
Special Ed. HS course work accepted: No
Separate application required for program services: No
# of students last year receiving services/accommodations for:
  LD: 60-70
Contact Information
Name of program or department: Student Disability Services
Telephone: 405-744-7116
Fax: 405-744-8380

Oklahoma State University

Additional Information

Services could include test accommodations, course substitutions, and independent study. The underlying philosophy of this program is to provide assistance to students to facilitate their academic progress. Student Disability Services (SDS) also acts as a resource for faculty and staff.. Student Support Services, also known as Project Threshold on the OU campus, is a Federally funded program. It is one of seven TRIO programs designed to serve students who are either first generation, economically disadvantaged or disabled. Camp Crimson is a OU's official orientation camp. It is a three day and two night experience, with an attendance of around 2,500 students per year.

GENERAL ADMISSIONS

Very important factors considered include: class rank, academic GPA, standardized test scores. *Important factors considered include:* application essay. *Other factors considered include:* recommendation(s). *Freshman Admission Requirements:* High school diploma is required and GED is accepted. *Academic units required:* 4 English, 3 math, 3 science, 3 science labs, 2 social studies, 1 history.

ACCOMMODATION OR SERVICES

Accommodations are decided upon an individual basis after a thorough review of appropriate, current documentation. The accommodations requests must be supported through the documentation provided and must be logically linked to the current impact of the condition on academic functioning.

FINANCIAL AID

Students should submit: FAFSA. The Princeton Review suggests that all financial aid forms be submitted as soon as possible after October 1. *Need-based scholarships/grants offered:* College/university scholarship or grant aid from institutional funds; Federal Pell; Private scholarships; SEOG; State scholarships/grants. *Loan aid offered:* Direct PLUS loans; Direct Subsidized Stafford Loans; Direct Unsubsidized Stafford Loans. Federal Work-Study Program available. Institutional employment available.

CAMPUS LIFE

Activities: Campus Ministries; Choral groups; Concert band; Dance; Drama/theater; International Student Organization; Jazz band; Literary magazine; Marching band; Music ensembles; Musical theater; Opera; Pep band; Radio station; Student government; Student newspaper; Symphony orchestra; Television station. **Organizations:** 300 registered organizations, **Athletics (Intercollegiate):** *Men:* baseball, basketball, cross-country, football, golf, tennis, track/field (outdoor), wrestling. *Women:* basketball, cross-country, equestrian sports, golf, soccer, softball, tennis, track/field (outdoor). **On-Campus Highlights:** Colvin Recreational Center, Gallagher/Iba Arena and Museum, Student Union Building, Edmon Low Library, ConocoPhillips Alumni Center.

ACCOMMODATIONS

Allowed in exams:	
Calculators	Yes
Dictionary	Yes
Computer	Yes
Spell-checker	Yes
Extended test time	Yes
Scribe	Yes
Proctors	Yes
Oral exams	Yes
Note-takers	Yes
Support services for students with	
LD	Yes
ADHD	Yes
ASD	Yes
Distraction-reduced environment	Yes
Recording of lecture allowed	Yes
Reading technology:	Yes
Audio books	Yes
Other assistive technology	WYNN software, Open Book, JAWS, MAGic, Dragon Naturally Speaking, CCTV, Braille printer
Priority registration	Yes
Added costs for services:	
For LD:	No
LD specialists	No
ADHD & ASD coaching	No
ASD specialists	No
Professional tutors	No
Peer tutors	No
Max. hours/week for services	Unlimited
How professors are notified of student approved accommodations	student and director

COLLEGE GRADUATION REQUIREMENTS

Course waivers allowed	No
Course substitutions allowed	No

The University of Tulsa

800 SOUTH TUCKER DRIVE, TULSA, OK 74104 • ADMISSIONS: 918-631-2307 • FAX: 918-631-5003

CAMPUS

Type of school	Private (nonprofit)
Environment	Metropolis
Support	CS

STUDENTS

Undergrad enrollment	3,316
% male/female	56/44
% from out of state	41
% frosh live on campus	80

FINANCIAL FACTS

Annual tuition	$40,484
Room and board	$11,116
Required fees	$540

GENERAL ADMISSIONS INFO

Application fee	$50
Priority deadline	1/15

Nonfall registration accepted. Admission may be deferred for a maximum of 1 year.

Range SAT EBRW	590–720
Range SAT Math	560–720
Range ACT Composite	25–32

ACADEMICS

Student/faculty ratio	11:1
% students returning for sophomore year	88
% students graduating within 4 years	50
% students graduating within 6 years	69

Most classes have 10–19 students.
Most lab/discussion sessions have 20–29 students.

PROGRAMS/SERVICES FOR STUDENTS WITH LEARNING DIFFERENCES

The Center for Student Academic Support (CSAS) provides support services to all students which will, in combination with the talents and resources of the student, provide opportunities to develop independence and achieve academic and personal success. We believe self-advocacy skills are acquired through support and encouragement promoting autonomy and lifelong learning.

ADMISSIONS

All students must meet the general admissions requirements. Students with disabilities are not required to disclose information about the disability, but may voluntarily disclose or request information from CSAS. The university does not consider disabilities in the decision-making process, even if there is knowledge of the disability, without a request and disclosure by the applicant. All students must meet the general admissions requirements. Students with disabilities are not required to disclose information about the disability, but may voluntarily disclose or request information from CSAS. The university does not consider disabilities in the decision-making process, even if there is knowledge of the disability, without a request and disclosure by the applicant. Students may provide verification of the disability that should be submitted directly to CSAS. General admission requirements include: 4 years of English, 3 years of math, 4 years of science, and 2 years of foreign language. No course substitutions are allowed. The average ACT is above 21 and for the SAT is 1080–1140. Students applying to the nursing or athletic training programs must submit a special application. Conditional admission is available for freshmen and probational admission is an option for transfer students.

ADMISSIONS INFO FOR STUDENTS WITH LEARNING DIFFERENCES

SAT/ACT required: Yes
Interview required: No
Essay required: Not Applicable
Additional application required: Yes
Documentation required for:
 LD: Self-report application form and documentation from health care professional with diagnosis and description of functional limitations.
 ADHD: Self-report application form and documentation from health care professional with diagnosis and description of functional limitations.
 ASD: Self-report application form and documentation from health care professional with diagnosis and description of functional limitations.
Documentation submitted to: Center for Student Academic Support
Special Ed. HS course work accepted: No
Separate application required for program services: No
# of students last year receiving services/accommodations for:
 LD: 82
 ADHD: 110
 ASD: 26
Contact Information
Name of program or department: Center for Student Academic Support
Telephone: 918-631-2315
Fax: 918-631-3459
Email: csas@utulsa.edu

The University of Tulsa

Additional Information
Coaches work one-on-one with students to provide accountability for coursework and partner with students to create individualized academic success plans as they pursue their academic goals. Academic coaching meetings typically occur once a week for around 30 minutes. Topics covered may include the following: Time management, Study skills, Test-taking skills, Test preparation, Prioritization, Motivation, Test anxiety, Learning styles, Memory and concentration, Presentation strategies, Stress management and anxiety, Organization, and Note-taking strategies.

GENERAL ADMISSIONS
Very important factors considered include: rigor of secondary school record, academic GPA, standardized test scores. *Important factors considered include:* class rank, application essay, recommendation(s), interview, level of applicant's interest. *Other factors considered include:* extracurricular activities, talent/ability, character/personal qualities, first generation, alumni/ae relation, racial/ethnic status, volunteer work, work experience. *Freshman Admission Requirements:* High school diploma is required and GED is accepted. *Academic units recommended:* 4 English, 4 math, 3 science, 3 science labs, 2 foreign language, 3 social studies, 1 computer science, 1 visual/performing arts.

ACCOMMODATION OR SERVICES
Accommodations are decided upon an individual basis after a thorough review of appropriate, current documentation. The accommodations requests must be supported through the documentation provided and must be logically linked to the current impact of the condition on academic functioning.

FINANCIAL AID
Students should submit: FAFSA. Applicants will be notified of awards on a rolling basis beginning 2/1. The Princeton Review suggests that all financial aid forms be submitted as soon as possible after October 1. *Need-based scholarships/grants offered:* College/university scholarship or grant aid from institutional funds; Federal Pell; Private scholarships; SEOG; State scholarships/grants. *Loan aid offered:* Direct PLUS loans; Direct Subsidized Stafford Loans; Direct Unsubsidized Stafford Loans. Federal Work-Study Program available. Institutional employment available.

CAMPUS LIFE
Activities: Campus Ministries; Choral groups; Concert band; Dance; Drama/theater; International Student Organization; Jazz band; Literary magazine; Marching band; Music ensembles; Musical theater; Opera; Pep band; Radio station; Student government; Student newspaper; Student-run film society; Symphony orchestra; Television station. **Organizations:** 245 registered organizations, 40 honor societies, 21 religious organizations. 7 fraternities, 9 sororities. **Athletics (Intercollegiate):** *Men:* basketball, cheerleading, cross-country, football, golf, soccer, tennis, track/field (outdoor), track/field (indoor). *Women:* basketball, cheerleading, crew/rowing, cross-country, golf, soccer, softball, tennis, track/field (outdoor), track/field (indoor), volleyball. **On-Campus Highlights:** Collins Fitness Center, Reynolds Center, McFarlin Library, Allen Chapman Student Union, Lorton Performance Center.

ACCOMMODATIONS

Allowed in exams:	
Calculators	Yes
Dictionary	Yes
Computer	Yes
Spell-checker	Yes
Extended test time	Yes
Scribe	Yes
Proctors	Yes
Oral exams	Yes
Note-takers	Yes

Support services for students with	
LD	Yes
ADHD	Yes
ASD	Yes
Distraction-reduced environment	Yes
Recording of lecture allowed	Yes
Reading technology:	Yes
Audio books	Yes
Other assistive technology	CART, CAN
Priority registration	Yes

Added costs for services:	
For LD:	Yes
LD specialists	Yes
ADHD & ASD coaching	Yes
ASD specialists	Yes
Professional tutors	Yes
Peer tutors	Yes
Max. hours/week for services	Varies
How professors are notified of student approved accommodations	Student

COLLEGE GRADUATION REQUIREMENTS

Course waivers allowed	Yes
In what courses	Any applicable courses.
Course substitutions allowed	Yes
In what courses	Any applicable courses.

Lewis & Clark College

0615 S.W. Palatine Hill Road, Portland, OR 97219-7899 • Admissions: 503-768-7040 • Fax: 503-768-7055

CAMPUS

Type of school	Private (nonprofit)
Environment	Metropolis
Support	S

STUDENTS

Undergrad enrollment	2,021
% male/female	41/59
% from out of state	88
% frosh live on campus	99

FINANCIAL FACTS

Annual tuition	$50,574
Room and board	$12,490
Required fees	$360

GENERAL ADMISSIONS INFO

Priority deadline	1/15
Regular application deadline	1/15

Nonfall registration accepted. Admission may be deferred for a maximum of One year.

Range SAT EBRW	620–710
Range SAT Math	590–680
Range ACT Composite	27–31

ACADEMICS

Student/faculty ratio	12:1
% students returning for sophomore year	83
% students graduating within 4 years	75
% students graduating within 6 years	80

Most classes have 10–19 students.

PROGRAMS/SERVICES FOR STUDENTS WITH LEARNING DIFFERENCES

Lewis & Clark is committed to serving the needs of our students with disabilities and learning differences. Professional staff in the office of Student Support Services are available to ensure that students receive all of the benefits of a comprehensive selection of services. Our office also provides advising and advocacy for students with disabilities and support for students who seek advice on academic strategies. Services, advising, and accommodations are always the result of an active partnership between students and Student Support Services staff.

ADMISSIONS

Lewis & Clark's is Test-Optional and the Portfolio Path allows students to achieve a more personal representation in the admissions process. The Portfolio Path provides an academic portfolio demonstrative of the student's intellectual curiosity, depth and breadth of curriculum, and overall preparation for college work. Applicants must also provide two academic teacher recommendations from grades 10-12 and a portfolio of graded academic work. An academic portfolio includes: One graded analytical writing (expository writing, essay exams, research papers... NOT creative writing). One sample of graded quantitative/scientific work (science lab report, math/statistics or science test or work). Sample should demonstrate student's ability to use numbers to work through a problem. . The average GPA is 3.85 and Of those submitted test scores the middle 50% scored between 1210-1390 on SAT* and 27-31 on ACT.

Additional Information

Student Support Services works with students on effective study strategies, test-taking skills, and curriculum planning that fits their learning style. The Writing Center has peer consultants to help with writing skills; There is free peer to peer tutoring. The Keck Interactive Learning Center provides drop-in assistance for all languages taught on campus.

ADMISSIONS INFO FOR STUDENTS WITH LEARNING DIFFERENCES

SAT/ACT required: No
Interview required: Not Applicable
Essay required: Not Applicable
Additional application required: Not Applicable
Documentation required for:
  LD: Full battery of diagnostic psycho-educational assessments with recommendation for accommodation.
  ADHD: Psycho-educational assessment or verification of diagnosis with recommendation for accommodation.
  ASD: Verification of diagnosis with recommendation for accommodation.
Documentation submitted to: Student Support Services
Special Ed. HS course work accepted: Not Applicable
Separate application required for program services: No
Contact Information
Name of program or department: Student Support Services
Telephone: 503-768-7192
Fax: 503-768-7197
Email: access@lclark.edu

Lewis & Clark College

GENERAL ADMISSIONS

Very important factors considered include: rigor of secondary school record, academic GPA. *Important factors considered include:* application essay, standardized test scores, recommendation(s), extracurricular activities, talent/ability, character/personal qualities, volunteer work, work experience. *Other factors considered include:* class rank, interview, first generation, alumni/ae relation, geographical residence, racial/ethnic status, level of applicant's interest. *Freshman Admission Requirements:* High school diploma is required and GED is accepted. *Academic units recommended:* 4 English, 4 math, 3 science, 2 science labs, 2 foreign language, 3 social studies, 1 visual/performing arts.

ACCOMMODATION OR SERVICES

Accommodations are decided upon an individual basis after a thorough review of appropriate, current documentation. The accommodations requests must be supported through the documentation provided and must be logically linked to the current impact of the condition on academic functioning.

FINANCIAL AID

Students should submit: CSS/Financial Aid PROFILE; FAFSA. Applicants will be notified of awards on a rolling basis beginning 1/30. The Princeton Review suggests that all financial aid forms be submitted as soon as possible after October 1. *Need-based scholarships/grants offered:* College/university scholarship or grant aid from institutional funds; Federal Pell; Private scholarships; SEOG; State scholarships/grants. *Loan aid offered:* Direct PLUS loans; Direct Subsidized Stafford Loans; Direct Unsubsidized Stafford Loans. Federal Work-Study Program available. Institutional employment available.

CAMPUS LIFE

Activities: Campus Ministries; Choral groups; Concert band; Dance; Drama/theater; International Student Organization; Jazz band; Literary magazine; Model UN; Music ensembles; Musical theater; Pep band; Radio station; Student government; Student newspaper; Symphony orchestra. **Organizations:** 70 registered organizations, 5 honor societies, 9 religious organizations. **Athletics (Intercollegiate):** *Men:* baseball, basketball, crew/rowing, cross-country, football, golf, swimming, tennis, track/field (outdoor). *Women:* basketball, crew/rowing, cross-country, golf, soccer, softball, swimming, tennis, track/field (outdoor), volleyball. **On-Campus Highlights:** Aubrey Watzek Library, Templeton Student Center, Pamplin Sports Center, Estate Gardens, Maggies Coffee Shop.

ACCOMMODATIONS

Allowed in exams:

Calculators	Yes
Dictionary	Yes
Computer	Yes
Spell-checker	Yes
Extended test time	Yes
Scribe	Yes
Proctors	Yes
Oral exams	Yes
Note-takers	Yes

Support services for students with

LD	Yes
ADHD	Yes
ASD	Yes
Distraction-reduced environment	Yes
Recording of lecture allowed	Yes
Reading technology:	Yes
Audio books	Yes
Other assistive technology	as needed per request
Priority registration	No

Added costs for services:

For LD:	No
For ADHD:	No
For ASD:	No
LD specialists	Yes
ADHD & ASD coaching	Yes
ASD specialists	No
Professional tutors	Yes
Peer tutors	Yes
Max. hours/week for services	16
How professors are notified of student approved accommodations	Director

COLLEGE GRADUATION REQUIREMENTS

Course waivers allowed	No
Course substitutions allowed	Yes
In what courses	Foreign Language

Oregon State University

104 Kerr Administration Building, Corvallis, OR 97331-2106 • Admissions: 541-737-4411 • Fax: 541-737-2482

CAMPUS

Type of school	Public
Environment	Town
Support	S

STUDENTS

Undergrad enrollment	24,921
% male/female	54/46
% from out of state	32
% frosh live on campus	90

FINANCIAL FACTS

Annual in-state tuition	$9,390
Annual out-of-state tuition	$28,365
Room and board	$12,855
Required fees	$1,776

GENERAL ADMISSIONS INFO

Application fee	$60
Priority deadline	2/1
Regular application deadline	9/1

Nonfall registration accepted. Admission may be deferred for a maximum of 1 year.

Range SAT EBRW	540–650
Range SAT Math	530–650
Range ACT Composite	22–28

ACADEMICS

Student/faculty ratio	18:1
% students returning for sophomore year	85
% students graduating within 4 years	33
% students graduating within 6 years	65

Most classes have 10–19 students.
Most lab/discussion sessions have 10–19 students.

PROGRAMS/SERVICES FOR STUDENTS WITH LEARNING DIFFERENCES

It is the policy of Oregon State University to comply with Sections 503 and 504 of the Rehabilitation Act of 1973, the Americans with Disabilities Act of 1990 (ADA), as amended by the ADA Amendments Act of 2008, and other applicable federal and state regulations that prohibit discrimination on the basis of disability. The Rehabilitation Act and the ADA require that no qualified person shall, solely by reason of disability, be denied access to, participation in, or the benefits of, any program or activity operated by the University. Each qualified person shall receive the reasonable accommodations needed to ensure equal access to employment, educational opportunities, programs, and activities in the most integrated setting feasible. Disability Access Services Mission: Disability Access Services facilitates access to University programs and services for students, faculty, staff and visitors with disabilities through accommodations, education, consultation and advocacy.

ADMISSIONS

Oregon State's admission requirements promote student success by assessing student preparedness and academic potential in the unique context of each student's personal experience. Admission assessment will consider all achievements, both academic and non-

Additional Information

Coaching sessions are available in the Academic Success Center to all students registered with DAS. Coaching provides students with individualized strategies based on the students' impacts. Individual sessions focus on strategies, techniques and resources. Some common topics may include time management, study skills, managing a course load, or navigating the college environment as a student with a disability. There is no set number of Coaching sessions, as they are based on the students need. Counseling and Psychological Services (CAPS) provides individual services that can help students develop effective habits to

ADMISSIONS INFO FOR STUDENTS WITH LEARNING DIFFERENCES

SAT/ACT required: Yes
Interview required: No
Essay required: Not Applicable
Additional application required: Yes
Documentation required for:
 LD: Psycho ed evaluation
 ADHD: ADD/ ADHD Guidelines A full detailed evaluation or diagnostic report of the condition and impact or limitations caused as a result of the condition(s).
 ASD: A full detailed evaluation or diagnostic report of the condition and impact or limitations caused as a result of the condition(s).
Documentation submitted to: Disability Access Services
Special Ed. HS course work accepted: No
Separate application required for program services: No
# of students last year receiving services/accommodations for:
 LD: 179
Contact Information
Name of program or department: Disability Access Services
Telephone: 541-737-4098
Fax: 541-737-7354
Email: disability.services@oregonstate.edu

compensate for poor focus, distractibility, disorganization, and/or difficulty completing tasks, whether caused by ADHD/ADD or by other conditions. They can also help with issues of poor self-esteem, lack of self-confidence, anxiety and/or depression that can accompany ADHD/ADD. CAPS also offers an ADHD support group that teaches specific skills for coping with ADHD, both in and out of the classroom. The group provides an environment for students to learn from each other and receive social support for the struggles that come with having ADHD.

GENERAL ADMISSIONS

Very important factors considered include: academic GPA. *Important factors considered include:* rigor of secondary school record, application essay, talent/ability, character/personal qualities, volunteer work, work experience. *Other factors considered include:* class rank, standardized test scores, recommendation(s), extracurricular activities, level of applicant's interest. *Freshman Admission Requirements:* High school diploma is required and GED is accepted. *Academic units required:* 4 English, 3 math, 3 science, 2 science labs, 2 foreign language, 3 social studies. *Academic units recommended:* 3 science labs,

ACCOMMODATION OR SERVICES

Accommodations are decided upon an individual basis after a thorough review of appropriate, current documentation. The accommodations requests must be supported through the documentation provided and must be logically linked to the current impact of the condition on academic functioning.

FINANCIAL AID

Students should submit: FAFSA. Applicants will be notified of awards on a rolling basis beginning 4/1. The Princeton Review suggests that all financial aid forms be submitted as soon as possible after October 1. *Need-based scholarships/grants offered:* College/university scholarship or grant aid from institutional funds; Federal Pell; Private scholarships; SEOG; State scholarships/grants. *Loan aid offered:* Direct PLUS loans; Direct Subsidized Stafford Loans; Direct Unsubsidized Stafford Loans. Federal Work-Study Program available. Institutional employment available.

CAMPUS LIFE

Activities: Campus Ministries; Choral groups; Concert band; Dance; Drama/theater; International Student Organization; Jazz band; Literary magazine; Marching band; Model UN; Music ensembles; Musical theater; Opera; Pep band; Radio station; Student government; Student newspaper; Student-run film society; Symphony orchestra; Television station; Yearbook. **Organizations:** 350 registered organizations, 29 honor societies, 23 religious organizations. 24 fraternities, 13 sororities. **Athletics (Intercollegiate):** *Men:* baseball, basketball, crew/rowing, football, golf, soccer, wrestling. *Women:* basketball, crew/rowing, cross-country, golf, gymnastics, soccer, softball, swimming, track/field (outdoor), volleyball. **On-Campus Highlights:** Memorial Union, Valley Library, Kelly Engineering Center, Dixon Recreation Center, Reser Stadium.

ACCOMMODATIONS

Allowed in exams:

Calculators	Yes
Dictionary	No
Computer	Yes
Spell-checker	Yes
Extended test time	Yes
Scribe	Yes
Proctors	Yes
Oral exams	Yes
Note-takers	Yes

Support services for students with

LD	Yes
ADHD	Yes
ASD	Yes
Distraction-reduced environment	Yes
Recording of lecture allowed	Yes
Reading technology:	Yes
Audio books	Yes

Other assistive technology   Etext (Kurzweil), LiveScribe Pen, Sonocent Audio Notetaker, Computers with various assistive technology for taking exams (eg: VTek).

Priority registration	Yes

Added costs for services:

For LD:	No
LD specialists	Yes
ADHD & ASD coaching	Yes
ASD specialists	No
Professional tutors	No
Peer tutors	No
Max. hours/week for services	Varies

How professors are notified of student
approved accommodations   Director

COLLEGE GRADUATION REQUIREMENTS

Course waivers allowed	No
Course substitutions allowed	Yes

In what courses   Math, foreign language.
Courses may only be substituted to meet core requirements not major requirements.

University of Oregon

1226 UNIVERSITY OF OREGON, EUGENE, OR 97403-1217 • ADMISSIONS: 541-346-3201 • FAX: 541-346-5815

PROGRAMS/SERVICES FOR STUDENTS WITH LEARNING DIFFERENCES

At the University of Oregon, the Accessible Education Center (AEC) promotes inclusive education and coordinates services and support to students with currently documented disabilities. During university orientation programs students discuss their needs, challenges, educational goals, and available services. Accommodations are determined on a case-by-case basis after admission and an individual appointment. A faculty notification letter outlining suggested accommodations is provided, and is shared at students' discretion. The University is actively engaged in universal design instructional strategies to minimize the need for individualized accommodations when possible. Successful students are motivated, hard working, and able to articulate their strengths and challenges.

ADMISSIONS

When making an admission decision UO considers: strength of academic course work; GPA; grade trend; ACT/SAT; senior-year courses; motivation demonstrated in the essay (there is a second optional essay); extracurricular activities , community service and work; diversity; academic potential; and special talents There is an alternative admission for applicants with a GPA below 3.00 not generally considered eligible for admission. However, they will still be reviewed for a combination of factors in a holistic fashion. It is critical to provide information in the "Special Circumstances" section of the application. If deficient in courses required, these may be fulfilled by doing one of the following: Take the following SAT Subject Tests: Math I or II and a second test of choice other than math. Earn a total score of 940 or above for the two tests; or take high school or college work to complete courses missed in high school. A one-term transferable college course of at least three credits (quarter system) is equal to one year of high school work.

University of Oregon

Additional Information

The Autism Interest Group (AIG) at the UO goal is to increase outreach efforts throughout the UO and the broader Eugene area and to make AIG more accessible to students, researchers, parents, and anyone interested in autism spectrum disorders. A range of supports and services are available through the Accessible Education Center to eligible students. In addition, support with academic planning and problem solving is available, as well as assistance with time management and organizational strategies.

GENERAL ADMISSIONS

Very important factors considered include: rigor of secondary school record, academic GPA. *Important factors considered include:* application essay, standardized test scores. *Other factors considered include:* class rank, extracurricular activities, talent/ability, character/personal qualities, first generation, geographical residence, state residency, racial/ethnic status, volunteer work, work experience. *Freshman Admission Requirements:* High school diploma is required and GED is accepted. *Academic units required:* 4 English, 3 math, 3 science, 2 foreign language, 3 social studies. *Academic units recommended:* 1 science labs.

ACCOMMODATION OR SERVICES

Accommodations are decided upon an individual basis after a thorough review of appropriate, current documentation. The accommodations requests must be supported through the documentation provided and must be logically linked to the current impact of the condition on academic functioning.

FINANCIAL AID

Students should submit: FAFSA. Applicants will be notified of awards on a rolling basis beginning 4/15. The Princeton Review suggests that all financial aid forms be submitted as soon as possible after October 1. *Need-based scholarships/grants offered:* College/university scholarship or grant aid from institutional funds; Federal Pell; Private scholarships; SEOG; State scholarships/grants. *Loan aid offered:* Direct PLUS loans; Direct Subsidized Stafford Loans; Direct Unsubsidized Stafford Loans. Federal Work-Study Program available. Institutional employment available.

CAMPUS LIFE

Activities: Campus Ministries; Choral groups; Concert band; Dance; Drama/theater; International Student Organization; Jazz band; Literary magazine; Marching band; Music ensembles; Musical theater; Opera; Pep band; Radio station; Student government; Student newspaper; Student-run film society; Symphony orchestra; Television station. **Organizations:** 250 registered organizations, 22 honor societies, 20 religious organizations. 12 fraternities, 10 sororities. **Athletics (Intercollegiate):** *Men:* baseball, basketball, cross-country, football, golf, tennis, track/field (outdoor). *Women:* basketball, cross-country, golf, gymnastics, lacrosse, soccer, softball, tennis, track/field (outdoor), volleyball. **On-Campus Highlights:** University of Oregon Duck Store, Knight Library, Erb Memorial Union, Laverne Krauss Gallery in Lawrence Hall, Watch sports at Autzen, Hayward, or Matt Knight Arena.

ACCOMMODATIONS

Allowed in exams:

Calculators	Yes
Dictionary	Yes
Computer	Yes
Spell-checker	Yes
Extended test time	Yes
Scribe	Yes
Proctors	Yes
Oral exams	Yes Note-takers Yes

Support services for students with

LD	Yes
ADHD	Yes
ASD	Yes
Distraction-reduced environment	Yes
Recording of lecture allowed	Yes
Reading technology:	Yes
Audio books	Yes

Other assistive technology Voice recognition software, text to speech software, smart pens.

Priority registration	Yes

Added costs for services:

For LD:	No
For ADHD:	No
For ASD:	No
LD specialists	No
ADHD & ASD coaching	Yes
ASD specialists	Yes
Professional tutors	Yes
Peer tutors	Yes
Max. hours/week for services	Varies

How professors are notified of student approved accommodations
Director and student

COLLEGE GRADUATION REQUIREMENTS

Course waivers allowed	No
Course substitutions allowed	Yes

In what courses In very compelling cases with thorough documentation supporting the modification to the requirement

Western Oregon University

345 N Monmouth Avenue, Monmouth, OR 97361 • Admissions: 503-838-8211 • Fax: 503-838-8067

CAMPUS

Type of school	Public
Environment	Village
Support	S

STUDENTS

Undergrad enrollment	4,696
% male/female	38/62
% from out of state	23
% frosh live on campus	87

FINANCIAL FACTS

Annual in-state tuition	$7,440
Annual out-of-state tuition	$23,895
Room and board	$10,203
Required fees	$1,758

GENERAL ADMISSIONS INFO

Application fee	$60

Nonfall registration accepted.

ACADEMICS

Student/faculty ratio	15:1
% students returning for sophomore year	72
% students graduating within 4 years	22
% students graduating within 6 years	44

Most classes have 10–19 students.
Most lab/discussion sessions have 10–19 students.

PROGRAMS/SERVICES FOR STUDENTS WITH LEARNING DIFFERENCES

The mission of the Office of Disability Services (ODS) is to remove barriers to learning for students with disabilities and to help ensure that these students access the tools and processes they need to create a successful experience at Western and beyond. These goals are realized by providing support services and information to help students develop skills such as self-advocacy, independence, identification and use of resources, appropriate use of problem-solving techniques, and accepting responsibility for one's actions. ODS strives to meet the individual needs of students with disabilities. The Student Enrichment Program (SEP) is designed to help students find success in college. The program's goals are to help SEP students develop writing, math, learning, and critical-thinking skills; maintain the necessary GPA to achieve individual goals; develop interpersonal communication skills; and achieve autonomy and maintain a sense of self-worth. Students who could benefit from SEP are those who enter the university without being completely prepared. SEP staff focuses on working with individual needs. Eligibility is based on federal guidelines determined by first-generation college-bound, financial need, or physical or learning disability; additionally, the student must have demonstrated academic need for the program.

ADMISSIONS

General admission requires a 2.75 GPA and ACT/SAT scores, which are used only as alternatives to the required GPA. A limited number of students who do not meet the regular admission requirements, alternatives, or exceptions may be admitted through special action of an Admissions Committee. Submit a letter of petition stating why they don't meet the admission requirements and what they are doing to make up deficiencies, and three letters of recommendation from school and community members.

ADMISSIONS INFO FOR STUDENTS WITH LEARNING DIFFERENCES

SAT/ACT required: No
Interview required: No
Essay required: No
Additional application required: No
Documentation required for:
 LD: Psycho ed evaluation to include: relevant historical info, instructional interventions, related services, age diagnosed, objective data (aptitude, achievement, info processing), test scores (standard, percentile and grade equivalents) and describe functional limitations.
 ADHD: Diagnosis based on DSM-V; history of behaviors impairing functioning in academic setting; diagnostic interview; history of symptoms; evidence of ongoing behaviors.
 ASD: Psycho ed evaluation
Documentation submitted to: Office of Disability Services
Special Ed. HS course work accepted: No
Separate application required for program services: Yes
# of students last year receiving services/accommodations for:
 LD: 60-70
Contact Information
Name of program or department: Office of Disability Services
Telephone: 503-838-8250
Fax: 503-838-8721

Western Oregon University

Additional Information

Skills classes are offered in academic survival strategies (no credit) and critical thinking (college credit). Other services include advocacy, computer stations, note-takers, readers and taping services, alternative testing, advisement, and assistance with registration. CEP offers counseling; basic math courses; advising; individualized instruction in reading, study skills, writing, and critical thinking; monitor programs; and workshops on study skills, research writing, math anxiety, rapid reading, note-taking, and time management. Services and accommodations are available for undergraduate and graduate students.

GENERAL ADMISSIONS

Very important factors considered include: rigor of secondary school record, class rank, academic GPA. *Important factors considered include:* recommendation(s), talent/ability. *Other factors considered include:* application essay, standardized test scores, character/personal qualities, first generation. *Freshman Admission Requirements:* High school diploma is required and GED is accepted. *Academic units required:* 4 English, 3 math, 2 foreign language, 3 social studies. *Academic units recommended:* 4 English, 3 math, 2 foreign language, 3 social studies.

ACCOMMODATION OR SERVICES

Accommodations are decided upon an individual basis after a thorough review of appropriate, current documentation. The accommodations requests must be supported through the documentation provided and must be logically linked to the current impact of the condition on academic functioning.

FINANCIAL AID

Students should submit: FAFSA. Applicants will be notified of awards on a rolling basis beginning 3/15. The Princeton Review suggests that all financial aid forms be submitted as soon as possible after October 1. *Need-based scholarships/grants offered:* College/university scholarship or grant aid from institutional funds; Federal Pell; Private scholarships; SEOG; State scholarships/grants; United Negro College Fund. *Loan aid offered:* Direct PLUS loans; Direct Subsidized Stafford Loans; Direct Unsubsidized Stafford Loans. Federal Work-Study Program available.

CAMPUS LIFE

Activities: Campus Ministries; Choral groups; Concert band; Dance; Drama/theater; International Student Organization; Jazz band; Literary magazine; Marching band; Model UN; Music ensembles; Musical theater; Pep band; Radio station; Student government; Student newspaper. **Organizations:** 50 registered organizations, 4 honor societies, 6 religious organizations. **Athletics (Intercollegiate):** *Men:* baseball, basketball, cheerleading, cross-country, football, track/field (outdoor). *Women:* basketball, cheerleading, cross-country, soccer, softball, track/field (outdoor), volleyball. **On-Campus Highlights:** Wayne and Lynn Hamersly Library, Neal Werner University Center, Paul Jensen Arctic Museum, Campbell Hall Art Gallery, Arbor Park Apartments.

ACCOMMODATIONS

Allowed in exams:	
Calculators	Yes
Dictionary	Yes
Computer	Yes
Spell-checker	Yes
Extended test time	Yes
Scribe	Yes
Proctors	Yes
Oral exams	Yes
Note-takers	Yes
Support services for students with	
LD	Yes
ADHD	Yes
ASD	Yes
Distraction-reduced environment	Yes
Recording of lecture allowed	Yes
Reading technology:	Yes
Audio books	Yes
Other assistive technology	Yes
Priority registration	Yes
Added costs for services:	
For LD:	No
For ADHD:	No
For ASD:	No
LD specialists	No
ADHD & ASD coaching	No
ASD specialists	No
Professional tutors	No
Peer tutors	Yes
Max. hours/week for services	Varies
How professors are notified of student approved accommodations	Student and director

COLLEGE GRADUATION REQUIREMENTS

Course waivers allowed	No
Course substitutions allowed	Yes
In what courses: Decisions are made on a case-by-case basis.	

Bucknell University

1 DENT DRIVE, LEWISBURG, PA 17837 • ADMISSIONS: 570-577-3000 • FAX: 570-577-3538

CAMPUS
Type of school	Private (nonprofit)
Environment	Village
Support	S

STUDENTS
Undergrad enrollment	3,588
% male/female	49/51
% from out of state	78
% frosh live on campus	100

FINANCIAL FACTS
Annual tuition	$55,788
Room and board	$13,662
Required fees	$304

GENERAL ADMISSIONS INFO
Application fee	$40
Regular application deadline	1/15

Nonfall registration accepted. Admission may be deferred for a maximum of 2 years.

Range SAT EBRW	620–700
Range SAT Math	630–720
Range ACT Composite	28–31

ACADEMICS
Student/faculty ratio	9:1
% students returning for sophomore year	94
% students graduating within 4 years	86
% students graduating within 6 years	90

Most classes have 10–19 students.
Most lab/discussion sessions have fewer than 10 students.

PROGRAMS/SERVICES FOR STUDENTS WITH LEARNING DIFFERENCES
The Office of Accessibility Resources (formerly referred to as the Office of Disability Services) exists to ensure access, provide support, and help to navigate or remove barriers for students, faculty, staff, and visitors to our campus. Our office is committed to providing a strong support system for individuals with disabilities, and is committed to ensuring that no otherwise qualified individual with a disability will be denied participation in or the benefits of any of our programs on the basis of a disability. Documentation required can be found on website.

ADMISSIONS
Students applying to the College of Arts & Sciences should select an intended major within the College of Arts & Sciences. If undecided about which major to pursue, select "Undecided Arts & Sciences" within the College of Arts & Sciences. The opportunities for students enrolled in the College of Arts & Sciences to transfer into the College of Engineering are quite limited, and enrollment in the Freeman College of Management is limited to students who were admitted directly into the Freeman College of Management at the time of their initial application to Bucknell. Students should apply directly to your preferred college. ACT or SAT required for admission. Subject Tests are not required but can be submitted.

Additional Information
The Office of Accessibility Resources (OAR) meet with students regarding academic concerns; consult regarding approved accommodations and make the appropriate referrals to on and off campus available resources when needed; discuss with registered students about how to talk to professors regarding accommodation needs; meet with registered students and professors to discuss the approved reasonable accommodations for specific academic needs; discuss assistive technology and other academic adjustments; and assist with arranging testing accommodations. The OAR Testing Center is a secondary option for registered students to take quizzes and tests.

ADMISSIONS INFO FOR STUDENTS WITH LEARNING DIFFERENCES
SAT/ACT required: Yes
Interview required: No
Essay required: Not Applicable
Additional application required: Yes
Documentation required for:
 LD: Educational Psychological evaluation
 ADHD: Educational Psychological evaluation
 ASD: Psychological evaluation
Documentation submitted to: Office of Accessability Resources
Special Ed. HS course work accepted: Yes
Separate application required for program services: No
# of students last year receiving services/accommodations for:
 LD: 208
Contact Information
Name of program or department: Office of Accessability Resources
Telephone: 570-577-1188
Fax: 570-577-1826

Bucknell University

GENERAL ADMISSIONS

Very important factors considered include: rigor of secondary school record, academic GPA, application essay, standardized test scores, talent/ability, character/personal qualities. *Important factors considered include:* recommendation(s), extracurricular activities, volunteer work, work experience. *Other factors considered include:* class rank, first generation, alumni/ae relation, geographical residence, religious affiliation/commitment, racial/ethnic status. *Freshman Admission Requirements:* High school diploma is required and GED is accepted. *Academic units required:* 4 English, 3 math, 2 science, 2 foreign language, 2 social studies, 2 history, 1 academic elective. *Academic units recommended:* 4 English, 4 math, 2 science, 2 science labs, 4 foreign language, 2 social studies, 2 history, 1 academic elective.

ACCOMMODATION OR SERVICES

Accommodations are decided upon an individual basis after a thorough review of appropriate, current documentation. The accommodations requests must be supported through the documentation provided and must be logically linked to the current impact of the condition on academic functioning.

FINANCIAL AID

Students should submit: CSS/Financial Aid PROFILE; FAFSA. Applicants will be notified of awards on or about 4/1. The Princeton Review suggests that all financial aid forms be submitted as soon as possible after October 1. *Need-based scholarships/grants offered:* College/university scholarship or grant aid from institutional funds; Federal Pell; Private scholarships; SEOG; State scholarships/grants. *Loan aid offered:* Direct PLUS loans; Direct Subsidized Stafford Loans; Direct Unsubsidized Stafford Loans. Federal Work-Study Program available. Institutional employment available.

CAMPUS LIFE

Activities: Campus Ministries; Choral groups; Concert band; Dance; Drama/theater; International Student Organization; Jazz band; Literary magazine; Model UN; Music ensembles; Musical theater; Opera; Pep band; Radio station; Student government; Student newspaper; Student-run film society; Symphony orchestra; Yearbook. **Organizations:** 150 registered organizations, 23 honor societies, 13 religious organizations, 12 fraternities, 8 sororities. **Athletics (Intercollegiate):** *Men:* baseball, basketball, cross-country, diving, football, golf, lacrosse, soccer, swimming, tennis, track/field (outdoor), track/field (indoor), water polo, wrestling. *Women:* basketball, crew/rowing, cross-country, diving, field hockey, golf, lacrosse, soccer, softball, swimming, tennis, track/field (outdoor), track/field (indoor), volleyball, water polo. **On-Campus Highlights:** Weis Center for the Performing Arts, Outdoor Primate Facilities, Uptown Night Club, Stadler Poetry Center, Library with Technology and Media Commons.

ACCOMMODATIONS

Allowed in exams:

Calculators	Yes
Dictionary	No
Computer	Yes
Spell-checker	Yes
Extended test time	Yes
Scribe	Yes
Proctors	Yes
Oral exams	Yes
Note-takers	Yes

Support services for students with

LD	Yes
ADHD	Yes
ASD	Yes
Distraction-reduced environment	Yes
Recording of lecture allowed	Yes
Reading technology:	Yes
Audio books	Yes

Other assistive technology   Site license for Read&Write Gold; LiveScribe Pens and Digital Voice Recorders for loan at Library; FM Systems; Loop System; JAWS (as needed); Magnification (as needed)

Priority registration	No

Added costs for services:

For LD:	No
For ADHD:	No
For ASD:	No
LD specialists	Yes
ADHD & ASD coaching	Yes
ASD specialists	Yes
Professional tutors	Yes
Peer tutors	Yes
Max. hours/week for services	Varies

How professors are notified of student approved accommodations   Director and student

COLLEGE GRADUATION REQUIREMENTS

Course waivers allowed	No
Course substitutions allowed	Yes
In what courses	Foreign Language

Chatham University

WOODLAND ROAD, PITTSBURGH, PA 15232 • ADMISSIONS: 412-365-1825 • FAX: 412-365-1609

CAMPUS

Type of school	Private (nonprofit)
Environment	Metropolis
Support	CS

STUDENTS

Undergrad enrollment	981
% male/female	25/75
% from out of state	21
% frosh live on campus	88

FINANCIAL FACTS

Annual tuition	$36,276
Room and board	$12,090
Required fees	$1,335

GENERAL ADMISSIONS INFO

Application fee	$35
Priority deadline	3/15
Regular application deadline	8/1

Nonfall registration accepted. Admission may be deferred for a maximum of 1 year.

Range SAT EBRW	540–640
Range SAT Math	510–600
Range ACT Composite	22–27

ACADEMICS

Student/faculty ratio	10:1
% students returning for sophomore year	85
% students graduating within 4 years	51
% students graduating within 6 years	63

Most classes have 10–19 students.
Most lab/discussion sessions have 10–19 students.

PROGRAMS/SERVICES FOR STUDENTS WITH LEARNING DIFFERENCES

The mission of the PACE Center is to create a support system that promotes academic access, student success and retention, self-advocacy, and lifelong learning for the Chatham student body. We do this through a holistic approach to disability support services, and a student-centered academic support model that provides peer-to-peer assistance across disciplines..The PACE Center also strives to create an inclusive campus environment that meets the accessibility needs of a diverse community. Collaboration with faculty, staff, and students within the Chatham community is essential to our mission.

ADMISSIONS

Chatham University has a test-optional policy. If the student chooses not to submit scores they should send the following (in addition to the application): Resume, graded writing sample, and on campus interview.

Additional Information

Academic accommodations for students with disabilities may include, but are not limited to: Alternate text formats,; Distraction-limited setting for testing; Extended time for testing; Note-taker services; and Screen reading software.. Other PACE services available for students with disabilities include: Academic skills coaching; Learning styles assessment; Procrastination management; Self-advocacy development; Study strategies analysis; Time management planning; Tutoring; and Supplemental Instruction.

ADMISSIONS INFO FOR STUDENTS WITH LEARNING DIFFERENCES

SAT/ACT required: Yes
Interview required: No
Essay required: Not Applicable
Additional application required: No
Documentation required for:
  LD: Documentation may consist of medical or educational records, and reports and assessments from health care providers, educational psychologists, teachers, or the educational system.
  ADHD: Documentation may consist of medical or educational records, and reports and assessments from health care providers, educational psychologists, teachers, or the educational system.
  ASD: No specific documentation is required but documentation must be provided by a qualified professional that states the diagnosis, functional limitations and recommendations for accommodations, adaptive devices, and support services.
Documentation submitted to: PACE Center
Special Ed. HS course work accepted: Yes
Separate application required for program services: No
# of students last year receiving services/accommodations for:
  LD: 35
  ADHD: 27
  ASD: 5
Contact Information
Name of program or department: PACE Center
Telephone: 412-365-1611
Fax: 412-365-1660

Chatham University

GENERAL ADMISSIONS

Very important factors considered include: rigor of secondary school record. *Important factors considered include:* academic GPA, application essay. *Other factors considered include:* class rank, standardized test scores, recommendation(s), interview, extracurricular activities, talent/ability, character/personal qualities, alumni/ae relation, volunteer work, work experience, level of applicant's interest. *Freshman Admission Requirements:* High school diploma is required and GED is accepted. *Academic units required:* 4 English, 2 math, 2 science, and 3 units from above areas or other academic areas. *Academic units recommended:* 4 English, 3 math, 3 science, 2 foreign language, 3 social studies.

ACCOMMODATION OR SERVICES

Accommodations are decided upon an individual basis after a thorough review of appropriate, current documentation. The accommodations requests must be supported through the documentation provided and must be logically linked to the current impact of the condition on academic functioning.

FINANCIAL AID

Students should submit: FAFSA. Applicants will be notified of awards on a rolling basis beginning 12/1. The Princeton Review suggests that all financial aid forms be submitted as soon as possible after October 1. *Need-based scholarships/grants offered:* College/university scholarship or grant aid from institutional funds; Federal Pell; Private scholarships; SEOG; State scholarships/grants. *Loan aid offered:* Direct PLUS loans; Direct Subsidized Stafford Loans; Direct Unsubsidized Stafford Loans. Federal Work-Study Program available. Institutional employment available.

CAMPUS LIFE

Activities: Campus Ministries; Choral groups; Drama/theater; International Student Organization; Literary magazine; Musical theater; Student government; Student newspaper; Student-run film society; Symphony orchestra. **Organizations:** 25 registered organizations, 10 honor societies, 6 religious organizations. **Athletics (Intercollegiate):** *Women:* basketball, cross-country, ice hockey, soccer, softball, swimming, tennis, volleyball, water polo. **On-Campus Highlights:** Cafe Rachel coffee shop and art gallery, Athletic and Fitness Center, Art and Design Center, Science Complex, The Carriage House - new student center.

ACCOMMODATIONS

Allowed in exams:	
Calculators	Yes
Dictionary	Yes
Computer	Yes
Spell-checker	Yes
Extended test time	Yes
Scribe	Yes
Proctors	Yes
Oral exams	Yes
Note-takers	Yes
Support services for students with	
LD	Yes
ADHD	Yes
ASD	Yes
Distraction-reduced environment	Yes
Recording of lecture allowed	Yes
Reading technology:	Yes
Audio books	Yes
Other assistive technology We have text-to-speech software, screen reading software and the capability to Braille.	
Priority registration	No
Added costs for services:	
For LD:	No
For ADHD:	No
For ASD:	No
LD specialists	No
ADHD & ASD coaching	Yes
ASD specialists	No
Professional tutors	Yes
Peer tutors	Yes
Max. hours/week for services	2
How professors are notified of student approved accommodations	Director and student

COLLEGE GRADUATION REQUIREMENTS

Course waivers allowed	No
Course substitutions allowed	Yes
In what courses	Physical Education

Drexel University

3141 CHESTNUT STREET, PHILADELPHIA, PA 19104 • ADMISSIONS: 215-895-2400 • FAX: 215-895-1285

PROGRAMS/SERVICES FOR STUDENTS WITH LEARNING DIFFERENCES
Drexel University does not have a specific learning disability program, but services are provided through the Office of Disability Resources (ODR). The professional staff works closely with the students who have special needs to ensure that they have the opportunity to participate fully in Drexel University's programs and activities. Drexel's ODR offers an individualized transition program for students with disabilities upon request. Students need to contact the ODR.

ADMISSIONS
The regular admission requirements are the same for all students, and there is no special process for students with learning disabilities or any other type of disability. Students are encouraged to-self disclose and provide current documentation of their disabilities to the ODR. General admission criteria include recommended courses of 4 years of English, 3 years of math, 1 year of science, 1 year of social studies, 7 electives (chosen from English, math, science, social studies, foreign language, history, or mechanical drawing). The average SAT score is 1180, and the average GPA is 3.4; an interview is recommended. For additional information, contact the Admissions Office at Drexel University directly.

Additional Information
Accommodations may be provided, if appropriate and reasonable, and may include extra time for exams, adaptive technologies, note-takers, priority scheduling, instruction modifications, reduced course loads, and course substitutions. All accommodation eligibility is determined on a case-by-case basis. Tutors are not an accommodation in college, but are available for all students at Drexel through the Learning Centers. Currently there are nearly 270 students with LD eligible for services and accommodations. The Drexel Autism Support Program (DASP) exists to provide a peer-mediated community of practice for current Drexel students that promotes academic excellence, self-advocacy, and social integration. DASP does not require its participants to provide documentation of a

diagnosis or disability. Disability Resources use the ClockWork system to process new student accommodations. Additionally, students will register to take exams with Disability Resources, request alternative format / accessible books and materials, and request note-taking services, using this system.

GENERAL ADMISSIONS

Very important factors considered include: rigor of secondary school record, class rank, academic GPA, standardized test scores. *Important factors considered include:* application essay, recommendation(s), character/personal qualities. *Other factors considered include:* interview, extracurricular activities, talent/ability, first generation, alumni/ae relation, volunteer work, work experience, level of applicant's interest. *Freshman Admission Requirements:* High school diploma is required and GED is accepted. *Academic units required:* 3 math, 1 science, 1 science lab. *Academic units recommended:* 1 foreign language.

ACCOMMODATION OR SERVICES

Accommodations are decided upon an individual basis after a thorough review of appropriate, current documentation. The accommodations requests must be supported through the documentation provided and must be logically linked to the current impact of the condition on academic functioning.

FINANCIAL AID

Students should submit: CSS/Financial Aid PROFILE; FAFSA. Applicants will be notified of awards on or about 4/1. The Princeton Review suggests that all financial aid forms be submitted as soon as possible after October 1. *Need-based scholarships/grants offered:* College/university scholarship or grant aid from institutional funds; Federal Pell; Private scholarships; SEOG; State scholarships/grants. *Loan aid offered:* Direct PLUS loans; Direct Subsidized Stafford Loans; Direct Unsubsidized Stafford Loans. Federal Work-Study Program available. Institutional employment available.

CAMPUS LIFE

Activities: Campus Ministries; Choral groups; Concert band; Dance; Drama/theater; Jazz band; Literary magazine; Model UN; Music ensembles; Musical theater; Pep band; Radio station; Student government; Student newspaper; Student-run film society; Symphony orchestra; Television station; Yearbook. **Organizations:** 136 registered organizations, 8 honor societies, 8 religious organizations. 12 fraternities, 11 sororities. **Athletics (Intercollegiate):** *Men:* basketball, cheerleading, crew/rowing, diving, golf, lacrosse, soccer, swimming, tennis, wrestling. *Women:* basketball, cheerleading, crew/rowing, diving, field hockey, lacrosse, soccer, softball, swimming, tennis, volleyball. **On-Campus Highlights:** Drexel Recreation Center, Barnes & Noble University Bookstore, Creese Student Center, Handschumacher Dining Center, The Quad.

ACCOMMODATIONS

Allowed in exams:

Calculators	Yes
Dictionary	No
Computer	Yes
Spell-checker	Yes
Extended test time	Yes
Scribe	Yes
Proctors	Yes
Oral exams	Yes
Note-takers	Yes

Support services for students with

LD	Yes
ADHD	Yes
ASD	Yes
Distraction-reduced environment	Yes
Recording of lecture allowed	Yes
Reading technology:	Yes
Audio books	Yes

Other assistive technology Textbooks can be transformed into the required medium, i.e. audio books

Priority registration	No

Added costs for services:

For LD:	No
For ADHD:	No
For ASD:	No
LD specialists	
ADHD & ASD coaching	Yes
ASD specialists	Yes
Professional tutors	Yes
Peer tutors	Yes
Max. hours/week for services	Varies
How professors are notified of student approved accommodations	Student

COLLEGE GRADUATION REQUIREMENTS

Course waivers allowed	No
Course substitutions allowed	No

East Stroudsburg University of Pennsylvania

200 PROSPECT STREET, EAST STROUDSBURG, PA 18301-2999 • ADMISSIONS: 570-422-3542 • FAX: 570-422-3933

CAMPUS

Type of school	Public
Environment	Village
Support	CS

STUDENTS

Undergrad enrollment	6,274
% male/female	45/55
% from out of state	25
% frosh live on campus	80

FINANCIAL FACTS

Annual in-state tuition	$5,804
Annual out-of-state tuition	$14,510
Room and board	$6,658
Required fees	$1,974

GENERAL ADMISSIONS INFO

Application fee	$35
Regular application deadline	4/1

Nonfall registration accepted.

Range SAT EBRW	440–530
Range SAT Math	460–550
Range ACT Composite	19-24

ACADEMICS

Student/faculty ratio	17:1
% students returning for sophomore year	78
% students graduating within 4 years	32
% students graduating within 6 years	48

Most classes have 10–19 students.
Most lab/discussion sessions have 10–19 students.

PROGRAMS/SERVICES FOR STUDENTS WITH LEARNING DIFFERENCES

East Stroudsburg University of Pennsylvania is committed to providing equal educational access to otherwise qualified students with disabilities. Individuals with disabilities are guaranteed certain protections and rights of equal access to programs and services under section 504 of the Rehabilitation Act of 1973 and the Americans with Disability Act (ADA). Therefore, East Stroudsburg University of Pennsylvania recognizes the responsibility of the university community to provide equal educational access and full participation in any university program and activity. East Stroudsburg University of Pennsylvania believes that an individual's access to opportunities for achievement and personal fulfillment must be determined solely on the basis of the person's ability and interest. East Stroudsburg University of Pennsylvania and the Pennsylvania State System of Higher Education promotes a broad definition of diversity that appreciates disability as an integral part of the human experience.

ADMISSIONS

Students with LD file the general application and are encouraged to complete the section titled "Disabilities Information" and forward documentation of their disability to the Office of Disability Services. For general admission, academic achievement is the primary factor considered in the selection process. ESU looks for a good match between what each applicant can contribute to the university and how the university can meet each applicant's expectations through a whole-person assessment. ESU is interested in student contributions to their school and community, activities and achievements, aspirations, and anything else that would help evaluate potential success at ESU. SAT or ACT are used as a common yardstick to help in the selection process. SAT Subject Tests are not required.

ADMISSIONS INFO FOR STUDENTS WITH LEARNING DIFFERENCES

SAT/ACT required: Yes
Interview required: No
Essay required: Yes
Additional application required: No
Documentation required for:
  LD: Psychoeducational evaluation; reevaluation done within 3 years; must have been completed no earlier than 10th grade and functional limitation impact on learning.
  ADHD: Psychoeducational evaluation and/or medical evaluation that includes medical history, diagnostic assessment instruments, diagnosis, and functional limitations.
  ASD: Psycho ed evaluation
Documentation submitted to: Office of Disability Services
Special Ed. HS course work accepted: Yes
Separate application required for program services: No
# of students last year receiving services/accommodations for:
  LD: 90
Contact Information
Name of program or department: Office of Disability Services
Telephone: 570-422-3954
Fax: 717-422-3898

East Stroudsburg University of Pennsylvania

Additional Information

Students with learning disabilities may work individually or in groups with the disabilities specialist. All students enrolled in the university have the opportunity to take skills classes in reading, composition, and math. Other services include workshops in time management and test-taking strategies that are offered to all students. The Learning Center provides individual and group tutoring by peer tutors free of charge to ESU students. Tutors are assigned on a first-come, first-served basis, and students must complete and submit a request form in order to receive tutoring. East Stroudsburg University is the home of the Alpha Chapter of Delta Alpha Pi International Honor Society, an international honor society for students with disabilities who have achieved academic success. Services and accommodations are available for undergraduate and graduate students.

GENERAL ADMISSIONS

Very important factors considered include: rigor of secondary school record, class rank, academic GPA, standardized test scores. *Freshman Admission Requirements:* High school diploma is required and GED is accepted. *Academic units recommended:* 4 English, 4 math, 3 science, 2 science labs, 2 foreign language, 3 social studies.

ACCOMMODATION OR SERVICES

Accommodations are decided upon an individual basis after a thorough review of appropriate, current documentation. The accommodations requests must be supported through the documentation provided and must be logically linked to the current impact of the condition on academic functioning.

FINANCIAL AID

Students should submit: FAFSA. Applicants will be notified of awards on or about 4/1. The Princeton Review suggests that all financial aid forms be submitted as soon as possible after October 1. *Need-based scholarships/grants offered:* College/university scholarship or grant aid from institutional funds; Federal Pell; Private scholarships; SEOG; State scholarships/grants. *Loan aid offered:* Direct PLUS loans; Direct Subsidized Stafford Loans; Direct Unsubsidized Stafford Loans. Federal Work-Study Program available. Institutional employment available.

CAMPUS LIFE

Activities: Campus Ministries; Choral groups; Concert band; Dance; Drama/theater; International Student Organization; Jazz band; Literary magazine; Marching band; Music ensembles; Musical theater; Pep band; Radio station; Student government; Student newspaper; Symphony orchestra. **Organizations:** 110 registered organizations, 28 honor societies, 3 religious organizations. 5 fraternities, 5 sororities. **Athletics (Intercollegiate):** *Men:* baseball, basketball, cross-country, football, soccer, tennis, track/field (outdoor), track/field (indoor), wrestling. *Women:* basketball, cross-country, field hockey, golf, lacrosse, soccer, softball, swimming, tennis, track/field (outdoor), track/field (indoor), volleyball. **On-Campus Highlights:** Recreation Center, Java CIty, University Center, Stoney Acres, The Quad.

ACCOMMODATIONS

Allowed in exams:	
Calculators	Yes
Dictionary	Yes
Computer	Yes
Spell-checker	Yes
Extended test time	Yes
Scribe	Yes
Proctors	No
Oral exams	No
Note-takers	Yes
Support services for students with	
LD	Yes
ADHD	Yes
ASD	Yes
Distraction-reduced environment	Yes
Recording of lecture allowed	Yes
Reading technology:	Yes
Audio books	Yes
Other assistive technology	Yes
Priority registration	Yes
Added costs for services:	
For LD:	No
For ADHD:	No
For ASD:	No
LD specialists	Yes
ADHD & ASD coaching	No
ASD specialists	No
Professional tutors	Yes
Peer tutors	Yes
Max. hours/week for services	2
How professors are notified of student approved accommodations	Student

COLLEGE GRADUATION REQUIREMENTS

Course waivers allowed	No
Course substitutions allowed	No

Edinboro University of Pennsylvania

200 EAST NORMAL STREET, EDINBORO, PA 16444 • ADMISSIONS: 814-732-2761 • FAX: 814-732-2420

CAMPUS

Type of school	Public
Environment	Rural
Support	CS

STUDENTS

Undergrad enrollment	6,301
% male/female	44/56
% from out of state	11
% frosh live on campus	77

FINANCIAL FACTS

Annual in-state tuition	$5,554
Annual out-of-state tuition	$8,332
Room and board	$7,130
Required fees	$1,762

GENERAL ADMISSIONS INFO

Application fee	$30

Nonfall registration accepted. Admission may be deferred for a maximum of 1 year.

Range SAT EBRW	415–520
Range SAT Math	410–520
Range ACT Composite	17–23

ACADEMICS

% students returning for sophomore year	75
% students graduating within 4 years	27
% students graduating within 6 years	48

Most classes have 10–19 students.

PROGRAMS/SERVICES FOR STUDENTS WITH LEARNING DIFFERENCES

Edinboro is actively involved in providing services for students with learning disabilities. The Office for Students with Disabilities (OSD) provides services that are individually directed by the program staff according to expressed needs. There are different levels of services offered depending on the student's needs. Level 1 offers supervised study sessions with trained peer advisors up to 10 hours per week; writing specialist by appointment one to two hours weekly; required appointment every two weeks with professional staff to review progress; and all services in Basic Service. Level 2 includes peer advising up to three hours weekly and all services in Basic Service. Basic Service provides assistance in arranging academic accommodations, including alternate test arrangements; priority scheduling; consultation with staff; and an alternate format of textbooks. Level 1 and 2 are fee-for-service levels.

ADMISSIONS

Students with LD submit the general application form. Upon receipt of the application by the Admissions Office, it is suggested that students identify any special services that may be required and contact the OSD so that a personal interview may be scheduled. Occasionally, OSD staff are asked for remarks on certain files, but it is not part of the admission decision. Students must provide a multifactored educational assessment; grade-level scores in reading, vocabulary and comprehension, math, and spelling; an individual intelligence test administered by a psychologist, including a list of the tests given; and a list of recommended accommodations. Evaluations submitted must have been completed recently (recommend within 3 years) and should meet the guidelines as published College Board, www.collegeboard.org. Students are reviewed for academic promise, motivation, and positive attitude.

Additional Information

The Office for Students with Disabilities has developed the Boro Autism Support Initiative for Success (BASIS) program in order to provide opportunities to otherwise qualified degree seeking college students with Autism Spectrum Disorders (ASD) to achieve excellence in all areas of their university experience. BASIS is an individualized support program available for enrolled Edinboro University students. The BASIS team will work with students to identify individual needs and provide support in 5

ADMISSIONS INFO FOR STUDENTS WITH LEARNING DIFFERENCES

SAT/ACT required: Yes
Interview required: No
Essay required: No
Additional application required: No
Documentation required for:
 LD: Psychological evaluation
 ADHD: Psychological evaluation
 ASD: Psychological evaluation
Documentation submitted to: OSD
Special Ed. HS course work accepted: Yes
Separate application required for program services: No
# of students last year receiving services/accommodations for:
 LD: 270
Contact Information
Name of program or department: Office for Students with Disabilities (OSD)
Telephone: 814-732-2462
Fax: 814-732-2866

Edinboro University of Pennsylvania

key areas: Academics, Communication, Daily Living Skills, Employment Readiness, Social Skills. BASIS is a fee based program: $2500 per semester.

GENERAL ADMISSIONS
Very important factors considered include: rigor of secondary school record, class rank, academic GPA, standardized test scores. *Other factors considered include:* application essay, recommendation(s), interview, extracurricular activities, talent/ability, character/personal qualities, volunteer work, work experience. *Freshman Admission Requirements:* High school diploma is required and GED is accepted. *Academic units recommended:* 4 English, 3 math, 3 science, 2 foreign language, 4 social studies, 1 computer science.

ACCOMMODATION OR SERVICES
Accommodations are decided upon an individual basis after a thorough review of appropriate, current documentation. The accommodations requests must be supported through the documentation provided and must be logically linked to the current impact of the condition on academic functioning.

FINANCIAL AID
Students should submit: FAFSA. Applicants will be notified of awards on a rolling basis beginning 3/22. The Princeton Review suggests that all financial aid forms be submitted as soon as possible after October 1. *Need-based scholarships/grants offered:* College/university scholarship or grant aid from institutional funds; Federal Pell; Private scholarships; SEOG; State scholarships/grants. *Loan aid offered:* Direct Subsidized Stafford Loans; Direct Unsubsidized Stafford Loans. Federal Work-Study Program available. Institutional employment available.

CAMPUS LIFE
Activities: Campus Ministries; Choral groups; Dance; Drama/theater; International Student Organization; Jazz band; Literary magazine; Marching band; Music ensembles; Opera; Radio station; Student government; Student newspaper; Student-run film society; Television station. **Organizations:** 157 registered organizations, 13 honor societies, 4 religious organizations. 10 fraternities, 7 sororities. **Athletics (Intercollegiate):** *Men:* basketball, cross-country, football, swimming, track/field (outdoor), track/field (indoor), wheel-chair basketball, wrestling. *Women:* basketball, cross-country, lacrosse, soccer, softball, swimming, track/field (outdoor), track/field (indoor), volleyball. **On-Campus Highlights:** Tilles Center for the Performing Arts, Hillwood Commons, Pratt Recreation Center, Equestrian Center, Entrepreneurship Lab.

ACCOMMODATIONS

Allowed in exams:

Calculators	Yes
Dictionary	Yes
Computer	Yes
Spell-checker	Yes
Extended test time	Yes
Scribe	Yes
Proctors	Yes
Oral exams	Yes
Note-takers	No

Support services for students with

LD	Yes
ADHD	Yes
ASD	Yes
Distraction-reduced environment	Yes
Recording of lecture allowed	Yes
Reading technology:	Yes
Audio books	Yes
Other assistive technology	Assistive Tech Center and training.
Priority registration	Yes

Added costs for services:

For LD:	No
For ADHD:	No
For ASD:	Yes
LD specialists	Yes
ADHD & ASD coaching	No
ASD specialists	No
Professional tutors	No
Peer tutors	Yes
Max. hours/week for services	8
How professors are notified of student approved accommodations	Student

COLLEGE GRADUATION REQUIREMENTS

Course waivers allowed	No
Course substitutions allowed	Yes
In what courses	Case-by-case basis

Gannon University

109 University Square, Erie, PA 16541 • Admissions: 814-871-7240 • Fax: 814-871-5803

CAMPUS

Type of school	Private (nonprofit)
Environment	City
Support	SP

STUDENTS

Undergrad enrollment	2,616
% male/female	43/57
% from out of state	29
% frosh live on campus	75

FINANCIAL FACTS

Annual tuition	$31,180

GENERAL ADMISSIONS INFO

Application fee	$25

Nonfall registration accepted. Admission may be deferred for a maximum of 1 year.

Range SAT EBRW	450–560
Range SAT Math	470–570
Range ACT Composite	20–26

ACADEMICS

Student/faculty ratio	12:1
% students returning for sophomore year	85
% students graduating within 4 years	53
% students graduating within 6 years	68

Most classes have 10–19 students. Most lab/discussion sessions have 10–19 students.

PROGRAMS/SERVICES FOR STUDENTS WITH LEARNING DIFFERENCES

Gannon's Program for Students with Learning Disabilities (PSLD) provides special support services for students who have been diagnosed with either LD or ADHD who are highly motivated for academic achievement. PSLD faculty are committed to excellence and strive to offer each student individually designed instruction. Students in the program may select any academic major offered by the university. Freshman-year support includes weekly individual sessions with instructor-tutors and a writing specialist. They also provide an advocacy seminar course that includes participation in small group counseling. Students should check the appropriate box on the admissions application if this service applies.

ADMISSIONS

Admissions is based on several factors including academic courses, grades, rank in class, and counselor recommendation. ACT/SAT test required. The minimum GPA and test scores required very based on the academic program and the university will notify the applicants if they do not meet the minimum requirements. Personal statement/essay is optional but recommended as it assists the university in evaluating eligibility beyond test scores and academic record. Courses required include 16 units of which 4 must be in English. Students diagnosed with a learning disability and who are interested in the Gannon's PSLD Program will also need: personal letters of recommendation from teachers, counselor or school administrators, WAIS/WISC scores and sub scores (abbreviate WISC/WAIS scores are not accepted). The WAIS/WISC are not required if the primary diagnosis is ADHD. Records from any professional with whom the student has worked, such as psychologist, physician, reading specialist or math specialist. Students admitted conditionally must enter as undeclared majors until they can achieve a 2.0 GPA.

Additional Information

Specific features of the program include biweekly or more as needed, tutoring sessions with the program instructors and tutors to review course material, and focus on specific needs; weekly sessions with the writing specialist for reviewing, editing, and brainstorming. Additional services available are taping of classes, extended time on exams, scribes as prescribed. Basic services are free, and there is a $600 yearly fee for support services.

ADMISSIONS INFO FOR STUDENTS WITH LEARNING DIFFERENCES

SAT/ACT required: Yes
Interview required: No
Essay required: Recommended
Additional application required: No
Documentation required for:
  LD: Diagnosing physician report and recommendations
  ADHD: Diagnosing physician report and recommendations
  ASD: Diagnosing physician report and recommendations
Documentation submitted to: Office of Disability Services
Special Ed. HS course work accepted: No
Separate application required for program services: No
# of students last year receiving services/accommodations for:
  LD: 50
Contact Information
Name of program or department: Office of Disability Services
Telephone: 814-871-5522
Fax: 814-871-7422

Gannon University

GENERAL ADMISSIONS

Very important factors considered include: rigor of secondary school record, academic GPA, standardized test scores. *Other factors considered include:* class rank, application essay, recommendation(s), interview, extracurricular activities, character/personal qualities, alumni/ae relation, work experience. *Freshman Admission Requirements:* High school diploma is required and GED is accepted. *Academic units required:* 4 English, 2 math, 2 science, 2 science labs, 2 social studies, 1 history, 3 academic electives. *Academic units recommended:* 4 English, 4 math, 4 science, 3 science labs, 2 foreign language, 2 social studies, 1 history, 3 academic electives, 1 computer science, 1 visual/performing arts.

ACCOMMODATION OR SERVICES

Accommodations are decided upon an individual basis after a thorough review of appropriate, current documentation. The accommodations requests must be supported through the documentation provided and must be logically linked to the current impact of the condition on academic functioning.

FINANCIAL AID

Students should submit: FAFSA. Applicants will be notified of awards on a rolling basis beginning 11/1. The Princeton Review suggests that all financial aid forms be submitted as soon as possible after October 1. *Need-based scholarships/grants offered:* College/university scholarship or grant aid from institutional funds; Federal Nursing Scholarships; Federal Pell; Private scholarships; SEOG; State scholarships/grants. *Loan aid offered:* Direct PLUS loans; Direct Subsidized Stafford Loans; Direct Unsubsidized Stafford Loans. Federal Work-Study Program available. Institutional employment available.

CAMPUS LIFE

Activities: Campus Ministries; Choral groups; Concert band; Dance; Drama/theater; International Student Organization; Literary magazine; Model UN; Pep band; Radio station; Student government; Student newspaper. **Organizations:** 71 registered organizations, 11 honor societies, 6 religious organizations. 5 fraternities, 5 sororities. **Athletics (Intercollegiate):** *Men:* baseball, basketball, cheerleading, cross-country, football, golf, soccer, swimming, water polo, wrestling. *Women:* basketball, cheerleading, cross-country, golf, lacrosse, soccer, softball, swimming, volleyball, water polo. **On-Campus Highlights:** Waldron Campus Center, Friendship Green, Student Recreation Center, Knight Club, Hammermill Center.

ACCOMMODATIONS

Allowed in exams:

Calculators	No
Dictionary	No
Computer	Yes
Spell-checker	No
Extended test time	Yes
Scribe	Yes
Proctors	Yes
Oral exams	No
Note-takers	Yes

Support services for students with

LD	Yes
ADHD	Yes
ASD	Yes
Distraction-reduced environment	Yes
Recording of lecture allowed	Yes
Reading technology:	Yes
Audio books	Yes
Other assistive technology	Not Applicable
Priority registration	Yes

Added costs for services:

For LD:	Yes
For ADHD:	No
For ASD:	No
PSLD:	Yes
LD specialists	Yes
ADHD & ASD coaching	Yes
ASD specialists	No
Professional tutors	Yes
Peer tutors	Yes
Max. hours/week for services	Varies

How professors are notified of student approved accommodations
    Student and director

COLLEGE GRADUATION REQUIREMENTS

Course waivers allowed	No
Course substitutions allowed	Yes
In what courses	Foreign language

Kutztown University of Pennsylvania

PO Box 730, Kutztown, PA 19530-0730 • Admissions: 610-683-4060 • Fax: 610-683-1375

CAMPUS
Type of school	Public
Environment	Rural
Support	CS

STUDENTS
Undergrad enrollment	8,329
% male/female	45/55
% from out of state	12
% frosh live on campus	90

FINANCIAL FACTS
Annual in-state tuition	$7,492
Annual out-of-state tuition	$11,238
Room and board	$10,282
Required fees	$2,495

GENERAL ADMISSIONS INFO
Application fee	$35
Priority deadline	12/1

Nonfall registration accepted. Admission may be deferred for a maximum of 1 year.

Range SAT EBRW	490–580
Range SAT Math	480–560
Range ACT Composite	18–24

ACADEMICS
Student/faculty ratio	18:1
% students returning for sophomore year	74
% students graduating within 4 years	35
% students graduating within 6 years	53

Most classes have fewer than 10 students. Most lab/discussion sessions have 10–19 students.

PROGRAMS/SERVICES FOR STUDENTS WITH LEARNING DIFFERENCES

Kutztown University welcomes academically qualified students with disabilities to participate in its educational programs and is committed to providing access to its programs and services for all qualified individuals. Disability status is not a consideration in the admissions process at Kutztown University. The admissions process and criteria are the same for all students applying to Kutztown University. Upon acceptance to Kutztown University, students should complete and submit the Accommodation Request Form from the Disability Service Office (DSO). This form is the means by which a student self-discloses a disability and is the first step in the process for requesting accommodations at KU. At Kutztown University, reasonable accommodations are determined and an individual accommodation plan is developed on a case-by-case basis through an interactive process with the Disability Services Office (DSO).

ADMISSIONS INFO FOR STUDENTS WITH LEARNING DIFFERENCES

SAT/ACT required: Yes
Interview required: No
Essay required: Not Applicable
Additional application required: Not Applicable
Documentation required for:
  ADHD: A current evaluation (within the past 3 years) by a psychiatrist, neurologist, licensed psychologist or other qualified medical professional that includes: • A statement of the diagnosis of ADHD or ADD, based on the DSM-V diagnostic criteria. • A description of the current substantial limitation to learning, living or working. Include information from the diagnostic interview and third party input. • Clinical instruments and/or procedures used to determine the diagnosis including results from cognitive or achievement measures. • Recommendations for prescriptive treatments, environmental management, and reasonable accommodations.
  ASD: A current evaluation (within the past 5 years) by a licensed psychologist or neuropsychologist, psychiatrist, physician, or other health professional experienced and certified in the diagnosis and treatment of the specific condition that includes: • A clear statement of the diagnosis that conforms to diagnostic criteria for Autism according to the DSM-V. • A history of and current functional limitations of major life activities including communication or language skills, social interaction, restricted, repetitive or other patterns of behavior and activities, sensory functioning, and sensitivity to environmental conditions. • Results and interpretation of assessment measures. • A history of accommodations and services used previously, and recommendations for reasonable accommodations in the learning, living or working environment.
Documentation submitted to: Disability Services Office (DSO)
Special Ed. HS course work accepted: No
Separate application required for program services: No
Contact Information
Name of program or department: Disability Services Office (DSO)
Telephone: 610-683-4108
Fax: 610-683-1520
Email: DSO@kutztown.edu

Kutztown University of Pennsylvania

ADMISSIONS

There is no special admissions process for students with learning disabilities. All applicants are expected to meet the same admission criteria. Course requirements include: 4 years English, 3 years math, 3 years social studies. Conditional Admission is available.

Additional Information

The director of Disability Services for ADA is the initial resource person and record keeper who validates the existence of a disability and the need for any specific accommodations. Academic assistance is provided through the Department of Academic Enrichment. Students with LD are eligible to receive services and accommodations prescribed in the psychoeducational evaluation, extended time on exams, use of a recorder, use of calculator, testing in a separate location, readers, spell check and grammar check on written assignments, scribes, alternative texts, tutorial assistance, early advisement and priority registration, computer assistive technology, and referrals. Tutors are available to all students, and arrangements are made at no cost to the student.

GENERAL ADMISSIONS

Very important factors considered include: rigor of secondary school record, class rank, standardized test scores. *Other factors considered include:* academic GPA, recommendation(s), talent/ability. *Freshman Admission Requirements:* High school diploma is required and GED is accepted. *Academic units required:* 4 English, 3 math, 3 science, 2 science labs, 3 social studies.

ACCOMMODATION OR SERVICES

Accommodations are decided upon an individual basis after a thorough review of appropriate, current documentation. The accommodations requests must be supported through the documentation provided and must be logically linked to the current impact of the condition on academic functioning.

FINANCIAL AID

Students should submit: FAFSA. Applicants will be notified of awards on a rolling basis beginning 3/30. The Princeton Review suggests that all financial aid forms be submitted as soon as possible after October 1. *Need-based scholarships/grants offered:* College/university scholarship or grant aid from institutional funds; Federal Pell; Private scholarships; SEOG; State scholarships/grants. *Loan aid offered:* Direct PLUS loans; Direct Subsidized Stafford Loans; Direct Unsubsidized Stafford Loans. Federal Work-Study Program available. Institutional employment available.

CAMPUS LIFE

Activities: Campus Ministries; Choral groups; Concert band; Dance; Drama/theater; International Student Organization; Jazz band; Literary magazine; Marching band; Model UN; Music ensembles; Musical theater; Radio station; Student government; Student newspaper; Student-run film society; Symphony orchestra; Television station; Yearbook. **Organizations:** 218 registered organizations, 15 honor societies, 11 religious organizations. 9 fraternities, 8 sororities. **Athletics (Intercollegiate):** *Men:* baseball, basketball, cross-country, football, tennis, track/field (outdoor), track/field (indoor), wrestling. *Women:* basketball, bowling, cross-country, field hockey, golf, lacrosse, soccer, softball, swimming, tennis, track/field (outdoor), track/field (indoor), volleyball. **On-Campus Highlights:** Taylor and Burnes Gourmet Coffee, Student Rec Center, Alumni Plaza-new walkway with outdoor amphitheater, Pennsylvania German Cultural Heritage Center, Academic Forum.

ACCOMMODATIONS

Allowed in exams:	
Calculators	Yes
Dictionary	Not Applicable
Computer	Yes
Spell-checker	Yes
Extended test time	Yes
Scribe	Yes
Proctors	Yes
Oral exams	No
Note-takers	Yes
Support services for students with	
LD	Yes
ADHD	Yes
ASD	Yes
Distraction-reduced environment	Yes
Recording of lecture allowed	Yes
Reading technology:	Yes
Audio books	Yes
Other assistive technology JAWS, Zoomtext, Natural Reader, Dragon, MAC computer	
Priority registration	Yes
Added costs for services:	
For LD:	No
For ADHD:	No
For ASD:	No
LD specialists	No
ADHD & ASD coaching	No
ASD specialists	No
Professional tutors	Yes
Peer tutors	Yes
Max. hours/week for services	3
How professors are notified of student approved accommodations	Student

COLLEGE GRADUATION REQUIREMENTS

Course waivers allowed	No
Course substitutions allowed	Yes
In what coursesOnly with strong diagnostic recommendation and departmental approval - foreign language and math	

Lehigh University

27 Memorial Drive West, Bethlehem, PA 18015 • Admissions: 610-758-3100 • Fax: 610-758-4361

CAMPUS

Type of school	Private (nonprofit)
Environment	City
Support	CS

STUDENTS

Undergrad enrollment	5,057
% male/female	55/45
% from out of state	73
% frosh live on campus	99

FINANCIAL FACTS

Annual tuition	$50,320
Room and board	$13,120
Required fees	$420

GENERAL ADMISSIONS INFO

Application fee	$70
Regular application deadline	1/1

Nonfall registration accepted. Admission may be deferred for a maximum of 1 year.

Range SAT EBRW	620–700
Range SAT Math	650–730
Range ACT Composite	29–32

ACADEMICS

Student/faculty ratio	9:1
% students returning for sophomore year	96
% students graduating within 4 years	76
% students graduating within 6 years	86

Most classes have 10–19 students.
Most lab/discussion sessions have 10–19 students.

PROGRAMS/SERVICES FOR STUDENTS WITH LEARNING DIFFERENCES

Lehigh University is committed to ensuring reasonable accommodations to students who are substantially limited by a diagnosed disability. Students requesting academic accommodations are required to submit for review current documentation of their disability. If a student is not certain whether he or she has a learning disability, the Director of Academic Support Services can conduct a comprehensive intake interview and screening process. If a complete diagnostic evaluation seems appropriate, the student will be provided with referrals to community-based professionals who can perform a comprehensive evaluation at the student's expense. The ultimate goal is to ensure that students with disabilities have an opportunity to grow independently to their fullest potential at a competitive university. It is the responsibility of students with disabilities to identify themselves to the appropriate university contact person and provide the required documentation to receive accommodations. Given the specific nature of each person's disability, reasonable accommodations will be determined on an individual basis by the appropriate university contact person. Students who are eligible for accommodations must sign a professor notification and accommodation form at the beginning of each semester that students are requesting accommodations.

ADMISSIONS

There is no special admission process for students with learning disabilities. All applicants must meet the same admission criteria. Applicants must submit either the SAT Reasoning Test or the ACT with the optional Writing section. An on-campus interview is recommended. Applicants' evaluations are based on many factors, including a challenging college-prep curriculum that included AP and honors courses.

ADMISSIONS INFO FOR STUDENTS WITH LEARNING DIFFERENCES

SAT/ACT required: Yes
Interview required: No
Essay required: Not Applicable
Additional application required:No
Documentation required for:
  LD:Psycho ed evaluation to include: relevant historical info, instructional interventions, related services, age diagnosed, objective data (aptitude, achievement, info processing), test scores (standard, percentile and grade equivalents) and describe functional limitations.
  ADHD: Diagnosis based on DSM-V; history of behaviors impairing functioning in academic setting; diagnostic interview; history of symptoms; evidence of ongoing behaviors.
  ASD: Students requesting support services are required to provide the Dean of Students/Academic Support Services with current documentation of a diagnosed Autism Spectrum Disorder or Asperger's Syndrome from a recognized authority. If documentation of ASD has been established during the time that the student attended K-12 school, then the diagnosis will generally be sufficient. However, a description of the current functional limitations of the disorder should be provided.
Documentation submitted to: Support Program/Services
Special Ed. HS course work accepted: No
Separate application required for program services:No
# of students last year receiving services/accommodations for:
  LD: 74
  ADHD: 132
Contact Information
Name of program or department: Academic Support Services
Telephone: 610-758-4152
Fax: 610-758-5293

Additional Information

The Peer Mentor Program assists first-year students with the transition from high school to a competitive university. The peer mentors are composed of upperclass students who have a diagnosed learning disability or attention deficit hyperactivity disorder. Each mentor has demonstrated leadership capability and has been academically successful at Lehigh University. First- year students are matched with a peer mentor by college and/or major. The rationale for matching students in this manner is because upperclass students of the same major and/or college have most likely taken the same courses and professors and have experienced the same challenges as the freshman with whom they have been matched. The first-year students who have participated in the Peer Mentor Program and who have worked with the Office of Academic Support Services have traditionally performed significantly better than students who have not participated in support services. Program participation is voluntary, and students may choose to withdraw from the program at any time. The Center for Writing and Math provides assistance with any writing assignments, including brainstorming, rough-draft preparations, and critiques of final draft and assistance in calculus and other math courses. The Center for Academic Success has peer tutors available in most freshman- and sophomore-level courses. Ten free hours of tutoring per course per semester are provided. The tutors provide assistance with study skills, note-taking skills, and time management techniques.

GENERAL ADMISSIONS

Very important factors considered include: rigor of secondary school record, academic GPA, recommendation(s), extracurricular activities, character/personal qualities. *Important factors considered include:* application essay, standardized test scores, talent/ability, volunteer work.level of applicant's interest. *Other factors considered include:* class rank, interview, first generation, alumni/ae relation, geographical residence, racial/ethnic status, work experience. *Freshman Admission Requirements:* High school diploma is required and GED is accepted. *Academic units required:* 4 English, 3 math, 2 science, 2 science labs, 2 foreign language, 2 social studies, 3 academic electives. *Academic units recommended:* 4 math, 4 science, 2 science labs.

ACCOMMODATION OR SERVICES

Accommodations are decided upon an individual basis after a thorough review of appropriate, current documentation. The accommodations requests must be supported through the documentation provided and must be logically linked to the current impact of the condition on academic functioning.

FINANCIAL AID

Students should submit: Business/Farm Supplement; CSS/Financial Aid PROFILE; FAFSA; Noncustodial PROFILE. Applicants will be notified of awards on or about 3/30. The Princeton Review suggests that all financial aid forms be submitted as soon as possible after October 1. *Need-based scholarships/grants offered:* College/university scholarship or grant aid from institutional funds; Federal Pell; Private scholarships; SEOG; State scholarships/grants. *Loan aid offered:* Direct PLUS loans; Direct Subsidized Stafford Loans; Direct Unsubsidized Stafford Loans. Federal Work-Study Program available. Institutional employment available.

ACCOMMODATIONS

Allowed in exams:	
Calculators	No
Dictionary	No
Computer	Yes
Spell-checker	No
Extended test time	Yes
Scribe	Yes
Proctors	No
Oral exams	Yes
Note-takers	Yes
Support services for students with	
LD	Yes
ADHD	Yes
ASD	Yes
Distraction-reduced environment	Not Applicable
Recording of lecture allowed	Yes
Reading technology:	Yes
Audio books	Yes
Other assistive technology	Yes
Priority registration	Yes
Added costs for services:	
For LD:	No
For ADHD:	No
For ASD:	No
LD specialists	Yes
ADHD & ASD coaching	
ASD specialists	Yes
Professional tutors	Yes
Peer tutors	Yes
Max. hours/week for services	Varies
How professors are notified of student approved accommodations	Student

COLLEGE GRADUATION REQUIREMENTS

Course waivers allowed	No
Course substitutions allowed	No

Mercyhurst University

501 E. 38TH STREET, ERIE, PA 16546 • ADMISSIONS: 814-824-2202 • FAX: 814-824-2071

CAMPUS

Type of school	Private (nonprofit)
Environment	City
Support	SP

STUDENTS

Undergrad enrollment	2,680
% male/female	44/56
% from out of state	48
% frosh live on campus	93

FINANCIAL FACTS

Annual tuition	$29,600
Room and board	$10,800
Required fees	$1,885

GENERAL ADMISSIONS INFO

Application fee	$30
Priority deadline	5/1

Nonfall registration accepted. Admission may be deferred for a maximum of 1 year.

Range SAT EBRW	470–580
Range SAT Math	470–570
Range ACT Composite	21–26

ACADEMICS

Student/faculty ratio	14:1
% students returning for sophomore year	79
% students graduating within 4 years	62
% students graduating within 6 years	68

Most classes have 20–29 students.
Most lab/discussion sessions have 20–29 students.

PROGRAMS/SERVICES FOR STUDENTS WITH LEARNING DIFFERENCES

The Learning Differences program at Mercyhurst College is designed to assist students who have been identified as having LD. The emphasis is on students' individual strengths, abilities and interests, as well as learning deficits. This program consists of a structured, individualized set of experiences designed to assist students with LD, ADHD and ASD to get maximum value from their educational potential and earn a college degree. Students selecting the structured program for students with learning differences pay an additional fee for this service and must submit a recent psychological evaluation that includes the WAIS or WISC scores (completed with the past 5 years); three letters of recommendation; SAT/ACT scores; and a written statement from a professional which documents the student's disability. Students choosing the structured program (Level II) have the option to attend summer sessions prior to entrance; classes may include guided practice while enrolled in actual college class, learning strategies, and use of assistive technology. The program lasts 3 weeks and costs approximately $1,600 (includes room, board and tuition). Students with learning differences who feel that they do not require a structured program may opt to receive support services through level I program at no additional charge. Our AIM program supports ASD students in all areas of the college experience, including campus life as well as class work. Students are evaluated in key domains that are essential to higher education and vocational success.

ADMISSIONS

To be eligible for any of the services at Mercyhurst, students with LD must adhere to the regular admission requirements and meet the regular admission criteria. Students who do not meet the regular admissions standards are referred to Mercyhurst—McAuley and/or Mercyhurst—North East for consideration into the two-year division. Some students may be admitted on probation pending the completion of developmental course work. The college reserves the right to reject any student not meeting admission standards. The admission decisions are made jointly by the director of Programs for Students with Learning Differences and the Office of Admission. Upon acceptance to the college, if the student wishes special services, she/he must identify herself/himself to the

ADMISSIONS INFO FOR STUDENTS WITH LEARNING DIFFERENCES

SAT/ACT required: No
Interview required: No
Essay required: Recommended
Additional application required: Yes
Documentation required for:
   ASD: Thorough history by a developmental pediatrician or a developmental medical doctor Comprehensive neuropsychological examination, within the past three years, including a discussion of the individual's current functioning as it impacts the educational environment Academic testing of standardized achievement tests, including scores; and a review of the academic record Current social/emotional functioning; if not in neuropsychological evaluation, then by separate evaluator Integrated summary, including impact of symptoms on learning, ability to functioning deficits as relevant to post secondary education Clear identification of DSM-IV criteria An interview including a description of the presenting problem(s) including any significant developmental, medical, psychosocial and employment issues
Documentation submitted to: Learning Differences Program
Special Ed. HS course work accepted: No
Contact Information
Name of program or department: Learning Differences Program
Telephone: 814-824-3048
Fax: 814-824-2589

Mercyhurst University

Admissions Office and, at that time, choose to receive services in one of two options available to students with documented learning differences. These programs are a structured program and a basic service program. Admission to Mercyhurst University does not guarantee admission to AIM, as applications to the university and to this highly selective support program are separate and distinct processes.

Additional Information

The Structured Program for Students with Learning Differences provides special services, advocacy, alternative testing, Assisstive Technology, community skills, drop-in services, Kurzweil 3000, electronic text book search, midterm progress reports, notetakers, peer tutoring, professional advising/priority registration, special three-week Summer Orientation Program prior to freshman year, optional study hall (required of all freshmen), and a support group.

GENERAL ADMISSIONS

Very important factors considered include: rigor of secondary school record, class rank, academic GPA, standardized test scores. *Important factors considered include:* application essay, recommendation(s), interview, extracurricular activities, talent/ability, character/personal qualities. *Other factors considered include:* alumni/ae relation, geographical residence, state residency, religious affiliation/commitment, racial/ethnic status, volunteer work, work experience, level of applicant's interest. *Freshman Admission Requirements:* High school diploma is required and GED is accepted. *Academic units required:* 4 English, 3 math, 2 science, 1 science lab, 2 foreign language, 5 social studies. *Academic units recommended:* 4 English, 3 math, 3 science, 2 science labs, 2 foreign language, 5 social studies.

ACCOMMODATION OR SERVICES

Accommodations are decided upon an individual basis after a thorough review of appropriate, current documentation. The accommodations requests must be supported through the documentation provided and must be logically linked to the current impact of the condition on academic functioning.

FINANCIAL AID

Students should submit:. Applicants will be notified of awards on a rolling basis beginning 2/15. The Princeton Review suggests that all financial aid forms be submitted as soon as possible after October 1. *Need-based scholarships/grants offered:* College/university scholarship or grant aid from institutional funds; Federal Pell; Private scholarships; SEOG; State scholarships/grants. *Loan aid offered:* Direct PLUS loans; Direct Subsidized Stafford Loans; Direct Unsubsidized Stafford Loans. Federal Work-Study Program available. Institutional employment available.

CAMPUS LIFE

Activities: Campus Ministries; Choral groups; Dance; Drama/theater; International Student Organization; Jazz band; Literary magazine; Model UN; Music ensembles; Musical theater; Pep band; Radio station; Student government; Student newspaper; Television station; Yearbook. **Organizations:** 9 honor societies, 2 religious organizations. **Athletics (Intercollegiate):** *Men:* baseball, basketball, cheerleading, crew/rowing, cross-country, football, golf, ice hockey, lacrosse, soccer, tennis, volleyball, water polo, wrestling. *Women:* basketball, cheerleading, crew/rowing, cross-country, field hockey, golf, ice hockey, lacrosse, soccer, softball, tennis, volleyball, water polo. **On-Campus Highlights:** Performing Arts Center, Mercyhurst Athletic Center, Library, Student Union, Ice Rink.

ACCOMMODATIONS

Allowed in exams:

Calculators	Yes
Dictionary	No
Computer	Yes
Spell-checker	Yes
Extended test time	Yes
Scribe	Yes
Proctors	Yes
Oral exams	Yes
Note-takers	Yes

Support services for students with

LD	Yes
ADHD	Yes
ASD	Yes
Distraction-reduced environment	Yes
Recording of lecture allowed	No
Reading technology:	Yes
Audio books	No

Other assistive technology Kurzweil Screen Reader, Speech-to-text, Inspiration

Priority registration	Yes

Added costs for services:

For LD:	No
For ADHD:	No
For ASD:	No
LD specialists	Yes
ADHD & ASD coaching	Yes
ASD specialists	Yes
Professional tutors	Yes
Peer tutors	Yes
Max. hours/week for services	3

How professors are notified of student approved accommodations
Director and student

COLLEGE GRADUATION REQUIREMENTS

Course waivers allowed	Yes

In what courses   foreign languages, and only on an individual basis.

Course substitutions allowed	No

Messiah College

One College Avenue, Mechanicsburg, PA 17055 • Admissions: (717) 691-6000 • Fax: 717-691-2307

CAMPUS

Type of school	Private (nonprofit)
Environment	Village
Support	S

STUDENTS

Undergrad enrollment	2,759
% male/female	41/59
% from out of state	36
% frosh live on campus	95

FINANCIAL FACTS

Annual tuition	$34,320
Room and board	$5,570
Required fees	$840

GENERAL ADMISSIONS INFO

Application fee	$50

Nonfall registration accepted.

Range SAT EBRW	560–660
Range SAT Math	540–650
Range ACT Composite	22–29

ACADEMICS

Student/faculty ratio	12:1
% students returning for sophomore year	88
% students graduating within 4 years	76
% students graduating within 6 years	81

Most classes have 20–29 students.
Most lab/discussion sessions have 10–19 students.

PROGRAMS/SERVICES FOR STUDENTS WITH LEARNING DIFFERENCES

Messiah College is a Christian college committed to providing reasonable accommodations to qualified students with disabilities. Students who feel they may qualify for services should meet with the Office of Disability Service's (ODS) staff. At that meeting, ODS staff will discuss the documentation process, services available, and their educational goals. Services and accommodations rendered will be based on the individualized needs of the students. Such services/accommodations are granted to create an equal opportunity for student success, but do not in any way waive class expectations. Therefore, classroom success is not guaranteed. To be recognized as a student with a disability, students are required to submit documentation from a qualified educational evaluator stating their diagnosis, how such a diagnosis creates a "substantial impairment" and in which life activities, and a list of accommodations that will be needed by the student in order to benefit from the program. Students who do not have documentation but who think they may have a disability may seek assistance from ODS by locating screening services. Any costs incurred for an evaluation are the responsibility of the student. ODS finds most students registered with the office to be motivated, hardworking, and interested and willing to meet their educational goals.

ADMISSIONS

All applicants must meet the same admission criteria. There is an extensive application process including: letters of recommendation; ACT/SAT; high school transcript; essays, and a review by the Admissions officer/committee. Admission requirements include a high school transcript, SAT or ACT scores, and four English, two math, two natural sciences, two social studies, and six electives (prefer that two of these be in foreign language), and a Christian life recommendation. Messiah College makes all efforts to avoid any possible prejudice in the admission process. Students with disabilities are encouraged to self-disclose and request an interview with the ODS Director, but not to include documentation of the disability in the actual admissions packet.

ADMISSIONS INFO FOR STUDENTS WITH LEARNING DIFFERENCES

SAT/ACT required: Yes
Interview required: No
Essay required: No
Additional application required: No
Documentation required for:
  LD: Complete psychoeducational report from a qualified examiner, to include all test details; IEP/504 service plan suggested with few exceptions, report should be less than three years old.
  ADHD: Complete psychoeducational report from a qualified examiner, to include all test details; IEP/504 service plan suggested with few exceptions, report should be less than three years old.
  ASD: evaluation from school psychologist, neuropsychologist, medical professional or counselor
Documentation submitted to: Support Program/Services
Special Ed. HS course work accepted: Yes
Separate application required for program services: No
# of students last year receiving services/accommodations for:
  LD: 25-30
Contact Information
Name of program or department: Office of Disability Services
Telephone: 717-796-5382
Fax: 717-796-5217

Additional Information

Documentation should include a recent multi-disciplinary evaluation appropriate to the disability claimed. Neither an IEP nor a written 504 plan is sufficient to determine eligibility, but may be helpful when included along with a comprehensive evaluation report. Commonly provided accommodations by the Office of Disability Services include: extended time for test-taking; proctored exams in an alternate location; assistance with getting notes; disability coaching support; advocacy with instructors; alternate format textbooks;transition services; peer tutoring; referral source for other required services. Other accommodations are considered on an individual basis. Additionally, The Learning Center offers assistance with time management, motivation, goal setting, reading skills, note-taking, learning theory, and taking exams, in addition to providing a range of tutorial services through trained peer tutors. The Writing Center provides peer tutors for written projects. Other supports include math tutors and Supplemental Instruction, primarily in the sciences. Personal counseling is available through the Engle Health Center. The staff at ODS encourages and develops students self advocacy, but may act as a liaison between students and faculty when needed.

GENERAL ADMISSIONS

Very important factors considered include: rigor of secondary school record, class rank, academic GPA, standardized test scores, extracurricular activities, talent/ability, character/personal qualities, religious affiliation/commitment. *Important factors considered include:* application essay, volunteer work. *Other factors considered include:* recommendation(s), alumni/ae relation, racial/ethnic status, work experience, level of applicant's interest. *Freshman Admission Requirements:* High school diploma is required and GED is accepted. *Academic units required:* 4 English, 2 math, 2 science, 2 science labs, 2 foreign language, 2 social studies, 4 academic electives. *Academic units recommended:* 4 English, 3 math, 3 science, 3 science labs, 2 foreign language, 2 social studies, 2 history, 4 academic electives.

ACCOMMODATION OR SERVICES

Accommodations are decided upon an individual basis after a thorough review of appropriate, current documentation. The accommodations requests must be supported through the documentation provided and must be logically linked to the current impact of the condition on academic functioning.

FINANCIAL AID

Students should submit: FAFSA. Applicants will be notified of awards on a rolling basis beginning 12/1. The Princeton Review suggests that all financial aid forms be submitted as soon as possible after October 1. *Need-based scholarships/grants offered:* College/university scholarship or grant aid from institutional funds; Federal Nursing Scholarships; Federal Pell; Private scholarships; SEOG; State scholarships/grants. *Loan aid offered:* Direct PLUS loans; Direct Subsidized Stafford Loans; Direct Unsubsidized Stafford Loans. Federal Work-Study Program available. Institutional employment available.

CAMPUS LIFE

Activities: Campus Ministries; Choral groups; Concert band; Dance; Drama/theater; International Student Organization; Jazz band; Literary magazine; Music ensembles; Musical theater; Pep band; Radio station; Student government; Student newspaper; Student-run film society; Symphony orchestra; Yearbook.

ACCOMMODATIONS

Allowed in exams:	
Calculators	Yes
Dictionary	Not Applicable
Computer	Yes
Spell-checker	Yes
Extended test time	Yes
Scribe	Yes
Proctors	Yes
Oral exams	Yes
Note-takers	Yes
Support services for students with	
LD	Yes
ADHD	Yes
ASD	Yes
Distraction-reduced environment	Yes
Recording of lecture allowed	Yes
Reading technology:	Yes
Audio books	No
Other assistive technology Kurzweil, JAWS, and Dragon Naturally Speaking are on limited computers in ODS, electronic textbooks for students who qualify	
Priority registration	Yes
Added costs for services:	
For LD:	No
For ADHD:	No
For ASD:	No
LD specialists	No
ADHD & ASD coaching	No
ASD specialists	Yes
Professional tutors	Yes
Peer tutors	Yes
Max. hours/week for services	Varies
How professors are notified of student approved accommodations	Student

COLLEGE GRADUATION REQUIREMENTS

Course waivers allowed	No
Course substitutions allowed	Yes
In what courses	
If documentation is clear, students may be afforded a foreign language substitution.	

Millersville University of Pennsylvania

P.O. Box 1002, Millersville, PA 17551-0302 • Admissions: 717-871-4625 • Fax: 717-871-2147

CAMPUS
Type of school	Public
Environment	Village
Support	S

STUDENTS
Undergrad enrollment	6,613
% male/female	43/57
% from out of state	6
% frosh live on campus	80

FINANCIAL FACTS
Annual in-state tuition	$9,270
Annual out-of-state tuition	$18,730
Room and board	$13,440
Required fees	$2,588

GENERAL ADMISSIONS INFO
Application fee	$50

Nonfall registration accepted. Admission may be deferred for a maximum of 1 year.

Range SAT EBRW	490–590
Range SAT Math	480–570
Range ACT Composite	19–24

ACADEMICS
Student/faculty ratio	18:1
% students returning for sophomore year	77
% students graduating within 4 years	36
% students graduating within 6 years	62

Most classes have 30–39 students.
Most lab/discussion sessions have fewer than 10 students.

PROGRAMS/SERVICES FOR STUDENTS WITH LEARNING DIFFERENCES

The Office of Learning Services promotes and encourages the unique learning styles of all Millersville University students through advocacy, assistive technology, collaboration, and direct services with the University community. Through excellence in service delivery, the Office of Learning Services fosters a climate that ensures student access and equity at Millersville University.

ADMISSIONS

Typical first year students have achieved a solid B average in high school and earned an above average ACT or SAT. The University has their own application form online.

Additional Information

The Office of Learning Services coordinates academic accommodations and related services for students with learning and physical disabilities. Students must complete a Special Assistance Request Form. For a student with learning disabilities the first page and the page labeled Learning Disability are required together with a complete psychoeducational, psychological, neuropsychological, or evaluation report as the official documentation.

ADMISSIONS INFO FOR STUDENTS WITH LEARNING DIFFERENCES

SAT/ACT required: Yes
Interview required: No
Essay required: Not Applicable
Additional application required: No
Documentation required for:
  LD: Evaluation/ Re-evaluation report
  ADHD: Evaluation/ Re-evaluation report
  ASD: Evaluation/ Re-evaluation report
Documentation submitted to: Support Program/Services
Special Ed. HS course work accepted: Not Applicable
Separate application required for program services: No
# of students last year receiving services/accommodations for:
  LD: 185
  ADHD: 149
Contact Information
Name of program or department: Office of Learning Services
Telephone: 717-871-5554
Fax: 717-871-7943
Email: Learning.Services@millersville.edu

Millersville University of Pennsylvania

GENERAL ADMISSIONS

Very important factors considered include: rigor of secondary school record, class rank, academic GPA. *Important factors considered include:* application essay, standardized test scores, talent/ability, character/personal qualities. *Other factors considered include:* recommendation(s), extracurricular activities, first generation, racial/ethnic status, volunteer work, work experience, level of applicant's interest. *Freshman Admission Requirements:* High school diploma is required and GED is accepted. *Academic units required:* 4 English, 3 math, 3 science, 2 science labs, 3 social studies, 2 history. *Academic units recommended:* 4 English, 3 math, 3 science, 2 science labs, 2 foreign language, 3 social studies, 2 history, 4 academic electives.

ACCOMMODATION OR SERVICES

Accommodations are decided upon an individual basis after a thorough review of appropriate, current documentation. The accommodations requests must be supported through the documentation provided and must be logically linked to the current impact of the condition on academic functioning.

FINANCIAL AID

Students should submit: FAFSA. Applicants will be notified of awards on a rolling basis beginning 3/19. The Princeton Review suggests that all financial aid forms be submitted as soon as possible after October 1. *Need-based scholarships/grants offered:* College/university scholarship or grant aid from institutional funds; Federal Pell; Private scholarships; SEOG; State scholarships/grants. *Loan aid offered:* Direct PLUS loans; Direct Subsidized Stafford Loans; Direct Unsubsidized Stafford Loans. Federal Work-Study Program available. Institutional employment available.

CAMPUS LIFE

Activities: Campus Ministries; Choral groups; Concert band; Dance; Drama/theater; International Student Organization; Jazz band; Literary magazine; Marching band; Music cnscmbles; Musical theater; Radio station; Student government; Student newspaper; Student-run film society; Symphony orchestra; Television station. **Organizations:** 120 registered organizations, 11 honor societies, 12 religious organizations. 9 fraternities, 10 sororities. **Athletics (Intercollegiate):** *Men:* baseball, basketball, cross-country, football, golf, soccer, tennis, track/field (outdoor), track/field (indoor), wrestling. *Women:* basketball, cheerleading, cross-country, field hockey, lacrosse, soccer, softball, swimming, tennis, track/field (outdoor), track/field (indoor), volleyball. **On-Campus Highlights:** Student Memorial Center, The Francine G. McNairy Library and Learning Forum, Roddy and Caputo Science and Technology Buildings, Biemesderfer Executive Center, Gordinier Dining Hall.

ACCOMMODATIONS

Allowed in exams:	
Calculators	Yes
Dictionary	Yes
Computer	Yes
Spell-checker	Yes
Extended test time	Yes
Scribe	Yes
Proctors	Yes
Oral exams	Yes
Note-takers	Yes
Support services for students with	
LD	Yes
ADHD	Yes
ASD	Yes
Distraction-reduced environment	Yes
Recording of lecture allowed	Yes
Reading technology:	Yes
Audio books	Yes
Other assistive technology	Screen readers, speech to text, text magnification.
Priority registration	Yes
Added costs for services:	
For LD:	No
For ADHD:	No
For ASD:	No
LD specialists	Yes
ADHD & ASD coaching	Yes
ASD specialists	Yes
Professional tutors	Yes
Peer tutors	Yes
Max. hours/week for services	3
How professors are notified of student approved accommodations	Director

COLLEGE GRADUATION REQUIREMENTS

Course waivers allowed	Yes
In what courses	Foreign Language and others determined by academic departments
Course substitutions allowed	Yes
In what courses	Foreign Language and others determined by academic departments

Misericordia University

301 Lake Street, Dallas, PA 18612 • Admissions: 570-674-6264 • Fax: 570-675-2441

CAMPUS

Type of school	Private (nonprofit)
Environment	Town
Support	SP

STUDENTS

Undergrad enrollment	2,100
% male/female	33/67
% from out of state	27
% frosh live on campus	84

FINANCIAL FACTS

Annual tuition	$31,530
Room and board	$13,960
Required fees	$1,710

GENERAL ADMISSIONS INFO

Nonfall registration accepted. Admission may be deferred for a maximum of 1 year.

Range SAT EBRW	520–610
Range SAT Math	510–595
Range ACT Composite	22–26

ACADEMICS

Student/faculty ratio	12:1
% students returning for sophomore year	85
% students graduating within 4 years	71
% students graduating within 6 years	76

Most classes have 20–29 students.

PROGRAMS/SERVICES FOR STUDENTS WITH LEARNING DIFFERENCES

In 1979, the Alternative Learners Project (ALP) was founded as the first of its kind in Pennsylvania to provide support to students with learning disabilities. With a dedicated Alternative Learning Manager, a professional staff of highly qualified full time coordinators and an abundance of cooperation and support from an exceptional faculty and administration, the ALP serves a population of approximately 40 students with disabilities per year. All students who participate in ALP are enrolled in regular college courses and are supported by an assortment of services delivered by a specially trained full time staff. Services include "Learning Strategies" which are designed to make students more efficient learners, and accommodations designed to work around students' disabilities whenever possible. Upon entry, each student develops a program of accommodation (POA), and participates in individual weekly meetings with a Program Coordinator. The ultimate goal of ALP is to help students with learning differences succeed independently in college.

ADMISSIONS

Misericordia University's experience with students with learning disabilities is that students who are highly motivated and socially mature have an excellent chance to be successful. Each applicant has to submit a standard application to the Admissions Office. In addition, students must send a written cover letter to the ALP Manager summarizing the disability, and indicate a desire to participate in the ALP. Additionally, a copy of the psycho-educational report should be submitted along with the high school transcript and three letters of recommendation (one should be written by a special education professional, if appropriate). Class rank is usually above the top 60 percent. Although ACT/SAT scores are required by the university for traditional admissions, they are not used in the ALP Admissions decision. Students and their parents will be invited to campus for an interview. Following the interview, the ALP Manager reviews all information and notifies the student directly regarding admission to the program.

ADMISSIONS INFO FOR STUDENTS WITH LEARNING DIFFERENCES

SAT/ACT required: Yes
Interview required: Yes
Essay required: Yes
Additional application required: No
Documentation required for:
  LD: Psycho ed evaluation to include: relevant historical info, instructional interventions, related services, age diagnosed, objective data (aptitude, achievement, info processing), test scores (standard, percentile and grade equivalents) and describe functional limitations.
  ADHD: Diagnosis based on DSM-V; history of behaviors impairing functioning in academic setting; diagnostic interview; history of symptoms; evidence of ongoing behaviors.
  ASD: P sycho ed evaluation
Documentation submitted to: ALP Office
Special Ed. HS course work accepted: No
Separate application required for program services: Yes
Contact Information
Name of program or department: Alternative Learners Project (ALP)
Telephone: 570-674-6205
Fax: 570-674-3026

Misericordia University

Additional Information
The ALP students can participate in the BRIDGE Program. The BRIDGE program brings ALP students to campus one week prior to the start of freshman year and features a series of assessments and workshops designed to assist students in identifying both strengths and needs in their learning styles. They receive training in the use of the Learning Strategies Curriculum, designed to help students become more effective and efficient learners. The ALP staff works with students to establish their Program of Accommodations.

GENERAL ADMISSIONS
Very important factors considered include: rigor of secondary school record, academic GPA, standardized test scores, character/personal qualities. *Important factors considered include:* class rank, extracurricular activities, talent/ability, volunteer work. *Other factors considered include:* application essay, recommendation(s), interview, first generation, alumni/ae relation, work experience, level of applicant's interest. *Freshman Admission Requirements:* High school diploma is required and GED is accepted. *Academic units required:* 4 English, 4 math, 4 science, 4 social studies.

ACCOMMODATION OR SERVICES
Accommodations are decided upon an individual basis after a thorough review of appropriate, current documentation. The accommodations requests must be supported through the documentation provided and must be logically linked to the current impact of the condition on academic functioning.

FINANCIAL AID
Students should submit: FAFSA. Applicants will be notified of awards on a rolling basis beginning 3/15. The Princeton Review suggests that all financial aid forms be submitted as soon as possible after October 1. *Need-based scholarships/grants offered:* College/university scholarship or grant aid from institutional funds; Federal Nursing Scholarships; Federal Pell; Private scholarships; SEOG; State scholarships/grants. *Loan aid offered:* Direct PLUS loans; Direct Subsidized Stafford Loans; Direct Unsubsidized Stafford Loans. Federal Work-Study Program available. Institutional employment available.

CAMPUS LIFE
Activities: Campus Ministries; Choral groups; Dance; Drama/theater; Jazz band; Literary magazine; Music ensembles; Radio station; Student government; Student newspaper; Television station; Yearbook. **Organizations:** 27 registered organizations, 1 honor society, 1 religious organization. **Athletics (Intercollegiate):** *Men:* baseball, basketball, cross-country, golf, lacrosse, soccer, swimming, tennis, track/field (outdoor). *Women:* basketball, cheerleading, cross-country, field hockey, lacrosse, soccer, softball, swimming, tennis, track/field (outdoor), volleyball. **On-Campus Highlights:** Anderson Sports and Health Center, Banks Student Life Center, Mangelsdorf Field, Bevevino Library, Insalaco Hall.

ACCOMMODATIONS

Allowed in exams:	
Calculators	Yes
Dictionary	Yes
Computer	Yes
Spell-checker	Yes
Extended test time	Yes
Scribe	Yes
Proctors	Yes
Oral exams	Yes
Note-takers	Yes
Support services for students with	
LD	Yes
ADHD	Yes
ASD	Yes
Distraction-reduced environment	Yes
Recording of lecture allowed	Yes
Reading technology:	Yes
Audio books	Yes
Other assistive technology	Yes
Priority registration	No
Added costs for services:	
For LD:	No
For ADHD:	No
For ASD:	No
LD specialists	Yes
ADHD & ASD coaching	No
ASD specialists	No
Professional tutors	No
Peer tutors	Yes
Max. hours/week for services	10
How professors are notified of student approved accommodations	By Program Coordinators

COLLEGE GRADUATION REQUIREMENTS

Course waivers allowed	No
Course substitutions allowed	No

Neumann University

ONE NEUMANN DRIVE, ASTON, PA 19014-1298 • ADMISSIONS: 610-558-5616 • FAX: 610-361-2548

CAMPUS

Type of school	Private (nonprofit)
Environment	Metropolis
Support	S

STUDENTS

Undergrad enrollment	1,997
% male/female	34/66
% from out of state	31
% frosh live on campus	82

FINANCIAL FACTS

Annual tuition	$28,710
Room and board	$12,520
Required fees	$1,340

GENERAL ADMISSIONS INFO

Application fee	$35

Nonfall registration accepted. Admission may be deferred for a maximum of 2 semesters.

Range SAT EBRW	450–550
Range SAT Math	440–530
Range ACT Composite	15–20

ACADEMICS

Student/faculty ratio	15:1
% students returning for sophomore year	77
% students graduating within 4 years	38
% students graduating within 6 years	57

Most classes have 10–19 students. Most lab/discussion sessions have 10–19 students.

PROGRAMS/SERVICES FOR STUDENTS WITH LEARNING DIFFERENCES

Neumann University, consistent with its Mission Statement, is committed to providing equal educational opportunities to all qualified students with disabilities. In accordance with Section 504 of the Rehabilitation Act of 1973 and the Americans with Disabilities Act of 1990, Neumann University will provide appropriate and reasonable accommodations which allow equal access to its educational programs. A student with disabilities is defined as anyone having one or more physical or mental impairments that limit major life activities. Some examples would be vision impairments, hearing impairments, learning disabilities, and orthopedic or mobility impairments. Students are responsible for declaring their disabilities to the University in order to be eligible for accommodations or special services.

ADMISSIONS

Neumann University's undergraduate admissions have a rolling admissions policy. Interviews are not required, but strongly recommended.

Additional Information

A student declares his/her disability to Neumann University by providing the Disabilities Services Coordinator of the John C. Ford Academic Resource Center (ARC) with current documentation of the disability by a recognized authority. The declaration remains confidential unless the student provides the Coordinator with written permission to release

ADMISSIONS INFO FOR STUDENTS WITH LEARNING DIFFERENCES

SAT/ACT required: Yes
Interview required: No
Essay required: Not Applicable
Additional application required: Yes
Documentation required for:
  LD: A letter from a physician, on official letterhead, signed by the physician, that details the diagnosis of ADHD, together with the patient's history of the condition, the prescribed treatment of the condition, and any side effects of the condition that may affect postsecondary study.
  ADHD: An Evaluation Report (Psychological, Psychoeducational, Psychiatric, or Neuropsychological) that shows an appropriate diagnosis of ASD with the record of tests taken, the interpretation of those tests, and interviews that lead to the diagnosis.
  ASD: Students are required to provide an evaluation report (Psychological, Psychoeducational, Psychiatric, or Neuropsychological) documenting an appropriate diagnosis of ASD with the record of tests taken, the interpretation of those tests, and interviews that lead to the diagnosis.
Documentation submitted to: ARC - Disabilities Services Office
Special Ed. HS course work accepted: Yes
Separate application required for program services: Yes
# of students last year receiving services/accommodations for:
  LD: 76
  ADHD: 64
Contact Information
Name of program or department: ARC - Disabilities Services Office
Telephone: 610-361-5471
Fax: 610-358-4564
Email: disAbilities@neumann.edu

Neumann University

this information. Once the documentation of the disability is on record, Neumann University will provide reasonable accommodations to assist the student in fulfilling his/her academic pursuits. By law, the University is not responsible for making special accommodations for a student who has not declared and documented his/her disabilities. If a student wishes to appeal a decision regarding an academic matter, the student must follow the grievance procedure as stated in the Academic Information of the University catalog. Once the documentation of the disability has been filed, the student is also responsible for communicating his/her particular needs to the Disabilities Services Coordinator prior to the start of each semester. At this time, the student may fill out and sign a Disclosure and Notification Form, which gives ARC personnel permission to contact the appropriate faculty member(s) regarding the student's particular needs. Students are also invited and encouraged to discuss their needs with their teachers, the Director of Counseling, and the Director of Health Services.

GENERAL ADMISSIONS

Very important factors considered include: rigor of secondary school record, academic GPA, standardized test scores. *Important factors considered include:* interview. *Other factors considered include:* application essay, recommendation(s), extracurricular activities, talent/ability, character/personal qualities, first generation, alumni/ae relation, volunteer work, work experience, level of applicant's interest. *Freshman Admission Requirements:* High school diploma is required and GED is accepted. *Academic units required:* 4 English, 2 math, 2 science, 2 foreign language, 2 social studies, 4 academic electives. *Academic units recommended:* 4 English, 2 math, 3 science, 2 science labs, 2 foreign language, 2 social studies, 4 academic electives.

ACCOMMODATION OR SERVICES

Accommodations are decided upon an individual basis after a thorough review of appropriate, current documentation. The accommodations requests must be supported through the documentation provided and must be logically linked to the current impact of the condition on academic functioning.

FINANCIAL AID

Students should submit: FAFSA; State aid form. Applicants will be notified of awards on a rolling basis beginning 3/1. The Princeton Review suggests that all financial aid forms be submitted as soon as possible after October 1. *Need-based scholarships/grants offered:* College/university scholarship or grant aid from institutional funds; Federal Pell; Private scholarships; SEOG; State scholarships/grants. *Loan aid offered:* Direct PLUS loans; Direct Subsidized Stafford Loans; Direct Unsubsidized Stafford Loans. Federal Work-Study Program available.

CAMPUS LIFE

Activities: Campus Ministries; Choral groups; Dance; Drama/theater; Jazz band; Literary magazine; Music ensembles; Musical theater; Pep band; Radio station; Student government; Student newspaper; Symphony orchestra; Television station. **Organizations:** 14 registered organizations, 4 honor societies, 2 religious organizations. **Athletics (Intercollegiate):** *Men:* baseball, basketball, cross-country, golf, ice hockey, lacrosse, soccer, tennis. *Women:* basketball, cross-country, field hockey, ice hockey, lacrosse, soccer, softball, tennis, volleyball. **On-Campus Highlights:** Neumann Media Radio Station, Knight's Cafe, Library, Mirenda Center, Residence Halls.

ACCOMMODATIONS

Allowed in exams:	
Calculators	Yes
Dictionary	No
Computer	Yes
Spell-checker	Yes
Extended test time	Yes
Scribe	Yes
Proctors	Yes
Oral exams	Yes
Note-takers	Yes
Support services for students with	
LD	Yes
ADHD	Yes
ASD	Yes
Distraction-reduced environment	Yes
Recording of lecture allowed	Yes
Reading technology:	Yes
Audio books	Yes

Other assistive technologyTake-home exams or other testing accommodations, early syllabus, priority seating, proofreading services, accommodations counseling, adaptive technology, paratransit, text-to-speech software, speech-to-text software, ZoomText software, Kurzweil 3000 softw

Priority registration	Yes
Added costs for services:	
For LD:	No
For ADHD:	No
For ASD:	No
LD specialists	No
ADHD & ASD coaching	Yes
ASD specialists	Yes
Professional tutors	Yes
Peer tutors	Yes
Max. hours/week for services	Varies
How professors are notified of student approved accommodations	Director and student

COLLEGE GRADUATION REQUIREMENTS

Course waivers allowed	Yes

In what courses As a last resort, students with certain documented disabilities, such as severe dyslexia or dyscalculia, can, with the approval of the Vice President for Academic Affairs, receive waivers for certain specific courses for those courses required.

Course substitutions allowed	Yes

In what courses
Students with certain documented disabilities, such as severe dyslexia or dyscalculia, can, with the approval of the Vice President for Academic Affairs, substitute certain specific courses required for graduation, particularly for math or foreign language.

Penn State University Park

201 Old Main, University Park, PA 16802 • Admissions: 814-865-5471 • Fax: 814-863-7590

CAMPUS
Type of school	Public
Environment	Town
Support	S

STUDENTS
Undergrad enrollment	40,552
% male/female	53/47
% from out of state	34
% frosh live on campus	NR

FINANCIAL FACTS
Annual in-state tuition	$17,416
Annual out-of-state tuition	$33,820
Room and board	$11,570
Required fees	$1,038

GENERAL ADMISSIONS INFO
Application fee	$65
Priority deadline	11/30

Nonfall registration accepted. Admission may be deferred for a maximum of One year.

Range SAT EBRW	580–660
Range SAT Math	580–680
Range ACT Composite	25–30

ACADEMICS
Student/faculty ratio	16:1
% students returning for sophomore year	93
% students graduating within 4 years	67
% students graduating within 6 years	85

Most classes have 10–19 students.
Most lab/discussion sessions have 10–19 students.

PROGRAMS/SERVICES FOR STUDENTS WITH LEARNING DIFFERENCES
The goal of Penn State's academic support services for students with learning disabilities is to ensure that students receive appropriate accommodations so that they can function independently and meet the academic demands of a competitive university. Students with learning disabilities should be able to complete college-level courses with the help of support services and classroom accommodations. To receive any of the support services, students must submit documentation of their learning disability to the learning disability specialist in the Office for Disability Services (ODS). Documentation should be a psychoeducational report from a certified or licensed psychologist completed within the past 3 years. The report should include measures of intellectual functioning and measures of achievement that describe current levels of functioning in reading, mathematics, and written language. Students with ADHD should have the professional who diagnosed them complete the ADHD Verification Form and submit it to the Office for Disability Services.

ADMISSIONS
There is no special application process for students with learning disabilities or attention deficit hyperactivity disorder, and these students are considered for admission on the same basis as other applicants. The minimum 50 percent of admitted students have a GPA between 3.52 and 3.97 and an ACT score between 26 and 30 or an SAT score between 1750 and 1990. Course requirements include 4 years of English, 3 years of math, 3 years of science, 2 years of a foreign language, and 3 years of social studies. If the applicant's high school grades and test scores are low, students may submit a letter explaining why their ability to succeed in college is higher than indicated by their academic records. The Admissions Office will consider this information as it is voluntarily provided. The acceptable ACT or SAT score will depend on the high school grades and class rank of the student. Two-thirds of the evaluation is based on high school grades and one-third on test scores. Once admitted, students must submit documentation of their learning disability to receive support services. Students may seek admission as a provisional or nondegree student if they do not meet criteria required for admission as a degree candidate. Any student may enroll as a nondegree student.

ADMISSIONS INFO FOR STUDENTS WITH LEARNING DIFFERENCES
SAT/ACT required: Yes
Interview required: Not Applicable
Essay required: Not Applicable
Additional application required: Not Applicable
Documentation required for:
  LD: See: http://equity.psu.edu/student-disability-resources/guidelines/learning-disorders
  ADHD: See: http://equity.psu.edu/student-disability-resources/guidelines/ad-hd
  ASD: See: http://equity.psu.edu/student-disability-resources/guidelines/asd
Documentation submitted to: Support Program/Services
Special Ed. HS course work accepted: Not Applicable
Separate application required for program services: Not Applicable
Contact Information
Name of program or department: Student Disability Resources
Telephone: 814-863-1807
Fax: 814-863-3217
Email: http://equity.psu.edu/student-disability-resources/contact

Penn State University Park

Additional Information

Students with LD are encouraged to participate in the Buddy Program; incoming students are matched with a senior buddy who is a current student with a disability and is available to share experiences with a junior buddy. Other services include providing audiotaped textbooks, arranging course substitutions with academic departments (when essential requirements are not involved), providing test accommodations, and providing individual counseling. Assistance with note-taking is offered through the ODS. Services are offered in a mainstream setting. The Learning Assistance Center operates a Math Center, Tutoring Center, Writing Center, and Computer Learning Center. Students may receive academic help either individually or in small groups for a number of different courses. One-on-one academic assistance is available through the Office of Disability Services. Graduate clinicians provide individual assistance with study skills, time management, and compensatory learning strategies.

GENERAL ADMISSIONS

Very important factors considered include: academic GPA, standardized test scores. *Important factors considered include:* rigor of secondary school record. *Other factors considered include:* class rank, application essay, extracurricular activities, talent/ability, character/personal qualities, alumni/ae relation, geographical residence, state residency, volunteer work, work experience. *Freshman Admission Requirements:* High school diploma is required and GED is accepted. *Academic units required:* 4 English, 3 math, 3 science, 2 foreign language, 3 social studies. *Academic units recommended:* 3 foreign language.

ACCOMMODATION OR SERVICES

Accommodations are decided upon an individual basis after a thorough review of appropriate, current documentation. The accommodations requests must be supported through the documentation provided and must be logically linked to the current impact of the condition on academic functioning.

FINANCIAL AID

Students should submit: FAFSA. The Princeton Review suggests that all financial aid forms be submitted as soon as possible after October 1. *Need-based scholarships/grants offered:* College/university scholarship or grant aid from institutional funds; Federal Pell; Private scholarships; SEOG; State scholarships/grants. *Loan aid offered:* Direct PLUS loans; Direct Subsidized Stafford Loans; Direct Unsubsidized Stafford Loans. Federal Work-Study Program available. Institutional employment available.

CAMPUS LIFE

Activities: Campus Ministries; Choral groups; Concert band; Dance; Drama/theater; International Student Organization; Jazz band; Literary magazine; Marching band; Model UN; Music ensembles; Musical theater; Opera; Pep band; Radio station; Student government; Student newspaper; Student-run film society; Symphony orchestra; Television station; Yearbook. **Organizations:** 784 registered organizations, 34 honor societies, 49 religious organizations. 58 fraternities, 32 sororities. **Athletics (Intercollegiate):** *Men:* baseball, basketball, cheerleading, cross-country, diving, fencing, football, golf, gymnastics, lacrosse, soccer, swimming, tennis, track/field (outdoor), track/field (indoor), volleyball, wrestling. *Women:* basketball, cheerleading, cross-country, diving, fencing, field hockey, golf, gymnastics, lacrosse, soccer, softball, swimming, tennis, track/field (outdoor), track/field (indoor), volleyball. **On-Campus Highlights:** Hetzel Union Building, Pattee/Paterno Library, The Creamery, Old Main, The Lion Shrine.

ACCOMMODATIONS

Allowed in exams:

Calculators	Yes
Dictionary	Not Applicable
Computer	Yes
Spell-checker	Yes
Extended test time	Yes
Scribe	Yes
Proctors	Yes
Oral exams	Yes
Note-takers	Yes

Support services for students with

LD	Yes
ADHD	Yes
ASD	Yes
Distraction-reduced environment	Yes
Recording of lecture allowed	Yes
Reading technology:	Yes
Audio books	No
Other assistive technology	Live Scribe pens for note-taking.
Priority registration	Yes

Added costs for services:

For LD:	No
For ADHD:	No
For ASD:	No
LD specialists	No
ADHD & ASD coaching	No
ASD specialists	No
Professional tutors	Yes
Peer tutors	Not Applicable
Max. hours/week for services	Varies
How professors are notified of student approved accommodations	Student

COLLEGE GRADUATION REQUIREMENTS

Course waivers allowed	No
Course substitutions allowed	Yes
In what courses	Foreign Language

Saint Joseph's University (PA)

5600 City Avenue, Philadelphia, PA 19131 • Admissions: 888-BE-A-HAWK • Fax: 610-660-1314

CAMPUS

Type of school	Private (nonprofit)
Environment	Metropolis
Support	CS

STUDENTS

Undergrad enrollment	5,004
% male/female	45/55
% from out of state	53
% frosh live on campus	96

FINANCIAL FACTS

Annual tuition	$44,793
Room and board	$14,840
Required fees	$180

GENERAL ADMISSIONS INFO

Application fee	$50
Priority deadline	2/1

Nonfall registration accepted. Admission may be deferred.

Range SAT EBRW	560–640
Range SAT Math	550–650
Range ACT Composite	23–28

ACADEMICS

Student/faculty ratio	11:1.
% students returning for sophomore year	91
students graduating within 4 years	76
students graduating within 6 years	82

Most classes have 20-29 students.

PROGRAMS/SERVICES FOR STUDENTS WITH LEARNING DIFFERENCES

The Success Center offers a variety of programs and services to meet the academic needs of the undergraduate and graduate students. There is an Office of Learning Resources within the SDS, that runs the College Transition Coaching program to assist students in navigating the transition from high school to college. In the summer, this Office offers a summer pre-college program, too.

ADMISSIONS

True to the Jesuit Tradition, the admission process is designed to get to know the applicant as a whole person—not just numbers without context. The application is reviewed on the basis of academic and personal accomplishments, with primary consideration given to the high school record and strong academic performance in college preparatory courses. The university will also consider the personal essay, letter of academic recommendation, and extracurricular involvement. Submission of standardized test scores is optional. The average GPA is 3.5. Applicants to Jefferson's 3+3 Doctorate of Physical Therapy and 3+2 Master's of Occupational Therapy programs must have test scores on file in order to be reviewed for academic eligibility. Students may still be reviewed as a test-optional applicant for admission to SJU only. Interviews are open to high school seniors to meet one-on-one with a representative from admissions. However, interviews are not required and those who cannot interview are not at a disadvantage.

Additional Information

Peer tutoring is offered in multiple subjects and there is supplemental instruction session in 6 subjects. They also help to organize study groups. There are appointments available for strategy development in approaching academic classes. There are note taker available, books in alternative formats and exams in alternative formats.

APPLICATION REQUIREMENTS FOR SERVICES

SAT/ACT required: No
Interview required: No
Essay required: No
Additional application required: No
Documentation required for:
  LD: Psycho ed evaluation to include: relevant historical info, instructional interventions, related services, age diagnosed, objective data (aptitude, achievement, info processing), test scores (standard, percentile and grade equivalents) and describe functional limitations.
  ADHD: Diagnosis based on DSM-V; history of behaviors impairing functioning in academic setting; diagnostic interview; history of symptoms; evidence of ongoing behaviors.
  ASD: Psycho ed evaluation.
Documentation submitted to: Disability Services
Separate application required for program services: No
Contact Information
Name of program or department: Office of Student Disability Services
Telephone: 610-660-1774
Fax: 610-660-3053

Saint Joseph's University (PA)

GENERAL ADMISSIONS

Very important factors considered include: rigor of secondary school record, class rank, academic GPA. Important factors considered include: application essay, standardized test scores, recommendation(s). Other factors considered include: interview, extracurricular activities, talent/ability, character/personal qualities, first generation, alumni/ae relation, geographical residence, racial/ethnic status, volunteer work, work experience, level of applicant's interest. Freshman Admission Requirements: High school diploma is required and GED is accepted Academic units required: 4 English, 3 math, 3 science, 2 foreign language, 3 social studies, 5 academic electives,

ACCOMMODATION OR SERVICES

Accommodations are decided upon an individual basis after a thorough review of appropriate, current documentation. The accommodations requests must be supported through the documentation provided and must be logically linked to the current impact of the condition on academic functioning.

FINANCIAL AID

Students should submit: FAFSA. Applicants will be notified of awards on a rolling basis beginning 3/31.. The Princeton Review suggests that all financial aid forms be submitted as soon as possible after October 1. Need-based scholarships/grants offered: College/university scholarship or grant aid from institutional funds; Federal Pell; Private scholarships; SEOG; State scholarships/grants Loan aid offered: Direct PLUS loans; Direct Subsidized Stafford Loans; Direct Unsubsidized Stafford Loans Federal Work-Study Program available. Institutional employment available.

CAMPUS LIFE

Activities: Campus Ministries; Choral groups; Dance ; Drama/theater; International Student Organization; Jazz band; Literary magazine; Music ensembles; Musical theater; Pep band; Radio station ; Student government; Student newspaper; Student-run film society; Yearbook Organizations: 100 registered organizations, 20 honor societies, 4 fraternities, 4 sororities, Athletics (Intercollegiate): Men: baseball, basketball, crew/rowing, cross-country, golf, lacrosse, soccer, tennis, track/field (outdoor), track/field (indoor) Women: basketball, crew/rowing, cross-country, field hockey, lacrosse, soccer, softball, tennis, track/field (outdoor), track/field (indoor). On-Campus Highlights: Campion / The Perch, Post Learning Commons, Hagan Arena, Merion Hall, Hawks Landing.

ACCOMMODATIONS

Allowed in exams:

Calculators	Yes
Dictionary	Yes
Computer	Yes
Spell-checker	Yes
Extended test time	Yes
Scribe	Yes
Proctors	Yes
Oral exams	Yes
Note-takers	Yes

Support services for students with

LD	Yes
ADHD	Yes
ASD	Yes
Distraction-reduced environment	Yes
Recording of lecture allowed	Yes
Reading technology:	Yes
Audio books	Yes

Other assistive technology livescribe, screen readers, enlarged print, braille, closed captioning, interpreting services

Priority registration	Yes

Added costs of services:

For LD:	No
For ADHD:	No
For ASD:	No
LD specialists	No
ADHD & ASD coaching	Yes
ASD specialists	Yes
Professional tutors	Yes
Peer tutors	Yes
Max. hours/week for services	1
How professors are notified of student approved accommodations	Director

COLLEGE GRADUATION REQUIREMENTS

Course waivers allowed	Yes

In what courses
   Must be approved for the waiver. foreign language

Course substitutions allowed	Yes

In what courses
   Must be approved for the waiver. foreign language

Seton Hill University

1 S<small>ETON</small> H<small>ILL</small> D<small>RIVE</small>, G<small>REENSBURG</small>, PA 15601 • A<small>DMISSIONS</small>: 724-838-4255 • F<small>AX</small>: 724-830-1294

CAMPUS

Type of school	Private (nonprofit)
Environment	Town
Support	S

STUDENTS

Undergrad enrollment	1,650
% male/female	35/65
% from out of state	23
% frosh live on campus	81

FINANCIAL FACTS

Annual tuition $35,248	
Room and board	$11,884
Required fees	$500

GENERAL ADMISSIONS INFO

Application fee	$35
Priority deadline	5/1
Regular application deadline	8/15

Nonfall registration accepted. Admission may be deferred for a maximum of 1 year.

Range SAT EBRW	510–610
Range SAT Math	510–610
Range ACT Composite	20–27

ACADEMICS

Student/faculty ratio	14:1
% students returning for sophomore year	84
% students graduating within 4 years	48
% students graduating within 6 years	58

Most classes have 20–29 students.
Most lab/discussion sessions have 10–19 students.

P<small>ROGRAMS</small>/S<small>ERVICES FOR</small> S<small>TUDENTS WITH</small> L<small>EARNING</small> D<small>IFFERENCES</small>

The Office of Disability Services offers academic support services to students with disabilities. The office works closely with students to assess individual needs and prepare a plan of accommodation, which may include note-takers, preferential seating, readers, extended time for testing, distraction-reduced testing environments, and access to special adaptive equipment and technology.

A<small>DMISSIONS</small>

Students with documented learning disabilities may request course substitutions for deficiencies in entrance courses based on the LD. Pre admission interviews are not required but are recommended. The admissions office can also determine if an applicant might be appropriate to be admitted through the C.A.P.S Program. Within the C.A.P.S. Program there are two academic support programs, the pre-freshman year Opportunity Program and Student Support Services. The Admissions Office primarily determines acceptance into these two programs. Students who feel they would benefit from the C.A.P.S. Program services may also apply by submitting an application that can be obtained through the C.A.P.S. Program Office.

Additional Information

There is a summer program that targets English and study skills. These are required programs for students with weak transcripts or SAT/ACT scores who otherwise meet admissions standards. The Opportunity Program is a weeklong learning experience that prepares students for the University's demanding academic culture. It is designed to provide students with

ADMISSIONS INFO FOR STUDENTS WITH LEARNING DIFFERENCES

SAT/ACT required: Yes
Interview required: No
Essay required: No
Additional application required: No
Documentation required for:
  LD: Psycho ed evaluation to include: relevant historical info, instructional interventions, related services, age diagnosed, objective data (aptitude, achievement, info processing), test scores (standard, percentile and grade equivalents) and describe functional limitations.
  ADHD: Diagnosis based on DSM-V; history of behaviors impairing functioning in academic setting; diagnostic interview; history of symptoms; evidence of ongoing behaviors.
  ASD: Psycho ed evaluation.
Documentation submitted to: Disability Services
Special Ed. HS course work accepted: No
Separate application required for program services: No
Contact Information
Name of program or department: Disability Services
Telephone: 724-838-4295
Fax: 724-830-4233
Email: bassi@setonhill.edu

Seton Hill University

an academic experience that will ease their transition from high school to college. The program provides services that assist the students in maximizing and enhancing academic potential. Accommodations once in the college may include, but are not limited to, preferential seating, note-taking services, tape-recorded lectures, extended time for projects, extended time for quizzes and tests, testing in distraction-reduced environments, alternative testing formats, tutoring, counseling, course substitutions, use of assisted technologies (e.g., spellcheckers), computer-based programs, and scribe services. Students are responsible for notifying professors about their disability and requesting accommodations. Course substitution requests are reviewed and considered on an individual basis. Skills classes for college credit are offered in time management techniques, note-taking strategies, test-taking strategies, and text reading.

GENERAL ADMISSIONS

Very important factors considered include: rigor of secondary school record, academic GPA, interview. *Important factors considered include:* class rank, standardized test scores, extracurricular activities, talent/ability, character/personal qualities. *Other factors considered include:* application essay, recommendation(s), alumni/ae relation, volunteer work, work experience, level of applicant's interest. *Freshman Admission Requirements:* High school diploma is required and GED is accepted. *Academic units required:* 4 English, 2 math, 1 science, 1 science lab, 2 social studies, 4 academic electives. *Academic units recommended:* 4 English, 2 math, 1 science, 1 science lab, 2 foreign language, 2 social studies, 4 academic electives.

ACCOMMODATION OR SERVICES

Accommodations are decided upon an individual basis after a thorough review of appropriate, current documentation. The accommodations requests must be supported through the documentation provided and must be logically linked to the current impact of the condition on academic functioning.

FINANCIAL AID

Students should submit: FAFSA; Institution's own financial aid form; State aid form. Applicants will be notified of awards on a rolling basis beginning 11/30. The Princeton Review suggests that all financial aid forms be submitted as soon as possible after October 1. *Need-based scholarships/grants offered:* College/university scholarship or grant aid from institutional funds; Federal Pell; Private scholarships; SEOG; State scholarships/grants. *Loan aid offered:* Direct PLUS loans; Direct Subsidized Stafford Loans; Direct Unsubsidized Stafford Loans. Federal Work-Study Program available. Institutional employment available.

CAMPUS LIFE

Activities: Campus Ministries; Choral groups; Concert band; Dance; Drama/theater; International Student Organization; Jazz band; Literary magazine; Marching band; Music ensembles; Musical theater; Pep band; Student government; Student newspaper; Symphony orchestra. **Organizations:** 53 registered organizations, 4 honor societies, 7 religious organizations. **Athletics (Intercollegiate):** *Men:* baseball, basketball, cross-country, football, lacrosse, soccer, track/field (outdoor), track/field (indoor), wrestling. *Women:* basketball, cross-country, equestrian sports, field hockey, golf, lacrosse, soccer, softball, tennis, track/field (outdoor), track/field (indoor), volleyball. **On-Campus Highlights:** Griffin's Cove, McKenna Recreation Center, Sullivan Lounge, Residence Halls, Lowe Dining Hall.

ACCOMMODATIONS

Allowed in exams:	
Calculators	Yes
Dictionary	Yes
Computer	Yes
Spell-checker	Yes
Extended test time	Yes
Scribe	Yes
Proctors	Yes
Oral exams	Yes
Note-takers	Yes
Support services for students with	
LD	Yes
ADHD	Yes
ASD	Yes
Distraction-reduced environment	Yes
Recording of lecture allowed	Yes
Reading technology:	Yes
Audio books	No
Other assistive technology	Yes
Priority registration	Yes
Added costs for services:	
For LD:	No
For ADHD:	No
For ASD:	No
LD specialists	No
ADHD & ASD coaching	No
ASD specialists	No
Professional tutors	No
Peer tutors	Yes
Max. hours/week for services	Unlimited
How professors are notified of student approved accommodations	By student

COLLEGE GRADUATION REQUIREMENTS

Course waivers allowed   Yes
 In what coursesAll appropriate waivers are reviewed and considered. Essential elements of a student's program cannot be waived.
Course substitutions allowed   Yes
 In what courses   All appropriate substitutions are reviewed and considered. Essential elements of a student's program cannot be substituted.

Temple University

1801 North Broad Street, Philadelphia, PA 19122 • Admissions: 215-204-7200 • Fax: 215-204-5694

CAMPUS
Type of school	Public
Environment	Metropolis
Support	CS

STUDENTS
Undergrad enrollment	29,007
% male/female	47/53
% from out of state	21
% frosh live on campus	77

FINANCIAL FACTS
Annual in-state tuition	$16,080
Annual out-of-state tuition	$28,176
Room and board	$11,916
Required fees	$890

GENERAL ADMISSIONS INFO
Application fee $55. Priority deadline 11/1
Regular application deadline   2/1
Nonfall registration accepted. Admission
may be deferred for a maximum of 1 year.

Range SAT EBRW	570 –660
Range SAT Math	560 –650
Range ACT Composite	24 –29

ACADEMICS
Student/faculty ratio	14:1
% students returning for sophomore year	90
students graduating within 4 years	45
students graduating within 6 years	71

Most classes have 10-19 students.
Most lab/discussion sessions have 20-29 students.

PROGRAMS/SERVICES FOR STUDENTS WITH LEARNING DIFFERENCES

Disability Resources and Services   Vision Statement - We envision a learning community that values people with diverse abilities and demonstrates through its actions a deep commitment to the full inclusion of all its members. Mission Statement - To advance Temple University's commitment to diversity and inclusion, Disability Resources and Services provides leadership to the university community to ensure that students with a disability have full access to the university experience. Our Values - Disability Inclusion, Full Access, Disability Pride, Dignity, Ingenuity, Independence Students should submit the most current and comprehensive documentation available.   Students can access academic accommodations, housing access, orientation and placement assessment accommodations, communication access, assistive technology and alternate format materials, scholarships, career development, peer mentoring, and social skills development.

ADMISSIONS INFO FOR STUDENTS WITH LEARNING DIFFERENCES
SAT/ACT required: No
Interview required: No
Essay required: No
Additional application required: No
Documentation required for:
  ADHD: Documentation should be current and relevant to higher education and answer the following questions: What is the disability or condition for which you are seeking services? How does the disability impact you in a higher education environment? What evaluations, tests or assessments were used to diagnose the disability and/or demonstrate its impact? What accommodations have been recommended or used in the past?   Some examples of documentation that may support a request for accommodations include: Psycho-educational evaluations Medical evaluations Speech or hearing evaluations IEPs or 504 plans Other professional evaluations that are specific to the disability
  ASD: Documentation should be current and relevant to higher education and answer the following questions: What is the disability or condition for which you are seeking services? How does the disability impact you in a higher education environment? What evaluations, tests or assessments were used to diagnose the disability and/or demonstrate its impact? What accommodations have been recommended or used in the past?   Some examples of documentation that may support a request for accommodations include: Psycho-educational evaluations Medical evaluations Speech or hearing evaluations IEPs or 504 plans Other professional evaluations that are specific to the disability
Documentation submitted to: Support Program/Services
Special Ed. HS course work accepted: No
Separate application required for program services: No
# of students last year receiving services/accommodations for:
  LD: 368
  ADHD: 505
  ASD: 81
Contact Information
Name of program or department: Disability Resources and Services
Telephone: 215-204-1280
Fax: 215-204-6794
Email: drs@temple.edu

Temple University

ADMISSIONS

When applying for admission to Temple, students with disabilities should follow the standard application process. The presence of a disability is not considered in admissions. Temple University is test optional (Temple Option). The Temple Option is an admissions path for talented students whose potential for academic success is not accurately captured by standardized test scores. Students who choose the Temple Option will submit self-reflective, short-answers to a few specially designed, open-ended questions instead of their SAT or ACT scores.

ADDITIONAL INFORMATION

Professors can distribute documents from the classroom through an electric version posted on Blackboard. This allows students to download it and use assistive technologies to read it. Professors can provide a calendar at the beginning of the semester, showing all dates for exams and important assignments. This availability helps those with tie management challenges keep up with their assignments.

GENERAL ADMISSIONS

Very important factors considered include: rigor of secondary school record, academic GPA. *Important factors considered include:* class rank. *Other factors considered include:* application essay, standardized test scores, recommendation(s), extracurricular activities, talent/ability, character/personal qualities, alumni/ae relation, geographical residence, state residency, volunteer work, work experience. *Freshman Admission Requirements:* High school diploma is required and GED is accepted *Academic units required:* 4 English, 3 math, 2 science, 1 science labs, 2 foreign language, 2 social studies, 1 history, 1 academic electives, 1 visual/performing arts, *Academic units recommended:* 4 English, 4 math, 3 science, 2 science labs, 2 foreign language, 2 social studies, 1 history, 3 academic electives, 1 visual/performing arts,

ACCOMMODATION OR SERVICES

Accommodations are decided upon an individual basis after a thorough review of appropriate, current documentation. The accommodations requests must be supported through the documentation provided and must be logically linked to the current impact of the condition on academic functioning.

FINANCIAL AID

Students should submit: FAFSA. Applicants will be notified of awards on a rolling basis beginning 2/1.. The Princeton Review suggests that all financial aid forms be submitted as soon as possible after October 1. *Need-based scholarships/grants offered:* College/university scholarship or grant aid from institutional funds; Federal Nursing Scholarships; Federal Pell; Private scholarships; SEOG; State scholarships/grants; United Negro College Fund *Loan aid offered:* Direct PLUS loans; Direct Subsidized Stafford Loans; Direct Unsubsidized Stafford Loans Federal Work-Study Program available. Institutional employment available.

CAMPUS LIFE

Activities: Choral groups; Concert band ; Dance ; Drama/theater; International Student Organization; Jazz band; Literary magazine; Marching band; Model UN; Music ensembles; Musical theater; Opera; Pep band; Radio station ; Student government; Student newspaper; Student-run film society; Symphony orchestra ; Television station; Yearbook Organizations: 232 registered organizations, 12 honor societies, 24 religious organizations. 11 fraternities, 9 sororities.

ACCOMMODATIONS

Allowed in exams:	
Calculators	Yes
Dictionary	Yes
Computer	Yes
Spell-checker	Yes
Extended test time	Yes
Scribe	Yes
Proctors	Yes
Oral exams	Yes
Note-takers	Yes
Support services for students with	
LD	Yes
ADHD	Yes
ASD	Yes
Distraction-reduced environment	Yes
Recording of lecture allowed	Yes
Reading technology:	Yes
Audio books	Yes
Other assistive technology	Smart pen,
software for reading, writing, organization, time management, books in alternate format	
Priority registration	Yes
Added costs for services:	
For LD:	No
For ADHD:	No
For ASD:	No
LD specialists	Yes
ADHD & ASD coaching	Yes
ASD specialists	Yes
Professional tutors	Yes
Peer tutors	Yes
Max. hours/week for services	
How professors are notified of student approved accommodations	Student

COLLEGE GRADUATION REQUIREMENTS

Course waivers allowed	Yes
In what courses	Math
Course substitutions allowed	Yes
In what courses	
Foreign language, other courses as appropriate	

University of Pittsburgh—Pittsburgh Campus

4200 FIFTH AVENUE, PITTSBURGH, PA 15260 • ADMISSIONS: 412-624-7488 • FAX: 412-648-8815

CAMPUS

Type of school	Public
Environment	City
Support	CS

STUDENTS

Undergrad enrollment	19,134
% male/female	49/51
% from out of state	28
% frosh live on campus	97

FINANCIAL FACTS

Annual in-state tuition	$18,130
Annual out-of-state tuition	$31,102
Room and board	$11,050
Required fees	$950

GENERAL ADMISSIONS INFO

Application fee	$45

Nonfall registration accepted. Admission may be deferred for a maximum of 1 year.

Range SAT EBRW	620–700
Range SAT Math	620–718
Range ACT Composite	27–32

ACADEMICS

Student/faculty ratio	15:1
% students returning for sophomore year	93
% students graduating within 4 years	65
% students graduating within 6 years	81

Most classes have 10–19 students. Most lab/discussion sessions have 20–29 students.

PROGRAMS/SERVICES FOR STUDENTS WITH LEARNING DIFFERENCES

The University of Pittsburgh is committed to providing equal opportunities in higher education to academically qualified students with disabilities. Students with disabilities will be integrated as completely as possible into the University experience. Disability Resources and Services (DRS) shares with you, the student, the responsibility for creating equal access toward achievement of your academic goals.

ADMISSIONS

Students with learning disabilities must meet the same admission criteria established for all applicants. It is important to have applications reviewed based on more than just the high school record and SAT/ACT scores. U Pitt recommends that students submit any supplemental information that they feel will help the committee get to know them better. The committee is looking for students who are well-rounded both in and out of the classroom. The Personal Essay is optional. However, applicants should definitely submit a personal essay if they want: scholarship consideration; consideration into the guaranteed admission to graduate/professional school; special consideration in the review process due to extenuating circumstances affecting a term or so of grades; and they would like the committee to review more than just the high school transcript and SAT/ACT scores. Likewise, while not required, letter(s) of recommendation from a person or people who knows the student well can help the admission office get to know the student better. Additional Information DRS individually designs and recommends services to enhance the skills and personal development of the student. Services available may include: exam accommodations, use of calculators, computer or spell checker in exams, scribes, proctors, controlled environments, alternative format, instructional strategy assistance, and assistive technology. There are three disability specialists on staff.

ADMISSIONS INFO FOR STUDENTS WITH LEARNING DIFFERENCES

SAT/ACT required: Yes
Interview required: Not Applicable
Essay required: Not Applicable
Additional application required: No
Documentation required for:
  LD: Psycho ed evaluation to include: relevant historical info, instructional interventions, related services, age diagnosed, objective data (aptitude, achievement, info processing), test scores (standard, percentile and grade equivalents) and describe functional limitations.
  ADHD: Diagnosis based on DSM-V; history of behaviors impairing functioning in academic setting; diagnostic interview; history of symptoms; evidence of ongoing behaviors.
  ASD: Documentation from a psychologist or psychiatrist which outlines diagnosis, duration and severity of symptoms, impact on academics.
Documentation submitted to: Disability Resources and Services
Special Ed. HS course work accepted: Not Applicable
Separate application required for program services: No
# of students last year receiving services/accommodations for:
  LD: 81
  ADHD: 131
  ASD: 23
Contact Information
Name of program or department: Disability Resources and Services
Telephone: 412-648-7890
Fax: 412-624-3346
Email: lculley@pitt.edu

University of Pittsburgh—Pittsburgh Campus

GENERAL ADMISSIONS

Very important factors considered include: rigor of secondary school record, academic GPA, standardized test scores. *Important factors considered include:* application essay. *Other factors considered include:* class rank, recommendation(s), extracurricular activities, talent/ability, character/personal qualities, first generation, alumni/ae relation, geographical residence, state residency, racial/ethnic status, volunteer work, work experience, level of applica *Freshman Admission Requirements:* High school diploma is required and GED is not accepted. *Academic units required:* 4 English, 3 math, 3 science, 3 science labs, 2 foreign language, 2 social studies, 3 academic electives. *Academic units recommended:* 4 English, 4 math, 4 science, 4 science labs, 3 foreign language, 3 social studies, 5 academic electives.

ACCOMMODATION OR SERVICES

Accommodations are decided upon an individual basis after a thorough review of appropriate, current documentation. The accommodations requests must be supported through the documentation provided and must be logically linked to the current impact of the condition on academic functioning.

FINANCIAL AID

Students should submit: FAFSA; State aid form. Applicants will be notified of awards on a rolling basis beginning 2/1. The Princeton Review suggests that all financial aid forms be submitted as soon as possible after October 1. *Need-based scholarships/grants offered:* College/university scholarship or grant aid from institutional funds; Federal Nursing Scholarships; Federal Pell; Private scholarships; SEOG; State scholarships/grants. *Loan aid offered:* Direct PLUS loans; Direct Subsidized Stafford Loans; Direct Unsubsidized Stafford Loans. Federal Work-Study Program available. Institutional employment available.

CAMPUS LIFE

Activities: Campus Ministries; Choral groups; Concert band; Dance; Drama/theater; International Student Organization; Jazz band; Literary magazine; Marching band; Model UN; Music ensembles; Musical theater; Pep band; Radio station; Student government; Student newspaper; Student-run film society; Symphony orchestra; Television station. **Organizations:** 395 registered organizations, 17 honor societies, 20 fraternities, 16 sororities. **Athletics (Intercollegiate):** *Men:* baseball, basketball, cross-country, diving, football, soccer, swimming, track/field (outdoor), wrestling. *Women:* basketball, cross-country, diving, gymnastics, soccer, softball, swimming, tennis, track/field (outdoor), volleyball. **On-Campus Highlights:** Cathedral of Learning, William Pitt Union, Heinz Chapel, Petersen Event Center, Sennott Square.

ACCOMMODATIONS

Allowed in exams:

Calculators	No
Dictionary	Yes
Computer	Yes
Spell-checker	Yes
Extended test time	Yes
Scribe	Yes
Proctors	Yes
Oral exams	No
Note-takers	Yes

Support services for students with

LD	Yes
ADHD	Yes
ASD	Yes
Distraction-reduced environment	Yes
Recording of lecture allowed	Yes
Reading technology:	Yes
Audio books	Yes

Other assistive technology   Kurzweil, JAWS and MAGic are all available in campus computing labs.

Priority registration	No

Added costs for services:

For LD:	No
For ADHD:	No
For ASD:	No
LD specialists	Yes
ADHD & ASD coaching	No
ASD specialists	Yes
Professional tutors	Yes
Peer tutors	Yes

Max. hours/week for services

How professors are notified of student approved accommodations Director and student

COLLEGE GRADUATION REQUIREMENTS

Course waivers allowed	No
Course substitutions allowed	Yes

In what coursesThere is a process in place for students to request a course substitution if their disability supports the request.

Widener University

ONE UNIVERSITY PLACE, CHESTER, PA 19013 • ADMISSIONS: 610-499-4126 • FAX: 610-499-4676

CAMPUS

Type of school	Private (nonprofit)
Environment	Town
Support	CS

STUDENTS

Undergrad enrollment	3,427
% male/female	44/56
% from out of state	40
% frosh live on campus	87

FINANCIAL FACTS

Annual tuition	$43,296
Room and board	$14,024
Required fees	$870

GENERAL ADMISSIONS INFO

Priority deadline 2/15.
Nonfall registration accepted. Admission may be deferred for a maximum of 1 academic year.

Range SAT EBRW	510–590
Range SAT Math	510–590
Range ACT Composite	20–25

ACADEMICS

Student/faculty ratio	14:1
% students returning for sophomore year	80
% students graduating within 4 years	44
% students graduating within 6 years	57

Most classes have 10–19 students.
Most lab/discussion sessions have 20–29 students.

PROGRAMS/SERVICES FOR STUDENTS WITH LEARNING DIFFERENCES

Disabilities Services is a structured mainstream support service designed to assist students enrolled in one of Widener's standard academic programs. Students wishing to use Disabilities Services must submit documentation that describes the nature of the learning disability including relevant evaluations and assessments. Each student at Disabilities Services has the option of meeting once or twice a week with a learning specialist in our academic coaching program. Typically, academic coaching sessions focus on time management, study skills, social and emotional adjustment, and academic planning. Disabilities Services serves as a campus advocate for the needs of students with LD by making sure that accommodations are provided when appropriate. Participation in our services is included in the basic tuition charge. Thus, there is no extra fee.

ADMISSIONS

Students with learning disabilities submit the general application form. Admission decisions are made by the Office of Admissions. Students should submit their application, an essay, and recommendations. ACT scores range between 17 and 27 and SAT scores range between 750 and 1300. There are no specific course requirements for admissions. High school GPA range is 2.0–4.0.

Additional Information

Disabilities Services is a personalized academic support and counseling service designed to help students with learning disabilities who meet university entrance requirements cope with the rigors of academic life. Students can sign up for academic coaching to meet with counselors who can help them understand and accept their disabilities; individualize learning strategies; teach self-advocacy; and link the students with the other Academic Support Services available at Widener. This office assures that professors understand which accommodations are needed. The Writing Center provides assistance with writing assignments and is staffed by professors. The Math Center offers individualized and group tutoring and is staffed by professors and experienced tutors. In addition, the Tutoring Office provides individual and group tutoring for the majority of undergraduate Widener courses.

ADMISSIONS INFO FOR STUDENTS WITH LEARNING DIFFERENCES

SAT/ACT required: Yes
Interview required: No
Essay required: Yes
Additional application required: No
Documentation required for:
  LD: Psycho ed evaluation to include: relevant historical info, instructional interventions, related services, age diagnosed, objective data (aptitude, achievement, info processing), test scores (standard, percentile and grade equivalents) and describe functional limitations.
  ADHD: Diagnosis based on DSM-V; history of behaviors impairing functioning in academic setting; diagnostic interview; history of symptoms; evidence of ongoing behaviors.
  ASD: Psycho ed evaluation.
Documentation submitted to: Enable
Special Ed. HS course work accepted: Yes
Separate application required for program services: No
# of students last year receiving services/accommodations for:
  LD: 200
Contact Information
Name of program or department: Disabilities Services
Telephone: 610-499-1266
Fax: 610-499-1192

Widener University

GENERAL ADMISSIONS

Very important factors considered include: rigor of secondary school record, class rank, academic GPA, standardized test scores. *Other factors considered include:* application essay, recommendation(s), interview, extracurricular activities, talent/ability, character/personal qualities, alumni/ae relation, volunteer work, level of applicant's interest. *Freshman Admission Requirements:* High school diploma is required and GED is accepted. *Academic units required:* 4 English, 3 math, 3 science, 2 foreign language, 3 social studies, 3 academic electives. *Academic units recommended:* 4 English, 4 math, 4 science, 2 science labs, 2 foreign language, 4 social studies, 3 academic electives.

ACCOMMODATION OR SERVICES

Accommodations are decided upon an individual basis after a thorough review of appropriate, current documentation. The accommodations requests must be supported through the documentation provided and must be logically linked to the current impact of the condition on academic functioning.

FINANCIAL AID

Students should submit: FAFSA. Applicants will be notified of awards on a rolling basis beginning 1/30. The Princeton Review suggests that all financial aid forms be submitted as soon as possible after October 1. *Need-based scholarships/grants offered:* College/university scholarship or grant aid from institutional funds; Federal Pell; Private scholarships; SEOG; State scholarships/grants. *Loan aid offered:* Direct PLUS loans; Direct Subsidized Stafford Loans; Direct Unsubsidized Stafford Loans. Federal Work-Study Program available. Institutional employment available.

CAMPUS LIFE

Activities: Campus Ministries; Choral groups; Concert band; Dance; Drama/theater; International Student Organization; Jazz band; Literary magazine; Marching band; Music ensembles; Pep band; Radio station; Student government; Student-run film society; Television station; Yearbook. **Organizations:** 80 registered organizations, 29 honor societies, 3 religious organizations. 7 fraternities, 3 sororities. **Athletics (Intercollegiate):** *Men:* baseball, basketball, cross-country, football, golf, lacrosse, soccer, swimming, tennis, track/field (outdoor), track/field (indoor). *Women:* basketball, cheerleading, cross-country, field hockey, lacrosse, soccer, softball, swimming, tennis, track/field (outdoor), track/field (indoor), volleyball. **On-Campus Highlights:** University Center, Java City and Residential Restaurant, Schwartz Athletic Center, Observatory, Art Gallery.

ACCOMMODATIONS

Allowed in exams:	
Calculators	Yes
Dictionary	Yes
Computer	Yes
Spell-checker	Yes
Extended test time	Yes
Scribe	Yes
Proctors	Yes
Oral exams	Yes
Note-takers	Yes
Support services for students with	
LD	Yes
ADHD	Yes
ASD	Yes
Distraction-reduced environment	Yes
Recording of lecture allowed	Yes
Reading technology:	Yes
Audio books	No
Other assistive technology	Yes
Priority registration	Yes
Added costs for services:	
For LD:	No
For ADHD:	No
For ASD:	No
LD specialists	Yes
ADHD & ASD coaching	No
ASD specialists	No
Professional tutors	Yes
Peer tutors	Yes
Max. hours/week for services	Unlimited
How professors are notified of student approved accommodations	By student

COLLEGE GRADUATION REQUIREMENTS

Course waivers allowed	No
Course substitutions allowed	No

Brown University

ONE PROSPECT STREET, PROVIDENCE, RI 02912 • ADMISSIONS: 401-863-2378 • FAX: 401-863-9300

CAMPUS
Type of school	Private (nonprofit)
Environment	City
Support	CS

STUDENTS
Undergrad enrollment	6,670
% male/female	47/53
% from out of state	94
% frosh live on campus	100

FINANCIAL FACTS
Annual Tuition	$54,320
Room and board	$14,670
Required fees	$1,236

GENERAL ADMISSIONS INFO
Application fee	$75
Regular application deadline	1/1

Nonfall registration accepted. Admission may be deferred for a maximum of 1 year.

Range SAT EBRW	705–780
Range SAT Math	700–790
Range ACT Composite	31–35

ACADEMICS
Student/faculty ratio	7:1
% students returning for sophomore year	98
% students graduating within 4 years	86
% students graduating within 6 years	95

Most classes have fewer than 10 students. Most lab/discussion sessions have 10–19 students.

PROGRAMS/SERVICES FOR STUDENTS WITH LEARNING DIFFERENCES
Brown has a long history of providing accommodations and services to students with learning disabilities. There are no specific general education requirements which can be helpful to students for whom a particular area may be very challenging. Documentation guidelines are available on the SEAS website as well as information about services and accommodations: http://www.brown.edu/campus-life/support/accessibility-services/

ADMISSIONS
Brown has a long history of providing accommodations and services to students with learning disabilities. There are no specific general education requirements which can be helpful to students for whom a particular area may be very challenging. Documentation guidelines are available on the SEAS website as well as information about services and accommodations: http://www.brown.edu/campus-life/support/accessibility-services/

Additional Information
Brown University has as its primary aim the education of a highly qualified and diverse student body. Brown's commitment to students with disabilities is based on awareness of what students require for success and seeks to foster an environment in which that success may be achieved. Group tutoring is offered for introductory courses in science, math, economics, and statistics. Students are assigned to small groups that meet weekly to review important or difficult topics covered in class that week. Tutors have either taken the course or proven competency, and have been trained by the Academic Support Staff. Students can receive assistance with quick questions in introductory and intermediate biology, chemistry, and physics. Students with disabilities who believe they may need accommodations should self-identify by registering with SEAS. SEAS staff will conduct a review and analysis prior to making a recommendation regarding the provision of reasonable accommodations. Requests for accommodations are evaluated individually, based on documentation, and completion of the registration process.

ADMISSIONS INFO FOR STUDENTS WITH LEARNING DIFFERENCES
SAT/ACT required: Yes
Interview required: No
Essay required: No
Additional application required: Not Applicable
Documentation required for:
  LD: A current, complete psycho-educational evaluation is required and will hopefully have been done when the student could be evaluated using adult scales. Aptitude testing such as the WAIS III; achievement testing such as the Woodcock-Johnson IV; and information processing as appropriate are required.
  ADHD: We prefer to have the same documentation that we request for documenting a learning disability. We require that the evaluation come from a qualified provider and that they use objective measures to make the diagnosis.
  ASD: The same documentation provided for LD/ADHD is often helpful, but sometimes documentation comes from a therapist.
Documentation submitted to: Support program/services
Special Ed. HS course work accepted: No
Separate application required for program services: No
Contact Information
Name of program or department: Student and Employee Accessibility Services
Telephone: 401-863-9588
Fax: 401-863-1444
Email: SEAS@brown.edu

Brown University

GENERAL ADMISSIONS

Very important factors considered include: rigor of secondary school record, class rank, academic GPA, application essay, standardized test scores, recommendation(s), talent/ability, character/personal qualities. *Important factors considered include:* extracurricular activities. *Other factors considered include:* interview, first generation, alumni/ae relation, geographical residence, state residency, racial/ethnic status, volunteer work, work experience. *Freshman Admission Requirements:* High school diploma is required and GED is accepted. *Academic units required:* 4 English, 3 math, 3 science, 2 science labs, 3 foreign language, 2 history, 1 academic elective. *Academic units recommended:* 4 English, 4 math, 4 science, 3 science labs, 4 foreign language, 1 social studies, 2 history, 1 academic elective, 1 visual/performing arts.

ACCOMMODATION OR SERVICES

Accommodations are decided upon an individual basis after a thorough review of appropriate, current documentation. The accommodations requests must be supported through the documentation provided and must be logically linked to the current impact of the condition on academic functioning.

FINANCIAL AID

Students should submit: CSS/Financial Aid PROFILE; FAFSA; Noncustodial PROFILE. Applicants will be notified of awards on or about 4/1. The Princeton Review suggests that all financial aid forms be submitted as soon as possible after October 1. *Need-based scholarships/ grants offered:* College/university scholarship or grant aid from institutional funds; Federal Pell; Private scholarships; SEOG; State scholarships/grants. *Loan aid offered:* Direct PLUS loans; Direct Subsidized Stafford Loans; Direct Unsubsidized Stafford Loans. Federal Work-Study Program available. Institutional employment available.

CAMPUS LIFE

Activities: Campus Ministries; Choral groups; Concert band; Dance; Drama/theater; International Student Organization; Jazz band; Literary magazine; Marching band; Model UN; Music ensembles; Musical theater; Opera; Pep band; Radio station; Student government; Student newspaper; Student-run film society; Symphony orchestra; Television station; Yearbook. **Organizations:** 400 registered organizations, 3 honor societies, 20 religious organizations. 8 fraternities, 2 sororities. **Athletics (Intercollegiate):** *Men:* baseball, basketball, crew/rowing, cross-country, diving, fencing, football, golf, ice hockey, lacrosse, soccer, squash, swimming, tennis, track/field (outdoor), track/field (indoor), water polo, wrestling. *Women:* basketball, crew/rowing, cross-country, diving, equestrian sports, fencing, field hockey, golf, gymnastics, ice hockey, lacrosse, skiing (downhill/alpine), soccer, softball, squash, swimming, tennis, track/field (outdoor), track/field (indoor), volleyball. **On-Campus Highlights:** The College Green (Main Green), Nelson Fitness Center, Libraries - including the John Hay Library, Orwig Music Library, Rockefeller Library, Sciences Library., Stephen Robert '62 Campus Center, Granoff Center for the Creative Arts.

ACCOMMODATIONS

Allowed in exams:	
Calculators	Yes
Dictionary	Not Applicable
Computer	Yes
Spell-checker	Yes
Extended test time	Yes
Scribe	Yes
Proctors	Yes
Oral exams	No
Note-takers	Yes
Support services for students with	
LD	Yes
ADHD	Yes
ASD	Yes
Distraction-reduced environment	Yes
Recording of lecture allowed	Yes
Reading technology:	Yes
Audio books	Yes
Other assistive technology ZoomText, JAWS, Inspiration, Naturally Speaking, Kurzweil 3000	
Priority registration	Not Applicable
Added costs for services:	
For LD:	Not Applicable
For ADHD:	Not Applicable
For ASD:	Not Applicable
LD specialists	Not Applicable
ADHD & ASD coaching	Yes
ASD specialists	Yes
Professional tutors	Yes
Peer tutors	Yes
Max. hours/week for services	2
How professors are notified of student approved accommodations	Student

COLLEGE GRADUATION REQUIREMENTS

Course waivers allowed	Not Applicable
In what courses	
Course substitutions allowed	Not Applicable
In what courses	

Bryant University

1150 Douglas Pike, Smithfield, RI 02917-1291 • Admissions: 401-232-6100 • Fax: 401-232-6731

CAMPUS
Type of school	Private (nonprofit)
Environment	Village
Support	CS

STUDENTS
Undergrad enrollment	3,449
% male/female	61/39
% from out of state	86
% frosh live on campus	95

FINANCIAL FACTS
Annual tuition	$43,076
Room and board	$15,702
Required fees	$897

GENERAL ADMISSIONS INFO
Application fee	$50
Regular application deadline	2/1

Nonfall registration accepted. Admission may be deferred for a maximum of 1 year.

Range SAT EBRW	560–630
Range SAT Math	560–650
Range ACT Composite	24–29

ACADEMICS
Student/faculty ratio	13:1
% students returning for sophomore year	90
% students graduating within 4 years	73
% students graduating within 6 years	79

Most classes have 10–19 students.
Most lab/discussion sessions have 10–19 students.

PROGRAMS/SERVICES FOR STUDENTS WITH LEARNING DIFFERENCES

Bryant University offers services for students with learning disabilities. The Academic Center for Excellence (ACE) is dedicated to helping Bryant students achieve their goal of academic success. Basically, the center provides study skills training to help students become self-reliant, independent, and confident learners. This is achieved through an internationally accredited peer tutoring program and study skills instruction by professional staff. Group sessions as a mode of instruction are encouraged and the staff engages in a partnership with students to help them achieve their goals. The Learning Specialist provides support for students with LD. In keeping with the philosophy of empowering Bryant students to achieve their goals of academic success, they also will receive assistance in learning how to access the comprehensive academic support services offered by the Academic Success Programs.

ADMISSIONS

Students are encouraged to self-disclose a learning challenge. All documentation should be sent to ACE. General admission criteria include an average GPA of 3.0. ACT/SAT are not required as Bryant is Test-Optional. A minimum of 16 units with the following courses is recommended: 4 years of English; 4 years of college prep math, including a year beyond Algebra II; 2 years of history or social science; 2 years of lab sciences; 2 years of foreign language. Interviews are not required but are encouraged.

Additional Information

Students with documented learning differences need to submit documentation and request academic accommodations through Access Services in the Academic Center for Excellence. Comprehensive documentation completed within the past three years must address the current impact of disability on the academic performance. Students are encouraged to submit their documentation after their acceptance and decision to enroll at Bryant. At the start of each semester, students will need to meet with someone from the ACE staff to discuss academic needs and request reasonable accommodations. The Academic Success Programs provide access to learning specialists who provide individualized assistance and group workshops on college-level study skill development.

ADMISSIONS INFO FOR STUDENTS WITH LEARNING DIFFERENCES
SAT/ACT required:
Interview required: Not Applicable
Essay required: Not Applicable
Additional application required: Not Applicable
Documentation required for:
  LD:Psycho ed evaluation to include: relevant historical info, instructional interventions, related services, age diagnosed, objective data (aptitude, achievement,
info processing), test scores (standard, percentile and grade equivalents) and describe functional limitations.
  ADHD: Diagnosis based on DSM-V; history of behaviors impairing functioning in academic setting; diagnostic interview; history of symptoms; evidence of ongoing behaviors.
  ASD: Psycho ed evaluation
Documentation submitted to: Support program/services
Special Ed. HS course work accepted: Not Applicable
Separate application required for program services: Yes
Contact Information
Name of program or department: Academic Center for Excellence
Telephone: 401-232-6532

Bryant University

Examples of some of the programs and services offered include: The Academic Center for Excellence, which is staffed by professional math specialists and peer tutors. The peer tutors are trained and certified by The College Reading and Learning Association and offer both one-on-one and group appointments for a variety of academic subjects. Learning Labs allow students to work with a specialist or peer tutor on math, economics, finance or accounting assignments. The Writing Center provides one-on-one services with professional writing specialists and student writing consultants, who are also CRLA trained and certified. The Writing Center staff work with students at all stages of the writing process, including brainstorming, outlining, thesis development, and draft editing. As a liaison among students, faculty, and administration, ACE encourages students with LD requiring special accommodations to schedule an appointment with a Learning Specialist as soon as they register for courses each semester.

GENERAL ADMISSIONS

Very important factors considered include: rigor of secondary school record, academic GPA. *Important factors considered include:* class rank, application essay, standardized test scores, recommendation(s). *Other factors considered include:* interview, extracurricular activities, talent/ability, character/personal qualities, first generation, alumni/ae relation, geographical residence, state residency, racial/ethnic status, volunteer work, work experience, level of applicant's interest. *Freshman Admission Requirements:* High school diploma is required and GED is accepted. *Academic units required:* 4 English, 4 math, 2 science, 2 science labs, 2 foreign language, 2 history. *Academic units recommended:* 4 English, 4 math, 3 science, 2 science labs, 2 foreign language, 3 history.

ACCOMMODATION OR SERVICES

Accommodations are decided upon an individual basis after a thorough review of appropriate, current documentation. The accommodations requests must be supported through the documentation provided and must be logically linked to the current impact of the condition on academic functioning.

FINANCIAL AID

Students should submit: FAFSA. Applicants will be notified of awards on or about 3/24. The Princeton Review suggests that all financial aid forms be submitted as soon as possible after October 1. *Need-based scholarships/grants offered:* College/university scholarship or grant aid from institutional funds; Federal Pell; Private scholarships; SEOG; State scholarships/grants. *Loan aid offered:* Direct PLUS loans; Direct Subsidized Stafford Loans; Direct Unsubsidized Stafford Loans. Federal Work-Study Program available. Institutional employment available.

CAMPUS LIFE

Activities: Campus Ministries; Choral groups; Dance; Drama/theater; International Student Organization; Jazz band; Literary magazine; Music ensembles; Musical theater; Pep band; Radio station; Student government; Student newspaper; Television station; Yearbook. **Organizations:** 87 registered organizations, 6 honor societies, 5 religious organizations. 6 fraternities, 2 sororities. **Athletics (Intercollegiate):** *Men:* baseball, basketball, cross-country, football, golf, lacrosse, soccer, swimming, tennis, track/field (outdoor), track/field (indoor). *Women:* basketball, cross-country, field hockey, lacrosse, soccer, softball, swimming, tennis, track/field (outdoor), track/field (indoor), volleyball. **On-Campus Highlights:** Fisher Student Center, Academic Center for Innovation, Chase Athletics and Wellness Center, Bello Center for Information andTechnology, Unistructure Rotunda.

ACCOMMODATIONS

Allowed in exams:

Calculators	Yes
Dictionary	No
Computer	Yes
Spell-checker	Yes
Extended test time	Yes
Scribe	Yes
Proctors	Yes
Oral exams	Yes
Note-takers	Yes

Support services for students with

LD	Yes
ADHD	Yes
ASD	Yes
Distraction-reduced environment	Yes
Recording of lecture allowed	Yes
Reading technology:	Yes
Audio books	Yes
Other assistive technology	Yes
Priority registration	No

Added costs for services:

For LD:	No
For ADHD:	No
For ASD:	No
LD specialists	Yes
ADHD & ASD coaching	No
ASD specialists	No
Professional tutors	Yes
Peer tutors	Yes
Max. hours/week for services	Varies
How professors are notified of student approved accommodations	Student and director

COLLEGE GRADUATION REQUIREMENTS

Course waivers allowed	No
Course substitutions allowed	No

Providence College

1 Cunningham Square, Providence, RI 02918 • Admissions: 401-865-2535 • Fax: 401-865-2826

CAMPUS
Type of school	Private (nonprofit)
Environment	City
Support	CS

STUDENTS
Undergrad enrollment	4,233
% male/female	45/55
% from out of state	91
% frosh live on campus	98

FINANCIAL FACTS
Annual Tuition	$49,600
Room and board	$14,700
Required fees	$790

GENERAL ADMISSIONS INFO
Application fee	$65.
Regular application deadline	1/15

Nonfall registration accepted. Admission may be deferred for a maximum of 1 year.

Range SAT EBRW	580–660
Range SAT Math	580–670
Range ACT Composite	26–30

ACADEMICS
Student/faculty ratio	12:1
% students returning for sophomore year	92
% students graduating within 4 years	80
% students graduating within 6 years	84

Most classes have 20–29 students. Most lab/discussion sessions have 20–29 students.

PROGRAMS/SERVICES FOR STUDENTS WITH LEARNING DIFFERENCES
The director of the Office of Academic Services and the faculty of the college are very supportive and are diligent about providing comprehensive services. The goal of the college is to be available to assist students whenever help is requested. After admission, the assistant director for Disability Services meets with the learning disabled students during the summer, prior to entry, to help them begin planning for freshman year. Students are monitored for four years. The college makes every effort to provide "reasonable accommodations."

ADMISSIONS
There is no special admissions process for students with learning disabilities. However, an interview is highly recommended, during which individualized course work is examined. General course requirements include four years English, three years math, three years foreign language, two years lab science, two years social studies, and two years electives. Students with learning disabilities who have lower test scores but a fairly good academic record may be accepted. The admission committee has the flexibility to overlook poor test scores for students with learning disabilities. Those who have higher test scores and reasonable grades in college-prep courses (C-plus/B) may also gain admission. Students should self-identify as learning disabled on their application.

Additional Information
The following services and accommodatations are available for students presenting appropriate documentation: the use of calculators, dictionaries and computers during exams; extended time on tests; distraction-free testing environment; scribes; proctors; oral exams; note-takers; tape recorders in class; assistive technology; and priority registration. Skills seminars (for no credit) are offered in study techniques and test-taking strategies. All students have access to the Tutorial Center and Writing Center. Services and accommodations are available for undergraduate and graduate students.

ADMISSIONS INFO FOR STUDENTS WITH LEARNING DIFFERENCES
SAT/ACT required: No
Interview required: Not Applicable
Essay required: Not Applicable
Additional application required: Not Applicable
Documentation required for:
  LD: Psycho ed evaluation to include: relevant historical info, instructional interventions, related services, age diagnosed, objective data (aptitude, achievement, info processing), test scores (standard, percentile and grade equivalents) and describe functional limitations.
  ADHD: Diagnosis based on DSM-V; history of behaviors impairing functioning in academic setting; diagnostic interview; history of symptoms; evidence of ongoing behaviors.
  ASD: Psycho ed evaluation
Documentation submitted to: Office of Academic Services
Special Ed. HS course work accepted: Not Applicable
Separate application required for program services: Not Applicable
Contact Information
Name of program or department: Office of Academic Services - OAS
Telephone: (401) 865-2494
Fax: (401) 865-1219
Email: OAS@providence.edu

Providence College

GENERAL ADMISSIONS

Very important factors considered include: rigor of secondary school record, academic GPA, application essay. *Important factors considered include:* recommendation(s), extracurricular activities, character/personal qualities. *Other factors considered include:* class rank, standardized test scores, talent/ability, first generation, alumni/ae relation, geographical residence, racial/ethnic status, volunteer work, work experience, level of applicant's interest. *Freshman Admission Requirements:* High school diploma is required and GED is not accepted. *Academic units required:* 4 English, 4 math, 3 science, 2 science labs, 3 foreign language, 2 social studies, 2 history. *Academic units recommended:* 4 English, 4 math, 4 science, 2 science labs, 4 foreign language, 2 social studies, 2 history.

ACCOMMODATION OR SERVICES

Accommodations are decided upon an individual basis after a thorough review of appropriate, current documentation. The accommodations requests must be supported through the documentation provided and must be logically linked to the current impact of the condition on academic functioning.

FINANCIAL AID

Students should submit: CSS/Financial Aid PROFILE; FAFSA. Applicants will be notified of awards on or about 3/15. The Princeton Review suggests that all financial aid forms be submitted as soon as possible after October 1. *Need-based scholarships/grants offered:* College/university scholarship or grant aid from institutional funds; Federal Pell; Private scholarships; SEOG; State scholarships/grants; United Negro College Fund. *Loan aid offered:* Direct PLUS loans; Direct Subsidized Stafford Loans; Direct Unsubsidized Stafford Loans. Federal Work-Study Program available. Institutional employment available.

CAMPUS LIFE

Activities: Campus Ministries; Choral groups; Concert band; Dance; Drama/theater; International Student Organization; Jazz band; Literary magazine; Music ensembles; Musical theater; Pep band; Radio station; Student government; Student newspaper; Student-run film society; Television station; Yearbook. **Organizations:** 112 registered organizations, 18 honor societies, 2 religious organizations. **Athletics (Intercollegiate):** *Men:* basketball, cross-country, diving, ice hockey, lacrosse, soccer, swimming, track/field (outdoor), track/field (indoor). *Women:* basketball, cross-country, diving, field hockey, ice hockey, soccer, softball, swimming, tennis, track/field (outdoor), track/field (indoor), volleyball. **On-Campus Highlights:** Ryan Center for Business Studies, Ruane Center for the Humanities, McPhail's Entertainment Facility, Concannon Fitness Center, Slavin Center - Student Center.

ACCOMMODATIONS

Allowed in exams:	
Calculators	Yes
Dictionary	Yes
Computer	Yes
Spell-checker	Yes
Extended test time	Yes
Scribe	Yes
Proctors	Yes
Oral exams	Yes
Note-takers	Yes
Support services for students with	
LD	Yes
ADHD	Yes
ASD	Yes
Distraction-reduced environment	Yes
Recording of lecture allowed	Yes
Reading technology:	No
Audio books	No
Other assistive technology	
Priority registration	Yes
Added costs for services:	
For LD:	No
For ADHD:	No
For ASD:	No
LD specialists	Yes
ADHD & ASD coaching	No
ASD specialists	No
Professional tutors	Yes
Peer tutors	Yes
Max. hours/week for services	Varies
How professors are notified of student approved accommodations	Student

COLLEGE GRADUATION REQUIREMENTS

Course waivers allowed	Yes
In what courses	Varies
Course substitutions allowed	Yes
In what courses	Varies

Rhode Island College

600 Mount Pleasant Avenue, Providence, RI 02908 • Admissions: 401-456-8234 • Fax: 401-456-8817

CAMPUS
Type of school	Public
Environment	City
Support	CS

STUDENTS
Undergrad enrollment	6,903
% male/female	31/69
% from out of state	14
% frosh live on campus	41

FINANCIAL FACTS
Annual in-state tuition	$7,637
Annual out-of-state tuition	$20,150
Room and board	$11,335
Required fees	$1,139

GENERAL ADMISSIONS INFO
Application fee	$50
Regular application deadline	3/15

Nonfall registration accepted.

Range SAT EBRW	450–560
Range SAT Math	430–530
Range ACT Composite	15–22

ACADEMICS
Student/faculty ratio	14:1
% students returning for sophomore year	75
% students graduating within 4 years	20
% students graduating within 6 years	46

PROGRAMS/SERVICES FOR STUDENTS WITH LEARNING DIFFERENCES

Rhode Island College strives to create and promote an environment that is conducive to learning for all students. Necessary accommodations require that administration, faculty, and staff be consistent and use flexibility in making adaptations, and that the students be flexible in adapting to and using alternative modes of learning and instruction. Students with disabilities may self-identify at any point, but are encouraged to do so at admission. A registration card is sent to all new students. Filling out this card and returning it to the Office of Student Life starts the process. Faculty is responsible for stating at the beginning of each semester verbally or in writing that the instructor is available to meet individually with students who require accommodations. The college wants students to feel comfortable requesting assistance, and faculty and fellow students are encouraged to be friendly and supportive. The college feels that the presence of students with individual ways of learning and coping serves as a learning experience for the professor, student, and class.

ADMISSIONS

Admission requirements are the same for all applicants. Freshman requirements include 4 years of English, 2 years of a foreign language, 3 years of mathematics (Algebra I, Algebra II, and geometry), 2 years of social studies, 2 years of science (biology and chemistry or physics), 0.5 unit in the arts, and 4.5 additional college-preparatory units. Most accepted students rank in the upper 50 percent of their class. SAT or ACT scores required. Students with LD/ADHD should submit the general application for admission. If a student does not meet admission requirements and is considered as a conditional admit, this would be done regardless of having an LD or ADHD.

Additional Information

The Paul V. Sherlock Center on Disabilities, founded at Rhode Island College in 1993, is a University Center on Excellence in Developmental Disabilities Education, Research, & Service. Since 1963, University Centers on Excellence in Developmental Disabilities

ADMISSIONS INFO FOR STUDENTS WITH LEARNING DIFFERENCES

SAT/ACT required: Yes
Interview required: No
Essay required: No
Additional application required: No
Documentation required for:
  LD: Psycho ed evaluation to include: relevant historical info, instructional interventions, related services, age diagnosed, objective data (aptitude, achievement, info processing), test scores (standard, percentile and grade equivalents) and describe functional limitations.
  ADHD: Diagnosis based on DSM-V; history of behaviors impairing functioning in academic setting; diagnostic interview; history of symptoms; evidence of ongoing behaviors.
  ASD: Psycho ed evaluation
Documentation submitted to: Both admissions and office of Student Life
Special Ed. HS course work accepted: No
Separate application required for program services: Yes
# of students last year receiving services/accommodations for:
  LD: 177
Contact Information
Name of program or department: Disability Services, Student Life Office
Telephone: 401-456-8061
Fax: 401-456-8702

(UCEDDs) have worked towards a shared vision that individuals with disabilities participate fully in their communities. Independence, productivity, and community inclusion are key components of this vision. The Certificate of Undergraduate Study (CUS) in College and Career Attainment at Rhode Island College offers students with intellectual disability (ID) the opportunity to self-direct academic coursework and internships to enhance their skills and knowledge critical to a variety of career choices. The CUS includes internships extending student knowledge and skills across four vocational internship experiences. The CUS is designed to include students with ID who are still eligible for special education through their local school district and students who have already graduated from high school.

General Admissions

Very important factors considered include: rigor of secondary school record, class rank, academic GPA. *Important factors considered include:* application essay, standardized test scores, recommendation(s). *Other factors considered include:* interview, extracurricular activities, talent/ ability, alumni/ae relation, volunteer work, work experience. *Freshman Admission Requirements:* High school diploma is required and GED is accepted. *Academic units required:* 4 English, 3 math, 2 science, 2 science labs, 2 foreign language, 2 social studies, 5 academic electives.

Accommodation or Services

Accommodations are decided upon an individual basis after a thorough review of appropriate, current documentation. The accommodations requests must be supported through the documentation provided and must be logically linked to the current impact of the condition on academic functioning.

Financial Aid

Students should submit: FAFSA; Institution's own financial aid form. Applicants will be notified of awards on a rolling basis beginning 2/15. The Princeton Review suggests that all financial aid forms be submitted as soon as possible after October 1. *Need-based scholarships/grants offered:* College/university scholarship or grant aid from institutional funds; Federal Pell; Private scholarships; SEOG; State scholarships/grants. *Loan aid offered:* Direct PLUS loans; Direct Subsidized Stafford Loans; Direct Unsubsidized Stafford Loans. Federal Work-Study Program available. Institutional employment available.

Campus Life

Activities: Choral groups; Concert band; Dance; Drama/theater; International Student Organization; Jazz band; Literary magazine; Music ensembles; Musical theater; Radio station; Student government; Student newspaper; Student-run film society; Symphony orchestra; Television station.

ACCOMMODATIONS

Allowed in exams:

Calculators	Yes
Dictionary	Yes
Computer	Yes
Spell-checker	Yes
Extended test time	Yes
Scribe	Yes
Proctors	No
Oral exams	Yes
Note-takers	Yes

Support services for students with

LD	Yes
ADHD	Yes
ASD	Yes
Distraction-reduced environment	Yes
Recording of lecture allowed	Yes
Reading technology:	Yes
Audio books	Yes
Other assistive technology	Larger

screen monitors, network printers, adjustable computer tables, a clearview optiplex enlarger and various specialized software

Priority registration	Yes

Added costs for services:

For LD:	No
For ADHD:	No
For ASD:	No
LD specialists	Yes
ADHD & ASD coaching	No
ASD specialists	No
Professional tutors	No
Peer tutors	Yes
Max. hours/week for services	Unlimited

How professors are notified of student approved accommodations
Student and director

COLLEGE GRADUATION REQUIREMENTS

Course waivers allowed	Yes

In what courses: English and others if not required by student's major.

Course substitutions allowed	Yes

In what courses English and others if not required by student's major.

University of Rhode Island

Newman Hall, Kingston, RI 02881 • Admissions: 401-874-7100 • Fax: 401-874-5523

CAMPUS

Type of school	Public
Environment	Village
Support	CS

STUDENTS

Undergrad enrollment	13,993
% male/female	43/57
% from out of state	46
% frosh live on campus	95

FINANCIAL FACTS

Annual in-state tuition	$12,002
Annual out-of-state tuition	$28,252
Room and board	$12,274
Required fees	$1,790

GENERAL ADMISSIONS INFO

Application fee	$65
Regular application deadline	2/1

Nonfall registration accepted. Admission may be deferred for a maximum of 1 year.

Range SAT EBRW	550–630
Range SAT Math	530–620
Range ACT Composite	23–27

ACADEMICS

Student/faculty ratio	17:1
% students returning for sophomore year	85
% students graduating within 4 years	47
% students graduating within 6 years	66

Most classes have 20–29 students.
Most lab/discussion sessions have 20–29 students.

PROGRAMS/SERVICES FOR STUDENTS WITH LEARNING DIFFERENCES

Disability Services for Students will assist students in arranging accommodations, facilitate communication between students and professors, and help them to develop effective coping skills like time management, study skills, stress management, etc. Accommodations are provided case-by-case to meet the specific needs of individual students. Students are encouraged to have an on-going relationship with DSS and the professional staff is able to meet with students as often as desired. Students with LD/ADHD who want to access services or accommodations must provide DSS with current documentation and communicate what needs are requested. Students are also expected to keep up with their requested accommodations (pick up, deliver and return letters in timely manner) and be involved in the decision-making process when it comes to their needs. Students are encouraged to make accommodation requests as early as possible and/or prior to the beginning of each semester.

ADMISSIONS

All applicants are expected to meet the general admission criteria. There is not a special process for students with LD/ADHD. General admission requirements expect students to rank in the upper 50% of their high school class and complete college preparatory courses including English, math, social studies, science and foreign language. If there is current documentation of a language-based LD there is a waiver for the foreign language admissions requirement, but students must self-disclose during the admission process.

Additional Information

Students need to provide the Disability Services for Students office with current documentation of their disability that includes: psycho-educational testing completed by a professional evaluator (see www.uri.edu/disability_services for more information). DSS will assist students in arranging for accommodations, help to facilitate communication between students and professors, work with students to develop effective coping strategies,

ADMISSIONS INFO FOR STUDENTS WITH LEARNING DIFFERENCES

SAT/ACT required: Yes
Interview required: No
Essay required: No
Additional application required: No
Documentation required for:
  LD: Full psychoeducational testing including aptitude, achievement, and information processing
  ADHD: Same as above or full diagnostic letter from Psychiatrist or Neurologist
  ASD: Psycho ed evaluation
Documentation submitted to: Disability Services for Students
Special Ed. HS course work accepted: No
Separate application required for program services: No
# of students last year receiving services/accommodations for:
  LD: 159
  ADHD: 242
  ASD: 36
Contact Information
Name of program or department: Disability Services for Students
Telephone: 401-874-2098
Fax: 401-874-5694

University of Rhode Island

assist students with identifying appropriate resources and provide referrals, and offer support for various issues, such as academic skill enhancement, and mentoring for 1st year students. Accommodations are based solely on documented disabilities and eligible students have access to services such as: priority registration, extended time on exams, permission to tape record lectures and access to a note taker. The university is one of 22 institutions nationwide to receive U.S. Dept of Education Grants that trains faculty and administrators to promote inclusion of students with disabilities.

GENERAL ADMISSIONS

Very important factors considered include: rigor of secondary school record, academic GPA. *Important factors considered include:* class rank, standardized test scores. *Other factors considered include:* application essay, recommendation(s), extracurricular activities, talent/ability, character/personal qualities, first generation, alumni/ae relation, geographical residence, state residency, racial/ethnic status, volunteer work, work experience, level of *Freshman Admission Requirements:* High school diploma is required and GED is accepted. *Academic units required:* 4 English, 3 math, 2 science, 1 science lab, 2 foreign language, 2 social studies, 5 academic electives.

ACCOMMODATIONS OR SERVICES

Accommodations are decided upon an individual basis after a thorough review of appropriate, current documentation. The accommodations requests must be supported through the documentation provided and must be logically linked to the current impact of the condition on academic functioning.

FINANCIAL AID

Students should submit: FAFSA. Applicants will be notified of awards on a rolling basis beginning 3/15. The Princeton Review suggests that all financial aid forms be submitted as soon as possible after October 1. *Need-based scholarships/grants offered:* College/university scholarship or grant aid from institutional funds; Federal Pell; Private scholarships; SEOG; State scholarships/grants. *Loan aid offered:* Direct PLUS loans; Direct Subsidized Stafford Loans; Direct Unsubsidized Stafford Loans. Federal Work-Study Program available. Institutional employment available.

CAMPUS LIFE

Activities: Campus Ministries; Choral groups; Concert band; Dance; Drama/theater; International Student Organization; Jazz band; Literary magazine; Marching band; Music ensembles; Musical theater; Opera; Pep band; Radio station; Student government; Student newspaper; Student-run film society; Television station; Yearbook. **Organizations:** 100 registered organizations, 40 honor societies, 5 religious organizations, 11 fraternities, 9 sororities. **Athletics (Intercollegiate):** *Men:* baseball, basketball, cheerleading, cross-country, football, golf, soccer, track/field (outdoor), track/field (indoor). *Women:* basketball, cheerleading, crew/rowing, cross-country, diving, soccer, softball, swimming, tennis, track/field (outdoor), track/field (indoor), volleyball. **On-Campus Highlights:** Ryan Center and Boss Ice Arena, Fascitelli Wellness & Fitness Center, Memorial Student Union, Multicultural Center, Hope Dining Commons.

ACCOMMODATIONS

Allowed in exams:	
Calculators	Yes
Dictionary	Yes
Computer	Yes
Spell-checker	No
Extended test time	Yes
Scribe	Yes
Proctors	Yes
Oral exams	Yes
Note-takers	Yes
Support services for students with	
LD	Yes
ADHD	Yes
ASD	Yes
Distraction-reduced environment	Yes
Recording of lecture allowed	Yes
Reading technology:	Yes
Audio books	Yes
Other assistive technology FM assistive listening systems, smart pens, digital recorders, residential alert devices, speech to text technology, etc	
Priority registration	Yes
Added costs for services:	
For ASD:	No
LD specialists	Yes
ADHD & ASD coaching	Yes
ASD specialists	Yes
Professional tutors	Yes
Peer tutors	Not Applicable
Max. hours/week for services	varies
How professors are notified of student approved accommodations	
Director and student	

COLLEGE GRADUATION REQUIREMENTS

Course substitutions allowed	Yes
In what courses	Foreign Language

Clemson University

105 Sikes Hall, Clemson, SC 29634-5124 • Admissions: 864-656-2287 • Fax: 864-656-2464

CAMPUS
Type of school	Public
Environment	Village
Support	S

STUDENTS
Undergrad enrollment	19,172
% male/female	51/49
% from out of state	35
% frosh live on campus	98

FINANCIAL FACTS
Annual in-state tuition	$13,186
Annual out-of-state tuition	$32,738
Room and board	
Required fees	$1,132

GENERAL ADMISSIONS INFO
Application fee	$70
Priority deadline	12/1
Regular application deadline	5/1

Nonfall registration accepted.

Range SAT EBRW	620–690
Range SAT Math	600–700
Range ACT Composite	27–31

ACADEMICS
Student/faculty ratio	16:1
% students returning for sophomore year	59
% students graduating within 6 years	82

Most classes have 10–19 students.
Most lab/discussion sessions have 10–19 students.

PROGRAMS/SERVICES FOR STUDENTS WITH LEARNING DIFFERENCES

Student Disability Services coordinates the provision of reasonable accommodations for students with disabilities. All reasonable accommodations are individualized, flexible, and confidential based on the nature of the disability and the academic environment. Students requesting accommodations must provide current documentation of the disability from a physician or licensed professional. High school IEP, 504 plan, and/or letter from a physician or other professional will not be sufficient to document some disabilities. While such documentation can be helpful in establishing the student's learning history, a recent (typically less than 3 years old) evaluation is still necessary to confirm current needs. Reasonable accommodations can be made in the instructional process to ensure full educational opportunities. The objective is to provide appropriate services to accommodate the student's learning differences, not to change scholastic requirements.

ADMISSIONS

All students must satisfy the same admission criteria for the university. There is no separate application process for students with disabilities. Students may request a waiver of the foreign language requirement by submitting a request to the exception committee. It is recommended that students self-disclose their learning disability if they need to explain the lack of a foreign language in their background or other information that will help admissions to understand their challenges.

Additional Information

Appropriate accommodations are discussed with each student individually and confidentially. Some of the accommodations offered are assistive technology; note-takers, readers, and transcribers; course substitutions; exam modifications, including computers, extended time, private and quiet rooms, readers, and scribes; priority registration; and recorded lectures. All students have access to peer tutoring, supplemental instruction, a writing lab, and departmental tutoring. Assistive technology available includes screen readers, and scanners. Study skills instruction is available in topics such as time management techniques and test strategies. Peer mentoring is available. There are

ADMISSIONS INFO FOR STUDENTS WITH LEARNING DIFFERENCES

SAT/ACT required: Yes
Interview required: No
Essay required: No
Additional application required: No
Documentation required for:
  LD: Psycho ed evaluation to include: relevant historical info, instructional interventions, related services, age diagnosed, objective data (aptitude, achievement, info processing), test scores (standard, percentile and grade equivalents) and describe functional limitations.
  ADHD: Diagnosis based on DSM-V; history of behaviors impairing functioning in academic setting; diagnostic interview; history of symptoms; evidence of ongoing behaviors.
  ASD: Psycho ed evaluation
Documentation submitted to: Student Disability Services
Special Ed. HS course work accepted: Yes
Separate application required for program services: No
Contact Information
Name of program or department: Student Disability Services
Telephone: (864) 656-6848
Fax: (864) 656-6849

Clemson University

currently 135 students with learning disabilities and 345 students with ADHD receiving services. The ClemsonLIFE Program offers a 2-year Basic Program that incorporates functional academics, independent living, employment, social/ leisure skills, and health/wellness skills in a public university setting with the goal of producing self-sufficient young adults. ClemsonLIFE Program offers a 2-year Advanced Program for students that have demonstrated the ability to safely live independently, sustain employment, and socially integrate during the Basic Program. The Advanced Program progresses with an emphasis on workplace experience, community integration, and independent living with transitionally reduced supports. Students who successfully complete the Basic or Advanced program will receive a corresponding certificate of postsecondary education.

GENERAL ADMISSIONS

Very important factors considered include: rigor of secondary school record, class rank, academic GPA, standardized test scores, state residency. *Important factors considered include:* alumni/ae relation. *Other factors considered include:* application essay, recommendation(s), extracurricular activities, talent/ability. *Freshman Admission Requirements:* High school diploma is required and GED is accepted. *Academic units required:* 4 English, 3 math, 3 science, 3 science labs, 2 foreign language, 1 social studies, 1 history, 2 academic electives, 1 computer science, 1 visual/performing arts, and 1 unit from above areas or other academic areas. *Academic units recommended:* 4 math, 4 science labs, 3 foreign language.

ACCOMMODATIONS OR SERVICES

Accommodations are decided upon an individual basis after a thorough review of appropriate, current documentation. The accommodations requests must be supported through the documentation provided and must be logically linked to the current impact of the condition on academic functioning.

FINANCIAL AID

Students should submit: FAFSA. Applicants will be notified of awards on a rolling basis beginning 4/1. The Princeton Review suggests that all financial aid forms be submitted as soon as possible after October 1. *Need-based scholarships/grants offered:* College/university scholarship or grant aid from institutional funds; Federal Nursing Scholarships; Federal Pell; Private scholarships; SEOG; State scholarships/grants. *Loan aid offered:* Direct PLUS loans; Direct Subsidized Stafford Loans; Direct Unsubsidized Stafford Loans. Federal Work-Study Program available. Institutional employment available.

CAMPUS LIFE

Activities: Choral groups; Concert band; Dance; Drama/theater; Jazz band; Literary magazine; Marching band; Music ensembles; Pep band; Radio station; Student government; Student newspaper; Television station; Yearbook. **Organizations:** 292 registered organizations, 23 honor societies, 24 religious organizations. 26 fraternities, 17 sororities. **Athletics (Intercollegiate):** *Men:* baseball, basketball, cheerleading, cross-country, diving, football, golf, soccer, swimming, tennis, track/field (outdoor), track/field (indoor). *Women:* basketball, cheerleading, crew/rowing, cross-country, diving, soccer, swimming, tennis, track/field (outdoor), track/field (indoor), volleyball. **On-Campus Highlights:** SC Botanical Garden/ Discovery Center/Geology Muse, Hendrix Student Center - Clemson Ice Cream, Conference Center and Inn at Clemson/ Walker Golf C, Fort Hill - John C. Calhoun House, Lee Art Gallery.

ACCOMMODATIONS

Allowed in exams:

Calculators	Yes
Dictionary	Yes
Computer	Yes
Spell-checker	Yes
Extended test time	Yes
Scribe	Yes
Proctors	Yes
Oral exams	Yes
Note-takers	Yes

Support services for students with

LD	Yes
ADHD	Yes
ASD	Yes
Distraction-reduced environment	Yes
Recording of lecture allowed	Yes
Reading technology:	Yes
Audio books	Yes
Other assistive technology	Yes
Priority registration	Yes

Added costs for services:

For LD:	No
For ADHD:	No
For ASD:	No
LD specialists	No
ADHD & ASD coaching	Yes
ASD specialists	Yes, January 2019
Professional tutors	No
Peer tutors	Yes
Max. hours/week for services	Unlimited
How professors are notified of student approved accommodations	Student

COLLEGE GRADUATION REQUIREMENTS

Course waivers allowed	No
Course substitutions allowed	No

College of Charleston

66 GEORGE STREET, CHARLESTON, SC 29424 • ADMISSIONS: 843-953-5670 • FAX: 843-953-6322

CAMPUS

Type of school	Public
Environment	City
Support	S

STUDENTS

Undergrad enrollment	9,599
% male/female	37/63
% from out of state	33
% frosh live on campus	89

FINANCIAL FACTS

Annual in-state tuition	$11,998
Annual out-of-state tuition	$30,386
Room and board	NR
Required fees	$460

GENERAL ADMISSIONS INFO

Application fee	$50
Priority deadline	2/15
Regular application deadline	2/15

Nonfall registration accepted. Admission may be deferred.

Range SAT EBRW	550–630
Range SAT Math	520–600
Range ACT Composite	22–27

ACADEMICS

Student/faculty ratio	15:1
% students returning for sophomore year	78
% students graduating within 4 years	56
% students graduating within 6 years	69

Most classes have 10–19 students.
Most lab/discussion sessions have 10–19 students.

PROGRAMS/SERVICES FOR STUDENTS WITH LEARNING DIFFERENCES

Please refer to our website for details. The Center for Disability Services is dedicated to •Ensuring that all programs and services of the College of Charleston are accessible; •Providing reasonable and effective accommodations while promoting independence in the student; •Offering educational opportunities to students, faculty and staff that enhance understanding of the various types of disabilities, promoting an environment respectful of all; •Serving as a resource center for faculty, staff, students and the community.

ADMISSIONS

When you apply, the College of Charleston admissions committee looks at many things in your application, including your academic preparation, GPA, rank in class, SAT/ACT scores, talents and leadership qualifications. We want you to do well here, so we will.

Additional Information

The Center for Student Disabilities (CSD) offers SNAP - Students Needing Access Parity. SNAP Provides assistance and guidance to students with a documented disability to ensure equal access to all programs and services of the College; Once the CSD complete application packet is turned in, a SNAP administrator evaluates the completeness of the application and supporting documentation and makes a recommendation of SNAP approval or denial. A letter of approval or denial will be e-mailed to your College of Charleston email account approximately one week from receipt of your application packet. Included within this e-mail are the Student's Guide to SNAP Services and a set of forms to be completed by the student. Reasonable accommodations will be provided once the

ADMISSIONS INFO FOR STUDENTS WITH LEARNING DIFFERENCES

SAT/ACT required: Yes
Interview required: No
Essay required: Not Applicable
Additional application required: Yes
Documentation required for:
  LD: A current psychoeducational evaluation administered by an appropriately credentialed professional.
  ADHD: The student must submit a report that meets the following guidelines: 1.Completed within the last three years 2.Administered by one of the following: Licensed psychologist or neuropsychologist Licensed school psychologist Psychiatrist M.D. specializing in the diagnosis and treatment of attention deficits Please Note: Evaluations administered by a relative are not accepted. 3.Includes: A diagnosis of ADHD based on the DSM criteria (code required) Comprehensive educational, developmental, and medical history relevant to the disability Results/copies of a Continuous Performance Test (CPT) or a set of norm-referenced behavior ratings from the student, and preferably a parent, spouse, teacher, or significant other Assessment ruling out or addressing potentially confounding conditions (e.g., anxiety, depression, hyperthyroidism, substance abuse) Results/copies of behavior ratings or CPT An explanation of the current functional impact of the disability The evaluator's signature, credentials, and licensing number
  ASD: A current evaluation administered by an appropriately credentialed professional.
Documentation submitted to: Center for Disability Services
Special Ed. HS course work accepted: No
Contact Information
Name of program or department: Center for Disability Services
Telephone: 843-953-1431
Fax: 843-953-7731
Email: SNAP@cofc.edu

College of Charleston

completed forms have been returned to SNAP. Students applying for alternative courses will receive an additional e-mail one to two weeks after the initial approval e-mail notifying them of their alternative status. If denied, you may appeal to the Director of the Center for Disability Services.

Additional Information
Please see our website for details. Once the complete application packet is turned in, a SNAP administrator evaluates the completeness of the application and supporting documentation and makes a recommendation of SNAP approval or denial. A letter of appr

GENERAL ADMISSIONS
Very important factors considered include: rigor of secondary school record, academic GPA, standardized test scores. *Important factors considered include:* class rank, talent/ability, character/personal qualities, first generation, state residency. *Other factors considered include:* application essay, recommendation(s), extracurricular activities, alumni/ae relation, geographical residence, racial/ethnic status, volunteer work, work experience, level of applicant's interest. *Freshman Admission Requirements:* High school diploma is required and GED is accepted. *Academic units required:* 4 English, 4 math, 3 science, 3 science labs, 3 foreign language, 2 social studies, 1 history, 3 academic electives, 1 visual/performing arts, and 1 unit from above areas or other academic areas. *Academic units recommended:* 4 English, 4 math, 2 history, 1 computer science.

ACCOMMODATIONS OR SERVICES
Accommodations are decided upon an individual basis after a thorough review of appropriate, current documentation. The accommodations requests must be supported through the documentation provided and must be logically linked to the current impact of the condition on academic functioning.

FINANCIAL AID
Students should submit: FAFSA. Applicants will be notified of awards on a rolling basis beginning 4/10. The Princeton Review suggests that all financial aid forms be submitted as soon as possible after October 1. *Need-based scholarships/grants offered:* College/university scholarship or grant aid from institutional funds; Federal Pell; Private scholarships; SEOG; State scholarships/grants. *Loan aid offered:* Direct PLUS loans; Direct Subsidized Stafford Loans; Direct Unsubsidized Stafford Loans. Federal Work-Study Program available. Institutional employment available.

CAMPUS LIFE
Activities: Campus Ministries; Choral groups; Dance; Drama/theater; International Student Organization; Jazz band; Literary magazine; Model UN; Music ensembles; Musical theater; Pep band; Radio station; Student government; Student newspaper; Symphony orchestra; Yearbook. **Organizations:** 120 registered organizations, 19 honor societies, 16 religious organizations. 13 fraternities, 12 sororities. **Athletics (Intercollegiate):** *Men:* baseball, basketball, cross-country, diving, golf, sailing, soccer, swimming, tennis. *Women:* basketball, cross-country, diving, equestrian sports, golf, sailing, soccer, softball, swimming, tennis, track/field (outdoor), track/field (indoor), volleyball. **On-Campus Highlights:** The Cistern Yard, TD Arena, Liberty Fresh Food Company and City Bistro, Addlestone Library / Starbucks / Rivers Green, Harbor Walk.

ACCOMMODATIONS
Allowed in exams:

Calculators	Yes
Dictionary	Yes
Computer	Yes
Spell-checker	Yes
Extended test time	Yes
Scribe	Yes
Proctors	Yes
Oral exams	Yes
Note-takers	Yes

Support services for students with

LD	Yes
ADHD	Yes
ASD	Yes
Distraction-reduced environment	Yes
Recording of lecture allowed	Yes
Reading technology:	Yes
Audio books	Yes

Other assistive technology Dragon Naturally Speaking JAWS Zoomtext TextHelp Read/ Write Gold Reading Made Easy Livescribe SmartPens ZoomTwix

Priority registration	Yes

Added costs for services:

For LD:	No
For ADHD:	No
For ASD:	No
LD specialists	Yes
ADHD & ASD coaching	Yes
ASD specialists	Yes
Professional tutors	Yes
Peer tutors	Yes
Max. hours/week for services	2

How professors are notified of student
approved accommodations   Student

COLLEGE GRADUATION REQUIREMENTS

Course waivers allowed	No
Course substitutions allowed	Yes
In what courses	Math/logic
	Foreign Language

Limestone College

1115 COLLEGE DRIVE, GAFFNEY, SC 29340-3799 • ADMISSIONS: 864-488-4549 • FAX: 864-487-8706

CAMPUS

Type of school	Private (nonprofit)
Environment	Town
Support	CS

STUDENTS

Undergrad enrollment	1,052
% male/female	62/38
% from out of state	42
% frosh live on campus	88

FINANCIAL FACTS

Annual tuition	$25,025
Room and board	$8,808
Required fees	NR

GENERAL ADMISSIONS INFO

Application fee	$25
Priority deadline	6/1
Regular application deadline	8/25

Nonfall registration accepted. Admission may be deferred for a maximum of 18 months.

Range SAT EBRW	480–560
Range SAT Math	480–550
Range ACT Composite	17-22

ACADEMICS

Student/faculty ratio	13:1
% students returning for sophomore year	57
%students graduating within 4 years	12
%students graduating within 6 years	24

Most classes have 10–19 students. Most lab/discussion sessions have 10–19 students.

PROGRAMS/SERVICES FOR STUDENTS WITH LEARNING DIFFERENCES

In addition to free disability services offered by all institutions, the Program for Alternative Learning Styles (PALS) was developed to comprehensively service students with learning disabilities. Therefore, only students with documented learning disabilities are eligible to receive program services. For program purposes, LD refers to students with average to above average intelligence (above 90) who have a discrepancy between measured intelligence and achievement. PALS's biggest advantage is the follow-up system that is in place for the PALS students. Each student is very carefully monitored as to his or her progress in each course he or she takes. The students who are not successful are typically those students who do not take advantage of the system. Deliberate accountability helps students remain aware of their status and offers assistance to improve on negative reports. The tracking system is specifically designed to keep PALS personnel, the professors and the students informed about their progress toward a degree from Limestone College.

ADMISSIONS

Students who self-disclose their LD and want the services of PALS must first be admitted to Limestone College either fully or conditionally. Students must submit a high school transcript with a diploma or GED certificate, SAT or ACT scores (though a minimum score is not required to seek admission via PALS), and the general college application. The minimum GPA is a 2.0. To receive services through PALS, students must submit their most recent psychological report (completed within the past 3 years) documenting an LD. In addition, only intelligence test scores from the Stanford Binet and/or Wechsler Scales will be acceptable. All available information is carefully reviewed prior to acceptance. Students may be admitted provisionally via PALS, if approved by the PALS Admissions Committee and enrolled in PALS. Students interested in PALS must arrange for an interview with the director of PALS to learn what will be expected of the student and what the program will and will not do for the student. After the interview is completed, students will be

ADMISSIONS INFO FOR STUDENTS WITH LEARNING DIFFERENCES

SAT/ACT required: No
Interview required: Yes
Essay required: No
Additional application required: No
Documentation required for:
 LD: Psycho ed evaluation to include: relevant historical info, instructional interventions, related services, age diagnosed, objective data (aptitude, achievement, info processing), test scores (standard, percentile and grade equivalents) and describe functional limitations.
 ADHD: D iagnosis based on DSM-V; history of behaviors impairing functioning in academic setting; diagnostic interview; history of symptoms; evidence of ongoing behaviors.
 ASD: Psycho ed evaluation
Documentation submitted to: Program for Alternative Learning Styles
Special Ed. HS course work accepted: Yes
Separate application required for program services: No
# of students last year receiving services/accommodations for:
 LD + PALS: 150
Contact Information
Name of program or department: Program for Alternative Learning Styles (PALS)
Telephone: 864-488-8377
Fax: 864-487-8706

Limestone College

notified of their eligibility for PALS and be given the opportunity to sign a statement indicating their wish to participate or not to participate.

Additional Information
During the regular academic year, students will receive special instruction in the area of study skills. Students are required to participate in a minimum of ten hours per week of supervised study hall. PALS personnel are in constant communication with students concerning grades, tutors, professors, accommodations, time management, and study habits. Tutorial services are provided on an individual basis so that all students can reach their maximum potential. Skills classes are offered in math and reading. Other services include counseling, personal test proctors, time management skills, and screening for the best ways to make accommodations. PALS does not offer training in social skills. The cost of the program is $2500 per semester.

GENERAL ADMISSIONS
Very important factors considered include: rigor of secondary school record, academic GPA, standardized test scores. *Important factors considered include:* class rank. *Other factors considered include:* recommendation(s), interview. *Freshman Admission Requirements:* High school diploma is required and GED is accepted. *Academic units required:* 4 English, 3 math, 2 science, 2 science labs, 3 social studies.

ACCOMMODATIONS OR SERVICES
Accommodations are decided upon an individual basis after a thorough review of appropriate, current documentation. The accommodations requests must be supported through the documentation provided and must be logically linked to the current impact of the condition on academic functioning.

FINANCIAL AID
Students should submit: FAFSA. Applicants will be notified of awards on a rolling basis beginning 1/15. The Princeton Review suggests that all financial aid forms be submitted as soon as possible after October 1. *Need-based scholarships/grants offered:* College/university scholarship or grant aid from institutional funds; Federal Pell; Private scholarships; SEOG; State scholarships/grants. *Loan aid offered:* Direct PLUS loans; Direct Subsidized Stafford Loans; Direct Unsubsidized Stafford Loans. Federal Work-Study Program available. Institutional employment available.

CAMPUS LIFE
Activities: Campus Ministries; Choral groups; Concert band; Drama/theater; Jazz band; Literary magazine; Marching band; Music ensembles; Musical theater; Pep band; Student government; Yearbook. **Organizations:** 2 religious organizations. **Athletics (Intercollegiate):** *Men:* baseball, basketball, cross-country, golf, lacrosse, soccer, swimming, tennis, track/field (outdoor), volleyball, wrestling. *Women:* basketball, cross-country, field hockey, golf, lacrosse, soccer, softball, swimming, tennis, track/field (outdoor), volleyball. **On-Campus Highlights:** Dixie Lodge Student Center, Stephenson Dining Hall, Timken Gym and Pool, Eastwood Library, Curtis Administration Building.

ACCOMMODATIONS	
Allowed in exams:	
Calculators	Yes
Dictionary	Yes
Computer	Yes
Spell-checker	Yes
Extended test time	Yes
Scribe	Yes
Proctors	Yes
Oral exams	Yes
Note-takers	Yes
Support services for students with	
LD	Yes
ADHD	Yes
ASD	Yes
Distraction-reduced environment	Yes
Recording of lecture allowed	Yes
Reading technology:	Yes
Audio books	Yes
Other assistive technology	Yes
Priority registration	No
Added costs for services:	
For LD:	No
For ADHD:	No
For ASD:	No
PALS:	Yes
LD specialists	Yes
ADHD & ASD coaching	No
ASD specialists	No
Professional tutors	Yes
Peer tutors	Yes
Max. hours/week for services	Unlimited
How professors are notified of student	
approved accommodations	PALS Staff

COLLEGE GRADUATION REQUIREMENTS	
Course waivers allowed	No
In what courses	Foreign Language not required at Lmestone.
Course substitutions allowed	No

Southern Wesleyan University

WESLEYAN DRIVE, CENTRAL, SC 29630-1020 • ADMISSIONS: 864-644-5550 • FAX: 864-644-5972

CAMPUS

Type of school	Private (nonprofit)
Environment	Town
Support	S

STUDENTS

Undergrad enrollment	1,444
% male/female	40/60
% from out of state	28
% frosh live on campus	71

FINANCIAL FACTS

Annual tuition	$19,950
Room and board	$8,410
Required fees	$600

GENERAL ADMISSIONS INFO

Application fee	$25
Regular application deadline	8/1

Nonfall registration accepted. Admission may be deferred for a maximum of 1 semester.

Range SAT EBRW	430–540
Range SAT Math	445–550
Range ACT Composite	18–22

ACADEMICS

Student/faculty ratio	18:1
% students returning for sophomore year	70
% students graduating within 4 years	38
% students graduating within 6 years	44

Most classes have 20–29 students.
Most lab/discussion sessions have 10–19 students.

PROGRAMS/SERVICES FOR STUDENTS WITH LEARNING DIFFERENCES

Southern Wesleyan University offers services to students with disabilities by coordinating the efforts of faculty, staff, under the director of the Student Success Coordinator in the Student Success Center. This is free academic assistance that includes peer tutors, writing coaches, online tutoring and Supplemental instruction. Supplemental Instruction (SI) is an academic assistance program designed to increase retention, improve student grades and increase graduation rates. SI accomplishes these goals by helping students learn to solve problems, organize classroom materials, develop effective study strategies and meet personal and faculty expectations. Supplemental Instruction is intended to be a semester-long series of weekly group study sessions led by an SI leader. The SI leader is an undergraduate who has successfully completed the course with an "A" average. All SI leaders are recommended by faculty. The SI leader attends the weekly lecture, takes notes, meets with the course instructor regularly, and then holds three study sessions weekly to provide support to students currently enrolled in the course.

ADMISSIONS

All applicants must meet the same admission criteria. Courses taken in high school should include at least: must have: 4 years of English, 2 years of science, 2 years of social studies, and 2 years of math. Applicants should have a GPA of 2.3 (or rank in upper half of your graduating class at time of acceptance) and a composite SAT score of 860 (based on the critical reading/verbal and math sections) or an ACT score of 18.

Additional Information

Documentation of a disability goes to the student Learning Services Coordinator. The student must request services each semester by discussing with the coordinator what accommodations are appropriate and needed in each course. The coordinator sends a letter to the professor of each course the student has identified for needed accommodation. The student also receives a copy and arranges the logistics and details with

ADMISSIONS INFO FOR STUDENTS WITH LEARNING DIFFERENCES

SAT/ACT required: Yes
Interview required: No
Essay required: No
Documentation required for:
 LD: Psycho ed evaluation to include: relevant historical info, instructional interventions, related services, age diagnosed, objective data (aptitude, achievement, info processing), test scores (standard, percentile and grade equivalents) and describe functional limitations.
 ADHD: Diagnosis based on DSM-V; history of behaviors impairing functioning in academic setting; diagnostic interview; history of symptoms; evidence of ongoing behaviors.
 ASD: Psycho ed evalaution
Documentation submitted to: Student Services Learning Coordinator
Separate application required for program services: No
Contact Information
Name of program or department: Services to Students with Disabilities
Telephone: 864-644-5036
Fax: 864-644-5979

Southern Wesleyan University

professors. We emphasize that students must initiate the request and the arrangements. We encourage the student to develop the highest degree of independence possible during their college years and become prepared to compete successfully in their chosen career. There is a liaison person between faculty and students. Professors are available to students after class. Modifications can be made in test-taking, which could include extended time and a quiet place to take exams. Additionally, students may receive assistance with note-taking. All services are offered in response to students' requests.

GENERAL ADMISSIONS

Very important factors considered include: academic GPA, standardized test scores. *Important factors considered include:* rigor of secondary school record, class rank, talent/ability, character/personal qualities. *Other factors considered include:* recommendation(s). *Freshman Admission Requirements:* High school diploma is required and GED is accepted. *Academic units recommended:* 4 English, 2 math, 2 science, 2 social studies.

ACCOMMODATIONS OR SERVICES

Accommodations are decided upon an individual basis after a thorough review of appropriate, current documentation. The accommodations requests must be supported through the documentation provided and must be logically linked to the current impact of the condition on academic functioning.

FINANCIAL AID

Students should submit: FAFSA; Institution's own financial aid form. Applicants will be notified of awards on a rolling basis beginning 2/1. The Princeton Review suggests that all financial aid forms be submitted as soon as possible after October 1. *Need-based scholarships/grants offered:* College/university scholarship or grant aid from institutional funds; Federal Pell; Private scholarships; SEOG; State scholarships/grants. *Loan aid offered:* Direct PLUS loans; Direct Subsidized Stafford Loans; Direct Unsubsidized Stafford Loans. Federal Work-Study Program available. Institutional employment available.

CAMPUS LIFE

Activities: Campus Ministries; Choral groups; Concert band; Drama/theater; Jazz band; Literary magazine; Music ensembles; Musical theater; Student government; Yearbook. **Organizations:** 12 registered organizations, 2 honor societies, 3 religious organizations. **Athletics (Intercollegiate):** *Men:* baseball, basketball, cross-country, golf, soccer *Women:* basketball, cross-country, soccer, softball, volleyball. **On-Campus Highlights:** Jennings Campus Center, Java City Coffee Shop, Historic Tysinger Gymnasium, Student Apartment Complex.

ACCOMMODATIONS

Allowed in exams:	
Calculators	Yes
Dictionary	Yes
Computer	Yes
Spell-checker	Yes
Extended test time	Yes
Scribe	Yes
Proctors	Yes
Oral exams	Yes
Note-takers	Yes
Support services for students with	
LD	Yes
ADHD	Yes
ASD	Yes
Distraction-reduced environment	Yes
Recording of lecture allowed	Yes
Reading technology:	Yes
Audio books	Yes
Other assistive technology voice recognition program	
Priority registration	No
Added costs for services:	
For LD:	No
For ADHD:	No
For ASD:	No
LD specialists	No
ADHD & ASD coaching	No
ASD specialists	No
Professional tutors	Yes
Peer tutors	Yes
Max. hours/week for services	Varies
How professors are notified of student approved accommodations	Student and coordinator

COLLEGE GRADUATION REQUIREMENTS

Course waivers allowed	No
Course substitutions allowed	No

University of South Carolina–Columbia

OFFICE OF UNDERGRADUATE ADMISSIONS, COLUMBIA, SC 29208 • ADMISSIONS: 803-777-7700 • FAX: 803-777-0101

CAMPUS

Type of school	Public
Environment	City
Support	CS

STUDENTS

Undergrad enrollment	25,950
% male/female	46/54
% from out of state	40
% frosh live on campus	94

FINANCIAL FACTS

Annual in-state tuition	$11,862
Annual out-of-state tuition	$31,962
Room and board	$10,008
Required fees	$400

GENERAL ADMISSIONS INFO

Application fee	$65
Priority deadline	12/1
Regular application deadline	12/1

Nonfall registration accepted. Admission may be deferred for a maximum of 1 year.

Range SAT EBRW	590–660
Range SAT Math	580–670
Range ACT Composite	25–30

ACADEMICS

Student/faculty ratio	17:1
% students returning for sophomore year	89
% students graduating within 4 years	59
% students graduating within 6 years	75

Most classes have 20–29 students. Most lab/discussion sessions have 20–29 students.

PROGRAMS/SERVICES FOR STUDENTS WITH LEARNING DIFFERENCES

The university's Student Disability Resource Center (ODS) provides educational support and assistance to students with LD who have the potential for success in a competitive university setting. The Student Disability Resource Center is specifically designed to empower them with the confidence to become self-advocates and to take an active role in their education. The university works with each student on an individualized basis to match needs with appropriate services. The services are tailored to provide educational support and assistance to students based on their specific needs. Student Disability Resource Center recommends and coordinates support services with faculty, administrators, advisors, and deans. The nature and severity of LD may vary considerably. All requests are based on documented diagnostic information regarding each student's specific learning disability. The first step in accessing services from the Office of Disability Services is to self-disclose the disability and arrange an interview. During the interview, staff members will discuss the student's educational background and determine which services best fit his or her needs.

ADMISSIONS

There is no special application or admission process for students with LD. Required scores on the SAT and ACT vary with class rank. Applicants must have a cumulative C-plus average on defined college-preparatory courses, including 4 years of English, 3 years of math, 3 years of science, 2 years of the same foreign language, 4 years of electives, and 1 year of physical education, as well as a 1200 SAT or 27 ACT. If they are denied admission or feel they do not meet the required standards, students may petition the Admissions Committee for an exception to the regular admissions requirements. Once admitted, students should contact the Educational Support Services Center to arrange an interview to determine which services are necessary to accommodate their needs.

ADMISSIONS INFO FOR STUDENTS WITH LEARNING DIFFERENCES

SAT/ACT required: Yes
Interview required: Yes
Essay required: No
Additional application required: No
Documentation required for:
 LD: Psycho ed evaluation to include: relevant historical info, instructional interventions, related services, age diagnosed, objective data (aptitude, achievement, info processing), test scores (standard, percentile and grade equivalents) and describe functional limitations.
 ADHD: Diagnosis based on DSM-V; history of behaviors impairing functioning in academic setting; diagnostic interview; history of symptoms; evidence of ongoing behaviors.
 ASD: Psycho ed evalaution
Documentation submitted to: ODS
Special Ed. HS course work accepted: No
Separate application required for program services: No
# of students last year receiving services/accommodations for:
 LD: 500
Contact Information
Name of program or department: Office of Student Disability Services
Telephone: 803-777-6142
Fax: 803-777-6741

University of South Carolina–Columbia

ADDITIONAL INFORMATION

Services are individually tailored to provide educational support and assistance. All requests are based on documented diagnostic information. The program is designed to provide educational support and assistance, including analysis of learning needs to determine appropriate interventions, consulting with the faculty about special academic needs, monitoring of progress by a staff member, study skills training, and tutorial referrals. Special program accommodations may include a reduced course load of 9–12 hours, waivers/substitutions for some courses, and expanded pass/fail options. Special classroom accommodations may include tape recorders, note-takers, and extended time on tests. General Admissions *Very important factors considered include:* rigor of secondary school record, academic GPA, standardized test scores. *Other factors considered include:* class rank, application essay, recommendation(s), extracurricular activities, talent/ability, character/personal qualities, first generation, state residency, racial/ethnic status, volunteer work, work experience. *Freshman Admission Requirements:* High school diploma is required and GED is accepted. *Academic units required:* 4 English, 4 math, 3 science, 3 science labs, 2 foreign language, 2 social studies, 1 history, 1 academic elective, 1 visual/performing arts, and 1 unit from above areas or other academic areas.

ACCOMMODATIONS OR SERVICES

Accommodations are decided upon an individual basis after a thorough review of appropriate, current documentation. The accommodations requests must be supported through the documentation provided and must be logically linked to the current impact of the condition on academic functioning.

FINANCIAL AID

Students should submit: FAFSA. Applicants will be notified of awards on a rolling basis beginning 4/1. The Princeton Review suggests that all financial aid forms be submitted as soon as possible after October 1. *Need-based scholarships/grants offered:* College/university scholarship or grant aid from institutional funds; Federal Nursing Scholarships; Federal Pell; Private scholarships; SEOG; State scholarships/grants; United Negro College Fund. *Loan aid offered:* Direct PLUS loans; Direct Subsidized Stafford Loans; Direct Unsubsidized Stafford Loans. Federal Work-Study Program available. Institutional employment available.

CAMPUS LIFE

Activities: Campus Ministries; Choral groups; Concert band; Dance; Drama/theater; International Student Organization; Jazz band; Literary magazine; Marching band; Music ensembles; Musical theater; Opera; Pep band; Radio station; Student government; Student newspaper; Student-run film society; Symphony orchestra; Television station. **Organizations:** 300 registered organizations, 25 honor societies, 32 religious organizations. 20 fraternities, 14 sororities. **Athletics (Intercollegiate):** *Men:* baseball, basketball, diving, football, golf, racquetball, soccer, softball, swimming, tennis, track/field (outdoor). *Women:* basketball, cross-country, diving, equestrian sports, golf, racquetball, soccer, softball, swimming, tennis, track/field (outdoor), volleyball. **On-Campus Highlights:** Strom Thurmond Wellness & Fitness Center, Russell House University Union, Greek Village, Williams-Brice Stadium - Home of the 2012 Outback Bowl Champs, Historic Horseshoe.

ACCOMMODATIONS

Allowed in exams:	
Calculators	Yes
Dictionary	Yes
Computer	Yes
Spell-checker	Yes
Extended test time	Yes
Scribe	Yes
Proctors	Yes
Oral exams	No
Note-takers	Yes
Support services for students with	
LD	Yes
ADHD	Yes
ASD	Yes
Distraction-reduced environment	Yes
Recording of lecture allowed	Yes
Reading technology:	Yes
Audio books	Yes
Other assistive technology	Yes
Priority registration	Yes
Added costs for services:	
For LD:	No
For ADHD:	No
For ASD:	No
LD specialists	Yes
ADHD & ASD coaching	No
ASD specialists	No
Professional tutors	No
Peer tutors	No
Max. hours/week for services	Yes
How professors are notified of student approved accommodations	Student

COLLEGE GRADUATION REQUIREMENTS

Course waivers allowed	Yes

In what courses: Students with learning disabilities may petition their college for substitution of the required foreign language if the requirement is not an intregal part of the degree program.

Course substitutions allowed	Yes

In what courses: Students with learning disabilities may petition their college for substitution of the required foreign language if the requirement is not an intregal part of the degree program.

South Dakota State University

1015 Campanile Ave., Brookings, SD 57007 • Admissions: 605-688-4121 • Fax: 605-688-6891

CAMPUS
Type of school	Public
Environment	Village
Support	S

STUDENTS
Undergrad enrollment	9,725
% male/female	49/51
% from out of state	47

FINANCIAL FACTS
Annual in-state tuition	$7,191
Annual out-of-state tuition	$10,439
Room and board	$7,744
Required fees	$1,250

GENERAL ADMISSIONS INFO
Application fee	$20

Nonfall registration accepted.

Range SAT EBRW	480–630
Range SAT Math	500–630
Range ACT Composite	20–26

ACADEMICS
Student/faculty ratio	16:1
% students returning for sophomore year	77
% students graduating within 4 years	29
% students graduating within 6 years	54

Most classes have 10–19 students.

PROGRAMS/SERVICES FOR STUDENTS WITH LEARNING DIFFERENCES
South Dakota State University is committed to providing equal opportunities for higher education to academically qualified students with LDs. All students, including those with disabilities, have access to skill development courses in the areas of general academic success skills, English composition, and mathematics. Free tutoring is available for all students in a wide variety of subject areas. They provide, through the Wintrode Tutoring Program , small group tutoring and walk-in review sessions in select courses, and it's from peers who have been through the same classes.

ADMISSIONS
Students with learning disabilities must meet the same admission criteria as all applicants. For admission to SDS they
look for one of the following academic achievements: 1) An ACT composite score of 18 or higher (SAT of 870 or higher) 2) a high school cumulative GPA of 2.6 or higher or 3) rank in the top 60 percent of the class. Students should also complete the following core courses with a "C" average or above: 4 years of English (or ACT English sub-score of 18) 3 years of advanced math—Algebra I and higher (or ACT math sub-score of 20), 3 years of laboratory science (or ACT science reasoning sub-score of 17), 3 years of social science (or ACT reading sub-score of 17), 1 year of fine arts (includes vocal, instrumental and studio arts), and basic computer skills (students should have basic keyboarding, word processing, spreadsheet and internet skills).

Additional Information
The Office of Disability Services provides assistance for students with a wide range of disabilities. The first step is to fill out the application for disability services. Along with this application, students need to send documentation of the disability. After that, ODS will set up an appointment to discuss services provided that will enhance the students learning experiences at SDSU. Some of the services include: alternative

ADMISSIONS INFO FOR STUDENTS WITH LEARNING DIFFERENCES
SAT/ACT required: Yes
Interview required: No
Essay required: No
Additional application required: No
Documentation required for:
 LD: Psycho ed evaluation to include: relevant historical info, instructional interventions, related services, age diagnosed, objective data (aptitude, achievement, info processing), test scores (standard, percentile and grade equivalents) and describe functional limitations.
 ADHD: Diagnosis based on DSM-V; history of behaviors impairing functioning in academic setting; diagnostic interview; history of symptoms; evidence of ongoing behaviors.
 ASD: Psycho ed evaluation
Documentation submitted to: DS
Special Ed. HS course work accepted: No
Contact Information
Name of program or department: Disability Services
Telephone: 605-688-4504
Fax: 605-688-4987

South Dakota State University

text formats, note taker, assistive technology, alternative accommodations for exams (testing in a distraction-free environment or providing readers for exams),extended time for testing, and referrals to other resources. Tutoring and Supplemental Instruction (SI) is offered to all SDSU students through the Wintrode Tutoring & SI Program. SI offers a series of weekly review sessions for students.

GENERAL ADMISSIONS
Very important factors considered include: rigor of secondary school record, class rank, academic GPA, standardized test scores. *Other factors considered include:* application essay, recommendation(s). *Freshman Admission Requirements:* High school diploma is required and GED is accepted. *Academic units required:* 4 English, 3 math, 3 science, 3 science labs, 3 social studies, 1 visual/performing arts.

ACCOMMODATIONS OR SERVICES
Accommodations are decided upon an individual basis after a thorough review of appropriate, current documentation. The accommodations requests must be supported through the documentation provided and must be logically linked to the current impact of the condition on academic functioning.

FINANCIAL AID
Students should submit: FAFSA. Applicants will be notified of awards on a rolling basis beginning 4/1. The Princeton Review suggests that all financial aid forms be submitted as soon as possible after October 1. *Need-based scholarships/grants offered: Loan aid offered:* Federal Work-Study Program available. Institutional employment available.

CAMPUS LIFE
Activities: Choral groups; Concert band; Dance; Drama/theater; International Student Organization; Jazz band; Literary magazine; Marching band; Model UN; Music ensembles; Musical theater; Pep band; Radio station; Student government; Student newspaper; Symphony orchestra; Yearbook. **Organizations:** 200 registered organizations, 32 honor societies, 14 religious organizations. 6 fraternities, 4 sororities. **Athletics (Intercollegiate):** *Men:* baseball, basketball, cross-country, diving, football, golf, swimming, tennis, track/field (outdoor), track/field (indoor), wrestling. *Women:* basketball, cross-country, diving, equestrian sports, golf, soccer, softball, swimming, tennis, track/field (outdoor), track/field (indoor), volleyball. **On-Campus Highlights:** Performing Arts Center, Dairy Bar, University Student Union, Frost Arena, South Dakota Art Museum.

ACCOMMODATIONS

Allowed in exams:

Calculators	Yes
Dictionary	No
Computer	Yes
Spell-checker	Yes
Extended test time	Yes
Scribe	Yes
Proctors	Yes
Oral exams	Yes
Note-takers	Yes
Support services for students with	
LD	Yes
ADHD	Yes
ASD	Yes
Distraction-reduced environment	Yes
Recording of lecture allowed	Yes
Reading technology:	Yes
Audio books	Yes
Other assistive technology	Yes
Priority registration	No
Added costs for services:	
For LD:	No
For ADHD:	No
For ASD:	No
LD specialists	No
ADHD & ASD coaching	No
ASD specialists	No
Professional tutors	Yes
Peer tutors	Yes
Max. hours/week for services	Unlimited
How professors are notified of student approved accommodations	Through

Accommodations letters student presents to professors.

COLLEGE GRADUATION REQUIREMENTS

Course waivers allowed	No
Course substitutions allowed	No

The University of South Dakota

414 East Clark St, Vermillion, SD 57069 • Admissions: 605-677-5434 • Fax: 605-677-6323

CAMPUS

Type of school	Public
Environment	Village
Support	CS

STUDENTS

Undergrad enrollment	6,166
% male/female	38/62
% from out of state	35
% frosh live on campus	85

FINANCIAL FACTS

Annual in-state tuition	$7,191
Annual out-of-state tuition	$10,438
Room and board	$4,113
Required fees	$8,030

GENERAL ADMISSIONS INFO

Application fee	$20

Nonfall registration accepted.

Range SAT EBRW	510–590
Range SAT Math	500–630
Range ACT Composite	20–25

ACADEMICS

Student/faculty ratio	17:1
% students returning for sophomore year	72
% students graduating within 4 years	39
% students graduating within 6 years	57

Most classes have 10–19 students.
Most lab/discussion sessions have 10–19 students.

PROGRAMS/SERVICES FOR STUDENTS WITH LEARNING DIFFERENCES

The University of South Dakota Disability Services (USDDS) operates on the premise that students at the university are full participants in the process of obtaining appropriate accommodations for their disabilities. Students are encouraged to make their own decisions and become self-advocates for appropriate accommodations or services. The three main goals are to: (1) help students become self-advocates; (2) provide better transition services into and out of college; and (3) to provide better instructional and support services. The university strives to ensure that all individuals with legally defined disabilities have access to the full range of the university's programs, services, and activities.

ADMISSIONS

For Freshmen Admission, students must have a minimum 2.6 GPA on a 4.0 scale in all high school courses, or be in the top 50 percent of their high school graduating class, or have a minimum 21 Composite Score on the ACT (minimum 990 SAT score), and complete the following courses with a cumulative grade point average of a C or higher (2.0 on a 4.0 scale): four years of English, three years of advanced math (algebra I or higher), three years of social science, three years of lab science, and one year of fine arts. Other requirements apply for Transfer Admission and Non-Traditional Admission. Non-Traditional Admission requirements apply for students who are age 24 or over and for those who did not graduate from high school. Please contact the Office of Admissions at 1-877-COYOTES [1-877-269-6837] for more information.

Additional Information

Services are individualized for each student's learning needs. USDDS staff provides the following activities: planning, developing, delivering, and evaluating direct service programs; meeting individually with students ensuring that students receive reasonable and appropriate accommodations

ADMISSIONS INFO FOR STUDENTS WITH LEARNING DIFFERENCES

SAT/ACT required: Yes
Interview required: No
Essay required: No
Additional application required: No
Documentation required for:
 LD: Psycho ed evaluation to include: relevant historical info, instructional interventions, related services, age diagnosed, objective data (aptitude, achievement, info processing), test scores (standard, percentile and grade equivalents) and describe functional limitations.
 ADHD: Diagnosis based on DSM-V; history of behaviors impairing functioning in academic setting; diagnostic interview; history of symptoms; evidence of ongoing behaviors.
 ASD: Psycho ed evaluation
Documentation submitted to: Disability Services
Special Ed. HS course work accepted: Yes
Separate application required for program services: No
Contact Information
Name of program or department: Disability Services (DS)
Telephone: 605-688-4504
Fax: 605-688-4987

The University of South Dakota

that match their needs; consulting with faculty; and providing academic, career, and personal counseling referrals. Classroom accommodations include test modification, note-taking assistance, readers, books on tape, specialized computer facilities, and tutors.

GENERAL ADMISSIONS

Very important factors considered include: rigor of secondary school record, class rank, academic GPA, standardized test scores. *Other factors considered include:* application essay, recommendation(s), extracurricular activities, talent/ability, character/personal qualities, geographical residence, state residency, racial/ethnic status, volunteer work, work experience. *Freshman Admission Requirements:* High school diploma is required and GED is accepted. *Academic units required:* 4 English, 3 math, 3 science labs, 3 social studies. *Academic units recommended:* 4 math, 4 science, 2 foreign language, 1 unit from above areas or other academic areas.

ACCOMMODATIONS OR SERVICES

Accommodations are decided upon an individual basis after a thorough review of appropriate, current documentation. The accommodations requests must be supported through the documentation provided and must be logically linked to the current impact of the condition on academic functioning.

FINANCIAL AID

Students should submit: FAFSA. The Princeton Review suggests that all financial aid forms be submitted as soon as possible after October 1. *Need-based scholarships/grants offered:* College/university scholarship or grant aid from institutional funds; Federal Pell; Private scholarships; SEOG; State scholarships/grants; United Negro College Fund. *Loan aid offered:* Direct PLUS loans; Direct Subsidized Stafford Loans; Direct Unsubsidized Stafford Loans. Federal Work-Study Program available. Institutional employment available.

CAMPUS LIFE

Activities: Campus Ministries; Choral groups; Concert band; Dance; Drama/theater; International Student Organization; Jazz band; Marching band; Music ensembles; Musical theater; Opera; Pep band; Radio station; Student government; Student newspaper; Student-run film society; Symphony orchestra; Television station. **Organizations:** 120 registered organizations, 6 honor societies, 6 religious organizations. 8 fraternities, 3 sororities. **Athletics (Intercollegiate):** *Men:* basketball, cross-country, diving, football, golf, swimming, track/field (outdoor), track/field (indoor). *Women:* basketball, cross-country, diving, golf, soccer, softball, swimming, tennis, track/field (outdoor), track/field (indoor), volleyball. **On-Campus Highlights:** Al Neuharth Media Center, The National Music Museum, The Dakota Dome, Belbas Student Service Center, Muenster University Center.

ACCOMMODATIONS

Allowed in exams:	
Calculators	Yes
Dictionary	Yes
Computer	Yes
Spell-checker	Yes
Extended test time	Yes
Scribe	Yes
Proctors	Yes
Oral exams	Yes
Note-takers	Yes
Support services for students with	
LD	Yes
ADHD	Yes
ASD	Yes
Distraction-reduced environment	Yes
Recording of lecture allowed	Yes
Reading technology:	Yes
Audio books	Yes
Other assistive technology	Yes
Priority registration	No
Added costs for services:	
For LD:	No
For ADHD:	No
For ASD:	No
LD specialists	Yes
ADHD & ASD coaching	No
ASD specialists	No
Professional tutors	No
Peer tutors	Yes
Max. hours/week for services	Unlimited
How professors are notified of student approved accommodations	Student

COLLEGE GRADUATION REQUIREMENTS

Course waivers allowed	No
Course substitutions allowed	No

Lee University

P.O. Box 3450, Cleveland, TN 37320-3450 • Admissions: 423-614-8500 • Fax: 423-614-8533

CAMPUS

Type of school	Private (nonprofit)
Environment	Town
Support	CS

STUDENTS

Undergrad enrollment	4,265
% male/female	38/62
% from out of state	55
% frosh live on campus	86

FINANCIAL FACTS

Annual tuition	$17,040
Room and board	$8,300
Required fees	$650

GENERAL ADMISSIONS INFO

Application fee	$25
Priority deadline	4/15

Nonfall registration accepted. Admission may be deferred for a maximum of 1 semester.

Range SAT EBRW	510–630
Range SAT Math	490–610
Range ACT Composite	21–28

ACADEMICS

Student/faculty ratio	16:1
% students returning for sophomore year	81
% students graduating within 4 years	37
% students graduating within 6 years	52

Most classes have 10–19 students.

PROGRAMS/SERVICES FOR STUDENTS WITH LEARNING DIFFERENCES

The Academic Support Office acts as a liaison between students with disabilities and the Lee University academic community. In compliance with Section 504 of the Rehabilitation Act of 1973, as amended, and the Americans with Disabilities Act (ADA) of 1990, and the amended ADA of 2011, the Academic Support Office works to ensure that students with disabilities, (physical, sensory, learning, and/or emotional), have equal access to educational opportunities.

ADMISSIONS

Students who think they may qualify for these accommodations should contact the Office of Academic Support to set up accommodations. There is no special admission process for students with LD. All students must meet the same general admission requirements. Course substitutions are not allowed. Students are encouraged to self-disclose a disability in a personal statement during the admission process, although this is not required.

Additional Information

Accommodations meeting with Director of Academic Support as long as proper documentation is provided. Students are encouraged to initiate contact with the DAC coordinator early in the semester to determine the necessary accommodations. Once enrolled in courses students schedule regular meetings with the coordinator in order to monitor progress and/or determine the need for adjustments to the accommodations. Services/resources provided include orientation to the DAC; orientation to the Adaptive Technology Center; assistance with the admission process; advising and strategic scheduling of classes; early registration of classes; tutorial services; test accommodations; note- takers, readers, scribes, books on tape; exploration of time management/note-taking strategies; career planning and employment strategies; and resume preparation. The Adaptive Technology Center provides training support for students, with disabilities in the use of adaptive/assistive technology application and devices. All disability documentation is confidential and is not released without the consent of the student.

ADMISSIONS INFO FOR STUDENTS WITH LEARNING DIFFERENCES

SAT/ACT required: Yes
Interview required: Not Applicable
Essay required: Not Applicable
Additional application required: Yes
Documentation required for:
 LD: Full adult psychological evaluation completed within the last 3 years.
 ADHD: Full adult psychological evaluation completed within the last 3 years.
 ASD: Full adult psychological evaluation completed within the last 3 years.
Documentation submitted to: Academic Support Office
Special Ed. HS course work accepted: No
Separate application required for program services: Yes
# of students last year receiving services/accommodations for:
 LD: 39
Contact Information
Name of program or department: Academic Support Office
Telephone: 423-614-8181
Email: academicsupport@leeuniversity.edu

Lee University

GENERAL ADMISSIONS

Very important factors considered include: rigor of secondary school record, academic GPA, standardized test scores. *Important factors considered include:* class rank, character/personal qualities, level of applicant's interest. *Other factors considered include:* application essay, recommendation(s), interview, extracurricular activities, talent/ability, first generation, alumni/ae relation. *Freshman Admission Requirements:* High school diploma is required and GED is accepted. *Academic units required:* 4 English, 3 math, 2 science, 1 foreign language, 2 social studies, 1 history. *Academic units recommended:* 4 English, 3 math, 2 science, 1 foreign language, 2 social studies, 1 history, 1 computer science.

ACCOMMODATIONS OR SERVICES

Accommodations are decided upon an individual basis after a thorough review of appropriate, current documentation. The accommodations requests must be supported through the documentation provided and must be logically linked to the current impact of the condition on academic functioning.

FINANCIAL AID

Students should submit: FAFSA. Applicants will be notified of awards on a rolling basis beginning 2/1. The Princeton Review suggests that all financial aid forms be submitted as soon as possible after October 1. *Need-based scholarships/grants offered:* College/university scholarship or grant aid from institutional funds; Federal Pell; Private scholarships; SEOG; State scholarships/grants. *Loan aid offered:* Direct PLUS loans; Direct Subsidized Stafford Loans; Direct Unsubsidized Stafford Loans. Federal Work-Study Program available. Institutional employment available.

CAMPUS LIFE

Activities: Campus Ministries; Choral groups; Concert band; Drama/theater; International Student Organization; Jazz band; Literary magazine; Model UN; Music ensembles; Musical theater; Opera; Pep band; Student government; Student newspaper; Symphony orchestra; Yearbook. **Organizations:** 72 registered organizations, 16 honor societies, 10 religious organizations. 5 fraternities, 4 sororities. **Athletics (Intercollegiate):** *Men:* baseball, basketball, cheerleading, cross-country, golf, soccer, tennis. *Women:* basketball, cheerleading, cross-country, soccer, softball, tennis, volleyball. **On-Campus Highlights:** Paul Conn Student Union-Bookstore, Chick-fil-a, Conn Center-Home of Chapels, Concerts, etc., Dixon Center plays, recitals, community events, De Vos Recreation Center, Dunkin Donuts, Einstein Bros., Subway.

ACCOMMODATIONS

Allowed in exams:	
Calculators	Yes
Dictionary	Yes
Computer	Yes
Spell-checker	Yes
Extended test time	Yes
Scribe	Yes
Proctors	Yes
Oral exams	Yes
Note-takers	Yes
Support services for students with	
LD	Yes
ADHD	Yes
ASD	Yes
Distraction-reduced environment	Yes
Recording of lecture allowed	Yes
Reading technology:	Yes
Audio books	Yes
Other assistive technology Braille embosser; Dragon naturally speaking, Jaws; Mac Program	
Priority registration	Yes
Added costs for services:	
For LD:	No
For ADHD:	No
For ASD:	No
LD specialists	Yes
ADHD & ASD coaching	Yes
ASD specialists	Yes
Professional tutors	Yes
Peer tutors	Yes
Max. hours/week for services	2
How professors are notified of student approved accommodations	Student

COLLEGE GRADUATION REQUIREMENTS

Course waivers allowed	No
Course substitutions allowed	No

Middle Tennessee State University

1301 E Main Street, Murfreesboro, TN 37132 • Admissions: 615-898-2111 • Fax: 615-898-5478

Programs/Services for Students with Learning Differences

The Disability & Access Center (DAC) is a cultural, social, and academic support hub for students at Middle Tennessee State University. This office serves as an initial point of contact, conduit of information, and provisioner in matters related to disability accommodation, access, and awareness. By keeping abreast of emerging trends, the Disability & Access Center will effectively and efficiently respond to the needs of the population it serves. To request accommodations, students should complete a registration application to begin the process. They are required to provide documentation of disability from a healthcare provider. Documentation is reviewed by DAC for completeness and appropriateness. Student meets with DAC staff to discuss accommodation needs. Appropriate accommodations are determined and displayed in a letter format.
Students are responsible for notifying instructors and provides them copies of accommodation letters. Student and faculty discuss the best ways to implement the accommodations.

Admissions

The admission requirements are the same for all students. There is no special admission process for students with LD. All students must meet the same general admission requirements. The minimum GPA is a 2.8 and/or ACT 20. Students should have four years of English, three years of math, two years of science, two years of social studies, two years of foreign language, and one year of visual/performing arts. Course substitutions are not allowed. Students are encouraged to self-disclose a disability in a personal statement during the admission process, although this is not required.

Additional Information

The Disability & Access Center supports student success by promoting independence, cultural awareness, access, advocacy, universal design principles, and technological advances culminating in the understanding that disability is a natural part of the life. Students automatically receives Early Class Registration, each semester, after registering with DAC. Early

Middle Tennessee State University

registration allows students the opportunity to be in the first group of students to register for courses each semester.

GENERAL ADMISSIONS

Very important factors considered include: academic GPA, standardized test scores. *Other factors considered include:* rigor of secondary school record, application essay, recommendation(s), extracurricular activities, talent/ability, character/personal qualities, volunteer work, work experience, level of applicant's interest. *Freshman Admission Requirements:* High school diploma is required and GED is accepted. *Academic units required:* 4 English, 4 math, 3 science, 1 science lab, 2 foreign language, 1 social studies, 1 history, 1 visual/performing arts.

ACCOMMODATIONS OR SERVICES

Accommodations are decided upon an individual basis after a thorough review of appropriate, current documentation. The accommodations requests must be supported through the documentation provided and must be logically linked to the current impact of the condition on academic functioning.

FINANCIAL AID

Students should submit: FAFSA. Applicants will be notified of awards on a rolling basis beginning 2/6. The Princeton Review suggests that all financial aid forms be submitted as soon as possible after October 1. *Need-based scholarships/grants offered:* College/university scholarship or grant aid from institutional funds; Federal Pell; Private scholarships; SEOG; State scholarships/grants. *Loan aid offered:* Direct PLUS loans; Direct Subsidized Stafford Loans; Direct Unsubsidized Stafford Loans. Federal Work-Study Program available. Institutional employment available.

CAMPUS LIFE

Activities: Campus Ministries; Choral groups; Concert band; Dance; Drama/theater; International Student Organization; Jazz band; Literary magazine; Marching band; Model UN; Music ensembles; Musical theater; Pep band; Radio station; Student government; Student newspaper; Student-run film society; Symphony orchestra; Television station. **On-Campus Highlights:** Student Union, Recreation Center, Library, Bragg Building (Recording Industry), Science Building.

ACCOMMODATIONS

Allowed in exams:

Calculators	Yes
Dictionary	Yes
Computer	Yes
Spell-checker	Yes
Extended test time	Yes
Scribe	Yes
Proctors	Yes
Oral exams	Yes
Note-takers	Yes

Support services for students with

LD	No
ADHD	No
ASD	No
Distraction-reduced environment	Yes
Recording of lecture allowed	Yes
Reading technology:	Yes
Audio books	Yes

Other assistive technology Adaptive technology center in the library including : Screen reading software, reading software, writing software, specialized mice, assistive technology computer stations, braille embossers, etc.

Priority registration	Yes

Added costs for services:

For LD:	No
For ADHD:	No
For ASD:	No
LD specialists	No
ADHD & ASD coaching	No
ASD specialists	No
Professional tutors	Yes
Peer tutors	Yes
Max. hours/week for services	44

How professors are notified of student approved accommodations
Director and student

COLLEGE GRADUATION REQUIREMENTS

Course waivers allowed	Yes

In what courses
Math, Foreign Language, public speaking on a case-by-case basis

Course substitutions allowed	Yes

In what courses
Math, Foreign Language, public speaking on a case-by-case basis

The University of Memphis

101 WILDER TOWER, MEMPHIS, TN 38152 • ADMISSIONS: 901-678-2111 • FAX: 901-678-3053

CAMPUS

Type of school	Public
Environment	Metropolis
Support	CS

STUDENTS

Undergrad enrollment	16,741
% male/female	39/61
% from out of state	10
% frosh live on campus	48

FINANCIAL FACTS

Annual in-state tuition	$9,317
Annual out-of-state tuition	$21,029
Room and board	$9,366

GENERAL ADMISSIONS INFO

Application fee	$25
Regular application deadline	7/1

Nonfall registration accepted.

Range SAT EBRW	440–570
Range SAT Math	440–590
Range ACT Composite	20–25

ACADEMICS

Student/faculty ratio	14:1
% students returning for sophomore year	76
% students graduating within 4 years	19
% students graduating within 6 years	43

Most classes have 20–29 students.
Most lab/discussion sessions have 10–19 students.

PROGRAMS/SERVICES FOR STUDENTS WITH LEARNING DIFFERENCES

The university's LD/ADHD/ASD Program is designed to enhance academic strengths, provide support for areas of weakness, and build skills to help students with Learning, ADHD and Autism Spectrum Disorders compete in the college environment. The program encourages development of life-long learning skills as well as personal responsibility for academic success. Training in college survival skills and regular meetings with the staff are emphasized during the first year to aid in the transition to college. Specific services are tailored to individual needs, considering one's strengths, weaknesses, course requirements, and learning styles. Students are integrated into regular classes and are held to the same academic standards as other students; however, academic accommodations are available to assist them in meeting requirements. The LD/ADHD/ASD program places responsibility on students to initiate services and follow through with services once they are arranged. Most students who use the appropriate services are successful in their academic pursuits.

ADMISSIONS

The LD/ADHD/ASD services are open to any student admitted to the university who provides current, appropriate psycho-educational and other relevant medical information sufficient to establish the existence of a disability which causes substantial limitation.

Additional Information

Some services are available to all students registered with DRS, however, academic services and accommodations are individually determined and are based on the student's current functional limitations outlined in the medical or professional documentation, the student's compensatory skills and the requirements of a particular course or program. The following general services are available to all students registered with DRS: Early registration, orientation to using disability services, assistance with

ADMISSIONS INFO FOR STUDENTS WITH LEARNING DIFFERENCES

SAT/ACT required: Yes
Interview required: No
Essay required: No
Additional application required: No
Documentation required for:
 LD: Psycho ed evaluation to include: relevant historical info, instructional interventions, related services, age diagnosed, objective data (aptitude, achievement, info processing), test scores (standard, percentile and grade equivalents) and describe functional limitations.
 ADHD: Diagnosis based on DSM-V; history of behaviors impairing functioning in academic setting; diagnostic interview; history of symptoms; evidence of ongoing behaviors.
 ASD: Psycho ed evaluation
Documentation submitted to: Disability Resources for Students
Special Ed. HS course work accepted: No
Separate application required for program services: No
Contact Information
Name of program or department: Disability Resources for Students
Telephone: 901-678-2880
Fax: 901-678-3070

The University of Memphis

strategic class scheduling to enhance academic success, semester plan for accommodations and services, memos to faculty about disability needs, advocacy relating to disability access issues, information and guidance on academic, social, career, and personal issues; orientation to and use of the Assistive Technology Lab, referral to other university departments and community agencies, liaison with state and federal rehabilitation agencies, and information about specific opportunities for students with disabilities.

GENERAL ADMISSIONS

Very important factors considered include: rigor of secondary school record, academic GPA, standardized test scores. *Other factors considered include:* application essay, recommendation(s), talent/ability, character/personal qualities, first generation, work experience. *Freshman Admission Requirements:* High school diploma is required and GED is accepted. *Academic units required:* 4 English, 3 math, 2 science, 1 science lab, 2 foreign language, 1 social studies, 1 history, 1 visual/performing arts.

ACCOMMODATIONS OR SERVICES

Accommodations are decided upon an individual basis after a thorough review of appropriate, current documentation. The accommodations requests must be supported through the documentation provided and must be logically linked to the current impact of the condition on academic functioning.

FINANCIAL AID

Students should submit: FAFSA. Applicants will be notified of awards on a rolling basis beginning 3/15. The Princeton Review suggests that all financial aid forms be submitted as soon as possible after October 1. *Need-based scholarships/grants offered:* College/university scholarship or grant aid from institutional funds; Federal Pell; Private scholarships; SEOG; State scholarships/grants. *Loan aid offered:* Direct PLUS loans; Direct Subsidized Stafford Loans; Direct Unsubsidized Stafford Loans. Federal Work-Study Program available. Institutional employment available.

CAMPUS LIFE

Activities: Campus Ministries; Choral groups; Concert band; Dance; Drama/theater; International Student Organization; Jazz band; Literary magazine; Marching band; Music ensembles; Musical theater; Opera; Pep band; Radio station; Student government; Student newspaper; Symphony orchestra. **Organizations:** 140 registered organizations, 20 honor societies, 12 religious organizations. 14 fraternities, 11 sororities. **Athletics (Intercollegiate):** *Men:* baseball, basketball, cross-country, football, golf, riflery, soccer, tennis, track/field (outdoor). *Women:* basketball, cross-country, golf, riflery, soccer, softball, tennis, track/field (outdoor), volleyball. **On-Campus Highlights:** Rose Theater Lecture Hall, FedEx Institute of Technology, Finch Recreation Facility, Harris Concert Hall, Newly opened University Center.

ACCOMMODATIONS

Allowed in exams:

Calculators	Yes
Dictionary	Yes
Computer	Yes
Spell-checker	Yes
Extended test time	Yes
Scribe	Yes
Proctors	Yes
Oral exams	Yes
Note-takers	Yes

Support services for students with

LD	Yes
ADHD	Yes
ASD	Yes
Distraction-reduced environment	Yes
Recording of lecture allowed	Yes
Reading technology:	Yes
Audio books	Yes
Other assistive technology	Yes
Priority registration	Yes
Added costs for services:	
For LD:	No
For ADHD:	No
For ASD:	No
LD specialists	Yes
ADHD & ASD coaching	Yes- Academic Coaching for Excellence Program
ASD specialists	No
Professional tutors	Yes
Peer tutors	No
Max. hours/week for services	Varies
How professors are notified of student approved accommodations	Student

COLLEGE GRADUATION REQUIREMENTS

Course waivers allowed	No
Course substitutions allowed	Yes

In what courses: Course substitutions may be granted for foreign language requirements. Students with questions about specific course substitutions outside of foreign language should consult with their coordinator.

University of Tennessee—Chattanooga

615 McCallie Avenue, Chattanooga, TN 37403 • Admissions: 423-425-4662 • Fax: 423-425-4157

CAMPUS

Type of school	Public
Environment	City
Support	CS

STUDENTS

Undergrad enrollment	10,097
% male/female	44/56
% from out of state	6
% frosh live on campus	78

FINANCIAL FACTS

Annual in-state tuition	$6,888
Annual out-of-state tuition	$23,006
Room and board	$8,786
Required fees	$1,776

GENERAL ADMISSIONS INFO

Application fee	$30
Regular application deadline	5/1

Nonfall registration accepted. Admission may be deferred for a maximum of 1 semester.

Range SAT EBRW	530–630
Range SAT Math	510–610
Range ACT Composite	21–26

ACADEMICS

Student/faculty ratio	14:1
% students returning for sophomore year	73
% students graduating within 4 years	22
% students graduating within 6 years	45

Most classes have 10–19 students.
Most lab/discussion sessions have 10–19 students.

PROGRAMS/SERVICES FOR STUDENTS WITH LEARNING DIFFERENCES

Disability Resource Center (DRC) at The University of Tennessee at Chattanooga is committed to ensuring that each individual has equal access to all educational opportunities and maximizes their potential regardless of the impact of their disability. OSD is also committed to supporting the ongoing development of an accessible university that embraces diversity. This mission is accomplished by: creating a physically, programmatically and attitudinally accessible environment where people are accepted and expected to participate fully regardless of their disability, and encouraging the development of an educational culture that embraces and celebrates people's differences.

ADMISSIONS

Students with disabilities submit a general application to the Admissions Office. If a course deficiency is due to impact of disability, an Appeals Committee will sometimes allow a probationary admittance if DRC works with prospective student to develop an accommodation plan. Students admitted on condition must earn at least a 2.0 GPA their first semester or suspension will result. The Dean of Admissions or Admission Committee may recommend conditions for acceptance. In order to receive accommodations in the classroom, students with disabilities need to submit application and documentation (listed above) to the Disability Resource Center. Application to the Disability Resource Center is a separate process and is not relevant to the admissions process.

ADMISSIONS INFO FOR STUDENTS WITH LEARNING DIFFERENCES

SAT/ACT required: No
Interview required: No
Essay required: No
Additional application required: No
Documentation required for:
 LD: Psycho ed evaluation to include: relevant historical info, instructional interventions, related services, age diagnosed, objective data (aptitude, achievement, info processing), test scores (standard, percentile and grade equivalents) and describe functional limitations.
 ADHD: Diagnosis based on DSM-V; history of behaviors impairing functioning in academic setting; diagnostic interview; history of symptoms; evidence of ongoing behaviors.
 ASD: Psycho ed evaluation
Documentation submitted to: DRC
Special Ed. HS course work accepted: No
Separate application required for program services: Yes
# of students last year receiving services/accommodations for:
 LD: 850
Contact Information
Name of program or department: Disability Resource Center
Telephone: 423-425-4006
Fax: 423-425-2288

University of Tennessee—Chattanooga

Additional Information

DRC does not, as a matter of policy, seek on a student's behalf a waiver of any course work. Students admitted conditionally may be required to carry a reduced course load, take specific courses, have a specific advisor, and take specific programs of developmental study. Social skills development activities may involve video and role-playing situations in group form as well as during informal gatherings. There is a monthly publication, The CAPsule, for CAP students and parents. UTC offers developmental math and English courses for institutional credit. Services and accommodations are available for undergraduate and graduate students.

GENERAL ADMISSIONS

Very important factors considered include: rigor of secondary school record, academic GPA, standardized test scores. *Important factors considered include:* character/personal qualities. *Other factors considered include:* application essay, recommendation(s), extracurricular activities, talent/ability, volunteer work, work experience. *Freshman Admission Requirements:* High school diploma is required and GED is accepted. *Academic units required:* 4 English, 4 math, 3 science, 3 science labs, 2 foreign language, 2 history, 1 visual/performing arts.

ACCOMMODATIONS OR SERVICES

Accommodations are decided upon an individual basis after a thorough review of appropriate, current documentation. The accommodations requests must be supported through the documentation provided and must be logically linked to the current impact of the condition on academic functioning.

FINANCIAL AID

Students should submit: FAFSA. Applicants will be notified of awards on a rolling basis beginning 1/20. The Princeton Review suggests that all financial aid forms be submitted as soon as possible after October 1. *Need-based scholarships/grants offered:* College/university scholarship or grant aid from institutional funds; Federal Pell; Private scholarships; SEOG; State scholarships/grants. *Loan aid offered:* Direct PLUS loans; Direct Subsidized Stafford Loans; Direct Unsubsidized Stafford Loans. Federal Work-Study Program available. Institutional employment available.

CAMPUS LIFE

Activities: Campus Ministries; Choral groups; Concert band; Dance; Drama/theater; International Student Organization; Jazz band; Literary magazine; Marching band; Model UN; Music ensembles; Musical theater; Opera; Pep band; Radio station; Student government; Student newspaper; Student-run film society; Symphony orchestra; Television station. **Organizations:** 130 registered organizations, 34 honor societies, 8 religious organizations. 7 fraternities, 7 sororities. **Athletics (Intercollegiate):** *Men:* basketball, cross-country, football, golf, tennis, track/field (outdoor), wrestling. *Women:* basketball, cross-country, golf, soccer, softball, tennis, track/field (outdoor), volleyball. **On-Campus Highlights:** Aquatic and Recreation Center, New UTC Library, The Crossroads, Challenger Center.

ACCOMMODATIONS

Allowed in exams:

Calculators	Yes
Dictionary	Not Applicable
Computer	Yes
Spell-checker	Yes
Extended test time	Yes
Scribe	Yes
Proctors	Yes
Oral exams	Yes
Note-takers	Yes

Support services for students with

LD	Yes
ADHD	Yes
ASD	Yes
Distraction-reduced environment	Yes
Recording of lecture allowed	Yes
Reading technology:	Yes
Audio books	Yes
Other assistive technology	Yes
Priority registration	Yes

Added costs for services:

For LD:	No
LD specialists	Yes
ADHD & ASD coaching	No
ASD specialists	No
Professional tutors	No
Peer tutors	No
Max. hours/week for services	Varies
How professors are notified of student approved accommodations	Student

COLLEGE GRADUATION REQUIREMENTS

Course waivers allowed	No
Course substitutions allowed	Yes

University of Tennessee, Knoxville

527 Andy Holt Tower, Knoxville, TN 37996-0230 • Admissions: 865-974-1111 • Fax:

CAMPUS

Type of school	Public
Environment	City
Support	CS

STUDENTS

Undergrad enrollment	22,151
% male/female	50/50
% from out of state	13
% frosh live on campus	90

FINANCIAL FACTS

Annual in-state tuition	$11,110
Annual out-of-state tuition	$29,300
Room and board	$10,696
Required fees	$1,896

GENERAL ADMISSIONS INFO

Application fee	$50
Priority deadline	11/11

Nonfall registration accepted.

Range SAT EBRW	580–660
Range SAT Math	560–650
Range ACT Composite	24–30

ACADEMICS

Student/faculty ratio	17:1
% students returning for sophomore year	86
% students graduating within 4 years	46
% students graduating within 6 years	70

Most classes have 20–29 students.
Most lab/discussion sessions have 20–29 students.

Programs/Services for Students with Learning Differences

The mission of the Office of Disability Services is to provide each student with a disability an equal opportunity to participate in the university's programs and activities. Students who are requesting support services are required to submit documentation to verify eligibility under the ADA of 1990. The documentation must include medical or psychological information from a certified professional. It is each student's responsibility to meet the essential qualifications and institutional standards; disclose the disability in a timely manner to ODS; provide appropriate documentation; inform ODS of accommodation needs; talk with professors about accommodations in the classroom, as needed; inform ODS of barriers to a successful education; maintain and return borrowed equipment; keep all appointments with ODS staff members or all to cancel or reschedule; be involved in their academic planning and course selection; and monitor their own progress toward graduation.

Admissions

There is no special admission process for students with learning disabilities. The Office of Admissions makes every attempt to judge each application on its academic merits. Applicants believe that their academic record does not accurately reflect their situation, do not include documentation with admission materials. Applicants feel more information is needed to compete at an equal level with others seeking admission, they consider voluntarily self-identifying the disability and the circumstances to the Admissions Office. Qualified candidates with a disability will not be denied admissions solely on the basis of their disability.

ADMISSIONS INFO FOR STUDENTS WITH LEARNING DIFFERENCES

SAT/ACT required: Yes
Interview required: Not Applicable
Essay required: Not Applicable
Additional application required: Not Applicable
Documentation required for:
 LD: Documentation may be required to establish disability, to determine functional limitations, and as guidance on the most appropriate accommodations. SDS meets with students, reviews any documentations provided, and then determines what, if any, additional documentation is needed.
 ADHD: Documentation may be required to establish disability, to determine functional limitations, and as guidance on the most appropriate accommodations. SDS meets with students, reviews any documentations provided, and then determines what, if any, additional documentation is needed.
 ASD: Documentation may be required to establish disability, to determine functional limitations, and as guidance on the most appropriate accommodations. SDS meets with students, reviews any documentations provided, and then determines what, if any, additional documentation is needed.
Documentation submitted to: Student Disability Services
Special Ed. HS course work accepted: Not Applicable
Separate application required for program services: Not Applicable
Contact Information
Name of program or department: Student Disability Services
Telephone: 865-974-6087
Fax: 865-974-9552
Email: sds@utk.edu

University of Tennessee, Knoxville

Additional Information

The goals of ODS are to provide access to appropriate accommodations and support services; provide referrals and information for a variety of campus resources, including transportation and housing; encourage and assist students with disabilities to develop greater independence; increase faculty and staff understanding of the various needs of students with disabilities; and assist the university in interpreting legal mandates that address students with disabilities. Disability Services works with each student on a case-by-case basis to determine and implement appropriate accommodations based on documentation. Services could include note-takers, alternative testing arrangements such as extra time, books on tape, computers with speech input, separate testing rooms, tape recorders, and foreign language substitutions. Content tutors are available on campus through different departments.

GENERAL ADMISSIONS

Very important factors considered include: rigor of secondary school record, academic GPA, standardized test scores. *Important factors considered include:* application essay, recommendation(s), extracurricular activities, talent/ability, character/personal qualities, first generation, alumni/ae relation, volunteer work, work experience. *Other factors considered include:* class rank, level of applicant's interest. *Freshman Admission Requirements:* High school diploma is required and GED is accepted. *Academic units required: Academic units recommended:* 4 English, 4 math, 3 science, 3 science labs, 2 foreign language, 1 social studies, 1 history, 1 visual/performing arts.

ACCOMMODATIONS OR SERVICES

Accommodations are decided upon an individual basis after a thorough review of appropriate, current documentation. The accommodations requests must be supported through the documentation provided and must be logically linked to the current impact of the condition on academic functioning.

FINANCIAL AID

Students should submit: FAFSA. Applicants will be notified of awards on a rolling basis beginning 3/15. The Princeton Review suggests that all financial aid forms be submitted as soon as possible after October 1. *Need-based scholarships/grants offered:* College/university scholarship or grant aid from institutional funds; Federal Pell; Private scholarships; SEOG; State scholarships/grants. *Loan aid offered:* Direct PLUS loans; Direct Subsidized Stafford Loans; Direct Unsubsidized Stafford Loans. Federal Work-Study Program available.

CAMPUS LIFE

Activities: Campus Ministries; Choral groups; Concert band; Dance; Drama/theater; International Student Organization; Jazz band; Literary magazine; Marching band; Model UN; Music ensembles; Musical theater; Opera; Pep band; Radio station; Student government; Student newspaper; Student-run film society; Symphony orchestra; Television station; Yearbook. **Organizations:** 450 registered organizations, 90 honor societies, 30 religious organizations. 23 fraternities, 18 sororities. **Athletics (Intercollegiate):** *Men:* baseball, basketball, cheerleading, cross-country, diving, football, golf, swimming, tennis, track/field (outdoor), track/field (indoor). *Women:* basketball, cheerleading, crew/rowing, cross-country, diving, golf, soccer, softball, swimming, tennis, track/field (outdoor), track/field (indoor), volleyball. **On-Campus Highlights:** Neyland Stadium, Student Union, Ayres Hall and the Hill, Johnson-Ward Pedestrian Mall and Walkway, T-Recs (Student Recreation Center).

ACCOMMODATIONS	
Allowed in exams:	
Calculators	Yes
Dictionary	Yes
Computer	Yes
Spell-checker	Yes
Extended test time	Yes
Scribe	Yes
Proctors	Yes
Oral exams	Yes
Note-takers	Yes
Support services for students with	
LD	Yes
ADHD	Yes
ASD	Yes
Distraction-reduced environment	Yes
Recording of lecture allowed	Yes
Reading technology:	Yes
Audio books	Yes
Other assistive technology	
Priority registration	Yes
Added costs for services:	
For LD:	No
LD specialists	Yes
ADHD & ASD coaching	Yes
ASD specialists	No
Professional tutors	Yes
Peer tutors	Yes
Max. hours/week for services	Varies
How professors are notified of student	
approved accommodations	Student

COLLEGE GRADUATION REQUIREMENTS	
Course waivers allowed	No
Course substitutions allowed	Yes
In what courses	Math,
Foreign Language, Other	

University of Tennessee at Martin

554 UNIVERSITY STREET, MARTIN, TN 38238 • ADMISSIONS: 731-881-7020 • FAX: 731-881-7029

CAMPUS

Type of school	Public
Environment	Village
Support	SP

STUDENTS

Undergrad enrollment	5,525
% male/female	42/58
% from out of state	8
% frosh live on campus	61

FINANCIAL FACTS

Annual in-state tuition	$8,052
Annual out-of-state tuition	$14,092
Room and board	$6,164
Required fees	$1,460

GENERAL ADMISSIONS INFO

Application fee	$30
Priority deadline	8/1

Nonfall registration accepted. Admission may be deferred for a maximum of 1 year.

Range ACT Composite	20–25

ACADEMICS

Student/faculty ratio	15:1
% students returning for sophomore year	76
% students graduating within 4 years	23
% students graduating within 6 years	50

Most classes have 10–19 students.
Most lab/discussion sessions have fewer than 10 students.

PROGRAMS/SERVICES FOR STUDENTS WITH LEARNING DIFFERENCES

The university believes students with learning disabilities can achieve success in college without academic compromise and can become productive, self-sufficient members of society. Students must self-identify with ODS by completing the "ODS Introductory Questionnaire" and sending this back to the Office with the appropriate documentation. ODS has a list of "reasonable accommodations" and are willing to work with the student to access what is needed. ODS is designed to complement and supplement existing university support services available for all students.

ADMISSIONS

Basically, applicants must meet regular admission criteria. Qualified students with learning disabilities should apply to ODS once they have received an acceptance from the Office of Admissions.. Documentation should be sent to ODS. Applicants are selected on the basis of intellectual potential (average to superior), motivation, academic preparation, and willingness to work hard.

Additional Information

Students make an appointment with the ODS office and meet with an ODS advisor. The advisor will determine what reasonable accommodations and

ADMISSIONS INFO FOR STUDENTS WITH LEARNING DIFFERENCES

SAT/ACT required: Yes
Interview required: Yes
Essay required: Not Applicable
Additional application required: Yes
Documentation required for:
 LD: A letter form a licensed psychologist, psychiatrist, neurologist or other qualified medical professional detailing the diagnosis, functional limitations, and recommended accommodations. We consider all requests for accommodations on an individual basis. We research any available medical/ professional documentation, past IEP or 504 plans, and notes from one-on-one interviews.
 ADHD: A letter form a licensed psychologist, psychiatrist, neurologist or other qualified medical professional detailing the diagnosis, functional limitations, and recommended accommodations. We consider all requests for accommodations on an individual basis. We research any available medical/ professional documentation, past IEP or 504 plans, and notes from one-on-one interviews.
 ASD: A letter form a licensed psychologist, psychiatrist, neurologist or other qualified medical professional detailing the diagnosis, functional limitations, and recommended accommodations. We consider all requests for accommodations on an individual basis. We research any available medical/ professional documentation, past IEP or 504 plans, and notes from one-on-one interviews.
Documentation submitted to: Disabilites Services Office
Special Ed. HS course work accepted: No
Separate application required for program services: Yes
# of students last year receiving services/accommodations for:
 LD: 43
 ADHD: 76
Contact Information
Name of program or department: Disabilites Services Office
Telephone: 731-881-7719
Fax: 731-881-1886
Email: success@utm.edu

University of Tennessee at Martin

services will be needed and the procedures for receiving services. Students with appropriate documentation may be eligible to receive the following services: extended testing times; distraction-free testing environments; use of calculators, dictionaries, computers, and spellcheckers during exams; proctors; oral exams; note-takers; taper recorders in class; books on tape; and tutoring. Services and accommodations are provided to undergraduate and graduate students.

GENERAL ADMISSIONS

Very important factors considered include: rigor of secondary school record, academic GPA, standardized test scores. *Freshman Admission Requirements:* High school diploma is required and GED is accepted. *Academic units required:* 4 English, 4 math, 3 science, 1 science lab, 2 foreign language, 1 social studies, 1 history, 1 visual/performing arts.

ACCOMMODATIONS OR SERVICES

Accommodations are decided upon an individual basis after a thorough review of appropriate, current documentation. The accommodations requests must be supported through the documentation provided and must be logically linked to the current impact of the condition on academic functioning.

FINANCIAL AID

Students should submit: FAFSA. Applicants will be notified of awards on a rolling basis beginning 3/15. The Princeton Review suggests that all financial aid forms be submitted as soon as possible after October 1. *Need-based scholarships/grants offered:* College/university scholarship or grant aid from institutional funds; Federal Pell; Private scholarships; SEOG; State scholarships/grants. *Loan aid offered:* Direct PLUS loans; Direct Subsidized Stafford Loans; Direct Unsubsidized Stafford Loans. Federal Work-Study Program available. Institutional employment available.

CAMPUS LIFE

Activities: Campus Ministries; Choral groups; Concert band; Dance; Drama/theater; International Student Organization; Jazz band; Literary magazine; Marching band; Model UN; Music ensembles; Musical theater; Pep band; Radio station; Student government; Student newspaper; Student-run film society; Television station; Yearbook. **Organizations:** 100 registered organizations, 27 honor societies, 11 religious organizations. 12 fraternities, 8 sororities. **Athletics (Intercollegiate):** *Men:* baseball, basketball, cross-country, football, golf, riflery, rodeo *Women:* basketball, cheerleading, cross-country, equestrian sports, riflery, rodeo, soccer, softball, tennis, volleyball. **On-Campus Highlights:** Boling University Center, Paul Meek Library, Student Recreation Center, Elam Center and Intramural facilities, Quad.

ACCOMMODATIONS

Allowed in exams:	
Calculators	Yes
Dictionary	Yes
Computer	Yes
Spell-checker	Yes
Extended test time	Yes
Scribe	Yes
Proctors	Yes
Oral exams	Yes
Note-takers	Yes
Support services for students with	
LD	Yes
ADHD	Yes
ASD	Yes
Distraction-reduced environment	Yes
Recording of lecture allowed	Yes
Reading technology:	Yes
Audio books	Yes
Other assistive technologyJAWS, Zoom Text, FM Amplifier, Braille embossers, ABYY Fine Reader, Read and Write Gold, Livescribe	
Priority registration	No
Added costs for services:	
For LD:	No
LD specialists	No
ADHD & ASD coaching	No
ASD specialists	Yes
Professional tutors	Yes
Peer tutors	Yes
Max. hours/week for services	120
How professors are notified of student approved accommodations	
Director and student	

COLLEGE GRADUATION REQUIREMENTS

Course waivers allowed	No
Course substitutions allowed	Yes
In what courses	
This varies and is subject to faculty approval.	

Abilene Christian University

ACU Box 29100, Abilene, TX 79699 • Admissions: 325-674-2650 • Fax: 325-674-2130

CAMPUS

Type of school	Private (nonprofit)
Environment	City
Support	CS

STUDENTS

Undergrad enrollment	3,655
% male/female	41/59
% from out of state	11
% frosh live on campus	96

FINANCIAL FACTS

Annual tuition	$33,280
Room and board	$10,378
Required fees	$50

GENERAL ADMISSIONS INFO

Application fee	$50
Regular application deadline	2/15
Nonfall registration accepted.	

Range SAT EBRW	510–620
Range SAT Math	515–600
Range ACT Composite	21–26

ACADEMICS

Student/faculty ratio	13:1
% students returning for sophomore year	77
% students graduating within 4 years	47
% students graduating within 6 years	60

PROGRAMS/SERVICES FOR STUDENTS WITH LEARNING DIFFERENCES

ACU has a tradition and a vision for academic excellence for all of its students—including those with disabilities. SOAR -- Student Opportunities, Advocacy, and Resources --is a recommendation program designed to assist ACU students and connect them to resources available to support their path to success. SOAR is a partnership with faculty, staff, parents and students to build a caring community and create a safe environment for students to discuss challenges and obstacles they face.

ADMISSIONS

All students must be admitted to the university and meet the same criteria for admission. There is no special admission process for students with learning disabilities. Regular admissions criteria include 20 ACT or 930-plus SAT; college preparatory courses including 4 years of English, 3 years of math, 3 years of science, and 2 years of a foreign language; and no specific GPA. Some students not meeting the admission criteria may be admitted conditionally. Students admitted conditionally must take specified courses in a summer term and demonstrate motivation and ability.

Additional Information

Alpha Scholars Program provides opportunities for individual instruction in basic skills areas such as writing, math, or study skills; assessment of learning preferences, strengths, and weaknesses; instruction and tutoring designed to fit the student's particular learning preferences and strengths and academic needs; classroom help if needed such as readers, note-takers, alternative testing arrangements; personal, career, and academic counseling; and workshops on topics such as time management skills, resume writing, career placement, and study skills.

ADMISSIONS INFO FOR STUDENTS WITH LEARNING DIFFERENCES

SAT/ACT required: Yes
Interview required: No
Essay required: Not Applicable
Additional application required: Yes
Documentation required for:
  LD: Full psychoeducational assessment (with subscores)
  ADHD: Psychoeducational assessment or response to documentation form from qualified professional
  ASD: documentation of previous services
Documentation submitted to: Alpha Scholars Program
Special Ed. HS course work accepted: No
Separate application required for program services: No
  LD: 193
  ADHD: 117
Contact Information
Name of program or department: Alpha Scholars Program
Telephone: 325-674-2667
Fax: 325-674-6847

Abilene Christian University

GENERAL ADMISSIONS

Very important factors considered include: rigor of secondary school record, class rank, academic GPA, standardized test scores. *Important factors considered include:* talent/ability, character/personal qualities. *Other factors considered include:* application essay, recommendation(s), extracurricular activities, first generation, alumni/ae relation, volunteer work, work experience, level of applicant's interest. *Freshman Admission Requirements:* High school diploma is required and GED is accepted. *Academic units recommended:* 4 English, 3 math, 3 science, 2 science labs, 2 foreign language, 1 history, 1 unit from above areas or other academic areas.

ACCOMMODATIONS OR SERVICES

Accommodations are decided upon an individual basis after a thorough review of appropriate, current documentation. The accommodations requests must be supported through the documentation provided and must be logically linked to the current impact of the condition on academic functioning.

FINANCIAL AID

Students should submit: FAFSA. Applicants will be notified of awards on a rolling basis beginning 4/1. The Princeton Review suggests that all financial aid forms be submitted as soon as possible after October 1. *Need-based scholarships/grants offered:* College/university scholarship or grant aid from institutional funds; Federal Pell; Private scholarships; SEOG; State scholarships/grants. *Loan aid offered:* Direct PLUS loans; Direct Subsidized Stafford Loans; Direct Unsubsidized Stafford Loans. Federal Work-Study Program available. Institutional employment available.

CAMPUS LIFE

Activities: Campus Ministries; Choral groups; Concert band; Dance; Drama/theater; International Student Organization; Jazz band; Literary magazine; Marching band; Model UN; Music ensembles; Musical theater; Opera; Pep band; Radio station; Student government; Student newspaper; Symphony orchestra; Television station. **Organizations:** 108 registered organizations, 14 honor societies, 16 religious organizations. 4 fraternities, 7 sororities. **Athletics (Intercollegiate):** *Men:* baseball, basketball, cross-country, football, tennis, track/field (outdoor), track/field (indoor). *Women:* basketball, cross-country, soccer, softball, tennis, track/field (outdoor), track/field (indoor), volleyball. **On-Campus Highlights:** Student Recreation and Wellness Center, Learning Commons in Brown Library, Jacob's Dream Sculpture, World Famous Bean in McGlothlin Campus Cntr., Hunter Welcome Center.

ACCOMMODATIONS

Allowed in exams:	
Calculators	Yes
Dictionary	Yes
Computer	Yes
Spell-checker	Yes
Extended test time	Yes
Scribe	Yes
Proctors	Yes
Oral exams	No
Note-takers	Yes
Support services for students with	
LD	Yes
ADHD	Yes
ASD	Yes
Distraction-reduced environment	Yes
Recording of lecture allowed	Yes
Reading technology:	Yes
Audio books	Yes
Other assistive technology	Captioning, copies of teachers slides, preferential seating
Priority registration	No
Added costs for services:	
For LD:	No
For ADHD:	No
For ASD:	No
LD specialists	Yes
ADHD & ASD coaching	Yes
ASD specialists	Yes
Professional tutors	Yes
Peer tutors	Yes
Max. hours/week for services	20
How professors are notified of student approved accommodations	Student

COLLEGE GRADUATION REQUIREMENTS

Course waivers allowed	No
Course substitutions allowed	No

Lamar University

LAMAR STATION, BEAUMONT, TX 77710 • ADMISSIONS: 409-880-8888 • FAX: 409-880-8463

PROGRAMS/SERVICES FOR STUDENTS WITH LEARNING DIFFERENCES

The Disability Resource Center (DRC) assures qualified students access to Lamar University's academic activities, programs, resources, and services. Students with disabilities may qualify for accommodations, academic adjustments and/or assistive technology. Students are encouraged to contact the DRC to schedule an appointment with the Director or Communication Access Coordinator and complete an Accommodation Request Form and submit appropriate disability documentation that supports the accommodation requests. Individualized accommodation plans are developed for each student based on the needs identified.

ADMISSIONS

Applicants with learning disabilities and/or ADHD must meet the general admission requirements. Services will be offered to enrolled students who notify The Disability Resource Center. Students must be in top half of their class and complete 14 "solid" credits to be admitted unconditionally, including four years English, three years math (algebra I–II and geometry or higher), two years science (physical science, biology, chemistry, physics, or geology), two and a half years social science, and two and a half years electives (foreign language is recommended). A very limited number of applicants not meeting the prerequisites may be admitted on "individual approval." Those not in the top half must achieve a minimum composite score of 1000 SAT/21 ACT. Some students may be considered on an Individual Approval basis if they fail to meet Unconditional Admission. These students are subject to mandatory advisement; six-credit limit in summer and 14 in fall term, and must successfully complete nine hours with 2.0 GPA; students must meet these provisions or leave for one year.

Additional Information

The Disability Resource Center offers a variety of services designed to assure qualified students access to the university's academic activities, programs, resources, and services. Services or accommodations could include priority registration; alternative testing accommodations; copying of class notes; classroom accommodations; note-takers; readers and textbooks on tape. Professional staff assist students with questions, problem solving, adjustment, decision making, goal planning, and testing. Skills classes in study skills are offered, including developmental writing, reading, and math for credit. Students are referred to other offices and personnel in accord with the needs and intents of the individual. Services and accommodations are available for undergraduate and graduate students.

GENERAL ADMISSIONS

Freshman Admission Requirements: High school diploma is required and GED is accepted; High school diploma is required and GED is not accepted. *Academic units recommended:* 4 English, 3 math, 2 science, 2 social studies, 2 academic electives.

ACCOMMODATIONS OR SERVICES

Accommodations are decided upon an individual basis after a thorough review of appropriate, current documentation. The accommodations requests must be supported through the documentation provided and must be logically linked to the current impact of the condition on academic functioning.

FINANCIAL AID

Students should submit: FAFSA; Institution's own financial aid form; State aid form. The Princeton Review suggests that all financial aid forms be submitted as soon as possible after October 1. *Loan aid offered:* Federal Work-Study Program available. Institutional employment available.

CAMPUS LIFE

Activities: Student government; Student newspaper. **Organizations:** 145 registered organizations, 11 fraternities, 8 sororities. **Athletics (Intercollegiate):** *Men:* baseball, basketball, cross-country, golf, tennis, track/field (outdoor). *Women:* basketball, cross-country, golf, tennis, track/field (outdoor), volleyball.

ACCOMMODATIONS

Allowed in exams:

Calculators	Yes
Dictionary	Yes
Computer	Yes
Spell-checker	Yes
Extended test time	Yes
Scribe	Yes
Proctors	Yes
Oral exams	Yes
Note-takers	Yes
Support services for students with	
LD	Yes
ADHD	Yes
ASD	Yes
Distraction-reduced environment	Yes
Recording of lecture allowed	Yes
Reading technology:	Yes
Audio books	Yes
Other assistive technology computer screen reader, screen enlarger, Braille	
Priority registration	Yes
Added costs for services:	
For LD:	No
For ADHD:	No
For ASD:	No
LD specialists	No
ADHD & ASD coaching	No
ASD specialists	No
Professional tutors	No
Peer tutors	Yes
Max. hours/week for services	15
How professors are notified of student approved accommodations	Student

COLLEGE GRADUATION REQUIREMENTS

Course waivers allowed	No
Course substitutions allowed	Yes

In what courses Appropriateness of a core course substitution is determined by the Coordinating Board of the State of Texas; other subsitutions are determined by student's academic department.

Schreiner University

2100 MEMORIAL BOULEVARD, KERRVILLE, TX 78028-5697 • ADMISSIONS: 830-792-7217 • FAX: (830) 792-7226

CAMPUS

Type of school	Private (nonprofit)
Environment	Town
Support	SP

STUDENTS

Undergrad enrollment	1,165
% male/female	42/58
% from out of state	2
% frosh live on campus	75

FINANCIAL FACTS

Annual tuition	$24,990
Room and board	$10,152
Required fees	$1,910

GENERAL ADMISSIONS INFO

Application fee	$25
Priority deadline	5/1
Regular application deadline	8/1

Nonfall registration accepted. Admission may be deferred for a maximum of 1 semester.

Range SAT EBRW	480–580
Range SAT Math	480–560
Range ACT Composite	19–24

ACADEMICS

Student/faculty ratio	13:1
% students returning for sophomore year	71
% students graduating within 4 years	41
% students graduating within 6 years	48

Most classes have 10–19 students. Most lab/discussion sessions have 10–19 students.

PROGRAMS/SERVICES FOR STUDENTS WITH LEARNING DIFFERENCES

Students admitted to the Learning Support Services program must be highly motivated, have the intellectual potential for success in a rigorous academic program, and have the ability to meet the demands of college life. Extensive learning support is given to each student, and the ultimate goal is for students to be able to succeed without special help. The Learning Support Services (LSS) program is staffed by LD specialists and many tutors. Students with learning disabilities are enrolled in regular college courses and receive individual tutorial assistance in each subject. Students in the program are held to the same high standards and complete the same curriculum requirements as all other degree candidates. In addition to the LSS staff, the Schreiner University faculty is dedicated to helping students realize their full potential.

ADMISSIONS

Proof of high school diploma and all significant materials relevant to the specific learning disability must be submitted. Applicants should be enrolled in regular, mainstream English courses in high school. We recommend that students take a college-preparatory curriculum. However, admission would not be denied to a qualified candidate if some course work was not included. The Woodcock-Johnson Achievement Battery is preferred, but other tests are accepted. An interview is required and is an important part of the admissions decision. Applicants are considered individually and selected on the basis of their intellectual ability, motivation, academic preparation, and potential for success. For a candidate to be considered for admission, the following are required: all secondary school transcripts (transfer students must also supply transcripts of all attempted college work); medical or psychological statement of specific learning disability or attention deficit hyperactivity disorder; written report of the results of the WAIS-IV, including all subtest scores and verbal, performance, and full-scale IQ scores taken within 12 months of application for admission; current individual achievement test results showing level of proficiency in reading comprehension, word identification, word attack, spelling, writing (written language), math calculation, and applied mathematics;

ADMISSIONS INFO FOR STUDENTS WITH LEARNING DIFFERENCES

SAT/ACT required: Yes
Interview required: Yes
Essay required: Required
Additional application required: Not Applicable
Documentation required for:
LD:Psycho ed evaluation to include: relevant historical info, instructional interventions, related services, age diagnosed, objective data (aptitude, achievement, info processing), test scores (standard, percentile and grade equivalents) and describe functional limitations.
ADHD: Diagnosis based on DSM-V; history of behaviors impairing functioning in academic setting; diagnostic interview; history of symptoms; evidence of ongoing behaviors.
ASD: Psycho ed evaluation
Documentation submitted to: Support Program/Services
Special Ed. HS course work accepted: Yes
Separate application required for program services: Not Applicable
# of students last year receiving services/accommodations for:
LD: 65
Contact Information
Name of program or department: Learning Support Services
Telephone: 830-792-7258

Schreiner University

and a completed application with application fee must be submitted to the Office of Admissions.

Additional Information

The Learning Support Services Program is tailored to meet the needs of each participating student. Each LSS staff member is committed to helping students develop the independent study skills and strategies that are necessary for academic success. Individualized services may include study skills development; regularly scheduled tutoring for all classes; testing accommodations, including readers, scribes, and extended time; use of recorded textbooks; arrangements made for note-takers in lecture classes; and a freshman seminar class that addresses issues of specific concern to college students with learning disabilities.

GENERAL ADMISSIONS

Very important factors considered include: class rank, academic GPA, standardized test scores. *Important factors considered include:* rigor of secondary school record, application essay, character/personal qualities, volunteer work, work experience, level of applicant's interest. *Other factors considered include:* recommendation(s), interview, extracurricular activities, talent/ability. *Freshman Admission Requirements:* High school diploma is required and GED is accepted. *Academic units recommended:* 4 English, 3 math, 3 science, 2 science labs, 2 foreign language, 2 social studies, 2 history, 3.5 academic electives, 1 computer science, 1 visual/performing arts, 2.5 units from above areas or other academic areas.

ACCOMMODATIONS OR SERVICES

Accommodations are decided upon an individual basis after a thorough review of appropriate, current documentation. The accommodations requests must be supported through the documentation provided and must be logically linked to the current impact of the condition on academic functioning.

FINANCIAL AID

Students should submit: FAFSA. Applicants will be notified of awards on a rolling basis beginning 2/15. The Princeton Review suggests that all financial aid forms be submitted as soon as possible after October 1. *Need-based scholarships/grants offered:* College/university scholarship or grant aid from institutional funds; Federal Pell; Private scholarships; SEOG; State scholarships/grants. *Loan aid offered:* Direct PLUS loans; Direct Subsidized Stafford Loans; Direct Unsubsidized Stafford Loans. Federal Work-Study Program available. Institutional employment available.

CAMPUS LIFE

Activities: Campus Ministries; Choral groups; Dance; Drama/theater; Literary magazine; Music ensembles; Musical theater; Pep band; Student government; Student newspaper; Symphony orchestra. **Organizations:** 35 registered organizations, 5 honor societies, 7 religious organizations. 2 fraternities, 2 sororities. **Athletics (Intercollegiate):** *Men:* baseball, basketball, golf, soccer, tennis. *Women:* basketball, cheerleading, golf, soccer, softball, tennis, volleyball. **On-Campus Highlights:** Caillioux Campus Activity Center, Logan Library, Griffin Welcome Center, Schriner Event Center, Mountaineer Fitness Center.

ACCOMMODATIONS

Allowed in exams:	
Calculators	Yes
Dictionary	Yes
Computer	Yes
Spell-checker	Yes
Extended test time	Yes
Scribe	Yes
Proctors	Yes
Oral exams	Yes
Note-takers	Yes
Support services for students with	
LD	Yes
ADHD	Yes
ASD	Yes
Distraction-reduced environment	Yes
Recording of lecture allowed	Yes
Reading technology:	Yes
Audio books	Yes
Other assistive technology	Yes
Priority registration	No
Added costs for services:	
For LD:	No
For ADHD:	No
For ASD:	No
ADHD & ASD coaching	Yes
ASD specialists	No
Professional tutors	Yes
Peer tutors	No
Max. hours/week for services	Unlimited
How professors are notified of student approved accommodations	student and director

COLLEGE GRADUATION REQUIREMENTS

Course waivers allowed	No
Course substitutions allowed	No

Southern Methodist University

P.O. Box 750181, Dallas, TX 75275-0181 • Admissions: 214-768-2058 • Fax: 214-768-0103

CAMPUS
Type of school	Private (nonprofit)
Environment	Metropolis
Support	CS

STUDENTS
Undergrad enrollment	6,427
% male/female	50/50
% from out of state	55
% frosh live on campus	97

FINANCIAL FACTS
Annual tuition	$48,365
Room and board	$16,845
Required fees	$6,128

GENERAL ADMISSIONS INFO
Application fee	$60
Priority deadline	1/15
Regular application deadline	1/15

Nonfall registration accepted. Admission may be deferred for a maximum of 1 year.

Range SAT EBRW	630–710
Range SAT Math	640–730
Range ACT Composite	28–32

ACADEMICS
Student/faculty ratio	11:1
% students returning for sophomore year	91
% students graduating within 4 years	71
% students graduating within 6 years	81

Most classes have 20–29 students. Most lab/discussion sessions have 10–19 students.

PROGRAMS/SERVICES FOR STUDENTS WITH LEARNING DIFFERENCES
The goal of Disability Accommodations & Success Strategies (DASS) is to provide students with documented disabilities services or reasonable accommodations in order to reduce the effects that a disability may have on their performance in a traditional academic setting. DASS provides individual attention and support for students needing assistance with various aspects of their campus experience such as notifying professors, arranging accommodations, referrals, and accessibility.

ADMISSIONS
There is no special admission process to the university for students with LD. If their standardized tests were administered under non-standard conditions, this will not weigh unfavorably into the admission decision. In addition to GPA and SAT or ACT scores, the admission committee weighs many factors during the course of the application process, including classroom performance, rigor of high school curriculum, quality of essays and recommendations, extracurricular activities, talents, character and life experiences. Please note SAT II scores are recommended for some home-school students. if a student plans to major or minor in music, dance, or theater, an audition is a requirement for admission.

Additional Information
All students have access to tutoring, writing centers, study skills workshops, and classes to improve reading rate, comprehension, and vocabulary. Skills classes are offered in time management, test strategies, notetaking strategies, organizational skills, concentration, memory, and test anxiety. There are two learning specialists available to work with students with learning differences free of charge. There are currently 380 students with learning disabilities and/or ADHD receiving services. DASS also offers academic coaching for students with diagnosed learning disabilities, a study and reading skills course called ORACLE and a student-run organization called Students for New Learning. DASS does also collaborate with Residence Life and student housing regarding special needs of the student. Incoming students are encouraged to start

ADMISSIONS INFO FOR STUDENTS WITH LEARNING DIFFERENCES
SAT/ACT required: Yes
Interview required: No
Essay required: No
Additional application required: No
Documentation required for:
 LD: A full psychoeducational assessment conducted, preferably, in the last three years. Needs to use comprehensive measures of potential and achievement.
 ADHD: Report from either a licensed psychologist or physician trained in diagnosing ADHD. Evaluation needs to be conducted, preferably, within three years of the time student seeks accommodations. Documentation guidelines are posted on website.
 ASD: Documentation from a licensed professional, detailing the diagnosed condition, its impact on the student, and recommendations in an academic setting.
Documentation submitted to: Disability Accommodations & Success
Special Ed. HS course work accepted: Yes
Separate application required for program services: No
Contact Information
Name of program or department: Disability Accommodations & Success Strategies
Telephone: 214-768-1470
Fax: 214-768-1255
Email: dass@smu.edu

Southern Methodist University

the process of requesting services before classes begin. Attend a DASS session during orientation or meet with our office during a campus visit.

GENERAL ADMISSIONS

Very important factors considered include: rigor of secondary school record, academic GPA, application essay, standardized test scores, recommendation(s). *Important factors considered include:* class rank, extracurricular activities, talent/ability, character/personal qualities. *Other factors considered include:* first generation, alumni/ae relation, racial/ethnic status, volunteer work, work experience, level of applicant's interest. *Freshman Admission Requirements:* High school diploma is required and GED is not accepted. *Academic units required:* 4 English, 3 math, 3 science, 2 science labs, 2 foreign language, 3 social studies. *Academic units recommended:* 4 English, 4 math, 3 science, 2 science labs, 3 foreign language, 3 history, 3 academic electives.

ACCOMMODATIONS OR SERVICES

Accommodations are decided upon an individual basis after a thorough review of appropriate, current documentation. The accommodations requests must be supported through the documentation provided and must be logically linked to the current impact of the condition on academic functioning.

FINANCIAL AID

Students should submit: CSS/Financial Aid PROFILE; FAFSA; Noncustodial PROFILE. Applicants will be notified of awards on or about 1/20. The Princeton Review suggests that all financial aid forms be submitted as soon as possible after October 1. *Need-based scholarships/grants offered:* College/university scholarship or grant aid from institutional funds; Federal Pell; Private scholarships; SEOG; State scholarships/grants. *Loan aid offered:* Direct PLUS loans; Direct Subsidized Stafford Loans; Direct Unsubsidized Stafford Loans. Federal Work-Study Program available. Institutional employment available.

CAMPUS LIFE

Activities: Campus Ministries; Choral groups; Concert band; Dance; Drama/theater; International Student Organization; Jazz band; Literary magazine; Marching band; Model UN; Music ensembles; Musical theater; Opera; Pep band; Radio station; Student government; Student newspaper; Student-run film society; Symphony orchestra; Television station; Yearbook. **Organizations:** 180 registered organizations, 15 honor societies, 27 religious organizations. 15 fraternities, 13 sororities. **Athletics (Intercollegiate):** *Men:* basketball, diving, football, golf, soccer, swimming, tennis, volleyball, water polo. *Women:* basketball, crew/rowing, cross-country, diving, equestrian sports, golf, soccer, swimming, tennis, track/field (outdoor), volleyball, water polo. **On-Campus Highlights:** Dallas Hall, Meadows Museum, Hughes Trigg Student Center, Gerald J Ford Stadium, Fondren Library.

ACCOMMODATIONS

Allowed in exams:	
Calculators	Yes
Dictionary	Yes
Computer	Yes
Spell-checker	Yes
Extended test time	Yes
Scribe	Yes
Proctors	Yes
Oral exams	Yes
Note-takers	Yes
Support services for students with	
LD	Yes
ADHD	Yes
ASD	Yes
Distraction-reduced environment	Yes
Recording of lecture allowed	Yes
Reading technology:	Yes
Audio books	Yes
Other assistive technologyKurzweil 3000 and Firefly remote version available on campus	
Priority registration	Yes
Added costs for services:	
For LD:	No
LD specialists	Yes
ADHD & ASD coaching	Yes
ASD specialists	No
Professional tutors	Yes
Peer tutors	Yes
Max. hours/week for services	Varies
How professors are notified of student approved accommodations	Student

COLLEGE GRADUATION REQUIREMENTS

Course waivers allowed	No
Course substitutions allowed	Yes
In what courses	Foreign Language

Texas A&M University–College Station

P.O. Box 30014, College Station, TX 77843-3014 • Admissions: (979) 845-1060 • Fax: (979) 458-1808

CAMPUS

Type of school	Public
Environment	City
Support	S

STUDENTS

Undergrad enrollment	52,571
% male/female	52/48
% from out of state	4
% frosh live on campus	

FINANCIAL FACTS

Annual in-state tuition	$7,406
Annual out-of-state tuition	$33,074
Room and board	$10,436
Required fees	$3,562

GENERAL ADMISSIONS INFO

Application fee	$75
Regular application deadline	12/1

Nonfall registration accepted.

Range SAT EBRW	570–670
Range SAT Math	570–690
Range ACT Composite	25–30

ACADEMICS

Student/faculty ratio	21:1
% students returning for sophomore year	92
% students graduating within 4 years	54
% students graduating within 6 years	82

Most classes have 10–19 students.
Most lab/discussion sessions have fewer than 10 students.

Programs/Services for Students with Learning Differences

Disability Services offers accommodations coordination, evaluation referral, disability-related information, assistive technology services, sign language interpreting and transcription services for academically related purposes. Although Disability Services does not offer disability evaluation and/or testing, tutoring, personal expenses, attendants or scholarships, Disability Services will provide resources and referral information
DS provides a one page handout, "Requesting Accommodations" (on our forms page), that can be printed out for review and reference. Students may submit information at any time during the semester. However, it may take up to 2-3 weeks for the information to be reviewed and accommodations to be put in place.
Student information will be reviewed on an individual, case-by-case basis in the order that it is received. Students can check on the status of their review at: Tracker Online. After the review, an Access Coordinator will contact student to set up an appointment to discuss possible accommodations. The student will meet with their Access Coordinator to discuss Disability Services policies and procedures as well as possible accommodations and resources available. If necessary, the Access Coordinator will advise the student of any additional information needed.

Admissions

Students ranked in the top 10 percent of their class are automatically admissible if they have taken the required courses. Students not in the top 10 percent but ranked in the top 25 percent must have a 1300 on the SAT with a score of 600-plus in math and verbal or a 30 on the ACT and have the course requirements. Applicants with learning disabilities submit the general application form and are considered under the same guidelines as all applicants. Students may have their application reviewed by requesting special consideration based on their disability and by providing letters of recommendation from their high school counselor stating what accommodations are needed in college to be successful. Admissions will be affected by the student's record indicating success with provided accommodations along with any activities and leadership skills. Students not meeting academic criteria for automatic admission may be offered admission to a summer provisional program. These students must take 9–12 credits and receive a grade of C in each of the courses.

Additional Information

Accommodations are provided on an individual basis as needs arise. Disability Services is a resource for information, including, but not

ADMISSIONS INFO FOR STUDENTS WITH LEARNING DIFFERENCES

SAT/ACT required: Yes
Interview required: Not Applicable
Essay required: Not Applicable
Additional application required: Not Applicable
Documentation required for:
 LD: Psycho ed evaluation
 ADHD: Psycho ed evaluation
 ASD: Psycho ed evaluation
Documentation submitted to: Disability Services
Special Ed. HS course work accepted: Not Applicable
Separate application required for program services: No
Contact Information
Name of program or department: Disability Service
Telephone: 979-845-1637
Fax: 979-458-1214
Email: disability@tamu.edu

Texas A&M University–College Station

limited to, tutoring services, study and time management skills training, community resources, disability awareness, and various university services. Skills classes in math, reading, and writing are offered to the entire student body though the Student Learning Center. Some of these classes may be taken for college credit. Services and accommodations are available for undergraduate and graduate students. Services include an adaptive technology laboratory equipped with state-of-the-art technology for students with disabilities, including text-to-speech scanning for personal use. The Academic Success Center has tutors available for support and Academic Coaches. They can be reached at 979-845-4900.

GENERAL ADMISSIONS

Very important factors considered include: rigor of secondary school record, class rank, academic GPA, standardized test scores, extracurricular activities, talent/ability. *Important factors considered include:* application essay, first generation, geographical residence, state residency, volunteer work, work experience. *Other factors considered include:* recommendation(s), character/personal qualities, level of applicant's interest. *Freshman Admission Requirements:* High school diploma is required and GED is accepted. *Academic units required:* 4 English, 3 math, 3 science, 1 science lab, 2 foreign language, 3 social studies, 5 academic electives, 1 visual/performing arts, and 1 unit from above areas or other academic areas. *Academic units recommended:* 4 English, 4 math, 4 science, 2 science labs, 2 foreign language, 4 social studies, 7 academic electives, 1 visual/performing arts, 1 unit from above areas or other academic areas.

ACCOMMODATIONS OR SERVICES

Accommodations are decided upon an individual basis after a thorough review of appropriate, current documentation. The accommodations requests must be supported through the documentation provided and must be logically linked to the current impact of the condition on academic functioning.

FINANCIAL AID

Students should submit: FAFSA. Applicants will be notified of awards on a rolling basis beginning 2/25. The Princeton Review suggests that all financial aid forms be submitted as soon as possible after October 1. *Need-based scholarships/grants offered:* College/university scholarship or grant aid from institutional funds; Federal Pell; Private scholarships; SEOG; State scholarships/grants. *Loan aid offered:* Direct PLUS loans; Direct Subsidized Stafford Loans; Direct Unsubsidized Stafford Loans. Federal Work-Study Program available. Institutional employment available.

CAMPUS LIFE

Activities: Campus Ministries; Choral groups; Concert band; Dance; Drama/theater; International Student Organization; Jazz band; Literary magazine; Marching band; Music ensembles; Musical theater; Radio station; Student government; Student newspaper; Student-run film society; Symphony orchestra; Television station; Yearbook. **Organizations:** 725 registered organizations, 34 honor societies, 77 religious organizations. 33 fraternities, 23 sororities. **Athletics (Intercollegiate):** *Men:* baseball, basketball, cross-country, diving, football, golf, riflery, swimming, tennis, track/field (outdoor), track/field (indoor). *Women:* basketball, cross-country, diving, equestrian sports, golf, riflery, soccer, softball, swimming, tennis, track/field (outdoor), track/field (indoor), volleyball. **On-Campus Highlights:** Student Recreation Center, Kyle Field, Corps of Cadets, George Bush Presidential Library/Museum, Research Park.

ACCOMMODATIONS

Allowed in exams:

Calculators	Yes
Dictionary	Yes
Computer	Yes
Spell-checker	Yes
Extended test time	Yes
Scribe	Yes
Proctors	Yes
Oral exams	Yes
Note-takers	Yes

Support services for students with

LD	Yes
ADHD	Yes
ASD	Yes
Distraction-reduced environment	Yes
Recording of lecture allowed	Yes
Reading technology:	Yes
Audio books	Yes

Other assistive technology — Notetaking technology (audio recorders, smart pens), magifiers, electronic text with text-to-speech software, voice recognition software

Priority registration	Yes

Added costs for services:

For LD:	No
For ADHD:	No
For ASD:	No
LD specialists	
ADHD & ASD coaching	Yes
ASD specialists	Yes
Professional tutors	Yes
Peer tutors	Not Applicable
Max. hours/week for services	Varies
How professors are notified of student approved accommodations	Student

COLLEGE GRADUATION REQUIREMENTS

Course waivers allowed	No
Course substitutions allowed	Yes

In what courses   Math, foreign language, Handled on a case-by-case depending on the nature of the disability and requirements fo the major.

Texas A&M University—Kingsville

MSC 105, Kingsville, TX 78363 • Admissions: 361-593-2315 • Fax: 361-593-2195

PROGRAMS/SERVICES FOR STUDENTS WITH LEARNING DIFFERENCES

The university is committed to providing an environment in which every student is encouraged to reach the highest level of personal and educational achievement. Students with disabilities may have special concerns and even special needs. Services vary according to the nature of the disability and are provided by the Center for Life Services and Wellness. Counseling services offer educational, vocational, and personal consultations, as well as tutoring, testing, and academic advising. Students with LD have access to note-takers, readers, writers, and other assistance that the university can provide. All students entering college as freshmen (or transfers with less than 30 hours) have the university's commitment to improve student achievement, retention, depth, and quality of instruction and services.

ADMISSIONS

All applicants must meet the same general admission criteria. Admission is very similar to open door admissions, and thus, most applicants are admitted either conditionally or unconditionally or on probation. Average ACT scores are 16-plus; for the SAT, they are 610-plus. Students with LD are encouraged to self-disclose during the application process. There are two types of admission plans: conditional and unconditional. Unconditional admission is met by achieving 970-plus on the SAT. Conditional admission is achieved by scoring 810–960 on the SAT.

Additional Information

Each freshman receives academic endorsement; developmental educational classes in writing, math, or reading (if necessary); access to tutoring or study groups; and academic rescue programs for students in academic jeopardy. Skills classes are offered for no credit in stress management and test anxiety. Letters are sent to faculty each semester, hand delivered by the student. DRC provides tutoring on a limited basis. Students are responsible for registering with the DRC office EACH SEMESTER. Testing accommodations are available, but students are responsible for scheduling the tests. Accommodations

Texas A&M University-Kingsville

include extended testing times, private rooms, scribes, and readers. DRC will also proctor the exam and return the test to the instructor. DRC relies on a volunteer program for note-takers. Services and accommodations are available to undergraduate and graduate students.

GENERAL ADMISSIONS

Important factors considered include: rigor of secondary school record, class rank, standardized test scores. *Freshman Admission Requirements: Academic units recommended:* 4 English, 3 math, 3 science, 3 foreign language, 4 social studies, 3 history, 3 academic electives.

ACCOMMODATIONS OR SERVICES

Accommodations are decided upon an individual basis after a thorough review of appropriate, current documentation. The accommodations requests must be supported through the documentation provided and must be logically linked to the current impact of the condition on academic functioning.

FINANCIAL AID

Students should submit: FAFSA. The Princeton Review suggests that all financial aid forms be submitted as soon as possible after October 1.

CAMPUS LIFE

Activities: Choral groups; Concert band; Dance; Drama/theater; Jazz band; Marching band; Music ensembles; Musical theater; Pep band; Radio station; Student government; Student newspaper; Television station.

ACCOMMODATIONS

Allowed in exams:	
Calculators	Yes
Dictionary	Yes
Computer	Yes
Spell-checker	Yes
Extended test time	Yes
Scribe	Yes
Proctors	Yes
Oral exams	Yes
Note-takers	Yes
Support services for students with	
LD	Yes
ADHD	Yes
ASD	Yes
Distraction-reduced environment	Yes
Recording of lecture allowed	Yes
Reading technology:	Yes
Audio books	Yes
Other assistive technology	Yes
Priority registration	Yes
Added costs for services:	
For LD:	No
For ADHD:	No
For ASD:	No
LD specialists	No
ADHD & ASD coaching	No
ASD specialists	No
Professional tutors	No
Peer tutors	Yes
Max. hours/week for services	Varies
How professors are notified of student approved accommodations	Student

COLLEGE GRADUATION REQUIREMENTS

Course waivers allowed	Yes
In what courses: Case-by-case decision made by provost	
Course substitutions allowed	Yes
In what courses: Case-by-case decision made by provost.	

Texas State University

601 University Drive, San Marcos, TX 78666 • Admissions: 512-245-2364 • Fax: 512-245-8044

CAMPUS

Type of school	Public
Environment	Town
Support	CS

STUDENTS

Undergrad enrollment	34,180
% male/female	43/57
% from out of state	2
% frosh live on campus	92

FINANCIAL FACTS

Annual in-state tuition	$7,750
Annual out-of-state tuition	$19,990
Room and board	$9,132
Required fees	$2,468

GENERAL ADMISSIONS INFO

Application fee	$75
Priority deadline	3/1
Regular application deadline	5/1

Nonfall registration accepted. Admission may be deferred.

Range SAT EBRW	510–610
Range SAT Math	510–590
Range ACT Composite	20–26

ACADEMICS

Student/faculty ratio	21:1
% students returning for sophomore year	78
% students graduating within 4 years	27
% students graduating within 6 years	54

Most classes have 10–19 students.
Most lab/discussion sessions have 20–29 students.

PROGRAMS/SERVICES FOR STUDENTS WITH LEARNING DIFFERENCES

The Office of Disability Services will strive to become a model program serving students with disabilities in higher education. We are committed to developing a society in which individuals with disabilities thrive and participate fully. These individuals will be challenged to become responsible decision-makers, problem solvers and self-advocates in charge of their own destiny. We envision a campus community where all individuals are seen as valued and contributing members of society. Respect for all will encompass everything we do. To register for accommodations: 1.) Fill out the Confidential Student Information Form. Registration for services with ODS requires this form. 2.) Send any available documentation of the student's disability to our office, email ODS, or fax at 512.245.3452. You may upload your documentation when you fill out the confidential student information form. 3.) The ODS will review the need for accommodations and support services based on the student's disability documentation and disability-based need.* 4.) The ODS will notify the student to set up an appointment via email after determining appropriate accommodations in accordance with Section 504 of the 1973 Rehabilitation Act, the Americans with Disabilities Act Amendments Act of 2008 and university policy.

ADMISSIONS

Students with LD must meet the same admission requirements as other applicants. A student whose educational and/or personal goals for success have been negatively impacted by a disability may address any challenges in the essay with their application for admission. This information may be considered during the application process. This enables the ODS to inform the applicant as to whether or not they will qualify for accommodations at SWT based on the SWT disability guidelines, available from the ODS upon request. Freshmen applicants whose test scores do not meet the minimum requirements for their class rank are eligible for a PAS review if they rank in the top three-quarters of their class. Students in the fourth quarter are not eligible for this review. A limited number of students whose academic record demonstrates potential for academic success at SWT will

ADMISSIONS INFO FOR STUDENTS WITH LEARNING DIFFERENCES

SAT/ACT required: Yes
Interview required: No
Essay required: No
Additional application required: No
Documentation required for:
 LD: Psycho ed evaluation to include: relevant historical info, instructional interventions, related services, age diagnosed, objective data (aptitude, achievement, info processing), test scores (standard, percentile and grade equivalents) and describe functional limitations.
 ADHD: Diagnosis based on DSM-V; history of behaviors impairing functioning in academic setting; diagnostic interview; history of symptoms; evidence of ongoing behaviors.
 ASD: Psycho ed evaluation
Documentation submitted to: Office of Disability Services
Special Ed. HS course work accepted: No
Separate application required for program services: No
# of students last year receiving services/accommodations for:
 LD: 527
Contact Information
Name of program or department: Office of Disability Services
Telephone: 512-245-3451
Fax: 512-245-3452
Email: ods@txstate.edu

be offered admission. Factors considered in the review process include specific class rank, size of the graduating class, quality and competitive level of high school courses taken and grades earned, and the applicant's individual verbal and math scores on ACT or SAT.

Additional Information

Specialized support services are based on the individual student disability-based needs. Services available could include special groups registration, recorded textbooks, recording of textbooks not available on tape, arranging for special testing accommodations including extended time and reader services, assistance in accessing adaptive computer equipment, assistance in locating volunteer readers and note-takers, liaison and advocacy between students, faculty and staff, referral for tutoring, disability management counseling, and information and referral to on and off-campus resources.

GENERAL ADMISSIONS

Very important factors considered include: class rank, standardized test scores. *Other factors considered include:* rigor of secondary school record, application essay, extracurricular activities, talent/ability, first generation. *Freshman Admission Requirements:* High school diploma is required and GED is accepted. *Academic units required:* 4 English, 4 math, 4 science, 2 science labs, 2 foreign language, 2 social studies, 2 history, 6 academic electives, 1 visual/performing arts, and 1 unit from above areas or other academic areas. *Academic units recommended:* 4 English, 4 math, 4 science, 2 science labs, 2 foreign language, 2 social studies, 2 history, 6 academic electives, 1 visual/performing arts, 1 unit from above areas or other academic areas.

ACCOMMODATIONS OR SERVICES

Accommodations are decided upon an individual basis after a thorough review of appropriate, current documentation. The accommodations requests must be supported through the documentation provided and must be logically linked to the current impact of the condition on academic functioning.

FINANCIAL AID

Students should submit: FAFSA. Applicants will be notified of awards on a rolling basis beginning 5/1. The Princeton Review suggests that all financial aid forms be submitted as soon as possible after October 1. *Need-based scholarships/grants offered:* College/university scholarship or grant aid from institutional funds; Federal Pell; Private scholarships; SEOG; State scholarships/grants. *Loan aid offered:* Direct PLUS loans; Direct Subsidized Stafford Loans; Direct Unsubsidized Stafford Loans. Federal Work-Study Program available. Institutional employment available.

CAMPUS LIFE

Activities: Campus Ministries; Choral groups; Concert band; Dance; Drama/theater; International Student Organization; Jazz band; Literary magazine; Marching band; Model UN; Music ensembles; Musical theater; Opera; Pep band; Radio station; Student government; Student newspaper; Student-run film society; Symphony orchestra; Yearbook. **Organizations:** 254 registered organizations, 16 honor societies, 27 religious organizations. 18 fraternities, 14 sororities. **Athletics (Intercollegiate):** *Men:* baseball, basketball, cheerleading, cross-country, football, golf, track/field (outdoor). *Women:* basketball, cheerleading, cross-country, golf, soccer, softball, tennis, track/field (outdoor), volleyball. **On-Campus Highlights:** LBJ Student Center, Alkek Library, Student Recreation Center, The Quad, Sewell Park.

ACCOMMODATIONS

Allowed in exams:	
Calculators	Yes
Dictionary	Yes
Computer	Yes
Spell-checker	Yes
Extended test time	Yes
Scribe	Yes
Proctors	Yes
Oral exams	Yes
Note-takers	Yes
Support services for students with	
LD	Yes
ADHD	Yes
ASD	Yes
Distraction-reduced environment	Yes
Recording of lecture allowed	Yes
Reading technology:	Yes
Audio books	Yes
Other assistive technology	
Priority registration	Yes
Added costs for services:	
For LD:	No
For ADHD:	No
For ASD:	No
LD specialists	Yes
ADHD & ASD coaching	Yes
ASD specialists	Yes
Professional tutors	Yes
Peer tutors	Yes
Max. hours/week for services	Varies
How professors are notified of student approved accommodations	
Director and student	

COLLEGE GRADUATION REQUIREMENTS

Course waivers allowed	No
Course substitutions allowed	Yes
In what courses	
Substitutions are primarily considered for Math and Foreign Language courses.	

Texas Tech University

Box 45005, Lubbock, TX 79409-5005 • Admissions: 806-742-1480 • Fax: 806-742-0062

CAMPUS

Type of school	Public
Environment	City
Support	S

STUDENTS

Undergrad enrollment	30,330
% male/female	54/46
% from out of state	6
% frosh live on campus	93

FINANCIAL FACTS

Annual in-state tuition	$8,220
Annual out-of-state tuition	$20,670
Required fees	$2,825

GENERAL ADMISSIONS INFO

Application fee	$75
Priority deadline	2/1
Regular application deadline	8/1

Nonfall registration accepted.

Range SAT EBRW	540–620
Range SAT Math	530–620
Range ACT Composite	22–27

ACADEMICS

Student/faculty ratio	21:1
% students returning for sophomore year	84
% students graduating within 4 years	35
% students graduating within 6 years	59

Most classes have 10–19 students.
Most lab/discussion sessions have 10–19 students.

PROGRAMS/SERVICES FOR STUDENTS WITH LEARNING DIFFERENCES

It is the philosophy of Texas Tech University to serve each student on a case-by-case basis. All services rendered are supported by adequate documentation. We firmly believe that all students should be and will become effective self advocates. Students with disabilities attending Texas Tech will find numerous programs designed to provide services and promote access to all phases of university activity. Such programming is coordinated through the Dean of Students Office with the assistance of an advisory committee of both disabled and non-disabled students, faculty, and staff. Services to disabled students are offered through a decentralized network of university and nonuniversity resources. This means that many excellent services are available, but it is up to the student to initiate them. Each student is encouraged to act as his or her own advocate and take the major responsibility for securing services and accommodations. The Disabled Student Services team, Dean of Students's Office, faculty, and staff are supportive in this effort.

ADMISSIONS

There is no special admissions process for students with LD, and all applicants must meet the same criteria. All students must have 4 years of

ADMISSIONS INFO FOR STUDENTS WITH LEARNING DIFFERENCES

SAT/ACT required: Yes
Interview required: Not Applicable
Essay required: Not Applicable
Additional application required: Yes
Documentation required for:
 LD: Written evaluation including a narrative with history, cognitive evaluation (with all subtest scores), tests of achievement (with a full print-out of age-normed scores) discussion of the findings, a diagnostic conclusion, and recommendations for academic accommodations. Evaluations must have been completed during the student's ninth grade year of school or later or after the age of 14. If the initial diagnosis or the re-evaluation of the learning disability occurred prior to the student's ninth grade year of high school, or prior to the age of 14, the student can still be granted accommodations if the student demonstrated a continual need for accommodations during their high school career. This would be established through providing copies of either the Admission Review and Dismissal (ARD) Committee reports or the Section 504 Committee reports that documented the use of specific accommodations throughout high school.
 ADHD: Current diagnosis, as defined by the DSM-IV, and any additional psychological or neurological testing results. If the diagnosis was made before the student's ninth grade year of school or prior to the age of 14, then a letter from the current treating physician will suffice as long as the letter includes the following: (1) A statement of diagnosis and (2) a current method of treatment. The diagnosis should also include a discussion of how the student's symptoms affect learning and academic achievement to the level of a disability. Specific recommendations for classroom accommodations should be included as well.
 ASD: Psycho ed evaluation
Documentation submitted to: Student Disability Services
Special Ed. HS course work accepted: No
# of students last year receiving services/accommodations for:
 LD: 600
Contact Information
Name of program or department: Student Disability Services
Telephone: 806-742-2405
Fax: 806-742-4837
Email: sds@ttu.edu

Texas Tech University

English, 3 years of math, 2.5 years of social studies, 2 years of science, and 3.5 years of electives. Any applicant who scores a 1200 on the SAT or a 29 on the ACT is automatically admitted regardless of class rank. Some students are admissible who do not meet the stated requirements, but they must have a 2.0 GPA for a provisional admission. After a student is admitted, Disabled Student Services requires documentation that provides a diagnosis and an indication of the severity of the disability and offers recommendations for accommodations for students to receive services.

Additional Information

Support services through Disabled Student Services include academic support services, which can help students develop habits enabling them to get a good education. Students may receive academic support services in the PASS (Programs for Academic Support Services) Center, which is open to all students on campus. Services offered free of charge include tutor referral services (paid by student); study skills group; hour-long workshops that target a variety of subjects from overcoming math anxiety to preparing for finals; a self-help learning lab with videotapes; computer assisted instruction; individual consultations assisting students with specific study problems; and setting study skills improvement goals. All students with LD are offered priority registration. Services and accommodations are available for undergraduate and graduate students.

GENERAL ADMISSIONS

Very important factors considered include: rigor of secondary school record, class rank, academic GPA, standardized test scores. *Important factors considered include:* application essay, recommendation(s), extracurricular activities, talent/ability, character/personal qualities, volunteer work, work experience. *Other factors considered include:* first generation, geographical residence, level of applicant's interest. *Freshman Admission Requirements:* High school diploma is required and GED is accepted. *Academic units required:* 4 English, 3 math, 3 science, 3 science labs, 2 foreign language, 5 academic electives, 1 visual/performing arts, and 4 units from above areas or other academic areas. *Academic units recommended:* 4 English, 4 math, 4 science, 4 science labs, 2 foreign language, 6 academic electives, 1 visual/performing arts, 5.5 units from above areas or other academic areas.

ACCOMMODATIONS OR SERVICES

Accommodations are decided upon an individual basis after a thorough review of appropriate, current documentation. The accommodations requests must be supported through the documentation provided and must be logically linked to the current impact of the condition on academic functioning.

FINANCIAL AID

Students should submit: FAFSA. The Princeton Review suggests that all financial aid forms be submitted as soon as possible after October 1. *Need-based scholarships/grants offered:* College/university scholarship or grant aid from institutional funds; Federal Pell; Private scholarships; SEOG; State scholarships/grants. *Loan aid offered:* Direct PLUS loans; Direct Subsidized Stafford Loans; Direct Unsubsidized Stafford Loans. Federal Work-Study Program available. Institutional employment available.

CAMPUS LIFE

Activities: Campus Ministries; Choral groups; Concert band; Dance; Drama/theater; International Student Organization; Jazz band; Literary magazine; Marching band; Model UN; Music ensembles; Musical theater; Opera; Pep band; Radio station; Student government; Student newspaper; Student-run film society; Symphony orchestra; Television station; Yearbook. **Organizations:** 399 registered organizations, 33 honor societies, 35 religious organizations. 25 fraternities, 18 sororities.

ACCOMMODATIONS	
Allowed in exams:	
Calculators	Yes
Dictionary	No
Computer	Yes
Spell-checker	Yes
Extended test time	Yes
Scribe	Yes
Proctors	Yes
Oral exams	Yes
Note-takers	Yes
Support services for students with	
LD	Yes
ADHD	Yes
ASD	Yes
Distraction-reduced environment	Yes
Recording of lecture allowed	Yes
Reading technology:	Yes
Audio books	Yes
Other assistive technology	
Priority registration	Yes
Added costs for services:	
For LD:	No
For ADHD:	No
For ASD:	No
LD specialists	Yes
ADHD & ASD coaching	Yes
ASD specialists	Yes
Professional tutors	Yes
Peer tutors	Yes
Max. hours/week for services	7
How professors are notified of student approved accommodations	Student

COLLEGE GRADUATION REQUIREMENTS	
Course waivers allowed	No
Course substitutions allowed	Yes
In what courses Math, Foreign Language, and Physical Education.	

University of Houston

4800 Calhoun Road, Houston, TX 77204-2023 • Admissions: 713-743-1010 • Fax: 713-743-7542

CAMPUS

Type of school	Public
Environment	Metropolis
Support	CS

STUDENTS

Undergrad enrollment	36,088
% male/female	51/49
% from out of state	1
% frosh live on campus	46

FINANCIAL FACTS

Annual in-state tuition	$9,888
Annual out-of-state tuition	$25,338
Room and board	$9,984
Required fees	$1,002

GENERAL ADMISSIONS INFO

Application fee	$75
Priority deadline	11/15
Regular application deadline	6/15

Nonfall registration accepted.

Range SAT EBRW	560–640
Range SAT Math	550–640
Range ACT Composite	23–27

ACADEMICS

Student/faculty ratio	22:1
% students returning for sophomore year	85
% students graduating within 4 years	25
% students graduating within 6 years	54

Most classes have 10–19 students.
Most lab/discussion sessions have 10–19 students.

PROGRAMS/SERVICES FOR STUDENTS WITH LEARNING DIFFERENCES

The Center for Students with DisABILITIES provides a wide variety of academic support services to students with all types of disabilities. Our goal is to help ensure that these otherwise qualified students are able to successfully compete with non-disabled students by receiving equal educational opportunities in college as mandated by law. Through advocacy efforts and a deliberate, ongoing, public education program, the staff strives to heighten the awareness of disability issues, educational rights, and abilities of persons who have disabilities.

ADMISSIONS

Admission is automatic for Texas residents in the top 15 percent of the class. Applicants who do not meet these admissions criteria will be reviewed in light of the applicant's academic rigor, community service, extracurricular activities, and surmounting obstacles to pursue higher education. Letters of reference from high school teachers, counselors, supervisors and activity leaders along with personal statements are welcome additions to an applicant's file.

Additional Information

Students who come from an educationally and/or economically disadvantaged background may be eligible to participate in the UH `Challenger Program' which is designed to provide intense support to students who face obstacles in their efforts to successfully complete college. Services to all students include: tutoring, counseling, financial aid advisement, and social enrichment. Remedial reading, writing, and study skills courses for three hours of non-college credit are offered. There are also remedial courses for credit in English and college algebra. Other services include assistance with petitions for course substitutions, peer

ADMISSIONS INFO FOR STUDENTS WITH LEARNING DIFFERENCES

SAT/ACT required: Yes
Interview required: Not Applicable
Additional application required: Yes
Documentation required for:
 LD: Assessment must be within the last 36 months. It should include 1. Diagnosis 2. IQ Battery 3. Achievement Testing 4. Information Processing 5. Diagnostic Interview 6. Accommodation recommendations.
 ADHD: Assessment must be within the last 36 months. It should include 1. Diagnostic Information 2. Clinical Assessment 3. Treatment 4. Functional limitations 5. Accommodation Recommendations.
 ASD: Diagnosis and functional limitations.
Documentation submitted to: Center for Students with Disabilities
Special Ed. HS course work accepted: No
Separate application required for program services: No
# of students last year receiving services/accommodations for:
 LD: 226
Contact Information
Name of program or department: Center for Students with Disabilities
Telephone: 713-743-5400
Fax: 713-743-5396
Email: uhcsd@central.uh.edu

University of Houston

support groups, free carbonized paper for note-taking, textbooks and class handouts put on tape by office staff or volunteer readers, and advocacy for student's legal rights to "reasonable and necessary accommodations" in their course work. Extended tutoring is available at the Learning Support Services and Math Lab.

GENERAL ADMISSIONS

Very important factors considered include: rigor of secondary school record, class rank, academic GPA, standardized test scores. *Other factors considered include:* application essay, recommendation(s), extracurricular activities, talent/ability, first generation, volunteer work, work experience. *Freshman Admission Requirements:* High school diploma is required and GED is accepted. *Academic units required:* 4 English, 3 math, 3 science, 2 science labs, 3 social studies. *Academic units recommended:* 4 math, 4 science, 2 foreign language, 1 history, 1 visual/performing arts.

ACCOMMODATIONS OR SERVICES

Accommodations are decided upon an individual basis after a thorough review of appropriate, current documentation. The accommodations requests must be supported through the documentation provided and must be logically linked to the current impact of the condition on academic functioning.

FINANCIAL AID

Students should submit: FAFSA. Applicants will be notified of awards on a rolling basis beginning 3/1. The Princeton Review suggests that all financial aid forms be submitted as soon as possible after October 1. *Need-based scholarships/grants offered:* College/university scholarship or grant aid from institutional funds; Federal Pell; Private scholarships; SEOG; State scholarships/grants. *Loan aid offered:* Direct PLUS loans; Direct Subsidized Stafford Loans; Direct Unsubsidized Stafford Loans. Federal Work-Study Program available. Institutional employment available.

CAMPUS LIFE

Activities: Campus Ministries; Choral groups; Concert band; Dance; Drama/theater; International Student Organization; Jazz band; Literary magazine; Marching band; Music ensembles; Musical theater; Opera; Pep band; Radio station; Student government; Student newspaper; Student-run film society; Symphony orchestra; Television station; Yearbook. **Organizations:** 350 registered organizations, 25 honor societies, 39 religious organizations. 21 fraternities, 19 sororities. **Athletics (Intercollegiate):** *Men:* baseball, basketball, cross-country, football, golf, track/field (outdoor), track/field (indoor). *Women:* basketball, cross-country, diving, soccer, softball, swimming, tennis, track/field (outdoor), track/field (indoor), volleyball. **On-Campus Highlights:** Student Center, Campus Recreation and Wellness Center, Student Center Satellite, Blaffer Gallery, Center for Student Involvement.

ACCOMMODATIONS

Allowed in exams:

Calculators	Yes
Dictionary	Yes
Computer	Yes
Spell-checker	Yes
Extended test time	Yes
Scribe	Yes
Proctors	Yes
Oral exams	Yes
Note-takers	Yes

Support services for students with

LD	Yes
ADHD	Yes
ASD	Yes
Distraction-reduced environment	Yes
Recording of lecture allowed	Yes
Reading technology:	Yes
Audio books	Yes

Other assistive technology CCTV's, a variety of hardware and software, dragon naturally speaking

Priority registration	Yes

Added costs for services:

For LD:	No
For ADHD:	No
For ASD:	No
LD specialists	Yes
ADHD & ASD coaching	Yes
ASD specialists	Yes
Professional tutors	Yes
Peer tutors	Yes
Max. hours/week for services	Varies
How professors are notified of student approved accommodations	Student

COLLEGE GRADUATION REQUIREMENTS

Course waivers allowed	No
Course substitutions allowed	Yes
In what courses	Foreign Language

The University of Texas at Austin

P.O. Box 8058, Austin, TX 78713-8058 • Admissions: 512-475-7399 • Fax: 512-471-8102

CAMPUS

Type of school	Public
Environment	Metropolis
Support	CS

STUDENTS

Undergrad enrollment	39,965
% male/female	47/53
% from out of state	6
% frosh live on campus	65

FINANCIAL FACTS

Annual in-state tuition	$10,606
Annual out-of-state tuition	$37,480
Room and board	$10,804

GENERAL ADMISSIONS INFO

Application fee	$75
Regular application deadline	12/1

Nonfall registration accepted.

Range SAT EBRW	620–720
Range SAT Math	610–740
Range ACT Composite	26–33

ACADEMICS

Student/faculty ratio	18:1
% students returning for sophomore year	95
% students graduating within 4 years	58
% students graduating within 6 years	83

Most classes have 10–19 students.
Most lab/discussion sessions have 10–19 students.

PROGRAMS/SERVICES FOR STUDENTS WITH LEARNING DIFFERENCES

Services for Students with Disabilities (SSD) provides a program of support and advocacy for students with LD. Services offered include assistance with learning strategies, note-takers for lectures, scribe/readers, and extended time for in-class work. There is also a Tutoring and Learning Center whose free services include study skill assistance, subject area tutoring, life management skills, exam reviews, peer mentoring, and distance tutoring.

ADMISSIONS

Students with disabilities are expected to meet the same admissions criteria as all other students. It is up to the student whether he/she wants to self-identify during the admissions process as having a disability. Please note that disability-related documentation sent to the Office of Admissions is not automatically forwarded to SSD. For students not otherwise eligible to enter due to grades or scores, a study skills class is required plus other courses from a course list.

Additional Information

To receive services, students must meet an SSD coordinator. Students need to provide current documentation from an appropriate licensed professional. Services offered to students, when appropriate, assistance

ADMISSIONS INFO FOR STUDENTS WITH LEARNING DIFFERENCES

SAT/ACT required: Yes
Interview required: No
Essay required: No
Additional application required: No
Documentation required for:
 LD: Students seeking support services from Services for Students with Disabilities (SSD) on the basis of a previously diagnosed learning disorder (LD) must submit documentation that verifies their eligibility under Section 504 of the Rehabilitation Act, the Americans with Disabilities Act (ADA) and the ADA Amendments Act. For more information on documentation required, see: http://diversity.utexas.edu/disability/guidelines-for-documenting-learning-disabilities/
 ADHD: Students seeking support services from Services for Students with Disabilities (SSD) on the basis of a previously diagnosed Attention-Deficit/Hyperactivity Disorder (ADHD) must submit documentation that verifies their eligibility under Section 504 of the Rehabilitation Act, the Americans with Disabilities Act (ADA) and the ADA Amendments Act. For more information on documentation required, see: http://diversity.utexas.edu/disability/adhd-2/
 ASD: Students seeking support services from Services for Students with Disabilities (SSD) on the basis of a previously diagnosed Autism Spectrum Disorder (ASD) must submit documentation that verifies their eligibility under Section 504 of the Rehabilitation Act, the Americans with Disabilities Act (ADA) and the ADA Amendments Act. For more information on documentation required, see: http://diversity.utexas.edu/disability/autism-spectrum-disorder-documentation-guidelines/
Documentation submitted to: Services for Students with Disabilities
Special Ed. HS course work accepted
Separate application required for program services: No
# of students last year receiving services/accommodations for:
 LD: 305
Contact Information
Name of program or department: Services for Students with Disabilities
Telephone: 512-471-6259
Fax: 512-475-7730
Email: ssd@austin.utexas.edu

The University of Texas at Austin

with learning strategies, and priority registration. The Assistive Technology gives students access to various supports to help them with their studies and testing with screen readers and other technology. There is a support group for UT students with ASD. Classroom accommodations include note-takers, assistive technology, scribes, readers, and extended testing times. In the Tutoring and Learning Center, students can access study skills assistance, subject area tutoring, life management skills assistance, and a special needs room with state of the art technology. Currently there are 305 students with LD and 745 with ADHD receiving services. Students may request that instructors make course materials displayed on Power Point slides available for review.

GENERAL ADMISSIONS

Very important factors considered include: rigor of secondary school record, class rank. *Important factors considered include:* application essay, standardized test scores, extracurricular activities, talent/ability, volunteer work, work experience. *Other factors considered include:* recommendation(s), character/personal qualities, first generation, state residency, racial/ethnic status, level of applicant's interest. *Freshman Admission Requirements:* High school diploma is required and GED is accepted. *Academic units required:* 4 English, 4 math, 4 science, 2 foreign language, 4 social studies, 6 academic electives.

ACCOMMODATIONS OR SERVICES

Accommodations are decided upon an individual basis after a thorough review of appropriate, current documentation. The accommodations requests must be supported through the documentation provided and must be logically linked to the current impact of the condition on academic functioning.

FINANCIAL AID

Students should submit: FAFSA; Institution's own financial aid form. Applicants will be notified of awards on a rolling basis beginning 3/15. The Princeton Review suggests that all financial aid forms be submitted as soon as possible after October 1. *Need-based scholarships/grants offered:* College/university scholarship or grant aid from institutional funds; Federal Pell; Private scholarships; SEOG; State scholarships/grants. *Loan aid offered:* Direct PLUS loans; Direct Subsidized Stafford Loans; Direct Unsubsidized Stafford Loans. Federal Work-Study Program available. Institutional employment available.

CAMPUS LIFE

Activities: Campus Ministries; Choral groups; Concert band; Dance; Drama/theater; International Student Organization; Jazz band; Literary magazine; Marching band; Model UN; Music ensembles; Musical theater; Radio station; Student government; Student newspaper; Student-run film society; Symphony orchestra; Television station; Yearbook. **Organizations:** 900 registered organizations, 15 honor societies, 95 religious organizations. 26 fraternities, 22 sororities. **Athletics (Intercollegiate):** *Men:* baseball, basketball, cross-country, diving, football, golf, swimming, tennis, track/field (outdoor). *Women:* basketball, crew/rowing, cross-country, diving, golf, soccer, softball, swimming, tennis, track/field (outdoor), volleyball. **On-Campus Highlights:** The Tower, Darrell K Royal-Texas Memorial Stadium, LBJ Presidential Library, Blanton Museum of Art, Student Activities Center.

ACCOMMODATIONS

Allowed in exams:	
Calculators	Yes
Dictionary	Yes
Computer	Yes
Spell-checker	Yes
Extended test time	Yes
Scribe	Yes
Proctors	Yes
Oral exams	Yes
Note-takers	Yes
Support services for students with	
LD	Yes
ADHD	Yes
ASD	Yes
Distraction-reduced environment	Yes
Recording of lecture allowed	Yes
Reading technology:	Yes
Audio books	Yes
Other assistive technology test conversion, speech to text, screen reader software, braille	
Priority registration	Yes
Added costs for services:	
For LD:	No
For ADHD:	No
For ASD:	No
LD specialists	No
ADHD & ASD coaching	No
ASD specialists	Yes
Professional tutors	Yes
Peer tutors	Yes
Max. hours/week for services	Varies
How professors are notified of student approved accommodations	Student

COLLEGE GRADUATION REQUIREMENTS

Course waivers allowed	No
Course substitutions allowed	Yes
In what courses foreign language (only if criteria is met and process is followed)	

Brigham Young University (UT)

BRIGHAM YOUNG UNIVERSITY, PROVO, UT 84602-1110 • ADMISSIONS: 801-422-2507 • FAX: 801-422-0005

CAMPUS
Type of school	Private (nonprofit)
Environment	City
Support	CS

STUDENTS
Undergrad enrollment	31,233
% male/female	51/49
% from out of state	64
% frosh live on campus	70

FINANCIAL FACTS
Annual tuition	$5,620
Room and board	$7,530

GENERAL ADMISSIONS INFO
Application fee	$35
Regular application deadline	12/15

Nonfall registration accepted. Admission may be deferred.

Range SAT EBRW	610–710
Range SAT Math	600–700
Range ACT Composite	27–32

ACADEMICS
Student/faculty ratio	20:1
% students returning for sophomore year	90
% students graduating within 4 years	23
% students graduating within 6 years	83

Most classes have 10–19 students.
Most lab/discussion sessions have 10–19 students.

PROGRAMS/SERVICES FOR STUDENTS WITH LEARNING DIFFERENCES
The University Accessibility Center works to provide individualized programs to meet the specific needs of each student with a disability, assisting in developing strengths to meet the challenges, and making arrangements for accommodations and special services as required.

ADMISSIONS
There is no special admission process for students with learning disabilities. Suggested courses include: four years English, three to four years math, two to three years science, two years history or government, two years foreign language, and two years of literature or writing. Evaluations are made on an individualized basis with a system weighted for college-prep courses and core classes.

Additional Information
Non-credit workshops and a study skill class are offered for all student and often recommended to students with learning concerns. The following topics are some examples: math anxiety, memory, overcoming procrastination, self-appreciation, stress management, test-taking, textbook comprehension, time management, and communication. Additional services include counseling support and advising. Services and accommodations are available for undergraduate and graduate students. There are academic learning services available through the Academic Learning Department. There is a Reading Center, Writing Center, Math Study Center, and a Study Skills Center. They are provided at no extra cost. There are several opportunities for obtaining tutors. An excellent volunteer program, also many of the general education classes offer labs where students can receive help free of charge.

ADMISSIONS INFO FOR STUDENTS WITH LEARNING DIFFERENCES
SAT/ACT required: Yes
Interview required: No
Essay required: No
Additional application required: No
Documentation required for:
 LD: Psycho ed evaluation to include: relevant historical info, instructional interventions, related services, age diagnosed, objective data (aptitude, achievement, info processing), test scores (standard, percentile and grade equivalents) and describe functional limitations.
 ADHD: Diagnosis based on DSM-V; history of behaviors impairing functioning in academic setting; diagnostic interview; history of symptoms; evidence of ongoing behaviors.
 ASD: Psycho ed evaluation
Documentation submitted to: Support Program/Services
Special Ed. HS course work accepted: No
Separate application required for program services: No
# of students last year receiving services/accommodations for:
 LD: 110-130
Contact Information
Name of program or department: University Accessibility Center
Telephone: 801-422-2767
Fax: 801-422-0174

Brigham Young University (UT)

GENERAL ADMISSIONS

Very important factors considered include: rigor of secondary school record, academic GPA, application essay, standardized test scores, recommendation(s), extracurricular activities, talent/ability, character/personal qualities, religious affiliation/commitment, volunteer work, work experience. *Important factors considered include:* first generation, racial/ethnic status. *Other factors considered include:* level of applicant's interest. *Freshman Admission Requirements:* High school diploma is required and GED is accepted; High school diploma is required and GED is not accepted. *Academic units recommended:* 4 English, 4 math, 3 science, 2 foreign language, 2 history.

ACCOMMODATIONS OR SERVICES

Accommodations are decided upon an individual basis after a thorough review of appropriate, current documentation. The accommodations requests must be supported through the documentation provided and must be logically linked to the current impact of the condition on academic functioning.

FINANCIAL AID

Students should submit: FAFSA. The Princeton Review suggests that all financial aid forms be submitted as soon as possible after October 1. *Need-based scholarships/grants offered:* College/university scholarship or grant aid from institutional funds; Federal Pell; Private scholarships *Loan aid offered:* Direct PLUS loans; Direct Subsidized Stafford Loans; Direct Unsubsidized Stafford Loans.

CAMPUS LIFE

Activities: Choral groups; Concert band; Dance; Drama/theater; Jazz band; Literary magazine; Marching band; Music ensembles; Musical theater; Opera; Pep band; Radio station; Student government; Student newspaper; Student-run film society; Symphony orchestra; Television station. **Organizations:** 390 registered organizations, 22 honor societies, 25 religious organizations. **Athletics (Intercollegiate):** *Men:* baseball, basketball, cheerleading, cross-country, diving, football, golf, swimming, tennis, track/field (outdoor), track/field (indoor), volleyball. *Women:* basketball, cheerleading, cross-country, diving, golf, gymnastics, soccer, softball, swimming, tennis, track/field (outdoor), track/field (indoor), volleyball. **On-Campus Highlights:** Monte L. Bean Life Science Museum, The Museum of Art, Gordon B. Hinckley Alumni & Visitors Cen, Harold B. Lee Library, Wilkinson Student Center.

ACCOMMODATIONS

Calculators	Yes
Dictionary	Yes
Computer	Yes
Spell-checker	Yes
Extended test time	Yes
Scribe	Yes
Proctors	Yes
Oral exams	Yes
Note-takers	Yes
Support services for students with	
LD	Yes
ADHD	Yes
ASD	Yes
Distraction-reduced environment	Yes
Recording of lecture allowed	Yes
Reading technology:	Yes
Audio books	Yes
Other assistive technology	Yes
Priority registration	Yes
Added costs for services:	
For LD:	No
For ADHD:	No
For ASD:	No
LD specialists	Yes
ADHD & ASD coaching	No
ASD specialists	No
Professional tutors	No
Peer tutors	Yes
Max. hours/week for services	Varies
How professors are notified of student approved accommodations	
Student and director	

COLLEGE GRADUATION REQUIREMENTS

Course waivers allowed	No
Course substitutions allowed	Yes

In what courses: General education, foreign language, and/or math.

Southern Utah University

351 W University Blvd, Cedar City, UT 84720 • Admissions: 435-586-7740 • Fax: 435-865-8223

CAMPUS

Type of school	Public
Environment	Village
Support	S

STUDENTS

Undergrad enrollment	6,849
% male/female	46/54
% from out of state	17
% frosh live on campus	24

FINANCIAL FACTS

Annual in-state tuition	$5,918
Annual out-of-state tuition	$19,530
Room and board	$7,067
Required fees	$758

GENERAL ADMISSIONS INFO

Application fee	$50
Priority deadline	12/1
Regular application deadline	5/1

Nonfall registration accepted. Admission may be deferred for a maximum of 5 semesters.

Range SAT EBRW	510–620
Range SAT Math	500–600
Range ACT Composite	20–27

ACADEMICS

Student/faculty ratio	19:1
% students returning for sophomore year	71
% students graduating within 4 years	19
% students graduating within 6 years	37

Most classes have 10–19 students.

PROGRAMS/SERVICES FOR STUDENTS WITH LEARNING DIFFERENCES

The Disability Support Office at Southern Utah University continuously provides support and services to students with disabilities who are overcoming different educational difficulties because of their individual challenges. Reasonable accommodations are offered to participants in the program, giving them access to services requested by law. We encourage self-direction, resourcefulness, academic skill development and personal advancement. Cooperation between faculty, students and community assures an atmosphere of understanding and acceptance.

ADMISSIONS

Students with learning disabilities submit the general application form. Students must have at least a 2.0 GPA and show competency in English, math, science, and social studies. The university uses an admissions index derived from the combination of the high school GPA and results of either the ACT or SAT. If students are not admissible through the regular process, special consideration by a Committee Review can be gained through reference letters and a personal letter. The university is allowed to admit 5 percent in "flex" admission. These applications are reviewed by a committee consisting of the Director of Support Services and representatives from the Admissions Office. Students are encouraged to self-disclose their learning disability and submit documentation.

ADMISSIONS INFO FOR STUDENTS WITH LEARNING DIFFERENCES

SAT/ACT required: Yes
Interview required: No
Essay required: No
Additional application required: No
Documentation required for:
 LD: Psycho ed evaluation to include: relevant historical info, instructional interventions, related services, age diagnosed, objective data (aptitude, achievement, info processing), test scores (standard, percentile and grade equivalents) and describe functional limitations.
 ADHD: Diagnosis based on DSM-V; history of behaviors impairing functioning in academic setting; diagnostic interview; history of symptoms; evidence of ongoing behaviors.
 ASD: Psycho ed evaluation
Documentation submitted to: Disability Support Center
Special Ed. HS course work accepted: No
Separate application required for program services: No
# of students last year receiving services/accommodations for:
 LD: 94
Contact Information
Name of program or department: Disability Support Center
Telephone: (435) 865-8022
Fax: (435) 865-8235

Southern Utah University

Additional Information
Students with disabilities are evaluated by the Office of Students with Disabilities to determine accommodations or services. The following accommodations or services may be available on a case-by-case basis for students with appropriate documentation: the use of calculators, dictionary, computer or spell checker in exams; extended testing time; scribes; proctors; oral exams; note-takers; distraction-free testing environments; tape recorders in class; books on tape; assistive technolgy; and priority registration. Tutoring is available in small groups or one-to-one, free of charge. Basic skills classes, for credit, are offered in English, reading, math, math anxiety, language, and study skills.

GENERAL ADMISSIONS
Very important factors considered include: academic GPA, standardized test scores. *Important factors considered include:* level of applicant's interest. *Freshman Admission Requirements:* High school diploma is required and GED is accepted. *Academic units recommended:* 4 English, 3 math, 3 science, 1 science lab, 2 foreign language, 3 social studies.

ACCOMMODATIONS OR SERVICES
Accommodations are decided upon an individual basis after a thorough review of appropriate, current documentation. The accommodations requests must be supported through the documentation provided and must be logically linked to the current impact of the condition on academic functioning.

FINANCIAL AID
Students should submit: FAFSA; Institution's own financial aid form. Applicants will be notified of awards on a rolling basis beginning 3/14. The Princeton Review suggests that all financial aid forms be submitted as soon as possible after October 1. *Need-based scholarships/grants offered:* College/university scholarship or grant aid from institutional funds; Federal Pell; Private scholarships; SEOG; State scholarships/grants. *Loan aid offered:* Direct PLUS loans; Direct Subsidized Stafford Loans; Direct Unsubsidized Stafford Loans. Federal Work-Study Program available. Institutional employment available.

CAMPUS LIFE
Activities: Campus Ministries; Choral groups; Concert band; Dance; Drama/theater; International Student Organization; Jazz band; Literary magazine; Marching band; Music ensembles; Musical theater; Opera; Pep band; Radio station; Student government; Student newspaper; Student-run film society; Symphony orchestra; Television station. **Organizations: Athletics (Intercollegiate):** *Men:* baseball, basketball, cross-country, football, golf, track/field (outdoor). *Women:* basketball, cross-country, gymnastics, softball, tennis, track/field (outdoor). Shakespeare Festival, Carter Carillon, Student Center, Library.

ACCOMMODATIONS	
Allowed in exams:	
Calculators	No
Dictionary	Yes
Computer	Yes
Spell-checker	Yes
Extended test time	Yes
Scribe	Yes
Proctors	Yes
Oral exams	Yes
Note-takers	Yes
Support services for students with	
LD	Yes
ADHD	Yes
ASD	Yes
Distraction-reduced environment	Yes
Recording of lecture allowed	Yes
Reading technology:	Yes
Audio books	Yes
Other assistive technology	Yes
Priority registration	Yes
Added costs for services:	
For LD:	No
LD specialists	No
ADHD & ASD coaching	No
ASD specialists	No
Professional tutors	No
Peer tutors	No
Max. hours/week for services	Varies
How professors are notified of student approved accommodations	Student and director as well as by letter

COLLEGE GRADUATION REQUIREMENTS	
Course waivers allowed	No
Course substitutions allowed	No

University of Utah

201 S. PRESIDENTS CIRCLE, SALT LAKE CITY, UT 84112 • ADMISSIONS: 801-581-8761 • FAX: 801-585-7864

CAMPUS
Type of school	Public
Environment	Metropolis
Support	CS

STUDENTS
Undergrad enrollment	23,402
% male/female	54/46
% from out of state	19
% frosh live on campus	50

FINANCIAL FACTS
Annual in-state tuition	$7,997
Annual out-of-state tuition	$27,990
Room and board	$10,262
Required fees	$1,225

GENERAL ADMISSIONS INFO
Application fee	$55
Priority deadline	12/1
Regular application deadline	4/1

Nonfall registration accepted. Admission may be deferred for a maximum of 7 semesters.

Range SAT EBRW	560–670
Range SAT Math	550–680
Range ACT Composite	22–29

ACADEMICS
Student/faculty ratio	16:1
% students returning for sophomore year	91
% students graduating within 4 years	31
% students graduating within 6 years	67

Most classes have 10–19 students.
Most lab/discussion sessions have 10–19 students.

PROGRAMS/SERVICES FOR STUDENTS WITH LEARNING DIFFERENCES

The Center for Disability Services is dedicated to students with disabilities by providing the opportunity for success and equal access at the University of Utah. We are committed to providing reasonable accommodations as outlined by Federal and State law. We also strive to create an inclusive, safe and respectful environment. By promoting awareness, knowledge and equity, we aspire to impact positive change within individuals and the campus community. The Center for Disability Services is the designated office at the University of Utah which evaluates disability documentation, determines eligibility, and implements reasonable accommodations for enrolled students as guided by Section 504 of the Rehabilitation Act, the Americans with Disabilities Act, and University policy.

ADMISSIONS

There is no special application process for students with learning disabilities. All applicants to the university must meet the general admission requirements. Students who do not meet the admission requirements as a direct result of their disability may be admitted on the condition that course deficiencies are filled prior to earning 30 semester hours at the university. Conditional admission is determined by the Center for Disability Services and the Admissions Office. Students must provide appropriate information regarding their disability and any services they received in high school due to their disability. Self-disclosure is recommended only if the student needs to inform the Admissions Office they are working with the Center for Disability Services to consider conditional admission. Otherwise disclosure is not recommended, but it is left to the student to make the decision.

Additional Information

The University of Utah is committed to providing reasonable accommodations to students whose disabilities may limit their ability to function in the academic setting. To meet the needs of students and to make university activities, programs, and facilities accessible, the Center for Disability Services can provide the following services to students who provide documentation of a disability: assistance with admissions, registration, and graduation; orientation to the campus; referrals to campus and community services; guidelines for obtaining CDS services; general and academic advising related to disability; investigation of

ADMISSIONS INFO FOR STUDENTS WITH LEARNING DIFFERENCES

SAT/ACT required: Yes
Interview required: Not Applicable
Essay required: Not Applicable
Additional application required: Yes
Documentation required for:
LD: Psycho ed evaluation
ADHD: Psycho ed evaluation
ASD: Psycho ed evaluation
Documentation submitted to:Center of Disability Services
Special Ed. HS course work accepted: Not Applicable
Separate application required for program services: No
# of students last year receiving services/accommodations for:
LD: 370
Contact Information
Name of program or department: Center for Disability Services
Telephone: 801-581-5020
Fax: 801-581-5487
Email: info@disability.utah.edu

academic strengths and weaknesses; develop effective learning strategies; coordinate with academic and departmental advisors regarding program goals; coordinate reasonable accommodations of disability-related limitations with faculty and staff; liaison between student and faculty or staff; provide readers, scribes, note-takers, textbooks, and printed material recorded onto cassettes; and arrange for exam accommodations. The Center for Disability Services has the right to set procedures to determine whether the student qualifies for services and how the services will be implemented. Additionally, the center has the responsibility to adjust or substitute academic requirements that unfairly discriminate against the student with a disability and that are not essential to the integrity of a student's academic program. Students must provide appropriate documentation.

GENERAL ADMISSIONS

Very important factors considered include: rigor of secondary school record, academic GPA. *Important factors considered include:* standardized test scores. *Other factors considered include:* class rank, extracurricular activities, talent/ability, character/personal qualities, first generation, alumni/ae relation, geographical residence, state residency, racial/ethnic status, volunteer work, work experience. *Freshman Admission Requirements:* High school diploma is required and GED is accepted. *Academic units required:* 4 English, 2 math, 3 science, 1 science lab, 2 foreign language, 1 history, 4 academic electives.

ACCOMMODATIONS OR SERVICES

Accommodations are decided upon an individual basis after a thorough review of appropriate, current documentation. The accommodations requests must be supported through the documentation provided and must be logically linked to the current impact of the condition on academic functioning.

FINANCIAL AID

Students should submit: FAFSA. Applicants will be notified of awards on a rolling basis beginning 3/1. The Princeton Review suggests that all financial aid forms be submitted as soon as possible after October 1. *Need-based scholarships/grants offered:* College/university scholarship or grant aid from institutional funds; Federal Nursing Scholarships; Federal Pell; Private scholarships; SEOG; State scholarships/grants. *Loan aid offered:* Direct PLUS loans; Direct Subsidized Stafford Loans; Direct Unsubsidized Stafford Loans. Federal Work-Study Program available. Institutional employment available.

CAMPUS LIFE

Activities: Campus Ministries; Choral groups; Concert band; Dance; Drama/theater; International Student Organization; Jazz band; Literary magazine; Marching band; Music ensembles; Musical theater; Opera; Pep band; Radio station; Student government; Student newspaper; Student-run film society; Symphony orchestra; Television station. **Organizations:** 238 registered organizations, 41 honor societies, 9 religious organizations. 7 fraternities, 6 sororities. **Athletics (Intercollegiate):** *Men:* baseball, basketball, cheerleading, diving, football, golf, skiing (downhill/alpine), skiing (nordic/cross-country), swimming, tennis. *Women:* basketball, cheerleading, cross-country, diving, gymnastics, skiing (downhill/alpine), skiing (nordic/cross-country), soccer, softball, swimming, tennis, track/field (outdoor), track/field (indoor), volleyball. **On-Campus Highlights:** Rice Eccles Stadium, Jon M. Huntsman Center, University Union, Marriott Library, Student Life Center.

ACCOMMODATIONS

Allowed in exams:	
Calculators	Yes
Dictionary	Yes
Computer	Yes
Spell-checker	Yes
Extended test time	Yes
Scribe	Yes
Proctors	Yes
Oral exams	Yes
Note-takers	Yes
Support services for students with	
LD	Yes
ADHD	Yes
ASD	Yes
Distraction-reduced environment	Yes
Recording of lecture allowed	Yes
Reading technology:	
Audio books	Yes
Other assistive technology	Kurzweil 3000 reading software, Tape Recorders
Priority registration	Yes
Added costs for services:	
For LD:	No
For ADHD:	No
For ASD:	No
LD specialists	Yes
ADHD & ASD coaching	No
ASD specialists	Yes
Professional tutors	Yes
Peer tutors	Yes
Max. hours/week for services	Varies
How professors are notified of student approved accommodations	Student

COLLEGE GRADUATION REQUIREMENTS

Course waivers allowed	No
Course substitutions allowed	Yes
In what courses	Math Foreign Language

Utah State University

OLD MAIN HILL, LOGAN, UT 84322-0160 • ADMISSIONS: 435-797-1079 • FAX: 435-797-3708

CAMPUS

Type of school	Public
Environment	Town
Support	CS

STUDENTS

Undergrad enrollment	21,473
% male/female	48/52
% from out of state	27
% frosh live on campus	

FINANCIAL FACTS

Annual in-state tuition	$6,105
Annual out-of-state tuition	$19,657
Room and board	$6,060
Required fees	$1,070

GENERAL ADMISSIONS INFO

Application fee	$50

Nonfall registration accepted. Admission may be deferred for a maximum of 2 years.

Range SAT EBRW	490–600
Range SAT Math	510–620
Range ACT Composite	21–27

ACADEMICS

Student/faculty ratio	
% students returning for sophomore year	69
% students graduating within 4 years	18
% students graduating within 6 years	48

Most classes have 10–19 students.
Most lab/discussion sessions have 10–19 students.

PROGRAMS/SERVICES FOR STUDENTS WITH LEARNING DIFFERENCES

The mission of the Disability Resource Center (DRC) is to provide persons with disabilities equal access to University programs, services, and activities. This is accomplished by fostering an environment which supports the understanding and acceptance of persons with disabilities throughout the University community, and the provision of reasonable and appropriate accommodations. The DRC affirms the right of persons with disabilities to obtain access in a manner promoting dignity and independence.

ADMISSIONS

All students must submit the regular application and meet the established admissions requirements. A minimum 2.5 high school GPA, 17 ACT, and 90 admissions index are the minimum requirements for admission into a 4-year Bachelor Degree program. Applicants with a least a 2.0 high school GPA, 14 ACT, and 85 index score may be admitted into a 2-year Associate Degree program. In the 2-year degree program, the student can either earn an AS degree or an AA degree, or change to a 4-year bachelor degree after completing 24 credits with a minimum 2.5 GPA at USU. Please note that applicants must apply at least two months prior to the beginning of classes to be considered for admission into this associate degree program, and students cannot begin this associate degree program in summer.

Additional Information

The Disability Resource Center provides the following services: registration assistance and priority registration, note takers, textbooks in alternative formats, accommodations for exams, including extended time and distraction reduced rooms with scribes/readers if appropriate. Basic skills courses are offered to all students by the Academic Resource Center (ARC) in time management, learning strategies, reading, math, and study strategies. Tutoring in math and supplemental instruction for some classes are also offered free of charge to all students by the ARC. The DRC has developed an assistive technology lab with computers and

ADMISSIONS INFO FOR STUDENTS WITH LEARNING DIFFERENCES

SAT/ACT required: Yes
Interview required: No
Essay required: No
Additional application required: No
Documentation required for:
 LD: Psycho ed evaluation to include: relevant historical info, instructional interventions, related services, age diagnosed, objective data (aptitude, achievement, info processing), test scores (standard, percentile and grade equivalents) and describe functional limitations.
 ADHD: Diagnosis based on DSM-V; history of behaviors impairing functioning in academic setting; diagnostic interview; history of symptoms; evidence of ongoing behaviors.
 ASD: Psychological evaluation preferred but letter from professional or copy of IEP/504 might suffice
Documentation submitted to: Disability Resource Center
Special Ed. HS course work accepted: Yes
Separate application required for program services: Yes
# of students last year receiving services/accommodations for:
 LD: 712
Contact Information
Name of program or department: Disability Resource Center
Telephone: 435-797-2444
Fax: 435-797-0130
Email: drc@usu.edu

adaptive equipment to promote independence in conducting research and completing class assignments. If eligible, some DRC students may also access services provided by USU's Student Support Services program (TRIO). Workshops and individual services are also offered by the Health and Wellness Center and the Counseling and Psychological Services office.

GENERAL ADMISSIONS

Very important factors considered include: academic GPA, standardized test scores. *Other factors considered include:* rigor of secondary school record, class rank, recommendation(s). *Freshman Admission Requirements:* High school diploma is required and GED is accepted. *Academic units required: Academic units recommended:* 4 English, 4 math, 3 science, 3 science labs, 2 foreign language, 3.5 social studies.

ACCOMMODATIONS OR SERVICES

Accommodations are decided upon an individual basis after a thorough review of appropriate, current documentation. The accommodations requests must be supported through the documentation provided and must be logically linked to the current impact of the condition on academic functioning.

FINANCIAL AID

Students should submit: FAFSA. Applicants will be notified of awards on a rolling basis beginning 4/1. The Princeton Review suggests that all financial aid forms be submitted as soon as possible after October 1. *Need-based scholarships/grants offered:* College/university scholarship or grant aid from institutional funds; Federal Pell; Private scholarships; SEOG; State scholarships/grants. *Loan aid offered:* Direct PLUS loans; Direct Subsidized Stafford Loans; Direct Unsubsidized Stafford Loans. Federal Work-Study Program available. Institutional employment available.

CAMPUS LIFE

Activities: Campus Ministries; Choral groups; Concert band; Dance; Drama/theater; International Student Organization; Jazz band; Marching band; Music ensembles; Musical theater; Opera; Pep band; Radio station; Student government; Student newspaper; Student-run film society; Symphony orchestra; Television station. **Organizations:** 194 registered organizations, 32 honor societies, 8 religious organizations. 5 fraternities, 3 sororities. **Athletics (Intercollegiate):** *Men:* basketball, cross-country, football, golf, tennis, track/field (outdoor), track/field (indoor). *Women:* basketball, cross-country, gymnastics, soccer, softball, tennis, track/field (outdoor), track/field (indoor), volleyball. **On-Campus Highlights:** Aggie Recreation Center, Dee Glen Smith Spectrum, Merrill-Cazier Library, Taggart Student Center, The Quad.

ACCOMMODATIONS

Allowed in exams:

Calculators	Yes
Dictionary	Yes
Computer	Yes
Spell-checker	Yes
Extended test time	Yes
Scribe	Yes
Proctors	Yes
Oral exams	Yes
Note-takers	Yes

Support services for students with

LD	Yes
ADHD	Yes
ASD	Yes
Distraction-reduced environment	Yes
Recording of lecture allowed	Yes
Reading technology:	Yes
Audio books	Yes

Other assistive technologyUSU offers a wide variety of assistive technology as well as the ability to purchase additional technology based on the needs of individual students

Priority registration	Yes

Added costs for services:

For LD:	No
For ADHD:	No
For ASD:	No
LD specialists	Yes
ADHD & ASD coaching	No
ASD specialists	No
Professional tutors	Yes
Peer tutors	Yes
Max. hours/week for services	Varies

How professors are notified of student approved accommodations
Director and student

COLLEGE GRADUATION REQUIREMENTS

Course waivers allowed	Yes
In what courses	Varies

Under certain circumstances

Course substitutions allowed	Yes

In what courses
General Education math requirements may be substituted with other courses when a student can demonstrate that there is a substantial limitation that necessitates such an accommodation.

Champlain College

PO Box 670, Burlington, VT 05402-0670 • Admissions: 802-860-2727 • Fax: 802-860-2767

CAMPUS

Type of school	Private (nonprofit)
Environment	Town
Support	S

STUDENTS

Undergrad enrollment	2,216
% male/female	63/37
% from out of state	79
% frosh live on campus	95

FINANCIAL FACTS

Annual tuition	$40,910
Room and board	$15,354
Required fees	$100

GENERAL ADMISSIONS INFO

Regular application deadline   1/15
Nonfall registration accepted. Admission may be deferred for a maximum of 1 year.

Range SAT EBRW	560–670
Range SAT Math	530–630
Range ACT Composite	23–29

ACADEMICS

Student/faculty ratio	14:1
% students returning for sophomore year	79
% students graduating within 4 years	50
% students graduating within 6 years	60

Most classes have 10–19 students.
Most lab/discussion sessions have 10–19 students.

PROGRAMS/SERVICES FOR STUDENTS WITH LEARNING DIFFERENCES

Champlain College does not offer a special program for students with LD. Support services and academic accommodations are available when needed. Students with LD meet individually with a counselor at the start of the semester and are assisted in developing a plan of academic support. The counselor acts as liaison between the student and faculty. The college offers peer tutoring, writing assistance, accounting lab, math lab, and an oral communications lab. Mental health counseling is offered as is academic coaching. Students must provide documentation of the disability to the Office of Disability Services in the Counseling Department, which should include the most recent educational evaluation performed by a qualified individual, and a letter from any educational support service provider who has recently worked with the student would be most helpful. The letter should include information about the nature of the disability and the support services and/or program modifications provided.

ADMISSIONS

There is no special admissions procedure for students with LD. The admissions process is fairly competitive. The most important part of the application is the high school transcript. Upward grade trend and challenging course work are looked on favorably. Recommendations and college essay are required. All admission decisions are based on an assessment of the academic foundation needed for success in the required courses at the bachelor's degree level. Strong writing skills are important for all applicants. Minimum recommended preparation includes successful completion of a college preparatory curriculum. Students are expected to take a full course load of challenging academic subjects senior year. Applicants are evaluated based on the demands of their secondary school curriculum, grades earned, rank in class, standardized test scores, writing ability, teacher and counselor recommendations, and academic growth. Strong writing skills are important for all applicants.

ADMISSIONS INFO FOR STUDENTS WITH LEARNING DIFFERENCES

SAT/ACT required: Yes
Interview required: No
Essay required: Yes
Additional application required: No
Documentation required for:
 LD: Psycho ed evaluation to include: relevant historical info, instructional interventions, related services, age diagnosed, objective data (aptitude, achievement, info processing), test scores (standard, percentile and grade equivalents) and describe functional limitations.
 ADHD: Diagnosis based on DSM-V; history of behaviors impairing functioning in academic setting; diagnostic interview; history of symptoms; evidence of ongoing behaviors.
 ASD: Psycho education evaluation
Documentation submitted to: Accommodation Services
Special Ed. HS course work accepted: No
Contact Information
Name of program or department: Accommodation Services
Telephone: 802-651-5961

Champlain College

Additional Information

Students with learning disabilities who self-disclose receive a special needs form after they have enrolled in college courses from the Counseling Department. The coordinator meets with each student during the first week of school. The first appointment includes a discussion about the student's disability and the academic accommodations that will be needed. Accommodations could include, but are not limited to, tutoring, extended time for tests, readers for tests, use of computers during exams, peer note-takers, tape recording lectures, and books on tape. With the student's permission, faculty members receive a letter discussing appropriate accommodations. The coordinators will continue to act as a liaison between students and faculty, consult with tutors, monitor students' academic progress, and consult with faculty as needed.

GENERAL ADMISSIONS

Very important factors considered include: rigor of secondary school record, academic GPA, talent/ability. *Important factors considered include:* application essay, standardized test scores, recommendation(s), extracurricular activities, character/personal qualities, first generation, racial/ethnic status, level of applicant's interest. *Other factors considered include:* class rank, alumni/ae relation, volunteer work, work experience. *Freshman Admission Requirements:* High school diploma is required and GED is accepted. *Academic units required:* 4 English, 3 math, 3 science, 3 science labs, 2 foreign language, 4 history, 4 academic electives. *Academic units recommended:* 4 math, 4 science, 4 foreign language.

ACCOMMODATIONS OR SERVICES

Accommodations are decided upon an individual basis after a thorough review of appropriate, current documentation. The accommodations requests must be supported through the documentation provided and must be logically linked to the current impact of the condition on academic functioning.

FINANCIAL AID

Students should submit: FAFSA. Applicants will be notified of awards on a rolling basis beginning 3/1. The Princeton Review suggests that all financial aid forms be submitted as soon as possible after October 1. *Need-based scholarships/grants offered:* College/university scholarship or grant aid from institutional funds; Federal Pell; Private scholarships; SEOG; State scholarships/grants. *Loan aid offered:* Direct PLUS loans; Direct Subsidized Stafford Loans; Direct Unsubsidized Stafford Loans. Federal Work-Study Program available. Institutional employment available.

CAMPUS LIFE

Activities: Choral groups; Drama/theater; International Student Organization; Literary magazine; Musical theater; Radio station; Student government; Student newspaper. **Organizations:** 40 registered organizations, 2 honor societies, 1 religious organization. **On-Campus Highlights:** Sr. Leahy Center for Digital Forenics, Center for Communication and Creative Media, Student Life Center, Emergent Media Center & Maker Lab, Miller Information Commons.

ACCOMMODATIONS

Allowed in exams:	
Calculators	Yes
Dictionary	Yes
Computer	Yes
Spell-checker	Yes
Extended test time	Yes
Scribe	Yes
Proctors	Yes
Oral exams	Yes
Note-takers	Yes
Support services for students with	
LD	Yes
ADHD	Yes
ASD	Yes
Distraction-reduced environment	Yes
Recording of lecture allowed	Yes
Reading technology:	Yes
Audio books	Yes
Other assistive technology	Yes
Priority registration	Yes
Added costs for services:	
For LD:	No
For ADHD:	No
For ASD:	No
LD specialists	No
ADHD & ASD coaching	No
ASD specialists	No
Professional tutors	Yes
Peer tutors	Yes
Max. hours/week for services	Varies
How professors are notified of student approved accommodations	By student with a letter generated by the Disabilities Services Office

COLLEGE GRADUATION REQUIREMENTS

Course waivers allowed	No
Course substitutions allowed	No

Green Mountain College

ONE BRENNAN CIRCLE, POULTNEY, VT 05764-1199 • ADMISSIONS: 802-287-8000 • FAX: 802-287-8099

CAMPUS

Type of school	Private (nonprofit)
Environment	Rural
Support	S

STUDENTS

Undergrad enrollment	457
% male/female	43/57
% from out of state	82
% frosh live on campus	98

FINANCIAL FACTS

Annual tuition	$35,560
Room and board	$11,722
Required fees	$1,442

GENERAL ADMISSIONS INFO

Application fee	$30
Priority deadline	3/1

Nonfall registration accepted. Admission may be deferred for a maximum of 1 year.

Range SAT EBRW	450–560
Range SAT Math	475–615
Range ACT Composite	21–26

ACADEMICS

Student/faculty ratio	14:1
% students returning for sophomore year	74
% students graduating within 4 years	41
% students graduating within 6 years	51

Most classes have 20–29 students. Most lab/discussion sessions have 20–29 students.

PROGRAMS/SERVICES FOR STUDENTS WITH LEARNING DIFFERENCES

Green Mountain College provides accommodations for students with documented learning differences. The college believes that every student has the potential for academic success and strives to support students while teaching them independence and self-advocacy skills. The Calhoun Learning Center (CLC) functions as the primary source of information regarding academic issues relating to disabilities. Students seeking academic accommodations must self-identify and submit valid documentation of their learning needs. The CLC staff determines which students are eligible for academic accommodations and works with the student and staff to develop and implement an accommodation plan that will allow the student an opportunity to succeed at college. The CLC has six main functions: to provide academic support, primarily through one-on-one, small group, general content area tutoring; to serve as the campus Writing Center; to support courses specifically designed for underprepared students; to provide support for foreign students; to be the campus center for academic issues relating to disabilities; and to provide workshops and seminars and events with the goal of improving learning skills.

ADMISSIONS

There is no special admissions process for students with learning disabilities. Students face the same admission criteria. All applications are carefully considered with the best interest of both the student and the college in mind.

ADMISSIONS INFO FOR STUDENTS WITH LEARNING DIFFERENCES

SAT/ACT required: No
Interview required: No
Essay required: Not Applicable
Additional application required: No
Documentation required for:
  ADHD: Evaluators must be properly credentialed to evaluate the specific needs of the individual for whom they are recommending accommodations. Psychologists may provide documentation regarding mental health concerns possibly including mood disorders, anxiety disorders, pervasive developmental disorders, cognitive impairment, or the like. Psychologists could not, for example, provide documentation for a student seeking accommodations for a hearing impairment; an audiologist would be a more appropriate evaluator in that case. The credentials of the evaluator will depend on the type of condition that impacts learning.
  ASD: Evaluators must be properly credentialed to evaluate the specific needs of the individual for whom they are recommending accommodations. Psychologists may provide documentation regarding mental health concerns possibly including mood disorders, anxiety disorders, pervasive developmental disorders, cognitive impairment, or the like. Psychologists could not, for example, provide documentation for a student seeking accommodations for a hearing impairment; an audiologist would be a more appropriate evaluator in that case. The credentials of the evaluator will depend on the type of condition that impacts learning.
Documentation submitted to: The Calhoun Learning Center (CLC)
Special Ed. HS course work accepted: Yes
Separate application required for program services: No
Contact Information
Name of program or department: The Calhoun Learning Center (CLC)
Telephone: 802-287-2180
Fax: 802-287-8288
Email: fabreyc@greenmtn.edu

Green Mountain College

Additional Information

The Learning Center provides support services to all students which include: academic counseling for students on an individual basis and, when appropriate, making referrals to related college departments; offering and facilitating group sessions for students experiencing similar academic concerns; coordinating the delivery of services for students with disabilities that impact academic performance including responding to requests for reasonable and appropriate accommodations; conducting educational workshops designed to facilitate the mastery of study strategies and learning skills and to improve overall academic performance; coordinating the college tutorial program in consultation with individual academic departments; and collaborating with existing college components. The tutoring program uses a three-tiered approach: a drop-in clinic for immediate but temporary academic assistance; individually scheduled tutoring; or a more extensive schedule of one, two, or three tutoring sessions per week for tutorial help throughout a course. All new students take placement tests to assess their achievement in mathematics. Students underprepared in math are advised to take Intro to College Math and tutoring is available.

GENERAL ADMISSIONS

Very important factors considered include: academic GPA, recommendation(s). *Important factors considered include:* rigor of secondary school record, class rank, application essay, standardized test scores, interview, extracurricular activities, volunteer work.level of applicant's interest. *Other factors considered include:* talent/ability, character/personal qualities, alumni/ae relation, religious affiliation/commitment, racial/ethnic status, work experience. *Freshman Admission Requirements:* High school diploma is required and GED is accepted. *Academic units required:* 4 English, 3 math, 3 science, 2 science labs, 1 foreign language, 3 social studies, 1 history, 5 academic electives. *Academic units recommended:* 4 math, 4 science, 2 foreign language, 2 history.

ACCOMMODATIONS OR SERVICES

Accommodations are decided upon an individual basis after a thorough review of appropriate, current documentation. The accommodations requests must be supported through the documentation provided and must be logically linked to the current impact of the condition on academic functioning.

FINANCIAL AID

Students should submit: FAFSA. Applicants will be notified of awards on a rolling basis beginning 12/16. The Princeton Review suggests that all financial aid forms be submitted as soon as possible after October 1. *Need-based scholarships/grants offered:* College/university scholarship or grant aid from institutional funds; Federal Pell; Private scholarships; SEOG; State scholarships/grants. *Loan aid offered:* Direct PLUS loans; Direct Subsidized Stafford Loans; Direct Unsubsidized Stafford Loans. Federal Work-Study Program available. Institutional employment available.

CAMPUS LIFE

Activities: Choral groups; Concert band; Drama/theater; International Student Organization; Jazz band; Literary magazine; Model UN; Music ensembles; Student government; Student newspaper; Student-run film society. **Organizations:** 25 registered organizations, 2 honor societies, 2 religious organizations. **Athletics (Intercollegiate):** *Men:* basketball, cross-country, golf, lacrosse, skiing (downhill/alpine), soccer, tennis. *Women:* basketball, cross-country, lacrosse, skiing (downhill/alpine), soccer, softball, tennis, volleyball. **On-Campus Highlights:** Griswold Library, Cerridwen Farm, Withey Student Center, Moses Coffeehouse, Poultney River.

ACCOMMODATIONS

Allowed in exams:	
Calculators	Yes
Dictionary	Yes
Computer	Yes
Spell-checker	Yes
Extended test time	Yes
Scribe	Yes
Proctors	Yes
Oral exams	Yes
Note-takers	Yes
Support services for students with	
LD	Yes
ADHD	Yes
ASD	Yes
Distraction-reduced environment	Yes
Recording of lecture allowed	Yes
Reading technology:	Yes
Audio books	Yes
Other assistive technology Dragon Naturally Speaking, tape recorders, Livescribe pens	
Priority registration	Yes
Added costs for services:	
For LD:	No
For ADHD:	No
For ASD:	No
LD specialists	Yes
ADHD & ASD coaching	Yes
ASD specialists	Yes
Professional tutors	Yes
Peer tutors	Yes
Max. hours/week for services	
How professors are notified of student approved accommodations Director and student	

COLLEGE GRADUATION REQUIREMENTS

Course waivers allowed	No
Course substitutions allowed	Yes
In what courses	math

Northern Vermont University

337 COLLEGE HILL, JOHNSON, VT 05656-9408 • ADMISSIONS: 802-635-1219 • FAX: 802-635-1230

PROGRAMS/SERVICES FOR STUDENTS WITH LEARNING DIFFERENCES

Northern Vermont University provides services to students with disabilities through the Learning Specialist at the Academic Support Service Program. The fundamental purpose is to provide students with the appropriate services necessary to allow access to Northern Vermont University academic programs. Students with disabilities are integrated fully into the college community. In addition, students with disabilities may also be eligible for the TRiO program, which provides additional supports and services through the Learning Resource Center. The Learning Resource Center provides a friendly and supportive environment for any student who is academically struggling or underprepared to meet his or her educational goals. Services may include group and peer tutoring; professional tutoring in writing and math

ADMISSIONS

Students with disabilities who demonstrate the academic ability to be successful at the post-secondary level are eligible for acceptance. Applicants with a disability are encouraged to contact the Admissions Office so that accommodations can be made available, where appropriate, throughout the admission process. Course requirements include four years of English, three years of college preparatory mathematics, three years of social sciences, and two years of science (one course with a lab).

Additional Information

Academic Support Services provides tutoring, academic advising, personal counseling and mentoring, career exploration, college survival skills workshops, and assistance with establishing appropriate and reasonable accommodations. Students should be self-advocates and are responsible for notifying instructors to arrange for providing the approved accommodations.

Northern Vermont University

General Admissions

Very important factors considered include: rigor of secondary school record, standardized test scores. *Important factors considered include:* class rank, academic GPA, application essay, recommendation(s), talent/ability, character/personal qualities. *Other factors considered include:* interview, extracurricular activities, volunteer work, work experience. *Freshman Admission Requirements:* High school diploma is required and GED is accepted. *Academic units required:* 4 English, 2 math, 2 science, 1 science lab, 3 social studies, 2 history. *Academic units recommended:* 4 English, 3 math, 3 science, 2 science labs, 1 foreign language, 3 social studies, 3 history.

Accommodations or Services

Accommodations are decided upon an individual basis after a thorough review of appropriate, current documentation. The accommodations requests must be supported through the documentation provided and must be logically linked to the current impact of the condition on academic functioning.

Financial Aid

Students should submit: FAFSA; State aid form. Applicants will be notified of awards on a rolling basis beginning 4/1. The Princeton Review suggests that all financial aid forms be submitted as soon as possible after October 1. *Need-based scholarships/grants offered:* College/university scholarship or grant aid from institutional funds; Federal Pell; Private scholarships; SEOG; State scholarships/grants. *Loan aid offered:* Direct PLUS loans; Direct Subsidized Stafford Loans; Direct Unsubsidized Stafford Loans. Federal Work-Study Program available. Institutional employment available.

Campus Life

Activities: Choral groups; Concert band; Dance; Drama/theater; Jazz band; Literary magazine; Music ensembles; Musical theater; Radio station; Student government; Student newspaper; Yearbook. **Organizations:** 30 registered organizations, 1 honor society, 4 religious organizations. **Athletics (Intercollegiate):** *Men:* basketball, cross-country, golf, lacrosse, soccer, tennis. *Women:* basketball, cross-country, soccer, softball, tennis, volleyball. **On-Campus Highlights:** Dibden Center For the Arts, Snowboarding Hill, Movie Cinema, Disc Golf Course, SHAPE Athletic Facility.

ACCOMMODATIONS

Allowed in exams:	
Calculators	Yes
Dictionary	Yes
Computer	Yes
Spell-checker	Yes
Extended test time	Yes
Scribe	Yes
Proctors	Yes
Oral exams	No
Note-takers	Yes
Support services for students with	
LD	Yes
ADHD	Yes
ASD	Yes
Distraction-reduced environment	Yes
Recording of lecture allowed	Yes
Reading technology:	Yes
Audio books	Yes
Other assistive technology	Kurzweil 3000, Inspiration Mapping Software, Dragon Naturally-Speaking Text Help, Read and Write Gold, digital recorders, Victor Vibe, Smart Pen
Priority registration	No
Added costs for services:	
For LD:	No
For ADHD:	No
For ASD:	No
LD specialists	Yes
ADHD & ASD coaching	No
ASD specialists	No
Professional tutors	Yes
Peer tutors	Yes
Max. hours/week for services	Unlimited
How professors are notified of student approved accommodations	Student

COLLEGE GRADUATION REQUIREMENTS

Course waivers allowed	No
Course substitutions allowed	Yes

In what courses: Lower math may be substituted for one of the two math requirements if there is a math LD only.

Landmark College

P.O. Box 820, Putney, VT 05346-0820 • Admissions: 802-387-6718 • Fax: 802-387-6868

CAMPUS

Type of school	Private (nonprofit)
Environment	Rural
Support	SP

STUDENTS

Undergrad enrollment	487
% male/female	68/32
% from out of state	95
% frosh live on campus	100

FINANCIAL FACTS

Annual tuition	$48,210
Room and board	$8,620
Required fees	$500

GENERAL ADMISSIONS INFO

Application fee	$75
Priority deadline	5/15

Nonfall registration accepted. Admission may be deferred for a maximum of 1 year.

ACADEMICS

Student/faculty ratio	6:1
% students returning for sophomore year	90
% students graduating within 4 years	28
% students graduating within 6 years	30

Most classes have 10–19 students.

PROGRAMS/SERVICES FOR STUDENTS WITH LEARNING DIFFERENCES

For three decades, Landmark College has been the leader in creating successful learning strategies for students who learn differently. When Landmark College opened in 1985, we were the first institution of higher education to pioneer college-level studies for students with dyslexia. Today, we are known throughout the world for our innovative educational model, where students become confident, empowered, and independent learners. Landmark College is the only accredited college in the country designed exclusively for students of average to superior intellectual potential with dyslexia, attention deficit hyperactivity disorder (ADHD), or specific learning disabilities. Life- changing experiences are commonplace at Landmark College. Simply put, Landmark College knows how to serve students who learn differently better than any other place on earth. Landmark's beautiful campus offers all the resources students might expect at a high quality higher education institution, including a new athletic center, a student center, dining facility, cafe, residence halls, and academic resource center (library). The college has also invested substantially in technology, and offers a wireless network in all of its classrooms, along with LAN, telephone, and cable connections in all the residence rooms. Entering students are expected to bring a notebook computer, as these are used in nearly every class session. The college's programs extensively integrate assistive technologies, such as Dragon Naturally Speaking and Kurzweil text-to-speech software. What makes Landmark unique, though, is its faculty and staff. The college's 100+ full time faculty members are all highly experienced in serving students with learning disabilities and attention deficit disorders. Over 100 staff members provide an array of support services that are unusually comprehensive for a student population of less than 450 students.

ADMISSIONS

Applicants to Landmark College must have a diagnosis of dyslexia, attention deficit disorder, or other specific learning disability. The college offers rolling admissions, and enrolls academic semester students for fall and spring semesters. Enrolled students can earn up to 12 credits during the summer. A four-week skills development program is offered in the summer. A high school program, for students aged 16–18, is also offered in the summer. Diagnostic testing within the last three years is required, along with a diagnosis of a learning disability or AD/HD. One of the Wechsler Scales (WAIS-III or WISC-III) administered within three years of application is required. Scores, sub-test scores and their analysis are required to be submitted as well. Alternately, the Woodcock-Johnson Cognitive Assessment may be substituted if administered within three years of application.

ADMISSIONS INFO FOR STUDENTS WITH LEARNING DIFFERENCES

SAT/ACT required: No
Interview required: Yes
Essay required: Required
Additional application required: No
Documentation required for:
 LD: Same documentation for all students.
 ADHD: Same documentation for all students.
 ASD: Same documentation for all students.
Documentation submitted to: Office of Admissions
Special Ed. HS course work accepted: No
Separate application required for program services: No
Contact Information
Name of program or department: Landmark College
Telephone: 802-387-6718
Fax: 802-387-6868
Email: admissions@landmark.edu

Landmark College

Additional Information

The Landmark College Transition Program is a 2-week program for high school graduates and college students. A typical summer term includes pre-credit course work to develop skills and strategies to be successful in college credit work. Summer students work with professional faculty to: develop a writing process based on multi-modal writing techniques; to learn, integrate, and practice research-proven study skills; and to complete a communication or math course designed to integrate strategies and practice. Additionally there are small Group Individualized Instruction seminars, specific to strategy integration; Assistive technology training; and athletics and other activities. The Landmark Study Abroad Program has developed programs with students' diverse learning styles in mind. Faculty design and teach experiential courses in their specific disciplines that fulfill Landmark core requirements while helping students gain confidence and independence in new academic structures. Faculty accompany students abroad, providing them with the Landmark College academic experience in an international setting. Landmark also offers a 3-week summer session for high school students between the ages of 16 and 18 introducing students to the skills and strategies in reading and study skills -understanding and remembering readings; writing process—from pre- writing to final drafting—the Landmark way; and communication - self-advocacy, collaboration, and effective communication.

GENERAL ADMISSIONS

Very important factors considered include: recommendation(s), interview. *Important factors considered include:* character/personal qualities, level of applicant's interest. *Other factors considered include:* rigor of secondary school record, class rank, academic GPA, application essay, standardized test scores, extracurricular activities, talent/ability. *Freshman Admission Requirements:* High school diploma is required and GED is accepted. *Academic units recommended:* 4 English, 3 math, 3 science, 1 foreign language, 3 social studies, 3 history, 1 academic elective, 1 visual/performing arts.

ACCOMMODATIONS OR SERVICES

Accommodations are decided upon an individual basis after a thorough review of appropriate, current documentation. The accommodations requests must be supported through the documentation provided and must be logically linked to the current impact of the condition on academic functioning.

FINANCIAL AID

Students should submit: FAFSA. Applicants will be notified of awards on a rolling basis beginning 3/15. The Princeton Review suggests that all financial aid forms be submitted as soon as possible after October 1. *Need-based scholarships/grants offered:* College/university scholarship or grant aid from institutional funds; Federal Pell; Private scholarships; SEOG; State scholarships/grants. *Loan aid offered:* Direct PLUS loans; Direct Subsidized Stafford Loans; Direct Unsubsidized Stafford Loans. Federal Work-Study Program available. Institutional employment available.

CAMPUS LIFE

Activities: Choral groups; Dance; Drama/theater; Jazz band; Literary magazine; Music ensembles; Radio station; Student government; Student newspaper.

ACCOMMODATIONS

Allowed in exams:	
Calculators	Yes
Dictionary	Yes
Computer	Yes
Spell-checker	Yes
Extended test time	Yes
Scribe	No
Proctors	No
Oral exams	Yes
Note-takers	No
Support services for students with	
LD	Yes
ADHD	Yes
ASD	Yes
Distraction-reduced environment	Yes
Recording of lecture allowed	Yes
Reading technology:	Yes
Audio books	No
Other assistive technology	Yes
Priority registration	Not Applicable
Added costs for services:	
For LD:	No
For ADHD:	No
For ASD:	No
LD specialists	Yes
ADHD & ASD coaching	Yes
ASD specialists	Yes
Professional tutors	Yes
Peer tutors	Not Applicable
Max. hours/week for services	Varies
How professors are notified of student approved accomodations	Director

COLLEGE GRADUATION REQUIREMENTS

Course waivers allowed	No
Course substitutions allowed	No

Norwich University

158 HARMON DRIVE, NORTHFIELD, VT 05663 • ADMISSIONS: 802-485-2001 • FAX: 802-485-2032

CAMPUS

Type of school	Private (nonprofit)
Environment	Rural
Support	CS

STUDENTS

Undergrad enrollment	2,201
% male/female	74/26
% from out of state	84
% frosh live on campus	94

FINANCIAL FACTS

Annual tuition	$30,048
Room and board	$10,976
Required fees	$1,734

GENERAL ADMISSIONS INFO

Application fee	$35
Priority deadline	2/1

Nonfall registration accepted. Admission may be deferred for a maximum of 1 term.

Range SAT EBRW	480–580
Range SAT Math	500–640
Range ACT Composite	21–26

ACADEMICS

Student/faculty ratio	14:1
% students returning for sophomore year	85
% students graduating within 4 years	51
% students graduating within 6 years	59

Most classes have 10–19 students.

PROGRAMS/SERVICES FOR STUDENTS WITH LEARNING DIFFERENCES

Services for students with disabilities, available if you have a suspected or documented disability, are provided by the Coordinator of Specialized Student Services. The Coordinator of Specialized Student Services: helps you with the process of properly documenting your disability; orients you to your Educational Profile and Academic Accommodations; provides training and information about assistive technology; facilitates communication with faculty, staff, and family members, with your permission; provides academic coaching and counseling; and meets with you on an as-needed or regular basis.

ADMISSIONS

Students with learning disabilities submit a general application. Admission criteria include high school GPA of a C or better; an SAT score of 850 or equivalent ACT; participation in activities; and strong college recommendations from teachers, counselors, or coaches. There are no course waivers for admission. The university is flexible on ACT/SAT test scores. If grades and other indicators are problematic is recommended that students provide detailed information to give a better understanding the disability. A complete psychodiagnostic evaluation is required. A small number of students who do not meet the general admission requirements may be admitted if they show promise. An interview is highly recommended. There are limited provisional admission slots.

Additional Information

A telephone conversation or personal meeting with the LSC support personnel is encouraged prior to the start of college, so that work can begin immediately on preparing an individualized program. Students are responsible for meeting with each professor to discuss accommodations. Services begin with Freshman Placement Testing designed to assess each individual's level of readiness for college-level math. Other services include course advising with an assigned academic advisor and advocacy for academic petitions. Services and accommodations are available for undergraduate and graduate students.

ADMISSIONS INFO FOR STUDENTS WITH LEARNING DIFFERENCES

SAT/ACT required: Yes
Interview required: No
Essay required: No
Additional application required: No
Documentation required for:
LD: Psycho ed evaluation to include: relevant historical info, instructional interventions, related services, age diagnosed, objective data (aptitude, achievement, info processing), test scores (standard, percentile and grade equivalents) and describe functional limitations.
ADHD: Diagnosis based on DSM-V; history of behaviors impairing functioning in academic setting; diagnostic interview; history of symptoms; evidence of ongoing behaviors.
ASD: Psycho ed evaluation
Documentation submitted to: Academic Achievement Center
Special Ed. HS course work accepted: No
Separate application required for program services: No
Contact Information
Name of program or department: Academic Achievement Center (AAC)
Telephone: 802-485-2130
Fax: 802-485-2684

Norwich University

GENERAL ADMISSIONS

Very important factors considered include: rigor of secondary school record, academic GPA, standardized test scores. *Other factors considered include:* class rank, application essay, recommendation(s), interview, extracurricular activities, talent/ability, character/personal qualities, alumni/ae relation, volunteer work, work experience. *Freshman Admission Requirements:* High school diploma is required and GED is accepted. *Academic units recommended:* 4 English, 4 math, 4 science, 3 science labs, 2 foreign language, 3 social studies, 3 history.

ACCOMMODATIONS OR SERVICES

Accommodations are decided upon an individual basis after a thorough review of appropriate, current documentation. The accommodations requests must be supported through the documentation provided and must be logically linked to the current impact of the condition on academic functioning.

FINANCIAL AID

Students should submit: FAFSA. Applicants will be notified of awards on a rolling basis beginning 2/15. The Princeton Review suggests that all financial aid forms be submitted as soon as possible after October 1. *Need-based scholarships/grants offered:* College/university scholarship or grant aid from institutional funds; Federal Pell; Private scholarships; SEOG; State scholarships/grants. *Loan aid offered:* Direct PLUS loans; Direct Subsidized Stafford Loans; Direct Unsubsidized Stafford Loans. Federal Work-Study Program available. Institutional employment available.

CAMPUS LIFE

Activities: Campus Ministries; Dance; Drama/theater; International Student Organization; Jazz band; Marching band; Model UN; Radio station; Student government; Student newspaper; Yearbook. **Organizations:** 40 registered organizations, 8 honor societies, 4 religious organizations. **Athletics (Intercollegiate):** *Men:* baseball, basketball, cross-country, diving, football, ice hockey, lacrosse, riflery, rugby, soccer, swimming, track/field (outdoor), volleyball, wrestling. *Women:* basketball, cross-country, diving, riflery, rugby, soccer, softball, swimming, track/field (outdoor), volleyball.

ACCOMMODATIONS

Allowed in exams:	
Calculators	Yes
Dictionary	Yes
Computer	Yes
Spell-checker	Yes
Extended test time	Yes
Scribe	Yes
Proctors	Yes
Oral exams	Yes
Note-takers	No
Support services for students with	
LD	Yes
ADHD	Yes
ASD	Yes
Distraction-reduced environment	Yes
Recording of lecture allowed	Yes
Reading technology:	Yes
Audio books	Yes
Other assistive technology	Yes
Priority registration	Limited
Added costs for services:	
For LD:	No
For ADHD:	No
For ASD:	No
LD specialists	Yes
ADHD & ASD coaching	No
ASD specialists	No
Professional tutors	Yes
Peer tutors	30
Max. hours/week for services	Varies
How professors are notified of student approved accommodations	Student and director

COLLEGE GRADUATION REQUIREMENTS

Course waivers allowed	No
Course substitutions allowed	Yes

In what courses: Foreign language, only with proof of inability to successfully function and after having gone through a lengthy petition process.

Saint Michael's College

ONE WINOOSKI PARK, COLCHESTER, VT 05439 • ADMISSIONS: 802-654-3000 • FAX: 802-654-2906

CAMPUS

Type of school	Private (nonprofit)
Environment	City
Support	CS

STUDENTS

Undergrad enrollment	1,759
% male/female	45/55
% from out of state	85
% frosh live on campus	98

FINANCIAL FACTS

Annual tuition	$45,050
Room and board	$12,220
Required fees	$325

GENERAL ADMISSIONS INFO

Application fee	$50.
Priority deadline	11/1
Regular application deadline	2/1

Nonfall registration accepted. Admission may be deferred.

Range SAT EBRW	580–660
Range SAT Math	570–650
Range ACT Composite	25–29

ACADEMICS

Student/faculty ratio	13:1.
% students returning for sophomore year	83
% students graduating within 4 years	71
% students graduating within 6 years	78

Most classes have 20-29 students.
Most lab/discussion sessions have 10-19 students.

PROGRAMS/SERVICES FOR STUDENTS WITH LEARNING DIFFERENCES

Saint Michael's College, through the Office of Accessibility Services, has an academic support consultant who helps with study skills, picking out classes, and time management skill development. In addition they offer guidance with note and test taking skills and facilitate peer study groups. Students are encouraged to speak with their professors if they are experiencing any difficulty with the particular course, The Academic Support Center also offers free tutoring for many different subjects.

ADMISSIONS

Support is provided through the Office of Accessibility Services located in the Academic Enrichment Commons. The Director promotes self-awareness for students with disabilities by educating them about their rights so that they can independently advocate and make choices to meet or exceed the academic standards expected of them. All eligible students are invited and encouraged to seek access to the services provided.

Additional Information

This is a fee-based service that is a holistic, highly focused approach to helping students define and achieve their academic goals. This one-to-one coaching model helps students identify their learning objectives, find their own solutions, and follow their plans through to completion. Students own their own learning when participating in Collaborative Educational Consulting. Students wanting individual tutors must first meet with their professors outside of class and attend at least one group or drop-in session. Students are also encouraged to form their own study groups. Requests for tutors are considered after meeting with the Assistant Director of Academic Support. An academic support consultant will work with students on personal choices, study skills, and time management in relation to their academic performance. The writing coaches are trained peers.

ADMISSIONS INFO FOR STUDENTS WITH LEARNING DIFFERENCES

SAT/ACT required: No
Interview required: No
Essay required: No
Additional application required: No
Documentation required for:
LD: Psycho ed evaluation to include: relevant historical info, instructional interventions, related services, age diagnosed, objective data (aptitude, achievement, info processing), test scores (standard, percentile and grade equivalents) and describe functional limitations.
ADHD: Diagnosis based on DSM-V; history of behaviors impairing functioning in academic setting; diagnostic interview; history of symptoms; evidence of ongoing behaviors.
ASD: Psycho ed evaluation
Documentation submitted to: Support Program/Services
Separate application required for program services: No
Contact Information
Name of program or department: Office of Accessibility Services
Telephone: 802-654-2467
Fax: 802-654-2974

Saint Michael's College

General Admissions

Very important factors considered include: rigor of secondary school record, class rank, academic GPA. *Important factors considered include:* application essay, standardized test scores, recommendation(s), talent/ability, character/personal qualities. *Other factors considered include:* interview, extracurricular activities, first generation, alumni/ae relation, geographical residence, state residency, racial/ethnic status, volunteer work, work experience, level of applicant's interest. *Freshman Admission Requirements:* High school diploma is required and GED is accepted *Academic units required:* 4 English, 4 math, 3 science, 2 science labs, 2 foreign language, 3 social studies, 3 history, *Academic units recommended:* 4 English, 4 math, 4 science, 3 science labs, 4 foreign language, 4 social studies, 4 history,

Accommodation or Services

Accommodations are decided upon an individual basis after a thorough review of appropriate, current documentation. The accommodations requests must be supported through the documentation provided and must be logically linked to the current impact of the condition on academic functioning.

Financial Aid

Students should submit: FAFSA. Applicants will be notified of awards on a rolling basis beginning 1/30.. The Princeton Review suggests that all financial aid forms be submitted as soon as possible after October 1. *Need-based scholarships/grants offered:* College/university scholarship or grant aid from institutional funds; Federal Pell; Private scholarships; SEOG; State scholarships/grants *Loan aid offered:* Direct PLUS loans; Direct Subsidized Stafford Loans; Direct Unsubsidized Stafford Loans Federal Work-Study Program available. Institutional employment available.

Campus Life

Activities: Campus Ministries; Choral groups; Concert band ; Dance ; Drama/theater; International Student Organization; Jazz band; Literary magazine; Music ensembles; Musical theater; Radio station ; Student government; Student newspaper; Yearbook Organizations: 50 registered organizations, 11 honor societies, 1 religious organizations. **Athletics (Intercollegiate):** *Men:* baseball, basketball, cross-country, diving, golf, ice hockey, lacrosse, skiing (downhill/alpine), skiingnordiccross-country, soccer, swimming, tennis *Women:* basketball, cross-country, diving, field hockey, ice hockey, lacrosse, skiing (downhill/alpine), skiingnordiccross-country, soccer, softball, swimming, tennis, volleyball. **On-Campus Highlights:** Dion Family Student Center, McCarthy Arts Center, Chapel of Saint Michael the Archangel, Vincent C. Ross Sports Center, Tarrant Student Recreational Center.

ACCOMMODATIONS

Allowed in exams:	
Calculators	Yes
Dictionary	Yes
Computer	Yes
Spell-checker	Yes
Extended test time	Yes
Scribe	Yes
Proctors	Yes
Oral exams	No
Note-takers	Yes
Support services for students with	
LD	Yes
ADHD	Yes
ASD	Yes
Distraction-reduced environment	Yes
Recording of lecture allowed	Yes
Reading technology:	Yes
Audio books	Yes
Other assistive technology	The College is open to purchasing what assistive technology works best for students including software like "Writing Works" and "Dragon Naturally Speaking"
Priority registration	No
Added costs of services:	
For LD:	No
For ADHD:	No
For ASD:	No
LD specialists	No
ADHD & ASD coaching	Yes
ASD specialists	No
Professional tutors	Yes
Peer tutors	Yes
Max. hours/week for services	Varies
How professors are notified of student approved accommodations	Director

COLLEGE GRADUATION REQUIREMENTS

Course waivers allowed	No
Course substitutions allowed	Yes
In what courses	
There are course substitutions for the Modern Languages requirement and a modified math course.	

University of Vermont

South Prospect Street, Burlington, VT 05401-3596 • Admissions: 802-656-3370 • Fax: 802-656-8611

CAMPUS

Type of school	Public
Environment	Town
Support	CS

STUDENTS

Undergrad enrollment	10,513
% male/female	42/58
% from out of state	71
% frosh live on campus	98

FINANCIAL FACTS

Annual in-state tuition	$15,936
Annual out-of-state tuition	$40,176
Room and board	$12,022
Required fees	$2,340

GENERAL ADMISSIONS INFO

Application fee	$55
Regular application deadline	1/15

Nonfall registration accepted. Admission may be deferred for a maximum of 1 year.

Range SAT EBRW	600–680
Range SAT Math	580–670
Range ACT Composite	25–30

ACADEMICS

Student/faculty ratio	17:1
% students returning for sophomore year	86
% students graduating within 4 years	62
% students graduating within 6 years	75

Most classes have 10–19 students.
Most lab/discussion sessions have 10–19 students.

PROGRAMS/SERVICES FOR STUDENTS WITH LEARNING DIFFERENCES

ACCESS provides Accommodations, Consultation, Collaboration, and Educational Support Services to students with documented disabilities. Among our extensive programs and services, ACCESS offers: exam accommodations, note taking, ebooks, meetings with Disability Specialists to receive advisement and advocacy around disability-related matters, as well as use of adaptive technology, unique opportunities for engagement and education related to identity development.

ADMISSIONS

Students submit a common application to admissions. Documentation of a student's disability is sent directly to ACCESS. Students are encouraged to voluntarily provide documentation of their disability. ACCESS reviews documentation and may consult with Admissions if/when necessary as to how a student's disability has affected their academic record. Upon request, if time and resources allow, students may request a review of their documentation to assess for eligibility and/ or entrance requirements if they feel their disability has impacted them in such a way that they are missing a requirement such as Foreign Language. Students with LD/ADHD should submit a current educational evaluation that includes a comprehensive measure of both cognitive and achievement functioning. Course requirements include 4 years English, 3 years Social Science, 3 years Math, 2 years Physical Sciences and 2 years Foreign Language. Self-disclosing in the application is a matter of personal choice. At UVM, disclosing a disability will absolutely not have a negative impact on a student's admissibility.

ADMISSIONS INFO FOR STUDENTS WITH LEARNING DIFFERENCES

SAT/ACT required: Yes
Interview required: No
Essay required: No
Additional application required: No
Documentation required for:
 LD: Recent Individualized Education Plan (IEP) A summary of performance (SOP) Section 504 Accommodation Plan (504) A letter from a qualified professional providing prior diagnosis.
 ADHD: A letter from a qualified professional providing prior diagnosis IEP SOP 504.
 ASD: Psycho ed evalaution
Documentation submitted to: ACCESS
Special Ed. HS course work accepted: No
Separate application required for program services: No
# of students last year receiving services/accommodations for:
 LD: 425
 ADHD: 350
Contact Information
Name of program or department: Student Accessibility Services
Telephone: 802-656-7753
Fax: 802-656-0739
Email: access@uvm.edu

Additional Information

UVM provides a multidisciplinary program for students with LD /ADHD emphasizing development of advocacy and reasonable and appropriate use of academic accommodations including: note-taking, reduced course load, extended test time, alternative test and media formats, technology use, audio format, readers/scribes, computer/spellchecker, tutoring, reading and writing skill development, academic advising and course selection, priority registration, learning strategies and study skills training, LD/ADHD support via peer and community leadership building opportunities, faculty consultation, trainings, diagnostic screenings/info sessions and evaluation referral.

GENERAL ADMISSIONS

Very important factors considered include: rigor of secondary school record. *Important factors considered include:* class rank, academic GPA, application essay, standardized test scores, character/personal qualities, state residency. *Other factors considered include:* recommendation(s), extracurricular activities, talent/ability, first generation, alumni/ae relation, geographical residence, racial/ethnic status, volunteer work, work experience, level of applicant's interest. *Freshman Admission Requirements:* High school diploma is required and GED is accepted. *Academic units required:* 4 English, 3 math, 2 science, 1 science lab, 2 foreign language, 3 social studies.

ACCOMMODATIONS OR SERVICES

Accommodations are decided upon an individual basis after a thorough review of appropriate, current documentation. The accommodations requests must be supported through the documentation provided and must be logically linked to the current impact of the condition on academic functioning.

FINANCIAL AID

Students should submit: FAFSA. Applicants will be notified of awards on a rolling basis beginning 3/15. The Princeton Review suggests that all financial aid forms be submitted as soon as possible after October 1. *Need-based scholarships/grants offered:* College/university scholarship or grant aid from institutional funds; Federal Pell; Private scholarships; SEOG; State scholarships/grants. *Loan aid offered:* Direct PLUS loans; Direct Subsidized Stafford Loans; Direct Unsubsidized Stafford Loans. Federal Work-Study Program available. Institutional employment available.

CAMPUS LIFE

Activities: Campus Ministries; Choral groups; Concert band; Dance; Drama/theater; International Student Organization; Jazz band; Literary magazine; Music ensembles; Musical theater; Pep band; Radio station; Student government; Student newspaper; Student-run film society; Symphony orchestra; Television station. **Organizations:** 140 registered organizations, 30 honor societies, 10 religious organizations. 9 fraternities, 6 sororities. **Athletics (Intercollegiate):** *Men:* basketball, cross-country, ice hockey, lacrosse, skiing (downhill/alpine), skiing (nordic/cross-country), soccer, track/field (outdoor), track/field (indoor). *Women:* basketball, cross-country, diving, field hockey, ice hockey, lacrosse, skiing (downhill/alpine), skiing (nordic/cross-country), soccer, swimming, track/field (outdoor), track/field (indoor). **On-Campus Highlights:** Davis Student Center, Bailey-Howe Library, Henderson's Cafe, Athletic Complex/Fitness Center, Campus Green.

ACCOMMODATIONS

Allowed in exams:	
Calculators	Yes
Dictionary	Yes
Computer	Yes
Spell-checker	Yes
Extended test time	Yes
Scribe	Yes
Proctors	Yes
Oral exams	Yes
Note-takers	Yes
Support services for students with	
LD	Yes
ADHD	Yes
ASD	Yes
Distraction-reduced environment	Yes
Recording of lecture allowed	Yes
Reading technology:	Yes
Audio books	Yes
Other assistive technology Smart Pens Live scribe Recordings Transcripts Zoomtext Dragon Read Write Gold-text to speech software Mobile Apps	
Priority registration	Yes
Added costs for services:	
For LD:	No
For ADHD:	No
For ASD:	No
LD specialists	Yes
ADHD & ASD coaching	No
ASD specialists	No
Professional tutors	Yes
Peer tutors	Yes
Max. hours/week for services	1
How professors are notified of student approved accommodations	Director

COLLEGE GRADUATION REQUIREMENTS

Course waivers allowed	No
Course substitutions allowed	No

College of William and Mary

P.O. Box 8795, Williamsburg, VA 23187-8795 • Admissions: 757-221-4223 • Fax: 757-221-1242

CAMPUS

Type of school	Public
Environment	Town
Support	CS

STUDENTS

Undergrad enrollment	6,243
% male/female	42/58
% from out of state	30
% frosh live on campus	100

FINANCIAL FACTS

Annual in-state tuition	$17,434
Annual out-of-state tuition	$38,735
Room and board	$12,236
Required fees	$5,966

GENERAL ADMISSIONS INFO

Application fee	$75
Regular application deadline	1/1

Nonfall registration accepted. Admission may be deferred for a maximum of 1 year.

Range SAT EBRW	660–740
Range SAT Math	640–740
Range ACT Composite	29–33

ACADEMICS

Student/faculty ratio

% students returning for sophomore year	95
% students graduating within 4 years	85
% students graduating within 6 years	91

Most classes have 20–29 students.
Most lab/discussion sessions have 10–19 students.

PROGRAMS/SERVICES FOR STUDENTS WITH LEARNING DIFFERENCES

Disability Services at the College of William and Mary are available to all students with disabilities. Reasonable accommodations upon request are evaluated on an individual and flexible basis. Program goals include fostering independence, encouraging self-determination, emphasizing accommodations over limitations, and creating an accessible environment to ensure that individuals are viewed on the basis of ability and not disability. Individual accommodations needs are considered on a case-by-case basis in consultation with the student. The staff works with students and faculty to implement reasonable supports. Students anticipating the need for academic support must provide pertinent documentation in a timely manner in order to facilitate the provision of the service. Additional documentation may be requested and accommodation requests can be denied if they do not seem to be substantially supported. Documentation for LD/ADHD must include a comprehensive report of psychoeducational or neuropsychological assessment. The documentation must demonstrate the impact of the disability on major life activities and support all the recommended accommodations.

ADMISSIONS

Students go through a regular admissions process. Students must take either the SAT or ACT and three SAT Subject Tests are recommended. Results of non-standardized test administrations and documentation of disability may be submitted in support of any application, but are not essential for full consideration. Once admitted, students are fully mainstreamed and are expected to maintain the same academic standards as all other students.

Additional Information

The staff of Student Accessibility Services (SAS) seeks to create a barrier-free environment for students with disabilities by considering reasonable

ADMISSIONS INFO FOR STUDENTS WITH LEARNING DIFFERENCES

SAT/ACT required: Yes
Interview required: No
Essay required: Not Applicable
Additional application required: Not Applicable
Documentation required for:
LD:Psycho ed evaluation to include: relevant historical info, instructional interventions, related services, age diagnosed, objective data (aptitude, achievement, info processing), test scores (standard, percentile and grade equivalents) and describe functional limitations.
 ADHD:Diagnosis based on DSM-V; history of behaviors impairing functioning in academic setting; diagnostic interview; history of symptoms; evidence of ongoing behaviors.
 ASD: Psycho ed evaluation
Documentation submitted to: Support Program/Services
Special Ed. HS course work accepted: No
Separate application required for program services: No
# of students last year receiving services/accommodations for:
 LD: 235
Contact Information
Name of program or department: Student Accessibility Services
Telephone: 757-221-2509
Fax: 757-221-2538
Email: sas@wm.edu

College of William and Mary

accommodations upon request. The staff works closely with all college departments to identify appropriate options for accommodating students with disabilities. Additionally, they offer services when students need special housing accommodations.

GENERAL ADMISSIONS

Very important factors considered include: rigor of secondary school record, class rank, academic GPA, application essay, standardized test scores, recommendation(s), extracurricular activities, talent/ability, character/personal qualities, state residency, volunteer work, work experience. *Other factors considered include:* interview, first generation, alumni/ae relation, geographical residence, racial/ethnic status, level of applicant's interest. *Freshman Admission Requirements:* High school diploma or equivalent is not required *Academic units recommended:* 4 English, 4 math, 4 science, 3 science labs, 4 foreign language, 4 social studies.

ACCOMMODATIONS OR SERVICES

Accommodations are decided upon an individual basis after a thorough review of appropriate, current documentation. The accommodations requests must be supported through the documentation provided and must be logically linked to the current impact of the condition on academic functioning.

FINANCIAL AID

Students should submit: CSS/Financial Aid PROFILE; FAFSA. Applicants will be notified of awards on or about 3/15. The Princeton Review suggests that all financial aid forms be submitted as soon as possible after October 1. *Need-based scholarships/grants offered:* College/university scholarship or grant aid from institutional funds; Federal Pell; Private scholarships; SEOG; State scholarships/grants. *Loan aid offered:* Direct PLUS loans; Direct Subsidized Stafford Loans; Direct Unsubsidized Stafford Loans. Federal Work-Study Program available. Institutional employment available.

CAMPUS LIFE

Activities: Campus Ministries; Choral groups; Concert band; Dance; Drama/theater; International Student Organization; Jazz band; Literary magazine; Model UN; Music ensembles; Musical theater; Opera; Pep band; Radio station; Student government; Student newspaper; Student-run film society; Symphony orchestra; Television station; Yearbook. **Organizations:** 375 registered organizations, 32 honor societies, 32 religious organizations. 18 fraternities, 11 sororities. **Athletics (Intercollegiate):** *Men:* baseball, basketball, cheerleading, cross-country, diving, football, golf, gymnastics, soccer, swimming, tennis, track/field (outdoor), track/field (indoor). *Women:* basketball, cheerleading, cross-country, diving, field hockey, golf, gymnastics, lacrosse, soccer, swimming, tennis, track/field (outdoor), track/field (indoor), volleyball. **On-Campus Highlights:** Wren Building (oldest academic building), Muscarelle Museum of Art, Lake Matoaka/College Woods, Sadler Center, Sunken Garden.

ACCOMMODATIONS

Allowed in exams:

Calculators	Yes
Dictionary	Yes
Computer	Yes
Spell-checker	Yes
Extended test time	Yes
Scribe	Yes
Proctors	Yes
Oral exams	Yes
Note-takers	Yes

Support services for students with

LD	Yes
ADHD	Yes
ASD	Yes
Distraction-reduced environment	Yes
Recording of lecture allowed	Yes
Reading technology:	Yes
Audio books	Yes
Other assistive technology	Yes
Priority registration	Yes

Added costs for services:

For LD:	No
For ADHD:	No
For ASD:	No
LD specialists	No
ADHD & ASD coaching	Yes
ASD specialists	Yes
Professional tutors	Yes
Peer tutors	Yes
Max. hours/week for services	Varies

How professors are notified of student approved accommodations
Director and student

COLLEGE GRADUATION REQUIREMENTS

Course waivers allowed	No
Course substitutions allowed	Yes

In what courses
Documentation must exist that evidences impairment in specific area for consideration by the college's Committee on Degrees (which grants exception to school policy)

George Mason University

4400 University Drive, Fairfax, VA 22030-4444 • Admissions: 703-993-2400 • Fax: 703-993-4622

CAMPUS

Type of school	Public
Environment	City
Support	CS

STUDENTS

Undergrad enrollment	24,372
% male/female	50/50
% from out of state	10
% frosh live on campus	67

FINANCIAL FACTS

Annual in-state tuition	$9,060
Annual out-of-state tuition	$32,250
Room and board	$11,460
Required fees	$3,402

GENERAL ADMISSIONS INFO

Application fee	$70.
Priority deadline	11/1
Regular application deadline	1/15

Nonfall registration accepted. Admission may be deferred for a maximum of 1 year.

Range SAT EBRW	560–650
Range SAT Math	540–640
Range ACT Composite	24–30

ACADEMICS

Student/faculty ratio	17:1.
% students returning for sophomore year	88
% students graduating within 4 years	49
% students graduating within 6 years	71

Most classes have 20-29 students. Most lab/discussion sessions have 10-19 students.

PROGRAMS/SERVICES FOR STUDENTS WITH LEARNING DIFFERENCES

Disability Services implements and coordinates accommodations. Through their Learning Services students can explore a range of academic concerns. There is individualized study skills counseling and tutoring.

ADMISSIONS

Admission is competitive and is done using a holistic approach that includes the high school transcript, standardized test scores, essays, and letters of recommendation, and other supplemental material. The personal statement explaining why the student wants to go to college is optional but strongly recommended. Some majors are very selective. The Art and Visual Technology, Computer Game Design, Dance, Film and Video Studies, Music and Theater majors in the College of Visual and Performing Arts require portfolio or audition. Nursing is also competitive. Engineering applicants are required to attain a 550 on the Math section of the SAT, or a 24 on the Math section of the ACT, and have taken or be enrolled in 4 years of high school mathematics, including a course beyond Algebra II by their senior year. ACT or SAT scores may be self-reported. Mid 50% SAT is 1130-1310 or ACT 24-29.

Additional Information

Mason's Autism Support Initiative is part of George Mason's Disability Service which is part of University Life. This is a comprehensive program that provides intensive support services to students on the autism spectrum beyond the typical higher education accommodations. Enrolled students are paired with a peer mentor to help them socially acclimate to campus, and a learning strategist who supports the student's academic, time management and organizational skills.

ADMISSIONS INFO FOR STUDENTS WITH LEARNING DIFFERENCES

SAT/ACT required: Yes
Interview required: No
Essay required: No
Additional application required: Yes
Documentation required for:
LD: Psycho ed evaluation
ADHD: Psycho ed evaluation
ASD: Psycho ed evaluation.
Documentation submitted to: Support Program/Services
Special Ed. HS course work accepted: Not Applicable
Separate application required for program services: Yes
Contact Information
Name of program or department: Disability Services
Telephone: 703-993-2474
Fax: 703-993-4306

George Mason University

ACCOMMODATION OR SERVICES

Accommodations are decided upon an individual basis after a thorough review of appropriate, current documentation. The accommodations requests must be supported through the documentation provided and must be logically linked to the current impact of the condition on academic functioning.

FINANCIAL AID

Students should submit: FAFSA. Applicants will be notified of awards on a rolling basis beginning 4/1.. The Princeton Review suggests that all financial aid forms be submitted as soon as possible after October 1. *Need-based scholarships/grants offered:* College/university scholarship or grant aid from institutional funds; Federal Pell; Private scholarships; SEOG; State scholarships/grants *Loan aid offered:* Direct PLUS loans; Direct Subsidized Stafford Loans; Direct Unsubsidized Stafford Loans Federal Work-Study Program available. Institutional employment available.

CAMPUS LIFE

Activities: Campus Ministries; Choral groups; Concert band ; Dance ; Drama/theater; International Student Organization; Jazz band; Literary magazine; Model UN; Music ensembles; Musical theater; Opera; Pep band; Radio station ; Student government; Student newspaper; Student-run film society; Symphony orchestra ; Television station; Yearbook Organizations: 250 registered organizations, 7 honor societies, 29 religious organizations. 22 fraternities, 13 sororities, **Athletics (Intercollegiate):** *Men:* baseball, basketball, cheerleading, cross-country, diving, golf, soccer, swimming, tennis, track/field (outdoor), track/field (indoor), volleyball, wrestling *Women:* basketball, cheerleading, crew/rowing, cross-country, diving, lacrosse, soccer, softball, swimming, tennis, track/field (outdoor), track/field (indoor), volleyball. **On-Campus Highlights:** Johnson Center, Aquatic and Fitness Center, Center for the Arts, Eagle Bank Arena, Hylton Performing Arts Center.

ACCOMMODATIONS

Allowed in exams:

Calculators	Yes
Dictionary	Yes
Computer	Yes
Spell-checker	Yes
Extended test time	Yes
Scribe	Yes
Proctors	Yes
Oral exams	Yes
Note-takers	Yes

Support services for students with

LD	Yes
ADHD	Yes
ASD	Yes
Distraction-reduced environment	Yes
Recording of lecture allowed	Yes
Reading technology:	Yes
Audio books	Yes
Other assistive technology	Use of

SmartPens, Closed-Circuit Television, Text-to-speech/Speech-to-text software, and Scantron scribes are allowed when appropriate

Priority registration	Yes

Added costs of services:

For LD:	No
For ADHD:	No
For ASD:	Yes
LD specialists	Yes
ADHD & ASD coaching	Yes
ASD specialists	Yes
Professional tutors	Yes
Peer tutors	Not Applicable

Max. hours/week for services

How professors are notified of student
approved accommodations   Student

COLLEGE GRADUATION REQUIREMENTS

Course waivers allowed	Yes

In what courses
Mainly Math, however Disability Services will evaluate all requests.

Course substitutions allowed	Yes

In what courses
Mainly foreign language, however Disability Services will evaluate all requests.

Hampton University

Hampton University, Hampton, VA 23668 • Admissions: 757-727-5328 • Fax: 757-727-5095

CAMPUS
Type of school	Private (nonprofit)
Environment	City
Support	S

STUDENTS
Undergrad enrollment	3,799
% male/female	33/67
% from out of state	73
% frosh live on campus	98

FINANCIAL FACTS
Annual tuition	$23,762
Room and board	$11,778
Required fees	$2,940

GENERAL ADMISSIONS INFO
Application fee	$35
Priority deadline	3/1

Nonfall registration accepted. Admission may be deferred for a maximum of 1 year.

Range SAT EBRW	500–570
Range SAT Math	480–550
Range ACT Composite	20–24

ACADEMICS
Student/faculty ratio	13:1
% students returning for sophomore year	77
% students graduating within 4 years	37
% students graduating within 6 years	54

Most classes have 20–29 students.
Most lab/discussion sessions have 10–19 students.

PROGRAMS/SERVICES FOR STUDENTS WITH LEARNING DIFFERENCES
The University is fully committed to complying with all requirements of the Americans with Disabilities Act of 1990 (ADA) and Section 504 of the Rehabilitation Act of 1973. In class accommodations may be provided to students with a documented physical, mental, or learning disability. It is in the student's best interest to request accommodations within the first week of classes, understanding that accommodations are not retroactive. Temporary accommodations are also available to students who may experience a temporary impairment, such as a broken limb or surgery recovery. To obtain accommodations or to receive more information please contact the Office of the Director of Compliance and Disability Services at 757-727-5493 or visit the office located in The Student Success Center.

ADMISSIONS
There is no special admission process for students with learning disabilities. Students are encouraged to send documentation directly to the Office of the Director of Compliance and Disability Services and not combine it with their application for admission to the university.

ADMISSIONS INFO FOR STUDENTS WITH LEARNING DIFFERENCES
SAT/ACT required: Yes
Interview required: No
Essay required: No
Additional application required: No
Documentation required for:
 LD: Learning Disabilities- Documentation must be within the last three years Documentation submitted must include the following: 1. Diagnosis of disability 2. Diagnosis by a qualified professional 3. Diagnostic Interview 4. Intelligence test score (WAIS-R) 5. Measurement of Cognitive Processing (Woodcock-Johnson) 6. Aptitude Achievement test date 7. DSM IV diagnosis 8. Evaluation of ability to function in a competitive college setting 9. Recommendations for academic support based on diagnosis.
 ADHD: ADHD or other Attention/Concentration/Processing Disorder- Documentation must be within the last three years Documentation submitted must include the following: 1. Diagnosis by a qualified professional 2. Test date and assessment tools used to make diagnosis 3. Medication and treatment plan 4. Recommendations for academic accommodations in a competitive college environment
 ASD: Any documentation received must be typewritten on letterhead and signed by the appropriate licensed personnel.
Documentation submitted to: of Compliance and Disability Services
Special Ed. HS course work accepted: Yes
Separate application required for program services: No
# of students last year receiving services/accommodations for:
 LD: 30-40
Contact Information
Name of program or department: University Testing, Office of Compliance and Disability Services
Telephone: 757-727-5493
Fax: 757-728-6973

Hampton University

Additional Information

Accommodations in the classroom could include permission to record lectures, use of calculators, extended time for assignments and note sharing. Accommodations in an examination could include reduced-distraction environment, extended time, alternative test formats, readers/scribes, printed copies of oral instructions, and oral proctors. A student who would like to receive accommodations must contact the Office of the Director of Compliance and Disability Services and provide documentation of the disability that is not older than 3 years. The director is responsible for qualifying students with disabilities for reasonable academic accommodations within the university.

GENERAL ADMISSIONS

Very important factors considered include: rigor of secondary school record, academic GPA, application essay, character/personal qualities. *Important factors considered include:* class rank, recommendation(s). *Other factors considered include:* interview, extracurricular activities, talent/ability, volunteer work, work experience, level of applicant's interest. *Freshman Admission Requirements:* High school diploma is required and GED is accepted. *Academic units required:* 4 English, 3 math, 2 science, 2 science labs, 2 social studies, 6 academic electives. *Academic units recommended:* 2 foreign language.

ACCOMMODATIONS OR SERVICES

Accommodations are decided upon an individual basis after a thorough review of appropriate, current documentation. The accommodations requests must be supported through the documentation provided and must be logically linked to the current impact of the condition on academic functioning.

FINANCIAL AID

Students should submit: FAFSA. Applicants will be notified of awards on a rolling basis beginning 4/15. The Princeton Review suggests that all financial aid forms be submitted as soon as possible after October 1. *Need-based scholarships/grants offered:* College/university scholarship or grant aid from institutional funds; Federal Pell; Private scholarships; SEOG; State scholarships/grants; United Negro College Fund. *Loan aid offered:* Direct PLUS loans; Direct Subsidized Stafford Loans; Direct Unsubsidized Stafford Loans. Federal Work-Study Program available.

CAMPUS LIFE

Activities: Campus Ministries; Choral groups; Concert band; Dance; Drama/theater; International Student Organization; Jazz band; Literary magazine; Marching band; Music ensembles; Musical theater; Opera; Pep band; Radio station; Student government; Student newspaper; Symphony orchestra; Television station; Yearbook. **Organizations:** 85 registered organizations, 16 honor societies, 3 religious organizations. 6 fraternities, 3 sororities. **Athletics (Intercollegiate):** *Men:* basketball, cross-country, football, golf, sailing, tennis, track/field (outdoor), track/field (indoor). *Women:* basketball, bowling, cross-country, golf, sailing, softball, tennis, track/field (outdoor), track/field (indoor), volleyball. **On-Campus Highlights:** Emancipation Oak, Memorial Chapel, Huntington Memorial Museum, Booker T. Washington Monument, Student Center: bowling, fitness and movie.

ACCOMMODATIONS

Allowed in exams:

Calculators	Yes
Dictionary	Yes
Computer	Yes
Spell-checker	Yes
Extended test time	Yes
Scribe	Yes
Proctors	Yes
Oral exams	Yes
Note-takers	Yes

Support services for students with

LD	Yes
ADHD	Yes
ASD	Yes
Distraction-reduced environment	Yes
Recording of lecture allowed	Yes
Reading technology:	No
Audio books	No
Priority registration	Yes

Added costs for services:

For LD:	No
LD specialists	No
ADHD & ASD coaching	Yes
ASD specialists	No
Professional tutors	Yes
Peer tutors	Yes
Max. hours/week for services	Unlimited

How professors are notified of student approved accommodations
Director and student

COLLEGE GRADUATION REQUIREMENTS

Course waivers allowed	Yes
In what courses	Foreign language
Course substitutions allowed	Yes
In what courses	Foreign language

James Madison University

800 South Main Street, Harrisonburg, VA 22807 • Admissions: 540-568-5681 • Fax: 540-568-3332

PROGRAMS/SERVICES FOR STUDENTS WITH LEARNING DIFFERENCES

ODS collaborates with the JMU community providing programs and services that support the university in creating inclusive, equitable environments that value disability, diversity and accessibility. Vision To be the strategic campus partner for removing barriers and building capacity to ensure inclusion and equity for people with disabilities. Values Innovation Excellence Ethical Reasoning/Integrity Universal Design Academic Quality Student-Focus Confidentiality Statement All information obtained in diagnostic and medical reports will be maintained and used in accordance with applicable confidentiality requirements. All contact information and documentation received in Disability Services is kept in separate confidential files within the office. No information concerning inquiries about accommodations or documentation will be released without written consent by the student.

ADMISSIONS

During the admissions process, the admissions team at JMU is highly sensitive and knowledgeable concerning students with learning disabilities. Admission decisions are made without regard to disabilities and all prospective students are expected to present academic credentials that are competitive. After admission to JMU, the student should forward his or her documentation to ODS. Current recommendations for post-secondary accommodations are crucial for providing appropriate services in college. There are no specific courses required for admission into James Madison; however, students are expected to complete a solid college-prep curriculum. ODS is not involved in the JMU admission process unless we are contacted by the Office of Admissions.

James Madison University

Additional Information

The Office of Disability Services offers a number of services to students with disabilities including classroom accommodations such as extended time on tests, interpreters and other classroom accommodations for deaf and hard of hearing students, assistive technology labs; test proctoring; alternative texts and peer mentoring. Learning Strategies Instruction and Screening & Assessment services are available to all students, regardless of disability status. Additional on-campus services include: Learning Resource Centers (LRC). LRC consists of the following programs, tutoring and services available to all enrolled students: Communication Resource Center, Science & Math Learning Center, University Writing Center, Supplemental Instruction, Counseling and Student Development Center, and Career & Academic Planning.

GENERAL ADMISSIONS

Very important factors considered include: rigor of secondary school record, academic GPA. *Other factors considered include:* application essay, standardized test scores, recommendation(s), extracurricular activities, talent/ability, character/personal qualities, first generation, alumni/ae relation, geographical residence, state residency, racial/ethnic status, volunteer work, *Freshman Admission Requirements:* High school diploma is required and GED is accepted. *Academic units required:* 4 English, 4 math, 3 science, 3 foreign language, 2 social studies, 3 history. *Academic units recommended:* 4 English, 4 math, 3 science, 3 foreign language, 2 social studies, 3 history.

ACCOMMODATIONS OR SERVICES

Accommodations are decided upon an individual basis after a thorough review of appropriate, current documentation. The accommodations requests must be supported through the documentation provided and must be logically linked to the current impact of the condition on academic functioning.

FINANCIAL AID

Students should submit: FAFSA. Applicants will be notified of awards on a rolling basis beginning 4/1. The Princeton Review suggests that all financial aid forms be submitted as soon as possible after October 1. *Need-based scholarships/grants offered:* College/university scholarship or grant aid from institutional funds; Federal Pell; Private scholarships; SEOG; State scholarships/grants. *Loan aid offered:* Direct PLUS loans; Direct Subsidized Stafford Loans; Direct Unsubsidized Stafford Loans. Federal Work-Study Program available. Institutional employment available.

CAMPUS LIFE

Activities: Campus Ministries; Choral groups; Concert band; Dance; Drama/theater; International Student Organization; Jazz band; Literary magazine; Marching band; Music ensembles; Musical theater; Opera; Pep band; Radio station; Student government; Student newspaper; Student-run film society; Symphony orchestra; Yearbook. **Organizations:** 298 registered organizations, 28 honor societies, 28 religious organizations, 15 fraternities, 9 sororities. **Athletics (Intercollegiate):** *Men:* baseball, basketball, cheerleading, football, golf, soccer, tennis. *Women:* basketball, cheerleading, cross-country, diving, field hockey, golf, lacrosse, soccer, softball, swimming, tennis, track/field (outdoor), volleyball. **On-Campus Highlights:** Quad, Taylor Down Under, University Recreation Center, East Campus Dining Hall, Student Success Center.

ACCOMMODATIONS

Allowed in exams:	
Calculators	Yes
Dictionary	Yes
Computer	Yes
Spell-checker	Yes
Extended test time	Yes
Scribe	Yes
Proctors	Yes
Oral exams	Yes
Note-takers	Yes
Support services for students with	
LD	Yes
ADHD	Yes
ASD	Yes
Distraction-reduced environment	Yes
Recording of lecture allowed	No
Reading technology:	Yes
Audio books	Yes
Other assistive technology	All
accommodations for all students with disabilities are determined on a case by case basis relevant to the functional limitations experienced by the student and the concurrent need for mitigation by accommodation	
Priority registration	Yes
Added costs for services:	
For LD:	No
For ADHD:	No
For ASD:	No
LD specialists	No
ADHD & ASD coaching	Yes
ASD specialists	Yes
Professional tutors	No
Peer tutors	Yes
Max. hours/week for services	Varies
How professors are notified of student approved accommodations	Student

COLLEGE GRADUATION REQUIREMENTS

Course waivers allowed	Yes
In what courses	
All accommodations for all students with disabilities are determined on a case by case basis. Generally, Math requirements cannot be.	
Course substitutions allowed	Yes
In what courses	
All accommodations for all students with disabilities are determined on a case by case basis. Generally, Math requirements cannot be.	

Liberty University

1971 University Boulevard, Lynchburg, VA 24515 • Admissions: 434-582-2000 • Fax: 800-628-7977

CAMPUS

Type of school	Private (nonprofit)
Environment	Town
Support	CS

STUDENTS

Undergrad enrollment	13,748
% male/female	46/54
% from out of state	61
% frosh live on campus	93

FINANCIAL FACTS

Annual tuition	$22,000
Room and board	$9,306
Required fees	$1,020

GENERAL ADMISSIONS INFO

Application fee	$50
Priority deadline	1/31

Nonfall registration accepted. Admission may be deferred for a maximum of 1 year.

Range SAT EBRW	530–640
Range SAT Math	510–600
Range ACT Composite	21–28

ACADEMICS

Student/faculty ratio	
% students returning for sophomore year	86
% students graduating within 4 years	38
% students graduating within 6 years	60

Most classes have fewer than 10 students. Most lab/discussion sessions have 10–19 students.

PROGRAMS/SERVICES FOR STUDENTS WITH LEARNING DIFFERENCES

The Office of Disability Academic Support, a component of the Center for Academic Support and Advising Services, was created to coordinate academic support services for Liberty University students who have documented disabilities. The Bruckner Learning Center helps all students plan, develop and maintain quality, university-wide academic support services.

ADMISSIONS

All applicants must submit an official transcript from an accredited high school and/or college, an official copy of a state high school equivalency diploma, or an official copy of the GED test results. The minimum acceptable unweighted GPA is 2.0. Applicants who fail to meet the minimum required GPA will be evaluated using other indicators of collegiate ability and may be admitted on Academic Warning. All applicants must submit ACT or SAT prior to admission. The minimum acceptable scores are SAT 800 or ACT 17.

Additional Information

If a student's entrance test scores indicate a deficiency in English or math, then the student will enroll in a basic composition class or fundamentals of math class. With the student's permission, instructors are provided with written communication providing information about the student's disability and suggestions of appropriate accommodations. Students with a specific learning disability can be assigned to a faculty advisor who has had training in LD. This person acts as a liaison between instructors and students regarding classroom accommodations. The Bruckner Learning Center provides individualized peer tutoring in most subjects on a weekly or drop-in basis. The Academic Opportunity Program (AOP) assists incoming freshmen in the adjustment of the rigors of college academically in their first semester. Students will be placed in groups of about 20 and have the same basic schedule. The AOP student schedule is created for the first semester to provide maximum success, allowing connections and study groups to be formed.

ADMISSIONS INFO FOR STUDENTS WITH LEARNING DIFFERENCES

SAT/ACT required: Yes
Interview required: No
Essay required: No
Additional application required: No
Documentation required for:
 LD: Their latest IEP and/ or psychological testing profile or other written information that describes the learning disability.
 ADHD: Diagnosis from a qualified professional
 ASD: Psycho ed evaluation
Documentation submitted to: Support program
Special Ed. HS course work accepted: No
Separate application required for program services: No
# of students last year receiving services/accommodations for:
 LD: 300
Contact Information
Name of program or department: Office of Disability Academic Support
Telephone: 434-582-2159
Fax: 434-582-2297

Liberty University

General Admissions

Very important factors considered include: rigor of secondary school record, academic GPA. *Important factors considered include:* standardized test scores, character/personal qualities. *Other factors considered include:* class rank, application essay, recommendation(s), extracurricular activities, talent/ability, level of applicant's interest. *Freshman Admission Requirements:* High school diploma is required and GED is accepted. *Academic units recommended:* 4 English, 3 math, 2 science, 2 science labs, 2 foreign language, 2 social studies, 4 academic electives.

Accommodations or Services

Accommodations are decided upon an individual basis after a thorough review of appropriate, current documentation. The accommodations requests must be supported through the documentation provided and must be logically linked to the current impact of the condition on academic functioning.

Financial Aid

Students should submit: FAFSA; State aid form. Applicants will be notified of awards on a rolling basis beginning 3/15. The Princeton Review suggests that all financial aid forms be submitted as soon as possible after October 1. *Need-based scholarships/grants offered:* College/university scholarship or grant aid from institutional funds; Federal Pell; Private scholarships; SEOG; State scholarships/grants. *Loan aid offered:* Direct PLUS loans; Direct Subsidized Stafford Loans; Direct Unsubsidized Stafford Loans.

Campus Life

Activities: Campus Ministries; Choral groups; Concert band; Drama/theater; Literary magazine; Marching band; Music ensembles; Musical theater; Pep band; Radio station; Student government; Student newspaper; Symphony orchestra; Television station; Yearbook. **Organizations:** 25 registered organizations, 8 honor societies, 10 religious organizations. **Athletics (Intercollegiate):** *Men:* baseball, basketball, cheerleading, cross-country, football, golf, soccer, tennis, track/field (outdoor), track/field (indoor), wrestling. *Women:* basketball, cheerleading, cross-country, soccer, softball, tennis, track/field (outdoor), track/field (indoor), volleyball. **On-Campus Highlights:** LaHaye Student Center, Bookstore, Hangar (Food Court), ILRC Computer Lab, LaHaye Ice Center (Ice Arena).

ACCOMMODATIONS

Allowed in exams:	
Calculators	Yes
Dictionary	Yes
Computer	Yes
Spell-checker	Yes
Extended test time	Yes
Scribe	Yes
Proctors	Yes
Oral exams	Yes
Note-takers	Yes
Support services for students with	
LD	Yes
ADHD	Yes
ASD	Yes
Distraction-reduced environment	Yes
Recording of lecture allowed	Yes
Reading technology:	Yes
Audio books	No
Other assistive technology	Yes
Priority registration	Yes
Added costs for services:	
For LD:	No
For ADHD:	No
For ASD:	No
LD specialists	Yes
ADHD & ASD coaching	No
ASD specialists	No
Professional tutors	No
Peer tutors	Yes
Max. hours/week for services	Varies
How professors are notified of student approved accommodations	Director

COLLEGE GRADUATION REQUIREMENTS

Course waivers allowed	No
Course substitutions allowed	No

Old Dominion University

5115 Hampton Boulevard, Norfolk, VA 23529-0050 • Admissions: 757-683-3685 • Fax: 757-683-3255

CAMPUS
Type of school	Public
Environment	Metropolis
Support	CS

STUDENTS
Undergrad enrollment	19,540
% male/female	45/55
% from out of state	8
% frosh live on campus	75

FINANCIAL FACTS
Annual in-state tuition	$10,830
Annual out-of-state tuition	$29,370
Room and board	$12,318
Required fees	$310

GENERAL ADMISSIONS INFO
Application fee	$50
Priority deadline	12/1
Regular application deadline	2/1

Nonfall registration accepted. Admission may be deferred for a maximum of 1 year.

Range SAT EBRW	500–610
Range SAT Math	480–590
Range ACT Composite	19–26

ACADEMICS
Student/faculty ratio	18:1
% students returning for sophomore year	80
% students graduating within 4 years	27
% students graduating within 6 years	54

Most classes have 10–19 students.

PROGRAMS/SERVICES FOR STUDENTS WITH LEARNING DIFFERENCES

The Office of Educational Accessibility is a welcoming, engaging, and supportive environment which offers dynamic educational support services for students who experience disabilities so they can be successfully accommodated and included in the rich diversity of university life. The office offers a wide variety of accommodations and supports to students based on their individual needs so they will have equal access to the university environment. The office also works collaboratively with partners across campus to ensure that all aspects of campus are inclusive in nature.

ADMISSIONS

Admission to Old Dominion is based solely on the entrance requirements as described in the University Catalog. Disclosure of a disability during the admissions process is not required; neither the nature nor the severity of an individual's disability is used as criterion for admission. Recommended high school course work includes 4 years of English, 4 years of Mathematics, 3 years of Science, 3 years of Social Studies, and 3 years of Foreign Languages. For more information about the university and the admissions process, contact the Office of Admissions at (757) 683-3685.

Additional Information

Accommodations are based upon the documentation that the student presents and the discussion that the student has with the office of Educational Accessibility professionals. The accommodations may have to be adjusted during the course of the academic career of the student at the University. Students are encouraged to seek out the Office each semester for any learning needs not being accommodated. Counseling and advising; study skills instruction; reading, writing, and math instruction; and tutorial assistance are available. Program staff design support services that focus on students' learning styles and special needs. There is a special section of Spanish for students with learning disabilities to meet the foreign language requirements, as well as developmental math, reading, spelling, and writing classes.

ADMISSIONS INFO FOR STUDENTS WITH LEARNING DIFFERENCES

SAT/ACT required: Yes
Interview required: No
Essay required: Not Applicable
Additional application required: No
Documentation required for:
  LD: Please see the documentation guidelines listed on the office website: https:// www.odu.edu/educationalaccessibility.
  ADHD: Please see the documentation guidelines listed on the office website: https:// www.odu.edu/educationalaccessibility.
  ASD: Please see the documentation guidelines listed on the office website: https:// www.odu.edu/educationalaccessibility.
Documentation submitted to: Office of Educational Accessibility
Special Ed. HS course work accepted: Yes
Separate application required for program services: No
Contact Information
Name of program or department: Office of Educational Accessibility
Telephone: 757-683-4655
Fax: 757-683-5356
Email: oea@odu.edu

Old Dominion University

GENERAL ADMISSIONS

Very important factors considered include: rigor of secondary school record, academic GPA, standardized test scores. *Important factors considered include:* application essay, recommendation(s), extracurricular activities, volunteer work, work experience. *Other factors considered include:* class rank, talent/ability, character/personal qualities, first generation, alumni/ae relation, level of applicant's interest. *Freshman Admission Requirements:* High school diploma is required and GED is accepted. *Academic units required:* 4 English, 3 math, 3 science, 3 foreign language, 3 social studies. *Academic units recommended:* 4 English, 4 math, 3 science, 3 foreign language, 3 social studies.

ACCOMMODATIONS OR SERVICES

Accommodations are decided upon an individual basis after a thorough review of appropriate, current documentation. The accommodations requests must be supported through the documentation provided and must be logically linked to the current impact of the condition on academic functioning.

FINANCIAL AID

Students should submit: FAFSA. Applicants will be notified of awards on a rolling basis beginning 3/1. The Princeton Review suggests that all financial aid forms be submitted as soon as possible after October 1. *Need-based scholarships/grants offered:* College/university scholarship or grant aid from institutional funds; Federal Nursing Scholarships; Federal Pell; Private scholarships; SEOG; State scholarships/grants; United Negro College Fund. *Loan aid offered:* Direct PLUS loans; Direct Subsidized Stafford Loans; Direct Unsubsidized Stafford Loans. Federal Work-Study Program available. Institutional employment available.

CAMPUS LIFE

Activities: Campus Ministries; Choral groups; Concert band; Dance; Drama/theater; International Student Organization; Jazz band; Marching band; Model UN; Music ensembles; Musical theater; Pep band; Radio station; Student government; Student newspaper; Student-run film society; Symphony orchestra. **Organizations:** 155 registered organizations, 16 honor societies, 25 religious organizations. 14 fraternities, 10 sororities. **Athletics (Intercollegiate):** *Men:* baseball, basketball, diving, football, golf, sailing, soccer, tennis, wrestling. *Women:* basketball, crew/rowing, diving, field hockey, golf, lacrosse, sailing, soccer, tennis. **On-Campus Highlights:** Webb Student Center, Student Recreation Center, University Village, Constant Convocation Center, Kaufman Mall.

ACCOMMODATIONS

Allowed in exams:

Calculators	Yes
Dictionary	Yes
Computer	Yes
Spell-checker	Yes
Extended test time	Yes
Scribe	Yes
Proctors	Yes
Oral exams	Yes
Note-takers	Yes

Support services for students with

LD	Yes
ADHD	Yes
ASD	Yes
Distraction-reduced environment	Yes
Recording of lecture allowed	Yes
Reading technology:	Yes
Audio books	Yes

Other assistive technologyJAWS, Zoom Text, Read & Write Gold is available to students as well as other assistive technology that is require for access to classes

Priority registration	Yes

Added costs for services:

For LD:	No
For ADHD:	No
For ASD:	No
LD specialists	Not Applicable
ADHD & ASD coaching	Yes
ASD specialists	No
Professional tutors	Yes
Peer tutors	Yes
Max. hours/week for services	Varies
How professors are notified of student approved accommodations	Student

COLLEGE GRADUATION REQUIREMENTS

Course waivers allowed	No
Course substitutions allowed	Yes

In what courses Foreign language substitutions are available with sufficient documentation of a language processing disability.

Radford University

801 East Main Street, Radford, VA 24142 • Admissions: 540-831-5371 • Fax: 540-831-5038

CAMPUS

Type of school	Public
Environment	Village
Support	S

STUDENTS

Undergrad enrollment	8,376
% male/female	43/57
% from out of state	6
% frosh live on campus	96

FINANCIAL FACTS

Annual in-state tuition	$7,922
Annual out-of-state tuition	$19,557
Room and board	$9,406
Required fees	$3,288

GENERAL ADMISSIONS INFO

Priority deadline	2/1

Nonfall registration accepted. Admission may be deferred for a maximum of 1 year.

Range SAT EBRW	480–580
Range SAT Math	460–540
Range ACT Composite	17–23

ACADEMICS

Student/faculty ratio	16:1
% students returning for sophomore year	76
% students graduating within 4 years	38
% students graduating within 6 years	55

Most classes have 10–19 students.
Most lab/discussion sessions have 10–19 students.

PROGRAMS/SERVICES FOR STUDENTS WITH LEARNING DIFFERENCES

The Center for Accessibility Services (CAS) is committed to the ongoing goal of access and inclusion so that all individuals on campus can fully participate in the university experience. CAS Promotes equal Access in curricular and co-curricular activities within the university setting, empowers students to self-advocate for needed resources and creates environments that are accessible, diverse, and Inclusive.

ADMISSIONS

General admissions requirements must be met.

Additional Information

The Learning Assistance and Resource Center helps student achieve academic success. In individual or group tutoring sessions, students acquire support from College Reading and Learning Association certified trained tutors. Writing tutors aid students with writing assignments for any discipline. Additionally, students can improve their learning skills through one-on-one consultations. With a learner-centered approach, the staff and tutors seek to meet each Radford University student's academic needs.

ADMISSIONS INFO FOR STUDENTS WITH LEARNING DIFFERENCES

SAT/ACT required:
Interview required: No
Essay required: Not Applicable
Additional application required: Yes
Documentation required for:
  LD: Documentation of the Diagnosis from provider with Functional limitations and severity.
  ADHD: Diagnosis from individual performing assessment complete with functional limitations, severity, impact on learning environment, recommended academic and testing accommodations.
  ASD: Documentation of DSM Diagnosis from provider on letterhead from care provider or diagnosing professional
Documentation submitted to: Center for Accessibility Services
Special Ed. HS course work accepted: Not Applicable
Separate application required for program services: No
Contact Information
Name of program or department: Center for Accessibility Services
Telephone: 540-831-6350
Fax: 540-831-6525
Email: cas@radford.edu

Radford University

GENERAL ADMISSIONS

Very important factors considered include: rigor of secondary school record. *Important factors considered include:* academic GPA. *Other factors considered include:* class rank, application essay, standardized test scores, recommendation(s), interview, extracurricular activities, talent/ability, character/personal qualities, first generation, alumni/ae relation, volunteer work, work experience, level of applicant's in *Freshman Admission Requirements:* High school diploma is required and GED is accepted. *Academic units recommended:* 4 English, 4 math, 4 science, 4 science labs, 4 foreign language, 2 social studies, 2 history.

ACCOMMODATIONS OR SERVICES

Accommodations are decided upon an individual basis after a thorough review of appropriate, current documentation. The accommodations requests must be supported through the documentation provided and must be logically linked to the current impact of the condition on academic functioning.

FINANCIAL AID

Students should submit: FAFSA. Applicants will be notified of awards on a rolling basis beginning 4/15. The Princeton Review suggests that all financial aid forms be submitted as soon as possible after October 1. *Need-based scholarships/grants offered:* College/university scholarship or grant aid from institutional funds; Federal Pell; Private scholarships; SEOG; State scholarships/grants. *Loan aid offered:* Direct PLUS loans; Direct Subsidized Stafford Loans; Direct Unsubsidized Stafford Loans. Federal Work-Study Program available. Institutional employment available.

CAMPUS LIFE

Activities: Campus Ministries; Choral groups; Concert band; Dance; Drama/theater; International Student Organization; Jazz band; Literary magazine; Model UN; Music ensembles; Musical theater; Opera; Pep band; Radio station; Student government; Student newspaper; Student-run film society; Yearbook. **Organizations:** 237 registered organizations, 14 honor societies, 10 religious organizations. 15 fraternities, 10 sororities. **Athletics (Intercollegiate):** *Men:* baseball, basketball, cheerleading, cross-country, golf, soccer, tennis, track/field (outdoor), track/field (indoor). *Women:* basketball, cheerleading, cross-country, diving, field hockey, golf, soccer, softball, swimming, tennis, track/field (outdoor), track/field (indoor), volleyball. **On-Campus Highlights:** new Student Recreation & Wellness Center (opened fall 2014), College of Business & Economics building (Kyle Hall) (opened fall 2012), College of Humanities & Behaivoral Science building and Starbucks (2016), Hurlburt Student Center, including food court,.

ACCOMMODATIONS

Allowed in exams:	
Calculators	Yes
Dictionary	Yes
Computer	Yes
Spell-checker	Yes
Extended test time	Yes
Scribe	Yes
Proctors	Yes
Oral exams	Yes
Note-takers	Yes
Support services for students with	
LD	Yes
ADHD	Yes
ASD	Yes
Distraction-reduced environment	Yes
Recording of lecture allowed	Yes
Reading technology:	Yes
Audio books	Yes
Other assistive technology Various types of Assistive Technology including but not limited to SMART PENS, Video phone for ASL Users, IPAD, Reader software, Dictation Software, Recording devices, Assistive Listening Devices, FM Loop Systems,	
Priority registration	Yes
Added costs for services:	
For LD:	No
For ADHD:	No
For ASD:	No
LD specialists	Yes
ADHD & ASD coaching	Yes
ASD specialists	Yes
Professional tutors	Yes
Peer tutors	Yes
Max. hours/week for services	3
How professors are notified of student approved accommodations	Student

COLLEGE GRADUATION REQUIREMENTS

Course waivers allowed	No
Course substitutions allowed	Yes
In what courses	

These are determined on a case by case basis and students living with the above disabilities may not be granted substitutions.

Roanoke College

221 COLLEGE LANE, SALEM, VA 24153-3794 • ADMISSIONS: 540-375-2270 • FAX: 540-375-2267

PROGRAMS/SERVICES FOR STUDENTS WITH LEARNING DIFFERENCES

Accessible Education Services strives to meet the needs of students with documented disabilities in alignment with Roanoke College's commitment to providing equal access to educational opportunities for all students. Individuals with disabilities are encouraged to visit Roanoke College after their acceptance of admission. A personal visit enables the student and college representatives to meet and determine how the college can accommodate the student's physical and learning needs. All requests are handled on a case-by-case basis. Students are encouraged to submit their documentation shortly after being admitted to the College to ensure that their accommodations are in place prior to the beginning of their first term.

ADMISSIONS

Admission to Roanoke College is based on individual qualifications. No separate standards are used for students with documented disabilities.

Additional Information

All services are accessed through the Disability Support Services office and the Goode-Pasfield Center for Learning & Teaching. Any special considerations or accommodations requested by the student will not be allowed until testing results have been received and reviewed by the Coordinator of Disability Support Services. All requests are handled on a case by case basis. Students are encouraged to submit their documentation shortly after being admitted to the College. The College does not permit substitutions for language, statistics or mathematics requirements.

GENERAL ADMISSIONS

Very important factors considered include: rigor of secondary school record, academic GPA, character/personal qualities. *Important factors considered include:* class rank, standardized test scores, interview, extracurricular activities, level of applicant's interest. *Other factors considered include:* application essay, recommendation(s), talent/ability, alumni/ae relation, racial/ethnic status, volunteer work, work experience. *Freshman Admission Requirements:* High school diploma is required and GED is accepted. *Academic units required:* 4 English, 3 math, 2 science, 2 science labs, 2 foreign language, 2 social studies, 5 academic electives. *Academic units recommended:* 2 foreign language.

ACCOMMODATIONS OR SERVICES

Accommodations are decided upon an individual basis after a thorough review of appropriate, current documentation. The accommodations requests must be supported through the documentation provided and must be logically linked to the current impact of the condition on academic functioning.

FINANCIAL AID

Students should submit: FAFSA; State aid form. Applicants will be notified of awards on a rolling basis beginning 12/15. The Princeton Review suggests that all financial aid forms be submitted as soon as possible after October 1. *Need-based scholarships/grants offered:* College/university scholarship or grant aid from institutional funds; Federal Pell; Private scholarships; SEOG; State scholarships/grants. *Loan aid offered:* Direct PLUS loans; Direct Subsidized Stafford Loans; Direct Unsubsidized Stafford Loans. Federal Work-Study Program available. Institutional employment available.

CAMPUS LIFE

Activities: Campus Ministries; Choral groups; Concert band; Dance; Drama/theater; International Student Organization; Jazz band; Literary magazine; Model UN; Music ensembles; Pep band; Radio station; Student government; Student newspaper; Student-run film society. **Organizations:** 85 registered organizations, 30 honor societies, 7 religious organizations. 4 fraternities, 4 sororities. **Athletics (Intercollegiate):** *Men:* baseball, basketball, cross-country, golf, lacrosse, soccer, tennis, track/field (outdoor), track/field (indoor). *Women:* basketball, cross-country, field hockey, lacrosse, soccer, softball, tennis, track/field (outdoor), track/field (indoor), volleyball. **On-Campus Highlights:** Cregger Center & Belk Fitness Center, Kerr Stadium, Fintel Library (& Little Green Hive coffee shop), Colket Center, New Hall (new residence hall).

ACCOMMODATIONS

Allowed in exams:	
Calculators	Yes
Dictionary	Yes
Computer	Yes
Spell-checker	Yes
Extended test time	Yes
Scribe	Yes
Proctors	Yes
Oral exams	Yes
Note-takers	Yes
Support services for students with	
LD	Yes
ADHD	Yes
ASD	Yes
Distraction-reduced environment	Yes
Recording of lecture allowed	Yes
Reading technology:	No
Audio books	Yes
Other assistive technology	Live scribe pens
Priority registration	No
Added costs for services:	
For LD:	No
For ADHD:	No
For ASD:	No
LD specialists	No
ADHD & ASD coaching	Yes
ASD specialists	No
Professional tutors	Yes
Peer tutors	Yes
Max. hours/week for services	20
How professors are notified of student approved accommodations	Student

COLLEGE GRADUATION REQUIREMENTS

Course waivers allowed	No
Course substitutions allowed	No

University of Virginia

OFFICE OF ADMISSION, CHARLOTTESVILLE, VA 22906 • ADMISSIONS: 434-982-3200 • FAX: 434-924-3587

CAMPUS
Type of school	Public
Environment	City
Support	CS

STUDENTS
Undergrad enrollment	16,089
% male/female	46/54
% from out of state	27
% frosh live on campus	100

FINANCIAL FACTS
Annual in-state tuition	$14,722
Annual out-of-state tuition	$45,623
Room and board	$11,220
Required fees	$2,845

GENERAL ADMISSIONS INFO
Application fee	$60
Regular application deadline	1/1

Nonfall registration accepted. Admission may be deferred for a maximum of 1 year.

Range SAT EBRW	650–730
Range SAT Math	640–740
Range ACT Composite	29–33

ACADEMICS
Student/faculty ratio	15:1
% students returning for sophomore year	97
% students graduating within 4 years	88
% students graduating within 6 years	95

Most classes have 20–29 students.
Most lab/discussion sessions have 20–29 students.

PROGRAMS/SERVICES FOR STUDENTS WITH LEARNING DIFFERENCES

The Student Disability Access Center (SDAC) is the University of Virginia's designated access agency for students with disabilities. We support UVA students in the work of creating access to the full University experience. Our primary role is to determine eligibility and to provide reasonable academic accommodations for students with disabilities in line with Section 504 of the Rehabilitation Act of 1973, the Americans with Disabilities Act of 1990, and the Americans with Disabilities Amendments Acts of 2008. These federal laws ensure that institutions of higher learning provide equal access to students with disabilities who are "otherwise qualified" to meet the essential demands of the academic program. The SDAC provides services to two groups of students: those who have been previously diagnosed with a disability; and those who have never been diagnosed, but find themselves struggling academically, and seek advice and support on their difficulties. Mission and Vision The mission of the Student Disability Access Center is to support the University's commitment to accessible education. For UVA's students with disabilities, we encourage self-determination and independence via accommodations, education, consultation, and advocacy with the goal of building an equitable academic experience. Our vision is for individuals with disabilities to have full access to the physical, educational, social, cultural and political milieu of the University of Virginia. The staff of the Student Disability Access Center (SDAC) embrace the values of The University (accountability, diversity, integrity, respect, social responsibility) and the values of the Student Affairs Office (knowledge, humanity, responsibility, integrity, community), particularly as they have bearing on accessibility, equal opportunity, collaboration and learning. SDAC strives to promote accessibility for all individuals with disabilities including faculty, staff, family, friends, guests of the University, and members of the community.

ADMISSIONS

The students with learning disabilities go through the same admissions procedure as all incoming applicants. After admission to the university, students must contact the SDAC to receive services. Students with learning disabilities admitted to the university have qualified for admission because of their abilities. No criteria for admission are waived because of a disability. All applicants to UVA have outstanding grades, a high rank

ADMISSIONS INFO FOR STUDENTS WITH LEARNING DIFFERENCES
SAT/ACT required: Yes
Interview required: No
Essay required: Not Applicable
Additional application required: Not Applicable
Documentation required for:
 LD: Psycho ed evaluation to include: relevant historical info, instructional interventions, related services, age diagnosed, objective data (aptitude, achievement, info processing), test scores (standard, percentile and grade equivalents) and describe functional limitations.
 ADHD: Diagnosis based on DSM-V; history of behaviors impairing functioning in academic setting; diagnostic interview; history of symptoms; evidence of ongoing behaviors.
 ASD: Psycho ed evaluation
Documentation submitted to: Student Disability Access Center
Special Ed. HS course work accepted: No
Separate application required for program services: No
Contact Information
Name of program or department: Student Disability Access Center
Telephone: 434-243-5180
Fax: 434-243-5188
Email: sdac@virginia.edu

University of Virginia

in their high school class, excellent performance in advanced placement and honor courses, superior performance on ACT/SAT Reasoning and SAT Subject Tests, extracurricular success, special talents, and interests and goals. Letters of recommendation are required.

Additional Information

Upon acceptance to the University, students are encouraged to apply for SDAC services online through the SDAC website: http://studenthealth.virginia.edu/sdac. Students are strongly encouraged to consult the Guidelines for Documentation of a Learning Disorder or ADHD available in the Information section of the SDAC website. Services and accommodations are available for undergraduate and graduate students.

General Admissions

Very important factors considered include: rigor of secondary school record, class rank, academic GPA, recommendation(s), character/personal qualities, state residency. *Important factors considered include:* application essay, standardized test scores, extracurricular activities, talent/ability. *Other factors considered include:* first generation, alumni/ae relation, geographical residence, racial/ethnic status, volunteer work, work experience. *Freshman Admission Requirements:* High school diploma is required and GED is accepted. *Academic units required:* 4 English, 4 math, 2 science, 2 foreign language, 1 social studies. *Academic units recommended:* 5 math, 4 science, 5 foreign language, 4 social studies.

Accommodations or Services

Accommodations are decided upon an individual basis after a thorough review of appropriate, current documentation. The accommodations requests must be supported through the documentation provided and must be logically linked to the current impact of the condition on academic functioning.

Financial Aid

Students should submit: CSS/Financial Aid PROFILE; FAFSA. Applicants will be notified of awards on or about 4/5. The Princeton Review suggests that all financial aid forms be submitted as soon as possible after October 1. *Need-based scholarships/grants offered:* College/university scholarship or grant aid from institutional funds; Federal Nursing Scholarships; Federal Pell; Private scholarships; SEOG; State scholarships/grants. *Loan aid offered:* Direct PLUS loans; Direct Subsidized Stafford Loans; Direct Unsubsidized Stafford Loans. Federal Work-Study Program available. Institutional employment available.

Campus Life

Activities: Campus Ministries; Choral groups; Concert band; Dance; Drama/theater; International Student Organization; Jazz band; Literary magazine; Marching band; Model UN; Music ensembles; Musical theater; Opera; Pep band; Radio station; Student government; Student newspaper; Student-run film society; Symphony orchestra; Television station; Yearbook. **Organizations:** 7 honor societies, 44 religious organizations. 28 fraternities, 15 sororities. **Athletics (Intercollegiate):** *Men:* baseball, basketball, cross-country, diving, football, golf, lacrosse, soccer, swimming, tennis, track/field (outdoor), track/field (indoor), wrestling. *Women:* basketball, crew/rowing, cross-country, diving, field hockey, golf, lacrosse, soccer, softball, swimming, tennis, track/field (outdoor), track/field (indoor), volleyball. **On-Campus Highlights:** Rotunda/Academical Village (orig campus), Alderman and Clemons Libraries, John Paul Jones Arena, Football, Baseball, and Soccer Stadiums, Aquatic and Fitness Center.

ACCOMMODATIONS

Allowed in exams:

Calculators	Yes
Dictionary	Yes
Computer	Yes
Spell-checker	Yes
Extended test time	Yes
Scribe	Yes
Proctors	Yes
Oral exams	Yes
Note-takers	Yes

Support services for students with

LD	Yes
ADHD	Yes
ASD	Yes
Distraction-reduced environment	Yes
Recording of lecture allowed	Yes
Reading technology:	Yes
Audio books	Yes

Other assistive technology Sonocent Audio Notetaker, Read & Write Gold

Priority registration	Yes

Added costs for services:

For LD:	No
For ADHD:	No
For ASD:	No
LD specialists	Yes
ADHD & ASD coaching	Yes
ASD specialists	Yes
Professional tutors	Yes
Peer tutors	No
Max. hours/week for services	Varies

How professors are notified of student approved accommodations
  Director and student

COLLEGE GRADUATION REQUIREMENTS

Course waivers allowed	No
Course substitutions allowed	Yes

In what courses course substitution request. Additionally, students are required to demonstrate a "good faith effort" to fulfill the foreign language requirement before a course substitution would be considered.

Eastern Washington University

526 FIFTH STREET, CHENEY, WA 99004 • ADMISSIONS: 509-359-6692 • FAX: 509-359-6692

CAMPUS

Type of school	Public
Environment	Town
Support	S

STUDENTS

Undergrad enrollment	10,500
% male/female	47/53
% from out of state	5
% frosh live on campus	68

FINANCIAL FACTS

Annual in-state tuition	$6,379
Annual out-of-state tuition	$23,501
Room and board	$12,056
Required fees	$939

GENERAL ADMISSIONS INFO

Application fee	$50
Priority deadline	2/15
Regular application deadline	5/15

Nonfall registration accepted. Admission may be deferred for a maximum of 1 year.

Range SAT EBRW	440–530
Range SAT Math	430–560
Range ACT Composite	17–24

ACADEMICS

Student/faculty ratio	21:1
% students returning for sophomore year	76
% students graduating within 4 years	25
% students graduating within 6 years	52

Most classes have 20–29 students.
Most lab/discussion sessions have 10–19 students.

PROGRAMS/SERVICES FOR STUDENTS WITH LEARNING DIFFERENCES

Although the university does not offer a specialized curriculum, personnel work with students to modify programs to meet individual needs. Disability Support Services (DSS) is dedicated to the coordination of appropriate and reasonable accommodations for students with disabilities. These accommodations are based on individual needs so that each student may receive an equal opportunity to learn to participate in campus life, to grow emotionally and socially, and to successfully complete a program of study that will enable him or her to be self-supporting and remain as independent as possible. This is facilitated through support services, information sharing, advisement, and referral when requested. Students who require services and support need to contact DSS so that the disability can be verified, specific needs determined, and timely accommodations made. In most cases, documentation by a professional service provider will be necessary. Information is kept strictly confidential. However, it is important to share information that will enable DSS staff to provide appropriate, reasonable, and timely services tailored to individual needs.

ADMISSIONS

Individuals with disabilities are admitted via the standard admissions criteria that apply to all students. General admissibility is based on an index using GPA and test scores. The minimum GPA accepted is a 2.0. Required courses include 4 years of English, 3 years of math, 3 years of social science, 2 years of science (1 year of lab), 2 years of a foreign language (American Sign Language accepted), and 1 year of arts or academic electives. Special education courses are acceptable if they are courses that are regularly taught in the high school. However, all applicants must complete the required core courses. Students who do not meet the grade and test score admission scale may provide additional information to the Admission Office and request consideration through the special talent admissions process.

Additional Information

Examples of services for students with specific learning disabilities include alternative format textbooks; equipment loans; alternative testing

ADMISSIONS INFO FOR STUDENTS WITH LEARNING DIFFERENCES

SAT/ACT required: Yes
Interview required: No
Essay required: Yes
Additional application required: No
Documentation required for:
 LD: Psycho ed evaluation to include: relevant historical info, instructional interventions, related services, age diagnosed, objective data (aptitude, achievement, info processing), test scores (standard, percentile and grade equivalents) and describe functional limitations.
 ADHD: Diagnosis based on DSM-V; history of behaviors impairing functioning in academic setting; diagnostic interview; history of symptoms; evidence of ongoing behaviors.
 ASD: Psycho ed evaluation
Documentation submitted to: Admissions Office and DSS
Special Ed. HS course work accepted: Yes
Separate application required for program services: No
# of students last year receiving services/accommodations for:
 LD: 200
Contact Information
Name of program or department: Disabiltiy Support Services
Telephone: 509-359-4796

Eastern Washington University

arrangements such as oral exams, extended time on tests, relocation of testing site; note-takers; tutorial assistance (available to all students); referral to a Learning Skills Center, Writers' Center, and/or Mathematics Lab; accessible computer stations; and a Kurzweil Reader. Examples of services for students with ADHD are consultation regarding reasonable and effective accommodations with classroom professors; alternative testing; alternative format textbooks; note-takers; taped lectures; equipment loans; referrals to a Learning Skills Center, a Math Lab, a Writers' Center, and counseling and psychological services; information on ADHD; and informal counseling. Skills classes for credit are offered in math, reading, time management, study skills, and writing skills. FOCUS is a structured first-year experience for selected, provisionally admitted students. The experience includes advising; academic instruction in math, English, and study strategies; and professional mentoring. Services and accommodations are offered to undergraduate and graduate students.

GENERAL ADMISSIONS

Very important factors considered include: academic GPA, standardized test scores. *Important factors considered include:* rigor of secondary school record, application essay. *Other factors considered include:* recommendation(s), extracurricular activities, talent/ability, character/ personal qualities, volunteer work, work experience. *Freshman Admission Requirements:* High school diploma or equivalent is not required *Academic units required:* 4 English, 3 math, 2 science, 2 science labs, 2 foreign language, 3 social studies, 1 visual/performing arts, and 1 unit from above areas or other academic areas.

ACCOMMODATIONS OR SERVICES

Accommodations are decided upon an individual basis after a thorough review of appropriate, current documentation. The accommodations requests must be supported through the documentation provided and must be logically linked to the current impact of the condition on academic functioning.

FINANCIAL AID

Students should submit:. The Princeton Review suggests that all financial aid forms be submitted as soon as possible after October 1. *Need-based scholarships/grants offered: Loan aid offered:* Federal Work-Study Program available. Institutional employment available.

CAMPUS LIFE

Activities: Campus Ministries; Choral groups; Concert band; Dance; Drama/theater; International Student Organization; Jazz band; Literary magazine; Marching band; Model UN; Music ensembles; Musical theater; Pep band; Radio station; Student government; Student newspaper; Student-run film society; Symphony orchestra. **Organizations:** 100 registered organizations, 14 honor societies, 10 religious organizations. 5 fraternities, 5 sororities. **Athletics (Intercollegiate):** *Men:* basketball, cross-country, football, golf, tennis, track/field (outdoor), track/field (indoor). *Women:* basketball, cross-country, golf, soccer, tennis, track/ field (outdoor), track/field (indoor), volleyball. **On-Campus Highlights:** Roos Stadium: "The Inferno" red turf, URC- New Recreaton Center, JFK Library, PUB- Pence Union Building, Central Campus mall.

ACCOMMODATIONS

Calculators	Yes
Dictionary	Yes
Computer	Yes
Spell-checker	Yes
Extended test time	Yes
Scribe	Yes
Proctors	Yes
Oral exams	Yes
Note-takers	Yes
Support services for students with	
LD	Yes
ADHD	Yes
ASD	Yes
Distraction-reduced environment	Yes
Recording of lecture allowed	Yes
Reading technology:	Yes
Audio books	Yes
Other assistive technology	Yes
Priority registration	Yes
Added costs for services:	
For LD:	No
For ADHD:	No
For ASD:	No
LD specialists	No
ADHD & ASD coaching	No
ASD specialists	No
Professional tutors	Yes
Peer tutors	Yes
Max. hours/week for services	Varies
How professors are notified of student approved accommodations	Student and director

COLLEGE GRADUATION REQUIREMENTS

Course waivers allowed	No
Course substitutions allowed	No

The Evergreen State College

2700 Evergreen Pkwy NW, Olympia, WA 98505 • Admissions: 360-867-6170 • Fax: 360-867-5114

CAMPUS

Type of school	Public
Environment	City
Support	S

STUDENTS

Undergrad enrollment	3,560
% male/female	43/58
% from out of state	20
% frosh live on campus	76

FINANCIAL FACTS

Annual in-state tuition	$6,825
Annual out-of-state tuition	$25,335
Room and board	$11,346
Required fees	$849

GENERAL ADMISSIONS INFO

Application fee	$50
Priority deadline	2/1

Nonfall registration accepted. Admission may be deferred for a maximum of One quarter.

Range SAT EBRW	500–630
Range SAT Math	460–560
Range ACT Composite	19–27

ACADEMICS

Student/faculty ratio	21:1
% students returning for sophomore year	61
% students graduating within 4 years	42
% students graduating within 6 years	57

Most classes have 10–19 students.
Most lab/discussion sessions have 10–19 students.

PROGRAMS/SERVICES FOR STUDENTS WITH LEARNING DIFFERENCES

For almost forty years, The Evergreen State College has consistently provided an integrated learning community for students. Instead of taking four or five separate, unrelated classes each quarter, students take one program that unifies these classes around a central theme, taught by two or three faculty members from different academic disciplines. Many programs continue for two or three consecutive quarters. This allows students to build specific skills to produce highly sophisticated work, even in introductory offerings. And, because learning is too important to be reduced to an arbitrary number or letter grade, students receive a narrative evaluation from the faculty. The student's accomplishments and achievements will be detailed to provide graduate schools and employers with a comprehensive overview of his or her undergraduate education.

ADMISSIONS

Students entering Evergreen directly from high school will be considered for admission on the following basis: Completion of college-preparatory course work in high school; Grade point average (GPA) and ACT or SAT test scores. A 2.8 cumulative GPA is recommended; a 2.0 cumulative GPA is required for admission consideration. The SAT writing test and subject tests are not required; Good standing in any college-level work attempted while in high school or after high school graduation. The quality of the college work will be taken into consideration as well. A personal statement is an important part of the application, too. This statement is desired from all applicants. However, Home School applicants must submit a personal statement. More information about the admission application process and the personal statement can be found on the web at admissions.evergreen.edu/application.

ADMISSIONS INFO FOR STUDENTS WITH LEARNING DIFFERENCES

SAT/ACT required: Yes
Interview required: No
Essay required: Not Applicable
Additional application required: Yes
Documentation required for:
 LD: The use of a single test and/or instrument (such as Slingerland, and Scopotic Sensitivity Screening) is not acceptable for the purposes of diagnosis.
 ADHD: Documentation should show current impact of the disability.
ASD: Documentation must be from a provider who is qualified to make the diagnosis. Documentation must: Identify the diagnosis and include the DSM IV or DSM V diagnostic code; identify the functional limitations and/or challenges and barriers the student experiences in an academic environment.
Documentation submitted to: Access Services
Special Ed. HS course work accepted: No
Contact Information
Name of program or department: Access Services
Telephone: (360) 867-6348
Email: inocenc@evergreen.edu

The Evergreen State College

Additional Information

The Evergreen State College is committed to providing equal access, accommodations, and educational support for qualified students with disabilities. It is our goal to invite and celebrate diversity within our campus community. Our approach is designed to be holistic and to empower by promoting: self reliance, effective problem solving skills, enhanced academic and personal development, and equal access to college programs and activities for qualified students with disabilities.

GENERAL ADMISSIONS

Very important factors considered include: rigor of secondary school record, academic GPA, application essay. *Important factors considered include:* standardized test scores, first generation, level of applicant's interest. *Other factors considered include:* recommendation(s), interview, extracurricular activities, volunteer work, work experience. *Freshman Admission Requirements:* High school diploma is required and GED is accepted. *Academic units required:* 4 English, 3 math, 2 science, 2 science labs, 2 foreign language, 3 social studies, 1 academic elective, and 1 unit from above areas or other academic areas.

ACCOMMODATIONS OR SERVICES

Accommodations are decided upon an individual basis after a thorough review of appropriate, current documentation. The accommodations requests must be supported through the documentation provided and must be logically linked to the current impact of the condition on academic functioning.

FINANCIAL AID

Students should submit: FAFSA. Applicants will be notified of awards on a rolling basis beginning 4/1. The Princeton Review suggests that all financial aid forms be submitted as soon as possible after October 1. *Need-based scholarships/grants offered:* College/university scholarship or grant aid from institutional funds; Federal Pell; Private scholarships; SEOG; State scholarships/grants. *Loan aid offered:* Direct PLUS loans; Direct Subsidized Stafford Loans; Direct Unsubsidized Stafford Loans. Federal Work-Study Program available. Institutional employment available.

CAMPUS LIFE

Activities: Campus Ministries; Choral groups; Dance; Drama/theater; Jazz band; Literary magazine; Music ensembles; Pep band; Radio station; Student government; Student newspaper; Student-run film society; Television station. **Organizations:** 61 registered organizations, 3 religious organizations. **Athletics (Intercollegiate):** *Men:* basketball, cross-country, soccer, track/field (outdoor), track/field (indoor). *Women:* basketball, cross-country, soccer, track/field (outdoor), track/field (indoor), volleyball. **On-Campus Highlights:** College Activities Building, Trans & Queer Center, Organic Farm, The Flaming Eggplant-Student run cafe, Evergreen beach and woods.

ACCOMMODATIONS

Allowed in exams:

Calculators	Yes
Dictionary	Yes
Computer	Yes
Spell-checker	Yes
Extended test time	Yes
Scribe	No
Proctors	No
Oral exams	No
Note-takers	Yes

Support services for students with

LD	Yes
ADHD	Yes
ASD	Yes
Distraction-reduced environment	Yes
Recording of lecture allowed	Yes
Reading technology:	Yes
Audio books	Yes

Other assistive technology Peer support and advocacy, counseling referrals, tests available on tape or computer. Evergreen also offers an Assistive Technology lab that features computers with scanners, on adjustable height tables, loaded with the following software: Read & Write

Priority registration	Yes

Added costs for services:

For LD:	No
For ADHD:	No
For ASD:	No
LD specialists	Yes
ADHD & ASD coaching	Yes
ASD specialists	No
Professional tutors	Yes
Peer tutors	Not Applicable
Max. hours/week for services	Varies
How professors are notified of student approved accommodations	Director and student

COLLEGE GRADUATION REQUIREMENTS

Course waivers allowed	No
Course substitutions allowed	No

Washington State University

PO Box 645910, Pullman, WA 99164-1067 • Admissions: 509-335-5586 • Fax: 509-335-4902

CAMPUS

Type of school	Public
Environment	Town
Support	S

STUDENTS

Undergrad enrollment	20,286
% male/female	48/52
% from out of state	13
% frosh live on campus	82

FINANCIAL FACTS

Annual in-state tuition	$9,720
Annual out-of-state tuition	$23,956
Room and board	$11,398
Required fees	$1,864

GENERAL ADMISSIONS INFO

Application fee	$50
Priority deadline	1/31

Nonfall registration accepted.

Range SAT EBRW	510–610
Range SAT Math	510–610
Range ACT Composite	20–26

ACADEMICS

Student/faculty ratio	15:1
% students returning for sophomore year	81
% students graduating within 4 years	38
% students graduating within 6 years	62

Most classes have 10–19 students.
Most lab/discussion sessions have 20–29 students.

Programs/Services for Students with Learning Differences

The Access Center (AC) assists students who have a disability by providing academic accommodations. The program may also refer students to other service programs that may assist them in achieving their academic goals. AC will help students overcome potential obstacles so that they may be successful in their area of study. All academic adjustments are authorized on an individual basis. The program offers academic coaching. To be eligible for assistance, students must be currently enrolled at Washington State University. They also must submit documentation of their disability. For a learning disability, the student must submit a written report that includes test scores and evaluation. It is the student's responsibility to request accommodations if desired. It is important to remember that even though two individuals may have the same disability, they may not necessarily need the same academic adjustments. AC works with students and instructors to determine and implement appropriate academic adjustments. Many adjustments are simple, creative alternatives for traditional ways of learning.

Admissions

All students must meet the general admission requirements. The university looks at the combination of scores on the ACT/SAT and the applicant's high school GPA. The standard admission criteria are based on an index score determined by 75 percent GPA and 25 percent SAT/ACT. Courses required include 4 years of English, 4 years of math, 2 years of science, 2 years of a foreign language, 3 years of social studies, 1 year of art. Only 15 percent of new admissions may be admitted under special admission. Documentation of the learning disability and diagnostic tests are required if requesting accommodations or services.

Additional Information

General assistance to students with learning disabilities includes pre-admission counseling; information about disabilities; referral to appropriate community resources; academic, personal, and career counseling; information about accommodations; information about

ADMISSIONS INFO FOR STUDENTS WITH LEARNING DIFFERENCES

SAT/ACT required: Yes
Interview required: No
Essay required: No
Documentation required for:
 LD: Psycho ed evaluation to include: relevant historical info, instructional interventions, related services, age diagnosed, objective data (aptitude, achievement, info processing), test scores (standard, percentile and grade equivalents) and describe functional limitations.
 ADHD: Diagnosis based on DSM-V; history of behaviors impairing functioning in academic setting; diagnostic interview; history of symptoms; evidence of ongoing behaviors.
 ASD: Psycho ed evaluation
Documentation submitted to: Access Center, Division of Student Affairs
Special Ed. HS course work accepted: Yes
Separate application required for program services: No
# of students last year receiving services/accommodations for:
 LD: 125
Contact Information
Name of program or department: Access Center, Division of Student Affairs
Telephone: 509-335-3417
Email: access.center@wsu.edu

Washington State University

the laws pertaining to individuals with disabilities; and self-advocacy. Typical academic adjustments for students with learning disabilities may include note-takers and/or audiotape class sessions; alternative testing arrangements; alternate print (mp3 files or text files); extended time for exams; essay exams taken on computer; and use of computers with voice output and spellcheckers. Services and accommodations are available for undergraduate and graduate students.

GENERAL ADMISSIONS

Very important factors considered include: academic GPA, standardized test scores. *Important factors considered include:* rigor of secondary school record, class rank. *Other factors considered include:* application essay, recommendation(s), extracurricular activities, talent/ability, character/ personal qualities, volunteer work, work experience. *Freshman Admission Requirements:* High school diploma is required and GED is accepted. *Academic units required:* 4 English, 3 math, 2 science, 2 foreign language, 3 social studies, 1 visual/performing arts, and 1 unit from above areas or other academic areas. *Academic units recommended:* 4 English, 4 math, 2 science, 2 foreign language, 3 social studies, 1 visual/performing arts, 1 unit from above areas or other academic areas.

ACCOMMODATIONS OR SERVICES

Accommodations are decided upon an individual basis after a thorough review of appropriate, current documentation. The accommodations requests must be supported through the documentation provided and must be logically linked to the current impact of the condition on academic functioning.

FINANCIAL AID

Students should submit: FAFSA;; State aid form. Applicants will be notified of awards on a rolling basis beginning 4/15. The Princeton Review suggests that all financial aid forms be submitted as soon as possible after October 1. *Need-based scholarships/grants offered:* College/university scholarship or grant aid from institutional funds; Federal Nursing Scholarships; Federal Pell; Private scholarships; SEOG; State scholarships/grants. *Loan aid offered:* Direct PLUS loans; Direct Subsidized Stafford Loans; Direct Unsubsidized Stafford Loans. Federal Work-Study Program available. Institutional employment available.

CAMPUS LIFE

Activities: Campus Ministries; Choral groups; Concert band; Dance; Drama/theater; International Student Organization; Jazz band; Literary magazine; Marching band; Model UN; Music ensembles; Musical theater; Opera; Pep band; Radio station; Student government; Student newspaper; Student-run film society; Symphony orchestra; Television station; Yearbook. **Organizations:** 300 registered organizations, 36 honor societies, 19 religious organizations. 26 fraternities, 13 sororities. **Athletics (Intercollegiate):** *Men:* baseball, basketball, cross-country, football, golf, track/field (outdoor). *Women:* basketball, crew/rowing, cross-country, golf, soccer, swimming, tennis, track/field (outdoor), volleyball. **On-Campus Highlights:** Compton Union Building (CUB), Terrell Friendship Mall, Student Recreation Center, Beasley Performing Arts Coliseum, Martin Stadium.

ACCOMMODATIONS

Allowed in exams:	
Calculators	Yes
Dictionary	Yes
Computer	Yes
Spell-checker	Yes
Extended test time	Yes
Scribe	Yes
Proctors	Yes
Oral exams	Yes
Note-takers	Yes
Support services for students with	
LD	Yes
ADHD	Yes
ASD	Yes
Distraction-reduced environment	Yes
Recording of lecture allowed	Yes
Reading technology:	Yes
Audio books	Yes
Other assistive technology	Yes
Priority registration	Yes
Added costs for services:	
For LD:	No
LD specialists	No
DHD & ASD coaching	No
SD specialists	No
Professional tutors	No
Peer tutors	No
Max. hours/week for services	5-10
How professors are notified of student approved accommodations	Student

COLLEGE GRADUATION REQUIREMENTS

Course waivers allowed	No
Course substitutions allowed	No

Whitman College

345 Boyer Avenue, Walla Walla, WA 99362 • Admissions: 509-527-5176 • Fax: 509-527-4967

CAMPUS
Type of school	Private (nonprofit)
Environment	Town
Support	CS

STUDENTS
Undergrad enrollment	1,468
% male/female	43/57
% from out of state	66
% frosh live on campus	100

FINANCIAL FACTS
Room and board	NR
Required fees	NR

GENERAL ADMISSIONS INFO
Application fee	$50.
Priority deadline	11/15
Regular application deadline	1/15

Nonfall registration accepted. Admission may be deferred for a maximum of 1 year.

Range SAT EBRW	510–690
Range SAT Math	510–680
Range ACT Composite	26–31

ACADEMICS
Student/faculty ratio	9:1.
% students returning for sophomore year	94
% students graduating within 4 years	79
% students graduating within 6 years	88

Most classes have 10-19 students.
Most lab/discussion sessions have 10-19 students.

PROGRAMS/SERVICES FOR STUDENTS WITH LEARNING DIFFERENCES

Whitman College is committed to the education of all qualified students, regardless of disability status. The American with Disabilities Act and subsequent updates to that legislation require that the College ensures that all programs and services provided by the College are genuinely accessible and offered to all qualified students. Academic Resource Center staff members work with staff and faculty colleagues to ensure that materials and instructions can be accessed and understood and that students are able to demonstrate their knowledge and interest appropriately as well. Our office and our campus partners are committed to reducing or circumventing the barriers to access that people with disabilities face, and welcome your feedback and cooperation as we work towards achieving equity for all students. Documentation requirements and available resources were covered in the responses above.

ADMISSIONS

Whitman is committed to the education of all qualified students, regardless of disability status. If a student needs accommodations during their application process or while they are visiting our campus, they should contact the Assistant Director of Academic Resources: Disability Support Services, who can assist in making the appropriate arrangements.

Additional Information

The Academic Resource Center offers academic coaching. One-on-one sessions are designed with particular goals in mind. Strategies and topics can include goal setting, time management, reading and study strategies, and overcoming procrastination. Regular meetings also encourage accountability and can build towards establishing personal accountability. There are also skill building workshops and sessions that have common topics such as: time management, note taking, critical reading skills, test-taking strategies, and managing test anxiety. Student Academic Advisers (SAs) are students who live in the first-year residence halls and provide guidance and support.

ADMISSIONS INFO FOR STUDENTS WITH LEARNING DIFFERENCES

SAT/ACT required: No
Interview required: No
Essay required: No
Additional application required: No
Documentation required for:
  LD: Psycho ed evaluation
  ADHD: Written repoPsycho ed evaluation
  ASD: Psycho ed evaluation
Documentation submitted to: Disabililty Support Services
Separate application required for program services:
Contact Information
Name of program or department: Disabililty Support Services
Telephone: (509) 527-5767
Fax: (509) 526-4701

Whitman College

GENERAL ADMISSIONS

Very important factors considered include: rigor of secondary school record, academic GPA, application essay. *Important factors considered include:* recommendation(s), extracurricular activities, talent/ability, character/personal qualities. *Other factors considered include:* class rank, standardized test scores, interview, first generation, alumni/ae relation, geographical residence, state residency, religious affiliation/commitment, racial/ethnic status, volunteer work, work experience, level of applicant's interest. *Freshman Admission Requirements:* High school diploma is required and GED is accepted   *Academic units recommended:* 4 English, 4 math, 3 science, 3 science labs, 2 foreign language, 2 social studies, 2 history,

ACCOMMODATION OR SERVICES

Accommodations are decided upon an individual basis after a thorough review of appropriate, current documentation. The accommodations requests must be supported through the documentation provided and must be logically linked to the current impact of the condition on academic functioning.

FINANCIAL AID

Students should submit: CSS/Financial Aid PROFILE; FAFSA; Noncustodial PROFILE;. Applicants will be notified of awards on or about 4/1.. The Princeton Review suggests that all financial aid forms be submitted as soon as possible after October 1. *Need-based scholarships/grants offered:* College/university scholarship or grant aid from institutional funds; Federal Pell; Private scholarships; SEOG; State scholarships/grants *Loan aid offered:* Direct PLUS loans; Direct Subsidized Stafford Loans; Direct Unsubsidized Stafford Loans Federal Work-Study Program available. Institutional employment available.

CAMPUS LIFE

Activities: Campus Ministries; Choral groups; Concert band ; Dance ; Drama/theater; International Student Organization; Jazz band; Literary magazine; Model UN; Music ensembles; Musical theater; Radio station ; Student government; Student newspaper; Student-run film society; Symphony orchestra ; Yearbook Organizations: 80 registered organizations, 3 honor societies, 7 religious organizations. 4 fraternities, 3 sororities, **Athletics (Intercollegiate):** *Men:* baseball, basketball, cross-country, golf, soccer, swimming, tennis *Women:* basketball, cross-country, golf, soccer, swimming, tennis, volleyball. **On-Campus Highlights:** Reid Campus Center, Ankeny Field (Main Quad), Baker Ferguson Fitness Center, Penrose Library, Harper Joy Theatre.

ACCOMMODATIONS

Allowed in exams:	
Calculators	Yes
Dictionary	Yes
Computer	Yes
Spell-checker	Yes
Extended test time	Yes
Scribe	Yes
Proctors	Yes
Oral exams	Yes
Note-takers	Yes
Support services for students with	
LD	No
ADHD	No
ASD	No
Distraction-reduced environment	Yes
Recording of lecture allowed	Yes
Reading technology:	Yes
Audio books	Yes
Other assistive technologyStudents can loan technology including audio recorders, SmartPens, Iris scanning pens. Also have software technology including Dragon and Mathematica	
Priority registration	No
Added costs of services:	
For LD:	No
For ADHD:	No
For ASD:	No
LD specialists	
ADHD & ASD coaching	Yes
ASD specialists	
Professional tutors	Yes
Peer tutors	Yes
Max. hours/week for services	1
How professors are notified of student approved accommodations	Director

COLLEGE GRADUATION REQUIREMENTS

Course waivers allowed	No
Course substitutions allowed	No

Whitworth University

300 West Hawthorne Road, Spokane, WA 99251 • Admissions: 509-777-4786 • Fax: 509-777-3758

CAMPUS

Type of school	Private (nonprofit)
Environment	City
Support	S

STUDENTS

Undergrad enrollment	2,227
% male/female	40/60
% from out of state	33
% frosh live on campus	90

FINANCIAL FACTS

Annual tuition	$42,540
Room and board	$11,496
Required fees	$1,100

GENERAL ADMISSIONS INFO

Priority deadline	3/1
Regular application deadline	8/1

Nonfall registration accepted. Admission may be deferred for a maximum of 1 year.

Range SAT EBRW	550–660
Range SAT Math	540–650
Range ACT Composite	23–29

ACADEMICS

Student/faculty ratio	11:1.
% students returning for sophomore year	85
% students graduating within 4 years	65
% students graduating within 6 years	75

Most classes have fewer than 10 students.

PROGRAMS/SERVICES FOR STUDENTS WITH LEARNING DIFFERENCES

Whitworth University will not exclude otherwise qualified applicants or students with disabilities from participation in, or access to, its academic, housing, or extracurricular programs. The phrase "Otherwise qualified" refers to students who, without consideration of disability, are admissible to the university. Program participation will not be denied to a student with a disability when that person, with a reasonable accommodation, can perform the essential functions required of that program.

ADMISSIONS

We seek to evaluate all students ability to succeed academically at Whitworth University. In the case of students with documented learning disabilities, we make that assessment in light of the educational support services available at Whitworth University to accommodate their learning disabilities.

Additional Information

Whitworth University has a long history of supporting students with disabilities. We are committed to making our campus accessible to the whole community. However, it is only through voluntary disclosure of disability and request for accommodation that Whitworth University can make adjustments to meet the specific needs of an individual. Whitworth University expects all students to play an active role in their education. It is a student's responsibility to familiarize him or herself with the university's policies and with specific course requirements. All students should take the initiative to seek the support, advice, and resources available to them. Students with disabilities who want academic adjustments in order to achieve access to programs and activities must contact Educational Support Services.

ADMISSIONS INFO FOR STUDENTS WITH LEARNING DIFFERENCES

SAT/ACT required: No
Interview required: No
Essay required: No
Additional application required: No
Documentation required for:
  ASD: WAIS-R ,Woodcock-Johnson
Documentation submitted to: Educational Support Services
Special Ed. HS course work accepted: Not Applicable
Separate application required for program services: No
Contact Information
Name of program or department: Educational Support Services
Telephone: 509-777-3380
Fax: 509-777-3821

Whitworth University

GENERAL ADMISSIONS

Very important factors considered include: academic GPA, application essay, recommendation(s). *Important factors considered include:* rigor of secondary school record, standardized test scores, interview, extracurricular activities, character/personal qualities. *Other factors considered include:* talent/ability, first generation, alumni/ae relation, geographical residence, state residency, racial/ethnic status, volunteer work, work experience, level of applicant's interest. *Freshman Admission Requirements:* High school diploma is required and GED is accepted *Academic units recommended:* 4 English, 3 math, 3 science, 2 science labs, 2 foreign language, 2 social studies, 2 history,

ACCOMMODATION OR SERVICES

Accommodations are decided upon an individual basis after a thorough review of appropriate, current documentation. The accommodations requests must be supported through the documentation provided and must be logically linked to the current impact of the condition on academic functioning.

FINANCIAL AID

Students should submit: FAFSA. Applicants will be notified of awards on a rolling basis beginning 1/17.. The Princeton Review suggests that all financial aid forms be submitted as soon as possible after October 1. *Need-based scholarships/grants offered:* College/university scholarship or grant aid from institutional funds; Federal Pell; Private scholarships; SEOG; State scholarships/grants *Loan aid offered:* Direct PLUS loans; Direct Subsidized Stafford Loans; Direct Unsubsidized Stafford Loans Federal Work-Study Program available. Institutional employment available.

CAMPUS LIFE

Activities: Campus Ministries; Choral groups; Concert band ; Dance ; Drama/theater; International Student Organization; Jazz band; Literary magazine; Music ensembles; Musical theater; Radio station ; Student government; Student newspaper; Symphony orchestra ; Yearbook Organizations: 50 registered organizations, 5 honor societies, **Athletics (Intercollegiate):** *Men:* baseball, basketball, cheerleading, cross-country, football, golf, soccer, swimming, tennis, track/field (outdoor) *Women:* basketball, cheerleading, cross-country, golf, soccer, softball, swimming, tennis, track/field (outdoor), volleyball. **On-Campus Highlights:** Hixson Student Union Building Mind & Hearth Coffee Shop, University Rec Center, Robinson Science Center, Cowles Music Center, Fieldhouse.

ACCOMMODATIONS

Allowed in exams:	
Calculators	Yes
Dictionary	Yes
Computer	Yes
Spell-checker	Yes
Extended test time	Yes
Scribe	Yes
Proctors	Yes
Oral exams	Yes
Note-takers	Yes
Support services for students with	
LD	Yes
ADHD	Yes
ASD	Yes
Distraction-reduced environment	Yes
Recording of lecture allowed	Yes
Reading technology:	Yes
Audio books	Yes
Other assistive technology	FM System;
Specialized Software	
Priority registration	No
Added costs of services:	
For LD:	No
For ADHD:	No
For ASD:	No
LD specialists	No
ADHD & ASD coaching	Yes
ASD specialists	No
Professional tutors	Yes
Peer tutors	Yes
Max. hours/week for services	Varies
How professors are notified of student	
approved accommodations	Both

COLLEGE GRADUATION REQUIREMENTS

Course waivers allowed	Yes
In what courses Determined case by case.	
Course substitutions allowed	Yes
In what courses	
Determined case by case.	

Marshall University

ONE JOHN MARSHALL DRIVE, HUNTINGTON, WV 25755 • ADMISSIONS: 304-696-3160 • FAX: 304-696-3135

CAMPUS

Type of school	Public
Environment	Town
Support	SP

STUDENTS

Undergrad enrollment	8,554
% male/female	43/57
% from out of state	20

FINANCIAL FACTS

Annual in-state tuition	$6,676
Annual out-of-state tuition	$16,734
Room and board	$9,254
Required fees	$1,122

GENERAL ADMISSIONS INFO

Application fee	$40

Nonfall registration accepted. Admission may be deferred for a maximum of 1 year.

Range SAT EBRW	490–608
Range SAT Math	470–560
Range ACT Composite	19–25

ACADEMICS

Student/faculty ratio	19:1
% students returning for sophomore year	72
% students graduating within 4 years	29
% students graduating within 6 years	49

Most classes have 10–19 students.

PROGRAMS/SERVICES FOR STUDENTS WITH LEARNING DIFFERENCES

Higher Education for Learning Problems (H.E.L.P.) is a comprehensive and structured tutoring support program for college students who have a diagnosed Specific Learning Disability and/or Attention-deficit Disorder. Both academic and remedial tutoring is available. The academic tutoring is done by graduate assistants so that we have the expertise in the subject matter. The remedial tutoring is done by Learning Disabilities Specialists. Through the academic component, students receive tutoring in the classes they are taking as well as receiving the needed accommodations in testing. The remedial component addresses skills areas such as reading, written expression, math, study skills, time management and organizational skills. H.E.L.P. encourages a feeling of camaraderie among the students enrolled in the program. Students attend class with all other students at Marshall University and they must meet the same standards as all other students. The H.E.L.P. Program boasts a high success rate with students.

ADMISSIONS

Students must apply to both Marshall University and to the H.E.L.P. Program. Students applying to H.E.L.P. must have a diagnosed Specific Learning Disability and/or Attention-deficit Disorder. These students must submit: an application; updated psychological and educational evaluation; one-page, handwritten statement by the student (no assistance) regarding why college is desirable; and two recommendations stating why they feel the student should attend college. An interview with H.E.L.P. is required. It is best if students apply to H.E.L.P. at least six months in advance of the proposed entry date to college. There is a required 5-week summer HELP Program for incoming freshmen. Marshall University admission requires minimum GPA of 2.0, ACT 19, or SAT 910, plus 4 years English, 3 years social studies, 4 years math (including Algebra 1 and at least two higher units), and 3 years of laboratory science.

Additional Information

The Summer Prep Learning Disabilities Program is offered through H.E.L.P. for our incoming freshmen. Students take one Marshall

ADMISSIONS INFO FOR STUDENTS WITH LEARNING DIFFERENCES

SAT/ACT required: Yes
Interview required: Yes
Essay required: Required
Additional application required: Not Applicable
Documentation required for:
 LD: Psychoeducational testing with a diagnosis of ADHD and/or SLD. Testing must include an intelligence test given under adult norms and be no more than three years old. In addition, an individually administered educational evaluation assessing reading, math, and written language must be provided that is no older than one year. Provisional admission to College H.E.L.P. is possible pending updated testing.
 ADHD: Physician's statement.
 ASD: Psycho ed evaluation
Documentation submitted to: H.E.L.P. Program
Special Ed. HS course work accepted: Yes
Separate application required for program services: Yes
# of students last year receiving services/accommodations for:
 LD: 200
Contact Information
Name of program or department: H.E.L.P. Program (Higher Education for Learning Problems)
Telephone: 304-696-6252
Fax: 304-696-6252
Email: help@marshall.edu

Marshall University

University class in the morning for credit, and receive one hour of tutoring daily for that class. In the afternoons, the students attend three hours of College Prep. Students are assigned to three, one hour sessions based on their areas of greatest need. The areas covered are basic reading skills, reading comprehension, written expression, study skills and math. The program is taught by Learning Disabilities Specialists. Students are taught in small groups, generally with five to six students per group. The cost for the Summer Prep Program is $1,000 for West Virginia residents, $1,400 for Metro area residents, and $2,200 for non-West Virginia residents. This does not include registration for classes students take through the university or housing. Students sign a release allowing H.E.L.P. to talk to professors and parents. The College Program for Students with Autism Spectrum Disorder was established in 2002. Students participating in the program have met acceptance criteria for Marshall University and have been admitted to The College Program through a separate application process. The program uses a positive behavior support approach to assist participating students. Social, communication, academic, leisure and personal living skills are assessed through person-centered planning. Personal goals are identified and strategies are developed based on the individual needs of each student. The program seeks to help students learn skills which will help them earn a college degree, work in their chosen field, and live a productive, independent, and quality life. The program fee for The College Program is $4,500 per semester.

GENERAL ADMISSIONS

Very important factors considered include: academic GPA, standardized test scores. *Other factors considered include:* rigor of secondary school record. *Freshman Admission Requirements:* High school diploma is required and GED is accepted. *Academic units required: Academic units recommended:* 4 English, 4 math, 3 science, 3 science labs, 2 foreign language, 3 social studies, 1 visual/performing arts.

ACCOMMODATIONS OR SERVICES

Accommodations are decided upon an individual basis after a thorough review of appropriate, current documentation. The accommodations requests must be supported through the documentation provided and must be logically linked to the current impact of the condition on academic functioning.

FINANCIAL AID

Students should submit: FAFSA; State aid form. Applicants will be notified of awards on a rolling basis beginning 4/1. The Princeton Review suggests that all financial aid forms be submitted as soon as possible after October 1. *Need-based scholarships/grants offered:* College/university scholarship or grant aid from institutional funds; Federal Nursing Scholarships; Federal Pell; Private scholarships; SEOG; State scholarships/grants. *Loan aid offered:* Direct PLUS loans; Direct Subsidized Stafford Loans; Direct Unsubsidized Stafford Loans.

CAMPUS LIFE

Activities: Campus Ministries; Choral groups; Concert band; Dance; Drama/theater; International Student Organization; Jazz band; Literary magazine; Marching band; Model UN; Music ensembles; Musical theater; Opera; Pep band; Radio station; Student government; Student newspaper; Symphony orchestra; Television station. **Organizations:** 100 registered organizations, 11 honor societies, 10 religious organizations. 12 fraternities, 7 sororities. **Athletics (Intercollegiate):** *Men:* baseball, basketball, cross-country, football, golf, soccer, track/field (outdoor). *Women:* basketball, cross-country, golf, soccer, softball, swimming, tennis, track/field (outdoor), volleyball.

ACCOMMODATIONS

Allowed in exams:

Calculators	Yes
Dictionary	Not Applicable
Computer	Yes
Spell-checker	Yes
Extended test time	Yes
Scribe	Yes
Proctors	Yes
Oral exams	Yes
Note-takers	No

Support services for students with

LD	Yes
ADHD	Yes
ASD	Not Applicable
Distraction-reduced environment	Yes
Recording of lecture allowed	Yes
Reading technology:	Yes
Audio books	Yes
Other assistive technology	Kurzweil 3000
Ginger Software	
Priority registration	Yes

Added costs for services:

For LD:	No
For ADHD:	No
For ASD:	No
LD specialists	Yes
ADHD & ASD coaching	Yes
ASD specialists	No
Professional tutors	Yes
Peer tutors	No
Max. hours/week for services	Varies
How professors are notified of student approved accommodations	Director

COLLEGE GRADUATION REQUIREMENTS

Course waivers allowed	No
Course substitutions allowed	Yes
In what courses	Math, Foreign Language

West Virginia University

Presidents Office, Morgantown, WV 26506-6009 • Admissions: 304-293-2121 • Fax: 304-293-3080

CAMPUS

Type of school	Public
Environment	Town
Support	S

STUDENTS

Undergrad enrollment	21,705
% male/female	53/47
% from out of state	43
% frosh live on campus	85

FINANCIAL FACTS

Annual in-state tuition	$8,856
Annual out-of-state tuition	$24,950

GENERAL ADMISSIONS INFO

Application fee	$45
Priority deadline	3/1
Regular application deadline	8/1

Nonfall registration accepted. Admission may be deferred for a maximum of 1 year.

Range SAT EBRW	510-610
Range SAT Math	510-600
Range ACT Composite	21–27

ACADEMICS

Student/faculty ratio	
% students returning for sophomore year	80
% students graduating within 4 years	32
% students graduating within 6 years	57

Most classes have 20–29 students.
Most lab/discussion sessions have 20–29 students.

PROGRAMS/SERVICES FOR STUDENTS WITH LEARNING DIFFERENCES

The Office of Accessibility Services (OAS) is dedicated to enhancing the educational opportunities for students with temporary and permanent disabilities at West Virginia University (WVU) and all of its campuses. To ensure access to University programs, accessibility specialist work individually with students to help them achieve academic success. Academic Accommodations are only authorized for lecture, online and some lab type classes.

ADMISSIONS

There is no special admissions process for students with LD and ADHD. Students must meet admissions requirements. In-state students must have a 2.0 GPA and out-of-state students must have a 2.25 GPA and either a composite ACT of 20 or a combined SAT score of 950 to be considered for admission. Additionally, all applicants must have four years of English, three years of social studies, four years of math, three years of lab science, two years of same foreign language and one year of fine art. Students are not encouraged to self-disclose a disability in a personal statement during the application process. Appropriate services/accommodations will be determined after the student is admitted.

Additional Information

Requirements for the documentation of a LD include the following: a signed, dated comprehensive psychoeducational evaluation report indicating how the LD impacts academic performance and contributes to a "significant impairment" in academic functioning. The report should address Aptitude, Achievement, Processing, and should include the WAIS and full Woodcock-Johnson Battery. A description of the

ADMISSIONS INFO FOR STUDENTS WITH LEARNING DIFFERENCES

SAT/ACT required: Yes
Interview required: No
Essay required: Not Applicable
Additional application required: No
Documentation required for:
  LD: Comprehensive Psychoeducation report
  ADHD: Comprehensive evaluation report
  ASD: Comprehensive Psychoeducation evaluation report
Documentation submitted to: Accessibility Services
Special Ed. HS course work accepted: No
Separate application required for program services: Yes
# of students last year receiving services/accommodations for:
  LD: 500
Contact Information
Name of program or department: Accessibility Services
Telephone: 304-293-6700
Fax: 304-293-3861
Email: access2@mail.wvu.edu

West Virginia University

functional limitations, which impact against the educational effort, must be included in the diagnostic report. Additionally, a documented history of previous accommodations received should be included. Documentation of ADHD must be in the form of a signed and dated report, by either a psychiatrist, neuropsychologist or licensed psychologist trained in the differential diagnosis. Additional information is required. There are no LD specialists on staff; however, counselors are available to provide services to all students. Some accommodations that are available with appropriate documentation include: priority registration, extended testing time, note-takers, distraction-free environments, books on tape, and assistive technology.

GENERAL ADMISSIONS

Very important factors considered include: academic GPA, standardized test scores. *Important factors considered include:* rigor of secondary school record, state residency. *Other factors considered include:* extracurricular activities, talent/ability. *Freshman Admission Requirements:* High school diploma is required and GED is accepted. *Academic units required:* 4 English, 4 math, 3 science, 3 science labs, 2 foreign language, 3 social studies, 1 visual/performing arts.

ACCOMMODATIONS OR SERVICES

Accommodations are decided upon an individual basis after a thorough review of appropriate, current documentation. The accommodations requests must be supported through the documentation provided and must be logically linked to the current impact of the condition on academic functioning.

FINANCIAL AID

Students should submit: FAFSA. Applicants will be notified of awards on a rolling basis beginning 3/15. The Princeton Review suggests that all financial aid forms be submitted as soon as possible after October 1. *Need-based scholarships/grants offered:* College/university scholarship or grant aid from institutional funds; Federal Nursing Scholarships; Federal Pell; Private scholarships; SEOG; State scholarships/grants. *Loan aid offered:* Direct PLUS loans; Direct Subsidized Stafford Loans; Direct Unsubsidized Stafford Loans. Federal Work-Study Program available. Institutional employment available.

CAMPUS LIFE

Activities: Campus Ministries; Choral groups; Concert band; Dance; Drama/theater; International Student Organization; Jazz band; Literary magazine; Marching band; Model UN; Music ensembles; Musical theater; Pep band; Radio station; Student government; Student newspaper; Symphony orchestra. **Organizations:** 370 registered organizations, 31 honor societies, 28 religious organizations. 14 fraternities, 9 sororities. **Athletics (Intercollegiate):** *Men:* baseball, basketball, diving, football, riflery, soccer, swimming, wrestling. *Women:* basketball, crew/rowing, cross-country, diving, gymnastics, riflery, soccer, swimming, tennis, track/field (outdoor), track/field (indoor), volleyball. **On-Campus Highlights:** Student Recreation Center, Mountainlair (Student Union), Personal Rapid Transit (PRT), Mountaineer Field, Historic Woodburn Circle.

ACCOMMODATIONS

Allowed in exams:

Calculators	Yes
Dictionary	Yes
Computer	Yes
Spell-checker	Yes
Extended test time	Yes
Scribe	Yes
Proctors	Yes
Oral exams	Yes
Note-takers	Yes

Support services for students with

LD	Yes
ADHD	Yes
ASD	Yes
Distraction-reduced environment	Yes
Recording of lecture allowed	Yes
Reading technology:	Yes
Audio books	Yes

Other assistive technology Kurzwell, Dragon, Jaws, VRI, Remote transcribing, tape recorders, fm loops

Priority registration	Yes

Added costs for services:

For LD:	No
For ADHD:	No
For ASD:	No
LD specialists	Yes
ADHD & ASD coaching	No
ASD specialists	Yes
Professional tutors	Yes
Peer tutors	Yes
Max. hours/week for services	Varies

How professors are notified of student
approved accommodations   Student

COLLEGE GRADUATION REQUIREMENTS

Course waivers allowed	No
Course substitutions allowed	Yes
In what courses	Foreign Language

West Virginia Wesleyan College

59 College Avenue, Buckhannon, WV 26201 • Admissions: 304-473-8510 • Fax: 304-473-8108

CAMPUS
Type of school	Private (nonprofit)
Environment	Village
Support	SP

STUDENTS
Undergrad enrollment	1,304
% male/female	44/56
% from out of state	38
% frosh live on campus	90

FINANCIAL FACTS
Annual tuition	$28,574
Room and board	$8,248
Required fees	$1,178

GENERAL ADMISSIONS INFO
Application fee	$35
Priority deadline	2/1
Regular application deadline	8/15

Nonfall registration accepted. Admission may be deferred for a maximum of 1 year.

Range SAT EBRW	470–590
Range SAT Math	485–580
Range ACT Composite	19–25

ACADEMICS
Student/faculty ratio	13:1
% students returning for sophomore year	74
% students graduating within 4 years	38
% students graduating within 6 years	50

Most classes have 10–19 students.
Most lab/discussion sessions have 10–19 students.

PROGRAMS/SERVICES FOR STUDENTS WITH LEARNING DIFFERENCES

West Virginia Wesleyan College is strongly committed to providing excellent support to students with documented learning disabilities and attention difficulties. Our comprehensive program provides a solid foundational service delivered by master level professionals and two fee-based, optional programs assisting with the transition to college level academics. The Mentor Advantage Program provides an innovative, individualized support developed from research on the transition and persistence of post-secondary students with learning disabilities and from self-regulated learning theory. It is designed to create a bridge to academic regulation in the college environment. The program is composed of several elements: one-to-one professional organizational mentoring and academic strategic content tutoring, and Day-time and Evening Check-In. Taken together, the Day-Time and Evening Check-In provide 12.5 hours, each weekday, of study time in a quiet environment with access to a professional mentor. Students may enroll in the program as a package or sign up for various components separately, depending on the student need. In addition, Wesleyan offers an individualized clinical learning program that focuses on the improvement of reading skills and language comprehension. Although the program is not an official site certified and endorsed by Lindamood-Bell ®, students work with instructors who have been trained in Lindamood-Bell ® Learning Techniques. Consistent application with this approach will improve skills required for accurate decoding, quick word recognition, and comprehension for the increased volume of information facing today's college student. Test scores and improved academic performance have validated a record of success with our students.

ADMISSIONS INFO FOR STUDENTS WITH LEARNING DIFFERENCES
SAT/ACT required: Yes
Interview required: No
Essay required: Recommended
Additional application required: No
Documentation required for:
  LD: The Wechsler Adult Intelligence Scale or the Woodcock-Johnson Tests of Cognitive Ability plus the Woodcock Johnson Achievement Battery. All testing must be completed no more than 2 years prior to application. Both narrative and numeric reporting is necessary.
  ADHD: Psychological or medical documentation on professional letterhead describing the diagnosis, how the disability interferes with academic and everyday functioning, and recommendations for accommodations.
  ASD: Recent aptitude and achievement testing and a diagnosis by a licensed or school psychologist using the DSM-IV-TR/DSM-5 criteria for ASD. Also, a description of how the applicant's academic and everyday functioning is impacted by the disorder should be included in the evaluation.
Documentation submitted to: The Learning Center
Special Ed. HS course work accepted: Not Applicable
Separate application required for program services: No
# of students last year receiving services/accommodations for:
  LD: 40-45
Contact Information
Name of program or department: The Learning Center
Telephone: 304-473-8563
Fax: 304-473-8497

West Virginia Wesleyan College

ADMISSIONS

The Director of the Learning Center reviews and decides the application outcome of students who disclose a disability. Applicants are encouraged to submit a psychoeducational evaluation if they believe it will help develop an accurate picture of student potential.

Additional Information

West Virginia Wesleyan College provides excellent support programs to students with diagnosed learning disabilities, attention disorders, and other special needs. The heart of the program is the student relationship with the Comprehensive Advisor. Students work with their Comprehensive Advisor to cover the following areas: specialized academic advising; preferential preregistration for the first three semesters; implementation of accommodations to be used for college classes; development of academic, organizational, and self-monitoring strategies; discussion of priorities and motivational outlook; self-advocacy and social coaching, as needed; assistive technology lab with state-of-the-art software, test taking Lab including readers, scribes, and word-processing, as needed; and note takers, as needed. General Admissions

Very important factors considered include: rigor of secondary school record, academic GPA, talent/ability. *Important factors considered include:* class rank, standardized test scores, extracurricular activities, character/personal qualities, volunteer work, work experience, level of applicant's interest. *Other factors considered include:* application essay, recommendation(s), interview. *Freshman Admission Requirements:* High school diploma is required and GED is accepted. *Academic units required:* 4 English, 3 math, 3 science, 1 science lab, 3 social studies. *Academic units recommended:* 2 foreign language.

ACCOMMODATIONS OR SERVICES

Accommodations are decided upon an individual basis after a thorough review of appropriate, current documentation. The accommodations requests must be supported through the documentation provided and must be logically linked to the current impact of the condition on academic functioning.

FINANCIAL AID

Students should submit: FAFSA. Applicants will be notified of awards on a rolling basis beginning 3/1. The Princeton Review suggests that all financial aid forms be submitted as soon as possible after October 1. *Need-based scholarships/grants offered:* College/university scholarship or grant aid from institutional funds; Federal Nursing Scholarships; Federal Pell; Private scholarships; SEOG; State scholarships/grants. *Loan aid offered:* Direct PLUS loans; Direct Subsidized Stafford Loans; Direct Unsubsidized Stafford Loans. Federal Work-Study Program available. Institutional employment available.

CAMPUS LIFE

Activities: Campus Ministries; Choral groups; Concert band; Dance; Drama/theater; International Student Organization; Jazz band; Literary magazine; Marching band; Music ensembles; Musical theater; Opera; Pep band; Radio station; Student government; Student newspaper; Yearbook. **Organizations:** 75 registered organizations, 31 honor societies, 6 religious organizations, 6 fraternities, 5 sororities. **Athletics (Intercollegiate):** *Men:* baseball, basketball, cross-country, football, golf, soccer, softball, swimming, tennis, track/field (outdoor), track/field (indoor). *Women:* basketball, cross-country, golf, lacrosse, soccer, swimming, tennis, track/field (outdoor), track/field (indoor), volleyball. **On-Campus Highlights:** David E. Reemsnyder Research Center, Sunny Bucks (Convienence Store), Wesley Chapel, Sleeth Art Gallery, Virginia Thomas Law Center for the Performing Arts.

ACCOMMODATIONS

Allowed in exams:	
Calculators	Yes
Dictionary	Yes
Computer	Yes
Spell-checker	Yes
Extended test time	Yes
Scribe	Yes
Proctors	Yes
Oral exams	Yes
Note-takers	Yes
Support services for students with	
LD	Yes
ADHD	Yes
ASD	Yes
Distraction-reduced environment	Yes
Recording of lecture allowed	Yes
Reading technology:	Yes
Audio books	Yes
Other assistive technology	State of the art assistive technology
Priority registration	Yes
Added costs for services:	
For LD:	No
For ADHD:	No
For ASD:	No
LD specialists	Yes
ADHD & ASD coaching	Yes
ASD specialists	No
Professional tutors	Yes
Peer tutors	Yes
Max. hours/week for services	Varies
How professors are notified of student approved accommodations	Student

COLLEGE GRADUATION REQUIREMENTS

Course waivers allowed	No
In what courses	

There is no foreign language requirement. We have only one math requirement and a student can fill this with a college level Math for the Liberal Arts class.

Course substitutions allowed	Not Applicable
In what courses	

There is no foreign language requirement. We have only one math requirement and a student can fill this with a college level Math for the Liberal Arts class.

Alverno College

P.O. Box 343922, Milwaukee, WI 53234-3922 • Admissions: 414-382-6101 • Fax: 414-382-6055

CAMPUS
Type of school	Private (nonprofit)
Environment	Metropolis
Support	S

STUDENTS
Undergrad enrollment	1,283
% male/female	0/100
% from out of state	7
% frosh live on campus	37

FINANCIAL FACTS
Annual tuition	$27,552
Room and board	$8,546
Required fees	$750

GENERAL ADMISSIONS INFO
Nonfall registration accepted. Admission may be deferred for a maximum of 1 year.

Range ACT Composite	17–22

ACADEMICS
Student/faculty ratio	10:1
% students returning for sophomore year	71
% students graduating within 4 years	12
% students graduating within 6 years	45

Most classes have 20–29 students. Most lab/discussion sessions have 20–29 students.

PROGRAMS/SERVICES FOR STUDENTS WITH LEARNING DIFFERENCES
The Office for Student Accessibility supports students who have a physical, sensory, learning, and/or psychological disability that substantially limits a major life activity such as learning, communicating, walking, seeing, hearing, or breathing. Many of these disabilities are hidden or less visible, such as anxiety, depression, learning disabilities, arthritis, or other health impairments. The goal of Student Accessibility is to provide academic and physical access by accommodating the disability, promoting student independence and maximizing academic potential.

ADMISSIONS
Students need to provide appropriate documentation of a disability based on the following documentation guidelines: Must come from a licensed professional with their name, title, professional credentials, place of employment, address and phone number of the professional should be clearly stated in the documentation. It should be typed, printed on letterhead and signed. It should establish that you have a disability that substantially limits a major life activity. It should describe how the disability impacts your participation in campus activities and programs. It should recommend accommodations that are appropriate and effective and allow you equal access to campus activities and programs. All students must meet regular admission standards and submit the general application form.

ADMISSIONS INFO FOR STUDENTS WITH LEARNING DIFFERENCES
SAT/ACT required: No
Interview required: No
Essay required: No
Additional application required: Not Applicable
Documentation required for:
 LD: If the applicant wishes to access accommodations and services, ideally, in addition to a high school IEP, a current psychoeducational evaluation is provided from a relevant professional to assist the Coordinator to identify appropriate supports and accommodations to assist the student with her academic work.
 ADHD: No documentation is required for admissions, but if accommodations and services are requested, documentation from a relevant professional identifying a history of presenting attentional symptoms, including evidence of impulsive, hyperactive or inattentive behavior that has significantly impaired functioning over time.
 ASD: Psycho ed evaluation
Documentation submitted to: Student Accessibility
Special Ed. HS course work accepted: Not Applicable
Separate application required for program services: No
# of students last year receiving services/accommodations for:
 LD: 45
Contact Information
Name of program or department: Student Accessibility
Telephone: 414-382-6026
Fax: 414-382-6354

Alverno College

Additional Information

It's suggested that students contact the Coordinator for Student Accessibility at least one semester prior to admission; or immediately following diagnosis of a disability. Be prepared to provide written documentation to verify disability and to identify appropriate accommodations.

Contact local Vocational Rehabilitation office (and the Social Security Administration as appropriate) to seek possible funding for educational costs and for other disability-related services. Remember to Identify and observe all deadlines (e.g. admissions, housing, financial aid, disability services) and keep a record of all correspondence and documents relevant to your education.

GENERAL ADMISSIONS

Very important factors considered include: academic GPA, standardized test scores. *Important factors considered include:* rigor of secondary school record. *Other factors considered include:* application essay, recommendation(s), interview, extracurricular activities, talent/ability, character/personal qualities, volunteer work, work experience, level of applicant's interest. *Freshman Admission Requirements:* High school diploma is required and GED is accepted. *Academic units required:* 4 English, 3 math, 3 science, 3 social studies, 4 academic electives. *Academic units recommended:* 2 foreign language.

ACCOMMODATIONS OR SERVICES

Accommodations are decided upon an individual basis after a thorough review of appropriate, current documentation. The accommodations requests must be supported through the documentation provided and must be logically linked to the current impact of the condition on academic functioning.

FINANCIAL AID

Students should submit: FAFSA. Applicants will be notified of awards on a rolling basis beginning 11/1. The Princeton Review suggests that all financial aid forms be submitted as soon as possible after October 1. *Need-based scholarships/grants offered:* College/university scholarship or grant aid from institutional funds; Federal Pell; Private scholarships; SEOG; State scholarships/grants. *Loan aid offered:* Direct PLUS loans; Direct Subsidized Stafford Loans; Direct Unsubsidized Stafford Loans. Federal Work-Study Program available. Institutional employment available.

CAMPUS LIFE

Activities: Campus Ministries; Choral groups; Dance; Drama/theater; International Student Organization; Literary magazine; Model UN; Music ensembles; Radio station; Student government; Student newspaper. **Organizations:** 37 registered organizations, 1 honor society, 1 religious organization. 2 sororities. **Athletics (Intercollegiate):** *Women:* basketball, cross-country, soccer, softball, tennis, volleyball. **On-Campus Highlights:** Inferno Cafe, Alverno Library, Alexia Hall, Nursing Simulation Center, Galleria, LaVerna Commons.

ACCOMMODATIONS

Allowed in exams:	
Calculators	Yes
Dictionary	Yes
Computer	Yes
Spell-checker	Yes
Extended test time	Yes
Scribe	Yes
Proctors	Yes
Oral exams	Yes
Note-takers	Yes
Support services for students with	
LD	Yes
ADHD	Yes
ASD	Yes
Distraction-reduced environment	Yes
Recording of lecture allowed	Yes
Reading technology:	Yes
Audio books	Yes
Other assistive technology	
Priority registration	No
Added costs for services:	
For LD:	No
For ADHD:	No
For ASD:	No
LD specialists	No
ADHD & ASD coaching	No
ASD specialists	No
Professional tutors	No
Peer tutors	Yes
Max. hours/week for services	Varies
How professors are notified of student approved accommodations	
Director and student	

COLLEGE GRADUATION REQUIREMENTS

Course waivers allowed	No
Course substitutions allowed	No

Beloit College

700 College St., Beloit, WI 53511 • Admissions: 608-363-2500 • Fax: 608-363-2075

CAMPUS
Type of school	Private (nonprofit)
Environment	Town
Support	CS

STUDENTS
Undergrad enrollment	1,324
% male/female	48/52
% from out of state	85
% frosh live on campus	98

FINANCIAL FACTS
Annual tuition	$49,564
Room and board	$8,830
Required fees	$476

GENERAL ADMISSIONS INFO
Priority deadline	1/15

Nonfall registration accepted. Admission may be deferred for a maximum of 1 year.

Range SAT EBRW	510–650
Range SAT Math	530–660
Range ACT Composite	24–30

ACADEMICS
Student/faculty ratio	11:1
% students returning for sophomore year	85
% students graduating within 4 years	75
% students graduating within 6 years	86

Most classes have fewer than 10 students. Most lab/discussion sessions have fewer than 10 students.

PROGRAMS/SERVICES FOR STUDENTS WITH LEARNING DIFFERENCES

The Learning Enrichment and Disability Services office provides academic enrichment opportunities (i.e. tutoring, one- on-one assistance) and support for all Beloit College students. For students with documented disabilities, we ensure that appropriate accommodations are implemented while educating the campus community regarding disability related laws, issues and concerns. In addition, we work with students with academic challenges and concerns (i.e. alert slips, academic probation) to assist them in implementing appropriate strategies to achieve personal and academic success. To accomplish these goals, we collaborate with faculty, staff and students and operate with a philosophy of student self-advocacy.

ADMISSIONS

There is no special admissions procedure for students with learning disabilities. Each student is reviewed individually, and the final decision is made by the Office of Admissions. The college is competitive in admissions, but there are no absolute GPA or test scores. A minimum of sixteen academic courses are required for admission. Courses recommended include 4 years of English, 4 years of math, 3 years of laboratory science, 2 years of a foreign language, and 3 years of social science or history.

Additional Information

Beloit College Learning Enrichment and Disability Services offers additional resources to all students in the areas of tutoring (most courses, including math and science), reading strategies, study strategies, time management, study groups, advising, mentoring, as well as assistance with computer usage and assistive technology. Improvement of writing and research skills as well as personal counseling, career guidance, and crisis intervention are also available at the college. Individual assistance and small group workshops are offered each semester.

Summer Bridge:

The Summer Bridge program at Beloit College is an educational pre-college orientation program designed to provide a smooth and successful transition to college. Students develop personal, academic, and social skills necessary for college success. Students learn Beloit College standards and expectations. Complete assessments that will help set and achieve goals. The program creates a network of faculty, staff, and peer connections in a supportive environment.

ADMISSIONS INFO FOR STUDENTS WITH LEARNING DIFFERENCES

SAT/ACT required: No
Interview required: No
Essay required: Not Applicable
Additional application required: No
Documentation required for:
 LD: Information from an appropriate professional which indicates the impact of the LD on this student.
 ADHD: Information from an appropriate professional which indicates the impact of the ADHD on this student.
 ASD: Psycho ed evaluation
Documentation submitted to: The Learning Enrichment and Disability Services Office
Special Ed. HS course work accepted: Yes
Contact Information
Name of program or department: The Learning Enrichment and Disability Services Office
Telephone: 608-363-2572
Fax: 608-363-7059

Beloit College

GENERAL ADMISSIONS

Very important factors considered include: rigor of secondary school record, academic GPA, application essay, recommendation(s). *Important factors considered include:* class rank, extracurricular activities, talent/ability. *Other factors considered include:* standardized test scores, interview, character/personal qualities, first generation, alumni/ae relation, racial/ethnic status, volunteer work, work experience. *Freshman Admission Requirements:* High school diploma is required and GED is accepted. *Academic units recommended:* 4 English, 3 math, 3 science, 3 science labs, 2 foreign language, 3 social studies.

ACCOMMODATIONS OR SERVICES

Accommodations are decided upon an individual basis after a thorough review of appropriate, current documentation. The accommodations requests must be supported through the documentation provided and must be logically linked to the current impact of the condition on academic functioning.

FINANCIAL AID

Students should submit: FAFSA. The Princeton Review suggests that all financial aid forms be submitted as soon as possible after October 1. *Need-based scholarships/grants offered:* College/university scholarship or grant aid from institutional funds; Federal Pell; Private scholarships; SEOG; State scholarships/grants. *Loan aid offered:* Direct PLUS loans; Direct Subsidized Stafford Loans; Direct Unsubsidized Stafford Loans. Federal Work-Study Program available. Institutional employment available.

CAMPUS LIFE

Activities: Campus Ministries; Choral groups; Dance; Drama/theater; International Student Organization; Jazz band; Literary magazine; Model UN; Music ensembles; Musical theater; Radio station; Student government; Student newspaper; Television station. **Organizations:** 95 registered organizations, 6 honor societies, 3 religious organizations. 3 fraternities, 3 sororities. **Athletics (Intercollegiate):** *Men:* baseball, basketball, cross-country, football, golf, soccer, swimming, tennis, track/field (outdoor), track/field (indoor). *Women:* basketball, cross-country, soccer, softball, swimming, tennis, track/field (outdoor), track/field (indoor), volleyball. **On-Campus Highlights:** Logan Museum of Anthropology, Wright Museum of Art, Center for the Sciences, Hendricks Center for the Performing Arts, Laura H. Idrich Neese Theatre Complex.

ACCOMMODATIONS

Allowed in exams:	
Calculators	Yes
Dictionary	No
Computer	Yes
Spell-checker	No
Extended test time	Yes
Scribe	No
Proctors	No
Oral exams	No
Note-takers	No
Support services for students with	
LD	Yes
ADHD	Yes
ASD	Yes
Distraction-reduced environment	No
Recording of lecture allowed	No
Reading technology:	Yes
Audio books	Yes
Other assistive technology	
Accommodations are provided on an individual basics	
Priority registration	Yes
Added costs for services:	
For LD:	No
For ADHD:	No
For ASD:	No
LD specialists	No
ADHD & ASD coaching	No
ASD specialists	Yes
Professional tutors	Yes
Peer tutors	Yes
Max. hours/week for services	Varies
How professors are notified of student approved accommodations	Student

COLLEGE GRADUATION REQUIREMENTS

Course waivers allowed	Not Applicable
In what courses	Students do not receive waivers, but substitutions are considered on an individual basis.
Course substitutions allowed	Yes
In what courses	Substitutions are considered on an individual basis. They depend on the impact of the disability.

Edgewood College

1000 EDGEWOOD COLLEGE DRIVE, MADISON, WI 53711-1997 • ADMISSIONS: 608-663-2294 • FAX: 608-663-2214

CAMPUS
Type of school	Private (nonprofit)
Environment	City
Support	S

STUDENTS
Undergrad enrollment	1,521
% male/female	27/73
% from out of state	8
% frosh live on campus	85

FINANCIAL FACTS
Annual tuition	$29,500
Room and board	$11,020

GENERAL ADMISSIONS INFO
Application fee	$30
Priority deadline	3/1
Regular application deadline	8/15

Nonfall registration accepted. Admission may be deferred for a maximum of 1 year.

Range SAT EBRW	550–590
Range SAT Math	510–630
Range ACT Composite	21–25

ACADEMICS
Student/faculty ratio	9:1
% students returning for sophomore year	78
% students graduating within 4 years	38
% students graduating within 6 years	61

Most classes have 10–19 students.
Most lab/discussion sessions have fewer than 10 students.

PROGRAMS/SERVICES FOR STUDENTS WITH LEARNING DIFFERENCES
Sponsored by the Sinsinawa Dominicans, Edgewood College is a community of learners that affirms both its Catholic heritage and its respect for other religious traditions. The liberal arts are the foundation of all our curricular offerings in the humanities, arts, sciences, and professional programs. Committed to excellence in teaching and learning, we seek to develop intellect, spirit, imagination, and heart. We welcome women and men who reflect the rich diversity of the world's cultures and perspectives. We foster open, caring, thoughtful engagement with one another and an enduring commitment to service, all in an educational community that seeks truth, compassion, justice and partnership.

ADMISSIONS
Candidates for the Cutting-Edge program are encouraged to begin the admissions process a year in advance. To be considered for the program, the student and family are encouraged to submit all application materials by December.

Additional Information
The Cutting Edge is an individualized approach to education and inclusion in college for students with intellectual developmental disabilities. These are individuals who have either traditionally not been able to meet the standard admissions criteria for college, or require additional supports in order to be successful in college. Edgewood College is the first four-year college in Wisconsin to offer such a program to students who have intellectual developmental disabilities.

ADMISSIONS INFO FOR STUDENTS WITH LEARNING DIFFERENCES
SAT/ACT required: Yes
Interview required: No
Essay required: Not Applicable
Additional application required: Yes
Documentation required for:
  LD: Woodcock-Johnson –III Test of Cognitive Ability, Wechsler Adult Intelligence Scale –IV (WAIS-IV)
  ADHD: Brown Attention Deficit Disorder Scale, Kaufman Adolescent and Adult Intelligence Test
  ASD: Diagnostic and Statistical Manual of Mental Disorders (DSM-5)
Documentation submitted to: Student Accessibility and Disability
Special Ed. HS course work accepted: Yes
Separate application required for program services: No with the exception of the Cutting Edge Program.
Contact Information
Name of program or department: Student Accessibility and Disability Services
Telephone: (608) 663-8347
Fax: (608) 663-2278

Edgewood College

General Admissions

Very important factors considered include: class rank, academic GPA, standardized test scores. *Other factors considered include:* application essay, recommendation(s). *Freshman Admission Requirements:* High school diploma is required and GED is accepted. *Academic units required:* 4 English, 2 math, 2 science, 1 science lab, 2 foreign language, 2 social studies, 1 history. *Academic units recommended:* 4 English, 2 math, 2 science, 1 science lab, 2 foreign language, 2 social studies, 1 history.

Accommodations or Services

Accommodations are decided upon an individual basis after a thorough review of appropriate, current documentation. The accommodations requests must be supported through the documentation provided and must be logically linked to the current impact of the condition on academic functioning.

Financial Aid

Students should submit: FAFSA. Applicants will be notified of awards on a rolling basis beginning 12/15. The Princeton Review suggests that all financial aid forms be submitted as soon as possible after October 1. *Need-based scholarships/grants offered:* College/university scholarship or grant aid from institutional funds; Federal Pell; Private scholarships; SEOG; State scholarships/grants. *Loan aid offered:* Direct PLUS loans; Direct Subsidized Stafford Loans; Direct Unsubsidized Stafford Loans. Federal Work-Study Program available. Institutional employment available.

Campus Life

Activities: Campus Ministries; Choral groups; Concert band; Dance; Drama/theater; International Student Organization; Jazz band; Literary magazine; Model UN; Music ensembles; Musical theater; Student government; Student newspaper; Symphony orchestra. **Organizations:** 45 registered organizations, 4 honor societies, 1 religious organization. **Athletics (Intercollegiate):** *Men:* baseball, basketball, cross-country, golf, soccer, tennis, track/field (outdoor), track/field (indoor). *Women:* basketball, cross-country, golf, soccer, softball, tennis, track/field (outdoor), track/field (indoor), volleyball. **On-Campus Highlights:** Wingra Cafe, Commons, Phil's, Lake Wingra Boardwalk, The Stream, Sonderegger Science Center.

ACCOMMODATIONS

Allowed in exams:

Calculators	Yes
Dictionary	Yes
Computer	Yes
Spell-checker	Yes
Extended test time	Yes
Scribe	Yes
Proctors	Yes
Oral exams	Yes
Note-takers	Yes

Support services for students with

LD	Yes
ADHD	Yes
ASD	Yes
Distraction-reduced environment	Yes
Recording of lecture allowed	Yes
Reading technology:	Yes
Audio books	Yes
Other assistive technology	Smart Pens, tape recorders, Ipads, etc
Priority registration	Yes

Added costs for services:

For LD:	No
For ADHD:	No
For ASD:	No
LD specialists	No
ADHD & ASD coaching	Yes
ASD specialists	No
Professional tutors	Yes
Peer tutors	Yes
Max. hours/week for services	Varies
How professors are notified of student approved accommodations	Director and student

COLLEGE GRADUATION REQUIREMENTS

Course waivers allowed	No
Course substitutions allowed	Yes
In what courses	Foreign Language

Marian University

45 South National Avenue, Fond du Lac, WI 54935 • Admissions: 920-923-7650 • Fax: 920-923-8755

CAMPUS
Type of school	Private (nonprofit)
Environment	Town
Support	S

STUDENTS
Undergrad enrollment	1,903
% male/female	25/75
% from out of state	7
% frosh live on campus	72

FINANCIAL FACTS
Annual tuition	$19,590
Room and board	$5,380
Required fees	$350

GENERAL ADMISSIONS INFO
Application fee	$20
Priority deadline	4/1

Nonfall registration accepted. Admission may be deferred.

Range SAT EBRW	490-530
Range SAT Math 4	90-540
Range ACT Composite	17–22

ACADEMICS
Student/faculty ratio	12:1
% students returning for sophomore year	71
% students graduating within 4 years	31
% students graduating within 6 years	48

Most classes have 10–19 students.

PROGRAMS/SERVICES FOR STUDENTS WITH LEARNING DIFFERENCES
Marian University is committed to providing equal educational opportunities to students with learning disabilities and/or ADD/ADHD. The Coordinator for Disability Services and Academic Support is housed in the Center for Academic Support and Excellence, (CASE) Office. The Coordinator for Disability Services and Academic Support is dedicated to providing personal and academic support to students with disabilities from freshman year to graduation.

ADMISSIONS
There is no special application or admissions procedure for students with learning disabilities. Admission criteria include a 2.0 GPA, a class rank within top 50 percent, and an ACT score of 18. All students, not just those with LD, are asked to meet two-thirds of these criteria. Students who do not meet two-thirds may be admitted on probation through a program called EXCEL. Students will be asked to submit 3 letters of recommendation supporting their ability to succeed in college-level course work. Students also may be asked to schedule a visit to Marian for a pre-admission interview during which their skills, attitudes, motivation, and self-understanding will be informally assessed. Students admitted provisionally may be admitted with limited credit status and may be required to take a freshman seminar course. Special education course work is accepted, but students are encouraged to be fully mainstreamed by senior year with minimal monitoring. Students who self-disclose their disability are given information on services available through the Center for Academic Support and Excellence (CASE) office.

Additional Information
Disability Services offers the following services and accommodations to students who disclose a disability and submit appropriate documentation: notetakers, audio books, audio players, scan and read software, distraction-free test environments, extended exam times, and test readers/scribes. The following support is also provided: organizational and study skills training, liaison with instructors/advisors, consultation, advocacy, referrals, and

ADMISSIONS INFO FOR STUDENTS WITH LEARNING DIFFERENCES
SAT/ACT required: Yes
Interview required: No
Essay required: No
Additional application required: No
Documentation required for:
 LD: Psycho ed evaluation to include: relevant historical info, instructional interventions, related services, age diagnosed, objective data (aptitude, achievement, info processing), test scores (standard, percentile and grade equivalents) and describe functional limitations.
 ADHD: Diagnosis based on DSM-V; history of behaviors impairing functioning in academic setting; diagnostic interview; history of symptoms; evidence of ongoing behaviors.
 ASD: Psycho ed evaluation
Documentation submitted to: Disability Services
Special Ed. HS course work accepted: No
Separate application required for program services: No
Contact Information
Name of program or department: Disability Services
Telephone: 920-923-8951
Fax: 920-923-8135

Marian University

resource materials. The peer tutoring program helps students gain the confidence and skills necessary to successfully complete course work. Other services include information on community, state, and national resources, and course scheduling. Calculators are allowed in exams for students with a documented disability in math. Assistance is determined for each individual based on assessment. All students have access to the tutoring program, and the Learning and Writing Center. Services are available for undergraduate and graduate students. The EXCEL Program provides freshman with support as they transition to the college environment. The program offers smaller class sizes and encouragement and exposure to campus resources and services. To participate in the program, students must attend the EXCEL Summer Bridge Program and meet with an academic advisor bi-weekly. All first-year students are also assigned a Student Mentor to help them get acclimated.

GENERAL ADMISSIONS

Very important factors considered include: rigor of secondary school record, class rank, academic GPA, standardized test scores. *Important factors considered include:* interview, character/personal qualities, level of applicant's interest. *Other factors considered include:* application essay, recommendation(s), extracurricular activities, talent/ability, alumni/ae relation, volunteer work, work experience. *Freshman Admission Requirements:* High school diploma is required and GED is accepted. *Academic units required:* 4 English, 2 math, 1 science, 1 science lab, 1 history. *Academic units recommended:* 3 math, 2 science, 2 foreign language.

ACCOMMODATIONS OR SERVICES

Accommodations are decided upon an individual basis after a thorough review of appropriate, current documentation. The accommodations requests must be supported through the documentation provided and must be logically linked to the current impact of the condition on academic functioning.

FINANCIAL AID

Students should submit: FAFSA; Institution's own financial aid form. Applicants will be notified of awards on a rolling basis beginning 3/1. The Princeton Review suggests that all financial aid forms be submitted as soon as possible after October 1. *Need-based scholarships/grants offered:* College/university scholarship or grant aid from institutional funds; Federal Pell; Private scholarships; SEOG; State scholarships/grants. *Loan aid offered:* Federal Work-Study Program available. Institutional employment available.

CAMPUS LIFE

Activities: Campus Ministries; Choral groups; Concert band; Dance; Drama/theater; Jazz band; Literary magazine; Model UN; Music ensembles; Pep band; Student government; Student newspaper; Symphony orchestra. **Organizations:** 40 registered organizations, 6 honor societies, 1 religious organization. 1 fraternity, 2 sororities. **Athletics (Intercollegiate):** *Men:* baseball, basketball, cross-country, golf, ice hockey, soccer, tennis. *Women:* basketball, cross-country, golf, ice hockey, soccer, softball, tennis, volleyball. **On-Campus Highlights:** Housing, Coffee House, Student Center, Stayer Center, Library and Academic buildings.

ACCOMMODATIONS

Allowed in exams:	
Calculators	Yes
Dictionary	No
Computer	Yes
Spell-checker	Yes
Extended test time	Yes
Scribe	Yes
Proctors	Yes
Oral exams	Yes
Note-takers	Yes
Support services for students with	
LD	Yes
ADHD	Yes
ASD	Yes
Distraction-reduced environment	Yes
Recording of lecture allowed	Yes
Reading technology:	Yes
Audio books	Yes
Other assistive technology	Yes
Priority registration	Yes
Added costs for services:	
For LD:	No
For ADHD:	No
For ASD:	No
LD specialists	No
ADHD & ASD coaching	Yes
ASD specialists	No
Professional tutors	Yes
Peer tutors	Yes
Max. hours/week for services	Unlimited
How professors are notified of student approved accommodations	By coordinator of Disability Services

COLLEGE GRADUATION REQUIREMENTS

Course waivers allowed	No
Course substitutions allowed	Yes
In what courses:	Foreign language. Students must attempt required course.

Marquette University

P.O. Box 1881, Milwaukee, WI 53201-1881 • Admissions: 414-288-7302 • Fax: 414-288-3764

CAMPUS

Type of school	Private (nonprofit)
Environment	Metropolis
Support	S

STUDENTS

Undergrad enrollment	8,093
% male/female	47/53
% from out of state	69
% frosh live on campus	95

FINANCIAL FACTS

Annual tuition	$41,290
Room and board	$11,890
Required fees	$580

GENERAL ADMISSIONS INFO

Priority deadline	12/1
Regular application deadline	12/1

Nonfall registration accepted. Admission may be deferred for a maximum of 1 semester.

Range SAT EBRW	570–660
Range SAT Math	560–650
Range ACT Composite	24–29

ACADEMICS

Student/faculty ratio	14:1
% students returning for sophomore year	89
% students graduating within 4 years	89
% students graduating within 6 years	81

Most classes have 10–19 students.
Most lab/discussion sessions have 10–19 students.

PROGRAMS/SERVICES FOR STUDENTS WITH LEARNING DIFFERENCES

The Office of Disability Services (ODS) is the designated office at Marquette University to coordinate accommodations for all students with identified and documented disabilities. Accommodations are determined on a case-by-case basis, but the student must seek assistance prior to the need for accommodation. Relevant documentation from an appropriate licensed professional that gives a diagnosis of the disability and how it impacts on participation in courses, programs, jobs, activities and facilities at Marquette is required. The student and a staff member from ODS will discuss the student's disability and how it will impact on the requirements of the student's courses. Based upon this evaluation the ODS Coordinator provides a range of individualized accommodations.

ADMISSIONS

There is no special admissions process for students with LD and ADD. All applicants for admission must meet the same admission criteria. Marquette requires applicants to have 4 years of English, 2-4 years of math and science, 2 -3 years of social studies.

Additional Information

ODS provides a number of accommodations for students with LD and AD/HD including texts in alternate formats and alternative testing arrangements. If a student's disability requires a backup note taker, ODS assists students in locating or hiring note taker. Other methods of acquiring class material may include use of a tape recorder in class, and photocopying class notes or copies of lecture notes. Advance notice of assignments, alternative ways of completing an assignment, computer technology, taped textbooks and course or program modifications are also available. To assist students with reading-related disabilities, the Kurzweil Omni 3000 Education System is available. Students also have access to the campus Writing Center, tutors and general study skills assistance from the Office of Student Educational Services.

ADMISSIONS INFO FOR STUDENTS WITH LEARNING DIFFERENCES

SAT/ACT required: Yes
Interview required: No
Essay required: Not Applicable
Additional application required: Not Applicable
Documentation required for:
  LD: Psychoeducational Evaluation
  ADHD: Documentation completed by psychologist or psychiatrist that includes diagnosis, functional limitations, and accommodation suggestions.
  ASD: Documentation completed by psychologist or psychiatrist that includes diagnosis, functional limitations, and accommodation suggestions.
Documentation submitted to: Support Program/Services
Special Ed. HS course work accepted: Not Applicable
Separate application required for program services: No
Contact Information
Name of program or department: Office of Disability Services
Telephone: 414-288-1645
Fax: 414-288-5799
Email: ods@marquette.edu

Marquette University

General Admissions

Very important factors considered include: rigor of secondary school record, academic GPA. *Important factors considered include:* application essay, standardized test scores, extracurricular activities, volunteer work. *Other factors considered include:* class rank, recommendation(s), talent/ability, character/personal qualities, first generation, alumni/ae relation, racial/ethnic status, work experience. *Freshman Admission Requirements:* High school diploma is required and GED is accepted. *Academic units required:* 4 English, 2 math, 2 science, 2 science labs, 2 social studies, 2 academic electives. *Academic units recommended:* 4 English, 4 math, 4 science, 3 science labs, 2 foreign language, 3 social studies, 2 history, 5 academic electives.

Accommodations or Services

Accommodations are decided upon an individual basis after a thorough review of appropriate, current documentation. The accommodations requests must be supported through the documentation provided and must be logically linked to the current impact of the condition on academic functioning.

Financial Aid

Students should submit: FAFSA. Applicants will be notified of awards on a rolling basis beginning 1/9. The Princeton Review suggests that all financial aid forms be submitted as soon as possible after October 1. *Need-based scholarships/grants offered:* College/university scholarship or grant aid from institutional funds; Federal Pell; Private scholarships; SEOG; State scholarships/grants. *Loan aid offered:* Direct PLUS loans; Direct Subsidized Stafford Loans; Direct Unsubsidized Stafford Loans. Federal Work-Study Program available. Institutional employment available.

Campus Life

Activities: Campus Ministries; Choral groups; Concert band; Dance; Drama/theater; International Student Organization; Jazz band; Literary magazine; Model UN; Music ensembles; Musical theater; Pep band; Radio station; Student government; Student newspaper; Symphony orchestra; Television station; Yearbook. **Organizations:** 230 registered organizations, 21 honor societies, 11 religious organizations. 11 fraternities, 11 sororities. **Athletics (Intercollegiate):** *Men:* basketball, cheerleading, cross-country, golf, soccer, tennis, track/field (outdoor), track/field (indoor). *Women:* basketball, cheerleading, cross-country, soccer, tennis, track/field (outdoor), track/field (indoor), volleyball. **On-Campus Highlights:** The Raynor Memorial Library and the Law, Gesu Church, Haggerty Museum of Art, Al McGuire Center, Helfaer Recreation Center.

ACCOMMODATIONS

Allowed in exams:

Calculators	Yes
Dictionary	Yes
Computer	Yes
Spell-checker	Yes
Extended test time	Yes
Scribe	Yes
Proctors	Yes
Oral exams	Yes
Note-takers	Yes

Support services for students with

LD	Yes
ADHD	Yes
ASD	Yes
Distraction-reduced environment	Yes
Recording of lecture allowed	Yes
Reading technology:	Yes
Audio books	Yes

Other assistive technology   All of the above services depend on the student's documented disability and the class learning objectives

Priority registration	Yes

Added costs for services:

For LD:	No
For ADHD:	No
For ASD:	No
LD specialists	No
ADHD & ASD coaching	No
ASD specialists	No
Professional tutors	Yes
Peer tutors	Yes
Max. hours/week for services	1
How professors are notified of student approved accommodations	Student

COLLEGE GRADUATION REQUIREMENTS

Course waivers allowed	No
Course substitutions allowed	Yes

In what courses
Foreign language, math. Depends on the diagnosis.

Ripon College

PO Box 248, Ripon, WI 54971 • Admissions: 920-748-8337 • Fax: 920-748-8335

CAMPUS

Type of school	Private (nonprofit)
Environment	Village
Support	S

STUDENTS

Undergrad enrollment	740
% male/female	46/54
% from out of state	30
% frosh live on campus	98

FINANCIAL FACTS

Annual tuition	$43,508
Room and board	$8,400
Required fees	$300

GENERAL ADMISSIONS INFO

Application fee	$30
Priority deadline	3/15

Nonfall registration accepted. Admission may be deferred for a maximum of 1 year.

Range SAT EBRW	520–610
Range SAT Math	520–650
Range ACT Composite	20–26

ACADEMICS

Student/faculty ratio	14:1
% students returning for sophomore year	71
% students graduating within 4 years	62
% students graduating within 6 years	68

Most classes have 10–19 students.

PROGRAMS/SERVICES FOR STUDENTS WITH LEARNING DIFFERENCES

The Student Support Services (SSS) provides a wide variety of services on the campus, including academic and personal counseling, study skills information, and tutoring. Although the focus of the program is on first generation students, students of higher need, and students who are learning disabled, other students who feel they might qualify are encouraged to contact the SSS office. SSS is a voluntary program that has been in existence at Ripon College since 1974. For the many students who have used its services, SSS has provided a network of support for academic, financial, and personal concerns. A group of peer contacts serves SSS by meeting regularly with students to facilitate communication between SSS participants and the office staff. For students who qualify, SSS offers free tutoring in specific subject areas. (All campus tutoring is also available.) The tutors are upperclass students who have been recommended by their professors and trained by the SSS staff. These tutors serve as a supplement to faculty assistance. The aim of the tutoring program is to help students develop independent learning skills and improve their course grades. Although federal guidelines require a restriction on who "qualifies," the door to SSS remains open to all eligible students.

ADMISSIONS

Students with learning disabilities are screened by admissions and must meet the same admission criteria as all other applicants. There is no set GPA required; courses required include four years English, algebra and geometry, two years natural science, two years social studies, and seven additional units. Students with learning disabilities who self-disclose are referred to Student Support Services when making prospective visits to the campus in order to ascertain specific needs and abilities of the student.

Additional Information

SSS provides tutoring in subject areas; skills classes for no credit in time management, note-taking, test-taking strategies, reading college texts,

ADMISSIONS INFO FOR STUDENTS WITH LEARNING DIFFERENCES

SAT/ACT required: Yes
Interview required: Yes
Essay required: No
Additional application required: No
Documentation required for:
 LD: Psycho ed evaluation to include: relevant historical info, instructional interventions, related services, age diagnosed, objective data (aptitude, achievement, info processing), test scores (standard, percentile and grade equivalents) and describe functional limitations.
 ADHD: Diagnosis based on DSM-V; history of behaviors impairing functioning in academic setting; diagnostic interview; history of symptoms; evidence of ongoing behaviors.
 ASD: Psycho ed evaluation
Documentation submitted to: Student Support Services
Special Ed. HS course work accepted: No
Separate application required for program services: No
# of students last year receiving services/accommodations for:
 LD: 10
Contact Information
Name of program or department: Student Support Services
Telephone: 920-748-8107
Fax: 920-748-8382

Ripon College

writing papers, studying for and taking exams, and setting goals; and counseling/guidance. Student Support Services provides intensive study groups, LD support and internships. SSS provides students with peer contacts who provide students with one-on-one support and is useful in helping students adjust to college life, to provide a contact for the student to go to with problems or issues, organize group tutoring, and to help students open their minds and see hope in their future.

General Admissions

Very important factors considered include: rigor of secondary school record, interview. *Important factors considered include:* class rank, academic GPA, extracurricular activities, character/personal qualities. *Other factors considered include:* application essay, standardized test scores, recommendation(s), talent/ability, volunteer work. *Freshman Admission Requirements:* High school diploma is required and GED is accepted. *Academic units required:* 4 English, 2 math, 2 science, 2 social studies. *Academic units recommended:* 4 math, 4 science, 2 foreign language, 4 social studies.

Accommodations or Services

Accommodations are decided upon an individual basis after a thorough review of appropriate, current documentation. The accommodations requests must be supported through the documentation provided and must be logically linked to the current impact of the condition on academic functioning.

Financial Aid

Students should submit: FAFSA. Applicants will be notified of awards on a rolling basis beginning 3/1. The Princeton Review suggests that all financial aid forms be submitted as soon as possible after October 1. *Need-based scholarships/grants offered:* College/university scholarship or grant aid from institutional funds; Federal Pell; Private scholarships; SEOG; State scholarships/grants. *Loan aid offered:* Direct PLUS loans; Direct Subsidized Stafford Loans; Direct Unsubsidized Stafford Loans. Federal Work-Study Program available. Institutional employment available.

Campus Life

Activities: Campus Ministries; Choral groups; Concert band; Dance; Drama/theater; International Student Organization; Jazz band; Literary magazine; Music ensembles; Musical theater; Pep band; Radio station; Student government; Student newspaper; Student-run film society; Symphony orchestra; Television station; Yearbook. **Organizations:** 45 registered organizations, 13 honor societies, 2 religious organizations. 5 fraternities, 3 sororities. **Athletics (Intercollegiate):** *Men:* baseball, basketball, cross-country, cycling, football, golf, soccer, swimming, tennis, track/field (outdoor), track/field (indoor). *Women:* basketball, cross-country, cycling, golf, soccer, softball, swimming, tennis, track/field (outdoor), track/field (indoor), volleyball. **On-Campus Highlights:** Ceresco Prairie Conservancy, Caestecker Art Gallery, Great Hall, Willmore Center, Lounge and Starbucks Coffee.

ACCOMMODATIONS

Allowed in exams:

Calculators	Yes
Dictionary	No
Computer	Yes
Spell-checker	Yes
Extended test time	Yes
Scribe	Yes
Proctors	Yes
Oral exams	Yes
Note-takers	Yes

Support services for students with

LD	Yes
ADHD	Yes
ASD	Yes
Distraction-reduced environment	Yes
Recording of lecture allowed	Yes
Reading technology:	Yes
Audio books	Yes
Other assistive technology	

Interactive computer technology speech recognition and Kurzweil Reading technology

Priority registration	No

Added costs for services:

For LD:	No
LD specialists	No
ADHD & ASD coaching	No
ASD specialists	No
Professional tutors	No
Peer tutors	Yes
Max. hours/week for services	3hrs/week/class

How professors are notified of student approved accommodations
Both student and director

COLLEGE GRADUATION REQUIREMENTS

Course waivers allowed	No
Course substitutions allowed	No

University of Wisconsin—Eau Claire

105 GARFIELD AVENUE, EAU CLAIRE, WI 54701 • ADMISSIONS: 715-836-5415 • FAX: 715-831-4799

CAMPUS

Type of school	Public
Environment	City
Support	CS

STUDENTS

Undergrad enrollment	9,905
% male/female	39/61
% from out of state	30
% frosh live on campus	94

FINANCIAL FACTS

Annual in-state tuition	$7,361
Annual out-of-state tuition	$15,637
Room and board	$7,813
Required fees	$1,459

GENERAL ADMISSIONS INFO

Application fee	$50
Priority deadline	12/1
Regular application deadline	8/20

Nonfall registration accepted.

Range SAT EBRW	510–640
Range SAT Math	530–650
Range ACT Composite	21–26

ACADEMICS

Student/faculty ratio	22:1
% students returning for sophomore year	82
% students graduating within 4 years	34
% students graduating within 6 years	67

Most classes have 20–29 students.
Most lab/discussion sessions have 20–29 students.

PROGRAMS/SERVICES FOR STUDENTS WITH LEARNING DIFFERENCES

The University of Wisconsin—Eau Claire is committed to providing all students with an equal opportunity to fully participate in all aspects of the university community. Services for Students with Disabilities will work with students, faculty, staff, and community partners in a cooperative manner to review policies and procedures and to facilitate the provision of services and accommodations that will ensure that university facilities, programs, and activities are universally accessible.

ADMISSIONS

Individuals with disabilities must complete the standard university application form. Applicants should carefully review the university's published admission criteria, including math and foreign language requirements. If an applicant with a disability wishes to request an exception to any admission requirements, s/he must: 1) include with the application a letter requesting the exception and explaining the rationale for the request, and 2) submit to the Services for Students with Disabilities Office appropriate documentation establishing both the existence of a disability and a resulting need for the exception being requested. Any information regarding a disability is treated as confidential information as defined by the Family and Educational Rights and Privacy Act (FERPA) at: http://www.ed.gov/offices/OII/fpco/ferpa/.

ADMISSIONS INFO FOR STUDENTS WITH LEARNING DIFFERENCES

SAT/ACT required: Yes
Interview required: Not Applicable
Essay required: Not Applicable
Additional application required: Yes
Documentation required for:
 LD: Copies of neuropsychological, psychoeducational and learning disabilities specialist reports, with names, titles and license numbers of the evaluators and dates of testing. Subtest and Standard Scores from assessments such as Wechsler Adult Intelligence Scale, Stanford-Binet Tests, Woodcock-Johnson, Kaufman, Scholastic Abilities Tests, Stanford tests, learning aptitude tests, and tests recommended by ETS and AHEAD.
 ADHD: A clear diagnostic statement with information on the severity of the condition and the resulting impact on a major life activity, completed by a licensed physician, psychologist, or credentialed professional with no personal relationship with the client. Copies of neuro-psychological and psycho-educational testing, rating scales, aptitude and cognitive ability testing, and individual educational plans based on approved state department of education criteria.
 ASD: Diagnosis or diagnostic statement from a licensed physician, psychiatrist, clinical psychologist, or licensed professional that includes license or credential information. Assessment data and interpretive reports helpful in determining appropriate accommodations.
Documentation submitted to: Support Program/Services
Special Ed. HS course work accepted: Yes
Separate application required for program services: No
Contact Information
Name of program or department: Services for Students with Disabilities
Telephone: 715-836-5800
Fax: 715-831-2651
Email: ssd@uwec.edu

University of Wisconsin—Eau Claire

Additional Information

Students must provide documentation prior to receiving appropriate accommodations. Some of the accommodations provided with appropriate documentation could include tutoring individually or in groups, readers, scribes, note-takers, taped textbooks, proofreaders, and exam accommodations, including extended time, readers, and separate testing rooms. The Academic Skills Center offers individualized tutoring in math preparation and background, composition, reading, and study skills. Many departments on campus provide tutors to help students with course content. Students take a form identifying appropriate accommodation requests completed by SSD staff to instructors. Students who are denied accommodations can appeal any denial by filing a complaint with the Affirmative Action Review Board. Services and accommodations are available to undergraduate and graduate students.

GENERAL ADMISSIONS

Very important factors considered include: rigor of secondary school record, class rank, academic GPA. *Important factors considered include:* application essay, standardized test scores. *Other factors considered include:* recommendation(s), interview, extracurricular activities, talent/ability, character/personal qualities, first generation, geographical residence, state residency, racial/ethnic status, volunteer work, work experience, level of applicant's interest. *Freshman Admission Requirements:* High school diploma is required and GED is accepted. *Academic units required:* 4 English, 3 math, 3 science, 3 social studies, 4 academic electives.

ACCOMMODATIONS OR SERVICES

Accommodations are decided upon an individual basis after a thorough review of appropriate, current documentation. The accommodations requests must be supported through the documentation provided and must be logically linked to the current impact of the condition on academic functioning.

FINANCIAL AID

Students should submit: FAFSA. Applicants will be notified of awards on a rolling basis beginning 4/15. The Princeton Review suggests that all financial aid forms be submitted as soon as possible after October 1. *Need-based scholarships/grants offered:* College/university scholarship or grant aid from institutional funds; Federal Nursing Scholarships; Federal Pell; Private scholarships; SEOG; State scholarships/grants. *Loan aid offered:* Direct PLUS loans; Direct Subsidized Stafford Loans; Direct Unsubsidized Stafford Loans. Federal Work-Study Program available. Institutional employment available.

CAMPUS LIFE

Activities: Campus Ministries; Choral groups; Concert band; Dance; Drama/theater; International Student Organization; Jazz band; Literary magazine; Marching band; Model UN; Music ensembles; Musical theater; Opera; Pep band; Radio station; Student government; Student newspaper; Student-run film society; Symphony orchestra; Television station. **Organizations:** 240 registered organizations, 30 honor societies, 16 religious organizations. 2 fraternities, 3 sororities. **Athletics (Intercollegiate):** *Men:* basketball, cross-country, diving, football, golf, ice hockey, swimming, tennis, track/field (outdoor), track/field (indoor), wrestling. *Women:* basketball, cross-country, diving, golf, gymnastics, ice hockey, soccer, softball, swimming, tennis, track/field (outdoor), track/field (indoor), volleyball. **On-Campus Highlights:** Chippewa River Footbridge, Davies Center (Student Center/Union), McPhee Center (Athletic Facility), Hass Fine Arts Center, Higher Ground (Recreational Facility).

ACCOMMODATIONS

Allowed in exams:

Calculators	Yes
Dictionary	Yes
Computer	Yes
Spell-checker	Yes
Extended test time	Yes
Scribe	Yes
Proctors	Yes
Oral exams	Yes
Note-takers	Yes

Support services for students with

LD	Yes
ADHD	Yes
ASD	Yes
Distraction-reduced environment	Yes
Recording of lecture allowed	Yes
Reading technology:	Yes
Audio books	Yes

Other assistive technology   Alternative textbook format, screen readers, Live Scribe Smart Pens, Closed Captioning, Listen Technology FM Systems, Speech to Text software, use of iPads and individual assistance with computer software

Priority registration	Yes

Added costs for services:

For LD:	No
For ADHD:	No
For ASD:	No
LD specialists	Yes
ADHD & ASD coaching	Yes
ASD specialists	Yes
Professional tutors	Yes
Peer tutors	Yes
Max. hours/week for services	4
How professors are notified of student approved accommodations	Student

COLLEGE GRADUATION REQUIREMENTS

Course waivers allowed	No
Course substitutions allowed	Yes

In what courses   Physical Activity Courses and some general education courses

University of Wisconsin—Madison

161 BASCOM HALL, MADISON, WI 53715–1007 • ADMISSIONS: 608-262-3961 • FAX: 608-262-7706

CAMPUS
Type of school	Public
Environment	City
Support	CS

STUDENTS
Undergrad enrollment	29,931
% male/female	49/51
% from out of state	34
% frosh live on campus	92

FINANCIAL FACTS
Annual in-state tuition	$9,273
Annual out-of-state tuition	$33,523
Required fees	$1,260

GENERAL ADMISSIONS INFO
Application fee	$60
Regular application deadline	2/1

Nonfall registration accepted. Admission may be deferred for a maximum of 1 year.

Range SAT EBRW	620–690
Range SAT Math	660–760
Range ACT Composite	27–31

ACADEMICS
Student/faculty ratio	18:1
% students returning for sophomore year	95
% students graduating within 4 years	61
% students graduating within 6 years	87

Most classes have 10–19 students.
Most lab/discussion sessions have 10–19 students.

PROGRAMS/SERVICES FOR STUDENTS WITH LEARNING DIFFERENCES

The McBurney Disability Resource Center provides students with disabilities equal access to the programs and activities of the University. Over 1,000 students with disabilities are currently registered with the McBurney Center. Students with disabilities who tend to do well have graduated from competitive high school or college programs and are reasonably independent, proactive in seeking assistance, and use accommodations similar to those offered here. For complete information about the McBurney Center, please visit our web site at www.mcburney.wisc.edu.

ADMISSIONS

The admission review process is the same for all applicants. Factors in the review process may include self-disclosed disability information in the written statement, grades, rank, test scores, course requirements completed, and potential for success. Disclosure of disability will not have a negative effect on a student's admission application. If a student wishes to disclose a disability they may do so in the "additional statement" on the application. Suggested information to include is the date of diagnosis or the onset of the disability and the ramifications of the disability on course requirements, attendance, and academic performance. This information will be considered during the admission review by trained admission counselors. Any documentation about the disability should be submitted to the McBurney Disability Resource Center.

Additional Information

The documentation must be completed by a professional qualified to diagnose an LD. The report must include results of a clinical interview and descriptions of the testing procedures; instruments used; test and subtest results reported in standard scores, as well as percentile rank and grade scores where useful; and interpretation and recommendations based on data gathered. It must be comprehensive and include test results where applicable in intelligence, reading, math, spelling, written language,

ADMISSIONS INFO FOR STUDENTS WITH LEARNING DIFFERENCES

SAT/ACT required: Yes
Interview required: No
Essay required: Not Applicable
Additional application required: No
Documentation required for:
 LD: Recent psychometric assessment with test analysis and interpretation
 ADHD: Current comprehensive ADHD diagnostic evaluation report (within approximately the last three years)
 ASD: Psycho ed evaluation
Documentation submitted to: McBurney Disability Resource Center
Special Ed. HS course work accepted: No
Separate application required for program services: Yes
# of students last year receiving services/accommodations for:
 LD: 675
Contact Information
Name of program or department: McBurney Disability Resource Center
Telephone: 608-263-2741
Fax: 608-265-2998
Email: mcburney@studentlife.wisc.edu

University of Wisconsin—Madison

language processing, and cognitive processing skills. Testing should carefully examine areas of concern/weakness, as well as areas of strengths; documentation should include a clear diagnostic statement based on the test results and personal history. Students may be eligible for advocacy/liaison with faculty and staff, alternative testing accommodations, curriculum modifications, disability management advising, learning skills training, liaison with vocational rehab, access to the McBurney Learning Resource Room, note-takers, peer support groups, priority registration, taped texts, and course materials.

GENERAL ADMISSIONS

Very important factors considered include: rigor of secondary school record, class rank, academic GPA. *Important factors considered include:* application essay, standardized test scores, state residency. *Other factors considered include:* recommendation(s), extracurricular activities, talent/ability, character/personal qualities, first generation, alumni/ae relation, racial/ethnic status, volunteer work, work experience, level of applicant's interest. *Freshman Admission Requirements:* High school diploma is required and GED is accepted. *Academic units required:* 4 English, 4 math, 3 science, 3 foreign language, 3 social studies, and 2 units from above areas or other academic areas. *Academic units recommended:* 4 English, 4 math, 4 science, 4 foreign language, 4 social studies, 2 units from above areas or other academic areas.

ACCOMMODATIONS OR SERVICES

Accommodations are decided upon an individual basis after a thorough review of appropriate, current documentation. The accommodations requests must be supported through the documentation provided and must be logically linked to the current impact of the condition on academic functioning.

FINANCIAL AID

Students should submit: FAFSA. Applicants will be notified of awards on a rolling basis beginning 3/1. The Princeton Review suggests that all financial aid forms be submitted as soon as possible after October 1. *Need-based scholarships/grants offered:* College/university scholarship or grant aid from institutional funds; Federal Pell; Private scholarships; SEOG; State scholarships/grants. *Loan aid offered:* Direct PLUS loans; Direct Subsidized Stafford Loans; Direct Unsubsidized Stafford Loans. Federal Work-Study Program available. Institutional employment available.

CAMPUS LIFE

Activities: Choral groups; Concert band; Dance; Drama/theater; International Student Organization; Jazz band; Literary magazine; Marching band; Music ensembles; Musical theater; Opera; Pep band; Radio station; Student government; Student newspaper; Student-run film society; Symphony orchestra; Television station; Yearbook. **Organizations:** 685 registered organizations, 27 honor societies, 26 fraternities, 11 sororities. **Athletics (Intercollegiate):** *Men:* basketball, cheerleading, crew/rowing, cross-country, football, golf, ice hockey, soccer, swimming, tennis, track/field (outdoor), wrestling. *Women:* basketball, cheerleading, crew/rowing, cross-country, golf, ice hockey, soccer, softball, swimming, tennis, track/field (outdoor), volleyball. **On-Campus Highlights:** Allen Centennial Gardens, Kohl Center, Memorial Union Terrace, Chazen Museum of Art, Babcock Hall Dairy Plant and Store.

ACCOMMODATIONS

Allowed in exams:

Calculators	Yes
Dictionary	Yes
Computer	Yes
Spell-checker	Yes
Extended test time	Yes
Scribe	Yes
Proctors	No
Oral exams	Yes
Note-takers	Yes
Support services for students with	
LD	Yes
ADHD	Yes
ASD	Yes
Distraction-reduced environment	Yes
Recording of lecture allowed	Yes
Reading technology:	Yes
Audio books	Yes
Other assistive technology	Yes
Priority registration	Yes
Added costs for services:	
For LD:	No
LD specialists	Yes
ADHD & ASD coaching	No
ASD specialists	Yes
Professional tutors	No
Peer tutors	Yes
Max. hours/week for services	5
How professors are notified of student approved accommodations	Student

COLLEGE GRADUATION REQUIREMENTS

Course waivers allowed	No
Course substitutions allowed	No

University of Wisconsin—Milwaukee

P.O. Box 413, Milwaukee, WI 53211 • Admissions: 414-229-2222 • Fax: 414-229-6940

CAMPUS
Type of school	Public
Environment	Metropolis
Support	CS

STUDENTS
Undergrad enrollment	20,000
% male/female	49/51
% from out of state	11
% frosh live on campus	74

FINANCIAL FACTS
Annual in-state tuition	$8,090
Annual out-of-state tuition	$9,685
Room and board	$10,560
Required fees	$1,444

GENERAL ADMISSIONS INFO
Application fee	$50
Priority deadline	3/1
Regular application deadline	8/11

Nonfall registration accepted. Admission may be deferred for a maximum of 1 year.

Range ACT Composite 20-25

ACADEMICS
Student/faculty ratio	19:1
% students returning for sophomore year	72
% students graduating within 4 years	15
% students graduating within 6 years	41

Most classes have 10–19 students.
Most lab/discussion sessions have 10–19 students.

PROGRAMS/SERVICES FOR STUDENTS WITH LEARNING DIFFERENCES
The Accessibility Resource Center (ARC) offers a wide range of academic support services to students with learning disabilities, attention deficit hyperactivity disorders, Autism Spectrum Disorder and traumatic brain injuries. Our mission is to create an accessible university community for students with disabilities that fosters the development of each student's full potential. There is no waiting list or caps on participation. This program is well suited for students who are fairly independent and willing to seek the support services they need. Recommended academic accommodations are based on documentation of disability and disability related needs. The accommodations may include but are not limited to: note-taking assistance, exam accommodations, alternate format textbooks, priority registration. In addition to academic accommodations, staff is available to meet individually with students to work on study strategies, time management issues, and organization.

ADMISSIONS
Admission into UWM is necessary for participation. Students apply directly to Enrollment Services or online. Online applications are encouraged. Apply online at apply.wisconsin.edu. The Accessibility Resource Center does not make admission decisions. Disability Documentation should be sent directly to the Accessibility Resource Center. Students need to apply online, and submit ACT scores, high school transcripts. Accommodations can be requested to take the placement tests by contacting the LD Program and submitting documentation of disability.

Additional Information
Students who meet eligibility criteria receive individual counseling and guidance. In addition, students may be eligible for academic accommodations based upon specific disability-related needs. These accommodations may include but are not limited to: Priority registration, note-taking assistance, exam accommodations, taped textbooks, and use of computer. To use the Computer & Assistive Technology Lab students

ADMISSIONS INFO FOR STUDENTS WITH LEARNING DIFFERENCES
SAT/ACT required: Yes
Interview required: No
Essay required: No
Additional application required: No
Documentation required for:
 LD: Comprehensive and current psycho-educational or neuro-psychological assessment. Recommended testing instruments include the WAIS III and Wodcock-Johnson Tests of Achievement
 ADHD: Preferred is a comprehensive and current psycho-educational or neuro- psychological assessment. Also accepted is completion of UWM's form of Certification of ADHD completed by a psychiatraist or psychologist.
 ASD: Psycho ed evaluation
Documentation submitted to: Accessibility Resource Center
Special Ed. HS course work accepted: Yes
Separate application required for program services: Yes
Contact Information
Name of program or department: Accessibility Resource Center
Telephone: 414-229-6287
Fax: 414 229-2237

University of Wisconsin—Milwaukee

must have an initial screening of the need for assistive technology. Specific, individualized recommendations for each student are evaluated. Eligible students will have portable, flexible access to technology. Assistive Technology is based on student need and there is training in the use of Assistive Technology.

GENERAL ADMISSIONS

Very important factors considered include: rigor of secondary school record, academic GPA, standardized test scores. *Important factors considered include:* application essay. *Other factors considered include:* class rank, recommendation(s), interview, extracurricular activities, talent/ ability, character/personal qualities, first generation, racial/ethnic status, volunteer work, work experience. *Freshman Admission Requirements:* High school diploma is required and GED is accepted. *Academic units required:* 4 English, 3 math, 3 science, 1 science lab, 3 social studies, 4 academic electives. *Academic units recommended:* 4 English, 4 math, 4 science, 1 science lab, 2 foreign language, 4 social studies, 4 academic electives.

ACCOMMODATIONS OR SERVICES

Accommodations are decided upon an individual basis after a thorough review of appropriate, current documentation. The accommodations requests must be supported through the documentation provided and must be logically linked to the current impact of the condition on academic functioning.

FINANCIAL AID

Students should submit: FAFSA. Applicants will be notified of awards on a rolling basis beginning 3/15. The Princeton Review suggests that all financial aid forms be submitted as soon as possible after October 1. *Need-based scholarships/grants offered:* College/university scholarship or grant aid from institutional funds; Federal Pell; Private scholarships; SEOG; State scholarships/grants. *Loan aid offered:* Direct PLUS loans; Direct Subsidized Stafford Loans; Direct Unsubsidized Stafford Loans. Federal Work-Study Program available. Institutional employment available.

CAMPUS LIFE

Activities: Campus Ministries; Choral groups; Concert band; Dance; Drama/theater; International Student Organization; Jazz band; Literary magazine; Model UN; Music ensembles; Musical theater; Opera; Pep band; Radio station; Student government; Student newspaper; Student-run film society; Symphony orchestra. **Organizations:** 250 registered organizations, 1 honor society, 4 religious organizations. 8 fraternities, 4 sororities. **Athletics (Intercollegiate):** *Men:* baseball, basketball, cross-country, diving, soccer, swimming, track/field (outdoor). *Women:* basketball, cross-country, soccer, swimming, tennis, track/field (outdoor), volleyball. The Grind Coffee Shop, Student Union, Klotche Recreation Center, Golda Meier Library, Sandburg Residence Hall.

ACCOMMODATIONS

Allowed in exams:

Calculators	No
Dictionary	Yes
Computer	Yes
Spell-checker	Yes
Extended test time	Yes
Scribe	Yes
Proctors	Yes
Oral exams	Yes
Note-takers	Yes

Support services for students with

LD	Yes
ADHD	Yes
ASD	Yes
Distraction-reduced environment	Yes
Recording of lecture allowed	Yes
Reading technology:	Yes
Audio books	Yes
Other assistive technology	Yes
Priority registration	Yes

Added costs for services:

For LD:	No
For ADHD:	No
For ASD:	No
LD specialists	Yes
ADHD & ASD coaching	No
ASD specialists	No
Professional tutors	No
Peer tutors	Yes
Max. hours/week for services	3
How professors are notified of student approved accommodations	Student

COLLEGE GRADUATION REQUIREMENTS

Course waivers allowed	No
Course substitutions allowed	Yes

In what courses

On an individual basis for math and foreign language.

University of Wisconsin—Oshkosh

800 Algoma Boulevard, Oshkosh, WI 54901 • Admissions: 920-424-0202 • Fax: 920-424-1098

CAMPUS

Type of school	Public
Environment	City
Support	SP

STUDENTS

Undergrad enrollment	10,771
% male/female	43/57
% from out of state	3
% frosh live on campus	88

FINANCIAL FACTS

Annual in-state tuition	$7,360
Annual out-of-state tuition	$14,934
Room and board	$6,926

GENERAL ADMISSIONS INFO

Application fee	$44

Nonfall registration accepted. Admission may be deferred.

Range ACT Composite	20–24

ACADEMICS

Student/faculty ratio	22:1
% students returning for sophomore year	75
% students graduating within 4 years	19
% students graduating within 6 years	52

PROGRAMS/SERVICES FOR STUDENTS WITH LEARNING DIFFERENCES

Project Success is a language remediation project that is based on mastering the entire sound structure of the English language. These students are academically able and determined to succeed, in spite of a pronounced problem in a number of areas. Help is offered in the following ways: direct remediation of deficiencies through the Orton-Gillingham Technique, one-on-one tutoring assistance, math and writing labs, guidance and counseling with scheduling course work and interpersonal relations, extended time, and by providing an atmosphere that is supportive. The goal is for students to become language independent in and across all of these major educational areas: math, spelling, reading, writing, comprehension, and study skills. As full-time university students, they will acquire language independence by mastering the entire phonetic structure of the American English language.

ADMISSIONS

Students may apply to Project Success in their junior year of high school. Applicants apply by writing a letter, in their own handwriting, indicating interest in the program and why they are interested. Applications are processed on a first- come, first-served basis. Those interested should apply at least 1 to 2 years prior to the student's desired entrance semester. Students and parents will be invited to interview. The interview is used to assess family dynamics in terms of support for the student and reasons for wanting to attend college. The director is looking for motivation, stability, and the ability of the students to describe the disability. Acceptance into Project Success does not grant acceptance into the university. Admission to the university and acceptance into Project Success is a joint decision, but a separate process is required for each. General admissions procedures must be followed before acceptance into Project Success can be offered. ACT/SAT or GPA are not critical. Students who are admitted to UW --Oshkosh and Project Success not in full standing (all high school units completed, top 40 percent of graduating class, and ACT of 22-plus) must attend the Project Success summer program prior to freshman year.

ADMISSIONS INFO FOR STUDENTS WITH LEARNING DIFFERENCES

SAT/ACT required: Yes
Interview required: No
Essay required: Yes
Additional application required: No
Documentation required for:
 LD: Psycho ed evaluation to include: relevant historical info, instructional interventions, related services, age diagnosed, objective data (aptitude, achievement, info processing), test scores (standard, percentile and grade equivalents) and describe functional limitations.
 ADHD: Diagnosis based on DSM-V; history of behaviors impairing functioning in academic setting; diagnostic interview; history of symptoms; evidence of ongoing behaviors.
 ASD: Psycho educational evaluation
Documentation submitted to: Admissions Office and Project Success Project Success
Special Ed. HS course work accepted: Yes
Separate application required for program services: Yes
# of students last year receiving services/accommodations for:
 LD: 350
Contact Information
Name of program or department: Project Success
Telephone: 920-424-3100
Fax: 920-424-0858

University of Wisconsin—Oshkosh

Additional Information

Incoming freshmen to Project Success must participate in an 6-week summer school program consisting of simultaneous multisensory instructional procedures (SMSIP). This program is used to teach study skills, reading, spelling, writing, and mathematical operations. The Project Success program offers the following remedial and support services for all students enrolled in its program: organizational tutors, mathematics courses/tutoring, remedial reading and spelling courses, English/written expression courses/tutoring, and content area tutoring. Additionally, students are eligible for extended time testing opportunities. Although Project Success does not offer taped texts, students are not prohibited from using them. Student requesting taped texts are referred to the UW --Oshkosh Disability Services office. Services and accommodations are available for undergraduate and graduate students.

GENERAL ADMISSIONS

Very important factors considered include: rigor of secondary school record, class rank, academic GPA, standardized test scores. *Important factors considered include:* application essay, recommendation(s), first generation. *Other factors considered include:* interview, extracurricular activities, talent/ability, character/personal qualities, alumni/ae relation, volunteer work, work experience. *Freshman Admission Requirements:* High school diploma is required and GED is accepted. *Academic units required:* 4 English, 3 math, 3 science, 3 science labs, 3 social studies, 2 history, 4 academic electives. *Academic units recommended:* 4 math, 4 science, 4 science labs, 2 foreign language, 4 social studies, 1 history, 1 visual/performing arts.

ACCOMMODATIONS OR SERVICES

Accommodations are decided upon an individual basis after a thorough review of appropriate, current documentation. The accommodations requests must be supported through the documentation provided and must be logically linked to the current impact of the condition on academic functioning.

FINANCIAL AID

Students should submit: FAFSA. Applicants will be notified of awards on or about 4/15. The Princeton Review suggests that all financial aid forms be submitted as soon as possible after October 1. *Need-based scholarships/grants offered:* College/university scholarship or grant aid from institutional funds; Federal Nursing Scholarships; Federal Pell; Private scholarships; SEOG; State scholarships/grants; United Negro College Fund. *Loan aid offered:* Direct PLUS loans; Direct Subsidized Stafford Loans; Direct Unsubsidized Stafford Loans. Federal Work-Study Program available. Institutional employment available.

CAMPUS LIFE

Activities: Campus Ministries; Choral groups; Concert band; Dance; Drama/theater; International Student Organization; Jazz band; Literary magazine; Model UN; Music ensembles; Musical theater; Pep band; Radio station; Student government; Student newspaper; Student-run film society; Television station. **Organizations:** 175 registered organizations, 15 honor societies, 6 religious organizations. 8 fraternities, 5 sororities. **Athletics (Intercollegiate):** *Men:* baseball, basketball, cross-country, diving, football, soccer, swimming, tennis, track/field (outdoor), track/field (indoor), wrestling. *Women:* basketball, cross-country, diving, golf, gymnastics, soccer, softball, swimming, tennis, track/field (outdoor), track/field (indoor), volleyball. Sage Hall - LEEDS certification, Horizon Village - State of Art res hall.

ACCOMMODATIONS

Allowed in exams:

Calculators	Yes
Dictionary	Yes
Computer	Yes
Spell-checker	No
Extended test time	Yes
Scribe	No
Proctors	Yes
Oral exams	No
Note-takers	Yes

Support services for students with

LD	Yes
ADHD	Yes
ASD	Yes
Distraction-reduced environment	Yes
Recording of lecture allowed	Yes
Reading technology:	Yes
Audio books	Yes
Other assistive technology	Yes
Priority registration	Yes

Added costs for services:

For LD:	No
For ADHD:	No
For ASD:	No
LD specialists	Yes
ADHD & ASD coaching	No
ASD specialists	No
Professional tutors	No
Peer tutors	Yes
Max. hours/week for services	Varies
How professors are notified of student approved accommodations	Student and director

COLLEGE GRADUATION REQUIREMENTS

Course waivers allowed	Yes

In what courses: UW—Oshkosh has special accommodations in place relating to the foreign language requirement.

Course substitutions allowed	Yes

In what courses: Foreign language and several others in select areas.

University of Wisconsin—Stevens Point

2100 Main Street, Stevens Point, WI 54481 • Admissions: 715-346-2441 • Fax: 715-346-3296

CAMPUS
Type of school	Public
Environment	Town
Support	S

STUDENTS
Undergrad enrollment	8,684
% male/female	48/52
% from out of state	11
% frosh live on campus	90

FINANCIAL FACTS
Annual in-state tuition	$7,674
Annual out-of-state tuition	$15,940
Room and board	$3,414
Required fees	$1,374

GENERAL ADMISSIONS INFO
Nonfall registration accepted.

Range SAT EBRW	405–565
Range SAT Math	410–523
Range ACT Composite	20–25

ACADEMICS
Student/faculty ratio	21:1
% students returning for sophomore year	74
% students graduating within 4 years	33
% students graduating within 6 years	65

Most classes have 20–29 students.
Most lab/discussion sessions have 10–19 students.

PROGRAMS/SERVICES FOR STUDENTS WITH LEARNING DIFFERENCES
The Disability & Assistive Technology Center (DATC) at the University of Wisconsin-Stevens Point. The DATC is comprised of the Disability Services and Assistive Technology programs. The DATC provides accessibility, accommodation, and assistive technology services to students with disabilities, working individually with qualified students to identify, design, and implement an accommodation plan that will aid them in acquiring equal access to their education.

The DATC aims to create a learning environment that will help maximize opportunities for our students to succeed. The goal is to develop a rapport with students, so they feel welcome communicating with staff. The program seeks to meet not only the letter-of-the-law in providing access and accommodations, but also to go beyond that measure by making sure students receive the best support services possible.

ADMISSIONS
There is no separate admission procedure for students with learning disabilities. However, students are encouraged to make a pre-admission inquiry and talk to the director of DATC.

Additional Information
The DATC serves current and future UW-Stevens Point students needing to arrange accommodations who have documented disabilities, including: ADD/ADHD; Autism Spectrum Disorders; Brain Injuries; Health Impairments; Hearing Disorders; Learning Disabilities; Psychological Disorders; Physical Disabilities; Temporary Disabilities; Visual Impairments.

ADMISSIONS INFO FOR STUDENTS WITH LEARNING DIFFERENCES
SAT/ACT required: No
Interview required: No
Essay required: Not Applicable
Additional application required: No
Documentation required for:
  LD: High school psychological report or other psychological report documenting a learning disorder
  ADHD: Medical or psychological report identifying ADHD
  ASD: Medical or psychological documentation completed by a professional qualified to document ASD.
Documentation submitted to: Disability and Assistive Technology Center
Special Ed. HS course work accepted: Not Applicable
Separate application required for program services: No
Contact Information
Name of program or department: Disability and Assistive Technology Center
Telephone: 715 346-3365
Fax: 715 346-4143
Email: datctr@uwsp.edu

University of Wisconsin—Stevens Point

GENERAL ADMISSIONS

Very important factors considered include: rigor of secondary school record, class rank, academic GPA, standardized test scores. *Important factors considered include:* application essay, recommendation(s), talent/ability, first generation. *Other factors considered include:* interview, extracurricular activities, character/personal qualities, alumni/ae relation, geographical residence, state residency, racial/ethnic status, volunteer work, work experience. *Freshman Admission Requirements:* High school diploma is required and GED is accepted. *Academic units required:* 4 English, 3 math, 3 science, 3 social studies, 4 academic electives. *Academic units recommended:* 4 English, 4 math, 4 science, 4 social studies, 4 academic electives.

ACCOMMODATIONS OR SERVICES

Accommodations are decided upon an individual basis after a thorough review of appropriate, current documentation. The accommodations requests must be supported through the documentation provided and must be logically linked to the current impact of the condition on academic functioning.

FINANCIAL AID

Students should submit: FAFSA. Applicants will be notified of awards on a rolling basis beginning 3/1. The Princeton Review suggests that all financial aid forms be submitted as soon as possible after October 1. *Need-based scholarships/grants offered:* College/university scholarship or grant aid from institutional funds; Federal Pell; Private scholarships; SEOG; State scholarships/grants. *Loan aid offered:* Direct PLUS loans; Direct Subsidized Stafford Loans; Direct Unsubsidized Stafford Loans. Federal Work-Study Program available. Institutional employment available.

CAMPUS LIFE

Activities: Campus Ministries; Choral groups; Dance; Drama/theater; International Student Organization; Jazz band; Model UN; Music ensembles; Musical theater; Opera; Pep band; Radio station; Student government; Student newspaper; Student-run film society; Symphony orchestra; Television station. **Organizations:** 185 registered organizations, 12 honor societies, 9 religious organizations. 4 fraternities, 3 sororities. **Athletics (Intercollegiate):** *Men:* baseball, basketball, cross-country, diving, football, ice hockey, swimming, track/field (outdoor), wrestling. *Women:* basketball, cross-country, diving, golf, ice hockey, soccer, softball, swimming, tennis, track/field (outdoor), volleyball. **On-Campus Highlights:** University Center/Brewhouse, Schmeeckle Reserve/Wisconsin Conservation Hall of, Health Enhancement Center, Allen Recreation Center, Fine Arts Building.

ACCOMMODATIONS

Allowed in exams:

Calculators	Yes
Dictionary	No
Computer	Yes
Spell-checker	Yes
Extended test time	Yes
Scribe	Yes
Proctors	Yes
Oral exams	Not Applicable
Note-takers	Yes

Support services for students with

LD	Yes
ADHD	Yes
ASD	Yes
Distraction-reduced environment	Yes
Recording of lecture allowed	Yes
Reading technology:	Yes
Audio books	Yes
Other assistive technology	text-to-voice and voice-to-text services
Priority registration	Yes

Added costs for services:

For LD:	No
For ADHD	No
For ASD:	No
LD specialists	No
ADHD & ASD coaching	No
ASD specialists	No
Professional tutors	Yes
Peer tutors	Yes
Max. hours/week for services	Varies
How professors are notified of student approved accommodations	Student

COLLEGE GRADUATION REQUIREMENTS

Course waivers allowed	No
Course substitutions allowed	Yes
In what courses	
Substitutions mostly granted for foreign language, speech and math.	

University of Wisconsin—Whitewate

800 West Main Street, Whitewater, WI 53190-1791 • Admissions: 262-472-1440 • Fax: 262-472-1515

CAMPUS

Type of school	Public
Environment	Village
Support	CS

STUDENTS

Undergrad enrollment	8,999
% male/female	50/50
% from out of state	4
% frosh live on campus	90

FINANCIAL FACTS

Annual in-state tuition	$5,568
Annual out-of-state tuition	$13,042
Room and board	$4,322
Required fees	$710

GENERAL ADMISSIONS INFO

Application fee	$35
Priority deadline	1/1

Nonfall registration accepted. Admission may be deferred for a maximum of 3 terms.

Range ACT Composite	20–24

ACADEMICS

Student/faculty ratio	22:1
% students returning for sophomore year	74
% students graduating within 4 years	32
% students graduating within 6 years	62

Most classes have 10–19 students.

PROGRAMS/SERVICES FOR STUDENTS WITH LEARNING DIFFERENCES

The University of Wisconsin --Whitewater Center for Students with Disabilities, Project ASSIST program offers support services for students with learning disabilities and ADD/ADHD. The Project ASSIST Summer Transition Program is a four- week program in which students enroll in a three credit study skills class, one credit New Student Seminar and non-credit Project ASSIST class. Areas addressed include learning strategies, comprehension concerns, written language skills, study habits, time management and self-advocacy skills. The philosophy of the program is that students with learning disabilities can learn strategies to become independent learners.

The University of Wisconsin-Whitewater also offers the LIFE (Learning is for Everyone) program will provide a complete college experience for young adults between the ages of 18-25 who have an intellectual disability. With ample supports, specialized instruction, on-campus residential living, and community integration, the program serves a critical need in our region and community. The program will have two components, which includes a Basic Program (2 years) and an Advanced Program (2 years) that are designed to facilitate independent living and employment success for persons with significant cognitive limitations.

ADMISSIONS

All applicants must meet the same criteria for admission. Students should apply to both the university and the Center for Students with Disabilities. General criteria include: Students apply to the university admissions and the Center for Students with Disabilities at the same time. Program staff review the documentation and application regarding eligibility for academic accommodations and Project ASSIST. Programs of Opportunity and Conditional admission to a limited number of students may be possible depending on review of documentation and reason for admission denial.

ADMISSIONS INFO FOR STUDENTS WITH LEARNING DIFFERENCES

SAT/ACT required: Yes

Interview required: No

Essay required: Yes

Additional application required: No

Documentation required for:

LD: Diagnostic interview, assessment of aptitude (WAIS III), academic achievement (Woodcock-Johnson), information processing, specific diagnosis and test scores should be included in the summary report along with recommendations for accommodations. Response to Intervention, 504 Plans, and IEPs are helpful

ADHD: History of early impairment, evidence of current impairment, diagnostic interview, any relevant testing, clearly stated specific diagnosis, rationale for specific accommodations

ASD: A specific diagnosis that conforms to DSM-IV criteria for Autism, Asperger's Syndrome, or Pervasive Developmental Disorder- Not Otherwise Specified. Documentation from psychologist, physician, psychiatrist or other appropriate professional. Response to Intervention, 504 Plans, and IEP documents can be helpful.

Documentation submitted to: Center for Students with Disabilities

Special Ed. HS course work accepted: Yes

Separate application required for program services: Yes

Contact Information

Name of program or department: Center for Students with Disabilities

Telephone: 262-472-4711

Fax: 262-472-4865

University of Wisconsin—Whitewater

Students applying to the LIFE program will complete an application. Applications will be screened that the prospective student will be contacted by the program staff with an invitation for a face to face interview or notice that the student is not being considered for admission.

Additional Information

Tutoring services are provided in a one-to-one setting where students work with tutors on study, math and written language strategies in the context of specific course work. In addition, organizational tutoring is offered to assist students with time management and organization. Computer lab with assistive technology, small group support and academic advising available. Study areas available for student use with daytime and evening hours. In addition, drop-in tutoring is available each weekday and early evening. Access to copies of class notes to qualified students through Hawknotes system.

General Admissions

Very important factors considered include: rigor of secondary school record, class rank, standardized test scores. *Other factors considered include:* academic GPA, application essay, recommendation(s), interview, extracurricular activities, talent/ability, character/personal qualities, first generation, geographical residence, state residency, racial/ethnic status, volunteer work, work experience, leve *Freshman Admission Requirements:* High school diploma is required and GED is accepted. *Academic units required:* 4 English, 3 math, 3 science, 1 science lab, 3 social studies, 4 academic electives. *Academic units recommended:* 4 math, 4 science, 2 foreign language, 4 social studies.

Accommodations or Services

Accommodations are decided upon an individual basis after a thorough review of appropriate, current documentation. The accommodations requests must be supported through the documentation provided and must be logically linked to the current impact of the condition on academic functioning.

Financial Aid

Students should submit: FAFSA. Applicants will be notified of awards on a rolling basis beginning 4/1. The Princeton Review suggests that all financial aid forms be submitted as soon as possible after October 1. *Need-based scholarships/grants offered:* College/university scholarship or grant aid from institutional funds; Federal Pell; Private scholarships; SEOG; State scholarships/grants. *Loan aid offered:* Direct PLUS loans; Direct Subsidized Stafford Loans; Direct Unsubsidized Stafford Loans.

Campus Life

Activities: Choral groups; Concert band; Dance; Drama/theater; Jazz band; Literary magazine; Marching band; Music ensembles; Musical theater; Opera; Radio station; Student government; Student newspaper; Symphony orchestra; Television station. **Organizations:** 130 registered organizations, 4 honor societies, 8 religious organizations. 9 fraternities, 8 sororities. **Athletics (Intercollegiate):** *Men:* baseball, basketball, cross-country, diving, football, soccer, swimming, tennis, track/field (outdoor), track/field (indoor), wrestling. *Women:* basketball, bowling, cross-country, diving, golf, gymnastics, soccer, softball, swimming, tennis, track/field (outdoor), track/field (indoor), volleyball. **On-Campus Highlights:** New Kachel Field House, University Center, Underground Dance Club, Ritazza Coffee Shop, Warhawk Room.

ACCOMMODATIONS

Allowed in exams:	
Calculators	Yes
Dictionary	Yes
Computer	Yes
Spell-checker	Yes
Extended test time Y	es
Scribe	Yes
Proctors	Yes
Oral exams	Yes
Note-takers	Yes
Support services for students with	
LD	Yes
ADHD	Yes
ASD	Yes
Distraction-reduced environment	Yes
Recording of lecture allowed	Yes
Reading technology:	Yes
Audio books	Yes
Other assistive technology	Yes
Priority registration	Yes
Added costs for services:	
For LD:	No
For ADHD:	No
For ASD:	No
LD specialists	Yes
ADHD & ASD coaching	No
ASD specialists	No
Professional tutors	Yes
Peer tutors	Yes
Max. hours/week for services	Varies
How professors are notified of student approved accommodations	Student

COLLEGE GRADUATION REQUIREMENTS

Course waivers allowed	No
Course substitutions allowed	Yes
In what courses	

some math requirements, communications, foreign language.

University of Wyoming

1000 E. University Ave, Laramie, WY 82071 • Admissions: 307-766-5160 • Fax: 307-766-4042

CAMPUS
Type of school	Public
Environment	Town
Support	CS

STUDENTS
Undergrad enrollment	9,623
% male/female	50/50
% from out of state	33
% frosh live on campus	84

FINANCIAL FACTS
Annual in-state tuition	$10,320
Annual out-of-state tuition	$15,480
Room and board	$10,320
Required fees	$1,347

GENERAL ADMISSIONS INFO
Application fee	$40
Regular application deadline	8/10

Nonfall registration accepted. Admission may be deferred for a maximum of 1 year.

Range SAT EBRW	520–650
Range SAT Math	520–640
Range ACT Composite	22–27

ACADEMICS
Student/faculty ratio	15:1
% students returning for sophomore year	78
% students graduating within 4 years	27
% students graduating within 6 years	55

Most classes have 10–19 students.
Most lab/discussion sessions have fewer than 10 students.

PROGRAMS/SERVICES FOR STUDENTS WITH LEARNING DIFFERENCES
Accommodations are not automatically initiated: they must be requested for each course and each semester for which they are needed. Faculty are not required to provide accommodations without notification from the DSS.

ADMISSIONS
Applicants are admitted who have a cumulative, unweighted high school GPA of 3.0 (on a 4.0 scale), and a minimum composite ACT score of 21 or SAT score of 1060. Courses required (Success Curriculum) include: 4 years English, 4 years Math (Algebra I, Algebra II, and geometry), 4 years Science (One year must be from the physical sciences: physics, chemistry, or a college preparatory physical science course. and the remaining years may be a combination of biological, life, physical, or earth/space science courses.), 3 years Social Science, 2 years of same Foreign Language, and 2 years additional coursework chosen from fine and performing arts, social and behavioral studies, humanities, additional foreign language or career-technical courses. Some math and foreign language requirements may be met in grades 7 and 8. If coursework is not indicated on your high school transcript, please submit an official junior high school transcript. Admission with Support applicants are high school seniors or graduates who satisfy the following: Submit ACT/SAT and have a cumulative unweighted GPA of: 2.5 - 2.99 -Or- 2.25 - 2.49 and a minimum composite ACT score of 20 or SAT score of 1020 (math/critical reasoning combined), and completion of the success curriculum with no more than two deficiencies. Both deficiencies cannot occur in the same curriculum category. To foster academic success, students admitted with support participate in UW's nationally recognized Fall Bridge Program or other academic transition programs.

Additional Information
Students can have alternative accommodations through DSS. There are notetakers, priority registration, advocacy with faculty and staff, and more. The student becomes the primary person responsible for asking for assistance, and for providing the necessary documentation and information to justify the services requested. The parent does not have access to student records without the student's written consent. Students with disabilities must seek out tutoring resources available to all college students. Students are expected to manage their own time and complete assignments independently.

ADMISSIONS INFO FOR STUDENTS WITH LEARNING DIFFERENCES
SAT/ACT required: Yes
Interview required: No
Essay required: Not Applicable
Additional application required: No
Documentation required for:
  LD: Psycho ed evaluation
  ADHD: Psycho ed evaluation
  ASD: Psycho ed evaluation
Documentation submitted to: University Disability Support Services
Special Ed. HS course work accepted: No
Separate application required for program services: Yes
Contact Information
Name of program or department: University Disability Support Services
Telephone: 307-766-6189
Fax: 307-766-4010

University of Wyoming

General Admissions

Very important factors considered include: rigor of secondary school record, academic GPA, standardized test scores. *Other factors considered include:* application essay. *Freshman Admission Requirements:* High school diploma is required and GED is accepted. *Academic units required:* 4 English, 4 math, 4 science, 3 science labs, 2 foreign language, 3 social studies, 2 academic electives, and 2 units from above areas or other academic areas. *Academic units recommended:* 4 English, 4 math, 4 science, 3 science labs, 2 foreign language, 3 social studies, 2 academic electives, 2 units from above areas or other academic areas.

Accommodations or Services

Accommodations are decided upon an individual basis after a thorough review of appropriate, current documentation. The accommodations requests must be supported through the documentation provided and must be logically linked to the current impact of the condition on academic functioning.

Financial Aid

Students should submit: FAFSA. Applicants will be notified of awards on a rolling basis beginning 3/16. The Princeton Review suggests that all financial aid forms be submitted as soon as possible after October 1. *Need-based scholarships/grants offered:* College/university scholarship or grant aid from institutional funds; Federal Pell; Private scholarships; SEOG; State scholarships/grants. *Loan aid offered:* Direct PLUS loans; Direct Subsidized Stafford Loans; Direct Unsubsidized Stafford Loans. Federal Work-Study Program available. Institutional employment available.

Campus Life

Activities: Campus Ministries; Choral groups; Concert band; Dance; Drama/theater; International Student Organization; Jazz band; Literary magazine; Marching band; Model UN; Music ensembles; Musical theater; Opera; Pep band; Radio station; Student government; Student newspaper; Student-run film society; Symphony orchestra; Television station. **Organizations:** 223 registered organizations, 41 honor societies, 17 religious organizations. 8 fraternities, 6 sororities. **Athletics (Intercollegiate):** *Men:* basketball, cheerleading, cross-country, diving, football, golf, swimming, track/field (outdoor), track/field (indoor), wrestling. *Women:* basketball, cheerleading, cross-country, diving, golf, soccer, swimming, tennis, track/field (outdoor), track/field (indoor), volleyball. **On-Campus Highlights:** Wyoming Student Union, Half Acre Gym, Geology Museum, Buchanan Center for the Performing Arts, American Heritage Center and Art Museum.

ACCOMMODATIONS

Allowed in exams:

Calculators	Yes
Dictionary	No
Computer	Yes
Spell-checker	Yes
Extended test time	Yes
Scribe	Yes
Proctors	Yes
Oral exams	No
Note-takers	Yes

Support services for students with

LD	Yes
ADHD	Yes
ASD	Yes
Distraction-reduced environment	Yes
Recording of lecture allowed	Yes
Reading technology:	Yes
Audio books	Yes

Other assistive technology   Smart Pen loan, access to MTC computer lab for specialized software, Kurzweil

Priority registration	Yes

Added costs for services:

For LD:	No
For ADHD:	No
For ASD:	No
LD specialists	No
ADHD & ASD coaching	No
ASD specialists	No
Professional tutors	Yes
Peer tutors	No
Max. hours/week for services	Varies

How professors are notified of student approved accommodations
  Director and student

COLLEGE GRADUATION REQUIREMENTS

Course waivers allowed	No
Course substitutions allowed	No

INDEPENDENT LIVING OPTIONS

School	Program Overview	Contact Information
Anchor to Windward, Inc.	Structured living experience	Anchor to Windward, Inc. 600 Loring Avenue Salem, MA 09\1970 P.O. Box 813 Marblehead, MA 01945 978-740-0013 www.anchor-to-windward.com
Bancroft NeuroHealth	Various therapeutic services for children and adults with autism, and other neurological impairments.	Bancroft Admissions Office Haddonfield Campus 425 Kings Highway East P.O. Box 20 Haddonfield, NJ 08033-0018 Ph.: 856-429-0010 www.bancroftneurohealth.org
Berkshire Hills Music Academy	Post-secondary school providing young adults with learning and developmental disabilities to live in a college setting while developing musical potential. Two-year certificate program.	Berkshire Hills Music Academy 48 Woodbridge Street South Hadley, MA 01075 Ph: 413-540-9720 www.berkshirehills.org
Berkshire Center	College Internship Program and the Aspire Program – both are independent living experiences. Aspire for those with Asperger's and Non-verbal learning differences. (Also Brevard)	Admissions Director 18 Park Street Lee, MA 01238 Ph: (877) Know-CIP http://www.berkshirecenter.org/academicsupport.html
Bethesda College program at Concordia in WI program	It is a two-year program designed to meet the higher education needs of students with intellectual, developmental, and other complex disabilities. It gives students with disabilities the ability to experience the full range of college learning and life and provides a "blended" model of instruction centered on the intellectual, vocational, social, personal, and spiritual growth of students.	Concordia Wisconsin Campus 12800 N Lake Shore Drive Mequon, WI 53097 Ph: Phone: 262-243-2183 https://www.cuw.edu/about/offices/bethesda.html
Casa de Amma	Young adults who function independently but require assistance and structure in daily living. Life-long residential community.	Casa de Amma 27231 Calle Arroyo San Juan Capistrano, CA 92675 Ph: (949) 496-9901
Center for Adaptive Learning	18+ with a neurological disability, supportive living program.	Center for Adaptive Learning 3227 Clayton Road Concord, CA 94519 Ph: (925) 827-3863 www.centerforadaptivelearning.org
Chapel Haven	Residential program teaching independent living to young adults.	1040 Whalley Avenue New Haven, CT 06151 Ph: (203) 397-1714 Ext 113 or 148 www.chapelhaven.org

Chapel Haven West	Residential program teaching independent living to young adults.	1701 N. Park Ave Tucson, AZ 85719 University of Arizona Tucson, Arizona 85719 Ph: 877-824-9378 Cdecarlo@chapelhaven.org http://chapelhavenwest.org/
College of Charleston REACH Program	The REACH Program at the College of Charleston is a four-year, fully inclusive certificate program for students with mild intellectual and/or developmental disabilities that promotes the advancement of knowledge and skill in Academics, Socialization, Independent Living and Career Development.	College of Charleston 66 George Street Charleston, SC 29424 Ph:843.953.4849 REACHProgram@cofc.edu
College Excel	Support programs for young adults 18-27 years of age who are ready to begin or continue in college. Program provides college-accredited courses, skill development classes, tutoring, life skills education, and life coaching.	College Excel 86 SW Century Drive Box 199 Bend, OR 97702 Ph: 541 (388 – 3043 http://www.collegeexcel.com/
College Internship Programs	Post-secondary academic, internship and independent living experiences for age 18-25 with Asperger's and non-verbal learning differences. Students participate in the College Internship Programs and can also attend classes at local colleges or community colleges.	CIP Bloomington Center 425 N. College Ave Bloomington, Indiana 47404 Ph: 812-323-0600 X 22 http://www.cipbloomington.org lmanagrum@cipbloomington.org CIP Berkshire 40 Main St. Suite 3 Lee, MA 01238 Ph: (413) 243-2576 X34 lhubbard@cipberkshire.org www.cipberkshire.org CIP Brevard 3692 N. Wickham Road Melbourne, FL 32935 Ph: 321-259-1900 X11 sbrown@cipbrevard.org http://www.brevard.org CIP Berkeley Center 2020 Kittredge Street, Suite B Berkeley, CA 94704 Ph: 510-704-4476 X104 mpaul@cipberkeley.org www.cipberkeley.org CIP Amherst 4500 Harlem Rd Amherst, NY 14226 Ph: 716-839-2620 X 14 jcovert@cipamherst.org www.cipamherst.org CIP Long Beach 4510 E. Pacific Highway Long Beach, CA 90804 Ph: 562-961-9250 X 223 CIP National Admissions Office 18 Park Street Lee, MA 01238 admissions@cipworldwide.org

College Living Experience	College program for students with autism spectrum disorders, Asperger's nonverbal learning disorder, ADD/ADHD and other learning disabilities	National Admissions 7150 Columbus Gateway Suite J Columbia MD 21046 Ph: 800-486-5058 CLE Fort Lauderdale 6555 Nova Drive Suite 300 Fort Lauderdale, FL 33317 Ph: (800) 486 – 5058 http://www.experiencecle.com/loca-tions/ft_lauderdale.aspx CLE Austin TX 11801Stonehollow Dr. Suite 100 Austin, TZX 78758 Ph: 800-486-5058 http://www.cleinc.net/locations/austin.aspx CLE Denver CO 1391 Speer Blvd. Suite 400 Denver. CO 80204 Ph: 800-486-5058 http://www.cleinc.net/locations/denver.aspx CLE Monterey CA 787 Munras Ave. Suite 201 Montery, CA 93940 Ph: 800-486-5058 http://www.cleinc.net/locations/monte-rey.aspx CLE Washington DC 401 North Washington St. Suite 420 Rockville Maryland 20850 http://www.cleinc.net/locations/wash-ington_dc.aspx CLE Costa Mesa, CA 2183 Fairview Road Suite 101 Costa Mesa, CA 92627 Ph: 800-486-5058 http://www.experiencecle.com/loca-tions/Costa_Mesa.aspx http://www.experiencecle.com/loca-tions/Costa_Mesa.aspx7150 Columbia Gateway, Suite J Columbia, MD 2104 7150 Columbia Gateway, Suite J Columbia, MD 21046 Toll-free: 800-486-5058

Drexel Academic and Career Program	Two-year non-degree postsecondary experience for young adults with autism spectrum disorder (ASD).. Students will receive a Certificate of Achievement upon program completion from the A.J. Drexel Autism Institute.	A.J. Drexel Autism Institute (215) 571-3401 3020 Market Street, Suite 560 Philadelphia, PA 19104-3734 autisminstitute@drexel.edu
Edgewood College	Cutting-Edge Program Individualized program to education and inclusion for students with intellectual developmental disabilities	Edgewood College 1255 Deming Way Madiso, Wisc 53717 608-663-2340 cuttingedge@edgewood.edu
Elmhurst Life Skills Academy ELSA	Program assists students with special needs in completing college and transitioning into independent adults. Locations in Florida, Colorado and Texas.	Elmhurst Life Skills Academy 190 Prospect Avenue Elmhurst, Illinois 60126 Ph: (630) 617-3752 http://public.elmhurst.edu/elsa
Evaluation & Development Center	Center provides services to anyone 16+ who is vocationally handicapped to attain greater productivity and self-sufficiency.	Evaluation & Development Center 500 C. Lewis Lane Carbondale, Il 62901 Ph: (618) 453-2331 rehab@siu.edu
Gersh College Experience at Daemen College	Post-secondary, undergraduate program for students with neurobiological disorders, e.g. Asperger's ADHD, OCD, Tourette's Syndrome, Anxiety or Depression, Autism Spectrum and Nonverbal Learning disorders.	150 Broad Hollow Rd Suite 120 Mellville NY 11747 Ph: (631) 385-3342 http://www.gershacademy.org/index. php/schools/the-gersh-experience
The Horizons School	Young adults with learning disabilities to live self-sufficient lives. Non-degree program focused on life and social skills and career development.	The Horizons School 2018 15th Ave. South Birmingham, AL 35205 Ph: (800)-822- 6242 www.horizonsschool.org
Independence Center	Young adults 18-30 transitional residential program.	Independence Center 3640 S. Sepulveda Blvd., Ste. 102 Los Angeles, CA 90034 Ph: (310) 202-7102 www.independencecenter.com
Kent State University Career and Community Studies	To create meaningful experiences for students with intellectual and developmental disabilities by maximizing opportunities in order to equip them to become self-determined and autonomous adults.	Career & Community Studies, 218 White Hall yhale@kent.edu 330-672-0725 https://www.kent.edu/ehhs/ccs
Lesley University	Threshold Program is a comprehensive two year non-degree campus-based program for highly motivated young adults with diverse learning disabilities and other special needs.	Threshold Program Lesley University 29 Everett Street Cambridge, MA 02138 – 2790 Ph: 617-868-9600 http://www.lesley.edu/threshold/admissions.html
Life Development Institute	High school and post-secondary programs teaching independence.	Life Development Institute 18001 N. 79th Ave., E-71 Glendale, AZ 85308 Ph: (623) 773-2774 www.life-development-inst.org

LIFE Skills, Inc.	Young adults 18+ with developmental disabilities, brain injury or mental illness. Services to enhance higher levels of independence.	LIFE Skills, Inc. 483 Highway I West Iowa City, Iowa 52246-4205 Ph: (319) 354-2121 www.lifeskills-inc.com
Maplebrook School	11-21 residential and day school consisting of vocational and college programs.	Maplebrook School 5142 Route 22 Amenia, NY 12501 Ph: (845) 373-9511 www.maplebrookschool.org
The Mason LIFE Program at George Mason University	The Program is an innovative post-secondary program for young adults with intellectual and developmental disabilities who desire a university experience in a supportive academic environment.	Helen A. Kellar Institute for Human Disabilities Graduate School of Education 4400 University Drive, MSN 1F2 Fairfax, Virginia 22030 Ph: : (703)993-3905 https://masonlife.gmu.edu/
Minnesota Life College	Apartment living instructional program for young adults whose learning disabilities pose serious challenges to their independence. Must be 18+ and have completed K-12 education. Vocational skills and workforce readiness.	Minnesota Life College 7501 Logan Ave. South Suite 2A Richfield, MN 55423 Ph: (612) 869-4008 www.minnesotalifecollege.com
New York Institute of Technology Vocational Independence Program	18+ with significant learning disabilities and have received special education services during high school years. 3 year certificate program for vocational major or degree program.	VIP Program NY Institute of Technology Central Islip Campus 300 Carleton Avenue Central Islip, NY 11722-9029 Ph: (631) 348-3354 http://www.nyit.edu/vip/
OPTIONS at Brehm	Young adults with complex learning disabilities. Certificate. 2 year and 4 year degree programs.	OPTIONS at Brehm 1245 East Grand Avenue Carbondale, Il 62901 Ph: (618) 457-0371 www.brehm.org/options
PACE Program at National Louis University	18-30 years with cognitive and provides integrated services to empower students to become independent adults within the community.	PACE National Louis University 5202 Old Orchard Road Skokie, Il 60077 Ph: 224-233-2670 http://www.nl.edu/pace/
Pathway at UCLA	Two year certificate program for students with developmental disabilities providing a blend of educational, social and vocational experiences.	Pathway UCLA Extension 10995 Le Conte Avenue Suite 639 Los Angeles, CA 90024 Ph: (310) 794-1235 pathway@uclaextension.edu
Riverview School	Ages 12-20 in secondary program, 19-23 in post secondary program (GROW). Co-ed residential school for students with complex language, learning and cognitive disabilities.	Riverview School Admissions Office 551 Route 6A East Sandwich, MA 02537 Ph: (508) 888-0489 www.riverviewschool.org

Shepherds College	Three-Year post-secondary program for students with intellectual disabilities.	Ph: 262-878-5620 1805 15th Ave, Union Grove, WI 53182 https://www.shepherdscollege.edu/
University of Iowa	R.E.A.C.H Realizing Educational and Career Hopes A 2-year certificate for students with multiple learning and cognitive disabilities	N297 Lindquist Center The University of Iowa Iowa City, IA 52242-1529 319-384-2127 REACH@uiowa.edu
The University of Wisconsin-Whitewater LIFE (Learning is for Everyone) program	The Program provides a complete college experience for young adults between the ages of 18-25 who have an intellectual disability. With ample supports, specialized instruction, on-campus residential living, and community integration, the program serves a critical need in our region and community.	College of Education & Professional Studies Winther Hall 2031 800 W. Main Street Whitewater, WI 53190 Ph: 262-472-1905 http://www.uww.edu/coeps/departments/life-program
Vista Vocational & Life Skills Center	Three year post-secondary training program for 18+ with neurological disabilities.	Vista Vocational & Life Skills Center 1358 Old Clinton Road Westbrook, CT Ph: (800) 399-8080 www.vistavocational.org
The Washington State University College of Education ROAR (Responsibility, Opportunity, Advocacy, and Respect) Program	Two-year secondary program that provides educational opportunities and a college experience to young adults from around the country with intellectual or developmental disabilities. It closely follows WSU's land-grant mission of access, engagement, and service to the community.	160 Cleveland Hall PO Box 642114 1155 College Ave. Pullman, WA 99164-2114 Ph: 509-335-2525 www.education.wsu.edu/WSUROAR
Wellspring Foundation	Intensive residential treatment for various populations including girls 13-18 and adults. Highly structured programs designed to treat a wide range of emotional and behavioral problems including affective, personality, attachment, eating and traumatic stress disorders.	The Wellspring Foundation, Inc. 21 Arch Bridge Road P.O. Box 370 Bethlehem, CT 06751 Ph: (203) 266-8000 www.wellspring.org

RECOMMENDED WEBSITES

Independent Educational Consultants Association
> www.IECAonline.com

LDA of America
> www.ldanatl.org

Council for Exceptional Children
> www.cec.sped.org

Council for Learning Disabilities
> www.cldinternational.org

ALPHABETICAL LIST OF COLLEGES BY LEVEL OF SUPPORT SERVICES

SP: STRUCTURED PROGRAMS

College/University	State	Support
Adelphi Univeristy	New York	SP
American International College	Massachusetts	SP
American University	District of Columbia	SP
Augsburg University	Minnesota	SP
Barry University	Florida	SP
Beacon College	Florida	SP
Brenau University	Georgia	SP
Curry College	Massachusetts	SP
Fairleigh Dickinson University, College at Florham	New Jersey	SP
Fairleigh Dickinson University, Metropolitan Campus	New Jersey	SP
Florida Agriculture and Mechanical University	Florida	SP
Gannon University	Pennsylvania	SP
Georgian Court University	New Jersey	SP
Hofstra University	New York	SP
Iona College	New York	SP
Landmark College	Vermont	SP
Long Island University	New York	SP
Loras College	Iowa	SP
Louisiana College	Louisiana	SP
Lynn University	Florida	SP
Manhattanville College	New York	SP
Marist College	New York	SP
Marshall University	West Virginia	SP
Marymount Manhattan College	New York	SP
Mercyhurst University	Pennsylvania	SP
Misericordia University	Pennsylvania	SP
Mitchell College	Connecticut	SP
Mount St. Joseph University	Ohio	SP
Muskingum University	Ohio	SP
New Jersey City University	New Jersey	SP
Northeastern University	Massachusetts	SP
Reinhardt University	Georgia	SP
Rochester Institute of Technology	New York	SP
Schreiner University	Texas	SP
Southern Illinois University Carbondale	Illinois	SP
St. Thomas Aquinas College	New York	SP
University of Arizona	Arizona	SP
University of Denver	Colorado	SP
University of Indianapolis	Indiana	SP
University of the Ozarks	Arkansas	SP
University of Tennessee at Martin	Tennessee	SP
University of Wisconsin-Oshkosh	Wisconsin	SP
Ursuline College	Ohio	SP

Westminster College (MO)	Missouri	SP
West Virginia Wesleyan College	West Virginia	SP

CS: COORDINATED SERVICES

College/University	State	Support
Abilene Christian University	Texas	CS
Adrian College	Michigan	CS
Anderson University (IN)	Indiana	CS
Appalachian State University	North Carolina	CS
Arizona State University at the Tempe campus	Arizona	CS
Boston College	Massachusetts	CS
Boston University	Massachusetts	CS
Brevard College	North Carolina	CS
Brigham Young University (UT)	Utah	CS
Brown University	Rhode Island	CS
Bryant University	Rhode Island	CS
California Polytechnic State University	California	CS
California State Polytechnic University, Pomona	California	CS
California State University, Fresno	California	CS
California State University, Fullerton	California	CS
California State University–Long Beach	California	CS
California State University, Northridge	California	CS
California State University–San Bernardino	California	CS
Calvin College	Michigan	CS
The Catholic University of America	District of Columbia	CS
Central Ohio Technical College	Ohio	CS
Chatham University	Pennsylvania	CS
Clark University	Massachusetts	CS
Colby-Sawyer College	New Hampshire	CS
Colgate University	New York	CS
College of William and Mary	Virginia	CS
Concordia College (NY)	New York	CS
Davidson College	North Carolina	CS
DePaul University	Illinois	CS
Drexel University	Pennsylvania	CS
Duke University	North Carolina	CS
East Carolina University	North Carolina	CS
Eastern Kentucky University	Kentucky	CS
East Stroudsburg University of Pennsylvania	Pennsylvania	CS
Edinboro University of Pennsylvania	Pennsylvania	CS
Emerson College	Massachusetts	CS
Emory University	Georgia	CS
Fairfield University	Connecticut	CS
Ferris State University	Michigan	CS
Flagler College	Florida	CS

Florida Atlantic University	Florida	CS
Florida State University	Florida	CS
George Mason University	Virginia	CS
The George Washington University	District of Columbia	CS
Georgia Southern University	Georgia	CS
Georgia State University	Georgia	CS
Grand View University	Iowa	CS
Illinois State University	Illinois	CS
Indiana University Bloomington	Indiana	CS
Iowa State University	Iowa	CS
James Madison University	Virginia	CS
Kansas State University	Kansas	CS
Kean University	New Jersey	CS
Kent State University- Kent Campus	Ohio	CS
Kutztown University of Pennsylvania	Pennsylvania	CS
Lee University	Tennessee	CS
Lehigh University	Pennsylvania	CS
Liberty University	Virginia	CS
Limestone College	South Carolina	CS
Louisiana State University	Louisiana	CS
Loyola University of Chicago	Illinois	CS
Manchester University	Indiana	CS
McDaniel College	Maryland	CS
Menlo College	California	CS
Miami University	Ohio	CS
Michigan State University	Michigan	CS
Michigan Technological University	Michigan	CS
Monmouth University (NJ)	New Jersey	CS
Montana Tech of the University of Montana	Montana	CS
Morningside College	Iowa	CS
New England College	New Hampshire	CS
New York University	New York	CS
Northern Illinois University	Illinois	CS
North Carolina State University	North Carolina	CS
Northern Vermont University	Vermont	CS
Northwestern University	Illinois	CS
Norwich University	Vermont	CS
Oberlin College	Ohio	CS
The Ohio State University–Columbus	Ohio	CS
Old Dominion University	Virginia	CS
Pittsburg State University	Kansas	CS
Providence College	Rhode Island	CS
Regis University	Colorado	CS
Rhode island College	Rhode Island	CS
Rider University	New Jersey	CS

Rocky Mountain College	Montana	CS
Roosevelt University	Illinois	CS
Saint Joseph's University (PA)	Pennsylvania	CS
Saint Michael's College	Vermont	CS
San Diego State University	California	CS
San Francisco State University	California	CS
San Jose State University	California	CS
Santa Clara University	California	CS
Seton Hall University	New Jersey	CS
Southern Connecticut State University	Connecticut	CS
Southern Illinois University Edwardsville	Illinois	CS
Southern Methodist University	Texas	CS
St. Ambrose University	Iowa	CS
St. Andrews University	North Carolina	CS
Stanford University	California	CS
State University of New York - Alfred State College	New York	CS
State University of New York–Stony Brook University	New York	CS
St. Catherine University	Minnesota	CS
Stetson University	Florida	CS
Syracuse University	New York	CS
Temple University	Pennsylvania	CS
Texas State University	Texas	CS
Towson University	Maryland	CS
University of California–Berkeley	California	CS
University of California, Los Angeles	California	CS
University of California–San Diego	California	CS
University of California–Santa Barbara	California	CS
University of Central Florida	Florida	CS
University of Cincinnati	Ohio	CS
University of Colorado at Colorado Springs	Colorado	CS
University of Colorado Boulder	Colorado	CS
University of Connecticut	Connecticut	CS
University of Dayton	Ohio	CS
University of Delaware	Delaware	CS
University of Florida	Florida	CS
University of Georgia	Georgia	CS
University of Hartford	Connecticut	CS
University of Houston	Texas	CS
University of Illinois at Urbana-Champaign	Illinois	CS
University of Iowa	Iowa	CS
University of Kansas	Kansas	CS
University of Kentucky	Kentucky	CS
University of Maryland, College Park	Maryland	CS
University of Massachusetts Amherst	Massachusetts	CS
The University of Memphis	Tennessee	CS

College/University	State	Support
University of Michigan–Ann Arbor	Michigan	CS
University of Missouri	Missouri	CS
University of Nevada, Las Vegas	Nevada	CS
University of New Hampshire	New Hampshire	CS
The University of North Carolina at Chapel Hill	North Carolina	CS
The University of North Carolina at Greensboro	North Carolina	CS
University of North Carolina at Charlotte	North Carolina	CS
University of North Carolina–Wilmington	North Carolina	CS
University of Oregon	Oregon	CS
University of Pittsburgh–Pittsburgh Campus	Pennsylvania	CS
University of Rhode Island	Rhode Island	CS
University of Saint Francis	Indiana	CS
University of San Francisco	California	CS
University of Southern California	California	CS
University of South Carolina–Columbia	South Carolina	CS
The University of South Dakota	South Dakota	CS
University of Tennessee-Chattanooga	Tennessee	CS
University of Tennessee, Knoxville	Tennessee	CS
The University of Texas at Austin	Texas	CS
The University of Tulsa	Oklahoma	CS
University of Utah	Utah	CS
University of Vermont	Vermont	CS
University of Virginia	Virginia	CS
University of Wisconsin-Madison	Wisconsin	CS
University of Wisconsin–Milwaukee	Wisconsin	CS
University of Wisconsin-Whitewater	Wisconsin	CS
University of Wyoming	Wyoming	CS
Utah State University	Utah	CS
Utica College	New York	CS
Wake Forest University	North Carolina	CS
Washington University in St. Louis	Missouri	CS
Western Carolina University	North Carolina	CS
Western Connecticut State University	Connecticut	CS
Western Illinois University	Illinois	CS
Western Kentucky University	Kentucky	CS
Whitman College	Washington	CS
Widener University	Pennsylvania	CS
Wright State University	Ohio	CS
Xavier University	Ohio	CS

S: SERVICES

College/University	State	Support
Alverno College	Wisconsin	S
Arkansas State University	Arkansas	S
Auburn University at Montgomery	Alabama	S

Barnard College	New York	S
Beloit College	Wisconsin	CS
Bowling Green State University	Ohio	S
Bradley University	Illinois	S
Bucknell University	Pennsylvania	S
Canisius College	New York	S
Case Western Reserve University	Ohio	S
Cedarville University	Ohio	S
Champlain College	Vermont	S
Clarkson University	New York	S
Clemson University	South Carolina	S
College of Charleston	South Carolina	S
Colorado State University-Pueblo	Colorado	S
Cornell College	Iowa	S
Cornell University	New York	S
Drake University	Iowa	S
Eastern Illinois University	Illinois	S
Eastern Washington University	Washington	S
Edgewood College	Wisconsin	S
Elon University	North Carolina	S
The Evergreen State College	Washington	S
Farmingdale State College	New York	S
Fitchburg State University	Massachusetts	S
Frostburg State University	Maryland	S
Grand Valley State University	Michigan	S
Green Mountain College	Vermont	S
Grinnell College	Iowa	S
Guilford College	North Carolina	S
Hampton University	Virginia	S
Hobart and William Smith Colleges	New York	S
Indiana University-Purdue University Indianapolis	Indiana	S
Kennesaw State University	Georgia	CS
Lake Superior State University	Michigan	S
Lamar University	Texas	S
Le Moyne College	New York	S
Lenoir Rhyne University	North Carolina	S
Lewis & Clark College	Oregon	S
Loyola Marymount University	California	S
Marian University	Wisconsin	S
Marquette University	Wisconsin	S
Messiah College	Pennsylvania	S
Middle Tennessee State University	Tennessee	S
Millersville University of Pennsylvania	Pennsylvania	S
Minnesota State University Moorhead	Minnesota	S
Montana State University Billings	Montana	S

Montclair State University	New Jersey	S
Neumann University	Pennsylvania	S
New College of Florida	Florida	S
New Mexico Institute of Mining and Technology	New Mexico	S
New Mexico State University	New Mexico	S
Nicholls State University	Louisiana	S
Northern Arizona University	Arizona	S
Northern Michigan University	Michigan	S
North Dakota State University	North Dakota	S
Occidental College	California	S
Ohio University–Athens	Ohio	S
Oklahoma State University	Oklahoma	S
Oregon State University	Oregon	S
Pace University	New York	S
Penn State University Park	Pennsylvania	S
Radford University	Virginia	S
Ripon College	Wisconsin	S
Rivier University	New Hampshire	S
Roanoke College	Virginia	S
Saint Louis University	Missouri	S
Salisbury University	Maryland	S
Savannah College of Art and Design	Georgia	S
Seton Hill University	Pennsylvania	S
Smith College	Massachusetts	S
Sonoma State University	California	S
Southern Maine Community College	Maine	S
Southern Utah University	Utah	S
Southern Wesleyan University	South Carolina	S
South Dakota State University	South Dakota	S
SUNY at Binghamton (Binghamton University)	New York	S
State University of New York—Potsdam	New York	S
University at Albany—SUNY	New York	S
St. Bonaventure University	New York	S
St. Lawrence University	New York	S
St. Olaf College	Minnesota	S
Texas A&M University–College Station	Texas	S
Texas A&M University-Kingsville	Texas	S
Texas Tech University	Texas	S
Thomas More College	Kentucky	SP
Tulane University	Louisiana	S
The University of Alabama in Huntsville	Alabama	S
The University of Alabama-Tuscaloosa	Alabama	S
University of Alaska Anchorage	Alaska	S
University of Alaska Fairbanks	Alaska	S
University of Arkansas	Arkansas	S

University of Illinois Springfield	Illinois	S
University of Jamestown	North Dakota	S
University of Maine	Maine	S
University of Minnesota, Morris	Minnesota	S
University of Missouri–Kansas City	Missouri	S
The University of Montana - Missoula	Montana	S
The University of Montana-Western	Montana	S
University of Nebraska–Lincoln	Nebraska	S
University of New England	Maine	S
University of New Haven	Connecticut	S
University of New Orleans	Louisiana	S
University of Northern Colorado	Colorado	S
University of Northern Iowa	Iowa	S
University of North Carolina at Asheville	North Carolina	S
University of Notre Dame	Indiana	S
University of the Pacific	California	S
University of Southern Indiana	Indiana	S
University of St. Francis	Illinois	S
University of Wisconsin-Eau Claire	Wisconsin	CS
University of Wisconsin-Stevens Point	Wisconsin	S
Wabash College	Indiana	S
Washington State University	Washington	S
Wayne State College	Nebraska	S
Western Colorado University	Colorado	S
Western Oregon University	Oregon	S
West Virginia University	West Virginia	S
Wheaton College (IL)	Illinois	S
Wheaton College (MA)	Massachusetts	S
Whittier College	California	S
Whitworth University	Washington	S
Winona State University	Minnesota	S

INDEX

Get More (Free) Content

1 Go to **PrincetonReview.com/guidebooks**.

2 Enter the following ISBN for your book: 9780525567899.

3 Answer a few simple questions to set up an exclusive Princeton Review account. (If you already have one, you can just log in.)

4 Click the "Student Tools" button, also found under "My Account" from the top toolbar. You're all set to access your bonus content!

Once you've **registered**, you can...

- Take a full-length practice SAT.
- Take a full-length practice ACT.
- Get valuable advice about applying to college.

Need to report a **technical** issue?

Contact **TPRStudentTech@review.com** and provide:

- your full name
- email address used to register the book
- full book title and ISBN
- computer OS (Mac/PC) and browser (Firefox, Safari, etc.)

NOTES

NOTES

NOTES

NOTES

NOTES

NOTES

NOTES

NOTES

NOTES

NOTES

NOTES

NOTES

NOTES

NOTES

ABOUT THE AUTHORS

Marybeth Kravets, MA, is the President of Marybeth Kravets & Associates LLC providing educational and college consulting to students with and without learning differences and is also the Director of College Counseling at Wolcott School, Chicago Illinois. She received her BA in Education from the University of Michigan in Ann Arbor, and her MA in Counseling from Wayne State University in Detroit, Michigan. She is a Past President of the National Association for College Admission Counseling (NACAC) and also served as the President of the Illinois Association for College Admission Counseling. Marybeth Kravets is a recipient of the Harvard University Club of Chicago Community Service Award for her lifelong dedication to serving students who are economically challenged or challenged with learning differences.. For additional information or to contact Marybeth Kravets for consultation email or call:

Marybeth Kravets
847-212-3687- Cell
Marybeth@kravets.net

Imy Wax is a Psychotherapist, Licensed Clinical Professional Counselor (LCPC), National Board Certified Counselor (NBCC), Certified Educational Planner (CEP), and a Therapeutic and Educational Consultant. As a consultant, Imy travels 100,000 miles a year visiting programs, schools, colleges and post-secondary options for children, adolescents and young adults throughout the U.S. and Internationally, often as a guest speaker.

Imy is a frequent presenter at professional and parental conferences. She has authored and been quoted in numerous journal articles and conducts workshops for parents and school districts. She is also a wife, mother to four, and grandmother to seven. Her daughter was the inspiration for this book.

Imy is often called upon by mental health professionals and attorneys to assist them in identifying appropriate education and program alternatives for their students and clients. She is the founder and President of The Aspire Group (www.theaspiregroup.com). For over 30 years, Imy and her team continue to be that "objective voice," guiding, supporting, and empowering families in making an informed decision that will secure and enhance their child's future. Imy believes that there should never be a "closed door" to one's Hopes and Dreams and that today is but a stepping stone to a better tomorrow; and that each child's journey is unique to them.

For additional information or to contact Imy Wax for consultation, email or phone:

IMY WAX
847-945-0913 (office)
844-945-0913 (toll free)
+1 224-619-3558 (Skype # -International)
Imy@TheAspireGroup.com

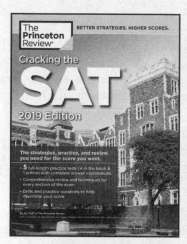
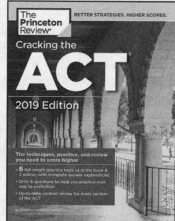